UPLAND KENYA
WILD FLOWERS

UPLAND KENYA
WILD FLOWERS

A FLORA OF THE FERNS
AND HERBACEOUS FLOWERING PLANTS
OF UPLAND KENYA

BY

A. D. Q. AGNEW

OXFORD UNIVERSITY PRESS
1974

Oxford University Press, Ely House, London W.1

GLASGOW NEW YORK TORONTO MELBOURNE WELLINGTON
CAPE TOWN IBADAN NAIROBI DAR ES SALAAM LUSAKA ADDIS ABABA
DELHI BOMBAY CALCUTTA MADRAS KARACHI LAHORE DACCA
KUALA LUMPUR SINGAPORE HONG KONG TOKYO

ISBN 0 19 854503 7

© OXFORD UNIVERSITY PRESS 1974

PRINTED IN GREAT BRITAIN BY
WILLIAM CLOWES & SONS LTD.,
LONDON COLCHESTER AND BECCLES

PREFACE

THIS Book aims to give amateurs and specialists a means of identifying the herbs and climbers of Kenya above 3000 ft (approximately 1000 metres) altitude. It is meant to fill the gap left by I. R. Dale and P. J. Greenway's *Kenya trees and shrubs* (Buchanan's Kenya Estates, 1961) and A. V. Bogdan's *A revised list of Kenya grasses* (Kenya Government printer, 1958). Both of these books are still available and give an adequate account of their plant groups. A work which is continuing is the *Flora of tropical East Africa*, edited and largely written by botanists at the Royal Botanic Gardens, Kew, England, with the co-operation of local scientists. This is a very full and useful work, but has several disadvantages for the general enquirer. Firstly, it is incomplete, and looks like staying incomplete for a number of years. Second, the whole work will run to several thousand pages and be too bulky and expensive for any but the most serious student, since it treats of all East Africa and not simply Kenya. Finally the sedges (Cyperaceae) have all recently been ordered and keyed by the late Miss D. M. Napper in the *Journal of the East Africa Natural History Society* Nos. 106 (**24**, 1963), 109 (**24**, 1964), 110 (**25**, 1965), 113 (**26**, 1966) and 124 (**28**, 1971). They are therefore omitted from this book.

Here then is the first relatively concise account of the Kenya wild flowers and ferns. It includes everything that we have had access to of herbs and climbers, as well as those shrubs omitted from *Kenya trees and shrubs*. It is by no means complete, for new discoveries are continually being made and new research will yield a better understanding of existing material, but I expect it to cover over 90 per cent of the total.

The area covered is roughly central and western Kenya, especially the high altitude centres of population. This area was chosen after much consultation as being that area which could be covered in the field from Nairobi. Two major areas not covered (although naturally most of the species are common to our area) are the coast and the Taita Hills. The area is delimited in the map on p. 2.

While I have been responsible for the editing of this work and its general preparation, its completion would not have been possible without help from numerous experts who have generously given their time. The principal contributor in terms of numbers of entire families is undoubtedly Mr. M. A. Hanid who was my research assistant in the University of Nairobi during 1965-1968 and who was jointly responsible for the 1966 Check List. He wrote the accounts of the following families: Capparidaceae, Chenopodiaceae, Elatinaceae, Liliaceae (except *Aloe*), Linaceae, Lythraceae, Hernandiaceae, Malpighiaceae, Naiadaceae, Onagraceae, Pontederiaceae, Portulacaceae, Smilacaceae, Tiliaceae, Trapaceae, Turneraceae, Zygophyllaceae.

Because researchers may like to refer questions to individual authors, I list below the groups which have been dealt with by every contributing expert.

CONTRIBUTORS

Author	Address	Groups dealt with
Archer, P.	Box 12309, Nairobi.	*Ceropegia*
Earle-Smith, C.	U.S.D.A., New Crops, Research Branch, Beltsville, Maryland 20705. U.S.A.	*Vernonia* sect. Stengelia

Author	Address	Groups dealt with
Faden, R. B.	Botany Department Washington University, St Louis, Mo 63130 U.S.A.	Commelinaceae, Pteridophytes
Gillett, J. B.	East African Herbarium, PO Box 45166, Nairobi.	*Indigofera, Vigna, Tephrosia, Sesbania, Trifolium* and smaller genera in the Papilionaceae
Griffiths, R.	University College of Wales Aberystwyth, Wales.	Primulaceae
Hepper, F. N.	Royal Botanic Gardens, Kew, Richmond, Surrey, England.	Lemnaceae
Ihlenfeldt, H. D.	Freie und Hansestadt Hamburg, 2000 Hamburg 36, Jungiusstrasse 6–8.	Pedaliaceae
Kabuye, C. H. S.	East Africa Herbarium, PO Box 45166, Nairobi.	Oxalidaceae, Boraginaceae (in part)
Kibe, S. K.	Kenya National Parks PO Box 2076, Nairobi.	Ericaceae (in part), Oleaceae, Apocynaceae, Caprifoliaceae, Valerianaceae, Dipsacaceae, Rosaceae, Celastraceae (in part), Balanophoraceae, Rhamnaceae, Sapindaceae
Kokwaro, J. O.	University of Nairobi PO Box 30197, Nairobi.	Geraniaceae
Lye, Kåre	Botanical Institute of Norway, 1432 Vollebekk, Norway.	Aponogetonaceae
Napper, D. M.		Acanthaceae (in part) and Typhaceae
Peterson, B.	Goteborgs Universitet, Botaniska Museet, Frolundagatan 22, Goteborg, Sweden.	Thymeliaceae
Polhill, R.	Royal Botanic Gardens, Kew, Richmond, Surrey, England.	*Crotalaria*, smaller genera, and key to Papilionaceae
Stewart, Joyce	Botany Department, University of Natal, Box 375, Pietermaritzburg, S.A.	Cruciferae (in part), Orchidaceae
Verdcourt, B.	Royal Botanic Gardens, Kew, Richmond, Surrey, England.	Convolvulaceae
De Wilde, W. J. J. O.	Rijksherbarium, Schelpenkade 6, Leiden, Netherlands.	*Adenia*

Author	Address	Groups dealt with
Wood, D.	Royal Botanic Gardens, Edinburgh 3. Scotland.	Hydnoraceae

ILLUSTRATIONS

All illustrations are referred to in the text as well as in the index. The line drawings which accompany the text were all drawn by Mrs. E. M. Tweedie except for two (*Chlorophytum macrophyllum* and *C. gallabatense*) which are the work of M. A. Hanid. They are all half natural size, except for the few 'habit' drawings of large plants such as Aloes, and these are self-evident.

The plates were made up by Mrs. Tweedie using the Check List as a guide for species order and occurrence. Naturally changes in species concepts and taxonomic groupings have led to some of them being in a different arrangement from that finally adopted in the text. Thus some drawings are widely separated from their descriptions, and there are some plates which group together an odd assortment of plants. Again the coverage of species illustrated is patchy. Some families (especially Orchidaceae) have most of their species illustrated while others have very few plates devoted to them. This uneven treatment resulted partly from the varying availability of material for Mrs. Tweedie to draw, and partly to the prior existence of a collection of drawings, made by her over a number of years, which naturally reflected her special interests. The production of a uniform illustrated coverage of the Kenya flora is a task which will occupy some future enthusiast for a much longer time than available for the preparation of this work.

The writing of this book has been hard but enjoyable. I hope that it will give as much pleasure to its users as it has to me.

Aberystwyth   A.D.Q.A.
October, 1973

ACKNOWLEDGEMENTS

THERE are so many to whom I owe a debt of gratitude that this section is likely to be a long one; I would like to acknowledge all the help that I have received during all phases of the preparation of this book from the start of collecting and working in Kenya to writing the account and the final publication. And because none of this work would have become generally available without the last step of publication I shall start with that. For, quite simply, this book would never have appeared without the generosity of a group of donors who were informed of the need for it by Mr. L. A. S. Grumbley and Mr. R. Houghton. Mr. Grumbley is a keen naturalist who elicited great generosity from commercial firms of Nairobi (including his own of Brooke-Bond Liebig Kenya Ltd.) as well as from the Kenya Horticultural Society. Mr. Houghton of the Oxford University Press (East Africa) has consistently encouraged this book's publication. Sir Michael Blundell K.B.E. also kindly assisted in attracting donors. All of them spent a great deal of time and energy on behalf of this book; its publication is their vindication and I am sincerely grateful to them.

The following institutions and individuals have contributed:

The Kenya Horticultural Society
Brooke-Bond Liebig Kenya Ltd.
Hoechst E.A. Ltd.
Shell Chemical Co. of E.A. Ltd.
Twiga Chemical Industries Ltd.
E.A. Natural History Society
Kenya Breweries Ltd.
Barclays Bank International Ltd.
Steel Supplies of Kenya Ltd.
Mrs. E. D. Polhill
Dr. R. R. Scott

Dried plant (herbarium) specimens from the East African Herbarium at Nairobi, the Herbarium of the University of Nairobi, as well as, in certain cases, those of other herbaria have been used. We have drawn freely on advice and knowledge of others, and stand in their debt. This is particularly the case with those herbarium workers who made sense of so many puzzling groups before we started work. Principally these are Dr. P. J. Greenway, Dr. B. Verdcourt, Mr. P. R. O. Bally, and Mr. J. B. Gillett. This book could not have been written without their earlier work, and it gives me pleasure to acknowledge it here.

The Flora project was started in 1965 with a generous grant from the Ford Foundation through the East Africanisation Committee of the University of East Africa. In 1966 a Check List was issued in mimeographed form which listed nearly 3000 species. This was written under the joint authorship of myself and Mr. M. A. Hanid, who has also been responsible for so many of the families in this work.

I am most grateful to the Ford Foundation and its executors, the University of East Africa, who had the foresight to provide the funds, and to the University of Nairobi who provided working space and facilities. The successive Botanists-in-Charge of the East African Herbarium (Bernard Verdcourt, Jan Gillett, and Christine Kabuye), and through them the East African Agriculture and Forestry Research Organisation, have afforded every opportunity for me and my students to work on their premises and use their collections. I would like to mention especially the debt I owe to Mr. J. B. Gillett who has been involved in consultation on this flora since its inception. He has exerted an influence far beyond the contribution he has made to the Papilionaceae.

The staff of the Herbarium of the Royal Botanic Gardens, Kew have always been my friends and mentors. Many of them have contributed parts of this book and this acknowledgement is an inadequate return for the time they have spent on it. Of those who are not recorded through writing an account I would like to mention the following who each helped with the families given after their name: G. Lucas (Malvaceae), R. Taylor (Lentibulariaceae), C. Jeffrey (Compositae) and B. Verdcourt (Rubiaceae) while Roger and Diana Polhill have provided friendly encouragement and much help throughout. One member of Kew staff who is sadly no longer with us is Miss Diana Napper who died so tragically in 1972. Diana entered enthusiastically into the project and provided most of the account of the Acanthaceae.

I would also like to thank Dr. Bengt Jonsell of the Institute of Systematic Botany, Uppsala for help with the Cruciferae.

So much for the written work. The drawings that will, I hope, make this work of value to amateurs, students and beginners were executed by Mrs. Marjorie Tweedie of Kitale. Mrs. Tweedie also contributed by collection, annotation, and textual criticism while the writing was being completed. She is responsible for the treatment of western Kenya plants being much fuller and more complete than it would otherwise have been. The other major aid has come from the Kenya Science Teachers' College, where Dr. Ake Strid and others provided rich herbarium material, and tested the keys as they were produced. During the production of the Check List and enumeration many of my students were involved. Only one of these has been able to complete a family (S. K. Kibe) and his name is thus recorded, but the contribution of the others was essential and important and I should like to record their names here: Mr. H. Adenya, Mr. I. R. Aggundey, Mr. P. M. B. Champsi, Miss P. K. Cheema, Mr. C. Dhatemwa, Miss C. Khatri, Mr. A. Mendes, Mr. J. C. Ngethe, Mr. L. Nhwani.

Staff of the University College Nairobi who have given care and attention to my demands on behalf of this flora are Mrs. S. Sachdeva and Miss Phyllis Wakaba who have typed the bulk of the manuscript, and Mr. S. Kiniaruh and Mr. S. G. Mathenge who have assisted with the collection and collation of many thousands of herbarium specimens. Miss H. Bigwood has spent much time collating the manuscript and typescript and has helped with proof reading. The Clarendon Press have been very sympathetic and helpful, and have increased my pleasure in seeing the book take shape. Clearly I have received a great deal of help and these words are a poor expression of my gratitude.

Finally, without the help and encouragement of my wife, in the field, in the herbarium, and with production, this work would never have been completed.

THE LAYOUT
OF THE FLORA

WITH over two and a half thousand species to be dealt with, many from families which require thorough revision in East Africa, it must always be remembered that this is a first attempt, which will, I hope, become more useful as it becomes more amended. The object has been to present an account of as many of the total number of species present in our area as possible. The species must be defined and identifiable through this book, and thus I have laid emphasis on the keys. These are all strictly dichotomous (asking only two questions at every point) and balanced between the pairs of questions. To the beginner, the number of specialized terms used appears formidable, and although I have attempted to keep these down to the minimum, it is inevitable that the names of leaf shapes, for instance, should be initially unfamiliar. However, even a trained botanist needs to learn to use a new key and I hope that perseverance will yield faster identifications with these keys.

Family descriptions are given here mainly for the benefit of students. Generic descriptions are given for the aid of serious naturalists who may discover new species of a genus or specimens which do not quite 'fit' a key, and who wish to check the generic identification of their plant. Specific descriptions are kept to a short habit description. In some families this is longer than in others, and there is some inconsistency here. For instance the Curcurbitaceae have very short descriptions because the account follows closely that of C. Jeffrey (1967) in FTEA whereas the Orchidaceae have been given longer specific descriptions because of the intricate nature of distinctions within that group. In general I have tried to avoid repeating too many of the characters used in the specific keys within their descriptions.

After the description there is a short statement of the habitat and abundance of the species followed by a number of letters which indicate its recorded range in Upland Kenya. These follow a subdivision of our area into smaller areas which are ecologically more or less homogeneous. The citation of these areas starts in the highlands (prefix H) and continues with the lowlands, giving north-west first and south-east last.

These areas are shown on the map and are defined as follows:

HE :   (Highlands Elgon) Kenya Elgon above 6000 ft.
HC :   (Highlands Cherangani) Cherangani above 6000 ft on east and 7000 ft on west, bounded on south by line east-west across narrowest point. Includes Mt. Seker over 7000 ft.
HT :   (Highlands Tinderet) Plateau and Tinderet highlands above 6000 ft on east (with the exception of the section between the Nakuru/Baringo district boundary and the Nakuru–Kisumu Railway where the 7000 ft contour is used) and 7000 ft on west, bounded on north by HC and on south by Nakuru–Kisumu railway.
HM :   (Highlands Mau) 7000 ft contour defines except in the north where it bounds on HT.
HL :   (Highlands Loita) Loita hills above 7000 ft.
HA :   (Highlands Aberdares) Aberdare range above 7000 ft on the west (extended along scarp to Ngong in south and straightened to include Marmanet forest in the north). On the east boundary from the north is the 7000 ft contour until the Laikipia/Nyeri boundary which it follows to the Nanyuki railway and then the latter to the 5000 ft contour. This contour is taken south to Fort Hall where the rail line is again used south to the Nairobi extra-provincial boundary, which is taken north and west of Nairobi until an undemarcated 'loop' can extend round the Ngong hills.
HK: (Highlands Kenya) Mt. Kenya above 5000 ft on the south and east, and 7000 ft on the north and west. South-west is the boundary with HA along the railway.

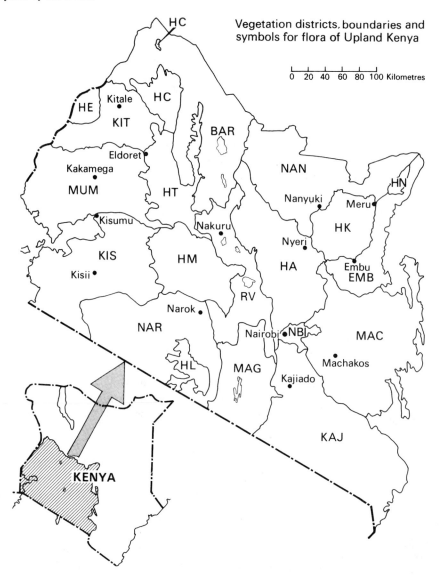

Vegetation districts, boundaries and symbols for flora of Upland Kenya

HN : (Highlands Nyambeni) Nyambeni hills over 5000 ft.
KIT : (Kitale) Below 7000 ft (where it borders on HE, HC, and HT), the West Pokot/Trans Nzoia boundary in the north, the Uganda border in the west, and the Eldoret–Tororo railway in the south.
MUM : (Mumias—after the early kingdom) Below 7000 ft (where it borders on HT) and north of the Kisumu–Nakuru railway, its eastern boundary is the Uganda border and Lake Victoria.
KIS : (Kisii) Below 7000 ft (where it borders on HM), the southern boundary is the Tanzania border, its eastern boundary is the Narok/Nyanza administrative boundary (the old Nyanza/Masai provinces or K5/K6 in FTEA).
NAR : (Narok) Below 7000 ft (which defines the boundary with HM and HL), on the west it adjoins KIS, on the south Tanzania, and in the East the boundary extends north from the Nguruman escarpment to the Ewaso Nyiro and thence up the Siyabei river to 7000 ft.
BAR : (Baringo) In the north the administrative boundary with Turkana and Northern Frontier provinces, in the east the 5000 ft contour, and in the south the 6000 ft contour (adjoining HT

and eastern HC) except for the boundary between Nakuru/Baringo districts in the east, and, in the west, the 7000 ft contour on the northern Cheranganis.

RV : (Rift Valley) This is delimited in the south by the 5000 ft contour, and on all other sides by boundaries with NAR, HM, HT, BAR, and HA.

MAG : (Magadi) This adjoins the already delimited NAR in the west, and the remainder of its boundary is given by the Tanzania border and the 5000 ft contour.

NAN : (Nanyuki) This adjoins BAR, HA, HK, and HN as already delimited in the south and east, while the northern edge follows the northern frontier/central province boundary until the 3000 ft contour is reached in the east, which is thereafter followed. The area boundary with EMB is not shown on a map and is simply drawn so as to divide EMB from NAN.

EMB : (Embu) In the east the 3000 ft contour and in the south the Tana River bound this area. The adjoining NAN, HN, and HK have already been delimited.

MAC : (Machakos) The boundaries with EMB and HA have already been stated. In the east the 3000 ft contour delimits the area while in the south the railway (which is also the old central province/Masai boundary, or K4/K6).

NBI : Nairobi extra provincial area.

KAJ : (Kajiado) This is bounded by MAG, RV, HA, MAC, and by the 3000 ft contour in the east, and the Tanzania border in the south.

Lastly, at the end of each species description, is a list of specimens which are cited by the collector's name and number on a herbarium sheet which has been seen by the author and compared with other material from Kenya. This is to allow future workers to use these authentic specimens for an exact revision of the names and concepts used. Mostly two specimens are cited, one from the East African herbarium and one from the herbarium of the University College Nairobi, except in those families which have been written by workers outside Kenya. These include the *Thymeliaceae, Papilionaceae, Convolvulaceae, Pedaliaceae,* and *Lemnaceae,* and within these families specimens are cited from Kew or the East African herbarium only.

Sometimes reference is made to the fact that a species or genus has been mentioned in one of the source works for our area. The titles of these works are abbreviated as follows:

FTA–*Flora of tropical Africa* edited by D. Oliver *et al.,* 1868 and later dates.

FTEA–*Flora of tropical East Africa* edited by W. B. Turrill and E. Milne–Redhead *et al.,* 1952 onwards.

FWTA–*Flora of west tropical Africa* by J. Hutchinson and J. M. Dalziel, edited by R. W. J. Keay and F. N. Hepper, 1954 and later dates.

KTS–*Kenya trees and shrubs* by I. R. Dale and P. J. Greenway, 1961.

Specimens are often cited as 'in EAH' when they are to be found in the East African Herbarium, of which the official abbreviation in the World List of Herbaria (*Index Herbariorum* (1954–9) by Lanjouw and Staflew) is EA.

In the preparation of this book we issued a cyclostyled 'Check List' in 1966 which was widely circulated to schools in East Africa and to scientists overseas. Thus in some places it has been necessary to refer to names that have been used in this list.

Serious students of the flora of Kenya will have to consult the above works from time to time. Beginners who are unfamiliar with botanical terms will find *A Luo-English botanical dictionary of plant names and uses* by J. O. Kokwaro (1972, E. A. Publishing House) extremely useful. The order of families follows J. Hutchinson's *The families of flowering plants, Dicotyledons* (1926) and *Monocotyledons* (1934).

KEY TO THE
FAMILIES OF HERBS
IN UPLAND KENYA

THIS key is strictly artificial and deals only with those plants which are not in Dale and Greenway's *Kenya trees and shrubs*. Thus it is not useful for all plants found in Upland Kenya, and although it should be possible to look up most herbs or climbers, small shrubs may or may not key out successfully.

Flowering and fruiting material will be needed to key out most families, but one might be able to obtain a short list of the possibilities with incomplete material. If your plant is a fern or bears spores, turn to p. 13.

1 Plants parasitic; (without green colour if growing out of the ground or often with green colour if growing out of tree branches)   2
    Plants not parasitic   7

PARASITES

2 Plants climbing with suckers   3
    Plants erect, not climbing   4

3 Flowers aggregated
            85. Convolvulaceae (530)
    Flowers solitary   1. Lauraceae (75)

4 Plants growing out of the ground   5
    Plants attached to tree branches
            62. Loranthaceae (326)

5 Flowers solitary   8. Hydnoraceae (84)
    Flowers in racemes or dense aggregations   6

6 Flowers yellow or blue, in racemes
            87. Orobanchaceae (567)
    Flowers crimson, in masses
            64. Balanophoraceae (338)

7 Floating or submerged aquatics, sometimes closely appressed to rocks in moving streams   8
    Terrestrial plants or, if growing in flooded soil, then with emergent leaves   26

AQUATIC PLANTS

8 Plants free-floating, without soil anchorage   9
    Plants rooted in the soil or on rocks   16

9 Plants completely submerged   10
    Plants with leaves floating or emergent   13

10 Plants with tiny bladders; stem with alternately arranged branches
            88. Lentibulariaceae (569)

    Plants without bladders; leaves whorled or opposite   11

11 Leaf blade flat   94. Hydrocharitaceae (648)
    Leaf blade cylindrical or of fine divisions, not flat   12

12 Leaves simple, opposite
            98. Najadaceae (652)
    Leaves divided, whorled
            4. Ceratophyllaceae (81)

13 Plants stemless   14
    Plants with a distinct stem and swollen roots
            36. Onagraceae (155)

14 Plants consisting of a rosette of leaves, erect or spreading from a centre   15
    Plants consisting of green floating fragments
            107. Lemnaceae (706)

15 Leaves with a distinct petiole and lamina
            37. Trapaceae (157)
    Leaves without a distinct petiole and lamina
            106. Araceae (701)

16 Plants appressed to rocks in fast-moving water
            20. Podostemaceae (109)
    Plants rooted in mud   17

17 Leaves orbicular, mostly floating   18
    Leaves linear to ovate, floating or immersed   19

18 Flowers with many petals and stamens, solitary   5. Nympheaceae (81)
    Flowers with only 5 petals and stamens, in small clusters   78. Gentianaceae (501)

19 Stems elongated, leafy   20
    Plants stemless except for the inflorescence stalk   24

20 Leaves pinnate, in whorls
            38. Haloragaceae (158)

Leaves undivided, opposite or alternate   **21**

21 Leaves stipulate
                    97. Potamogetonaceae (652)
Leaves without stipules   **22**

22 Swollen pithy roots present; leaves over 2 cm
    long   36. Onagraceae (155)
Roots fibrous; leaves less than 2 cm long   **23**

23 Leaves serrate   94. Hydrocharitaceae (648)
Leaves entire   36. Onagraceae (155)

24 Flowers enclosed in a spathe, at least in bud,
    or solitary   **25**
Flowers in a spike-like inflorescence
                    96. Aponogetonaceae (650)

25 Leaves floating, ovate or heart-shaped;
    flowers solitary, bisexual
                    86. Scrophulariaceae (549)

Leaves mostly immersed, linear or oblong;
    flowers unisexual, solitary or in a spathe
                    94. Hydrocharitaceae (648)

26 Leaves opposite or whorled   **27**
Leaves alternate or spiral on the stem or
    plants with a rosette of leaves and no
    visible stem   **70**

LEAVES OPPOSITE

27 Plants with milky latex immediately visible if
    stem is punctured   **28**
Plants without milky latex   **30**

28 'Flowers' surrounded by sticky glands, with
    minute stamens within, and frequently
    with the ovary emergent after pollination
                    53. Euphorbiaceae (210)
'Flowers' without sticky glands or emergent
    ovaries   **29**

29 Stamens clearly separable from the stigma
                    71. Apocynaceae (365)
Stamens fused to or very intimately attached
    to the stigma   72. Asclepiadaceae (367)

30 Stipules fused between the opposite petioles
    or leaves constantly in whorls of 4 or more
                    73. Rubiaceae (396)
Stipules absent or if present free from each
    other at a node; leaves in whorls of 3 or 3
    and 4 on the same plant   **31**

31 Flowers sessile in flat or hemispherical heads
                                          32
Flowers in elongated inflorescences or soli-
    tary, if held at the same level then clearly
    pedicellate   **35**

32 Central flowers of the head with rounded
    petal lobes   **33**

Central flowers of the head without petals or
    with acute petal lobes   **34**

33 Leaves with parallel submarginal veins;
    stamens with a joint below the anther
                    46. Melastomataceae (180)
Leaves without parallel submarginal veins;
    stames without joints
                    76. Dipsacaceae (414)

34 Petals absent; sepals free, narrow
                    28. Amaranthaceae (130)
Petals present, fused in a tube; sepals absent
                    77. Compositae (416)

35 Flowers reduced, in a fleshy spike, difficult
    to separate from each other
                    9. Piperaceae (84)
Flowers free from each other   **36**

36 Ovary inferior, below the attachment of the
    sepals   **37**
Ovary superior   **40**

37 Calyx obscure at flowering time, enlarging
    later   75. Valerianaceae (412)
Calyx always distinguishable   **38**

38 Leaves pinnate   74. Caprifoliaceae (412)
Leaves simple   **39**

39 Petals and sepals 4   36. Onagraceae (155)
Petals and sepals 5
                    82. Campanulaceae (509)

40 Flowers zygomorphic (bilaterally sym-
    metrical)   **41**
Flowers regular (radially symmetrical)   **48**

41 Leaves with submarginal parallel veins; fila-
    ments with a distinct joint below the
    anther; corolla almost regular, with spread-
    ing lobes   46. Melastomataceae (180)
Leaves without submarginal parallel veins;
    filaments without a joint except where (in
    Salvia) the corolla is 2-lipped   **42**

42 Fruit a capsule, if indehiscent then winged or
    spiny   **44**
Fruit a berry or dry, splitting into 1-seeded
    portions when ripe, never winged or spiny
                                          43

43 Flowers mostly in spikes; corolla rarely bila-
    biate; style apical on ovary
                    92. Verbenaceae (611)
Flowers mostly in axillary cymes; corolla
    mostly bilabiate; style attached to base of
    centre of ovary and surrounded by the 4
    1-seeded nutlets   93. Labiatae (616)

44 Flowers spurred   34. Balsaminaceae (149)
Flowers without spurs   **45**

45 Ovary and capsule with parietal placentation

of ovules and with only one chamber
89. Gesneriaceae (571)
Ovary and capsule with axile placentation of ovules and with 2 or more chambers   **46**

46   Flowers solitary; pedicels with 2 glands at base; fruits often winged or armed
90. Pedaliaceae (572)
Flowers mostly in groups; pedicels without glands at base; fruits never winged or armed   **47**

47   Fruit hard, widest at the middle or below and gradually narrowed above into a sterile beak   91. Acanthaceae (573)
Fruit usually leathery, always blunt at apex
86. Scrophulariaceae (549)

48   Leaves thick, fleshy   **49**
Leaves thin, not fleshy   **51**

49   Ovaries of 5 free carpels
18. Crassulaceae (104)
Ovary single within the flower   **50**

50   Sepals 2   24. Portulacaceae (119)
Sepals 5   23. Aizoaceae (115)

51   Stamens numerous (more than 3 times the number of petals)   **52**
Stamens up to 3 times the number of petals **53**

52   Leaves divided; flowers white to purple
3. Ranunculaceae (75)
Leaves simple; flowers yellow
48. Hypericaceae (183)

53   Sepals, which may resemble petals, and petals (if present) borne at the top of a tube around the ovary   **54**
Sepals and petals (if present) borne at the same level as the ovary, ovary superior   **56**

54   Perianth in only one whorl, coloured
41. Nyctaginaceae (161)
Perianth in two whorls (sepals and petals) or, if only one whorl, then green or brown   **55**

55   Woody climbers or shrubs; fruit winged, indehiscent   47. Combretaceae (183)
Herbs or shrubs; fruit unwinged, dehiscent
35. Lythraceae (153)

56   Petals absent   **57**
Petals present (often very small)   **62**

57   Stipules present   **58**
Stipules absent   **59**

58   Leaves entire   22. Caryophyllaceae (110)
Leaves serrate at margins
59. Urticaceae (320)

59   Flowers solitary, sessile, axillary
39. Callitrichaceae (158)

Flowers in terminal or axillary clusters   **60**

60   Flowers densely crowded, touching one another in the cluster
28. Amaranthaceae (130)
Flowers in loose clusters, not touching one another   **61**

61   Leaves linear; ovary with free-central placentation   22. Caryophyllaceae (110)
Leaves mostly broader than linear; ovary with axile placentation   23. Aizoaceae (115)

62   Stamens 2   70. Oleaceae (364)
Stamens more than 4   **63**

63   Stamens opposite the petals, alternate with the sepals; ovary with free-central placentation   79. Primulaceae (505)
Stamens alternating with the petals   **64**

64   Petals joined to each other
78. Gentianaceae (501)
Petals free from each other   **65**

65   Plant annual; flowers several together in inflorescences   **66**
Plant perennial or, if annual, then flowers solitary   **67**

66   Flowers yellow, in terminal cymes; leaves whorled   30. Linaceae (139)
Flowers minutely pink, in axillary clusters; leaves opposite   21. Elatinaceae (110)

67   Ovary divided into three, with 3 stigmas   **68**
Ovary divided into five, with 5 stigmas   **69**

68   Plant climbing by twining branches; leaves glabrous   60. Celastraceae (325)
Plant without twining branches; leaves hairy
52. Malpighiaceae (209)

69   Fruit spiny or plant with spines at leaf-bases
31. Zygophyllaceae (139)
Fruit smooth, plant unarmed
32. Geraniaceae (140)

LEAVES ALTERNATE

70   Leaves simple, linear, with veins parallel to each other, without veinlets joining the larger ones   **71**
Leaves simple or compound, veins forming a network in the leaf   **85**

LEAVES WITH PARALLEL VENATION
(MOST MONOCOTYLEDONS)

71   Flowers entirely brown or green, with dry perianth or scales which do not shrivel when dry   **72**
Flowers coloured or, if brown or green, with a fleshy perianth which shrivels on drying
75

72 Flowers crowded but individually distinguishable; petals and sepals larger than bracts
    115. Juncaceae (802)
    Flowers crowded on spikes or spikelets; petals and sepals absent or much smaller than the bracts **73**

73 Inflorescence of one spike with male flowers at the top, female flowers below **74**
    Inflorescence compound or of bisexual flowers
    Cyperaceae (not dealt with in this book)

74 Leaves flat 108. Typhaceae (707)
    Leaves channelled
    Cyperaceae (not dealt with in this book)

75 Flowers in heads, sessile **76**
    Flowers pedicellate or, if sessile, in spikes **77**

76 Flowers black or white, unisexual
    101. Eriocaulaceae (669)
    Flowers yellow, bisexual
    100. Xyridaceae (669)

77 Ovary inferior, borne below the insertion of the perianth **78**
    Ovary superior, borne above the insertion of the perianth **82**

78 Stamens 3 110. Iridaceae (712)
    Stamens 1 or 2 or hardly identifiable **79**

79 Flowers zygomorphic (bilaterally symmetrical **80**
    Flowers regular (radially symmetrical) **81**

80 Stamen 1, with powdery pollen in normal pollen-sacs which enclose the style
    102. Zingiberaceae (669)
    Stamens 2 or 1, hardly recognisable as such, consisting of sticky pollen-masses attached to the much larger style
    114. Orchidaceae (726)

81 Flowers in an umbel with a paper-thin bract at the base, inner flowers the last to open
    109. Amaryllidaceace (708)
    Flowers in cymes (that is the centre flower opening first), with a leafy bract at base
    113. Hypoxidaceae (724)

82 Perianth of 6 parts, all similar in colour and texture **83**
    Perianth of 3 outer green sepals and 3 inner coloured petals
    99. Commelinaceae (653)

83 Stamens 3 104. Pontederiaceae (700)
    Stamens 6 **84**

84 Leaves fleshy, entire, erect from ground level or plants woody climbers or trees
    112. Agavaceae (722)

Leaves spreading or scale-like, if fleshy then with marginal prickles
    103. Liliaceae (671)

85 Leaves compound **86**
    Leaves simple **103**

ALTERNATE COMPOUND LEAVES

86 Flowers crowded on a central spike, subtended and partially surrounded by a spathe 106. Araceae (701)
    Flowers not crowded on a spike or subtended by an enclosing spathe **87**

87 Flowers without petals (although sepals may be coloured); stamens numerous
    3. Ranunculaceae (75)
    Flowers with sepals and petals (often both green); stamens usually definite in number **88**

88 Flowers with petals and sepals in fours **89**
    Flowers with 5 sepals and/or petals **93**

89 Flowers zygomorphic (bilaterally symmetrical) or with fewer stamens than petals **90**
    Flowers regular (radially symmetrical) **91**

90 Corolla spreading; stamens 8; fruit inflated
    67. Sapindaceae (347)
    Corolla tubular; stamens 2; fruit not inflated
    11. Fumariaceae (88)

91 Mostly climbers with tendrils; ovary inferior or almost so 66. Vitaceae (340)
    Herbs without tendrils; ovary superior **92**

92 Ovary and fruit sessile in the flower
    14. Cruciferae (92)
    Ovary and fruit shortly stalked in the flower
    13. Capparaceae (90)

93 Flowers zygomorphic **94**
    Flowers actinomorphic **95**

94 Upper petal inside the two below in bud; stamens free of the petals
    55. Caesalpiniaceae (230)
    Upper petal outside the two below in bud; stamens enclosed in loosely coherent petals
    57. Papilionaceae (237)

95 Inflorescence an umbel **96**
    Inflorescence a panicle or raceme or flowers solitary, never an umbel **97**

96 Ovary superior 33. Oxalidaceae (144)
    Ovary inferior 68. Umbelliferae (348)

97 Flowers unisexual; plants usually with tendrils 43. Cucurbitaceae (166)
    Flowers bisexual; plants without tendrils **98**

98 Ovary inferior   2. Hernandiaceae (75)
    Ovary superior   **99**

99 Stamens 2   70. Oleaceae (364)
    Stamens more than 2   **100**

100 Stipules absent; stamens 8
               67. Sapindaceae (347)
    Stipules present; stamens more than 8   **101**

101 Leaves bipinnate; fruit a pod   **102**
    Leaves simply pinnate or palmate; fruit of separate 1-seeded carpels
               54. Rosaceae (225)

102 Leaves not sensitive; pods winged
            55. Caesalpiniaceae (230)
    Leaves often sensitive; pods unwinged
              56. Mimosaceae (236)

ALTERNATE SIMPLE LEAVES

103 Flowers small; sepals and petals green or brown or absent   **104**
    Flowers with white or coloured petals or sepals   **128**

104 Leaves with a stipule at base of petiole which encloses the stem above the axil
          25. Polygonaceae (122)
    Leaves with free stipules or none   **105**

105 Flowers in leafless spikes or racemes   **106**
    Flowers solitary or in cymes or clusters along the stem, or in heads, never in simple racemes ,   **114**

106 Flowers very reduced so that it is impossible to distinguish the perianth of individual flowers   **107**
    Flowers frequently crowded but with distinguishable perianths to each flower   **108**

107 Spikes surrounded and subtended by an enlarged bract (spathe)   106. Araceae (701)
    Spikes without a subtending modified leaf
              9. Piperaceae (84)

108 Petals present   **109**
    Petals absent   **110**

109 Plant a weak woody climber; inflorescence pendulous   61. Icacinaceae (326)
    Plant an erect herb; inflorescence erect
              16. Resedaceae (100)

110 Perianth of paper-like acute sepals which do not wrinkle when dry; fruit with one seed
          28. Amaranthaceae (130)
    Perianth soft, wrinkling when dry; fruit either of 1-seeded carpels or with many-seeded carpels   **111**

111 Flowers bisexual   **112**
    Flowers unisexual   **113**

112 Flowers in leafless racemes
          26. Phytolaccaceae (127)
    Flowers in clusters or, if solitary, then subtended by leaves
          27. Chenopodiaceae (127)

113 Perianth segments in threes; fruit of 1–3 free carpels, each with one large curved seed
          6. Menispermaceae (82)
    Perianth segments in fives; fruit of 3 fused carpels, each with 1 or 2 ovoid seeds
          53. Euphorbiaceae (210)

114 Flowers sunk in flat fleshy heads
          58. Moraceae (318)
    Flowers in other types of inflorescence   **115**

115 Ovary below the origin of the sepals and stamens   **116**
    Ovary above the insertion of the sepals and stamens   **121**

116 Inflorescence an umbel or with all flowers held at the same level   **117**
    Inflorescence of groups of flowers at the nodes or in racemes   **118**

117 Often tendrillate climbers; flower parts in fours   66. Vitaceae (340)
    Mostly herbs, never tendrillate; flower parts in fives   68. Umbelliferae (348)

118 Petals very small, held just under anthers
          65. Rhamnaceae (335)
    Petals absent   **119**

119 Leaves stipulate   54. Rosaceae (225)
    Leaves without stipules   **120**

120 Leaves with crenate or serrate margins; flowers crowded in terminal panicles or axillary   38. Haloragaceae (158)
    Leaves entire; flowers solitary or in groups of 2–3, not crowded   63. Santalaceae (334)

121 Stipules present   **122**
    Stipules absent   **124**

122 Stigmas 2   59. Urticaceae (320)
    Stigmas 3   **123**

123 Petals absent; stigmas often forked; ovary with 3–6 ovules   53. Euphorbiaceae (210)
    Petals present, small; stigmas entire; ovary with 1 ovule   22. Caryophyllaceae (110)

124 Flowers unisexual   6. Menispermaceae (82)
    Flowers bisexual   **125**

125 Petals absent   **126**
    Petals present   61. Icacinaceae (326)

126 Perianth stiff and papery, drying without collapsing   28. Amaranthaceae (130)
    Perianth soft, fleshy   **127**

127 Sepals fused into a tube at base; ovary with more than 1 ovule   23. Aizoaceae (115)
Sepals free; ovary with 1 ovule
27. Chenopodiaceae (127)

128 Flowers zygomorphic (bilaterally symmetrical) or with fewer stamens than petal lobes   **129**
Flowers actinomorphic (radially symmetrical)   **144**

LEAVES ALTERNATE, SIMPLE;
FLOWERS ZYGOMORPHIC

129 Flowers with a spur at base   **130**
Flowers without a spur at base   **134**

130 Flowers in a raceme   **131**
Flowers solitary or in axillary groups   **133**

131 Petals fused into a tube; ovary one, with axile placentation   **132**
Petals free; ovary of 1–3 free carpels
3. Ranunculaceae (75)

132 Leaves borne on the erect stems
86. Scrophulariaceae (549)
Leaves either difficult to distinguish or all in a basal rosette
88. Lentibulariaceae (569)

133 Sepals intergrading with petals; stamens fused in a 'hood' around the stigma; stipules absent   34. Balsaminaceae (149)
Sepals never petaloid; stamens free from each other; stipules present 15. Violaceae (100)

134 One pair of sepals enlarged to enclose most of the flower   17. Polygalaceae (101)
All sepals more or less the same size, if distinguishable, or not enlarged   **135**

135 Flowers in heads; sepals reduced to scales or a pappus of hairs   77. Compositae (416)
Flowers not in heads, or if so then sepals not reduced   **136**

136 Ovary inferior; stamens joined round the style   **137**
Ovary superior; stamens free or fused to petals only   **138**

137 Anthers sessile around the style column and fused to it   7. Aristolochiaceae (84)
Stamens with filaments, only loosely coherent around the style
82. Campanulaceae (509)

138 Stamens 5 or fewer   **139**
Stamens more than 5   **141**

139 Flower parts in twos or fours; filaments 2
11. Fumariaceae (88)
Flower parts in fives   **140**

140 Ovules attached to the walls of the ovary
89. Gesneriaceae (571)
Ovules attached to the centre of the ovary
86. Scrophulariaceae (549)

141 Leaves without stipules; petals lobed
16. Resedaceae (100)
Leaves stipulate; petals entire or the uppermost slightly notched   **142**

142 Petals and sepals 4   13. Capparaceae (90)
Petals and sepals 5   **143**

143 Stamen filaments joined in a tube
57. Papilionaceae (237)
Stamen filaments free
55. Caesalpiniaceae (230)

LEAVES ALTERNATE, SIMPLE;
FLOWERS REGULAR

144 Plants climbing or scrambling   **145**
Plants erect, unsupported   **153**

145 Plants with tendrils or prickly stems   **146**
Plants without tendrils, unarmed   **148**

146 Leaves stipulate   **147**
Leaves without stipules
43. Cucurbitaceae (166)

147 Tendrils paired at each node
105. Smilacaceae (700)
Tendrils single at each node
42. Passifloraceae (163)

148 Flowers in spikes or racemes   **149**
Flowers in heads, cymes or solitary   **151**

149 Flowers unisexual; perianth with 6 lobes
111. Dioscoreaceae (720)
Flowers bisexual; perianth with 5 lobes   **150**

150 Plant woody with trailing shoots from a tuberous rootstock; flowers green
61. Icacinaceae (326)
Plant herbaceous with twining stems; flowers white   29. Basellaceae (139)

151 Flowers in heads, sessile
77. Compositae (416)
Flowers in cymes or solitary, mostly pedicellate   **152**

152 Flowers unisexual; petals free
44. Begoniaceae (178)
Flowers bisexual; petals joined
85. Convolvulaceae (530)

153 Anthers fused in a tube around the style; flowers in a head   77. Compositae (416)
Flowers not in a head and/or with anthers not forming a tube around the style   **154**

154 Flowers unisexual, with fertile anthers and no

ovary, or with style and stigma but no fertile anthers   **155**
Flowers bisexual with anthers and stigma **157**

155 Leaves stipulate   **156**
Leaves without stipules
                    43. Cucurbitaceae (166)

156 Ovary inferior; stigma forked; stamens numerous   44. Begoniaceae (178)
Ovary superior; stigma entire; stamens 5
                    42. Passifloraceae (163)

157 Ovary inferior   **158**
Ovary superior   **161**

158 Plant fleshy; petals in more than one row
                    45. Cactaceae (180)
Plant not fleshy; petals in one row   **159**

159 Flowers in umbels or apparently in heads if sessile   68. Umbelliferae (348)
Flowers in racemes, spikes or solitary   **160**

160 Petals 4, free   36. Onagraceae (155)
Petals 5, joined   82. Campanulaceae (509)

161 Leaves stipulate   **162**
Leaves without stipules   **169**

162 Stipules forming a sheath around the stem above the node   25. Polygonaceae (122)
Stipules not forming a sheath   **163**

163 Stamens many, with filaments fused into a sheath around the style
                    51. Malvaceae (193)
Filaments free, or fused at base only, in bundles   **164**

164 Stamens 5   **165**
Stamens more than 5   **168**

165 Flowers with a corona of petaloid organs in one or more whorls together with the stamens   42. Passifloraceae (163)
Flowers without a corona   **166**

166 Stamens borne on a delicate cylinder which may bear staminodes between the filaments   50. Sterculiaceae (190)
Stamens free or borne on a central column in the flower   **167**

167 Leaves with sticky hairs which trap insects; stellate hairs absent
                    19. Droseraceae (109)
Leaves without glandular hairs; stellate hairs present   49. Tiliaceae (187)

168 Fruit with a long sterile beak
                    32. Geraniaceae (140)
Fruit a drupe or capsule, without a long sterile beak above   49. Tiliaceae (187)

169 Sepals 2, 3,or 4   **170**
Sepals 5   **175**

170 Sepals 3   **171**
Sepals 2 or 4   **172**

171 Petals 4–6   10. Papaveraceae (88)
Petals 3   95. Alismataceae (650)

172 Sepals 4   **173**
Sepals 2   **174**

173 Flowers crowded in a spike; petals joined in a tube at base; stamens 4
                    81. Plantaginaceae (508)
Flowers in racemes; petals free; stamens 6
                    14. Cruciferae (92)

174 Sepals caducous; petals 4–6
                    10. Papaveraceae (88)
Sepals persistent; petals 5
                    24. Portulacaceae (119)

175 Petals fused into a tube at least at base **176**
Petals free from each other   **185**

176 Leaves needle-like   69. Ericaceae (362)
Leaves flat, broad, or fleshy   **177**

177 Ovary of 4–5 separate carpels, each with many ovules   18. Crassulaceae (104)
Ovary simple, or if lobed, then style single
                                    178

178 Fruit of 4 hard nutlets
                    83. Boraginaceae (517)
Fruit a capsule or indehiscent, not divided into nutlets   **179**

179 Flowers in heads   **180**
Flowers in cymes or racemes   **181**

180 Stamens attached to perianth tube
                    40. Thymelaeaceae (159)
Stamens free   80. Plumbaginaceae (508)

181 Stamens opposite the petals
                    79. Primulaceae (505)
Stamens alternating with the petals   **182**

182 Perianth tube bearing petal-like lobes at its mouth   40. Thymelaeaceae (159)
Petals not borne on a perianth tube   **183**

183 Sepals free   85. Convolvulaceae (530)
Sepals fused at least at the base   **184**

184 Plants with a rosette of leaves and flowers on erect scapes with or without sterile bracts at base, or plants with creeping stems and leafless flowering stalks
                    86. Scrophulariaceae (549)
Plants with leafy, erect, or at least aerial stems   84. Solanaceae (523)

185 Ovary of free carpels   **186**
Ovary simple   **187**

186 Leaves fleshy   18. Crassulaceae (104)
Leaves not fleshy   3. Ranunculaceae (75)

187 Leaves with sticky glands which trap and hold
    insects   19. Droseraceae (109)
    Leaves without sticky glands   188

188 Flowers blue, yellow or orange   189
    Flowers pink, red or white
                        23. Aizoaceae (115)

189 Sepals forming a tube at base; ovary with 3
    stigmas and parietal placentation
                        12. Turneraceae (89)
    Sepals free; ovary with 4–5 stigmas and axile
    placentation   30. Linaceae (139)

PTERIDOPHYTES
(FERNS AND FERN-ALLIES)[†]

SPOROPHYTES free-living, generally medium-sized (20–200 cm long), containing vascular tissue variously arranged, producing sporangia which contain spores; gametophytes free-living or rarely saprophytic, always small (less than 2 cm long) and generally inconspicuous (often passed over as liverworts), lacking vascular tissue, containing antheridia and/or archegonia.

The Pteridophytes do not constitute a single natural group of plants. They are therefore difficult to characterize in any meaningful way. The two subgroups, ferns and fern-allies, into which they are commonly divided, while not necessarily natural assemblages themselves, are much easier to delineate. Each is described below.

FERN-ALLIES (GENERA 1–4)

Stems usually elongate (except *Isoetes*), glabrous or occasionally hairy, never scaly; leaves numerous, simple, one-nerved, generally small (up to 2·5 cm long, except in *Isoetes*), sometimes with a small appendage called the ligule near the base on the upper (adaxial) side (*Selaginella, Isoetes*); sporangia solitary and borne in the axils of leaves termed sporophylls (*Lycopodium, Selaginella*), or solitary and sunken in the base of a sporophyll (*Isoetes*), or several and borne on the underside of umbrella-shaped sporangiophores (*Equisetum*); sporophylls and sporangiophores often grouped into cone-like strobili; sporangia, spores and gametophytes either of one kind (*Lycopodium, Equisetum*) or of two kinds (*Selaginella, Isoetes*).

FERNS (GENERA 5–67)

Stems (which are called rhizomes) usually densely to sparsely covered by scales and/or hairs; leaves (which are called fronds) several to many, simple or compound, with several to many veins; young fronds (of most ferns) uncurling at the apex, the hook-like tip being called a crozier or fiddlehead; sporangia borne on the lower (abaxial) surface or margins of the fronds, usually in distinctively shaped clusters called sori or, less commonly, completely covering the lower surface of the frond; sori uncovered, or covered by special structures called indusia, or covered by reflexed frond margins (false indusia); sporangia, spores and gametophytes generally of one kind (of two kinds in *Marsilea, Salvinia*, and *Azolla*).

Pteridophytes occur in almost all habitats but are most abundant in moist, montane forests, particularly along streams and rivers. Most species are shade-loving and many are epiphytic. Economically these plants are of no importance with the exception of the naturalized *Salvinia auriculata* which has become an important weed in Lake Naivasha. The cultivated *Nephrolepis cordifolia* and *Adiantum raddianum* have also become naturalized in places.

CLASSIFICATION OF THE PTERIDOPHYTES AND AN INDEX TO THE GENERA

As yet there is no general agreement among fern specialists as to family limits in certain groups of ferns. As a result of this and the necessity to use microscopic characters in distinguishing most families, a key to the families and family descriptions have been omitted. These may be found in any of the African fern floras cited below, the most generally useful in our area being Schelpe's 'Pteridophyta' in '*Flora Zambesiaca*'. Even the generic boundaries in some families, notably the Hymenophyllaceae and Thelypteridaceae, are still far from decided. An outline of the classification of the pteridophyte families and genera used in this book is given below.

FAMILY	GENERA	FAMILY	GENERA
1. Lycopodiaceae	1. *Lycopodium*	3. Isoetaceae	3. *Isoetes*
2. Selaginellaceae	2. *Selaginella*	4. Equisetaceae	4. *Equisetum*

† By R. B. Faden.

FAMILY	GENERA	FAMILY	GENERA
5. Ophioglossaceae	5. *Ophioglossum*		39. *Polystichum*
6. Marattiaceae	6. *Marattia*		40. *Arachniodes*
7. Osmundaceae	7. *Osmunda*		41. *Ctenitis*
8. Schizaeaceae	8. *Anemia*		42. *Tectaria*
	9. *Mohria*	16. Lomariopsidaceae	43. *Elaphoglossum*
9. Gleicheniaceae	10. *Gleichenia*		44. *Lomariopsis*
	11. *Dicranopteris*		45. *Bolbitis*
10. Hymenophyllaceae	12. *Hymenophyllum*	17. Thelypteridaceae	46a. *Macrothelypteris*
	13. *Trichomanes*		46b. *Ampelopteris*
11. Dennstaediaceae	14. *Microlepia*		46c. *Cyclosorus*
	15. *Hypolepis*		46d. *Leptogramma*
	16. *Pteridium*		46e. *Thelypteris*
	17. *Blotiella*	18. Athyriaceae	47. *Cystopteris*
	18. *Histiopteris*		48. *Athyrium*
12. Adiantaceae	19. *Coniogramme*		49. *Diplazium*
	20. *Pityrogramma*		50. *Dryoathyrium*
	21. *Anogramma*	19. Blechnaceae	51. *Blechnum*
	22. *Adiantum*	20. Aspleniaceae	52. *Asplenium*
	23. *Pteris*		53. *Ceterach*
	24. *Notholaena*	21. Polypodiaceae	54. *Platycerium*
	25. *Cheilanthes*		55. *Pyrrosia*
	26. *Doryopteris*		56. *Drynaria*
	27. *Pellaea*		57. *Loxogramme*
	28. *Aspidotis*		58. *Phymatodes*
	29. *Actiniopteris*		59. *Pleopeltis*
13. Davalliaceae	30. *Nephrolepis*		60. *Microsorium*
	31. *Arthropteris*	22. Grammitidaceae	61. *Grammitis*
	32. *Oleandra*		62. *Xiphopteris*
	33. *Davallia*	23. Vittariaceae	63. *Antrophyum*
14. Cyatheaceae	34. *Cyathea*		64. *Vittaria*
15. Aspidiaceae	35. *Didymochlaena*	24. Marsileaceae	65. *Marsilea*
	36. *Dryopteris*	25. Salviniaceae	66. *Salvinia*
	37. *Hypodematium*	26. Azollaceae	67. *Azolla*
	38. *Phanerophlebia*		

REFERENCES WHICH ARE USEFUL FOR
IDENTIFYING PTERIDOPHYTES

ALSTON, A. H. G. (1959). *The ferns and fern-allies of west tropical Africa* (Suppl. to 2nd edn, FWTA). London. (Good keys but few illustrations.)

TARDIEU-BLOT, M.-L. (1953). Les ptéridophytes de l'Afrique intertropicale Française. *Mém. Inst. Fr. Afr. Noire* **28**, 1–241; (1957) **50**, 11–49. (Well illustrated but many of the names are out of date; the second part contains the aquatic ferns and the fern-allies and the whole volume in which it was published must be purchased.)

—— (1964). Ptéridophytes *in* Aubréville, A. (ed.), *Flore du Cameroun*. Paris. (Well illustrated but lacks many of our species.)

—— (1964). Ptéridophytes *in* Aubréville, A. (ed.) *Flore du Gabon*. Paris. (Well illustrated, many of the plates being the same as in the above two works, but shorter and generally less useful than the previous book.)

SCHELPE, E. A. C. L. E. (1969). Reviews of Tropical African Pteridophyta. 1. *Contrib. Bolus Herb.* 1, 1–132. (No illustrations; contains the families Grammitidaceae, Azollaceae, Salviniaceae, Vittariaceae, Lomariopsidaceae, Adiantaceae, Polypodiaceae.)

—— (1970). Pteridophyta *in* Exell, A. W. and Launert E. (ed.), *Flora Zambesiaca.* London. (Well illustrated; the most useful published work for our area.)

GLOSSARY

acroscopic: on the side towards the apex.

anastomosis (*pl.* **anastomoses**): the joining of vein branches, usually to form a reticulate venation.

antheridium (*pl.* **antheridia**): the male reproductive organ which contains male gametes; produced by the gametophyte.

archegonium (*pl.* **archegonia**): the female reproductive organ which contains a single female gamete; produced by the gametophyte.

areole: a portion of the lamina, usually polygonal in shape, completely surrounded by veinlets, in a reticulate venation.

basiscopic: on the side towards the base.

clathrate: having the appearance of a lattice; said of scales in which the peripheral walls of the cells are thick and opaque while the central part (lumen) is thin and transparent.

coenosorus: a sorus formed by the confluence of smaller sori.

costa (*pl.* **costae**): the midvein of a pinna.

costule: the midvein of a pinnule, a branch of a costa.

crozier: the hook-like apex of a young fern frond.

decompound: several times compound.

dichotomous: repeatedly dividing into two equal parts.

dimidiate: said of pinnae in which the costae run along the basiscopic margin for some distance, the costae thus dividing the pinnae into very unequal parts.

exindusiate: lacking an indusium.

frond: the leaf of a fern.

gametophyte: the generation which bears the sexual organs (antheridia and archegonia in pteridophytes).

gemma (*pl.* **gemmae**): an asexual bud produced on a fern frond which gives rise to a new plant.

hydathode: a dot-like pore in leaves through which water is exuded.

indusiate: having an indusium.

indusium (*pl.* **indusia**): an outgrowth of the lower epidermis in ferns which covers the sorus. The reflexed margin which covers the sori in some ferns is called a 'false indusium'.

lamina (*pl.* **laminae**): the blade or expanded green portion of a leaf.

ligulate: having a ligule.

ligule: a small appendage borne on the adaxial surface near the base of a leaf in *Selaginella* and *Isoetes.*

lumina (*sing.* **lumen**): the transparent, window-like areas of the cells in clathrate scales.

megasporangium: a sporangium which contains megaspores.

megaspore: when two types of spores are produced, the larger of the two. This gives rise to a female gametophyte.

microsporangium: a sporangium which contains microspores.

microspore: when two types of spores are produced, the smaller of the two. This gives rise to a male gametophyte.

palea (*pl.* **paleae**): the scales which are frequently found on fern rhizomes and fronds.

paleate: having paleae.

palmate; palmately compound: said of a lamina which is divided to the base into segments which are attached at one point.

palmatifid: similar to palmate but the segments joined near their bases.

paraphysis (*pl.* **paraphyses**): a sterile stalk produced among the sporangia in a sorus.

phyllopodium (*pl.* **phyllopodia**): a peg-like structure which is left attached to the rhizome in some ferns when the frond falls off. This is the persistent stipe base.

pinna (*pl.* **pinnae**): the primary division of a compound frond; a leaflet of a frond.

pinnate; pinnately compound: said of a lamina which is divided to the midvein into segments (pinnae) which are arranged like the barbs of a feather. The midvein in such a leaf is called a rachis.

pinnate-pinnatifid: when used in this way, terms such as these are not averaged but are additive. A frond which is pinnate-pinnatifid has the lamina pinnate with pinnatifid pinnae.

pinnatifid: similar to pinnate but the segments joined near their bases.

pinnule: a division of a pinna.

rachis: the midvein of the lamina in a compound leaf; the continuation of the petiole in a compound leaf or frond to which the leaflets or pinnae are attached.

reticulate: forming a network.

rhizophore: a white, root-like branch in *Selaginella* which arises from a fork of two leafy shoots. The rhizophore produces roots.

segment: in a highly dissected frond, the smallest division of the lamina. When small pinnules are very similar to the lobes of larger pinnules, the term segment refers to both of these.

sinus: the space between two adjacent lobes of the lamina.

soboliferous: bearing soboles, which are sprouting shoots that arise just above the base of a stem and grow horizontally. They are slender, have reduced leaves and long internodes, and give rise to new plants vegetatively.

sorus (*pl.* **sori**): a cluster of sporangia on a fern frond.

sporangiophore: an umbrella-shaped structure in *Equisetum* which bears sporangia on its underside. The cap is hexagonal in outline.

sporangium (*pl.* **sporangia**): the case or sac which contains the spores. Sporangia vary in size from barely visible to several millimetres in length.

sporocarp: the structure in *Marsilea, Salvinia,* and *Azolla* which contains the sori and sporangia.

sporophyll: a leaf or modified leaf which bears one or more sporangia on its base or in its axil.

sporophyte: the generation which produces spores asexually.

stipe: the petiole of a fern frond.

strobilus (*pl.* **strobili**): a dense, cone-like cluster of sporangium-bearing structures (sporophylls or sporangiophores).

synangium (*pl.* **synangia**): a structure in *Marattia* composed of laterally fused sporangia.

vascular bundle; strand: a collection of water- and food-conducting tissue (xylem and phloem). A vascular bundle is circular or elliptic in cross-section while a vascular strand is oblong, linear or variously shaped, but not circular or elliptic.

velum: a flap of tissue on the sporophyll in some species of *Isoetes* which partially or completely covers the sporangium.

USING THE KEYS

The keys are intended for use in the field with living plants. Therefore microscopic characters have been omitted. A 10x or 20x lens and a sharp knife (for making cross-sections of stipes) are essential however. A familiarity with the use of keys and a general knowledge of the more common botanical terms are assumed. There are however a number of terms which are used primarily or exclusively for pteridophytes or are used in a different sense for these plants than they are for flowering plants. For this reason a short glossary has been included.

WHAT TO LOOK FOR BEFORE ATTEMPTING TO KEY OUT A FERN

Rhizome: Is it erect or creeping? Is it covered with hairs and/or scales? Are the scales clathrate or not?

Fronds: Are the fronds simple or compound? Is the venation free or reticulate? Are the fertile and sterile fronds (or pinnae) uniform or dimorphic? Are the stipes or pinnae articulated at or near their bases?

Stipe: What are the shape and arrangement of the vascular bundles or strands in a cross-section (not easily determined in small fronds)?

Sporangia and sori: Are the sporangia in sori? What is the shape of the sorus? Are the sori in any distinctive position, e.g. marginal, submarginal? Is there an indusium? A false indusium?

1	Aquatic plants	2
	Terrestrial or epiphytic plants	9
2	Plants floating	3
	Plants rooted	4

3 Leaves in whorls of 3, the upper 2 entire and usually more than 1 cm long, the lower one submersed and divided into numerous root-like segments

66. *Salvinia auriculata*

Leaves alternate, less than 0·3 cm long, each with a floating green (sometimes tinged with red) lobe and a submersed colourless lobe

67. *Azolla*

4 Leaves grass-like, each with 4 longitudinal air channels; sporangia sunken in the swollen, fleshy basal part of the leaf   3. *Isoetes*

Leaves not grass-like; sporangia not sunken in the basal part of the leaf   **5**

5 Stems jointed; leaves simple, sessile, whorled, less than 1 cm long, fused laterally into a tube-like sheath; sporangia in terminal strobili   4. *Equisetum ramosissimum*

Stems not jointed; leaves (fronds) compound, petiolate (stipitate), alternate or spirally arranged, more than 3 cm long; sporangia not in strobili   **6**

6 Fronds with 4 obdeltoid to obovate pinnae clustered at the summit of the stipe; sporangia in seed-like sporocarps arising from the rhizome or the bases of the stipes   65. *Marsilea*

Fronds pinnate to bipinnate; sporangia on the fronds   **7**

7 Fronds bipinnate; fertile pinnae without a lamina, bearing clusters of large sporangia; stipe with one vascular strand   7. *Osmunda regalis*

Fronds pinnate or bipinnatifid; fertile pinnae with a lamina, bearing small sporangia; stipes with 2-several vascular bundles or strands at least at the base   **8**

8 Fronds leathery; sporangia completely covering the underside of the fertile fronds; stipes with several vascular bundles arranged in a U-shape   45. *Bolbitis heudelotii*

Fronds not leathery; sporangia in round sori; stipes with 2 C-shaped vascular strands at the base, uniting above to form a single U-shaped strand   46. *Thelypteris* Group

9 Leaves up to 2 cm long, if longer, then grass-like, usually numerous, each with a single vein; sporangia axillary or sunken in the swollen base of the leaf, or borne on the underside of umbrella-shaped sporangiophores in terminal strobili   **10**

Leaves (fronds) larger, usually few, never grass-like, each with several to many veins; sporangia borne on the undersides or margins of the leaves   **14**

10 Leaves whorled, fused laterally into a tube-like sheath; stems jointed and grooved; sporangia borne on the undersides of umbrella-shaped sporangiophores in terminal strobili   4. *Equisetum ramosissimum*

Leaves spirally arranged, free; stems neither jointed nor grooved; sporangia axillary or sunken in the base of the leaf   **11**

11 Stems not elongate; leaves grass-like, more than 3 cm long   3. *Isoetes*

Stems elongate; leaves not grass-like, less than 2·5 cm long   **12**

12 Vegetative leaves dimorphic, arranged in 4 ranks   2. *Selaginella*

Vegetative leaves uniform, arranged in 6-many ranks or not obviously in ranks   **13**

13 Sporangia and spores of two kinds; leaves ligulate; plants of rock crevices   2. *Selaginella*

Sporangia and spores uniform; leaves not ligulate; plants of various habitats but not of rock crevices   1. *Lycopodium*

14 Stem erect, woody, 1-10 m tall; fronds 1-3·5 m long; tree ferns   34. *Cyathea*

Stem (rhizome) various, if erect then less than 1 m tall; frond length various but usually less than 2 m (except *Marattia*)   **15**

15 Undersurface of frond densely covered with white or brown matted hairs or with brown or whitish stellate scales which obscure the surface in places (if surface obscured by dense, lanceolate, clathrate scales, see 53. *Ceterach cordatum*)   **16**

Undersurface of frond hairy or glabrous, but the surface clearly visible   **18**

16 Undersurface of frond covered with white or brown matted hairs; plants terrestrial   24. *Notholaena inaequalis*

Undersurface of frond covered with stellate scales; plants usually epiphytic   **17**

17 Fronds tufted, completely hiding the rhizome, strongly dimorphic, up to 100 cm long and 50 cm wide (often much less in herbarium specimens); fertile frond obovate-cuneate   54. *Platycerium angolense*

Fronds widely spaced on a thin, long-creeping rhizome, uniform, lanceolate to oblanceolate, up to 30 cm long and 2·5 cm wide   55. *Pyrrosia schimperana*

18 Undersurface of frond covered with white or orange powder   **19**

Undersurface green   **20**

19 Undersurface with white powder   25. *Cheilanthes*

Undersurface with orange powder   20. *Pityrogramma aurantiaca*

20 Fertile fronds simple, unlobed, or lobed less than halfway to the midvein, or if more deeply lobed then fronds up to 0·5 cm wide   **21**

Fertile fronds compound to decompound, or

simple and lobed more than halfway to the midvein and fronds more than 0·5 cm wide
32

21 Fronds dimorphic, the fertile ones long stipitate, without a lamina, bearing two rows of large sporangia near the apex, the stipe attached to the stipe or lamina of the sterile frond; rhizome erect   5. *Ophioglossum*
Fronds uniform or occasionally dimorphic, the fertile one always with a lamina; sporangia either covering the undersurface of the fertile frond or else in sori; fertile frond always separate from the sterile frond (if fronds dimorphic); rhizome creeping to erect   **22**

22 Sporangia completely covering the underside of the fertile fronds; stipes articulated a short distance above the rhizome
43. *Elaphoglossum*
Sporangia in sori; stipes not articulated or articulated at the rhizome, rarely a short distance above the rhizome (*Oleandra, Microsorium*)   **23**

23 Fronds one cell layer thick, often shallowly lobed; sori marginal; indusium conical
13. *Trichomanes erosum*
Fronds thicker, unlobed (except *Xiphopteris* and a form of *Pleopeltis macrocarpa*); sori not marginal; indusium absent or, if present, then not conical   **24**

24 Sori elongate   **25**
Sori round to elliptic or more or less confluent in the upper part of the frond   **28**

25 Indusium present; venation free
52. *Asplenium* sp. *A*
Indusium absent; venation reticulate   **26**

26 Fronds linear, less than 0·5 cm wide; sori 2, parallel to and just within the margin
64. *Vittaria volkensii*
Fronds lanceolate to ovate, more than 1 cm wide; sori few–numerous, not parallel to the margin   **27**

27 Stipe longer than the blade; blade ovate; sori forking and frequently anastomosing; venation prominent
63. *Antrophyum mannianum*
Stipe much shorter than the blade; blade lanceolate; sori separate; venation not prominent   57. *Loxogramme lanceolata*

28 Indusium present; veins free and mostly forked; rhizome often free from the substrate for much of its length, often pendent
32. *Oleandra distenta*
Indusium absent; venation reticulate or free; rhizome firmly attached to the substrate, never pendent   **29**

29 Venation free; fronds up to 7 cm long and 0·5 cm wide, tufted on an erect rhizome   **30**
Venation reticulate; fronds at least 8 cm long and 1 cm wide, tufted on a short-creeping rhizome or widely spaced on a long-creeping rhizome   **31**

30 Fronds lobed, at least in the lower part, the upper, sori-bearing part being serrate to entire   62. *Xiphopteris*

Fronds entire   61. *Grammitis* sp. *A*

31 Sori in one row on each side of and parallel to the midvein; fronds up to 30 cm long and 2·5 cm wide   59. *Pleopeltis*
Sori numerous and scattered; fronds 60–100 cm long and 4–6 cm wide
60. *Microsorium punctatum*

32 Rachis or lamina dichotomously branched or divided   **33**
Rachis and lamina palmately or pinnately branched or divided   **34**

33 Rachis absent; lamina dichotomously divided, fan-shaped or wedge-shaped; fronds of determinate growth, without buds, up to 30 cm long; sori elongate; plants of rock crevices   29. *Actiniopteris*
Rachis dichotomously branched, the segments without a lamina or with a deeply pinnatifid lamina; fronds with continuous growth, with buds, sometimes 100 cm long or longer; sori round; plants of disturbed ground, e.g. roadside banks
11. *Dicranopteris linearis*

34 Fronds pinnatifid to pinnate, the pinnae sometimes lobed or toothed   **35**
Fronds palmatifid or bipinnatifid to decompound   **48**

35 Sporangia covering the entire lower surface of the fertile frond   **36**
Sporangia in sori   **37**

36 Venation free   44. *Lomariopsis warneckei*
Venation reticulate   45. *Bolbitis heudelotii*

37 Sori marginal or submarginal, usually covered by the reflexed margin   **38**
Sori medial to subcostal or rarely submarginal
40

38 Fronds lacking a terminal pinna, often rooting at the apex; pinnae trapezoidal; young fronds often reddish; sori borne on the inner faces of reflexed marginal lobes
22. *Adiantum incisum*

Fronds with a terminal pinna similar to the lateral pinnae, never rooting at the apex; pinnae lanceolate to elliptic or oblong; young fronds green; sori borne on the lamina beneath the reflexed margins **39**

39 Fronds glabrous; stipes reddish or straw-coloured **23. *Pteris***
Fronds hairy or glabrous; stipes shiny black to reddish-brown **27. *Pellaea***

40 Sori elongate **41**
Sori round to elliptic or semilunar **44**

41 Indusium absent **42**
Indusium present **43**

42 Fronds pinnatifid, to 15 cm long, tufted on the rhizome, densely covered with lanceolate, clathrate scales on the lower surface; plants of banks and rock crevices, not usually associated with water
53. *Ceterach cordatum*
Fronds pinnate to bipinnate, 50–150 cm long, spaced on the rhizome, without scales on the lower surface; plants of stream banks and the vicinity of waterfalls
19. *Coniogramme africana*

43 Pinnae uniform; margins usually toothed, rarely revolute; sori at an angle to the costa; scales clathrate **52. *Asplenium***
Fertile pinnae usually much narrower than the sterile pinnae; margins revolute, usually entire; sori parallel to the costa and usually more or less confluent, forming one long coenosorus on both sides; scales not clathrate **51. *Blechnum***

44 Indusium present; fronds pinnate, the pinnae stalked or narrowly attached to the rachis
45
Indusium absent; fronds pinnatifid or if pinnate then pinnae broadly attached to the rachis and their bases contiguous **46**

45 Pinnae articulated; veins free; indusium reniform; sori in 2 submarginal rows on each pinna **30. *Nephrolepis***
Pinnae not articulated; venation reticulate; indusium peltate; sori in many rows or irregularly scattered on the pinnae
38. *Phanerophlebia caryotidea*

46 Fronds 0·5–2 cm wide; venation free (usually obscure) **62. *Xiphopteris flabelliformis***
Fronds 10–30 cm wide; venation reticulate **47**

47 Fronds dimorphic, the fertile ones large and stipitate, texture herbaceous, the sterile ones much smaller and sessile, texture ±

coriaceous; pinnae with 2 rows of subcostal sori **56. *Drynaria volkensii***
Fronds uniform, stipitate, slightly fleshy; pinnae with 4–6 (rarely 2) rows of sori
58. *Phymatodes scolopendria*

48 Fronds with buds at the bases of the pinnae
10. *Gleichenia elongata*
Fronds without buds at the bases of the pinnae **49**

49 Fronds strongly dimorphic, the fertile fronds or pinnae without a lamina **50**
Fronds not at all to rarely slightly dimorphic, the fertile fronds always with a lamina **51**

50 Fronds bipinnate, glabrous; rhizome erect; plants usually growing near water
7. *Osmunda regalis*
Fronds pinnate, the lower pinnae bipinnatifid, hairy; rhizome shortly creeping; plants of dry situations **8. *Anemia schimperana***

51 Sporangia covering the lower surface of the fertile fronds; fronds pinnate with pinnatifid pinnae, fleshy, glabrous; venation reticulate; plants usually growing on rocks in rivers
45. *Bolbitis heudelotii*
Sporangia in sori; cutting of frond and texture various; venation free or reticulate; fronds glabrous or hairy; plants of various habitats
52

52 Sporangia large and united into elliptic synangia which are borne in two submarginal rows on each pinnule; stipules present at the base of the stipe; fronds bipinnate, fleshy, to 3 m long
6. *Marattia fraxinea*
Sporangia separate or too small to be readily seen without a lens; stipules absent; frond cutting and texture various; size various **53**

53 Sori marginal; indusium cup-shaped to conical or tubular **54**
Sori marginal or not, if marginal then indusium absent, or if present, then not cup-shaped to conical or tubular **57**

54 Fronds one cell layer thick (except *Trichomanes radicans*); rhizome and often fronds hairy, without scales **55**
Fronds thicker; rhizome scaly, without hairs; fronds glabrous but often with scales **56**

55 Indusium cup-shaped, 2-lipped, the lips ± equalling the cup-shaped part in length
12. *Hymenophyllum*
Indusium conical or tubular, usually broadened at the apex but not 2-lipped (except *T.* sp. *A*) **13. *Trichomanes***

56 Rhizome long-creeping; fronds spaced; stipes

articulated a short distance above the rhizome; indusium with horn-like projections of the lamina on both sides; scales not clathrate   33. *Davallia chaerophylloides*
Rhizome ± erect; fronds ± tufted; stripes not articulated; indusium with a horn-like projection on one side or without horn-like projections; scales clathrate 52. *Asplenium*

57 Stipes jointed; fronds pinnate; pinnae deeply pinnatifid, articulated to the rachis; rhizome rampant with widely spaced fronds; upper surface of frond often with white calcareous nodules along the margin; sori round
31. *Arthropteris*
Stipes not jointed; frond cutting various; pinnae not articulated (sometimes the pinnules are articulated); rhizome rampant to erect; calcareous nodules absent; sori various   **58**

58 Sporangia large (about 0·5 mm in diameter), easily seen with the unaided eye, marginal or submarginal and often protected by reflexed marginal lobes; indusium absent; fronds narrowly lanceolate to narrowly elliptic, to 40 cm long, tufted on a short-creeping rhizome; rachis densely scaly and hairy   9. *Mohria caffrorum*

Sporangia small (usually less than 0·2 mm in diameter); frond shape, length, and arrangement on rhizome various; indusium present or absent; rachis glabrous or hairy or scaly, rarely hairs mixed with scales   **59**

59 Rhizome hairy on young parts (hairs mixed with scales in *Histiopteris*), often rampant with spaced fronds (short with tufted fronds in *Blotiella*), sometimes deeply buried; fronds hairy (except *Histiopteris*), without scales, 1–3 m long (occasionally less in dwarfed forms of *Hypolepis rugosula*); sori marginal or submarginal   **60**

Rhizome scaly on young parts, rarely rampant, never deeply buried; fronds glabrous or hairy, with or without scales; size various; sori various   **64**

60 Fronds glabrous, often glaucous beneath; pinnae with basal pair of pinnules usually reduced and stipule-like; rhizome covered with hairs and scales 18. *Histiopteris incisa*
Fronds hairy; basal pair of pinnules rarely stipule-like (sometimes so in *Pteridium*); rhizome covered with hairs only   **61**

61 Rhizome thick, woody, densely covered with long, shaggy, red or golden hairs; fronds tufted; venation reticulate   17. *Blotiella*

Rhizome thin, herbaceous, sparsely hairy; fronds spaced; venation free   **62**

62 Sori marginal, very elongate; texture coriaceous; vascular bundles and strands in the stipe numerous and arranged in an irregular pattern   16. *Pteridium aquilinum*
Sori submarginal to marginal, round to ovate or elliptic; texture membranaceous, sometimes firmly so; vascular strands 1–several, arrangement in a U-shape   **63**

63 Indusium cup-shaped, opening outwards
14. *Microlepia speluncae*
Indusium absent, but sori often covered by reflexed marginal lobes   15. *Hypolepis*

64 Pinnules wedge-shaped, fan-shaped or trapezoidal; all pinnules stalked; sori borne on reflexed marginal flaps   22. *Adiantum*
Pinnules variously shaped but seldom any of the above shapes; at least the ultimate pinnules usually sessile; sori borne on the lamina, sometimes covered by the reflexed margins   **65**

65 Stipes with a single vascular strand, often wiry and shiny reddish-brown to black; sori either submarginal and without a true indusium but covered by reflexed margins, or else elongate on the veins and frequently forking   **66**
Stipes with 2–many vascular bundles or strands *near the base*, usully green to dull brown; sori with or without an indusium, neither covered by reflexed margins nor forking   **72**

66 Sori elongate along the vein, often forking **67**
Sori submarginal and covered by the reflexed margins   **68**

67 Rhizome erect; fronds tufted, up to 15 cm long
21. *Anogramma leptophylla*
Rhizome rampant; fronds spaced, 50–150 cm long   19. *Coniogramme africana*

68 Blade deltoid, tri- to quadripinnatifid
26. *Doryopteris*
Blade variously shaped, seldom deltoid, bi- to tripinnate   **69**

69 Sori interrupted along the margin, not more than twice as long as wide   **70**
Sori ± continuous along the margin, often at least 5 times longer than wide   **71**

70 Fronds glabrous, ovate-deltoid; marginal teeth pointed; sori covered by thin, scarious, reflexed marginal lobes very distinct in texture from the lamina; recorded only from Kacheliba   28. *Aspidotis schimperi*

Fronds glabrous or hairy, variously shaped but if ovate-deltoid, then hairy; marginal teeth rounded; sori covered by reflexed marginal lobes similar in texture to the rest of the lamina; widespread   25. *Cheilanthes*

71 Fronds up to 50 cm long; stipes shiny reddish-brown to black   27. *Pellaea*
Fronds 40–200 cm long; stipes green to dull brown or rarely reddish or castaneous
     23. *Pteris*

72 Vascular bundles near the base of the stipe several– many, arranged in a U-shape   73
Vascular strands near the base of the stipe 2, each usually C-shaped   79

73 Sori elliptic; pinnules trapezoidal and articulated   35. *Didymochlaena truncatula*
Sori round; pinnules neither trapezoidal nor articulated   74

74 Venation reticulate; gemmae often present
     42. *Tectaria gemmifera*
Venation free; gemmae rarely present (present only in *Dryopteris manniana*, *Polystichum volkensii* and *P. magnificum*)   75

75 Fronds pinnate, the pinnae deeply pinnatifid into oblong pinnules; margins entire or crenulate; rachis and costae densely and finely pubescent above 41. *Ctenitis cirrhosa*
Fronds bi- to quadripinnate; margins serrate to dentate, rarely crenulate; rachis and costae glabrous or pubescent above   76

76 Fronds lanceolate to elliptic; rachis and stipe densely scaly and hairy; indusium round, peltate; marginal teeth often ending in bristles   39. *Polystichum*
Fronds deltoid to ovate or ovate-lanceolate, rarely lanceolate; rachis and stipe sparsely to densely hairy or scaly; indusium, if present, round-reniform; marginal teeth rarely ending in bristles   77

77 Frond axes densely hairy; texture membranaceous; marginal teeth rounded; indusium with a few long hairs
     41. *Ctenitis lanuginosa*
Frond axes glabrous or sparsely hairy, sometimes with numerous narrow scales; texture herbaceous, rarely membranaceous; marginal teeth rounded or pointed; indusium, if present, glabrous   78

78 Fronds deltoid to ovate; basal pair of pinnae usually much larger than the other pinnae; upper basal pinnule much larger than the other pinnules on the upper side of the pinna; marginal teeth terminating in a short bristle   40. *Arachniodes foliosa*

Fronds ovate-lanceolate to deltoid; basal pair of pinnae only slightly larger than the pinna pair above, or more commonly, slightly smaller than the next 1 or 2 pinna pairs; upper basal pinnule ± equal in size to the next pinnule on the upper side of the pinna; marginal teeth rounded or pointed, rarely terminating in a short bristle 36. *Dryopteris*

79 Vascular strands joining in the stipe to form a single X-shaped strand; sori elliptic to linear; scales clathrate   80
Vascular strands joining to form a single U-shaped strand; sori variously shaped; scales not clathrate   81

80 Indusium present; sori usually easily seen
     52. *Asplenium*
Indusium absent; sori often covered by dense scales   53. *Ceterach cordatum*

81 Sori elongate, submarginal and covered by the reflexed margins   23. *Pteris cretica*
Sori variously shaped, rarely submarginal, not covered by reflexed margins   82

82 Fronds ovate-deltoid, densely and finely pubescent on both surfaces, lacking scales except at the base of the stipe; indusium large, persistent, broadly reniform, pubescent; recorded only from south Nyanza
     37. *Hypodematium crenatum*
Frond shape and pubescence various; scales present or absent; indusium variously shaped, rarely reniform, hairy or glabrous, persistent or caducous; widespread   83

83 Costae grooved above or not grooved, if grooved, the groove not continuous with the groove of the rachis; rhizome scales often ciliate; sori round or rarely oblong-elliptic; indusium, if present, round-reniform and attached at the sinus
     46. *Thelypteris* Group
Costae always grooved above, the groove continuous with the groove of the rachis; rhizome scales not ciliate; sori round, elliptic to linear, J-shaped or horseshoe shaped; indusium present, cup-shaped, elliptic to linear, J-shaped or horseshoe shaped, rarely round-reniform   84

84 Sori ± round or ovate   85
Sori elliptic to linear or J-shaped or horseshoe shaped   86

85 Fronds 100–150 cm long; pinnules of middle pinnae 4·5–7 cm long; indusium round-reniform   50. *Dryoathyrium boryanum*

Fronds 10–30 cm long; pinnules of middle pinnae 0·5–2 cm long; indusium cup-shaped
47. *Cystopteris fragilis*

86 At least some sori J-shaped or horseshoe shaped, the distal end crossing the veinlet to which the sorus is attached   48. *Athyrium*
Sori all elliptic to linear, never crossing the veinlet   49. *Diplazium*

1. LYCOPODIUM *L.*

Small to large, terrestrial or epiphytic herbs; roots adventitious; stems erect, prostrate or pendent, sometimes rhizomatous, covered with numerous, small, spirally-arranged, 1-nerved leaves; ligules absent; sporophylls uniform, similar to the vegetative leaves or strongly differentiated from them, sometimes arranged in strobili; sporangia large, reniform or globose, solitary in the axils of the sporophylls, dehiscent longitudinally into two valves.

1 Plants terrestrial with long, trailing stems or rhizomes, producing upright branches; sporophylls in strobili abruptly distinct from the vegetative shoot and often stalked (sessile in *L. cernuum*); leaves less than 1 mm broad   **2**
Plants terrestrial and erect (moorland plants) or pendent and epiphytic; sporophylls not in distinct strobili, or if so, then these not stalked; leaves more than 1 mm wide (except *L. verticillatum*)   **4**

2 Strobili sessile, up to 10 mm long and 3 mm wide, borne on the lateral branches of the upright shoots   1. *L. cernuum*
Strobili stalked, 20–50 (rarely to 80) mm long and 5–7 mm wide, terminal on the upright shoots   **3**

3 Upright branches uniformly leafy until the junction with the rhizome; leaves ending in a bristle; sporophylls lanceolate-ovate to ovate   2. *L. clavatum*
Upright branches nearly leafless for a short distance from the junction with the rhizome; leaves acuminate but not ending in a bristle; sporophylls lanceolate
3. *L. aberdaricum*

4 Sporophylls in 4 ranks, decussate, strongly differentiated from the vegetative leaves; vegetative leaves tapered at both ends, ellip-

tic to lanceolate-elliptic or, less commonly, lanceolate   4. *L. ophioglossoides*
Sporophylls in 6 or more ranks, or the ranks not easily counted; sporophylls strongly, or weakly or not at all differentiated from the vegetative leaves; leaves broadest at or just above the base, linear-lanceolate to lanceolate   **5**

5 Leaves less than 10 mm long and 1 mm wide; sporangia up to 1 mm wide
5. *L. verticillatum*
Some or all leaves more than 10 mm long and 1 mm wide; sporangia 1·5–2 mm wide   **6**

6 Sporophylls not differentiated from the vegetative leaves; sporophylls arranged in many ill-defined ranks; leaf apex acute or acuminate; plants terrestrial, erect, occurring in moorland   6. *L. saururus*
Sporophylls gradually reduced in size from the vegetative leaves; sporophylls arranged in 6 or 8 usually distinct ranks; leaf apex attenuate; plants epiphytic, pendent, occurring in forest   7. *L. dacrydioides*

1. Lycopodium cernuum *L.*

A herb with Christmas-tree-like upright shoots with a main axis and drooping lateral branches.

This is a plant of disturbed ground such as roadsides, and usually grows in full sun, 4000–8000 ft. It may also occur at swamp edges and is often associated with the fern *Dicranopteris linearis*. HM, HA, HN, NAR, RV, EMB, MAC, NBI. Also in the Taita hills.

Greenway 13814; Glover and Samuel 3345.

2. Lycopodium clavatum *L.*

Upright shoots with ascending branches and often lacking a main axis.

This species occurs in high-altitude forests, often in the bamboo zone, and is frequent on roadside banks at the forest edge, occurring 6500–9250 ft. HE, HC, HT, HM, HA, HK, KIS. Also in the Taita hills.

Napper 665; Bally 4803.

3. Lycopodium aberdaricum *Chiov.*

The nearly leafless base of the upright shoots suggests a subterranean rhizome which would be unique among African species of *Lycopodium*.

The type and sole collection is from the Aberdares (Kinangop). HA.

Balbo 475.

4. Lycopodium ophioglossoides *Lam.*

A pendent epiphyte, when fully developed bearing dichotomously branched strobili which are often interrupted by small groups of vegetative leaves.

A plant of high-altitude wet forest, 5000–8200 ft. HC, HM, HA, HK, KIS. Also in the Taita hills.

Faden 69/092; Bally 4804.

5. Lycopodium verticillatum *L.f.*

A pendent epiphyte 20–180 cm long with filiform leaves.

This is another high-altitude, wet-forest plant. HA, HK. Also in the Taita hills.

Balbo 819; Faden 71/91.

6. Lycopodium saururus *Lam.*

A somewhat succulent herb with numerous, densely tufted, rigidly erect shoots with incurved thick leaves.

A characteristic moorland species, 8300–15 100 ft, it also occurs less commonly in more shaded habitats in the ericaceous zone. HE, HC, HA, HK.

Hedberg 1627; Faden 70/113.

7. Lycopodium dacrydioides *Bak.*

As broadly interpreted here, a very variable species in which the vegetative leaves are narrowly lanceolate and often somewhat falcate and pass gradually into the shorter and relatively broader sporophylls.

A forest species occurring 5000–9300 ft. HT, HM, HA, HK, KIT, MUM, KAJ. Also in the Taita and Sagala hills and on Mt. Kasigau.

Bally 4855; Mainwaring 2503.

2. SELAGINELLA *Beauv.*

Terrestrial herbs with rhizophores; stems erect to prostrate, sometimes soboliferous, with numerous, small, 1-veined leaves; leaves ligulate, spirally arranged, either uniform and not clearly arranged in ranks or dimorphic and distinctly 4-ranked; sporophylls distinct from the vegetative leaves, 4-ranked (in our species), uniform or dimorphic, arranged in terminal strobili; sporangia dimorphic, the megasporangia and microsporangia solitary in the axils of the sporophylls, usually both kinds present in the strobilus, sporangia dehiscent into two valves; spores dimorphic, the megaspores borne in the larger megasporangia and the microspores in the smaller microsporangia.

1 Leaves uniform, linear lanceolate, not in obvious ranks   2
  Leaves dimorphic, 4-ranked, the lateral ones elliptic to oblong   3
2 Branches dorsiventral; megaspores densely reticulate   1. *S. caffrorum*

Branches not dorsiventral; megaspores faintly rugose   2. *S. phillipsiana*
3 Leaf margin white, long-ciliate; branches recurved when dry; plants of dry situations   3. *S. yemensis*
  Leaf margin green, denticulate to ciliolate; branches not recurved; plants of wet situations   4
4 Plants usually frond-like, soboliferous; rhizophores produced only at the base; median leaves ending in a bristle; sporophylls dimorphic   4. *S. abyssinica*
  Plants not frond-like, not soboliferous, usually forming a carpet on the forest floor; rhizophores produced along the length of the stem; median leaves attenuate at the apex, not ending in a bristle; sporophylls uniform   5. *S. kraussiana*

1. Selaginella caffrorum (*Milde*) *Hieron.*

A mat-forming species with branches strongly incurved when dry.

A plant of frequently-moist rock crevices at moderate altitudes (4750–7500 ft). HC, HT, KIT, RV, MAC. Also at Maralal and in the Taita hills.

Agnew 10089; Faden and Evans 69/169.

2. Selaginella phillipsiana (*Hieron.*) *Alston*

A mat-forming species in which the leaves have long white tips.

This grows in rock crevices in generally drier situations than *S. caffrorum* and the two never occur together (3000–6850 ft). BAR, RV, KAJ. Common in northern Kenya. The somewhat similar-looking species in the Tsavo area is *S. dregei* (Presl) Hieron.

Verdcourt, Napper, Glover, and Oledonet 4161; Faden 70/864.

3. Selaginella yemensis *Decne*

This is the only dry-rock-crevice species (in our area) with dimorphic leaves.

This plant is known in Kenya only from the Kabarnet Escarpment, 5000–6000 ft. BAR.

Tweedie 2276; Faden 70/861.

4. Selaginella abyssinica *Spring*

Unlike the other forest species *S. kraussiana*, this does not form a continuous carpet, but colonies consist of many individual, frond-like plants.

Found in wet forests or, less commonly, moist thickets, usually occurring on rocks or banks, 4000–8000 ft. HE, HC, HM, HK, KIT, MUM, KIS, NAR, MAC. Also on Mt. Kasigau.

Faden 67/579; Greenway 9554.

5. Selaginella kraussiana (*Kunze*) A. Br.

A carpet-forming herb with generally longer leaves than in *S. abyssinica.*

A frequently abundant plant of the forest floor in wet forests and in the bamboo zone, 4250–10 200 ft, but most common above 8500 ft. HE, HM, HA, HK, HN, MUM, KIS, MAC. Also in the Taita and Sagala hills on Mt. Kasigau.

Polhill and Verdcourt 266; Hedberg 1517.

3. ISOETES *L.*

Small terrestrial herbs of seasonally wet places; stem a subterranean, 2–4 lobed, fleshy corm; roots arising from the furrows between the lobes; leaves ligulate, tubular, grass-like, 1-nerved, with 4 longitudinal air channels; sporophylls similar to the vegetative leaves, each with a single large, septate sporangium sunken in its base; spores of two kinds, megaspores and microspores, borne in separate sporangia.

1. Velum absent; leaves of well-developed plants 1·0–1·6 mm thick   1. *I. abyssinica*
   Velum present, blackish; leaves 0·8 mm thick   2. *I. tenuifolia*

1. Isoetes abyssinica *Chiov.*

A small, sedge-like plant with tufted leaves 4–20 cm long which are ± semicircular in cross-section.

This plant occurs in sunny, seasonally wet places which remain wet well into the dry season. It often grows in shallow soil over rocks. It sometimes forms part of a 'miniflora' of tiny herbs such as *Ilysanthes* spp. and *Eriocaulon abyssinicum* among larger sedges. Recorded 5000–7850 ft. HE, HM, MAC, NBI.

Napper and Faden 1867; Faden and Evans 71/449.

2. Isoetes tenuifolia *Jermy*

The leaves of this species are generally shorter and more slender than those of *I. abyssinica* and are more nearly circular in cross-section. The velum completely covers the sporangium.

This grows in the same habitat as *I. abyssinica* and was on one occasion found growing with that species. It was known from only two seasonal pools in Thika (5000 ft) one of which has recently been destroyed. MAC.

Faden 71/544; Faden and Kabuye 71/550.

4. EQUISETUM *L.*

Medium-sized, rhizomatous, terrestrial herbs; rhizome subterranean, black; stems green, jointed, hollow, finely ridged longitudinally, often with whorls of similar branches from the nodes; leaves small, 1-nerved, whorled, fused laterally and forming a tube-like sheath ending in small black teeth; sporangia borne on umbrella-shaped sporangiophores, each with 5–10 sporangia on the underside of the hexagonal cap; sporangiophores in dense whorls and forming a terminal strobilus.

Equisetum ramosissimum *Desf.*

A rough-stemmed, colony-forming plant 0·6–1·0 m tall.

This species occurs along streams and river banks. It is rare in our area, occurring 1800–6500 ft, but is more common in the Tsavo area where it occurs down to 500 ft altitude. NAR, RV, NAN, MAC.

Greenway 13100; Archer 654.

5. OPHIOGLOSSUM *L.*

Small perennial, terrestrial (in our area) herbs producing annual fronds; rhizome subterranean, vertical (in our species); fronds simple, fleshy, glabrous, 1–several per plant, margin entire; venation reticulate; fertile frond (spike) without a lamina, its stipe attached to the upper part of the stipe or lower part of the lamina of the sterile frond; sporangia large, borne in two rows on the upper part of the fertile frond; indusium absent.

Note that frequently two or more species are found growing together so that, when one species is found, one should look for others.

1 Frond base cordate; venation prominent
        1. *O. reticulatum*
  Frond base cuneate to rarely somewhat truncate; venation prominent or not   2
2 Fronds narrowly lanceolate to linear-lanceolate; lamina 0·2–0·7 cm wide; apex acute to acuminate   2. *O. lusoafricanum*
  Fronds lanceolate to ovate; width various; apex obtuse-mucronate to acute   3
3 Lamina more than 2·5 cm long   4
  Lamina less than 2·5 cm long   5
4 Fertile spike usually attached to the lower part of the sterile lamina; base of sterile lamina always cuneate; old stipe bases persistent; fronds 1–4 per plant; plants of grassland, bushland or seasonally waterlogged, shallow soil; below 7200 ft
        3. *O. polyphyllum*
  Fertile spike attached to the upper part of the stipe of the sterile frond; base of sterile lamina usually cuneate but sometimes truncate; old stipe bases not persistent; fronds 1 or less commonly 2 per plant; plants of forest glades or edges; generally above 7200 ft   4. *O. vulgatum*
5 Stipe less than 2 cm long; plants of low to medium altitudes in shallow, seasonally waterlogged soil   5. *O. rubellum*

Stipe 3-4 cm long; plants of high altitude, tussock-sedge bogs   6. *O.* sp. *A*

1. Ophioglossum reticulatum *L.*

This plant has the broadest fronds (up to about 6 cm wide) of any of our species and can be confused only with *O. vulgatum* which sometimes has a truncate but never a truly heart-shaped frond base.

It is recorded from forest edges and damp pockets of soil on rock outcrops but probably occurs in other habitats as well. HE, ?HT, MAC, KAJ. Also in the Shimba hills.

Archer 503; Faden and Evans 71/453.

2. Ophioglossum lusoafricanum *Prantl*

The narrow, grass-like fronds which can reach 9 cm in length readily distinguish this from all other Upland Flora 'adder's tongues'.

Grows in seasonally waterlogged depressions in grassland and in damp pockets of soil on rock outcrops at medium altitudes, always in full sun; very easily overlooked. HT, HM, NBI, KAJ. Also at Dandu.

Faden and Evans 71/448; Faden 72/18.

3. Ophioglossum polyphyllum *A. Br.* (see p. 26)

Our only moderately large (sterile lamina up to 5 cm long and 2 cm wide) species which regularly has several fronds per plant. The consistent attachment of the fertile spike to the sterile lamina instead of to the stipe is unique among Kenya species.

This is the most commonly collected Kenya species and occurs in dry bushland, damp depressions in grassland and shallow, seasonally waterlogged soil over rocks up to 6850 ft. HE, HK, KIT, RV, MAC, KAJ.

Faden 68/857; Polhill and Paulo 1017.

4. Ophioglossum vulgatum *L.*

The absence of a cordate leaf-base distinguishes this species from *O. reticulatum*. The smaller number of larger fronds is the best character to separate this species from *O. polyphyllum*.

This is a plant primarily of forest glades and edges at high altitudes, but in the lower part of its range it occurs in damp depressions in grassland. HE, HM, HA, HK, RV. Also in Taita hills.

Faden and Evans 71/454; Napper 1480.

5. Ophioglossum rubellum *A. Br.*

The tiny (about 1 cm long) ovate-elliptic sterile lamina is a distinctive bluish-green colour and is generally prostrate on the ground. The plants reproduce by root buds and tend to form dense colonies. Very easily overlooked because of its small size.

This plant occurs in seasonally waterlogged pockets of soil on granitic outcrops. It has been collected only once in our area but should be looked for on hills in the Kitui district. MAC. Also in the Tsavo area.

Napper 1605.

6. Ophioglossum *sp.* **A.**

The plants in the single collection of this species look like small delicate specimens of *O. vulgatum*. Whether they represent a distinct species or not can be decided only after further collections have been obtained.

This is recorded as growing in hollows between the tussocks in a *Carex monostachya* bog at 11 000 ft (higher than any record of *O. vulgatum*). HA.

Agnew 7233.

6. MARATTIA *Swartz*

Large terrestrial herbs; rhizome short, stout, erect; fronds tufted; stipes rough near the base, with a pair of persistent stipules at the base, vascular bundles numerous; lamina bipinnate (in our plant), glabrous; margins serrate; venation free; sporangia large, fused laterally into elliptic synangia which are borne dorsally on the veins in two submarginal rows on each pinnule; synangia opening by a longitudinal slit.

Marattia fraxinea *Sm.*

The massive rhizome (up to 40 x 30 cm) and very large fronds readily distinguish this species. The oblong pinnules are up to 16 cm long with long-acuminate apices.

This is a species of moist, montane forests, usually occurring along streams, 5000-7500 ft. HA, HK, HN, MUM, KIS. Also in the Taita and Sagala hills and on Mt. Kasigau.

Polhill and Verdcourt 264; Fries 1856.

7. OSMUNDA *L.*

Medium to large terrestrial herbs; rhizome large, erect, without scales or hairs, covered by a thick mass of black, wiry roots (the 'Osmunda fibre' of orchid growers); fronds tufted, dimorphic; stipes glabrous, with a single U-shaped bundle; lamina bipinnate, glabrous when mature; venation free; margins crenulate; fertile frond completely separate from the sterile frond or else only the upper pinnae of some fronds fertile; fertile pinnae without a lamina; sporangia large (about 0·5 mm), dehiscing by an apical slit; indusium absent.

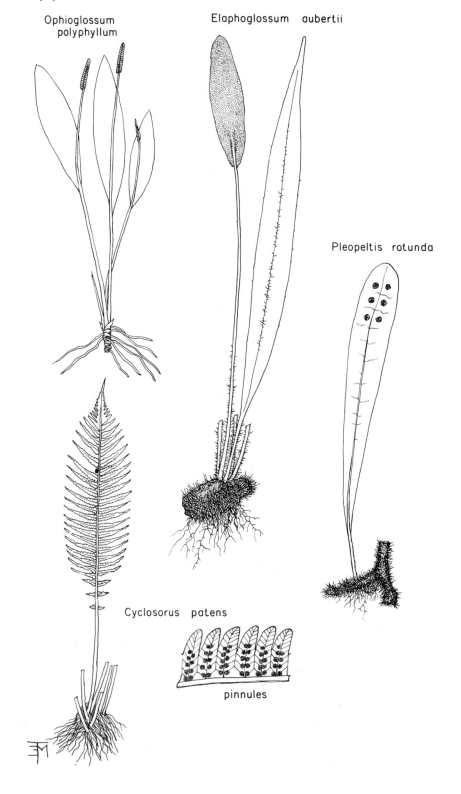

Ophioglossum
polyphyllum

Elaphoglossum   aubertii

Pleopeltis   rotunda

Cyclosorus   patens

pinnules

Osmunda regalis *L.*

The Royal Fern. A very distinctive plant with opposite or subopposite pinnae and elliptic to lanceolate, subsessile pinnules, to about 1 m tall in Kenya.

An uncommon plant of swamps and river banks, growing either in full sun or partial shade, 4750–8500 ft. HC, HT, HM, HA, HK, KIT, NAR, MAC.

Agnew and Faden 9989; Bally 4788.

8. ANEMIA *Swartz*

Small terrestrial herbs; rhizome short-creeping, densely hairy, without scales; fronds tufted, dimorphic; stipes densely hairy, with a single U-shaped bundle; lamina hairy, ovate to ovate-lanceolate, pinnate to bipinnatifid; venation free (in our plant); lowest pair of pinnae of the fertile fronds strongly erect and long stalked, without a lamina, bearing numerous large (about 0·5 mm) sporangia; indusium absent.

Anemia schimperana *Presl*

Fronds to 30 cm long of which about half is stipe.

An apparently rare plant of rock crevices in dry areas, 3000–5400 ft. BAR, MAC. Also from the Garri hills.

Napper 1642; Faden, Evans, and Rathbun 69/400.

9. MOHRIA *Swartz*

Small terrestrial herbs; rhizome short-creeping, densely covered with pale, narrow scales; fronds tufted; stipes densely scaly and hairy; lamina narrowly lanceolate to narrowly elliptic, pinnate to bipinnatifid, hairy and scaly; venation free; sporangia large (about 0·5 mm), single on the ends of veinlets, marginal or submarginal, often protected by reflexed marginal lobes; indusium absent.

Mohria caffrorum *(L) Desv.*

This plant has a superficial resemblance to *Cheilanthes hirta* which however is more finely divided, has much smaller sporangia, and lacks scales on the lamina.

Occurs rarely in high-altitude grassy areas, sometimes in rock crevices, usually fully exposed. HC, KAJ (Ol Doinyo Orok). Also in the Taita hills.

Tweedie 3107; Faden 71/489.

10. GLEICHENIA *Sm.*

Medium-sized terrestrial herbs; rhizome long-creeping, wiry, naked except at the apex; fronds widely spaced, of indeterminate growth; stipes olivaceous, brittle, glabrous; lamina tripinnate (in our plant); pinnae opposite, each with a bud at the base; costules hairy beneath (in our plant); ultimate segments small, about as wide as long; venation free; sori dorsal on the veins, one on each of the ultimate segments, each sorus round and consisting of several large sporangia; indusium absent.

Gleichenia elongata *Bak.*

Stiffly erect plants to 1 m tall forming dense colonies.

Known in Kenya only from the ericaceous zone on the crater rim of Kirui, north-east Mt. Kenya, 8200–8500 ft. HK.

Faden 70/91; Faden, Temba, Karanja, and Gurley 69/527.

11. DICRANOPTERIS *Bernh.*

Medium to large terrestrial herbs; rhizome long-creeping, glabrous or sparsely hairy; fronds widely spaced, of indeterminate growth; stipe glabrous; rachis dichotomously branched; bud present at the base of each dichotomy; pinnules deeply pinnatifid; pinnule lobes oblong and retuse or emarginate at the apex, margins entire; venation free; sori dorsal on the veins, arranged in two rows on each pinnule lobe, ± round and consisting of several large sporangia; indusium absent.

Dicranopteris linearis *(Burm. f.) Underw.*

A colonial fern with stiff fronds which are usually glaucous beneath.

A plant of exposed situations, usually on disturbed soil, e.g. roadside banks, 4000–6000 ft, often associated with *Lycopodium cernuum*. HN, RV, NAR, NBI. Also in the Taita hills and on Mt. Kasigau.

Verdcourt 850; Faden, Evans and Worth 69/707.

12. HYMENOPHYLLUM *Sm.*

Small, usually epiphytic herbs; rhizome long-creeping, covered with hairs or glabrous; fronds bipinnatifid (in our species), one cell layer thick; venation free; sori marginal, terminal on a vein; indusium cup-shaped, 2-lipped at the apex, the lips ± equal to the cup in length; receptacle not exserted.

1	Fronds with stellate hairs	2
	Fronds glabrous	3
2	Rachis winged for its entire length	1. *H. splendidum*
	Rachis not winged, or winged only in the upper half of the frond	2. *H. capillare*
3	Margins toothed	3. *H. tunbrigense*
	Margins entire	4. *H. kuhnii*

1. Hymenophyllum splendidum *v. d. Bosch*
Fronds pendent, flaccid, linear, with the hairs more or less confined to the margins and veins.

This plant grows on moist, shaded rocky banks and tree trunks in wet forests, 6500–7500 ft (in our area). HK. Also on Mt. Kasigau.

Faden 71/105; Faden and Holland 72/186.

2. Hymenophyllum capillare *Desv.*
Fronds pendent, flaccid, linear. It is much more common than the previous species and has more densely hairy fronds.

This plant is epiphytic in wet montane forests and is either epiphytic or terrestrial along streams in the bamboo and ericaceous zones, 6500–10 000 ft (in our area). HA, HK, HN, KIS. Also in the Taita hills and on Mt. Kasigau.

Faden and Evans 69/799; Verdcourt 2947.

Hymenophyllum capillare *Desv.* var. **alternialatum** (*Pic. Ser.*) *Faden* **comb. nov.** (*Sphaerocionium capillare* (Desv.) Copel. var. *alternialatum* Pic. Ser., Webbia **23**, 196 (1968)).

Differs from the typical variety in having the pinnules slightly decurrent on the rachis. The rachis may thus be winged in the upper part of the frond. Small fronds can have the rachis completely winged and can be confused with *H. splendidum* which occurs at much lower altitudes.

Epiphytic or terrestrial, this variety occurs at generally higher altitudes than the typical variety, 9800–11 000 ft. HA, HK.

Schelpe 2592; Agnew, Hedberg, and Mmari 9640.

3. Hymenophyllum tunbrigense (*L.*) *Sm.*
A medium-sized filmy fern with fronds to 10 cm long and indusium lobes toothed at the apex.

This is an uncommon plant of wet montane forests where it occurs as an epiphyte or on rocks, 6500–8250 ft. HK, HN.

Faden, Temba, Karanja, and Gurley 69/516; Faden, Evans and Worth 69/692.

4. Hymenophyllum kuhnii *C. Chr.*
In addition to its generally longer fronds with entire margins, this species also differs from the previous one in the indusium lobes being entire at the apex.

This is the most common species of *Hymenophyllum* in Kenya, occurring in wet montane forests where apparently it is always epiphytic, 6300–8500 ft (in our area). HM, HA, HK, HN, KIS. Also in the Taita hills and on Mt. Kasigau.

Faden 69/115; Polhill and Verdcourt 303.

13. TRICHOMANES *L.*
Small, commonly epiphytic herbs; rhizome long-creeping (in our species), covered with hairs or glabrous; fronds simple to decompound, usually one cell layer thick (except *T. radicans*); venation free (false marginal vein of *T. erosum* may make veins appear reticulate); sori marginal, terminal on a vein; indusium tubular or conical, usually broadened at the apex, rarely 2-lipped; receptacle frequently exserted.

1   Fronds simple, sometimes irregularly lobed; false marginal vein present   1. *T. erosum*
    Fronds palmatifid or pinnatifid to decompound; false marginal vein absent   **2**
2   Rhizome more than 1 mm thick; fronds to 50 cm long, bi- to tripinnate   2. *T. radicans*
    Rhizome less than 1 mm thick; fronds to 15 cm long, palmatifid, or pinnatifid to pinnate or tripinnatifid   **3**
3   Fronds palmatifid; stipes frequently proliferous   3. *T. mannii*
    Fronds palmatifid to tripinnatifid; stipes never proliferous   **4**
4   Indusium bilabiate, not dilated at the mouth; rhizome hairs branched   4. *T.* sp. *A*
    Indusium dilated at the mouth, not bilabiate; rhizome hairs unbranched   **5**
5   Longitudinal drying folds (appearing like veins) absent; rhizome hairs brown; indusium narrowly tubular, 2–3 times longer than wide   5. *T. borbonicum*
    Longitudinal drying folds present; rhizome hairs blackish; indusium up to 2 times longer than wide   **6**
6   Fronds palmately divided   6. *T. chevalieri*
    Fronds bi- to tripinnatifid
        7. *T. melanotrichum*

1. Trichomanes erosum *Willd.*
Fronds 1–6·5 cm in length, in our area mostly linear to oblanceolate and frequently shallowly and irregularly lobed.

An uncommon plant in our area which grows on rocky banks, usually near streams, in wet forests, 7000–7850 ft (in our area). HA, HK. Also in the Taita and Shimba hills and on Mt. Kasigau.

Agnew 9003; Faden, Temba, Karanja, and Gurley 69/499.

2. Trichomanes radicans *Swartz*
The large fronds and thick rhizome readily distinguish this species from all others in our area. Most African specimens determined as *T. giganteum* belong here (Pichi-Sermolli *in lit.*).

This plant is known in Kenya from a single collection from the cave behind Thika Falls (not

Chania Falls) in Thika at 4800 ft. MAC. Faden 68/822A.

3. Trichomanes mannii *Hook.*

The small, palmately divided fronds are darker green and have narrower lobes than the fronds of *T. chevalieri,* the only other Kenya species with similar frond cutting.

This is another wet forest species and is usually epiphytic. In our area it is known from a single collection at 6850 ft. KIS. Also on Mt. Kasigau at 4000 ft.

Faden and Cameron 72/313.

4. Trichomanes *sp.* A.

This filmy fern has fronds to 14 cm long and in general looks like *T. melanotrichum* with which it may occur and from which it may be distinguished by the shape of the indusium. The branched rhizome hairs are not found in any other species of *Trichomanes* in East Africa.

A low epiphyte on tree trunks in moist forests, 5300–6850 ft. MUM, KIS. Also from the Taita hills and Mt. Kasigau.

Faden 69/2045A; Faden and Grumbley 72/338.

5. Trichomanes borbonicum *v. d. Bosch*

The fronds of this species can reach 15 cm in length. The shape of the indusium and the absence of vein-like folds easily distinguish this species from *T. melanotrichum.*

A moist-forest plant which grows on wet, rocky banks (rarely on tree trunks), often near streams. Although little collected, it is probably common in the Aberdares and on Mt. Kenya between 7500 ft and 8500 ft. HA, HK. Also in the Taita hills and on Mt. Kasigau.

Napper 711; Faden, Temba, Karanja, and Gurley 69/500.

6. Trichomanes chevalieri *Christ*

The small, palmately divided fronds distinguish this plant from all others in our area except *T. mannii.* The latter has proliferating fronds which are absent in *T. chevalieri.*

A moist-forest plant, usually epiphytic, but occasionally growing on rocks. It is known in Kenya only from the Kakamega forest, the Kericho area, and Thika, altitudes 4750–6850 ft. MUM, KIS, MAC.

Faden 69/2009; Gillett 16689.

7. Trichomanes melanotrichum *Schlechtend.*

The presence of vein-like folds in the dry state and a conical indusium distinguish this plant. In the dry season it may be found curled up.

This is the most widespread filmy fern in Kenya. It is usually found on tree trunks, uncommonly found growing on rocks. Although found in wet forests, it often occurs in wet places in dry forests, and frequently it is the only Hymenophyllacean present. Occurs 4750–10 000 ft in our area. HE, HC, HT, HA, HK, HN, KIT, MUM, KIS, MAC, NBI. Also in the Taita, Maungu, and Sagala hills and on Mts. Kasigau and Marsabit.

Faden 69/2008; Mabberley and McCall 27.

14. MICROLEPIA *Presl*

Medium to large, terrestrial herbs; rhizome thin, creeping, hairy; fronds spaced; stipes hairy, green, with a single U-shaped vascular strand; lamina bi- to tripinnate, the pinnae bi- to tripinnatifid, thin textured, hairy; venation free; sori ± round, terminal on the veins, submarginal; indusium cup-shaped, opening outwards, attached at the base and sides.

Microlepia speluncae (*L.*) *Moore*

Plants with large ovate fronds with alternate pinnae.

Fairly common in open swampy spots in the Kakamega forest, rare elsewhere, 5300–6000 ft. MUM, RV.

Faden 69/2011; Faden and Evans 69/2036.

15. HYPOLEPIS *Bernh.*

Medium to large, terrestrial herbs; rhizome thin, long-creeping, hairy; fronds widely spaced, often of indeterminate growth; stipes hairy; lamina thin-textured, hairy, bipinnatifid to quadripinnate; venation free; sori small, marginal to submarginal, covered by reflexed lobes of the margin; indusium absent.

1 Stipe and rachis reddish-purple with a rough, red pubescence 1. *H. rugosula*
Stipe and rachis green (above the base) with a soft grey pubescence to nearly glabrous
2. *H. sparsisora*

1. Hypolepis rugosula (*Labill.*) *J. Sm.* (see p. 31)

The finely-dissected fronds of this plant are generally about 1 m long and, in contrast to *H. sparsisora,* usually have determinate growth. Plants from exposed situations at high altitudes are often dwarfed.

This is primarily found in the bamboo zone, extending up into the ericaceous zone and occasionally into the moorland. It occurs in the open, along forest edges, and along paths, never in dense shade; most common 8800–9800 ft. HE, HL, HA, HK.

Faden 70/116; Verdcourt 3727.

2. Hypolepis sparsisora (*Schrad.*) *Kuhn*

A rank species with large (to about 1·5 m long), finely-dissected fronds of indeterminate growth.

A common plant of open areas (usually derived from forest) at high altitudes. It often occurs intermixed with bracken fern (*Pteridium aquilinum*) and is frequently overlooked for that reason. It is occasionally found growing with *H. rugosula*, but it generally occurs at lower altitudes than that species. HA, HK, HN. Also in the Taita hills and on Mt. Kasigau.

Faden 71/888; Verdcourt 3989.

16. PTERIDIUM *Scop.*

Medium to large, terrestrial herbs; rhizome subterranean, long-creeping, hairy; fronds widely spaced; stipes with numerous, scattered vascular bundles and strands; lamina coriaceous, deltoid, tripinnate, hairy; venation free; sori continuous along the margin, protected by a double indusium, an inner true indusium and the reflexed margin.

Pteridium aquilinum (*L.*) *Kuhn*

A rank species with erect to semi-scandent fronds up to 3 m in length.

The bracken fern, the most abundant fern in Upland Kenya, occurs in large colonies in open areas, at forest edges and along forest paths from 900 ft (Shimba hills) to 8650 ft, being most common at higher elevations. HE, HC, HT, HM, HA, HK, KIT, NAR, RV, MAC, KAJ.

Hedberg 157; Faden 67/703.

17. BLOTIELLA *Tryon*

Medium to large, terrestrial herbs; rhizome thick, woody, ascending to short-creeping, densely covered with long, shaggy, reddish or golden, multicellular hairs; fronds tufted, with determinate growth; stipes grooved above, with several vascular strands arranged in a U-shape; lamina bipinnate to tripinnate, densely hairy; venation reticulate; sori marginal, in the sinuses between marginal lobes, covered by the reflexed margin; indusium absent.

1   Veins raised on the upper surface of the frond; axes with numerous, strongly curved, dark-tipped hairs; pinnules of middle pinnae mostly stalked; rhizome hairs red   1. *B. stipitata*
     Veins flush with or impressed in the upper surface; axes without dark-tipped hairs or with a few spreading ones only; pinnules stalked or sessile; rhizome hairs golden   2
2   Veins impressed in the upper surface of the frond; all pinnules sessile; dark-tipped hairs absent   2. *B. glabra*
     Veins flush with the surface; some pinnules stalked; dark-tipped hairs sometimes present   3. *B. sp. A*

1. Blotiella stipitata (*Alston*) Faden **comb. nov.**
Lonchitis stipitata Alston, Bol. Soc. Brot., sér. 2A, **30**, 19 (1956). (see p. 31)

The fronds can reach 2 m in length. The cutting of the fronds is *extremely variable* and small plants are often fertile. It is generally safe to assume that small plants of this genus associated with large ones which can be identified, belong to the same species, since different species seldom grow intermixed.

A common plant of moist, montane forests, about 5900–7500 ft. This plant usually occurs in dense shade and often forms large colonies. HA, HK, HN. Also in the Taita and Sagala hills and on Mt. Kasigau.

Faden 70/75; Verdcourt and Polhill 2978.

2. Blotiella glabra (*Bory*) *Tryon* (see p. 31)

This plant is similar in size to the previous one. The pinnules have a marked tendency to curl, which is distinctive.

Another moist forest plant, it occurs generally at somewhat higher altitudes than the last species, reaching the lower part of the bamboo zone. It grows in dense shade or fully exposed. HA, HK. Also on Mt. Kasigau.

Faden and Evans 69/896; Perdue and Kibuwa 8301.

3. Blotiella *sp.* **A**

This species is exactly intermediate between the last two species, and may represent a hybrid between them.

The only definite locality for this plant is near the base of volcanic cone Kirui, north-east Mt. Kenya. Several plants were found in this moist, montane forest as were *B. glabra* and *B. stipitata*. HK.

Faden *et al.* 69/536; Faden 70/80.

18. HISTIOPTERIS (*Agardh*) *J. Sm.*

Medium to large, terrestrial herbs; rhizome long-creeping, densely covered with scales and hairs; fronds widely spaced; stipe glabrous; lamina bipinnate-pinnatifid to tripinnate, glabrous, of indeterminate growth; venation reticulate or sometimes nearly free; sori continuous along the margin, covered by the reflexed margin; indusium absent.

Histiopteris incisa (*Thunb.*) *J. Sm.*

A colonial plant with fronds glaucous on the lower surface, with opposite pinnae.

This is a plant primarily of the bamboo zone, occurring usually in glades or clearings, 8250–10 500 ft. HA, HK.

Faden 71/876; Mearns 1741.

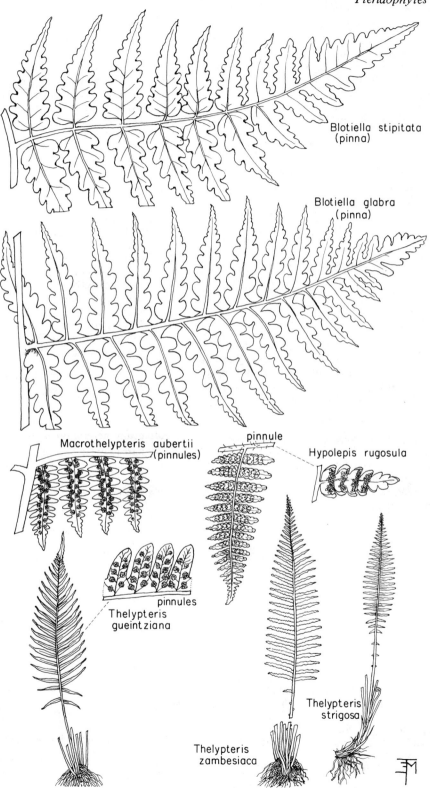

Blotiella stipitata
(pinna)

Blotiella glabra
(pinna)

Macrothelypteris aubertii
(pinnules)

pinnule

Hypolepis rugosula

pinnules

Thelypteris
gueintziana

Thelypteris
strigosa

Thelypteris
zambesiaca

19. CONIOGRAMME *Fée*

Medium to large, terrestrial herbs; rhizome long-creeping, densely scaly; fronds spaced; stipes green, glabrous, with a single U-shaped vascular strand; lamina glabrous, pinnate to tripinnate (at the base), margin serrate; venation free, prominent; sori elongate along the veins, sometimes forking; indusium absent.

Coniogramme africana *Hieron.*

Fronds 0·5–1·5 m long with large, unlobed, lanceolate to lanceolate-elliptic pinnae in the upper two-thirds; lower pinnae pinnatifid to bipinnate with lateral veins numerous and ± parallel.

In Kenya this uncommon species occurs along streams and in the spray zone of waterfalls, generally at medium altitudes. HA, HK, MUM, EMB, MAC.

Faden 69/1982; Fries 2041.

20. PITYROGRAMMA *Link*

Medium-sized terrestrial herbs; rhizome short-creeping, densely covered with dark brown scales; fronds tufted; stipes polished brown, glabrous, with a single vascular strand; lamina bi- to tripinnate with small, rounded segments, glabrous above, densely covered with yellow to orange powder beneath (in our plant); venation free; sori elongate along the veins; indusium absent.

Pityrogramma aurantiaca (*Hieron.*) *C. Chr.*

A striking plant because of its orange lower surface. The lanceolate fronds grow to 80 cm long.

Known in Kenya from a single collection in sheltered spots among rocks in moorland at 8300 ft (crater floor of volcanic cone Kirui, north-east Mt. Kenya). HK.

Faden 70/115.

21. ANOGRAMMA *Link*

Small terrestrial herbs; rhizome erect, densely scaly; fronds tufted; stipes glabrous, with a singular vascular strand; lamina bipinnatifid to tripinnate, glabrous; venation free; sori elongate along the veins and often forking with them; indusium absent.

Anogramma leptophylla (*L.*) *Link*

Plant small, delicate with finely-dissected fronds to 15 cm long (often much smaller) and with stipes reddish-brown at the base and green above.

This species occurs on moist, shaded banks and in sheltered rock crevices, 4900–11 200 ft, being most common above 8000 ft. At higher elevations it is usually found near streams. HE, HC, HA, HK, KIT, RV, MAC.

Faden 67/652; Bogdan AB3599.

22. ADIANTUM *L.*

Small to medium terrestrial herbs; rhizome erect to short-creeping, densely scaly; fronds tufted or shortly spaced; stipes polished reddish-brown to black, with two vascular strands at the base, uniting above to form a single T-shaped, lunular or trapezoidal strand; lamina pinnate to quadripinnate, glabrous or hairy; pinnae and pinnules all stalked; pinnae (of pinnate fronds) and pinnules trapezoidal, fan-shaped or wedge-shaped; venation free (in our species); sori borne on the inner face of reflexed marginal lobes; indusium absent; maidenhair ferns.

1   Fronds pinnate, often proliferous at the apex of the rachis   1. *A. incisum*
    Fronds pedate or bi- to quadripinnate, never proliferous   2
2   Fronds pedate; axes hairy   2. *A. hispidulum*
    Fronds bi- to quadripinnate; axes glabrous   3
3   Pinnules mostly fan-shaped, articulated and falling off with age   3. *A. thalictroides*
    Pinnules mostly wedge-shaped, not articulated, persistent   4
4   Pinnules 3·5–9 (–13) mm long; reflexed marginal lobes reniform to round-reniform   4. *A. raddianum*
    Pinnules (8–) 10–20(–27) mm long; reflexed marginal lobes square or oblong   5. *A capillus-veneris*

1. Adiantum incisum *Forsk.* (see p. 42)

Fronds narrowly-lanceolate to about 30 cm long and 4 cm wide; pinnae hairy, the largest 1·5–2 cm long.

This plant has the lowest moisture requirement of any Kenya species of *Adiantum*; hence it is the most widespread. It grows in moist thickets, and on damp, shady banks in dry forests, sometimes near streams, about 2500–5000 ft. KIS, BAR, EMB, MAC, KAJ. Also in the Taita hills, on Mts. Marsabit and Kasigau, and at Moyale.

Faden, Evans, and Napper 69/254; Napper 491.

2. Adiantum hispidulum *Swartz*

The somewhat fan-like arrangement of the pinnae makes this fern unmistakable; fronds about 30 cm long, pinnules up to 1 cm long, sparsely hairy.

This beautiful fern is associated with streams and waterfalls, 4000–5400 ft, growing in dense shade. MUM, EMB, MAC. Also in the Taita hills and on Mt. Marsabit.

Faden 69/2108; Schelpe 2403.

3. Adiantum thalictroides *Schlechtend.* (see p. 42)

Except for an occasional record of *A. capillus-veneris*, this is the only high-altitude forest maidenhair fern. Fronds finely-dissected up to 80 cm long, with pinnules up to 2 cm wide.

Occurs chiefly in dry, montane forests, extending along streams up into the ericaceous zone, and rarely down into moist, intermediate forests. Recorded 5300–9800 ft, but rare under 7000 ft. HE, HC, HT, HM, HA, HK, KIT, MUM, KIS, BAR, RV, KAJ. Also on Mt. Kulal and in the Murua Nysigar hills.

Verdcourt 2501; Hedberg 65.

4. Adiantum raddianum *Presl* (see p. 42)

The finely-dissected fronds have much smaller pinnules than the native *A. capillus-veneris*, and the veins of the sterile pinnules do not end in marginal teeth as they do in that species.

This tropical American species is commonly cultivated and has become naturalized at Thika (4750 ft) near Chania Falls where it grows with *A. capillus-veneris*. It should be looked for in other localities. MAC.

Faden 68/765, 68/849.

5. Adiantum capillus-veneris *L.* (see p. 42)

This species can be distinguished from both *A. thalictroides* and *A. raddianum* by the veins of the sterile pinnules ending in marginal teeth.

It occurs on rocks in rivers, near waterfalls, and in rock crevices with seepage either in partial shade or full sun. It occurs 3000–8500 ft, but is rare above 5900 ft. HM, HA, RV, NAR, MAG, EMB, MAC, NBI, KAJ. Also in the Taita hills and on Mts. Marsabit and Nyiru.

Greenway 441; Gardner in CM 13093.

23. PTERIS *L.*

Medium to moderately large, terrestrial herbs; rhizome usually stout, woody and short-creeping to ascending, rarely thin and rampant, densely and persistently scaly, or rarely the scales caducous; stipe with one U-shaped vascular strand (rarely with two C-shaped strands at the base uniting above into a U-shape); lamina pinnate to quadripinnate, glabrous and without scales; venation free or rarely (in our species) with a few anastomoses along the costules; costae and costules sometimes with short spines on the upper surface; sori elongate, marginal, covered by the reflexed margins; indusium absent.

1	Fronds pinnate, the upper pinnae always unlobed	2
	Fronds pinnate-pinnatifid to decompound	3
2	Pinnae 20–40 pairs; lowest pinnae reduced, never lobed	1. *P. vittata*
	Pinnae 2–8 pairs; lowest pair of pinnae not conspicuously reduced, always lobed	2. *P. cretica*

3 At least some veins anastomosing along the costules; rhizome creeping with spaced fronds   3. *P. buchananii*
Veins all free; rhizome usually ascending with tufted fronds, rarely creeping with spaced fronds   **4**

4 Pinnules or pinnule lobes toothed at the apex **5**
Pinnules or pinnule lobes entire at the apex **7**

5 Rachis castaneous, beset with numerous sharp spines up to 3 mm long   4. *P. intricata*
Rachis variously coloured, not spiny   **6**

6 Fronds tripartite, the 3 nearly equal divisions of the frond each pinnate-pinnatifid with oblong pinnule lobes   5. *P. pteridioides*
Fronds bipinnate, the basal pinnae bipinnatifid and much larger than the others but not equal to the rest of the frond   6. *P. dentata*

7 Fronds gemmiferous   7. *P. preussii*
Fronds not gemmiferous   **8**

8 Pinnae 16–18 pairs; fronds stiffly erect; costules without spines; plants of swamp forest   8. *P. mohasiensis*
Pinnae 6–13 pairs (occasionally more in some plants from western Kenya); fronds ascending to stiffly erect; costules with or without spines; plants of various habitats, but not of swamp forest   9. *P. catoptera*

1. Pteris vittata *L.*

This species is more likely to be confused with *Pellaea* species than with other species of *Pteris*. It can be distinguished from the former by the rachis being scaly (not hairy), dull brown (not polished dark brown or black) and the upper pinnae sessile. The narrowly lanceolate pinnules are 4–10 cm long.

This is an uncommon plant in Kenya, occurring near streams either in dense shade or full sun, 4000–5250 ft. MUM, BAR, MAC. Also in the Taita hills.

Tweedie 2960; Faden and Evans 69/953.

2. Pteris cretica *L.* (see p. 34)

Fronds to about 60 cm long, somewhat dimorphic with the pinnae of the fertile fronds being much narrower than the pinnae of the sterile fronds; sterile pinnae with coarsely serrate margins.

This is a plant of dry or moist, montane forests, usually occurring in dense shade 4900–8800 ft (rare below 5900 ft). It is much less common east of the Rift Valley than west of it. HE, HC, HT, HM, HA, HK, KIT, KIS, EMB, KAJ.

Hedberg 308; Faden and Grumbley 72/357.

Pteris cretica

3. Pteris buchananii *Bak. ex Sim*

Fronds thin-textured, to 2 m long, tripinnate (those of the similar-looking *P. dentata* are never more than bipinnate). The anastomosing venation does not occur in any other Upland Kenya species of *Pteris*. The pinnule lobes have serrate margins.

This is an uncommon plant of moist, intermediate to montane forests, occurring in dense shade, 5000–7650 ft. HA, HK, EMB, MUM.

Faden 70/388; Balbo 816.

4. Pteris intricata *C. H. Wright*

The large (up to 2 m long), ovate fronds are tripinnate and, because of the long spines on all of the axes, are unmistakable.

The sole Kenya collection of this species came from a swampy spot in a small stream, in the dense shade of a moist, montane forest at 6250 ft altitude. HK.

Faden and Holland 72/196.

5. Pteris pteridioides *(Hook.) Ballard*

Fronds 1–2 m long with the middle one of the three divisions somewhat longer than the lateral two; sori short (a quarter to a half the length of the lobe), medial on the pinnule lobes.

This is a plant of moist, intermediate to montane forests, where it grows in dense shade, 5000–6850 ft. It is uncommon east of the Rift Valley. HA, HK, MUM, KIS, KAJ. Also in the Taita hills.

Faden 69/1990; Bally 1137.

6. Pteris dentata *Forssk.*

Fronds thin-textured, light green, up to 1·75 m long, lanceolate to broadly ovate; margins coarsely serrate. Some high-altitude plants are unusual in having creeping rhizomes and shortly spaced fronds instead of the normal ascending rhizomes and tufted fronds.

It occurs in moist shady places in a great variety of habitats, 3250–9800 ft. It is particularly abundant in open *Podocarpus milanjianus* forests and in some pine plantations. HM, HA, HK, KIT, MUM, KIS, RV, NAN, MAC, NBI, KAJ. Also in the Taita, Sagala, and Maungu hills and on Mt. Kasigau.

Verdcourt 3266; Schelpe 2375.

7. Pteris preussii *Hieron.*

Almost identical to medium-altitude (5000–7000 ft) plants of *P. catoptera* but for the presence of a gemma on the upper part of the rachis of every frond. Where the two species occur together, the fronds of *P. preussii* have more pinnae.

A plant of moist, intermediate to montane forests, growing in dense shade, 5250–6650 ft. This is the most common species of *Pteris* in the Kakamega forest. MUM, KIS.

Faden 69/1978; Faden and Cameron 72/293.

8. Pteris mohasiensis *Hieron.*

This species can be distinguished from the occasional plants of *P. catoptera* with more than 13 pairs of pinnae by its stiffly erect habit. The veins in the pinnules tend to fork about one-third of the distance from the costule to the margin instead of forking near the base as in *P. catoptera.*

This plant grows in swamp forest characterized by the tree *Voacanga thouarsii* (Apocynaceae). The sole Kenya locality is the Kabras (Malava) forest (5250 ft). MUM.

Faden 69/2042.

9. Pteris catoptera *Kunze* (see p. 36)

As broadly construed here, this is a rather heterogeneous species. Medium altitude plants have arching, lanceolate fronds with only the basal pair of pinnae forked. High altitude plants have stiffly-erect, lanceolate-ovate fronds which are more divided. Intermediates occur. The fronds are commonly 1–1·5 m long.

It occurs in wet or dry forests, extending up into the bamboo zone, 3250–10 000 ft. It is most often found in dense shade but tolerates full sun. HE, HC, HT, HM, HA, HK, HN, KIT, MUM, KIS, EMB, MAC, NBI, KAJ. Also in the Taita and Sagala hills and on Mts. Kasigau and Marsabit.

Faden 70/121; Bogdan AB4209.

24. NOTHOLAENA *R. Br.*

Small terrestrial herbs; rhizome short-creeping, densely covered with long, narrow, light brown scales; stipes polished black, hairy, with a single vascular strand; lamina coriaceous, bipinnate, hairy above, densely woolly beneath; venation free; sori continuous along the margin which is not reflexed; indusium absent.

Notholaena inaequalis *Kunze* (see p. 38)

A plant with tufted fronds to 30 cm long in which the pinnae, upon drying, curl upwards, leaving the white or brown, woolly lower surface exposed.

This is an uncommon plant in Kenya which grows in moist, exposed rock crevices, about 5900–8300 ft. HC, HT, NAN, MAC.

Napper 1315; Tweedie 66/366.

25 CHEILANTHES *Swartz*

Small to medium-sized, terrestrial or rarely epiphytic herbs, often of rocky places and roadside banks; rhizome short-creeping, densely scaly;

Pteris catoptera

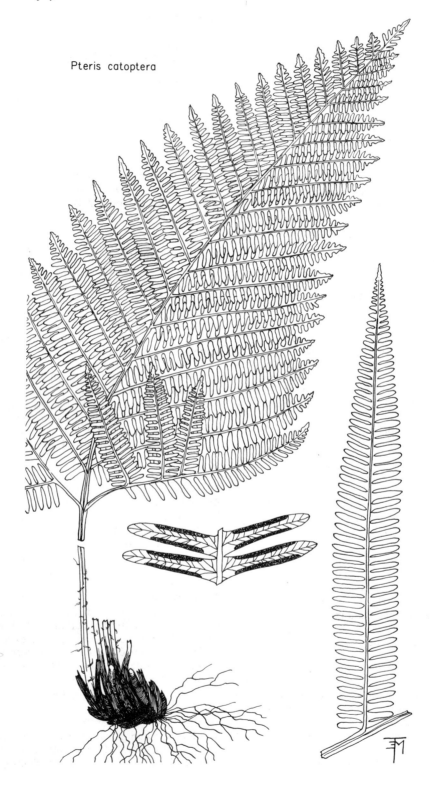

fronds tufted; stipes usually a polished reddish-brown, with a single U-shaped, V-shaped or triangular vascular strand; lamina bipinnatifid to quadripinnate, hairy or glabrous, sometimes with white powder on the lower surface; venation free; sori marginal, short or elongate, covered by a thin reflexed margin or marginal lobes; indusium absent.

1 Lamina covered with white powder beneath 2
  Lamina lacking white powder beneath **4**
2 Upper surface bullate; reflexed margin more than 1 mm wide, more or less continuous; plants occurring only above 8170 ft elevation (in our area) 1. *C. sp. A*
  Upper surface not bullate; reflexed margin less than 1 mm wide, regularly lobed almost to the base; plants occurring at various altitudes **3**
3 Lamina narrowly elliptic to oblong; middle pinnae lanceolate-ovate; plants occurring above 9000 ft. 2. *C. sp. B*
  Lamina lanceolate; middle pinnae lanceolate to lanceolate-oblong; plants occurring below 9000 ft. 3. *C. farinosa*
4 Lamina glabrous 4. *C. multifida*
  Lamina hairy **5**
5 Lamina ovate to deltoid; forest plants
  5. *C. bergiana*
  Lamina narrowly elliptic to oblong; plants of rock crevices or roadside banks
  6. *C. hirta*

1. Cheilanthes *sp.* A

The broad, continuous, reflexed margin is the best character for separating this from the other two 'white-backed' *Cheilanthes* species.

Occurs near streams and waterfalls in the moorland, extending down into the bamboo zone, 8000–12 000 ft. Occurs with *C. sp. B* but not with *C. farinosa*. HE, HA, HK, HN.

Faden 71/69; Hedberg 897.

2. Cheilanthes *sp.* B

A plant of this species is best distinguished from the two other 'white-backed' *Cheilanthes* by elimination: if it is growing at too high an altitude for *C. farinosa* and lacks a continuous reflexed margin, so it is not *C. sp. A*, then it must be *C. sp. B*.

It occurs with *C. sp. A* in the moorland but does not extend into the bamboo zone, 9750–12 000 ft. This plant is much less common than *C. sp. A*. HE, HA.

Faden and Evans 69/792; Hedberg 897a.

3. Cheilanthes farinosa (*Forssk.*) *Kaulf.* (see p. 38)

This is the only 'white-backed' *Cheilanthes* throughout most of its altitudinal range. For distinctions from *C. sp. A* and *C. sp. B* see above. The fronds are up to 60 cm long.

This species is terrestrial or occasionally epiphytic. It occurs in a variety of situations but most commonly along streams and near waterfalls. It is also frequent on moist roadside banks. Occurs 5000–9000 ft. HE, HC, HT, HM, HK, KIT, MUM, KIS, MAC, KAJ. Also in the Taita and Murua Nysigar hills.

Faden 67/583; Verdcourt 938.

4. Cheilanthes multifida (*Swartz*) *Swartz*

Fronds finely-dissected, tri- to quadripinnate, up to 50 cm long; lamina lanceolate to lanceolate-ovate.

This is a common plant of dry forests and moist bushland, occurring on banks and in rock crevices, usually in partial shade, 3250–8300 ft. HC, HT, HA, KIS, NAR, RV, NAN, MAC, KAJ. Also in the Taita and Murua Nysigar hills, on Mt. Kasigau, and at Furroli.

Glover, Gwynne, and Samuel 3073; Gardner 1036.

5. Cheilanthes bergiana *Kunze*

Fronds finely dissected, ovate to deltoid, tripinnate with a lamina up to about 30 cm long and wide.

Occurs on moist, shaded banks in moist, intermediate to montane forests, about 5250–7500 ft. Uncommon. ?HE, ?HM, MUM, KIS. Also occurs in the Taita hills.

Faden 69/2111; Faden and Cameron 72/322.

6. Cheilanthes hirta *Swartz* (see p. 38)

The narrow, finely-dissected, hairy fronds which grow to 30 cm long (in our area) can be confused only with *Mohria caffrorum*. They differ from those of that species, which is known from only one locality in western Kenya, in being more dissected and in lacking scales on the rachis and costae.

This is a species of moist, usually exposed, rock crevices and roadside banks, about 6400–8300 ft. HC, HT, KIT, KIS, BAR.

Tweedie 67/39; Faden 70/897.

26. DORYOPTERIS *J. Sm.*

Small terrestrial herbs; rhizome short-creeping to erect, densely scaly; fronds tufted; stipes polished brown, with a single vascular strand; lamina deltoid, shorter than the stipe, tripinnatifid; venation free; sori marginal, interrupted or continuous,

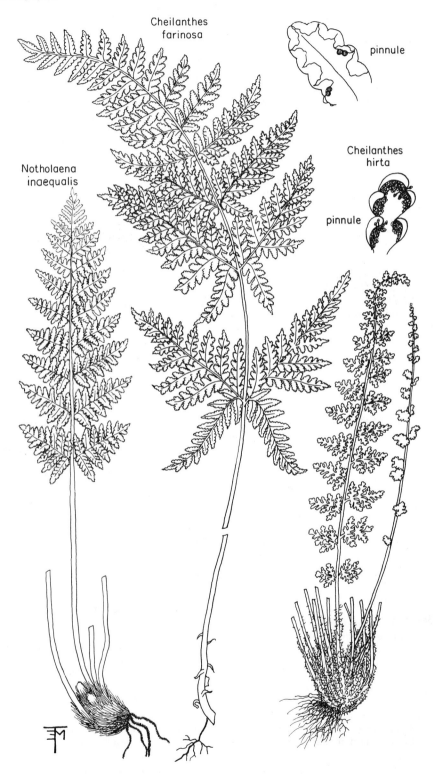

Cheilanthes
farinosa

pinnule

Cheilanthes
hirta

pinnule

Notholaena
inaequalis

partially covered by the thin reflexed margin or marginal lobes; indusium absent.

1   Reflexed margin discontinuous
                 1. *D. concolor*
   Reflexed margin continuous, interrupted only at the sinuses and frequently at the apices of the pinnules
                 2. *D. nicklesii*

1. Doryopteris concolor (*Langsd. & Fisch.*) *Kuhn* (see p. 42)

(see p. 42)

An attractive fern with tufted fronds to 30 cm long.

This is a characteristic plant of dry forest, but also occurs in wet forest (e.g. Kakamega), being recorded 3250–7500 ft. Grows in dense shade. HC, HT, HM, HA, KIT, MUM, KIS, NAR, EMB, MAC, NBI, KAJ. Occasional in mountains outside our area.

Faden 71/856; Hedberg 290.

2. Doryopteris nicklesii *Tard.*

In addition to the key character of the reflexed margin, this species may be distinguished from *D. concolor* by its somewhat dimorphic fronds, the fertile ones having much longer stipes than the sterile ones.

Known in Kenya from a single collection. It was found growing on shaded, mossy banks in evergreen thickets along the Tiva River near Kitui at 3900 ft. MAC.

Faden 71/377.

27. PELLAEA *Link*

Small to medium sized, terrestrial herbs; rhizome short-creeping, densely scaly; fronds tufted; stipes polished reddish-brown to black, with a single U-shaped vascular strand; lamina pinnate to quadripinnate, glabrous or hairy; venation free or reticulate; sori continuous along the margin and covered by the reflexed margin; indusium absent.

1   Fronds pinnate (rarely bipinnate at the base); terminal pinnule articulated   2
   Fronds bi- to quadripinnate; terminal pinnule articulated or not   4
2   Pinnae glabrous; venation free 1. *P. doniana*
   Pinnae hairy; venation free or reticulate   3
3   Venation free (sometimes the pinnae have to be cleared in order for this character to be seen); scales on crozier and base of stipe black   2. *P. longipilosa*
   Venation reticulate; scales tan
             3. *P. schweinfurthii*
4   Terminal pinnules articulated   5

Terminal pinnules not articulated   6
5   Pinnules grey-green, rhomboidal, hastate at base; rachis glabrous   4. *P. calomelanos*
   Pinnules green, lanceolate, cordate at base; rachis puberulous on the upper side
                 5. *P. boivinii*
6   Rachis and stipe with numerous, spreading, brown, hair-like scales; venation not clearly visible   6. *P. involuta*
   Rachis without scales; stipe scaly only at the base; venation clearly visible   7
7   Fronds ovate to deltoid, tri- to quadripinnate, usually coriaceous 7. *P. quadripinnata*
   Fronds lanceolate to ovate, rarely deltoid, bipinnate to tripinnate, texture herbaceous   8
8   Fronds deltoid; plants of wet forest
                 8. *P.* sp. *A*
   Fronds lanceolate to ovate; plants of bushland, thicket, or forest
9   Rachis with tan, scarious ridges on the upper side; segments mostly rounded at the apex; fronds lanceolate to ovate
              9. *P. adiantoides*
   Rachis lacking scarious ridges; segments acute at apex; fronds lanceolate-elliptic
              10. *P. viridis*

1. Pellaea doniana *Hook.*

The venation is much more easily seen in this species than in the related *P. longipilosa* and *P. schweinfurthii*. The pinnules tend to be longer (up to 10 x 2 cm in our area).

In our area this uncommon plant occurs in shaded, moist thickets and on banks, usually in riverine forest at about 5000 ft. MAC. Also sporadic in lowland rain forest along the coast.

Faden 68/915; Opiko 324.

2. Pellaea longipilosa *Bonap.* (see p. 41)

(see p. 41)

Fronds to about 30 cm long. Extremely similar to *P. schweinfurthii* and separated for certain only by its free venation. The venation can be seen in young fronds by placing them in front of a strong light (e.g. the sun). For old plants use the scale colour in the field.

A species of dry, usually fully exposed, rock crevices, occurring 2000–7850 ft. When this species occurs in the same area as *P. schweinfurthii*, the latter is found to grow in the moister, more sheltered situations. BAR, EMB, MAC. Also on Mt. Kasigau and on scattered hills in northern Kenya.

Faden, Temba, and Karanja 69/494; Napper 492.

3. Pellaea schweinfurthii (*Hieron.*) *Diels*

Fronds up to 40 cm long. For distinctions from *P. longipilosa* see above. Old pinnules can be cleared by placing them in a 5–10 per cent solution of sodium or potassium hydroxide for 1–2 days.

Occurs in moist rock crevices, either in shade or full sun, about 2800–6500 ft. KIT, NAN, MAC, KAJ. Also in the Taita hills, the Mathews range, and on Mt. Kasigau.

Faden and Evans 69/165; Napper 1607.

4. Pellaea calomelanos (*Swartz*) *Link* (see p. 41)

The colour and shape of the pinnules make this the most easily recognized *Pellaea* in Kenya. The lamina is ovate to deltoid, bipinnate and up to 30 cm long. The venation is obscure.

A common plant of dry or moist, rock crevices and roadside banks in full sun, 5000–8800 ft. HC, NAR, BAR, RV, NAN, MAC, KAJ. Also on hills in northern Kenya.

Verdcourt 3567; Bally 5442.

5. Pellaea boivinii *Hook.*

Fronds lanceolate-ovate, tripinnate at the base, bipinnate above, venation free.

Only collected once in our area, growing in rock crevices at about 6850 ft on Ol Doinyo Orok (Mt. Namanga). KAJ.

Archer in EAH 15086.

6. Pellaea involuta (*Swartz*) *Bak.*

In frond-cutting this plant resembles *P. adiantoides* but lacks the scarious ridges on the rachis. The fronds reach about 30 cm in length (in our area).

This is an uncommon plant (in our area), occurring in rock crevices and moist thickets up to about 6250 ft. HK, MUM, KIS, RV, MAC. Also in the Taita hills, on Mt. Kulal, and sporadically in dry coastal forests.

Faden and Evans 69/305; Kerfoot 3452.

7. Pellaea quadripinnata (*Forssk.*) *Prantl*

This is the most finely-dissected Kenya species of *Pellaea*. The glabrous pinnules are 1–2 cm long.

Occurs on banks and along roadsides in moist montane forests and in the bamboo zone. It grows in partial shade or full sun, about 4250–8000 ft (rare below 6850 ft in our area). HE, HC, HT, HM, HA, HK, HN, RV, KAJ. Also on the Taita and Sagala hills.

Faden, Evans, and Worth 69/701; Bally 352.

8. Pellaea sp. A.

The deltoid fronds, with long (up to about 8 cm), linear-lanceolate segments readily distinguish this species, which is sometimes considered to be only a variety of *P. viridis*.

Plants of forest edges, occurring 4000–5600 ft. Collected only once in our area. HN. Also in the Taita and Sagala hills.

Faden, Evans and Worth 69/710.

9. Pellaea adiantoides (*Willd.*) *J. Sm.* (see p. 41)

This is *Pellaea viridis* var. *glauca* of Schelpe (1970). Fronds up to 50 cm long with segments usually 1–2 cm long.

Grows in dry bushland and dry rocky places, frequently in full sun, 2000–7300 ft; never found in forest. HC, HA, KIT, KIS, BAR, RV, NAN, EMB, MAC, NBI, KAJ. This is one of the most common ferns in Kenya and occurs in suitable habitats everywhere except the coastal strip.

Glover 3733; Hemming 245.

10. Pellaea viridis (*Forssk.*) *Prantl* (see p. 42)

Fronds 30–50 cm long, with segments usually 1·5–4 cm long.

This is generally a plant of moist thickets and dry forests, where it often occurs along paths and on banks. It occasionally grows in the open or along streams. Common in Kenya, occurring about 3000–7500 ft. HM, HA, HN, KIT, MUM, KIS, NAR, NAN, EMB, MAC, NBI, KAJ. Also in the Taita, Sagala, and Murua Nysigar hills and on Mts. Kasigau and Marsabit.

Faden 67/710; Hanid 307.

28. ASPIDOTIS (*Hook.*) *Copel.*

Small terrestrial herbs; rhizome short-creeping, densely scaly; fronds tufted; stipes glabrous, polished brown, with a single vascular strand; lamina deltoid, glabrous, tripinnate, the pinnules bipinnatifid; segments acute; venation free; sori in sinuses between marginal teeth, covered by whitish, scarious, reflexed marginal lobes; indusium absent.

Aspidotis schimperi (*Kunze*) *Pic. Ser.*

The finely-dissected fronds are 20–50 cm long, with the stipes longer than the laminae.

A plant of woodland, forest or exposed sites, often in rocky places; in our area recorded from 'hill tops, desert country, rock crevices'. BAR (Kacheliba).

van Someren 633.

29. ACTINIOPTERIS *Link*

Small, terrestrial herbs; rhizome short-creeping, densely scaly, often with a scent of bitter almonds when freshly cut; fronds tufted; stipe scaly, grey or green above, grooved, below 3-ridged, with a broad, brown median ridge separated by grooves

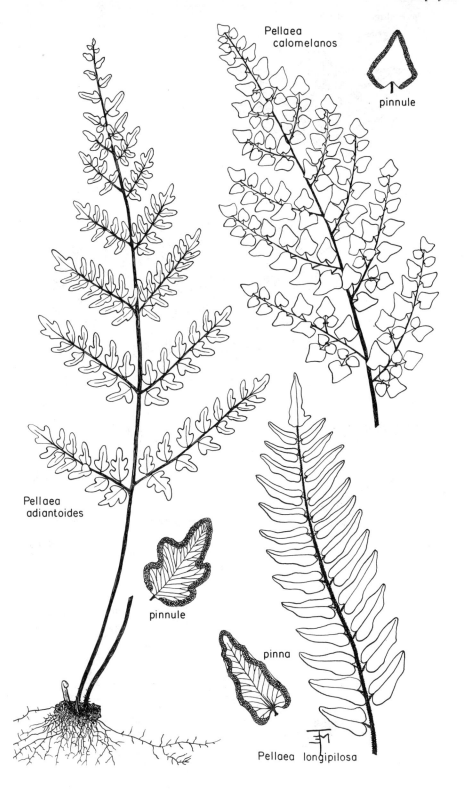

Pellaea
calomelanos

pinnule

Pellaea
adiantoides

pinnule

pinna

Pellaea longipilosa

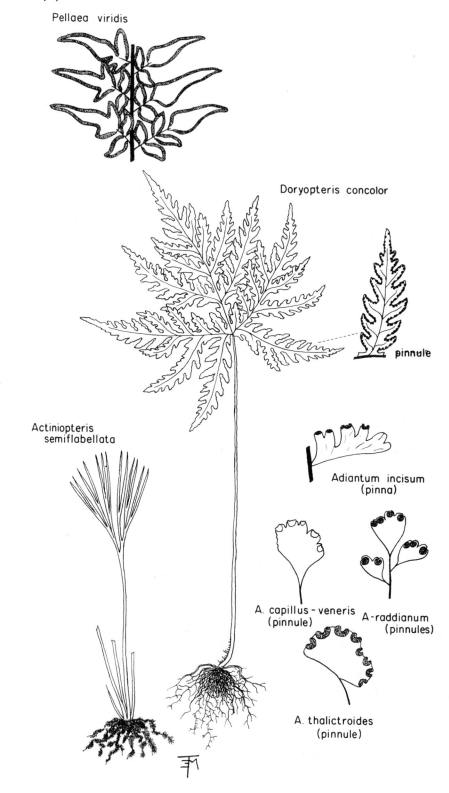

Pellaea viridis

Doryopteris concolor

pinnule

Actiniopteris
semiflabellata

Adiantum incisum
(pinna)

A. capillus-veneris
(pinnule)

A-raddianum
(pinnules)

A. thalictroides
(pinnule)

from 2 outer, grey or green ridges; vascular bundle 1, U-shaped; lamina shorter than the stipe, fan-shaped or wedge-shaped, scaly, dichotomously divided into linear or narrowly wedge-shaped segments; sori sub-marginal, covered by the reflexed margins; indusium absent.

1   All fronds wedge-shaped to broadly obdeltoid, each segment ending in a single hard point   1. *A. semiflabellata*
     Some or all of the fronds broadly fan-shaped; segments of at least the sterile fronds ending in several teeth   2
2   Fronds dimorphic; segments of the fertile fronds ending in a single point, sometimes bordered by small teeth   2. *A. dimorpha*
     Fronds uniform; segments of the fertile fronds ending in several teeth
                 3. *A. radiata*

1. Actiniopteris semiflabellata *Pic. Ser.*

Fertile fronds up to 30 cm long. This is the only *Actiniopteris* in which the segments of all fronds end in one hard point. Small secondary teeth may occur lateral to the main point on some or all segments.

This is a common fern in Kenya and is the most common *Actiniopteris*. It occurs in dry or moist, shaded or exposed, rock crevices, 2000–6850 ft. HK, KIS, NAR, BAR, RV, NAN, EMB, MAC, NBI, KAJ. Also occurs in many localities in eastern and northern Kenya.

Faden 67/653; Gillett 17289.

2. Actiniopteris dimorpha *Pic. Ser.*

The sterile fronds are similar in cutting to those of *A. radiata* (they tend to have more teeth per segment than in that species), while the fertile fronds resemble those of *A. semiflabellata*.

Dry rock crevices, 1750–3000 ft. Uncommon in our area. MAC, KAJ. Also known from Mts. Kasigau and Tsavo and Meru National Parks.

Verdcourt 3881; Faden 72/17.

3. Actiniopteris radiata *(Swartz) Link*

Distinguished from both of the above species in having both the fertile and sterile fronds with segments ending in several ± equal teeth.

Occurs in dry rock crevices, growing on the whole in somewhat drier situations than *A. semiflabellata*, although the two not infrequently occur together. Occurs about 100–6250 ft. BAR, RV, MAG, EMB, MAC, KAJ. Also occurs in many localities in eastern and northern Kenya.

Faden 67/645; Verdcourt 2642.

30. NEPHROLEPIS *Schott*

Medium to large, terrestrial herbs; rhizome erect, scaly, producing numerous stolons, sometimes producing subterranean tubers; fronds tufted; stipes with several vascular bundles; lamina pinnate, the pinnae articulated to the rachis; margins serrate; venation free; sori round, terminal on the veins, borne in two rows on each pinna; indusium semi-lunular to round-reniform.

1   Pinnae without basal auricles; indusium facing the margin of the pinna; middle pinnae 7–15 (–23) cm long; tubers absent
                 1. *N. biserrata*
     Pinnae with basal auricles; indusium facing the apex of the pinna; middle pinnae 1·5–5 cm long; tubers usually present   2
2   Rhizome annual; fronds one to few, annual; rachis glabrous or nearly so 2. *N. undulata*
     Rhizome perennial; fronds numerous, perennial; rachis hairy   3. *N. cordifolia*

1. Nephrolepis biserrata *(Swartz) Schott*

Fronds usually 1–2 m long; pinnae oblong, sessile, with rounded to truncate bases and acuminate apices; indusium round-reniform with a very narrow sinus.

This is a plant of moist forests. It is rare in our area. HE, HA, RV. Also occurs sporadically in coastal forests.

Polhill 3; Glover 3542.

2. Nephrolepis undulata *(Swartz) J. Sm.*

Rhizome very slender and, like the fronds, annual, only the subterranean, easily-detached, ellipsoid tubers persisting during the dry season.

This species forms dense colonies in moist thickets at moderate altitudes in western Kenya. Supposed records east of the Rift Valley almost certainly refer to the next or some other cultivated species. HC, KIT, MUM.

Williams 572; Faden 71/462.

3. Nephrolepis cordifolia *(L.) Presl*

The perennial rhizome and narrow fronds readily distinguish this from the two native species of *Nephrolepis*. Subterranean tubers are sometimes present. The fronds may be erect, or (in moist, shaded situations) arching or pendent.

A native of tropical America and tropical Asia, this plant is commonly cultivated. It is naturalized at Thika (near Chania and Thika Falls, altitude 4850 ft) and perhaps elsewhere. MAC.

Faden 68/904.

31. ARTHROPTERIS *J. Sm.*

Medium-sized, terrestrial or epiphytic herbs; rhizome thin, long-creeping, scaly; fronds widely spaced; stipes finely hairy, articulated above the base, sometimes above the middle, the articulation usually noted as a swelling, lamina pinnate, the pinnae pinnatifid and articulated to the rachis; venation free; sori ± round, terminal on the veins; indusium round-reniform.

1   White calcareous dots present on the upper surface of the lobes; sporangia 1–8 on each lobe; stipe articulation usually above the middle   1. *A. orientalis*
      White dots absent; sporangia 1 on each lobe; stipe articulation usually below the middle
                                          2. *A. monocarpa*

1. Arthropteris orientalis (*Gmel.*) *Posth.*

Fronds generally 25–40 cm long; lamina lanceolate to lanceolate-elliptic.

This is a plant of dry forests and dry or moist thickets. It grows in partial shade on rocks or on the ground, and is rarely epiphytic, occurring about 2950–7850 ft. HC, ?HL, ?HK, HN, MUM, KIS, RV, MAC, KAJ. Also in the Taita hills and on Mt. Kasigau.

Agnew, Kibe, and Mathenge 10360; Faden, Evans and Worth 69/706.

2. Arthropteris monocarpa (*Cordem.*) *C. Chr.*

The fronds are thinner textured than those of *A. orientalis* and are usually somewhat longer than them.

Ecologically this species is absolutely distinct from *A. orientalis*, occurring in moist, montane forest, sometimes near streams, and extending up into the bamboo zone. It can be either terrestrial or epiphytic, but if the latter, then the rhizome is rooted in the ground and ascends the tree trunks. HE, HA, HK, KIS.

Napper 717; Faden and Grumbley 72/343.

32. OLEANDRA *Cav.*

Epiphytic or, rarely, terrestrial herbs; rhizome long-creeping, densely covered by appressed scales; fronds simple, widely spaced; stipes with several vascular bundles, articulated a short distance above the point of attachment to the rhizome; lamina oblong to oblong-elliptic; venation free, prominent; sori round, dorsal on the veins, subcostal; indusium round-reniform.

Oleandra distenta *Kunze*

Stems stiff, free of roots for a great length and often hanging from the trees; fronds with entire margins and abruptly acuminate apices.

A plant of wet forests, 5000–8200 ft. HA, HK, RV. Also occurs on Mt. Kasigau.

Greenway 13815; Faden 69/017.

33. DAVALLIA *Sm.*

Medium sized, epiphytic or, rarely, terrestrial herbs; rhizome long-creeping, densely scaly; stipes articulated a short distance above the attachment to the rhizome, with several vascular bundles; lamina glabrous, ovate to deltoid, about quadripinnate; venation free; sori marginal, terminal on the veins; indusium cup-shaped, fixed at the base and sides, flanked by horn-like projections of the lamina.

Davallia chaerophylloides (*Poir.*) *Steud.*

A finely divided, usually pendent epiphyte with alternate pinnae.

This species has been collected in our area only once; it was found along the Yala River. MUM. Also in the Maungu hills and along the coast.

Agnew, Waithaka *et al.* 10034.

34. CYATHEA *Sm.*

Tree ferns with unbranched trunks 1–10 m tall, rarely shorter; stipe bases persistent or not, if not, then leaf scars very prominent; fronds clustered at the top of the trunk, 1–3.5 m long; stipes scaly at the base, with numerous vascular bundles; lamina pinnate or bipinnate; venation free (in our species); sori spherical, dorsal on the veins; indusium, if present, surrounding the sorus and attached at its base, often cup-shaped.

1   Fronds pinnate, up to 1·5 m long; pinnae deeply pinnatifid   1. *C. stuhlmannii*
      Fronds bipinnate, 2–3·5 m long; pinnules deeply pinnatifid   2
2   Stipe bases finely muricate; scales uniformly coloured; old dead fronds pendent below the living ones; cross-section of trunk with about 10–12 vascular strands; costae usually glabrous above, sometimes with long, fine hairs   2. *C. dregei*
      Stipe bases very spiny; scales with broad pale margins; old fronds never pendent; cross-section of trunk with about 5–6 vascular strands; costae densely and finely hairy above   3. *C. manniana*

1. Cyathea stuhlmannii *Hieron.*

Trunk up to about 2 m high, diameter 4–5 cm, with about 5 vascular strands; stipe bases not persistent.

This is a rare plant in our area and grows in moist, montane forest, about 5250–6500 ft. HK, HN. Also in the Taita hills.

Schelpe 2427; Faden, Evans, and Worth 69/705.

2. Cyathea dregei *Kunze*

The old stipe bases persist on the trunk, but they are broken up and fibrous, not whole and spiny as in *C. manniana*. The trunks can reach about 6 m in height and about 20 cm in diameter. The stipe base scales are longer and much narrower than those of *C. manniana*.

This plant occurs in dense shade along streams and is rare in our area. Recorded about 4250–5900 ft. HN. Also in the Taita hills.

H. D. van Someren 328.

3. Cyathea manniana *Hook.*

As broadly interpreted here, this plant has trunks which grow to about 10 m tall and 15 cm in diameter. Spiny stipe bases persistent, (or very rarely not), the spaces between them becoming filled with epiphytic mosses and ferns (particularly *Asplenium hypomelas*).

This is the common tree fern in Kenya, and forms dense stands in steep, forested valleys along rivers in the Aberdares and on Mt. Kenya. It is rarely found far from water (in our area). Young plants often grow on exposed roadside banks but they never mature. Occurs about 5000–8200 ft. HC, HM, HA, HK, HN, KIS. Also in the Taita and Sagala hills.

Faden 70/387; Mabberley and McCall 19.

35. DIDYMOCHLAENA *Desv.*

Large terrestrial herbs; rhizome large, woody, erect, densely scaly; fronds tufted; stipe with several vascular bundles arranged in a U-shape; lamina lanceolate-elliptic to narrowly oblong, bipinnate; pinnules trapezoidal, articulated; margin crenulate; venation free; sori submarginal, elliptic, terminal on the veins; indusium the same shape as the sorus, attached in the centre and at the base, free at the sides and apex.

Didymochlaena truncatula (*Swartz*) *J. Sm.* (see p. 59)

A handsome plant with fronds to 2 m long, easily recognized by its *Albizia*-like pinnules.

This is a rather uncommon plant, of wet forests, occurring about 5000–6850 ft. HA, HK, HN, KIS, KAJ. Also in the Taita hills and on Mt. Kasigau.

Bally 1142; Agnew 9011.

36. DRYOPTERIS *Adans.*

Medium to large, terrestrial herbs; rhizome thick, woody, short-creeping to erect; fronds tufted; stipes densely scaly at the base, with several vascular bundles arranged in a U-shape; lamina bipinnate to tripinnate; margin toothed; rachis and costae scaly; venation free; sori round, dorsal on the veins; indusium, if present, round-reniform, attached at its sinus.

1 Fronds gemmiferous; indusium absent
          1. *D. manniana*
  Fronds not gemmiferous; indusium present or absent   2

2 Rachis with numerous, spreading, reddish-brown, hair-like scales; stipes with dense, narrow, spreading white scales (turning brown with age or upon drying)
         2. *D. squamiseta*
  Rachis and stipe scales various but not as above   3

3 Pinnules obliquely cuneate at the base 4
  Pinnules rounded to truncate at the base 5

4 Pinnae strongly ascending; texture coriaceous to firmly herbaceous; plants of wooded grassland   3. *D. athamantica*
  Pinnae at ± right angles to the rachis; texture herbaceous; forest plants   4. *D. sp. A*

5 Fronds tripinnate; lamina deltoid to ovate-deltoid; rhizome and stipe base scales dark brown with entire margins; costules with ovate, bullate scales   5. *D. kilemensis*
  Fronds bipinnate (rarely tripinnate); lamina lanceolate-ovate to ovate; rhizome and stipe base scales various; costules with scales lanceolate or narrower, bullate or not   6

6 At least some lower stipe scales dark brown with pale margins; fronds with shortly-aristate, spreading teeth on margin
         6. *D. callolepis*
  Lower stipe scales uniformly coloured; fronds with short, nonaristate, incurved teeth on margin   7

7 Stipe bases swollen, polished black with caducous scales; lower stipe scales much paler than the dark brown rhizome scales; rhizome and stipe scales with ± entire margins; pinnules of middle pinnae ± parallel sided, with truncate lobes and rounded apices   7. *D. schimperana*
  Stipe bases swollen or not, brown, scales usually persistent; lower stipe scales similar in colour to the rhizome scales; rhizome and stipe scales with entire to ciliate or lacerate margins; pinnules of middle pinnae lanceolate to lanceolate-ovate, with rounded to subtruncate lobes and acute to acuminate apices   8

8 Rhizome scales pale brown; stipe base scales with numerous lateral processes; costules with long, pale, twisted, hair-like scales beneath, bullate scales absent; indusium persistent   8. *D. inaequalis*

Rhizome scales dark brown; stipe base scales entire or with one to several lateral processes; costules with lanceolate, bullate scales beneath; long, twisted, hair-like scales absent; indusium persistent or caducous   9. *D. pentheri*

1. Dryopteris manniana (*Hook.*) *C. Chr.*

Fronds with one to several gemmae present on the upper part of the rachis (in our area); large fronds may have an additional gemma near the apex of each basal pinna; pinnules of the middle pinnae rounded at the apex.

This plant grows in dense shade in moist, montane forests, 5000–7500 ft. It is common east of the Rift valley. HA, HK, HN, MUM. Also in the Taita and Sagala hills and on Mt. Kasigau. Verdcourt and Polhill 2929; Faden 69/020.

2. Dryopteris squamiseta (*Hook.*) *O. Kuntze*

Lamina tripinnate, ovate and thin-textured; pinnule lobes rounded; sori large with a persistent indusium.

This is primarily a plant of the moister parts of the bamboo zone, occasionally extending down into moist, montane forest. It occurs in dense shade, 6900–9500 ft. HA, HK. Faden *et al.* 69/765; Verdcourt 2050.

3. Dryopteris athamantica (*Kunze*) *O. Kuntze* (see p. 47)

Rhizome subterranean, frequently branched: characters not found in other Kenya species of *Dryopteris*. Fronds about 1 m tall, with the pinnule lobes often somewhat falcate.

This is the only grassland species of *Dryopteris*. It occurs in moist, broad-leaved, deciduous, wooded grassland (*Terminalia mollis* a characteristic tree) in the Kitale area. The buried rhizome is a protection against fire. KIT. Tweedie 2855; Faden 70/898.

4. Dryopteris sp. A.

Fronds about 40 cm long; rhizome scales light brown. The taxonomic status of this plant remains uncertain; it is most closely related to *D. inaequalis*.

The single collection is from shaded stream banks in moist, intermediate forest at about 5250 ft. MUM (Kakamega forest). Faden 69/2054.

5. Dryopteris kilemensis (*Kuhn*) *O. Kuntze*

This is the largest and perhaps most common species of *Dryopteris* in Kenya. The fronds can reach a length of about 2 m and a width of nearly half that. The rhizome is thick and ascending.

This plant is common in moist, montane forests and in the bamboo zone. It occurs in dense shade, about 6500–9800 ft. HA, HK, HN, KIS. Also in the Taita hills.

Napper 647; Faden and Holland 71/871.

6. Dryopteris callolepis *C. Chr.*

Rhizome scales with entire margins; fronds generally up to 70 cm long; pinnules often with a tendency to curl; indusium persistent.

This is a species of the bamboo, ericaceous and *Hagenia-Hypericum* zones, occurring in shade, about 8300–10 350 ft. HA, HK.

Fries 2554; Faden 71/883.

7. Dryopteris schimperana (*A. Br.*) *C. Chr.*

Rhizome and stipe base scales with ± entire margins (sometimes with one lateral process); scales on undersides of costules lanceolate, never bullate. Neither the name nor the circumscription of this species is very certain.

Extending from moist, montane forests into the moorland. Recorded 6850–11 200 ft. HE, HA, HK.

Faden and Evans 69/802; Coe and Kirika 396.

8. Dryopteris inaequalis (*Schlechtend.*) *O. Kuntze*

In eastern Kenya this is a clearly circumscribed species both morphologically and ecologically. The pinnae may be spreading or strongly erect (when growing in full sun). The freshly cut rhizome shows dark streaks in longitudinal section.

This is a plant of moist, forest edges at medium altitudes. It sometimes grows on roadside banks. It is found in partial shade or full sun. Occurs 4900–8200 ft. HA, HN, KIT, KIS, MAC. Also in the Taita hills.

Faden, Evans, and Worth 69/649; Faden and Evans 69/191.

9. Dryopteris pentheri (*Krasser*) *C. Chr.*

The bullate scales on the costules distinguish this from all other Kenya *Dryopteris* species except *D. kilemensis* which has a broader, more dissected lamina. Fronds grow to about 1·5 m tall and are bi- to tripinnate. The freshly-cut rhizome lacks dark streaks in longitudinal section.

This is a plant of moist, montane forests and the bamboo zone. It grows in dense shade, about 6750–8350 ft. HA, HM, HK.

Faden 71/68, 69/907.

37. HYPODEMATIUM *Kunze*

Small to medium-sized, terrestrial herbs; rhizome short-creeping, densely covered with long, narrow, lustrous, brown scales; fronds tufted; stipes scaly at base, finely hairy above, with 2 vascular strands;

Dryopteris athamantica

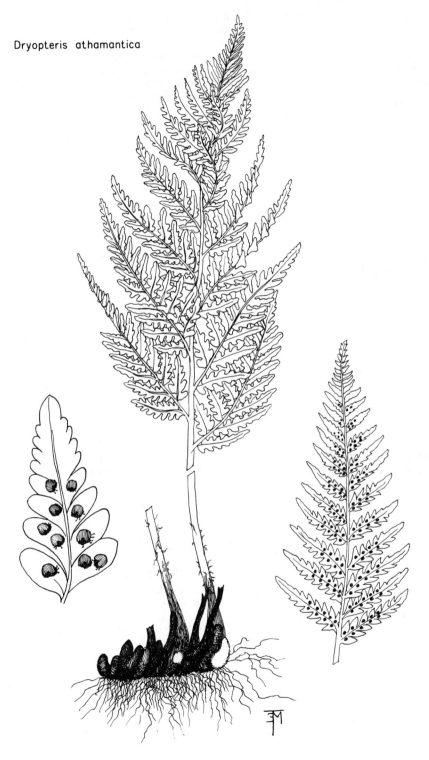

lamina ovate-deltoid, bi- to tripinnate, finely and densely hairy on both surfaces and on the axes; venation free; sori slightly elongate to somewhat curved, dorsal on the veins; indusium large, reniform, but usually asymmetrical, densely and finely hairy, persistent.

Hypodematium crenatum (*Forssk.*) *Kuhn*

The absence of scales on the lamina and axes easily distinguishes this species from all similar looking ones.

This plant grows in rock crevices. It has been collected only once in Kenya. KIS (Kanam, Mt. Homa, altitude 4000 ft).

Turner in CM/3632.

38. PHANEROPHLEBIA *Presl*

Medium-sized terrestrial herbs; rhizome erect, densely scaly; fronds tufted; stipes with several vascular bundles arranged in a U-shape; lamina oblong, pinnate with 5–9 pairs of pinnae, margin finely serrate; venation reticulate without included veinlets; sori round, numerous and scattered on the pinnae but often in apparent rows; indusium round, peltate.

Phanerophlebia caryotidea (*Hook. & Grev.*) *Copel.* (see p. 59)

This plant resembles a weak, thin-textured form of the cultivated Holly Fern (*Phanerophlebia* (*Cyrtomium*) *falcata*).

This is a rare forest plant occurring 5000–6000 ft. HA, MUM, KIS, EMB, NBI.

Faden 69/2105; Agnew 7934.

39. POLYSTICHUM *Roth*

Medium to large, terrestrial herbs; rhizome thick, woody, erect to ascending, densely scaly; fronds tufted; stipes densely scaly, with several vascular bundles arranged in a U-shape; lamina lanceolate, bipinnate, the pinnules unlobed to bipinnatifid; margin toothed, the teeth often aristate; axes densely scaly and hairy; venation free; sori round, dorsal on the veins; indusium round, peltate, persistent.

1 Pinnules toothed to shallowly lobed; teeth aristate; rachis never gemmiferous
                              1. *P. fuscopaleaceum*
   Pinnules pinnatifid to bipinnatifid; teeth not aristate; rachis gemmiferous   2
2 Pinnules rounded at apex, pinnatifid
                              2. *P. magnificum*
   Pinnules acute at apex, bipinnatifid
                              3. *P. volkensii*

1. Polystichum fuscopaleacum *Alston*

Pinnules with long marginal bristles.

This plant grows in dense shady moist montane forests, especially along streams and rivers, from 5000 ft up to the moorland at 13 500 ft. The plants at lower altitudes constitute a distinct variety with long attenuate apices of pinnae and dark brown scales on the rachis, while the high-altitude variety has abruptly acute pinnae and pale scales. Widespread and local it is often common at high altitudes. HE, HC, HM, HA, HK, HN, KIS, ?KIT, EMB, ?KAJ.

Hedberg 1933; Faden 70/114; Faden 71/464; Verdcourt and Moggi 2486.

2. Polystichum magnificum *Ballard*

Fronds up to 110 cm long and 25 cm wide; stipe base scales golden-brown or straw-coloured, up to 3 cm long and 0·9 cm wide.

This plant is known in East Africa only from moorland in the crater of Mt. Elgon at 11 500 ft. It has been collected only once on the Kenya side of the border. HE.

Tweedie s.n. (Nov. 1932).

3. Polystichum volkensii (*Hieron.*) *C. Chr.* (*P. barbatum* C. Chr.) (see p. 59)

A beautiful fern with fronds growing to at least 1 m tall. The finely dissected, gemmiferous fronds are unmistakable.

This plant is known in Kenya only from Mt. Kinangop at about 10 800 ft. It occurs in the *Hagenia–Hypericum* zone. HA. Elsewhere only on Kilimanjaro.

Fries 2735; Rabb and Nightingale 7.

40. ARACHNIODES *Blume*

Medium-sized terrestrial herbs; rhizome woody, short-creeping, densely scaly; fronds tufted to shortly-spaced; stipes arcuate-ascending, with several vascular bundles arranged in a U-shape; lamina deltoid to ovate-deltoid, bi- to tripinnate; marginal teeth aristate; venation free; sori round, dorsal to subterminal on the veins; indusium round-reniform.

Arachniodes foliosa (*C. Chr.*) *Schelpe*

An attractive fern with numerous, pale, narrow scales and hairs on the axes and costules.

This plant is frequent in wet forests, occurring 5000–8500 ft. HE, HT, HM, HA, HK, HN, RV, EMB, KAJ. Also in the Taita hills and on Mt. Kasigau.

Hedberg 151; Faden 71/875.

41. CTENITIS *C. Chr.*

Medium to large, terrestrial herbs; rhizome woody, erect to ascending (in our species), densely scaly; fronds tufted (in our species); stipes with several vascular bundles arranged in a U-shape; lamina pinnate to tripinnate; axes with scattered bullate scales (in our species) and with numerous multi-cellular hairs; venation free; sori round, dorsal or terminal on the veins; indusium round-reniform, slightly hairy.

1 Fronds lanceolate to lanceolate-elliptic, pinnate, the pinnae deeply pinnatifid; sori dorsal on the veins   1. *C. cirrhosa*
  Fronds deltoid, tripinnate at base, bipinnate in the middle; sori terminal on the veins
                  2. *C. lanuginosa*

1. Ctenitis cirrhosa (*Schumach.*) *Ching*

Stipe covered (more densely towards the base) with spreading, dark brown, hair-like scales; pinnae oblong-lanceolate, up to 20 cm long.

This is a rare plant in our area, occurring in shady places near streams in moist, intermediate forests, about 4900–5500 ft. EMB, MUM. Also in the Taita hills.
Faden 69/1981; Balbo 815.

2. Ctenitis lanuginosa (*Kaulf.*) *Copel.*

Rhizome thick, erect, bearing large (to about 2 m tall), softly hairy fronds; lamina finely-dissected, thin-textured.

This uncommon plant occurs in dense shade along streams in moist, montane forests, about 4900–7300 ft. HA, HK, HN. Also in the Taita hills and on Mt. Kasigau.
Faden *et al.* 69/763; Faden, Evans, and Worth 69/683.

42. TECTARIA *Cav.*

Medium-sized terrestrial herbs; rhizome woody, erect to ascending (in our plant), densely scaly; fronds tufted (in our plant); stipes with several vascular bundles arranged in a U-shape; lamina ovate (in our plant), bipinnate at the base, bipinnatifid above; costae very finely hairy above and below; venation reticulate with included veinlets; sori round; indusium round-reniform.

Tectaria gemmifera (*Fée*) *Alston* (see p. 50)
This plant can be recognized by the presence of gemmae or their scars on the upper surface of the rachis at junctions with costae. They sometimes occur on the lower surface as well. The lamina is ovate.
This is a common forest plant, 3900–8200 ft. HT, HM, HA, HK, HN, KIT, MUM, EMB, MAC, KAJ. Also in the Taita hills and on Mts. Kasigau and Marsabit.
Tweedie 2926; Faden 68/770.

43. ELAPHOGLOSSUM *J. Sm.*

Small to medium-sized, terrestrial or epiphytic herbs; rhizome erect or creeping, densely scaly; fronds tufted or spaced, usually dimorphic; stipes articulated a short distance above the base, leaving peg-like phyllopodia when they fall; lamina simple, spathulate to linear, most commonly oblong to oblong-elliptic, often densely scaly; margin entire; venation free; fertile laminae usually different in size and/or shape from the sterile laminae; sporangia covering the entire lower surface of the fertile laminae; indusium absent.

1 Sterile lamina without scales or with minute, dot-like scales only, margins never scaly 2
  Sterile lamina scaly on the margins and/or surfaces   5
2 Rhizome scales reddish-brown; fronds shortly spaced on the rhizome, coriaceous, to 5 cm wide; frond apex always round; sterile lamina at least 1·5 times as wide as the fertile lamina   1. *E. lastii*
  Rhizome scales pale to dark brown; fronds shortly to widely spaced on the rhizome, firmly herbaceous, to 3·5 cm wide; frond apex acute to acuminate (sometimes obtuse in some specimens of *E. conforme*); sterile lamina usually less than 1·5 times as wide as the fertile lamina (sometimes more in *E. acrostichoides*)   3
3 Rhizome scales ovate, appressed, light brown; sterile lamina with a conspicuous translucent margin about 0·5 mm broad; apex acuminate   2. *E. angulatum*
  Rhizome scales lanceolate, spreading, medium brown to dark brown; sterile lamina without a translucent margin; apex acuminate to obtuse   4
4 Frond apex acuminate; rhizome scales dark brown   3. *E. acrostichoides*
  Frond apex acute to obtuse; rhizome scales medium brown   4. *E conforme*
5 Scales on lamina with entire or serrulate margins, not forming a mat on the lamina   6
  Scales on lamina with conspicuously ciliate margins, often forming a mat on the lamina   9
6 Sterile lamina linear, with conspicuous, black, submarginal hydathodes on the upper surface; stipe of sterile frond 0·2–0·4 (–0·7) times the length of the lamina   5. *E. aubertii*
  Sterile lamina elliptic to oblong or lanceolate-oblong, or oblanceolate to spathulate; hydathodes absent or not clearly seen; stipe of sterile frond 0·5–1·5 times the length of the lamina   7
7 Sterile lamina oblanceolate to spathulate; fronds up to 8 cm long and 0·9 cm wide   6. *E. spathulatum*

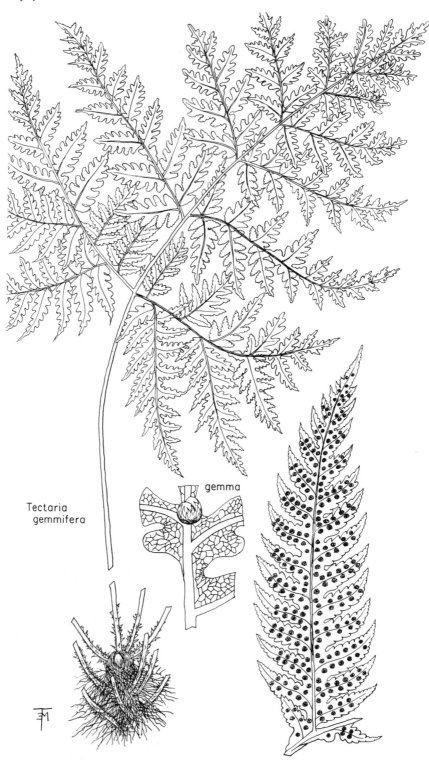

Tectaria
gemmifera

gemma

Sterile lamina elliptic to oblong or lanceolate-oblong; fronds 8–50 cm long and 2–5 cm wide   **8**

8 Rhizome scales blackish; scales of the sterile lamina blackish and ± confined to the margins and midvein   7. *E. hybridum*

Rhizome scales light brown; scales of the sterile lamina orange-brown, scattered on both surfaces   8. *E. mildbraedii*

9 Rhizome thin, long-creeping with widely spaced fronds; rhizome scales 3–5 mm long; lamina of sterile frond 4–12 cm long   9. *E. subcinnamomeum*

Rhizome thick, short-creeping with shortly spaced fronds; rhizome scales more than 5 mm long (sometimes shorter in *E. ruwenzorii*); lamina of sterile frond 15–100 cm long   **10**

10 Lamina scales mostly honey-coloured; marginal hairs of stipe scales mostly shorter than the width of the scale   10. *E. tanganjicense*

Lamina scales mostly reddish, or reddish on one surface and honey-coloured on the other; marginal hairs of stipe scales 1–2 times as long as the width of the scales   **11**

11 Rhizomes scales with ± entire margins; sterile fronds of mature plants up to 40 cm long   11. *E. ruwenzorii*

Rhizome scales ciliate; sterile fronds 40–100 cm long   12. *E. deckenii*

1. Elaphoglossum lastii (*Bak.*) *C. Chr.* (*E. volkensii* Hieron., *E. convolutum* Chiov.)

Fronds up to 70 cm in length; sterile lamina either shorter or longer than the stipe; fertile fronds usually longer than the sterile fronds.

This common species is an erect epiphyte, usually growing high up on trees (rarely low or terrestrial). It tends to be gregarious, and grows in moist, montane forests, 4900–8500 ft. HM, HA, HK, KIS. Also in the Taita hills and on Mt. Kasigau.

Verdcourt, Polhill, and Lucas 3036A; Balbo 769.

2. Elaphoglossum angulatum (*Blume*) *Moore*

Fronds up to 35 cm long; sterile lamina oblong-elliptic and, in large plants, equalling or slightly exceeding the stipe in length; fertile lamina similar in shape to the sterile one but somewhat smaller.

This rare plant is terrestrial or epiphytic. It occurs in the bamboo and ericaceous zones, 8000–8500 ft. HA, HK.

Faden and Evans 70/89; Faden 71/201.

3. Elaphoglossum acrostichoides (*Hook. & Grev.*) *Schelpe*

This is easily recognized, being the only *Elaphoglossum* in our area with non-scaly laminae attenuate at both ends. The fronds may be shortly or widely spaced on the rhizome, and they are up to 50 cm in length.

This species occurs in moist, montane forest. It is almost always epiphytic, and frequently occurs with *E. lastii*, but is less common than that species. Occurs about 5750–8500 ft. HA, HK, HN, KIT, KIS. Also in the Taita hills.

Faden and Evans 69/545; Faden and Cameron 72/309.

4. Elaphoglossum conforme (*Swartz*) *Schott*

Rhizome thin, with the widely spaced fronds usually 20–30 cm long; lamina oblong-elliptic to narrowly elliptic.

This is a species of the ericaceous and *Hagenia-Hypericum* zones. It is apparently terrestrial along streams and has been collected at 9000 ft. HA, HK.

Schelpe 2302; Agnew 9060.

5. Elaphoglossum aubertii (*Desv.*) *Moore* (see p. 26)

Sterile fronds normally about 30 cm long; fertile fronds with shorter laminae and longer stipes than sterile fronds. The narrow, sterile fronds with short stipes and scattered brown scales on the laminae readily distinguish this species.

Moist, montane forest is the habitat of this plant. It is terrestrial or epiphytic (seldom more than 5 m above the ground) and usually occurs near streams in dense shade. Recorded 4900–8500 ft. HA, HK, KIS. Also occurs on Mt. Kasigau.

Faden *et al.* 69/528; Faden and Grumbley 72/340.

6. Elaphoglossum spathulatum (*Bory*) *Moore*

The small size of the fronds and their shape make this species unmistakable. The fronds are ± tufted. The fertile lamina is ovate-elliptic and is shorter than the sterile lamina.

The single Kenya collection of this species came from a moss- and liverwort-covered rock about 1·5 km downstream from the Sasumua Dam, at 8000 ft. HA.

Faden 71/74.

7. Elaphoglossum hybridum (*Bory*) *Brack.*

Fronds clustered on the rhizome and generally 20–30 cm long; sterile lamina oblong to oblong-elliptic; fertile lamina smaller, longer-stalked, lanceolate-elliptic. Even small, sterile plants are easily recognized by the black scales on the margin and along the midvein.

This species extends from the moist montane forest up into the moorland. It is usually terrestrial and is found along streams or beside waterfalls. It occurs 6500–11 000 ft. HE, HA, HK, KIS.

Hedberg 904; Faden and Grumbley 72/350.

8. Elaphoglossum mildbraedii *Hieron.*

Sterile fronds up to 43 cm long, but some fertile plants with much smaller fronds; sterile lamina oblong-elliptic to 21 cm long and 4·5 cm wide with the apex acuminate (large plants) or rounded (small plants); fertile frond much shorter than sterile frond and with much shorter lamina.

This is a plant of moist, shaded, rock crevices and grows in moist, montane forest along rivers at 6500 ft. It is found in the Kericho area, below Salt Lick Falls on the Kiptoget River. KIS.

Faden and Grumbley 72/334.

9. Elaphoglossum subcinnamomeum (*Christ*) *Hieron.*

This plant is easily recognized by its small fronds with ciliate, greyish scales on the narrowly elliptic laminae. Terrestrial and commonly growing on rocks, this is primarily a moorland plant, extending down into either the ericaceous or *Hagenia–Hypericum* zone, occurring 9800–11 500 ft. HE, HK.

Hedberg 993; Schelpe 2605.

10. Elaphoglossum tanganjicense *Pic. Ser.*

Fronds flaccid, to 100 cm long, 5 cm wide; apex often obtusely acute; fertile lamina shorter and much narrower than the sterile lamina.

This is a pendent epiphyte in moist, montane forests. It is very common in the south-west Mau forest along the larger rivers but occurs nowhere else in our area. Occurs in Kenya 4900–7500 ft. HM, KIS. Also on Mt. Kasigau.

Kerfoot 4034; Faden and Grumbley 72/339.

11. Elaphoglossum ruwenzorii *Pirotta*

The smaller fronds with somewhat sparser scales and more abruptly acuminate apices serve to distinguish this species from *E. deckenii*. The two may prove to be conspecific.

This is a terrestrial or epiphytic plant, occurring primarily in moist, montane forests and the bamboo zone, occasionally extending up into the ericaceous zone. Occurs about 7200–8500 ft. HM, HA, HK.

Faden and Evans 70/99; Bally 4897.

12. Elaphoglossum deckenii (*Kuhn*) *C. Chr.*

Apex of sterile lamina acute or acuminate; fertile fronds always shorter than the sterile fronds.

This appears to be a plant primarily of the ericaceous and *Hagenia–Hypericum* zones. It can be either a pendulous epiphyte or terrestrial. Occurs 8000–10 800 ft., but is rare below 9000 ft. HE, HA, HK.

Hedberg 1635; Fries 2726.

44. LOMARIOPSIS *Fée*

Medium-sized herbs rooted in the ground but the rhizomes typically climbing trees; rhizomes elongate, dorsiventral, scaly; fronds widely spaced, dimorphic; stipes decurrent on the rhizome, with several vascular bundles arranged in a U-shape; lamina pinnate, lateral pinnae articulated to the rachis; venation free; fertile fronds with very contracted pinnae; sporangia covering the lower surface of the fertile pinnae; indusium absent.

Lomariopsis warneckei (*Hieron.*) *Alston*

This plant, which has fronds to 100 cm long with 14–19 pairs of oblong pinnae, has not yet been observed climbing trees (in our area), although Faden 69/2024 is fully fertile.

This is a moist forest plant of deep shade known in our area only from the Kakamega forest and south-east Mt. Kenya, 5250–6250 ft. HK, MUM. Also occurs in the Taita and Sagala hills and on Mt. Kasigau.

Faden 70/7, 69/2024.

45. BOLBITIS *Schott*

Small or medium-sized, terrestrial herbs; rhizome long-creeping (in our plant), scaly; fronds spaced, dimorphic; stipes with several vascular bundles; blade pinnate to pinnate-pinnatifid (in our plant), glabrous; venation reticulate; fertile fronds similar in cutting to sterile fronds but smaller; sporangia covering the entire lower surface of the fertile pinnae; indusium absent.

Bolbitis heudelotii (*Fée*) *Alston*

A dark green, fleshy plant growing to 70 cm tall and occurring in colonies. Much smaller, deeply bipinnatifid, submerged fronds are known from outside our area.

This plant grows on rocks in rivers; known in Kenya only from the Isiukhu River at the northern edge of the Kakamega forest (altitude 5300 ft). MUM.

Faden 69/2101.

46. THELYPTERIS GROUP (*Thelypteridaceae*)

Medium to large, terrestrial herbs; rhizome erect to long-creeping, densely or sparsely scaly; rhizome scales not clathrate, usually ciliate; fronds tufted to widely spaced; stipes with two vascular strands near the base, uniting above to form one U-shaped strand; lamina usually hairy, rarely with scales (*Thelypteris confluens*), usually pinnate (bipinnate in *Macrothelypteris*), the pinnae lanceolate or oblong-lanceolate to linear and regularly crenate, pinnately lobed or deeply pinnatifid; venation free (*Macrothelypteris, Leptogramma, Thelypteris*), or one or more pairs of veinlets joined below the sinuses (*Ampelopteris, Cyclosorus*); sori round or slightly elongate, dorsal on the veins; indusium absent or round-reniform, persistent or caducous.

The generic limits in the Thelypteridaceae are currently in a state of flux. Hence the above description is of the family, not of any particular genus. The generic limits used here are those Alston (1959) with the exception of *Macrothelypteris* being segregated from *Thelypteris*.

1 Fronds bipinnate; stipe bases of young fronds with numerous, spreading scales which are colourless in living plants but turn brown on drying   1. *Macrothelypteris aubertii*
   Fronds pinnate; stipe bases without scales or with appressed, brown scales only   2
2 Fronds arching and producing gemmae and young plants on the rachis at irregular intervals; lamina glabrous; several pairs of veinlets united below the sinuses; paraphyses present (dissecting microscope required)   2. *Ampelopteris prolifera*
   Fronds either not gemmiferous or, if so, then producing a single gemma on the upper part of the rachis; lamina usually hairy; veinlets free or united; paraphyses absent 3
3 One or more pairs of veinlets joined below the sinus (*Cyclosorus*)   4
   Veinlets all free, the lowest pair sometimes meeting at the sinus   9
4 Rhizome erect; fronds gemmiferous; 2–4 pairs of veinlets joined below the sinus   3. *Cyclosorus madagascariensis*
   Rhizome erect or short- to long-creeping; fronds not gemmiferous; 1–2 pairs of veinlets joined below the sinus   5
5 Two pairs of veinlets joined below the sinus; pinnae cut one-quarter to one-third the distance to the costa; rhizome long-creeping   4. *C.* sp. *A*
   One pair of veinlets joined below the sinus; pinnae cut one-third to three-quarters the distance to the costa; rhizome long-creeping, short-creeping or erect   6
6 Rhizome long-creeping with widely spaced fronds; costae glabrous or sparsely hairy above; plants usually of swamps and marshes   7
   Rhizome short-creeping or erect; fronds shortly-spaced or tufted; costae densely

hairy above; plants of forests or stream banks, but rarely of swamps or marshes   8
7 Pinnae cut one-third to one-half the distance to the costa; pinna lobes triangular, pointed   5. *C. interruptus*
   Pinnae cut one-half to three-quarters the distance to the costa; pinna lobes oblong, rounded   6. *C. striatus*
8 Rhizome erect or ascending; fronds tufted; lower pinnae only slightly reduced, the lowermost never auriculiform; united veinlets below the sinuses always meeting at an obtuse angle   7. *C. quadrangularis*
   Rhizome short-creeping; fronds shortly spaced; lower pinnae gradually reduced in size, the lowermost often reduced to auricles; united veinlets below the sinuses meeting at an acute or, less commonly, obtuse angle   8. *C. dentatus*
9 Sori elliptic, exindusiate; sporangia ciliate (microscope required)   9. *Leptogramma pozoi*
   Sori all round, indusiate or exindusiate; sporangia not ciliate (*Thelypteris*)   10
10 Fronds glabrous or nearly so; costae with ovate scales beneath; rhizome thin and long-creeping with widely spaced fronds   10. *Thelypteris confluens*
   Fronds hairy; costae without scales; rhizome erect, ascending or rarely long-creeping; fronds tufted or rarely widely spaced   11
11 Lower pinnae ± abruptly reduced into a long series of auricles   12
   Lower pinnae only slightly reduced or gradually reduced and only the lowermost auriculiform   13
12 Rhizome creeping; fronds spaced; indusium hairy   11. *T. friesi*
   Rhizome erect; fronds tufted; indusium glabrous   12. *T. longicuspis*
13 Indusium large, persistent; lower few pairs of pinnae only slightly reduced (rarely regularly reduced and the lowermost auriculiform)   14
   Indusium absent or small and caducous; lower pinnae regularly and gradually reduced in size, the lowermost auriculiform   15
14 Rhizome creeping; fronds spaced   13. *T. chaseana*
   Rhizome erect or ascending; fronds tufted   14. *T. gueintziana*
15 Pinnae with hooked hairs on the undersides of the lobes; large, sessile, yellow or red glands absent from the costules on the lower surface; sori submarginal to medial on the lobes   15. *T. bergiana*

Pinnae lacking hooked hairs beneath; large, sessile, yellow or red glands (sometimes very few) present on the lower surface of the costules; sori medial   16. *T. strigosa*

1. Macrothelypteris aubertii (*Desv.*) *Pic. Ser.* (see p. 31)

Rhizome erect with tufted fronds which reach 1·5 m long; pinnules with acuminate to attenuate apices; sori round, exindusiate.

This is an uncommon plant of moist, montane forests. It generally occurs along streams in dense shade. HA, HK, HN, KIS. Also in the Taita hills.
Faden 69/214; Faden, Evans and Worth 69/682.

2. Ampelopteris prolifera (*Retz.*) *Copel.*

Rhizome creeping with shortly spaced fronds, often of indeterminate growth; pinnae oblong with crenate or shallowly lobed margins; sori (not yet seen in our area) circular to elongate, exindusiate.

This plant occurs along rivers and in marshy places in full sun. The sole Kenya record is from just outside our area (along the Tana River at Seven Forks, about 3000 ft altitude).
Mrs. J. Brown s.n.

3. Cyclosorus madagascariensis (*Fée*) *Ching* (*C. patens* (Fée) Copel.) (see p. 26)

The large (generally 2–3 m long), gemmiferous fronds readily distinguish this species. The linear-oblong pinnae are crenate or shallowly lobed. The circular sori are subcostular and exindusiate.

This is a common plant of moist, montane forests and the bamboo zone. It is usually gregarious and grows along streams, 4900–8200 ft. HA, HK, HN, KIT, MUM, KIS. Also in the Taita hills and on Mount Kasigau.
Verdcourt and Polhill 2930; Faden and Grumbley 72/347.

4. Cyclosorus sp. A.

The widely spaced fronds have the lowest pinnae only slightly reduced. In the latter character this species resembles *C. quadrangularis* but that species has an erect rhizome with tufted fronds and only one pair of veins joined below the sinus.

This is a species of moist, intermediate or lowland forests. It occurs along streams in dense shade at about 5250 ft (in our area). MUM. Also in the Shimba hills.
Faden 70/23; Agnew and Musumba 8558.

5. Cyclosorus interruptus (*Willd.*) *H. Itô* (*C. tottus* (Thunb.) Pic. Ser., *C. gongylodes* (Schkuhr) Link)

Fronds coriaceous, normally 40–60 cm long; lower pinnae not reduced; rhizome black.

This is a gregarious plant of marshes, usually growing in full sun. It occasionally occurs along streams in forests. Uncommon in our area. HN, KIS, MAC. Also in the Taita hills and along the coast.
Faden, Evans, and Worth 69/652; Hanid and Kiniaruh 693.

6. Cyclosorus striatus (*Schumach.*) *Ching*

This species is very similar to *C. interruptus* and differs primarily in having larger fronds (to about 1·5 m tall) with larger, more deeply cut pinnae.

This is a plant of papyrus swamps, and occurs around Lake Victoria. MUM, KIS.
Agnew and Musumba 8603; Ayieko 65.

7. Cyclosorus quadrangularis (*Fée*) *Tard.*

Fronds normally 30–60 cm long, lanceolate to lanceolate-elliptic in outline. The frond shape and erect rhizome resemble *Thelypteris gueintziana* but that species has free veins.

This plant grows in moist, lowland or intermediate forests usually along streams. Apparently it is rare in our area. MUM (Kakemega forest). Also in the Taita and Shimba hills.
Faden 69/2012, 70/21A.

8. Cyclosorus dentatus (*Forssk.*) *Ching* (see p. 55)

This is the only species of *Cyclosorus* in our area with a short-creeping rhizome and the pinnae regularly decreasing in length towards the base of the frond. The lamina is narrowly elliptic in outline.

This common species grows along streams and in other wet situations in forests up to 6850 ft. It usually grows in partial shade but tolerates full sun. HE, HA, HK, KIT, MUM, KIS, MAG, EMB, MAC. Also in the Taita hills, on Mt. Kasigau and along the coast.
Faden 68/989; Verdcourt and Greenway 440.

9. Leptogramma pozoi (*Lagasca*) *Heywood*

Rhizome erect; fronds tufted, generally 25–40 cm long; the lower few pairs of pinnae decreasing in length towards the base of the frond but never auriculiform; middle pinnae lobed about halfway to the costae.

Although primarily a species of the bamboo zone, it extends down into the moist, montane forest and up into the ericaceous zone. It grows in dense shade from 6650–11 000 ft. HE, HC, HA, HK, KIS. Also in the Taita hills.
Turner 3225; Faden 70/931.

Cyclosorus dentatus

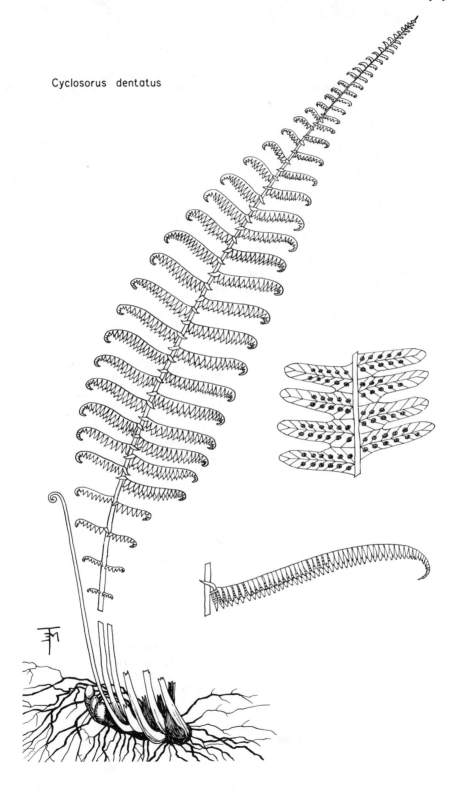

10. Thelypteris confluens (*Thunb.*) *Morton*

This is the only species of Thelypteridaceae in our area with scales on the lamina and with the veinlets of the sterile pinnules frequently forking before reaching the margin. The lower pinnae are only slightly reduced and the margins of the pinnules are often revolute.

This is a gregarious plant of marshes and river banks, growing in full sun or, less commonly, in partial shade, about 4000–6850 ft. HA, HN, KIT, MUM, MAC. Also in the Taita hills.

Verdcourt 429; Faden, Evans, and Worth 69/654.

11. Thelypteris friesii (*Brause*) *Schelpe*

This is our only species of *Thelypteris* with the pinnae greatly reduced towards the frond base which has a creeping rhizome. The occasional specimens which have the lower pinnae gradually instead of abruptly reduced can be distinguished from *T. bergiana* and *T. strigosa* by the creeping rhizome and persistent, hairy indusium.

This plant is known from only one locality in Kenya, the edge of a marsh at Sandum's Bridge near Kitale at 6000 ft. KIT.

Faden 71/458; Tweedie 2863.

12. Thelypteris longicuspis (*Bak.*) *Schelpe* (*T. zambesiaca* (Bak.) Tard.) (see p. 31)

This is the largest species of *Thelypteris* in our area with fronds up to 2 m long and 60 cm wide. The pinnae reach about 30 x3 cm and are cut almost to the costae.

This species is widespread in Kenya but is nowhere common. It occurs along streams in forests at moderate altitudes. HE, HC, HK, HN, ?KIT, MUM, MAC. Also occurs in the Taita hills.

Faden 68/988; Isaac in EAH 12619.

13. Thelypteris chaseana *Schelpe*

This species is indistinguishable from the much more common *T. gueintziana* in the absence of the rhizome (see key). The lower pinnae are somewhat reduced but are never auriculiform.

Plants are recorded from two quite different habitats in Kenya: edge of a large marsh in partial shade (Sandum's Bridge, 6000 ft); along a small stream in dense shade in moist, intermediate forest (Taita hills, 4900 ft). KIT.

Tweedie 66/241; Faden 71/456.

14. Thelypteris gueintziana (*Mett.*) *Schelpe* (see p. 31)

Plants of this species look very similar to *Thelypteris chaseana* and *Cyclosorus quadrangularis*. For distinctions from the former see key. From the latter they may be separated by their free veins.

Occasional plants may have the lowermost pinnae auriculiform and may be distinguished from *T. bergiana* and *T. strigosa* by the hairy, persistent indusium.

This is a common riverside plant at moderate altitudes, occurring in full sun or partial shade. It also occurs in other wet situations (e.g. moist, roadside banks), but it is apparently absent from undisturbed forests or open, marshy places. MUM, NAR, BAR, EMB, MAC, NBI. Also occurs in the Taita hills and on Mt. Kasigau.

Faden 68/832; Glover *et al.* 2608.

15. Thelypteris bergiana (*Schlechtend.*) *Ching*

Fronds to about 1·2 m tall and 25 cm wide. This plant is most readily distinguished from the very similar *T. strigosa* by its larger fronds (they do overlap in size however) on which the sori are frequently submarginal.

This is a common plant of moist, montane forests and the bamboo zone, occurring down to about 5900 ft. It is usually found along streams and rivers. HE, HA, HK, HN, KIT, KIS. Also in the Taita hills.

Faden 69/101; Faden and Pócs 71/900.

16. Thelypteris strigosa (*Willd.*) *Tard.* (see p. 31)

Fronds up to about 1 m long and 15 cm wide. Large plants must be studied carefully (preferably with a dissecting microscope) to distinguish them from *T. bergiana* (see key).

This plant occurs primarily in the bamboo zone, extending down into the montane forest and up into the ericaceous zone. It is commonly found along streams, often growing with *T. bergiana,* and is recorded 6250–9650 ft. HE, HT, HM, HA, HK, HN, KIT. Also in the Taita hills.

Faden 69/080; Faden *et al.* 69/762.

47. CYSTOPTERIS *Bernh.*

Small terrestrial herbs; rhizome short-creeping, densely scaly; fronds shortly spaced to tufted; stipes glabrous; lamina glabrous, lanceolate to narrowly elliptic, bipinnate or less commonly pinnate; venation free; sori ovate or round, dorsal on the veins; indusium cup-shaped, attached at the base of the receptacle and opening outwards.

Cystopteris fragilis (*L.*) *Bernh.*

Fragile fern or Brittle fern. Fronds delicate, thin-textured, acuminate, up to 30 cm in length; pinnae lanceolate, acuminate, acute or rarely obtuse at the apex.

This is primarily a plant of the bamboo zone and above, but has been recorded 5500–11 800 ft altitude in Kenya. HE, HT, HM, HA, HK, KIS, NBI.

Hedberg 898; Gardner 978.

48. ATHYRIUM *Roth*

Medium-sized terrestrial herbs; rhizome creeping or erect, somewhat fleshy, densely scaly; fronds tufted or spaced; stipes glabrous, scaly at the base, with two C-shaped vascular strands near the base, uniting above into a single U-shaped strand; lamina elliptic to lanceolate-elliptic, bi- to tripinnate, ± glabrous; margins sharply toothed; venation free; sori dorsal on the veinlets, either elongate on one side of the veinlet or else the distal end crossing the veinlet, making the sorus J-shaped or horseshoe-shaped; indusium attached to the veinlet and the same shape as the sorus, persistent.

1 Rhizome thin, creeping; fronds spaced, elliptic, mostly bipinnate   1. *A. schimperi*
   Rhizome thick, erect; fronds tufted, lanceolate-elliptic, mostly tripinnate
                    2. *A. scandicinum*

1. Athyrium schimperi *Fée*

Fronds about 25–40 cm long with the lower pinnae slightly reduced. The stipe base is brown.

This plant is known in Kenya from a single locality on Mt. Elgon at about 7850 ft. It was found at the edge of montane forest with *Juniperus procera* and *Olinia usambarensis* being two common trees. HE.

Tweedie 1882; Faden 71/452.

2. Athyrium scandicinum (*Willd.*) *Presl* (see p. 59)

Fronds very variable in size, reaching at least 1·2 m in length, but sometimes fertile when no more than 20 cm long. The stipe bases are pink or green. Two ± distinct varieties may be recognized, one with stipe bases pink is the typical one, the other has green stipe bases.

The first is primarily a plant of the bamboo zone but extends down along rivers and streams into the montane forest and up into the ericaceous zone, occurring 5250–9800 ft. HA, HK, MUM, KIS.

Faden 70/104; 69/1977.

The variety with green stipe bases tends to have the marginal teeth more spreading and the pinnules broader, longer-stalked and more obtuse than the typical variety. It does not extend into the montane forest and is recorded 8300–10 500 ft. HA, HK.

Faden 69/078; Schelpe 2716.

49. DIPLAZIUM *Swartz*

Large terrestrial herbs; rhizome thick, erect to ascending, densely scaly; fronds tufted; stipes glabrous, swollen just above the base, with two C-shaped vascular strands near the base, uniting above into a single U-shaped strand; lamina ovate, bipinnate (in our species), the pinnules deeply pinnatifid or bipinnatifid, ± glabrous; margins toothed; venation free (in our species); sori elongated along the veinlets, elliptic to linear, either on one or both sides of the veinlet; indusium the same shape as the sorus and attached to the veinlet, caducous or persistent.

1 Fronds of mature plants bipinnate-pinnatifid;
   sori mostly oblong   1. *D. hylophilum*
   Fronds bipinnate-bipinnatifid; sori mostly
   elliptic or oblong-elliptic   2
2 Indusium never completely covering the
   sorus, not splitting, caducous
                  2. *D. zanzibaricum*
   Indusium completely covering the sorus,
   splitting irregularly, persistent
                  3. *D. velaminosum*

1. Diplazium hylophilum (*Hieron.*) *C. Chr.*

Fronds about 1·2 m long; pinnules lanceolate with acuminate apices; indusium broad and persistent.

This is a rare species of moist, montane forests and occurs in dense shade in swampy spots, about 5000–6250 ft. HK. Also occurs in the Taita hills.

Faden and Holland 72/193.

2. Diplazium zanzibaricum (*Bak.*) *C. Chr.*

Fronds large (about 1·5 m long); pinnules oblong with attenuate apices; sori about 1–1·5 mm long.

This is an uncommon plant of moist, montane forests. HK, HN; also in the Taita hills.

Faden, Evans, and Worth 69/665; Faden *et al.* 69/764.

3. Diplazium velaminosum (*Diels*) *Pic. Ser.* (see p. 59)

The fronds are almost identical to those of *D. zanzibaricum* in size and cutting, and it is somewhat doubtful whether this represents a good species.

This plant grows along streams in dense shade of moist, intermediate forests. It is known in Kenya only from the Kakamega forest. MUM.

Faden 69/1976, 70/10.

50. DRYOATHYRIUM *Ching*

Large terrestrial herbs; rhizome erect, densely scaly; fronds tufted; stipes swollen just above the base, with two C-shaped vascular strands at the base, uniting above into a single U-shaped strand; lamina ovate, bipinnate, the pinnules deeply pinnatifid to bipinnatifid; venation free; sori dorsal on the veinlets, round or ovate; indusium ovate to round-reniform.

Dryoathyrium boryanum (*Willd.*) *Ching* (see p. 59)

This species has large (to 1·5 m long), thin-textured fronds which closely resemble those of

Diplazium zanzibaricum from which they differ chiefly in the shape of the sori.

This is a widespread, but uncommon, moist-forest plant, usually found along streams, 4750–8350 ft. HM, HA, HK, HN, MUM, KIS, MAC.

Faden 69/2026; Glover, Gwynne, and Samuel 1167.

51. BLECHNUM *L.*

Medium-sized, terrestrial or epiphytic herbs (rarely small trees); rhizome erect, sometimes forming a trunk, densely scaly; fronds tufted to slightly spaced, dimorphic; stipes with several vascular strands; lamina pinnate to deeply pinnatifid; margin entire to serrate, often revolute; venation free, veins parallel, once or twice forked; fertile pinnae contracted; sori linear, close to and parallel to the costa or nearly covering the whole under-surface of the contracted, fertile pinnae; indusium linear, opening towards the costa, rarely vestigial.

1   Bases of middle and lower sterile pinnae not
    adnate to the rachis   1. *B. australe*
    Bases of middle and lower sterile pinnae
    adnate to the rachis   2
2   Sterile pinnae narrowed at the base; bases of
    middle sterile pinnae quite separate from
    each other; rhizome usually trunk-like
        2. *B. tabulare*
    Sterile pinnae broadest at the base; bases of
    middle sterile pinnae in contact with each
    other; rhizome not trunk-like   3
3   Margins entire; fronds coriaceous, to 150 cm
    long, slightly spaced on an elongate
    rhizome   3. *B. attenuatum*
    Margins crenulate; fronds herbaceous, to 35
    cm long, tufted on a short rhizome
        4. *B. ivohibense*

1. Blechnum australe *L.*

Fronds up to 40 cm long and 8 cm wide; pinnae mucronate at the apex. Fronds may have all pinnae sterile, all fertile or the upper fertile and the lower sterile.

This plant is terrestrial in the bamboo zone and is very local, occurring at about 8000 ft. HM, HA. Cameron 18; Faden 71/71.

2. Blechnum tabulare (*Thunb.*) *Kuhn*

Rhizome to about 100 cm tall and 10 cm in diameter; rhizome scales linear-lanceolate, up to 3·5 cm long; fronds dimorphic, 50–100 cm long with oblong pinnae.

This terrestrial species occurs principally in the bamboo zone but is also recorded from one locality in the ericaceous zone. In partial or dense shade, at about 8000–8500 ft. HA, HK. Faden and Evans 69/903; Faden *et al.* 69/539.

3. Blechnum attenuatum (*Swartz*) *Mett.*

Fronds with the pinnae gradually reduced towards the base with the lowermost auriculiform; middle pinnules acuminate and distinctly broadened at the base.

Plants are either terrestrial, or else the rhizomes climb tree fern trunks (to a height of at least 5 m) and bear fronds only at the summit. This is the common *Blechnum* in Kenya, occurring in moist, montane forests and the bamboo zone. HM, HA, HK, KIS. Also in the Taita hills and on Mt. Kasigau.

Bally 4814; Faden and Grumbley 72/345.

4. Blechnum ivohibense *C. Chr.*

Lower pinnae reduced but not auriculiform (in our area); middle pinnae up to 4 cm long; young fronds often reddish.

This terrestrial species is known from only one locality in our area: the base of volcanic cone Kirui, north-east Mt. Kenya. It grows in moist, montane forests. HK. Also in the Taita hills and on Mt. Kasigau.

Faden *et al.* 69/773, 69/495.

52. ASPLENIUM *L.*

Small to medium, terrestrial or epiphytic herbs; rhizome erect to long-creeping, densely covered with clathrate scales; fronds tufted to widely spaced; stipes with two vascular strands near the base, uniting above to form an X-shape; lamina simple to quadripinnate, with sparse to dense clathrate scales; venation free; sori elliptic to linear, borne on one side of a veinlet; indusium cup-shaped or elliptic to linear, attached to the veinlet.

1   Fronds simple   1. *A.* sp. *A*
    Fronds pinnate to quadripinnate   2
2   Fronds pinnate, pinnae toothed to lobed   3
    Fronds pinnate-pinnatifid to quadripinnate
        25
3   Terminal segment absent, the rachis
    elongated and proliferous at the apex
        2. *A. sandersonii*
    Terminal segment present   4
4   Terminal segment similar to the lateral pinnae
        5
    Terminal segment unlike the lateral pinnae   8
5   Fronds gemmiferous   6
    Fronds not gemmiferous   7
6   Gemma present on the upper (adaxial) side of
    the costa of the terminal pinna, about
    half way between the base and apex; pinnae
    2–4 pairs   3. *A. angolense*
    Gemma present at the base of the terminal
    pinna; pinnae usually 5–10 pairs
        4. *A. gemmiferum*

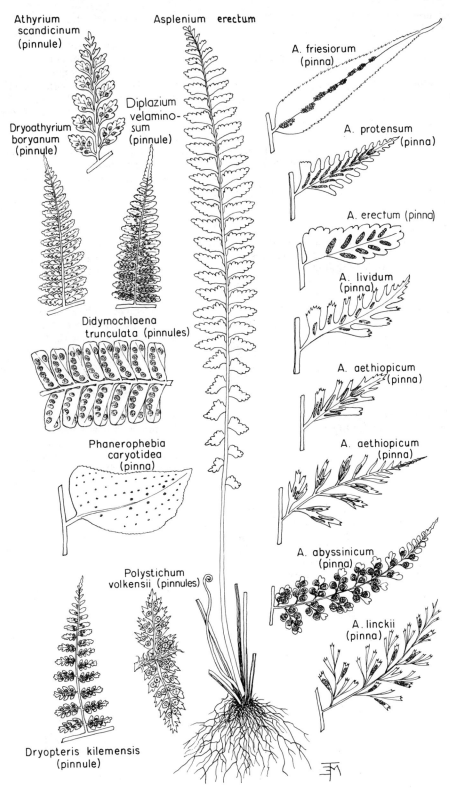

Athyrium
scandicinum
(pinnule)

Dryoathyrium
boryanum
(pinnule)

Diplazium
velamino-
sum
(pinnule)

Asplenium **erectum**

A. friesiorum
(pinna)

A. protensum
(pinna)

A. erectum (pinna)

A. lividum
(pinna)

A. aethiopicum
(pinna)

A. aethiopicum
(pinna)

A. abyssinicum
(pinna)

A. linckii
(pinna)

Didymochlaena
trunculata (pinnules)

Phanerophlebia
caryotidea
(pinna)

Polystichum
volkensii (pinnules)

Dryopteris kilemensis
(pinnule)

7   Plants epiphytic; indusium about 0·5 mm
    wide; sori usually medial or slightly sub-
    costal   5. *A. ceii*
    Plants terrestrial; indusium about 1 mm wide;
    sori subcostal   4. *A. gemmiferum*

8   Rachis gemmiferous   9
    Rachis not gemmiferous (if stipe gemmi-
    ferous see *A. monanthes*)   15

9   Rachis hairy; pinnae margins usually deeply
    toothed or lobed   10
    Rachis   glabrous   (although   sometimes
    paleate); margins crenate to doubly serrate
                                            11

10 Pinnae normally 20–55 pairs, lanceolate to
    oblong; frond apex gradually acuminate;
    costae of mature fronds prominent above,
    not grooved   6. *A. protensum*
    Pinnae 8–20 pairs, lanceolate to deltoid;
    frond apex abruptly acuminate; costae
    grooved, not prominent above
                               7. *A. adamsii*

11 Stipes a uniform lustrous brown or reddish
    brown; pinnae to 1·5 cm long, dimidiate
                               8. *A. normale*
    Stipes green or green on the adaxial surface
    and black on the abaxial surface, dull;
    pinnae 1·5–12 cm long   12

12 Sori 2–3·5 mm long; indusium elliptic to
    oblong-elliptic   13
    Sori 3–10 mm long; indusium narrowly
    oblong to linear   14

13 Margin coarsely and doubly serrate
                               9. *A. boltonii*
    Margin finely serrate   10. *A. elliottii*

14 Pinnae 7–10 pairs, widely spaced, usually
    without a prominent basal auricle
                               11. *A. christii*
    Pinnae 10–20 pairs, usually close together,
    with a prominent basal auricle
                           12. *A. macrophlebium*

15 Pinnae cuneate-lacerate with an abruptly
    caudate apex; rachis lustrous brown,
    usually brittle; plants usually epiphytic
                               13. *A. megalura*
    Pinnae variously shaped but not as above;
    rachis green to lustrous brown or black,
    seldom brittle; plants usually terrestrial
    (except *A. friesiorum* and *A.* sp. *B*) 16

16 Rachis hairy   7. *A. adamsii*
    Rachis glabrous (sometimes paleate)   17

17 Rhizome long-creeping with spaced fronds
                                            18
    Rhizome erect or short-creeping with ±
    tufted fronds   19

18 Pinnae dimidiate, to 5 cm long, oblong; sori
    medial; plants terrestrial, usually growing

near waterfalls or streams
                           14. *A. unilaterale*
    Pinnae not dimidiate, 5·5–14 cm long,
    narrowly lanceolate; sori subcostal; plants
    epiphytic or less commonly terrestrial, not
    primarily associated with streams or water-
    falls   15. *A. friesiorum*

19 Lower pinnae regularly reduced towards the
    base of the frond, the lowermost ones
    deltoid   20
    Lower pinnae only slightly smaller than the
    ones above them   23

20 Upper margins of middle pinnae laciniate, cut
    more than half the width of the pinnae
                               16. *A. formosum*
    Upper margins of middle pinnae crenate to
    shallowly lobed   21

21 Stipe and rachis lustrous brown; middle
    pinnae elliptic to oblong; margin crenate;
    pinnae with basal auricle (when present)
    not separated from the rest of the pinna by
    a sinus   22
    Stipe and rachis dull, green or brown; middle
    pinnae mostly lanceolate; margin crenate
    to lobed; pinnae with basal auricle fre-
    quently separated from the rest of the
    pinna by a sinus   19. *A. erectum*

22 Pinnae dimidiate, with a prominent basal
    auricle; middle pinnae 0·8–1·6 (–1·9) cm
    long; sori usually 1–3 (sometimes up to 6)
    per pinna and confined to the lower half of
    the pinna; stipes sometimes gemmiferous
                               17. *A. monanthes*
    Pinnae not dimidiate, usually without a basal
    auricle; middle pinnae 0·3–0·9 cm long;
    sori (1–) 2–10 per pinna, in approximately
    equal numbers in both halves of the pinna;
    stipes never gemmiferous
                               18. *A. trichomanes*

23 Pinnae acuminate; rhizome and stipes fleshy;
    croziers and often stipe bases covered with
    a tangle of hair-like scales; indusium 1–1·5
    mm broad   20. *A.* sp. *B*
    Pinnae obtuse to acute; rhizome and stipes
    not fleshy; croziers and stipe bases without
    hair-like scales; indusium less than 1 mm
    broad   24

24 Middle pinnae 1·2–1·8 cm long; lower margin
    of pinna toothed only in the outer quarter
    to third of its length
                               21. *A. suppositum*
    Middle pinnae 2–5 cm long; lower margin of
    pinna toothed in the outer half to three-
    quarters of its length
                               22. *A. inaequilaterale*

25 Sori one on each segment; segments linear to

narrowly oblong-elliptic (sometimes slightly broadened towards the apex); apex of segment rounded and entire; indusium often reaching the margin, often cup-shaped **26**

Sori more than one on each segment (often one on *some* segments of *A. abyssinicum* and *A. linckii*); segments usually cuneate and toothed at the apex (entire in *A. abyssinicum*); indusium not reaching the margin, never cup-shaped **35**

26 Fronds dimorphic: stolon-like, gemmiferous fronds of indeterminate growth and lacking a lamina produced in addition to the normal fronds; normal fronds 3–16 cm long; lamina narrowly deltoid, widest at the base 23. *A. mannii*

Fronds uniform, if gemmiferous, then the gemmae borne on the upper part of the rachis; frond length and shape various; lamina widest above the base (sometimes widest at the base in *A. theciferum*) **27**

27 Fronds gemmiferous **28**

Fronds not gemmiferous **32**

28 Pinnae 1·3–3 (–4·5) cm long; bases of pinnae very asymmetric with the basiscopic pinnule opposite the sinus between the second–third to fourth–fifth acroscopic pinnules 24. *A. dregeanum*

Pinnae 3–11 cm long; bases of pinnae more symmetrical; first basiscopic pinnule opposite the sinus between the first–second acroscopic pinnules **29**

29 Sori confined to the pinnule and pinna lobes; basal acroscopic pinnules of middle pinnae pinnatifid, forming a winged costule less than or equal to the pinnule lobes in width **30**

Sori extending from the lobes into the winged costal or costular part of the lamina (rarely confined to the lobes in some pinnules); basal acroscopic pinnules of middle pinnae lobed to pinnatifid, if forming a winged costule, then this greater than the pinnule lobes in width **31**

30 Middle pinnae lanceolate to narrowly deltoid, gradually tapering from the base to an acute or acuminate apex 25. *A. bugoiense*

Middle pinnae oblong to lanceolate-oblong; apex abruptly acute 26. *A. sp. C*

31 Basal acroscopic pinnule of middle pinnae much more developed than the basal basiscopic pinnule; basal basiscopic pinnule usually slightly smaller than the next basiscopic pinnule

27. *A. pseudoauriculatum*

Basal acroscopic pinnule of middle pinnae only slightly more developed than the basal basiscopic pinnule; basal basiscopic pinnule equal to or slightly larger than the next basiscopic pinnule 28. *A. sp. D*

32 Fronds tri- to quadripinnate; croziers and stipe bases covered with a dense, matted, hair-like indumentum; plants usually epiphytic on tree-fern trunks

29. *A. hypomelas*

Fronds pinnate-pinnatifid to rarely pinnate-bipinnatifid; hair-like indumentum usually absent (sometimes present in *A. loxoscaphoides*); plants terrestrial or epiphytic **33**

33 Sori terminal or subterminal on the segments; indusium terminal on a veinlet; pinnae 6–12 pairs; pinnules 2–7 pairs

30. *A. theciferum*

Sori lateral on the segments; indusium lateral on a veinlet; pinnae 12–42 pairs; pinnules 8–25 pairs **34**

34 Sori borne in the middle to upper part of the pinnules; pinnae rounded to acute at the apex, with 8–11 pairs of pinnules (in our area); stipe bases and croziers without a matted, hair-like indumentum; plants drying green; plants of dry or riverine forest, 2500–8100 ft 31. *A. rutifolium*

Sori borne in the middle to lower part of the pinnules; pinnae acuminate to acute at the apex, with 14–25 pairs of pinnules; stipe bases and croziers sometimes with a matted, hair-like indumentum; plants usually drying grey or grey-green; plants chiefly of moist forests and the bamboo zone, 6800–12 200 ft 32. *A. loxoscaphoides*

35 Fronds gemmiferous 33. *A. blastophorum*

Fronds not gemmiferous **36**

36 Stipes dark brown, bases swollen and green

34. *A. adiantum-nigrum*

Stipes variously coloured, bases neither swollen nor green **37**

37 Stipes lustrous, reddish or brown; margins entire; texture membranaceous; fronds bi- to tripinnate 35. *A. abyssinicum*

Stipes green, brown or black; margins toothed; texture firmly herbaceous to coriaceous, rarely membranaceous; fronds pinnate-pinnatifid to tripinnate **38**

38 Stipes entirely green; fronds to 15 cm long; texture membranaceous 36. *A. varians*

Stipes entirely brown or black, or, more commonly, green on the adaxial surface and black on the abaxial surface; fronds of various lengths, but usually more than 15 cm long; texture firmly herbaceous to coriaceous   **39**

39 Fronds tripinnate   **40**
     Fronds pinnate-pinnatifid to bipinnate   **41**

40 Lamina ovate-lanceolate to deltoid; fronds ± tufted to shortly spaced; plants of montane forests   37. *A. linckii*
     Lamina lanceolate to oblong-lanceolate; fronds widely spaced; plants of the bamboo zone   38. *A. praegracile*

41 Rhizome erect; fronds tufted; stipe bases with numerous hair-like scales
                            39. *A. aethiopicum*
     Rhizome short- or long-creeping; fronds shortly to widely spaced; stipe bases with or without hair-like scales   **42**

42 Fronds pinnate-pinnatifid   **43**
     Fronds bipinnate-pinnatifid   **46**

43 Pinnae sessile or subsessile, deltoid, usually clearly discolourous; frond narrowly oblong   40. *A. stuhlmannii*
     Pinnae distinctly stalked, usually lanceolate, rarely a few deltoid, not at all to only slightly discolourous; fronds lanceolate to oblong   **44**

44 Croziers and stipes with two kinds of scales, appearing as if a mixture of long hairs and scales   39. *A. aethiopicum*
     Croziers and stipes with only one kind of scale   **45**

45 Rhizome scales brown; stipes 0·25–0·5 times the length of the lamina; plants found below 6700 ft   41. *A. lividum*
     Rhizome scales black; stipes 0·6–2 times the length of the lamina; plants found above 9850 ft   42. *A. uhligii*

46 Rhizome scales copper-coloured; moorland plants   43. *A.* sp. *E*
     Rhizome scales dark brown to black; plants of various habitats   **47**

47 Rhizome scales uniformly coloured; scales of the stipe bases uniform, linear-lanceolate, not mixed with hair-like scales; fronds usually widely spaced on the rhizome; moorland plants   **48**
     Rhizome scales black with narrow brown margins; scales of the stipe base dimorphic, the linear-lanceolate ones mixed with few to many (rarely none) hair-like scales; fronds shortly spaced on the rhizome; plants of various habitats, but rarely of moorland   **49**

48 Rachis with numerous, minute stalked glands; rhizome scales dark brown or black; lumina yellow   44. *A. actiniopteroides*
     Rachis without glands; rhizome scales black; lumina colourless   42. *A. uhligii*

49 Fronds lanceolate-ovate to deltoid, conspicuously discolorous; stipe bases with few or no hair-like scales; plants apparently always terrestrial; not recorded above 6700 ft elevation   45. *A. buettneri*
     Fronds lanceolate to narrowly oblong, slightly discolorous; stipe bases with numerous hair-like scales; plants terrestrial or epiphytic, recorded up to 12 000 ft
                            39. *A. aethiopicum*

1. Asplenium *sp.* A.

The strap-shaped fronds, about 25 cm long, tufted on a short, fleshy rhizome, readily distinguish this species. It has sometimes been named *A. holstii* Hieron., a species occurring in the Taita and Sagala hills and on Mt. Kasigau, but the rhizome scales are different.

Only a single collection of this plant has been made in Kenya. It was epiphytic along the Yala River in the Kakamega forest, which is of a moist, intermediate type, at 5000 ft. MUM.

Faden 70/39.

2. Asplenium sandersonii *Hook.* (see p. 66)

Rhizome erect with tufted fronds to about 15 cm long and 2·5 cm wide; fronds arching producing new plants where in contact with the substrate.

This is a common, gregarious epiphyte of moist, montane, and intermediate forests. It occasionally grows in moister spots in dry forests, occurring 3600–8000 ft. HC, HT, HM, HA, HK, HN, MUM, KIS, NAR, MAC, KAJ. Also in the Taita hills and on Mts. Kasigau and Marsabit.

Gillett 16540; Faden 69/095.

3. Asplenium angolense *Bak.*

The position of the gemma is constant and is unique among the East African species of *Asplenium*. The fronds reach a length of about 30 cm and the lateral pinnae a length of 5 cm.

This terrestrial plant grows in dense shade in moist, intermediate forests, 5250–5500 ft. It is known in Kenya only from the Kakamega forest. MUM.

Faden 69/2112, 70/1.

4. Asplenium gemmiferum *Schrad.* (see p. 63)

Rhizome erect; fronds tufted, somewhat fleshy, up to 80 cm long; pinnae up to 12 cm long; sori 1·5 cm long. Some fronds lack gemmae, but it is likely that every plant has at least some gemmiferous fronds.

This is a rather uncommon plant in our area. It is terrestrial in dense shade in moist, intermediate forests, reaching the lower edge of the moist, montane forest in places and occurring

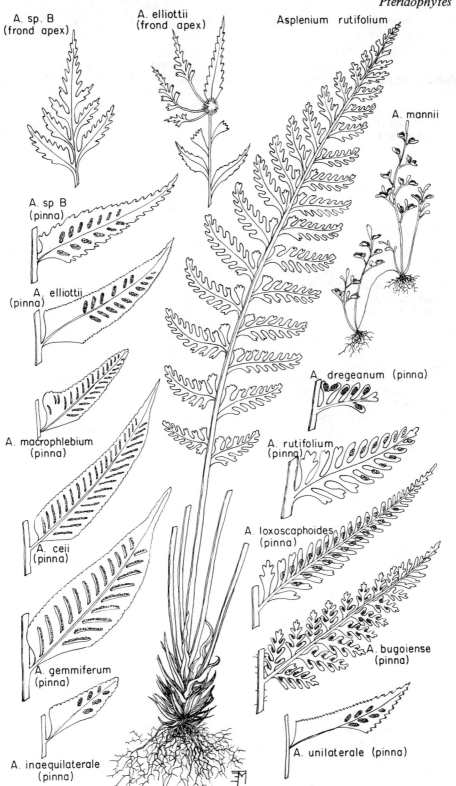

A. sp. B
(frond apex)

A. elliottii
(frond apex)

Asplenium rutifolium

A. mannii

A. sp. B
(pinna)

A. elliottii
(pinna)

A. macrophlebium
(pinna)

A. dregeanum (pinna)

A. rutifolium
(pinna)

A. ceii
(pinna)

A. loxoscaphoides
(pinna)

A. gemmiferum
(pinna)

A. bugoiense
(pinna)

A. inaequilaterale
(pinna)

A. unilaterale (pinna)

4900–7500 ft. ?HK, HN, KIS, EMB, KAJ. Also on Mts. Kulal and Marsabit.

Faden and Evans 69/579; Verdcourt 2242.

5. Asplenium ceii *Pic. Ser.* (*A. atroviride* Schelpe) (see p. 63)

The erect rhizome, tufted fronds and large pinnae are all very similar in size and general appearance to *A. gemmiferum*. Fronds of *A. ceii* never have gemmae.

In our area *A. ceii* is always epiphytic, occurring in dense shade in moist, intermediate forests, about 5250–5500 ft. The altitude of the single collection from Mt. Elgon (8000 ft, Gardner 1028) is probably erroneous. ?HE, MUM.

Faden 69/2014; Verdcourt 1671.

6. Asplenium protensum *Schrad.* (see p. 59)

Rhizome erect, bearing narrowly oblong-elliptic, gemmiferous fronds which grow to about 60 cm in length; pinnae deeply lobed with subcostal sori. The freshly cut rhizome has a characteristic odour of oil of wintergreen (methyl salicylate).

This is a common plant of moist, montane and intermediate forests. It may be either terrestrial or a low-level epiphyte and is recorded about 4750–9500 ft. HE, HC, HA, HK, HN, KIT, MUM, KIS, BAR, EMB, MAC, KAJ. Also on Mt. Marsabit and in the Murua Nysigar hills.

Verdcourt and Moggi 2503; Faden and Grumbley 72/342.

7. Asplenium adamsii *Alston*

The small (up to 20 cm long), oblong-elliptic fronds occasionally are gemmiferous and are tufted on an erect rhizome.

This is a plant of moorland and the upper part of the ericaceous zone. It grows on rocky banks near waterfalls, 9750–11 200 ft. HE, HA.

Faden and Evans 69/795; Taylor 3735.

8. Asplenium normale *D. Don*

Fronds narrowly oblong to linear, tufted, up to 30 cm long. Plants closely resemble the much more common *A. monanthes* but can usually be distinguished by the presence of gemmae on the upper part of the rachis in some fronds. In the absence of gemmae, the smaller, more numerous sori per pinna in *A. normale* are sufficient to separate the two species.

This is uncommon in our area. It is terrestrial and grows in dense shade in moist, intermediate, and montane forests from 3250–8000 ft. HA, HK. Locally common in the Taita hills and on Mt. Kasigau.

Faden 71/284; Faden and Holland 72/180.

9. Asplenium boltonii *Schelpe*

Plants of this species can be distinguished from the much more common *A. sp. B* only by the presence of gemmae on the fronds. Both have an erect fleshy rhizome and tufted fleshy fronds which can reach a length of about 70 cm. In both the sori are elliptic with a broad indusium.

The sole unambiguous record from our area is from the bamboo zone at 9000 ft. In the Taita hills this plant occurs at about 5300–7000 ft and is terrestrial. HK, ?MAC.

White 1346.

10. Asplenium elliottii *C. H. Wright* (see p. 63)

Rhizomes erect; fronds generally 30–60 cm (occasionally more than 100 cm) long. The basiscopic halves of the middle pinnae bases are less cuneate than in *A. boltonii* and *A. sp. B*.

This is a very common, often gregarious, moist montane-forest plant which extends down into moist intermediate forests and up into the bamboo zone. It is consistently terrestrial except in the Kericho area where it occasionally grows as a low-level epiphyte. Recorded 4000–8750 ft. HE, HT, HM, HA, HK, HN, KIT, MUM, KIS, EMB, MAC, KAJ. Also in the Taita hills and on Mt. Kasigau.

Faden 69/087; Fries 1233.

11. Asplenium christii *Hieron.*

Plants of this species resemble small plants of *A. elliottii* in their erect rhizomes, tufted, gemmiferous fronds and general cutting of the lamina. They differ most clearly in their longer (up to 8 mm long), linear sori and narrower (up to 0·8 mm wide) indusium. The fronds of plants in our area appear to be uniform while those of Taita and Sagala hills' plants are dimorphic.

This is an uncommon plant of moist, intermediate forests. It is terrestrial in dense shade, 4750–6250 ft. ?HK, MUM, EMB.

Faden 69/2004; Schelpe 2395.

12. Asplenium macrophlebium *Bak.* (see p. 63)

Rhizome erect; fronds tufted, oblong-lanceolate, gemmiferous up to about 30 cm long; basal auricle never separated from the rest of the pinna by a sinus.

This plant is terrestrial in moist, intermediate forests. It occurs about 5250–6000 ft and is common in the Kakamega forest. MUM. Also in the Taita hills.

Faden 69/1999, 69/2021.

13. Asplenium megalura *Hieron.*

Fronds tufted with an oblong lamina. The wedge-shaped pinnae make this species unmistakable.

This is usually a pendulous epiphyte (rarely terrestrial) in moist, intermediate, and montane forests. Occurs 3000–8000 ft. Common in the Kericho area, but apparently uncommon elsewhere. HT, HM, HN, KIS, KIT. Also in the Taita, Sagala, and Maungu hills and on Mt. Kasigau.

Faden, Evans, and Worth 69/708; Faden and Cameron 72/300.

14. Asplenium unilaterale *Lam.* (see p. 63)

Fronds 20–30 cm long with the lower pinnae only slightly reduced; pinnae often with sori confined to the outer quarter or third.

This species occurs along streams and near waterfalls in riverine and moist, intermediate forests 4400–5500 ft. HA, MUM, EMB, MAC. Also in the Taita hills.

Faden 68/821; Schelpe 2404.

15. Asplenium friesiorum *C. Chr.* (see p. 59)

Fronds 60–100 cm long with narrowly lanceolate pinnae with attenuate apices and coarsely serrate to deeply lobed margins. The arrangement of the sori in two rows very close to the costa is distinctive.

Common in moist, montane forests, particularly *Ocotea* (camphorwood) forests, where it grows high on trees with other ferns such as *Elaphoglossum lastii*, *Drynaria volkensii*, and *Oleandra distenta*. It also grows in the bamboo zone and moist, intermediate forests, occurring at 4600–9000 ft. HM, HA, HK, HN, KIS. Also in the Taita and Sagala hills and on Mt. Kasigau.

Lucas 227; Faden and Grumbley 72/341.

16. Asplenium formosum *Willd.*

Fronds tufted, to 15 cm long and 2·5 cm wide. This species differs from *A. erectum* var. *usambarense* in having generally smaller fronds with more deeply lobed pinnae.

This rare (in our area) fern was found in partially shaded rock crevices at the northern end of the Kakamega forest at 5400 ft. MUM.

Faden 69/2113.

17. Asplenium monanthes *L.* (see p. 66)

Fronds linear, 25–40 cm long; sori are parallel to the basiscopic margins of the oblong pinnae.

A common plant of the bamboo zone, it also occurs in dry, montane forests. It is sometimes found along streams and may grow in dense shade or full sun, 6850–11 200 ft. HE, HC, HT, HM, HA, HK, KIS.

Greenway and Kanuri 13868; Schelpe 2590.

18. Asplenium trichomanes *L.*

Fronds narrowly oblong, up to 15 cm long and 1·8 cm wide; pinnae rounded at apex and less than twice as long as wide.

This uncommon species occurs in moist, shaded rock crevices, 7000–8000 ft. HT, HM, RV. Also in Murua Nysigar hills.

Glover, Gwynne, and Samuel 1720; Faden 70/859.

19. Asplenium erectum *Willd.* (see p. 59)

Fronds generally 25–40 cm long.

This species extends from moist intermediate forests up into the bamboo zone, in dense shade. It can be divided into two varieties: the typical one differing from var. *usambarense* (Hieron.) Schelpe by its acute pinnae, costa often whitish (not dark) above and the sori more than 2 mm from the margin. These occur in the same zone but the typical variety is mainly western in its distribution; 4300–9000 ft. HE, HT, HM, HA, HK, HN, KIT, MUM, KIS, EMB, MAC, NBI, KAJ.

Hedberg 90; Faden and Cameron 72/308; Faden, Evans, and Worth 69/674; Gardner in Batiscombe 966.

20. Asplenium *sp.* B. (see p. 63)

For similarities to and distinctions from *A. boltonii*, see that species (above).

Unlike *A. boltonii*, this plant is strictly epiphytic. It occurs in moist, montane forests and in the bamboo zone, about 4900–9800 ft. HT, HM, HA, HK, HN, KIT, KIS, ?EMB.

Faden and Evans 69/895; Verdcourt and Polhill 2988.

21. Asplenium suppositum *Hieron.*

The smaller, more finely toothed and more numerous pinnae give this plant a different 'look' from *A. inaequilaterale*, and I consider them distinct species. Both are terrestrial and were found growing side by side in the Lower Imenti forest near Meru. The narrowly oblong fronds of *A. suppositum* reach to 30 cm.

A plant of moist, intermediate forests, occurring along streams at about 4000 ft. It has been collected only twice in Kenya. EMB.

Faden 70/124; Balbo 781.

22. Asplenium inaequilaterale *Willd.* (see p. 63)

Fronds generally 20–30 cm long. For distinctions from *A. suppositum* see above and key. It differs from *A. unilaterale* chiefly in its erect rhizome and tufted fronds.

A species of moist, intermediate forests occurring in dense shade near streams and rivers, but occasionally found far from running water. There are also two collections from dry, intermediate forests and one from moist, montane forest. Recorded about 4000–6500 ft, but rare above

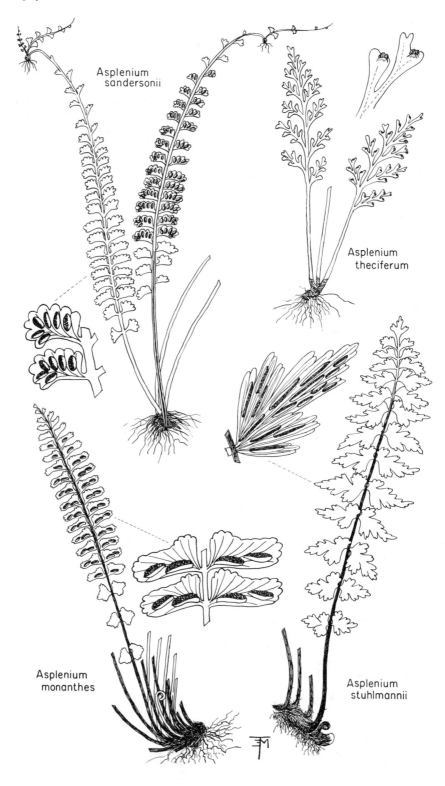

Asplenium
sandersonii

Asplenium
theciferum

Asplenium
monanthes

Asplenium
stuhlmannii

5900 ft. MUM, KIS, EMB, NBI. Also in the Taita hills and on Mt. Kasigau.
Faden 69/2005; Agnew 7571.

23. **Asplenium mannii** *Hook.* (see p. 63)
The pinnae of the normal fronds are alternate as are the gemmae of the gemmiferous fronds, which can reach a length of at least 45 cm.

A gregarious epiphyte of moist, intermediate, and montane forests. Generally uncommon except in the Kericho area, occurring about 5300–8000 ft. HT, HM, HA, HK, MUM, KIS. Also in the Taita hills and on Mt. Kasigau.
Kerfoot 2977; Faden and Holland 72/187.

24. **Asplenium dregeanum** *Kunze* (see p. 63)
Fronds tufted, generally 25–40 cm long. The numerous, small, crowded pinnae with very unequal-sided bases readily distinguish this species.

This plant is terrestrial in dense shade in moist, intermediate forests. It is known in our area only from the Kakamega forest at 5600 ft. MUM. Also on Mt. Kasigau, 3250–3600 ft.
Faden 69/2018, 69/2103.

25. **Asplenium bugoiense** *Hieron.* (see p. 63)
The finely-dissected fronds with narrowly triangular middle pinnae are not likely to be confused with any other species except *A.* sp. *C.* Both are recorded from the Aberdares and Mt. Kenya, and some intermediates have been collected, e.g. Faden 69/023. Plants from western Kenya are all *A. bugoiense*.

This plant grows in moist, montane forests in dense shade, usually near streams. It is generally terrestrial and is recorded about 6500–8800 ft. HE, HM, HA, HK, HN, KIT, KIS.
Maas Geesteranus 5659; Faden and Cameron 72/289.

26. **Asplenium** *sp.* **C.**
In typical plants of this species, the segments are narrower than in *A. bugoiense*. The distal, unlobed pinnules of the middle pinnae are often at an angle of 70–90° to the costa, while those in *A. bugoiense* are usually at an angle of 45–60°.

This is another terrestrial plant of moist montane forests, perhaps extending down into moist, intermediate forests in the Meru area. It occurs in dense shade near streams. HA, HK, EMB.
Gardner 1266; Balbo 776.

27. **Asplenium pseudoauriculatum** *Schelpe*
This species differs from *A. bugoiense*, *A.* sp. *C* and *A.* sp. *D* in having the basal acroscopic pinnule much larger than the next acroscopic pinnule and the basal basiscopic pinnule. It differs from *A.*

dregeanum in having generally larger fronds (up to about 60 cm long) with larger pinnae having more numerous pinnules and a more symmetrical base. The fronds are tufted.

Known only from moist, intermediate forests, in dense shade; it generally occurs near streams and is recorded at c. 5400 ft. MUM (Kakamega forest and Kaimosi).
Gillett 16703; Faden 69/2117.

28. **Asplenium** *sp.* **D.**
This species is intermediate in frond cutting between *A. bugoiense* and *A. pseudoauriculatum*, the pinnae being narrowly triangular but less divided than *A. bugoiense*. The fronds are tufted. Since this species has only been collected once, the limits of its variation are uncertain.

Known only from the Kakamega forest, which is of a moist, intermediate type, this terrestrial plant was found growing in dense shade at 5400 ft. MUM.
Faden 69/2019.

29. **Asplenium hypomelas** *Kuhn*
The large (up to about 100 cm long), finely-dissected fronds with small, cup-shaped indusia are unmistakable.

The association of this species with the tree fern *Cyathea manniana* is, in the author's experience, absolute. The *Asplenium* may be epiphytic on the trunks or may be growing on the ground below the tree ferns, perhaps having fallen off one. The habitat is the same as for the *Cyathea*: moist, montane forests generally along rivers. Occurs about 5000–7500 ft. HA, HK, HN, KIS, ?EMB. Also in the Taita hills.
Kabuye 48; Faden and Grumbley 72/346.

30. **Asplenium theciferum** *(Kunth) Mett.* (see p. 66)
Fronds tufted, somewhat fleshy, up to about 35 cm long; lamina generally narrowly oblong-elliptic, but in some plants from western Kenya (Tweedie 2970; Faden and Evans 69/2057) ovate-deltoid. The latter are close to *A. cornutum* Alston of West Africa.

This is a very common and widespread fern in Kenya and grows in a variety of habitats. It is epiphytic in moist, intermediate and montane forests and in the bamboo zone, frequently growing on isolated trees or clumps of trees. It occurs about 2900–9500 ft. HE, HC, HT, HM, HA, HK, HN, KIT, MUM, KIS, NAR, MAC, KAJ. Also on forested hills east and north of our area.
Bally 4810; Faden 69/1853.

31. Asplenium rutifolium (*Berg.*) *Kunze* (see p. 63)

Fronds arching, fleshy, tufted on an erect rhizome and generally 30–40 cm long.

Occurring in dry or riverine forests, usually on banks or in rock crevices or occasionally epiphytic in the wettest places. HA, KIS, ?EMB, MAC, NBI, KAJ. Also on the forested hills to the east and north of our area.

Faden 67/510; Opiko 327.

32. Asplenium loxoscaphoides *Bak.* (see p. 63)

Fronds fleshy, tufted on an erect rhizome, either rigidly erect or arching, to 75–120 cm tall. Plants of the Kericho area are smaller (fronds 30–65 cm long) and brighter green than higher altitude plants and may represent a distinct variety.

This is primarily a plant of the bamboo zone, but it extends into moist, montane forests in some areas. It is terrestrial everywhere except in the Kericho area. HE, HC, HM, HA, HK, KIS, KAJ.

Hedberg 116; Faden and Cameron 72/299.

33. Asplenium blastophorum *Hieron.*

Fronds narrowly deltoid, bipinnate and shortly spaced on a short-creeping rhizome. In habit and cutting of the fronds, this species most closely resembles the non-gemmiferous *A. buettneri*, but in that species the pinnae are more dissected.

A terrestrial species in moist, intermediate forests, occurring at c. 5400 ft. MUM (Kakamega and Malava forests).

Faden 69/2040, 69/2114.

34. Asplenium adiantum-nigrum *L.*

Fronds bi- to tripinnate, about 25 cm in length and tufted on a short rhizome. Lamina deltoid and usually coriaceous in our area.

In our area this is primarily a species of the ericaceous zone and moorland, occurring 9800–12 500 ft. Terrestrial, growing in dense shade, frequently near streams. HE, HC, HA, HK. Occurs at much lower altitudes in the Taita and Sagala hills.

Faden and Evans 69/801; Schelpe 2563.

35. Asplenium abyssinicum *Fée* (see p. 59)

Fronds commonly 30–40 cm long and tufted on an erect rhizome; lower pinnae reduced in size; rachis lacking scales and hairs.

This is primarily a plant of the bamboo zone and occurs in dense shade along streams. It extends up into the moorland and down into moist, montane forest, occurring about 6000–11 500 ft. HE, HT, HA, HK, HN.

Faden 69/109; Verdcourt 2048.

36. Asplenium varians *Hook. & Grev.*

Fronds delicate, tufted on an erect rhizome with a narrowly elliptic bipinnate lamina.

This uncommon fern grows in rock crevices in dry forests, about 5000–5600 ft. ?HE, KIS, BAR, RV, NBI.

Faden and Evans 69/2080; Mabberley and McCall 104.

37. Asplenium linckii *Kuhn* (see p. 59)

Rhizome creeping with shortly spaced fronds generally 30–50 cm long; lamina finely dissected bearing small, wedge-shaped segments to 3 mm wide. with marginal teeth 1–2 mm long.

This very attractive fern is a species of moist, montane forests. It is usually terrestrial (occasionally growing on the bases of trees) and grows in dense shade, about 5650–8200 ft. HT, HA, HK, HN, ?EMB. Also in the Taita hills.

Polhill, Verdcourt, and Lucas 323; Faden 69/003.

38. Asplenium praegracile *Rosenst.*

The sole Kenya collection looks like a large, deeply-cut plant of *A. aethiopicum* but differs most clearly in its long-creeping rhizome with widely spaced fronds. The correct name for this species is uncertain.

This plant was found in the bamboo zone in dense shade near a stream at 9600 ft. HA.

Faden 71/880.

39. Asplenium aethiopicum (*Burm. f.*) *Becherer* (see p. 59)

As broadly interpreted here, this species is very variable. Rhizome erect with tufted fronds or short-creeping with shortly spaced fronds; fronds generally 30–60 cm long; pinnae deltoid to narrowly lanceolate and pinnatifid to pinnate-pinnatifid. The presence of two types of scales on the stipe bases and croziers is characteristic.

This is the most common and widespread species of *Asplenium* in Kenya. It occurs in dry and moist forests, moist bushland, and extends up into the moorland, occurring 4700–11 800 ft. It can be terrestrial or epiphytic. HE, HC, HT, HM, HA, HK, HN, KIT, MUM, KIS, NAR, RV, NAN, NBI, MAC, KAJ. Also on forested hills to the east and north of our area.

Greenway and Kanuri 13866; Faden and Grumbley 72/348.

40. Asplenium stuhlmannii *Hieron.* (see p. 66)

Fronds shortly spaced on long-creeping rhizomes, generally 30–45 cm long and rigidly erect and coriaceous; middle and lower pinnae strictly opposite.

This plant grows in somewhat sheltered rock crevices generally in grassland, less commonly at the edges of riverine forests. It grows in partial shade or full sun, about 3000–7300 ft. HC, HT, KIT, MUM, MAC. Also in the Taita hills.

Greenway 8538; Faden 70/127.

41. Asplenium lividum *Kuhn* (see p. 59)

Fronds of this species resemble narrow, pinnate-pinnatifid fronds of *A. aethiopicum* in size and shape of the lamina, but differ in having lanceolate pinnae which are very asymmetric at the base. Fronds to about 30 cm long, with the lobes of the pinnae subequal except for a much enlarged and often oblong basal acroscopic lobe.

This local and uncommon plant occurs in riverine and moist intermediate forests, about 4800–5400 ft. It grows in dense shade, either on rocks or trees. KIS, MUM, MAC, NBI, KAJ.

Gillett 16698; Faden 68/834.

42. Asplenium uhligii *Hieron.*

This species along with *A. actiniopteroides*, *A.* sp. *E* and *A. kassneri* Hieron. (the last not definitely recorded from Kenya) form a group of closely related species which occur primarily in the moorland, extending down in the *Hagenia–Hypericum* zone. They are either terrestrial or epiphytic. All of these species have thin, long-creeping rhizomes with widely spaced fronds which generally have long stipes. *A. uhligii* is recognized by its black rhizome scales with entire margins and colourless lumina.

Since the species limits in this group are still uncertain, the distributions given here are subject to revision. HK.

Meinertzhagen in AH 9477; Furnari s.n.

43. Asplenium *sp. E.*

The copper-coloured scales readily distinguish this plant. It is the common species of this group on Mt. Kenya (see notes under *A. uhligii*). HE, HA, HK.

Hedberg 1833; Agnew, Hedberg, and Mmari 9625.

44. Asplenium actiniopteroides *Peter*

The lamina is usually ovate-deltoid and more finely dissected than the other species in this group (see *A. uhligii*). The dark scales and glandular rachis are the best characters for recognizing this species. HE, HK.

Hedberg 954; Schelpe 2848.

45. Asplenium buettneri *Hieron.*

Fronds shortly spaced on a short-creeping rhizome and generally 25–40 cm long. Best distinguished from *A. aethiopicum* by the shape of the lamina,

and from *A. blastophorum* by the lamina being more finely dissected and lacking gemmae on the rachis.

A characteristic plant of dry and riverine forests at medium altitudes, also occurring in moist, intermediate forests. It is terrestrial and grows in dense shade from sea level to about 5500 ft. HA, MUM, KIS, MAC, NBI. Also in the Taita hills and along the coast.

Faden 68/813; Napper 490.

53. CETERACH *Garsault*

Small terrestrial plants; rhizome erect, densely covered with clathrate scales; stipes very short, with two vascular strands at the base uniting to form an X-shape above; lamina pinnatifid to rarely tripinnatifid, densely covered on the lower surface with light brown, clathrate scales; venation free (in our plant); sori elongate along one side of a veinlet; indusium absent.

Ceterach cordatum *(Thunb.) Desv.*

Fronds tufted to 15 cm long, with rounded frond and pinnae apices; fronds curling when dry.

Plants are usually found in partially shaded rock crevices in bushland or woodland, 5000–6000 ft. HA, NAR, BAR, RV, NAN, MAC, NBI. Also at Maralal.

Mabberley and McCall 89; Glover, Gwynne, and Paulo 493.

54. PLATYCERIUM *Desv.*

Medium to large, epiphytic or rarely terrestrial herbs; rhizome short and concealed by the fronds, covered with non-clathrate scales; fronds simple, dimorphic; sterile (nest) fronds sessile and cordate-clasping the rhizome, lobed or unlobed, appressed to the substrate; fertile fronds stipitate, obovate, unlobed (in our plant) or dichotomously forked; fronds densely stellate pubescent; venation reticulate with included veinlets; sori completely covering specialized areas on the fertile fronds; indusium absent.

Platycerium angolense *Bak.*

A large epiphyte with elephant-ear-shaped nest fronds; fertile fronds with a single large area of sporangia near the apex.

Usually grows on trees in forests, at forest edges or in the open. The single record for this area must be considered somewhat doubtful. KIT. Also occurs occasionally along the coast.

Jack 563.

55. PYRROSIA *Mirb.*

Small terrestrial or epiphytic herbs; rhizome thin, long-creeping, densely covered with non-clathrate scales; fronds widely spaced; stipes articulated to the rhizome; lamina simple, unlobed, lanceolate to oblanceolate (in our plant), densely covered on the lower surface with stellate scales; margin entire; venation reticulate with included veinlets; sori round, separate or more or less confluent in the distal part of the frond; indusium absent.

Pyrrosia schimperana *(Mett.) Alston*

Fronds pendent, flaccid, whitish-brown beneath.

A locally common plant of riverine and moist, intermediate forests, occurring 2000–6400 ft. It grows on rocks and trees. MUM, KIS, NAR, MAC. Also on Ol Doinyo Sabachi (Lolokwi).

Lucas 92; Glover, Gwynne, and Samuel 47.

56. DRYNARIA *(Bory) J. Sm.*

Large epiphytic herbs; rhizome long-creeping, thick, densely covered with ciliate scales; fronds widely spaced, glabrous, dimorphic; sterile fronds sessile, pinnately lobed, without chlorophyll; fertile fronds stipitate, the stipe articulated to the rhizome, lamina pinnatifid, the pinnae broadly attached and articulated to the rachis; venation reticulate with included veinlets; sori round, in two subcostal rows on each pinna of the fertile frond; indusium absent.

Drynaria volkensii *Hieron.*

Fertile fronds to 1 m; sterile, bracket-like fronds much smaller, retaining falling debris; rhizome scales dark brown.

A locally common species of moist, montane forests, particularly *Ocotea* (camphorwood) forests, commonly associated with other epiphytic ferns such as *Elaphoglossum lastii, Oleandra distenta* and *Asplenium friesiorum*. It occasionally persists on isolated trees in cultivated, formerly forested areas. Occurs 5250–7500 ft. HM, HA, HK, MUM, KIS.

Bally 4871; Faden 69/1861.

57 LOXOGRAMME *(Blume) C. Presl*

Small epiphytic or terrestrial herbs; rhizome thin, long-creeping, densely covered with clathrate scales; fronds widely spaced, stipitate; lamina simple, unlobed, oblanceolate, glabrous, tapered at both ends; margin entire; venation reticulate with included veinlets; sori elongate, oblique to the midvein and arranged in two rows near it; indusium absent.

Loxogramme lanceolata *(Swartz) C. Presl*

The fronds are slightly fleshy, and the lateral veins are inconspicuous.

One of the most common ferns in Kenya, occurring in dry and wet forests, about 3000–8200 ft; it is usually epiphytic but occasionally grows on rocks. HE, HC, HT, HM, HA, HK, HN, KIT, MUM, KIS, MAC, KAJ. Also in the Taita and Sagala hills and on Mts. Kasigau and Marsabit.

Verdcourt 1672; Faden, Evans, and Worth 69/664.

58. PHYMATODES *C. Presl*

Medium-sized, epiphytic or terrestrial herbs; rhizome long-creeping, fleshy, nearly naked except near the apex where covered with peltately-attached, lanceolate, clathrate scales with ciliolate margins; fronds widely spaced, glabrous, fleshy, simple (in young plants) to deeply pinnatifid with 3–8 pairs of opposite segments; stipes articulated to the rhizome; lamina ovate; margin entire to slightly sinuate; venation reticulate with included veinlets; sori round to elliptic, somewhat sunken in the lamina, in 4(–2) rows in each of the segments; indusium absent.

Phymatodes scolopendria *(Burm. f.) Ching*

Fronds to about 80 cm in length, slightly less than half of which is the stipe.

A terrestrial or epiphytic species of forests and thickets, it has been collected only once in our area. MUM (Samia hills, hill behind Nangina mission, altitude 4750 ft). Also in the Maungu hills, on Mt. Kasigau, and along the coast.

Dekker in EAH 14728.

59. PLEOPELTIS *Willd.*

Small epiphytic herbs; rhizome long-creeping, thin or thick, densely to sparsely covered with clathrate, peltate scales; fronds widely spaced; stipes articulated to the rhizome; lamina simple, lanceolate to narrowly elliptic or linear, with or without peltate scales on the lower surface, margin entire (rarely slightly sinuate or pinnately-lobed); venation reticulate with included veinlets; sori round to slightly elliptic, borne in two rows parallel to the midvein; indusium absent.

1 Mature fronds with numerous peltate scales on the lower surface; rhizomes thin
                          1. *P. macrocarpa*
  Mature fronds without peltate scales on the lower surface; rhizomes thin or thick   2
2 Rhizome thin; rhizome scales 2–3 mm long, black with paler margins   2. *P. schraderi*
  Rhizome thick; rhizome scales 2·5–7·5 mm long, brown and uniformly coloured or somewhat darker towards the centre   3
3 Apex of frond rounded   3. *P. rotunda*
  Apex of frond acute   4. *P. excavata*

1. Pleopeltis macrocarpa (*Willd.*) *Kaulf.*

Rhizomes densely covered with small (about 3 mm long) scales having a central dark area and broad, pale, lacerate margins; fronds narrowly lanceolate-elliptic, generally 10–20 cm long. A form with pinnately lobed fronds occurs around Nairobi, growing with the normal type.

This is one of the most common and widespread ferns in Kenya. It occurs in dry or moist forests, riverine forests, the bamboo zone, and occasionally in the moorland. It is usually epiphytic, though sometimes found on rocks, and is recorded about 3000–11 800 ft. HE, HC, HT, HM, HL, HA, HK, HN, KIT, MUM, KIS, NAR, NAN, MAC, NBI, KAJ. Also on forested hills east and north of our area.

Lucas 91; Verdcourt 2430; Isaac 3004; B.Sc. students s.n.

2. Pleopeltis schraderi (*Mett.*) *Tard.*

This species resembles *P. macrocarpa* in its frond shape and thin rhizome. It can be distinguished from that species in having much darker rhizome scales and in lacking peltate scales on the lower surface of the fronds.

This is an uncommon epiphyte in moist, intermediate and montane forests, occurring about 5500–7650 ft. HT, HA, MUM. Also occurs in the Taita hills.

Agnew, Hanid *et al.* 7467; Faden 69/1987.

3. Pleopeltis rotunda (*Bonap.*) *Tard.* (see p. 26)

Like all members of the *P. excavata* complex, this species has a thick rhizome which is glaucous in places where the scales have fallen off. The manifestly rounded apex of the linear-oblanceolate fronds and the large, pale rhizome scales seem sufficiently distinct to maintain this as a species.

This epiphyte occurs primarily in the ericaceous and *Hagenia–Hypericum* zones but extends down into the moist montane forest. It is recorded about 6250–10 000 ft. HC, HA, HK, HN.

Faden 70/98; Mearns 1771.

4. Pleopeltis excavata (*Willd.*) *Sledge*

This species includes all plants with thick rhizomes which do not fit into *P. rotunda*. It is polymorphic but cannot be further divided satisfactorily at this stage of our knowledge. Additional collections are greatly needed.

An epiphyte of moist, intermediate, and montane forests. HE, HC, HM, HA, KIT, KIS, KAJ. Also in the Taita and Sagala hills and on Mt. Kasigau.

Mabberley and McCall 25; Agnew and Musumba 7432.

60. MICROSORIUM *Link*

Medium-sized epiphytic or, less commonly, terrestrial herbs; rhizome thick, short-creeping, covered with black, caducous, clathrate scales; fronds ± tufted, sessile (the base sometimes considered to be a winged stipe); lamina simple (in our plant), glabrous; margin entire; venation reticulate with included veinlets; sori small, round, superficial, very numerous and scattered, occurring at the junctions of veinlets; indusium absent.

Microsorium punctatum (*L.*) *Copel.*

Fronds large, leathery, strap-shaped, tapered at both ends reaching 100 cm in length.

A species of moist thickets (in our area) where it is terrestrial. KIT, KIS. Also occurs as an epiphyte in coastal forests.

Faden 69/1612; Serbai in Faden 69/1718.

61. GRAMMITIS *Swartz*

Small epiphytic herbs; rhizome erect (in our plant), short- or, rarely, long-creeping, densely covered with non-clathrate scales; fronds tufted or shortly to widely spaced; stipes not articulated to the rhizome (in our plant); lamina simple, linear to lanceolate or oblanceolate; margins entire (in our plant) to crenate or rarely somewhat lobed; venation free (in our plant); sori round to elliptic, in a single row on each side of the midvein; indusium absent.

Grammitis *sp.* A.

A minute species with tufted, linear-oblanceolate fronds to 6 cm long and 0·4 cm wide. The persistently hairy fronds distinguish this species from the only other Kenya species, *G. nanodes* (Peter) Ching, of the Taita hills and Mt. Kasigau.

A middle- and possibly high-level epiphyte in *Ocotea* (camphorwood) forests; known from a single collection at 7000 ft. HA.

Faden 71/280.

62. XIPHOPTERIS *Kaulf.*

Small epiphytic or, less commonly, terrestrial herbs; rhizome erect to long-creeping, densely covered with scales; fronds tufted or widely spaced; stipes not articulated; lamina simple, linear to narrowly oblong or lanceolate, shallowly lobed to pinnatifid, glabrous or hairy; venation free, usually obscure (in our species); sori round, separate or ± confluent in the upper part of the frond; indusium absent.

1   Rhizome long-creeping; fronds widely spaced, coriaceous, pinnatifid, 5–20 mm wide; upper part of the frond not conspicuously less deeply lobed than the lower part
                          1. *X. flabelliformis*

Rhizome erect; fronds tufted, herbaceous, 1·5–5 mm wide, pinnatifid in the lower part, serrate to entire towards the apex (of fertile fronds)   2

2   Lobes of sterile part of frond oblong, to 2 mm long; fertile part of frond serrate
2. *X. strangeana*

Lobes of sterile part of frond ovate-deltoid, to 1 mm long; fertile part of frond crenate to entire   3. *X.* sp. *B*

1. Xiphopteris flabelliformis (*Poir.*) *Schelpe*

Rhizome scales lustrous grey-brown; lamina glabrous with several sori per lobe.

This plant occurs primarily in the ericaceous and *Hagenia–Hypericum* zones but extends into the moorland and occasionally into the bamboo zone. Usually epiphytic except in the moorland and is recorded 7300–11 500 ft (most commonly above 9300 ft). HC, HM, HA, HK.

Faden *et al.* 69/518; Verdcourt 2019.

2. Xiphopteris strangeana *Pic. Ser.*

A minute species with fronds to about 6 cm long. It is the species which is usually called *X. myosuroides* (Swartz) Kaulf. in African floras, but the African plants are not conspecific with American plants of that species.

An epiphyte in moist, montane and intermediate forests. Grows high up on tall, forest trees, so it is perhaps much more common than the few collections would suggest; occurs 4900–7000 ft. HA, KIS. Also occurs in the Taita hills and on Mt. Kasigau.

Strange 220; Faden 71/729.

3. Xiphopteris sp. B.

Plants of this species are similar in size and general appearance to the last. The lobing of the lamina must be studied carefully in order to distinguish the two species (see key).

This species is epiphytic and is known only from the rim of volcanic cone Kirui, north-east Mt. Kenya, at about 8350 ft. It was growing in the ericaceous zone and was very uncommon. HK.

Faden *et al.* 69/524; Faden 70/97.

63. ANTROPHYUM *Kaulf.*

Small or medium, epiphytic or lithophytic herbs; rhizome fleshy, short-creeping, densely covered with dark brown, clathrate scales; fronds shortly spaced, somewhat fleshy (in our plant), glabrous; stipes long (in our plant) with two vascular strands, not articulated; lamina simple, ovate (in our plant), without a midvein; venation prominently anastomosing, without included veinlets; sori elongate along the veins and usually anastomosing with them; indusium absent.

Antrophyum mannianum *Hook.*

Fronds up to 45 cm in length of which more than half is the stipe; frond apex acuminate.

This species grows on rocks and tree trunks in dense shade near streams. It occurs in moist, intermediate forests. MUM (Kakamega forest).

Faden 69/2027; Reichstein *et al.* 3006A.

64. VITTARIA *Sm.*

Small to medium, epiphytic herbs; rhizome short- to long-creeping, densely covered with clathrate scales; fronds shortly spaced; stipes absent or short; lamina simple, linear to linear-lanceolate, unlobed, pendent, glabrous; venation reticulate, consisting of the midvein, two submarginal veins parallel to the midvein and a single row of very elongate areoles (usually obscure), without included veinlets, between the midvein and each of the submarginal veins; sori two, elongate along each of the submarginal veins; indusium absent.

Vittaria volkensii *Hieron.*

Fronds characteristically very narrow, linear (2–4·5 mm wide) reaching 50 cm or more long; stipes black; rhizome scales lustrous, ending in long, hair-like points.

This is a species of moist, montane forests, occurring from 5650–7350 ft. HT, HM, HA, HK, HN, KIT, KIS. Also occurs in the Taita hills.

Faden, Evans, and Worth 69/711; Agnew *et al.* 7443.

65. MARSILEA *L.*

Small or medium, aquatic herbs; rhizome short- to long-creeping, sparsely to densely hairy, much branched; fronds shortly to widely spaced; stipe long in comparison to the lamina, usually sparsely hairy; lamina consisting of two subequal pairs of obdeltoid to obovate pinnae, the four of them clustered at the summit of the stipe and arranged in the form of a cross; pinnae sparsely hairy; margins entire to crenate or lobed; venation reticulate; sporangia borne inside seed-like, pedicellate, brown or black sporocarps which are attached singly (in our area) or in clusters to the rhizome or stipe; sporocarps containing sporangia and spores of two kinds: megasporangia which contain megaspores and microsporangia which contain microspores.

Because of the vegetative similarity of all species, sporocarps are essential for their identification. These are produced only by plants which have become stranded following a drop in the water level. Sporocarps are capable of enduring long periods of drought, and consequently some species of *Marsilea* are able to grow in areas of very low rainfall.

1   Sporocarps attached in a single row to the basal part of the stipe   1. *M. minuta*
    Sporocarps attached singly to the base of the stipe or attached to the rhizome   2
2   Pedicels of mature sporocarps hairy; sporocarps brown, 5·5–7·5 mm long   3
    Pedicels of mature sporocarps glabrous or nearly so; sporocarps black or dark brown, 3·5–5 mm long   4
3   Sporocarps with spreading hairs (sometimes mixed with appressed hairs) which curl when dry, giving the sporocarp a farinose appearance; upper tooth of sporocarp prominent (in our area)   2. *M. farinosa*
    Sporocarps with appressed hairs only; upper tooth of sporocarp not prominent   3. *M. macrocarpa*
4   Pedicels 3–7 mm long, growing upright to ascending   1. *M. minuta*
    Pedicels 8–15 mm long, usually growing horizontally or downwards and burying the sporocarp in the mud   4. *M. gibba*

1. Marsilea minuta *L.*

Pinnae of terrestrial plants usually with crenate margins; sporocarps appressed pubescent when young but ± glabrous when mature; pedicel attached to the sporocarp at ± right angles to the long axis of the sporocarp.

This species, the most widespread *Marsilea* in Kenya, grows in small, seasonal streams, seasonal water holes and at the edges of dams. MAC. Also at Isiolo, in the Tsavo area and along the coast.

Faden and Evans 69/934; Perkins in EAH 11052.

2. Marsilea farinosa *Launert*

This species is very close to *M. macrocarpa*, and the difference in the hairs on the sporocarps is the only safe way to separate the two. Fresh sporocarps of *M. farinosa* look fuzzy.

This plant has been found growing in a seasonal water hole and in a seasonal stream, both in the Lukenya–Doinyo Sapuk area. MAC.

Greenway and Napper 13597; Faden, Evans, and Msafiri 70/902.

3. Marsilea macrocarpa *Presl*

This is the largest and most pubescent species in our area: pinnae of terrestrial plants usually lobed at the apex; sporocarps persistently appressed pubescent.

This is the most common species of *Marsilea* in the Nairobi area, and the only one recorded in Nairobi district. It grows in roadside ditches,

seasonal pools, and streams and at the edges of permanent streams and rivers. MAC, NBI, KAJ.

Gillett 17331; Faden 72/78.

4. Marsilea gibba *A. Br.*

Vegetatively this species is very similar to *M. minuta*. Sporocarps ellipsoid to suborbicular in lateral view and elliptic in dorsiventral sections; pedicel attached to the sporocarp ± parallel to the long axis of the sporocarp.

This plant occurs in seasonal pools and streams and in roadside ditches. KIS, NAR, RV, NAN, MAC.

Faden and Evans 69/541; Glover *et al.* 1819.

66. SALVINIA *Adans.*

Small, floating, aquatic herbs; rhizome horizontal, branched; roots absent; leaves simple, petiolate, arranged in whorls of three, the upper two normal and floating, the lower one dissected into root-like segments and submersed; lower surface (and often the upper) of floating leaves densely hairy; sporocarps borne on the submersed leaves, each enclosing a basal columnar receptacle to which the sporangia are attached; sporangia and spores of two kinds, megasporangia which contain megaspores and microsporangia which contain microspores.

Salvinia auriculata *Aubl.*

Floating leaves ovate to oblong, 1–2·5 cm long and densely hairy on both surfaces. The correct name of this plant is still in doubt.

This is an introduced plant from tropical America which has become an important weed in Lake Naivasha. KIT, RV, ?NBI.

Bogdan 5316; Barnley in EA H170/57.

67. AZOLLA *Lam.*

Small, floating, aquatic herbs; rhizome horizontal, pinnately branched, covered with small imbricate leaves; roots present; leaves alternate, in 2 rows, each leaf bilobed, the upper lobe green and photosynthetic, normally resting on the water, the lower lobe submersed and colourless, usually inhabited by blue-green algae; sporocarps borne on the submersed leaf lobes, dimorphic, the larger containing microsporangia and microspores, the smaller containing megasporangia each containing a single megaspore.

1   Plants to 15 cm long (often much smaller); leaves with broad whitish margins, and never tinged with red   1. *A. nilotica*

Plants to 3 cm long; leaves with narrow whitish margins, or margins not whitish; leaves sometimes tinged with red

2. *A. pinnata*

1. Azolla nilotica *Decne.*

Large plants of this species often have branches which are held up above the surface of the water. The rhizome is up to 2 mm thick.

This species occurs on lakes and ponds and in slow flowing streams. KIS, ?NAR, BAR, KAJ. Also in scattered localities to the east of our area.

Leippert 5243; Kenya Exploration Society 53.

2. Azolla pinnata *R. Br.*

The plants are generally deltoid, and branches are never held above the surface of the water.

This species grows on stagnant water including rice paddies. HT, KIS, MUM, KAJ.

Verdcourt 3109; Kokwaro 2538.

FLOWERING PLANTS

1. LAURACEAE†

Trees or shrubs, very rarely (as ours) twining parasites, with aromatic glands and alternate simple exstipulate leaves; flowers small, not brightly coloured, often in panicles, bisexual or unisexual, regular; sepals 6, in two whorls, perigynous; petals 0; stamens usually 12, in 4 whorls of 3, the inner 1-2 whorls often sterile, with valvate dehiscence, the two outer whorls dehiscing inwards, the inner whorls usually dehiscing outwards; ovary superior, usually surrounded by the receptacular tube, with one loculus and one ovule; fruit a berry, drupe, or achene.

1. CASSYTHA *L.*

Yellowish parasitic twiners with reduced leaves; inflorescence racemose; flowers bisexual, with an ovoid receptacular tube which enlarges to enclose the fruit; sepals as in the family; stamens as in the family, the third whorl dehiscing outwards, the innermost whorl of staminodes; fruit enclosed in the succulent receptacle.

Cassytha filiformis *L.*
Parasitic herb with yellowish-green trailing stems with haustoria and young stems covered with reddish tomentum; flowers cream; fruit black.

A common coastal plant, parasitic on shrubs and herbs, which occurs in our area only in the drier south. It can easily be mistaken for a *Cuscuta.* MAC, KAJ.
Napper 1620.

2. HERNANDIACEAE‡

Trees or shrubs, very rarely woody climbers, with alternate simple or digitately compound exstipulate leaves; flowers bisexual, or monoecious, or polygamous by abortion, regular, in axillary corymbose or paniculate cymes, with or without bracts; calyx with 3-5 sepals in two whorls or sometimes 4-8 in one whorl; stamens 3-5 in a single whorl, often 4; staminodes glandular, in one or two whorls outside the stamens, or absent; ovary inferior, 1-celled; ovule single. Fruit dry, somewhat ribbed, with 2-4 wings, or wingless but enclosed in the inflated receptacle; seed non-endospermous, with large cotyledons.

1. ILLIGERA *Blume*

Illigera pentaphylla *Welw.*
Shrubby climber with mostly 5-foliate leaves, leaflets ovate-elliptic; flowers greenish-white in axillary, paniculate cymes; fruit spheroidal, 2-winged.

A strong forest liane growing at roadsides and forest edges over bushes, recorded only from Kakamega forest. Sheds its winged fruits copiously. MUM.
Lucas 136.

3. RANUNCULACEAE§

Mainly herbs, some climbers and occasional shrubs; leaves opposite or alternate with sheathing base, exstipulate, often compound, often palmate, inflorescence various, flowers regular or zygomorphic; sepals free; petals present or absent, free, sometimes bearing a nectary; stamens indefinite or variable in number; ovary superior of 1–many free carpels, each 1–many-seeded; fruits mostly dry achenes or follicles, rarely fleshy; seeds without arils, with endosperm.

1	Leaves opposite	2
	Leaves alternate or in a rosette	3
2	Climbers or trailing shrubs	1. *Clematis*
	Erect herbs or subshrubs	
		2. *Clematopsis scabiosifolia*
3	Flowers zygomorphic	6. *Delphinium*
	Flowers regular	4
4	Carpels more than 5	5
	Carpels less than 5	
		3. *Thalictrum rhynchocarpum*
5	Pedicels with a ring of 3 reduced leaves some distance below the solitary flowers; sepals pinkish outside; petals absent	
		4. *Anemone thomsonii*
	Pedicels with no ring of reduced leaves; flowers often numerous; sepals green or yellow; petals present, yellow or white	
		5. *Ranunculus*

1. CLEMATIS *L.*

Climbers, weakly shrubby or herbaceous, with opposite pinnate leaves, whose petiole and rachis twines round the support; flowers regular, in a paniculate inflorescence; sepals 4, petaloid; petals

---

† By A. D. Q. Agnew.
‡ By M. A. Hanid.

§ By A. D. Q. Agnew.

and nectaries absent; stamens numerous, sometimes grading into staminodes on the outside; carpels numerous, indefinite, each with one fertile ovule, the style elongating into a plumose or naked awn in fruit.

1   Leaflets suborbicular to ovate, irregularly dentate, some or all leaflets lobed
1. *C. hirsuta*

Leaflets ovate to ovate-lanceolate, entire or regularly dentate, lower leaflets not lobed, upper leaflets sometimes with 1-2 lobes
2. *C. simensis*

1. Clematis hirsuta *Guill. & Perr.* (*C. brachiata* Thunb. in Check List) (see p. 77)
Climber bearing leaves with 5-7 suborbicular to ovate leaflets; inflorescence paniculate; sepals cream or white.

An extremely variable species common in forest edges and in wooded grassland. HE, HC, HM, HA, KIT, MUM, KIS, NAR, RV, NAN, MAC, NBI, KAJ.
Hanid 274; Greenway 7851.

2. Clematis simensis *Fres.* (see p. 77)
Shrubby climber bearing leaves with up to 5 leaflets, often reduced in the paniculate inflorescence; sepals cream or white.

A variable plant common in forest edges and at roadsides in upland rain-forest, often behaving as a strong liane. Its leaves tend to be dark shiny green which distinguishes it immediately from *C. hirsuta.* HE, HC, HT, HA, HK, KIT, MUM, KIS, NAR, MAC, KAJ.
Tweedie 66/330; Hedberg 2000.

2. CLEMATOPSIS *Hutch.*
Similar to *Clematis* except that these are erect perennial herbs, with no twining leaf petiole or rachis, and have more often simple leaves and usually solitary flowers.

Clematopsis scabiosifolia (*DC.*) *Hutch.* (see p. 79)
Perennial herb with simple or trifoliolate leaves; flowers solitary or in few-flowered inflorescences; sepals white, cream, mauve, or pink.

A variable plant of burnt grassland principally in the west of Kenya, often on stony soil. HC, KIT, MUM, KIS.
Hanid and Kiniaruh 830; Thorold 3211.

3. THALICTRUM *L.*
Herbs with compound, alternate leaves, the basal sheath sometimes bearing a stipule-like structure; flowers small, in paniculate inflorescences; sepals

3-5, green or petaloid, caducous; petals and nectaries absent; stamens few to many, indefinite, carpels 1 to many, with one ovule; fruit an achene.

Thalictrum rhynchocarpum *Dillon & A. Rich.*
Glabrous perennial herb bearing much divided leaves with orbicular segments; inflorescences diffuse, with nodding, green flowers; carpels usually solitary; pedicels elongating in fruit.

A soft, often glaucous-looking plant common in forest edges and pathsides in upland rain forest, the leaves looking very like those of the fern *Adiantum thalictroides.* HE, HC, HM, HA, MUM, NAR, KAJ.
Agnew and Harris 5051; Verdcourt 2041.

4. ANEMONE *L.*
Perennial herbs with divided leaves; pedicel with a ring of 3 reduced leaves below the flower; flowers regular, in ours solitary; sepals variable in number, petaloid; petals absent; stamens numerous, sometimes grading into staminodes on the outside; carpels numerous, indefinite, with one ovule each; fruit with a persistent, plumose or naked style, on an elongated receptacle.

Anemone thomsonii *Oliv.*
Rhizomatous silky-tomentose perennial with much-dissected leaves, the ultimate segments oblong-dentate; sepals white or pale pink.

A common plant in moist or boggy (often rocky) situations on peat soil above 9000 ft. HE, HC, HA, HK, KIT.
Hanid 175; Hedberg 1678.

5. RANUNCULUS *L.*
Annual or perennial herbs with alternate, often palmate leaves; flowers solitary or inflorescence paniculate; flowers regular; sepals (3-) 5 in ours, herbaceous; petals often yellow, 5, free, with a basal nectary in a pit or below a scale on the upper side; stamens numerous, indefinite; carpels numerous, indefinite; fruit of achenes.

1   Leaves entire   4. *R. volkensii*
    Leaves divided or cut   2
2   Leaves simply pinnate   1. *R. oreophytus*
    Leaves compound pinnate or ternate or trifoliolate   3
3   Sepals spreading at anthesis   4
    Sepals reflexed downwards at anthesis   7
4   Petals white   5. *R. stagnalis*
    Petals yellow   5
5   Achenes very numerous (50-100) on a cylindrical receptacle; annual   3. *R. sceleratus*
    Achenes fewer (less than 50) on rounded heads; perennial   6

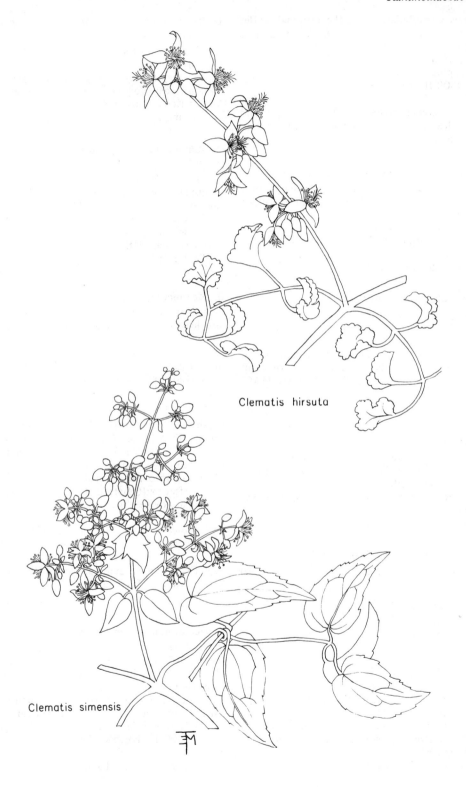

Clematis hirsuta

Clematis simensis

6   Leaves trifoliolate, with the terminal leaflet
petiolate   8. *R. aberdaricus*
Leaves trisect, with no petiole to the terminal
leaflet   7. *R. cryptanthus*
7   Creeping perennial of high altitudes (above
9000 ft); basal leaves trifoliolate
6. *R. keniensis*
Erect annual or perennial of 9000 ft and
below; basal leaves ternate, with ternate or
pinnate segments   2. *R. multifidus*

1. Ranunculus oreophytus *Del.* (see p. 79)

Perennial rosette herb with pinnate, usually glossy
leaves; flowers solitary, yellow, in fruit becoming
buried by the reflexion of the pedicel.

The most common alpine buttercup, found in
close wet turf at altitudes above 9000 ft. HE, HC,
HM, HA, HK.

Agnew 8161; Coe and Kirika 319.

2. Ranunculus multifidus *Forsk.* (see p. 79)

Perennial herb, sometimes stoloniferous, with
bipinnate or bipinnatifid leaves; flowers numerous,
yellow.

Our commonest 'buttercup' of streamsides at
4-8000 ft, also growing as a roadside weed in
upland rain forest. HE, HC, HT, HA, NAN, MAC,
NBI.

Strid 2469; Gillett 16272.

3. Ranunculus sceleratus *L.*

Annual herb with deeply 3-lobed leaves; flowers
numerous, yellow; achenes very numerous, forming a cylindrical head.

An introduced weed of mud left by retreating
water, not yet common. HA, RV, NBI.

Hanid and Kiniaruh 430; Gillett 16802.

4. Ranunculus volkensii *Engl.*

Stoloniferous creeping perennial with orbicular to
reniform leaves; flowers solitary, yellow.

An uncommon alpine buttercup, apparently a
pioneer of eroded wet hollows in peaty grassland,
above 10 000 ft. HE, HM, HA, HK.

Agnew 7229; Polhill 12034.

5. Ranunculus stagnalis *A. Rich.*

Perennial rosette herb with ternately palmatisect
to trifoliolate leaves; flowers numerous, white;
fruiting pedicels reflexed.

An uncommon alpine or subalpine buttercup
with white flowers, growing in marshy places near
streams. HE, HK.

Hanid 146A; Hedberg 994.

6. Ranunclus keniensis *Milne-Redhead & Turrill*

Creeping perennial herb, with rosettes of trifoliolate leaves; flowers 1-3 together, hardly exceeding
the leaves, yellow.

A creeping buttercup of wet ground near
streams, easily overlooked, in the alpine zone of
Mount Kenya only. HK.

Coe and Kirika 362; Moreau 128.

7. Ranunculus cryptanthus *Milne-Redhead & Turrill*

Similar to *R. keniensis* except for the heavier
creeping stem, incompletely divided leaves, spreading sepals, and the fully reflexed pedicels in fruit.

A little-known buttercup confined to alpine
Elgon where it grows in disturbed wet soil, often
amongst rocks. HE.

Taylor 3542.

8. Ranunculus aberdaricus *Ulbr.*

Perennial stoloniferous rosette herb, with trifoliolate leaves and orbicular leaflets; flowers solitary,
yellow.

A rare alpine buttercup of the Aberdares, need-
ing confirmation on Mt. Kenya. HA, HK.

Kerfoot 1406A; Strid 2266.

6. DELPHINIUM *L.*

Perennial herbs with alternate, palmate-nerved
leaves; flowers usually racemose, zygomorphic,
usually blue; sepals 5, petaloid, the posterior sepal
produced into a spur; petals 2-5, the two posterior
elongated into the spur; stamens indefinite, often
9-15, often with flattened filaments; carpels 3-5,
with many ovules; fruit of follicles.

1   Flowers 4·5-6 cm diam., sweetly scented   2
Flowers 2·5-3 cm diam., with no smell
1. *D. macrocentrum*
2   Flowers 6 cm diam., sepals white 2. *D. leroyi*
Flowers 4·5 cm diam., sepals blue or mauve
3. *D. wellbyi*

1. Delphinium macrocentrum *Oliv.* (see p. 80)

Erect herb, bearing deeply dissected, orbicular
leaves; inflorescence 3-10-flowered; flowers with
blue and/or metallic-green sepals and an ascending,
stout spur.

A local but conspicuous plant when in flower
with a most curious metallic-green sepal colour,
which is found in moist (often rocky) grassland
above 5000 ft. HE, HC, HM, HA, HK, KIT, KIS,
NBI.

Leippert 5157; Lind and Harris 5099.

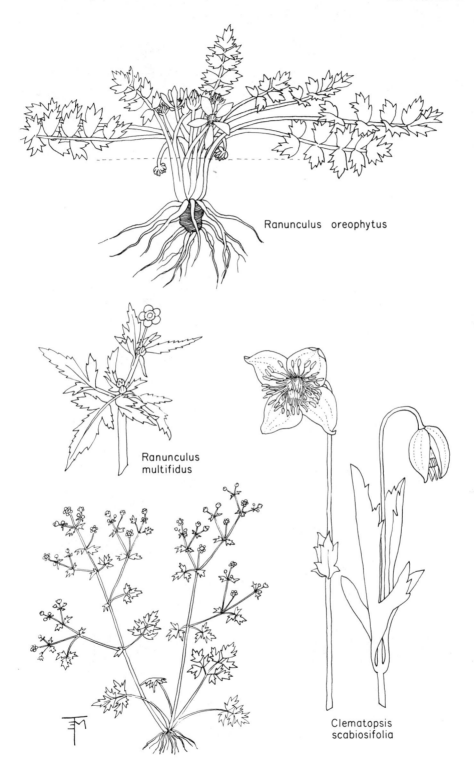

Ranunculus oreophytus

Ranunculus multifidus

Clematopsis scabiosifolia

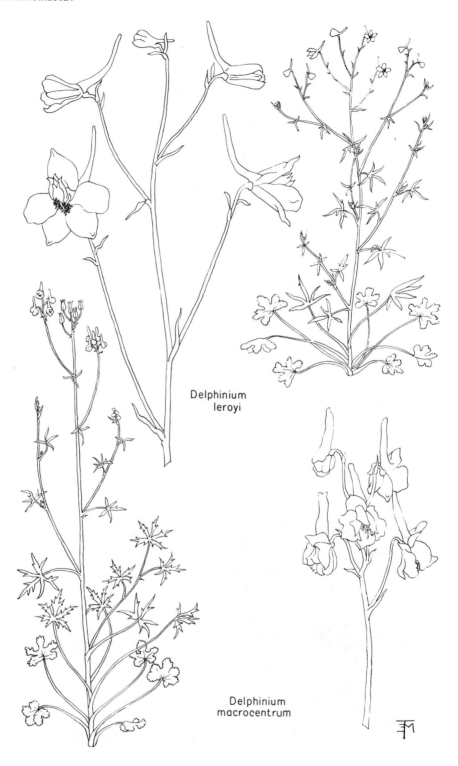

Delphinium
leroyi

Delphinium
macrocentrum

2. Delphinium leroyi *Hutch.* (see p. 80)

Perennial herb bearing palmatifid or palmatisect leaves; flowers 4-9 in each raceme, with white sepals and upcurving spur.

An uncommon sweet-scented *Delphinium* of burnt savannah woodland. MUM, KAJ.

Greenway and Doughty 8532.

3. Delphinium wellbyi *Hemsl.*

Perennial herb, with palmatisect, orbicular leaves; flowers 3-7 in each raceme, with blue sepals and ascending spur.

A local plant so far only collected from the Meru district in upland grassland. HN, EMB

Bader 260.

4. CERATOPHYLLACEAE†

Submerged aquatic herbs with verticillate, divided leaves; flowers unisexual, monoecious, solitary in the whorls of leaves, sessile, the male and female at separate nodes; sepals green, numerous in one whorl; male flowers with 10-20 stamens, each with a produced, often coloured connective above the anthers; female flowers without staminodes, with one unilocular ovary with a pendulous ovule; fruit a spiny achene; seed without endosperm.

1. CERATOPHYLLUM *L.*

The only genus in the family, with the characters of the family.

1 Leaves twice forked (rarely 3-forked in occasional leaves within a plant); fruit smooth, with an apical spine and usually with two basal spines   1. *C. demersum*
  Leaves 3-times, rarely 4-times forked; fruit rough, warty, with an apical spine but no basal spines   2. *C. submersum*

1. Ceratophyllum demersum *L.*

Trailing, submerged glabrous herb, leaves mostly 10 in each whorl, twice forked, the segments toothed.

A common aquatic plant of slow-flowing streams and lakes below 8000 ft, usually free from the substrate, dying at the base as it grows at the apex. HT, MUM, RV, MAC.

Polhill 203; Agnew 5894.

2. Ceratophyllum submersum *L.*

Similar to *C. demersum* except for the leaves and fruits.

Rare, but probably overlooked, aquatic, only recorded from Amboseli. KAJ.

Verdcourt 3108.

† By A. D. Q. Agnew.

5. NYMPHAEACEAE‡

Aquatic, anchored herbs with usually floating, exstipulate, long-petiolate, simple, peltate leaves; flowers emergent from the water, bisexual; sepals 4-6; petals numerous, spiral, often intergrading with sepals or stamens; stamens numerous, spiral, with longitudinal anther dehiscence, and often with an appendage continuing the connective; carpels numerous, in one whorl, sunk in the receptacle, but nevertheless mostly free from each other; ovules 1-many in each carpel, often scattered on the walls; fruit often fleshy; seeds with fleshy arils.

1. NYMPHAEA *L.*

Aquatic herbs, often with tuberous rhizome; leaves palmate-nerved, hardly peltate but deeply cordate; sepals 4; petals 5-numerous; stamens perigynous, with petaloid filaments; anthers often appendaged at apex; carpels with many ovules; fruit fleshy, ripening under water; seeds small.

1 Leaves toothed; flowers white   1. *N. lotus*
  Leaves entire or sinuate; flowers blue or mauve   2
2 Leaves sinuate at margin with 8-11 primary nerves on each side of the midrib; stamens more than 100   2. *N. capensis*
  Leaves entire at margin or sinuate towards the base, with 5-8 primary nerves on each side of the midrib; stamens often less than 100   3. *N. caerulea*

1. Nymphaea lotus *L.*

Glabrous herb with tuberous rhizome and floating orbicular or suborbicular leaves; flowers white or cream.

An uncommon waterlily found in Lake Victoria. MUM, KIS.

Napier 5279.

2. Nymphaea capensis *Thunb.*

Similar to *N. lotus* except for the small leaves sinuate at margin, and the blue or mauve flowers.

One of our common blue water lilies. HA, KIT, MAC, NBI.

van Someren 3033.

3. Nymphaea caerulea *Savigny*

Similar to *N. capensis* except for the key characters.

One of our common blue water lilies. These two latter species are often difficult to distinguish, and further work is required to confirm their separation. HE, HT, MUM, RV.

Verdcourt 3100; Lind 5589.

‡ By A. D. Q. Agnew.

6. MENISPERMACEAE†

Dioecious, twining herbs or shrubs (rarely erect), with simple exstipulate leaves; flowers unisexual, small, usually in bracteate compound racemes; male flowers with 3-12 free green sepals, 0-6 petals, 3-6 or numerous stamens, the latter free or united; female flowers with sepals and petals as in the male flowers, stamens 0, carpels 3-6 (rarely 1) free; carpels with 2 ovules, becoming 1–seeded; fruit of free drupes, each carpel becoming circular by eccentric growth with a basal style, the bony endocarp being characteristically ridged; seed curved into a horse-shoe shape, with or without endosperm.

1	Leaves peltate	2
	Leaves not peltate	3
2	Leaves usually glabrous, with the petiole inserted, on some leaves at least, more than 1 cm from the margin	5. *Stephania*
	Leaves hairy, with the petiole never inserted more than 5 mm from the margin	6. *Cissampelos*
3	Leaves glabrous, at least when fully expanded	4
	Leaves hairy even when mature	6
4	Leaves cordate	4. *Tinospora caffra*
	Leaves not cordate	5
5	Pulvinus (a more or less swollen, ridged area) present on petiole below the lamina	1. *Tiliacora*
	No pulvinus present, the petiole smooth throughout	2. *Cocculus pendulus*
6	Flowers in one cluster or solitary at each node	2. *Cocculus*
	Flowers in raceme or clustered along a raceme	7
7	Leaves soft, often lobed, cordate with a parallel-sided or acute sinus	3. *Chasmanthera dependens*
	Leaves more or less stiff, never lobed, not cordate, or, if so, then the sinus obtuse, never acute	6. *Cissampelos*

1. TILIACORA *Colebr.*

Woody climbers, glabrous or glabrescent, leaves simple, with a pulvinus on the petiole below the blade, and thus held horizontally however the branch is orientated; male inflorescence of racemes of condensed cymes, few-flowered; male flowers with 6-12 sepals in several whorls, 3-6 petals, 3-9 free or partly united stamens; female inflorescences as the male, but sometimes spikes of solitary flowers; female flowers with sepals and petals similar to the male, and 6-30 carpels on a gyno-

† By A. D. Q. Agnew.

phore; drupes ovate, stipitate, the endocarp being compressed and furrowed.

1	Female inflorescence of spikes of solitary flowers; leaves long acuminate	1. *T. keniensis*
	Female inflorescence of racemes of 3-9-flowered cymes; leaves not long acuminate	2. *T. funifera*

1. Tiliacora keniensis *Troupin*

Glabrous woody climber with ovate-oblong leaves; male plants unknown; female inflorescences from old wood, of spikes of solitary flowers.

Obviously a rare plant that needs more collecting to establish its characters, for it may prove to be but a variant of the next species. MUM, MAC.

Faden, s.n.

2. Tiliacora funifera (*Miers*) *Oliv.*

Woody climber with ovate-oblong to ovate leaves; inflorescences of either solitary axillary cymes or in 3-9-cymed clusters on racemes from the old wood.

Uncommon, in lowland rain-forest west of the Rift, collected from Kakamega; also one specimen exists from Emali Hill. MUM, KAJ.

van Someren 91; Dale 3130.

2. COCCULUS *DC.*

Woody climbers; leaves simple, entire or lobed; male inflorescences of short pedunculate cymes either solitary or clustered, on leafy or leafless branches; male flowers with 6 sepals in two whorls, 6 petals auriculate and ± surrounding the outer stamens, and 6-9 free stamens; female inflorescences similar to the male; female flowers similar to the male, with staminodes present or absent, and 3-6 carpels with spathulate stigmas; endocarp of fruit crested or not.

1	Leaf lamina usually glabrous or slightly pubescent, with 3 basal nerves	1. *C. pendulus*
	Leaf lamina usually tomentose or pubescent, with 5 basal nerves	2. *C. hirsutus*

1. Cocculus pendulus (*J. R. & G. Forst.*) *Diels*

Woody climber with ovate to elliptical leaves; inflorescences axillary of short-peduncled cymes of sessile flowers.

An uncommon climber of riverine vegetation in dry bushland of northern Kenya, only doubtfully found in our area. NAN.

Verdcourt 3789.

2 Cocculus hirsutus (*L.*) *Diels*

Large woody climber with ovate to elliptic leaves, otherwise similar to *C. pendulus.*

An uncommon climber found in the dry areas of Kenya, particularly in riverine vegetation in *Acacia/Commiphora* bushland. MAG.

Glover and Samuel 3259.

3. CHASMANTHERA *Hochst*

Woody climbers; leaves simple or obscurely lobed, suborbicular with palmate nervation; male inflorescences of pendulous racemes of spaced clusters of short-pedicellate cymes subtended by filiform bracts; male flowers with 6 sepals in two whorls, 6 rather fleshy petals and 6 stamens with fused filaments; female inflorescences of pendulous racemes; female flowers similar to the male, with 6 staminodes and 3 carpels; endocarp of fruit 3-toothed at apex, ridged down centre line and with 2 narrow lateral wings.

Chasmanthera dependens *Hochst.*

Woody tomentose climber with soft, almost succulent stems, and orbicular or obscurely lobed leaves.

An uncommon climber of the Kitui district in *Acacia/Combretum/Commiphora* woodland on sandy soils. MAC.

Gillett 16944.

4. TINOSPORA *Miers*

Woody or herbaceous climbers or shrubs; leaves simple, entire, with palmate nervation; male inflorescences of racemes or panicles of 2–4-flowered cymes; male flowers with 6 sepals in two whorls, 6 fleshy petals, and 3–6 fused or free stamens; female inflorescences of racemes of solitary flowers; female flowers similar to the male, sometimes with staminodes, with 3 carpels; endocarp of fruit rough on outside, with a large cavity on inner face.

Tinospora caffra (*Miers*) *Troupin*

Herbaceous or woody glabrous climber with orbicular to ovate leaves, inflorescences sometimes panicled.

A widespread but local climber, sometimes trailing over rocks, in dry woodlands. KIT, MUM, KIS, BAR, MAC.

Agnew 8091; Bally 11417.

5. STEPHANIA *Lour.*

Herbaceous, woody or succulent climbers; leaves simple, mostly orbicular, more or less deeply peltate; male inflorescences paniculate or umbel-like, male flowers with 6–8 sepals, 3–4 free petals (rarely absent), and 2–6 stamens inserted on a stalked disc; female inflorescences similar to the male; female flowers with 3–6 sepals, 2–4 free petals, staminodes absent, and 1 carpel; endocarp of fruit with 2–4 rows of tubercles, prickles, or ribs.

1   Stem succulent   1. *S. cyanantha*
    Stem woody or herbaceous, not succulent
                                       2. *S. abyssinica*

1. Stephania cyanantha *Hiern*

Glabrous succulent climber with triangular to orbicular, acuminate leaves; inflorescences in apparent umbels on leafless stems.

Rare plant of montane forest edges. HE, HN, KIS.

Kerfoot 4375.

2. Stephania abyssinica (*Dillon & A. Rich.*) *Walp.*

Similar to *S. cyanantha* but not succulent, and with tuberculate, not ribbed, fruit endocarp.

The commonest member of the Menispermaceae found in mountain rain forest, extending through the bamboo zone. The species is variable, the hairy individuals being known as var. *tomentella.* HE, HT, HM, HA, HK, MUM, KIS, KIT, NAR, KAJ.

Williams 604; Agnew 8673.

6. CISSAMPELOS *L.*

Woody or herbaceous twining climbers; leaves simple, peltate or almost so, entire; male inflorescences similar to those in *Stephania*; male flowers with 4–5 sepals, fused petals forming a cup, 4–10 stamens fused together, female inflorescences of short-pedicelled cymes spaced out on a hanging raceme with specialized bracts, or axillary; female flowers of 1 sepal, 1 petal, and 1 lateral carpel; drupes hairy or glabrous, with a dorsally ridged endocarp.

1   Leaves acuminate, rounded or cuneate at
    base, not cordate   1. *C. friesiorum*
    Leaves obtuse or rounded at apex, truncate
    to cordate at base   2
2   Leaves orbicular or suborbicular, usually not
    acutely cordate, apex often retuse, soft
    papery, usually nearly concolorous on
    both surfaces   2. *C. pareira*
    Leaves heart-shaped or subreniform, usually
    cordate, never retuse at apex, hard
    leathery, the lower side covered with a
    thick felty indumentum and usually paler
    than the upperside   3. *C. mucronata*

1. Cissampelos friesiorum *Diels*

Climbing tomentose herb with ovate leaves; male cymes axillary, clustered 2–3 together, female plants unknown.

A rare climber from the rain forest near Meru, badly in need of more collection. HK.

Conrads in EAH. 10434.

2. **Cissampelos pareira** *L.*

Herbaceous climber with peltate, orbicular or almost reniform leaves; male inflorescences of loose corymbose cymes, female inflorescences of 5–9-flowered axillary cymes.

The most common Menisperm of all forest and woodland areas outside the area of wetter montane forest. HE, HC, HA, MAC, NBI.

Verdcourt 636; Lugard 497.

3. **Cissampelos mucronata** *A. Rich.*

Herbaceous or woody hairy climber, with peltate heart-shaped leaves, male inflorescence of 3–6 clustered axillary cymes or racemes; female inflorescences with fused, often long-mucronate bracts.

A common swampland plant west of the Rift Valley, rarer in the east. The hard leathery leaves distinguish it immediately from *C. pareira.* HE, HA, KIT, MUM, KIS, NAR.

Gillett 16362; Agnew 9586.

7. ARISTOLOCHIACEAE†

Herbs or shrubs, often climbers, with alternate, simple, exstipulate leaves, often cordate at base; flowers bisexual, often zygomorphic, solitary, axillary, often with a foetid smell; sepals often produced in a long tube, often asymmetrically 3-lobed above; petals 0; stamens 6–many, fused to the style, with longitudinal dehiscence of the anthers; ovary inferior with 6 carpels, with the styles connate into a column above; ovules parietal or axile, numerous; seeds with much endosperm.

1. ARISTOLOCHIA *L.*

Herbs, shrubs or climbers; sepal tube dilated into a chamber below, and often zygomorphically dilated above; stamens 6 or more, fused to the styles; ovary inferior, with 6 carpels; placentation axile or parietal; fruit a capsule.

1 Climbing plant with entire leaves
1. *A. densivenia*
Prostrate or erect rhizomatous herb with crenulate leaf margins 2. *A. bracteata*

1. **Aristolochia densivenia** *Engl.*

Twining glabrous herb with ovate leaves; flowers green at base, blue above, borne on specialized raceme-like stems with sessile cordate bracts.

A rare plant of dry land, not yet definitely recorded for our area, but known from riversides near Meru.

Adamson 592.

† By A. D. Q. Agnew.

2. **Aristolochia bracteata** *Retz.*

Prostrate or erect rhizomatous glabrous herb, with orbicular to reniform leaves; flowers dark mauve to cream-coloured, solitary.

Also a rare plant, not yet definitely recorded for our area. A specimen from Marsabit (which cannot be from the mountain), may be from our area, and it should be looked for in the driest country. ?NAN.

Williams and Adamson in EAH 11011.

8. HYDNORACEAE‡

Evil-smelling parasites, without chlorophyll, growing on the roots of trees and shrubs by means of a pseudo-rhizome with haustoria; pseudo-rhizome warty, simple or branched, rounded or angled; leaves and scale-leaves 0; flowers large, solitary, epigeous; calyx thickened, fleshy, valvately 3–5 lobed; stamens 3–5, inserted on the calyx tube and united to form a ring around the stigma; anthers numerous, sessile; ovary inferior, 1-locular with numerous apical or parietal placentas, ovules numerous, stigma sessile or rudimentary; fruits underground, baccate; seeds numerous, very small, in glutinous pulp.

1. HYDNORA *Thunb.*

Pseudo-rhizomes brown externally, red internally, covered completely, or on londitudinal ridges only, by warts; flowers sessile on the pseudo-rhizome, 9–30 cm long, brown outside, bright-red or rose inside, calyx tubular, with lanceolate lobes which are often joined toward the summit; inner surface of lobes ciliate or glabrous; stigma 3–5-lobed.

Hydnora abyssinica *Schweinf.* (*H. johannis* Becc.)

A parasite with the underground pseudo-rhizome cylindrical or obscurely angled, completely covered with warts and large flowers with a very strong unpleasant smell; calyx very fleshy, 4-lobed, the inner surface apically cream and bright red and bristly below.

A very distinct and uncommon species of dry *Acacia* bushland, parasitic, often on *Acacia* roots, with only the flowers above the ground surface. MAG, NBI.

Napper 1220.

9. PIPERACEAE§

Herbs, sometimes shrubby, and climbers; leaves entire, alternate or opposite, stipulate or not, often fleshy; inflorescence a spike usually with

‡ By D. Wood.
§ By A. D. Q. Agnew.

crowded flowers; flowers bisexual or unisexual, subtended by a peltate bract; perianth absent (in ours) or present, in one whorl; stamens 2–6, with free filaments; ovary superior, with one ovule (in ours); fruit an indehiscent berry; seeds with much endosperm.

1 Trailing herbs, mostly epiphytic, without stipules; leaves not aromatic, often fleshy
                             1. *Peperomia*
Shrubby herbs or climbers with stipules adnate to petiole; leaves often aromatic when crushed, hardly fleshy   2. *Piper*

1. PEPEROMIA *Ruiz & Pav.*

Herbs, often epiphytic; leaves alternate or opposite, without stipules, not aromatic when crushed, often fleshy; flowers bisexual in usually dense spikes; perianth absent; stamens 2; fruit a berry, but the carpel wall always thin, sometimes glandular.

1 All or most leaves opposite or whorled   2
  All or most leaves alternate   3
2 Leaves glabrous, whorled usually in fours
                       1. *P. tetraphylla*
  Leaves hairy, opposite   2. *P. arabica*
3 Leaf lamina 2 cm long or smaller; creeping plants usually with decumbent flowering stems   4
  At least some leaf laminae more than 2 cm long; flowering shoots erect   5
4 Leaves orbicular; spikes not more than 1 cm long   3. *P. bangroana*
  Leaves elliptical; spikes more than 1 cm long, at least in fruit   4. *P. mannii*
5 Stems tomentose or glabrous; leaves constant in shape within one plant, elliptic, narrowing equally at base and apex, with the widest part often equidistant from both; fruits spherical, symmetrical
                      6. *P. butaguensis*
  Stems glabrous; leaves variable within one plant, usually oblanceolate or obcordate, cuneate at base, rounded or obtuse at apex, never *all* elliptic; fruits ellipsoid, asymmetric   5. *P. abyssinica*

1. Peperomia tetraphylla (*Forst.*) *Hook. & Arn.* (see p. 87)

Epiphytic, glabrous, creeping herb with fleshy, whorled, orbicular or elliptic leaves; spikes pubescent.

A common epiphyte of wet highland forest and occasionally found in the drier savannah edges of such forest forming mats on horizontal tree branches. HE, HC, HT, HM, HA, HN, KIT, MAC, KAJ.

Agnew 7915; Gillett 13893.

2. Peperomia arabica *Miq.*

Pubescent to tomentose fleshy herb, with opposite elliptic leaves.

A rare plant, restricted to certain drier districts, and found rarely as an epiphyte, more often growing on the ground amongst rocks. NAR, MAC.

Glover, Gwynne, and Samuel 12.

3. Peperomia bangroana *C. DC.*

Trailing tomentose epiphytic herb with small orbicular leaves; spikes to 1 cm long, exceeding the leaves.

Creeping, diffuse plant growing often amongst moss on horizontal tree branches. It seems curiously restricted in distribution, but may be overlooked. KIS.

Ossent 682; Glover, Gwynne, Samuel, and Tucker 2553.

4. Peperomia mannii *Hook. f.*

Trailing epiphytic herb with glabrescent, elliptic to obcordate leaves.

Rather uncommon epiphyte only found in the wettest highland forest, between 6500 and 8500 ft. HA, HK, HN.

Verdcourt and Polhill 2937; Agnew 5865A.

5. Peperomia abyssinica *Miq.* (see p. 87)

Glabrous herb, trailing at base, with ascending stems, and usually oblanceolate or obcordate leaves with the widest part above the middle; fruit asymmetric, ellipsoid.

The most common and most variable *Peperomia* in wet upland forest at nearly all altitudes below 9000 ft in our area. The plant often grows on the ground as well as epiphytically, as on the Ngong Hills. HE, HC, HT, HM, HA, HN, HK, KIT, MUM, KIS, RV.

Agnew 8767; Dale 54.

6. Peperomia butaguensis *De Wild*

Glabrous or tomentose herb similar to *P. abyssinica* except for the usually elliptic, acute leaves, mostly widest about the centre, and spherical, symmetrical fruits.

Apparently common in the wet highland forests west of the Rift Valley. HM, MUM, KIS.

Kerfoot 2724; Hanid and Kiniaruh 1041.

2. PIPER *L.*

Shrubby herbs or climbers, often glabrous with jointed nodes, leaves alternate, with stipules adnate to petiole, lamina aromatic when crushed; inflorescence a spike (in ours) or raceme of unisexual or bisexual flowers; flowers with no

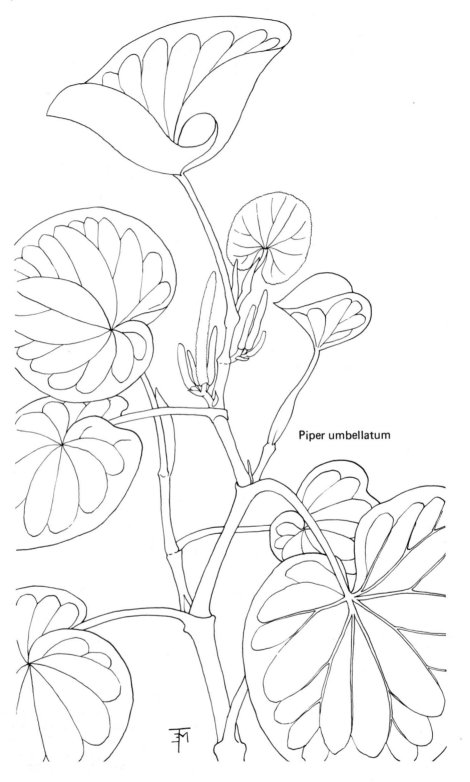

Piper umbellatum

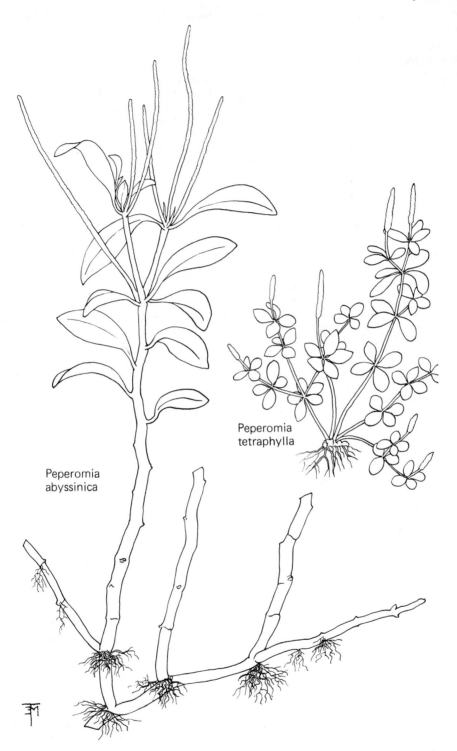

Peperomia
abyssinica

Peperomia
tetraphylla

perianth, 2-4 stamens; fruit a berry, stalked or sunk in the rachis of the spike.

1 Erect soft shrubs; fruits sessile 2
  Climber; fruits stalked 1. *P. guineense*
2 Spikes solitary; fruits exceeding the bracts
    2. *P. capense*
  Spikes 2-6 together; fruits not exceeding the bracts 3. *P. umbellatum*

1. Piper guineense *Schumach. & Thonn.*

Soft shrubby glabrous climber, with ovate leaves and solitary spikes.

A rare plant (in our area) only found in Kakamega forest and climbing by means of adventitious roots near the nodes. MUM.

Gillett 16682; Strid 2906.

2. Piper capense *L.*

Tall, soft shrub or herb, with broad-ovate to orbicular, cordate, sparsely tomentose leaves, and solitary whitish spikes.

A common undergrowth plant of wetter highland forests from 5000 to 9000 ft. HE, HM, HA, HK, HN, MUM, KIS, RV, EMB, MAC, KAJ.

Kabuye 64; Agnew 9810.

3. Piper umbellatum *L.* (see p. 86)

A soft shrub similar to *P. capense* from which it differs in being glabrous, and in having orbicular, hardly acuminate leaves, and spikes in axillary umbels of 2-6.

Common in the wetter forests of Kenya. HN, MUM.

Polhill and Verdcourt 290; Agnew 5884.

10. PAPAVERACEAE†

Herbs, rarely shrubs or small trees, with coloured latex; leaves exstipulate, alternate, rarely whorled, divided, rarely entire; flowers bisexual, regular; sepals 2-3, imbricate, green, usually free or calyptrate, caducous; petals showy, usually 4 or 6, imbricate, in 1-2 or 3 whorls, crumpled in the bud, deciduous; stamens mostly numerous; ovary superior, usually 1-celled; ovules numerous, parietal; fruit a capsule, dehiscing by valves or pores; seeds small, numerous, with fleshy or oily endosperm.

1. ARGEMONE *L.*

Glaucous often prickly herbs or shrubs; leaves sessile, pinnately lobed or incised; flowers large, solitary or cymose; sepals with a subterminal terete

horn, outer surface sparsely prickly; petals 6, in 2 whorls of 3, white or yellow; ovary with 3-7 carpels; capsule dehiscing by valves; seeds brown-black, pitted, up to 3 mm in diameter.

Argemone mexicana *L.*

Erect herb with yellow latex and amplexicaul, white-veined, roughly oblong leaves and bright-yellow flowers.

Weed of waste, dry places, roadsides and abandoned cultivated ground, this is the "Mexican Poppy" introduced from America. HA, NBI.

Verdcourt 3230; Agnew 8741.

11. FUMARIACEAE‡

Herbs, sometimes climbing; leaves exstipulate, alternate or radical, finely divided, sometimes ending in a branched tendril; flowers in racemes or spikes, rarely solitary, zygomorphic, bisexual; sepals usually 2, caducous; petals usually 4, one or both of outer ones spurred or saccate, inner segments often united at the apex; stamens 6 in 2 bundles; ovary 1-celled, with 2 parietal placentas, each with 1-many anatropous ovules; fruit a capsule or nutlet; seeds endospermous.

1 Flowers yellow, fruit an elongate capsule with many seeds 1. *Corydalis mildbraedii*
  Flowers white to pink; fruit a semi-globular nutlet 2. *Fumaria abyssinica*

1. CORYDALIS *Vent.*

Annual or perennial herbs with tap roots, tubers, or rhizomes; leaves alternate or rarely opposite, simple to variously divided; bracts persistent; flowers yellow, rarely red or purple; stigma persistent, flattened and lobed; style filiform; fruit a bicarpellate and 2-valved capsule; seeds numerous, orbicular to reniform, smooth to pitted, with a caruncle.

Corydalis mildbraedii *Fedde* (see p. 91)

Glabrous and glaucous perennial herb with much divided leaves; flowers yellow.

An uncommon plant found in upland forests, moors, and grasslands, often at forest edges or near streams from 7000-10 000 ft. HE, HM, HA, HK.

Verdcourt 2057; Agnew 9066.

2. FUMARIA *L.*

Annual herbs; leaves cauline, 2-4-pinnatisect; tendrils absent; petiolule and rachis sometimes prehensile; inflorescence in leaf-opposed racemes with persistent bracts; flowers white to pink, usually the 4 petals dark pink to purple at apex,

† By M. A. Hanid.

‡ By M. A. Hanid.

upper petals spurred, lower petals ± spathulate; ovule 1; fruit a nutlet, smooth or rugose when dry.

Fumaria abyssinica *Hamm.* (see p. 91)

Erect or straggling herb with 2–3-times pinnatisect glabrous leaves, leaflets oblong-lanceolate to linear-lanceolate; flowers pink; fruit spherical.

Uncommon plant found in upland rain-forest, bamboo-forest, and upland moor, often a weed of cultivation and more rarely of roadsides; 4000–9500 ft. HE, HT, HM, HA, HK.

Verdcourt 3207; Agnew 10119.

12. TURNERACEAE†

Herbs, shrubs or trees, with simple, usually ex-stipulate, alternate leaves; flowers bisexual, regular, often dimorphic, solitary to numerous, mostly axillary, in racemes, panicles, or cymes; calyx tubular, 5-merous, teeth imbricate; petals and stamens 5, both inserted on the calyx-tube; ovary superior, 1-celled with 3 parietal placentas; styles 3, stigma apically divided; fruit a 3-valved capsule; seeds arillate, pitted, endospermous, with 2-pored pits in ours.

1 Shrubs, 1–3 m tall   1. *Loewia*
   Herbs, 0·3–0·4 m tall   2
2 Seeds straight; capsule dehiscing irregularly, not from apex downwards
                2. *Wormskioldia*
   Seeds curved; capsule dehiscing from apex downwards   3. *Streptopetalum*

1. LOEWIA *Urb.*

Shrubs, indumentum glandular, densely hirsute or pubescent, often with stellate hairs; bracts foliaceous; flowers solitary in upper leaf axil, erect, trumpet-shaped, bibracteolate; calyx tubular for half its length or more; petals white, yellow, or bright orange, inserted near the opening of calyx-tube; capsule narrowly obovoid, dehiscing loculi-cidally from apex downwards, shortly beaked; seeds several, curved.

Loewia tanaensis *Urb.*

Small shrub with obovate leaves and orange flowers, found in dry bushland and doubtfully recorded for our area. KIS.

Steele 3979.

2. WORMSKIOLDIA *Schum. & Thonn.*

Herbs, pubescent or puberulous and setiferous; leaves sometimes glandular; inflorescences axillary or of scapose, one-sided racemes; bracteoles single or paired; pedicel accrescent, sometimes

† By M. A. Hanid.

curved; flowers erect, heterostylous; hypanthium 0·3–1·5 mm long; petals yellow to scarlet, each with a ligule at its base; stamens arising from the base of calyx tube, filaments winged, adnate to calyx for up to 2 mm, 2 shorter, 3 longer (in ours); capsules linear or narrowly ellipsoid, often held horizontally or reflexed, dehiscence not from apex downwards but irregular; seeds many, straight.

1 Leaves with a pair of pubescent glands at the base; bracteoles pubescent, up to 1 mm long; capsules glabrous   1. *W. lobata*
   Leaves without basal glands; bracteoles glabrous, 2–6 mm long; capsules shortly setiferous   2. *W. pilosa*

1. Wormskioldia lobata *Urb.*

Annual herb with elliptic leaves; inflorescence of 1–4 yellow flowers; capsule glabrous with 2–5 mm long beak.

A locally common plant of open situations in bushland amongst short grass on rocky outcrops, ironstone and sandy soils; more collections needed. BAR, MAC.

Napper 1600; Tweedie 67/624.

2. Wormskioldia pilosa (*Willd.*) *Urb.*

Annual herb with elliptic, pinnatipartite leaves; inflorescence of 2–4 yellow to orange flowers; capsules shortly setiferous with 4–7 mm long beak.

A plant of rocky places, roadsides, and culti-vated land, badly in need of collection. KIS.

Wilson 353.

3. STREPTOPETALUM *Hochst.*

Pubescent and setiferous herbs; leaves glandular or exstipulate; inflorescence axillary, 1- to many-flowered, usually in a one-sided raceme; bracteoles single or obscure; pedicels sometimes accrescent; flowers erect, sometimes heterostylous, hypan-thium ± 3 mm long; calyx tube hairy within for 3–6 mm from base, bearing 5 large tubercles above the insertion of stamens; petals yellow or orange, adnate to calyx for more than half the length of the tube, eligulate; filaments winged; capsules broadly ellipsoid, subovoid or suborbicular, erect, dehiscing loculicidally from apex; seeds numerous, curved.

1 Annual herb; stem-setae bulbous-based; heterophyllous; capsule shortly and regu-larly setiferous   1. *S. serratum*
   Perennial herb; stem-setae not bulbous-based; homophyllous; capsule pubescent and ir-regularly setiferous   2. *S. hildebrandtii*

1. Streptopetalum serratum *Hochst.*

Annual herb with narrowly elliptic leaves; inflorescence of 1–9 yellow or orange flowers; capsule broadly ellipsoid.

An infrequent herb of sandy soil among rocks in wooded grassland. BAR.

Bally 4531; Tweedie 67/263.

2. Streptopetalum hildebrandtii *Urb.*

Perennial herb with narrowly elliptic leaves; inflorescence of 3–5 yellow or orange flowers; capsule broadly ellipsoid.

An uncommon plant of open grassland and scattered-tree grassland. MAC, KAJ.

Gillett and Faden 18 256; Bally 24704.

13. CAPPARACEAE†

Herbs, shrubs, trees, or lianes; leaves mostly alternate, stipulate, simple or digitately 2–9-foliolate; inflorescences terminal or axillary, usually racemose, or flowers solitary or fascicled, often showy, regular, bisexual; sepals 4–8, free; petals 4–16 or absent; stamens few to many, borne on an androphore, staminodes present or absent; ovary sessile or borne on a gynophore, 1-celled or divided into 2 or more loculi by intrusive placentas; style short or absent; fruits various, mostly a capsule or berry, few- to many-seeded; seeds reniform or angular, usually non-endospermous, cotyledons folded or convolute.

1	Annual or perennial herbs **2**
	Trees, shrubs, or woody herbs **3**
2	Androphore absent, i.e. stamens not inserted on an elongated stalk *1. Cleome*
	Androphore longer than the corolla, i.e. stamens inserted on an elongated stalk *2. Gynandropsis gynandra*
3	Scrambling shrub with 2 stipular thorns at the base of each leaf, sepals dissimilar or unequal *3. Capparis*
	Spreading shrubs or woody herbs without thorns, sepals similar and equal *4. Maerua*

1. CLEOME *DC.*

Annual or perennial herbs, sometimes bushy and woody below; leaves petiolate, alternate, simple or digitately 3–9-foliolate, leaflets with very short petiolules; flowers ± zygomorphic, pedicellate, bracteolate, in terminal racemes; sepals 4; petals 4, equal or unequal, often long-clawed; androphore absent; stamens free; ovary 1-celled with many parietal ovules; fruit a siliquiform capsule with 2 dehiscing valves, smooth or longitudinally nerved.

† By A. D. Q. Agnew and M. A. Hanid.

1	Leaves simple	*1. C. monophylla*
	Leaves digitately compound	**2**
2	Plant glabrous, staminodes present	*2. C. angustifolia*
	Plant hairy, staminodes absent	**3**
3	All leaves 3-foliolate; gynophore absent or up to 2 mm long; all bracts nearly as long as the leaves	*4. C. schimperi*
	Some leaves more than 3-foliolate; gynophore present, more than 2 mm long; all or some bracts shorter than the leaves	**4**
4	Stem and leaves covered with bristly glandular hairs	*3. C. strigosa*
	Stem and leaves covered with gland-tipped hairs	**5**
5	Gynophore longer than the pedicel; stamens 6–8; seeds minutely puberulent	*5. C. allamanii*
	Gynophore shorter than the pedicel; stamens 10–12; seeds glabrous	*6. C. hirta*

1. Cleome monophylla *L.* (see p. 91)

Erect annual herb, usually branched, usually with lanceolate or oblong, pubescent leaves; petals usually pink or mauve; capsule with glandular and simple hairs.

A common plant in grassland, decidous woodland, bushland, and on lake-shores; often a weed of cultivated and disturbed ground. HE, HT, KIT, MUM, BAR, RV, EMB, MAC, NBI, KAJ.

Gillett 16605; Hanid 537.

2. Cleome angustifolia *Forsk.* (*C. diandra* Burch.)

Slender, glaucous, erect herb, with 3–9-foliolate leaves and filiform-linear leaflets; petals unequal, yellow, mauve at the base; capsule valves glabrous.

A handsome and distinct species found in bushland, grassland, and semi-desert scrub, with a tendency to become a weed of stony ground. HA, MAG, KAJ: below 3600 ft.

Rauh Ke 112; Isaac, December 1961.

3. Cleome strigosa (*Boj.*) *Oliv.* (see p. 91)

Eglandular annual with 3–5-foliolate leaves and obovate leaflets; petals purplish pink, upper pair yellow at the base.

Only one specimen collected by Dowson in 1914 from Nairobi area, possibly adventive from coast. NBI.

4. Cleome schimperi *Pax*

Annual with glandular or eglandular hairs and 3-foliolate leaves with elliptic leaflets; petals pink; capsules with gland-tipped hairs.

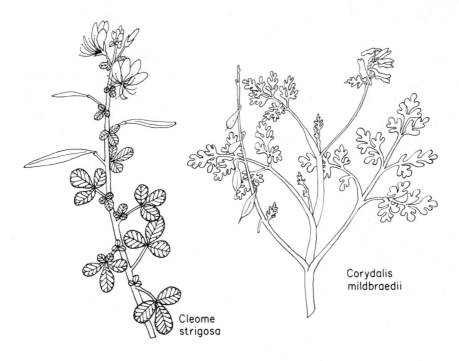

Cleome
strigosa

Corydalis
mildbraedii

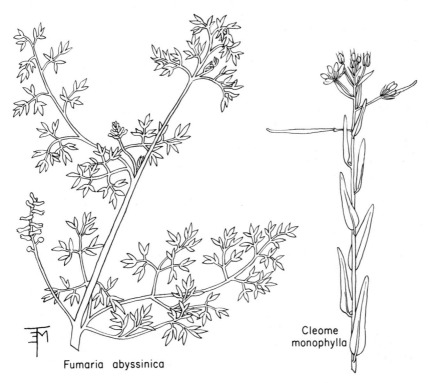

Fumaria abyssinica

Cleome
monophylla

A local plant of upland rain-forest margins, often a weed of cultivated land; 2000-6300 ft. HT, HM, HA, HN, MUM, KIS.

Polhill and Verdcourt 262.

5. Cleome allamanii *Chiov.*

Annual, glandular or glabrous, viscid, with 5-7-foliolate leaves and narrowly linear leaflets; petals magenta-pink, upper pair yellow-spotted.

A plant of dry areas growing on sandy and rocky ground. NAN, MAC.

Gillett 16418.

6. Cleome hirta (*Klotzsch*) *Oliv.* (see p. 93)

Annual or short-lived perennial glandular herb with 5-9-foliolate leaves and linear leaflets; petals purplish or pink, paler towards the base.

A common plant of open woodlands and grasslands, becoming a weed of roadsides and cultivated ground; below 5400 ft. HK, KIT, MUM, BAR, RV, MAG, NAN, MAC, NBI, KAJ.

Greenway and Kanure 12901; Tweedie 67/88.

2. GYNANDROPSIS *DC.*

Annual herbs, rarely rather shrubby; leaves petiolate, 3-7-foliolate; inflorescence a terminal raceme, bracts foliaceous; sepals 4; petals 4, clawed; androphore conspicuous, slender, elongate; stamens 6, free; staminodes absent; gynophore short; ovary 1-celled; ovules many, parietal; capsule dehiscent with 2 valves with persistent placentas; seeds reniform, testa reticulate or rugose.

Gynandropsis gynandra (*L.*) *Brig.* (see p. 93)

Glandular or glabrescent annual with obovate to elliptic leaflets; petals white, pale pink, or lilac.

A common weed of cultivated ground and roadsides, found below 7200 ft. HE, HC, HK, KIT, MUM, KIS, NAR, BAR, RV, MAC, NBI, KAJ.

Greenway 9674; Hanid 548.

3. CAPPARIS and 4. MAERUA

These genera are represented here mostly by shrubs, with several climbers and scramblers, all of which are dealt with in KTS, pp. 117-20 (*Capparis*) and pp. 123-7 (*Maerua*).

14. CRUCIFERAE†

Herbs or occasionally shrubs with alternate, exstipulate leaves and racemose inflorescences usually without bracts; sepals and petals 4; stamens 6, the two outer shorter than the 4 inner; ovary 2-locular, each loculus with 2 parietal placentas, the septum between usually membranous; style 1,

† By A. D. Q. Agnew and Joyce Stewart.

stigma 2-lobed or capitate; fruit usually a capsule, or not uncommonly indehiscent, but never fleshy; seeds 1-many, without endosperm.

A mainly Mediterranean family including many weeds which occasionally turn up in East Africa as rare casuals.

1 Fruit at least 3 times as long as broad 2
Fruit less than 3 times as long as broad 13
2 Leaves simple, entire, not clasping the stem
10. *Farsetia*
Leaves not simple, entire 3
3 Leaves all pinnate or trifoliolate
11. *Cardamine*
Leaves pinnatisect to dentate or, if lower leaves apparently pinnate then rachis winged and upper leaves simple 4
4 Perennials, mostly alpines 5
Annuals, seldom alpines 6
5 Trailing-stemmed plant with hairy leaves
13. *Arabis alpina*
Acaulescent plant with glabrous leaves
16. *Oreophyton falcatum*
6 Sepals more than 4.mm long 7
Sepals less than 4 mm long 8
7 Flowers yellow; fruit with dehiscing valves on the seed-containing portion 1. *Brassica*
Flowers white, red, or yellow; fruit without dehiscing valves on the seed-containing portion, either indehiscent or breaking into 1-seeded portions 3. *Raphanus*
8 Valves of capsule with no midrib; seeds in 2 rows in each loculus 14. *Rorippa*
Valves of capsule with a midrib; seeds usually in one row 9
9 Alpine plant to 10 cm tall; petals white
17. *Arabidopsis thaliana*
Lowland plant more than 10 cm tall; petals yellow 10
10 Stem leaves clasping the stem 11
Stem leaves not clasping the stem 12
11 Leaves simple 13. *Arabis glabra*
Leaves pinnatisect 12. *Barbarea intermedia*
12 Valves of fruit 3-veined; fruit without a persistent style (beak) at apex
15. *Sisymbrium*
Valves of fruit 1-veined, the lateral veins obscure; fruit with a persistent style (beak) at apex 2. *Erucastrum arabicum*
13 Small glabrous scapose alpine plant to 5 cm tall with entire, linear leaves
9. *Subularia monticola*
Larger plants with stem-leaves 14
14 Fruit indehiscent, spherical 4. *Crambe*
Fruit dehiscent or indehiscent, not spherical
15
15 Stem leaves clasping 16
Stem leaves not clasping 18

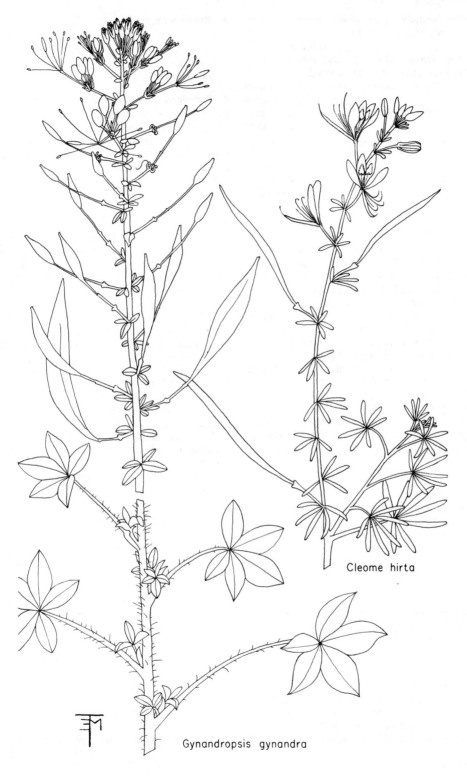

Cleome hirta

Gynandropsis gynandra

16 Leaves usually pinnatifid; capsule heart-shaped, broadest at the top, unwinged
8. *Capsella bursa-pastoris*
Leaves simple, dentate; capsule ellipsoid, broadest in the middle, winged   17
17 Capsule with septum across the broadest part
18. *Camelina alyssum*
Capsule with the septum across the narrowest part   7. *Thlaspi alliaceum*
18 Fruit of 2 globose lobes, hard, indehiscent and pitted; prostrate herb
6. *Coronopus didymus*
Fruit flat, unlobed, dehiscent; erect herbs
5. *Lepidium*

1. BRASSICA *L.*

Mostly annual herbs with erect, often branched stems, glabrous or with simple hairs; leaves often thick and glaucous; racemes bracteate; sepals erect, saccate; petals clawed, usually yellow; stamens 6, without appendages; ovary with a capitate or slightly 2-lobed stigma, the loculi continuing up into the style, forming a beak with 1-3 ovules; fruit a linear cylindrical capsule, the valves each with 1 prominent vein; seeds in 1 row.

An important genus of food plants including mustard, cabbage, turnip, etc., from which crops occasional individuals may escape and become adventive for a year or two. For this reason a key is given below, but a detailed description is made of only one, commonly weedy species, *B. rapa* L.

1 Upper leaves petiolate   1. *B. integrifolia*
Upper leaves sessile and clasping the stem   2
2 All leaves glabrous; stamens erect
2. *B. oleracea*
Lowest leaves always ± bristly; filaments of outer stamens curved at base   3
3 All leaves glaucous; buds held slightly higher than open flowers   3. *B. napus*
Lowest leaves grass-green; open flowers held higher than buds   4. *B. rapa*

1. Brassica integrifolia (*West*) *Ruprecht*

Found once in imported wheat seed. NBI.
Nattrass 1024.

2. Brassica oleracea *L.*

Abundantly cultivated and variable (as cabbage, kale, cauliflower, broccoli, brussels sprouts) this species has a long inflorescence with open flowers a long way below the buds. It has been found as an escape at NBI.
Nattrass 321.

3. Brassica napus *L.*

Not infrequently cultivated as swede, and as rape for the oily seeds. It has been found naturalized occasionally. HA.
van Someren s.n.

4. Brassica rapa *L.* (*B. campestris* L. of Check List)

Erect annual or biennial herb with swollen or thickened tap root and pinnatifid leaves with a large ovate terminal lobe; flowers bright yellow. Widely cultivated as turnip and for the oily seeds, and frequently found escaped. HM, HA, KIT, RV, NBI.
Bogdan 5576.

2. ERUCASTRUM (*DC.*) *Presl.*

Annual to perennial herbs with numerous simple hairs; leaves pinnatifid, not clasping the stem at base; sepals sometimes saccate; petals with limb and claw, yellow; stamens 6, without appendages; stigma simple or obscurely lobed; fruit a linear capsule, ± quadrangular in cross section, with keeled valves each with only one prominent dorsal vein, the beak of the fruit conical, with or (as in ours) without seeds; seeds ovoid or ellipsoid, ± one row in each loculus.

Erucastrum arabicum *Fisch. & Mey.*

An erect pubescent annual with oblanceolate pinnatifid leaves; petals yellow, rarely white with purple veins.

The commonest weedy Crucifer in Kenya, possibly introduced. HE, HT, HM, HA, HK, KIS, RV, NBI.
Wilkinson H41/40; Agnew and Azavedo 9317.

3. RAPHANUS *L.*

Annual to perennial herbs with simple stiff hairs and pinnatifid leaves; racemes bracteate; sepals erect, saccate; petals long-clawed, with a spreading limb, variable in colour; stamens 6, without appendages; ovary with a capitate or ± 2-lobed stigma; fruit elongated, jointed, the lowest portion corresponding to the valves of a 'normal' cruciferous fruit, seedless, resembling a stalk, while the upper portion (style or beak of other genera) contains a single row of seeds, without a septum.

1 Fruit very constricted between seeds and readily breaking up into 1-seeded portions, deeply ridged, the apical seedless portion more than twice the length of the last seeded portion   1. *R. raphanistrum*
Fruit not very constricted between seeds, indehiscent, shallowly ridged, the apical seedless portion up to twice the length of the last seeded portion   2. *R. sativus*

1. Raphanus raphanistrum *L.*

An erect annual with unswollen tap-root; leaves pinnatifid with the terminal lobe the largest; petals yellow, mauve, or white, often dark-veined; fruit ridged, constricted and dehiscent between the seeds, with a beak up to 4 times as long as the distance between constrictions.

An uncommon weed, probably not persistent, introduced from Southern Europe. HT, HM, HA, KIT, RV.

van Someren 549.

2. Raphanus sativus *L.*

Similar to the last species except for the swollen tap-root, the petals which are never yellow, and the fruit which is hardly constricted between seeds, almost smooth and shiny and indehiscent, with a shorter apical beak.

This is the common radish which occasionally escapes from cultivation. HA, RV.

Greenway 9735.

4. CRAMBE *L.*

Herbs with simple, often stiff hairs and entire or pinnatifid leaves; inflorescences usually much-branched, ebracteate; sepals spreading, hardly saccate; petals white, hardly clawed; stamens 6, the inner with toothed appendages; ovary with a capitate, sessile stigma; fruit indehiscent, 2-jointed, the lower one slender, stalk-like, seedless, the upper sphirical, 1-seeded.

1   Sepals over 1·9 mm long; fruits smooth
                                 1. *C. hispanica*
    Sepals under 1·5 mm long; fruits wrinkled or pitted   2. *C. abyssinica*

1. Crambe hispanica *L.*

An erect rough-hairy annual or biennial with pinnatisect leaves; petals white; fruits globose, smooth.

Apparently indigenous, though also found in Europe, this plant can be found in highland grassland from 6000–9000 ft. It is abundant along pathsides in the Ngong Hills. HA, KIT.

Lind and Agnew 5023; Gillett 16143.

2. Crambe abyssinica *R. E. Fries*

Similar to *C. hispanica* except for the smaller flowers, shorter fruiting pedicel, and regularly pitted-reticulate fruit surface.

This species is often found as a weed of cultivated and disturbed ground in grasslands from 5000–8000 ft. HM, HA, RV, KAJ.

Glover 3582; Agnew and Azavedo 9307.

5. LEPIDIUM *L.*

Herbs with simple hairs and often divided leaves; flowers in dense ebracteate racemes; sepals non-saccate; petals small, often shorter than the sepals or absent, whitish; stamens 6 or reduced in number, without appendages; ovary with 2 ovules, short style, and capitate stigma; fruit short, flat, usually winged, often retuse above or below, 2-seeded, with the septum across the narrowest part.

1   All leaves simple and entire or only the upper ones toothed   1. *L. africanum*
    All the leaves, or at least the lower ones, pinnatifid   2

2   Plant glaucous and glabrous; fruits 5–6 mm long   2. *L. sativum*
    Plant minutely hairy; fruits 2·5–4 mm long
                      3. *L. bonariense*

1. Lepidium africanum (*Burm. f.*) DC.

Perennial pubescent herb with narrow-oblanceolate to linear leaves and green flowers; capsule hardly winged, hardly retuse at apex so that the style protrudes shortly.

An uncommon indigenous plant, probably often overlooked, growing in grassland at medium altitudes. HA, NAR, NAN.

Napier 1525.

2. Lepidium sativum *L.*

A glabrous annual, with pinnatisect or simply pinnate leaves and white petals; capsule winged, retuse at apex without a projecting style.

An introduced plant from Southern Europe, often cultivated for green salad, and recorded as occurring as a weed in KIT and NBI.

Nattrass 201.

3. Lepidium bonariense *L.*

An erect, softly pubescent annual with twice pinnatisect or pinnate leaves and small greenish flowers; capsule winged, retuse at apex with the style shorter than the sinus.

A pernicious annual weed in lawns in highly populated areas of Kenya, introduced from South America. HT, HA, HK, NBI.

Verdcourt 2767; Harmsen 6546.

6. CORONOPUS *Boehm.*

Herbs with pinnatifid leaves and leaf-opposed ebracteate racemes; flowers small; sepals not saccate; petals whitish, sometimes absent; stamens 6 or fewer by reduction; ovary with 1 ovule in each loculus and a ± 2-lobed stigma; fruit short, wide, with the septum across the narrowest part, indehiscent, splitting into 1-seeded halves.

Coronopus didymus (*L.*) *Sm.*

A sparsely tomentose to pubescent annual with deeply pinnatisect leaves and small green flowers; stamens usually 2; fruit valves hard, spherical, pitted.

An introduced weed of arable farm land, found particularly along paths and around farm buildings. HT, HM, HA, NAR, RV, NBI.

Bogdan 5627; Agnew 9659.

7. THLASPI *L.*

Herbs, usually glabrous, with simple leaves, often clasping the stem; racemes without bracts; sepals not saccate; petals clawed, white to pink; stamens 6, without appendages; ovary with few ovules and a capitate stigma; fruit a short capsule, flattened, with the septum across the narrowest part, the valves keeled and often winged; seeds usually more than one in each cell.

Thlaspi alliaceum *L.*

A glabrous, unbranched annual with oblanceolate, often dentate leaves; petals white.

A rare species so far only found in the bamboo-forest on Mt. Kenya. HK.

Bally 3275; Strid 4668.

8. CAPSELLA *Medic.*

Annual (or biennial) herbs with simple and branched hairs and cauline leaves clasping the stem at base; sepals not saccate; petals white, clawed; stamens 6, without appendages; ovary with a short style, capitate stigma, and many ovules; fruit obcordate (to ovoid), flat, with the septum across the narrowest part and keeled valves.

Capsella bursa-pastoris (*L.*) *Medic.*

A glabrescent annual with a basal rosette of pinnatifid to oblanceolate leaves; petals white.

An introduced weed (from Europe) in the higher arable land of Kenya. HT, HM, HA, NBI.

Tweedie 66/290; Greenway 10206.

9. SUBULARIA *L.*

Small glabrous aquatic herbs, with leaves all in a basal rosette, linear; racemes ebracteate, scapose, few-flowered; sepals not saccate; petals white, often absent; stamens 6, without appendages; ovary a little sunk in the receptacle, its base surrounded by a fleshy ring, with a sessile, capitate stigma; fruit with few ovules, a short capsule with the septum across the widest portion and 1-veined valves.

Subularia monticola *Schweinf.*

A tufted herb of uncertain life span, with linear leaves and white flowers, often forming mats in water.

An alpine plant, growing above 10 000 ft in the water at stream edges, in permanent pools, and on lake edges. HE, HA, HK.

Hanid 96; Coe and Kirrika 283.

10. FARSETIA *Desv.*

Tough annuals or shrubby perennials with simple sessile leaves, most parts covered with medifixed white hairs; racemes ebracteate; sepals hardly saccate, caducous; petals exceeding the sepals, clawed, yellow to purple; stamens 6, sagittate at base, without appendages; ovary with many ovules and a capitate or 2-lobed stigma, the lobes often decurrent on the style; fruit a long capsule, flattened, with the septum along the long axis, with the valves 1-nerved and a persistent stigma; seeds flat, winged.

1   Annual herb with a straight pod; petals often
      acute   1. *F. stenoptera*
      Perennial shrub with a very undulate pod;
      petals rounded at apex   2. *F.* sp. *A*

1. Farsetia stenoptera *Hochst.*

An erect annual covered with white medifixed hairs, with linear to narrow-lanceolate leaves; petals twisting when not turgid, yellow or livid to red.

A common crucifer of dry country, and rather variable. The flowers open at night and thus are seldom observed to best advantage in sunlight, rather like *Silene burchellii*. RV, BAR, NAN, MAG, MAC, KAJ.

Bogdan 4888; Agnew 7297.

2. Farsetia sp. A.

An erect, loosely branched shrub with a ± dense covering of appressed medifixed hairs; leaves narrow-lanceolate, petals pink or purple with darker nerves.

Common in one part of the Rift Valley, on screes and cliffs. RV.

Glover 4522; Agnew and Azavedo 9300.

11. CARDAMINE *L.*

Annual or perennial herbs with pinnate leaves and simple hairs; sepals not saccate; petals white, pink, or purple, never yellow; stamens 4-6, without appendages; stigma entire or obscurely 2-lobed; fruit a long capsule with obscurely veined valves and seeds in one row in each loculus.

1   Leaves 3-foliolate   1. *C. africana*
      Leaves pinnate   2
2   Creeping plant rooting at nodes; petals more
      than 5 mm long   3. *C. obliqua*
      Annual erect plant; petals less than 3 mm
      long   3

3   Fruits less than 1 mm broad, erect on a
spreading pedicel, not crowded
2. *C. hirsuta*
Fruits 1–1·5 mm broad, held on straight
pedicels, crowded at tip of inflorescence
4. *C. trichocarpa*

1. Cardamine africana *L.* (see p. 98)
A pubescent rhizomatous perennial herb, with
trifoliolate leaves and ovate leaflets, petals white.
A widely distributed but never abundant plant of
highland forests, 8000–10 000 ft, growing on the
forest floor with other herbs and often found in
bamboo with *Sanicula elata.* HE, HM, HA, HK,
KAJ.
Agnew 7698; Bally 1190.

2. Cardamine hirsuta *L.*
Pubescent annual with pinnate leaves and 3–7
pairs of orbicular to linear leaflets; petals white or
absent.
A rare annual in disturbed soil in open places at
the upper forest levels and lower alpine zones on
the mountains of East Africa. The same species is a
common weed in Europe. HE, HA, HK.
Agnew 7182; Bogdan 4756.

3. Cardamine obliqua *A. Rich.*
A glabrescent perennial rhizomatous herb, often
also creeping, with leaves bearing 5–9 oblanceolate
to orbicular leaflets; petals white or pink, with red
veins.
A common plant of streamsides in the alpine
and highland forest zones, 7000–12 500 ft. HE,
HM, HA, HK.
Strid 3119; Burrows in EAH 10039.

4. Cardamine trichocarpa *Hochst.* (see p. 98)
A pubescent annual with leaves bearing usually 9
ovate leaflets; petals white, shorter than the sepals.
An uncommon plant of western Kenya,
growing in waste places in forest. HE, KIT.
Greenway 12125 (not from our area).

12. BARBAREA *R. Br.*
Herbs with erect stems, glabrous or with sparse
simple hairs and with amplexicaul stem leaves;
racemes ebracteate; sepals ± saccate; petals clawed,
yellow; stamens 6, without appendages; ovary with
many ovules, long style and obscurely 2-lobed
stigma; capsule long, 4-angled, the valves with
strong midrib; seeds in one row in each loculus,
unwinged.

Barbarea intermedia *Bor.*
An erect glabrous perennial herb with a rosette of
pinnatisect leaves; petals yellow.

A rare plant which has been found on the East
African mountains at the lower edge of the alpine
zone. HE, HA.
Dale 13275.

13. ARABIS *L.*
Annual to perennial herbs with simple and
branched hairs and sessile leaves; sepals often
saccate at base; petals with claw and limb; stamens
6, without appendages; ovary with short style and
entire stigma; fruit a compressed capsule with a
central indistinct midrib on each valve as well as a
lateral network of veins; seeds many, 1 or 2 rows
in each loculus.

1   Creeping perennial; flowers white; fruits
spreading   1. *A. alpina*
Erect biennial; flowers yellow; fruits erect
2. *A. glabra*

1. Arabis alpina *L.*
Perennial, stellate-pubescent stoloniferous herb
with obovate to oblong leaves.
A common alpine plant, growing above 10 000
ft altitude, often along streambanks and on cliffs.
HE, HA, HK.
Hanid 122; Newbould 6092.

2. Arabis glabra (*L.*) *Bernn.* (*Turritis glabra* L.)
An annual (in our area), pubescent with simple or
forked hairs, with basal obovate leaves in a rosette,
(dead at flowering time).
A locally abundant plant of highland grassland,
often on shallow, disturbed soil. HM, HA, HK.
Agnew 7663; Verdcourt 3206.

14. RORIPPA *Scop.*
Herbs, with simple hairs or glabrous, with
pinnatisect to pinnate leaves; racemes bracteate or
not; sepals saccate; petals clawed, yellow, or white;
stamens 6, without appendages; ovary with many
ovules, a style variable in length, and an entire
capitate stigma; fruit a long capsule, the valves
reticulately veined but with no midrib; seeds
usually in 2 rows in each loculus.

1   Leaves pinnate; flowers white
1. *R. nasturtium-aquaticum*
Leaves pinnatisect or almost simple; flowers
yellow   2
2   Flowers solitary axillary (or racemes
bracteate)   4. *R. cryptantha*
Flowers in ebracteate racemes   3
3   Petals 3–6 mm long; fruiting pedicels over
5 mm long   3. *R. nudiuscula*
Petals 1·5–2 mm long; fruiting pedicels less
than 4 mm long   2. *R. madagascariensis*

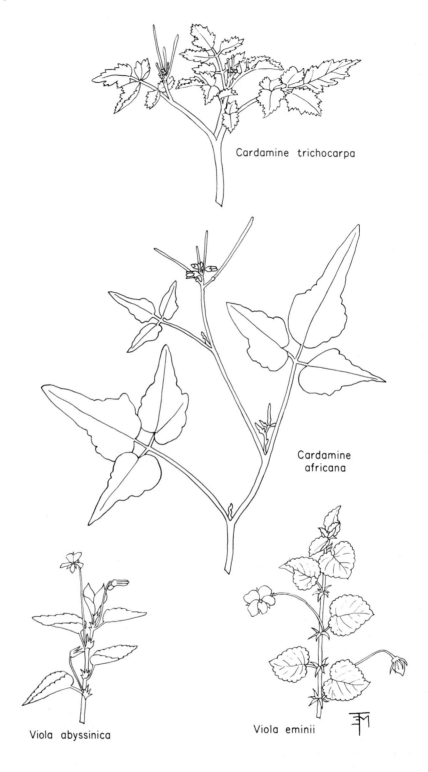

Cardamine trichocarpa

Cardamine africana

Viola abyssinica

Viola eminii

1. Rorippa nasturtium-aquaticum *(L.) Hayek* (*Nasturtium officinale* R. Br.)

A glabrescent trailing perennial herb, rooting at the nodes, with pinnate leaves bearing oblong-elliptic to suborbicular leaflets; flowers white.

Commonly grown for watercress (a green salad) and cosmopolitan in cooler streams. This plant is found in streamsides, often where disturbed by man's activities, and seldom in forest. HA, NBI.

Bally 8653; Hanid 16.

2. Rorippa madagascariensis *(DC.) Hara*

An annual, glabrous or pubescent, with pinnatisect leaves bearing oblong, often pinnatifid leaflets; petals yellow.

An uncommon plant of watersides in dry country. MAC.

Agnew 7507; Verdcourt 847.

3. Rorippa nudiuscula *(Sond.) Thell.*

A glabrescent perennial herb with spathulate, dentate, (sometimes lobed) leaves; petals yellow.

A rare plant only collected three times in Kenya and generally rather little known. HT, RV.

Harvey 5009.

4. Rorippa cryptantha *(A. Rich.) Robyns & Boutique*

A glabrescent annual, with twice pinnatisect leaves, the ultimate segments ± oblong; flowers solitary, yellow.

A rare plant found only once in Kenya, by Thomson's Falls, growing along the stream banks. HA.

Bogdan 4757.

15. SISYMBRIUM *L.*

Annual to perennial herbs with simple hairs and usually pinnatifid leaves; racemes with or (usually) without bracts; sepals not saccate; petals clawed, yellow or white; stamens 6, without appendages, stigma not 2-lobed; fruit a long capsule, the valves with a strong midrib and 2 weak lateral veins, and with the persistent stigma short or absent.

1   Fruit long-conical, narrowing to a point, appressed to the stem   1. *S. officinale*
Fruit long-cylindrical, parallel-sided, spreading
                         2. *S. erysimoides*

1. Sisymbrium officinale *(L.) Scop.*

An erect annual with pinnatifid leaves; petals yellow.

An introduced weed, possibly not maintaining itself. RV.

van Someren, December 1958.

2. Sisymbrium erysimoides *Desf.*

A sparsely pubescent annual with pinnatifid leaves; petals pale yellow.

A rare, introduced alien, from the Mediterranean region. RV.

Meinertzhagen 9309.

16. OREOPHYTON *O. E. Schulz*

A genus similar in all respects to *Rorippa*, except for the habit which is acaulescent and the embryo characters which are said to be different.

Oreophyton falcatum *(A. Rich.) O. E. Schulz*

A glabrous perennial herb with a rosette of pinnatisect leaves; flowers white in short racemes.

An alpine plant growing usually near streams from 11 500–14 500 ft. HE, HA, HK.

Hedberg 1702; Hanid 183.

17. ARABIDOPSIS *Heynh.*

Annual or perennial herbs with both simple and forked hairs; inflorescence corymbose; inner sepals not saccate; stamens 6, without appendages; style short, stigma entire or obscurely 2-lobed; fruit a many-ovuled capsule having 1-veined valves with prominent midribs and seeds in 1 row.

Arabidopsis thaliana *(L.) Heynh.*

A small annual rosette with elliptical or spathulate leaves; petals white.

A plant indigenous to the East African mountains but also found in Europe and Asia to Japan. HE, HM, HK.

Hanid, Agnew and Mendes 131; Hedberg 1814.

18. CAMELINA *Crantz*

Annual herbs with simple and forked hairs and erect stems with simple, amplexicaul, sessile leaves; raceme ebracteate; sepals not saccate; petals clawed, yellow or white; stamens 6, without appendages; ovary with many ovules, and a capitate stigma on a distinct style; fruit a capsule, short and broad, with convex, keeled, winged valves, each with a strong midrib which disappears above; septum across the broadest part; seeds in 2 rows in each loculus.

Camelina alyssum *(Mill.) Thell.*

An annual with coarsely dentate to pinnatifid leaves; petals white.

A weed of flax throughout the world which has been found only twice in Kenya, both times in KIT.

Dowson 698.

15. VIOLACEAE†

Herbs, shrubs, or trees, with alternate, or rarely opposite, stipulate simple leaves; flowers regular or zygomorphic, bisexual, solitary or in racemes; sepals 5, free; petals 5, free, the anterior one with a spur projecting between the adjacent sepals; stamens 5, all similar, or the anterior pair with appendages projecting into the spur; filaments free or united; ovary superior, sessile, unilocular usually with 3 parietal placentas and many ovules, with simple style and undivided stigma; fruit a capsule; seeds with endosperm, sometimes arillate.

1 Anterior petal with a long stalk; stipules
   entire   1. *Hybanthus enneaspermus*
   Anterior petal sessile; stipules dentate or
   laciniate   2. *Viola*

1. HYBANTHUS *Jacq.*

Herbs or shrubs with alternate or opposite, entire or serrate leaves; flowers solitary or rarely in racemes, zygomorphic; petals unequal, the anterior one either smaller than the others or, as in ours, much larger, and narrowly stalked, with a basal spur; 2 anterior stamens with spur appendages; ovary with 3 placentas, with few to many ovules; fruit a loculicidal capsule; seeds large and characteristically ornamented, with a small aril.

Hybanthus enneaspermus (*L.*) *F. Muell.*

A very variable hairy herb or shrub, with linear-lanceolate entire to ovate-elliptic serrate leaves and red or pink spurred flowers; seeds longitudinally ribbed and pitted, glabrous.

An extremely variable species, but usually found as a linear-leaved, strigose-hairy annual to 25 cm with pink flowers, in disturbed dry or subdesert bush. It is not very common. MUM, MAG, NBI, KAJ.
Isaac, December 1961; Verdcourt 2669.

2. VIOLA *L.*

Herbs (in ours) or shrubs, with alternate, usually serrate, leaves, flowers solitary, zygomorphic; sepals equal, sometimes with a basal appendage; petals unequal, the anterior spurred at base, the posterior ones erect; anterior filaments produced into the connective, and secreting nectar; ovary with 3 placentas and simple style and stigma; seeds usually smooth, with much endosperm, with or without an aril.

1 Leaves rounded at apex, glabrous or slightly
   hairy along midrib on upper surface
                                  1. *V. eminii*

Leaves pointed at apex, hirsute between the veins on the upper surface
                                  2. *V. abyssinica*

1. Viola eminii (*Engl.*) *R. E. Fries* (*V. duriprati* R. E. Fr. in Check List) (see p. 98)
Creeping, hairy, perennial herb with subcordate leaves and solitary blue to violet flowers.

A common violet, creeping often amongst rocks or on peaty soil at altitudes above 8000 ft, in the open or along forest paths and streamsides. HE, HC, HA, HK.
Agnew 8679; Glover 1099.

2. Viola abyssinica *Oliv.* (see p. 98)
Similar to *V. eminii* except for the leaves which are pointed and hairy above and sepals which are hardly appendiculate.

Found at lower altitudes (6000–9500 ft) than *V. eminii*; this species is also more rampant, and often has erect flowering stems. HE, HC, HM, HA, HK.
Agnew 8681; Kerfoot 2856.

16. RESEDACEAE‡

Usually herbs, rarely shrubs; leaves alternate, simple or divided, stipulate; inflorescence racemose, terminal; flowers bisexual (rarely unisexual) usually zygomorphic; sepals 4–6, usually 5, free; petals 4–7, usually 4–5, free, often divided or fringed; nectary disc often present, at least on one side; stamens definite to indefinite, often 10–15; anthers splitting longitudinally, introrse, 2-celled; ovary superior, of 2–6 (usually 5) free or slightly connate carpels, which often never completely close (thus the ovules resemble those of gymnosperms, but the pollen tube grows through the carpel wall in the normal angiosperm way); fruit a capsule or of follicles; seeds without endosperm.

1. CAYLUSEA *St.-Hill.*

Annual or short-lived perennial herbs with entire, often undulate, leaves; flowers bisexual, in dense bracteate racemes; sepals 5; petals 5, simple or digitate, with a short ligule between the spreading limb and dilated base; stamens 10–15; ovary of 5–6 whorled open carpels lightly connate at the base; fruit of open follicles with few seeds.

Caylusea abyssinica (*Fresen.*) *Fisch. & Mey.*

Annual or short-lived perennial herb, with linear-lanceolate, often undulate leaves and long racemes of whitish flowers.

---

† By A. D. Q. Agnew.

‡ By A. D. Q. Agnew.

A common weed of disturbed places in grassland, but not found in the driest or highest situations. It is allied to the European mignonette which it resembles. HT, HM, HA, HN, KIT, NAR, BAR, EMB, NBI, KAJ.

Strid 2724; Verdcourt 552.

17. POLYGALACEAE †

Herbs or woody trees, shrubs and climbers; leaves alternate, simple, entire, exstipulate; flowers zygomorphic, bisexual, usually in racemes; sepals 5, the two posterior laterals often enlarged and petaloid; petals 3-5, free or connate, the lower petal often forming an appendaged keel; stamens 5-8, with filaments united in a slit tube, rather similar to those of the Papilionaceae, anthers dehiscing by apical pores; ovary of 2 carpels, with one pendulous axile ovule in each; seeds usually arillate (the aril called a caruncle), endospermic.

1　Herbs, rarely shrubby at base; fruit a dry capsule　　　　　　　1. *Polygala*
　　Trees, shrubs or woody climbers; fruit not a dry capsule　　　　　　　　　2
2　Petals 5; stamens 5; fruit a drupe
　　　　　　　　　　　　　　　2. *Carpolobia*
　　Petals 3; stamens 8; fruit winged, indehiscent
　　　　　　　　　　　　　　　3. *Securidaca*

1. POLYGALA *L.*

Low shrubs or herbs; leaves and flowers as in the family; sepals 5, the two anterior fused or free, the two laterals enlarged and petaloid and termed *wings*; petals 3 or 5, the lowest forming a keel, often appendaged with a *crest* of filament-like threads, the lateral obscure or absent, the two posterior often as long as the keel and joined to it; stamens 8, or 6 + 2 sterile, the filaments fused in a tube around the ovary; fruit a flattened capsule, with 2 silky axile seeds, each with an aril, or *caruncle*, which may have papery appendages.

1　Anterior sepals (those next to the keel) fused
　　　　　　　　　　　　　　　　　　　2
　　Anterior sepals free　　　　　　　　3
2　Leaves rounded or obtuse, mucronate at tip; keel of flower with a tufted appendage
　　　　　　　　　　　　　1. *P. amboniensis*
　　Leaves with acute, needle-like tip; keel with no appendage　　　　2. *P. petitiana*
3　Inflorescences terminal and axillary　　4
　　Inflorescences axillary only　　　　　10
4　Usually annuals; racemes or raceme of clusters each with more than 20 flowers　5
　　Perennials; racemes with less than 20 flowers
　　　　　　　　　　　　　　　　　　　10

† By A. D. Q. Agnew.

5　Racemes exceeding the plant's leaves　6
　　Racemes overtopped by leaves　　　　8
6　Wings less than 2·0 mm wide
　　　　　　　　　　　　　3. *P. myriantha*
　　Wings more than 3·0 mm wide　　　　7
7　Stems and leaves pubescent or glabrous; pedicels and wings pubescent; wings with 5-7 nerves　　　　4. *P. ukirensis*
　　Stems and leaves with scattered hairs or glabrous; pedicels and wings glabrous; wings with 3 major nerves
　　　　　　　　　　　　　5. *P. abyssinica*
8　Racemes dense, spherical or shortly cylindrical　　　　　　　6. *P. arenaria*
　　Racemes or raceme of clusters elongate or long-cylindrical　　　　　　　　9
9　Wings orbicular, glabrous 7. *P. persicariifolia*
　　Wings elliptic, hairy at base　8. *P. albida*
10　Rachis of raceme longer than its subtending leaf　　　　　　　　　　　11
　　Rachis of racemes equal to or shorter than its subtending leaf　　　　　　　12
11　Wings orbicular　　　9. *P. sphenoptera*
　　Wings elliptical　　10. *P. ohlendorfiana*
12　Annual herb; wings with green midrib up to 2·5 mm broad　　11. *P. erioptera*
　　Perennial herbs; wings without green midrib, more than 3 mm broad　　　　13
13　Wings orbicular or triangular, more than 7·5 mm broad　　12. *P. senensis*
　　Wings elliptic, less than 5 mm broad
　　　　　　　　　　　　　13. *P. sadebeckiana*

1. Polygala amboniensis *Gürke*

Glabrescent annual or short-lived perennial herb, with oblong-linear leaves and green and pink or purple flowers.

A common *Polygala* of drier bushland in Kenya, extending to the coast. The flowers are not very colourful. RV, MAG, MAC.

Isaac, December 1961; Verdcourt and Napper 2168.

2. Polygala petitiana *A. Rich.* (see p. 102)

Glabrous or glabrescent annual with linear to narrow-elliptic leaves and elongated racemes of yellowish-green to dull-purple flowers.

The most easy to recognize of the annual, erect *Polygalas*. It grows in grassland, often on shallow soil, but not in the dry bush area or the highland forest zone. HE, HC, HT, KIT, MUM, KIS, MAC, NBI.

Tweedie 66/222; Symes 158.

3. Polygala myriantha *Chod.*

Puberulent, branched annual with elliptic to linear leaves and dense racemes of mauve or lilac flowers.

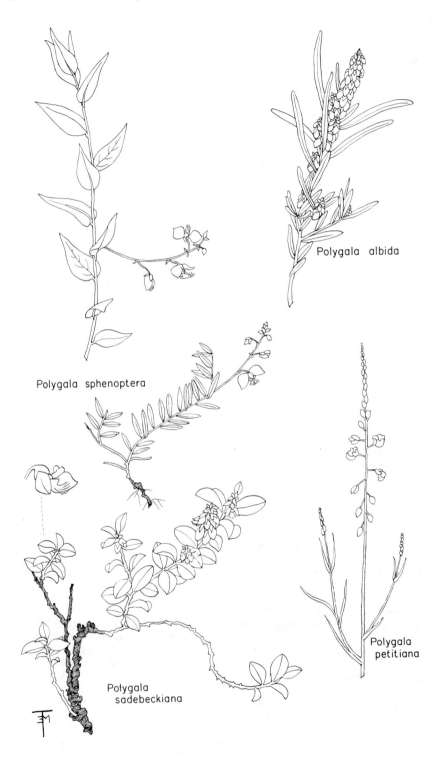

Polygala albida

Polygala sphenoptera

Polygala petitiana

Polygala
sadebeckiana

Apparently rare, but may be overlooked. Only recorded from upland grassland on grey soil near Kipkarren. KIT.

Brodhurst-Hill 361; Tweedie 68/133.

4. Polygala ukirensis *Gürke*

Pubescent annual with linear leaves and loose racemes of blue and yellow flowers.

Local but relatively common in the grasslands of Trans-Nzoia and thereabouts. KIT, MUM.

Dale 3182; Tweedie 67/211.

5. Polygala abyssinica *R.Br.*

A glabrous or sparsely hairy annual with linear leaves and loose racemes of white or flushed purple flowers.

Locally common plant found in dry grassland at medium altitudes. HM, HA, RV, NAN, MAC, KAJ.

Agnew and Humphry 5563; Kerfoot 4742.

6. Polygala arenaria *Willd.*

A sympodially branched, tomentose annual with elliptic to oblanceolate leaves and dense globular racemes of pinkish or white/cream flowers.

A rather rare *Polygala,* found at the coast and west of the Rift Valley, often associated with disturbed ground and cultivation. HA, KIS.

Hanid 649; Lucas 218.

7. Polygala persicariifolia *DC.*

A puberulous annual with linear, elliptic-acuminate or oblong-acute leaves and short racemes of cream to pale purplish flowers.

An uncommon plant of steep rocky hillsides and disturbed soils in wet forest of Kakamega, Nandi, lower Elgon, and Cherangani. HC, MUM.

Makin 321.

8. Polygala albida *Schinz* (see p. 102)

An erect puberulous annual with linear to elliptic-oblong leaves and short racemes bearing crowded green or white flowers.

A fairly common *Polygala* often found as a weed of fields and roadsides. HC, KIT, MUM, KIS, BAR, KAJ.

Agnew 8628; Symes 216.

9. Polygala sphenoptera *Fresen.* (see p. 102)

Perennial or annual shrubby herb, suffruticose or trailing, with linear, oblong or elliptic leaves, sometimes with revolute margins (especially in dry land forms), and lateral, axillary or extra-axillary, short, loose racemes of purple or pinkish-white flowers.

An extremely variable species, which is our commonest *Polygala* in Kenya. It grows apparently in dry bushland, grassland and upland grassland as well as along paths and clearings in the wetter highland forests. Perhaps future observations will show us how to split up the forms into units which make sense ecologically, but to this author it seems as though there is a continuously intergrading series from Magadi to Cherangani. Dry grass and bushland forms have narrow, revolute-margined leaves; white forms from wetter areas have broad, elliptic, acuminate leaves and often a trailing habit. HE, HC, HT, HM, HA, HK, KIT, MUM, KIS, NAR, BAR, RV, MAG, NAN, MAC, NBI, KAJ.

Agnew 8432; Leippert 5234.

10. Polygala ohlendorfiana *Eckl. & Zeyh.*

Glabrous or puberulent perennial herb from a woody rootstock, with elliptic leaves and red or purple flowers crowded in the terminal or lateral racemes.

A little-known plant in Kenya represented by scattered specimens from various habitats, but I am not quite convinced that all belong to one species. More collections are required, particularly fruiting specimens from the Aberdares above 9000 ft. HA, KIT, NAR.

Glover 5258; Jex-Blake B1259; Agnew 8129.

11. Polygala erioptera *DC.*

Annual or short-lived pubescent perennial with linear-oblong leaves and axillary clusters of white or red flowers.

Fairly common in rocky areas of bare soil in the dry grasslands of Kenya, especially on shallow soils. HE, MUM, KIS, RV, MAG, MAC, NBI.

Agnew 8227; Gillett 17329.

12. Polygala senensis *Klotzsch*

Erect, pubescent, shrubby perennial with oblanceolate to oblong leaves and axillary racemes of 1-4 pink to purple flowers.

A plant of dry bushland. This name has been applied to our material in the absence of any other. The species appears to be clear cut, but it remains probable that this is not the correct name for it. NAN, MAG.

Greenway 9519.

13. Polygala sadebeckiana *Gürke* (see p. 102)

Perennial herb or shrub, erect or decumbent, with elliptic to oblong leaves and axillary racemes of 8-12 (rarely more) orange-yellow to red flowers.

This name is used here for an uncommon but widespread group of plants which includes erect or trailing, red-flowered plants of forest edges and grassland, as well as prostrate, orange-yellow-flowered plants of bare grassland. More collecting is needed to determine whether one or two species are represented here. HM, HA, KIT, NAN, MAC, NBI.

Agnew 9149; Verdcourt 3171.

2. CARPOLOBIA and 3. SECURIDACA

Both these genera are dealt with in KTS., although *Securidaca welwitschii* Oliv. is a woody climber.

18. CRASSULACEAE†

Succulent, erect or creeping herbs and undershrubs; leaves opposite or alternate, exstipulate; flowers regular, bisexual, usually cymose; sepals free or united, often 4 or 5; petals as sepal number, free or united; stamens as many as or twice the number of petals; filaments free; ovary superior; carpels free, as many as petals, rarely loosely united in the middle, each with a nectary at the base; ovules few to many; fruit of membranous or leathery follicles, often surrounded by persistent membranous corolla; seeds minute, endospermous.

1	Leaves alternate above	2
	Leaves all opposite	3
2	Leaves peltate; corolla tubular	
	5. *Umbilicus botryoides*	
	Leaves simple; corolla lobes spreading	
	4. *Sedum*	
3	Corolla tubular, conspicuous, over 1 cm long; stamens 8-10	4
	Corolla small, rotate, less than 1 cm long; stamens 5	2. *Crassula*
4	Flower parts in fives; flowers pendulous	
	1. *Cotyledon barbeyi*	
	Flower parts in fours; flowers erect	
	3. *Kalanchoe*	

1. COTYLEDON *L.*

Herbs or shrubs with sessile opposite entire leaves and flowers in terminal corymbose cymes; calyx 5-lobed; corolla of 5 fused segments, forming a tube below with ± spreading lobes; stamens 10; follicles 5, free, many-seeded.

Cotyledon barbeyi *Schweinf.*

An erect, many-stemmed shrub with obovate to oblanceolate fleshy leaves; inflorescence glandular, of large pendulous red flowers.

Locally common and conspicuous in dry, stony bushland, especially on small hills. HM, NAR, NAN, RV, MAC, NBl, KAJ.

Strid 2808; Glover 3670.

2. CRASSULA *L.*

Fleshy herbs with opposite simple leaves and cymose inflorescences or solitary flowers; sepals 4-5 joined at base; petals 4-5, free; stamens 4-5

† By A. D. Q. Agnew.

alternating with scales which are opposite the petals and carpels; follicles 4-5, 1-many-seeded.

1	Leaves in a basal rosette often dying when the plant flowers; inflorescence a terminal corymbose cyme or raceme of cymes	2
	No basal rosette of leaves present; flowers all axillary	3
2	Flowers in a corymbose cyme	1. *C. alba*
	Flowers in a raceme of cymes	
		2. *C. nodulosa*
3	Leaves petiolate, narrowed to the base	4
	Leaves sessile, not or hardly narrowed to the base	5
4	Leaves round at apex; flowers white	
		3. *C. volkensii*
	Leaves acute at apex; flowers pink	
		4. *C. alsinoides*
5	Flowers solitary, axillary; pedicels longer than calyx	6
	Flowers in crowded axillary cymes; pedicels shorter than calyx	8
6	Plant of perennial streams and marshes which never dry up; leaves slightly wider in the middle than at base; seeds 1–4 in each follicle	7
	Plant of shallow temporary pools; leaves very narrow, parallel-sided; seeds more than 6 in each follicle	5. *C.* sp. *A*
7	Plant of Mt. Elgon above 9000 ft; seeds 4 in each follicle	6. *C.* sp. *B*
	Plant of other mountains and lowlands; seeds 1–2 in each follicle	7. *C. granvikii*
8	Plant annual; leaves never imbricate (overlapping one another)	8. *C.* sp. *C*
	Plant perennial; leaves imbricate on at least some shoots	9. *C. pentandra*

1. Crassula alba *Forsk.* (see p. 108)

An erect, probably biennial herb with a rosette of lanceolate fleshy basal leaves and opposite, reduced stem leaves; corymb of small white flowers.

Locally common plant found in dry rocky grassland. HC, HM, HK, KIT, NAR, RV, MAC, KAJ.

Agnew 10735; Glover 4238.

2. Crassula nodulosa *Schonl.*

A perennial herb with ovate-lanceolate rosette leaves and a cylindrical raceme of small whitish flowers.

Rare plant found in dry, stony grassland. NAN. Napper 1317.

3. Crassula volkensii *Engl.*

A glabrous or pubescent, loose perennial soft shrub or herb with spathulate to elliptic often-marked leaves and solitary white flowers on long pedicels.

Locally common, found in stony bushland, but not in the driest country. NAR, RV, NAN, MAC.
Lind in UCNH 13; Glover 4365.

4. Crassula alsinoides (*Hook. f.*) *Engl.* (see p. 108)

A sprawling or prostrate herb, glabrous except for a line of hairs on the internodes, with elliptic, acute, unmarked leaves and solitary pink flowers.

Locally common plant found in wet, rocky places in the montane forest area. HE, HM, HA, HK, MAC.
Agnew and Faden 9980; Mwangangi 330.

5. Crassula sp. A.

A trailing herb, possibly annual, with ascending or erect stems bearing linear leaves and solitary pink to white flowers.

Locally common plant found in ephemeral pools around Nairobi. MAC, NBI.
Archer 317; Agnew and Hanid 7525.

6. Crassula sp. B.

A glabrous, perennial, soft herb, with a trailing base and tufted, erect stems bearing linear leaves; flowers pinkish; follicles 4-seeded.

Only known from marshes in the moorlands of Mt. Elgon. HE.
Verdcourt 2474; Lugard 330.

7. Crassula granvikii *Mildbr.* (see p. 108)

Similar to the last species except for the often obtuse leaves (in *sp.* B. acute) and seed number.

This species is widespread and variable. Alpine forms on the Aberdares and Mt. Kenya are exceedingly small and tend to have 2-seeded follicles, but lowland forms can be very robust and their follicles are mostly 1-seeded. HE, HC, HT, HM, HL, HA, HK, KIT, RV, NBI.
Coe and Kirrika 263; Bally 11477.

8. Crassula sp. C.

A small, glabrous, erect, usually unbranched annual with linear leaves and axillary clusters of minute reddish flowers.

Locally common plant found on shallow soils. HC, RV, MAC.
Agnew, Kibe, and Mathenge 10314; Kerfoot 3582.

9. Crassula pentandra (*Edgeworth*) *Schonl.*

A glabrous perennial softly woody herb, trailing at base and with erect stems and triangular-ovate or lanceolate leaves; flowers pinkish-white in dense axillary clusters.

Common in stony upland grassland. HE, HC, HM, HA, HK, NAR, RV, NAN, MAC, NBI.
Lind and Agnew 5747; Verdcourt 3803.

3. KALANCHOE *Adans.*

Fleshy herbs or soft shrubs with opposite, entire or divided leaves and flowers in terminal corymbose cymes; calyx of 4 lobes joined at least at base; corolla of 4 joined petals, with a cylindrical tube; stamens 8, fused to corolla tube; follicles 4, many-seeded; seeds longitudinally ridged.

1   Leaves compound   2
     Leaves simple   3
2   Plant glabrous; calyx inflated with lobes shorter than the tube; flowers pendulous
                              1. *K. pinnata*
     Plant glandular-hairy; calyx not inflated, the tube shorter than the lobes; flowers erect
                              2. *K. rohlfsii*
3   Pedicels and calyx pubescent   4
     Pedicels and calyx glabrous   7
4   Plant glandular-hairy on the inflorescence   5
     Plant densely pubescent only, without glands
                              3. *K. citrina*
5   Leaves sessile; stem leaves oblong
                           4. *K. lanceolata*
     Stem and basal leaves ovate, petiolate   6
6   Sepals more than half as long as corolla tube; corolla lobes lanceolate, acute   5. *K. sp. A*
     Sepals less than half as long as corolla tube; corolla lobes ovate-elliptic, obtuse mucronate   6. *K. sp. B*
7   Leaves sessile; flowers white, over 5 cm long
                         7. *K. marmorata*
     Leaves petiolate; flowers yellow or orange, less than 4 cm long   8
8   Leaves auriculate, peltate at base; corolla over 2 cm long; anthers slightly exserted or visible in the mouth of the corolla tube
                          8. *K. lugardii*
     Leaves simple at base; corolla less than 2 cm long; anthers included in the corolla tube 9
9   Leaves cuneate at base, often spotted purple along the crenate margin; sepals fleshy, drying wrinkled   9. *K. glaucescens*
     Leaves rounded at base, never purple-spotted; sepals thin, drying flat and papery
                         10. *K. densiflora*

1. Kalanchoe pinnata (*Lam.*) *Pers.*

An erect, glabrous herb with pinnate leaves bearing elliptic leaflets and a diffuse inflorescence of large pendulous red flowers.

An introduced plant, escaped in parts of Nairobi. NBI.
Agnew 7617; Williams 716.

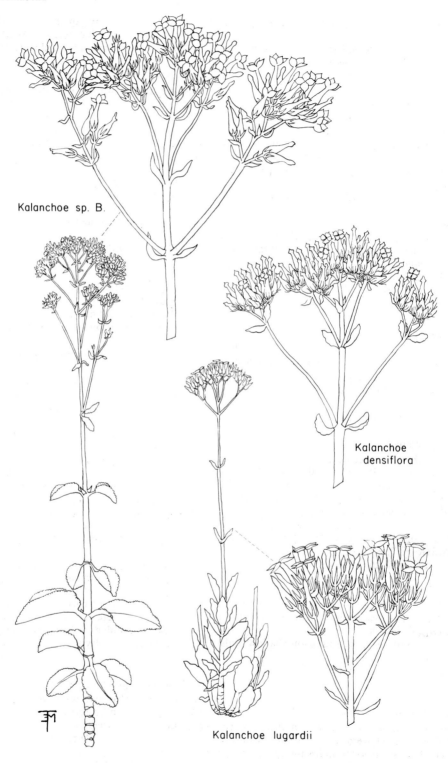

Kalanchoe sp. B.

Kalanchoe densiflora

Kalanchoe lugardii

2. Kalanchoe rohlfsii *Engl.*

An erect, glandular-pubescent, weak perennial with ternate leaves bearing lanceolate to ovate leaflets and a dense terminal corymb of yellow flowers.

Locally common plant found in rocky grassland, especially in the Rift Valley. RV, MAC, KAJ.
Agnew 10614.

3. Kalanchoe citrina *Schweinf.*

An erect, pubescent, weak perennial with oblanceolate to ovate deeply dentate leaves and a small dense terminal corymb of yellow flowers.

Locally common plant found in dry, rocky bushland. BAR, MAC.
Tweedie 68/141.

4. Kalanchoe lanceolata (*Forsk.*) *Pers.*

An erect, glandular-pubescent annual with almost glabrous, obovate to oblong, entire or dentate leaves and a dense corymb of yellow to orange-red flowers.

Locally common plant found in dry country. HE, KIT, MUM, BAR, RV, MAG, MAC, NBI, KAJ.
Strid 2709; Kokwaro 282.

5. Kalanchoe *sp.* A.

An ascending, glandular-pubescent, weak perennial with obovate crenate leaves and rather small corymbs of red flowers.

In bushed grassland in western Kenya. KIT, MUM.
Agnew, Musumba, and Kiniaruh 8059.

6. Kalanchoe *sp.* B. (see p. 106)

An erect glandular-pubescent perennial with ovate to orbicular leaves and corymbs of orange-red flowers.

Uncommon plant found in bushed grassland. HE, KIT.
Agnew, Kibe, and Mathenge 10592.

7. Kalanchoe marmorata *Bak.*

An erect, glabrous, weak perennial with sessile, obovate, often purple-blotched leaves and a loose terminal corymb of large white flowers.

Apparently not wild in our area but cultivated and escaped in western Kenya and around Nairobi. MUM, NBI.
Mathenge 349.

8. Kalanchoe lugardii *Bullock* (see p. 106)

An erect, glabrous herb, perennating from innovation shoots on the rootstock, or annual; with ovate to orbicular, peltate or auriculate, often purple-blotched leaves, and a corymb of pale orange to yellow flowers.

Uncommon plant found in dry, rocky bushland. HE, HT, KIT, BAR, MAG, NAN, MAC, KAJ.
Lugard 115; Agnew 10690.

9. Kalanchoe glaucescens *Britten*

A glabrous perennial, trailing at the base and with erect stems, with obovate to ovate-elliptic, petiolate leaves and small terminal corymbs of orange-yellow to yellow flowers.

Locally common plant found in stony bushland. MUM, NAR, BAR, RV, MAC.
Glover and Samuel 3377; Ehnbom in Strid 2706.

10. Kalanchoe densiflora *Rolfe* (see p. 106)

An erect, glabrous herb, perennating from innovation shoots on the rootstock, with orbicular to ovate, crenate, petiolate leaves and a dense terminal corymb of yellow flowers.

This is our commonest species of *Kalanchoe*, growing in disturbed places, 6000-9000 ft. HE, HT, HM, HA, RV, EMB, MAC, NBI, KAJ.
Glover, Gwynne, and Samuel 1279; Agnew 10796.

4. SEDUM *L.*

Erect or trailing herbs with entire, opposite or alternate fleshy leaves and cymose inflorescences; calyx of 5 fleshy segments of differing sizes; petals 5, free or nearly so; stamens 10, fused to the corolla at base; carpels 5, 1-many-seeded.

1 Petals white; follicles 1-seeded
       1. *S. crassularia*
 Petals yellow; follicles many-seeded 2
2 Leaves whorled at base of plant; anthers
  wedge-shaped, longer than broad
       2. *S.* sp. *A*
 Leaves mostly alternate at base of plant;
  anthers orbicular, as long as broad 3
3 Plant woody at base, with pustulated stems
       3. *S. ruwenzoriense*
 Plant herbaceous, with smooth stem
       4. *S. meyeri-johannis*

1. Sedum crassularia *R.-Ham.*

A small trailing plant forming cushions of blue-green fleshy leaves; flowers white- or purple-tinged, scattered.

Uncommon plant found in stony, solifluction soils in the alpine zone. HA, HK.
Hanid, Agnew, and Mendes 111; Hedberg 1552.

2. Sedum *sp.* A.

A spreading herb with cylindrical acute leaves and yellow flowers in a corymbose terminal cyme.

In stony soil at upper forest levels. HE.
Tweedie 67/305.

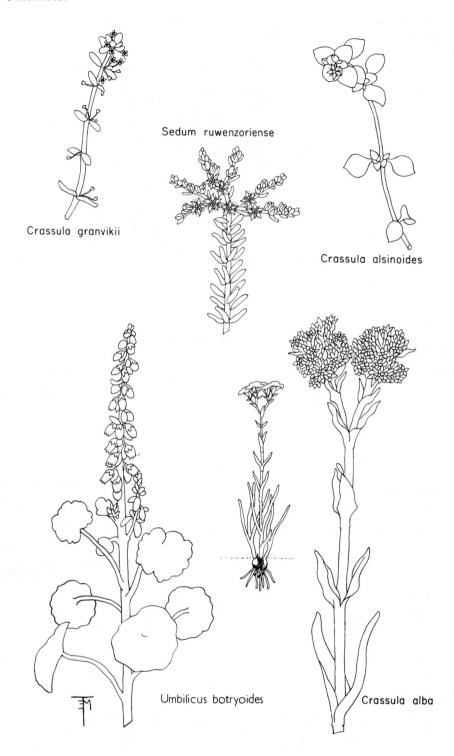

Crassula granvikii

Sedum ruwenzoriense

Crassula alsinoides

Umbilicus botryoides

Crassula alba

3. **Sedum ruwenzoriense** *Bak.* (see p. 108)

A trailing or erect, softly woody small shrub with blunt cylindrical leaves and diffuse terminal cymes.

Common in rock crevices in the heath and lower alpine zones. HE, HA, HK.

Mwangangi 387; Coe and Kirrika 252.

4. **Sedum meyeri-johannis** *Engl.*

A trailing herb, similar to *S. ruwenzoriense* in all respects except habit.

Locally common plant found in highland mist-forest as an epiphyte. HC, HM, HA.

Ivens 2057; Strid 2027.

5. UMBILICUS *DC.*

Perennial herbs with a tuberous root and alternate, peltate or cordate fleshy leaves; flowers in a terminal spike-like raceme; calyx of 5 nearly free lobes; corolla tubular, constricted at the mouth, of 5 fused petals; stamens 10; follicles 5, free, with numerous seeds.

Umbilicus botryoides *A. Rich.* (see p 108)

A small glabrous herb with peltate, circular, crenate, dimpled leaves and an erect raceme of pendulous white or greenish flowers.

Uncommon plant found in rock crevices in wet, montane forest. HE, HC, HM, HA, HK, RV.

Agnew 9067; Meinertzhagen 9325.

19. DROSERACEAE†

Herbs with alternate stipulate leaves; leaves bearing specialized hairs which trap and digest insects; inflorescences racemose or cymose; flowers bisexual, regular; sepals 4-8, connate at base, petals 4-8, free; stamens 5-20 (usually 5); ovary superior, of 3-5 connate carpels, with many ovules on parietal placentas; fruit a loculicidal capsule, seeds small, with endosperm.

1. DROSERA *L.*

Insectivorous herbs; leaves entire, with long sticky hairs; sepals and petals 5; stamens and ovary as in the family.

1 Plant with a trailing stem, the living leaves occupying an appreciable distance of it, internodes covered with reddish scarious stipules; sepals pilose-ciliate
   1. *D. madagascariensis*
   Plants with rosettes of leaves with no internodes visible; sepals not pilose-ciliate **2**
2 Peduncles glandular-pubescent; leaf lamina abruptly narrowing into the petiole
   2. *D. burkeana*

Peduncles pilose-glandular; leaf lamina gradually narrowing into the petiole
   3. *D. pilosa*

1. **Drosera madagascariensis** *DC.*

Trailing perennial, with spathulate leaves, the internodes covered by glossy, laciniate, reddish stipules; inflorescence an erect raceme of pink to purple flowers.

Like all the Droseras of Kenya, these are rare plants which should be studied at every opportunity. This is a distinctive one, recorded only from Soy. HT.

Bickford in Bally 6259.

2. **Drosera burkeana** *Planch.*

Perennial herb with a rosette of spathulate leaves and erect racemes of pink or white flowers.

Only recorded once from Kenya, at Kinangop, and doubtfully distinct from the next species, which is here kept separate merely to record the little which is known about Kenya sundews. More study is required on these plants. HA.

Agnew 7158.

3. **Drosera pilosa** *Exell*

This species differs from *D. burkeana* only in the key characters.

See note on *D. burkeana*.

Bally B4940.

20. PODOSTEMACEAE‡

Submerged aquatics of fast-flowing water, with very much modified vegetative and reproductive organisation; stems often thalloid; leaves present or absent; flowers bisexual or unisexual; perianth 0-5, free; stamens 1-many; ovary superior of 2-3 carpels, with axile or free-central placentation; stigmas sessile, 2-3, seeds minute, numerous.

1 Plant body with minute flat leaves in 3 ranks
   1. *Tristicha trifaria*
   Plant body erect or creeping, passing into capillary divisions and with no 3-ranked flat leaves   2. *Sphaerothylax abyssinica*

1. TRISTICHA *Thouars*

Moss-like herbs with 3-ranked leaves, each 1 cell thick; spathe at base of pedicel minute; flowers with 3 loosely coherent perianth segments, one stamen and erect ovary with 3 carpels and axile placentation.

Tristicha trifaria (*Bory*) *Spreng.*

A creeping herb, 1-4 cm tall, forming moss-like patches on rocks in fast flowing water. The reddish erect capsules look like those of a moss.

---

† By A. D. Q. Agnew.

‡ By A. D. Q. Agnew.

Locally common plant found in streams and rivers, and showing surprising tolerance to cold at higher altitudes. HE, HT, HA, MUM, BAR, MAC, KAJ.

Lind, Agnew, and Kettle 5902; Hedberg 47.

2. SPHAEROTHYLAX *Krauss*

Herbs, with or without leaves; flowers arising inverted from within a well-developed one-sided spathe; perianth of two minute linear segments, the filaments joined; ovary with free-central placentation and 2 stigmas; capsule longitudinally ribbed.

Sphaerothylax abyssinica *Warm.*

Plant with thalloid creeping portion and erect branching portion bearing capillary, divided segments; flowers arising from the thallus and from one upper node; filaments joined to close below the anthers.

Locally common plant found in rapids and waterfalls of larger rivers in warmer country. MUM, MAC.

Napper 409; Lind and Agnew 5901.

21. ELATINACEAE†

Herbs or low shrubs; leaves opposite or whorled, simple, with paired stipules; flowers solitary or in cymes, regular, bisexual, axillary, small; sepals 3–5, free, imbricate; petals as sepal number, free, imbricate, persistent; stamens equalling or twice as many as petals, free; ovary superior, 3–5 locular; styles 3–5, free; ovules numerous, axile; fruit a septicidal capsule; seeds exalbuminous.

1. BERGIA *L.*

Herbs or undershrubs, often pubescent or glandular-pubescent; leaves opposite, sessile or subsessile, entire or serrate; flowers pedicelled and fascicled (in ours); sepals 5 (in ours), keeled, with hyaline margins; petals equalling or slightly shorter than sepals; stamens usually 5 or 10; ovary usually 5-locular; carpels almost free; style one per carpel; fruit dehiscing from apex downwards; seeds brown or almost black, subcylindric, 3-angled or with rounded ends.

Bergia ammannioides *Roth*

Small erect or decumbent annual with sessile oblanceolate or oblong-elliptic leaves and white or pinkish flowers in dense verticillate clusters.

Herb of moist places, often a weed of cultivated land. More material desirable. EMB.

Bogdan 4443.

† By M. A. Hanid.

22. CARYOPHYLLACEAE‡

Mostly herbs, with simple, usually opposite, stipulate or exstipulate leaves; flowers mostly bisexual, regular, in cymose inflorescences; sepals 5, free or connate; petals 5, free, sometimes absent; stamens 5 or 10, free; ovary of 2–5 connate carpels, with free-central or rarely axile placentation; fruit a capsule or achene; seed curved, endospermic.

1	Leaves with stipules	2
	Leaves without stipules	7
2	Leaves alternate	6. *Corrigiola litoralis*
	Leaves opposite	3
3	Flowers densely packed at nodes of normal leaves, as well as, sometimes, terminal; fruits one-seeded, indehiscent, enclosed in red fleshy bracts	5. *Pollichia campestris*
	Flowers in terminal inflorescences, not densely packed at nodes of normal leaves; fruit a many-seeded dehiscent capsule, not enclosed in red fleshy bracts	4
4	Leaves all linear; styles free	4. *Spergula arvensis*
	Leaves not all linear; styles united	5
5	Leaves orbicular to ovate; sepals sticky in fruit	3. *Drymaria cordata*
	Leaves narrower than ovate; sepals not sticky in fruit	6
6	Sepals scarious, acute; leaves cylindrical, linear	1. *Polycarpaea*
	Sepals green, obtuse; leaves flat	2. *Polycarpon prostratum*
7	Sepals free	8
	Sepals connate	11
8	Plants prostrate, cushion- or rosette-forming; capsule teeth as many as style number	7. *Sagina*
	Plants erect or trailing, never forming a rosette or cushion; capsule teeth twice style number	9
9	Styles 4–5	8. *Cerastium*
	Styles 2–3	10
10	Petals entire to emarginate	9. *Arenaria foliacea*
	Petals deeply 2-lobed almost to base	10. *Stellaria*
11	Flowers solitary; calyx bell-shaped	11. *Uebelinia*
	Flowers in inflorescences; calyx tubular; erect plants	12. *Silene*

1. POLYCARPAEA *Lam.*

Annual or perennial herbs, or suffruticose; leaves opposite or apparently whorled, stipulate; inflorescences of terminal cymes; flowers bisexual,

‡ By A. D. Q. Agnew.

pentamerous; sepals entirely scarious, not keeled, white, brown to purple; petals small; stamens 5; ovary with few to many ovules on free-central placentation, and with a 3 lobed to simple style; fruit a 3-valved capsule.

1   Dorsal surface of sepals hairy, often lanate
                                             1. *P. eriantha*
     Dorsal surface of sepals glabrous
                                             2. *P. corymbosa*

1. Polycarpaea eriantha A. Rich.

An erect branched (at base) annual with hairy stem and linear glabrous leaves, bearing dense terminal corymbs of scarious white and red flowers.

An uncommon plant found in dry rocky places. The mature plant is almost umbrella-shaped, with the top covered with silvery white or pink flowers and stipules of the minute bracts. KIS, BAR, RV.

Glover 3764.

2. Polycarpaea corymbosa (L.) Lam.

Annual herb, erect to 40 cm, branching above into the inflorescence, otherwise similar to *P. eriantha* except for the sepals which are 3 mm long and glabrous, and the ovary which has 7–12 ovules.

A rare plant found in rocky places, only recorded from Machakos district. MAC.

Kirrika 134; Agnew 10084.

2. POLYCARPON L.

Annual or perennial herbs with opposite, often apparently whorled, stipulate leaves; flowers in cymes, terminating branches, bisexual, pentamerous; sepals 5, free, keeled; petals 5, shorter than the sepals; stamens 3–5; ovary with numerous free-central ovules, and one style with 3 stigmas; fruit a 3-valved capsule.

Polycarpon prostratum (Forsk.) Aschers. & Schweinf.

A glabrescent to pubescent annual herb, with ascending branches and spathulate or oblanceolate leaves; cymes small, terminal, of greenish-white flowers.

An apparently rare, recent introduction, only found so far at Limuru, but it may spread fast, and it may have been overlooked. HA.

Agnew 8292.

3. DRYMARIA Roem. & Schultes

Herbs, glabrous or hairy; leaves opposite, with expanded lamina, stipulate; flowers solitary or in terminal dichasial cymes; receptacle slightly perigynous; sepals 4–5, free; petals 4–5, bifid almost to base; stamens usually 5, the filaments shortly connate; ovary with 3 nearly free styles, and with 2-many ovules on free-central placentation; fruit a capsule with 3 valves.

Drymaria cordata (L.) Roem. & Schultes (see p. 113)

Straggling soft herb, usually glabrous, with broad-ovate cordate leaves and viscid-glandular inflorescences of white flowers.

A common herb in hedges, forest paths, and grassland edges in wetter forest zones from 4000–7500 ft in our area. Fruits and even young flowers are persistently picked up by one's trousers and on animals' coats, because of the viscid sepals. HE, HM, HA, HK, HN, KIT, MUM, EMB, MAC.

Agnew 5864; Kerfoot 4062.

4. SPERGULA L.

Annual herbs with linear, opposite, stipulate leaves; flowers in loose terminal dichasial cymes, pinkish or white, bisexual; sepals 5, free; petals 5, free; stamens 5; ovary with 3–5 free styles and free-central placentation of many ovules; fruit a capsule splitting into as many valves as there are styles.

1. Spergula arvensis L.

A prostrate or erect annual with apparently whorled, linear leaves and loose dichasia of pink or white flowers.

A local introduced weed of disturbed ground above 6000 ft. It is immediately recognized by its apparent whorls of linear leaves and sticky pink flowers. HT, HM, HA, RV.

Ivens 1131; Agnew 7148.

5. POLLICHIA Ait.

Trailing shrubs; leaves opposite, often appearing verticillate, stipulate; flowers bisexual, in dense sessile axillary cymes, surrounded by bracts of the cymes, pentamerous; sepals 5, free; petals 5, very small; stamens 1–2, borne with the perianth on a perigynous tube surrounding the 2-ovuled, single styled ovary; fruits in groups, surrounded by fleshy bracts and pedicels, each fruit one-seeded, indehiscent, surrounded by the persistent calyx.

Pollichia campestris Ait.

Straggling soft shrub or woody perennial, with apparently whorled, elliptic to lanceolate leaves; flowers green, fascicled axillary, turning red in fruit.

Fairly common, though never abundant, in disturbed grassland, waste places, and forest/grassland edges at medium altitudes, particularly in the Rift Valley. HM, HA, NAR, RV, MAC, NBI, KAJ.

Bally B8367; Agnew and Musumba 5478.

6. CORRIGIOLA *L.*

Decumbent herbs with alternate, stipulate leaves; flowers small, axillary or terminal, bisexual, pentamerous; petals present, small; ovary surrounded by a perigynous receptacle, with 3 stigmas and a solitary basal ovule; fruit indehiscent, enclosed in the persistent calyx.

Corrigiola litoralis *L.*

Prostrate, glabrous annual or short-lived perennial, with linear to narrow-oblanceolate leaves; sepals often turning red in fruit; petals pink-white.

A very local weedy plant of mountain roadsides and disturbed ground, above 7000 ft. HT, HA, HK.

Gillett 16661; Agnew 7150.

7. SAGINA *L.*

Tufted, rosette, cushion-like or procumbent herbs with linear exstipulate leaves; flowers small, in cymes, often green, bisexual, pentamerous; sepals 4–5, free, green; petals 4–5 or absent, always smaller than the sepals; stamens 5–10; ovary with 4–5 styles, free-central placentation and numerous ovules; fruit a capsule opening by as many valves as there are styles.

1   Plant forming cushions by means of close-packed short leafy stems; no petals
          1. *S. afroalpina*
     Plant forming rosettes, with no leafy shoots except for flowering shoots; petals present
          2. *S. abyssinica*

1. Sagina afroalpina *Hedb.*

A glabrous creeping perennial herb with short leafy stems usually forming a cushion; leaves linear, narrowing to a fine point; flowers 1–3 on axillary stems, green.

This pearlwort can be found along riverbanks and wet stony areas in the alpine belt above 9000 ft on Mt. Elgon, the Aberdares, and Mt. Kenya.

Coe 282.

2. Sagina abyssinica *A. Rich.*

Glabrous perennial herb with a rosette of leaves which usually hide the bases of the ascending flowering stems; flowers 5 to over 10 in loose dichasial cyme, green.

Often growing lower than *S. afroalpina* (7500–13 000 ft) this pearlwort is easily recognized by its distinct rosette habit, with the flowering stems appearing to come from below the rosette. It is found on the same three mountains as *S. afroalpina*, and it may be worth looking for on Cherangani. HE, HA, HK.

Kirrika 412.

8. CERASTIUM *L.*

Annual or perennial herbs, or suffrutescent; leaves sessile, opposite, exstipulate, entire; flowers bisexual in terminal dichasial cymes, or solitary; sepals 4–5, free; petals 4–5 or 0, emarginate or bifid, white; stamens 5–10; ovary with numerous free-central ovules and 4–5 styles; capsule cylindrical, often curved to one side with twice as many teeth as styles.

1   Lower 2–4 flowers of inflorescence solitary, apparently racemose; petals equal to or longer than calyx   1. *C. afromontanum*
     All flowers borne at ± the same height on the terminal cyme, crowded and touching one another, rarely but one solitary below the others and then in the first fork of the dichasium; petals longer or shorter than calyx   2

2   Largest leaves usually more than 10 mm broad; pedicels and calyx viscid, so that the flowers of the dichasium easily adhere to one another   2. *C. indicum*
     Largest leaves never more than 9 mm broad; pedicels and calyx viscid or not, but even if so, then flowers seldom adhering to one another   3

3   Erect or spreading annual; all leaves uniformly pilose below; petals absent or present, always bifid, shorter than the sepals
                              3. *C. octandrum*
     Creeping, stoloniferous perennial with ascending flowering stems; lower leaves glabrous except for the sometimes pilose midrib on lower side; petals present, shorter or longer than calyx, bifid to entire
                              4. *C. adnivale*

1. Cerastium afromontanum *T.C.E. Fr. & Weimark*

A pilose and glandular perennial or possibly annual herb, with prostrate or ascending branches to 10 cm, lanceolate-elliptic leaves and solitary lower flowers; upper flowers 2–3 in a weakly developed dichasium.

A rather variable plant which can be more or less hairy and glandular. It is common in open short grassland and stream edges from 7500 ft up to 13 000 ft. HE, HC, HT, HM, HA, HK.

Strid 3205B; Hedberg 1618.

2. Cerastium indicum *Wight & Arn.* (see p. 113)

Trailing perennial pilose herb with ovate amplexicaul leaves and dense inflorescences of glandular flowers with no solitary flowers at base; sepals often adhere to one another.

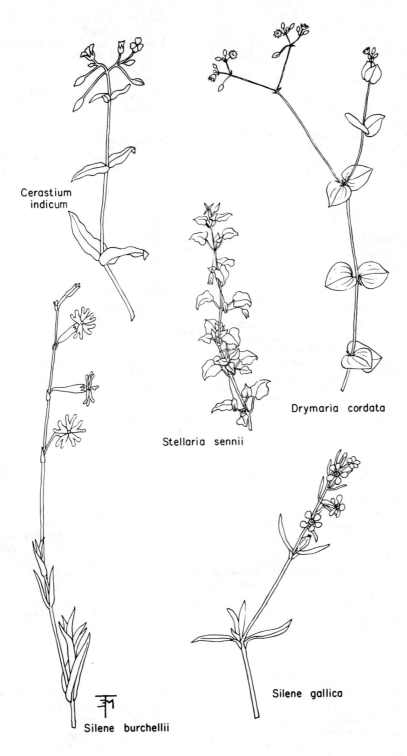

Cerastium
indicum

Stellaria sennii

Drymaria cordata

Silene burchellii

Silene gallica

A common trailing plant of hedgerows, forest edges, and wet grassland in the area of wet highland forest, but not found above 9000 ft. The white flowers are quite showy at times. HM, HA, HK, KAJ.

Agnew 7665; Kerfoot 2822.

3. Cerastium octandrum *A. Rich.*

Annual or perennial hairy herb, with oblong or lanceolate leaves and terminal dichasia of tetramerous or pentamerous flowers.

An uncommon plant found from 7000 ft to the lower alpine zone, often in disturbed places, in grassland and open woodland. HE, HC, HT, HM, HA, HK, KIT.

Knight 95; Hedberg 188; Tweedie 66/371.

4. Cerastium adnivale *Chiov.*

A creeping stoloniferous perennial, sometimes forming cushions, with lanceolate, sessile leaves and strictly dichotomous dichasia of short-pedicelled flowers.

A common plant of alpine zones, growing generally slightly higher than *C. afromontanum.* The species is delimited here with the knowledge that a lot more observations and experiments are needed before we really know about *Cerastium* in East Africa. The forms with long entire petals appear distinct from those with short bifid petals, but the capsules are rather variable. HM, HA, HK.

Coe 315; Hanid 119.

9. ARENARIA *L.*

Herbs or suffrutescent plants, often cushion-like; leaves entire, opposite, exstipulate; flowers solitary or in dichasia, pentamerous; sepals free; petals free, entire, white or pink; stamens 10 or fewer; ovary with 3 styles and many ovules, placentation free-central; fruit a capsule opening by 6 teeth.

Arenaria foliacea *Turrill*

Erect, glandular-hairy annual with ovate leaves and greenish-white flowers in lax dichasial cymes, subtended by leaf-like bracts.

A rare plant, only recently recorded for Kenya in the Chyulu Hills. KAJ.

Hanid 202.

10. STELLARIA *L.*

Annual or perennial, often weak, herbs; leaves opposite, exstipulate; flowers solitary or in terminal dichasia, bisexual, small, parts in 5s or rarely 4s; sepals free; petals always deeply bifid almost to base, white, rarely 0; stamens 10 or fewer; ovary with 3 stigmas (rarely 2) and numerous free central ovules; fruit a capsule with 3 or 6 valves.

1   All flowers in long-pedunculate dichasia, with reduced bracts   1. *S. mannii*
    Some or all flowers axillary or borne at branch forkings   2
2   Leaves truncate to cordate at base; sepals 4; styles 2   2. *S. sennii*
    Leaves cuneate to rounded at base; sepals 5; styles 3   3. *S. media*

1. Stellaria mannii *Hook. f.*

Prostrate or straggling, annual or perennial herb, sparsely glandular hairy throughout, with ovate leaves, and white flowers in glandular-sticky dichasia.

A rather rare plant found in shady pathsides and the floor of wet highland forest, recorded from south of Mt. Kenya and Chyulu in our area. HK, KAJ.

Kabuye 60.

2. Stellaria sennii *Chiov.* (see p. 113)

A weak, trailing, sparsely hairy herb with ovate or heart-shaped cordate leaves and solitary flowers, petals very small or absent.

An uncommon plant found in wet highland forest edges and paths, often in shade. HE, HT, HM, HA, HK.

Agnew 7696; Gillett 16757.

3. Stellaria media (*L.*) *Vill.*

Annual, sparsely pilose herb with elliptic leaves and solitary white flowers.

A locally abundant introduced weed in cultivation, especially gardens. HA, RV, NBI.

Gillett 16758.

11. UEBELINIA *Hochst.*

Herbs, prostrate or ascending; leaves opposite, exstipulate, flowers solitary, axillary, pentamerous; sepals connate; petals entire, white; stamens 10 or fewer; ovary with 3 or 4-5 styles and few, free-central ovules; capsule included within the persistent calyx, opening by as many septicidal valves as there are styles.

1   Stems ascending; calyx with minute spiny hairs and conical tube; petals much shorter and narrower than calyx lobes
                                        1. *U. abyssinica*
    Prostrate herbs; calyx softly hairy, with a bell-shaped tube; petals equal to or larger than calyx lobes   2
2   Fruit and ovary 1-seeded   2. *U. crassifolia*
    Fruit and ovary 3–4-seeded
                                        3. *U. rotundifolia*

1. Uebelinia abyssinica *Hochst.*

An ascending herb with obovate, often asymmetric leaves, and white flowers ± clustered at the stem apex; styles 4–5; fruit 5–8-seeded.

A rare plant of marshes, only found once near Gilgil in HA.

Agnew 10122.

2. Uebelinia crassifolia *T.C.E. Fries*

A creeping, sparsely soft-hairy herb with obovate to orbicular subsessile leaves and solitary axillary white flowers; styles 3; fruit 1-seeded.

Locally common in subalpine grassland, especially where disturbed. This is recorded from Mt. Kenya but we have only seen it from the Aberdares. HA, HK.

Agnew and Armstrong 8166; Dent 1306.

3. Uebelinia rotundifolia *Oliv.*

Similar to *U. crassifolia* but with rather smaller leaves and many seeds per capsule. This species has been found on Mt. Kilimanjaro and Mt. Kenya in disturbed heathland and upper mist forest zones. HK.

Verdcourt 1988; Strid 2265.

12. SILENE *L.*

Herbs or suffrutescent plants with opposite, entire, exstipulate leaves; inflorescence cymose or, by reduction, racemose; flowers bisexual or rarely unisexual; sepals 5, connate into a tube; petals 5, with a narrow claw (in the calyx tube) and a dilated, usually bifid, limb; stamens 10; ovary with 3–5 stigmas, often stipitate, with axile placentation at base and the septa breaking down above; capsule with many ovules, usually retained within the persistent calyx, opening by 3–6 valves.

1 Annuals with spreading hairs; calyx less than 1 cm long; petals entire   1. *S. gallica*
   Perennials, often suffrutescent, with appressed hairs or glabrous; calyx more than 1 cm long; petal limb deeply bifid   2
2 Plant short-hairy, not viscid   2. *S. burchellii*
   Plant glabrous, viscid on peduncle internodes   3. *S. macrosolen*

1. Silene gallica *L.* (see p. 113)

Erect pilose-glandular annual, with sessile spathulate or oblanceolate leaves and unbranched racemes of short-pedicelled white flowers.

An introduced weed in a few areas in Kenya, usually found along roadsides and in cultivation. HT, HM, HA, KIT, RV.

Mendes 19; Nattrass 1002.

2. Silene burchellii *DC.* (see p. 113)

Perennial herb with linear acute leaves and racemes of 3–9 flowers; petals pale pink, cream, or purple.

Our commonest *Silene* though by no means abundant. As is common in this genus, the petals open at night, and remain open during the following morning only, becoming darker and curling as mid-day approaches. The plant can grow from medium altitude grasslands up into the moorlands of the alpine zone. HE, HC, HM, HA, HK, KIT, RV, NBI, KAJ.

Agnew 5455; Bogdan 3677.

3. Silene macrosolen *A. Rich.*

A perennial herb similar to *S. burchellii* but larger in all its parts and completely glabrous; inflorescence with viscid patches on peduncle, pedicels and rachis.

Rather rare, and found in fairly well watered but low altitude grassland. HA, HK, RV, KAJ.

Hanid 263; Kabuye 7.

23. AIZOACEAE†

Herbs or shrubs, often succulent, with opposite or alternate, stipulate or exstipulate leaves; flowers bisexual, regular, solitary or cymose; sepals 5, connate or free; petals absent, often represented by petaloid staminodes; stamens 5-many; ovary variable, superior or inferior, of 1–2–5 united or free carpels, with axile placentation and 1–many ovules per loculus; fruit usually a capsule; seeds with a curved embryo.

This is a very vague and variable family, somehow held together (for the field botanist) by being plants near to, but obviously not of, the Caryophyllaceae and Portulacaceae/Phytolaccaceae.

1 Leaves linear or fleshy ± cylindrical   2
   Leaves broader than linear, flat, not cylindrical   5
2 Flowers on pedicels that are longer than the leaves   3
   Flowers sessile or pedicels shorter than the leaves   4
3 Perennial shrub   5. *Hypertelis bowkerana*
   Annual herb   4. *Mollugo cerviana*
4 Shrub; flowers white, 2–3 cm diameter   8. *Delosperma nakurense*
   Annual, but occasionally woody; flowers pink or red, less than 1 cm in diameter   6. *Trianthema*
5 Scapose annual with basal leaf rosette, and long-pedicellate flowers   4. *Mollugo nudicaulis*

† By A. D. Q. Agnew.

Herbs or shrubs with leafy stems; inflorescence various **6**

6 All leaves opposite **7**
   At least some leaves alternate **9**

7 Flowers in pedunculate umbels
   1. Gisekia pharnaceoides
   Flowers solitary or in sessile glomerules **8**

8 Style 1 *6. Trianthema*
   Styles 2 *7. Zaleya pentandra*

9 Ovary inferior; fruit spiny or softly ornamented with fleshy bristles *9. Tetragonia*
   Ovary superior; fruit unornamented **10**

10 Plant glabrous *10. Corbichonia decumbens*
   Plant hairy **11**

11 Some nodes with opposite leaves (often the alternate nodes); flowers fasciculate at nodes *3. Glinus*
   All nodes with single leaves; flowers in pedunculate cymes *2. Limeum viscosum*

1. GISEKIA *L.*

Annual herbs with opposite exstipulate subsucculent leaves; inflorescences axillary, of umbels or dichasia; flowers bisexual or unisexual, pedicellate; sepals 5, free; stamens 5-20; ovary of 3-6 or 10-15 superior, free, one-seeded carpels; fruit of free achenes.

Gisekia pharnaceoides *L.* (see p. 118)

Trailing or shortly erect glabrous annual with oblong-linear leaves and crowded umbels of bisexual red or pink flowers.

Common in the drier grasslands after rain, particularly in Machakos and the Rift Valley. The pink flowers in tiny umbels not more than 1 cm in diameter serve to distinguish this plant from all others. MUM, KIS, BAR, RV, MAC.

Tweedie 67/100; Napier 10643.

2. LIMEUM *L.*

Glabrous or hairy herbs or shrubs with opposite or alternate exstipulate leaves; inflorescences cymose; flowers bisexual, small; sepals 5, free; staminodes 5 or absent, if present arising from the base of the outer stamens; stamens 7 (5 + 2) or 5; ovary superior, of 2 carpels with 2 styles, bilocular with one seed in each loculus; fruit separating into 2 mericarps.

Limeum viscosum (*J. Gay*) *Fenzl*

A glandular-hairy annual with obovate or spathulate leaves, and axillary clusters of green flowers.

An uncommon species of sandy and shallow soils in *Commiphora* bushland, and found in our area only from Lukenia eastwards through Machakos district. MAC.

Napper 1279.

3. GLINUS *L.*

Annual herbs with opposite leaves alternating with solitary leaves; flowers bisexual, in clusters at the nodes, pedicellate; sepals 5, free; staminodes 0 to many, usually divided at apex, not always petaloid; ovary superior of 3-5 loculi with axile placentation, and 3-5 sessile stigmas; fruit a capsule; seeds with a white aril and a filiform appendage from the hylum.

1 Leaves stellate-hairy; pedicels shorter than flowers *1. G. lotoides*
   Leaves glabrescent, with simple hairs; pedicels longer than flowers *2. G. oppositifolius*

1. Glinus lotoides *L.*

A prostrate, stellate-pubescent annual with spathulate or elliptic leaves and 4-10 green flowers at each upper node.

A rather uncommon weed of sandy pond and riversides which grows in the dry weather after the water recedes. The flowers are green and inconspicuous. BAR, MAG, MAC, KAJ.

Mendes 1; Drummond and Hemsley 1249.

2. Glinus oppositifolius (*L.*) *DC.*

Erect or spreading, nearly glabrous subsucculent annual with oblanceolate leaves; flowers 4-12 at the nodes, on pedicels which are longer than the calyx.

In our area this species, as delimited here, is rare, only being found in Machakos, in the same type of habitat as *G. lotoides*. MAC.

There are many plants and populations of plants which show intermediate characters between these two species, and which may be hybrids. A study of these would be interesting. The putative hybrid is recorded from RV and NBI.

(Species) Kirrika 154; (Hybrid) Teesdale 26/461.

4. MOLLUGO *L.*

Annual herb with opposite or verticullate leaves, with or without small stipules; inflorescences cymose, often apparently umbelliform; flowers bisexual, inconspicuous; sepals 5, free; stamens usually 5, free; ovary superior, with 3-5 loculi and the same number of stigmas; ovules many, axile; fruit a capsule; seeds without an aril.

1 Scapose plant with a rosette of leaves at the base only *1. M. nudicaulis*
   Plant with whorls of leaves on the stem
   2. M. cerviana

1. Mollugo nudicaulis *Lam.*

A glabrous annual with a rosette of spathulate leaves, and a dichotomous or sub-umbelliform scape of pink or red flowers.

A small, easily overlooked annual of shallow soils in lower altitude grassland, not very common, but widespread. HM, KIS, NAR, BAR, RV, NBI.
Agnew 9270; Leippert 5275.

2. Mollugo cerviana *(L.) Ser.*

A small, much branched glabrous annual herb with spathulate to linear leaves in whorls; flowers borne in groups on long capillary pedicels at each node.

A beautiful but tiny plant, often found in sandy dry stream beds or bare ground. In our area only recorded near Machakos. MAC.
Lucas and Williams in EAH 12322; Agnew 10081.

5. HYPERTELIS *Fenzl.*

Herbs or low soft shrubs, with alternate or whorled, linear, succulent, stipulate leaves; stipules persistent, adnate to leaf base, membranous; inflorescences axillary of long-pedunculate simple umbels; sepals 5, free; stamens 3-15; ovary superior, 3-5-loculate, with numerous axile ovules; fruit a loculicidal capsule.

Hypertelis bowkerna *Sond.*

A perennial (or possibly annual) glabrous herb or soft shrub with opposite or alternate, linear, fleshy, stipulate leaves and single umbels of long-pedicellate green flowers.

A rather rare plant found in disturbed bare ground in sandy grassland or dry bushland at low altitudes. RV, MAG, KAJ.
Verdcourt 3557.

6. TRIANTHEMA *L.*

Herbs, usually annual, with opposite, succulent, often unequal leaves, obscurely stipulate; flowers axillary, solitary or in groups; sepals 5, connate, the lobes awned; stamens 5 to many, arising from the calyx tube; ovary of one carpel, with follicular placentation and one style; seeds 2 or more.

1 Leaves broad-elliptical or obovate, usually more than 3 cm long, densely pilose; flowers more than 8 mm long
                                  1. *T. ceratosepala*
   Leaves usually narrow-elliptical or linear, never more than 3 cm long, glabrous or sparsely papillose; flowers less than 5 mm long   2. *T. triquetra*

1. Trianthema ceratosepala *Volkens & Irmsch.*

Spreading or erect pilose woody annual or short-lived perennial, with obovate to elliptic leaves; flowers 1-3 together, bright purple or pink within.

Occasional in alkaline and subsaline soils, and certain localities (which may be alkaline) in *Acacia-Commiphora* bushland. In our area only known from Amboseli. KAJ.
Agnew 7307; Verdcourt 2540.

2. Trianthema triquetra *Willd.*

A crystalline-papillose annual with linear to orbicular leaves and reddish flowers in groups of 2-6, very shortly pedicellate or sessile.

On saline and alkaline clays and restricted to these areas. This plant is abundant where it occurs. BAR, MAG, KAJ.
Agnew 7306; Knight 5/65/2.

7. ZALEYA *Burm. f.*

Annual or perennial herbs with opposite, exstipulate leaves; flowers in nearly sessile axillary groups, bisexual; sepals 5, connate into a tube, the lobes with dorsal mucros; stamens 5-15, free, inserted on the calyx tube; ovary superior, of 2 united carpels, with 2 free stigmas, and 2 axile ovules per carpel; fruit a capsule.

Zaleya pentandra *(L.) Jeffrey*

A spreading or erect subsucculent annual with narrowly or broadly elliptic leaves which have the petiole base expanded into white-membranous wings, and with some bracts reduced to scarious leaf bases, resembling stipules; flowers subsessile at the nodes, crowded, pinkish.

Not uncommon in sands in hotter districts, especially near Lake Victoria in west Kenya. HE, MUM, KIS, NAR, BAR, RV, MAG, NAN, MAC.
Bally 19543; Hanid and Kiniaruh 746.

8. DELOSPERMA *N. E. Br.*

Perennial herbs, suffrutescent or stemless with opposite succulent ± cylindrical leaves without stipules and with no radiating hairs at their tips; flowers solitary, axillary or terminal; sepals 5, connate, with unequal lobes, succulent; staminodes many, petaloid, lanceolate; stamens many, free; ovary inferior, with 5 loculi and 5 stigmas; ovules many, parietal not axillary in each loculus; fruit a capsule, dehiscing at the top to expose the numerous seeds.

Delosperma nakurense *(Engl.) Herre* (see p. 118)

A glabrous shrubby perennial with sessile fleshy linear leaves and white or pink flowers.

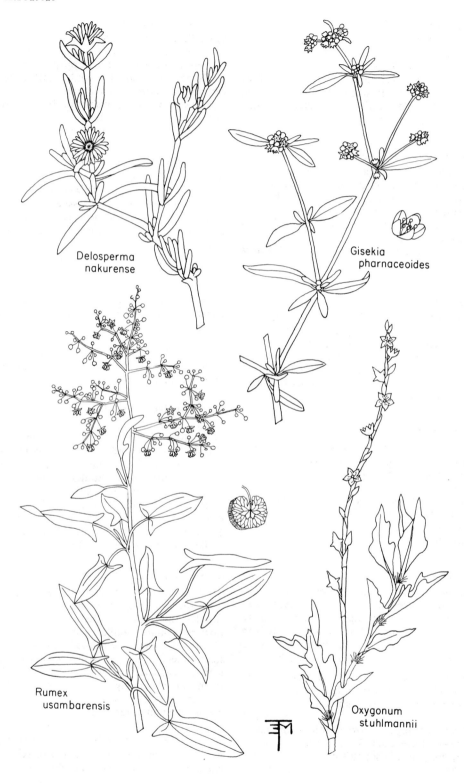

Delosperma
nakurense

Gisekia
pharnaceoides

Rumex
usambarensis

Oxygonum
stuhlmannii

Locally common in parts of the Rift Valley and occasionally elsewhere, this plant apparently likes to grow amongst loose friable rocks in dry bushland or grassland. HA, NAR, RV, MAC.

Agnew 9440; Glover 3617.

9. TETRAGONIA *L.*

Herbs or shrubs with entire alternate exstipulate leaves; flowers solitary or fasciculate, axillary; sepals 3–5, connate into a tube above the ovary; stamens few to many, alternate with the calyx lobes; ovary nearly or quite inferior, with 1–9 loculi, each with 1 ovule; fruit indehiscent, dry, often ornamented.

1 Fruit covered with soft fleshy spines
   1. T. acanthocarpa
   Fruit with 3–5 rather blunt horns
   2. T. tetragonioides

1. Tetragonia acanthocarpa *Adamson*

A semi-succulent papillose annual herb, with elliptic to rhombic leaves, and solitary greenish to pink flowers.

An uncommon weed, introduced from South Africa, but now naturalized in disturbed pastures in the Rift Valley, especially around Gilgil. RV.

Agnew and Azavedo 9311; Verdcourt 3233.

2. Tetragonia tetragonioides (*Pallas*) *O. Ktze.*

A succulent glabrous annual with ovate-rhombic leaves and axillary sessile yellow-green flowers.

A New Zealand plant, occasionally found as an escape from cultivation. RV.

Bally 12263.

10. CORBICHONIA *Scop.*

Herbs with alternate subsucculent exstipulate leaves; flowers bisexual, in pedunculate cymes; sepals 5, free; petaloid staminodes many; stamens many; ovary superior, with 5 styles, 5 loculi, and many ovules; fruit a loculicidal capsule.

Corbichonia decumbens (*Forsk.*) *Exell*

A usually prostrate glabrous annual or perennial herb, with obovate apiculate leaves and 5–10-flowered terminal dichasia of pinkish flowers.

An uncommon weed found in dry bushland, easily recognized by its glaucous apiculate leaves and pinkish stems. Only recorded from Lakes Baringo and Magadi in our district, but found just outside it at Mtito Andei. BAR, MAG.

Strid 2244; Glover 2960.

24. PORTULACACEAE†

Herbs or rarely shrubs, often succulent; leaves sessile or petiolate, alternate or opposite; stipules scarious or modified into setose axillary appendages or absent; flowers bisexual, regular, solitary or variously racemose, paniculate or cymose; sepals 2, imbricate, free or united at the base; petals 4–6, imbricate, free or connate up to halfway or more, usually fugacious; stamens as many as and opposite the petals or more numerous, free or epipetalous; ovary usually superior, 1-celled, placentation free-central or basal; fruit a capsule dehiscing by valves or by a transverse slit (circumscissile) rarely an indehiscent nutlet; seeds globose-reniform, endospermous.

1 Leaves with stipular hairs at the base
   1. Portulaca
   Leaves without stipules at the base   **2**
2 Plant less than 10 cm tall, a minute alpine herb; petals white   *2. Montia fontana*
   Plant over 10 cm tall, a robust lowland herb or shrub; petals yellow or purple
   3. Talinum

1. PORTULACA *L.*

Erect or prostrate herbs; leaves shortly petiolate or sessile; stipules usually divided into numerous hairs; flowers sessile, solitary or in small groups at the ends of branches and surrounded by 2-several leaves; sepals unequal, united at the base; petals marcescent and surrounding the ripe capsule; stamens 7–13 in ours, epipetalous or perigynous; ovary semi-inferior, 1-celled, usually multiovulate, capsule circumscissile; seeds smooth, tuberculate or granulate.

1 Stipular hairs very few, inconspicuous, caducous, about 1 mm long; leaves obovate-spathulate, apex rounded or truncate
   1. P. oleracea
   Stipular hairs usually numerous, persistent, more than 1 mm long; leaves various but not spathulate   **2**
2 Leaves terete or subterete, linear   **3**
   Leaves flattened, lanceolate-acuminate or elliptic to ovate   **5**
3 Seeds with sinuate edges to tubercles, interlocking as in a jigsaw puzzle   **4**
   Seeds with smooth, entire, straight edges to tubercles   *2. P. sp. A*
4 Stipular hairs few at nodes but numerous around flowers, about 3–5 mm long, seeds about 0·5 mm in diameter, shining grey-black with conical tubercles   *3. P. foliosa*

† By M. A. Hanid.

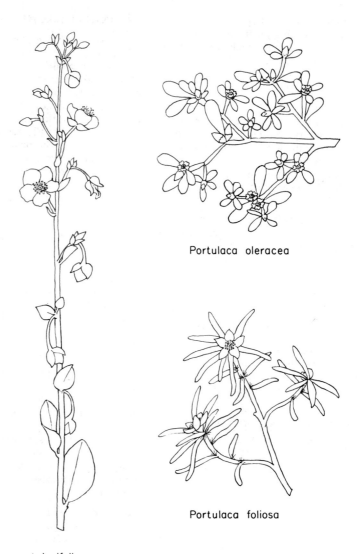

Portulaca oleracea

Portulaca foliosa

Talinum portulacifolium

Portulaca quadrifida

Stipular hairs numerous both at nodes and around flowers, 7–9 mm long, seeds about 1 mm in diameter, dull grey-black, with peg-like tubercles   4. *P. kermesina*
5   Stipules mostly broadened at the base, up to 7 mm long, silvery-white; tubercles of seeds raised with edges sinuate and interlocking like a jigsaw puzzle; a small erect herb to 5 cm tall   5. *P. parensis*
Stipules mostly filiform, 3–5 mm long, whitish; tubercles of seeds rounded with edges entire and not sinuate; a prostrate creeping annual herb to 30 cm long
          6. *P. quadrifida*

1. Portulaca oleracea *L.* (see p. 120)

A glabrous annual with numerous spreading branches bearing alternate obovate-spathulate leaves with inconspicuous stipular hairs; flowers yellow, in terminal clusters.

A widespread *Portulaca*, found as a nitrophilous weed of gardens, cultivation, railway tracks and roadsides. Flowers open only for a short time in the morning. HE, KIT, MUM, BAR, RV, MAC, NBI, KAJ.

Hanid and Kiniaruh 539; Pratt 315.

2. Portulaca *sp.* A.

Annual or perennial succulent herb with ascending branches and leaves clustered at branch apices; stipular hairs 3–5 mm long, golden; flowers yellow.

An uncommon plant so far collected from stony dry ground or rocks in Nanyuki area and dry grassland in Loita area, which is similar to *P. foliosa* except for the seeds. The above description is based on the three specimens recorded below. More collecting and careful field notes are needed to ascertain whether one or two species are represented here or whether these are variants or hybrids of other species. HL, NAN.

Moreau 69; Harger 35; Glover, Gwynne, Samuel, and Tucker 2234.

3. Portulaca foliosa *Ker-Gawl.* (see p. 120)

Annual or robust perennial herb or low shrub with subterete glaucous leaves and golden to white stipular hairs; flowers usually solitary, with pinkish sepals and yellow or orange petals.

A fairly common *Portulaca* of stony dry grassland and scrubland at medium altitudes. Appears to have wide ecological tolerance; more information needed on its ecology. KIS, NAR, BAR, MAC.

Lind, Agnew, and Beecher 5715; Napper 1560.

4. Portulaca kermesina *N. E. Br.*

Similar to *P. foliosa* but with the stipular hairs more numerous and longer (over 5 mm usually), and with yellow flowers.

On dry sandy or stony soils and on rocks in the hotter and drier southern parts of our area. More collection and field notes on habit, floral and fruit characters are needed. NAR, RV, MAC, NBI, KAJ.

Agnew and Tweedie 9281; Polhill 24.

5. Portulaca parensis *Poelln.*

A low annual or perennial herb with fleshy leaves and numerous, long silvery stipular hairs; flowers often solitary.

The most easy to recognize of the *Portulacae*, this species is apparently rare, but may have been overlooked. It is recorded only from Suswa on rocky ridges at 6000 ft. More collections and field notes on floral and fruit characters are required. RV.

Glover, Wateridge, Donet, and Sulbei 3439.

6. Portulaca quadrifida *L.* (see p. 120)

Prostrate annual herb up to 30 cm long; stems slender often rooting at the nodes; leaves opposite, up to 10 mm long but often much less, variable in size and shape, often lanceolate to elliptic-oblong, apex usually acute; stipular hairs numerous, 3–5 mm long, whitish; sepals united at the base; petals usually 4, yellow or orange, rarely pink or purplish, almost free; stamens 8–12; capsule conical-ovoid; seeds many, about 1 mm in diameter, dull grey, tubercles rounded.

Common in stony dry grassland and scrubland at medium altitudes; often a weed of cultivated land and roadsides. HE, HA, KIT, KIS, NAR, RV, MAC, NBI.

Agnew, Hanid, and Kiniaruh 9251; Verdcourt 3173.

2. MONTIA *L.*

Annual to perennial glabrous herbs with opposite, entire leaves and flowers solitary or in terminal cymes; sepals persistent; petals 3–5, free or united; stamens 3–5, at base fused to the petals; ovary superior; fruit a 3-valved capsule.

Montia fontana *L.*

A creeping tufted herb with narrow spathulate to obovate stem leaves and small white flowers in inconspicuous lateral cymes.

Locally common plant found in wet places in the alpine zone on Mt. Kenya. HK.

Borruso, January 1968.

3. TALINUM *Adans.*

Perennial herbs or shrubs with somewhat succulent, exstipulate, alternate or subopposite leaves; flowers in axillary or terminal cymes, racemes or panicles, rarely solitary; sepals 2, opposite; petals 5, free or joined at the base; stamens 5-indefinite; ovary superior, 1-celled, multiovulate; style 3-lobed; capsule globose or ovoid, dehiscing longitudinally into 3 valves; seeds with a distinct hilum, smooth or tuberculate, ridged or pitted.

1 Flowers purplish or purplish-pink; peduncles terminal bearing a long raceme or racemose panicle   1. *T. portulacifolium*
   Flowers yellow; peduncles axillary bearing 1–3 flowers   2
2 Seeds with prominent concentric ridges, without pits   2. *T. caffrum*
   Seeds with narrowly oblong tubercles with minute pits at the edges of tubercles
                                      3. *T. crispatulatum*

1. Talinum portulacifolium *(Forsk.) Schweinf.* (see p. 120)

Glabrous perennial herb or small shrub, with obovate to oblanceolate fleshy leaves and long terminal racemes of many purple to purple-pink flowers; pedicels recurved in fruit.

A common *Talinum* of drier bushland in Kenya, often with brightly coloured flowers. MUM, KIS, NAR, BAR, MAG, NAN, MAC, KAJ.
Hanid and Kiniaruh 761.

2. Talinum caffrum *(Thunb.) Eckl. & Zeyh.*

Glabrous perennial herb from a thickened fleshy root, with usually oblanceolate, elliptic-lanceolate or linear leaves and axillary solitary yellow flowers.

In open bushland or grassland below 6000 ft. NAR, MAG, NAN, MAC, KAJ.
Hanid and Kiniaruh 557; Napier 2353.

3. Talinum crispatulatum *Dinter*

Erect or suberect perennial succulent herb very similar to *T. caffrum*, except for the seeds which are without concentric ridges but with narrowly oblong, slightly raised tubercles arranged in concentric rings radiating from the hilum; seed tubercles with minute pits at their edges.

An uncommon plant of dry bushland or grassland and stream-side rocks which needs more collecting and careful field notes on habit and floral characters. MAG, MAC, KAJ.
Agnew, Kiniaruh, Ngethe, and Wyatt 8843; van Someren 2480.

25. POLYGONACEAE†

Plants variable in habit, but mostly herbs with alternate leaves in which the stipules are usually dilated into an amplexicaul cup around the stem at the insertion of the petiole; flowers regular, usually bisexual, usually in compound inflorescences of panicles of fascicles; sepals 3 or 6 (rarely 4–5), free; petals absent; stamens 5–9, (in ours) usually 6; ovary superior, sessile, with one loculus, one basal ovule and 2–3 styles with capitate stigmas; seeds with much endosperm.

1 Fruiting calyx with 3 hard radiating spines 2
   Fruit without 3 calyx spines   3
2 Fruits axillary from female flowers; male flowers in leafless racemes   1. *Emex*
   Fruits all from bisexual flowers in terminal leafless racemes   6. *Oxygonum*
3 Fruiting calyx or fruit bearing hooks or wings for dispersal; flowers mostly green   4
   Neither fruiting calyx nor fruit bearing hooks or wings; flowers mostly pink   5
4 Fruiting calyx winged or hooked, completely enclosing the unornamented fruit
                                       3. *Rumex*
   Fruiting calyx unspecialized, exceeded by the bristly fruit 2. *Harpagocarpus snowdenii*
5 Fruit much larger than fruiting calyx
                          5. *Fagopyrum esculentum*
   Fruit enclosed within fruiting calyx
                                   4. *Polygonum*

1. EMEX *Neck.*

Annual herbs, with stipular sheaths; flowers unisexual, the female axillary, the male on a narrow panicle; female flowers with 6 perianth segments in 2 series, all connate into a tube around the ovary, all becoming enlarged and woody in fruit, the outer forming 3 radiating simple spines; ovary with 3 fimbriate stigmas; male flowers with 6 sepals and 4–6 stamens.

1 Fruits 12–13 mm broad   1. *E. australis*
   Fruits 3–5 mm broad   2. *E. spinosus*

1. Emex australis *Steinh.*

An erect glabrous annual with ovate leaves and axillary sessile clusters of female flowers.

A rare weed at medium altitudes, not seen for 15 years. Possibly introduced from South Africa. HT, KIT, NBI.
Brodhurst-Hill 423.

2. Emex spinosus *(L.) Campd.*

Similar to *E. australis* from which it differs in the smaller fruits.

† By A. D. Q. Agnew.

A local weed of cultivation, often in wheat-growing areas. Introduced from the Mediterranean. HT, HA, NBI.

Krauss 320.

2. HARPAGOCARPUS *Hutch. & Dandy*

Climbing, nearly glabrous herbs with cordate entire leaves; flowers bisexual, sepals 5, 2 small and 3 large; stamens 8; ovary 3-angled, becoming bristly along the angles (the bristles having retrorse barbs) in fruit.

Harpagocarpus snowdenii *Hutch. & Dandy*

An almost glabrous perennial climbing or straggling herb with ovate to lanceolate sagittate acuminate leaves and erect inflorescences of fascicles of flowers; sepals enlarging in fruit; fruit orange, with red barbed bristles.

An uncommon plant of forest edges, clearings and streamsides in wetter highland forest below 8000 ft. HC, HK, HN.

Agnew and Coe 8781; Verdcourt and Polhill 2963.

3. RUMEX *L.*

Erect herbs or shrubs, with conspicuous sheathing stipules and leaves nearly always acid-tasting; flowers bisexual or unisexual, fascicled in panicles, sepals 6, in 2 series of 3, the inner whorl enlarging and often becoming ornamented in fruit; stamens 6; ovary with 3 feathery styles; fruit 3-angled, enclosed in the sepals.

1 Leaves hastate or sagittate at base 2
  Leaves neither hastate nor sagittate, the base rounded, truncate or cuneate 4
2 Flowers dioecious (unisexual); low herb to 30 cm with most leaves basal 1. *R. acetosella*
  Flowers bisexual; herbs more than 30 cm tall, or shrubs, with many stem leaves 3
3 Basal lobes of leaves less than 5 mm broad; plant shrubby, sometimes climbing
                   2. *R. usambarensis*
  Basal lobes of leaves more than 10 mm broad; a stout erect herb to 4 m 3. *R. abyssinicus*
4 Inner sepals toothed at edges in fruit, the teeth long and hooked 4. *R. bequaertii*
  Inner sepals entire or shallowly cut in fruit but with no teeth 5
5 Sepals in fruit entire, without a central tubercle 5. *R. ruwenzoriensis*
  Sepals in fruit entire or slightly dentate, with a central tubercle 6. *R. crispus*

1. Rumex acetosella *L.* (*Acetosella vulgaris* (Koch.) Fourr. *Rumex angiocarpus* Murb.)

An erect dioecious perennial herb with a basal rosette of lanceolate or oblong leaves.

An introduced weed, liable to occur in the wheat districts of Kenya, but not recently collected. It is rather unlike the rest of the *Rumex* species that we have here, and has been put into a separate genus, *Acetosella*. This genus contain a number of species, one of which (*Acetosella vulgaris*) is relatable to our material. HT, NBI.

Hocombe 1425.

2. Rumex usambarensis (*Dammer*) *Dammer* (see p. 118).

A glabrous weak shrub or climber often with fascicles of the oblong-elliptic hastate leaves; inflorescence a very complex panicle of reddish flowers; sepals enlarging to become orbicular and prominently net-veined in fruit.

A very beautiful plant in flower and fruit, with its red or crimson tresses of flowers. Common in most areas except the wetter forests and at higher altitudes, it is often seen along roadsides and is one of the shrubby plants which first invade cleared woodland around Nairobi. HM, HA, RV, MAC, KAJ.

Hanid 260; Glover 3588.

3. Rumex abyssinicus *Jacq.*

A large glabrescent erect perennial herb with triangular hastate leaves and an erect compound panicle of crowded green flowers; sepals becoming similar to those of *R. usambarensis* in fruit but smaller and straw-coloured.

Locally common in waste places, at higher altitudes than *R. usambarensis* although there is considerable overlap. HE, HT, HM, HA, KIT, NAR, RV, MAC, NBI, KAJ.

Strid 2723; Bogdan 5714.

4. Rumex bequaertii *De Wild.*

A glabrous erect perennial herb with narrow-lanceolate or linear-oblong leaves and erect racemes of fascicled flowers.

With *R. abyssinicus*, our commonest dock, growing in the area of upland forest and found on streamsides, pathsides, etc. HE, HC, HT, HM, HL, HA, HK, HN, KIS, MAC, NBI.

Harmsen 6551; Hedberg 1481.

5. Rumex ruwenzoriensis *Chiov.*

Erect or ascending sparsely pubescent perennial herb with oblong-lanceolate to ovate leaves; inflorescence similar to *R. bequaertii* but sepals ovate, obtuse, entire, without tubercles in fruit.

The common dock found above 7500 ft on the Aberdares and Mt. Kenya, often growing along streamsides. HA, HK.

Agnew 7030; Hedberg 1934.

6. Rumex crispus *L.*

An erect, almost glabrous, perennial (or possibly annual) herb similar to *R. bequaertii* except for the fruiting sepals.

A rare adventive from Southern Europe which has been collected once only (1948) on the banks of the Nairobi River. NBI.

Bally B 4621.

4. POLYGONUM *L.*

Herbs or shrubs with alternate leaves, the stipular sheaths often with terminal fringes of stiff bristles; flowers bisexual, usually in dense terminal racemes or spikes or heads; sepals usually 5, petaloid, persistent, not enlarging in fruit (in ours); stamens 5–8; ovary with 2 or 3 styles; fruit usually a black and glossy achene.

1 Twining climbers   2
  Erect or prostrate or scrambling herbs or
    shrubs   3
2 Sepals winged, the wings decurrent along the
    pedicel   1. *P. baldschuanicum*
  Sepals unwinged   2. *P. convolvulus*
3 Flowers in a pedunculate capitate head, with
    or without a clasping leaf around the base
    of the capitulum   4
  Flowers in a spike or raceme or axillary, not
    capitate   5
4 Leaf ovate, acuminate, with a winged petiole
                                3. *P. nepalense*
  Leaf elliptic, with a short unwinged petiole
                                4. *P. capitatum*
5 Flowers in clusters in the axils of foliage
    leaves   6
  Flowers in pedunculate leafless racemes   7
6 Perennial woody trailing shrub of altitudes
    above 8500 ft   5. *P. afromontanum*
  Annual erect herb, of altitudes lower than
    8000 ft   6. *P. aviculare*
7 Peduncles with stalked glandular hairs
                                7. *P. strigosum*
  Peduncles glabrous or hairy but without
    stalked glands   8
8 Plant annual; racemes interrupted, with a
    zig-zag axis; leaves ± linear
                                8. *P. salicifolium*
  Plant perennial; racemes crowded, hardly in-
    terrupted except sometimes at base; leaves
    usually broader   9
9 Plant robust; stipular sheaths truncate,
    usually without terminal bristles; fruit
    lens-shaped with dimpled or concave faces
                                9. *P. senegalense*
  Plant robust or not; stipular sheaths always
    fringed; fruits lens-shaped or 3-angled,
    always with convex faces   10

10 Leaves with over 22 pairs of lateral nerves,
    softly hairy below, usually with 2–3 longi-
    tudinal undulations in the narrow-lanceo-
    late lamina; flowers heterostylic; fruit
    always lens-shaped   10. *P. pulchrum*
  Leaves with less than 20 pairs of lateral
    nerves, glabrous or with stiff hairs below,
    flat, the lamina usually broad-lanceolate or
    almost ovate; flowers not heterostylic;
    fruit lens-shaped or 3-angled
                                11. *P. setosulum*

1. Polygonum baldschuanicum *Regel*

A cultivated ornamental which is only mentioned and keyed here since it may escape in places and has been recorded from Meru district.

2. Polygonum convolvulus *L.*

Climbing, twining, almost glabrous annual herb with ovate acuminate or triangular hastate leaves and fascicles of flowers in racemes or axillary; sepals enlarging to enclose the sharply 3-angled fruit.

Another introduced weed from Europe, now doing quite well in arable cultivation above 5500 ft. HE, HT, HM, HA, KIT, NBI.

Irwin 228.

3. Polygonum nepalense *Meisn.*

Glabrous or sparsely glandular-pilose straggling or erect annual, with triangular, often lobed leaves, and spicate or capitate inflorescences; flowers white or pink.

A plant of disturbed places in the area of high wet forest, occasionally growing as a field weed. HT, HM, HA, HK, KIS.

Kerfoot 4044; Agnew 8753.

4. Polygonum capitatum *Ham.*

A sparsely pilose prostrate herb, rooting at the nodes, with elliptic leaves and globular spikes of pink flowers.

Recorded once from 11 000 ft on the Aber-dares, this plant, which is otherwise Himalayan, needs further collection and study. Possibly it is an escape from cultivation which has died or will die out.

Polhill 84.

5. Polygonum afromontanum *Greenway*

A nearly glabrous scrambling or trailing shrub with elliptic leaves and axillary clusters of few pink flowers.

Fairly common in the forest edges at the tree line on Mt. Kenya and the Aberdares. HA, HK.

Agnew 8672; Gillett 16902.

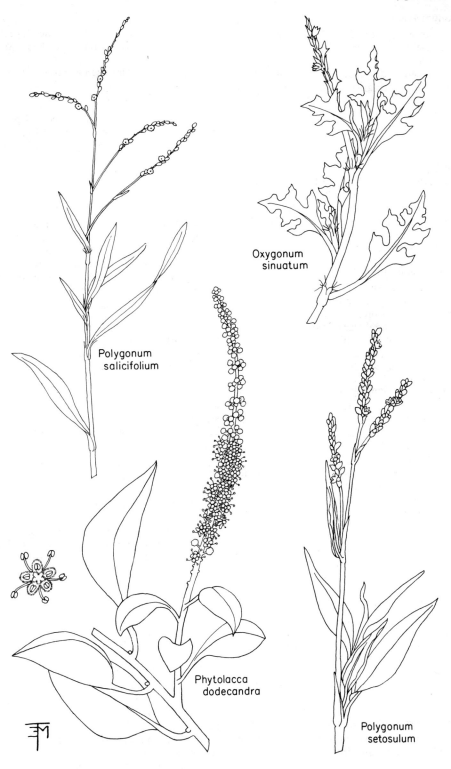

Polygonum
salicifolium

Oxygonum
sinuatum

Phytolacca
dodecandra

Polygonum
setosulum

6. Polygonum aviculare *L.*

A glabrous prostrate or ascending annual with sessile narrow-elliptic leaves and axillary groups of red-pink flowers.

An introduced and spreading weed of cultivation, above 7000 ft. Originally European. HT, HA, KIT.

Bogdan 5630; Mendes 21.

7. Polygonum strigosum *R. Br.*

Erect sparsely pilose, possibly annual herb sometimes trailing, with linear, oblong to lanceolate leaves often truncate or hastate at base; racemes of pink flowers often dichotomously branching.

A rare *Polygonum* which has occasionally turned up in many parts of Kenya. HC, HT, HA, NBI.

Lind 2290; Tweedie 67/336.

8. Polygonum salicifolium *Willd.* (see p. 125).

An erect glabrescent annual with elliptic, almost sessile, leaves and a terminal group of slender interrupted racemes of pink or white flowers.

A common waterside plant, particularly along streamsides up to 8000 ft. HC, HT, HM, HL, HA, KIT, MUM, NAR, RV, EMB, MAC, NBI.

Kerfoot 2611; Agnew 8297.

9. Polygonum senegalense *Meisn.*

An erect, variably hairy softly shrubby perennial, the stem often ± covered with the conspicuous, slightly inflated, brown stipular sheaths; leaves lanceolate, acute, glabrous or densely white-tomentose; racemes 2-6, of pink or white flowers.

A common herb of riversides, streamsides and marshes, up to 8500 ft in our area. There are two distinct forms which intergrade rarely, but apparently show no ecological preferences; var. *senegalense* is almost glabrous (except for the small yellow glands) while var. *albotomentosum* is densely white-tomentose. HT, HA, KIT, MUM, KIS, NAR, RV, EMB, MAC, NBI.

Glover 3984; Agnew and Musumba 5467.

10. Polygonum pulchrum *Blume*

A softly hairy perennial herb with narrow-lanceolate entire leaves, often with longitudinal undulations; racemes 1-5, terminal, of pink flowers.

A locally common waterside plant, often found around artificial dams; up to 7500 ft. HT, HM, HA, HK, KIT, MUM, KIS, NAR, RV, EMB, NBI.

Tucker 2292; Lind, Harris, and Agnew 5106.

11. Polygonum setosulum *A. Rich.* (see p. 125)

A roughly hairy perennial herb with lanceolate-ovate or elliptic leaves and inflorescences as in *P. pulchrum.*

A common waterside plant, often growing at higher altitudes than the other species, from 4000-9000 ft. HE, HM, HA, KIT, MUM, KIS, NAR, RV, NBI.

Glover 2083; Harmsen 6550.

5. FAGOPYRUM *Miller*

Erect annuals with sagittate leaves; stipular sheaths present, entire; flowers heterostylous, axillary or in raceme-like panicles; sepals 5, not thickening in fruit; stamens 8; styles 3; fruit much larger than the perianth, 3-angled.

Fagopyrum esculentum *Moench.*

A glabrous or puberulent erect annual with triangular hastate or cordate leaves and axillary long-pedunculate crowded racemes.

A rare escape from cultivation, when it is occasionally grown for chicken feed. HT, NBI.

Turner in Bally 5035.

6. OXYGONUM *Burch.*

Herbs with alternate leaves, and often extra-axillary branching; stipular sheaths present, the leaves emerging from their centre; inflorescence a narrow, interrupted raceme of groups of short-pedicelled flowers borne within the bracts which are reduced to stipular sheaths; flowers heterostylous, unisexual or bisexual; sepals forming a tube around the ovary becoming a hardened, often prickly, case in fruit.

1   Stipular sheaths with green photosynthetic
     ± spreading teeth at apex; leaves glabrous
                                    1. *O.* sp. A
     Stipular sheaths papery throughout; leaves
     mostly hairy   2
2   Leaves minutely undulate at margin, as well
     as often lobed; stigmas and anthers separated from each other in the flower by at
     least the length of an anther
                              2. *O. stuhlmannii*
     Leaves not or hardly undulate at margin, as
     well as often lobed ; stigmas and anthers
     touching or nearer to each other than one
     anther length   3. *O. sinuatum*

1. Oxygonum sp. A.

A glabrous perennial trailing shrub with ascending stems and linear to lanceolate leaves which usually bear one pair of lateral pointed lobes; flowers pink, not markedly heterostylic.

Locally common in dry country in shallow or rocky soils. MAC.

Lind and Agnew 5668; Strid 2138.

2. Oxygonum stuhlmannii *Dammer* (*O. maculatum* R. Grah.) (see p. 118)

A pubescent perennial or facultative annual herb with ovate to lanceolate to rhombic leaves; flowers pink, strongly heterostylic.

A variable plant as defined here, which includes annual and almost shrubby perennial forms which grow together in some areas (for example near Ulu), as well as the glabrous and pubescent-leaved forms which are separated in the FTEA into two distinct species. In our area we have intergrading plants between all of these forms and only more intensive field work can help us to understand the variation. This species is found in dry, sandy country from Narok and Machakos to the coast. NAR, MAC.

Verdcourt 2158; Agnew 9222.

3. Oxygonum sinuatum (*Meisn.*) *Dammer* (see p. 125)

An almost glabrous annual, with elliptic to ob-lanceolate or obovate leaves bearing 1-2 pairs of shallow lobes, or entire; flowers pink, not markedly heterostylic.

This species is only found (in Kenya) at medium altitudes, never at the Coast. It is our commonest *Oxygonum* with nasty prickly fruits, and is found in waste places generally. HM, HA, KIT, MUM, KIS, NAR, RV, MAG, EMB, MAC, NBI.

Bally B 8025; Hanid and Kiniaruh 742.

26. PHYTOLACCACEAE†

Herbs, trees, or shrubs, with alternate, entire ex-stipulate leaves; flowers in racemes, bisexual or rarely unisexual; bracts and bracteoles present; sepals usually 5, sometimes more; petals absent; stamens 5-30; anthers longitudinally dehiscent; ovary of 1-12 free or loosely connate carpels, with separate stigmas, each with one basal ovule; fruit fleshy, often of drupes; seed with a curved embryo surrounding the endosperm.

1   Annual herb with one carpel
                                    1. *Hilleria latifolia*
    Perennial shrubs with 8-12 carpels
                                    2. *Phytolacca*

1. HILLERIA *Vell.*

Herbs with terminal racemes; flower bisexual, with 4 unequal free sepals; stamens 4; ovary of one carpel with a sessile fringed stigma and one ovule; fruit lens-shaped with the fleshy pericarp ± fused to the black seed.

† By A. D. Q. Agnew.

Hilleria latifolia (*Lam.*) *Watt.*

Erect, sparsely pubescent annual with ovate-elliptic leaves and shortly pedunculate racemes.

An uncommon plant found in lowland damp conditions. HM, HK, MUM, NAR.

Glover, Gwynne and Samuel 389.

2. PHYTOLACCA *L.*

Shrubs or herbs, sometimes scrambling, with ± fleshy leaves and bisexual or unisexual flowers in terminal or leaf-opposed racemes; sepals 5; stamens 5-25, inserted on a fleshy disc; carpels 5-12, free or connate with free stigmas, forming a globose fleshy fruit of drupes.

1   Most pedicels longer than sepals; carpels free
                                    1. *P. dodecandra*
    All pedicels shorter than sepals; carpels con-
    nate   2. *P. octandra*

1. Phytolacca dodecandra *L'Herit.* (see p. 125)

A climbing, scrambling, or ± erect glabrous shrub with bluntly ovate-elliptic leaves and long terminal trailing racemes of pedicellate yellowish flowers.

A local plant of bushland and cleared forest at medium altitudes. Although often found as a low trailing shrub, it can grow as a strong liane in riverine forest. HE, HA, RV, NBI.

Agnew 9071; Kirrika 473.

2. Phytolacca octandra *L.*

A woody, glabrous soft shrub with lanceolate-elliptic leaves and leaf-opposed racemes of sub-sessile yellowish flowers.

A rare plant, possibly introduced from North America, to be found in waste places at medium altitudes. HT, HA, NBI.

Lind and Harris 5114; Kokwaro 312.

27. CHENOPODIACEAE‡

Annual or perennial herbs or shrubs, often halo-phytic, with alternate or rarely opposite, exstipu-late, simple leaves which are sometimes reduced to scales; flowers inconspicuous, greenish to grey, soli-tary and axillary, often clustered, usually regular, bisexual or unisexual; calyx usually 2-5-lobed, united below, persistent, often accrescent in fruit; petals absent; stamens as many as sepals or fewer, opposite to sepals; ovary superior, 1-celled, uni-ovulate; fruit indehiscent or circumscissile; seed with a curved peripheral embryo, endosperm present or absent.

1   Leaves terete   2
    Leaves flat   3

‡ By M. A. Hanid.

2   Leaves glabrous, not spine-tipped
                            4. *Suaeda monoica*
    Leaves hairy or spine-tipped   5. *Salsola*
3   Leaves with long woolly hairs
                            3. *Kochia indica*
    Leaves without woolly hairs   4
4   Leaves usually pinnatifid, and glandular-
    pubescent   1. *Chenopodium*
    Leaves usually dentate or entire, lobed and
    densely mealy   2. *A triplex*

1. CHENOPODIUM *L.*

Herbs, often glandular-pubescent, rarely glabrous,
with leaves alternate and mostly petiolate; flowers
in cymose clusters or glomeruli, with bisexual and
unisexual flowers mixed; bracteoles absent; calyx
usually 4–5-lobed, unchanged in fruit; stamens
1–5; style usually absent; fruits one-seeded with
membranous indehiscent pericarps; seeds vertically
or horizontally compressed, endospermous.

1   Plant more or less mealy, at least on young
    parts, with grey or whitish vesicular hairs,
    other sorts of hairs and glands absent   **2**
    Plant pubescent, and with yellow to amber
    glands, aromatic, without vesicular hairs **6**
2   Seeds sharply keeled on margin; testa marked
    with very close minute rounded pits; peri-
    carp very difficult to detach from seed
                            1. *C. murale*
    Seeds bluntly keeled on margin; testa not
    marked as above; pericarp readily rubbed
    or scraped from seed   **3**
3   Seeds 1–1·5 mm in diameter; testa marked
    with radial furrows, and often also with
    minute roughnesses in between, never
    closely pitted   **4**
    Seed 1·5–2 mm in diameter; testa furrowed
    or pitted   **5**
4   Upper leaves with acute teeth as well as ±
    acutely lobed at base   2. *C. album*
    Upper leaves with rounded lobes and a ±
    undulate leaf margin   3. *C. opulifolium*
5   Leaves below widest point cuneate and
    normally entire, sometimes broadly
    cuneate; teeth up to about 10 each side,
    usually fewer, not acuminate, usually
    directed upwards   2. *C. album*
    Leaves below widest point rounded in outline
    to subtruncate or even subcordate and
    distinctly toothed; teeth 7–60 each side,
    usually numerous, acuminate or acute,
    tending to be directed outwards
                            4. *C. fasciculosum*
6   Inflorescence built up of distinct though
    sometimes small dichasial cymes in the
    axils of leaves or bracts these cymes

usually aggregated as though into a spike;
seeds black or nearly so when ripe; stamens
1–2; lower and median leaves pinnately
divided, at least below; sepals always
keeled   **7**
Inflorescence built up of small sessile or
subsessile clusters of flowers in the axils of
leaves or bracts, flowers not in dichasial
cymes; seeds red-brown to blackish when
ripe; stamens 1–5; leaves and sepals various
                                            8
7   Seeds 0·9–1·1 mm in diam.; some glands
    shortly but distinctly stalked (use x20
    lens); lower part of leaves pinnately
    divided, (top part toothed but scarcely
    lobed) the lobes acute
                            5. *C. procerum*
    Seeds 0·7–0·8 mm in diam.; glands all sessile
    (use x20 lens); leaves pinnately divided
    throughout each side usually to within 2–3
    mm of midrib, the lobes usually rounded
                            6. *C. schraderanum*
8   Sepals keeled on the back, the keel wing-like
    and broadening upwards   7. *C. carinatum*
    Sepals rounded, not at all keeled on back **9**
9   Some seeds in each cluster 'vertical' others
    'horizontal', 0·5–1·25 mm in diam.;
    stamens 4–5; ovary glandular above; stig-
    mas 3–4, long   8. *C. ambrosioides*
    All seeds in each cluster 'vertical', 0·5–0·75
    mm in diam.; stamens 1; ovary not glan-
    dular; stigmas 2, short   9. *C. pumilio*

1. Chenopodium murale *L.*

Erect or spreading annual herb, mostly sparsely
mealy; leaves variable, usually rhombic-ovate with
5–15 coarse irregular ascending teeth at margin;
inflorescence of leafy, divaricately branched
cymes.

A common but variable weed of crops, old
cultivations and pasture land. RV, NBI.
    Greenway 12522; Lugard 272.

2. Chenopodium album *L.*

Annual grey-mealy herb; leaves very variable,
mostly longer than broad, rhombic to lanceolate;
inflorescences of dense rounded terminal clusters.

A common weed of cultivated land. HT, KIS,
RV, NBI.
    Agnew, Hanid, and Kiniaruh 7909; van
Someren 194.

3. Chenopodium opulifolium *Koch & Ziz*

Grey-mealy annual or perennial herb, often woody
below; leaves mostly broadly or shortly rhombic-
ovate, other characters as in *C. album*.

Our commonest *Chenopodium* species which is closely related to *C. album*. It is a weed of cultivation, roadsides, and settled areas at medium altitudes. HT, HM, HA, KIT, MUM, RV, MAC, NBI.

Agnew and Musumba 5354; van Someren 158.

4. Chenopodium fasciculosum *A ellen*

Mealy to glabrescent, much branched, erect or rarely spreading annual with ovate dentate leaves; inflorescences of divaricately branched cymes.

A common *Chenopodium* of upland evergreen forest, roadsides, and a weed of cultivation. There are two varieties which are separable according to the number of little teeth in mature leaves. One variety has few little teeth while in the other they are numerous. HT, HM, HA, KIT, KIS, NAR, BAR, RV, NAN, MAC, NBI, KAJ.

Bogdan 5711; Kerfoot 2871.

5. Chenopodium procerum *Moq.*

Erect glandular-pubescent annual herb with elliptic or ovoid-elliptic leaves; inflorescence of dichotomously branched axillary cymes usually aggregated into a leafy or nude continuous cylindrical terminal inflorescence.

A local *Chenopodium* of upland grasslands, and a weed of cultivated and waste places; below 8500 ft. HE, HC, HT, HM, HA, KIT, NAR, RV, NBI.

Njoroge 66; Agnew, Kibe, and Mathenge 10486.

6. Chenopodium schraderanum *Schult.*

Erect glandular-pubescent annual with elliptic to oblong pinnatifid leaves; inflorescence as in *C. procerum* but often smaller.

A locally common *Chenopodium* of medium altitudes which has become a weed of cultivation, waste places, and roadsides. HE, HT, HM, HA, KIT, NAR, RV, NAN, NBI.

Strid 2567; Bogdan 5666.

7. Chenopodium carinatum *R. Br.*

A trailing aromatic herb with ovate, obtusely lobed leaves and axillary glomerules of flowers.

This introduced plant smells of peppermint and is locally common in waste and disturbed rocky places. KIT, MAC, NBI.

Agnew and Haines 8238; Bogdan 5594.

8. Chenopodium ambrosioides *L.* (see p. 138)

Erect, strongly aromatic, pubescent annual with elliptic or obovate leaves; inflorescence a much branched panicle, ultimate branches with spicately arranged small sessile flower-clusters.

A common introduced weed of cultivation, disturbed land, dry grassland, roadsides, often near human habitations. HA, KIT, NAR, MAC, NBI.

Agnew and Tweedie 9293; Glover, Gwynne, and Samuel 179.

9. Chenopodium pumilio *R. Br.*

Annual pubescent-glandular herb, usually prostrate, sometimes erect, with elliptic to lanceolate, obscurely toothed or lobed leaves; inflorescence of small cymose glomeruli mostly at nodes, apically condensed into spike-like racemes.

A common weed of cultivation, disturbed land, often found by railways and roadsides; very common in some places. It seems to be variable in habit, size, leaves, and inflorescence, perhaps owing to habitat. Specimens from riverine forest may be 50 cm high and have toothed leaves up to 8 cm long, and smaller glomeruli, well-spaced on thin branches. HT, HM, HA, KIT, KIS, RV, MAC, NBI.

Agnew 8217; Bogdan 5666.

2. ATRIPLEX *L.*

Mealy annual or perennial herbs, shrubs or undershrubs, with vesicular hairs; leaves alternate or rarely opposite; flowers in axillary glomeruli or aggregated into terminal panicles or spikes, monoecious or dioecious; male flowers without bracteoles, with 3–5-lobed calyx and 3–5 stamens; female flowers with 2 accrescent bracteoles connate at the base; without calyx and staminodes; fruits enclosed in the persistent enlarged bracteoles, with membranous indehiscent pericarp; seeds laterally compressed, endospermous.

1   Plants with prostrate branches; mature leaves up to about 1 cm wide; fruit red, fleshy
1. *A. semibaccata*
    Plants with erect or ascending branches; mature leaves more than 1 cm wide; fruit dry, green   2
2   Inflorescences axillary; leaf-margins with 1–4 coarse teeth on each side   2. *A. muelleri*
    Inflorescence a terminal panicle; leaf-margins entire or with 1–2 small lateral lobes on each side   3. *A. halimus*

1. Atriplex semibaccata *R. Br.*

Mealy perennial undershrub with prostrate branches and oblanceolate to oblong-lanceolate or narrowly obovate leaves; inflorescences of small axillary cymose glomeruli; fruiting bracteoles cherry-coloured, sweet to the taste.

A weed of cultivated land, gardens, and roadsides which seems to prefer alkaline soils. The lower leaf surfaces are conspicuously mealy. It is mainly recorded from Naivasha area. RV, MAC.

Verdcourt 3597; Thomas 1421.

2. Atriplex muelleri *Benth.*

Erect annual herb or subshrub with ascending branches, and spathulate to elliptic or rhombic-ovate leaves; inflorescence of axillary glomeruli; fruiting bracteoles semicircular to triangular in outline with acute or subacute apex and 1–4 little teeth on each side.

An uncommon weed of cultivation which has been introduced from Australia. It is recorded from Elmenteita and Naivasha only. Information on habit needed. RV.

Bogdan 2021.

3. Atriplex halimus *L.*

Woody herb or shrub, much branched, densely mealy, with ovate to oblong or elliptic leaves; inflorescence a terminal panicle with ultimate branchlets spiciform and mostly leafless towards the top; fruiting bracteoles as broad as, or more often broader than, long, reniform to broadly deltoid-ovate with denticulate or almost lobed margins.

A rare but locally common plant which is recorded as growing on seasonally flooded saline soils with short sparse grass and on volcanic ash. It is recorded only from near Ol Tukai on raised beds of Lake Amboseli in our area, and is certainly worth looking out for in other areas of Kenya. KAJ.

Greenway 9203; Verdcourt 3118.

3. KOCHIA *Roth.*

Glabrous or hairy herbs or shrubs with sessile, alternate or rarely subopposite leaves; flowers small, sessile, axillary, solitary or clustered, bisexual and female; bracteoles absent; perianth 5-lobed, lobes horizontally winged outside and incurved; stamens 5; fruits depressed-globose; seeds orbicular.

Kochia indica *Wight*

Densely tomentose, silvery grey-green annual with narrowly elliptic to oblanceolate leaves and small axillary clusters of a few flowers; fruit with short thick broadly triangular-ovate wings.

A rare but locally common plant found in saline soils recorded only from Amboseli near Ol Tukai. KAJ.

Verdcourt 2536; Western 50.

4. SUAEDA *Scop.*

Suaeda monoica *J. F. Gmel.* is dealt with in KTS p. 139. KAJ.

5. SALSOLA *L.*

Herbs, shrubs, or undershrubs, more or less pubescent, leaves somewhat fleshy, alternate or rarely opposite, sessile, sometimes scale-like; flowers small, axillary, solitary or fascicled, bisexual, 2-bracteolate; sepals 4–5, each with a scarious horizontally spreading wing from above the middle in fruit; stamens 5 or fewer; stigmas usually 2; fruit with fleshy or membranous pericarp, enclosed in the calyx; seeds usually vertically compressed, non-endospermous, with membranous testa.

1   Pubescent or glabrescent shrub; leaves up to 4 mm long, apex without spine
                                   1. *S. dendroides*
    Spinescent woody herb; leaves more than 4 mm long, apex spine-tipped 2. *S. pestifera*

1. Salsola dendroides *Pallas*

Profusely and densely branched glabrescent shrub with small fleshy linear to boat-shaped or scale-like leaves and sessile flowers; fruit with transversely elliptic or deltoid-obovate wings, each over 2 mm long.

A plant of low rainfall areas found in semi-desert scrub and on sand near rivers. HE, NAN.

Nattrass 1495.

2. Salsola pestifera *A. Nels.*

Pubescent annual woody herb with spinescent linear-terete leaves and sessile flowers; fruit with 1–1·5 mm long wings.

A rare, but locally common, introduced weed of cultivation recorded only from a farm near Rumuruti. NAN.

Bumpus in Bogdan 4197.

28. AMARANTHACEAE†

Herbs, low shrubs, and a few climbers, with alternate or opposite, simple, usually entire, exstipulate leaves; inflorescences mainly dichasial cymes, and these often in racemes, or by reduction, racemes and spikes of solitary flowers; one bract and 2 bracteoles always present for each flower; flowers unisexual or (more often in ours) bisexual, some often sterile and involved in fruit dispersal; sepals 5, rarely fewer; petals 0; stamens 5, rarely fewer, often fused into a filament sheath at base, which may bear 5 staminodes; ovary superior of 1-many free-central ovules, pendulous or erect; fruit a capsule (often enclosed in the persistent calyx or even inflorescence) with circumscissile or irregular dehiscence; embryo usually curved round the endosperm.

1   Leaves, at least those above the first 2–3 nodes of the seedling, alternate   2
    Leaves opposite   7

† By A. D. Q. Agnew.

2   Leaves hairy on both surfaces   10. *Aerva*
    Leaves glabrous or at most ciliate on margins
    and lower nerves   **3**
3   Inflorescence of simple spikes of single
    flowers   **4**
    Inflorescence of cymes or of spike-like racemes
    of many-flowered cymes   **6**
4   Inflorescences axillary
    11. *Nothosaerva brachiata*
    Inflorescences terminal   **5**
5   Flowers green, imbricate; disseminule un-
    winged   12. *Psilotrichum schimperi*
    Flowers pink or white, not imbricate; dis-
    seminule winged with outgrowths from 2
    sterile flowers   3. *Digera muricata*
6   Erect or climbing herbs; flowers bisexual;
    sepals usually scarious; more than 1 seed
    per fruit   1. *Celosia*
    Erect or prostrate herbs, never climbers;
    flowers unisexual; sepals herbaceous; 1
    seed per fruit   2. *Amaranthus*
7   Inflorescence a simple spike of single fertile
    flowers (at least above the base of the
    spike)   **8**
    Inflorescence a spike or raceme of dichasial
    cymes, each cyme containing 2-several
    fertile flowers   **15**
8   Spikes axillary   **9**
    Spikes terminal   **11**
9   Spikes pedunculate   12. *Psilotrichum elliottii*
    Spikes sessile   **10**
10 Bracts lanceolate, scarious, glabrous
    15. *Alternanthera*
    Bracts semiorbicular, woolly
    10. *Aerva lanata*
11 Climber with fruiting spikes becoming long-
    hairy from a development of hairs in axils
    of bracteoles   4. *Sericostachys scandens*
    Erect herbs or shrubs, or if scrambling, then
    without long tufts of hairs in fruiting
    bracteole axils   **12**
12 Flowers reflexed in fruit   13. *Achyranthes*
    Flowers erect in fruit   **13**
13 Flowers enclosed and sepals hidden by keeled
    bracteoles   16. *Gomphrena celosioides*
    Flowers not enclosed by bracteoles; sepals
    evident   **14**
14 Annual herb   12. *Psilotrichum schimperi*
    Perennial shrub   14. *Achyropsis greenwayii*
15 Hooks or spines or bristles developed from
    sterile flowers, in axils of bracteoles and
    overtopping fruiting calyx; fruits usually
    adhesive   **16**
    No sterile flowers present; hooks never
    present, and if spines present on fruit then
    these short and developed from bracteoles
    19

16 Hooked bristles present, and fruit adhesive   **17**
    Bristles simple, without hooks   **18**
17 Hooks spreading in stellate rings on glabrous
    stalks, more or less flat on the surface of
    the fruiting glomerule
    8. *Pupalia lappacea*
    Hooks erect in all parts of the fruiting
    glomerule, never stellate   7. *Cyathula*
18 Bristles all short and spiny   7. *Cyathula*
    Bristles of two kinds, some long and soft,
    some shorter and spiny
    9. *Dasysphaera prostrata*
19 Cymes 3 (or more)-flowered, not hardened or
    woody in fruit, straw coloured or grey
    5. *Sericocomopsis*
    Cymes 2-flowered only, hardened and woody
    in fruit, usually bright red or carmine
    6. *Centemopsis rubra*

1. CELOSIA L.

Trailing plants, climbers, or erect herbs with alternate, usually entire leaves; inflorescence usually a
long terminal raceme of cymose groups, often
condensed; flowers bisexual; sepals often scarious;
stamens fused at base; staminodes absent; anthers
4-locular; ovary with 2 or 3 styles; ovules 1–8;
fruit a circumscissile capsule.

1   Inflorescence continuous, cylindrical, of
    close-packed, glossy flowers; sepals 7–9
    mm long   1. *C. argentea*
    Inflorescence interrupted, the flowers not
    close-packed except within the lateral
    cymes; sepals less than 4 mm long   **2**
2   Sepals scarious, ovate, delicate, white or pink;
    capsule ± equalling the sepals, widest
    below; stigmas 3   2. *C. trigyna*
    Sepals stiff, oblong, cream, capsule usually
    exceeding the sepals, or if equalling them,
    then the capsules cylindrical; stigmas 2 or
    3   **3**
3   Sepals drying dark brown or with a blackish
    line down the centre; capsule conical, not
    thickened above   3. *C. schweinfurthiana*
    Sepals drying straw-coloured; capsule ± cylin-
    drical, prominently thickened into two
    lobes above   4. *C. anthelmintica*

1. Celosia argentea L.

An erect glabrous annual with lanceolate-elliptic
leaves and terminal, spike-like, cylindrical, glossy,
white or pink inflorescences.

A rare plant of dry bushland in Kenya. This is
the wild relative of the fasciculated 'cock's comb'
of gardens. MAG, NAN.

Glover 3496.

2. Celosia trigyna *L.*

Erect glabrous or sparsely puberulent annual with ovate leaves and compound terminal racemes of widely spaced cymes of pink or white flowers.

An uncommon ruderal weed of waste places in the wetter lowlands of Kenya, and occurring in our area only in MUM, KIS, MAC.

Hanid and Kiniaruh 791; Dowson 455.

3. Celosia schweinfurthiana *Schinz.*

Annual or perennial, glabrous, prostrate, or scrambling herb with ovate to lanceolate leaves and terminal as well as accessory racemes of well-spaced cymes of pedicellate cream flowers.

A rare plant of wet lowland forests which grows also at the coast, often as a prostrate annual, but in Malaba forest as a climber at forest edges. MUM.

Strid 3389; Graham 21.

4. Celosia anthelmintica *Asch.* (*C. leptostachya* Benth. of Check List)

A glabrous or sparsely hairy scrambler on trees and shrubs, with ovate leaves and terminal racemes of widely scattered cymes of white (drying cream) flowers.

A common plant of the Magadi-Nairobi area and the adjacent Rift Valley, but hardly known outside this region. HA, NAR, BAR, RV, MAG, NAN, NBI, KAJ.

Agnew and Beecher 8285; Glover 3991.

2. AMARANTHUS *L.*

Usually annual, often glabrous herbs, with alternate exstipulate entire leaves prominently nerved below; inflorescences of glomerules of cymes, either axillary or in terminal spike-like racemes; flowers small, crowded, unisexual (in ours monoecious), usually overtopped by bracts and bracteoles in the cymes; sepals variable 2-5; stamens 3-5, exserted at anthesis, free, without staminodes, anthers 4-locular; styles 2-3; fruit 1-seeded, circumscissile or rupturing irregularly.

A genus, principally American, which has been widely cultivated and accidentally introduced, so that the following list is merely of species which have been already recorded, while more will probably be found in the future. The fact that so many species have hybridized makes the taxonomy difficult, and the conclusions of the present author will probably have to be drastically revised in the future.

1 Inflorescences terminal and axillary   2
  Inflorescences all axillary   6
2 Most nodes with a pair of divaricate sharp spines; leaves often darker below
                                    1. *A. spinosus*

Nodes without sharp spines; leaves concolorous   3
3 Fruit circumscissile   4
  Fruit rupturing irregularly or indehiscent
                                    2. *A. lividus*
4 Racemes never less than 7 mm (usually more than 10 mm) in diam. at their narrowest cylindrical parts, tapering abruptly into the apex, with a softly spiny appearance
                             3. *A. hybridus* ssp. *hybridus*
  Racemes less than 7·5 mm (usually 5 mm) in diam. at their narrowest cylindrical part, tapering gradually to the apex   5
5 Racemes sometimes nodding; capsule smooth, hemispherical above the line of dehiscence   4. *A. caudatus*
  Racemes never nodding; capsule wrinkled, conical above the line of dehiscence
                            3. *A. hybridus* ssp. *incurvatus*
6 Perianth longer than the fruit; fruiting inflorescence with a spiny appearance; fruit circumscissile   5. *A.* sp. *A*
  Perianth shorter than fruit; fruiting inflorescence without a spiny appearance; fruit circumscissile or not   7
7 Leaves emarginate or bifid; fruit indehiscent 8
  Leaves entire at apex except for a small mucro; fruit circumscissile
                                    6. *A. graecizans*
8 Annual or creeping perennial; leaves bifid; fruits rounded above, green
                                    7. *A. acutilobus*
  Annual; leaves emarginate; fruit narrowing to an acute apex, blackish when dry
                            8. *A. sparganiocephalus*

1. Amaranthus spinosus *L.*

An erect, sparsely branched, glabrous annual herb to 1 m; the pair of prophylls in the axil of every leaf frequently thickened into spines; leaves ovate-lanceolate; inflorescence a terminal panicle of spike-like racemes of cymes.

A common amaranth, easily recognized when it is spiny, but often difficult to spot when it is not. Widely distributed as a ruderal weed of hotter country below 6000 ft. HA, KIT, MUM, NAR, BAR, MAC, NBI.

Hanid and Kiniaruh 701; Glover, Gwynne, and Samuel 163.

2. Amaranthus lividus *L.*

An erect glabrescent annual, often rather sparsely branched, with ovate-elliptic leaves and axillary glomerules of flowers which coalesce to form a terminal spike-like raceme.

An uncommon wild plant but often cultivated by small arable farmers for a green spinach, and possibly also for chicken-food. The cultivated form has fruits from 2–2·5 mm long, as opposed to 1·5–2 mm long in the naturalised form, and larger leaves and is apparently plucked for eating and left to grow. In that case the terminal inflorescence may be lost leaving only axillary glomerules which sometimes exceed 4 cm in diam. HM, KIT, RV.

Turner 3516; Kerfoot 2784.

3. Amaranthus hybridus *L.* (*A. hypochondriacus* L. in Check List)

An erect glabrous annual with rhombic cuneate leaves and terminal and axillary spike-like racemes.

The commonest *Amaranthus* in Upland Kenya, this ruderal is found between 4000 and 8000 ft in all cultivation. The inflorescence has a characteristic 'spiny' look in the common subspecies, *A. hybridus* ssp. *hybridus*.

1 Bracts and bracteoles 4–5 mm long, twice as long as perianth segments; cymes, often with 1–2 mm long internodes, becoming monochasial above   ssp. *hybridus*
   Bracts and bracteoles ± equal to the sepals; cymes with short internodes, not monochasial above   ssp. *incurvatus*

ssp. hybridus
HC, HM, HA, HK, KIT, NAR, RV, NAN, MAC, NBI.

Strid 2570; Kerfoot 759.

ssp. incurvatus (*Gren. & Godr.*) *Brenan*
Rather rare, and very difficult to distinguish from *A. caudatus* on the one hand and *A. spinosus* (except for the absence of spines) on the other, so that the taxonomic position of these plants is a little doubtful. We have one sterile collection (rare in *Amaranthus* where seed is usually abundant) from the edge of our area at Mwingi (MAC) which may well be hybrid between this and *A. spinosus*. MUM.

Agnew and Musumba 8025.

4. Amaranthus caudatus *L.*

An erect glabrescent annual similar to *A. hybridus* except for the key characters.

There are but few specimens available of this species in Kenya, and this assessment may have to be altered as more are collected. The variety with a drooping, often brightly coloured (red) inflorescence, which may be rather thick at base and tapering throughout its length, has only been found at Kericho in a wild state, but is often cultivated. The variety with fewer, erect or spreading branches has been found at Embu. It may be cultivated as a leaf vegetable.

Graham 1726; Kerfoot 4719.

5. Amaranthus *sp.* A.

A glabrescent plant with prostrate or ascending sparsely pubescent stems and rhombic or elliptic leaves; flowers crowded in axillary cymes.

Only recorded once, from Ruiru; this plant should be searched for in that locality. HA.

James 2304.

6. Amaranthus graecizans *L.*

An erect or decumbent, sparsely pubescent annual with narrow-rhombic to elliptic leaves and axillary cymes of small green flowers.

A common plant of fields and disturbed places at medium altitudes in our area. HM, HA, KIT, NAR, BAR, RV, EMB, MAC, NBI, KAJ.

Kerfoot 2869; Agnew 7589.

7. Amaranthus acutilobus *Uline & Bray*

A glabrous erect annual or creeping perennial with elliptic to ovate leaves and axillary glomerules of flowers.

A recent arrival, apparently, in Nairobi, growing amongst lawn grass near Karura Forest; originally from Mexico. It should grow much larger than the specimens described here, which are all that have been found as yet. NBI.

Hughes-Rice in EAH 13377.

8. Amaranthus sparganiocephalus *Thell.*

Glabrous or glabrescent annual with ovate leaves and axillary glomerules of flowers.

A rare annual found in drier country, this plant has only once been recorded from our area, in Amboseli. KAJ.

Verdcourt 3127.

3. DIGERA *Forsk.*

Usually annual herbs with alternate leaves; inflorescence of simple spikes of sessile cymes, each cyme consisting of a central fertile bisexual flower with two accessory sterile flowers in the axils of the bracteoles, which are at length modified for fruit dispersal; stamens 5, not or hardly fused at base, without staminodes; anthers 4-locular; stigma 2-lobed; fruit 1-seeded.

Digera muricata (*L.*) *Mart.*

An erect, glabrous (often very tall) annual, usually unbranched below, with linear to lanceolate leaves and long terminal spikes of cymes; sterile flowers of each cyme forming green coriaceous wings.

An attractive annual of dry places in grassland, often on stony or sandy soil. KIS, BAR, NAN, MAG, MAC, KAJ.

Hanid and Kiniaruh 563; Glover and Samuel 2770.

4. SERICOSTACHYS *Gilg and Lopr.*

Climbing shrub with opposite entire leaves; inflorescence a terminal panicle of spikes; flowers sessile, bisexual, bracteate, with two bracteoles in the axil of each of which is a tuft of hairs representing a sterile flower which enlarges to long plumose structures in fruit; stamens 5, fused at base with 5 small glabrous truncate staminodes between the filaments; anthers 4-locular; stigma capitate; fruit 1-seeded.

Sericostachys scandens *Gilg & Lopr.*

A pilose or tomentose climbing shrub with ovate to elliptic leaves; inflorescence a large panicle of white spikes becoming feathery with the plumose sterile flowers in fruit.

An uncommon climber, only recorded from the western Kenya forests at Kakamega. It is very conspicuous in fruit, when it rather resembles *Clematis*. MUM.

Drummond and Hemsley 4751.

5. SERICOCOMOPSIS *Schinz*

Shrubs, usually densely hairy, with opposite leaves; inflorescence a raceme of dichasial cymes very similar to those of *Cyathula*, but without any sterile flowers subsequently involved in dispersal; any sterile flowers present result from arrested development within second order bracteoles; flower characters as in *Cyathula*.

1 Leaves ± spathulate, truncate at apex; hairs simple, bracts coriaceous, not membranous; bracteoles and sepals not plumose at tip   1. *S. hildebrandtii*
   Leaves ± elliptical, narrowed at apex; hairs stellate; bracts thin, membranous and transparent; bracteoles and sepals plumose at tip   2. *S. pallida*

1. Sericocomopsis hildebrandtii *Schinz*

A much-branched canescent bushy shrub with obovate to spathulate leaves and terminal racemes of sessile cymes.

A common shrubby amaranth of dry thornbush country especially on fine soils. The white inflorescences serve to distinguish it from the following species which has grey inflorescences, and the absence of hooks on the cymes from *Cyathula* sp. *A*. with which it is often confused. NAR, BAR, RV, MAG, NAN, MAC, KAJ.

Agnew 7619; Glover 4048.

2. Sericocomopsis pallida (*S. Moore*) *Schinz*

A much-branched stellate-canescent bushy shrub with ovate-elliptic leaves and terminal racemes of well separated, pedunculate, alternate greyish cymes.

A common shrub of dry thorn bush on shallow, often calcareous, soils. BAR, KAJ.

Agnew 7623; Vesey Fitzgerald 260.

6. CENTEMOPSIS *Schinz*

Usually erect annual or perennial herbs with opposite narrow leaves; inflorescence a spike of sessile reduced cymes; cymes with 1–3 flowers, without sterile flowers, becoming woody at base in fruit; flowers bisexual; stamens fused at base; staminodes present, ciliate; anthers 4-locular; stigma simple; fruit 1-seeded.

Centemopsis rubra (*Lopr.*) *Schinz* (inc. records of *C. kirkii* (Hook. f.) Schinz in Check List) (see p. 138)

Erect sparsely pubescent annual or facultative short-lived perennial with linear sessile leaves and reddish spikes of 2-flowered cymes.

A common plant of dry grassland at lower altitudes in our area, in the East only. MAC, NBI, KAJ.

Bally B4179; Tweedie 67/72.

7. CYATHULA *Lour.*

Erect or scrambling herbs or shrubs, nearly always hairy; leaves opposite, entire, petiolate; inflorescences of racemes of cymes, the cymes always more than 3-flowered, but variously developed, the ultimate unit being a central fertile flower with 2 lateral sterile ones which may be variously modified into hooked bristles or spines; sepals lanceolate, not thickened in fruit; filaments connate below into a tube, bearing 5 staminodes, of various shapes; anthers 4-locular; stigma capitate; fruit 1-seeded.

A large genus in which many of the names applied here are probably wrong and require revision.

1 Hooked bristles present on inflorescences; perennials   3
   Hooked bristles absent on inflorescences; annuals   2
2 Inflorescence a long raceme of sessile, globose cymes   1. *C. orthocantha*
   Inflorescence a short raceme of pedunculate globose cymes, or globose cymes solitary   2. *C. erinacea*
3 Shrubs or erect herbs (rarely scramblers); inflorescence a long raceme of cymes, interrupted towards the base   4

Scrambling or prostrate (rarely erect) herbs or shrubs; inflorescence a short or long continuous raceme of cymes, never interrupted   **5**

4 Erect herb; leaves cordate or rounded at base; racemes usually over 10 cm long
                                                  3. *C. schimperana*
   Shrub; leaves abruptly cuneate at base; inflorescences usually less than 10 cm long
                                                  4. *C.* sp. *A*

5 Racemes globose, densely covered with yellow hooked bristles   5. *C. uncinulata*
   Racemes cylindrical, with few hooks   **6**

6 Leaves mostly rounded at base; racemes grey-silvery, terminal, solitary, without divaricating branches bearing subsidiary racemes
                                                  6. *C. cylindrica*
   Leaves mostly cuneate at base; racemes golden-yellow, terminal and with subsidiary racemes on widely divaricate branches   7. *C. mannii*

1. Cyathula orthocantha (*Asch.*) *Schinz*

An erect pubescent to tomentose annual with ovate-elliptic or orbicular leaves and pedunculate terminal racemes of almost sessile cymes.

An uncommon annual of disturbed drier areas, often in *Acacia* bushland. KIS, BAR, MAG, NAN, KAJ.

Hanid and Kiniaruh 737; Bogdan 393.

2. Cyathula erinacea *Schinz*

Erect or trailing, sparsely pilose annual with ovate-lanceolate leaves and terminal short racemes of globose pedunculate heads of crowded cymes, ripening into spherical balls with straw-yellow spines appearing out of the felty tomentum.

An uncommon annual found in dry rocky bushland. The yellow fruiting heads are conspicuous and the stems are often reddish. MAG, KAJ.

Agnew 7643; Glover 2997.

3. Cyathula schimperana *Moq.* (*C. polycephala* Bak. in Check List)

A tomentose or woolly herb, with ascending or erect stems and ovate-elliptic, cordate or rounded leaves; inflorescence terminal, leafless, of crowded pedunculate cymes which are spaced out so that each may develop into a separate globose straw-coloured mass.

A common weed of upland grassland, especially where woodland has been recently cleared, 5000–9000 ft. A curious feature is that the flowers are either found with shrivelled, apparently empty anthers on short (about 1 mm) filaments, or with full anthers on 3 mm long

filaments. It would be interesting to know whether this was a constant feature of all populations helping cross-polination. HT, HM, HA, HK, MAC, NBI, KAJ.

Agnew 7541; Morley-Hewitt 1389.

4. Cyathula *sp.* A.

A small pubescent to tomentose shrub with ovate-elliptic leaves and terminal pedunculate interrupted white-glossy racemes.

A common bushy plant of rocky scarps and cliffs in dry country, especially abundant in the Rift Valley. HA, NAR, RV, MAG, MAC.

Agnew 7156; Nattrass 587.

5. Cyathula uncinulata (*Schrad.*) *Schinz.*

A softly tomentose prostrate or climbing herb or soft shrub (climbing by means of kneed petioles) with lanceolate to almost orbicular leaves; inflorescence a terminal condensed raceme forming a straw-coloured ball in fruit.

A rather variable species as defined here, and further work may allow separation between forms. It is found in medium-wet forest and forest edges, 4000 to 8000 ft. HE, HC, HM, HA, HK, KIT, NAR, MAC, NBI.

Kokwaro 227; Agnew *et al.* 8407.

6. Cyathula cylindrica *Moq.*

A pilose or tomentose scrambling perennial herb with lanceolate to ovate leaves and solitary terminal, cylindrical, uninterrupted, silvery-grey to hardly straw-coloured spikes.

Rather uncommon in the wetter high-level forests, 7500 to 10 000 ft; this trailer with its (usually) hanging silvery racemes is unmistakable. HE, HM, HA, HK.

Agnew 7163; Kerfoot 3861.

7. Cyathula mannii *Bak.*

A sparsely hairy scrambling or trailing perennial with elliptic leaves and short straw-coloured cylindrical uninterrupted spikes.

A common scrambler of the forest edge in regions of medium rainfall at medium altitudes, 5000–8000 ft; in fact this is usually the region of evergreen woodland. HM, HA, HK, NAR, RV, NBI, KAJ.

Glover 2265; Hanid 301.

8. PUPALIA *Juss.*

A genus very similar to *Cyathula* from which it differs in having alternately arranged cymes in the raceme, more highly developed sterile flowers of stellate hooks in fruit and no staminodes.

Pupalia lappacea *Juss.*

Annual or perennial, prostrate, scrambling or erect herb with elliptic or ovate leaves; racemes terminal, erect or pendulous with well-spaced, alternate, shortly pedunculate cymes, elongating in fruit.

An annoying plant producing highly adhesive burrs which stick on all clothing, and make life difficult in dry country. It is very variable, and although there are clearly defined forms growing in dry bush country (prostrate annual with sepals 3·5–5 mm long and seeds 2 mm long) and evergreen woodland (scrambler with sepals 6–9 mm long and seeds 4 mm long) intermediates do occur. HA, MUM, NAR, RV, MAG, EMB, MAC, NBI, KAJ.

  Agnew and Azavedo 9325; Kirrika 495.

9. DASYSPHAERA *Gilg*

Shrubs with opposite leaves; inflorescence a raceme of cymes; fertile flowers bisexual, each (except the central one of each dichasium) with a tuft of numerous bristles on either side in the axil of the bracteoles representing sterile flowers; stamens 5, the filaments fused at the base to form a tube (around the ovary) which is shortly free from the filaments above, but which bears no staminodal projections; anthers 4-locular; ovary 1-seeded, stigma capitate.

Dasysphaera prostrata (*Gilg*) *Cavaco*

A bristly-hairy suffruticose herb or shrub with lanceolate to triangular-cordate leaves and a loose terminal raceme of pedunculate cymes each forming a yellowish ball in fruit.

A somewhat rare plant found in alkaline areas. BAR, NAN, KAJ.

  Agnew 7641; Verdcourt 2555.

10. AERVA *Forsk.*

Usually woolly shrubs or herbs with alternate and sometimes opposite simple leaves; inflorescence a raceme of alternately arranged cymes, breaking within the cyme in fruit, or flowers directly inserted on the axis of a spike, not in cymose groups; bracts, bracteoles and sepals ± scarious with long woolly hairs giving a felty appearance to the whole inflorescence; flowers bisexual; stamens 5, shortly fused at base, or free; anthers with 4 loculi; staminodes present, entire; stigma 2-lobed; fruit 1-seeded.

1 Inflorescence terminal   1. *A. persica*
   Inflorescences all axillary   2. *A. lanata*

1. Aerva persica (*Burm. f.*) *Merrill*

A woolly erect perennial herb, sometimes suffruticose, with sessile lanceolate-elliptic leaves and a white terminal panicle of racemes.

A common plant of the driest thorn-bushland on finer soils. BAR, MAG.

  Harmsen 6475; Glover 2986.

2. Aerva lanata (*L.*) *Juss.*

Erect or trailing herb with usually rather few branches, lower leaves often opposite, the upper always alternate; leaves spathulate to obovate to elliptic; spikes axillary, 1–3 together, very variable, of crowded white-woolly flowers.

A common weed species of many open habitats in dry country at medium altitudes, although not found in the drier thorn-bushland. It is very variable but easily recognized. HM, HA, HK, HN, KIT, MUM, KIS, RV, NAN, EMB, MAC, NBI, KAJ.

  Glover 482; Strid 2612.

11. NOTHOSAERVA *Wight*

Herbs with alternate leaves; inflorescence a spike of sessile single flowers, the spikes axillary; bracts and sepals membranous, scarious; stamens 1–2, without a filament tube at base, anthers 4-locular; ovary with very short style and simple stigma; fruit 1-seeded.

Nothosaerva brachiata (*L.*) *Wight*

An erect glabrous annual, with elliptic leaves and axillary spikes of white or cream woolly flowers.

An inconspicuous rare annual, growing in seasonally wet, possibly alkaline, hollows in dry areas. BAR.

  Bogdan 4890.

12. PSILOTRICHUM *Blume*

Herbs or shrubs, hairy or glabrous with opposite, entire leaves; inflorescences axillary or terminal, of simple or panicled spikes of solitary flowers, without accessory sterile flowers; flowers bisexual; sepals 5, green, not scarious; stamens 5, the filaments united below, without staminodes, or with very short glabrous teeth between the filaments, anthers 4-locular; fruiting flower not reflexed, falling entire; stigma capitate; fruit 1-seeded.

1 Annual; leaves linear; spikes terminal and
     axillary   1. *Ps. schimperi*
   Perennials; leaves broader; spikes axillary
     only   2. *Ps. elliottii*

1. Psilotrichum schimperi *Baker*

A sparsely stiff-hairy, erect annual, with opposite or alternate, linear, stiffly ciliate leaves and terminal spikes of glabrous flowers.

An oddly local plant, often found in the Nairobi National Park, but infrequently elsewhere. MUM, NBI.

  Davidson 346; Agnew 5517.

2. Psilotrichum elliottii *Baker* (see p. 138)

Pilose to tomentose perennial shrub or scrambler with ovate to orbicular leaves and axillary simple spikes of imbricate green flowers.

A common plant of open bushland in the MAC area. It is rather variable and may grow as a bush or scrambler and be woolly or almost glabrous. NAR, MAC.

Agnew, Hanid, and Kiniaruh 9247; Glover 2030.

13. ACHYRANTHES *L.*

Herbs or shrubs similar to *Psilotrichum* but with staminodes and reflexed fruiting flowers.

1   Bracts, bracteoles and sepals shiny and glabrous in flower except for ciliate edges; flowers deflexed parallel to stem in fruit
                                          1. *A. aspera*
    Bracts, bracteoles and sepals woolly; flowers only partially deflexed in fruit to lie at 45° to the stem   2. *A. schinzii*

1. Achyranthes aspera *L.* (see p. 138)

An annual or perennial, tomentose or pubescent herb or shrub with ovate-obtuse to lanceolate-acute leaves and long spikes of reddish flowers.

A most variable plant which cannot yet be broken down satisfactorily to smaller, more ecologically natural units. The var. *aspera* has larger flowers (more than 5·5 mm long) and the bract longer than the bracteole and grows as a shrub along forest edges and waste places. The var. *sicula* has smaller flowers (less than 5 mm long) and the bract shorter than the bracteole and grows west of the Rift Valley at forest edges; it has an annual form which is a field weed. HE, HC, HT, HM, HA, HK, KIT, MUM, KIS, NAR, BAR, RV, EMB, MAC, NBI, KAJ.

Agnew 8046 ·Kerfoot 3503.

2. Achyranthes schinzii (*Standl.*) *Cuf.*

A tomentose woody scrambler with lanceolate leaves; spikes as in *A. aspera* but flowers set closer together.

A rare plant, only so far found in NAR, MAC, and NBI, in riverine woodland.

Verdcourt 3804; Agnew 10892.

14. ACHYROPSIS (*Moq.*) *Hook. f.*

A genus very similar to *Psilotrichum* from which it differs in the hard, shiny texture of the sepals and the long, ciliate staminodes.

Achyropsis greenwayii *Suessenguth*

A more or less canescent bushy shrub with lanceolate elliptic leaves and terminal green spikes.

A common shrub of dry grassland on black-cotton soil, in southern Kenya only. HA, NAR, MAC, NBI, KAJ.

Agnew and Musumba 5327; Verdcourt 1505.

15. ALTERNANTHERA *Forsk.*

Herbs, often prostrate, with opposite entire leaves; inflorescences of axillary spikes; flowers borne directly on the spike, not in dichasial cymes; sepals 5, sometimes hardened in fruit; stamens 5, with 2-locular anthers, fused into a ring at the base of the filaments, with staminodes (sometimes obscure); style short; stigma unlobed; ovary 1-seeded, globose or flattened, indehiscent.

1   Stems glabrous or with 2 lines of hairs only; calyx soft not spiny in fruit   1. *A. sessilis*
    Stem hairy all round; fruiting calyx hard and spiny   2
2   Glochidiate hairs only on inner pairs of fruiting calyx segments (rarely small tufts at base of outer segments) never showing between bracts of spike   2. *A. pungens*
    Glochidiate hairs on all members of fruiting calyx, showing as 'wool' between bracts of spike   3. *A. peploides*

1. Alternanthera sessilis (*L.*) *DC.*

A low herb, rooting at the nodes with ascending stems and oblanceolate to elliptic leaves; spikes axillary, globose or short-cylindrical, white.

Rather common in or near water in the hotter parts of our area. KIT, MUM, KIS, MAG, EMB, MAC, NBI.

Agnew 8013; Symes 342.

2. Alternanthera pungens *H. B. K.*

An annual herb with prostrate hairy stems from a thick ± fleshy taproot, and obovate-elliptic leaves; spikes sessile, straw-coloured.

A common unpleasant introduced weed of paths and roadsides, with spiny fruits. Found all over our area except in the wet highland forests. HT, HM, HA, KIS, NAR, BAR, MAC, NBI, KAJ.

Hanid and Kiniaruh 758; Glover 2020.

3. Alternanthera peploides (*H. & B.*) *Urban*

Similar to *A. pungens* but with smaller spikes and the differences mentioned in the key.

This species is also introduced from Central America, and is found in waste places, so far only in Nairobi and Thika. MAC, NBI.

Tweedie 66/60; Faden 67750.

16. GOMPHRENA *L.*

Herbs with erect or ascending stems; leaves opposite; inflorescence a terminal or lateral spike of imbricate flowers with keeled bracteoles; sepals

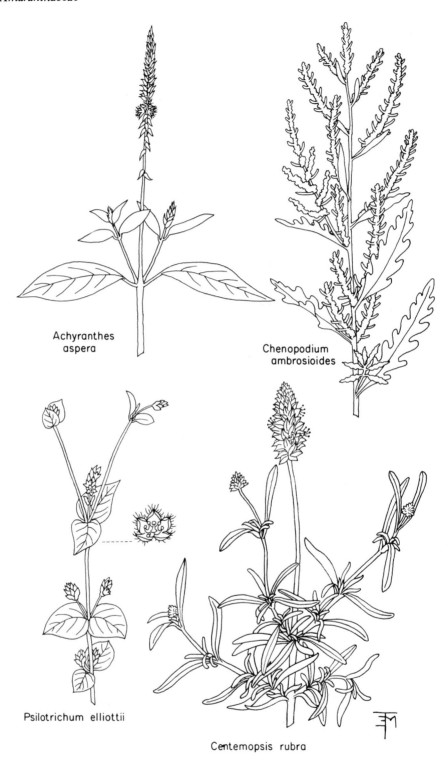

Achyranthes
aspera

Chenopodium
ambrosioides

Psilotrichum elliottii

Centemopsis rubra

5, equal; stamens 5, with 2-celled anthers sessile on the long filament tube; staminodes absent; style bifid; ovules 1; fruit indehiscent.

Gomphrena celosioides *Mart.*

A pilose perennial herb with prostrate or ascending branches and obovate to elliptic leaves; spikes terminal, pedunculate, white.

A common weed of roadsides and pathsides. HT, KIT, MUM, KIS, EMB, MAC, NBI, KAJ.

Agnew 7596; Boardman 10.

29. BASELLACEAE†

Twining climbers with alternate, ± fleshy, entire, exstipulate leaves; flowers bisexual, in spikes, racemes or panicles; bracteoles present, 2; sepals 5, free or united; petals absent; stamens 5, with free filaments, and porose or longitudinal dehiscence of the anthers; ovary superior, with one basal ovule and 3 stigmas; fruit indehiscent, surrounded by the calyx and often the bracteoles; seed with curved embryo and much endosperm.

1. BASELLA *L.*

Glabrous herbs with ovate, slightly fleshy leaves; flowers sessile, in spikes; bracteoles united to the sepals; sepals fused forming a fleshy tube with stamens inserted near the top; stamens with longitudinal dehiscence; ovary with 3 long filamentous stigmas on a short style.

Basella alba *L.* (see p. 148)

A glabrous climbing shrub with glossy, ovate-orbicular, cordate leaves and short spikes of white flowers.

A common species found in riverine forest at all altitudes from 7000 ft downwards. HE, HA, HK, KIT, RV, EMB, MAC, NBI.

Agnew 7747; Kabuye 46.

30. LINACEAE‡

Herbs, shrubs, lianes, or trees with simple, mostly stipulate, alternate or opposite leaves; stipules divided or entire, gland-like or interpetiolar; inflorescence mostly a terminal or axillary cyme; flowers regular, bisexual; sepals 4–5, free or connate below, imbricate, persistent; petals as sepal number, free or connate below, usually fugacious, contorted in bud, often clawed; stamens mostly as sepal number, sometimes staminodes present, filaments connate at the base; ovary superior, 3–5-celled, with 2 axile and pendulous ovules per loculus; fruit a septicidal capsule or drupe; seeds compressed, with or without endosperm.

† By A. D. Q. Agnew.
‡ By M. A. Hanid.

1. LINUM *L.*

Annual or perennial herbs, glabrous (in ours), often woody at the base; leaves sessile, alternate or whorled (in ours), with entire or shortly denticulate margin; stipules absent or glandular; inflorescence a terminal monochasial or dichasial cyme (in ours); sepals free; petals yellow or orange-yellow (in ours), shortly clawed; stamens alternating with petals; each loculus of ovary partly divided by a false septum; fruit 4–5-locular with valves twice the loculus number and 1 seed per loculus; seeds smooth, with scanty or no endosperm.

1	Leaves in whorls of 3 or 4	1. *L. keniense*
	Leaves alternate	2
2	Leaves with a pair of dark brown stipules, one on either side of base	2. *L. volkensii*
	Leaves exstipulate	3. *L. usitatissimum*

1. Linum keniense *T. C. E. Fries*

Prostrate or decumbent perennial herb with whorled, broadly elliptic to ovate leaves and terminal few-flowered dichasial cymes of tetramerous yellow flowers.

This rare species is our only tetramerous *Linum*. It is recorded from pathsides and edges of upland forests, possibly near streams. HE, HM, KIT.

Webster in EAH 10001; Glover, Gwynne, and Samuel 1462.

2. Linum volkensii *Engl.* (see p. 145)

Erect, sparsely branched annual with alternate linear-lanceolate leaves and a terminal loose corymbose cyme of pentamerous yellow flowers.

A common *Linum* of upland grasslands, often by streams and in marshes. HE, HC, HT, HM, HA, HK, KIT, MUM, KIS, RV, NAN, MAC, NBI, KAJ.

Hanid 234; Verdcourt 2256a.

3. Linum usitatissimum *L.*

An erect annual with alternate linear-lanceolate leaves and a terminal corymbose cyme of pentamerous blue or white flowers.

An introduced flax of waste places and abandoned cultivated ground. It is widely cultivated for its fibre and oily seeds and is easily recognized by its normally blue flowers and large capsules. KIT, EMB, NBI.

Bogdan 5710; Nattrass 318.

31. ZYGOPHYLLACEAE §

Herbs, shrubs, or undershrubs, rarely trees, with simple hairs; leaves opposite or alternate, usually pinnate or divided, stipulate; flowers solitary or

§ By M. A. Hanid.

rarely in cymes, regular or rarely zygomorphic, bisexual, pentamerous or rarely tetramerous; sepals and petals free, usually imbricate; stamens usually twice the petal number, more rarely the same or three times the number; ovary 4–5-locular, each loculus with 2 or more axile ovules, or very rarely 1 ovule per loculus or per fruit by abortion; style usually short or stigmas sessile; fruit a schizocarpous capsule or rarely a berry; seeds mostly endospermous with straight or slightly curved embryo.

1   Leaves simple, equal in each pair; stipules modified into 2 long and 2 short spines
       1. *Fagonia*
    Leaves pinnate, one of each pair longer than the other; stipules foliaceous   2. *Tribulus*

1. FAGONIA *L.*

Perennial herbs or small shrubs with opposite, often divided leaves, with stipules (in ours) modified into two long and two short spines at each node; flowers solitary, axillary, pentamerous; sepals membranous, imbricate, deciduous; petals longer than sepals, imbricate, vaducous, clawed, usually pink, red or purple; stamens 10; ovary 5-celled, with 5-angled style and simple stigma; ovules 2 per loculus; fruit an almost globular or pyramidal loculicidal capsule with furrows between the carpels; seeds compressed, mucilaginous.

Fagonia *sp.* **A.**

An erect, sparsely glandular, much branched woody herb with narrowly elliptic to narrowly oblanceolate leaves and solitary pink flowers.

A plant of hard diatomaceous lake beds or hard pans in dry areas where rainwater collects. It is recorded from Ol Orgesailie and Magadi only. MAG.

Lind 5576; Verdcourt 3711.

2. TRIBULUS *L.*

Annual or perennial herbs, very rarely shrubs, with prostrate or ascending branches; leaves opposite, paripinnate, one in each pair usually longer than the other, stipulate; leaflets opposite, sessile or very shortly petiolate, entire and somewhat oblique; stipules herbaceous; flowers solitary, axillary or in the dichotomies of the stem, pentamerous; sepals deciduous or sometimes persistent; petals (in ours) yellow, longer than sepals, spreading; stamens 10, those opposite the sepals with a gland at the base of each filament; ovary sessile, 5-lobed, each loculus with 1–5 ovules, densely covered with stiff erect hairs; stigmas 5; fruit hard, woody, each carpel dorsally tuberculate and armed with spines (in ours), schizocarpic; seeds without endosperm.

1   Peduncles usually shorter than or the same length as the subtending leaf; flowers up to about 17 mm in diameter; staminal glands free; style almost absent   1. *T. terrestris*
    Peduncles usually longer than the subtending leaf; flowers more than 17 mm in diameter; staminal glands connate and forming a shallow cup around base of ovary; style ± elongated   2. *T. cistoides*

1. Tribulus terrestris *L.* (see p. 145)

An often pubescent annual herb with prostrate branches and unequal leaves bearing 4–7 oblong to oblong-lanceolate leaflets; fruit globose in outline, each of the 5 mericarps having a pair of diverging bony spines in the upper part and 2 smaller ones in the lower.

A widespread ruderal growing on sandy soils, waste ground, near human habitation, and a troublesome weed of roadsides and cultivated land. HE, KIS, NAR, BAR, RV, NBI, KAJ.

Hanid and Kiniaruh 749; Glover, Gwynne, and Samuel 220.

2. Tribulus cistoides *L.*

Procumbent perennial, or rarely annual, herb similar to *T. terrestris* except for the key characters and the mericarps of the fruit, each of which has 4 or rarely 6 spines (sometimes reduced to thick warts) and a laterally compressed dorsal crest.

A weed of sandy soils recorded only from Kerio Valley, apparently overlooked and badly in need of more collection of flowering and fruiting material. BAR.

Brown in EAH 12805.

32. GERANIACEAE†

Herbs or shrubs, rarely arborescent; leaves alternate or opposite, stipulate, lobed or compound, rarely entire; inflorescences cymose or umbellate; flowers usually bisexual, generally 5-merous (occasionally 4- or 8-merous); calyx free or connate at the base, sometimes spurred; corolla free and usually unequal, imbricate, rarely contorted; stamens somewhat connate at the base, some occasionally sterile; disk glands often present; ovary superior, syncarpous, 3–5-locular with axile placentation, each chamber with 1–2 seeds; fruit schizocarpic.

1   Stamens 15   2. *Monsonia*
    Stamens 10   **2**
2   Flowers regular; sepals unspurred; anthers 10
       1. *Geranium*

† By J. O. Kokwaro.

Flowers zygomorphic; posterior sepal spurred (and fused to pedicel); anthers 2–7
                                    3. *Pelargonium*

1. GERANIUM *L.*

Annual or perennial herbs, sometimes tufted or woody below, with mostly opposite, palmately lobed or dissected leaves; flowers solitary or in axillary pairs or in a dichasium; calyx of 5 equal sepals; corolla of 5 mostly notched petals; stamens 10, all fertile; carpel beaks rolling upwards when ripe.

1 Stems armed with sharp prickles
                                    1. *G. aculeolatum*
   Stems without prickles   2
2 Lamina reniform in outline
                                2. *G. kilimandscharicum*
   Lamina pentagonal in outline   3
3 Stipules less than 2 mm wide
                                    3. *G. elamellatum*
   Stipules more than 2 mm wide   4
4 Annual, with some cleistogamous flowers
                                    4. *G. ocellatum*
   Perennial, without cleistogamous flowers   5
5 Stipules bifid; pedicels glandular
                                    5. *G. vagans*
   Stipules undivided; pedicels without glands
                                    6. *G. arabicum*

1. Geranium aculeolatum *Oliv.* (see p. 142)

A perennial trailing herb rooting at the nodes with sharp reflexed prickles and palmately lobed leaves; flowers mostly in pairs, white or mauve; mericarps smooth or pilose.

Found in montane forests and moist places such as river banks and marshy sides of valleys, also as a weed in cultivation above 8000 ft.

Napier 702; Agnew 7730.

2. Geranium kilimandscharicum *Engl.* (see p. 142)

A perennial prostrate stoloniferous herb, sometimes woody at base; leaves opposite but the basal ones sometimes in a rosette, frequently pink-red on the lower surface; flowers mostly solitary, pink-red to light pink; mericarps pilose.

Restricted to alpine belts of the high mountains at altitudes usually above 10 000 ft. HE, HA, HK.

Hedberg 1863; Hanid 162.

3. Geranium elamellatum *Kokwaro* (see p. 142)

A decumbent or erect glandular pubescent annual herb, with weak and hollow stems; leaves ovate, pinnatisect, sometimes alternate below; flowers pale lilac, mauve, or pink; mericarps wrinkled and usually with a raphe at the anterior end.

A rare herb confined to forest edges and moist shady areas of the montane forest belt. MUM, HE, HT, HA, HK.

Albrechtsen 2763; Agnew 10127.

4. Geranium ocellatum *Cambess.* (see p. 143)

An ascending, diffusely branched annual herb, with spreading hairs or glands; leaves orbicular palmatisect; flowers in pairs, chasmogamous and some cleistogamous, pink with dark almost black-purple centre; mericarps with shallow reticulate ridges.

Generally found in shade such as in caves or along the hillslopes and forest edges, also as a weed in cultivation. HE, HT, KIT, RV.

Bally B 918; Ables 122.

5. Geranium vagans *Bak.*

A perennial, decumbent, pilose to glandular herb, with orbicular palmatisect leaves alternate below and opposite above; sepals red or greenish, petals pink or mauve; mericarps pilose.

Found in grassland or montane forest belt and also in the alpine belt, usually along streambanks. HE, HA, HK.

Hedberg 844; Agnew 7208.

6. Geranium arabicum *Forsk.* (see p. 143)

A stoloniferous perennial herb, pilose or pubescent above to glabrescent below; leaves orbicular, palmatisect, opposite, ocasionally in basal rosettes; flowers white or purple with conspicuous red veins; mericarps pilose.

A widely distributed species found in the grassland region and the montane forest extending into the alpine belt. HE, HT, HA, HK.

Dowson 106; Agnew 7187.

2. MONSONIA *L.*

Annual or perennial, erect or decumbent herbs with dentate or crenate, sometimes lobed leaves; stipules filiform to subulate or rarely spinescent; flowers usually 2-several per peduncle, rarely solitary, mostly pentamerous and regular; stamens 15, all fertile; carpel beaks twisting spirally when ripe.

1 Petals 7–12 mm long; annual herbs
                                    1. *M. angustifolia*
   Petals 14–26 mm long; perennial herbs   2
2 Lamina hastate or trilobed; stipules 1·6–2 mm long   2. *M. longipes*
   Lamina lanceolate to ovate; anthers 2–2·5 mm long   3. *M. ovata*

1. Monsonia angustifolia *A. Rich.* (see p. 143)

An annual decumbent or erect herb with opposite or semi-opposite, narrowly oblong leaves; flowers 2–3 per peduncle; petals slightly longer than the sepals, mauve or white.

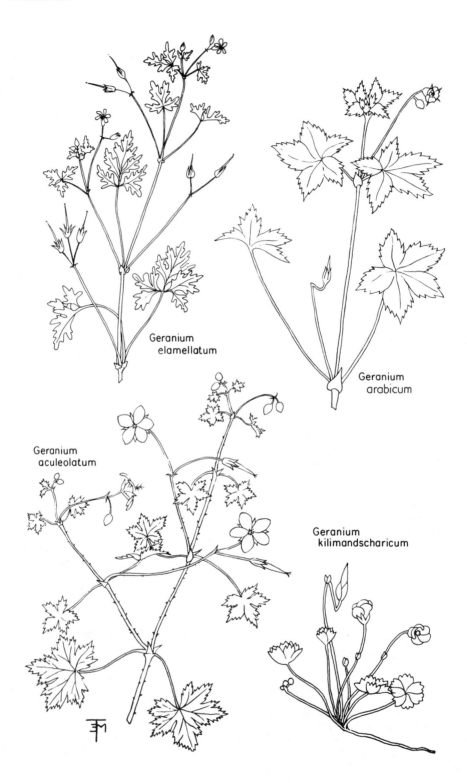

Geranium
elamellatum

Geranium
arabicum

Geranium
aculeolatum

Geranium
kilimandscharicum

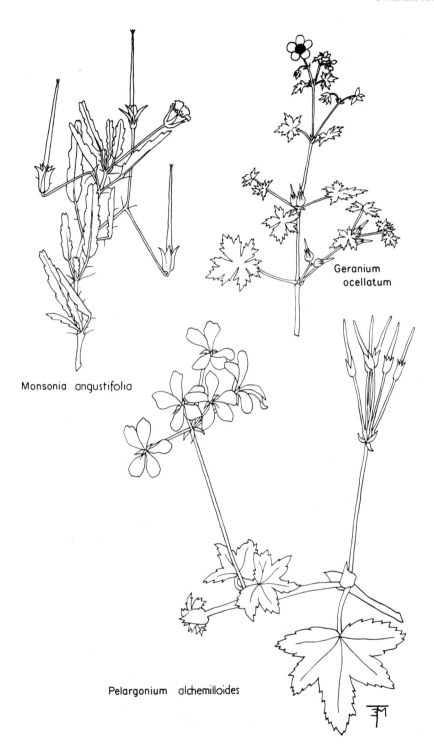

Monsonia angustifolia

Geranium
ocellatum

Pelargonium alchemilloides

In open woodland or wet grassland or more frequently as a weed in cultivated land. HE, KIT, HA, RV, MAC, KAJ.

Thorold 3203; Agnew and Musumba 5307.

2. Monsonia longipes *R. Knuth* (see p. 145)

A hairy, decumbent, profusely branched perennial herb with mostly opposite hastate leaves; peduncles usually 1–5-flowered; petals bright yellow or lemon but sometimes white.

Found in grassland or semi-seasonal swamps, particularly on sandy-loam hillsides. RV, NBI.

Verdcourt 3262; Ables 16.

3. Monsonia ovata *Cav.* (*M. glauca* Knuth)

Erect perennial herb with ± woody base and fleshy roots; leaves opposite to sub-opposite, narrowly lanceolate to ovate; flowers usually in pairs, white or lemon.

Can be found in open *Acacia* plains or wooded grassland on sandy or stony soils. RV, MAG, MAC.

Verdcourt and Napper 2171.

3. PELARGONIUM *Ait.*

Annual or perennial herbs or shrubs, sometimes with tuberous roots, erect or decumbent and sometimes acaulescent; leaves rarely entire, usually lobed to variously dissected or compound; flowers 2-many per peduncle, mostly pentamerous and zygomorphic; stamens 10, only 2–7 fertile; disk glands absent; carpel beak twisting spirally when ripe.

1   Leaves pinnate or 3-partite to 3-foliolata with
      terminal lobe or leaflet larger 1. *P. whytei*
      Leaves almost entire to 3–5(–7)-palmatilobed
      with ± equal lobes   2
2   Petals 4   2. *P. glechomoides*
      Petals 5   3
3   Petals greenish-yellow; lamina hastate
                              3. *P. quinquelobatum*
      Petals white, pink or red; lamina cordate
                                4. *P. alchemilloides*

1. Pelargonium whytei *Bak.*

A pubescent to almost glabrous, decumbent (occasionally tufted) perennial herb, with orbicular, variously dissected opposite leaves; flowers 2–5 per peduncle; petals 4, pink with red veins, antheriferous filaments 7.

Found in drier parts of the montane forest belt and the ericaceous belts, also in grassland regions. HE, HM, HN, RV, KAJ.

Rogers 260; Agnew *et al.* 10471.

2. Pelargonium glechomoides *A. Rich.*

A pubescent and glandular, rhizomatous ascending perennial herb with opposite and/or alternate ovate pinnatisect leaves; flowers 2–8 per peduncle; petals 4, pink or rose-red with crimson lines; antheriferous filaments 5.

A rare species in our area, found on cliffs and lava rock edges, usually under the shade of hill slopes or river banks. MAC.

Napier 18.

3. Pelargonium quinquelobatum *A. Rich.* (see p. 145)

A short-stemmed pubescent perennial herb with straggling branches and a tuberous root; leaves in basal rosettes on main stem, opposite or alternate on branches, orbicular, 3–5-lobed; flowers (2–)4–8 per peduncle; petals 5, greenish-yellow to pale-lemon; antheriferous filaments 7.

May be found as a farm weed, but commoner in the rocky soils of lava flows or especially in evergreen woodland edges. RV, NBI, KAJ.

Gillett 13467; Strid 2577.

4. Pelargonium alchemilloides (*L.*) *Ait.* (*P. multibracteatum* A. Rich.) (see p. 143)

A perennial pubescent herb with a slightly tuberous rootstock; leaves alternate below and opposite towards the apex, orbicular, 5–7-lobed; flowers (5–)7–16 per peduncle; petals 5, white but sometimes pink or dark red; antheriferous filaments 5 or 7.

Found along slopes of hills and mountains in grassland and savannah woodland, also extending into montane forest edges. HE, KIT, RV, NAN, MAC, NBI, KAJ.

Verdcourt 2769; Agnew 9452.

33. OXALIDACEAE†

Annual or perennial herbs (in ours); leaves basically alternate, exstipulate or stipulate, digitately or pinnately compound; flowers regular, pentamerous, bisexual, in axillary cymes, pseudo-umbels or solitary; sepals free; petals free or falsely connate near the base; stamens in two whorls; filaments fused at the base to form a tube, with alternate short (outer) filaments opposite the petals and long (inner) filaments opposite the sepals; anthers 2-celled, versatile, opening inwards; ovary 5-celled, styles 5, with 1 to many axile ovules in each loculus; fruit a capsule, often

† By C. H. S. Kabuye.

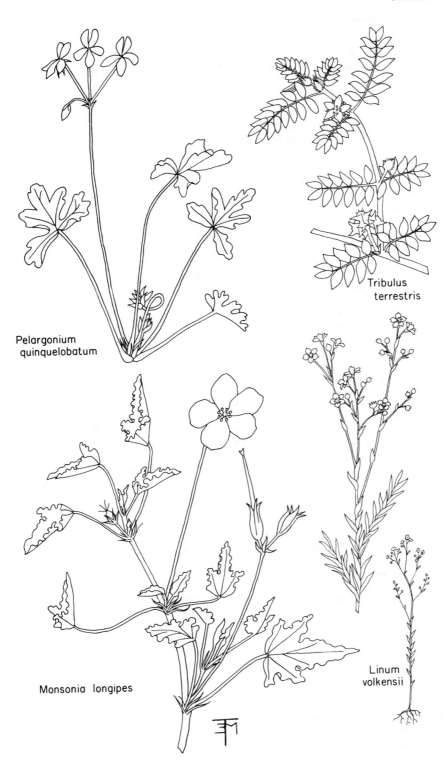

Pelargonium
quinquelobatum

Tribulus
terrestris

Monsonia longipes

Linum
volkensii

explosively dehiscent; seeds with a fleshy endosperm or non-endospermous.

1 Leaves digitately 3-foliolate   1. *Oxalis*
   Leaves pinnate and usually sensitive to touch
                                           2. *Biophytum*

1. OXALIS *L.*

Caulescent or acaulescent, annual or perennial herbs, bulbous or not; leaves trifoliolate, rather sensitive to light (leaflets drooping during its absence), petiolate with membranous stipules adnate to the petiole or without stipules; flowers pedicellate, subtended by bracts in pseudo-umbels, cymes or solitary, usually trimorphic heterostylous (largely homostylous in *O. corniculata*); sepals sometimes with apical thickenings; stigmas 5, free, capitate; seeds covered by a white fleshy aril which bursts elastically by contraction, expelling the seed when ripe.

1 Plants with branching stems, not bulbous;
      flowers yellow   2
   Plants bulbous; flowers pink to purple   3
2 Adnate stipules present at the base of petiole
                                        1. *O. corniculata*
   Stipules absent   2. *O. radicosa*
3 Vertical rhizome absent, the bulbs at or just
      below the soil surface with leaves and
      peduncles arising directly from them
                                        5. *O. latifolia*
   Vertical rhizome present, the bulbs at some
      depth below soil surface   4
4 Flowers solitary; lateral leaflets with 2–3
      similarly large veins   3. *O. obliquifolia*
   Flowers apparently in umbels; lateral leaflets
      with a well-marked midrib
                                        4. *O. anthelmintica*

1. Oxalis corniculata *L.* (see p. 147)

Annual or perennial much-branched herb with stems creeping, ascending and frequently rooting at the nodes; flowers yellow in 1–6-flowered pseudo-umbels or solitary.

A common weed of cultivation, disturbed ground, lawns and roadsides, which is also found in some subalpine grassland.

This species is very variable in mode of growth, size and pubescence of its parts. There are forms with purplish and purple-variegated leaves. HE, HC, HT, HM, HA, HK, KIT, MUM, KIS, NBI, KAJ.

The following varieties occur in our area:

var. *corniculata*. Stems creeping and ascending, leaflets up to over 15 mm long and 20 mm wide, usually thinly punctulate only beneath; capsule mostly much over 5 mm long.

Weed in cultivation, disturbed ground, lawns and roadsides.

Agnew, Hanid, and Kiniaruh 7870; Kerfoot 3919.

var. *repens* (Thumb.) Zucc. Stems creeping, prostrate, rooting almost at every node; leaflets very small up to 4 mm long and 5 mm wide, thickly punctulate on both sides; capsules almost globose, very short, rarely longer than 3–4 mm. Found in forest glades and moorlands.

Lind, Agnew, and Woodley 5757; Napier 713.

2. Oxalis radicosa *A. Rich.* (*O. stricta non* L.) (see p. 147)

A perennial herb with usually thin stems arising from a thick main rootstock; corolla usually appearing pinkish in bud.

Found in forest clearings, mountain slopes, weed in cultivation and roadsides. HT, HM, KIT.

Tweedie 66/94; Kokwaro 78.

3. Oxalis obliquifolia *A. Rich.* (see p. 147)

A bulbous herb with a vertical rhizome bearing a basal bulb and an apical rosette of leaves; flowers solitary on erect peduncles; petals pink or purple, sometimes with a yellowish base.

Found in shallow soils and grasslands at medium altitudes and occasionally as a weed of cultivation and roadsides, between 2500 and 9500 ft. HT, HM, KIT, KIS, BAR, NBI.

Ables 9; Rogers 201.

4. Oxalis anthelmintica *A. Rich.* (see p. 148)

Similar to *O. obliquifolia* but with the differences given in the key.

Occasional weed in grassland and edges of riverine forest, on sandy loam, appearing after rains, 2500–6500 ft. HE, HC, KIT, NBI, KAJ.

Hedberg 810.

5. Oxalis latifolia *H. B. & K.* (see p. 148)

Acaulescent herb with leaves and peduncles arising directly from an oval bulb, from which also arise stolons with membranous scales, the end of each stolon developing a bulbil which eventually forms a new plant; flowers in 5- to over 20-flowered pseudo-umbels, light pink-purple with a green throat.

Locally common and obnoxious introduced weed, very difficult to eradicate because of its formation of many bulbils. On cultivated land, waste places, usually in moist and well-shaded parts, 3800–7500 ft. HE, HM, KIT, MAC, NBI.

Williams 151; Mathenge 385.

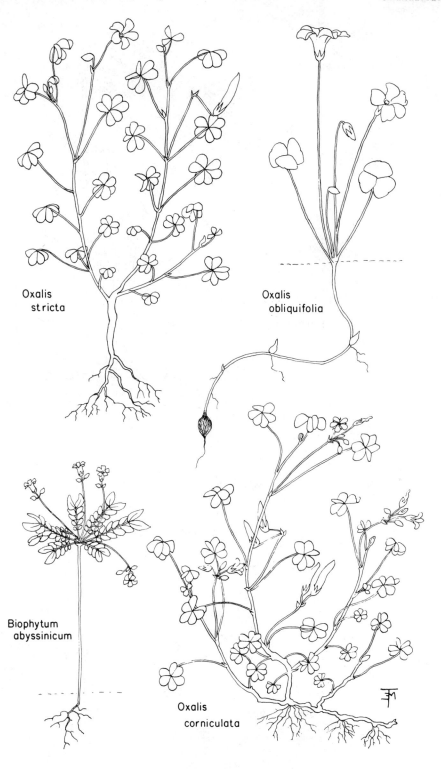

Oxalis
stricta

Oxalis
obliquifolia

Biophytum
abyssinicum

Oxalis
corniculata

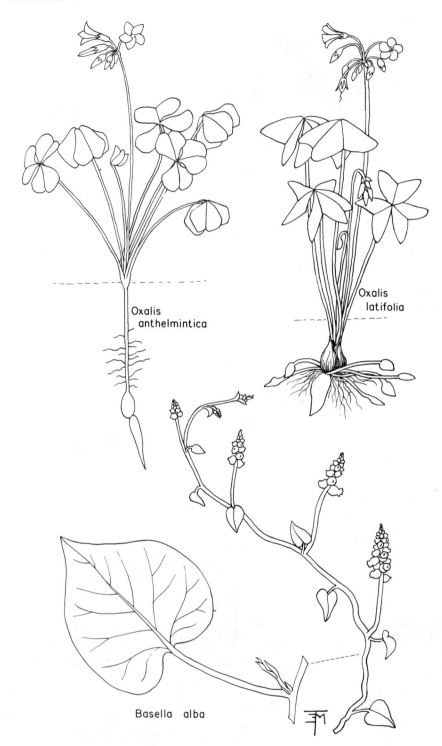

Oxalis
anthelmintica

Oxalis
latifolia

Basella alba

2. BIOPHYTUM *DC.*

Annual herbs with simple stems; leaves paripinnate, (the rachis ending in a bristle) fascicled or almost whorled at the top of the stem, sensitive to touch with leaflets closing downwards, leaflets inaequilateral, many, opposite or subopposite, obliquely rectangular or orbicular; flowers in pseudo-umbels; bracts small, persistent, forming an involucre at the base of pedicels; sepals strongly parallel-veined, those towards the centre of the pseudo-umbels narrower than the outer ones; petals free in bud but later adherent above the free base, pink (in ours); capsule globose.

1 Sepals up to 3 mm long   1. *B. abyssinicum*
   Sepals over 5 mm long   2. *B. petersianum*

1. Biophytum abyssinicum *A. Rich.* (see p.147)

A glabrescent annual with a rosette of sensitive, pinnate leaves held off the ground by the erect, unbranched stem; flowers pale pink or white in long-pedunculate pseudo-umbels.

Occasionally common in bare sandy ground in western Kenya, 5000–8000 ft. HE, HC, KIT, BAR, MAC.

Agnew, Kibe, and Mathenge 10247; Archer 231.

2. Biophytum petersianum *Klotzsch*

Similar to *B. abyssinicum* except for the stiffer leaflets with lateral nerves coming off the midrib strictly at right-angles.

Uncommon plant found in grassland in western Kenya. MUM, KIS.

Tweedie 67/251; Lind in EAH 10493.

34. BALSAMINACEAE†

Herbs or shrubs with opposite or alternate, exstipulate leaves; inflorescences racemose, usually axillary, or flowers solitary; flowers bisexual, zygomorphic, subtended by a bract but without bracteoles, twisted during development so that the posterior side appears anteriorly; sepals 3, rarely 5, petals 5, the anterior one keeled and held posteriorly, the others fused in lateral pairs, each lateral 2-lobed; stamens 5, alternating with the petals, the filaments connate above the ovary, forming a cap which usually must be removed (by a pollinator or by growth) before the stigmas can receive pollen; ovary superior, of 5 carpels, with axile placentation of many ovules; style short, simple; stigmas 1–5; fruit a capsule or berry; seed without endosperm and with a straight embryo.

† By A. D. Q. Agnew.

1. IMPATIENS *L.*

Herbs (often subsucculent) or shrubs commonly rooting at the nodes, with alternate, opposite or whorled leaves; leaves serrate at margin, with (in ours) tentacle-like hairs on the serration, sometimes extending into the petiole, all (in ours) lanceolate, elliptic or ovate, acute at apex; flowers solitary, in racemes, or in sessile or pedunculate umbels; posterior sepal spurred, other floral characters as in the family; fruit an explosively dehiscent loculicidal capsule, which throws the seeds out with great force, and which can be triggered by a light touch.

Floral features give a distinctive pattern to each species and are best seen in an illustration. Thus users of the key are urged to compare their flower with the illustration of the keyed species.

Note that in the key the words 'posterior' and 'anterior' are used to denote positions on the flower as it appears on the plant, the posterior being the upper side with the keeled petal, and the anterior being the lower side with the spurred sepal.

1 Inflorescences pedunculate, peduncle more than 1 cm long, or flowers solitary with a bract half way or more along the apparent pedicel   2
   Flowers fasciculate or solitary in the axils, with bracts at base of pedicel   7
2 Leaves apparently whorled; spur 4 cm long or more; flowers with 5 equally large petaloid limbs   1. *I. sodenii*
   Leaves alternate, or, if occasionally whorled, then spur less than 4 cm long; flowers with less than 5 petaloid limbs, or limbs of different size   3
3 Spur shortly bifid at tip; petals white with dark red spots and lines within   2. *I. elegantissima*
   Spur simple; petals white, red or pink, never white with many spots and lines within   4
4 Petioles with capillary 'glands'   5
   Petioles without capillary 'glands'   6
5 Spur narrow (to 3 mm wide at base), hairy, abruptly widening into the calyx limb; 2 lateral sepals   3. *I. stuhlmannii*
   Spur broad (over 3 mm wide at base), glabrous, gradually broadening into the calyx limb; 4 lateral sepals   4. *I. fischeri*
6 Anterior lobes of petals shorter than lateral lobes and shorter than posterior calyx limb   5. *I. nana*
   Anterior lobes of petals longer than lateral lobes and longer than posterior calyx limb   6. *I. telekii*
7 Spur about 3 mm wide at base, passing gradually into the calyx limb   8

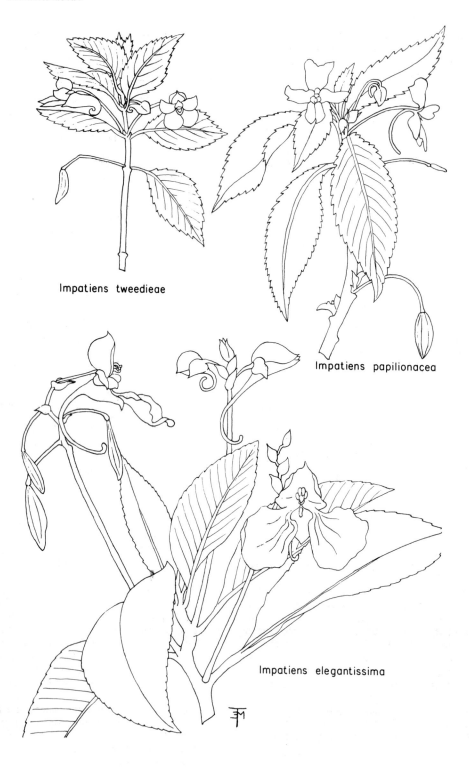

Impatiens tweedieae

Impatiens papilionacea

Impatiens elegantissima

Spur less than 2 mm wide at base, abruptly
widening into the calyx limb **11**

8 Spur coiled into a semicircle or full circle at
tip or bent through more than 90° **9**
Spur straight **7.** *I. phlyctidoceras*

9 Spur acute, and entire at apex **10**
Spur very bluntly 2-lobed at apex
8. *I. niamniamensis*

10 Leaves opposite **9.** *I. tweediae*
Leaves alternate **12.** *I. rubromaculata*

11 Spur shorter than its calyx limb **10.** *I. eminii*
Spur longer than its calyx limb **12**

12 Pedicel and sepals (with spur) glabrous; upper
surface of leaves without a line of hairs on
the major lateral veins, most hairs being
between them **11.** *I. hochstetteri*
Pedicel and sepals often hairy; upper surface
of leaves with a line of hairs along the
major lateral veins as well as between them
13

13 Posterior petal as large as, or larger than, any
of the other petal lobes; spur mostly
glabrous, gently curved
13. *I. papilionacea*
Posterior petal exceeded 2–4 times in length
by other petal lobes; spur mostly hairy,
usually abruptly bent so that the apex
approaches the calyx limb
12. *I. rubromaculata*

1. Impatiens sodenii *Engl. & Warb.*

An erect glabrous woody herb, unbranched or
branched from the base only, with 10–15 elliptic
to oblanceolate leaves in each whorl; petals nearly
equal, forming a flat, pink, red, or white suborbicular outline.

Locally common in escarpment zones and
waterfalls where mist is frequent. HE, HA, RV,
MAC.

Bogdan 496; Agnew and Hanid 8357.

2. Impatiens elegantissima *Gilg* (see p. 150)

An erect glabrous or glabrescent herb, 1–3 m tall,
with alternate elliptic leaves; flowers almost
trumpet-shaped, white with pink or red spots, with
very large anterior lobes, and bifid spur.

A common *Impatiens* in waterfalls and stream
banks in the wetter highland forest areas. HE, HC,
HT, HM, HA, HK, KIT, MUM.

Agnew, Azavedo, and Khatri 9547; Polhill 235.

3. Impatiens stuhlmannii *Warb.*

Pubescent herb to 1 m, with ascending stems and
ovate-elliptic leaves; flowers pink to red with large
anterior lobes.

A rare *Impatiens* of wet lowland forests,
recorded only from the Kakamega-Yala area. MUM.
It is occasionally cultivated.

Drummond and Hemsley 4767; Wyatt 30.

4. Impatiens fischeri *Warb.*

An erect, glabrous, sparsely branched herb with
alternate ovate leaves; flowers bright red to scarlet.

A common plant of wet highland forest but
seldom profusely flowering, which is a pity since it
is most attractive. HA, HK.

Verdcourt and Polhill 2986; Agnew and Lind
5618.

5. Impatiens nana *Eckl. & Warb.*

Glabrous or sparsely pubescent herb with ascending stems to 50 cm, rooting at the nodes, ovate-
elliptic leaves and usually solitary flowers; flowers
pink or white, sometimes with a yellow spot at the
base of the lateral petals.

A common plant of wet places in highland
forest at lower altitudes. HA, HK, HM, MAC.

Agnew 7674; Polhill and Verdcourt 265.

6. Impatiens telekii *T. C. E. Fries.*

A similar plant to *I. nana* but glabrous, with
usually 2 pink flowers on each peduncle.

This has only been found in the wet forest of
Mt. Kenya. HK.

Agnew and Coe 8756.

7. Impatiens phlyctidoceras *Bullock*

An erect pubescent herb with alternate ovate-
elliptic leaves and solitary scarlet-crimson flowers;
flowers with a small corolla and very long, thick
spur which is lobed at apex.

Rare plant found on Mt. Elgon and only once
collected. HE.

Lugard 313 (isotype).

8. Impatiens niamniamensis *Gilg*

A glabrous woody herb often (with support)
reaching to over 2 m tall, with ovate-lanceolate
leaves; flowers red, with small petals and big spur.

A rare plant only found in lowland wet forest,
and in our area only in MUM and KIS.

Bally B 6478; Gillett 16728.

9. Impatiens tweediae *E. A. Bruce* (see p. 150)

A pubescent trailing herb to 40 cm tall, the
ascending stems becoming somewhat woody at
base, with opposite, elliptic to suborbicular leaves;
flowers red.

A plant confined to forests on Mt. Elgon, where
is is not uncommon. It is named after Mrs. E. M.
Tweedie who drew the illustrations, and also made
many collections for this flora. HE.

Tweedie 67/11; Adamson 503.

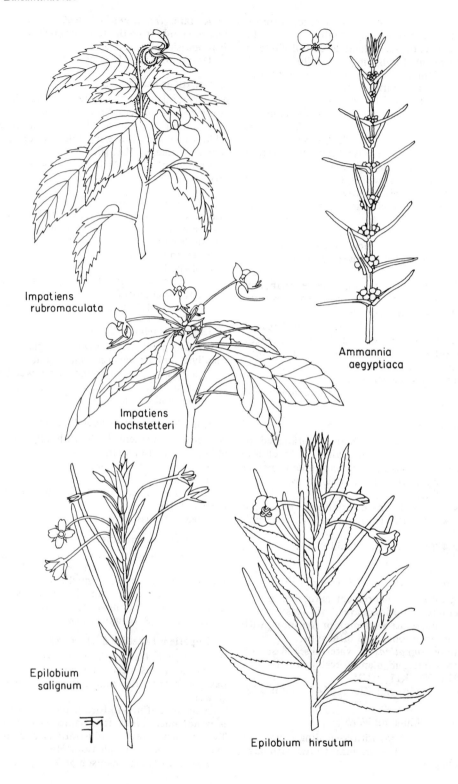

Impatiens
rubromaculata

Ammannia
aegyptiaca

Impatiens
hochstetteri

Epilobium
salignum

Epilobium hirsutum

10. Impatiens eminii *Warb.*

An erect, pubescent herb to 75 cm, with ovate-elliptic leaves; flowers usually cream, rather small.

A common herb by streamsides in wet lower altitude forests at Kakamega and Yala. MUM.

Strid 3355; Lucas 89.

11. Impatiens hochstetteri *Warb.* (*I. gilgii* T. C. E. Fries) (see p. 152)

Pubescent herb with ascending stems to 40 cm, rooting at the nodes, and with ovate-elliptic leaves; flowers with spreading white petals.

A common *Impatiens* of streamsides in wet forests. HE, HC, HM, HK, KIT, MUM, KIS, MAC.

Strid 3382; Kerfoot 4105.

12. Impatiens rubromaculata *Warb.* (*I. hoehnelii* T. C. E. Fries) (see p. 152)

A pubescent herb with ascending stems to 50 cm, rooting at the nodes, with alternate or rarely opposite or even whorled elliptic to subrhombic leaves; flowers bright pink, dominated by the spreading lateral petals.

A common and variable plant, defined here on the basis of the petal shape and not on variable features of the spur. The size of the flower varies considerably. It is common in upper levels of highland forest, in forest edges, and is found up to the tree-line in many places. HC, HM, HA, HK, HN, MAC.

Tweedie 66/390; Drummond and Hemsley 1226.

13. Impatiens papilionacea *Warb.* (*I. cruciata* T. C. E. Fries) (see p. 150)

A pubescent annual or perennial herb, with ascending stems to 40 cm, rooting at the nodes, and with ovate-elliptic alternate leaves; flowers pink, often with dark red spots in the centre.

A common *Impatiens* of the forest floor in highland forest, and also found in marshes. HE, HC, HM, HA, HK, KAJ.

Agnew 8734; Glover 993.

35. LYTHRACEAE†

Herbs, subshrubs, shrubs, or trees with opposite, rarely whorled or alternate leaves, mostly stipulate; inflorescence a cyme, very rarely a panicle or flowers solitary; flowers mostly regular, bisexual, 4–8-merous; sepals connate into a tube, valvate; petals free, inserted towards the top of the calyx-tube, and alternating with calyx-lobes, crumpled in bud, sometimes absent; stamens mostly 4 or 8, inserted on the calyx-tube below the petals; ovary

† By M. A. Hanid.

superior, completely or incompletely 2–6-celled, rarely 1-celled, with numerous axile ovules in each loculus; fruit a capsule with circumscissile, valvular, or irregular dehiscence; seeds small, without endosperm; embryo straight.

1　Flowers in a terminal leafless raceme
　　　　　　　　　　　　　4. Rotala repens
　Flowers all axillary, solitary or in inflorescences　　　　　　　　　　　2
2　Flowers solitary in each axil　　　　3
　Flowers (at least the majority of them) in sessile or pedunculate axillary cymes or heads　　　　　　　　　　　　　5
3　Petals over 4 mm long　　　　　　4
　Petals less than 2 mm long or absent
　　　　　　　　　　　　　　4. Rotala
4　Plant herbaceous, soft, trailing and rooting at the nodes　*2. Lythrum rotundifolium*
　Plant shrubby or with a woody rootstock, not rooting at the nodes　　*3. Nesaea*
5　Calyx over 2 mm long or flowers in capitate heads surrounded by two enlarged bracts
　　　　　　　　　　　　　　3. Nesaea
　Calyx less than 2 mm long; flowers in cymose clusters with obscure bracts
　　　　　　　　1. Ammannia and Rotala

1. AMMANNIA *L.*

Herbs of damp places with decussate, sessile or subsessile leaves and 4-angled stems and branches; inflorescences of short, dense axillary cymes, with 2 bracteoles at the base of each pedicel; flowers 4–6-merous; calyx usually bell-shaped, 8-nerved, with or without appendages; petals 4 or absent, caducous, white or purplish-pink; stamens 4 or 8; ovary sessile, 1–4-celled, style filiform, persistent, longer than the calyx-tube or absent; stigma capitate; capsule globose, included in the calyx-tube or exserted, dehiscing transversely or irregularly; seeds numerous, globular or triangular in outline, often concave on one side.

1　Leaf-bases auriculate-cordate　　　2
　Leaf-bases cuneate　　　　　　　3
2　Cymes distinctly pedunculate; flowers pedicellate, style slightly shorter or up to twice as long as the capsule　　*3. A. auriculata*
　Cymes without peduncles, flowers subsessile, style much shorter than the capsule
　　　　　　　　　　　　1. A. aegyptiaca
3　Stem spongy; appendage between calyx lobes elongate　　　　*4. A. sarcophylla*
　Stem not spongy; appendage between calyx lobes hardly evident　　　　　4
4　Capsule opening by apical valves
　　　　　　　　　　Rotala serpiculoides
　Capsule opening irregularly and transversely
　　　　　　　　　　　　2. A. baccifera

1. Ammannia aegyptiaca *Willd.* (see p. 152)
Erect annual with ascending to spreading branches and sessile lanceolate leaves.

A plant of river banks, marshes, and lake or pool margins; properly collected and carefully annotated material is needed. HE, KIT, MUM, NAN, MAC.

Dalton in CM 18058; Lugard 536.

2. Ammannia baccifera *L.*
Glabrous erect annual with simple or branched stem and linear-elliptic to narrowly oblanceolate leaves.

A small herb of marshy places. MAC, NBI.

Verdcourt 3634; Agnew 9419.

3. Ammannia auriculata *Willd.* (*A. prieureana* Guill. & Perr. of Check List.)
Glabrous, erect, with simple, or more often branched stems and linear-oblong or lanceolate leaves.

A herb, often small, of seasonally wet shallow soils overlying rocks, river banks, and margins of lakes and pools; sometimes a weed in irrigated land. HE, KIT, EMB, MAC, NBI.

Verdcourt 3250; Tweedie 67/231.

4. Ammannia sarcophylla *Hiern.*
Prostrate to erect, rooting at the nodes, with spongy stem bearing obovate, sessile glaucous leaves; cymes very shortly pedunculate or sessile.

A rare plant found in wet soils marginal to fresh-water lakes and pools; only one specimen recorded so far from Kisumu; this species is much in need of further collecting. KIS.

McMahon K 302.

2. LYTHRUM *L.*
Glabrous annual or perennial herbs with decussate, whorled or alternate leaves and solitary, axillary, subsessile and (in ours) tetramerous flowers; calyx tubular, with evident appendages between deltoid lobes; petals much longer than and alternating with calyx-lobes; stamens (in ours) 8, exserted; ovary sessile, 2-celled; style (in ours) longer than the calyx tube; capsule included in the calyx, 2-valved, septicidal; seeds many, small.

Lythrum rotundifolium *A. Rich.*
Trailing succulent herb with stem often tinged red and short ascending branches; leaves opposite, very shortly petiolate or sessile, ovate to rotund, base broadly cuneate to rounded or cordate-auriculate and amplexicaul; flowers solitary, axillary, purplish.

A fairly common, pretty little herb of wet places along streams, in swamps, and lake margins. HT, HM, HL, HA, KIT, MUM, RV, NAN, EMB.

Verdcourt 2493; Hanid and Kiniaruh 427.

3. NESAEA *Commers.*
Herbs, undershrubs, or shrubs with entire, sessile or shortly petioled, decussate, or whorled, or sometimes alternate leaves; flowers axillary, solitary or in stalked cymes or capitulum-like heads; bracteoles borne on peduncles; calyx campanulate or urceolate, persistent, with 4–8 lobes and as many appendages; petals as many as calyx-lobes, usually exserted, deciduous; stamens in 1–2 rows; ovary sessile, 2–5-celled; capsule enclosed in the calyx, membranous, dehiscing by valves or by irregular slits at the apex.

1   Flowers in bracteate heads; peduncles usually more than 3 mm long, with bracts at the top; bracts more than 1 mm long, enclosing the very short pedicels   2
    Flowers in 1–3-flowered cymes; peduncles usually up to 3 mm long, with bracts below the pedicels; bracts up to 1 mm long, not enclosing the distinct pedicels   3
2   Plant tomentose; calyx-lobes 6
                                 1. *N. floribunda*
    Plant glabrous; calyx-lobes 4   2. *N. erecta*
3   Leaf-apex usually acute; calyx-tube sub-globose-cylindrical, 6-lobed
                                 3. *N. lythroides*
    Leaf-apex usually rounded; calyx-tube turbinate, 4-lobed   4. *N. schinzii*

1. Nesaea floribunda *Sond.*
A tomentose annual herb with oblanceolate to ovate leaves and purplish pink flowers.

A plant of wet shallow soils, often growing amongst rocks in seeping water and near rivers in sandy places. HA, KIT, EMB, MAC.

Bally 11572; Archer 371.

2. Nesaea erecta *G. & P.*
A glabrous annual with narrowly elliptic to oblanceolate leaves and 3 to many lilac or magenta flowers, in heads.

A small plant of wet shallow soils, often near ephemeral pools. HA, KIT, MAC, NBI.

Faden 67/628; Verdcourt 3242.

3. Nesaea lythroides *Welw.*
A glabrous or hispid woody perennial herb or undershrub with sessile, narrowly lanceolate leaves and 1–3-flowered cymes; petals 6, pinkish to red.

A locally common plant of shallow soils overlying rocks and dry grassland, especially in the Nairobi area. A glabrous form with campanulate calyx-tube has been found at the bottom of the escarpment on the Nairobi–Naivasha road. HA, NAR, RV, MAG, MAC, NBI.

Agnew 7795 and 9190; Greenway 9168.

4. Nesaea schinzii *Koehne*

A glabrous, profusely branched, erect perennial herb with sessile lanceolate leaves and 1–3-flowered cymes; petals 4, pink.

A rare plant of western grasslands recorded only from Muhoroni in Lumbwa District. MUM.

Opiko 657.

4. ROTALA *L.*

Glabrous herbs, aquatic or growing in wet places, with decussate or whorled or rarely alternate simple leaves; flowers small, axillary and solitary or few together, sessile or subsessile, usually bibracteate; flowers 3–6-merous, sometimes dimorphic; calyx campanulate or urceolate-tubular, hemispherical in fruit, usually 4-lobed, rarely 5-lobed, appendages mostly absent or setiform; petals minute, persistent, as many as calyx-lobes or absent; stamens 1–5, usually 4, free; ovary incompletely 1–4-celled; capsule 2–4-valved, septicidal.

1 Plant submerged aquatic; leaves linear; flowers in terminal racemes   1. *R. repens*
   Plant with aerial stems; leaves broader than linear; flowers all axillary   2
2 Plant erect; leaves narrow-elliptic
                          2. *R. serpiculoides*
   Plant trailing; leaves oblong to obovate, often clasping the stem at the base   3
3 Calyx-lobes lanceolate; mature capsule half as long as calyx   4. *R. urundiensis*
   Calyx-lobes triangular-obtuse; mature capsule equalling calyx in length   3. *R. tenella*

1. Rotala repens (*Hochst.*) *Koehne*

Glabrous aquatic herb with anchored rhizome, submerged stems and filiform leaves; aerial racemes of white to pinkish flowers.

A rare plant found in streams, often growing on stones in stagnant water. It is recorded only from Suam River and is in need of further collection. KIT.

Taylor 3412.

2. Rotala serpiculoides *Hiern*

Glabrous erect annual herb, 3–20 cm high, with simple or slightly branched stem; superficially very similar to *Ammannia baccifera* L. but differing in having deltoid-acuminate calyx lobes and valvular dehiscence in the 4-valved capsule.

A small infrequent herb found in damp areas so far recorded from Kaptagat in rockpools, Nairobi National Park in vlei in forest area, and from Thika area in a temporary pool. HT, MAC, NBI.

Verdcourt 536; Faden 67/629.

3. Rotala tenella *Hiern*

Glabrous trailing perennial herb with ascending stems bearing obovate to oblong, sessile leaves which may reach 1·5 cm in length; capsule 2 mm long.

A rare herb found in wet places and seasonally flooded pools. EMB, MAC, NBI.

Faden 67632.

4. Rotala urundiensis *Fernandez & Diniz*

Similar to *Rotala tenella* but with the keyed differences, and smaller in all parts; capsule less than 2mm long.

A small herb of wet places, often growing in colonies to form cushions, so far recorded from Kitale area only. KIT.

Tweedie 67/23.

36. ONAGRACEAE†

Herbs, rarely shrubs or trees, with alternate or opposite or rarely whorled, stipulate or exstipulate, simple leaves; flowers solitary and axillary or sometimes aggregated into panicles or racemes, usually bisexual, regular or rarely irregular; sepals valvate, 2–7, mostly 4 or sometimes 5; petals free, as many as sepal number, contort or imbricate, fugacious, rarely absent; stamens the same as or twice the sepal number, very rarely fewer, in 1–2 rows; ovary inferior, mostly 4-celled, rarely 1–7-celled, with one to many axile ovules per cell; style simple; fruit a capsule, rarely a nut or berry; seeds without endosperm.

1 Seeds with a tuft of silky hairs at the top
                          1. *Epilobium*
   Seeds without any hairs   2
2 Sepals persistent above the fruit; fruit septicidal   2. *Ludwigia*
   Sepals not persistent above the fruit; fruit loculicidal   3. *Oenothera rosea*

1. EPILOBIUM *L.*

Annual or perennial herbs, sometimes thinly woody, with (in ours) denticulate or serrulate to subentire opposite leaves; stipules absent; flowers mostly regular, white to pink, red or purple; sepals and petals 4; hypanthium or receptacle not or hardly prolonged above the ovary; stamens 8; stigma entire or ± 4-cleft; ovary with uniseriate

† By M. A. Hanid.

ovules in each cell; capsule elongate, splitting
loculicidally into 4 valves from above; seeds
brown, ellipsoid, with an apical tuft of silky hairs.

1   Stem densely villous-hairy   1. *E. hirsutum*
    Stem subglabrous to puberulous, rarely
       pubescent   2
2   Leaves cuneate to narrowly rounded at base;
       young flowers white or cream, turning
       pink after opening   2. *E. salignum*
    Leaves broadly rounded to subcordate at
       base; flowers pink or mauve even before
       opening   3. *E. stereophyllum*

1. Epilobium hirsutum *L.* (see p. 152)

Erect rhizomatous herb 1·2 m high, with ascending
pale brown branches and densely villous or tomentose indumentum and with sessile, lanceolate to
elliptic leaves.

   A common plant of swampy and marshy places
by rivers, streams, lakes, and pools. HE, HT, HA,
KIT, RV, EMB, MAC.

   Hanid and Kiniaruh 1031; Bogdan 337.

2. Epilobium salignum *Hausskn.* (see p. 152)

Erect, slender, herbaceous or woody herb to 1·5 m
high, with reddish simple stem or often with a few
ascending branches above, appressed grey-
puberulous and with usually lanceolate leaves.

   A common plant of swampy and marshy places
near streams. HE, HC, HT, HA, KIT.

   Tweedie 66/186; Bogdan 4218.

3. Epilobium stereophyllum *Fres.*

Stoloniferous herb usually less than 1 m high
usually pubescent and with sessile, lanceolate
leaves.

   A farily common plant of swampy places in
upland moors, grasslands, and on moist ground
along streams and rivers. It is variable and has two
varieties, one with indumentum less than 0·25 mm
long and the other with indumentum 0·25-0·5
mm long. HE, HC, HT, HA, HK.

   Lind, Agnew, and Harris 5121; Hedberg 1080.

2. LUDWIGIA *L.*

Decumbent, creeping or erect, slender herbs sometimes shrubby, often growing in water, the under-
water parts often bearing aerenchymatous roots;
leaves mostly alternate, simple, entire (in ours);
stipules reduced or absent; flowers solitary,
clustered, or sometimes in a terminal head, usually
sessile, regular; hyphanthium not prolonged beyond
ovary; sepals 3-7, mostly 4-5, persistent; petals as
many as sepal number, caducous, yellow in ours,
aestivation contorted; stamens as many or twice as
many as sepals, epipetalous; stigma hemispherical

or capitate, often lobed, lobes as many as loculi;
loculi of ovary as many as sepal number, with
uniseriate or pluriseriate ovules in each cell; fruit a
capsule, mostly elongate, with variable dehiscence;
seeds rounded or elongate, free or surrounded by
endocarp, without hairs, usually with a large easily
visible raphe.

1   Stamens twice the sepal number   2
    Stamens as many as sepals   5
2   Seeds embedded in endocarp, uniseriate   3
    Seeds free, not embedded in endocarp,
       pluriseriate   4
3   Plants with spongy roots at nodes of floating
       branches; seeds firmly embedded in woody
       coherent endocarp, pendulous, appearing
       as rows of vertically elongated bumps be-
       tween ribs on capsule wall
                                      1. *L. stolonifera*
    Plants without spongy roots at nodes; seeds
       loosely embedded in horseshoe-shaped
       pieces of endocarp, horizontal, appearing
       as rows of horizontally elongated bumps
       between ribs on capsule wall
                                      2. *L. leptocarpa*
4   Sepals 3-6 mm long   3. *L. octovalvis*
    Sepals 10-14 mm long   4. *L. stenorraphe*
5   Capsule glabrous, terete, ribs obscure
                                      6. *L. abyssinica*
    Capsule puberulous or shortly pubescent,
       angled, ribs distinct   6
6   Sepals 1·3-3·5 mm long; capsule 1·3-1·9 cm
       long   5. *L. perennis*
    Sepals 6-13 mm long; capsule 2-4·3 cm long
                                      7. *L. jussiaeoides*

1. Ludwigia stolonifera (*Guill. & Perr.*) *Raven* (*Jussiaea repens* L. *p.p.*)

Glabrous to densely villous perennial herb with
prostrate or ascending stems rooting at the nodes,
and floating stems producing clusters of whitish to
pinkish swollen, spongy, fusiform, floating roots
from the nodes, the leaves shining green, cuneate.

   A common aquatic and floating plant of
swamps, pools, lakes, and rivers. This is the only
species of this genus (in our area) which produces
the very remarkable spongy roots or pneumato-
phores, apart from the adventitious roots, from
nodes of floating stems. HA, KIT, MUM, KIS,
NAR, RV, MAC, NBI.

   Hanid and Kiniaruh 715; Symes 352.

2. Ludwigia leptocarpa (*Nutt.*) *Hara*

Robust herb 0·4-2 m tall, with reclining or erect
woody base, well-branched stem, and with lanceolate leaves.

This plant is found along the shores or Lake Victoria, and in our area only in MUM and KIS.

Hanid and Kiniaruh 722; McMahon K297.

3. Ludwigia octovalvis *(Jacq.) Raven (L. pubescens* (L.) Hara, *Jussiaea suffruticosa* L.)

Well-branched robust herb or shrub up to 3·6 m tall, densely spreading-hairy, especially on younger parts, with usually narrow lanceolate leaves.

A highly polymorphic and variable species found in swampy places and damp areas by streams, rivers and lakes. It is recorded in our area only from south Nyanza and from Athi River, 20 miles beyond Thika, and is badly in need of further collection. KIS, MAC.

Hanid and Kiniaruh 779; Bally in CM 9202.

4. Ludwigia stenorraphe *(Brenan) Hara*

Erect much-branched robust suffructicose herb or shrub 1–3m high, with indumentum of dense or sparse, erect or appressed hairs and with often narrow elliptic leaves.

A very polymorphic species of *Ludwigia* found in swampy situations by watercourses, lakes, in flooded grasslands and on wet sandy river-beds. The sepals often turn reddish inside after anthesis, and are 6–9 mm long in ssp. *stenorraphe* and 10–14 mm long in ssp. *macrosepala*, but more material is required. HA, MUM, EMB.

Sunman 2219; Battiscombe 1122.

5. Ludwigia perennis *L. (Jussiaea perennis* (L.) Brenan)

Erect, slender, usually unbranched annual herb up to 50 cm high, subglabrous to minutely puberulous on younger parts, with very short tap-root and with elliptic to linear leaves.

A rare plant of swampy and wet places, such as the flood-plains of lakes and rivers. It is recorded in our area only from 18 miles SSW of Embu (Bogdan 4447); this record is from Raven (1963)†. EMB.

6. Ludwigia abyssinica *A. Rich. (L. erecta* of Check List)

Erect or straggling herb, often woody at base, up to 3 m tall, much branched, glabrous except for minute hairs on midribs and margin of younger lanceolate leaves.

A common plant of swampy situations along watercourses, and near pools and lakes. HE, HC, HA, KIT, MUM, KIS, NAR, MAC, NBI.

Agnew, Hanid, Musumba, and Kiniaruh 8462; Glover, Gwynne, Samuel, and Tucker 2405.

† Reinwardtia 6: 368.

7. Ludwigia jussiaeoides *Desr.*

Tall herb (up to 3 m), sometimes slightly woody, minutely puberulous or shortly pubescent, especially on young parts with lanceolate leaves.

A rare species of *Ludwigia* found in seasonally flooded places and disturbed ground. It is predominantly a coastal species, recorded only from Cherangani Hills (Tweedie B7617) in our area; this record is from Raven (1963)‡. HC.

3. OENOTHERA *L.*

Annual to perennial herbs with spirally arranged leaves and (in ours) solitary flowers in axils of upper leaves; hypanthium prolonged beyond the ovary, caducous after anthesis; flowers tetramerous; sepals strongly reflexed, caducous; petals contort, pink, white, or yellow; stamens 8; stigma entire or 4-lobed; fruit a capsule dehiscing loculicidally into 4 valves; seeds ellipsoid or elongated, free, usually with clearly visible raphe.

There are at least three introduced species of this American genus in our area, of which *O. rosea* is naturalised in NBI.

Two yellow-flowered species occur infrequently as casuals, escaping from gardens to waysides and waste places.

Oenothera rosea *Ait.*

A biennial to perennial erect herb up to about 60 cm high, tomentose, slightly woody and often reddish at the base, with elliptic to obovate leaves.

An American Evening Primrose naturalized locally and apparently spreading. So far it has only been recorded along the banks of Nairobi River. NBI.

Hanid 17; Verdcourt 3042.

37. TRAPACEAE§

Floating herbs with long-petioled alternate leaves; stipules small, long-linear, acuminate, scarious; petiole swollen above the middle; lamina deltoid-ovate with serrate margins; submerged stem with paired greenish root-like structures of unknown morphology, each structure pinnatisect into many filiform segments and arising one from either side of the leaf-scar; flowers solitary, axillary, pedicellate, bisexual, regular, tetramerous; sepals persistent, accrescent; petals longer than sepals, white; ovary semi-inferior, 2-celled, with one pendulous ovule per loculus; fruit a bony or coriaceous drupe, 1-seeded, 1-locular, with 2–4 horns derived from persistent sepals; seeds without endosperm, one large and thick, the other small and scale-like.

‡ *loc. cit.* p. 355.
§ By M. A. Hanid.

1. TRAPA *L.*

The only genus in the family, with the characters of the family.

Trapa natans *L.*

Shortly pubescent annual aquatic herb with leaves forming a rosette on water surface, floating by means of the inflated petioles; fruit with 4 horns varying in size, shape and direction.

An aquatic plant of still waters at lake edges. It is recorded only from Kisumu and Kendu Bay in our area. More flowering and fruiting material required. KIS.

McMahon K318.

38. HALORAGACEAE†

Herbs, often aquatic, with opposite, spiral or whorled leaves of variable shape, exstipulate or with intrapetiolar scales; inflorescences usually racemose; flowers small, inconspicuous, regular, never more than 4 each, sometimes one or both whorls absent; stamens 8, 4, or 2; ovary inferior, with 1 or 4 cells, with one ovule in each; styles 1-4, often short, each ending in a feathery or papillose stigma; fruit a nut or drupe; seeds with endosperm.

1 Leaves linear, sessile, almost entire
                           2. Laurembergia engleri
   Leaves not linear or entire   2
2 Leaves petiolate, simple, orbicular, serrate
                           1. Gunnera perpensa
   Leaves sessile, pinnate, oblong
                           3. Myriophyllum brasiliense

1. GUNNERA *L.*

Rhizomatous herbs, with (often very large) long-petiolate orbicular or ± peltate leaves with intrapetiolar scales; inflorescence a racemose panicle with male and female flowers on the same or separate panicles, and sometimes also with bisexual flowers; sepals 2-3 or absent; petals 2 or absent; stamens 1-2; ovary 1-celled, with 1 ovule, and with 2 styles and stigmas; fruit a 1-celled drupe.

Gunnera perpensa *L.*

A creeping perennial herb with a thick rhizome and orbicular shallowly lobed leaves; inflorescence a narrow panicle of sessile reddish spikes over-topping the leaves, female below and male above.

A rare plant of riverside marshes and low vegetation in the wettest highland forest, 7000-8500 ft. HA, HK.

Gardner 1882; Agnew and Lind 5868.

† By A. D. Q. Agnew.

2. LAUREMBERGIA *Berg.*

Small creeping herbs with simple, opposite or alternate leaves; flowers fasciculate in leaf axils, unisexual, both male and female together; male flowers with 4 sepals, 4 petals, and 4 nearly sessile anthers; female flowers with 4 sepals, petals absent and an inferior ovary with 4 nearly sessile stigmas; fruit globose, hard, indehiscent, 1-seeded, strongly warted on the outside.

Laurembergia engleri *Schindl.*

Prostrate creeping pubescent herb with ascending stems and linear or very narrowly oblanceolate leaves.

A rare plant only recorded from Kitale district, in grassy swamps. KIT.

Napper 790; Tweedie 67/21.

3. MYRIOPHYLLUM *L.*

Perennial aquatic herbs with whorled pinnate leaves, the segments capillary; flowers in bracteate terminal spikes, unisexual or bisexual; male flowers with 4 sepals, 4 petals and 4-8 stamens; female flowers with 4 obscure sepals, no petals and the ovary 4-celled, with 1 ovule in each cell, and 4-stigmas; fruit separating into 1-seeded nutlets.

Myriophyllum brasiliense *Cambess.*

Leaves glabrous, usually 5 in each whorl with 5-10 pairs of pinnae.

Apparently a rare escape from aquaria and recorded once from Nairobi. NBI.

Bond in EAH 13810.

39. CALLITRICHACEAE‡

Annual or perennial, creeping or aquatic herbs with small opposite entire exstipulate leaves; flowers axillary, unisexual (monoecious), solitary or in pairs, with bracteoles 2 or absent; sepals and petals 0; stamens 1, with only 1 pollen sac; ovary with 4 lobes, 2 styles, 4 loculi with one ovule in each; fruit separating into 4 winged or keeled druplets; seeds with endosperm.

1. CALLITRICHE *L.*

The only genus, with the characteristics of the family.

Callitriche stagnalis *Scop.*

A glabrous prostrate herb creeping and rooting at the nodes, with obovate to spathulate leaves and inconspicuous flowers.

A common plant in pools and wet paths in and above the bamboo zone to 14 000 ft, and rarely

‡ By A. D. Q. Agnew.

lower to the level of Nairobi. HE, HT, HA, HK, NBI.

Verdcourt 2000.

40. THYMELAEACEAE†

Trees, shrubs, or herbs with simple opposite or alternate leaves and strong phloem fibres which show as a silky fringe when the stem is broken; flowers mostly sessile in spikes or heads, bisexual, regular; calyx with a long cylindrical tube, the lower part persistent round the ovary in fruit, 4–5-lobed; corolla present as corona-like projections at the mouth of the calyx, or absent; stamens equal to or twice the number of the calyx lobes, included in the calyx tube, often at different levels; ovary superior 1–2-celled, with a single pendulous ovule in each cell; style often lateral; stigma capitate; fruit an achene or drupe.

The trees and shrubs of the genera *Dicranolepis*, *Englerodaphne* (= *Gnidia*), *Peddiea*, *Struthiola*, and *Synaptolepis* as well as some woody species of *Lasiosiphon* (= *Gnidia*) are dealt with in KTS. Only two genera have herbaceous members.

1 Leaves imbricate, glabrous with a fringed margin; flowers solitary
  1. *Struthiola thomsonii*
  Leaves not imbricate, glabrous or hairy but never hairy only on the margin; flowers in heads, rarely solitary   2. *Gnidia*

1. STRUTHIOLA *L.*

Low woody shrubs with solitary, axillary flowers; calyx with 4 lobes; petals 4–8; stamens 4; fruit dry.

Struthiola thomsonii *Oliv.* (see p. 160)
Dealt with in KTS p. 557.

2. GNIDIA *L.* (incl. *Lasiosiphon* Fres., *Arthrosolen* C. A. Mey., *Englerodaphne* Gilg)

Perennial herbs, shrubs, or trees with strong fibrous bark; leaves opposite or alternate, linear-lanceolate-oblong, without stipules; flowers 4–5-merous, shortly pedicelled, in ebracteate, few-flowered (2–8) fascicles (*G. subcordata*), or in bracteate few–many-flowered (2–50), terminal or axillary heads; calyx-tube cylindric, articulated above the ovary, with imbricate, coloured lobes; petals present or absent, membranous, fleshy, scaly or glandular; stamens 8 or 10 in two whorls; ovary sessile, 1-celled; style filiform, stigma capitate; hypogynous disc, usually minute, often

† By B. Peterson.

absent; fruit dry, enclosed in the persistent base of the calyx-tube.

1 Flowers with parts in 5s   2
  Flowers with parts in 4s   5
2 Petals 0   1. *G. latifolia*
  Petals 5   3
3 Suffrutescent herb up to 50 cm
      2. *G. kraussiana*
  Much branched shrub or tree   4
4 Tree to 15 m; leaves glaucous, glabrous or glabrescent   3. *G. glauca*
  Undershrub to 4 m; leaves densely pubescent
      4. *G. lamprantha*
5 Petals 0   5. *G. chrysantha*
  Petals present   6
6 Heads of flowers without bracts at the base
      6. *G. subcordata*
  Heads of flowers with bracts at the base   7
7 Calyx-tube hairy below the articulation, petals (often very small) 8 7. *G. fastigiata*
  Calyx-tube ± glabrous below the articulation, petals 4   8
8 Bracts broadly oblong–subrotund, brownish
      8. *G. buchananii*
  Bracts ovate, acute   9
9 Inflorescences terminal; unbranched perennial herb   9. *G. macrorrhiza*
  Inflorescences terminal and axillary; much branched, suffrutescent plant to 1 m
      10. *G. apiculata*

1. Gnidia latifolia (*Oliv.*) *Gilg*
Shrub to 6 m. Dealt with in KTS p. 556. MAC.

2. Gnidia kraussiana *Meisn.* (see p.160)
Perennial herb up to 50 cm with herbaceous or ligneous stems from a woody base, glabrous or pubescent; leaves lanceolate-ovate, 15–40 mm long, 4–12 mm wide, quite glabrous to densely pubescent; flowers in terminal heads, bracts foliaceous, lanceolate or ovate, calyx-tube pubescent outside and with long white silky hairs at the base.

A very variable plant ('Yellow-heads') found in grassland and on rocky banks. HC, HM, MUM.

Dale 3386; Archer 241.

3. Gnidia glauca (*Fres.*) *Gilg*
Shrub or tree to 15 m. Dealt with in KTS p. 556. HE, HC, HM, HA, HK.

4. Gnidia lamprantha *Gilg*
Shrub or tree to 5 m. Dealt with in KTS p. 556. HC, KIT, KIS.

5. Gnidia chrysantha (*Solms*) *Gilg* (see p. 160)
A glabrous perennial plant up to 60 cm, stems erect, sparingly branched; leaves linear, 10–25 mm long; flowers bright yellow, capitate, terminal,

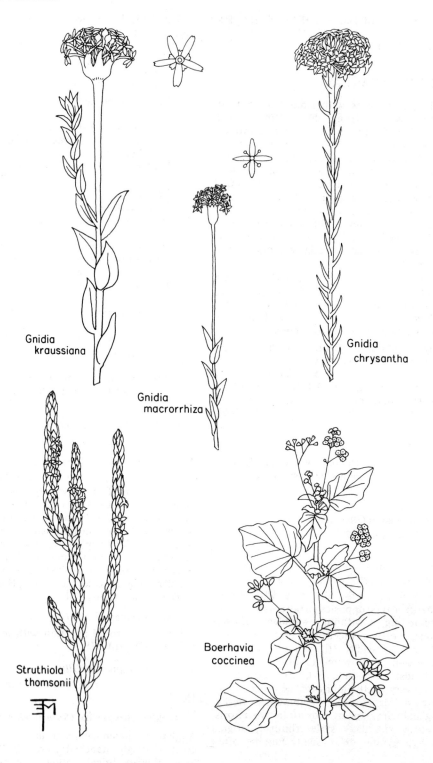

Gnidia
kraussiana

Gnidia
macrorrhiza

Gnidia
chrysantha

Struthiola
thomsonii

Boerhavia
coccinea

with ovate to lanceolate bracts, calyx-tube glabrous below the articulation, pubescent or glabrous above.

Rather common in vlei land. KIT.
Jex-Blake 1402; Symes 382.

6. Gnidia subcordata *Meisn.*

Much branched shrub up to 3·5 m. Dealt with in KTS p. 555. HT, HM, HL, HA, NAR, RV, NAN, NBI, KAJ.

7. Gnidia fastigiata *Rendle*

A low, shrubby herb with numerous little-branched stems from a woody base; leaves silky-hairy or glabrescent, linear-lanceolate; inflorescences with 1–3 cream or pale blue flowers.

Not uncommon in montane and subalpine grassland, 6000–9000 ft. HC, HT, HA.
Napier 1976; Irwin 231.

8. Gnidia buchananii *Gilg*

Suffrutescent plant with branched, glabrous stems to 50 cm; leaves 8–25 mm long, 2–5 mm wide, glabrous; inflorescences with 25–40 yellow flowers, bracts usually 5, quite glabrous, calyx-tube sparingly pubescent or glabrous above the articulation.

Rather common in grasslands. HC, RV, MAC, KAJ.
Ossent 283; Bally 11443.

9. Gnidia macrorrhiza *Gilg* (see p. 160)

Low, many-stemmed, unbranched, suffrutescent plant to 30 cm with glabrous, oblong-lanceolate leaves and terminal, bracteate inflorescences on leafless peduncles; flowers yellow or brownish-yellow.

Found in grassland. HT, KIT, BAR.
Dale 3176; Thorold 3247.

10. Gnidia apiculata (*Oliv.*) *Gilg*

Much branched woody herb up to 1 m; heads terminal and axillary with brownish, acute, involucral bracts; flowers yellow or greenish-yellow.

A rather variable species found in grasslands and on dry hillsides.
Archer 27; Rauh 328.

41. NYCTAGINACEAE †

Herbs, shrubs, or climbers, rarely trees, with alternate or opposite simple exstipulate leaves; inflorescences mostly cymose; bracts present, bracteoles often absent; sepals usually 5, fused and petaloid, forming a sheath round the ovary in fruit; petals 0;

† By A. D. Q. Agnew.

stamens 1-many with the filaments often fused into a cup at base and the anthers with only 2 loculi; ovary 1-celled, with a style and capitate stigma, and with one erect ovule; fruit indehiscent; seed with some endosperm and a straight or curved embryo.

1 Woody climber with axillary thorns
                    1. *Pisonia aculeata*
  Unarmed herbs   2
2 Flowers more than 3 cm long; flowers and fruit enclosed in bracts 4. *Mirabilis jalapa*
  Flowers less than 2 cm long; flowers and fruit not enclosed in bracts   3
3 Fruiting calyx with large raised glands, especially at apex, obscurely 9–11-ridged; flowers in apparent umbels or verticillate
                    3. *Commicarpus*
  Fruiting calyx with minute unicellular glands or glabrous, without glands, deeply 4–6-ridged; inflorescences terminating mostly in 3–5-flowered cymes   2. *Boerhavia*

1. PISONIA *L.*

Dioecious climbers or shrubs or trees with alternate or opposite entire leaves and small greenish flowers in loose corymbs; male flowers with a short perianth with spreading lobes and 5–10 exserted stamens with joined filaments; female flowers with a longer narrower perianth, rudimentary stamens and a sessile elongated ovary; style exserted; stigma divided; fruit surrounded by the hard, often bristly perianth.

Pisonia aculeata *L.*

A woody climber with large spines axillary to the oblong, acute, glabrous leaves; fruit club-shaped, with 5 rows of gland-tipped bristles.

Recently discovered in Kakamega forest. MUM.
Faden 70/19.

2. BOERHAVIA *L.*

Herbs, often prostrate, with opposite petiolate entire leaves; flowers often in paniculate cymes; sepals 5, spreading into the pink to white limb (± 2 mm long in ours) directly above the ovary; stamens usually 2–3; fruit with 4–6 (usually) pronounced ridges, narrowing at apex, with minute sticky glands or glabrous, never with large warty glands.

1 Fruits glabrous, sharply obconical, truncate at apex   1. *B. erecta*
  Fruits glandular, sticky, ellipsoid, tapered at the apex   2
2 Hairs on nodes and petioles over 1 mm long, large-celled (cells can be seen with a hand

lens); fruits broadest at apex; flowers in terminal panicles; perennial   2. *B. diffusa*

Hairs on nodes and petioles small, less than 1 mm long, cells invisible under a hand lens; fruits broadest in the middle; flowers in terminal panicles or in pedunculate small cymes; annual   **3**

3   Prostrate herb; axillary peduncles (except the terminal ones) with one cyme of 3–5 flowers   3. *B. repens*

Prostrate or scrambling herb; axillary peduncles with 2 or more cymes

4. *B. coccinea*

1. Boerhavia erecta *L.*

An erect or ascending annual herb to 60 cm, pubescent on all parts except the inflorescence with usually ovate leaves and white to pale purple flowers.

A local weed of disturbed ground in the drier parts of our area. HT, MAG.

Glover and Samuel 2989.

2. Boerhavia diffusa *L.*

A spreading or prostrate perennial herb with ascending stems to 30 cm, pubescent and long-hairy on the nodes and petioles, often glabrous elsewhere with elliptic-suborbicular leaves and pink flowers.

An uncommon plant of roadsides and waste places in the drier lowland areas. MUM, KAJ, MAC.

Agnew and Musumba 8052; Agnew and Lind 5660.

3. Boerhavia repens *L.*

A prostrate finely pubescent annual with elliptic to oblong leaves and cream flowers.

An uncommon weed found on dry lands, often in alkaline soils. KIS, BAR, MAG, MAC.

Greenway 9020.

4. Boerhavia coccinea *Mill.* (see p. 160)

A prostrate or scrambling glandular pubescent annual herb with usually ovate leaves and pink flowers.

An uncommon plant found in cultivation edges and disturbed ground in the drier and possibly more saline areas. The distinction between this species and *B. repens* is not very good, and this species itself seems variable, with a heavily glandular variety, its inflorescences almost entirely axillary, (principally coastal but also found in MAC) and an almost glabrous variety with a big terminal panicle (found in BAR). KIS, BAR, MAC.

Leippert 5270; Brown in EAH 12806.

3. COMMICARPUS *Standl.*

Herbs, sometimes shrubby at base and scrambling; leaves opposite, petiolate, often undulate and thick; flowers in whorls (reduced from cymes), often apparently umbellate; sepals 5, tubular at base spreading into a white, yellow, pink or purple limb above, at base thickened in fruit and with variously arranged, sticky, sessile or stalked, warty, often black glands, and usually obscurely 10-ridged; stamens 2–5, usually exserted; ovary with a peltate, glabrous stigma.

1   Flowers at anthesis less than 4·5 mm long
1. *C. stellatus*

Flowers at anthesis more than 6 mm long   **2**

2   Entire plant with sticky glandular hairs; raised glands in several whorls on fruiting calyx   2. *C. boissieri*

Plant without sticky glandular hairs; fruiting calyx with only one apical whorl of raised glands   **3**

3   Flowers pink, purple, or magenta
3. *C. pedunculosus*

Flowers white or cream   4. *C. plumbagineus*

1. Commicarpus stellatus (*Wight*) *Berhaut*

A perennial pubescent (sometimes glandular) trailing herb with ovate leaves and white flowers.

A common plant in dry bush country especially in eastern Kenya. BAR, MAG, MAC, KAJ.

Bogdan 411; Hanid 566.

2. Commicarpus boissieri (*Heim.*) *Cuf.*

An erect or prostrate, densely glandular, pubescent perennial herb to 40 cm tall; with ovate to suborbicular leaves and purple flowers.

A sharply defined species which is extremely sticky all over and which grows in drier bushland. BAR, MAC, KAJ.

Verdcourt 1491.

3. Commicarpus pedunculosus (*A. Rich.*) *Cuf.*

A shortly pubescent trailing herb, sometimes scrambling or with ascending branches to 50 cm, with ovate to suborbicular leaves and magenta flowers.

A common plant of thickets and riverine areas in the dry country of eastern Kenya. HA, NAR, RV, NAN, EMB, MAC, NBI, KAJ.

Hanid and Kiniaruh 763; Glover, Gwynne and Samuel 818.

4. Commicarpus plumbagineus (*Cav.*) *Standl.*

Similar to *C. pedunculosus* in habit but with white flowers and stalked glands on the fruit.

This species is found in similar situations to, but often in drier regions than *C. pedunculosus*, and it appears to be the more common of the two in the Rift Valley. MUM, KIS, BAR, RV, EMB, MAC, KAJ.

Hanid and Kiniaruh 750; Glover 4035.

4. MIRABILIS *L.*

Much-branched herbs with opposite simple leaves; inflorescence of terminal ± crowded cymes; flowers large, brightly coloured, surrounded by a calyx-like involucre of fused bracts; sepals totally petaloid with a long tube and a wide limb which separates from the expanded globose hard lower portion in fruit; stamens 5, fused into a short tube at the base of the filaments, which is usually persistent in fruit; fruit a hard globose 'nut' contained within the enlarged bracts.

Mirabilis jalapa *L.*

An erect dichotomous annual, sparsely pubescent at the nodes with ovate-acuminate leaves and yellow, pink, or magenta flowers.

An escaped garden plant, especially around Nairobi, though also recorded elsewhere; originally from Peru. HT, NBI.

Williams 417; Agnew 7611.

42. PASSIFLORACEAE†

Climbers with tendrils and usually palmately lobed stipulate, alternate leaves; flowers bisexual, usually in racemes or solitary, usually with a receptacular tube surrounding the base of the ovary; sepals 5, free; petals 5, free, or absent, often with a corona in 1–2 series; stamens 5; ovary of 3 carpels, with parietal placentation and many ovules; styles 3; stigmas capitate; fruit a berry or baccate capsule; seeds with much endosperm and a large embryo.

1 Flowers unisexual; plants spiny and/or leaves with large glands at top of petiole
                                1. *Adenia*
   Flowers bisexual; plants never spiny nor with large glands at top of petiole   **2**
2 Tendrils simple; flowers solitary, more than 3 cm in diameter   2. *Passiflora*
   Tendrils bearing inflorescences or at least with short branches; flowers less than 1·5 cm in diameter   3. *Tryphostemma*

1. ADENIA *Forsk.*

Herbs, shrubs or climbers, often with tendrils, often growing from a perennial rootstock or tuber; stipules minute, long-triangular or reniform; leaves alternate, simple, entire or lobed with 1–2 glands at the blade-base, on or near the apex of the petiole; tendrils axillary; inflorescences axillary, cymose, the middle (or the first three) flowers replaced by tendrils or not; flowers dioecious or

† By A. D. Q. Agnew and W. J. J. O. de Wilde (*Adenia.*).

rarely monoecious (outside Kenya sometimes bisexual or polygamous), mostly greenish to yellowish; flower stipe articulate at the base; sepals usually 5, free or partially connate into a tube, imbricate, persistent; petals usually 5, free, included in the calyx; corona (marking the upper rim of the ± cup-shaped receptacle tube, and often also present on the 5 septa connecting the hypanthium and the filament tube, opposite the petals) annular, or consisting of 5 cup-shaped parts or of a row of filamentous processes or hairs, or absent; disk-glands 5, capitate, inserted mostly at the bottom of the receptacle tube, alternating with the petals or absent; male flowers with stamens 5, inserted at the base of the hypanthium, free or partially connate into a tube; female flowers with superior shortly stipitate, subglobular to oblong, 1-celled ovary with 3 parietal placentas; ovules usually numerous; staminodes ± subulate; styles 3, free or partially united; stigmas reniform to subglobular, laciniate or plumose to densely woolly-papillose; fruit a stipitate 3-valved capsule, coriaceous to rather fleshy, greenish to bright red; seeds ± compressed, with crustaceous pitted testa, enclosed in a pulpy aril; endosperm horny; embryo large, straight; cotyledons foliaceous.

Male plants are more frequently found than female specimens. Most species are not common.

1 Shrubs (erect or scrambling) with many stems springing from a massive green globose or cylindrical tuber-like stem   **2**
   Shrubs or herbs, climbers or erect, with normal stems springing from the ground, never from a massive green base   **4**
2 Plants with spiny branches   **3**
   Plants unarmed   5. *A. venenata*
3 Main branches climbing or scrambling, not erect; thorns as long as or longer than the internodes; inflorescences scattered; seeds 3–6 per fruit   6. *A. globosa* ssp. *globosa*
   Main branches erect; thorns shorter than or as long as the internodes; inflorescences on branch apices; seeds 15–25 per fruit
               6. *A. globosa* ssp. *pseudoglobosa*
4 Gland at blade-base on a single, distinct, median, semi-hemispherical to spathulate narrowly attached appendage; corona absent or entire, or as 5 cup-shaped parts, or as a fleshy rim, never laciniate or composed of hairs; disk-glands absent from the flower   **5**
   Gland(s) at blade-base 1 or 2, (sub-)sessile, on the more or less peltate blade-base or on two auricles, never on a distinct spathulate appendage with narrow insertion; corona absent, or laciniate or consisting of (woolly) hairs; disk-glands present   **8**

5 Blade-glands all close to the axils of the
   nerves, rarely absent   1. *A. bequaertii*
   Blade-glands never restricted to the nerve
   axils, sometimes absent   **6**
6 Leaves broadly ovate to orbicular, not lobed;
   nerves neatly arching towards the apex of
   the blade; venation distinct   2. *A. stolzii*
   Leaves broadly ovate to orbicular, or ± triangular or bluntly 3-5 lobed; nerves ±
   straight, the upper pair ending in marginal
   glands, which are, in lobed leaves, the tips
   of the lobes   **7**
7 Leaves beneath with well-visible, finely
   netted, closed areolae between the large
   veins, on upper surface these reticulations
   well distinct   3. *A. gummifera*
   Veins on lower surface of leaf distinctly less
   regularly and finely netted, with coarser
   areolae of larger and less equal size; on
   upper surface reticulations just discernible
                              4. *A. cissampeloides*
8 Flowers over 8 mm long; sepals partially
   connate into a calyx tube   **9**
   Flowers less than 5 mm long; sepals free
                              14. *A. wightiana*
9 Plants with perennial stems, mostly shrubby
   climbers; leaves glabrous with entire
   margins; calyx lobes of male flowers entire
   or finely serrulate   **10**
   Plants herbaceous or low climbers; leaves
   mostly pubescent with ± dentate margin,
   or lobed-laciniate; calyx lobes of male
   flowers long-woolly   **13**
10 Receptacle tube (between the base of the
   flower and the petals) less than 5 mm
   wide, much narrower than the calyx tube
                                                11
   Receptacle tube (between the base of the
   flower and the petals) 5-15 mm wide,
   about as wide as the calyx tube   **12**
11 Calyx tube of male flowers 10-25 by 5-12
   mm; petals 10-18 mm long, feathery
   fimbriate; leaves ovate to suborbicular,
   with cordate to subtruncate base
                              7. *A. metriosiphon*
   Calyx tube of male flowers (4-)5-10 by 3-5
   mm; petals 5-9 mm, entire or serrulate;
   leaves ovate to oblong-lanceolate, with
   acute to rounded base   8. *A. lanceolata*
12 Anthers (5-)6-12 mm, much longer than the
   filaments; male flowers 10-35 mm long;
   fruits pear-shaped   9. *A. rumicifolia*
   Anthers 3·5-5 mm, shorter than the filaments; male flowers 8-15(-20) mm long;
   fruits subglobular to ellipsoid
                              10. *A. schweinfurthii*
13 Plant erect, without tendrils; male flowers

narrowed at the mouth, 8-18(-20) mm
wide; corona present   **14**
Plant mostly provided with tendrils; male
flowers long-tubular, 20-45 by 3-6 mm;
corona absent; leaves lobed, rarely entire,
rarely (sub-)glabrous; basal glands 2, situated on 2 auricles; anthers 5-6·5 mm
                              13. *A. ellenbeckii*
14 Leaves entire, more or less peltate; glands at
   blade-base 2, sessile; anthers 6-7 mm long
                              11. *A. keramanthus*
   Leaves 3-7 lobed, very rarely subentire; glands
   at blade-base 2, each on an auricle; anthers
   8-12 mm long   12. *A. volkensii*

1. Adenia bequaertii *Robyns & Lawalree*

Scrambling ± woody-stemmed herbs, or lianas;
leaves entire, ovate, acuminate, grey-glaucous
beneath; male flowers, including the 3-4 mm long
stipe, 10-17 mm; hypanthium 2·5-4·5 mm wide;
anthers 4-5 mm; female flowers 7-12 mm; fruits
ovate, 3-5 x 2-3 cm.
   Montane forests and scrub, 4500-7500 ft. HE,
HM.
   Jackson 433; Kerfoot 2836.

2. Adenia stolzii *Harms*

Lianas, ± woody-stemmed; leaves entire, orbicular
to ovate with obtuse to acute apex, grey-glaucous
beneath; male flowers, including the 2-3 mm long
stipe, 12-15 mm; hypanthium 2-4(-5) mm wide;
anthers 4·5-5 mm; female flowers *c.* 10 mm; fruits
ovate-oblong, 4-4·5 x 2-2·5 cm.
   Montane forests and scrub, 3000-6000 ft. HA.
   R.E. and Th. C.E. Fries (1958) (UPS), a sterile
specimen. The species is otherwise only known
from the highlands of south-west Tanzania.

3. Adenia gummifera *(Harvey) Harms*

Large, woody lianas; leaves entire or up to halfway
deeply 3-lobed, suborbicular to ovate or ± 3-5-
angled in outline, with ± rounded (obtuse) apex,
grey-green or glaucous beneath; male flowers, including the 2-8 mm long stripe, 11-20 mm;
hypanthium 2-4 mm wide; anthers (3-)4-6 mm;
female flowers 5·5-8 mm; fruits subglobular to
ovate, 2·5-4 x 1·75-3 cm.
   Often a vigorous climber in savannas, forest
edges, and on stony slopes 0-5500 ft. HN, KIT,
MUM, MAC, NBI.
   Agnew 7439; Verdcourt and Polhill 12117.

4. Adenia cissampeloides *(Benth.) Harms*

Climber up to 25 m long; leaves entire, suborbicular to faintly 5-angular, pale green to greyish-
green beneath; leaf apex obtuse; male flowers,

including the 2–4 mm long stipe, 10–15 mm; hypanthium 2–3 mm wide; anthers 3·5–5 mm; female flowers 6–10 mm; fruits broadly ovate to ellipsoid or ± fusiform, 2–3·5 x 1·5–2·5 cm.

Forests and forest-edges, gallery forest, 0–4500 ft. MUM (Kakamega forest). The species has its main distribution in tropical West Africa.

Maas Geesteranus s.n. (WAG).

5. Adenia venenata *Forsk.*

Climbers or shrublets, the branches growing from a pachypodous, fleshy, ± tapering trunk; leaves orbicular to broadly ovate, in outline shallowly to deeply 3–5(–7)-lobed, lobes with rounded apex; flowers in subsessile inflorescences along very short lateral shoots; male flowers ± infundibuliform, (20–)30–56 mm, the tube 2–3 mm wide; anthers 4–6 mm; female flowers 15–24 mm, the tube 3–4 mm wide; fruits ovate to ellipsoid-fusiform, often coarsely greenish- to purplish-veined, 2–4·5 x 1·5–3 cm.

Often leafless plants of savannas and steppe, scrub-vegetation, 0–4500 ft. HC, KIS, BAR, MAG.

Bally 12351; Harmsen 6476.

6. Adenia globosa *Engl.*

Straggling climber or with erect stems amongst other shrubs from a thick rock-like trunk; stems strongly thorny by transformed lateral twigs; leaves minute, caducous; inflorescences sessile, grouped in bundles or on short twigs axillary to the thorns along the shoots; flowers infundibuliform, the males 19–30 mm long; anthers 6–8 mm; female flowers (6–)8–12 mm; fruits sub-globular to ellipsoid, 1–1·8 cm long.

ssp. globosa

Dry rocky places in scrub-savanna, up to 4500 ft. MAC, KAJ.

Bally 12797; Opiko 309.

ssp. pseudoglobosa (*Verdc.*) *de Wilde*

Similar to the above except for the key characters, and confined to the Rift Valley.

Dry scrub and stony places, 2600–5600 ft. RV, MAG.

Bally 8639; Bogdan in EAH 77/60.

7. Adenia metriosiphon *de Wilde*

Slender, woody climber; leaves entire, suborbicular to ovate, with obtuse to sub-acute, mucronate apex; flowers ± tubular-urceolate, the males including the 4–4·5 mm long stipe 20–38 mm; petals densely feather-like, fimbriate; anthers 5·5–7 mm, mucronate; female flowers 15–20 mm; fruits subglobular, slightly fleshy, 4–5 x 3·5–4·5 cm.

Forest edges and scrub, 4500–6800 ft. Endemic to Kenya. HA, RV, MAC, NBI, KAJ.

Archer 11939; Napier 3244.

8. Adenia lanceolata *Engl.*

Trailing or suberect, herbaceous to woody plants, growing from a tuberous rootstock; leaves entire, ovate or obovate to lanceolate, with acute to obtuse apex; flowers more or less tubular, the males including the 1–6 mm long stipe 17–26 mm, the females 10–22 mm long; anthers 3·5–5 mm; fruits ovate-ellipsoid, 2–4 x 1·5–2·5 cm.

A variable species, growing in savannas, open woodland, rocky places, 1800–4000 ft. The roots are known as poisons. MAC, KAJ.

Battiscombe 887; Bally 7507.

9. Adenia rumicifolia *Engl. & Harms*

Robust, ± woody climber, sometimes with winged stems; leaves mostly large, mostly ± ovate, entire or shallowly 3-lobed, with acute apex; flowers large, broadly urceolate-campanulate, the males 15–35 mm; female flowers slightly smaller; anthers 6–12 mm, distinctly apiculate; fruits pear-shaped, 3–5 x 1·5–3 cm.

Forest edges, thickets, marshy gallery forest, 0–5500 ft. MUM, EMB.

Dale 3396; R. E. and Th. Ch. Fries 1958a.

10. Adenia schweinfurthii *Engl.*

Resembling *A. rumicifolia* but with mostly smaller, suborbicular leaves, and with smaller flowers, measuring (8–)10–15 mm; anthers 3·5–5(–6) mm, apiculate or not; fruits globular to ellipsoid, 3·5–5(–6) x 2·5–4 cm.

This climber has been found near Lake Victoria in secondary forest at 5300 ft. MUM.

Gillett 16701.

11. Adenia keramanthus *Harms*

Erect herb or shrublet without tendrils, up to 1 m tall, with a succulent main stem and branches; leaves suborbicular to ovate, densely pubescent, with ± rounded apex and dentate margin; flowers broadly tubular-urceolate; male and female flowers ± alike, 17–26 mm long, stipe 1–3 mm; anthers 6–7 mm; fruits ± fleshy, subglobose, 3·5–5 by 3–4·5 cm.

Rocky bushland, open woodland, up to *c.* 3000 ft. KAJ.

Bally 8660; Verdcourt 1850.

12. Adenia volkensii *Harms*

Herb or shrublet, without tendrils, 0·3–1·5 m tall from a buried tuber; leaves suborbicular to broadly ovate in outline, mostly deeply 3–7-lobed or dissected, with acute apex, mostly finely pubescent; flowers urceolate to broadly tubular-campanulate; male flowers including the 2–8 mm long stipe 20–35(–45) mm; anthers 8–12 mm; female flowers 16–25 mm; fruits ± fleshy, subglobose to ellipsoid, 3·5–5 x 3–4·5 cm.

Shrub vegetation, rocky places, 3000–6000 ft. HA, RV, MAG, NAN, EMB, MAC, NBI, KAJ. Adamson 520; Bally 1052.

13. Adenia ellenbeckii *Harms*

Resembling *A. volkensii* but mostly with more slender shoots and flowers and provided with tendrils; male flowers including the 1–3 mm long stipe 20–45 mm; anthers 5–6·5 mm; female flowers, including the 1–3 mm long stipe, 12–30 mm long; fruits subglobose, more or less fleshy, 2–4(–5) x 2–4(–4·5) cm.

Rocky places; open shrub-vegetation, 600–4500 ft. KAJ.
Greenway and Duvigneaud 12.622.

14. Adenia wightiana (*W. & A.*) *Engl.*

A perennial climber up to 8 m long; leaves variable, sub-orbicular to 3–5 lobed, with acutish apex and irregularly sinuate-dentate margin; male and female flowers ± alike, minute, including the (0·5–)1–2 mm long stipe 3–5 mm; anthers *c.* 0·5 mm long; fruits ovoid to ellipsoid, 1·5–3 x 1·25–2 cm.

Scrub-savanna and forest fringes, 3000–5500 ft. KAJ. Bally 8002; Greenway 5990.

2. PASSIFLORA *L.*

Climbers with branched or unbranched tendrils and usually palmately lobed or divided leaves with broad stipules; flowers usually solitary, axillary, with 3 bracts at base; sepals and petals 5, with a long or short petal tube, and a single corona of capillary filaments; stamens 5 borne beneath the ovary at the top of the gynophore; fruit an indehiscent berry, the seeds surrounded by a pulpy aril, often long-stalked.

A large genus of South American species some of which are grown as ornamentals or for their fruits and which have occasionally escaped. The following has been found wild in two areas in Kenya.

Passiflora eichlerana *Masters*

A glabrous climber with unbranched tendrils and tripalmatifid leaves with ovate lobes; bracts ovate to cordate at base; flowers white; fruit green, hardly juicy.

An escape found on disturbed ground recorded from Nairobi and Kericho. HM, MAC, NBI.
Hanid 46; Kerfoot 4874.

3. TRYPHOSTEMMA *Harv.*

Climbing or erect herbs or shrubs with entire or palmatifid, (usually 3-lobed) leaves with capillary stipules; inflorescences of short, axillary, 2-flowered racemes, the rachis continued into an apically thickened tendril; flowers bisexual, often small; sepals and petals 5, free, spreading; corona double, the outer fringed with numerous capillary appendages, separated from the inner by a disc, the inner simple, connate to the filaments within; stamens 5; fruit capsular, inflated, ellipsoid, stalked.

1 Leaves simple, linear-oblong
                               1. *T. longifolium*
   Leaves palmately lobed   2
2 Leaf lobes elliptic, broadest about the middle
   or above, glabrous below
                         2. *T. hanningtonianum*
   Leaf lobes lanceolate, broadest below the
   middle, sometimes hairy below
                                    3. *T.* sp. *A*

1. Tryphostemma longifolium *Harms*

A glabrous perennial with several ± unbranched ascending or erect stems to 40 cm from a woody rootstock and simple oblong obscurely dentate leaves; fruit 25–30 mm long.

A rare plant of dry places in the eastern lowlands of our area, and only recorded from the foot of the Chyulu Hills. KAJ.
Bally 8000.

2. Tryphostemma hanningtonianum *Masters*

A low glabrous climbing (or sometimes erect) annual with tripalmatifid leaves bearing elliptical obtuse lobes; fruit narrow, to 20 mm long.

Locally common in the bushland edges of the dry country to the east of our area. MAC.
Lind and Agnew 5649; Ossent 237.

3. Tryphostemma *sp.* A.

Similar to *T. hanningtonianum* but more robust, and with an indumentum; fruit to 16 mm long.

A rare plant, only found once in our area, at Donyo Sabuk, and also known from the coast, in forest edges and clearings. MAC.
Napper, Lind, Agnew, and Beecher 1716.

43. CUCURBITACEAE†

Mostly climbers with tendrils opposite the mostly palmatifid, serrate or dentate, alternate exstipulate leaves; probracts sometimes present at the base of

† By A. D. Q. Agnew.

the axillary branches; flowers unisexual, regular, obscurely or markedly zygomorphic on dioecious or monoecious plants, commonly racemose or solitary; receptacle of flower forming a tube (called simply the 'tube' or 'receptacular-tube' in the following generic descriptions) at the base of the flower, with 5 free sepals present as lobes at its apex and 5 free or connate petals; stamens basically 5, alternate with the petals, inserted at the top of or within the tube, but variably connate (often in 2 pairs with 1 free) to form a morphologically zygomorphic, functionally regular androecium, the thecae (pollen sacs) often contorted and folded; female flowers with an inferior ovary, with parietal (or rarely axillary) placentation, of mostly 3 carpels, with staminodes often on the tube above; stigmas 3 or 3-lobed; fruit usually a fleshy indehiscent berry, more rarely a dehiscent berry, dehiscent dry capsule or indehiscent samara.

A rather difficult family to deal with since the male and female flowers may not be found together, and these have the most important characters for identification. The leaves are characteristic but in fact are always difficult to describe and often variable.

1   Plants spiny, the spines mostly paired at the nodes   1. *Momordica spinosa*
    Plants unarmed   2
2   Plants without tendrils
          15. *Myrmecosicyos messorius*
    Plants with tendrils   3
3   Tendrils bifid at apex, spiralling above and below the point of branching; plants ± glabrous, with very zygomorphic flowers, dry capsules and winged seeds
         18. *Gerrardanthus lobatus*
    Tendrils simple or only spiralling above the branching point; fruits always succulent   4
4   Tendrils divided into 3–5 branches
             5. *Luffa cylindrica*
    Tendrils simple or bifid   5
5   Leaves compound or stems spotted and streaked with darker green   1. *Momordica*
    Leaves simple; stems uniformly green without darker spots   6
6   Tendrils bifid   7
    Tendrils simple   16
7   Petiole bearing a pair of glands at apex, or on the base of the lamina   2. *Lagenaria*
    Petiole without a pair of apical glands   8
8   Male or female flowers present   9
    Fruits present   12
9   Flowers over 4 cm long in last bud stage
          6. *Peponium vogelii*
    Flowers and buds under 4 cm long   10
10   Recurved scales at base or petals closing the

receptacle tube between the filaments; flower orange and black or white and black
         1. *Momordica*
    Recurved scales absent between filament bases; no black on flower   11
11   Peduncles of male racemes shorter than the pedicels or racemes sessile; ovary glabrous
         4. *Diplocyclos*
    Peduncles of male racemes longer than petioles and pedicels; ovary hairy
        16. *Kedrostis hirtella*
12   Ripe fruit hairy   13
    Ripe fruit glabrous or becoming glabrous   15
13   Fruit narrow-cylindrical, pointed at both ends   1. *Momordica boivinii*
    Fruit broader, rounded at both ends   14
14   Fruit setose to lanate, not densely velvety
         6. *Peponium vogelii*
    Fruit densely velvety 1. *Momordica calantha*
15   Fruit more than 4 cm long, with a long cylindrical beak at apex
        16. *Kedrostis hirtella*
    Fruit less than 3 cm long, rounded at apex or with a short conical beak   4. *Diplocyclos*
16   Leaves ± sessile, clasping the stem, pinnatifid or sinuate above
       7. *Cephalopentandra ecirrhosa*
    Leaves petiolate, not clasping the stem, always palmatifid   17
17   All flowers sessile 13. *Mukia maderaspatana*
    At least some flowers with appreciable pedicels   18
18   A suborbicular stipuliform bract present at the base of the petiole   19
    No stipuliform bract present, or if present, then not suborbicular   20
19   Petals linear, more than 10 mm long; seeds rounded   8. *Trochomeria macrocarpa*
    Petals triangular, less than 2 mm long; seeds angular   9. *Dactyliandra nigrescens*
20   Tendrils more than 1 at each node; fruits buried underground
      10. *Cucumis humifructus*
    Tendrils but 1 at each node; fruits not buried
                  21
21   Flowers, male or female, present   22
    Fruits present   30
22   Receptacle tube more than 13 mm long, narrow-cylindrical; petals linear, tapering from the base 8. *Trochomeria macrocarpa*
    Receptacle tube shorter, not narrow-cylindrical; petals broader   23
23   Flowers white, turning yellow with age
           14. *Zehneria*
    Flowers yellow or green   24
24   Disc at base of receptacle tube prominent, free from tube laterally and elevated and

subglobose or obconic in the male flower, forming a ring around the style in the female flower; stems rough hispid-hairy; male flowers solitary or fascicled   **25**

Disc not as above, obscure and **not** distinct from the walls of the ovary; stems usually not hispid-hairy but if so then male flowers in pedunculate racemes   **27**

25 At least the growing points with stiff brown hairs   *11. Oreosyce africana*

No stiff brown hairs on young parts   **26**

26 Male flowers solitary or 1–2 together; fruits often warted or spiny, usually more than 3 cm long   *10. Cucumis*

Male flowers 3–9 together, sometimes with a short peduncle; fruits smooth, often less than 3 cm long   *12. Cucumella engleri*

27 Flower from base of tube to top of petals less than 10 cm long   **28**

Flower from base of tube to top of petals more than 10 cm long   **29**

28 Male flower with a bract at base of pedicel; ovary with no basal cup   *16. Kedrostis*

Male flower with no bract at base of pedicel, or sometimes bract adherent to pedicel to half way; ovary developing a basal cup   *17. Corallocarpus*

29 Male flower with oblong sepals, over 2 mm broad; ovary hairy   *1. Momordica boivinii*

Male flower with much narrower sepals; ovary glabrous   *3. Coccinia*

30 Fruit cap separating pixidately from the cup-like base   *17. Corallocarpus*

Fruit cap not separating from base, either indehiscent or longitudinally valvate   **31**

31 Fruit beaked at apex (i.e. gradually narrowed into a point)   **32**

Fruit rounded at apex, not beaked   **35**

32 Fruit narrowed at base and apex   **33**

Fruit beaked at apex only   *16. Kedrostis*

33 Fruit stalk longer than 2·5 cm; stems not scabrid-hairy   *1. Momordica boivinii*

Fruit stalk shorter than 2·5 cm; stems scabrid-hairy   **34**

34 Fruit finely hairy   *12. Cucumella engleri*

Fruit glabrous   *14. Zehneria minutiflora*

35 Fruit globose or subglobose   **36**

Fruit ellipsoid to cylindrical to ovoid   **39**

36 Fruit glabrous   **37**

Fruit hairy   **38**

37 Fruit more than 15 mm long   *3. Coccinia microphylla*

Fruit less than 15 mm long   *14. Zehneria*

38 Fruit with fleshy protuberances and often with brown hairs   *11. Oreosyce africana*

Fruit smooth, without brown hairs   *10. Cucumis hirsutus*

39 Fruit ornamented with fleshy or spiny protuberances   **40**

Fruit smooth   **41**

40 Fruit densely hairy on the fleshy lobes   *11. Oreosyce africana*

Fruit glabrous or sparsely hairy   *10. Cucumis*

41 Stems rough-hairy; fruit often narrowed towards the base   *12. Cucumella engleri*

Stems almost glabrous, except for a few large spiny hairs sometimes present, smooth; fruit rounded at base   **42**

42 Seeds white, inflated, without a margin, almost globose   *8. Trochomeria macrocarpa*

Seeds cream, flattened, with a margin   *3. Coccinia*

1. MOMORDICA *L.*

Dioecious or monoecious herbaceous to woody climbers with a swollen or woody rootstock, tendrils simple or bifid near the base, and simple or divided leaves; flowers large, white to orange, often with black or orange spots of colour on sepals or petals; male flowers usually subumbellate, rarely solitary, often with a prominent suborbicular sheathing bract; receptacle tube short and broad with an incurved scale between each adjacent pair of filaments at base; petals free; stamens 3 (2 double 2-thecous, 1 single 1-thecous) or 2 (1 triple (2-) 3-thecous, 1 double 2-thecous), usually free, with the thecae curved, doubled or triplicate; female flowers solitary; ovules horizontal or pendulous or erect; fruit usually ellipsoid, often ornamented, red or orange, fleshy, indehiscent or dehiscent and 3-valved; seeds compressed with characteristic sculpturing in the thickened testa.

These plants usually have a nasty foetid smell when crushed.

1 Leaves simple   **2**

Leaves compound palmate or ternate   **5**

2 Paired spines at leaf base present   *1. M. spinosa*

Paired spines absent   **3**

3 Young stems spotted with darker green   *2. M. foetida*

Young stems concolorous   **4**

4 Sinus at leaf base wide, concave-semicircular on each side of the insertion of the petiole   *3. M. calantha*

Sinus at leaf base acute at insertion of petiole   *4. M. boivinii*

5 Young stems flecked with darker green   *5. M. cissoides*

Young stems concolorous   **6**

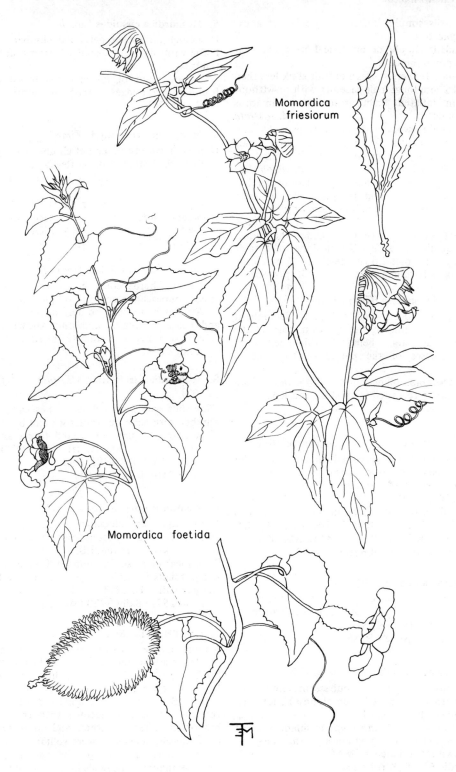

Momordica
friesiorum

Momordica foetida

6   Tendrils simple; leaflets ± rounded at apex,
       glabrous   7
     Tendrils simple or bifid, leaflets ± acute at
       apex pubescent   8
7   Female flowers subsessile; fruit-stalk less than
       15 mm long; male racemes with or without
       an inflated bract around the numerous
       buds   6. *M. rostrata*
     Female flowers with pedicels over 14 mm
       long; fruit-stalk over 2 cm long; male
       racemes with an inflated bract around the
       solitary flower   7. *M. trifoliolata*
8   Bract of male racemes longer than broad, less
       than 2·5 cm long; receptacle-tube of male
       flowers over 9 mm long; seeds ± globose
                                                  8. *M. friesiorum*
     Bract of male racemes broader than long,
       usually more than 2·5 cm long; receptacle
       tube of male flowers less than 7 mm long;
       seeds flattened   9. *M. pterocarpa*

1. Momordica spinosa (*Gilg*) *Chiov.*

Dioecious, tuberous-rooted, pubescent decumbent
spiny shrub or climber, the spines in pairs at the
nodes of older stems being the thickened blunt
persistent bases of the paired tendrils and/or
petioles.

An uncommon plant found in dry *Commiphora*
bushland, only recorded from M·AC and KAJ.
Bally 8741.

2. Momordica foetida *Schumach.* (see p. 169)

Dioecious pubescent perennial climber or trailer
with a woody rootstock, simple or bifid tendrils
and dark-green-spotted stems.

The common *Momordica* of forest edges, culti-
vation and disturbed places in wetter regions in
Upland Kenya up to 7000 ft. HE, HC, HT, HM,
HL, HA, HK, KIT, MUM, KIS, MAC, NBI, KAJ.
Agnew and Hanid 7906; Nattrass 920.

3. Momordica calantha *Gilg*

Monoecious pubescent climber with bifid tendrils.
An uncommon plant, but found near Nairobi in
forest margins. HA, HK, NBI.
Napier 5741; Agnew 8285.

4. Momordica boivinii *Baill.* (see p. 172)

Monoecious or dioecious, pubescent climber or
trailer, with a tuberous (often globose) rootstock
and simple or bifid tendrils.

Common in the *Combretum* bushland area of
Machakos district, creeping amongst the grass and
also known from the coast. MAC.
Tweedie 67/78; Kirrika 138.

5. Momordica cissoides *Planch*

Dioecious pubescent perennial climber or trailing
herb with dark-green-spotted stems and simple
tendrils.

A rare plant of lowland wet forest and only
found at forest edges of MUM in our area.
Rogers 708.

6. Momordica rostrata *A. Zimm.*

Dioecious woody perennial climber with perennial
white-barked stems from a fleshy rootstock which
often shows above the soil surface, and simple
tendrils.

Common in the drier parts of *Commiphora*
woodland areas and rocky places in grassland
below 5500 ft. RV, MAG, MAC, KAJ.
Agnew 7773; Glover 3969.

7. Momordica trifoliolata *Hook. f.*

Dioecious herbaceous perennial climber with
annual pubescent stems and simple tendrils.

A plant of riverine borders in the dry lowlands
and coast of Kenya, and only known from our
area by one specimen collected at Kitui. MAC.
Rauh 815.

8. Momordica friesiorum (*Harms*) C. *Jeffrey* (see p. 169)

Dioecious or monoecious pubescent perennial
climber with tuberous rootstock and bifid tendrils.

A common plant of upland forest and wetter
bushland 3500–8500 ft. HE, HC, HT, HM, HA,
HK, HN, NAR, RV, NBI, KAJ.
Strid 3108 B; Archer 81.

9. Momordica pterocarpa *A. Rich.*

Monoecious or dioecious pubescent perennial
climber from a tuberous rootstock, with (sometimes weakly) bifid tendrils.

A local plant so far found in Kenya only in the
forest relicts in the triangle bordered by Kikuyu–
Ngong–Thika. HA, MAC, NBI.
Strid 2571; Bally 9220 (May 1938).

2. LAGENARIA *Ser.*

Robust climbers with simple leaves bearing a pair
of glands at the apex of the petiole, and simple or
bifid tendrils; male flowers solitary or racemose,
large, the tube obconic to long-cylindrical and the
petals free, spreading; stamens 3 (2 double 2-
thecous, 1 single 1-thecous) with free filaments
but often coherent anthers and contorted, triplicate thecae; female flowers solitary, with a very
short tube; fruit large, hard-shelled, mainly
globose, indehiscent; seeds horizontal, compressed,

smooth, flat on the disc, with 2 flat submarginal ridges on either side.

1 Glands at the apex of the petiole strong, sticking out from the petiole at right angles to it   2
   Glands at the apex of the petiole weak, difficult to see, mostly on the base of the lamina, always directed downwards, parallel with the petiole   3
2 Receptacle-tube of male flower over 24 mm long; leaves glabrous beneath except for the major nerves   3. *L. breviflora*
   Receptacle-tube of male flower under 12 mm long; leaves puberulous beneath
       2. *L. sphaerica*
3 Receptacle-tube of male flower over 23 mm long; leaves usually prominently lobed, the lobes narrowed at the base
       4. *L. abyssinica*
   Receptacle-tube of male flower under 16 mm long; leaves obscurely lobed, and if lobed then the lobes widest at the base
       1. *L. siceraria*

1. Lagenaria siceraria (*Molina*) *Standley*

Monoecious climbing herb with bifid tendrils and glabrous to lanate stems, leaves with the glands at the base of the ± reniform lamina very short-conical, usually shorter than the indumentum and directed downwards along the petiole.

This is the cultivated bottle-gourd, which is apparently wild in some upland grassland and bushland in our area up to 6000 ft. KIS, KIT, HA, NBI.

Bally 7354.

2. Lagenaria sphaerica (*Sond.*) *Naud.*

Dioecious climbing herb with bifid tendrils similar to *L. abyssinica*, but with robust conical glands at junction of petiole with lamina, projecting at right angles to the petiole.

Riverine vegetation in drier districts below 6000 ft is favoured by this species. MUM, EMB, MAC.

Hanid and Kiniaruh 1051; Glasgow 46/38.

3. Lagenaria breviflora (*Benth.*) *G. Roberty*

Dioecious climber with glabrous stems and often bifid tendrils, the leaves with prominent conical glands at tip of petiole.

A rare plant found only once in Kenya at Kakamega. MUM.

Strid 2919.

4. Lagenaria abyssinica (*Hook. f.*) *C. Jeffrey*

Dioecious climber, often robust, with annual stems and bifid tendrils and with palmate leaves, the petiole glands small, tubular and pointing downwards.

The commonest *Lagenaria*, growing from bushland riverine forest to bamboo subalpine zones and in fact found wherever there are trees and water, 5000–9000 ft. HE, HC, HM, HA, HN, KIT, NAR, NBI, KAJ.

Strid 3620; Symes 96.

3. COCCINIA *Wight & Arn.*

Perennial climbers, usually from a tuberous rootstock, with simple leaves and simple or proximally bifid tendrils; flowers on separate plants, the males often racemose, orange-yellow to yellow; receptacle tube short, campanulate or funnel shaped; patals fused; stamens mostly 3 (all 2-thecous, or two 2-thecous, one 1-thecous) the filaments inserted near the top of the tube, the anthers and sometimes filaments connivent into a head in the centre of the flower, and with the thecae triplicate and often convoluted; ovary with horizontal ovules; fruit fleshy, cylindrical to globose, smooth, with a thin pericarp; seeds compressed ovate, not ornamented.

1 Leaves broader than long (measured from the top of the petiole to the top of the centre lobe); free petal lobes longer than the petal tube above the calyx   2
   Leaves longer (from the top of the petiole) than broad; free petal lobes shorter than the petal tube above the calyx
       1. *C. adoensis*
2 Leaves glabrous on lower side, ornamented on upper side with transparent hair-bases only; fruit concolorous, without clearly outlined darker or lighter streaks and blotches   2. *C. grandis*
   Leaves hairy below, and often roughly so on upper side; fruit with streaks and blotches of lighter colour   3
3 Stems annual, remaining concolorous; fruit cylindrical or ellipsoid   3. *C. trilobata*
   Stems perennial, becoming white-spotted by bark formation while still young; fruit subglobose or ellipsoid   4. *C. microphylla*

1. Coccinia adoensis (*A. Rich.*) *Cogn.* (see p. 172)

A perennial climber with a woody rootstock as well as root tubers, strigose-pubescent on all parts, stems annual, possibly rarely perennial, and with leaves ovate in outline, divided into seven oblong or even linear lobes.

Rare around Nairobi, this plant becomes very common in the north-west of our area, mainly in highland *Acacia* grassland. HE, HC, HT, HM, HA, KIT, MUM, MAC, KAJ.

Strid 2233; Polhill and Paulo 1013.

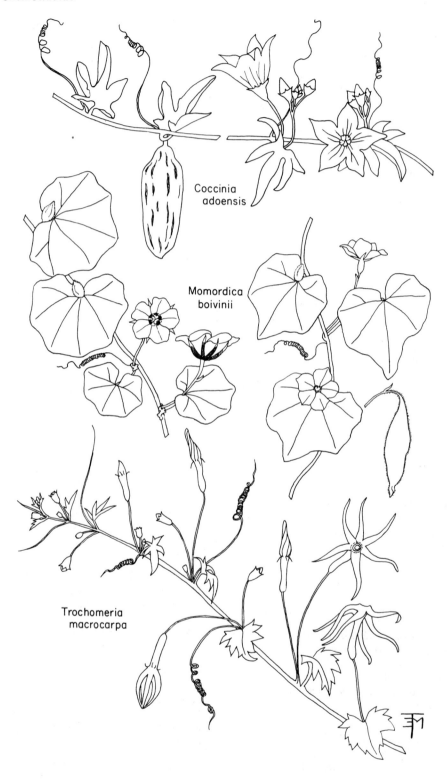

Coccinia
adoensis

Momordica
boivinii

Trochomeria
macrocarpa

2. Coccinia grandis (*L.*) *Voigt*

An almost glabrous perennial with a tuberous rootstock and perennial stems which become white-spotted with the development of cork even when quite young; the leaves are reniform, broader than long in outline, 3–5-lobed.

An uncommon plant found in dry *Commiphora* bushland. HM, MUM, KIS, MAG, NAN, NBI, KAJ.

Hanid and Kiniaruh 764; Kirrika 10.

3. Coccinia trilobata (*Cogn.*) *C. Jeffrey*

A perennial pubescent climber with a swollen fleshy rootstock and annual (occasionally perennial) stems; leaves reniform in outline and broader than long (from the top of the petiole), usually 5-lobed but sometimes simple.

A common plant around Nairobi in forest edges, and found in similar conditions east of, and in, the Rift Valley. HA, RV, NAN, MAC, NBI.

Agnew 8924; Kerfoot 1859.

4. Coccinia microphylla *Gilg*

Perennial climber with tuberous rootstock, perennial stems soon becoming white-spotted as cork forms; leaves reniform, broader than long in outline, palmatisect into seven lobes.

An uncommon plant found in dry bushland, particularly with *Combretum*. MAC, KAJ.

Verdcourt 3125.

4. DIPLOCYCLOS (*Endl.*) *von Post & O. Ktze.*

Perennial climber with bifid tendrils and characteristically shaped palmatifid leaves with broad-triangular spreading lower lobes; male and female flowers on the same plant; male flowers as in *Coccinia* except the stamens not fused in the centre; female flowers usually clustered, otherwise as in *Coccinia*; fruits usually clustered, subsessile, globose to ellipsoid, red with whitish stripes; seeds very bony, with a raised hemispherical disc and thick, 2-grooved margins.

1 Pedicels of male flowers 7–15 mm long; fruit subglobose, not beaked   1. *D. palmatus*
  Pedicels of male flowers 17–30 mm long; fruit with a short conical beak
                                        2. *D. schliebenii*

1. Diplocyclos palmatus (*L.*) *C. Jeffrey*

Perennial climber, glabrous except for sparse pubescence on nodes and young leaf bases; with leaves as in *D. schliebenii* but more deeply lobed.

Commoner than the next species, but local in medium altitude forest edges. HA, MUM, EMB, MAC, NBI.

Mainwaring 4857; Hanid and Kiniaruh 931.

2. Diplocyclos schliebenii (*Harms*) *C. Jeffrey*

Glabrous climber with annual stems and leaves with a 5-lobed lamina, the lobes ovate-triangular.

Uncommon plant found in the wettest forest zones. HA, HN.

Agnew 8737; Verdcourt and Polhill 2932.

5. LUFFA *Mill.*

Monoecious climbers with (usually) 3–6-fid tendrils and palmatifid, simple leaves; male flowers on a short raceme, with bracts small or absent, a short tube and free petals; stamens 5, all 1-thecous or by fusion apparently two double 2-thecous, 1 single 1-thecous, thecae much convoluted, the filaments free but anthers held together, exserted from the perianth; female flowers solitary with horizontal ovules; fruit smooth, ribbed or spiny, becoming dry and fibrous and dehiscing by an apical operculum; seeds compressed, smooth.

Luffa cylindrica (*L.*) *M. J. Roem.*

Annual or perennial herbaceous climber, sparsely hairy or glabrescent, with tendrils divided into 3–6 near the base, and with lobed leaves.

This is the cultivated 'loofah' which is used for scrubbing, and which is an apparent escape in the hotter parts of Kenya. MUM.

Agnew, Musumba, and Kiniaruh 8038.

6. PEPONIUM *Engl.*

Medium sized dioecious herbs with (usually) bifid tendrils and scarious probracts present in the axils; leaves simple, palmatifid; male flowers solitary or more usually in bracteate racemes with an elongated receptacle tube, entire calyx, free petals, and with 3 stamens (all 2-thecous or two 2-thecous, one 1-thecous, thecae triplicate) with anthers united into a head included in the tube; female flowers solitary with horizontal ovules; fruit thin-walled, smooth, fleshy, indehiscent, reddish; seeds small, elliptic, compressed, not sculptured.

Peponium vogelii (*Hook. f.*) *Engl.*

A large or small climber or trailer, hispid-hairy to glabrous on all parts with the leaf lamina reniform-orbicular in outline, ± deeply 5–7-palmatifid.

A local plant of rocky places and forest edges with a very wide ecological tolerance. The dry land, rocky country form growing in the *Commiphora* bush area has narrowly acute-lobed leaves and is almost glabrous on the stems, while the form from wet upland forest edges has broad, obtuse leaf-lobes and densely hairy stems. HT, HL, HA, KIT, MUM, NAR, RV, MAC, NBI, KAJ.

Agnew and Hanid 8381; van Someren 159.

7. CEPHALOPENTANDRA *Chiov.*

Dioecious tuberous-rooted climber with simple tendrils and pinnatifid sessile leaves; male flowers 1–2 together, with receptacle-tube cylindrical below, widened above, corolla lobes connate below, and 3 stamens (all 2-thecous) with triplicate thecae; female flowers solitary; fruit ellipsoid, smooth, fleshy, red; seeds horizontal, compressed with a concave disc, testa warted.

Cephalopentandra ecirrhosa (*Cogn.*) *C. Jeffrey*
Perennial glabrous climber from a hemispherical or elongate fleshy tuber projecting above the soil surface; sessile leaves of two types, one deeply pinnatifid with acute lobes, the other shallowly lobed, the lobes rounded and all leaves ± elliptic in outline.

In dry subdesert bushland and only recorded from Isiolo in our area. NAN.
Ritchie 1397.

8. TROCHOMERIA *Hook. f.*

Perennial dioecious herbs with root tubers, often climbing with simple tendrils, sometimes erect without tendrils, with annual stems and simple leaves; flowers with an elongated cylindrical receptacle tube, minute sepals and long, tapering petals; male flowers in clusters at nodes, pedunculate or not, with 3 stamens (2 double 2-thecous, 1 single 1-thecous) the anthers united into an oblong head within the tube, and with triplicate thecae; fruit fleshy, indehiscent, red; seeds large, subglobose, whitish, usually smooth and not sculptured.

Trochomeria macrocarpa (*Sond.*) *Hook. f.* (see p. 172)
Climbing or more usually trailing pubescent plant from a woody rootstock, with the leaves ± orbicular in outline usually deeply palmatifid to palmatisect.

A common plant of grassland in *Combretum* country. HC, HT, HA, KIT, MAC.
Polhill 414; Agnew and Tweedie 9289.

9. DACTYLIANDRA *(Hook. f.) Hook. f.*

Climbing herbs with annual stems and divided simple leaves, each with an expanded stipuliform bract at the base of the petiole; flowers as in *Diplocyclos* but the corolla free, small and with a (concave) disc present in the male flower; fruit globose, red, indehiscent, with a few horizontal seeds; seed with a smooth, thick testa with flat faces and angular margin.

Dactyliandra nigrescens *C. Jeffrey*
Strigose climber resembling *Diplocyclos palmatus* except for the usually 10 mm long suborbicular dentate stipuliform bract at each node.

A rare endemic only recorded from Isiolo, just inside our area in NAN, possibly also to be found near Kitui.
Kirrika 34.

10. CUCUMIS *L.*

Trailers or climbers without a swollen rootstock, usually with stiff hairs, tripalmatifid leaves and simple tendrils; male and female flowers usually on the same plant, yellow; male flowers in sessile or pedunculate groups, with a campanulate receptacle-tube, united petals, 3 stamens (2 double 2-thecous, 1 single 1-thecous) arising from the middle of the tube with free filaments and anthers, the thecae folded 3 times (triplicate), and with a basal nectary free from the tube; female flowers solitary yellow, with an annular disc surrounding the style; fruit fleshy, indehiscent, ellipsoid or globose, not narrowed or pointed at either end, seeds smooth, horizontal.

1	Tendrils more than 1 at each node; fruit buried 6. *C. humifructus*
	Tendrils solitary at each node; fruit not buried **2**
2	Fruit covered with fleshy, bristly-tipped projections **3**
	Fruit without projections, or with scattered hard spine-tipped projections **4**
3	Annual; leaves simple or obscurely lobed; fruit densely covered by fleshy projections 5. *C. dipsaceus*
	Perennial; leaves always palmatifid with oblong lobes; fruit surface visible between projections 4. *C. prophetarum*
4	Fruit without projections 7. *C. hirsutus*
	Fruit with projections or spines **5**
5	Fruit projections less than 1·5 mm high; fruit stalk not thickened at insertion of fruit; fruit usually less than 5 cm long 2. *C. ficifolius*
	Fruit projections more than 1·5 mm high; fruit stalk thickened at insertion of fruit; fruit more than 5 cm long when ripe **6**
6	Plant covered with thorn-like recurved hairs which are sharply distinct from rest of indumentum; fruit projections mamillate, ± flat-topped, with an apical spine 3. *C. aculeatus*
	Plant without hooked hairs, or, if present, then these intergrading with rest of indumentum; fruit projections conical, without an apical spine 1. *C. figarei*

1. Cucumis figarei *Naud.* (see p. 179)

Perennial herb with spiny hairs and soft bristles and tripalmatifid suborbicular leaves.

Uncommon plant found in dry *Acacia* country. KIS, BAR, MAG.

Hanid and Kiniaruh 685; Lucas 221.

2. Cucumis ficifolius *A. Rich.* (see p. 176)

Perennial herb with spiny and soft spreading hairs, the leaves similar to *C. figarei* but usually deeply lobed.

An uncommon plant found in upland grassland and pathsides, usually 5000–8000 ft in our area. HC, HT, HM, HA, NAR, RV, NBI.

Parsons in EAH 13696.

3. Cucumis aculeatus *Cogn.*

Perennial herb with spiny yellow-hooked hairs on stem ridges and major veins of lower leaf surface, these hairs differing sharply from the spreading indumentum of the leaves; leaves ovate, hardly suborbicular, deeply to shallowly lobed.

A common plant of grassland and bushland, 4000–6000 ft. HL, HA, NAR, RV, MAC, NBI, KAJ.

Strid 2048; Napier 739.

4. Cucumis prophetarum *L.*

Perennial herb with scabrid, but not spiny, hairs and deeply 3–5-palmatisect leaves.

A common species of the bushland and lower grassland of our area, particularly in *Combretum* and *Commiphora* country. BAR, MAG, EMB, MAC, KAJ.

Hanid 538; Verdcourt 3279.

5. Cucumis dipsaceus *Spach*

Annual herb with stiff, almost prickly, spreading hairs; leaves suborbicular-reniform in outline, hardly lobed.

A common species of dry bushland. BAR, MAG, EMB. MAC, KAJ.

Lind 5720; Glover 2823.

6. Cucumis humifructus *Stent*

Annual herb with soft spreading hairs and several weak tendrils in each axil, the leaves reniform, hardly lobed; fruit smooth, becoming buried in soil when ripe.

A rare but probably overlooked plant which turns up occasionally as a weed of cultivation at medium altitudes. RV, MAC, NBI.

Sydserff September 1940; Rishbeth October 1967.

7. Cucumis hirsutus *Sond.*

Perennial with a woody rootstock and coarse spreading hairs, the leaves ovate to lanceolate, hardly lobed.

A rare plant found in dry bushland recorded only from MAC.

No specimens seen.

11. OREOSYCE *Hook. f.*

Differing from *Cucumis* only in the straight or hooked anther thecae and in the fruit which is lobed and bristly-hairy.

Oreosyce africana *Hook. f.* (see p. 176)

Perennial climber with annual stems, all parts except leaves with brown bristly ± glossy hairs, the leaves pentagonal or shallowly lobed.

Common in the colder highland forests. HE, HM, HA, HK, KAJ.

Agnew and Kiniaruh 8893; Lucas 224.

12. CUCUMELLA *Chiov.*

Similar to *Cucumis*, differing only in the straight or apically hooked anther thecae and the fruit which is smooth, thin-skinned (so that when dry the seeds show through), and often tapered.

Cucumella engleri (*Gilg*) *C. Jeffrey*

Perennial herb with densely tomentose scabrid indumentum; leaves reniform or pentagonal.

Uncommon plant found in dry country. It was first collected at Nakuru over 50 years ago but has not been found there since. KIT, NAR, RV.

Glover 1736.

13. MUKIA *Arn.*

Perennial climbers with the aspect of *Zehneria* and similar to that genus except for the sessile flowers, the stamens 3 with two 2-thecous and one 1-thecous, and the densely hairy ovary.

Mukia maderaspatana (*L.*) *M. J. Roem.* (see p. 176)

Monoecious, hispid-hairy perennial climber with a woody rootstock and woolly growing apices; leaves with a ± hastate lamina.

A locally common plant along the shore of Lake Victoria in the west of our area, and also found on the Kenya coast, MUM, KIS.

Hanid and Kiniaruh 694.

14. ZEHNERIA *Endl.*

Climber similar to *Cucumis* except for the much smaller, often tubular flowers with the stamens all 2-thecous, the thecae arcuate or straight, the frequently clustered female flowers, and the usually

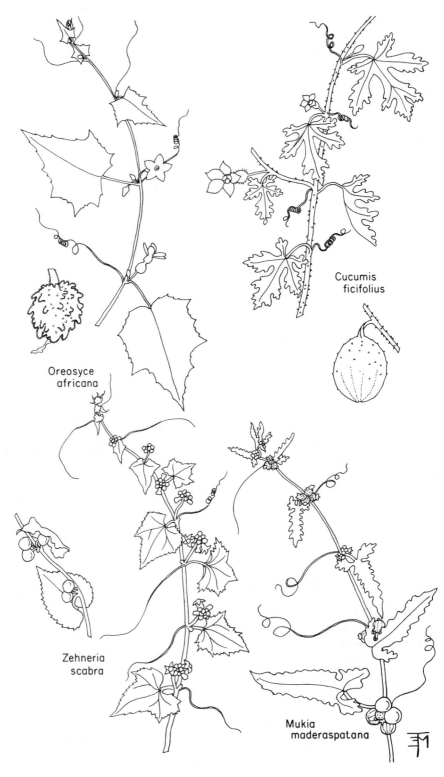

Oreosyce
africana

Cucumis
ficifolius

Zehneria
scabra

Mukia
maderaspatana

glabrous, smooth red fruit with a thin or leathery pericarp.

1   Stems and leaves glabrous   1. *Z. sp. A*
    Stems and/or leaves pubescent (sparsely in *Z. oligosperma*)   2
2   Leaves densely pubescent to tomentose below so that the lower side is lighter in colour than the upper   2. *Z. scabra*
    Leaves the same colour on both sides, or if lighter beneath then this not due to hairiness   3
3   Leaves scabrid-hairy beneath (and usually above)   4. *Z. minutiflora*
    Leaves almost glabrous except on the nerves below   3. *Z. oligosperma*

1. Zehneria *sp.* A.

Climber with glabrous stems and ovate leaves.

This plant has only been found once at Kinangop in bamboo forest. It is described as above in the FTEA by Jeffrey.

2. Zehneria scabra (*Linn. f.*) *Sond.* (see p. 176)

A dioecious pubescent perennial climber with stems becoming thick, white and jointed, and with ovate, often shallowly lobed, cordate leaves.

Probably our commonest Cucurbit, growing in forest edges and abandoned cultivation and bushland up to 10 000 ft, and often the only Cucurbit present in large areas of bamboo and secondary forest. HE, HC, HT, HM, HL, HA, HK, HN, KIT, MUM, KIS, NAR, RV, EMB, MAC, NBI, KAJ.
Strid 2815; Verdcourt 978.

3. Zehneria oligosperma *C. Jeffrey*

Dioecious, almost glabrous climber with annual stems and simple tendrils, drying light green, the leaves ovate cordate in outline, often simple, sometime palmatifid.

A rare plant of *Combretum* shrubland. MAC, KAJ.
Bally 1173; Agnew, Hanid, and Kiniaruh 9260.

4. Zehneria minutiflora (*Cogn.*) *C. Jeffrey*

Dioecious scabrid pubescent climber with herbaceous, often glabrous stems, and leaves ovate-pentagonal in outline, very scabrid.

An uncommon plant found in wet upland forest edges and swamps, 4000–10 000 ft. HC, HM, HA, KIT.
Hudson in EAH 13370; Agnew 8989.

15. MYRMECOSICYOS *C. Jeffrey*

Monoecious herbs with palmatisect leaves and no tendrils; male flowers few, axillary, fascicled, with short obscure tube and rounded free petals;

stamens 3, 2 double 2-thecous, 1 single 1-thecous, with lightly coherent anthers and arcuate, apically incurved thecae; female flowers sometimes co-axillary with males, with horizontal ovules; fruit small, fleshy; seeds ovoid, smooth.

Myrmecosicyos messorius *C. Jeffrey*

A prostrate herb from a woody rootstock, scabrid-hairy to pubescent on all parts, with the leaves deeply palmatisect into linear, fleshy lobes.

A rare endemic, recently described, apparently dependent upon harvester ants in dry country for its survival, for it has been found only on the bare ground around their nests. RV, KAJ.
Verdcourt and Polhill 4005.

16. KEDROSTIS *Medik.*

Shrubby or herbaceous climbers with simple or divided, entire or lobed leaves, and usually simple tendrils; flowers small, often greenish-yellow; male flowers usually in pedunculate racemes, with a campanulate receptacle tube and united petals; stamens 5, all 1-thecous, two pairs close together and 1 alone, the thecae straight or only slightly curved; disc basal, not distinct from tube and not surrounding base of style; female flowers usually solitary, with staminodes and a 2-lobed stigma; fruit usually solitary, fleshy, usually beaked, dehiscent or indehiscent; seeds horizontal, often ± globose, smooth.

1   Plant a woody climber with grooved, hard, stony, easily cracking bark   2
    Plant herbaceous, bark green, not stony nor easily cracking   3
2   Leaves palmate with 3 leaflets
                                      2. *K. pseudogijef*
    Leaves palmatifid with 3 lobes   1. *K. gijef*
3   Leaves simple, unlobed; fruit globose, less than 1·5cm long   3. *K. foetidissima*
    Leaves palmatifid; fruit cylindrical, more than 4 cm long   4. *K. hirtella*

1. Kedrostis gijef (*J. F. Gmel.*) *C. Jeffrey*

Woody climber with simple tendrils, roughly hairy, with stems soon becoming white- or pale-corky, smooth and ridged, and with palmatifid leaves.

A fairly common plant of dry *Commiphora* bushland in the west of our area. MAG, KAJ.
Harmsen 6485; Glover 3462.

2. Kedrostis pseudogijef (*Gilg*) *C. Jeffrey*

Similar to *K. gijef* except for the rough brown stems, trifoliolate leaves and much smaller flowers (to 2·25 mm long, half the size of those of *K. gijef*).

There is one record of this species within our area, from near the Chyulu hills. KAJ.
Agnew 9803.

3. Kedrostis foetidissima (*Jacq.*) *Cogn.*

Rarely glabrous, usually densely glandular-hairy, evil-smelling perennial climber with simple tendrils and orbicular, cordate leaves.

An uncommon plant found in dry *Commiphora* bushland country. MUM, MAC, NBI. KAJ.

Kokwaro 142; Harmsen 6468.

4. Kedrostis hirtella (*Naud.*) *Cogn.*

Perennial, strigose spreading-hairy climber with bifid tendrils and palmatifid leaves, orbicular-reniform in outline.

A common plant in the *Combretum* and general bush country of Machakos district but rather rare elsewhere. RV, NAN, MAC, KAJ.

Agnew 7627; van Someren 524.

17. CORALLOCARPUS *Hook. f.*

Climbing herbs very similar to *Kedrostis* but with the male flowers in short-racemose or ± capitate, ebracteate heads, without produced connectives in the stamens, and with the fruit dehiscent, the apical portion separating from the cup-like base in a pyxidate manner to expose the red seed-mass.

In general a genus in which much more collecting is required in Kenya, especially of fruits with the same species' male flowers.

1   Fruit conspicuously hairy; stems spreading, crisped-hairy   2. *C. boehmii*
    Fruit glabrous or only minutely hairy; stems ± glabrous   2
2   Fruit beak over 2 mm long; stems ± glabrous
                                            1. *C. epigeus*
    Fruit beak under 2 mm long; stem minutely hairy   3. *C. schimperi*

1. Corallocarpus epigeus (*Rottl.*) *C. B. Cl.*

Climbing, monoecious herb with ± glabrous glaucous stems and palmatifid leaves.

An uncommon plant found in *Commiphora* bushland. The male inflorescences are difficult to identify and a search should also be made for female flowers and fruits, the latter being most characteristic. A form with spherical, clustered fruits and short (3 mm) ornamented seeds occurs east of our area and may turn out to be another species. It should be looked for in Tsavo, east and west. RV, MAC.

Polhill in EAH 12009.

2. Corallocarpus boehmii (*Cogn.*) *C. Jeffrey*

A crisped-pubescent monoecious perennial similar to *C. epigeus.*

A rare plant found so far in *Combretum* savannah. MAC.

van Someren 105.

3. Corallocarpus schimperi (*Naud.*) *Hook. f.*

Similar to *C. epigeus* except for the short pubescence of the stem and leaves.

Recorded once from our area at Isiolo in FTEA. No specimens seen.

18. GERRARDANTHUS *Hook. f*

Dioecious climber with woody perennial stems and tendrils bifid towards the apex; leaves simple; flowers regular to zygomorphic; male flowers in few- to many-flowered panicles with 5 unequal petals, and 5 stamens, all 1-thecous in 2 pairs and one alone, the latter often sterile, the thecae straight; female flowers in few-flowered panicles, with a similar perianth to the male flowers; fruit a capsule, pendulous, dry, flask-shaped, opening by a triradiate apical slit to liberate the pendulous winged seeds.

Gerrardanthus lobatus (*Cogn.*) *C. Jeffrey*

Perennial climber with swollen succulent rootstock and ± fleshy, minutely pubescent stems, otherwise ± glabrous, with leaves orbicular or reniform.

A common plant in certain areas of *Commiphora* bushland and dry rocky places. NAR, RV, MAG, MAC, KAJ.

Thorold in EAH 17367.

44. BEGONIACEAE†

Mostly succulent herbs or soft shrubs, rarely climbers, with alternate simple or compound, often asymmetric stipulate leaves; flowers unisexual, regular; male flower with 2 sepals, 0–5 petals and numerous stamens with 2-loculate anthers; female flower similar but without stamens and with inferior 2–4- (usually 3-) locular ovary with axile placentation; stigmas 3, often twisted and divided; fruit a capsule or berry; seeds very numerous, minute, without endosperm.

1. BEGONIA *L.*

Sucoulent or subsucculent herbs or climbers with asymmetric leaves, with the characters of the family but with only 2 or fewer petals; fruit a berry or loculicidal capsule.

1   Fruits winged   2
    Fruits without wings   3
2   Leaf teeth acutely or obtusely angled; flowers over 3 cm diameter   4. *B. keniensis*
    Leaf teeth rounded; flowers under 3 cm diameter   5. *B. johnstonii*
3   Leaves lobed; plant erect   3. *B. oxyloba*
    Leaves unlobed; plant trailing or hanging   4

† By A. D. Q. Agnew.

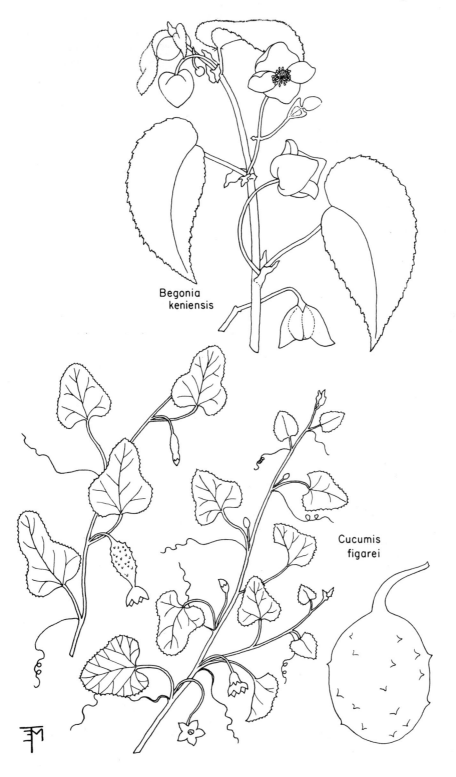

Begonia
keniensis

Cucumis
figarei

4   Leaves ± symmetrical at base; flowers usually
    more than five together in cymose inflor-
    escences   1. *B. meyeri-johannis*
    Leaves very asymmetric at base; flowers 1–3
    together, axillary   2. *B. eminii*

1. Begonia meyeri-johannis *Engl.*

A dioecious woody forest climber, glabrous except
for the lower leaf veins and petioles, with simple
ovate to suborbicular acuminate asymmetric
leaves; flowers in loose axillary cymes, white,
tinged pink; fruits hard and woody.

A common plant in the wettest highland forest,
5000–8000 ft. HM, HA, HK, HN.

Agnew 5845; Brunt 60/393.

2. Begonia eminii *Warb.*

A trailing epiphyte with woody stems and lanceolate-elliptic leaves; flowers white; fruits soft,
papery.

In Kakamega forest only. MUM.

Dale 3250.

3. Begonia oxyloba *Hook. f.*

A soft watery erect herb with 5–7-lobed, orbicular
leaves and axillary clusters of white and pink
flowers; fruits with a papery wall.

In Kakamega forest only. MUM.

Record from Faden *in litt.*

4. Begonia keniensis *Engl.* (see p. 179)

An erect tuberous-rooted herb to 1·5 m with
glabrous fleshy stems and suborbicular asymmetric,
serrate leaves; flowers 1–3 at the nodes, large, all
pinkish-white.

A rather rare plant of highland waterfalls where
it is continually wetted by spray. It is found in the
wet highland forest area and also at the Chania
Falls, Thika. HE, HK, MAC.

Agnew 7727; Battiscombe 136.

5. Begonia johnstonii *Oliv.*

Similar to *B. keniensis* but smaller throughout.

Rare plant found in wet riversides. NAR.

Bally 8038.

45. CACTACEAE †

Usually fleshy xerophytes with reduced leaves and
stems modified for water storage, usually spiny;
leaves entire, often modified to spines, exstipulate;
flowers usually solitary or in racemes or spikes,
bisexual, regular or zygomorphic; perianth usually
at apex of a receptacle-tube, usually of numerous
free parts showing a transition from green to
petaloid; stamens numerous; ovary inferior, of 2 to

† By A. D. Q. Agnew.

many carpels with parietal placentation, the ovules
on long, often branched funicles; style simple;
fruit a berry; seeds without endosperm.

1   Epiphyte; stem unarmed
                           1. *Rhipsalis baccifera*
    Herb or shrub; stem spiny, flattened
                           2. *Opuntia vulgaris*

1. RHIPSALIS *Gaert.*

Pendulous or erect epiphytes with cylindrical,
fleshy stems, tiny leaves and no·spines; flowers in
terminal spikes; outer perianth segments very
short, usually 3; inner perianth segments 6–10,
oblong; stamens about 20; ovary glabrous; stigma
4-lobed; fruit a small translucent berry.

Rhipsalis baccifera (*J. Mill.*) *Stearn*

A glabrous hanging epiphyte with narrow (to
6 mm diameter) stems and sessile pink flowers in
terminal spikes.

Rather a local epiphyte, but one which could
turn up anywhere in the upland forest area. HM,
HA, HK, KIS, NAR, NBI, KAJ.

Agnew 7798.

2. OPUNTIA *L.*

Fleshy succulents with terete, cylindrical or
flattened, spiny stems, without deep grooves and
ridges; leaves present, soon falling, linear to triangular; flowers with spiny ovary, many yellow
perianth segments and slightly zygomorphic
stamens; fruit a pear-shaped berry.

Opuntia vulgaris *L.*

Succulent shrub to 2·5 m, with flattened, jointed
stems, glabrous except for the tuft of hairs at the
base of each group of spines; flowers to 10 cm
long, yellow.

Introduced from Central America and occasionally escaped in dry ranching land. MAC.

Verdcourt 2623.

46. MELASTOMATACEAE‡

Trees, shrubs, or herbs with opposite simple exstipulate leaves usually with 3–7 parallel nerves;
inflorescence cymose or paniculate or flowers solitary; flowers usually regular, sometimes zygomorphic, with a receptacular tube at base which
may be partially fused to the ovary; sepals and
petals 4–5 from the top of the receptacle tube,
free; petals contort; stamens usually twice petal
number, with 2-celled, usually porose anthers, and
characteristic kneed or tubercled filaments; ovary
superior, often 5-celled, with axile placentation
and small seeds, rarely 1-celled; style and stigma 1,

‡ By A. D. Q. Agnew.

the latter capitate; fruit usually a dry capsule, rarely fleshy.

1 Flowers in a capitulum enclosed by woody persistent bracts
                           3. Tristemma incompletum
   Flowers not sessile in a capitulum, not enclosed in woody persistent bracts   **2**
2 Annual plants; stamens all similar
                           1. Antherotoma naudinii
   Perennials or annuals; stamens in 2 series, 4–5 large alternating with 4–5 small
                           2. Dissotis

1. ANTHEROTOMA *Hook. f.*

Herbs with square stems and leaves with 3–5 parallel nerves; flowers in condensed terminal dichasia; receptacle tube broadly fused to ovary to half-way or more; sepals 4–5, persistent; petals 4–5, pink to purple; stamens 8–10, all similar, all with 2 small lobes at the knee; ovary with a ring of bristles at tip; fruit and seeds as in *Dissotis*.

Antherotoma naudinii *Hook. f.* (see p. 189)

Annual herb with stiff, bristly, white hairs and ovate to lanceolate leaves; cymes almost sessile, of pink flowers.

A common plant of western Kenya, particularly the northern part of our area on shallow soils. HC, HM, KIT, MUM, KIS.
Agnew and Musumba 8568.

2. DISSOTIS *Benth.*

Herbs, shrubs, or rarely trees with square stems and leaves with 3–5 parallel nerves; inflorescences dichasially cymose or flowers solitary; receptacle tube cylindrical, simple- or stellate-hairy; sepals 4–5, deciduous or persistent; petals 4–5, usually blue to purple; stamens 8 or 10, all equal or 5 with long and 5 with short knees or with differently shaped knees on the filament, often all held in one plane so that the flower appears zygomorphic; receptacle tube fused to the ovary at base by 5 septa; ovary with 4–5 loculi, bristly-hairy above; fruit a censer capsule opening apically; seeds small, reniform in outline, smooth.

1 Flowers solitary; receptacle tube over 8 mm long   *1. D. speciosa*
   Flowers numerous in variously arranged inflorescences; receptacle tube under 8 mm long   **2**
2 Inflorescence subcapitate; flowers 4-merous and overtopped by the subtending leaves
                                       2. D. debilis
   Inflorescence elongate, the flowers mostly 5-merous, not overtopped by the subtending leaves or if so then flowers at

different levels, not in a globular or flat-topped head   **3**
3 Leaves parallel-sided, white-canescent on the lower side; receptacle-tube very shortly stellate-hairy; sepals persistent in fruit
                                       3. D. canescens
   Leaves ovate to lanceolate, not parallel-sided, hairy but not canescent on the lower side; receptacle-tube with simple hairs or conspicuously stellate-bristly, the bristles on lobes and protuberances; sepals deciduous in fruit   **4**
4 Stem with long spreading bristles
                                       4. D. senegambiensis
   Stem ± adpressed pubescent   *5. D. brazzae*

1. Dissotis speciosa *Taub.* (see p. 182)

A sericeous erect shrub with lanceolate subsessile leaves and solitary vivid blue-purple flowers.

A local plant of streamsides and marshes in west Kenya only. HE, KIT, MUM, KIS, NAR.
Tweedie, January 1966; Glover 2296.

2. Dissotis debilis (*Sond.*) *Triana*

An erect annual with adpressed or ascending hairs and lanceolate (to rarely ovate) leaves; inflorescence sub-capitate with 4 sessile cymes in the 2 upper pairs of leaves; flowers blue-purple.

A rare plant of grassland, where it has been found under medium to dry conditions at the coast and in KIT.
Brodhurst-Hill 367.

3. Dissotis canescens (*Graham*) *Hook. f.* (*D. incana* Triana) (see p. 182)

A pubescent perennial from a woody rootstock, with oblong-linear leaves; inflorescence a panicle of pedunculate cymes of sub-sessile purple flowers.

A common plant of burnt grassland in the Kitale region. HE, HC, HT, KIT, KIS.
Tweedie, January 1966; Symes 6200.

4. Dissotis senegambiensis (*Guill. & Perr.*) *Triana* (see p. 182)

An erect bristly annual or perennial herb with lanceolate to linear or even ovate leaves, cymes almost sessile to pedunculate at apices with shortly pedicellate purple flowers.

Our commonest *Dissotis*, turning up all over our area at medium altitudes (4000–8000 ft) usually on pathsides and in disturbed grasslands on basement complex rocks. It is also found by the hot springs and steam jets in the Rift Valley. HC, HT, HM, HA, HK, KIT, MUM, KIS, NAR, RV, EMB, MAC.
Strid 2822; Napier 10850.

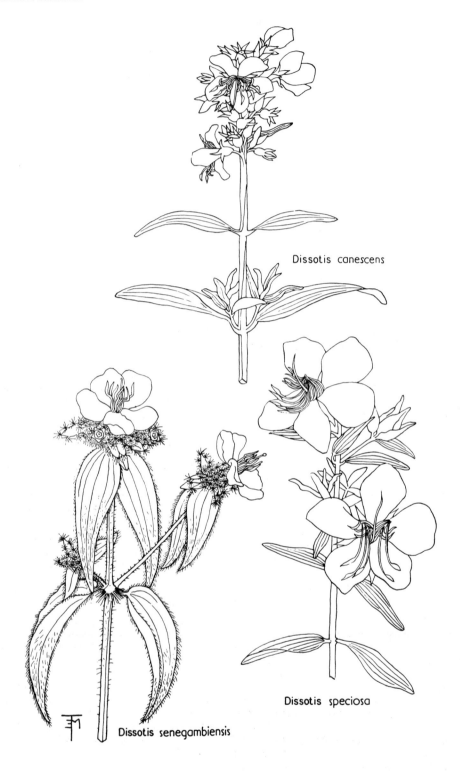

Dissotis canescens

Dissotis senegambiensis

Dissotis speciosa

5. Dissotis brazzae *Cogn.*

An erect pubescent perennial herb with broad ovate-elliptic leaves; inflorescence a paniculate raceme of pedunculate cymes with subsessile purple flowers.

Common in waste ground, forest edges, and grassland near Kakamega and towards Kitale. KIT, MUM.

Strid 3380; Webster 8750.

3. TRISTEMMA *Juss.*

Shrubs or herbs with vegetative and floral characteristics of *Dissotis* except for the inflorescence which is a capitulum of sessile flowers surrounded by 2 pairs of persistent hard woody bracts, the stamens which are all similar with the tuberculae at the 'knee' very close to the anther, and the ovary which adheres broadly (not by 5 septa) to the receptacle tube and which is not 5-valved but bursts irregularly in fruit.

Tristemma incompletum *R. Br.*

An erect stiff-haired short-lived soft shrub or herb with broad-elliptic leaves and subsessile heads of pink flowers.

An uncommon plant found in low-lying swamps in west Kenya. MUM.

Graham 62; Agnew and Musumba 8601.

47. COMBRETACEAE†

Trees, shrubs, or climbers with opposite simple exstipulate leaves; flowers in racemes, bisexual; receptacle often forming a tube; sepals 4–8, valvate; petals 0–5, small; stamens 4–10, in two series; ovary inferior, 1-locular, with a simple style and 2–6 pendulous ovules from the apex of the loculus; fruit often 1-seeded, winged, rarely dehiscent; seeds without endosperm.

A large family of tropical trees and shrubs which are dealt with in KTS. The only species remaining for us to consider are the climbers in the genus *Combretum*. Some of these occasionally grow as shrubs and so are described in KTS. Here therefore all climbing and scrambling species are keyed out but only those which do not appear in KTS are described.

1. COMBRETUM *Loefl.*

Shrubs, trees, or climbers with usually hairy leaves; flowers 4–5-merous, with or without a well-developed receptacle-tube which is often constricted above the basal nectary; stamens 8–10, in two whorls; ovary 1-celled with 2–6 ovules; fruit

indehiscent, usually 4–5-winged but sometimes merely angled.

Key to Upland Kenya climbers only :

1   Plant climbing by means of hooked, thorny, persistent petioles; flowers 5-merous; fruits 5-winged   2

    Plant twining, without hooks; flowers 4-merous; fruits 4-winged   3

2   Racemes with a few leaves at base bearing axillary flowers; fruit to 18 mm long   *1. C. aculeatum*

    Racemes without bracts or leaves, usually on leafless shoots; fruit over 20 mm long   *2. C. mossambicense*

3   Flowers with red petals and stamens protruding out of a receptacle-tube at least 5 mm long; fruits 2–3 cm long   *3. C. paniculatum*

    Flowers yellow-white, without a tube; fruits less than 1·7 cm long   *4. C. padoides*

1. Combretum aculeatum *Vent.*

Described in KTS p. 141. BAR, EMB, MAC, KAJ.

2. Combretum mossambicense (*Klotzsch*) *Engl.*

A pubescent shrub or loose climber with ovate-elliptic rounded leaves and racemes of crowded green, cream-pink or even crimson flowers.

A plant of *Commiphora* bushland, especially along water courses. KAJ.

Bally 1053.

3. Combretum paniculatum *Vent* (see p. 184)

A twining, woody climber with opposite leaves and glabrous or pubescent stems; racemes borne in axillary panicles on pendulous, non-twining branches; flowers red and very showy.

A local but most impressive plant, usually growing in riverine forest at lower altitudes but not at the Coast. HA, MUM, EMB, MAC, KAJ.

Agnew and Hanid 7526; Dale 3197.

4. Combretum padoides *Engl. & Diels*

Described in KTS p. 146. KAJ (Loitokitok).

48. HYPERICACEAE‡

Herbs, shrubs, or trees with opposite or rarely alternate simple exstipulate leaves, often glanddotted; inflorescence cymose or flowers solitary; flowers regular, bisexual; sepals 5, often glandular, free, without a tube at base; petals 5, free; stamens

† By A. D. Q. Agnew.

‡ By A. D. Q. Agnew.

Combretum paniculatum

Triumfetta rhomboidea

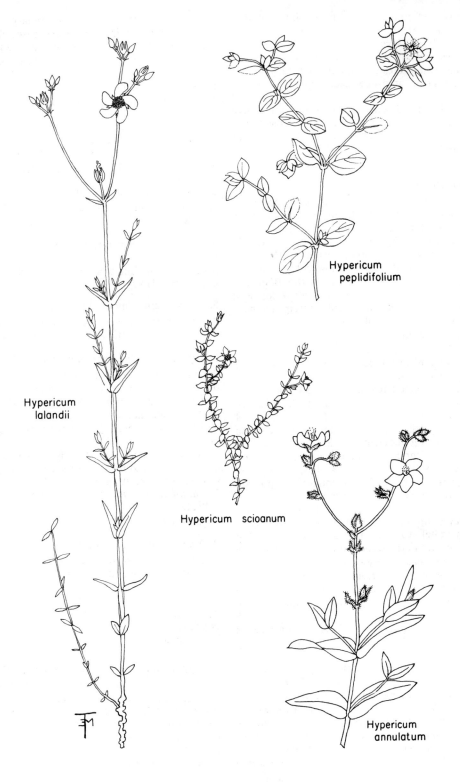

Hypericum
peplidifolium

Hypericum
lalandii

Hypericum   scioanum

Hypericum
annulatum

numerous, indefinite, often united into bundles opposite the sepals; anthers with 4 pollen sacs; ovary usually of 5 carpels, fused at base, with 5 free styles and stigmas; ovules and seeds usually numerous, sometimes solitary in each carpel; fruit a berry, capsule or drupe; seeds with little endosperm.

A family with 5 genera of trees found in Kenya which can be identified through KTS. One of the genera, *Hypericum*, includes a number of herbs which are treated here.

1. HYPERICUM L.

Trees, shrubs, or woody herbs with opposite, usually sessile, gland-dotted, entire leaves; flowers terminal, solitary or in dichasial cymes, often corymbose; sepals 5, often gland-dotted; petals 5, often asymmetric, yellow, often with black glands, persistent after flowering; stamens numerous, arranged in groups or the filaments fused into a ring around the ovary; styles 3–5; fruit usually a septicidal capsule, rarely an indehiscent berry; seeds minute, cylindrical.

1 Trees or shrubs   2
   Herbs   6
2 Flowers in corymbose cymes   3
   Flowers solitary   5
3 Leaves rounded at apex; styles 3 (–4)
           1. *H. kiboense*
   Leaves acute at apex; styles 5   4
4 Leaves with conspicuous reticulate venation visible on underside   2. *H. roeperianum*
   Leaves without reticulate venation visible on underside   3. *H. quartinianum*
5 Leaves up to 3–7 cm long with pinnate venation, the pinnate veins numerous
           4. *H. revolutum*
   Leaves up to 6 cm long, with most veins parallel to the midrib except for 2–4 pinnate in the upper half   5. *H. keniense*
6 Inflorescences many-flowered; styles 3–4   7
   Flowers solitary, often axillary; styles 4–5 **10**
7 Leaves pubescent; calyx with stalked glands **8**
   Leaves glabrous; calyx with sessile glands or none   **9**
8 Flowers ± capitate   6. *H. afromontanum*
   Flowers in a loose paniculate cyme
           7. *H. annulatum*
9 Leaves erect; sepals without marginal glands
           8. *H. lalandii*
   Leaves spreading; sepals with black marginal glands   9. *H. conjunctum*
10 Leaves with secondary nerves ± parallel, joining midrib at base; without black glands on leaf or sepal edges; fruit a capsule   10. *H. scioanum*

Leaves with pinnate secondary venation, joining midrib above the base; often with black glands on leaf and sepal edges; fruit fleshy   11. *H. peplidifolium*

1. Hypericum kiboense *Oliv.*

A small shrub to 3 m, described in KTS p. 235. HE, HA, HK.

2. Hypericum roeperianum *A. Rich.*

A shrub or small tree to 5 m, described in KTS p. 237. HM, HA, HK, NAR, NAN, MAC, NBI.

3. Hypericum quartinianum *A. Rich.*

A shrub to 5 m, described in KTS p. 237. HC, HE, HM, KIT.

4. Hypericum revolutum *Vahl* (*H. lanceolatum* Lam.)

A shrub or medium tree to 13 m, described in KTS p. 235. HE, HA, HK.

5. Hypericum keniense *Schweinf.*

A shrub or medium tree to 13 m, described in KTS p. 235. HE, HA, HK.

6. Hypericum afromontanum *Bullock*

Perennial pubescent to glabrescent herb with oblong-elliptic to lanceolate leaves; flowers few in a dense head supported by bracts with marginal stalked black glands forming a ring round the stem at their base; petals yellow with black glandular dots.

A rare endemic of Mt. Elgon and Mt. Kenya growing above 9000 ft in grassland. This may turn out to be merely a form of the next species, *H. annulatum*, when more material has been collected.

Gardner 2259.

7. Hypericum annulatum *Moris* (see p. 185)

A minutely pubescent perennial herb with ovate to lanceolate leaves and flowers in lax corymbs with very much reduced glandular-hairy bracts.

Locally common on sandy grassland, 3500–8000 ft. HT, HM, HA, HK, BAR, KIT, RV, NAN, MAC.

Tweedie 67/104; Glover 4217.

8. Hypericum lalandii *Choisy* (see p. 185)

A glabrous perennial herb with erect stems to 60 cm; leaves to 2 cm long, lanceolate-elliptic, often almost linear and few-leaved on the flowering stems; inflorescence a ± elongated cyme; bracts eglandular; sepals 5–7 mm long, ovate to lanceolate, glandular; petals to 10 mm long, yellow, without black dots.

Locally common in the Kitale district in seasonally flooded grassland. HC, HA, KIT.

Tweedie 66/79; Symes 615.

9. Hypericum conjunctum *N. Robson*

Probably perennial, possibly weakly scrambling glabrous herb with elliptic undulate leaves and paniculately cymose flowers.

A rare species only collected once from the Narok area, and one which should be searched for. NAR.

Rammell 3492.

10. Hypericum scioanum *Chiov.* (see p. 185)

Glabrous perennial trailing herb with suborbicular to ovate-elliptic leaves and solitary flowers; fruit a dry capsule.

An uncommon plant of montane grassland by streams, 6500–10 000 ft. HE, HT, HM, HA, KIT.

Agnew 9025; Napier 705.

11. Hypericum peplidifolium *A. Rich.* (see p. 185)

A glabrous creeping herb very similar to *H. scioanum* except for the larger leaves with the lateral nerves joining the midrib above the base and the fruit a conical berry.

A common plant of alpine and subalpine grassland and stream edges, also found down to 4000 ft in suitably wet places with short grass. HE, HC, HT, HM, HA, HK, KIT, MUM, KIS, RV, KAJ.

Hanid 230; Kerfoot 3991.

49. TILIACEAE†

Small trees or shrubs, rarely herbs, often with stellate hairs; leaves usually alternate, simple or rarely digitate, entire, toothed or lobed; stipules paired, usually small and deciduous; inflorescence usually a cyme, often leaf-opposed, sometimes a corymb or panicles, usually axillary, sometimes terminal; flowers regular, mostly bisexual; sepals 5, rarely 2–4, valvate; petals as many as sepals, alternate with them, rarely absent, often with a gland or appendage at base; stamens usually many, often on a distinct androgynophore, free or connate at base, all fertile or the outer sterile; ovary superior, 2–10-celled, with 1 to many axile ovules per cell; fruit a dry or fleshy drupe or schizocarp, 2–10-celled or 1-celled by abortion, sometimes transversely septate between seeds; seeds endospermous, with straight embryo.

1   Leaves with a pair of setaceous basal appendages   1. *Corchorus*
    Leaves without a pair of basal appendages   2

† By M. A. Hanid.

2   Flowers white to purple-pink; some stamens sterile, without anthers; pedicels articulated above the middle
                      2. *Sparrmannia ricinocarpa*
    Flowers yellow; all stamens fertile; pedicels not articulated   3. *Triumfetta*

1. CORCHORUS *L.*

Herbs or small shrubs with simple or stellate hairs; leaves alternate, serrate or deeply lobed, with a pair of setaceous basal-appendages (in ours); stipules lateral; inflorescences usually axillary or leaf-opposed bracteate pedunculate cymes; flowers small, yellow; sepals 4–5; petals 4–5, as long as sepals, usually with a short basal claw; stamens 7 to many; ovary 2–5-celled, borne on a short androgynophore; stigma mostly cup-shaped; fruit an elongated or subglobose capsule, smooth or prickly, loculicidally 2–5-valved, sometimes transversely septate within, 2- to many-seeded; seeds pendulous or horizontal, usually with curved embryo.

1   Capsule elongate, without any prickles   2
    Capsule globose, covered with prickles
                                  1. *C. hochstetteri*
2   Capsule terminated by a simple erect beak   3
    Capsule with 3 spreading horns at the apex
                                  2. *C. tridens*
3   Capsule 5-valved, beak about 12 mm long
                                  3. *C. olitorius*
    Capsule 3–4-valved, beak much shorter
                                  4. *C. trilocularis*

1. Corchorus hochstetteri *Milne-Redh.*

Erect hirsute annual herb with lanceolate to narrowly obovate leaves; inflorescences of 1–3 yellow flowers in cymes subopposite the leaves.

A plant of seasonally wet black-cotton soils, often found near rivers. It is easily identified by its echinate fruits. HA, KIS, MAC, NBI, KAJ.

Verdcourt 3176; Bogdan 4372.

2. Corchorus tridens *L.*

A glabrous to sparsely pilose, erect or prostrate annual similar to *C. hochstetteri* except for the oblong to lanceolate leaves; inflorescence of 1–3-flowered leaf-opposed cymes.

A weed of cultivation which so far has been recorded only from a swamp near Magadi in our area. MAG.

Williams B 5230.

3. Corchorus olitorius *L.*

Erect glabrescent annual with ovate to lanceolate leaves and 2–3-flowered cymes opposite the upper leaves.

A plant of seasonally wet ground but more often a weed of cultivation. It yields the 'Jute' fibre and is easily distinguished from other species of the genus in our area by its 5-valved capsule. KIS, MAG, NBI.

Bally 8021.

4. Corchorus trilocularis *L.*

A glabrous to setulose-pilose, herbaceous or woody annual with lanceolate to oblong or narrowly oblong leaves.

A common weed of wet areas especially along rivers and lakes. HM, KIT, MUM, KIS, NAR, EMB, NBI.

Kerfoot 4717.

2. SPARRMANNIA *L. f.*

Stellate-pubescent to softly tomentose or glabrescent shrubs or small trees; leaves alternate, petiolate, stipulate, deeply palmately lobed. palmately veined, with margins crenate-dentate to serrate; stipules deciduous, filiform; inflorescence an axillary or extra-axillary umbel on an elongated peduncle; bracts similar to stipules; flowers bisexual, regular, tetramerous; sepals lanceolate, deciduous; petals oblanceolate, eglandular; stamens numerous, free, outer ones sometimes sterile and moniliform; ovary 4-5-celled, with numerous ovules in each cell; stigma 4-5-toothed; capsule 4-5-valved, covered with rigid prickles.

Sparrmannia ricinocarpa (*Eckl. & Zeyh.*) *Kuntze*
(see p. 189)

A pubescent, much branched, erect or scrambling shrub with 3-7-lobed cordate suborbicular to ovate leaves; flowers white and purplish.

A common plant of high rainfall areas, often found at edges, along paths and in clearings of upland forests. HE, HC, HT, HM, HL, HA, HK, KIT, KIS, MAC, NBI, KAJ.

Lind and Agnew 5009; Gillett 18291.

3. TRIUMFETTA *L.*

Herbs or shrubs with entire or lobed, serrate or crenate, petiolate leaves, often many-nerved from base; stipules lateral; inflorescences in terminal cymes or at the nodes; sepals 5, each usually with a short appendage at or near the apex; stamens 4-10, inserted on an androgynophore or torus; ovary 2-5-celled with 2 ovules in each cell or falsely 10-celled by intrusion of false septa; fruit a capsule, 3-5-valved or indehiscent, usually globose, echinate or setose; seeds 1-2 per cell, with brown and somewhat leathery testa; embryo straight.

1 Leaves digitately 3-5-partite
1. *T. longicornuta*
   Leaves undivided or shallowly lobed   2

2 Fruit to 8 mm long including prickles   3
   Fruit 10 mm or more in diameter including prickles   5
3 Fruit globose; prickles spreading, glabrous
2. *T. rhomboidea*
   Fruit ovoid or conical; prickles incurved-ascending, hairy   4
4 Shrub; prickles terminated by one to several spinules, stellate-pubescent; sepals not hooded towards apex   3. *T. flavescens*
   Annual herb; prickles terminated by a single hooded spine, densely ciliate on one side; sepals hooded towards apex
4. *T. pentandra*
5 Petiole hairy on upper side only 5. *T. annua*
   Petiole densely hairy on all sides   6
6 Most prickles straight or slightly curved at apex   6. *T. tomentosa*
   Most prickles hooked or falcate at apex   7
7 Leaves mostly undivided, lanceolate; sepals 7-10 mm long   7. *T. pilosa*
   Leaves mostly tricuspidate, ovate; sepals 10-15 mm long   8. *T. macrophylla*

1. Triumfetta longicornuta *Hutch. & Moss*

A densely golden-stellate, much branched erect undershrub with digitately 3-5-lobed leaves and lanceolate or oblanceolate leaf segments; cymes crowded towards the apices of branches; capsule globose with very numerous and closely packed prickles each with 1-3 fine setae at apex which are easily rubbed off.

A locally common plant of open woodlands and grasslands, often along roadsides. It is much in need of further collection. EMB, MAC.

Lyne Watt 1165; Gillett 16836.

2. Triumfetta rhomboidea *Jacq.* (see p. 184)

Erect pubescent herb or undershrub with ovate to ovate-lanceolate, often 3-lobed leaves, and cymes in small crowded clusters at upper nodes; capsule with hooked glabrous prickles 1 mm long.

This polymorphic species commonly occurs along paths and roadsides in upland forests, dry country, and grassland. Often a weed of cultivation. HE, HC, HA, KIT, MUM, KIS, NAR, EMB, MAC, NBI.

Hanid and Kiniaruh 937; Faden 66233.

3. Triumfetta flavescens *A. Rich.*

A pubescent shrub with branches often densely covered with small black dots, leaves ovate to suborbicular, somewhat angular or slightly trilobed; inflorescences lax, of small clusters of cymes; capsule with incurved stellate-pubescent prickles 1 mm long.

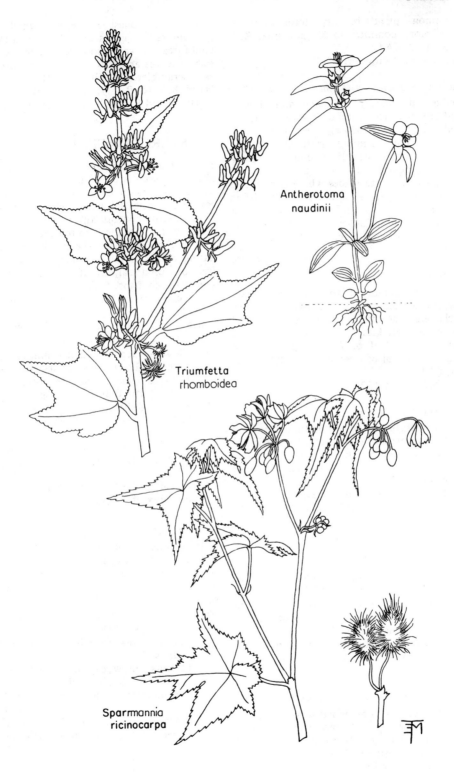

Antherotoma
naudinii

Triumfetta
rhomboidea

Sparrmannia
ricinocarpa

A common plant in dry bush country, apparently more common in Magadi area. KIS, RV, MAG, MAC, KAJ.

Harmsen 6481; Verdcourt 3867.

4. Triumfetta pentandra *A. Rich.*

Erect pubescent sparsely branched annual with rhomboid-orbicular to ovate or obovate, mostly undivided but often distinctly or obscurely 3-lobed leaves and terminal inflorescences of crowded cymes; capsule with ascending, densely ciliate hooked prickles 1–2 mm long.

A rare plant of waste places which is very like *T. rhomboidea* in general appearance. It differs from the latter in the fruit which is ovoid not globose and in the prickles which are densely ciliate below the uncinate apices. BAR, MAC.

Leippert 5070.

5. Triumfetta annua *L.*

Sparsely crisped pubescent to glabrescent erect annual with ovate leaves and inflorescences of 1–5 cymes clustered at nodes; fruit with hooked glabrous or pilose prickles 3–5 mm long.

A shade-loving plant of forest edges but also occurring as a ruderal or weed of cultivation. KIT, RV, NBI, KAJ.

Agnew 9421; Bally 117.

6. Triumfetta tomentosa *Boj.*

A low shrub with brown woolly indumentum and ovate or lanceolate-ovate, sometimes slightly 3-lobed leaves; cymes in crowded terminal panicles; capsule with slightly curved pilose or almost glabrous prickles 3–9 mm long.

A common plant of forest clearings and old cultivation. HE, HM, HA, KIT, MUM, EMB, MAC, NBI, KAJ.

Strid 2627; Bogdan 4845.

7. Triumfetta pilosa *Roth.*

An erect woody herb or small shrub with lanceolate to ovate-lanceolate leaves and loose terminal inflorescences of small yellow flowers crowded in leafy cymes at the nodes; capsule globose, mostly pilose with apically hooked prickles.

A locally common plant of forest margins and old cultivation. HA, KIT, MUM, EMB, KAJ.

Williams 278.

8. Triumfetta macrophylla *K. Schum.* (see p. 189)

A pubescent erect much-branched woody herb or shrub with ovate or lanceolate and often undivided leaves and large, sparsely leafy terminal panicles of numerous cymes; capsule with hooked glabrous or pilose prickles 3–7 mm long.

Our commonest *Triumfetta* which is mostly encountered at edges and along roadsides of upland forests. It varies considerably in the shape and size of leaves and also in habit as it often behaves as a scrambler. HE, HC, HM, HA, HK, HN, KIT, MUM, KIS, NAR, EMB, MAC, NBI.

Hanid and Kiniaruh 1053; Bogdan 4539.

50. STERCULIACEAE†

Herbs, shrubs, and trees with stellate hairs and alternate, stipulate, simple or rarely compound leaves; flowers in cymes or racemes, regular, bisexual or unisexual, pentamerous; sepals 5; petals 5 or absent, contort, often asymmetric; stamens 5–many, the filaments united into a ring below, if 5 then these opposite the petals and often alternating with staminodes; ovary of 5 (rarely fewer) free or fused carpels, if the latter, then often separating in fruit; fruit of follicles or a capsule; seeds few to many, with or without endosperm.

A family of many important trees in Kenya, which are dealt with in KTS. Here only the herbaceous genera are keyed out.

1 Flowers each less than 6 mm long, crowded into tight, usually axillary clusters   **2**

Flowers clearly separate from each other, rarely less than 6 mm long   **3**

2 Leaves stellate-pubescent or woolly; fruit enclosed within the petals

3. *Waltheria indica*

Leaves glabrescent or with simple hairs on veins only; fruit free from flower parts

4. *Melochia corchorifolia*

3 Epicalyx of 3 bracts present   2. *Melhania*

Epicalyx of 3 bracts absent   1. *Hermannia*

1. HERMANNIA *L.*

Herbs or small shrubs with stellate hairs and simple serrate leaves with prominent venation; flowers bisexual, racemose; sepals 5, connate at base; petals 5; stamens 5, opposite the petals, with sagittate anthers, the filaments ± connate at base; ovary sessile, of 5 connate carpels with axile placentation; fruit a capsule; seeds numerous.

1 Flowers pink or white; capsules awned at apex   **2**

Flowers yellow; capsules smooth at apex   **3**

2 Bracteoles clearly visible on upper half of pedicel; fruit with ascending awns

1. *H. viscosa*

Bracteoles absent from the articulation of the pedicel; fruit with spreading awns

2. *H. kirkii*

† By A. D. Q. Agnew.

3 Filaments expanded midway into two lateral
    lobes   3. *H.* sp. *A*
   Filaments simple   **4**
4 Inflorescence a terminal or lateral panicle of
    more than 40 flowers   **5**
   Inflorescence small, lateral, often umbelli-
    form, of fewer than 15 flowers
                                4. *H. uhligii*
5 Stipules ovate   5. *H. exappendiculata*
   Stipules linear   6. *H. oliveri*

1. Hermannia viscosa *Hiern*

An erect glandular-pilose annual or rarely perennating herb with ovate to lanceolate leaves and
axillary flowers; petals a little longer than sepals,
white with a pink base or pink, spreading.

   A rare plant found in dry country, mainly in
the Rift Valley. RV, MAG.
   Glover 4127.

2. Hermannia kirkii *Mast.*

Similar to the above except for the generally
narrower, lanceolate to oblong, rarely linear leaves;
the petals usually twice as long as the calyx and
usually pink-purple, and the awns on the capsule
spread at right angles to the axis, not ascending.

   An uncommon plant found in dry *Acacia* bushland, often in disturbed places. BAR.
   Bogdan 4241.

3. Hermannia sp. A. (see p. 192)

A stellate-pubescent, erect much branched shrub
with oblong leaves and panicles of yellow flowers.

   Common only around Machakos where it grows
within and at edges of *Combretum* woodland in
sandy soils on basement complex rocks. MAC.
   Agnew 9395; van Someren 4790.

4. Hermannia uhligii *Engl.* (Incl. *H. alhiensis* K. Schum. of Check List)

A grey-pubescent upright or semi-prostrate shrub
with oblong leaves and axillary panicles of 5–15
yellow flowers.

   A common and conspicuous plant after the
long rains in the dry grassland and bushland plains
around Nairobi. The large-flowered forms have
been named *H. alhiensis* K. Schum but these
appear to grade into the small-flowered specimens
which grow in the same places. NAR, RV, MAG,
MAC, NBI, KAJ.
   Heriz-Smith, March 1962; Verdcourt 3844.

5. Hermannia exappendiculata (*Mast.*) *K. Schum.*

Similar to *H. oliveri* but with broad stipules,
smaller leaves, and looser fewer-flowered panicles
usually glandular-pilose on the rachis and calyx.

   Locally common in *Commiphora* bushland in
dry areas. MAC, KAJ.
   Bally 712; Agnew and Hanid 8334.

6. Hermannia oliveri *K. Schum.*

A loose pubescent to grey-canescent shrub with
ovate-oblong leaves and large terminal panicles of
yellow flowers.

   A local plant of dry *Commiphora* bushland.
MAC, KAJ.
   Lind and Agnew 5694; Beckley 15.

2. MELHANIA *Forsk.*

Perennial herbs (sometimes short-lived) or shrubs,
usually densely stellate-tomentose, with entire,
serrate leaves; flowers bisexual, in axillary cymes or
solitary, yellow; epicalyx of 3 free bracts; sepals 5,
free; petals 5, asymmetric; stamens 5, opposite the
petals, connate at base and alternating with 5
ligulate staminodes; ovary sessile, tomentose, of 5
fused carpels, with axile placentation and 1-several
seeds per loculus; fruit a capsule; seeds with a
smooth or rough testa.

1 Young stems and leaves grey-white canescent;
    epicalyx bracts lanceolate   1. *M. ovata*
   Young stems and leaves reddish to orange
    tomentose; epicalyx bracts broad-ovate
                              2. *M. velutina*

1. Melhania ovata (*Cav.*) *Spreng.*

A grey-canescent woody herb or low shrub with
ovate or suborbicular leaves and axillary groups of
1–3 sulphur-yellow flowers.

   A common roadside weed in dry grassland,
where it can be mistaken for a *Sida* at first sight.
RV, EMB, MAG, KAJ.
   Agnew and Azavedo 9329.

2. Melhania velutina *Forsk.* (see p. 192)

A rusty-tomentose erect woody annual or short-
lived loose perennial with ovate-elliptic leaves and
axillary groups of 1–4 yellow flowers.

   A common weed in the drier areas of Kenya,
below 6000 ft. MUM, KIS, NAR, RV, NAN, MAC,
NBI, KAJ.
   Agnew 8742.

3. WALTHERIA *L.*

Herbs or small shrubs with stellate hairs and
simple, serrate leaves; flowers small, bisexual, in
crowded panicles, basically cymose, with bracts
and bracteoles; sepals 5, connate; petals 5, persistent; stamens 5, opposite the petals and with the
filaments united into a tube; ovary of one carpel,
with 2 ovules; fruit a follicle.

Waltheria indica *L.* (see p. 192)

An erect, stellate-pubescent woody annual or short-
lived herb with ovate-oblong leaves and terminal
clusters of yellow flowers.

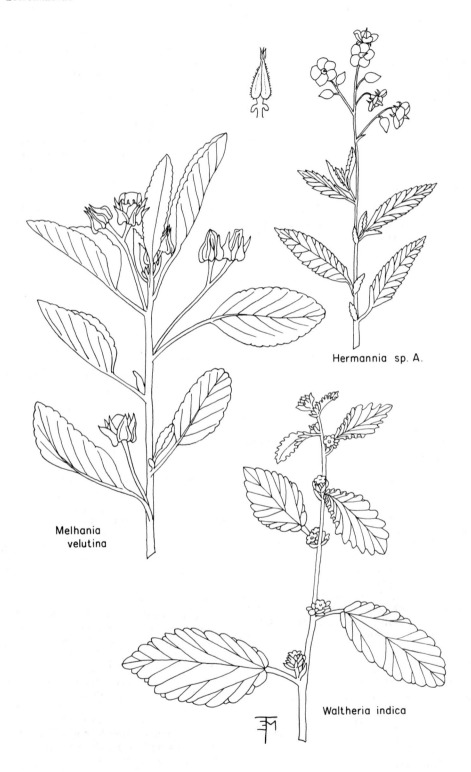

Hermannia sp. A.

Melhania
velutina

Waltheria indica

A common weed of dry places, 4500–7000 ft in our area, frequently in disturbed lands. It is very variable in habit. MUM, KIS, NAR, EMB, MAC, NBI, KAJ.

Hanid and Kiniaruh 664.

4. MELOCHIA *L.*

Herbs or shrubs with simple leaves and small bisexual flowers in dense cymose clusters; bracts and bracteoles present, linear; calyx ± inflated, 5-lobed; petals 5, free, deciduous in fruit; stamens 5, with filaments fused into a tube, without staminodes; ovary 5-celled, with 2 ovules in each cell; fruit a globose capsule.

Melochia corchorifolia *L.*

An erect, woody annual with glabrescent or sparsely simple-hairy ovate leaves, each subtending 2 lines of stellate hairs on the stem below the nodes; flowers in dense terminal or lateral clusters; petals white with a yellow base.

A tropical weed of the old world; rare in our area and only once recorded from Kisumu. KIS.

Kokwaro 1662.

51. MALVACEAE†

Herbs or shrubs, rarely trees, usually with stellate hairs and alternate, stipulate, palmately-nerved leaves; inflorescences racemose or more commonly the flowers solitary; flowers regular, bisexual; calyx 5, often with an epicalyx of a variable number of bracts below it; petals 5, contort, joined above the base to a hollow tube of filaments which is the staminal column; anthers many, 1-thecous; ovary superior, of fused or free carpels, with axile placentation when fused, each with axile-many ovules; fruit a capsule or of follicles or achenes; seeds with endosperm.

1 Epicalyx present   2
  Epicalyx absent   6
2 Epicalyx bracts connate into a lobed struc-
    ture resembling the true calyx; fruits of
    mericarps, densely covered with glochi-
    diate spines   6. *Urena lobata*
  Epicalyx of free bracts; fruit a capsule or of
    mericarps without or with 2–3 glochidiate
    spines only   3
3 Epicalyx of 3 bracts only   5. *Malva*
  Epicalyx of more than 3 bracts   4
4 Fruit a dehiscent capsule   5
  Fruit of 1-seeded mericarps   7. *Pavonia*
5 Flowers pink or purplish; fruit winged with
    1-seeded loculi   2. *Kosteletzkya*

† By A. D. Q. Agnew.

Flowers rarely pink or purplish; fruit seldom
    winged, always with more than 1 seed per
    loculus   1. *Hibiscus*
6 Upper leaves deeply tripalmatisect or tri-
    foliolate   7
  All leaves simple or shallowly lobed   8
7 Trailing herb of montane rain-forest; fruit of
    mericarps   3. *Sida ternata*
  Erect annual of dry bushland below 4000 ft;
    fruit a capsule   1. *Hibiscus*
8 Fruit of hard indehiscent mericarps   3. *Sida*
  Fruit of soft dehiscent mericarps   9
9 Fruit of 5 mericarps which are constricted in
    the middle and spreading at the apex;
    flowers less than 25 mm diameter
                          8. *Wissadula rostrata*
  Fruit of 10 or more mericarps which are not
    constricted; flowers usually more than 25
    mm in diameter   4. *Abutilon*

1. HIBISCUS *L.*

Annual or perennial herbs or shrubs with usually palmately lobed serrate leaves; flowers usually solitary, regular or, by declination of the staminal column, zygomorphic; pedicels usually articulated; epicalyx usually present; calyx sometimes enlarged in fruit; petals usually showy; ovary of 5 fused carpels with axile placentation; stigmas 5, free, capitate; fruit a loculicidal dry capsule with more than 2 seeds per loculus.

1 Epicalyx absent; upper leaves trifoliolate
                                1. *H. sidiformis*
  Epicalyx present; all leaves simple   2
2 Epicalyx bracts very narrow, stiff or subulate,
    not flat   3
  Epicalyx bracts flat   13
3 Capsule winged or apiculate when mature   4
  Capsule globose, without ornamentation   6
4 Capsule winged   5
  Capsule apiculate, the valves awned after
    dehiscence   2. *H. palmatus*
5 Pedicels articulated above the middle; flowers
    yellow with maroon centre   3. *H. vitifolius*
  Pedicels articulated below the middle; flowers
    pink to reddish-purple   4. *H.* sp. *D*
6 Calyx tube inflated in fruit, papery with
    purple veins   5. *H. trionum*
  Calyx tube sometimes enlarged in fruit, never
    inflated, nor papery with purple veins   7
7 Staminodes present at base of staminal
    column; blackish hairs prominent on bent
    articulation of pedicel and above, as well as
    often elsewhere on the plant   6. *H. fuscus*
  Staminodes absent; blackish hairs usually
    absent and if present then the pedicel not
    bent at the articulation   8

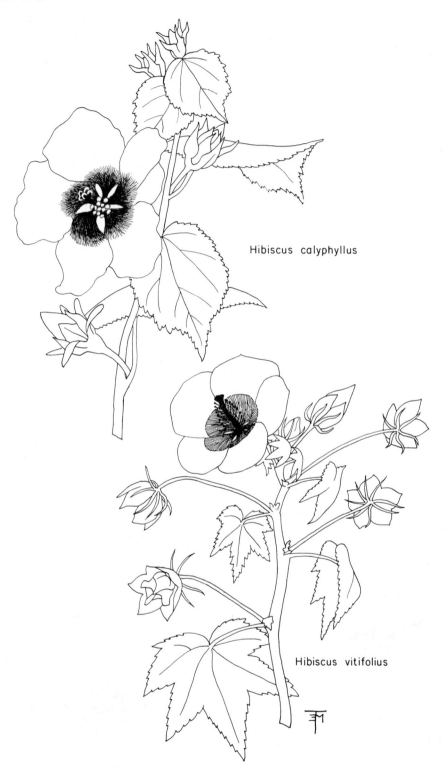

Hibiscus calyphyllus

Hibiscus vitifolius

8 Staminal column bearing stamens all the way
     down to the expanded base   **9**
   Staminal column with lower part smooth and
     without stamens   **10**
9 Petals crimson, more than 1 cm long, spread-
     ing at anthesis   7. *H. aponeurus*
   Petals pink or becoming pink, never crimson,
     usually less than 1 cm long, reflexed at
     anthesis   8. *H. micranthus*
10 Petals pink or turning pink with age   **11**
   Petals white or cream, not turning pink with
     age   **12**
11 Leaf surface obscured by thick tomentum of
     stellate hairs; calyx with dark brown in-
     dumentum at least at base   9. *H.* sp. *A*
   Leaf surface visible through a thin pu-
     bescence; calyx hairs white or colourless
                            8. *H. micranthus*
12 Petals more than 12 mm long; fruiting calyx
     longer than fruit   10. *H. flavifolius*
   Petals less than 10 mm long; fruiting calyx
     shorter than fruit   11. *H.* sp. *B*
13 Epicalyx bracts 5   **14**
   Epicalyx bracts 6 or more   **17**
14 Style and stigma over 4 cm long, almost
     equalling the petals   15. *H. macranthus*
   Style and stigma less than 4 cm long, much
     shorter than petals   **15**
15 Calyx enlarging in fruit to 3 cm long or more
                               13. *H.* sp. *C.*
   Calyx not enlarging in fruit   **16**
16 Epicalyx lobes elliptic, ± abruptly constricted
     below the middle and spreading or at least
     undulate   12. *H. calyphyllus*
   Epicalyx lobes linear-lanceolate, not abruptly
     constricted, not spreading nor undulate
                           14. *H. lunariifolius*
17 Stem with prickly hairs on enlarged bases;
     calyx with a large gland in the middle of
     each lobe   **18**
   Stem without spines; calyx without glands **21**
18 Stipules broad-ovate; epicalyx bracts bifid
                           16. *H. surattensis*
   Stipules linear; epicalyx bracts simple **19**
19 Erect annual, often single-stemmed to 1 m
                            17. *H. cannabinus*
   Shrubby perennial with spreading/ascending
     unbranched flowering stems   **20**
20 Stem-spines conical, woody, often 2 mm
     broad at base   18. *H. greenwayi*
   Stem-spines small, not conical, less than
     1 mm wide at base   19. *H. diversifolius*
21 Pedicels articulated at or above the middle **22**
   Pedicels articulated (obscurely) at base
                           20. *H. aethiopicus*
22 Epicalyx bracts spathulate; leaves tomentose
                           21. *H. panduriformis*

Epicalyx bracts linear; leaves almost glabrous
                                          23
23 Flowers in leafless terminal racemes
                           22. *H. corymbosus*
   Flowers **solitary**, axillary   23. *H. articulatus*

1. Hibiscus sidiformis *Baill.*

Erect tomentellous annual with orbicular, crenate,
simple lower leaves, and palmately trifoliolate
upper leaves; petals white or yellow.

A rare plant found in dry country, only once
doubtfully recorded for our area, at Koboko, so it
requires confirmation. KAJ.

Ossent 558.

2. Hibiscus palmatus *Forsk.*

Sparsely setose annual with deeply 5–7-
palmatisect leaves and solitary flowers; petals pale
yellow to orange, with pink or darker centre.

An uncommon plant found in dry bushland on
sandy soils, and entering our area only at the drier
eastern end. MAC, KAJ.

Verdcourt 2587B.

3. Hibiscus vitifolius *L.* (see p. 194)

A loose shrub with spreading branches, usually
glandular-pilose and stellate-hairy (the hairs
irritant as in *H. macranthus*); leaves suborbicular-
pentagonal in outline, shallowly 3–5-lobed;
flowers in loose terminal racemes; petals yellow
with maroon base.

Locally common in Upland Kenya at the edges
of drier forest formations. HC, HT, HA, HK,
MUM, NAR, BAR, RV, MAG, MAC, NBI, KAJ.

Harmsen 6522; Glover 3023.

4. Hibiscus *sp.* D.

Similar to *H. vitifolius* but an erect herb with
larger leaves and red/pink flowers with longer
petals (to 7 cm) and longer staminal tube (to
2·5 cm) on pedicels articulated below the middle;
seeds ± covered with fimbriate scales.

Replacing *H. vitifolius* in dry *Commiphora*
woodland and at the coast. MAC, KAJ.

Agnew and Lind 5697; Napper 1264.

5. Hibiscus trionum *L.*

Stellate-hispid annual herb with orbicular, deeply
3–7-palmatilobed leaves; flowers solitary, axillary;
petals white or yellow with a dark crimson spot at
base.

An uncommon weed found in disturbed places
in dry country below 7500 ft. HT, HM, HA, KIS,
BAR, MAG, NAN, MAC, NBI.

Gillett 16557; Napier 733.

6. Hibiscus fuscus *Garcke* (see p. 197)

An erect sparsely branched woody herb or shrub with brownish-black stellate hairs on stem, pedicels and calyx; colourless hairs on leaves and epicalyx; leaves ovate-triangular, simple or rarely 3-lobed; flowers solitary, axillary; petals white or pale purple.

Found from 5000 to 8000 ft in our area, this is a very common weed of disturbed ground where it appears to be a short-lived perennial with small flowers. It is also found in more natural surroundings in grassland, especially in the Rift Valley, as a branched shrub with large, sometimes coloured flowers. Further work is needed to elucidate the relationship between these two forms. HE, HC, HT, HM, HL, HA, HK, KIT, MUM, KIS, NAR, RV, NAN, EMB, MAC, NBI, KAJ.

Glover 2126; Agnew 5436.

7. Hibiscus aponeurus *Sprague & Hutch.* (see p. 198)

An erect short-lived perennial with an often dense indumentum of yellowish to occasionally brownish hairs; leaves oblong to ovate; flowers solitary, axillary, crimson.

Common in dry grasslands from 2000 to 6500 ft where its bright crimson flowers make it very conspicuous. HE, HC, HM, HA, KIT, MUM, KIS, NAR, RV, MAG, NAN, EMB, MAC, NBI.

Elliott 84 (syntype); Kerfoot 2230; Agnew and Musumba 5331.

8. Hibiscus micranthus *L. f.* (see p.198)

A stiff, slender, loosely pubescent perennial shrub, with oblong to ovate leaves; flowers solitary, axillary; petals white becoming pink, or pink with paler base.

A very variable species as defined here as there are two clear races with a few intermediates so that a consistent separation is apparently impossible. Further work is necessary to determine their relationship. The races are as follows:

1. Calyx lobes short-triangular, shorter than or as long as tube; staminal tube never more than 4 mm long with stamens present at base. Coastal and dry inland bushland. BAR, MAC, KAJ.

Napper 1260; Agnew 5667.

2. Calyx lobes lanceolate, longer than the tube; staminal tube always more than 4 mm long with naked base and stamens only at apex. Mostly inland dry grassland and rocky bushland to 4500 ft. MUM, KIS, BAR, RV, MAG, EMB, MAC, KAJ.

Greenway 9508; Agnew and Hanid 8350.

9. Hibiscus sp. A.

Erect shrub with dense felty tomentum on all parts and orbicular to subreniform leaves; flowers solitary, pink to red.

A rare plant found only in rocky dry grassland at the south end of our Rift Valley area (Kedong). RV.

Rogers 63.

10. Hibiscus flavifolius *Ulbr.* (see p. 200)

Similar to *H. aponeurus* in general, but bigger, with ovate-orbicular leaves and cream or white flowers.

Locally abundant in dry rocky grassland at medium altitudes. MUM, NAR, RV, MAC, KAJ.

Agnew and Musumba 5452; Glover 826.

11. Hibiscus sp. B.

Similar to *H. flavifolius*, but all parts smaller and the calyx lobes not enlarging in fruit, overtopped by the *c.* 8 mm diameter capsule.

Locally common in dry grassland, often growing with *H. flavifolius* but much less common than that species. MUM, KIS, RV, MAG, MAC.

Fox and Napier 6695; Agnew and Hanid 9262.

12. Hibiscus calyphyllus *Cav.* (see p. 194)

Tomentose shrub with ovate-cordate, simple or shallowly 3-lobed leaves; flowers solitary on short pedicels articulated at the base; petals yellow with a maroon patch at base of each.

Occasional in lowland dry woodland and evergreen woodland, 3000–6000 ft. HE, HA, KIT, MUM, NAR, RV, MAC, NBI, KAJ.

Agnew 7574; Padwa 30.

13. Hibiscus sp. C. (see p. 197)

Similar to *H. macranthus* except for the terminal leafless racemes and the parallel-sided calyx lobes which enlarge in fruit.

This shrub is very unpleasant to walk through or handle owing to its irritant hairs which break off in the skin. It is found in roadsides and cleared forest, 6600–9000 ft. HE, HT, HM, HA, HK, KIT.

Ables 86; Nattrass in EAH 10 237.

14. Hibiscus lunariifolius *Willd.*

Similar to *H. macranthus* except for the usually smaller leaves and key characters.

This plant is found in dry country, especially rocky bushland. MUM, KIS, RV, MAG, KAJ.

Greenway 8506.

15. Hibiscus macranthus *A. Rich.*

Usually a small shrub with erect branches, but sometimes larger and trailing, the whole plant pilose and with frequent sharp irritant hairs which

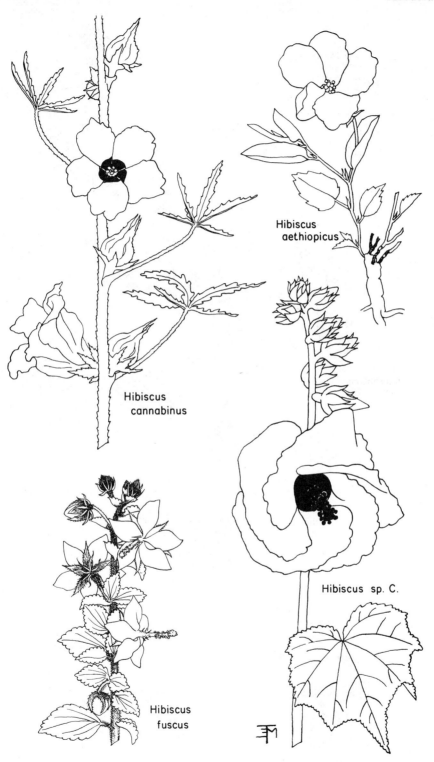

Hibiscus
aethiopicus

Hibiscus
cannabinus

Hibiscus sp. C.

Hibiscus
fuscus

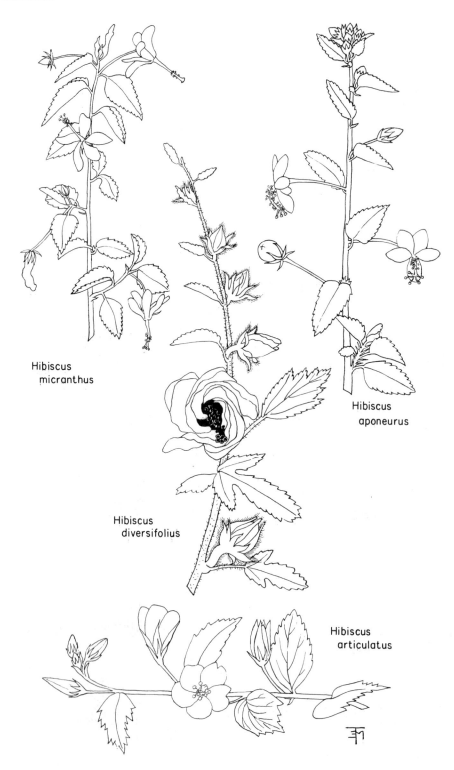

Hibiscus
micranthus

Hibiscus
aponeurus

Hibiscus
diversifolius

Hibiscus
articulatus

break off in the skin; leaves ovate-triangular to pentagonal, sometimes obscurely lobed; flowers in leafless racemes, or solitary axillary; petals yellow with maroon base.

A common *Hibiscus* with drooping flowers which never open fully, found 5000–8000 ft in cleared forest grassland. HE, HT, HM, HA, MUM, KIS, RV, KAJ.

Paulo 543; Agnew 8712.

16. Hibiscus surattensis *L.*

A large annual with small prickles on stem, petioles and leaf midrib; leaves orbicular to ovate, palmately 3–7-lobed; epicalyx lobes forked into an inner erect linear branch, and an outer spreading spathulate branch; petals yellow with purple base.

A rare weed, apparently not maintaining itself in our area, but found more commonly at the coast. HM, MAC, NBI.

Bogdan 4844.

17. Hibiscus cannabinus *L.* (see p. 197)

An erect pubescent annual with small spines on the stems; leaves orbicular, shallowly to deeply 3–5-palmatilobed; flowers pendulous in loose terminal racemes; petals grey-purple, purple, or yellow with maroon or purple base.

Locally common in dry grassland. HT, HA, KIT, MUM, KIS, NAR, RV, MAG, EMB, MAC, NBI.

Agnew and Musumba 7963.

18. Hibiscus greenwayi *Baker.*

A prickly-stemmed shrub with many long unbranched stems bearing orbicular 5–7-lobed leaves; flowers yellow with maroon centre.

Abundant in the dry coastal scrub, this species only enters our area in dry *Commiphora* woodland. EMB, MAC.

Lind and Agnew 5639; Napper 1657.

19. Hibiscus diversifolius *Jacq.* (see p. 198)

This species is similar to *H. cannabinus* but is a shrub (or even a small tree in some places), usually with shallowly lobed pilose leaves and a densely pilose calyx; petals mostly yellow.

This is, like the last species, a very variable plant with respect to its leaves and flower colour, and the woody, shrubby habit is the feature consistently distinguishing it from *H. cannabinus.* HE, HC, HT, HM, HL, HA, HK, KIT, RV, EMB, MAC, NBI.

Agnew and Hanid 8387; Nattrass 974.

20. Hibiscus aethiopicus *L.* (see p. 197)

Low perennial hispid herb, with elliptic-oblong, rarely 3-lobed leaves; flowers solitary on unarticulated pedicels, yellow.

A common plant of shallow soil or hard clay grassland, appearing only after rain, when the flowers are very ornamental. HC, HL, KIT, NAR, MAC, NBI, KAJ.

Agnew and Hanid 7515; Stewart 319.

21. Hibiscus panduriformis *Burm. f.*

Woody tomentose herb or soft shrub with ovate, pentagonal or shallowly lobed leaves; flowers on short pedicels articulated about the middle in loose terminal racemes; petals yellow with a purple centre.

Common near water in hot country, and at the coast. MUM, KIS, BAR, EMB.

Crowe 1147; Hanid and Kiniaruh 748.

22. Hibiscus corymbosus *Hochst.*

Perennial pubescent herb, rather variable in habit, with shortly ovate to oblong, simple or shallowly 3-lobed leaves; flowers in terminal racemes, yellow, sometimes externally flushed pink.

An uncommon plant found in burnt dry grassland in our area, where it has been picked up in a number of scattered localities. It much resembles a paler form of *H. aethiopicum* when it grows prostrate in shallow-soil grassland. MUM, KIS, EMB.

Verdcourt 3747; Hanid and Kiniaruh 807.

23. Hibiscus articulatus *Hochst.* (see p. 198)

A perennial herb with low, ascending stems to 30 cm, similar to *H. corymbosus* except for the habit, the almost glabrous leaves and the solitary axillary smaller flowers.

A rare plant found in burnt grassland on shallow or clay soils. MAC, KAJ.

Agnew 9150; Bally 7692.

2. KOSTELETZKYA *C. Presl*

Shrubs or herbs similar to *Hibiscus* but with the capsule winged with only one seed per loculus; epicalyx always present.

1   Stem with a line of dense pubescence on the internode, changing position at each node; petals 8–12 mm long   1. *K. adoensis*
Stem without a line of dense pubescence on the internode; petals 15–25 mm long
       2. *K. begoniifolia*

1. Kosteletzkya adoensis (*A. Rich.*) *Mast.* (see p. 200)

A perennial herb or low shrub with irritant stellate hairs and a line of dense pubescence on the internodes; leaves pentagonal to suborbicular, cordate; flowers solitary or fascicled; petals pink to purple, darker at base.

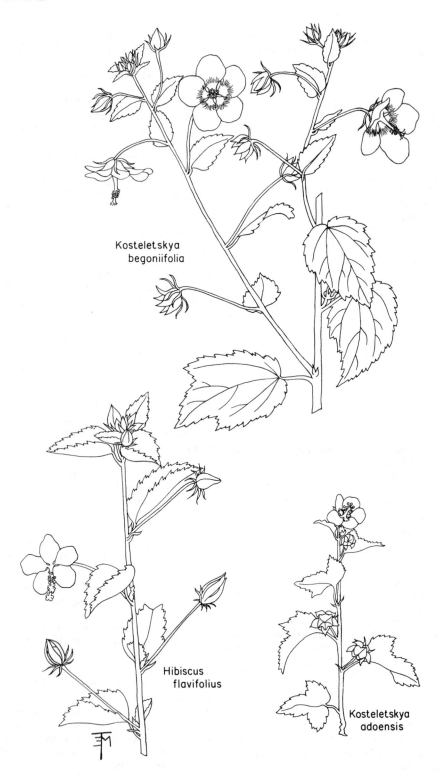

Kosteletskya
begoniifolia

Hibiscus
flavifolius

Kosteletskya
adoensis

Locally common at the edge of high forest and where high forest has been cleared, below 8000 ft. HE, HM, HA, HK, MUM, KIT, MAC.

Lind, Napper and Beecher 5509.

2. **Kosteletzkya begoniifolia** (*Ulbr.*) *Ulbr.* (see p. 200)

Similar to the last species but larger in all parts with irritant hairs and without the thick pubescent line between nodes.

Rare, found in the wetter savannah areas, especially near water. HE, KIT.

Tweedie 67/354.

3. SIDA *L.*

Annual to perennial herbs or low shrubs, with simple serrate leaves; flowers small, white to yellow or orange, solitary or fascicled or in racemes; epicalyx absent; calyx often campanulate; petals 5; staminal tube dilated at the base, giving rise to filaments only at the apex; ovary of 5-many carpels, with a similar number of style branches, each carpel 1-seeded; fruit of dehiscent or indehiscent mericarps.

1 Awns on mericarps overtopping the fruiting calyx, with retrorse barbs 1. *S. cordifolia*
  Mericarps awnless or awns not exceeding the calyx, never with retrorse barbs   **2**
2 Leaves cordate at base   **3**
  Leaves rounded to cuneate at base   **5**
3 Mericarps 8–12; leaves ± deeply 3-lobed
                      2. *S. ternata*
  Mericarps 5; leaves hardly lobed or simple   **4**
4 Calyx and leaves pilose; erect woody herb
                      3. *S. urens*
  Calyx and leaves sparsely pubescent; a trailing thin-stemmed plant   4. *S. veronicifolia*
5 Leaves entire except for an apical notch (or apically truncate) often with a small tooth in the centre of the notch   **6**
  Leaves serrate, not apically notched nor truncate   **7**
6 Leaves concolorous; mericarps smooth without reticulations on the dorsal or lateral faces   5. *S. cuneifolia*
  Leaves discolorous; mericarps with the dorsal (and often the lateral) faces reticulate
                    6. *S.* sp. *A*
7 Pedicels articulated less than 1·5 mm below the flowers   7. *S. ovata*
  Pedicels articulated more than 2 mm below the flowers   **8**
8 Calyx tube with 10 ridges at base; flowers less than 2 cm diameter; pedicels shorter than subtending leaf   **9**
  Calyx tube unridged at base; flowers more than 2 cm in diameter; pedicels longer than subtending leaf   8. *S.* sp. *B*
9 Petioles not more than a quarter the length of the lamina; mericarps thick-walled, indehiscent   **10**
  Petioles more than half the length of lamina; mericarps thin-walled at base, dehiscent
                    9. *S. alba*
10 Sepals acuminate; mericarps reticulately ornamented on the outside   10. *S. acuta*
  Sepals triangular; mericarps smooth on the outside   11. *S. rhombifolia*

1. **Sida cordifolia** *L.*

Erect woody pilose annual with ovate, cordate or rounded leaves and solitary, or often fascicled pale yellow flowers.

Found as a weed in the warmer parts of Kenya with an adequate rainfall. MUM, MAC.

Kirrika 210.

2. **Sida ternata** *L. f.* (see p. 202)

A low trailing almost glabrous herb, with ovate-pentagonal, 3–5-lobed leaves and solitary axillary white flowers.

Uncommon plant found in montane rain-forest. Often in the bamboo zone as an adventive in disturbed ground and pathsides. HE, HT, HM, HA, HK, KIT.

Agnew 7162; Nattrass 706.

3. **Sida urens** *L.*

An erect woody pilose annual with ovate cordate leaves and short axillary racemes of pale orange flowers.

Common in western Kenya, but nowhere else, as a weed of disturbed ground. MUM.

Davidson, July 1959; Agnew and Musumba 8076.

4. **Sida veronicifolia** *Lam.*

A trailing sparsely pilose herb, with leaves similar to *S. ternata* but suborbicular and hardly lobed, solitary white flowers.

A rare plant only recorded from swampy ground near Kisii. KIS.

Napier 5271.

5. **Sida cuneifolia** *Roxb.* (see p. 202)

An erect or spreading shrub with oblanceolate to narrowly-obtriangular to almost linear-oblong leaves and solitary yellow flowers.

Common in the dry grasslands of Kenya, 3000–8000 ft, and forming wiry bushes especially in overgrazed land. HM, KIS, NAR, RV, EMB, MAC, MAG, NBI, KAJ.

Hanid and Kiniaruh 936; Glover 2597.

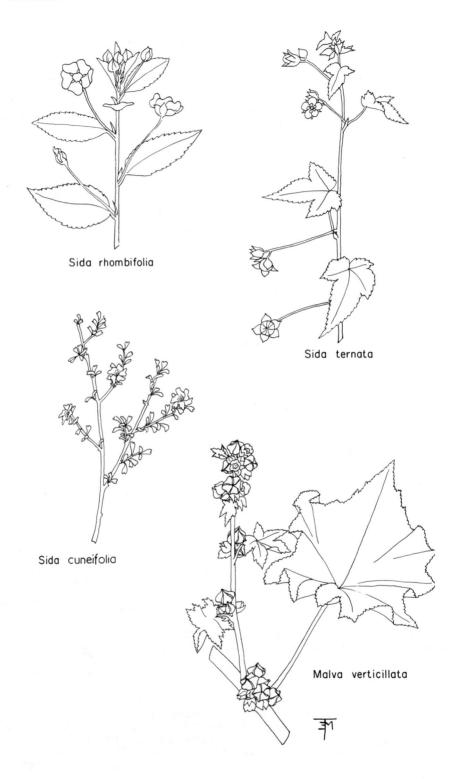

Sida rhombifolia

Sida ternata

Sida cuneifolia

Malva verticillata

6. Sida *sp.* A.

Very similar to *S. cuneifolia,* but a more tortuously branched plant with smaller leaves and usually densely pubescent on the lower side of the leaves and calyx, sometimes with much broader leaves, and with the fruit characteristics mentioned in the Key.

This species is found in similar situations to *S. cuneifolia* and is apparently as common. HC, KIT, NAR, RV, NAN, MAC, NBI, KAJ.

Hume 72; Agnew and Musumba 5338.

7. Sida ovata *Forsk.*

Densely pubescent, shrubby, short-lived perennial or woody annual with ovate elliptic leaves and solitary, pale orange-yellow flowers.

A common *Sida* in dry grassland areas. HA, HL, MUM, NAR, RV, NAN, MAC, NBI, KAJ.

Agnew and Azavedo 9330.

8. Sida *sp.* B.

Similar to *S. ovata* in all respects except for the following: pedicels usually longer than the leaves, articulated 4–7 mm below the flowers; sepals 8–10 mm long, not ridged at base; petals to 18 mm long, orange-yellow; mericarps awned, with ascending bristles, reticulate on the lower dorsal and lateral faces.

In dry grassland and bushland. MAC, KAJ.

Blencowe 26; Bally 742.

9. Sida alba *L.*

An erect pubescent woody annual, with ovate-elliptic to oblong leaves; flowers often on lateral racemes, or solitary, white or cream.

Uncommon plant found in disturbed places in dry grassland, 3000–6000 ft. MUM, KIS, NAR, BAR, MAC, NBI, KAJ.

Hanid and Kiniaruh 741; Bogdan 4734.

10. Sida acuta *Burm. f.*

Erect, short-lived, sparsely pubescent perennial with short-petiolate, lanceolate-oblong leaves and solitary cream or pale yellow flowers.

Not uncommon amongst cultivation in dry areas at the coast and again in west Kenya. KIS, MUM.

Hanid and Kiniaruh 676; Templer 29.

11. Sida rhombifolia *L.* (see p.202)

Erect, short-lived perennial with ovate-elliptic or rhombic leaves and yellow flowers in axillary racemes (or rarely fasciculate or solitary).

A common *Sida* below 6000 ft, often in places disturbed by man. HE, HC, HL, KIT, MUM, KIS, NAR, EMB, MAC, NBI.

van Someren in EAH 12281; Hanid and Kiniaruh 597.

4. ABUTILON *Mill.*

Herbs or shrubs with usually simple, ovate, cordate, acuminate leaves; flowers in terminal panicles or solitary or fascicled, usually yellow, opening usually mid-afternoon; epicalyx absent; sepals 5, connate at base; petals 5, often asymmetric; staminal tube markedly expanded at base, usually with stamens all crowded at the apex; ovary of 5–40 carpels, each with one style and stigma joined laterally to form a globose gynoecium; fruit of spreading, loosely coherent, 1–3-seeded mericarps; seeds glabrous or hairy.

1 Flowers blue, mauve, or white with purple base, in conical terminal panicles; staminal tube with reflexed simple crystalline hairs
          1. *A. longicuspe*
  Flowers yellow or orange, rarely in conical terminal panicles; staminal tube never with simple reflexed hairs   2

2 Mericarps less than 15, or shorter than 8 mm
          3
  Mericarps more than 15, or longer than 8 mm
          5

3 Pedicels 2–4 at apex of axillary peduncles; mericarps usually 8, with awns over 2 mm long   4. *A. ramosum*
  Pedicels solitary, axillary; mericarps usually 10 or more, with awns less than 1 mm long, or unawned   4

4 Annual plant; corolla more than 15 mm long; mericarps with a narrow awn above
          2. *A.* sp. *A*
  Perennial shrub; corolla less than 12 mm long; mericarps acute but not awned above
          3. *A. fruticosum*

5 Leaves bullate above; calyx lobes shorter than the tube; staminal tube glabrous
          6. *A. guineense*
  Leaves smooth above; calyx lobes usually longer than the tube; staminal tube stellate-hairy   6

6 Mericarps rounded or merely obtusely angled on the outside; inflorescence branches often viscid   5. *A. hirtum*
  Mericarps with a long acute point on the outside; inflorescence branches never viscid
          7

7 Both long spreading and short canescent hairs present; stipules filiform, straight
          8. *A. mauritianum*
  Indumentum without long spreading hairs; stipules strap-shaped, often curved
          7. *A. grandiflorum*

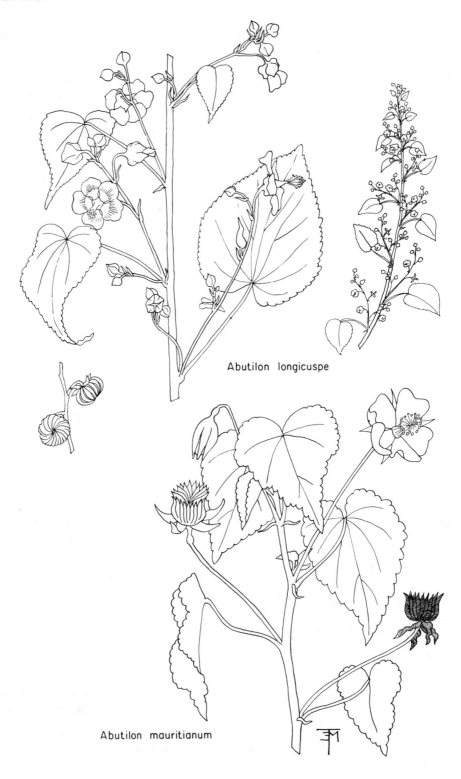

Abutilon longicuspe

Abutilon mauritianum

1. Abutilon longicuspe *A. Rich.* (see p. 204)

A perennial shrub with densely grey-pubescent stems and leaf undersides, bearing suborbicular cordate leaves; flowers in terminal conical panicles, mauve, lavender, or lilac with a darker **centre**; mericarps not awned.

A common plant of upland forest edges, 5000–9000 ft. HE, HT, HM, HA, HK, NAR, MAC, NBI.

Lind and Harris 5066; Dyson 456.

2. Abutilon *sp.* A.

Erect, densely pubescent, sparsely branched annual with ovate to lanceolate, cordate leaves and solitary yellow flowers; mericarps usually 10, with a short apical awn.

Locally common in dry grassland or bushland. MAG, MAC, KAJ.

Verdcourt 3890; Agnew 9777.

3. Abutilon fruticosum *Guill. & Perr.*

Woody, canescent, usually much-branched shrub, with ovate to suborbicular, shallowly cordate leaves; flowers solitary yellow; mericarps 10–12, with an apiculate angle on the top of the outer face.

A locally common plant of dry *Commiphora* bushland. MUM, BAR, MAG, EMB, KAJ.

Verdcourt 2750; Agnew and Musumba 7961.

4. Abutilon ramosum (*Cav.*) *Guill. & Perr.*

A loose shrub with densely pubescent stems and petioles and glabrescent, suborbicular, cordate leaves; flowers 2–4 on short axillary racemes, yellow; mericarps about 8, each with a 2 mm long awn.

A rare weed found in cultivation in dry country. BAR.

Tweedie 2301.

5. Abutilon hirtum (*Lam.*) *Sweet* (Incl. *A. figarianum* Webb of Check List.)

Erect, densely pubescent, sparsely branched woody herb or shrub with ovate to suborbicular, cordate leaves; flowers grouped on lateral, usually brown viscid-hairy branches or in loose terminal panicles, orange-yellow, with or without a dark red-purple spot at base; mericarps 20 or more, suborbicular, with or without an apiculate angle above.

A very variable plant as defined here, found in disturbed places in drier *Combretum* woodland as well as in dry *Commiphora* country. The sticky, viscid plant may be different from the non-viscid, often smaller-flowered plant, but more field work is required. BAR, MAG, NAN, KAJ.

Agnew 5394; Bogdan 4737.

6. Abutilon guineense (*Schum.*) *Bak. f.*

Similar to *A. mauritianum* except for the strap-shaped stipules and bullate leaves; sepal lobes shorter than the tube; mericarps as in *A. grandiflorum* but sericeous, overtopped by the fruiting sepals.

An uncommon plant found in dry disturbed country. KIT, MUM, KIS, BAR, KAJ.

Verdcourt 3847.

7. Abutilon grandiflorum *G. Don*

Similar to *A. mauritianum* except for the absence of long spreading hairs and the strap-shaped stipules; sepal lobes ± shorter than the tube; mericarps acutely pointed but hardly awned, with the lateral glabrous area rounded at the top, not pointed.

This species is hard to distinguish from *A. mauritianum*, but is found in drier regions. MUM, KAJ.

Verdcourt 2594.

8. Abutilon mauritianum (*Jacq.*) *Medic.*
(see p. 204)

A softly woody shrub with short dense pubescence and longer spreading hairs; leaves usually suborbicular, cordate; flowers solitary, yellow-gold; mericarps more than 20, each produced at the top into an acutely tapering awn, tomentose, the lateral glabrous areas pointed at the top.

The commonest species of *Abutilon* in our area, growing in red soils at forest and woodland edges and in disturbed ground. It is widely distributed and also found at the coast. HE, HC, HA, KIT, MUM, NAR, RV, EMB, MAC, NBI, KAJ.

Glover 3406; Harmsen 6430.

5. MALVA *L.*

Herbs, seldom woody, the leaves usually orbicular in outline; flowers racemose, sometimes fascicled; epicalyx present, usually of 3 bracts; sepals 5, connate at base; petals 5, pink, white or blue, seldom yellow; ovary of 9–15 1-ovuled carpels arranged around a central torus; fruit discoid, of mericarps which separate at maturity.

1   Epicalyx bracts oblong-ovate; sepals acute; mericarps scarcely sculptured, with rounded radial edges   1. *M. verticillata*

    Epicalyx bracts linear; sepals rounded-mucronate; mericarps deeply sculptured with raised radial edges   2. *M. parviflora*

1. Malva verticillata *L.* (see p. 202)

Annual, erect or ascending herb, bearing circular leaves with 5–7 short lobes; flowers fasciculate, axillary; petals exceeding calyx.

An introduced Mediterranean weed of waste land in upland areas. HE, HT, HA, HK, KIT, NAR, RV, NBI.

Agnew 7591; Kokwaro 36.

2. Malva parviflora *L.*

Similar to *M. verticillata* but often with decumbent branches; petals ± equalling calyx.

An introduced weed of cultivation at medium altitudes in the Rift Valley. RV.

Agnew and Azavedo 9313; Bogdan 5713.

6. URENA *L.*

Perennial woody herbs with simple leaves with conspicuous glands on the basal nerves; flowers axillary, solitary or fascicled; epicalyx of 5 lobes, connate at the base and campanulate; calyx 5-lobed; petals pink or mauve; ovary globose, of 5 1-ovuled carpels, each with 2 styles; fruit of 5 mericarps with dorsal glochidiate spines.

1. Urena lobata *L.* (see p. 207)

Erect tomentose herb with orbicular to oblong, simple to shallowly 3–7-lobed leaves; flowers pink; fruit globose.

Common in disturbed ground and cultivation in western Kenya. KIT, MUM, KIS.

Strid 2883.

7. PAVONIA *Cav.*

Shrubs or tough herbs with cordate, lobed or entire leaves; epicalyx present, or 5–6 bracts, often connate at base; petals variable in colour; staminal column (in ours) glabrous with the stamens at the apex; ovary with 5 carpels and 10 stigmas; fruit of 5 1-seeded mericarps, often ornamented or appendaged.

1 Epicalyx bracts filiform, 3–4 times longer than the calyx, forming a delicate 'basket' around the fruit   **2**
   Epicalyx bracts usually broad, up to 3 times as long as the calyx, not forming a 'basket' around the fruit   **4**
2 Leaves entire   **3**
   Leaves palmate   1. *P. zeylanica*
3 Flowers pink; mericarps unwinged
                                            2. *P. arabica*
   Flowers white; mericarps winged
                                            3. *P. sp. A*
4 Flowers yellow, sometimes maroon within at base   **5**
   Flowers pink or white or purple   **7**
5 Epicalyx bracts spreading, often rounded at apex; petals often with maroon spot at base   4. *P. patens*
   Epicalyx bracts appressed to calyx; petals concolorous   **6**

6 Epicalyx bracts linear-filiform; petals turning pink on drying.   5. *P. propinqua*
   Epicalyx bracts lanceolate; petals not turning pink on drying   6. *P. elegans*
7 Lower leaves oblong in outline; flowers solitary   7. *P. kilimandscharica*
   Lower leaves suborbicular in outline; flowers solitary or fascicled   8. *P. urens*

1. Pavonia zeylanica *Cav.*

Annual or short-lived perennial with viscid and simple hairs on all parts; leaves orbicular, 3–5-lobed; flowers solitary, pale yellow or cream.

A local plant of dry land after rain, found in *Commiphora* bushland. BAR, MAG, MAC.

Harmsen 6471; Bogdan 5130.

2. Pavonia arabica *Boiss.*

Glandular-pubescent annual or short-lived perennial, with ovate, cordate, entire leaves and pink flowers.

Found in dry country on sandy soils, this plant is easily confused with the next. BAR, EMB, MAC.

Edwards 138.

3. Pavonia *sp.* **A.**

Similar to *P. arabica* but smaller and not glandular, it can be further distinguished by its white flowers and winged fruits.

Uncommon plant found in dry country. MAC, KAJ.

Verdcourt 2580.

4. Pavonia patens (*Andr.*) *Chiov.* (see p. 208)

Stellate-pubescent trailing or erect shrub with ovate to orbicular cordate leaves and solitary flowers; petals yellow, with or without a dark spot at base within.

A most variable plant with (as defined here) a wide ecological tolerance, extending from *Commiphora* woodlands (where the form with long narrow acute epicalyx bracts and warty fruit is commonest) to upland wet forest margins (where the common plant has obovate, rounded epicalyx bracts and smooth fruits). More work is needed to settle the status of these forms, and at the moment it seems best to merge them in one. HE, HC, HT, HM, HA, HK, KIT, NAR, BAR, RV, MAG, NAN, MAC, NBI, KAJ.

Agnew and Kiniaruh 8858; Kokwaro 261.

5. Pavonia propinqua *Garcke* (*P. grewioides* Garcke) (see p. 207)

Stellate-pubescent shrub, with oblong or ovate rounded leaves and solitary flowers; petals yellow, usually turning pink with age.

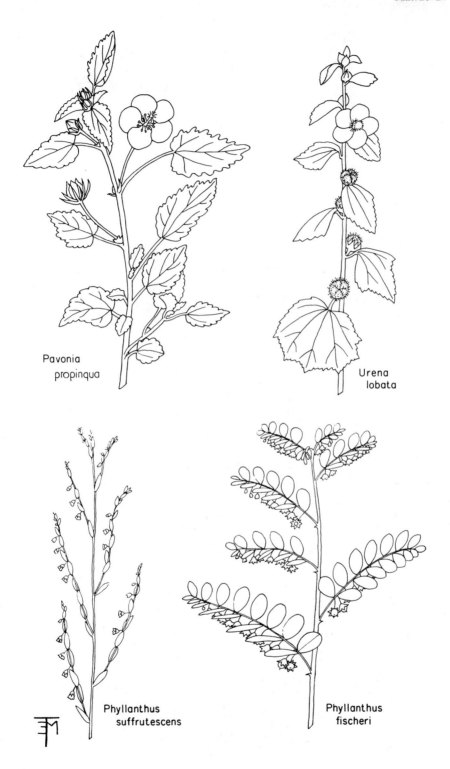

Pavonia
propinqua

Urena
lobata

Phyllanthus
suffrutescens

Phyllanthus
fischeri

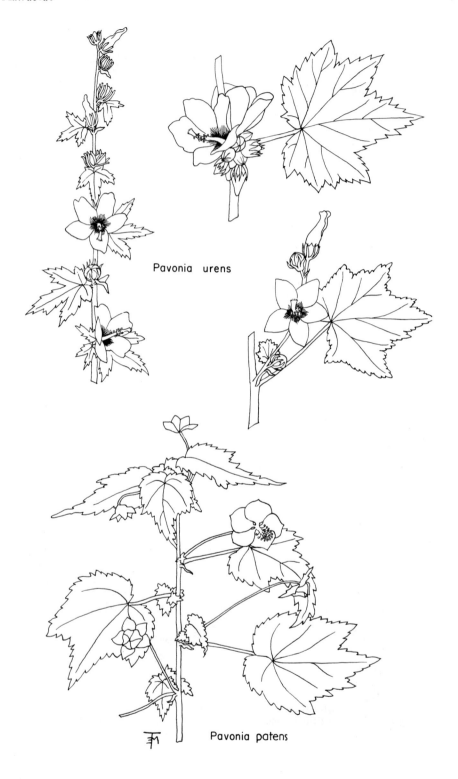

Pavonia urens

Pavonia patens

Locally common in dry *Commiphora* or *Combretum* country. MAG, MAC, KAJ.

Verdcourt 2584; Lind, Agnew, and Beecher 5710.

6. Pavonia elegans *Boiss.*

Similar to *P. propinqua* except for the leaves of which the lower are suborbicular and to 12 cm diameter and all of which are softly felty, the 6-8 lanceolate epicalyx bracts, the petals which do not fade to pink, and the mericarps which are densely sharp-tuberculate on the dorsal face and without lateral spines.

Locally common in dry country. MAC.

Hanid and Kiniaruh 496; Napper 1576.

7. Pavonia kilimandscharica *Guerke*

Sparsely pubescent shrub with oblong or elliptic leaves and solitary flowers; petals white to mauve, with purple spots within at base.

An uncommon plant found in forest edges, 6000-9000 ft. HM, HK, NAR, KAJ.

Honore 3048.

8. Pavonia urens *Cav.* (including *P. irakuensis* Ulbr. of Check List) (see p. 208)

Soft shrub, usually hairy, with suborbicular 5-7-triangular-lobed leaves; flowers clustered or solitary, on short pedicels; petals pink, mauve or white.

A highly variable species, as delimited here, which grows in upland forest edges and riverine communities in the drier regions above 5000 ft. A highland western Kenya type is densely golden-hairy, with dense clusters of almost sessile flowers, whilst a riverine-forest ecotype has solitary white flowers and is almost glabrous. There seem to be intermediates between all these types. HE, HC, HT, HM, HL, HA, HK, KIT, MUM, KIS, NAR, EMB, MAC, NBI, KAJ.

Baker 45; Harmsen 6527.

8. WISSADULA *Medic.*

Erect shrubs with mostly cordate, acuminate, entire leaves; flowers in panicles; epicalyx 0; petals orange to cream; ovary of 3-5 free carpels, each 2-3-ovulate with 3-5 style branches and capitate stigmas; fruit of 3-5 free beaked pubescent mericarps, each transversely divided and septicidal, eventually falling from the torus; seeds 1-3 per mericarp.

Wissadula rostrata (*Schumach.*) *Hook. f.*

A loose shrub with a cluster of ± unbranched stems bearing ovate-orbicular cordate leaves; flowers in loose axillary panicles, orange.

A rare plant of western Kenya, only found once amongst granite boulders in bushland. MUM.

Agnew, Musumba, and Kiniaruh 8087.

52. MALPIGHIACEAE

Woody climbers or small shrubs in ours, with unicellular appressed medifixed hairs; leaves opposite in ours, simple and entire, stipulate or exstipulate, with a pair of glands at the base of lamina or on petiole; inflorescences terminal or axillary corymbose racemes, sometimes paniculate; bracts and bracteoles present; flowers regular and bisexual in ours; sepals 5, free or connate at base, often biglandular outside; petals 5, frequently clawed, free, imbricate; stamens 10, filaments often connate at base; ovary superior, syncarpous, mostly 3-celled and 3-lobed, with a single axile ovule in each cell; styles as carpel number, separate, persistent; fruiting carpels winged in ours; seeds without endosperm, mostly with straight embryo.

1 Sepals closed over petals in bud
                1. *Flabellaria paniculata*
  Sepals open in bud, petals visible   2
2 Leaves ovate-cordate; ovary densely sericeous
                3. *Caucanthus auriculatus*
  Leaves elliptic to ovate, with rounded or cuneate base; ovary glabrous   2. *Triaspis*

1. FLABELLARIA *Cavan.*

Woody climbers with exstipulate leaves and terminal or axillary paniculate racemes; sepals closed over petals in bud, eglandular; petals entire, not clawed; lateral wings of samara connate at base and free at top.

A monospecific genus of tropical Africa.

Flabellaria paniculata *Cavan.*

A silky-tomentose to glabrescent woody climber with broadly elliptic to ovate leaves and leafy many-flowered inflorescences; petals white to light pink.

A rare plant of rain-forests, often riparian, and recorded only from Kakamega forest in our area. It is much in need of further collection with careful field notes. MUM.

Verdcourt in EAH 11554.

2. TRIASPIS *Burch.*

Erect, scandent or semiscandent, small shrubs with petiolate leaves in ours; leaf-lamina with 2-4 glands on under surface near the insertion of the petiole; inflorescences of terminal corymbs in ours; bracts and bracteoles deciduous; sepals without glands; petals with fringed or denticulate margins; pedicels articulated with the peduncles; wing of samara retuse at apex in ours.

1   Wings of fruit entire or slightly retuse at apex; leaves with ± prominent lateral nerves on lower surface   1. *T. erlangeri*
    Wings of fruit distinctly retuse at apex; leaves with indistinct lateral nerves
    2. *T. niedenzuiana*

1. Triaspis erlangeri *Engl.*

Canescent to glabrescent, much-branched, small, erect shrub with tips of branchlets twining and elliptic to ovate leaves; **inflorescences** terminal, loosely corymbose, of white to pinkish flowers.

A rare plant found in dry bush country, recorded only from Kitui District in our area. It is much in need of further collection. MAC.
    Edwards 151.

2. Triaspis niedenzuiana *Engl.*

A short-pilose to glabrescent, much branched semi-erect or scandent small shrub with broadly elliptic leaves and terminal inflorescences of loose corymbs of white to lilac or pink flowers.

A rare plant found in dry bush country, sometimes on rocky outcrops or stony hillsides, and recorded in our area only from Kitui District. More material with careful field notes needed. MAC.
    Edwards 54; Lind and Agnew 5653.

3. CAUCANTHUS *Forsk.*

Climbers with stipulate leaves bearing 2 large glands near the base; stipules very small, deciduous; sepals without glands; petals with wholly or partially fimbriate margins; each carpel of fruit completely surrounded by a wing.

Caucanthus auriculatus (*Radlk.*) *Niedenzu*

A pubescent or glabrescent climbing and twining shrub with ovate-cordate leaves and axillary and terminal corymbs of pale yellow evil-smelling flowers.

A plant of dry bush country, woodlands, and upland dry evergreen forests; often riparian or in rocky places. BAR, MAC, NBI, KAJ.
    Bogdan 4236; Lind and Agnew 5695.

53. EUPHORBIACEAE

Plants of every habit, with alternate or opposite, usually stipulate, usually simple leaves; flowers unisexual, monoecious or dioecious, regular, basically pentamerous but often irregular in numbers of parts; calyx rarely absent, often valvate; petals present, free or absent; glandular disc often present, sometimes variously lobed; male flowers with 5-numerous stamens, free or often

fused in a central column, and with or without a rudimentary ovary; female flowers with no staminodes, and usually with a 3-carpelled ovary with 1–2 axile ovules per loculus and dichotomous or divided stigmas; fruit usually a capsule or schizocarpic; seeds with aril and endosperm.

An abundant and important family, with small 'difficult' flowers. In the following account two pairs of genera are so similar (*Phyllanthus* and *Meineckia*, *Tragia* and *Tragiella*) that they are keyed out together.

1   Apparent flower (a cyathium) of stamens and ovary surrounded by a glandular cup; plants with milky latex   2
    Flowers separate, unisexual; plants without latex   3
2   Cyathia regular; involucral glands separate all round the involucre, or gland single, lateral
    11. *Euphorbia*
    Cyathia zygomorphic; gland continuous in a circle round the involucre except for a gap at one side through which the ovary is exserted   12. *Monadenium*
3   Leaves palmatifid or palmatisect   4
    Leaves simple   6
4   Twining climber with inflorescence held within a pair of light-coloured, 3-pointed bracts
    8. *Dalechampia ipomoeifolia*
    Erect shrubs or herbs   5
5   Flowers in a terminal panicle; male flowers with branched filaments; fruits usually softly spiny   7. *Ricinus communis*
    Flowers in axillary or terminal cymes; male flowers with simple filaments; fruit smooth
    9. *Jatropha*
6   Leaves entire   7
    Leaves serrate, dentate or sinuate   8
7   Leaves turning red or orange before falling
    10. *Clutia*
    Leaves falling while still green
    1. *Phyllanthus* (and 2. *Meineckia*)
8   Inflorescence of spikes or racemes of solitary or clustered flowers   9
    Inflorescence of dichasial cymes   9. *Jatropha*
9   Raceme very interrupted, with clusters of male and female flowers together along its length   3. *Micrococca*
    Raceme or spike with male flowers above, and female at base, or plants dioecious; male part of spike or raceme interrupted or not   10
10 Female flower with enlarging calyx in fruit; stinging hairs frequently present
    5. *Tragia* (and 6. *Tragiella*)
    Female flower with enlarging bract and inconspicuous sepals in fruit; stinging hairs never present   4. *Acalypha*

1. PHYLLANTHUS *L.*

Monoecious or dioecious shrubs or herbs, often with simple stipulate leaves on specialised branches of limited growth; flowers solitary or fasciculate with 4–6 sepals and an expanded disc; male flowers with 2–5 free or variously connate stamens; female flowers with an ovary with usually bifid or laciniate stigmas; fruit a berry or dry capsule with two seeds per loculus.

A common genus which includes a number of woody shrubs or trees which are described in KTS. Here all species are dealt with, not only because some of the woody species are often so low as to appear suffrutescent, but also because changes have been made to the names recorded in KTS.

1 Plants with specialized leafy branches of limited growth, and with only scale-leaves on main stem **4**
   Plants with leaves on main stem as well as on branches, the latter unlimited in growth, unspecialized **2**
2 Trees over 2 m in height   6. *Ph. discoideus*
   Shrubs or herbs under 1 m in height **3**
3 Leaves with a pale central blotch, acute, cuneate, or apiculate at apex
                                Meineckia phyllanthoides
   Leaves with no pale central blotch, rounded at apex   *Meineckia* sp. *A*
4 Sepals 4 or 5, occasionally a few flowers with 6 sepals **5**
   Sepals 6, occasionally a few flowers with 5 sepals **12**
5 Annual, erect herbs **6**
   Perennials **7**
6 Ovary warty   1. *Ph. leucocalyx*
   Ovary smooth   2. *Ph. amarus*
7 Plant low, creeping   3. *Ph.* sp. *A*
   Plant erect **8**
8 Pedicels over 8 mm long, often longer than their subtending leaves   4. *Ph. capillaris*
   Pedicels less than 8 mm long, always shorter than their subtending leaves **9**
9 Leaves oblong, less than 1 cm broad; stigmas entire or almost so   5. *Ph. guineensis*
   Leaves elliptic, always some over 1 cm broad; stigmas deeply bifid **10**
10 Leafy branches longer than 15 cm; fruits inflated, over 2 cm diameter
                                7. *Ph. inflatus*
   Leafy branches seldom over 10 cm long; fruit not inflated, to 5 mm diameter **11**
11 Stamens 4–5 all free   8. *Ph. muellerianus*
   Stamens 1–2 free, and 3 fused to a central column   9. *Ph. reticulatus*
12 Pedicels 5 mm or more long **13**
   Pedicels less than 5 mm long **14**

13 Leaves ovate; pedicels to 6·5 mm long
                                10. *Ph. glaucophyllus*
   Leaves elliptic; pedicel 7–14 mm long
                                11. *Ph.* sp. *B*
14 Upper leaves four times as long as broad; sepals obovate, with the hyaline margin narrow or absent   12. *Ph. maderaspatensis*
   Upper leaves up to three times as long as broad; sepals ovate or oblong, usually with a broad hyaline margin **15**
15 Outer sepals sub-orbicular, cordate at base; style fused in a central column
                                13. *Ph.* sp. *C*
   Outer sepals ovate to oblong, not cordate at base; styles free **16**
16 Leaves mostly oblong, some at least parallel-sided, rounded at base and apex, apiculate; sepals elliptic with a narrow midrib and broad hyaline margin
                                14. *Ph. odontadenius*
   Leaves elliptic or obovate, rarely apiculate; sepals often with a broad midrib **17**
17 Sepals with a broad white hyaline margin, as wide as or wider than the herbaceous central portion **20**
   Sepals with a hyaline margin narrower than the herbaceous central portion, or margin yellow or green, merging into the central portion **18**
18 Erect shrubs usually over 50 cm tall; leaves elliptic or obovate, over 5 mm wide **19**
   Erect spreading woody herbs, less than 50 cm tall; leaves elliptic, less than 5 mm wide
                                15. *Ph. suffrutescens*
19 Monoecious plant; sepals (especially of female flower) with yellow margins; fruit with a smooth outer wall   16. *Ph. fischeri*
   Dioecious plant; sepals with pale green margins; fruit with a reticulate pattern outside when dry   17. *Ph. sepialis*
20 Leaves elliptic, less than 5 mm wide; dioecious plants   15. *Ph. suffrutescens*
   Leaves oblong or obovate, often more than 5 mm wide; monoecious plants **21**
21 Leaves suborbicular to obovate, rounded at apex, sometimes minutely apiculate
                                18. *Ph. rotundifolius*
   Leaves oblong, occasionally obovate, broadly cuneate at apex, often apiculate
                                14. *Ph. odontadenius*

1. Phyllanthus leucocalyx (*Muell. Arg.*) *Hutch.*

An erect monoecious annual to 40 cm with elliptic acute leaves.

Rare plant found in western Kenya and at the coast. HA, MUM.

Graham H91/44; Agnew 10124.

2. Phyllanthus amarus *Schum. & Thonn.*

An erect, monoecious annual to 30 cm with oblong rounded leaves.

Uncommon plant found in marshes at the coast and in the west of our area. KIT.

Bally B 4828; Strid 3159.

3. Phyllanthus *sp.* **A.**

A low creeping monoecious perennial with red stems and obovate leaves.

Common on the Aberdares moorlands, 9000–10 750 ft. HA.

Agnew 8131; Verdcourt 4001.

4. Phyllanthus capillaris *Schum. & Thonn.*

An erect, tomentose or glabrous, monoecious or dioecious many-stemmed shrub to 2 m tall with suborbicular to broad-elliptic leaves.

Locally common in dry savannah woodland country, 6000–8000 ft. HE, HC, KIT, MUM, KAJ.

Agnew 9819; Napier 1997.

5. Phyllanthus guineensis *Pax*

A many-stemmed, erect, monoecious shrub to 3 m, with strictly oblong leaves and pinkish flowers.

Common at the edges of upland forest, 4500–6000 ft, and at the coast. HA, MUM, KIS, BAR, EMB, MAC, NBI.

Agnew and Faden 9977; Kerfoot 2164.

6. Phyllanthus discoideus *Pax*

A tree to 15 m tall, dioecious and without specially developed lateral leafy branches.

This species grows in upland woodland, 4000–6000 ft, and at the coast. HA, MUM, EMB, NBI.

Agnew 7784; Graham 1.

7. Phyllanthus inflatus *Hutch.*

A many-stemmed shrub or bushy tree to 10 m tall, with fascicled inflorescences and inflated fruits.

In wet upland forest. HN, KIS.

Polhill and Verdcourt 274.

8. Phyllanthus muellerianus (*Kuntze*) *Excell*

A tree or shrub to 3 m, with elliptic leaves; flowers monoecious, the males with 5 free stamens.

Only once recorded from our area, at Kakamega Forest, otherwise it is to be found at the coast. MUM.

Paulo 555.

9. Phyllanthus reticulatus *Poir.*

A monoecious shrub to 2 m, with elliptic to obovate leaves; male flowers with 5 stamens, 2 free and 3 connate.

Found in forest edges at the coast and only once recorded (at Bunyala) from our area. MUM. Makin 323.

10. Phyllanthus glaucophyllus *Sond.*

A low, shrubby, tufted, monoecious shrub to 40 cm tall, with glaucous, glabrous, cordate leaves.

Rare plant found in dry country. KIS, EMB, MAC, KAJ.

Hanid and Kiniaruh 825A; Bally 860.

11. Phyllanthus *sp.* **B.**

A shrub to 3 m, monoecious, with elliptic leaves and long-pedicelled flowers.

Only recorded from Fourteen Falls, on the Athi River. MAC.

Verdcourt 2608.

12. Phyllanthus maderaspatensis *L.*

A tufted monoecious woody annual or perennial to 40 cm with narrow elliptic to linear upper leaves and almost spathulate sepals to the female flowers.

It is the commonest *Phyllanthus* of grassland in dry country. HL, NAR, RV, MAG, EMB, MAC, NBI, KAJ.

Glover and Samuel 3168; Agnew and Hanid 7446.

13. Phyllanthus *sp.* **C.**

An erect monoecious annual or short-lived perennial to 30 cm, with suborbicular to elliptic leaves and cordate sepals.

In dry, sandy bushland. KAJ.

Agnew 9869A; Verdcourt 3862.

14. Phyllanthus odontadenius *Muell. Arg.*

An erect monoecious annual or short-lived perennial to 75 cm with oblong or obovate, apiculate or broadly cuneate leaves.

Common in open woodland grassland especially around Nairobi. HA, KIT, MUM, EMB, MAC, NBI.

Faden 67265; Agnew and Hanid 8376.

15. Phyllanthus suffrutescens *Pax* (see p. 207)

An erect, caespitose or much-branched, dioecious shrub to 40 cm with elliptic leaves and usually purple-nerved sepals.

Locally common in medium rainfall grassland, 3400–7000 ft. Plants from western Kenya usually have larger flowers than those from east of the Rift Valley, and since these two populations appear to be isolated from one another, they may be distinct enough to deserve separate names. HC, HT, KIT, MAC, NBI, KAJ.

Agnew 9223; Thorold 3252.

16. Phyllanthus fischeri *Pax* (see p. 207)

A monoecious shrub with erect or flexuous branches to 2 m (usually less), and elliptic leaves; sepals of the female flowers often yellowish.

Locally common at forest edges, 5000–8500 ft. HE, HT, HM, HA, HK, HN, KIT, RV, ENB, MAC, NBI.

Agnew 8779; Verdcourt 393.

17. Phyllanthus sepialis *Muell. Arg.* (*P. meruensis* of Check List)

An erect, many-stemmed, dioecious shrub to 3 m tall, with broad-elliptic leaves and wrinkled fruits.

Common in forest edges and riverine formations, 3000–8000 ft. MUM, NAR, BAR, RV, MAC, NBI, KAJ.

Bogdan 5243; Agnew 8833.

18. Phyllanthus rotundifolius *Willd.*

An erect branched annual or short-lived monoecious perennial, with obovate to suborbicular leaves and tiny flowers.

Common in dry country, especially grassland. KIS, NAR, RV, MAG, MAC, KAJ.

Hanid and Kiniaruh 825; Verdcourt 3174.

2. MEINECKIA *Baill.*

Monoecious herbs or shrubs with entire stipulate leaves; flowers fasciculate, with 5 sepals, 5 petals and a well-developed disc; male flowers with 5 stamens fused round a column which terminates in a rudimentary ovary; female flowers as in *Phyllanthus*.

1   Leaves with a pale central blotch, acute, cuneate or apiculate at apex
                                        1. *M. phyllanthoides*
    Leaves with no pale central blotch, rounded at apex   2. *M.* sp. A

1. Meineckia phyllanthoides *Baill.* (*Cluytiandra capillariformis* (Pax) Pax & Hoffm.)

An erect woody herb or low shrub to 50 cm with white-blotched leaves and long-pedicellate flowers.

Locally common, especially around Nairobi in open woodland, often beside rivers. MAC, NBI.

Agnew 7577; Greenway 8781.

2. Meineckia *sp.* A.

An erect monoecious annual to 50 cm with a pale-fissured bark and suborbicular leaves.

Rare plant found in dry, stony bushland. MAG, KAJ.

Agnew 9791; Glover 2957.

3. MICROCOCCA *Benth.*

Monoecious or dioecious herbs or shrubs with simple, serrate, stipulate leaves; inflorescences axillary, of long filiform interrupted racemes of glomeruli; male flowers with 3 valvate sepals, 3–20 free stamens and no sterile ovary; stamens often mixed with glands, the 2 anthers dehiscing longitudinally; female flowers with 3–4 sepals, 2–4-lobed disc **equalling** the calyx, and a 3-celled ovary; capsule or 3 chambers, each 1-seeded, opening loculicidally and septicidally and with hard, brittle valves and central column; seeds enclosed in a thin aril.

1   Shrub to 3 m tall in wet forests   1. *M. holstii*
    Annual herb to 50 cm tall in dry bushland
                                        2. *M. mercurialis*

1. Micrococca holstii (*Pax*) *Prain*

Dealt with in KTS p. 210. HA.

2. Micrococca mercurialis *Benth.*

A monoecious, glabrous to tomentose annual herb to 50 cm tall with lanceolate, cuneate leaves.

Rare plant found in dry country. BAR.

Bogdan 3847.

4. ACALYPHA *L.*

Dioecious or monoecious shrubs or herbs with simple, serrate leaves; inflorescences paniculate or spicate, often axillary, sometimes terminal; male flowers of 4 valvate sepals and usually 8 stamens, enclosed in bud, often fasciculate along catkinate racemes; female flowers surrounded by an often enlarged bract, 1–2 together, with 3–4 imbricate sepals; ovary with one ovule per loculus and filiform stigmas.

1   Female flowers axillary, sessile, at the base of the male raceme or found along the raceme
                                                         2
    Female flowers in terminal spikes, separate from the male raceme   12
2   Female flowers on 1–3·5 cm long peduncles, 2 together, surrounded by a bract almost completely divided into two flat, semi-orbicular lobes   1. *A. bipartita*
    Female flowers sessile or if pedunculate, not as above   3
3   Bracts of **female** flower deeply palmately divided to half way or more into oblong lobes   4
    Bracts of female flowers laciniate to crenate or entire, not palmatifid   5
4   Erect herb from perennial rootstock; leaves subsessile, rounded at base
                                        2. *A. stuhlmannii*

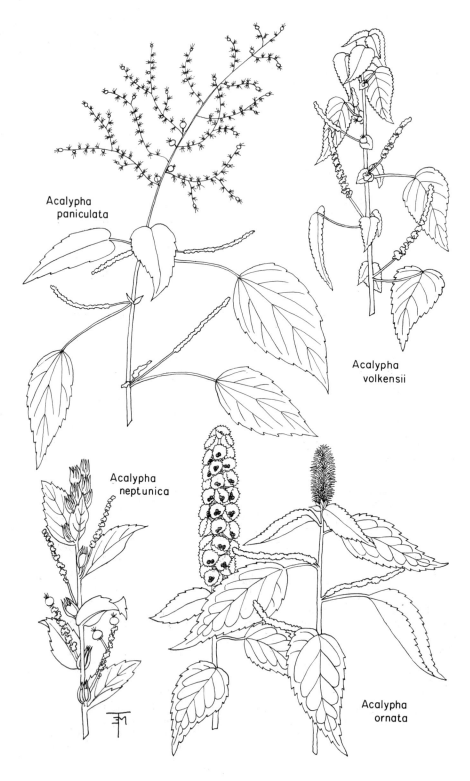

Acalypha
paniculata

Acalypha
volkensii

Acalypha
neptunica

Acalypha
ornata

Erect herb, generally annual; leaves long-
    petiolate, cordate at base
                                3. *A. psilostachya*
5   Annuals   **6**
    Perennial shrubs   **9**
6   Bracts of female flowers fringed at the margin
                                    4. *A. ciliata*
    Bracts of female flowers entire or crenate   **7**
7   Bracts of female flowers with long glandular
        hairs; leaf base cuneate   6. *A. lanceolata*
    Bracts of female flowers with eglandular hairs
        or glabrous; leaf base rounded   **8**
8   Female bracts 3–5 mm long; male glomerules
        intermixed with uppermost female bracts
        and extending at most up to 4 mm beyond
        them   7. *A. crenata*
    At least some female bracts over 5 mm long;
        male glomerules not intermixed with
        uppermost female bracts and extending
        more than 5 mm beyond them
                                    5. *A. indica*
9   Male racemes pedunculate; female flowers
        solitary axillary   8. *A. volkensii*
    Male racemes bearing glomeruli to base;
        female flowers on base of raceme   **10**
10 Undersurface of leaves with sessile, yellow,
        translucent resinous dots   9. *A. fruticosa*
    Undersurface of leaves without resinous dots
                                                    11
11 Leaves ovate, widest below the middle; male
        racemes less than 5 cm long   10. *A* sp. *A*
    Leaves obovate to oblanceolate to oblong,
        widest above the middle; male racemes
        usually over 5 cm long   12. *A. neptunica*
12 Female inflorescence paniculate
                                    13. *A. racemosa*
    Female inflorescence a spike   **13**
13 Female spike long cylindrical, seldom more
        than 7·5 mm diameter including the stig-
        mas at anthesis, enlarging to nearly 2 cm
        diameter in fruit   14. *A. ornata*
    Female spike globose or short cylindrical,
        seldom less than 1 cm diameter including
        the stigmas at anthesis, hardly wider than
        1·5 cm in fruit   11. *A. villicaulis*

1. Acalypha bipartita *Muell. Arg.*
A trailing shrub with the semiorbicular female
glomerules on peduncles 2–3 cm long.
    Rare, known only from one gathering from
Kombewa, near Kisumu. MUM.
    Agnew 8086.

2. Acalypha stuhlmannii *Pax*
A perennial monoecious herb with erect unbranched stems from a woody rootstock.

Common in savannah country in the north-west
of our area. HE, HC, KIT.
    Tweedie 66/29; Napier 1975.

3. Acalypha psilostachya *A. Rich.* (*A. brachy-
stachya* of Check List)
As defined here this is a most variable plant,
including single-stemmed, glandular-pubescent
annuals of roadsides and wet savannah, as well as
robust soft eglandular herbs of wet forest. HC,
HM, HK, KIT, MUM, KIS, KAJ.
    Agnew 8780 and 7898; Bally 291.

4. Acalypha ciliata *Forsk.*
Erect unbranched annual with short dense spikes.
    Occasional in dry country especially in eastern
Kenya. MUM, NAN, MAC, KAJ.
    Agnew 9854; Kirrika 11.

5. Acalypha indica *L.*
An erect annual with long inflorescences.
    Abundant in dry country on rocky soils. KIS,
MAG, MAC, KAJ.
    Hanid and Kiniaruh 736; Glover 2811.

6. Acalypha lanceolata *Willd.* (*A. glomerata* Hutch.)
An erect annual usually smaller than *A. indica*.
    Found at the coast and also occasionally inland.
Rare in our area. MUM, NBI.
    Napier 3422A; Agnew 9774.

7. Acalypha crenata *A. Rich.*
Similar to *A. glomerata* in habit but eglandular, or
with very few glandular hairs.
    Common around Nairobi in the National Park,
rare elsewhere. MUM, EMB, NBI, KAJ.
    Kokwaro 206.

8. Acalypha volkensii *Pax* (see p. 214)
A loose trailing shrub with red racemes of glabrous
male flowers.
    Found in upland grassland throughout our area.
HE, HC, HA, KIT, MUM, NAR, MAC, NBI, KAJ.
    Makin 4300; Agnew and Hanid 8378.

9. Acalypha fruticosa *Forsk.*
An erect, stiff shrub to 1·5 m, smelling resinous
when rubbed due to the glandular deposits on all
parts.
    Common in dry country. MUM, KIS, BAR,
MAG, MAC, KAJ.
    Agnew 9886; Bally 9037.

10. Acalypha sp. A.
An erect shrub very similar to *A. fruticosa* except
for the obscure glands and the more prominent
tertiary leaf-veins.

Common in dry country and often riverine. MUM, BAR, MAG, NAN, MAC, KAJ.

Agnew and Hanid 7530; Ibrahim 660.

11. Acalypha villicaulis *A. Rich.* (*A. senensis* of Check List)

Soft herb or weak shrub to 1 m with a pair of glands at the top of the petiole below the lanceolate lamina.

Uncommon plant found in warmer areas. MUM, KIS, KIT, EMB, MAC, NBI, KAJ.

Hanid and Kiniaruh 806; Dyson 455.

12. Acalypha neptunica *Muell. Arg.* (*A. subsessilis* in Check List) (see p. 214)

Robust shrub to 3 m with stiff, keeled stipules and stiff leaves.

It is an uncommon plant found in lowland wet forest and lowland gallery forest. HM, MUM, MAC.

Tweedie 67/116; Faden 66193.

13. Acalypha racemosa *Baill.* (*A. panicultata* Miq) (see p. 214)

A woody shrub or occasionally a soft herb, with terminal panicles of female flowers.

Locally common in upland forest edges, 5000–7000 ft, especially around Nairobi. HA, HK, EMB, MAC, NBI.

Hanid and Kiniaruh 1046; Faden 677.

14. Acalypha ornata *A. Rich.* (see p. 214)

A woody shrub to 3 m tall, with ovate leaves.

Rare plant found in warm wetter forest, 3000–5000 ft. MUM, KIS, KIT, NAR, EMB, MAC, KAJ.

Tweedie 66/88; Glover 5100.

5. TRAGIA *L.*

Herbs or climbers, often with stinging hairs, and with usually cordate leaves (in ours); flowers usually in axillary racemes with 1–3 female at base and many terminal male, but sometimes dioecious; male flowers bracteate, of 3 sepals and 3 free stamens; female flowers with 3 or 6 pinnate or palmate sepals becoming enlarged in fruit and 3-seeded ovary; stigmas 3, entire, joined at base.

1	Sepals of female flowers 3	2
	Sepals of female flowers 6	3
2	Plant erect; leaves subsessile, often clasping at base, coarsely dentate with teeth over 1 mm high	1. *Tragia subsessilis*
	Plant climbing; leaves conspicuously petiolate, cordate, finely serrate, the teeth up to 1 mm high	2. *Tragia scheffleri*
3	Leaves cordate at base	4
	Leaves rounded or truncate at base	5
4	Pinnae on female sepals 6–7, stiff, linear	3. *Tragia insuavis*
	Pinnae on female sepals 4–5, flexuous, capillary	4. *Tragia brevipes*
5	Erect shrub with ovate bracts to female flowers	5. *Tragia* sp. *A*
	Climbing plant with suborbicular bracts to female flowers	*Tragiella natalensis*

1. Tragia subsessilis *Pax*

An erect or spreading perennial suffruticose herb without stinging hairs, and with sessile or subsessile coarsely dentate oblong leaves, sometimes clasping the stem at base.

An uncommon plant found in dry *Commiphora* bushland. EMB, MAC.

Bogdan 4436.

2. Tragia scheffleri *Baker*

A climbing herb, not stinging, with ovate-oblong, cordate leaves.

Apparently so far recorded only from one specimen from the drier lakeside of west Kenya. MUM.

Agnew, Musumba, and Kiniaruh 8069.

3. Tragia insuavis *Prain*

A climbing or trailing perennial herb with stinging hairs especially on the stems, and with ovate, cordate, often almost glabrous leaves.

Rather uncommon in dry bushland, and very variable. NAR, MAG, MAC, KAJ.

Bogdan 413.

4. Tragia brevipes *Pax* (see p. 217)

A climbing herb, sometimes woody at base, with stinging hairs (especially on the fruits) and ovate to sub-orbicular, acuminate, cordate leaves.

Fairly common at edges of upland dry forest types, this plant is one of the principal stingers of Upland Kenya. HE, HC, HT, HA, KIT, MUM, KIS, NAR, NBI.

Strid 2879; Leippert 5229.

5. Tragia *sp.* **A.**

An erect shrub without stinging hairs, and with the leaves oblong, truncate at base.

This species has only been collected once, in black soil at Machakos. More material is badly needed. MAC.

Thomas 757.

6. TRAGIELLA *Pax & K. Hoffm.*

A genus very similar to *Tragia* but with the stigmas fused almost to the tip, forming a hollow entire column.

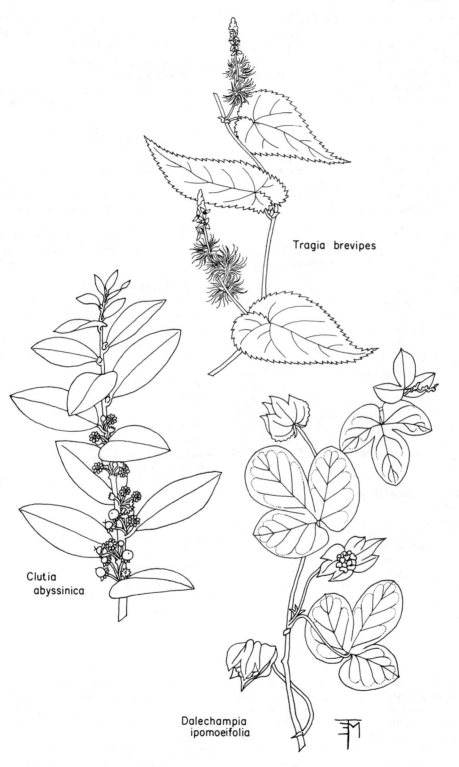

Tragia brevipes

Clutia
abyssinica

Dalechampia
ipomoeifolia

Tragiella natalensis (*Sond.*) *Pax & Hoffm.*

A twining climber, sometimes annual, with stinging hairs and elliptic-oblong leaves, widest in the middle and ± truncate at base.

Locally common in dry forest in Upland Kenya. HA, NAR, RV, NBI, KAJ.

van Someren 2409; Agnew 7925.

7. RICINUS *L.*

Herbs or shrubs with palmatisect, stipulate leaves; flowers in panicles, monoecious; male flowers with sepals 3–5, petals 0 and stamens very numerous borne on branching filaments; female flowers with caducous sepals and no disc; ovary with 3 ovules and a twice-divided stigma; seeds 3.

Ricinus communis *L.*

A tall annual or perennial herb, sometimes branching above, with large 5–9-palmatisect leaves; panicles terminal; capsule often softly prickly.

Widely cultivated (as Castor Oil) and spontaneous in dry country. HE, HA, MUM, NAR, RV, MAG, NBI.

Hanid and Kiniaruh 639.

8. DALECHAMPIA *L.*

Usually climbers with twining stems and alternate leaves; flowers monoecious, in dense axillary peduncled heads, subtended and ± enclosed by a pair of leafy bracts; male flowers without disc or petals, with 4–6 calyx lobes and 20–30 stamens fused into a central column; female flowers with 5–12 sepals becoming enlarged in fruit, and an entire stigma.

Dalechampia ipomoeifolia *Benth.* (*D. scandens* auct.) (see p. 217)

A twining perennial with 3–5-lobed palmatifid leaves; bracts subtending inflorescence often acutely 3-lobed at tip, ovate, yellow; fruit surrounded by 9–12 stiff-spreading calyx lobes.

A common plant in disturbed *Commiphora* bushland in dry country, often growing by roadsides or around habitations. The sepals in fruit develop extremely irritating stinging hairs. MAG, MAC, KAJ.

Agnew 5415.

9. JATROPHA *L.*

Herbs or shrubs, sometimes tuberous at base, usually with palmatifid leaves; flowers in terminal or axillary cymes, monoecious; male flowers with 5 sepals and petals and ± 5-lobed disc, and 8 stamens in two series (5 + 3) with connate filaments; female flowers similar to the male but without the stamens and with a usually 3-celled ovary, with connate, shortly bifid styles.

A genus of dry-land plants, rather rare in our area. *J. curcas* L. is cultivated as the 'physic-nut' for its medicinal qualities.

1   Plants with spiny stipules   2
    Plants unarmed   4
2   Spines in pairs only, each spine undivided   3
    Spines divided or in paired clusters
                               1. J. fissispina
3   Spines more than 15 mm long; leaves orbicular, densely woolly   *2. J. ferox*
    Spines less than 8 mm long; leaves obovate, alternate, sparsely pubescent to almost glabrous   *3. J. parvifolia*
4   Tree or shrub to 2 m or more; leaves stiff, shallowly lobed; stipules entire
                                 4. J. curcas
    Weak shrub to 1 m; leaves deeply palmatifid; stipules divided into capillary segments
                               5. J. spicata

1. Jatropha fissispina *Pax*

A shrub to about 1·5 m tall, with a soft, fleshy stem and orbicular, palmatifid, tomentose leaves; flowers green.

Rare plant found in the Magadi area. MAG. Bally 7138.

2. Jatropha ferox *Pax*

In KTS. p. 206. MAC.

3. Jatropha parvifolia *Chiov.*

A shrub to nearly 3 m, with clusters of sinuate, obovate small (to 4 cm long) leaves; flowers small, inconspicuous.

Rare plant found in the Magadi area. MAG. Bally B2646.

4. Jatropha curcas *L.*

Cultivated in MUM, MAC, and NBI.

5. Jatropha spicata *Pax*

A low shrub with swollen rootstock and deeply divided leaves; flowers green.

Uncommon plant found in dry country. MAG, KAJ.

Napper 1256A.

10. CLUTIA *L.*

Monoecious or dioecious herbs or shrubs (rarely small trees) with alternate, entire, stipulate leaves which turn conspicuously orange or red before falling; flowers in axillary fascicles with 5 sepals bearing glands at base, and 5 petals; disc usually present as glands under the petals in male flowers; male flowers with 5 stamens shortly declinate from a central column, the column with a terminal truncate sterile ovary; female flowers with usually free styles and once-divided stigmas, fruit with one red seed per loculus, dehiscent.

1 Leaves oblong to oblanceolate, pubescent; male flowers with 5 glands on disc at base of petals; female flowers with 3 stalked glands on base of sepals   1. *C. robusta*
   Leaves ovate to lanceolate or elliptic, rarely oblanceolate, commonly glabrous; male flowers with more than 5 glands on disc at base of petals; female flowers with 2 (often confluent) glands on base of sepals
                                         2. *C. abyssinica*

1. Clutia robusta *Pax*

A woody shrub to 2 m, dioecious or often with a few female flowers on each male plant; leaves oblong or oblanceolate, pubescent. Common in dry highland bushland, 8000–10 500 ft. HE, HT, HM, HA, HK.

Agnew, Azavedo, and Khatri 9520; Greenway 7850.

2. Clutia abyssinica *Jaub. & Spach* (*C. mollis, C. pedicellaris* of Check List) (see p. 217)

A dioecious woody shrub to 2 m with a variable leaf shape (ovate to oblanceolate or elliptic, obtuse or acute), a variable indumentum (nearly glabrous to densely velvety-pubescent) but with very constant floral characters as given in the Key. As here defined this is our commonest *Clutia*, occurring throughout the upland area at forest edges to 9000 ft. HE, HC, HT, HM, HA, HK, KIT, MUM, KIS, NAR, RV, NAN, NBI, KAJ.

Agnew, Azavedo, and Khatri 9560; Polhill and Lucas 11.

11. EUPHORBIA *L.*

Herbs, shrubs, or trees with simple alternate or opposite leaves, with or without stipules; flowers much reduced to single stamens (male flowers) and single gynoecium (female flowers) and crowded in a cymose capitulum with linear bracts, called a *cyathium*; cyathia solitary or arranged in dichasial cymes, each with one central female flower and many peripheral male flowers; involucre of cyathium regular, bearing 1–5 glands and 5 scale-teeth; fruit a capsule with 3 1-seeded loculi.

An abundant genus, including the succulent candelabra trees. In the following account only those species which may be taken for low shrubs or climbers, as well as all herbs, are keyed out. The remainder will be found in KTS pp. 181–222.

1 Plant unarmed   2
   Plant spiny   28
2 Plant stemless, flowering before the leaves; leaves in a rosette   1. *E. rubella*
   Plant with leaves at flowering time, with a stem; leaves not in a rosette   3
3 All leaves opposite   4
   At least the lower leaves alternate   11
4 Cyathia in axillary, pedunculate clusters
                                         2. *E. hirta*
   Cyathia solitary, axillary or at dichotomies 5
5 Leaves linear   3. *E. arabica*
   Leaves oblong to orbicular   6
6 Perennials with thickened rootstock; appendages of involucral glands orbicular, conspicuous, white or pink   7
   Annuals or weak perennials with appendages of involucral glands small, broader than long, inconspicuous   8
7 Leaves orbicular; peduncle less than 2·5 times as long as the involucre   5. *E. rivae*
   Leaves oblong; peduncle more than 2·5 times as long as the involucre   4. *E. zambesiaca*
8 Plant entirely glabrous   6. *E. inaequilatera*
   Plant hairy at least on the stem   9
9 Appendages of involucral glands white, lobed, visible under a lens; capsule often glabrous
                                   7. *E. mossambicensis*
   Appendages of involucral glands obscure, not lobed; capsule hairy   10
10 Stem hirsute all round   8. *E. granulata*
   Stem with a line of pubescence along the upper side only   9. *E. prostrata*
11 Annuals   12
   Perennials   17
12 Involucre with only one lateral gland
                                      10. *E. geniculata*
   Involucral glands more than one, regularly arranged   13
13 Petiole equalling half lamina-length; cyathia on axillary branchlets, never terminal to the main, monopodial branches
                                     11. *E. acalyphoides*
   Petioles shorter than half lamina-length; cyathia terminal on dichotomising, sympodial, principal branches   14
14 Majority of cyathia held in terminal corymbs
                                                    16
   Majority of cyathia solitary at nodes   15
15 Capsule tomentose, with spreading hairs
                                     12. *E. crotonoides*
   Capsule pubescent, with appressed hairs
                                      13. *E. systyloides*
16 Cyathia subtended by linear bracts; ovary pubescent   15. *E. agowensis*
   Cyathia subtended by triangular, orbicular to reniform bracts which clasp the stem; ovary glabrous   17
17 Glands of involucre divided into 4 or more branched processes 14. *E. pseudograntii*
   Glands of involucre entire or with only 2 points   18

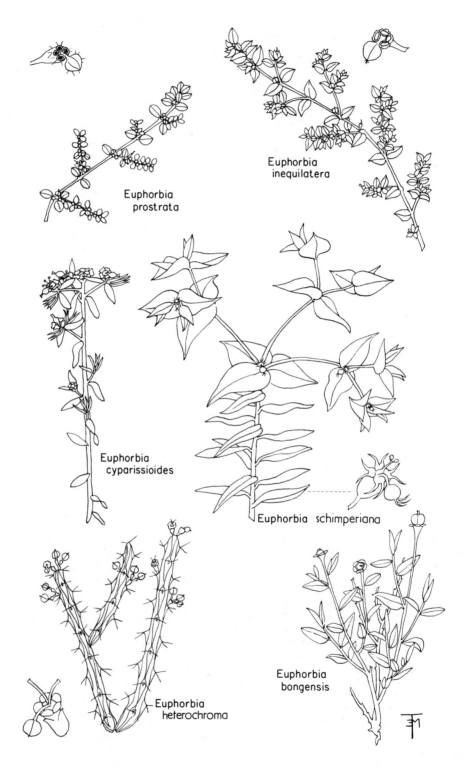

Euphorbia
prostrata

Euphorbia
inequilatera

Euphorbia
cyparissioides

Euphorbia schimperiana

Euphorbia
heterochroma

Euphorbia
bongensis

18 Involucral glands entire or obscurely crenate
22

Involucral glands **crescent-shaped** with two horns **19**

19 Bracts of the inflorescence triangular, pointed at the apex **20**

Bracts of the inflorescence reniform or orbicular, rounded at apex **21**

20 Involucral glands with two ± filamentous horns from a ± oval body
16. *E. schimperana*

Involucral glands with the body passing gradually into the abruptly tapering, awned horns 17. *E. repetita*

21 A many stemmed herb; leaves oblong to 3 cm long 18. *E. wellbyi*

A branched loose shrub; leaves elliptic to 20 cm long 19. *E. engleri*

22 A fleshy-stemmed climber; leaves soon falling
20. *E. gossypina*

Erect woody herbs or shrubs **23**

23 Leaves obovate, rounded at apex
21. *E. polyantha*

Leaves elliptic to oblong, if obovate-elliptic then acute at apex **24**

24 Capsule warty 22. *E. depauperata*
Capsule smooth **25**

25 Leaves obovate-elliptic 24. *E. ugandensis*
Leaves oblong or linear **26**

26 Cyathia glabrous externally; capsules glabrous
27

Cyathia finely pubescent externally; capsules spreading-pubescent 23. *E. bongensis*

27 Leaves obovate-elliptic, 2–8 cm long
24. *E. ugandensis*
Leaves narrow-oblong or linear, less than 2 cm long 25. *E. cyparissoides*

28 Spines solitary 26. *E. graciliramea*
Spines in pairs **29**

29 Spines forking more than half way up a common stalk 27. *E. glochidiata*

Spines separate from the base or with a short common stalk **30**

30 Stem irregularly lobed with wings or protuberances **31**

Stem quadrangular or cylindrical, not lobed
32

31 Stem with flattened portions, often semicircular at apex 28. *E. buruana*

Stem with fleshy spine-pointed lobes
29. *E. brevitorta*

32 Spines fused in pairs at base **33**
Spines free at base **34**

33 Spine shields horizontally prolonged with accessory hooked prickles at end of horizontal arms 30 *E. uhligiana*

Spine shields not horizontally prolonged, accessory prickles absent or, if any, straight
32. *E.* sp. *A*

34 Cartilaginous stem-margin (on which the spines are set) continuous **35**

Cartilaginous stem margin interrupted
32. *E.* sp. *A*

35 Stems ascending, less than 1·5 cm thick; heads dark red 33. *E.* sp. *B*

Stems erect, over 1·5 cm thick; heads yellow
31. *E. heterochroma*

1. Euphorbia rubella *Pax*

Perennial from a fleshy tuber with its apex at soil level; leaves suborbicular to elliptic, rounded at base and apex; bracts white and pink; involucral glands 6, yellow, entire.

A rare plant found in dry rocky country only recorded from south Elgon. HC, KIT.

Tweedie 69/12.

2. Euphorbia hirta *L.* (see p. 224)

An annual or weak perennial with prostrate branches and lanceolate-elliptic, often maculate leaves; cyathia in pedunculate clusters.

A common weed in the drier parts of our area. HE, KIT, MUM, KIS, BAR, RV, MAC, NBI, KAJ.

Hanid and Kiniaruh 814; Faden 67196.

3. Euphorbia arabica *Boiss.*

An erect glabrous annual to 30 cm tall, loosely branched above, with linear leaves.

Rare plant found in very dry country in the north of our area. BAR.

Leippert 5200.

4. Euphorbia zambesiaca *Benth.*

An often hairy perennial with a heavy woody rootstock and ascending stems to 20 cm; leaves oblong.

Rare plant found in upland grassland in the south of our area, this plant is found in Tanzania and Zambia. HL.

van Someren in EAH 12279.

5. Euphorbia rivae *Pax*

A perennial with a swollen fleshy rootstock and short prostrate branches, sparsely hairy, bearing orbicular leaves.

A local plant of shallow soils, particularly common around Nairobi. EMB, MAC, NBI.

Agnew 8813; Verdcourt 1962.

6. Euphorbia inaequilatera *Sond.* (see p. 220)

A prostrate or erect glabrous annual with asymmetric oblong leaves and very inconspicuous cyathia.

Common in waste ground and dry managed grassland and pastures. Said to be palatable to cattle. HE, HT, HM, KIT, MUM, KIS, NAR, RV, MAG, NBI, KAJ.

Hanid 251; Glover 2717.

7. Euphorbia mossambicensis (*Kl. & Gke.*) *Boiss.*

A prostrate annual with hairy stems and asymmetric leaves; the glandular appendages of the cyathia are difficult to see, and the distinctness of this species from the next needs confirmation.

Dry river beds in *Acacia* bushland. MAG.

Polhill and Greenway 451.

8. Euphorbia granulata *Forsk.*

A prostrate, sparsely hirsute annual with asymmetric leaves and inconspicuous cyathia.

Uncommon plant found in disturbed places in dry country, MAC, NBI.

Hanid and Kiniaruh 891; Faden 67195.

9. Euphorbia prostrata *Ait.* (see p. 220)

Very similar to the last species except for the line of pubescence only on the upper side of the stem.

Locally common as a weed of lawns and grassland throughout Kenya. KIS, KIT, NBI.

Tweedie 66/62; Bally 6571.

10. Euphorbia geniculata *Orteg.*

An erect, often unbranched, glabrescent annual with elliptic leaves; cyathia with only one, lateral, funnel-shaped gland.

An introduced common weed of cultivation in dry country. MUM, KIS, RV, MAC, NBI, KAJ.

Agnew 9673; Bally 8394.

11. Euphorbia acalyphoides *Boiss.*

An erect pubescent annual with ascending branches from the base, and petiolate, spathulate or obovate leaves; cyathia with hairy glands.

A rare *Euphorbia* of disturbed *Acacia* bushland. NAN, MAG.

Verdcourt 2757.

12. Euphorbia crotonoides *Boiss.* (see p. 224)

An erect, branched pubescent annual with lanceolate leaves narrowing into a short petiole; cyathia with entire, stalked glands; capsule with spreading white hairs, each hair almost half as long as the style.

The commonest annual weedy *Euphorbia* of cultivation and disturbed ground. HM, HA, KIT, MUM, NAR, RV, MAC, KAJ.

Agnew, Musumba, and Kiniaruh 7981; Verdcourt 1968.

13. Euphorbia systyloides *Pax*

Very similar to the last species except for the pubescent capsule with the hairs appressed.

Less common than *E. crotonoides* as a weed of cultivated ground and disturbed places in dry country. RV, MAC, NBI, KAJ.

Hanid and Kiniaruh 580; Bally 7704.

14. Euphorbia pseudograntii *Pax*

Herb or shrub with soft fleshy stems and oblanceolate leaves. It is dealt with in KTS p. 200. EMB, MAC.

15. Euphorbia agowensis *Boiss.*

An erect annual, branched above, with oblong or linear glabrous leaves; cyathia, at least the older ones, borne in groups of 2-5 in a loose corymb; involucral glands entire; capsule pubescent.

An uncommon *Euphorbia* of dry country. MAG, NAN, KAJ.

Agnew 9795; Glover and Samuel 2802.

16. Euphorbia schimperana *Scheele* (see p. 220)

An erect annual or short-lived perennial with usually narrowly elliptical leaves and deltoid triangular, clasping bracts, glabrous or hairy on all parts; involucral glands with a central crescent-shaped or oval body, abruptly joined to a filamentous horn at each end.

The commonest mountain *Euphorbia*, growing by roadsides and at forest edges. HE, HT, HM, HA, HK, KIT, KIS, RV, NBI, KAJ.

Hanid and Kiniaruh 605; Mathenge 198.

17. Euphorbia repetita *A. Rich.*

An erect perennial or, more rarely, annual with narrow-oblong leaves and long triangular bracts, often with a tuft of hairs below the nodes only; involucral glands narrowing gradually into a short, rapidly tapering incurved horn at each end.

Locally common in the drier highlands. HE, HT, HM, HA, HK, KIT.

Strid 3276; Napier 5957.

18. Euphorbia wellbyi *N. E. Br.*

Perennial from woody rhizomatous rootstock with erect, sparsely branched stems; leaves oblong, clasping at base; bracts of inflorescence orbicular.

An uncommon plant found in wet meadows within the upper forest limits. HE, HM, HA, HK.

Rauh Ke 518; Agnew 10002.

19. Euphorbia engleri *Pax*

A loose soft shurb with elliptic leaves; inflorescence an umbel of ± unbranched rays with orbicular bracts at intervals.

A common plant of shade within montane rain forest. HE, HM, HA, HK, HN, KIT, KAJ.

Mainwaring 2499; Agnew 8685.

20. Euphorbia gossypina *Pax*

A fleshy-stemmed shrub often trailing over trees, with oblong, acute, ephemeral leaves; inflorescence of umbellate cyathia which are white-woolly within.

Locally common in rocky bushland on shallow soils. HA, NAR, RV, NAN, MAC, NBI.

Wilkinson 313/60; Agnew, Hanid, and Kiniaruh 7865.

21. Euphorbia polyantha *Pax*

A much branched perennial shrub of dry *Commiphora* woodland dealt with in KTS p. 200. MAG, KAJ.

22. Euphorbia depauperata *A. Rich.* (see p. 224)

A perennial herb from a woody rootstock with ascending or erect branches and elliptic, mainly acute leaves; inflorescence bracts orbicular; ovary warty.

An uncommon plant of highland dry grassland. HE, HT, HM, HA, HK, KIT, RV.

Birch 61/64; Strid 2640.

23. Euphorbia bongensis *Peyr.* (see p. 220)

A low tortuous-branched shrub or, where burnt, herb with woody rootstock and oblong to narrowly elliptic, glabrous leaves; cyathia pubescent, solitary; capsules pubescent.

Rare plant found in western Kenya. KIT.

Brodhurst-Hill 469.

24. Euphorbia ugandensis *Pax*

An erect, much-branched shrub with elliptic leaves; inflorescence bracts reniform.

Uncommon plant found in montane rain-forest clearings and roadsides. HM, HA, HK.

Agnew and Lind 5634; Bally 1161.

25. Euphorbia cyparissoides *Pax* (see p. 220)

A perennial herb with many erect stems, usually densely covered with stiff narrow leaves.

Rare plant found in high altitude grassland. HC, HA, KIT.

Irwin 358.

26. Euphorbia graciliramea *Pax*

Perennial herb from a woody rootstock, with prostrate, succulent, ± cylindrical stems bearing 3 simple spines (2 small and 1 large) on each spine-shield.

Locally common in dry rocky country. This may eventually prove to be a subspecies of *E.*

triaculeata Forsk. NAR, RV, MAG, NAN, NBI, KAJ.

Hanid and Kiniaruh 897; Glover, Gwynne, and Samuel 1546.

27. Euphorbia glochidiata *Pax*

Perennial herb from a woody rootstock with trailing, rooting, succulent, ± cylindrical stems bearing 3 spines (2 small, 1 long and forked at apex) on each spine-shield.

Locally common in dry rocky country in the Athi River district. MAC, KAJ.

Agnew 5613; van Someren 4104.

28. Euphorbia buruana *Pax*

Perennial herb from a swollen fleshy root tuber, bearing many erect succulent, often variegated, irregularly winged stems with paired spines of various sizes.

Locally common in dry country. NAR, MAG, KAJ.

Classen 28.

29. Euphorbia brevitorta *Bally*

A densely tufted succulent with short unbranched spiny stems from a fleshy tuber.

Uncommon plant found in rocky grassland. NBI.

Classen 47.

30. Euphorbia uhligiana *Pax*

Perennial herb from a woody tap-root, with many erect succulent, angled-cylindrical stems bearing paired spines at apices of blunt lobes; spines fused at base.

Rare plant found in dry stony country. RV.

Glover 4066; Classen 52.

31. Euphorbia heterochroma *Pax* (see p. 224)

A low shrub dealt with in KTS p. 198. BAR, MAG, MAC, KAJ.

32. Euphorbia *sp.* A.

Similar to *E. uhligiana* except for the more cylindrical stems and with longer peduncles to the heads.

Rare plant found in dry rocky country. EMB, MAC.

Napper 1658.

33. Euphorbia *sp.* B.

Similar to *E. uhligiana* except for the spines which are well separated on the interrupted spine-shield.

Rare plant found in dry stony country. BAR, NAN.

Classen 68; Napper 1124.

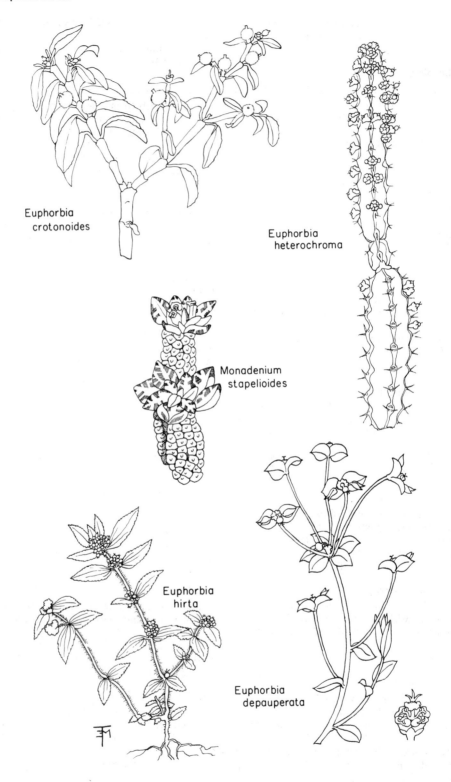

Euphorbia
crotonoides

Euphorbia
heterochroma

Monadenium
stapelioides

Euphorbia
hirta

Euphorbia
depauperata

12. MONADENIUM *Pax*

Succulent herbs or shrubs similar to *Euphorbia* except for the cyathium which is zygomorphic, held in two usually fused bracts, and with the involucre bearing a continuous glandular rim except for the abaxial side where a slot allows the female flower to hang free.

A curious group of plants which occur rarely in dry country. They are never abundant and have formed a number of endemics in East Africa.

1	Plant herbaceous, with annual stems	2
	Plant woody at base, with perennial stems	4
2	Cyathia held in pairs or threes	
		1. M. trinerve
	Cyathia solitary	3
3	Leaves crowded at stem apex and held on fleshy protuberances of the stem; cyathia 7-9 mm long	*2. M. rhizophorum*
	Leaves spaced along the cylindrical stem, not borne on protuberances; cyathia up to 6·5 mm long	*3. M. montanum*
4	Leaves held on fleshy, persistent protuberances of the stem, crowded	5
	Leaves spaced along the stem, not on fleshy protuberances	*4. M. invenustum*
5	Bract around cyathia whitish; gland of involucre red	*5. M. stapelioides*
	Bract around cyathia green; gland of involucre yellow	*6. M. yattanum*

1. Monadenium trinerve *Bally*

A perennial herb from a spherical tuber, with fleshy elliptic leaves and usually paired cyathia.

Rare plant found in dry country. MAC.
MacArthur in Bally E 109.

2. Monadenium rhizophorum *Bally*

A perennial erect succulent herb from a cylindrical tuber with fleshy elliptic leaves held on stem protuberances, and solitary cyathia.

Rare plant found in dry country. RV, MAC, KAJ.
Graham 2241; Agnew 10847.

3. Monadenium montanum *Bally*

Similar to *M. rhizophorum* but with the stems thinner, without protuberances, and with smaller cyathia.

Rare plant found in dry country. MAC, KAJ.
Record from P. R. O. Bally (1961) *The genus Monadenium*.

4. Monadenium invenustum *N. E. Br.*

A perennial, loose, fleshy shrub with a solitary, cylindrical stem arising from a globose tuber; leaves sub-orbicular to elliptical, thinly succulent; cyathia in cymes of 3-7.

Locally common, growing (never abundantly) in *Commiphora* bushland. MAC, KAJ.
Bally 592.

5. Monadenium stapelioides *Pax* (see p. 224)

A herb with short, fleshy, tuberculate, perennial stems arising from a tuberous rootstock; leaves elliptic to obovate; cyathia in pairs with a reddish involucral gland and pale bracts.

Locally common in dry rocky screes and cliffs in dry grassland. NAR, BAR, RV, MAG, NAN.
Bally 27.

6. Monadenium yattanum *Bally*

Very similar to *M. stapelioides* but differing in the less densely tuberculate stem and in the green cyathial bracts with a yellow involucral gland.

Rare plant found in the Machakos area. MAC.
Bally B9750.

54. ROSACEAE†

Trees, shrubs, or herbs with alternate, stipulate mostly serrate leaves; flowers usually in racemes, bisexual, regular, but with many exceptions, always with flower parts (except ovary) borne on a cup-shaped receptacle; calyx, sometimes with epicalyx, of 5 fused or free lobes; petals 5, free or absent; stamens usually many, rarely few; carpels 1-many, superior, free or sometimes united to the receptacle and inferior, many-seeded; fruit fleshy or dry.

1	Flowers conspicuous, with expanded coloured petals or plant spiny	2
	Flowers inconspicuous, petals absent; plant never spiny	4
2	Plant spiny	*4. Rubus*
	Plant unarmed	3
3	Petals yellow; fruit dry	*3. Potentilla hispanica*
	Petals white; fruit fleshy	*2. Fragaria vesca*
4	Shrub over 1 m tall, with glabrous leaves; flowers unisexual	*5. Cliffortia nitidula*
	Herbs or, if shrubby, then less than 1 m tall and the leaves hairy; flowers bisexual	*1. Alchemilla*

1. ALCHEMILLA *L.*

Perennial herbs or low shrubs with or without a basal leaf rosette; leaves palmate or palmately lobed, rounded in outline; inflorescence a simple or diffuse panicle of cymes; flowers small, bisexual, with parts in fours; epicalyx present; sepals 4, at the top of an obconical receptacle tube;

† By A. D. Q. Agnew and S. Kibe.

petals 0; stamens 4, with the disc partly closing the throat of the receptacle tube; carpels 2–12, free from each other, each with a basal style and capitate stigma; fruit of achenes retained within the receptacle tube.

1   Erect shrubs with sessile leaves   2
    Herbs or creeping shrubs with petiolate leaves
                                                3
2   Leaves deeply 3-lobed, with the central lobe apically broad and tridentate; lateral lobes lanceolate   1. *A. argyrophylla*
    Leaves unlobed, wedge-shaped, dentate or entire at the broad apex   2. *A. elgonensis*
3   Trailing shrubs or wiry herbs with leaves evenly distributed throughout the stems, and without leaf rosettes   4
    Herbs producing leaf rosettes as well as leafy trailing stolons   7
4   Stipules entirely papery; leaf lobes 9 or more, each triangular, acute   3. *A. hageniae*
    Stipules with a green leafy apex; leaf lobes 5 or fewer, rounded or notched   5
5   Stems woody at base; epicalyx much smaller than calyx lobes   4. *A. johnstonii*
    Stems herbaceous throughout; epicalyx almost as big as or bigger than the calyx   6
6   Receptacle, calyx, and epicalyx glabrous
                                        5. *A. ellenbeckii*
    Receptacle, calyx, and epicalyx hairy
                                        8. *A. cryptantha*
7   Epicalyx lobes longer than calyx lobes   8
    Epicalyx lobes shorter than or equal to calyx lobes   10
8   Leaves lobed to half the diameter or more, each lobe oblong to obovate bearing 9–13 teeth on each side of the midrib
                                        6. *A. kiwuensis*
    Leaves lobed to less than half the diameter; each lobe as wide as long, with up to 6 teeth on either side of the midrib   9
9   Stipules membranous, entire or with green teeth at apex; leaf lobes with 5–7 teeth
                                        7. *A. microbetula*
    Stipules with a green leafy apex; leaf lobes with 9–11 teeth at apex   8. *A. cryptantha*
10 Pedicels 3–50 mm long   11
    Pedicels 1 mm long or less   13
11 Underside of leaf glabrous and smooth except for major radiating veins; leaf lobes truncate   9. *A. cyclophylla*
    Underside of leaf hairy with a raised venation; leaf lobes rounded   12
12 Hairs on underside of leaf appressed and silky-white   10. *A. gracilipes*
    Hairs on underside of leaf spreading and brownish-white   11. *A. rothii*

13 Flowers in glomerules on pedunculate inflorescences   12. *A. fischeri*
    Flowers 1–2 hidden within the stipules
                                        7. *A. microbetula*

1. Alchemilla argyrophylla *Oliv.*

A low, much-branched shrub with the woody stems covered by brown stipules, and with silvery-hairy, deeply 3-lobed sessile leaves; flower clusters axillary.

Abundant and locally dominant, in well-drained alpine soils from 9000–14000 ft. HA, HK.

Agnew 7016; Kokwaro 32.

2. Alchemilla elgonensis *Mildbr.* (see p. 228)

Similar to *A. argyrophylla* except for the keyed leaf characters, this plant often flowers in its first year after fire. It replaces *A. argyrophylla* on Mount Elgon and Cheranganis.

Hedberg 224; Agnew, Kibe and Mathenge 10552.

3. Alchemilla hageniae *T. C. E. Fries*

A trailing wiry herb or soft shrub with silky hairs on all parts, and membranous stipules which almost cover the stem; leaves with acute shallow lobes; flowers in a pedunculate panicle.

Endemic on the Aberdares where it sometimes forms the dominant cover in *Philippia* woodland. HA.

Agnew and Menezes 7144; Polhill 168.

4. Alchemilla johnstonii *Oliv.*

A low woody straggling shrub with short erect glabrous or reddish-hairy branches and with small 3–5-lobed leaves; leaf lobes notched at apex; flowers on short slender lateral branches.

Common in wet alpine soils. HE, HC, HT, HA, HK.

Hedberg 2010; Isaac, March 1962.

5. Alchemilla ellenbeckii *Engl.*

Similar to *A. johnstonii* except for the keyed characters, this species is found in bare wet stony soils of streamsides and flushes in the alpine zone. HE, HC, HT, HM, HA, HK.

Lind 5173; Williams 558.

6. Alchemilla kiwuensis *Engl.*

A creeping, pubescent herb with rosettes of deeply 5–7-lobed leaves and raceme-like panicles of hairy flowers; fruits are nearly always present which inflate the receptacle tube in a characteristic way.

Locally common in highland grassland. HE, HT, HA, HK, MUM.

Verdcourt 601; Tweedie 68/59.

7. Alchemilla microbetula *Th. Fr. jr.*

Similar to *A. kiwuensis* but with the keyed differences and small, 1-2-flowered inflorescences almost hidden by the stipules.

Rare plant, only recorded for the Mount Elgon alpine zone. HE.

Hedberg 896.

8. Alchemilla cryptantha *A. Rich.*

Similar to *A. kiwuensis* but the basal rosette is often absent, and the leaves are more shallowly lobed.

Locally common in alpine and montane grassland. HE, HC, HT, HA, HK, KIT, NAR.

Bogdan 445; Tweedie 67/159.

9. Alchemilla cyclophylla *Th. Fr. jr.*

A prostrate herb with leafy stolons and rosettes of shallowly bluntly 5-9-lobed, almost glabrous leaves; flowers hairy, in short erect racemes.

Endemic to bare peaty soils on the Aberdares and Mount Kenya. HA, HK.

Verdcourt 3777; Agnew and Armstrong 8159.

10. Alchemilla gracilipes (*Engl.*) *Engl.*

Similar to *A. cyclophylla* except for the pointed leaf-lobes, the silky hairiness and the branched racemes.

Locally common in montane grassland. HC, HT, HM, HA, HK, RV.

Bogdan 338; Agnew, Azavedo and Khatri 9504.

11. Alchemilla rothii *Oliv.*

Similar to *A. cyclophylla* but with more hairy and rounded leaf lobes and (usually) branched inflorescences.

Locally common in the heath and bamboo zones of the mountains. HE, HM, HA, HK.

Battiscombe 1223; Agnew and Armstrong 8132.

12. Alchemilla fischeri *Engl.*

A trailing herb with rosettes of deeply 5-9-lobed, hairy leaves, the lobes obovate and rounded at apex; inflorescence a panicle of small masses of subsessile hairy flowers.

Endemic to the Aberdares and Mt. Kenya where it is common in *Philippia* woodland. HA, HK.

Agnew and Lind 5017; Verdcourt 3781.

2. FRAGARIA *L.*

Perennial stoloniferous herbs with trifoliolate or ternate leaves in a rosette; flowers in few-flowered cymes, pentamerous; epicalyx present; receptacle short, flat; petals 5, pink or white; stamens numerous; fruit a fleshy receptacle bearing scattered, dry achenes.

Fragaria vesca *L.*

A stoloniferous herb with ovate, serrate leaflets, hairy above; fruit covered with scattered achenes.

The strawberry. Once recorded from the Aberdares but never seen since. Possibly adventive from gardens. HA.

Record from FTEA.

3. POTENTILLA *L.*

Perenial herbs with pinnate or palmate leaves and solitary or cymose flowers; flowers bisexual; epicalyx present; sepals 5, on a short flat receptacle; petals 5, often showy; stamens numerous; carpels numerous, on a convex receptacle, each with a lateral style; fruit of dry achenes.

Potentilla pensylvanica *L.*

A tufted pubescent herb from a woody rootstock, with pinnate leaves and a terminal corymb of yellow flowers.

Possibly introduced and recently discovered on the Mau highlands in dry montane bush. HM.

Greenway and Kanuri 13582.

4. RUBUS *L.*

Shrubs or herbs with palmately divided leaves and (in ours) armed erect or scrambling stems; flowers bisexual in terminal compound panicles; epicalyx 0; sepals 5, on a shallow receptacle; stamens numerous; carpels inserted on a convex receptacle each with 2 ovules and subterminal style; fruit of 1-seeded drupes.

1	Stem glabrous	2
	Stem pubescent	4
2	Leaves 3-foliolate; leaflets whitish-tomentose beneath, glabrous above	1. *R. steudneri*
	Leaves more than 4-foliolate; leaflets glabrous on both surfaces	3
3	Petals shorter than calyx; calyx 5-8 mm long	2. *R. pinnatus*
	Petals longer than calyx; calyx 9-19 mm long	3. *R. scheffleri*
4	Stems annual, erect	5
	Stems perennial, scrambling, usually rooting on touching ground	6
5	Receptacle cylindrically elongate; stem to 75 cm tall, scarcely pubescent, without glands	4. *R. rosifolius*
	Receptacle globose; stem over 1 m tall, densely covered with capitate glandular hairs	5. *R. volkensii*
6	Petals always exceeding calyx	7
	Petals equal to or shorter than calyx or absent	8
7	Leaflets densely whitish-tomentose beneath, glabrous above; leaflets elliptic to elliptic-ovate, 5·5 x 3 cm	6. *R. friesiorum*

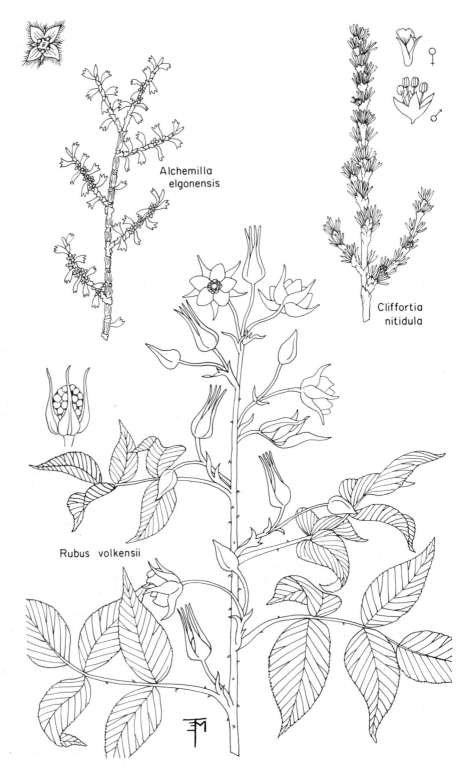

Alchemilla
elgonensis

Cliffortia
nitidula

Rubus volkensii

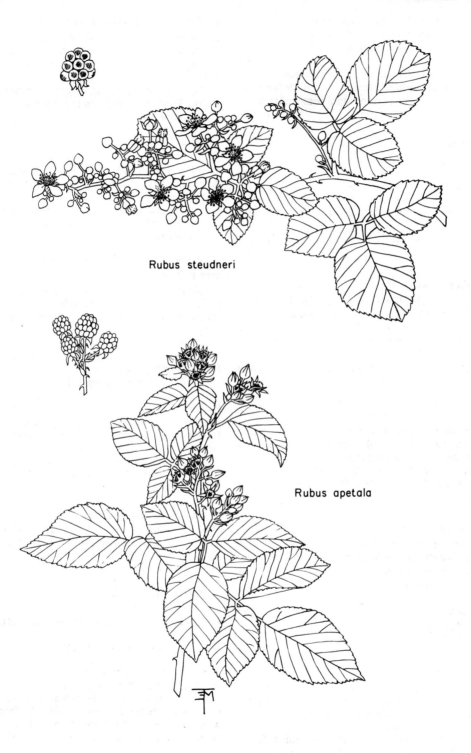

Rubus steudneri

Rubus apetala

Leaflets ± densely softly hairy and greenish beneath, pubescent above; leaflets broadly ovate to ovate-oblong 9·5 x 5·5 cm
                                          7. *R. keniensis*
8   Petals usually absent or fugaceous; leaves usually imparipinnate   8. *R. apetalus*
    Petals usually present and persistent; leaves usually trifoliolate   9. *R. rigidus*

1. Rubus steudneri *Schweinf.* (see p. 229)

A pubescent or tomentose scrambler with 3-foliolate leaves and purple flowers with large petals; drupes orange to dark red and glabrous.

Locally common in undergrowth in montane forest clearings and edges. HE, HC, HT, HM, HA, HK, KAJ.

Glover, Gwynne, and Samuel 1373; Tweedie 68/20.

2. Rubus pinnatus *Willd.*

A scrambling shrub with glabrous, glaucous stems and pinnate leaves; flowers pink in a lax panicle, petals shorter than sepals; drupes black, pubescent.

Locally common in upland rain-forest and bamboo. HE, HC, HT, HM, HA, HK.

Battiscombe 1191; Lind, Harris, and Agnew 5065.

3. Rubus scheffleri *Engl.*

Similar to *R. pinnatus* except for the key characters, the frequently trifoliolate leaves and the lack of glaucous bloom on the stem.

Uncommon plant found in upland rain-forest margins and glades. HC, HA, HN, KAJ.

Grant 1217; Agnew 9374.

4. Rubus rosifolius *Sm.*

An erect pubescent herb, with few prickles, pinnate leaves, and a leafy terminal inflorescence of white flowers; drupes very numerous becoming scarlet-red, succulent.

An introduced plant which appears to be spreading along stream banks in the Aberdares area. HA, MAC.

Faden 67576; Mathenge 232.

5. Rubus volkensii *Engl.* (see p. 228)

A large erect glandular (sticky) hairy herb with pinnate leaves and axillary as well as terminal small panicles of white flowers; drupes pubescent, orange-red, succulent.

Common in clearings within the upper forest and bamboo zones. HE, HA, HK.

Mwangangi 368; Agnew 8667.

6. Rubus friesiorum *C. E. Gust.*

A sub-erect pubescent to tomentose shrub with 3-foliolate leaves and a cylindrical terminal inflorescence of pinkish flowers; drupes glabrous or hairy.

Rare plant found at edges of montane rain-forest, 9000–10 000 ft, in the Aberdares. HA.

Hedberg 1996.

7. Rubus keniensis *Standl.*

A stout, scrambling, tomentose shrub with 3-foliolate leaves and whitish-pink flowers in a lax terminal panicle; drupes very large, turning orange, pubescent, watery and tasteless.

Locally common in wet montane forest on the Aberdares and Mt. Kenya. HA, HK.

Mathenge 383; Agnew 8736.

8. Rubus apetalus *Poir.* (*R. adolfi-friedericii* Engl.) (see p. 229)

A stout scrambling pubescent shrub with 5–7-foliolate leaves and a terminal inflorescence of green flowers; petals absent; drupes red or black, pubescent or glabrous.

A rather variable species of acid soils in drier montane forest and upland bushland. HE, HC, HA, HK, KIT, KIS, MAC.

Verdcourt 951; Agnew 9362.

9. Rubus rigidus *Sm.*

Similar to *R. friesiorum* except for its prickles (longer at 2 mm or more), puberulous leaflets and lanceolate (not obovate) petals.

Locally common at the edge of upland rain-forest, 3000–6500 ft. HA, HK, MUM, NBI, KAJ.

Verdcourt and Polhill 2976 (S).

5. CLIFFORTIA *L.*

Dioecious shrubs with trifoliolate or simple linear leaves and very reduced, solitary flowers; petals 0; stamens 3–50; fruit of 1–2 dry achenes enclosed by the calyx tube.

Cliffortia nitidula *R. E. & T. C. E. Fries* (see p. 228)

Described in KTS p. 401. HE, HC, HA, HK.

55. CAESALPINIACEAE†

Trees, shrubs, or herbs with alternate, stipulate, pinnate or bipinnate, rarely simple leaves; flowers bisexual, zygomorphic, in racemes; calyx of 5 free imbricate segments; corolla of 5 free petals, imbricate with the uppermost within the rest; stamens usually 10; ovary of one carpel, with a

† A. D. Q. Agnew.

terminal style and stigma; fruit a pod, dehiscent along opposite sides or indehiscent.

A large family of trees and shrubs. The genera and species keyed out in the following account are only those herbs, climbers, and shrubs which do not appear in KTS.

1   Plants spiny   2
    Plants without spines   3
2   Flowers white or cream, almost regular; pods winged, smooth   4. *Pterolobium stellatum*
    Flowers yellow, zygomorphic; pods unwinged, prickly   3. *Caesalpinia volkensii*
3   Climbers   1. *Tylosema fassoglensis*
    Erect or prostrate herbs or shrubs   2. *Cassia*

1. TYLOSEMA *(Schweinf.) Torre & Hillc.*

Climbers or trailers from a swollen rootstock with or without tendrils, and with simple bilobed leaves; flowers in racemes, yellow, heterostylic; sepals with the upper two fused, the rest free; petals 5, the uppermost smallest; stamens 10, but only two fertile; ovary with a long stalk; pods stalked, woody, 1–2-seeded.

Tylosema fassoglensis *(Schweinf.) Torre & Hillc.* (see p. 232)

A large trailing tendrillar climber with cordate, notched leaves; conspicuous flowers with yellow to pink crinkled petals.

Locally common in hot country where not too dry. HE, HC, KIT, MUM, KIS, NAR, NAN, MAC. Agnew, Musumba and Kiniaruh 7975; McDonald 914.

2. CASSIA *L.*

Annual or perennial herbs, shrubs, or trees with pinnate leaves, often with conspicuous glands on petiole and rachis; flowers in racemes, usually yellow; sepals 5, free; petals 5, the upper ones smaller; stamens 10, the upper ones sometimes staminodal, dehiscing by terminal pores or slits; pods variable, flat or cylindrical, woody to papery, indehiscent or dehiscent, with or without septa between the seeds.

1   Sepals rounded at apex   2
    Sepals acute at apex   7
2   Plant with glandular hairs   1. *C. absus*
    Plant without glandular hairs   3
3   Petiole and rachis of leaves with massive multicellular glands; pods straight and ± smooth   4
    Petiole and rachis of leaves without glands; pods curved and with a longitudinal crest   2. *C. italica*

4   Gland present on petiole base only   3. *C. occidentalis*
    Gland present on rachis between leaflets, never on petiole base   5
5   Leaflets acute at apex   4. *C. floribunda*
    Leaflets obtuse at apex   6
6   Pedicels of flowers over 1·5 cm long   5. *C. obtusifolia*
    Pedicels of flowers under 1·0 cm long   6. *C. bicapsularis*
7   Rachis of leaves winged between the insertion of the leaflets, so that it appears crenate or dentate once the leaflets fall   8
    Rachis of leaves unwinged, appearing entire after removal of leaflets   9
8   Plant perennial from a woody rootstock   8. *C.* sp. *B*
    Plant annual   7. *C. mimosoides*
9   Gland on petiole stalked   10
    Gland on petiole sessile   13
    (*N.B. Occasional specimens and leaves may be without glands and further searching may reveal them. If not, then both dichotomies of the key must be followed here.*)
10   Midrib of leaflet marginal, with lateral veins on one side only; glands with long stalks   9. *C. fallacina*
    Midrib of leaflet eccentric but with laterals on both sides; glands shortly stalked   11
11   Glands on petiole with stalk up to 1·5 times gland diameter; pods to 2·5 cm long; leaves to 2·2 cm long   10. *C. usambarensis*
    Glands longer-stalked; pods to 4 cm long; leaves up to 4·5 cm long   12
12   Accessory glands mostly present along rachis; upper leaf surface mostly glabrous; conspicuous vein anastomoses often present along leaflet margins   11. *C. grantii*
    Accessory glands absent; upper leaf surface densely pubescent or tomentose; anastomoses at margin of leaflets inconspicuous or absent   15. *C. hildebrandtii*
13   At least some leaflets more than 1·5 cm long; inflorescence subumbellate, of 3–5 flowers with peduncles less than 5 mm, and pedicels less than 5 mm; pods to 2·5 cm long   16. *C. nigricans*
    Leaflets rarely as long as 1·6 cm, inflorescence racemose or flowers solitary on longer pedicels; pods more than 2·5 cm long   14
14   Leaflets in 9–18 pairs; pods less than 3·5 cm long   17. *C. falcinella*
    At least some leaves with more than 20 pairs of leaflets; pods usually more than 3·5 cm long   15

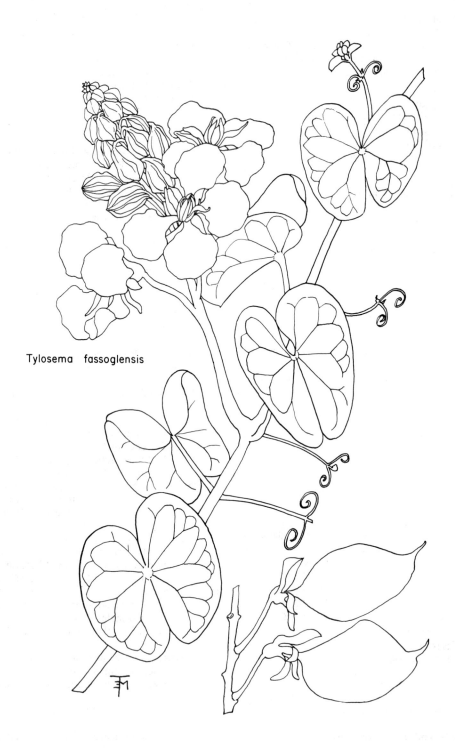

Tylosema fassoglensis

15 Annual 16
  Perennial 12. *C. parva*
16 Pedicels mostly over 10 mm long; petals
    usually over 8·5 mm long 13. *C. kirkii*
  Pedicels mostly under 10 mm long; petals
    usually under 8·5 mm long 14. *C. quarrei*

1. Cassia absus *L.*

An erect glandular pubescent annual with 3–5 asymmetric ovate leaflets to each leaf and small yellow to red flowers; pods flat, papery, dehiscent.

Locally common as a weed of dry country cultivation. HK, MUM, KIS, MAC.

Kokwaro 1803; Napier 2464.

2. Cassia italica (*Mill.*) *F. W. Andr.*

An erect glabrescent perennial herb or shrub with 4–8 pairs of oblong leaflets to each leaf and racemes of yellow flowers; pods flattened, curved or straight, with a ridge along centre of valve, papery, dehiscent.

The 'senna pods' of herbalists, this species is rare, found in dry bushland. NAR, BAR, MAC.

Knight B 14; Bally 3177.

3. Cassia occidentalis *L.* (see p. 234)

An annual or perennial, often robust, glabrous shrub with 4–7 pairs of ovate, acuminate leaflets to each leaf and short racemes of yellow flowers; pods long, with a raised bony ridge along each edge and constricted between the seeds, dehiscent.

Locally common as a weed of cultivation in the warmer districts. HA, MUM, KIS, BAR, MAC.

Hanid and Kiniaruh 660; Mainwaring 2192.

4. Cassia floribunda *Cav.*

Similar to *C. occidentalis* but with fewer leaflets and indehiscent, cylindrical pods.

Locally common, in cultivation in cleared forest. HT, MUM, KIS, NAR, EMB, MAC, NBI.

Strid 2618; Verdcourt 1481.

5. Cassia obtusifolia *L.*

An erect glabrescent annual with 2–3 pairs of obovate-elliptic leaflets to the leaf and solitary axillary yellow flowers; pod square in cross-section, long, curved, and narrowed towards the apex.

Locally common, as a weed of cultivation in warmer districts. KIT, KIS, MUM, BAR.

Hanid 683; Knight 7.

6. Cassia bicapsularis *L.*

An erect bushy woody glabrous shrub with 2–3 pairs of obovate to oblong leaflets on the leaf and short racemes of yellow flowers; pod cylindrical, indehiscent.

Locally common in disturbed, dry bushland. HE, MUM, KIS, BAR, RV.

Agnew, Musumba, and Kiniaruh 8008; Mwangangi 10.

7. Cassia mimosoides *L.* (see p. 235)

A prostrate or erect mostly pubescent wiry annual with parallel-sided leaves bearing over 30 leaflet-pairs, and solitary yellow flowers; pod flat, dehiscent.

Common in disturbed dry places and open habitats on shallow soil. HC, KIT, KIS, RV, MAG, MAC, NBI, KAJ.

Agnew 9843; Kerfoot 3935.

8. Cassia *sp.* **B.** *of FTEA*

Similar to *C. mimosoides* but with stems from a perennial rootstock.

Only once recorded from Donyo Sabuk. MAC.

Napier 3125.

9. Cassia fallacina *Chiov.*

A prostrate pubescent wiry shrub with tapering leaves bearing 9–27 pairs of very asymmetric leaflets and solitary yellow flowers.

Locally common in disturbed dry grassland. MAG, MAC, NBI.

Agnew 5607; Thomas 324.

10. Cassia usambarensis *Taub.*

A prostrate, pubescent perennial with annual branches from a thickened rootstock and ovate leaves bearing 5–11 pairs of leaflets; flowers solitary, long-pedicellate, yellow-orange.

Locally common in shallow soils within the upland forest area. HE, HC, HT, HM, HL, HA, KIT, RV, NAN, NBI.

Tweedie 67/130; Glover, Gwynne, and Samuel 790.

11. Cassia grantii *Oliv.*

A prostrate, sparsely pubescent perennial with annual branches from a woody rootstock and oblong leaves bearing 6–11 pairs of large, oblong, blunt leaflets; flowers yellow; in few-flowered axillary racemes.

Local in dry bushland. HK, NAR, RV, MAC, NBI, KAJ.

Blencowe 33; Bally 543.

12. Cassia parva *Steyaert*

An erect pubescent perennial with annual stems from a woody rootstock; leaves linear, with 8–35 pairs of lanceolate leaflets; flowers yellow, solitary or 2 together.

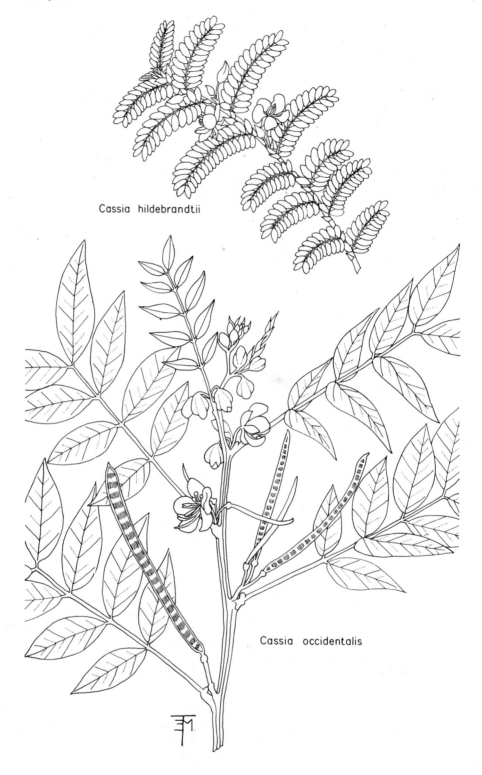

Cassia hildebrandtii

Cassia occidentalis

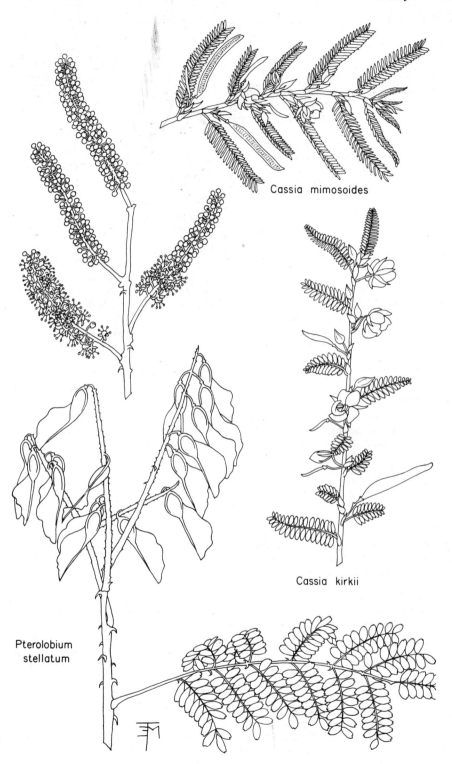

Cassia mimosoides

Cassia kirkii

Pterolobium
stellatum

Rare plant found in wooded grassland. HC, KAJ.

Tweedie 66/217; Bally 235)

13. Cassia kirkii *Oliv.* (see p. 235)

An erect pubescent annual with long linear-tapering leaves bearing 20–40 narrowly oblong leaflets and clustered yellow flowers at the upper nodes.

Common in tall grassland, especially where seasonally flooded. HE, HM, HA, KIT, MUM, KIS, NAR, MAC, NBI.

Tweedie 67/213; Kerfoot 5040.

14. Cassia quarrei (*Ghesq.*) *Steyaert*

Similar to *C. kirkii* but with prostrate or ascending stems and the key characters as given. HA, KIT.

Rare plant found in disturbed ground. ?HA.

Record from FTEA.

15. Cassia hildebrandtii *Vatke* (see p. 234)

Similar to *C. grantii* but usually much more hairy and with rather more, smaller leaflets.

Locally common in stony grassland at medium altitudes. HA, NAR, RV, MAC, NBI.

Agnew 9409; Napper 1565.

16. Cassia nigricans *Vahl*

An erect pubescent annual herb with oblong leaves bearing 7–15 pairs of oblong leaflets and 3–8-flowered supra-axillary racemes; flowers small, yellow.

Rare plant found in wooded grassland in western Kenya. KIS.

Napier 3450.

17. Cassia falcinella *Oliv.*

An erect or prostrate, pubescent, annual or perennial herb with ovate to elliptic leaves bearing 5–11 pairs of oblong leaflets and solitary yellow flowers.

Uncommon plant found in wooded or bushed grassland. HC, KIT, KAJ.

Agnew, Kibe, and Mathenge 10262; Brodhurst-Hill 50.

3. CAESALPINIA *L.*

Shrubs or climbers, usually prickly, with bipinnate leaves, without glands; flowers zygomorphic, in terminal racemes, usually bisexual; sepals imbricate; petals subequal except the uppermost; stamens 10, all fertile; ovary usually short-stalked; pods usually flat and compressed but variable, usually dehiscent.

1. Caesalpinia volkensii *Harms*

A woody climber with recurved prickles and rather large ovate, acuminate leaflets on the bipinnate leaves; flowers yellow, male and bisexual; pods flat, orbicular to oblong, covered with stiff bristles.

Locally common in lowland forest edges. HM, HA, MUM, KIS, MAC.

Mbonge 22.

4. PTEROLOBIUM *Wight & Arn.*

Prickly climbing shrubs with bipinnate leaves and small stipules; flowers almost regular, in panicles of racemes; sepals with the lowest overlapping all others; petals equal; stamens 10, all fertile; pods 1-seeded, winged on one side and terminally (a samara).

Pterolobium stellatum (*Forsk.*) *Brenan* (see p. 235)

A large trailing shrub with pegged prickles on the woody stems, recurved prickles on the leaves and petioles, and masses of whitish flowers or bright red fruits.

A common and annoying wait-a-bit thorn of drier forest and bushland edges, but not found with *Combretum* or *Commiphora*. HE, HT, HA, HK, KIS, NAR, BAR, RV, NBI, KAJ.

Strid 2397; Glover, Gwynne, and Samuel 2421.

56. MIMOSACEAE[†]

Trees, shrubs or rarely herbs with pinnate or bipinnate stipulate leaves and racemose or spicate inflorescences of regular, mostly bisexual flowers; sepals 5, usually united below to form a tube, valvate or imbricate; petals 5, valvate, mostly fused below into a tube; stamens 4–10-numerous, free or variously fused; pollen grains frequently compound; fruit a follicle (pod), dehiscent down two sides or indehiscent.

All species are dealt with in KTS except *Mimosa pudica*.

1. MIMOSA *L.*

Herbs or shrubs, often prickly, with bipinnate, often sensitive and motile leaves; flowers bisexual or male, sessile in globose heads (in ours); calyx very small; corolla with 3–6 lobes on a tube; stamens as many as or twice as many as the corolla lobes; pods flat, bristly or prickly (in ours), splitting into 1-seeded segments leaving the margins of the pod entire.

1 Leaves prickly on the petiole and rachis; pods densely bristly all over   1. *M. pigra*
   Leaves without prickles; pods prickly-hairy only on the margins   2. *M. pudica*

† By A. D. Q. Agnew.

1. Mimosa pigra *L.*

Dealt with in KTS p. 303. MUM, KIS.

2. Mimosa pudica *L.*

A prostrate or straggling woody annual or weak perennial with prickly stems; leaves with 2 pairs of pinnae from close together at the end of a long petiole and thus appearing palmate; flowers in heads, lilac or pink.

A rare introduced weed in our area (originally from South America) which occasionally turns up near towns. HA, NBI, KAJ.

Chauda, February 1967.

57. PAPILIONACEAE†

Herbs, trees, shrubs or climbers, often bearing root nodules of nitrogen-fixing bacteria; leaves stipulate (rarely stipules absent) alternate, simple or palmately or pinnately 1-many foliolate, the leaflets frequently with small stipules (*stipels*) at their junction with the *rachis* or continuation of the petiole; inflorescence racemose or fasciculate, rarely umbellate; bracts and bracteoles often present; flowers zygomorphic, bisexual; sepals 5, often connate into a tube; petals 5, free or loosely joined, the upper (*adaxial* or *posterior*, called the *standard* or *vexillum*) one enclosing the lateral petals (the *wings*) and within these the lower (*anterior*) petals which are often loosely joined together (the *keel*); stamens 9-10, free or the filaments fused into a tube (10) or with one adaxial filament free ((9) + 1); ovary of one carpel with marginal placentation; fruit a modified follicle (a *legume* or *pod*), indehiscent or dehiscent by two longitudinal valves or by transverse articulations; seeds without endosperm.

1   Leaves not present at flowering   2
    Leaves present at flowering   3
2   Flowers spreading; pod broadened upwards, 3-4 times as long as broad, pubescent
                34. *Rhynchosia pulchra*
    Flowers deflexed; pod ovate or elliptic-oblong up to twice as long as broad, covered with long hairs   35. *Eriosema*
3   Leaves all simple or 1-foliolate   4
    Leaves, or some of them, compound   9
4   Stipules sheathing, papery, sometimes connate, persistent; fruit narrowly sub-cylindrical, breaking into several 1-seeded segments; calyx scarious   15. *Alysicarpus*
    Stipules spreading; fruit not breaking into segments; calyx usually herbaceous   5

† By J. B. Gillett (Key and Genera 3-7, 26, 41-48), R. Polhill (Key and Genera 38-40), and A. D. Q. Agnew.

5   Anthers alternately long and short; pod inflated   38. *Crotalaria*
    Anthers uniform; pod not inflated   6
6   Anthers apiculate; hairs, or some of them, attached at their centres   4. *Indigofera*
    Anthers not apiculate; hairs simple or lacking
                           7
7   Standard pubescent or silky outside
                 3. *Tephrosia*
    Standard glabrous   8
8   Pod with more than 2 seeds   26. *Vigna*
    Pod with 1-2 seeds   34. *Rhynchosia alluaudii*
9   Leaves digitately 2-11-foliolate, the leaflets all arising from the same point and without any extension of the axis beyond them stipels usually absent   10
    Leaves pinnate, or pinnately trifoliolate (rachis prolonged beyond lateral leaflets), usually stipellate if trifoliolate   20
10   Leaflets slightly to conspicuously dentate or toothed; stipule base encircling the stem; stipels absent   11
    Leaflets entire; other characters not combined
                           12
11   Pod 3-4 times as long as the calyx, 10-15-seeded; peduncle 1-4-flowered
            42. *Parochetus communis*
    Pod usually shorter than the calyx, never as much as twice as long, 1-9-seeded; peduncles usually with more than 4 flowers   41. *Trifolium*
12   Leaflets 2 or 4; stipules and bracts conspicuous, produced below the point of insertion; fruits often bristly   11. *Zornia*
    Leaflets 3, 5 or more; stipules and bracts not so produced; fruits not bristly   13
13   Leaflets and calyx with sessile rounded resinous glands   14
    Leaflets and calyx without such glands   15
14   Shrub with fasciculate dense sessile inflorescences; pods bearing red globules of secretion which stain yellow
          36. *Flemingia grahamiana*
    Herbs, mostly with paniculate inflorescences; if inflorescences sessile then not agreeing in other characters; pods without secretory globules   35. *Eriosema vanderystii*
15   Anthers 4-5, basifixed, alternating with 5-6 shorter dorsifixed, or 5 only   16
    Anthers uniform, 10   4. *Indigofera cufodontii*
16   Calyx 2-lipped, the lower lip 3-fid   17
    Calyx not 2-lipped, or if slightly so the lower lobes much exceeding the united part   18
17   Leaflets 5-11; keel beaked
             39. *Lupinus princei*
    Leaflets 3; keel obtuse   40. *Argyrolobium*
18   Stipels present; pod linear, compressed, with

an upturned beak, with partitions of endocarp between the seeds; plant trailing or
twining   21. *Teramnus*
Stipels lacking; pod variously shaped but if
linear without an upturned beak, continuous within; plant never twining   **19**

19 Keel obtuse; lateral calyx lobes more united
with the upper than with the lower lobe
which is often narrower; 4 anthers large, 6
anthers small; pods only slightly inflated
                                    37. *Lotononis*
Keel beaked; calyx lobes subequal or the
three lower slightly more united or with
the upper 2 also slightly united to form 2
lips; 5 large anthers alternating with 5
small ones; pod inflated   38. *Crotalaria*

20 Leaves without a terminal leaflet or with the
terminal leaflet much smaller than the rest
                                                22
Leaves terminating in a leaflet as large as or
larger than the rest   **28**

21 Calyx 2-lipped; fruits with 1–28 1-seeded
joints which break up easily (in some
Aeschynomene species only one joint is
present which is straight above, strongly
rounded below and flattened)   **21**
Calyx not distinctly 2-lipped; fruits not
jointed   **27**

22 Inflorescences lax, never scorpioid, often
few-flowered; pods easily visible, well exserted from the calyx; bracts small
                                    7. *Aeschynomene*
Inflorescences mostly dense and scorpioid,
often almost cone-like; pods not visible,
folded like a concertina; bracts often large
                                                23

23 Stipules spurred; leaflets opposite with only 1
main nerve; bracts deciduous   8. *Smithia*
Stipules not spurred; leaflets alternate with
2–7 basal nerves; bracts persistent
                                        9. *Kotschya*

24 Herbs, shrubs or climbers without tendrils **25**
Herbs, with tendrils on leaves   **26**

25 Standard without appendages; pods oblong,
flattened, less than 3 cm long; seeds often
red and black   2. *Abrus*
Standard with appendages; pods cylindrical,
over 5 cm long; seeds not red and black
                                        5. *Sesbania*

26 Style pubescent on lower side, or on all sides,
or glabrous   50. *Vicia*
Style pubescent on upper side only
                                        51. *Lathyrus*

27 Leaves subsessile, the lowest pair of leaflets
sometimes resembling leafy stipules; stipules reduced to gland or absent   **28**
Leaves petiolate and/or stipulate   **29**

28 Pod straight, narrowly cylindrical, dehiscent
as a whole; leaflets 3–5   45. *Lotus*
Pod curved, composed of spherical, 1-seeded,
individually dehiscent segments; leaflets
3–11   46. *Antopetitia abyssinica*

29 Leaves 5–many-foliolate   **30**
Leaves all or mostly 3-foliolate   **40**

30 Anthers apiculate; hairs, or some of them,
attached at their centres; corolla usually
red in part   4. *Indigofera*
Anthers not apiculate; hairs basifixed; corolla
never red   **31**

31 Lower side of leaflets and calyx with
rounded, sessile, or shortly stalked glands
visible wherever the indumentum is not
dense   35. *Eriosema*
Leaflets and calyx without such glands   **32**

32 Standard over 2·5 cm long, much exceeding
the other petals; style hairy above; bracteoles large   18. *Clitoria ternatea*
Standard smaller, hardly exceeding other
petals; style glabrous or hairy only at tip;
bracteoles small   **33**

33 Standard pubescent or silky tomentose outside   3. *Tephrosia*
Standard glabrous or with small scattered
hairs mostly towards apex and margin **34**

34 Shrubs or woody climbers   **35**
Annual or perennial herbs   **37**

35 Leaflets mostly opposite; pods inflated
                              49. *Colutea abyssinica*
Leaflets mostly alternate; pods not inflated
                                                36

36 Leaves mostly in tufts; fruits covered with
stiff hairs   6. *Ormocarpum trichocarpum*
Leaves mostly borne separately along the
stem; ovaries and fruits glabrous
                                        1. *Dalbergia*

37 Pod of spherical 1-seeded segments; stipules
absent   46. *Antopetitia abyssinica*
Pod not segmented; stipules present, conspicuous   **38**

38 Stipules divided into 2–3 narrow lobes
                                        47. *Galega*
Stipules entire 48. *Astragalus atropilosulus*

39 Leaflets toothed   **40**
Leaflets entire   **41**

40 Pod spirally coiled   44. *Medicago*
Pod straight   43. *Melilotus*

41 Calyx truncate with no teeth
                                17. *Dumasia villosa*
Calyx teeth well developed   **42**

42 Undersides of leaflets and calyx covered with
yellow or orange gland-dots (often difficult
to see if densely hairy)   **43**
Undersides of leaflets and calyx without
gland-dots   **45**

43   Ovary 3–8-ovulate; pod grooved between the seeds   33. *Cajanus*
       Ovary 2-ovuled; pod not grooved between the seeds   **44**

44   Funicle (seeds stalk) inserted at centre of a circular hylum; flowers spreading; pod broadened upwards, 3–4 times as long as broad, covered with short, sometimes also with long hairs   34. *Rhynchosia*
       Funicle attached at one end of a linear hylum; flowers deflexed; pod ovate, or elliptic oblong, abruptly contracted to a stipe (stalk), up to twice as long as broad, always (in our area) with long hairs 35. *Eriosema*

45   Style flattened and spathulate at tip; standard glabrous   28. *Sphenostylis stenocarpa*
       Style apex various but not flattened, or if slightly so then standard hairy outside   **46**

46   Pods covered with irritant hairs; standard much shorter than other petals
                          22. *Mucuna*
       Pods without irritant hairs, although they may be bristly; standard usually longer than other petals   **47**

47   Standard hairy outside   **48**
       Standard glabrous outside   **50**

48   Flowers pink or orange   3. *Tephrosia*
       Flowers purple, cream or yellow   **49**

49   Inflorescences long-pedunculate   26. *Vigna*
       Inflorescences sessile at nodes of false racemes   19. *Ophrestia radicosa*

50   Alternate stamens sterile, lacking anthers; pods elongate, linear, distinctly turned up at the apex   21. *Teramnus*
       All stamens with anthers; pods without a distinctly upturned beak, or if beaked then very short and never linear   **51**

51   Fruit dividing into distinct articles, or if only one article then the calyx tube narrow, like a pedicel   **52**
       Fruit not dividing into distinct articles (sometimes transversely furrowed)   **53**

52   Calyx tube very slender, stalk-like; stamens all fused; stipels absent
             10. *Stylosanthes fruticosa*
       Calyx tube not so slender; stamens with one free; stipels present   12. *Desmodium*

53   Pods longitudinally 4–winged
             24. *Psophocarpus lancifolius*
       Pods not longitudinally winged   **54**

54   Style with reflexed appendage below the stigma   25. *Vatovaea pseudolablab*
       Style sometimes produced beyond the stigma but never reflexed as an appendage   **55**

55   Most pods over 15 cm long with 3 narrow ribs on the upper side   23. *Canavalia*
       All pods less than 8 cm long   **56**

56   Style with a distinct bulging callus at its junction with the ovary
             32. *Neorautanenia mitis*
       Style without a callus at its junction with the ovary   **57**

57   Style divided into a thin basal part and a thickened upper part   **58**
       Style either uniformly thick or uniformly thin or tapering but not of two distinct parts   **59**

58   Style with the apical bristly part thin and needle-like
       27. *Spathionema kilimandscharicum*
       Style with the apical bristly part thick
                      26. *Vigna*

59   Style distinctly thickened, conspicuous; standard with appendages inside near base
                          60
       Style not distinctly thickened, often short and inconspicuous; standard mostly without appendages   **61**

60   Style with a line of hairs near top of inner margin; stigma terminal, without a tuft of radiating hairs   31. *Lablab purpureus*
       Style glabrous except for the terminal stigma which has a tuft of spreading hairs
                    29. *Dolichos*

61   Pod inflated   13. *Pycnospora lutescens*
       Pod not inflated   **62**

62   Erect herbs or shrubs with small reddish-purple or white flowers; standard less than 1 cm long   14. *Pseudarthria*
       Climbers or, if erect, then flowers yellow; standard over 1 cm long   **63**

63   Bracteoles absent; bracts large and persistent
             16. *Amphicarpa africana*
       Bracteoles present; bracts caducous or inconspicuous   **64**

64   Corolla greenish yellow, cream or yellow, sometimes marked pink or purple; standard with 2 long linear appendages inside
             30. *Macrotyloma*
       Corolla purple or white; standard without appendages   20. *Glycine wightii*

1. DALBERGIA *L. f.*

Trees or woody climbers, with imparipinnate, petiolate leaves without stipels; inflorescences terminal and axillary, of diffuse panicles of small yellowish or flushed purple flowers; calyx bell-shaped, shortly 5-lobed; corolla glabrous or with scattered hairs; standard petal without scales; stamens 9–10, all united or with the upper stamen free; anthers small, erect; ovary with an incurved style and small terminal stigma; fruit indehiscent, oblong or linear, broadly-winged around the frequently thickened seed cavity.

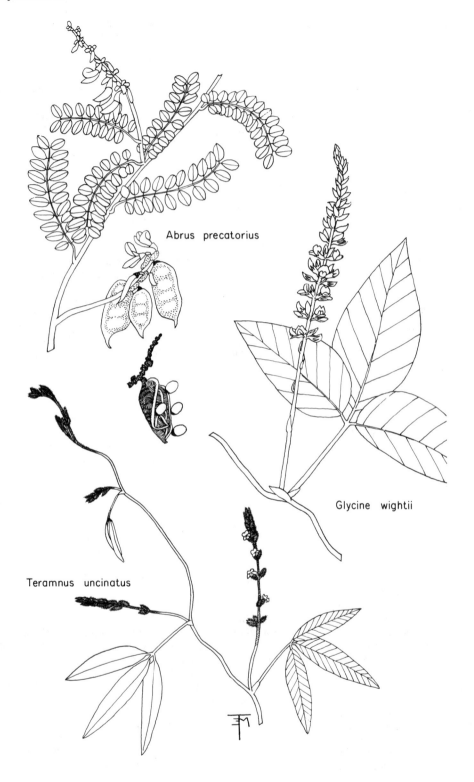

Abrus precatorius

Glycine wightii

Teramnus uncinatus

1 Branches with many short shoots, frequently with spines; leaves at the base of inflorescence branches   1. *D. melanoxylon*
Branches of long shoots, without spines and with inflorescences frequently modified into tendrils   2. *D. lactea*

1. Dalbergia melanoxylon *Guill & Perr.*
A tree, dealt with in KTS p. 362. MAC.

2. Dalbergia lactea *Vatke* (see p. 273)
A small tree or climber with branches and peduncles frequently modified into woody hooks and tendrils; leaves with 7–9 leaflets, oblong-elliptic, glabrous or pubescent; panicles on leafy branches, with crowded white, flushed mauve, flowers; pod 10–15 cm long, oblong.

Included here because it is a frequent climber. This is a plant of forest edges, especially riverine forest. HE, HA, HK, KIT, NAN, KAJ.

Elliot 12; Bally 8268.

2. ABRUS *Adans.*
Shrubs or climbers with pinnate leaves and numerous opposite leaflets; stipels minute, filiform; flowers in axillary or terminal racemes; bracts and bracteoles present; calyx almost truncate with 5 short teeth; stamens (9); anthers all similar; ovary subsessile, many-ovuled; style short, incurved, glabrous; stigma capitate; pods linear or oblong, more or less septate; seeds subglobose, usually glossy.

1 Seeds globose, black and red
                                   1. *A. precatorius*
Seeds not black and red, compressed   2
2 Bracts and bracteoles as long as or longer than the calyx   2. *A. canescens*
Bracts and bracteoles much shorter than the calyx   3. *A. schimperi*

1. Abrus precatorius *L.* (see p. 240)
A woody, glabrous or pubescent climber with oblong leaflets and pedunculate spikes of crowded white to pink flowers; pods with a hooked beak, densely hairy.

Locally common in dry or humid bushland. MUM, MAG, MAC.

Bogdan 912

2. Abrus canescens *Bak.*
A silky-hairy climber with oblong leaflets and sessile flowers in head-like fascicles; corolla dark red or purple.

Uncommon plant found along the lakeside in western Kenya. MUM.

Bogdan 237/61.

3. Abrus schimperi *Hochst.*
A loose, erect, glabrescent shrub with oblong leaflets and sessile flowers in sessile lateral spikes along the inflorescence; corolla variable in colour, cream to purple.

Locally common in dry bushland. MAC.

Bally 8248.

3. TEPHROSIA *Pers.*
Annual or, more often, perennial herbs or weak shrubs; hairs simple, often silky; leaves usually imparipinnate, less often unifoliolate or pinnately trifoliolate; stipels absent; leaflets entire, usually narrowed at the base and widest above the middle, the lateral nerves numerous, parallel, running through to form a marginal nerve; flowers usually pink or purple, occasionally orange or white, pedicellate, 2 or more together in the axils of the upper leaves or at the nodes of terminal or leaf-opposed pseudo-racemes, sometimes condensed to pseudo-umbels; bracteoles usually absent; lowest calyx lobe the longest, the upper pair often partly united; standard pubescent or silky outside; vexillar stamen lightly attached to the other 9, widened and often sharply bent a little above the base; intra-staminal disc usually present; ovary 2–22-ovulate, pubescent; pod nearly always several-seeded, linear or oblong, more or less flattened, not truly septate, never glabrous, ending in a beak (the persistent style-base), dehiscent, the valves twisting and scattering the seeds; seeds usually longitudinal (long axis parallel to the pod) sometimes transverse or oblique; funicle short; caruncle almost absent or variously developed.

1 Leaves all simple (1-foliolate)   2
Most leaves compound   3
2 Lateral calyx lobes not above 3 mm long, less than twice as long as tube; seeds longitudinal; caruncle minute
                                   1. *T. hildebrandtii*
Lateral calyx lobe over 3 mm long, more than twice as long as tube; seeds more or less transverse; caruncle large   4. *T. holstii*
3 Flowers in leaf axils only, never in panicles or pseudo-racemes   4
Flowers, or at least many of them, in terminal or leaf-opposed pseudo-racemes or panicles, sometimes also in upper leaf axils   5
4 Pod 5–9-seeded; claw of keel more than half as long as blade; style ribbon-shaped, not twisted, not, or hardly, penicillate, 1·5–2·5 mm long   2. *T. subtriflora*
Pod 10–14-seeded; claw of keel less than a third as long as blade; style tapering, twisted, penicillate, 2·5–3·5 mm long
                                   3. *T. uniflora*

Tephrosia
hildebrandtii

Tephrosia elata

Tephrosia interrupta

5   Style glabrous on both sides for most of its length, though often pubescent at the base and penicillate at the tip   **6**

Style pubescent, at least on one side, for most or all of its length   **16**

6   Leaflets 1–5, the terminal ones 3–7 cm long; seeds more or less transverse
           5. *T. paniculata*

Leaflets more than 5 (at least in the larger leaves), smaller than 6 cm long; seeds longitudinal   **7**

7   Calyx tube 3 mm long, about as long as the lower tooth   6. *T. emeroides*

Calyx tube less than 3 mm long, or if longer then much shorter than the lower tooth   **8**

8   Caruncle well-developed, yellowish, clasping one corner of the seed; leaflets linear, up to 4 (–6) mm wide; inconspicuous bracteoles appressed to calyx base
           7. *T. linearis*

Caruncle minute, inconspicuous; leaflets usually broader than above; bracteoles not present at calyx base   **9**

9   Hairs on calyx and pod sutures brown or black, or partly so; upper pair of calyx teeth united for at least half their length, not, or hardly, longer than the tube   **10**

Hairs on calyx and pod sutures white or yellowish; upper pair of calyx teeth united for less than half their length, often longer than the tube   **11**

10   Leaflets not more than 9, seven or more times as long as wide; stems rarely over 30 cm long; inflorescence rarely with more than 8 flowers   8. *T. athiensis*

Leaflets often more than 9, less than 6 times as long as wide; stems often over 30 cm long; inflorescence often with more than 8 flowers   9. *T. noctiflora*

11   Pod with appressed or stiffly spreading hairs which are rarely over 0·5 mm long and not dense enough to hide its surface   **12**

Pod with a dense felt of hairs which are often over 0·5 mm long, obscuring its surface   **15**

12   Distance between centres of adjacent seeds not more than width of pod; inflorescence rarely more than 5–6-flowered   **13**

Distance between centres of adjacent seeds greater than width of pod; inflorescences usually more than 6-flowered   **14**

13   Leaflets 5–7; standard 9–11 mm long; seeds 9–12   10. *T. lortii*

Leaflets 7–13, usually 9–11; standard under 8 mm long; seeds 8–14   11. *T. pumila*

14   Pod 4–6-seeded, usually strongly curved
           12. *T. drepanocarpa*

Pod 6–9-seeded, slightly curved
           13. *T. purpurea*

15   Lower calyx lobe usually under 8 mm long; pods slightly curved, spreading, ascending or slightly deflexed, their hairs rarely as much as 1 mm long; seeds up to 7, the distance between their centres more than the width of the pod; style more or less linear, not twisted; stigma not capitate
           14. *T. rhodesica*

Lower calyx lobe 8 mm or more long; pods strongly curved, deflexed, their basal part often parallel to the inflorescence-axis, their hairs often over 1 mm long; seeds 6–12, usually 8 or more, the distance between their centres less than the width of the pod; style twisted, tapering; stigma capitate   15. *T. villosa*

16   Pod less than 10 mm wide; keel usually glabrous   **17**

Pod 10 mm wide or more; keel pubescent near the lower margin   23. *T. vogelii*

17   Seeds longitudinal or strongly oblique; pod straight or curved slightly upward near the tip   **18**

Seeds transverse; pods straight or curved slightly downwards near the tip
           22. *T. nana*

18   Petiole usually more than 2·5 cm long and longer than the rest of the rachis; leaflets 3–11, rarely less than 5 times as long as wide   16. *T. lurida*

Petiole rarely exceeding 2·5 cm and if so then leaflets usually more than 13 and less than 5 times as long as wide   **19**

19   Midrib not impressed above; leaflets rarely truncate or rounded at the base   **20**

Midrib impressed above; leaflets truncate or rounded at the base   21. *T. aequilata*

20   Bracts persistent; leaflets pubescent above
           17. *T. reptans*

Bracts rarely persistent; leaflets usually glabrous above   **21**

21   Pseudo-raceme not markedly interrupted, with numerous nodes, the distance between which is less than or little more than the combined length of pedicel and calyx; larger leaflets usually 4 cm or more long **22**

Pseudo-raceme markedly interrupted with fewer nodes, the gaps between them usually greater than the combined length of pedicel and calyx; larger leaflets usually under 4 cm long   20. *T. interrupta*

22   Peduncle shorter than pseudo-raceme; bracts caducous, narrowly triangular or linear; upper half of style tapering, about 0·2–0·4 mm wide, pubescent on both sides; hairs on pod fulvous, never dark brown or black; caruncle up to 0·7 x 0·2 mm
           18. *T. elata*

Tephrosia pumila

Tephrosia emeroides

Peduncle usually longer than the very dense pseudo-raceme; bracts caducous, lanceolate or ovate-lanceolate; upper half of style linear, about 0·5–0·6 mm wide, pubescent on upper surface and margins only; hairs on pod sometimes dark; caruncle about 1·2 × 0·4 mm   19. *T. nyikensis*

1. Tephrosia hildebrandtii *Vatke* (*T. orientalis* Bak. f.) (see p. 242)

An erect or spreading perennial with 1-foliolate leaves; flowers reddish purple in the upper leaf axils and sometimes also in terminal pseudo-racemes; standard golden-brown, silky outside, 11–14 mm long; style glabrous, linear, not twisted.

In grassland and semi-evergreen bushland, 5000–6000 ft. A hybrid between this species and *T. emeroides* has been found (Gillett 16969). HA, RV, EMB, MAC, NBI, KAJ.

Gillett 16975; Graham 2291.

2. Tephrosia subtriflora *Bak.*

A prostrate or ascending annual or short-lived perennial; leaves with 5–13 leaflets, the terminal usually much longer than the rest; standard white-pubescent outside, 5–8 mm long; style linear, glabrous, not twisted.

A very variable species of *Acacia-Commiphora* open bushland and a weed in the drier cultivated areas up to 4500 ft. MAG, MAC, KAJ.

Milne-Redhead and Taylor 7006; Bogdan 2218.

3. Tephrosia uniflora *Pers.*

A semi-erect, short-lived perennial; leaves with 5–7 leaflets; flowers pink, in pairs in the leaf axils; standard white-pubescent outside, 9–11 mm long; style glabrous, twisted, tapering with a capitate, penicillate stigma.

Acacia-Commiphora bushland and dry grassland, often in rocky places, up to 4750 ft. MAG.

Bally in CM 7130; Faden and Napper 69240.

4. Tephrosia holstii *Taub.* (*T. kassneri* Bak. f.; *T. paniculata* Bak. ssp. *holstii* (Taub.) Brummitt) (see p. 246)

An annual or perennial, yellowish hairy herb with 1-foliolate leaves; flowers orange or brick red in short dense terminal pseudo-racemes, often also in the uppermost leaf axil; standard tomentose outside, 10–13 mm long; style glabrous, curved into a semicircle, penicillate.

Upland grassland and forest margins, 5000–8000 ft. HT, HM, KIT, MUM, EMB, MAC, KAJ.

Brodhurst-Hill 148; Bally in CM 8245.

5. Tephrosia paniculata *Bak.*

An erect annual or short-lived perennial differing from *T. holstii* in the leaves being 3–5-foliolate, the pseudo-racemes longer and the flowers rather larger, the standard up to 15 mm long.

In thicket margins, grassland, and swamps, 3500–7200 ft. HE, MUM, KIS.

Lugard 229; Brodhurst-Hill 512.

6. Tephrosia emeroides *A. Rich.* (see p. 244)

A softly woody, stiffly erect perennial with appressed hairs; leaves with 5–13 leaflets; flowers pink or rose in lax terminal pseudo-racemes and in many of the upper leaf axils; standard with appressed golden hairs outside, about 13 mm long.

In semi-evergreen bushland, 5000–6500 ft. HT, HA, MUM, NAR, RV, NAN, NBI.

Gillett 16976; Glover 3713.

7. Tephrosia linearis (*Willd.*) *Pers.*

A perennial with 5–15 leaflets to each leaf; flowers pink or orange in stiff pedunculate pseudo-racemes of usually 6–10 nodes.

Common in grassland and rocky, bushy slopes, especially in higher rainfall areas, 3000–8000 ft. HT, HM, HA, KIT, MUM, KIS, NAR, RV, EMB, MAC, KAJ. Specimens from EMB and MAC tend to be softer with more spreading indumentum and darker pods and may be varietally distinct.

Tweedie 2465; Verdcourt 3199.

8. Tephrosia athiensis *Bak. f.*

A perennial, with short, often prostrate, shoots from a woody base; leaflets 5–9; flowers pink, in pedunculate pseudo-racemes of 2–12 nodes, never in leaf axils; standard brown-tomentose outside, about 12 mm long.

Locally common in rocky grassland, 5500–9000 ft. Easily confused with *T. lurida*.

Gillett 16834; Nattrass 598.

9. Tephrosia noctiflora *Bak.*

A straggling, short-lived perennial; leaves with 15–25 leaflets; flowers purple, in terminal pseudo-racemes, rarely also in the upper leaf axils; standard densely brown-silky outside, 8–12 mm long.

In *Acacia-Commiphora* bushland up to 4500 ft. MAG, MAC.

Gillett 16168; Thomas 2091.

10. Tephrosia lortii *Bak. f.*

A straggling perennial; leaflets 3–7; flowers purple in short, open, terminal pseudo-racemes and in the upper leaf axils; standard grey-pubescent, about 10 mm long.

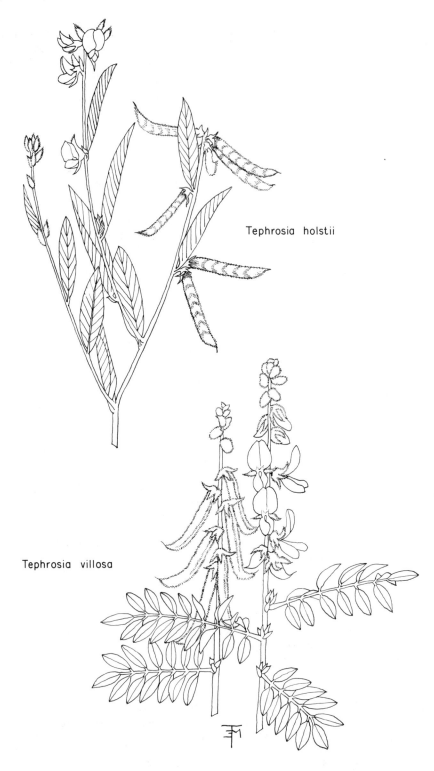

Tephrosia holstii

Tephrosia villosa

In *Acacia-Commiphora* bushland at about 3000 ft. MAG.

Verdcourt 2638.

11.   Tephrosia pumila (*Lam.*) *Pers.* (see p. 244)

An annual or short-lived perennial resembling *T. lortii* but with 7–13 leaflets and smaller flowers; standard under 8 mm long.

In *Acacia-Commiphora* open bushland, rocky grassland, and a weed in cultivation, up to 6000 ft. It is often confused with *T. purpurea* from which it is distinguished by the more numerous, more closely packed seeds and the sharply down-curved style base. MUM, KIS, BAR, MAC.

Napier 3433; Bogdan 1232 and 5197.

12. Tephrosia drepanocarpa *Bak.*

Closely resembling forms of *T. purpurea* from which it is distinguished by the shorter 4–6-seeded, more sharply curved pod.

Rare plant found in grassland and roadsides, 4750–5250 ft. MAC.

Bogdan 840; Thomas 1012.

13.   Tephrosia purpurea (*L.*) *Pers.*

An erect or more often spreading annual or short-lived perennial; leaflets 9–17; flowers reddish-purple or pink in slender, lax, leaf-opposed pseudo-recemes and in the upper leaf axils; standard white-pubescent outside, about 8 mm long.

In *Acacia-Commiphora* bushland and grassland, and as a weed up to 5000 ft. MAC.

Gillett 17196; Bogdan 3089.

14.   Tephrosia rhodesica *Bak. f.*

A short-lived perennial; 11–19 leaflets; flowers pink or mauve in rather dense terminal pseudo-racemes and also often in the upper leaf axils; standard tomentose, about 11 mm long.

Rare plant found in our area in open places amongst rocks up to 7000 ft. HL, MUM, MAC.

Bally 3861; Duemmer 1860.

15.   Tephrosia villosa (*L.*) *Pers.* (see p. 246)

An annual or short-lived perennial; leaflets 11–15; flowers purple in rather dense terminal pseudo-racemes and also often in the upper leaf axils; standard densely fulvous-tomentose, 11–13 mm long.

In *Acacia-Commiphora* bushland up to 5000 ft. MUM, RV, MAG, MAC.

Kokwaro 110; Glover *et al.* 2835.

16.   Tephrosia lurida *Sond.* (*T. dowsonii* Bak. f., *T. longipes* Meisn. var. *lurida* (Sond.) Gillett)

A perennial with a woody rootstock and prostrate or ascending stems; leaflets 3–5, rarely 1–11; flowers mauve-violet in terminal or leaf-opposed pseudo-racemes; standard golden-brown tomentose, 12–14 mm long.

In grassland and open bushland, 4500–7250 ft. HM, HA, MAC, NBI, KAJ.

Greenway 13095; Agnew 5533.

17.   Tephrosia reptans *Bak.*

A prostrate or weakly ascending perennial; leaflets 5–19; flowers purple in rather lax terminal or leaf-opposed racemes, usually shorter than the peduncle, never in the leaf axils; standard golden-pubescent, 14–16 mm long.

In open bushland and grassland, especially among rocks, 3000–6000 ft. BAR, RV, MAC.

Bogdan 3363; Gillett 18259.

18.   Tephrosia elata *Deflers* (*T. rigida* Bak. non Span., *T. heckmanniana* sensu Cronquist pp. non Harms.) (see p. 242)

A short-lived bushy perennial; leaflets 15–21; flowers pink or purple, numerous in rather dense terminal racemes which are usually longer than the peduncle; standard golden-pubescent, 14–16 mm long.

Grassland, former cultivation and thicket margins up to 6000 ft. HA, KIT, MUM, RV, MAG, EMB, MAC, NBI.

Glover *et al.* 3260; Perdue and Kibuwa 8383.

19.   Tephrosia nyikensis *Bak.*

A short-lived perennial differing from *T. elata* in the keyed characters. The inflorescence is sometimes branched.

Uncommon plant found in grassland, vleis, and scrub margins at about 5500 ft. MUM, KIS.

Napier 2882; Royston in CM 17712.

20.   Tephrosia interrupta *Engl.* (*T. atroviolacea* Bak. f.) (see p. 242)

A robust bushy woody herb; leaflets 9–21; flowers purple in terminal grey-, brownish- or blackish-tomentose pseudo-racemes with several flowers at each node and short lateral branches sometimes developed with the lower nodes well separated; standard brownish-tomentose 14–20 mm long.

Common in scrub margins and rocky outcrops, 5250–9250 ft. HE, HC, HT, HM, HA, HK, KIT, KIS, NAN, MAC, KAJ.

Gardner 1293; Lugard 43 and 539.

21. Tephrosia aequilata *Bak.*

A softly woody shrub; leaflets 13–21, rounded, truncate or cordate at the base; flowers purple in dense terminal, nearly sessile, subglobose white- or brown-tomentose inflorescences; standard silky, 13–17 mm long.

Rocky scrubland, 6000–7000 ft. HM, MAC.
Gardner 1414; Bogdan 1192.

22. Tephrosia nana *Kotschy & Schweinf.*

An annual or short-lived perennial; leaflets 7–19, larger towards the leaf apex; flowers pink or purple in pedunculate pseudo-racemes which may be short and dense or elongated, rarely a few in upper leaf axils; standard golden-brown silky, 14–16 mm long.

In grassland, fallow cultivation, and swamps up to 6000 ft. MUM, KIS.
Napier 5307; Davidson 263.

23. Tephrosia vogelii *Hook. f.*

A softly woody perennial; leaflets 13–29; flowers white or pale violet in dense terminal shortly pedunculate pseudo-racemes; standard white-silky, about 22 mm long.

Waste ground and former cultivation in high rainfall areas up to 7000 ft. This plant is cultivated as a fish poison and is probably not indigenous to Kenya. HE, HA.
Beckley in CM 6023; Gillett 16270.

4. INDIGOFERA *L.*

Erect or prostrate annual or perennial herbs or, less often, shrubs; hairs typically biramous, rarely simple through the suppression of one arm and in certain species erect multicellular, often glandular, hairs also occur; leaves usually imparipinnate, less often trifoliolate, conjugate, unifoliolate, or simple; stipels often present; flowers usually in axillary racemes, less often single in leaf axils or in panicles; bracteoles absent; corolla usually caducous, less often the standard persistent, usually red or pink at least in part, less than 18 mm long; standard usually pubescent outside, occasionally glabrous, longer than wide, narrowed gradually to the base; claw of wing, if distinct from the blade, less than ⅛th as long; keel gently curved below, spurred or, less often, merely somewhat pouched on each side; stamens persistent, the dorsal one free, the lower 9 united; anthers dorsifixed, apiculate, usually uniform, less often that on the dorsal stamen missing; pod usually dehiscent 2–many-seeded, rarely 1-seeded by abortion, usually cylindrical, tetragonal, or flattened, rarely as much as 3 mm wide, not inflated, occasionally oblong or oval; endocarp often spotted, forming septa between the seeds.

In the following account the 'width' of a pod is measured from suture to suture, the 'thickness' at right angles to this.

1	Rachis of inflorescence a spine	
		13. *I. spinosa*
	Rachis of inflorescence unarmed	2
2	Standard not glabrous outside	3
	Standard glabrous	43
3	Leaflets opposite	4
	Leaflets alternate	38
4	Flowers in congested panicles; pod oval, 1- or rarely 2-seeded	5
	Flowers in racemes; pod 2- or more seeded	6
5	Inflorescence at ends of shoots which are longer than the inflorescence is wide; fruiting calyx 6–8 mm long	3. *I. capitata*
	Inflorescences mostly lateral, sessile in leaf axils or on side shoots shorter than the width of the inflorescence; fruiting calyx *c.* 3 mm long	4. *I. congesta*
6	Stipules about 6 mm long and 2 mm wide at base; plant a woody white-pilose shrublet *c.* 65 cm tall	15. *I. thikaensis*
	Stipules much smaller	7
7	Pod flattened	8
	Pod not flattened	9
8	Bracts caducous; pod curved, 5–9-seeded	1. *I. hochstetteri*
	Bracts persistent; pod short, straight, 1–2-seeded	2. *I. demissa*
9	Pods erect or ascending	10
	Pods spreading or deflexed	18
10	Leaf rachis usually prolonged beyond lateral leaflets; filaments up to 6 mm long	11
	Leaf rachis not, or hardly prolonged beyond lateral leaflets; filaments 6 mm or more long	17
11	Fruiting pedicel over 2 mm long	5. *I. dendroides*
	Fruiting pedicel under 2 mm long	12
12	Leaflets with a translucent blister at each side and beneath the tip	6. *I. brevicalyx*
	Leaflets without translucent blisters	13
13	Inflorescence 1-flowered; stamens 2–2·7 mm long	7. *I. monanthoides*
	Inflorescence mostly 2- or more flowered; stamens over 3 mm long	14
14	Hairs on most young stems spreading	15
	Hairs on young stems appressed	16
15	Stipules *c.* 2 mm long; margins of young leaflets glandular; pods glabrous or nearly so	8. *I. tanganyikensis*
	Stipules *c.* 4 mm long; margins of leaflets not glandular; pods strigose-puberulent	9. *I. ambelacensis*
16	Calyx less than half as long as stamens; petiole 1–6 mm long	10. *I. vohemarensis*

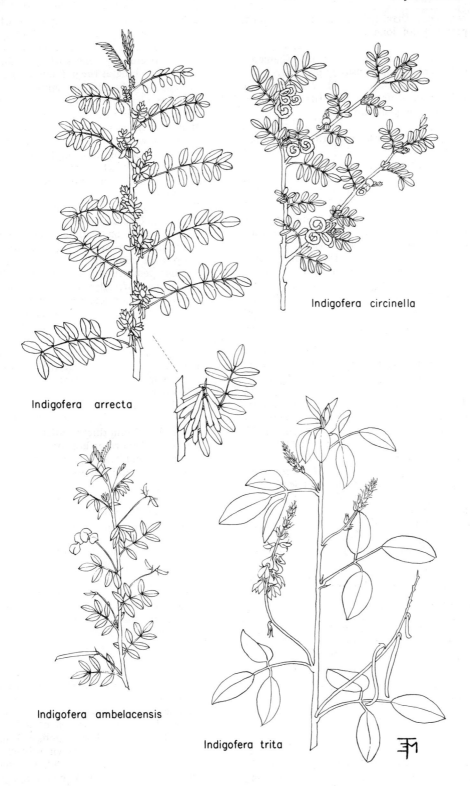

Indigofera circinella

Indigofera arrecta

Indigofera ambelacensis

Indigofera trita

Calyx more than half as long as stamens; petiole 1 mm long, or less

14. *I. subargentea*

17 Fruiting pedicel rarely over 2 mm, filaments 6–7 mm long; plant usually prostrate

11. *I. nairobiensis*

Fruiting pedicel up to 8 mm, filaments up to 13 mm long; plant erect

12. *I. hedyantha*

18 Pods spreading, with or without glandular hairs　　　　　　　　　　　　　　**19**

Pods deflexed, without glandular hairs　　**27**

19 Glandular hairs absent　　　　　　　　**20**

Glandular hairs present, at least on the pods

21

20 Pod under 2 mm wide, 15–20 mm long, not torulose, the suture *c.* 0·2 mm wide; leaflets appressed strigulose above

14. *I. subargentea*

Pod 2 mm or more wide, under 15 mm long, often rather torulose, the suture *c.* 0·5 mm wide; leaflets subglabrous or softly and laxly hairy above　　16. *I. vicioides*

21 Biramous hairs all white　　　　　　**22**

Some of the biramous hairs dark brown or black　　　　　　　23. *I. atriceps*

22 Pod 1–1·8 mm wide, usually over 6 mm long; flowers not held on only one side of the inflorescence　　　　　　　　**23**

Pod *c.* 2 mm wide, 4–6 mm long; flowers mostly held on only one side of the inflorescence　　　　22. *I. secundiflora*

23 Petiole usually shorter than basal leaflets; leaves rarely more than 9-foliolate

17. *I. mimosoides*

Petiole usually longer than basal leaflets; if shorter then leaflets more than 11　　**24**

24 Filaments 5–7 mm long　　21. *I. masaiensis*

Filaments up to 4·5 mm long　　　　**25**

25 Style 1·2–1·6 mm long, slightly curved, sloping upwards from its somewhat swollen base　　　　18. *I. colutea*

Style bent sharply upwards through 90° at the centre or near its base　　　　**26**

26 Leaflets without glandular hairs, usually more than 3 times as long as wide; glandular hairs on stems usually under 0·6 mm long; filaments 2·3–3 mm long; style 0·7–1 mm long　　　　20. *I. brachynema*

Leaflets with glandular hairs, not above twice as long as wide; glandular hairs on stems up to 2, 3, or even 4 mm long, on pods up to 1 or 1·2 mm; filaments 3·5–4·5 mm; style 2–3 mm long　　　19. *I. zenkeri*

27 Pod glabrous; stamens 8–12 mm long

24. *I. homblei*

Pod not glabrous; stamens usually shorter　**28**

28 Calyx not covered by long stiff spreading

hairs, shorter than the stamens which are 3–13 mm long; hairs on standard appressed and parallel giving a shiny appearance　**29**

Calyx covered by long stiff spreading hairs, about as long as the 4–5 mm long stamens; standard pubescent not shiny　　　**37**

29 Stamens 11–13 mm long　　25. *I. garckeana*

Stamens under 8 mm long　　　　**30**

30 Hairs on fruit mostly dark brown or if admixed with white then dense and somewhat spreading; stamens 4–6 mm long　**31**

Hairs on fruit white or if some dark then sparse and closely appressed; stamens up to 4 mm long　　　　　　**32**

31 Raceme almost sessile, shorter than subtending leaf; calyx teeth much shorter than tube; hairs on leaflets closely appressed, not dense enough to hide the surface; pod up to 22 mm long　　26. *I. emarginella*

Raceme pedunculate, usually longer than subtending leaf; calyx teeth about as long as tube; hairs on leaflets often spreading and dense enough to hide the surface; pod up to 35 mm long　　27. *I. swaziensis*

32 Pod more or less tetragonous; leaflets 3–9; calyx more than half as long as stamens　**33**

Pod not, or hardly tetragonous; leaflets 5–many; calyx less than half as long as stamens　　　　　　　　**35**

33 Pod 3·5–4 mm thick; leaflets 7–9

28. *I. lupatana*

Pod *c.* 1·5–2 mm thick; leaflets 3–9　**34**

34 Pod curved more or less into a semicircle, or circle; leaf rachis prolonged 0–2 mm beyond lateral leaflets

29 *I. cliffordiana*

Pod straight or slightly curved but not into a semi-circle; leaf rachis usually prolonged more than 2 mm beyond the lateral leaflets

30. *I. trita*

35 Pod torulose in plane of sutures, 1–4- or rarely 6-seeded; leaflets 5–9

31. *I. bogdanii*

Pod not torulose in plane of sutures or, if somewhat so, then seeds more numerous; leaflets usually 9 or more　　　**36**

36 Pod straight, *c.* 6-seeded, less than 2 cm long; hairs on inflorescence usually more or less brown　　　　32. *I. arrecta*

Pod curved or almost straight, over 2 cm long, 8–12-seeded; hairs on inflorescence whitish　　　　33. *I. tinctoria*

37 Petiole often under 4 mm long; peduncle usually longer than rest of inflorescence; seeds minutely dotted; pods *c.* 2 mm wide; hairs on calyx dark brown or black

34. *I. longibarbata*

Petiole usually over 4 mm long; peduncle

much shorter than rest of inflorescence; seeds coarsely pitted; pods *c.* 3 mm wide; hairs on calyx whitish   35. *I. astragalina*

38   Leaves 4- or more-foliolate or, if lower leaves with fewer leaflets occur, these do not subtend inflorescences; leaflets rarely over 3 cm long   39

     Lower leaves 1–3-foliolate, often subtending inflorescences; leaflets often over 3 cm long   40. *I. conjugata*

39   Pods straight, or almost so   40
     Pods curved   42

40   Calyx much less than half as long as corolla, the lobes little longer than the tube; standard densely covered with stiff appressed glistening hairs   36. *I. schimperi*

     Calyx at least half as long as corolla, the lobes much longer than the tube; hairs on standard relatively sparse and spreading   41

41   Hairs on stems, peduncles and leaf rachises more or less spreading at the tips; stipules narrow, pilose   37. *I. volkensii*

     Hairs on stems, peduncles, etc. all closely appressed; stipules with a wide scarious base glabrescent at the edges   38. *I. spicata*

42   Erect shrublet; leaflets 3–5; pod arcuate or circinate with flattened gaps between the seeds   29. *I. cliffordiana*

     Prostrate; leaflets 4–7; pod circinate, not flattened, with seeds close together
                         39. *I. circinella*

43   Bracts not persistent; fruiting pedicel under 2 mm long; deflexed; all stamens fertile; anthers without basal scales; leaflets 5–15   44

     Bracts persistent; fruiting pedicel often over 2 mm long, spreading; dorsal stamen sterile; anthers with basal scales; leaflets 1–13   45

44   Inflorescence pedunculate, longer than the subtending leaf, the peduncle longer than a leaflet   41. *I. costata*

     Inflorescence subsessile, shorter than the subtending leaf, the peduncle, if present, shorter than a leaflet   42. *I. parviflora*

45   Leaves all simple, silvery
                        43. *I. microcharoides*

     Leaves, or at least most of them, compound   46

46   Upper leaves digitately trifoliolate with more or less strigulose oblanceolate or obovate leaflets   44. *I. cufodontii*

     Leaves pinnate, subglabrous, the leaflets needle-shaped   45. *I. asparagoides*

1. Indigofera hochstetteri *Bak.* (*I. anabaptista* Bak.)

Strigose annual up to 50 cm tall; leaves 3–5-foliolate; rachis 16–40 mm long, of which half is petiole; raceme shortly pedunculate, many-

flowered, rather shorter than, or as long as the subtending leaf; calyx 2–3 mm long, deeply divided; stamens *c.* 3 mm long; pod deflexed, arcuate, flat, 5–9-seeded, about 2·4 mm wide, obtuse except for the persistent style base, appearing jointed because of transverse ridges formed by the septa.

Dry grassland, especially in stony places, and as a weed in cultivated areas up to 5400 ft. BAR, RV, MAC.

Bogdan 3039 and 3856; Bally 4450.

2. Indigofera demissa *Taub.*

Procumbent appressed-strigulose annual, or perhaps sometimes perennial, forming mats; leaves 5–7-foliolate, the rachis 8–15 mm long; raceme very short, almost sessile, 4–8-flowered, the bracts about 1 mm long, persistent; calyx and stamens 1·5–2 mm long; pod 1–2-seeded, 2·5–4 mm long, 2 mm wide.

Disturbed ground, *c.* 7800 ft. HA.

Nattrass 1285

Note: I. demissa may well have been casually introduced to its one known locality in Kenya, Sasumua dam, which is some 3300 ft higher than any locality known for the species elsewhere.

3. Indigofera capitata *Kotschy*

Erect rather woody branching annual up to 1 m tall; lower leaves *c.* 11-foliolate, upper 5–7-foliolate; leaflets oblanceolate, up to 2 cm long and 4 mm wide, rachis up to 3 cm long, including a petiole of *c.* 5 mm, not, or a little, prolonged beyond lateral leaflets; panicles subcapitate, at the ends of the branches, each with an involucre of 2–3 leaf-like outer bracts, inner bracts usually trifid, the segments resembling the calyx lobes; pedicel *c.* 1 mm long, erect in flower and fruit; calyx silky, divided to the base, the lobes linear-lanceolate; stamens *c.* 4 mm long.

Stony, grassy places, *c.* 4000 ft. MUM.

Kimani 168.

4. Indigofera congesta *Bak.*

Erect branching herb up to 1 m tall; leaves 3–7-foliolate, the rachis, including the 8–12 mm petiole, up to 3 cm long; flowers in dense subglobose axillary or terminal panicles; bracts 1–3-foliolate, ending in long stiff points; calyx *c.* 4 mm long, divided to the base; stamens *c.* 3·5 mm long; pod 1-, or rarely 2-seeded, *c.* 2·5 mm long and 1·5 mm wide.

Uncommon plant found in scattered tree grassland with *Combretum*, especially in seasonally waterlogged places, 3300–4500 ft. MUM, EMB.

Bogdan 3753 and 4033.

5. Indigofera dendroides *Jacq.*

Erect, sparsely appressed-strigulose annual up to 1·3 m tall; leaves 11-27-foliolate, the rachis, including the 1 mm petiole, up to 6 cm long; raceme often brownish-strigulose, 8-30-flowered, up to 13 cm long, including a peduncle of up to 5 cm; pedicels *c.* 3 mm long in flower, up to 5 mm in fruit; calyx *c.* 2·5 mm long, divided below the middle into triangular-subulate lobes; stamens 4-5 mm long; pod more or less erect, strigulose, 8-12-seeded, 2-3 cm long, *c.* 1·6 mm wide and thick.

Grassland and cultivated ground, up to 3600 ft. MUM, KIS.

Scott Elliot 7151; Lyne Watt 1546.

6. Indigofera brevicalyx *Bak. f.* (*I. pentaphylla* Auct. non Murr in L.; *I. glabra* Auct. non L.) (see p. 253)

Spreading sparsely appressed-strigulose perennial; leaf rachis, including the 1 mm petiole, up to 15 mm long; leaflets 5-13, each with 3 translucent blisters, one beneath each side and a third beneath the tip; raceme 2-3-flowered, up to 2 cm long; calyx *c.* 1·5 mm long, divided to the middle, each lobe with a blister; stamens 4-5 mm long; pod erect, strigulose, 8-12-seeded, up to 1-8 mm long, *c.* 1·8 mm wide, and 1·2 mm thick.

Short grassland, 4500-7000 ft. HE, HM, HA, KIT, KIS, NAR, RV, MAG, MAC, NBI, KAJ.

Napier 2604; Bogdan 2123.

7. Indigofera monanthoides *Gillett*

Erect annual about 12 cm tall; stipules filiform *c.* 3 mm long; leaflets 3-5, viscid at the margin; flowers solitary on glabrous peduncles 9-11 mm long; calyx 1·5 mm long; stamens 2-2·7 mm long; pod 8-12-seeded, glabrous, erect, 9-12 mm long.

Besides temporary rock pools in *Combretum*, etc. scattered-tree grassland, 5000 ft. MUM.

Brodhurst-Hill 35.

8. Indigofera tanganyikensis *Bak. f*

Stiffly erect herb up to 1 m tall, pubescent with many hairs spreading; leaf rachis, including the *c.* 1 mm petiole, up to 5 cm long, but usually much less; leaflets 7-15, channelled and viscid at the margins; raceme 2-3-flowered, up to 15 mm long; calyx *c.* 1·5 mm long, divided to the middle, the lobes usually gland-tipped; stamens 4-6 mm long; pod usually glabrous 7-10-seeded, 10-20 mm long, *c.* 1·8 mm wide and 1·4 mm thick.

Grassland and bushland, especially on sandy soil and among rocks, 3500-6600 ft. HM, MUM, KIS, NAR, RV, MAC, NBI.

Napper 1604; Bogdan 3384.

9. Indigofera ambelacensis *Schweinf.* (*I. pauciflora* De Wild. non E. & Z.; *I. wildemanii* Bak. f.; *I. conradsii* Bak. f.) (see p. 249)

Erect or spreading pubescent annual up to 80 cm tall; leaf rachis, including a petiole of under 1 mm, up to 2 cm long; stipules *c.* 4 mm long; leaflets 5-11, not viscid; raceme 2-4-flowered, up to 3 cm long; calyx pilose 2-3 mm long, divided below the middle into filiform lobes; stamens *c.* 4 mm long; pod 8-15-seeded, strigose-pubescent, 10-25 mm long, 1·7 mm wide, 1·3 mm thick.

Grassland and bushland, especially among rocks, 3500-5500 ft. KIT, MUM, MAC.

Tallantire 670; Bogdan 1364.

10. Indigofera vohemarensis *Baill.* (*I. pentaphylla* Auct. non Murr in L.; *I. suaveolens* Auct. non Jaub. & Spach; *I. uhehensis* Harms; *I. minimifolia* Chiov.)

Erect branching appressed-strigulose perennial up to 140 cm tall with a tap-root, smelling of coumarin; leaf rachis, including a 1-6 mm petiole, up to 2 cm long; leaflets (3-)5-7(-9); raceme 4-6-flowered, up to 2 cm long; calyx strigose, 1·5 mm long, divided to the middle, lobes triangular; stamens 4-5 mm long; pod appressed-strigulose, 8-14-seeded, 18-25 mm long, *c.* 2 mm wide and 1·7 mm thick.

Grassland and bushland, especially in rocky places, up to 5500 ft. HA, KIT, RV, EMB, MAC.

Bogdan 1549 and 2013.

11. Indigofera nairobiensis *Bak. f.*

Prostrate perennial with woody rootstock, hairs sparse or abundant, appressed or spreading at the tips; leaf rachis, including a 1 mm petiole, up to 15 or rarely 20 mm long, not, or hardly, prolonged beyond lateral leaflets; leaflets 5-11, often with red glandular hairs in their axils; raceme 7-15-flowered, 2-6 cm long; calyx tube 1 mm, lobes 1-3 mm long; stamens 6-7 mm long; pod sparsely strigulose, 6-13-seeded, 15-30 mm long, *c.* 2 mm wide and 1·7 mm thick.

Varies considerably in the density of the indumentum. Specimens collected in KIT and HA and near Thomson's Falls have shorter inflorescences and leaflets with viscid margins and have been described as subspecies *viscida* Gillett.

Grassland and stony places, 5000-6200 ft. HT, HA, HK, KIT, NBI, KAJ.

Bogdan 1608; Bally 7809.

12. Indigofera hedyantha *Eckl. & Zeyh.*

Stiffly erect rather woody herb up to 150 cm tall; leaf rachis, including a 1 mm petiole, up to 15 mm long, not prolonged beyond the lateral leaflets;

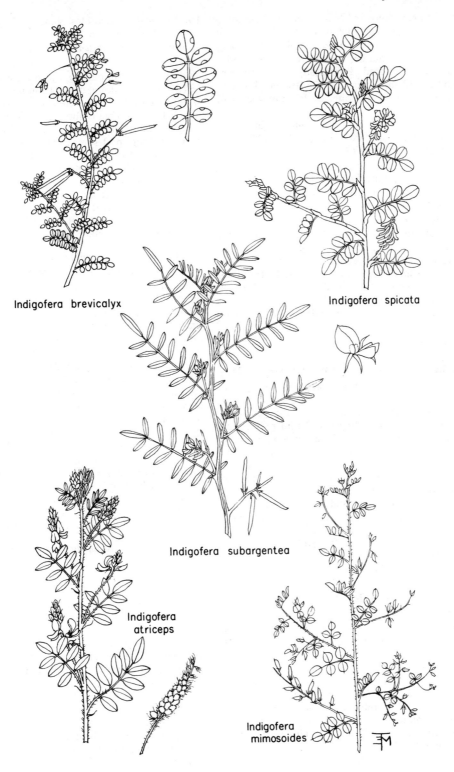

Indigofera brevicalyx

Indigofera spicata

Indigofera subargentea

Indigofera
atriceps

Indigofera
mimosoides

leaflets 7–11; raceme 5–17-flowered, 2–5 cm long, pedicels up to 8 mm long in fruit; calyx densely appressed blackish-strigulose, 3–4 mm long, divided to the middle, lobes triangular, indumentum on standard appressed, golden-brown; stamens 10–13 mm long; pod 7–10-seeded, black-strigulose, up to 4 cm long, *c.* 2·3 mm wide and thick.

Uncommon plant found on mountain slopes near forest margins, 4500–6500 ft. HA, KAJ.

Bally 245; Napier 2173.

13. Indigofera spinosa *Forsk.*

Intricate silvery shrublet up to 50 cm tall; hairs dense, appressed; leaflets 3; petiole 2–4 mm long; raceme with 2–3 flowers borne at, or above, the middle of the 6–25 mm long straw-coloured spinose axis; calyx *c.* 2·5 mm long, divided to the middle, lobes subulate at the tip; standard white-pubescent; stamens 5–6 mm long; pod ascending, strigulose, straight, 6–9-seeded, 15–20 mm long, *c.* 1·8 mm wide and 1·6 mm thick.

Subdesert and dry bushland; up to 3300 or rarely 4200 ft. MAG, MAC.

Bally 292; Bogdan 894.

14. Indigofera subargentea *De Wild.* (see p. 253)

Spreading or erect densely appressed-strigulose annual, with a tap-root, up to 60 cm tall; young stems and leaves of a characteristic yellowish green; leaf rachis, including a 1–2 mm petiole, up to 3 cm long; leaflets 7–17, linear-lanceolate, up to 12 mm long and 2 mm wide; raceme 7–20-flowered, 1–3 cm long, of which the peduncle is less than half; calyx 3–4 mm long, strigose, divided almost to the base into subulate-setaceous lobes; stamens 3–4 mm long; pod erect or spreading, densely strigulose, 7–11-seeded, 15–20 mm long, *c.* 1·8 mm wide and 1·4 mm thick.

Moist type grassland, 5500–6000 ft. HE, KIT, MUM, KIS.

Symes 771; Bogdan 3497.

15. Indigofera thikaensis *Gillett*

Erect woody white-pilose shrublet about 65 cm tall; leaves mostly crowded on short branches; stipules brownish about 6 mm long and up to 2 mm wide at the base; leaf rachis up to 14 mm long; leaflets 5–9, up to 9 mm long and 4 mm wide; racemes 3–12-flowered, 10–20 mm long; bracts lanceolate, up to 6 mm long; calyx 3 mm long; corolla white-pubescent; stamens 5·5 mm long; pods unknown, possibly a sterile hybrid.

Grassland and roadsides, at Thika. HA-MAC boundary, 4900 ft.

Faden 67/606, 67/726.

16. Indigofera vicioides Jaub. & Spach (*I. divaricata* De Wild. non Jacq.; *I. semlikiensis* Robyns & Boutique; *I. rogersii* R. E. Fries)

Spreading annual or perennial; leaf rachis, including a 1–7 mm petiole, up to 5 cm long; leaflets 5–13, elliptic-oblong, up to 15 mm long and 5 mm wide; raceme 5–15-flowered, up to 10 cm long of which the peduncle is about a third; calyx *c.* 2 mm long, deeply divided into subulate lobes; stamens *c.* 3 mm long; pod somewhat torulose with broad (0·5 mm) sutures, 4–8-seeded, 8–17 mm long, *c.* 2 mm wide and 1·8 mm thick.

Varies considerably in the amount of indumentum and whether it is appressed or spreading.

Uncommon plant found in grassland, 3600–5750 ft. KIT, MUM, EMB, MAC, NBI, KAJ.

Maher 1545; Bogdan 3365.

17. Indigofera mimosoides Bak. (*I. shirensis* Bak. f.; *I. brevipetiolata* Cronq.) (see p. 253)

Erect or spreading annual or short-lived perennial, up to 1 m tall, branches reddish with white biramous hairs and also weak spreading red, sometimes glandular, multicellular hairs up to 4 mm long, which are also found on the leaf rachis, inflorescence-axis and calyx but not on the leaflets; stipules setaceous-subulate up to 4 mm long; leaf rachis, including a 1–6 mm petiole, up to 25 mm long; leaflets 3–11; racemes lax, 10–30-flowered, up to 5 cm long including the *c.* 1 cm peduncle; calyx *c.* 3 mm long, divided nearly to the base into setaceous lobes; stamens 3–3·5 mm long; pod spreading, 2–5-seeded, sparsely covered with short appressed white biramous hairs as well as with short erect multicellular glandular hairs, up to 10 mm long, *c.* 1·2 mm wide and 1 mm thick.

Grassland, bushland, and forest margins, 5000–7000 ft. HE, HM, KIT, KIS, RV.

Tweedie 874 and 1318; Napier 2863.

18. Indigofera colutea (*Burm. f.*) Merrill (*I. viscosa* Lam.)

Erect or spreading annual or short-lived perennial up to 90 cm tall covered not very densely with white appressed or spreading biramous hairs and erect multicellular glandular hairs which are up to 1·2 or rarely 2 or 3 mm long on the stems and up to 0·6 mm on the pods, and also occur on the leaf-rachis, inflorescence-axis and leaflet margins; leaf rachis, including a petiole longer than a basal leaflet, up to 7 cm long; leaflets 9–15, 2–3 times as long as wide; raceme 8–20-flowered, as long as, or shorter than, the subtending leaf, the peduncle up to 8 or 12 mm long, shorter than the rest of the rachis; calyx deeply divided, 2/5–2/3 as long as the 3–4 mm stamens; style 1·2–1·6 mm long, sloping upwards from a somewhat thickened base; pod spreading, 8- 14-seeded, up to 18 or 23 mm long, *c*. 1·8 mm wide and thick.

Grassland and bushland, up to 5500 ft. KIT, MAG, EMB, MAC.

Bogdan 1346 and 2219.

19. Indigofera zenkeri *Bak. f.* (*I. multifoliolata* De Wild.; *I. viscosa* Auct. non Lam.; *I. colutea* sensu Gillett (1958) partly, non (Burm. f.) Merrill)

Differs from *I. colutea* as follows; up to 2 m tall; multicellular hairs up to 2 or even 3 or 4 mm long on the stems and 1 or 1·2 mm on the pod; leaves up to 15- or even 23-foliolate; raceme usually rather longer than subtending leaf; calyx from 1/2-9/10 as long as the 3·5-4·4 mm long stamens, style 2-3 mm long, rather abruptly bent through 90° in the middle, its base not swollen; pod 6- 10-seeded, up to 16 or rarely 18 mm long.

Scattered tree grassland, up to 5100 ft. KIT, KIS, NAR, MAC.

Tweedie 2581; Glover *et al.* 1830.

20. Indigofera brachynema *Gillett* (*I. colutea* (Burm. f.) Merrill var. *linearis* Gillett

Differs from *I. colutea* as follows: up to 30 cm tall; multicellular hairs on stems absent or if present under 0·6 mm or rarely up to 1 mm long; those on the leaf rachis up to 0·4 mm long; never present on leaflets; on pod up to 0·3 or rarely 0·7 mm long; leaflets 13-15, 2·6-6 times as long as wide; calyx from 2/3-1 times as long as the 2·3-3 mm stamens; style 0·7-1 mm long, bent up through 90° near the base; pod 12- 13-seeded, up to 18 mm long.

Open grassland on seasonally waterlogged black clay, 3000 ft. MAC.

Bogdan 4370.

21. Indigofera masaiensis *Gillett* (*I. colutea* (Burm f.) Merrill var. *grandiflora* Gillett)

Spreading annual or perennial differing from *I. colutea* as follows: leaflets 7-11 or rarely 13; calyx 2/7-3/5 as long as the 5-7 mm stamens; style about 3 mm long, bent through 90° near the middle.

Semidesert and dry, stony grassland, 2000-5500 ft. RV. MAG.

Bally 12642; Gillett 16180.

22. Indigofera secundiflora *Poir*

Stout erect annual up to 130 cm tall; stems covered both with rather spreading white biramous hairs and erect red, up to 5 mm long, multicellular hairs; leaf rachis, including the 10- 15 mm petiole, up to 5 cm long; leaflets 11-15; raceme dense, many-flowered, including the 2-2·5 cm peduncle

up to 8 cm long, the flowers all turned to one side ('secund'); calyx setose, *c.* 4 mm long; stamens *c.* 3·5 mm long; pod oval-oblong, 2-seeded, densely covered with short white biramous hairs and short erect multicellular hairs, *c.* 4 mm long, 2·4 mm wide, and 2 mm thick.

Scattered tree grassland, *c.* 3600 ft. MUM, EMB.

Scott Elliot 7115; Bogdan 4847.

23. Indigofera atriceps *Hook. f.* (*I. alboglandulosa* Engl.; *I. setosissima* Harms; *I. kaessneri* Bak. f.) (see p. 253)

Coarse branching sub-erect herb up to 2 m tall, strigose with many of the biramous hairs dark or black, except those on the leaflets; pale or reddish glandular multicellular hairs always present on the pods and usually also elsewhere; leaf rachis 1-6 cm long including a 1-13 mm petiole; leaflets 9-13, elliptical; racemes many-flowered, dense, pedunculate; calyx deeply divided, the lobes subulate-setaceous; standard dark-strigose; stamens 3-6 mm long; ovary shorter than the style; pod up to 10 mm long, 3-8-seeded, about 2 mm wide and thick.

Very variable: three subspecies may, with some difficulty, be distinguished in our area; ssp. *atriceps*, with appressed biramous hairs, and stamens 5 mm or more long, about 30 percent longer than calyx, reaches the highest altitudes; ssp. *setosissima* differing with stamens under 5 mm long and shorter pods, and ssp. *kaessneri* with spreading biramous hairs and stamens *c.* 4 mm long, hardly exceeding the calyx.

Moist type grassland, in bracken and at the edge of montane forest, 3600-8100 ft. HE, HC, HT, HM, HA, HK, KIT, MUM, KIS, RV, EMB, MAC, KAJ.

Irwin 100; McDonald 1085.

24. Indigofera homblei *Bak. f. & Martin* (see p. 256)

Softly woody shrub up to 2·5 m tall, stems 3-angled or winged; leaf rachis up to 14 cm long, including a petiole of *c.* 2 cm; leaflets 11- 17(- 19), elliptic-oblong, up to 45 mm long and 20 mm wide; raceme many-flowered, brown-strigulose, up to 16 cm long, including a peduncle of up to 6 cm; pedicels *c.* 2 mm long in flower, up to 4 or 5 mm and reflexed in fruit; calyx densely brown-strigulose, 1·5 mm long, the lobes triangular, shorter than the tube; stamens, in our area, 8-12 mm long; pod glabrous, reflexed, 6-8-seeded, up to 4·5 cm long, *c.* 3 mm wide and thick.

Scattered-tree grassland and forest edges, 4900-7800 ft. HE, HC, HA, KIT.

Bogdan 242 and 4276; Brodhurst-Hill 566.

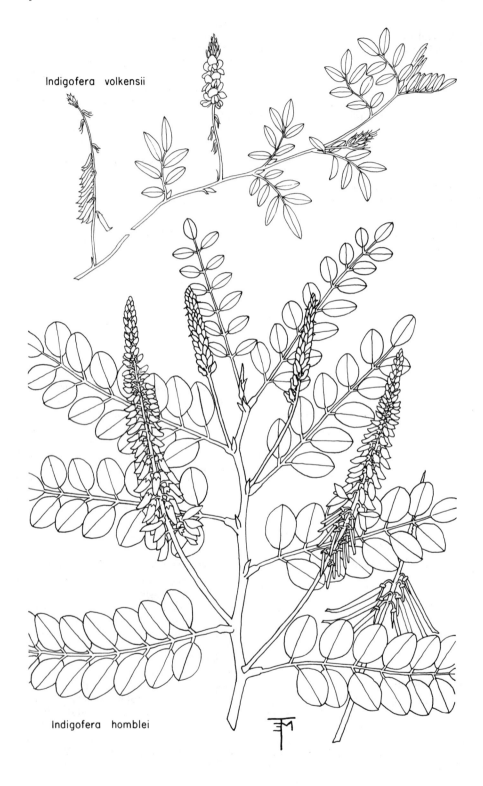

Indigofera volkensii

Indigofera homblei

25. Indigofera garckeana *Vatke* (KTS p. 366) (*I. tetragona* Lebrun & Taton)

Closely resembles *I. homblei*; differs in having fewer (5–9, or rarely –13) leaflets, slightly longer flowers (stamens 12–13 mm), strigulose pods, and pedicels rarely exceeding 3 mm even in fruit.

Scattered-tree grassland and forest margins, 3000–6750 ft. HC, KIS, EMB, MAC, KAJ.

Napier 3419; Graham 2113.

26. Indigofera emarginella *A. Rich.* (KTS p. 336)

Softly woody shrub up to 2 m tall; leaflets (5–)7–11, up to 2 cm long and 16 mm wide; racemes densely blackish or brownish strigulose, almost sessile, much shorter than the subtending leaf; calyx *c.* 1·5 mm long, the lobes broadly triangular, shorter than the tube; stamens 5–6 mm long; pod 15–22 mm long, *c.* 2 mm wide and 1·9 mm thick.

Grassland with *Combretum* etc., 4900–6300 ft. KIT, MUM, KIS, EMB.

Bogdan 3500; Verdcourt 3213.

27. Indigofera swaziensis *Bolus* (KTS p. 367) (*I. mearnsii* Standley; *I. oliveri* Harms)

Softly woody shrub up to 3 m tall; leaflets 9–15; raceme usually longer than subtending leaf including a 3–4 cm peduncle; calyx lobes pointed, as long as the tube; stamens 4–6 mm long; pod up to 35 mm long.

Scrub and forest margins, 3600–7200 ft. HM, HA, HK, KIS, NAR, NAN, MAC, NBI.

Bogdan 2453; Napier 454.

28. Indigofera lupatana *Bak. f.* (KTS p. 366) (*I. goniocarpa* Bak. f.; *I. commiphoroides* Chiov.)

Woody herb up to 2·5 m tall; leaflets (5–)7–9(–11), up to 20 mm long and 12 mm wide; raceme many-flowered, sessile or shortly pedunculate, 1–13 cm long; calyx 2·5 mm long, the lobes triangular-acuminate, twice as long as tube; stamens *c.* 3 mm long; pod markedly tetragonal, 3–4 cm long, *c.* 3·5 mm wide and 4 mm thick.

Bushland, especially in rocky places, 2550–4950 ft. MAG, EMB, MAC, KAJ.

Thomas 1073; Verdcourt and Napper 217.

29. Indigofera cliffordiana *Gillett*

Silvery shrublet *c.* 50 cm tall; leaflets usually 3, *c.* 12 mm long and 7 mm wide; raceme 10–20-flowered, up to 6 cm long including a peduncle of up to 2 cm; calyx *c.* 2·5 mm long, the lobes triangular-acuminate, rather longer than the tube; stamens *c.* 4 mm long; pod arcuate or circinate,

with flattened gaps between the 4–8 seeds, up to 3 cm long; 1·8 mm wide, and 1·4 mm thick.

Semidesert, *c.* 3100 ft. MAG.

Verdcourt 2758; Bogdan 3470.

30. Indigofera trita *L. f.* (*I. subulata* Poir.; *I. carinata* De Wild.; *I. scabra* Roth; *I. retroflexa* Baill.) (see p. 249)

Somewhat woody herb 1–2 m tall when erect but when subscandent among bushes reaching 5 m; indumentum white; leaflets 3 (var. *subulata*) or 5–9 (var. *scabra*), up to 3 cm long and 17 mm wide; racemes many-flowered, up to 27 cm long, including a peduncle of up to 3 cm; calyx 2·5–5 mm long, the lobes subulate-setaceous, much longer than the tube; stamens *c.* 4 mm long; pod more or less tetragonal, straight or gently curved, 2–2·5 cm long, *c.* 1·3 mm wide, and 2 mm thick.

Grassland, bushland, and forest margins, up to 5400 ft. HA, KIS, MAC, NBI, KAJ.

Bogdan 2442; Napier 449.

31. Indigofera bogdanii *Gillett*

Intricate appressed-strigulose shrublet up to 50 cm tall; leaf rachis 10–15 mm long; leaflets 5–9, up to 5 mm long and 3 mm wide; raceme 10–12-flowered, sessile, *c.* 10 mm long; calyx *c.* 1·5 mm long, the broadly triangular lobes shorter than the tube; stamens *c.* 4 mm long; pod 1–4(–6)-seeded, indehiscent, straight or slightly curved, up to 12 mm long, strongly torulose.

Rocky and saline places, dry grassland especially where overgrazed from 4500–6600 ft. What appear to be hybrids between *I. bogdanii* and *I. arrecta* occur. e.g. Gillett 18626. KIT, RV, NAN.

Drummond and Hemsley 4434; Napper 837.

32. Indigofera arrecta *A. Rich.* (KTS p. 366) (see p. 249)

Stout rather woody herb, 1–2 or rarely 3 m tall; leaf rachis up to 6 cm long, including a petiole of up to 15 mm; leaflets 7–17, up to 20 mm long and 7 mm wide; racemes many-flowered, sessile, up to 5 cm long, but usually much shorter; calyx brown-strigulose, *c.* 1·5 mm long, the lobes triangular, as long as the tube; stamens 3–4 mm long; pod brown, straight, 4–8-seeded, 12–17 mm long; *c.* 2·2 mm wide and 2·8 mm thick. Variable; high altitude forms have rather larger flowers and a greater proportion of brown or black hairs than those found at lower altitudes.

Grassland, bushland, and forest margins, up to 8100 ft. HE, HM, HA, HK, KIT, MUM, KIS, NAR, RV, MAG, EMB, MAC, NBI.

Kerfoot 1895; Napier 2432.

33. Indigofera tinctoria *L.*

Resembles *I. arrecta*, but the indumentum throughout is white, the stamens 4–5 mm long and the pod 8–12-seeded, often somewhat curved, up to 35 mm long and *c.* 2 mm wide and thick.

Alluvial ground near Lake Baringo, 3100 ft. BAR.

Bogdan 4107.

34. Indigofera longibarbata *Engl.*

Slightly woody annual, up to 1·3 m tall; leaf rachis up to 5 cm long, including a petiole of 2–6 mm; leaflets 9–13, up to 2 cm long and 1 cm wide; racemes stiffly dark brown-pilose, dense, many-flowered, up to 25 cm long, of which the peduncle is more than half; calyx stiffly brown- or black-pilose, *c.* 5 mm long, divided almost to the base into setaceous lobes; stamens *c.* 5 mm long; pod stiffly black-pilose, *c.* 3-seeded, up to 8 mm long, *c.* 1·8 mm long, *c.* 1·8 mm wide and 2 mm thick.

Moist grassland and forest margins, 4500–7200 ft. HE, HT, HM, HA, KIT, KIS, KAJ.

Brodhurst-Hill 260; Bogdan 3496.

35. Indigofera astragalina *DC.*

Stiffly brownish- or white-pilose spreading annual, up to 60 cm tall; leaf rachis up to 8 cm long, including a petiole of up to 2 cm; leaflets 3–9, up to 35 mm long and 16 mm wide; racemes dense, many-flowered, up to 12 cm long, including a peduncle of 2–25 mm; calyx and stamens *c.* 4 mm long; pod up to 6-seeded, 15–20 mm long, *c.* 3 mm wide and 3–4 mm thick.

Wooded grassland north of Kitale, 4500 ft. BAR.

Bogdan 3410; Tweedie 2894.

36. Indigofera schimperi *Jaub. & Spach* (*I. tettensis* Klotzsch; *I. baukeana* Vatke; *I. oblongifolia* Auct. non Forsk.)

Perennial with dense appressed silvery indumentum, *c.* 1 m or, rarely, up to 3 m tall; leaf rachis up to 6 cm long, including a petiole of *c.* 3 mm; leaflets 5–10, alternate, up to 25 mm long and 20 mm wide; raceme many-flowered, up to 20 cm long, including a peduncle of 1–2 cm; calyx 2–3 mm long with triangular lobes 1–2 times as long as the tube; standard glistening with a dense appressed silver or yellowish indumentum; stamens 5–7 mm long (var. *schimperi*) or 7–10 mm (var. *baukeana*); pod up to 12-seeded, up to 28 mm long, *c.* 2 mm wide and thick, usually bent abruptly outwards at the base in var. *baukeana*.

Grassland and bushland, often in areas with impeded drainage, up to 6300 ft. HM, HA, NAR, EMB, MAC, NBI, KAJ.

Napier 575; Verdcourt 2510.

37. Indigofera volkensii *Taub.* (*I. phillipsiae* sensu Bak. F. (1926) partly, non Bak. f. *I. subhirtella* Chiov.; *I. boranensis* Chiov.) (see p. 256)

Spreading perennial up to 40 cm tall with a white, rather dense, somewhat spreading indumentum; leaf rachis up to 25 mm long, including a 1–5 mm petiole; leaflets 3–7, the terminal usually much larger than the lateral; racemes many-flowered, up to 7 cm long including a 10–15 mm peduncle; calyx *c.* 4 mm long, divided nearly to the base into setaceous lobes; stamens *c.* 4 mm long; pod straight, rather tetragonal, 5–8-seeded, up to 15 mm long, *c.* 2 mm wide and thick.

Acacia-Commiphora bushland and grassland, up to 5700 ft. NAR, BAR, RV, MAG, NAN, MAC, NBI, KAJ.

Bogdan 2036; Edwards 98.

38. Indigofera spicata *Forsk.* (*I. hendecaphylla* (*endecaphylla*) Jacq.; *I. parvula* Auct. non Del.) (see p. 253)

Prostrate or ascending perennial; indumentum sparse, appressed; stems ridged, more or less flattened; stipules broad and scarious at the base with subglabrous margins; leaf rachis up to 3 cm long, including a 1–3 mm petiole; leaflets 5–11 varying from 3 to 30 mm in length; raceme dense, many-flowered, the fertile part at least twice as long as the 1–4 cm long peduncle; calyx 2–3 mm long, divided almost to the base; stamens *c.* 3·5 mm long; pod straight, or almost so, often torulose when immature, 5–8-seeded, 11–18 mm long, *c.* 1·7 mm wide, and 2 mm thick.

Grassland, especially in disturbed areas, up to 7500 ft. HE, HT, HM, HA, KIT, MUM, KIS, NAR, RV, EMB, MAC, NBI, KAJ.

Bogdan 2865; Brodhurst-hill 125.

39. Indigofera circinella *Bak. f.* (*I. spirocarpa* Harms) (see p. 249)

Procumbent perennial differing from small-leaved forms of *I. spicata* in the brown, subtorulose, spirally coiled, almost indehiscent fruits, the almost sessile inflorescence up to 15 mm long and the 2·5–3 mm long calyx and stamens.

Grassland, especially on shallow soil, 3500–6300 ft. HM, HA, KIT, MUM, KIS, NAR, BAR, MAC.

Gillett 16183; Greenway 8784.

40. Indigofera conjugata *Bak.*

Perennial with a stout woody rootstock and appressed indumentum; leaf rachis up to 4 cm long, including a petiole of up to 1 cm; leaflets 1–3 in lower leaves, up to 8 in upper leaves, glabrous above, except at the margin, up to 6 cm long and 12 mm wide; raceme many-flowered, up to 12 cm long, including a 0·5-2 cm peduncle; calyx divided almost to the base, *c.* 4 mm long; stamens 3-4 mm long; pod straight, brown, 5-8-seeded, 12-20 mm long, *c.* 2 mm wide, and 1·3 mm thick.

Wooded grassland, 3600-5700 ft. KIT, MUM. Bogdan 3683; Carroll H4.

41. Indigofera costata *Guill. & Perr.* (*Indigastrum macrostachyum* Jaub. & Spach; *Indigofera goniodes* Bak.)

Appressed strigulose annual *c.* 60 cm tall; leaf rachis up to 6 cm long, including a petiole of 2-4 mm; leaflets 9-15, glabrous above; raceme many-flowered, up to 20 cm long, including a peduncle of up to 5 cm; calyx 2-3 mm, the triangular teeth about as long as the tube, except the lowest, which is longer; corolla very pointed in the bud; stamens *c.* 4 mm long; pod slightly upturned at the tip, up to 4 cm long, *c.* 2·5 mm wide and 1·8 mm thick.

Grassland and bushland, up to 5700 ft. RV, MAG, MAC, NBI.
Verdcourt 3260; Thomas 1004.

42. Indigofera parviflora *Wight & Arn.* (*I. deflexa* A. Rich.)

Differs from *I. costata* in the inflorescence, which rarely exceeds 3 cm in length and is sessile or with a peduncle shorter than a leaflet, in the stamens *c.* 3 mm long and the pod *c.* 2 mm wide.

Acacia grassland, especially on black cotton soil, 3600-4500 ft. KIS, MAC, NBI.
Napier 6779; Bogdan 3076.

43. Indigofera microcharoides *Taub.* (*Rhynchotropis curtisiae* Johnst.)

Perennial, up to 50 cm tall; indumentum copious, white, stiff, rather spreading; leaf simple, up to 4 cm long and 2 cm wide; petiole *c.* 1 mm long; raceme 15-30-flowered, up to 12 cm long, including a 1-2 cm peduncle; bracts persistent *c.* 2 mm long; pedicels up to 7 mm long in fruit, spreading stiffly more or less at right angles to the axis; calyx nearly 4 mm long, the lobes narrowly triangular, longer than the tube; stamens about as long as calyx, the dorsal one sterile; anthers with translucent papery appendages at the base; pod often held parallel to the rachis, i.e. at right angles to the pedicel, *c.* 20-seeded, 3·5-5 cm long, *c.* 2 mm wide and 1·4 mm thick.

Subdesert, dry grassland, and bushland, 3000-6300 ft. NAR, RV, MAG, KAJ.
Verdcourt 2627; Glover *et al.* 1653.

44. Indigofera cufodontii *Chiov.*

Differs from *I. microcharoides* in the leaves which are digitately 3-foliolate and have a petiole up to 5 mm long.

Combretum etc. wooded grassland, 4000-5500 ft. HA, MAC.
Verdcourt 483; Bogdan 2859.

45. Indigofera asparagoides *Bak.*

Almost glabrous perennial; leaflets 5-13, more or less cylindrical, needle-like; raceme 2-10-flowered, up to 10 cm long including a peduncle up to 5 cm; bracts *c.* 1 mm long; pedicels up to 5 mm long; calyx *c.* 2 mm long, divided to the middle; stamens 2-3 mm long; pod 8-14-seeded, 12-25 mm long, *c.* 1·7 mm wide, and 1 mm thick.

Open, rocky places, 5700 ft. KIS.
Buxton in C. Mus. 6033.

5. SESBANIA *Adans.*

Erect herbs or softly woody short-lived shrubs or small trees, often producing a gummy juice when cut; hairs simple; stipules never spurred nor deeply lobed at the base; leaves abruptly pinnate with 4-many pairs of oblong entire leaflets; flowers in axillary 1-many-flowered racemes, bracts and bracteoles present but often very caducous; calyx bell-shaped, the teeth more or less equal, shorter than the tube; corolla glabrous, yellow, the standard often streaked and mottled with purple, with 2 vertical appendages at the base of the blade; wings transversely ribbed; dorsal stamen free, bent sharply near the base where it may be gripped between the appendages of the standard; 9 ventral filaments united for most of their length; anthers all alike; ovary and style usually glabrous; stigma small, globose or ovoid; pod long, narrow, dehiscent, rostrate, transversely septate, 8-50-seeded; seeds usually ellipsoid, the hilum circular or broadly elliptic at or near the centre of one side, often surrounded by a narrow white ring.

Found in places which are wet at least during the rains. In the Kenya uplands different species have not yet been seen growing together.

1 Appendages at base of standard with free tips 2 (or more) mm long; the blade about as wide as long, or wider, widest at or below the middle; pod elliptic in cross-section, the septa 4-6 mm apart; rachis of leaf and raceme not aculeate, except sometimes in *S. dummeri*   2

Appendages at base of standard without free tips or with free tips under 2 mm long; rachis of leaf and raceme usually more or less aculeate   5

2 Filament sheath 9-13 mm long; racemes 4-20-flowered   1. *S. sesban*
Filament sheath 15-24 mm long   3

3 Leaflets pubescent above and below, in 4-8 or rarely up to 12 pairs; stems pubescent; racemes 1-2-flowered   2. *S. goetzei*

Leaflets glabrous, rest of plant almost so   4

4   Racemes 1–2-flowered; leaflets in 4–9 or rarely up to 13 pairs   3. *S. keniensis*

Racemes 4–15-flowered; leaflets in 10–24 pairs   4. *S. dummeri*

5   Appendages at base of standard with short acute free tips, the blade longer than wide and widest above the middle; filament sheath 12–18 mm long; pod rectangular in cross-section with acute angles, the septa 5–5·5 mm apart   5. *S. quadrata*

Appendages at base of standard rounded, without free tips, the blade widest below the middle, wider than long; filament sheath 10–13 mm long; pod elliptic in cross-section, the septa 8–11 mm apart   6. *S. macrantha*

1. Sesbania sesban (*L.*) *Merr.*

Becoming a short-lived shrub or small tree, see KTS p. 376.

Usually by water or in places water-logged during the rains; below 5700 ft. HA, KIT, MUM, KIS, RV, MAC, NBI.

Bogdan 1788; Brodhurst-Hill 569.

2. Sesbania goetzei *Harms*

Becoming a short-lived shrub or small tree, see KTS p. 375.

At the margins of mildly alkaline lakes, abundant around Lake Nakuru, 3600–5500 ft. RV, KAJ.

Mettam 201; Gillett 18311.

3. Sesbania keniensis *Gillett*

Becoming a short-lived shrub or small tree, closely resembling *S. goetzei* but almost glabrous throughout; referred to as an apparent new species under *S. sesban* in KTS p. 376.

By fresh-water streams and lakes and at forest margins; 3600–7200 ft. HT, HM, HL, HA, HK, KIS, NAR, RV, NAN, NBI, KAJ.

Rayner 413; Kirrika in Bally 7757.

4. Sesbania dummeri *Phill. & Hutch.*

Tall herb, shrub or small tree up to 5 m tall, resembling *S. keniensis* but the racemes 4–15-flowered and leaflets in 10–20 pairs; the stems and leaf rachis may be sparsely aculeate.

Uncommon plant found in wet places, 5400–6000 ft. KIT.

Fulton in EAH 13871; Chater-Jack 134.

5. Sesbania quadrata *Gillett*

Annual herb, 1–3 m tall; leaf rachis usually minutely aculeate, and leaflets in 6–30 pairs, glabrous or with a few hairs at the margins;

racemes 5–12-flowered; pod usually purple-spotted at the septa, just as thick at the sutures as in the centre and thus quadrangular in cross-section.

Confused with *S. bispinosa*, a species found in the coastal province, in KTS p. 375.

Grassy places water-logged in the rains, 1500–3600 ft. KIS, MAG, MAC, KAJ.

Bally 12289; Gillett 17197.

6. Sesbania macrantha *Phill. & Hutch.*

Becoming a softly woody shrub or small tree up to 6 m tall; see KTS p. 375.

Uncommon plant found in areas once forested, 4200–6000 ft. MUM, HA.

Moore in Bally 8046; Battiscombe 8.

6. ORMOCARPUM *P. Beauv.*

Shrubs or small trees with normal white hairs and thick stiff ones, particularly on fruits and young twigs; leaves often fasciculate, imparipinnate, with striate, persistent, stipules no stipels, and ± alternate leaflets; flowers in few-flowered racemes or solitary, with bract and bracteoles persistent; calyx lobes longer than the tube, the upper lobes joined for over half their length; corolla glabrous, the standard with 2 ridges or scales at base; stamens usually joined laterally in two semicylinders of 5, but variable; ovary 3–9-ovulate, sometimes constricted between the seeds; becoming stiffly hairy in fruit.

1   Corolla persistent, pinkish or purple; fruit hairs under 1·5 mm long   2

Corolla caducous, cream or bluish; fruit hairs over 5 mm long   3. *O. trichocarpum*

2   Fruit more or less straight, protruding from corolla; standard blade not cordate; leaflet margins not revolute   2. *O. trachycarpum*

Fruit curved, hidden in corolla; standard blade cordate; leaflet margins revolute   1. *O. kirkii*

1. Ormocarpum kirkii *S. Moore*

Dealt with in KTS, p. 372. MAC, KAJ.

2. Ormocarpum trachycarpum (*Taub.*) *Harms* (*O. mimosoides* sensu KTS non S. Moore, *O. aromaticum* Bak. f.)

A shrub 1–6 m tall in KTS p. 373. Frequent in open bushland, 3200–6500 ft. HA, NAR, RV, NAN, MAC, NBI, KAJ.

3. Ormocarpum trichocarpum (*Taub.*) *Engl.* (see p. 262)

A much branched shrub, 1–5 m tall with whitish twigs, solitary flowers and cylindrical densely yellow-hairy fruit.

Uncommon plant found in dry bushland. MUM, KIS, BAR, NAR.

Trelawney 4327.

7. AESCHYNOMENE *L.*

Herbs or shrubs with pinnate leaves, no stipels and axillary racemes of usually showy yellow or orange flowers; calyx 2-lipped; corolla standard with appendages at the base of the claw; corolla wings with a lateral spur and a series of small pockets; stamens (9) + 1, or (10), sometimes in two groups of 5; anthers uniform; ovary linear, 2–18-ovuled; style inflexed, mostly glabrous; pods linear to elliptic, compressed, straight or curved, jointed between the seeds.

1 Pods with straight or crenate margins; seeds
    more than 3   2
   Pods of 1–3, 1-seeded portions, joined by
    narrow necks   7
2 Stems spiny; pods spirally coiled
                    3. *A. elaphroxylon*
   Stems not spiny; pods straight   3
3 Keel petals laciniate along lower margins   4
   Keel petals not laciniate along lower margins
                       2. *A. indica*
4 Inflorescences usually 1-flowered; calyx lips
    usually entire   5
   Inflorescences usually 2–8-flowered; calyx
    lips 2–3-toothed   6
5 Bracts present on pedicel; pods not constricted
    between seeds   4. *A. schimperi*
   Bracts absent; pods constricted between
    seeds   1. *A. uniflora*
6 Stems with soft glandular hairs; leaves with
    over 40 leaflets; pods linear   5. *A. cristata*
   Stems with stiff hairs; leaves with less than 40
    leaflets; pods oblong-elliptic   6. *A. pfundii*
7 Corolla wings entirely free; standard without
    swellings at base of lamina
                  7. *A. gracilipes*
   Corolla wings adhering to each other by
    basal appendages; standard with 2, often
    obscure, basal appendages   8
8 Main nerve of leaflets marginal or sub-
    marginal   8. *A. mimosifolia*
   Main nerve of leaflets central or nearly so
                  9. *A. abyssinica*

1. Aeschynomene uniflora *E. Mey.*

An erect shrubby often annual hairy herb; leaves with numerous sensitive leaflets; flowers solitary, yellow-white with a greenish keel.

Locally common in marshes in forest clearings below 4000 ft. MUM.

Tweedie 3618.

2. Aeschynomene indica *L.*

An erect, glabrous shrubby herb with over 20 pairs of oblong leaflets to each leaf, and small yellow flowers.

Locally common in ephemeral pool edges in hot country. MAC.

Hildebrandt 2853.

3. Aeschynomene elaphroxylon (*Guill. & Perr.*) *Taub.*

A spiny shrub or tree with 8–15 pairs of broad-oblong retuse leaflets to each spiny leaf and large solitary orange flowers.

Locally dominant in water edges in warmer country, the large pithy stems are used for boat-building on Lake Victoria. MUM.

Dummer 1782.

4. Aeschynomene schimperi *A. Rich.*

A softly bristly herb with 18–30 pairs of narrow oblong leaflets to each leaf and conspicuous orange and yellow flowers.

Common in marshes and riversides in the upland area. HE, HT, HA, HK, KIT, NAN, EMB, MAC, NBI.

Kabuye 84.

5. Aeschynomene cristata *Vatke*

An erect herb or shrub, glabrous (except for the calyx), with 10–24 pairs of oblong leaflets to the leaf and small racemes of orange and yellow flowers.

In marshes up to 3200 ft. MUM, BAR.

J. Leakey in EAH 14303, 14789.

6. Aeschynomene pfundii *Taub.*

A small shrub with pithy stems covered with golden hairs; flowers 3–7 together, orange-yellow; pod 1·1–1·7 cm wide.

Uncommon in lake edges. HA (Solai).

Richardson 25.

7. Aeschynomene gracilipes *Taub.*

A low spreading pubescent herb with 6–14 pairs of oblong leaflets to each leaf and small yellow flowers; pods with a long basal stalk.

Rare and only once collected in the Mbooni Hills. MAC.

Bogdan 1179.

8. Aeschynomene mimosifolia *Vatke*

An erect bristly wiry herb with 6–14 pairs of asymmetric, crowded leaflets to the leaf and small yellow flowers in long racemes.

Uncommon plant found in dry bushland. EMB, MAC.

Graham 2406.

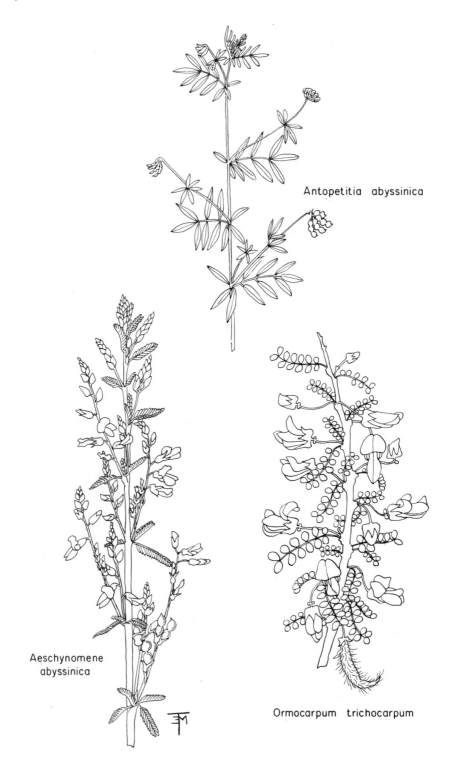

Antopetitia abyssinica

Aeschynomene
abyssinica

Ormocarpum trichocarpum

9. Aeschynomene abyssinica (*A. Rich.*) *Vatke* (see p. 262)

Similar to *A. mimosifolia* but larger in all parts and ± glabrous.

Locally common in forest edges and disturbed ground. HE, HC, HT, HM, HA, HK, KIT, KIS, RV, KAJ.

Bally 8211.

8. SMITHIA *Ait.*

Similar to *Kotschya* but with the keyed differences and the lateral appendages of the keel petals nearly as long as the claws.

Smithia elliotii *Bak. f.* (see p. 264)

A sparsely-hairy, weak woody-stemmed herb with 8–12 pairs of oblong-elliptic leaflets to each leaf and tight axillary umbels of mauve flowers.

Rare plant found in swamps within the montane forest area. HE.

Tweedie 1325.

9. KOTSCHYA *Endl.*

Herbs or shrubs with glandular hairs and pinnate leaves; leaflets alternate, asymmetric at the base; stipels absent; inflorescences mainly dense, axillary ± scorpioid, with reflexed, often distichous flowers; bracts entire; bracteoles free or connate; calyx scarious, 5-lobed, with a short tube; corolla small, white, yellow or blue; stamens (10); anthers uniform; ovary stalked, 2–9-ovuled; style glabrous; pods stalked, of 1–9-joints, the joints often folded together, enclosed in the calyx.

1   Plant annual; flowers in globose heads
                              4. *K. capitulifera*
     Plant perennial; flowers in elongated inflorescences   2
2   Claw of standard petal over half the length of the lamina; ovary glabrous
                              3. *K. aeschynomenoides*
     Claw of standard petal less than half the length of the lamina; ovary pubescent   3
3   Leaflets distinctly curved, in 4–9 pairs
                              2. *K. recurvifolia*
     Leaflets not curved, in 8–22 pairs
                              1. *K. africana*

1. Kotschya africana *Endl.*

An erect glandular-hairy shrub with numerous ovate leaflets and large yellow flowers terminating a raceme of sterile bracts.

This species much resembles an herbaceous *Cassia.* Rare plant found in upland grassland. HT, KIT, MUM.

Dowson 666.

2. Kotschya recurvifolia (*Taub.*) *F. White*

An erect bushy glandular shrub with recurved leaves and yellow flowers on condensed paniculate inflorescences.

Locally common in dry montane forest edges. HC, HM, HA, HK.

Gillett 16257.

3. Kotschya aeschynomenoides (*Bak.*) *Dewit & Duvign.*

An erect weak glandular shrub with over 10 pairs of oblong leaflets to each leaf; flowers white and purple, distichous, in viscid spikes.

Disturbed bushland in montane forest. HK, MAC.

Fries 1903.

4. Kotschya capitulifera (*Bak.*) *Dewit & Duvign.*

An erect pubescent eglandular annual with 6–12 pairs of asymmetric oblong leaflets to each leaf; flowers white, in globose heads.

Rare plant of shallow-soil grassland, only once recorded from Kenya in HT.

Williams 298.

10. STYLOSANTHES *Swartz*

Herbs or shrubs with trifoliolate leaves and dense, few-flowered, axillary or terminal inflorescences of subsessile yellow flowers; bracts 1-foliolate; subsidiary bracts hyaline; calyx 5-lobed; corolla wings and keels with a lateral basal spur and appendage and also with small pockets on the blade; stamens (10); anthers 5 longer and basifixed alternating with 5 shorter and versatile; ovary 2–3-ovuled; style filiform, breaking later, the lower part persistent, curved and dilated, simulating a stigma; pods oblong, compressed, beaked, 1–2-jointed but the upper or lower joints often aborted.

Stylosanthes fruticosa (*Retz.*) *Alston*

A small wiry pubescent shrub with elliptic, acute leaflets and subsessile yellow flowers.

Common in grassland and forest edges, especially in rocky soils. HA, MUM, KIS, BAR, RV, EMB, MAC, NBI.

Napper 1571; Mwangangi 284.

11. ZORNIA *J. F. Gmel.*

Herbs with palmately divided, 2–4 foliolate, mostly glandular leaves without stipels; inflorescence of terminal or axillary spikes; bracts paired, stipule-like, mostly peltate, enclosing the flowers; calyx 5-lobed, persistent; corolla mostly yellow or orange; stamens (10), all similar, ovary subsessile; pods sessile, 2–15-jointed, the joints glabrous to

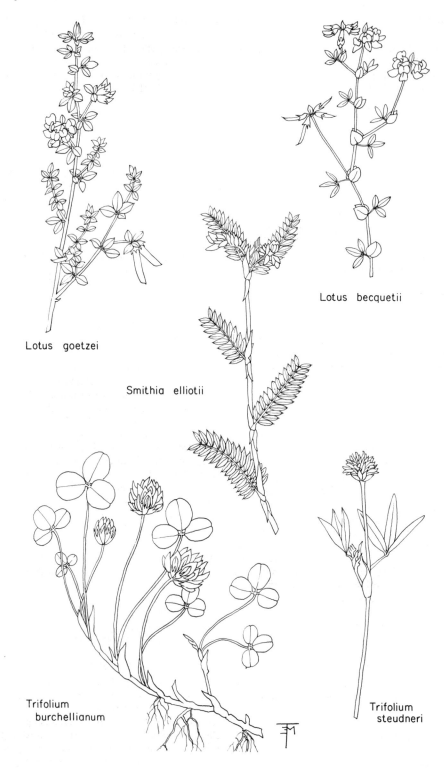

Lotus goetzei

Lotus becquetii

Smithia elliotii

Trifolium
burchellianum

Trifolium
steudneri

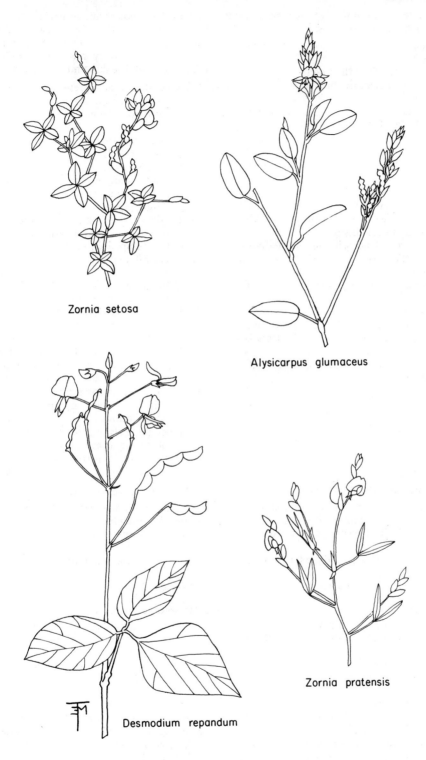

Zornia setosa

Alysicarpus glumaceus

Desmodium repandum

Zornia pratensis

pilose, mostly prominently nerved; seeds compressed, without appendages.

1 Leaflets 4   1. *Z. setosa*
   Leaflets 2   2
2 Flowers shorter than the bracts   3
   Flowers longer than the bracts   4
3 Plant perennial   2. *Z. albolutescens*
   Plant annual   3. *Z. glochidiata*
4 Leaflets linear; fruit hairs not sticky
                                          4. *Z. pratensis*
   Leaflets ovate; fruit sticky with retrorsely
      bristly hairs   5. *Z. apiculata*

1. Zornia setosa *Bak. f.* (see p. 265)

A trailing perennial herb with short-petiolate leaves; flowers orange or yellow or even pinkish in short axillary and terminal spikes.

Common in grassland with impeded drainage. HE, HC, HT, HM, HA, KIT, MUM, NAR, RV, MAC, NBI, KAJ.

Drummond and Hemsley 4478; Napier 1910.

2. Zornia albolutescens *Mohl.*

A trailing glandular perennial herb from a woody rootstock with 2 asymmetric elliptic leaflets on each leaf; flowers yellow.

Rare plant found in wooded grassland. MAC. Bogdan 4023.

3. Zornia glochidiata *DC.*

Very similar to *Z. albolutescens* but an annual with, in our area, fewer glands on the leaves.

Uncommon plant found in dry bushland. MUM, BAR.

Bogdan 2038.

4. Zornia pratensis *Milne-Redh.* (see p. 265)

A tufted perennial from a fibrous rootstock with prostrate branches bearing 2-foliolate leaves; leaflets linear-elliptic; flowers yellow and reddish-brown or orange.

Locally common in wooded grassland. HE, HT, KIT, MUM, NAR.

Tweedie 561; McDonald 1028.

5. Zornia apiculata *Milne-Redh.*

A semi-erect perennial similar to *Z. pratensis* except for the ovate-elliptic leaflets and the longer fruit bristles.

Locally common in dry, rocky bushland. MAC. Bogdan 3896; Verdcourt 701.

12. DESMODIUM *Desv.*

Herbs or low shrubs with simple hairs and without glands; leaves unifoliolate or trifoliolate, the leaflets stipellate, entire; flowers in terminal panicles or pseudo-racemes, pink or purplish, pedicellate,

without bracteoles, but sometimes with accessory bracts; calyx with 5 ± equal teeth; standard glabrous outside; stamens (9) + 1; anthers all fertile and similar; ovary sessile, with a filiform style; fruit flattened, breaking into 1-seeded joints.

1 Secondary bracts present   2
   Secondary bracts absent   6
2 Flowers over 10 mm long; fruits stipitate
                                         4. *D. repandum*
   Flowers less than 7·5 mm long; fruits sessile 3
3 Leaves 1-foliolate   4
   Leaves 3-foliolate   5
4 Leaflet margins mostly sinuate; stipules abruptly narrowed at base and with a long slender apex   5. *D. velutinum*
   Leaflets entire; stipules gradually narrowed throughout their length 6. *D. gangeticum*
5 Calyx 2-lipped, lips entire 7. *D. salicifolium*
   Calyx 5-lobed or lips with 2 and 3 lobes
                                        8. *D. dregeanum*
6 Calyx 5-lobed   9. *D. barbatum*
   Calyx 2-lipped   7
7 Racemes elongated, much exceeding the leaves, the lower internodes longer than the pedicels   8
   Racemes condensed, hardly exceeding the leaves, with the lower internodes much shorter than the pedicels   1. *D. triflorum*
8 Most pedicels longer than the corolla; fruit outline convex on both edges between constrictions   2. *D. setigerum*
   Most pedicels shorter than the corolla; fruit outline concave above, convex below, between the constrictions
                                       3. *D. ramosissimum*

1. Desmodium triflorum *(L.) DC.*

A trailing perennial herb with trifoliolate leaves bearing ± orbicular leaflets; flowers small, few, axillary towards the ends of the branches, purplish.

Locally common, found in stony grassland. MUM.

Tweedie 2614.

2. Desmodium setigerum *(E. Mey.) Harv.*

An erect or straggling herb with trifoliolate leaves bearing obovate leaflets; flowers small, mauve, in terminal racemes.

Rare, found in wet grassland. KIS. Buxton 6034.

3. Desmodium ramosissimum *G. Don*

Similar to *D. setigerum* but without the long hairs on the stem and with more oblong leaflets.

Recorded from grassland in Nairobi. NBI. Dowson 285.

4. Desmodium repandum (*Vahl*) *DC.* (see p. 265)

A loosely branched herb with trifoliolate leaves bearing ovate to rhomboid leaflets; flowers reddish-pink.

Common, in shade in forest, particularly by streams and along pathsides where its sticky fruits are easily picked up. HE, HT, HM, HA, KIT, MUM.

Paulo 508; Glover 2180.

5. Desmodium velutinum (*Willd.*) *DC.*

An erect woody herb or shrub with simple broad elliptic to rhombic leaves and axillary and terminal racemes of crowded pink to purple flowers.

Uncommon, found in forest edges and tall grassland. MUM.

Powell 28.

6. Desmodium gangeticum (*L.*) *DC.*

A trailing herb with simple ovate leaves and axillary and terminal racemes of pink to purple flowers.

Deciduous woodland and wet grassland. NBI.

White s.n.

7. Desmodium salicifolium (*Poir.*) *DC.*

An erect wiry herb with trifoliolate leaves bearing lanceolate-elliptic leaflets; flowers pinkish.

Locally common, found in shaded riverine habitats in western Kenya. KIT, KIS.

Tweedie 2858.

8. Desmodium dregeanum *Benth.*

A woody trailing herb with trifoliolate leaves bearing apparently sensitive, obovate, apiculate leaflets; inflorescence of dense spike-like racemes.

Uncommon, found in forest edges. MUM.

White s.n.

9. Desmodium barbatum (*L.*) *Benth.*

Similar to *D. triflorum* but with almost reniform leaflets and denser inflorescences which are definitely terminal.

In wooded grassland. MUM, KIS, NAR.

Tweedie 3533.

13. PYCNOSPORA *Wight & Arn.*

Woody herbs with pinnately trifoliolate stipellate leaves and terminal panicles of purplish flowers; bracts membranous, deciduous; bracteoles absent; calyx 5-lobed; corolla wings oblong, adherent to the keel; keel petals with small appendages near the base; stamens (9) + 1; anthers uniform; ovary many-ovuled; style subulate, glabrous; pod oblong, inflated, not septate.

Pycnospora lutescens (*Poir.*) *Schindl.*

A pubescent perennial with tufts of ascending stems from a woody rootstock and with oblong to broad-elliptic leaflets; flowers violet-blue in a terminal raceme-like panicle; pods ovoid, blackish.

Uncommon plant found in rocky, wooded grassland. MUM, KIS.

Kokwaro 58.

14. PSEUDARTHRIA *Wight & Arn.*

Erect perennial herbs or shrubs with pinnately trifoliolate stipellate leaves and paniculate terminal or axillary inflorescences; bracts narrow; bracteoles absent or soon falling; calyx 5-lobed, the lobes ± equal; corolla small, purple, pink, or white, glabrous; stamens (9) + 1; anthers uniform; ovary many-ovuled; style filiform, glabrous; stigma capitate; pods linear, compressed, and sinuate between the seeds but not breaking into 1-seeded joints.

1 Inflorescence dense, with pedicels hidden; flowers mostly in pairs; pods sessile, slightly curved   1. *P. confertiflora*
   Inflorescence lax with pedicels clearly visible; flowers in fascicles of 3–4, the middle one often reduced; pods mostly stipitate, straight   2. *P. hookeri*

1. Pseudarthria confertiflora (*A. Rich.*) *Bak.*

An erect densely pubescent woody herb with elliptic leaflets and crowded spike-like axillary inflorescences of pink flowers.

Uncommon plant found in upland wooded grassland. HE, HT, HM, HA, RV, KIT, NAN, EMB, MAC, NBI.

Graham 2180.

2. Pseudarthria hookeri *Wight & Arn.*

Similar to *P. confertiflora* but with looser inflorescences mostly in a terminal panicle.

Locally common in wooded grassland. HE, HC, HT, KIT, MUM, KIS, NAR, RV, MAC, KAJ.

Glover *et al.* 1805.

15. ALYSICARPUS *Desv.*

Herbs with simple or rarely trifoliolate leaves; flowers pinkish to purple in terminal panicles or false racemes; bracts present; bracteoles absent; calyx scarious, appearing 4-lobed; stamens (9) + 1, with alternate long and short filaments; anthers all similar; ovary sessile, many-ovuled; style glabrous, filiform; stigma capitate; pods linear-oblong, many-jointed, indehiscent, with straight or crenate margins.

1 Pods with straight margins, not constricted between the seeds   1. *A vaginalis*

Pods with definite constrictions between the
seeds   2
2   Individual portions of the pod smooth
                                                    2. *A. zeyheri*
     Individual portions of the pod sculptured   3
3   Calyx lobes overlapping at base, with white
     or rusty hairs   3. *A rugosus*
     Calyx lobes hardly overlapping at the base,
     never with rusty hairs   4
4   Individual portions of the pod with transverse
     ridges only   4. *A. glumaceus*
     Individual portions of the pod with a raised
     network of ridges   5. *A.* sp. *A*

1. Alysicarpus vaginalis (*L.*) *DC.*

A tufted perennial from a woody rootstock
with ovate to lanceolate or oblong-elliptic leaves
and long terminal false racemes of pinkish flowers;
pods cylindrical, much longer than the calyx.

Uncommon, found in dry bushland. MUM,
MAC.

Bogdan 3920.

2. Alysicarpus zeyheri *Harv.*

A tufted perennial from a woody rootstock with
linear-lanceolate leaves and pink to mauve flowers
in terminal false racemes; pods ± as long as the
calyx.

Locally common plant found in wooded grassland. HT, KIT, EMB, NBI.

Verdcourt 3170.

3. Alysicarpus rugosus (*Willd.*) *DC.*

Similar to *A. zeyheri* but with the keyed differences.

Locally common plant found in temporarily
flooded areas in dry country and in grassland with
impeded drainage. HE, HM, HA, KIT, KIS, NAR,
BAR, EMB, NBI, KAJ.

Buxton 1266.

4. Alysicarpus glumaceus (*Vahl*) *DC.* (see p. 265)

An erect annual with linear-lanceolate to elliptic
leaves and short terminal false racemes of pinkish-
buff flowers; fruit much longer than the calyx,
conspicuously lobed and roughened.

Common plant found in seasonally flooded
grassland, especially short grass on shallow soils.
HE, BAR, NAR, MAC, NBI, KAJ.

Glover *et al.* 1573.

5. Alysicarpus sp. A *of FTEA*

Similar to *A. glumaceus* but with shorter inflorescences and the keyed fruit differences.

Known from but one gathering on the Magadi
Road. MAG.

Bogdan 3472.

16. AMPHICARPA *Nuttall*

Climbing herbs with pinnately trifoliolate stipellate
leaves and axillary racemes; calyx tubular, appearing
4-toothed; corolla small, white, purple or blue;
stamens (9) + 1; anthers all similar or, in cleistogamous flowers, only 2–5 fertile; ovary ± sessile,
many-ovuled; style filiform, glabrous; pod linear or
falcate, compressed, not septate.

Amphicarpa africana (*Hook. f.*) *Harms* (see p. 269)

A perennial silky-hairy climber with suborbicular
to elliptic leaflets and false racemes of attractive,
violet flowers.

Locally common in montane forest edges. HE,
HM, HA, HK, KIT, MUM, KAJ.

Verdcourt 2300.

17. DUMASIA *DC.*

Climbers with pinnately trifoliolate stipellate leaves
and axillary racemose inflorescences of small
flowers; calyx cylindrical, mouth oblique, lobes
obsolete; stamens (9) + 1; anthers uniform; ovary
with a small stalk, 4–many-ovuled; style hairy
below, dilated and hollow near the middle,
cylindrical at apex; pods linear, compressed,
constricted between the seeds but not septate;
seeds blue-black, sub-globose.

Dumasia villosa *DC.*

A rusty-hairy climber with ovate leaflets and dense
or loose racemes of bright-yellow flowers.

Rare plant found in wet forest. HE, HN, MUM,
KAJ.

Irwin 126.

18. CLITORIA *L.*

Shrubs, climbers, herbs, or trees with pinnate
stipellate leaves bearing 3–9 leaflets; flowers solitary
or in racemes; bracts present, the upper pairs
connate; bracteoles large; calyx 5-lobed; corolla
large, red, white, or blue; standard much longer than
the other petals; stamens (9) + 1; anthers uniform or
5 dorsifixed alternating with 5 basifixed; ovary stipitate, 2–many-ovuled; style bearded on upper side;
pod linear, compressed, not septate; seeds subglobose.

Clitoria ternatea *L.* (see. p. 269)

A glabrescent climber; leaflets 5–7, often variable
in size and shape, linear to orbicular; flowers
axillary, solitary or paired, very attractive, blue.

This beautiful climber is found in warmer
country, in bushland. MAG, NAN, EMB, MAC,
KAJ.

Bogdan 3134.

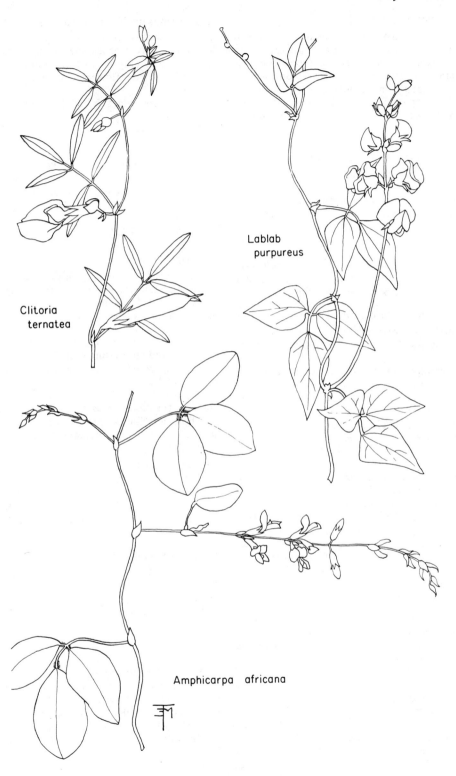

Lablab
purpureus

Clitoria
ternatea

Amphicarpa africana

19. OPHRESTIA *Forbes*

Climbing or erect herbs with pinnate 1–7-foliolate leaves, stipels minute or absent and flowers in false racemes or axillary clusters; calyx 5-lobed, the lobes equal; stamens (9) + 1; anthers uniform or alternating long and short; ovary subsessile 2–8-ovuled; style short, cylindrical, flattened, curved or hooked, hairy or glabrous; pods oblong-linear, compressed.

Ophrestia radicosa (*A. Rich.*) *Verdc.*

A perennial pubescent climber with trifoliolate leaves, leaflets lanceolate; flowers crowded at the nodes of false racemes, pale purple or cream.

Rare plant found in wooded grassland. KIT. Bogdan 3498.

20. GLYCINE *Willd.*

A genus similar (in our species) to *Amphicarpa* except for the 5-toothed calyx, smaller corolla and ± septate pod, constricted between the seeds.

Glycine wightii (*Wight & Arn.*) *Verdc.* (see p. 240)

A perennial climber with variable indumentum and axillary racemes of small white to blue or mauve flowers.

Very common and variable with large and small, hairy or glabrous forms, all over the upland area except where very dry. It grows in forest edges and disturbed ground. HA, HT, KIT, BAR, MAG, MAC, NBI, KAJ.

Dowson 471.

21. TERAMNUS *P. Br.*

Perennial climbing herbs, rarely erect shrubs, with trifoliolate stipellate leaves and axillary false racemes of small flowers; calyx 4–5-lobed, depending on whether the upper 2 lobes are free or united; corolla glabrous; stamens (9) + 1 or (10), 5 normal anthers alternating with 5 sterile ones; ovary many-ovuled, often with a tuft of hairs at the apex; style short and thick or obsolete, hidden in hair tuft; stigma capitate; pod linear, 8-seeded, hooked upwards at apex; seeds oblong.

1 Petiole shorter than leaflets; leaflets mostly oblong with the lateral nerves reaching the cartilaginous margin; raceme usually exceeding the subtending leaves; calyx covered by dark brown hairs
   1. *T. uncinatus*

   Petiole mostly longer than leaflets; leaflets mostly elliptic with the lateral nerves hardly reaching the scarcely thickened margin; raceme rarely exceeding the subtending leaf; calyx covered with cream or russet hairs   2. *T. labialis*

1. Teramnus uncinatus (*L.*) *Sw.* (see p. 240)

A wiry climber with russet or brown hairs on stems and nerves of leaflets; leaflets lanceolate to oblong, rarely elliptic, with pronounced nervation on the lower side; flowers white and mauve in long racemes.

Uncommon plant found in wooded grassland. KIT, KAJ.

Tweedie 1340.

2. Teramnus labialis (*L. f.*) *Spreng.*

A low twining pubescent perennial with elliptic leaflets and small whitish flowers in short racemes.

Uncommon plant found in dry country. KIT, KIS, NAR, MAC.

Glover *et al.* 1721.

22. MUCUNA *Adans.*

Mostly robust climbers with pinnately-trifoliolate often stipellate leaves and axillary, complex, often paniculate inflorescences; bracts and bracteoles present and deciduous; flowers large and showy, purple to greenish; calyx 4–5-lobed, 2-lipped; stamens (9) + 1; anthers in 2 series, the 5 larger basifixed and alternating with 5 smaller dorsifixed; ovary few-ovuled; style long, filiform, sometimes pubescent but not bearded; pods ovoid, oblong or linear, often covered with irritant bristles, septate between the seeds; seeds globose or oblong.

These are the *buffalo beans* which are often such a painful part of penetrating riverine forest in tropical Africa.

1 Plant erect   1. *M. stans*
   Plant climbing   2
2 Pod with two wings bordering the suture
                                       2. *M. gigantea*
   Pod without sutural wings   3. *M. poggei*

1. Mucuna stans *Bak.*

An erect shrub or tree with ± elliptic leaflets and purplish-black flowers; pods oblong, to 2 cm wide, densely rusty-hairy.

Uncommon plant found in wooded grassland. KIT.

Tweedie 854.

2. Mucuna gigantea *Bak.*

A robust climber with ovate acute or acuminate leaflets and long false racemes of greenish flowers; pods large, orbicular to oblong, over 3·5 cm wide, covered with irritant reddish hairs.

Uncommon plant found in riverine forest. MUM.

Glasgow 46/39.

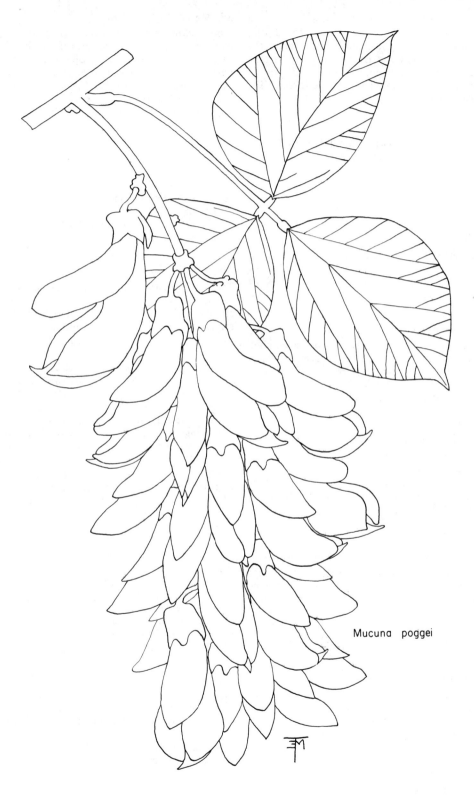

Mucuna poggei

3. Mucuna poggei *Taub.* (see p. 271)

A robust climber with broadly ovate to elliptic, acute leaflets and long false racemes of greenish-yellow flowers; calyx and fruit with rusty irritant hairs; pod over 3·5 cm wide.

Uncommon plant found in riverine forest. KIT. Tweedie 1893.

23. CANAVALIA *Adans.*

Herbs or climbers with pinnately trifoliolate stipellate leaves and axillary racemes of white to purple flowers; calyx 5-lobed, 2-lipped; corolla keel incurved, often twisted; stamens (10) or rarely (9) + 1; anthers all similar; ovary many-ovuled; style glabrous; pods linear or oblong, many-seeded, often winged or ridged along the top and elsewhere, seeds compressed.

1   Leaflets obtuse at apex; seeds white
                                    1. *C. ensiformis*
    Leaflets acute or acuminate at apex; seeds
    .not white   2. *C. virosa*

1. Canavalia ensiformis (*L.*) *DC.*

A glabrescent, annual or perennial robust climber with ovate-elliptic leaflets and long racemes of red to purple flowers; pods 15–30 cm long, with 3 narrow ribs on the upper side.

Cultivated and escaped. HA.
Bogdan 3984.

2. Canavalia virosa (*Roxb.*) *Wight & Arn.*

Similar to *C. ensiformis* but with the keyed differences.

This species is common around cultivation in warmer country in western Kenya. MUM, KIS.
Tweedie 2834.

24. PSOPHOCARPUS *DC.*

Herbs or shrubs with pinnately trifoliolate stipellate leaves (in ours) and axillary false racemes or fascicles of blue or purplish flowers; calyx 5-lobed; stamens (9) + 1; anthers 5 dorsifixed, alternating with 5 basifixed; ovary 3–8-ovuled; style bent above the ovary, flattened towards the apex, glabrous or bearded; stigma penicillate; pods oblong, 4-winged along the angles, dehiscent, ± septate.

Psophocarpus lancifolius *Harms* (see p. 273)

A pubescent climber with ovate to linear-oblong leaflets and axillary, shortly pedunculate, umbel-like groups of attractive violet-purple flowers.

Uncommon plant found in wooded grassland. KIT.
Bogdan 3545.

25. VATOVAEA *Chiov.*

Woody climbers with pinnately trifoliolate stipellate leaves and axillary false racemes of purplish flowers; calyx 5-lobed, 2-lipped; corolla wings with a long narrow spur; stamens (9) + 1; anthers uniform; ovary linear, 9–12-ovuled; style long, incurved, bearded within towards the apex and with a reflexed appendage above the oblique stigma; pod linear-oblong, dehiscent.

Vatovaea pseudolablab (*Harms*) *Gillett*

A woody glabrescent climber from a large woody tuber with ovate to orbicular, acute to emarginate leaflets and long racemes of purple flowers.

Locally common in dry grassland, especially on soils with impeded drainage. MAG, MAC, KAJ.
Bogdan 5133.

26. VIGNA *Savi.*

Twining, prostrate or erect herbs or, less often, subshrubs, usually from woody or tuberous root-stocks, with simple or pinnately trifoliolate leaves; stipels often present; inflorescence a raceme, usually much condensed so that it is nearly always much shorter than the peduncle and sometimes sub-umbellate; bracts and bracteoles more or less deciduous; calyx 2-lipped, the lower lip of 3 lobes, the upper of 2 usually wholly or partially united lobes; corolla small or medium-sized; the standard with inflexed auricles and usually with 2–4 appendages inside near the base; keel truncate, obtuse or, more often, beaked, the beak erect or incurved; ovary 3–many-ovulate; style with a thin lower and a thicker cartilaginous upper part which is barbate or hirsute on the inner surface and is often produced beyond the stigma; stigma completely lateral, oblique or rarely terminal; pods linear or linear-oblong, cylindrical or flattened, straight or curved, usually more or less septate.

Note in this key that purple denotes various shades from pink to dark blue, as contrasted with yellow-green; purple corollas may have yellow streaks on the standard and pale yellow bases to the petals, especially the keel. The left- and right-hand sides of the flower are stated with respect to the flower i.e. as though one were standing with one's back to the inflorescence-rachis.

1   Leaves simple   2
    Leaves 3-foliolate   3
2   Erect or ascending herb; peduncles longer than
        leaves   18. *V. monophylla*
    Twining herb; peduncles shorter than leaves
                                       14. *V.* sp. *B*
3   Standard densely pubescent outside   4
    Standard glabrous   5

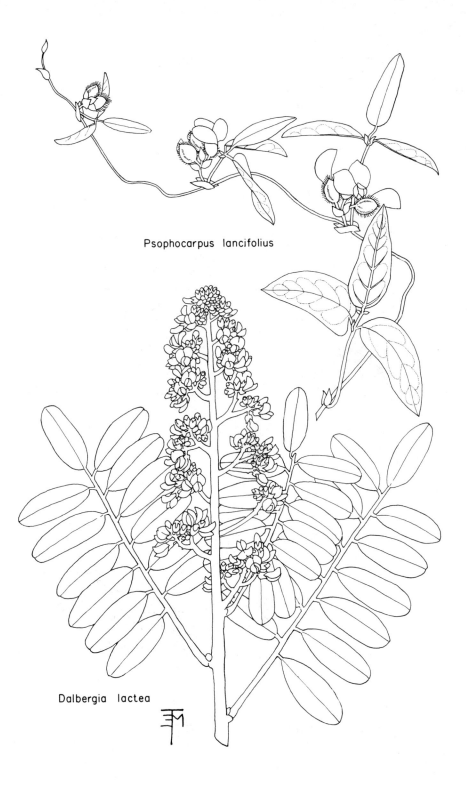

Psophocarpus lancifolius

Dalbergia lactea

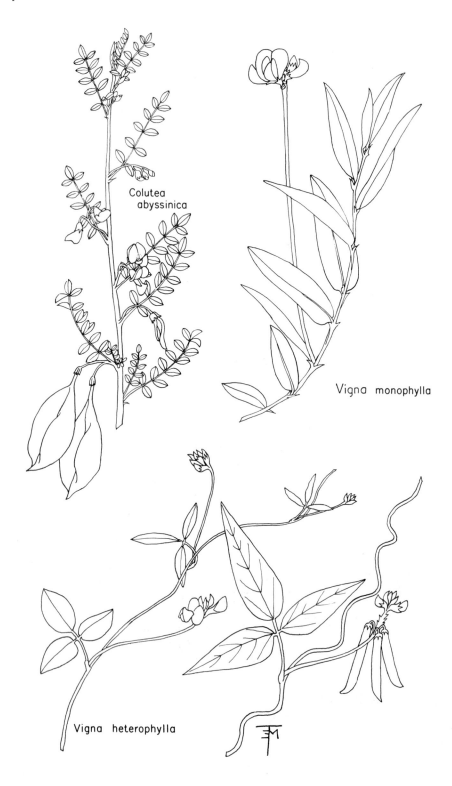

Colutea
abyssinica

Vigna monophylla

Vigna heterophylla

4   Calyx lobes longer than or equal to the tube and narrow; indumentum of calyx and fruit mostly spreading   6. *V. heterophylla*
     Calyx lobes short and wide, much shorter than the tube; indumentum of calyx and fruit mostly appressed   7. *V. ambacensis*

5   Keel prolonged into a narrow beak incurved through nearly 360°; inflorescence usually elongate with wide gaps between the nodes   17. *V. macrorhyncha*
     Beak of keel absent or much shorter and less incurved; inflorescence usually condensed   6

6   Anthers of the shorter stamens with paired glands at base (use × 10 lens)   19. *V. triphylla*
     Anthers of shorter stamens without glands   7

7   Corolla yellow-green; twiners   8
     Corolla red, blue, mauve or purple; sometimes ± erect   12

8   Pods ascending   3. *V. schimperi*
     Pods deflexed   9

9   Stipules truncate at base; pods 1–3-seeded   5. *V. comosa*
     Stipules more or less bilobed at base; pods nearly always more than 3-seeded   10

10   Corolla 0·5–1 cm long   4. *V. oblongifolia*
     Corolla well over 1 cm long   11

11   Pods sparsely or densely appressed-pubescent, 4–8 cm long, 6–9(–12)-seeded   1. *V. luteola*
     Pods densely covered with spreading red or orange hairs 3–5·5 cm long, *c.* 11-seeded   2. *V. fischeri*

12   Pods deflexed, 1–2·5 cm long, 2–5-seeded   8. *V. parkeri*
     Pods ascending, longer and with more seeds   13

13   Stipules peltate with a marked entire spur projecting below the base   14
     Stipules not peltate   15

14   Keel without a marked pocket; style with a very short ± reflexed projection beyond the stigma (native and cultivated)   11. *V. unguiculata*
     Keel with a distinct, upwardly directed pocket on left-hand side; style with a distinct beak beyond the stigma (cultivated)   16. *V. radiata*

15   Flowers often appearing before the leaves; style with a subulate beak *c.* 2 mm long projecting beyond the stigma   12. *V. frutescens*
     Flowers not appearing before the leaves; beak of style, if present, under 2 mm long   16

16   Stems erect or almost so; corolla 1–1·4 cm long   10. *V. friesiorum*

Stems twining or prostrate; corolla usually over 1·4 cm long   17

17   Keel with a distinct upwardly directed conical pocket on left-hand side   15. *V. vexillata*
     Keel without such a pocket   18

18   Tertiary venation of leaflets close and transversely parallel   13. *V. reticulata*
     Tertiary venation of leaflets more open   9. *V. membranacea*

1. Vigna luteola (*Jacq.*) *Benth.* (*V. nilotica* (Del.) Hook f.; *V. bukobensis* Harms)

Perennial twiner, stipules shortly bilobed at base; leaflets entire, sparsely pilose on both sides; inflorescence few-flowered; rachis 1·5–5 cm long; pedicels 4–9 mm long; calyx pubescent or glabrescent; tube 3–4 mm long; lobes deltoid, 2–4 mm long, the upper pair usually united; corolla greenish or yellow, glabrous, 13–25 mm long; beak of keel short, obtuse; pods 6–10-seeded, deflexed, sparsely or densely appressed-pubescent, 4–8 cm long; seeds up to 6 mm long, the rim-aril hardly developed.

Swampy grassland and forest margins, up to 5800 ft. HA, KIT, KIS, RV, MAC, NBI.
Symes 338; Napier 835.

2. Vigna fischeri *Harms*

Closely resembles *V. luteola* but more hairy throughout, and the pods, instead of the white appressed hairs about 1 mm long seen in *V. luteola*, have dense spreading rusty hairs about 2 mm long.

Rare plant found in swampy grassland and forest margins, 3300–6300 ft. HA, EMB, MAC.
Napier 1299; Battiscombe 1123.

3. Vigna schimperi *Bak.* (see p. 277)

Twiner with a large rootstock; stems velvety with appressed rust-coloured hairs, later glabrescent; leaflets entire, pubescent on both sides; stipules truncate or slightly bilobed at the base; inflorescence subumbellate, the rachis obsolete or up to 13 mm long; pedicels 2–7 mm long; calyx finely appressed-pubescent, the lower lobe 2·5–5 mm long, lateral lobes ovate or deltoid 2–3 mm long, shorter than the tube, upper lobes more or less united to form an acute lip; corolla glabrous, greenish yellow-orange or brownish, 18–25 mm long; pods erect, velvety with appressed rusty hairs, 4–9 cm long, *c.* 16-seeded; seeds up to 3·5 mm long, the rim-aril hardly developed.

Upland grassland and forest margins, 4800–7500 ft. HE, HT, HM, HA, HK, KIT, MUM, KIS, NAN, MAC, KAJ.

Bally 821; Harvey 206.

4. Vigna oblongifolia *A. Rich.* (*V. lancifolia* A. Rich.; *V. parviflora* Bak.)

Annual or perennial, twining or suberect; stems bristly pubescent; leaflets entire, sparsely appressed-pubescent on both sides; inflorescence 2-10-flowered, the rachis 5-25 mm long, pedicels 2-5 mm long; calyx pubescent, the tube 1·5-2 mm long, lobes triangular-lanceolate, 1-4 mm long, the lowest narrow, the upper pair more or less united; corolla glabrous, greenish-yellow, sometimes purple-flushed outside, 6-11 mm long, the beak of the keel short, not incurved; pods more or less deflexed, covered with bristly hairs, 23-65 mm long, 3-9-seeded; seeds up to 4·5 mm long, the rim-aril eccentric, fork-shaped with a short central prong.

Two well-marked varieties occur, var. *oblongifolia* with corolla 9-11 mm and pods over 4 cm long and var. *parviflora* (Bak.) Verdc., which is commoner in Kenya, with corolla 6-8 mm and pods under 4 cm long.

Grassland, often in damp places, and forest margins, 4500-6000 ft. HA, KIT, NAR, RV, MAC, NBI.

Bogdan 309; Glover 3705.

5. Vigna comosa *Bak.* (*V. micrantha* Harms)

Perennial, prostrate or twining, stems densely short white-pubescent; leaflets ovate to lanceolate often hastately lobed, pubescent or glabrescent; inflorescence-rachis 4-65 mm; pedicels 1-2 mm long; calyx pubescent, tube 1·5-2 mm long; lobes triangular, 0·6-1·5 mm long; corolla usually yellow, glabrous, 6-12 mm long, beak of keel short, scarcely incurved; pods deflexed, oblong-falcate, 10-25 mm long, 4-5 mm wide, sparsely pubescent, 1-3-seeded; seeds up to 5 mm long, the rim-aril rugulose, markedly eccentric.

Rare plant found in grassland and bushland, especially in rocky places, 5000 ft. KIT.

Brodhurst-Hill 369.

6. Vigna heterophylla *A. Rich.* (*V. micrantha* Chiov. non Harms; *V. chiovendae* Bak. f.; *V. heterophylla* A. Rich. var. *lanceolata* Wilczek.) (see p. 274)

Annual or perennial twiner, rarely suberect; leaflets entire, ovate or lanceolate, pubescent on both sides; inflorescence-rachis 7-20 mm long; pedicels 1-4 mm long; calyx pubescent with mostly dark-ferrugineous spreading bristly hairs; tube 2-2·5 mm long; lobes narrowly triangular-lanceolate, 3-4 mm long; corolla blue-violet; standard velvety outside, *c.* 11 mm long; pods deflexed, densely covered with dark spreading bristly hairs, 5-10-seeded, 15-43 mm long; seeds up to 4 mm long,

the rim-aril very eccentric, usually shorter and more cordate than in the next species.

Grassland, or a weed in wheat fields, 5400-6300 ft. HM, HA, KIT, RV.

Tweedie 79; Brodhurst-Hill 642.

7. Vigna ambacensis *Bak.* (*V. pubigera* Bak.; *V. abyssinica* Taub.; *V. stuhlmannii* Harms)

Doubtfully distinct from *V. heterophylla,* differing in the key characters only.

Grassland and bushland, 4500 ft. KIS.

Napier 3096.

8. Vigna parkeri *Bak.* (*V. gracilis* auct. non (G. & P.) Hook. f.; *V. maranguensis* (Taub.) Harms) (see p. 277)

Perennial, twining or prostrate, sometimes forming mats, the main root slender but tough; leaflets rounded or ovate, pubescent on both sides, the margins densely ciliate; inflorescence 2-5(-10)-flowered; rachis 5-25 mm long; pedicels 1-3 mm long; calyx sparsely pubescent; tube 1·5-2 mm long; lobes deltoid, ovate, or lanceolate, 1-1·5 mm long; corolla glabrous, in our area blue, 5-9(-12) mm long; pods deflexed, pubescent or glabrescent, 2-5-seeded, 1-2(-3) cm long; seeds up to 4 mm long, the rim-aril usually well developed and eccentric.

Montane grassland and openings in forest, 4500-8100 ft. HE, HT, HM, HA, HK, KIT, KIS, EMB.

Battiscombe 688; Symes 9.

9. Vigna membranacea *A. Rich.* (*V. mensensis* Schweinf. var. *hastata* Chiov.; *V. leptodon* Harms; *V. caesia* Chiov.; *V. macrodon* Robyns & Boutique; *V. membranaceoides* Robyns & Boutique) (see p. 277)

Annual or perennial twiner, rarely suberect; stems ridged, at first spreading-pilose with tubercle-based hairs, later glabrescent; leaflets often marked with a pale blotch, ovate or ovate-triangular in outline, rounded, truncate or subhastate at the base, often 3-lobed; inflorescence-rachis 3-20 mm long; pedicels 2-4 mm long; calyx glabrous or pilose with tubercle-based hairs, the tube 2-3 mm long, lobes deltoid to linear 2-17 mm long, often conspicuously long-ciliate at the margins, the upper pair almost free so that the calyx seems equally 5-fid; corolla glabrous, pink, blue, or mauve, 10-23 mm long, the keel sometimes twisted but the beak not incurved; pods erect, covered with very short tubercle-based or scale-like hairs, 3-9 cm long, 14-25-seeded; seeds up to 4·5 mm long, the rim-aril not developed.

Three forms occur in our area, ssp. *membranacea* with calyx lobes 5-9 mm and standard

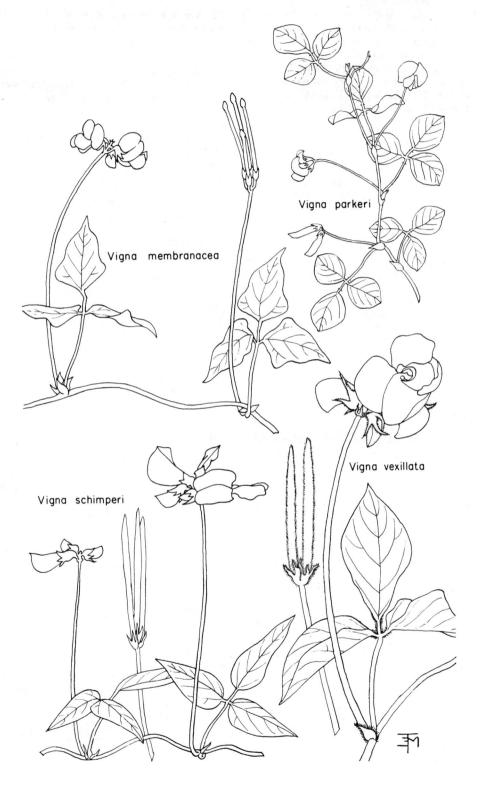

Vigna parkeri

Vigna membranacea

Vigna vexillata

Vigna schimperi

10–15 mm long, ssp. *macrodon* (Robyns & Boutique) Verdc. with calyx lobes 8–17 mm and standard 15–25 mm long and, in dry areas at lower altitudes, ssp. *caesia* (Chiov.) Verdc. with calyx lobes 1·5–7 mm and standard 20–23 mm long.

Grassland, bushland, and dry evergreen forest, up to 6500 ft. HE, HA, KIT, RV, MAC, NBI, KAJ.

Kerfoot 4109; Glover *et al.* 3971.

10.   **Vigna friesiorum** *Harms* (*V. ulugurensis* Harms; ? *V. pygmaea* sensu Bullock non Fries)

Erect or decumbent perennial, up to 30 cm tall, with a carrot-like rootstock; leaflets oblong, elliptic, or linear-lanceolate, glabrous, pubescent or pilose; inflorescence 1-several-flowered, subumbellate; pedicels 1–2 mm long; calyx tube glabrous or hairy, 2–3·5 mm long; lobes deltoid, as long as the tube, the upper pair joined for 2/3 of their length; corolla glabrous, yellowish green-mauve, 10–14 mm long; pods more or less erect, pubescent or with minute scale-like hairs, 4–6 cm long, 17–20-seeded; seeds up to 2·5 mm long, hilum minute, rim-aril not developed.

Two or three varieties occur differing in leaflet shape and pod indumentum. Uncommon, grassland, from 5400–7200 ft. HE, HK, KIT, NAR, MAG.

Harvey 64; Glover *et al.* 2247.

11. **Vigna unguiculata** (*L.*) *Walp.* (*V. sinensis* (L.) Hassk.; *V. catjang* (Burm.) Walp.; *V. caerulea* Bak.; *V. dekindtiana* Harms; *V. mensensis* Schweinf.)

Annual or perennial, erect, trailing, or climbing; stipules submedifixed; leaflets entire or lobed at the base, glabrous or sparsely pubescent on both sides; inflorescence-rachis 5–40 mm long; pedicels 1–2(–4) mm long; bracteoles spathulate, more or less persistent; calyx glabrous; tube 3–5·5 mm long; lobes 2·5–14 mm long, the upper pair joined at the base or for up to half their length; corolla blue or purple, at least in part, 12–33 mm long; pods glabrous or minutely verruculose, erect or eventually hanging in some cultivated forms, 10–16-seeded, 6–10 cm long, or up to 90 cm in some cultivated forms; seeds up to 5 mm long in wild and to 10 mm in cultivated forms; hilum eccentric; the rim-aril slightly developed.

Various cultivated forms of this 'Cowpea' are grown; wild forms in our area are ssp. *dekindtiana* (Harms) Verdc. with calyx lobes scarcely longer than the tube and ssp. *mensensis* (Schweinf.) Verdc. with calyx lobes much longer than the tube.

Uncommon plant found in bushland, up to 7500 ft. KIS, RV, KAJ.

Napier 2994; Bally 1008.

12. **Vigna frutescens** *A. Rich.* (*V. esculenta* (De Wild.) De Wild.; *V. fragrans* Bak. f.; *V. incana* Taub.; *V. keniensis* Harms; *V. taubertii* Harms)

Perennial with a woody tuber; stems densely pubescent, eventually prostrate or climbing but sometimes, after fires, producing flowers when under 20 cm tall and then erect and leafless; stipules cordate at the base; leaflets entire or 3-lobed, usually pubescent; inflorescences subumbellate, pedicels 2–4 mm long, bracteoles ovate-oblong, subpersistent; calyx (in our area) velvety pubescent, tube 3·5–5 mm long, lobes 2–10 mm long, the upper pair united for half their length; corolla glabrous, lilac-mauve, 15–26 mm long, beak of keel incurved; pods erect, 12–16-seeded, in our area pubescent with short appressed hairs, 6–11 cm long; seeds 3–5 mm long; hilum central; rim-aril not developed.

Two forms occur in our area; the commoner (ssp. *frutescens*) has calyx lobes 2–5·5 mm long; ssp. *incana* (Taub.) Verdc. has calyx lobes 5–10 mm long. Grassland and bushland, especially in rocky places, up to 7200 ft. HE, HC, HT, HM, HA, KIT, MUM, NAR, MAG, MAC, NBI, KAJ.

Bogdan 3477; Napier 1981.

13. **Vigna reticulata** *Hook. f.*

Annual or perennial trailing herb; stems densely covered with retrorse or spreading yellowish-brown hairs; stipules cordate; leaflets with appressed bristly hairs on both sides; tertiary veins prominent, closely parallel, at right angles to the midrib; inflorescence subumbellate, 2–6-flowered; pedicels 0–15 mm long; bracteoles lanceolate, deciduous; calyx with bristly white or brown hairs; tube 3–6 mm long; lobes narrowly triangular 6–16 mm long; corolla glabrous, lilac-mauve, 12–33 mm long; pods 6–10-seeded, erect, 4–7 cm long, bristly pubescent or hirsute; seeds 3–4 mm long; hilum eccentric; rim-aril greenish, well-developed.

Uncommon plant found on abandoned cultivation in scattered-tree grassland, 4200–5500 ft. KIT, MUM.

Brodhurst-Hill 476; Tweedie 2884.

14. **Vigna** *sp.* **B** of FTEA.

Resembles *V. reticulata* but the leaves are unifoliolate; calyx pilose; tube 2–2·5 mm long, lobes triangular, 4 mm long; corolla pinkish; pod erect 14–23 mm long; seeds 2 mm long, the rim-aril hardly developed.

Known from a single gathering, exact locality unknown? *c.* 4800 ft. KIT or MUM.

Irwin 138.

15. Vigna vexillata (*L.*) *A. Rich.* (see p. 277)

(see p. 277)

Perennial climber or trailer with a narrow woody rootstock; leaflets pubescent on both sides, rarely somewhat lobed, stipules subcordate; inflorescence 2–6-flowered, subumbellate; pedicels 1–2 mm long; bracteoles deciduous, lanceolate, 5–8 mm long; calyx with long bristly often brownish hairs and also short white hairs; tube 5–7 mm long; lobes 2–20 mm long, the keel asymmetric with a marked pocket on the left hand petal, the beak incurved and twisted; pods 10–18-seeded, erect, 4–14 cm long, covered with brown bristly hairs; seeds 2·5–4·5 mm long, the rim-aril hardly developed.

Var. *angustifolia* (Thonn.) Bak., less hairy than var. *vexillata*, has very narrow leaflets and calyx lobes 2–8 mm long. Grassland, bushland, and forest margins, up to 6600 ft. HE, HC, HT, HA, HL, KIT, MUM, RV, MAC, NBI.

Bogdan 3490; Verdcourt 507.

16. Vigna radiata (*L.*) *Wilczek*

Stems covered with long, spreading, yellowish-brown, bristly hairs; stipules peltate, ciliate at the margins; keel with an upward-directed conical pocket on the left-hand side; pods 10–14-seeded, ascending at first but sagging later, somewhat constricted between the seeds, bristly pubescent, 4–9 cm long; seeds up to 4·2 mm long, rim-aril not developed.

A cultivated plant, 'Mung' or 'Green gram', occasionally found as an escape in land formerly cultivated, up to 4800 ft. MUM, MAC.

Scott Elliot 6993; Bogdan 3092.

17. Vigna macrorhyncha (*Harms*) *Milne-Redhead* (*Phaseolus schimperi* Taub.; *P. macrorhynchus* Harms; *P. stenocarpus* Harms; *Vigna proboscidella* Chiov.)

Perennial twiner with a thick rootstock; stems glabrous or sparsely pubescent; stipules truncate at the base; leaflets entire, glabrous or sparsely hairy at the margins, with translucent veins; inflorescence lax, 2–7 cm long; pedicels 2–5 mm long; bracteoles ovate-lanceolate, persistent; calyx glabrous except at the margin; tube 2–3 mm long; lobes triangular, up to 2·5 mm long, the upper pair united, or almost so; corolla glabrous, pinkish-mauve, 9–13 mm long; keel with a long beak incurved through almost 360°; pods 8–15-seeded, spreading, glabrous, 5–11 cm long; seeds up to 6 mm long, hilum very small with a minute caruncle.

Uncommon plant found in grassland, especially among rocks and at forest margins, up to 5700 ft. KIT, MUM, KIS, KAJ.

Brodhurst-Hill 223; Tweedie 2002.

18. Vigna monophylla *Taub.* (*Haydonia monophylla* (Taub.) Wilczek) (see p. 274)

(see p. 274)

An erect, tufted herb from a tuberous or rhizomatous rootstock with glabrous, lanceolate to ovate leaves and head-like condensed racemes on very long peduncles which exceed the leaves; flowers yellow and mauve.

Locally common, in wooded grassland. KIT, MUM.

Bogdan 4067.

19. Vigna triphylla (*Wilczek*) *Verdc.* (*Haydonia triphylla* Wilczek)

A trailing, twining glabrescent herb with oblong leaflets and winged peduncles bearing heads of purple to pink flowers.

Only recorded from one specimen, 4500 ft. MUM.

Whyte, May 1900.

27. SPATHIONEMA *Taub.*

Woody climbers with pinnately trifoliolate stipellate leaves and axillary false racemes; calyx bell-shaped, 5-lobed, the upper pair of lobes joined; corolla green and purple; stamens (9) + 1, the 5 longer filaments dilated apically; anthers uniform; ovary 2–3-ovuled; style slender below, thickened above and bearded inside; pods oblong, not septate.

Spathionema kilimandscharicum *Taub.*

A woody climber with long-petiolate, often fasciculate leaves bearing ovate, emarginate leaflets; flowers blue-purple.

Locally common in *Commiphora* bushland. MAC.

Bogdan 3611.

28. SPHENOSTYLIS *E. Mey.*

Herbs or shrubs, climbing or not, with pinnately trifoliolate stipellate leaves and axillary false racemes; calyx 5-lobed, 2-lipped; stamens (9) + 1; 5 dorsifixed anthers alternating with 5 basifixed ones; ovary many-ovuled; style ± twisted, thickened basally, thin near the middle and then enlarged, flattened and spathulate near the apex, pubescent; pods linear, compressed, 5–many-seeded, ± septate.

Sphenostylis stenocarpa (*A. Rich.*) *Harms*

A glabrescent twining herb with lanceolate, acute leaflets and pedunculate groups of large showy pink, purple, and cream flowers.

Uncommon plant found in wooded grassland. KIT, MUM.

Bogdan 3544.

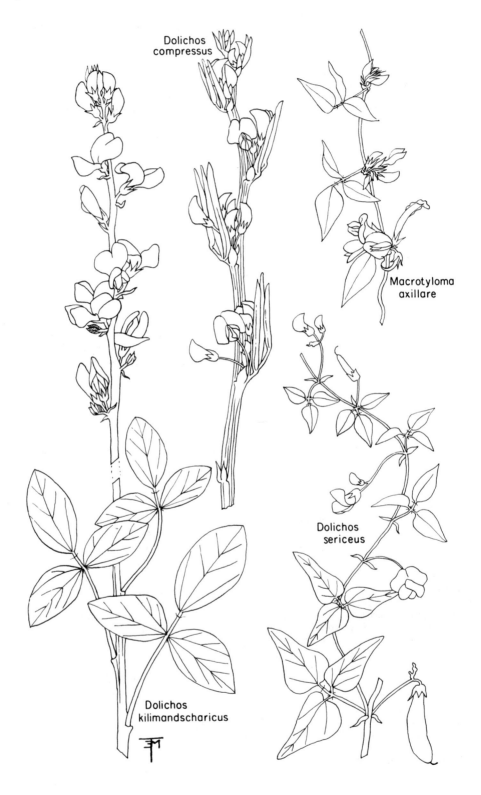

Dolichos
compressus

Macrotyloma
axillare

Dolichos
sericeus

Dolichos
kilimandscharicus

29. DOLICHOS *L.*

Climbing or erect herbs with pinnately trifoliolate stipellate leaves and axillary fascicles of yellow or purple flowers; calyx 5-lobed; corolla glabrous; corolla standard often with 2 mm long oblong appendages; corolla keel not twisted but often beaked; stamens (9) + 1; anthers uniform; ovary 3–12-ovuled; style swollen, tapering from the base, often twisted, usually glabrous and with a ring of hairs around the terminal capitate stigma; pods straight or curved, compressed.

1   Leaflets oblong-elliptic to ovate; (if linear-
        oblong then clearly 1-nerved from the
        base) with pinnate spreading venation   2
    Leaflets narrowly elliptic to linear-oblong,
        prominently 3-nerved from the base
                                    6. *D. compressus*
2   Flowers in umbel-like heads on a 4–20 cm
        long peduncle   1. *D. luticola*
    Flowers in axillary fascicles or in false
        racemes; peduncles mostly shorter   3
3   Erect herbs or shrubs or woody scramblers 5
    Climbers or scramblers with herbaceous stems
                                                4
4   Bracteoles up to 1·5 mm long, 1–3-nerved
                                    2. *D. trilobus*
    Bracteoles over 1·5 mm long, 3–7-nerved
                                    3. *D. sericeus*
5   Bracteoles 5-nerved   4. *D. oliveri*
    Bracteoles 1–3-nerved
                            5. *D. kilimandscharicus*

1. Dolichos luticola *Verdc.*

A small pubescent perennial herb with ovate-elliptic leaflets and long-peduncled umbels of mauve or purple flowers.

Locally common in black-cotton soil around Nairobi. MAC, NBI, KAJ.

Verdcourt 3008.

2. Dolichos trilobus *L.*

A pubescent twiner with ovate leaflets and small, solitary, pedunculate, mauve flowers.

Uncommon plant found in stony grassland in western Kenya. MUM.

Tweedie 1545.

3. Dolichos sericeus *E. Mey.* (see p. 280)

Similar to *D. trilobus* but with larger (over 12 mm long) and more numerous flowers, and usually larger in other parts as well.

This is a very variable species with distinct forms which appear not to intergrade in some places. Variation occurs in the hairiness and size of all parts, and the pods vary in shape and size.

Common in evergreen and montane forest edges and clearings. HE, HC, HT, HM, HA, KIT, MUM, NAR, RV, EMB, NBI, KAJ.

Gillett 17314.

4. Dolichos oliveri *Schweinf.*

An erect, silky-hairy shrub or woody herb from a tuberous rootstock with broadly ovate to rhomboid leaflets and solitary attractive blue flowers.

Locally common in dry bushland, especially where disturbed. KIT, MUM, NAR, BAR, RV, MAG, NAN, MAC, KAJ.

Tweedie 1916.

5. Dolichos kilimandscharicus *Taub.* (see p. 280)

A robust, tuberous-rooted herb with leafy stems bearing elliptic to suborbicular leaflets and terminal, often leafless false racemes of purple flowers.

Common in *Combretum* wooded grassland, especially in the Central Province of Kenya. HA, EMB, MAC, NBI, KAJ.

Bogdan 2884.

6. Dolichos compressus *Wilczek* (see p. 280)

An erect pubescent herb with linear leaflets often held upright and fascicles of pedicellate purple flowers.

Uncommon plant found in wooded grassland or bushland in western Kenya. KIT, MUM.

Tweedie 383.

30. MACROTYLOMA (*Wight & Arn.*) *Verdc.*

Herbs similar to *Dolichos* but with yellow-green flowers, very narrow corolla wings, and a filiform, pubescent, but not bearded style.

1   Climbers   2
    Erect herbs   5. *M. stipulosum*
2   Lower paired stipels (subtending leaflets at
        tip of petiole) 4–8 mm long, often twice as
        long as lateral petiolules
                                6. *M. maranguense*
    Lower paired stipels 1–3 mm long, usually
        not twice as long as lateral petiolules   3
3   Pods up to 5·5 mm wide   4
    Pods over 5·5 mm wide   5
4   Calyx teeth, at least the lower ones, 4–6 mm
        long; plant hairy   1. *M. uniflorum*
    Calyx teeth all 1–3 mm long; plant gla-
        brescent   3. *M. africanum*
5   Lower and lateral sepals attenuate into a
        hair-like point; flowers up to 10 mm long
                                    2. *M. daltonii*
    Lower and lateral sepals acuminate but with-
        out a hair-like point; flowers over 12 mm
        long   4. *M. axillare*

1. Macrotyloma uniflorum (*Lam.*) *Verdc.*

A pubescent twiner with elliptic leaflets and yellow flowers.

Locally common in hot, dry bushland. MAG, MAC.

Bogdan 3481.

2. Macrotyloma daltonii (*Webb*) *Verdc.*

Similar to *M. uniflorum* but with larger leaflets.

Uncommon plant found in dry bushland. KAJ.

Bally 96.

3. Macrotyloma africanum (*Wilczek*) *Verdc.*

Similar to *M. uniflorum* but glabrescent and with more ovate leaflets.

Uncommon plant found in wooded grassland. KIT.

Brodhurst-Hill 438.

4. Macrotyloma axillare (*E. Mey.*) *Verdc.* (see p. 280)

Similar to *M. uniflorum* but with rather larger flowers.

In evergreen forest edges and bushland at medium altitudes. HE, HT, HA, KIT, NAR, RV, MAC, KAJ.

Napper 422.

5. Macrotyloma stipulosum (*Bak.*) *Verdc.*

A pubescent herb from a woody rootstock with oblanceolate leaflets and shortly peduncled clusters of large yellow flowers.

Rare plant found in wooded grassland. HC, HT, KIT.

Symes 59.

6. Macrotyloma maranguense (*Taub.*) *Verdc.*

A pubescent perennial twiner from a woody rootstock with elliptic leaflets and long-pedunculate false racemes of small yellow flowers.

Uncommon plant found in dry grassland. MAC.

van Someren 30.

31. LABLAB *Adans.*

Climbing herbs with pinnately trifoliolate stipellate leaves and axillary, falsely racemose inflorescences; calyx bell-shaped, 2-lipped; corolla small, red to purple or white; standard with thickenings on the inner face; stamens (9) + 1; anthers uniform; ovary many-ovuled; style flat, parallel-sided, hairy within; pod oblong, compressed, with spongy divisions within; seeds ovoid.

Lablab purpureus (*L.*) *Sweet* (see p. 269)

A pubescent climber with ovate acute leaflets and axillary spikes of fascicles of pink and purple flowers.

This plant is frequently cultivated for its beans, but appears wild in riverine forest edges in dry country. HE, HT, KIT, MUM, NAR.

Tweedie 346.

32. NEORAUTANENIA *Schinz*

Prostrate, erect or climbing herbs with pinnately trifoliolate stipellate leaves and axillary false racemes or panicles of purplish flowers; bracts soon falling; bracteoles absent; calyx 5-lobed, 2-lipped; corolla rather small with long-spurred wings; stamens (9) + 1; anthers uniform; ovary 3–8-ovuled with a thickened glabrous swelling at the style base; style thickened below, angled, glabrous; pods linear-oblong, dehiscent, septate; seeds 3–8, compressed.

Neorautanenia mitis (*A. Rich.*) *Verdc.*

An erect woody herb or climber with entire or 3-lobed, ovate leaflets and simple or branched spikelike false racemes of purple flowers.

Locally common in dry bushland; very variable in leaf shape and indumentum. KIT, BAR, RV, MAG.

Mathenge 72.

33. CAJANUS *DC.*

Shrubs with pinnately 3-foliolate stipellate leaves gland-dotted; inflorescence a terminal panicle of subcapitate racemes; bracts present; bracteoles absent; calyx 5-lobed, the upper pair joined; standard petal auriculate; stamens (9) + 1; all anthers similar; ovary 4–6-ovuled; style thickened above and flattened below the capitate stigma; pod linear-oblong, inflated, with a long-persistent apex, 3–7-seeded.

Cajanus cajan (*L.*) *Millsp.*

An erect shrubby herb with elliptic leaflets and yellow and orange flowers.

This is the pigeon pea, widely cultivated in dry country and recorded as an escape. NBI.

Napier 1828.

34. RHYNCHOSIA *Lour.*

Climbing, prostrate or erect herbs or shrubs with pinnately trifoliolate or simple stipellate leaves gland-dotted below; inflorescences mostly axillary, racemose; bracts present; bracteoles absent; calyx 5-lobed, the upper pair ± joined; standard petal auricled; stamens (9) + 1 with all anthers similar; ovary 1–2-ovuled; style hairy below; pods circular to oblong, flat or rarely inflated, 1–2-seeded; seeds reddish-brown to blue-black.

1   Flowers usually appearing before the leaves; leaflets deeply lobed   9. *R. pulchra*

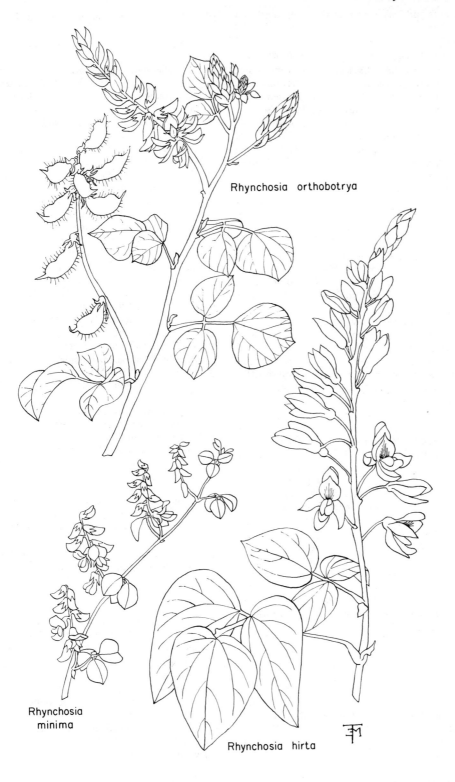

Rhynchosia orthobotrya

Rhynchosia
minima

Rhynchosia hirta

Flowers and leaves present together; leaflets ±
entire   2

2   Leaflets 3   3
Leaflets 1   14. *R. alluaudii*

3   Flowers in dense, ± sessile inflorescences, not
very sticky; sepals with conspicuous dark
or orange dots   2. *R. densiflora*
Flowers in laxer pedunculate inflorescences
or if dense and sessile then very sticky and
sepals without dots   4

4   Seeds persistent, globose, blue-black; corolla
drying reddish   1. *R. hirta*
Seeds falling, compressed, brown; corolla
drying brown   5

5   Erect plants, sometimes scrambling, never
twining or prostrate   6
Twining or prostrate plants   9

6   Calyx and undersurface of leaflets covered
with dense, greyish-white velvety indumentum which hides the gland dots
16. *R. albissima*
Calyx and leaves not so densely covered with
hairs   7

7   Leaflets rhomboid, with long-acuminate or
acute apices, distinctly paler beneath;
calyx saccate; indumentum yellow and
very sticky   4. *R. resinosa*
Leaflets oblate or rounded and very shortly,
abruptly apiculate; calyx not saccate   8

8   Inflorescence ± half as long as leaves; fruit
softly hairy; hairs up to 1 mm long;
stipules ± 4 x 1 mm   7. *R. nyasica*
Inflorescence ± as long as the leaves; fruit
with bristly, yellow, 1·5–2 mm long hairs;
stipules ± 7 x 2·5 mm   6. *R. orthobotrya*

9   Pods with fine, sparse to dense pubescence of
short hairs less than 0·5 mm long without
an admixture of longer hairs; stem and
inflorescence hairs not, or hardly, sticky-
glandular   10
Pods with longer, sometimes sticky hairs in
addition to fine pubescence and gland
dots; stem hairs sometimes long and glandular; if pod almost without long hairs the
inflorescence very glandular and sticky   16

10 Pod inflated, club-shaped   15. *R. sublobata*
Pod compressed   11

11 Calyx as long as or longer than the corolla
19. *R. minima*
Calyx shorter than the corolla   12

12 Corolla ± 1·5 cm long; leaflets with conspicuous grey hairs on the veins (and often
elsewhere) beneath   17. *R. holstii*
Corolla up to 1·2 cm long or leaflets glabrescent or very finely pubescent beneath   13

13 Corolla 5–8 mm long   14
Corolla 10–12 mm long   15

14 Calyx pale with conspicuous midribs
19. *R. minima*
Calyx drying purplish with midribs obscure
12. *R. usambarensis*

15 Corolla pale yellow without dark markings
18. *R. malacophylla*
Corolla with red and purple markings
19. *R. minima*

16 Leaflets ± twice as long as wide; inflorescence
lax and few-flowered   13. *R. totta*
Leaflets wider and inflorescence often dense
17

17 Pods up to 15 mm long; inflorescences not
densely glandular-hairy   18
Pods over 15 mm long or inflorescences with
dense yellow glandular hairs   19

18 Stipules over 8 mm long
20. *R. kilimandscharica*
Stipules less than 5 mm long   19. *R. minima*

19 All or some leaflets with pale areas along
midrib and main nerves above
12. *R. usambarensis*
All leaflets concolorous   20

20 Calyx asymmetrically saccate   4. *R. resinosa*
Calyx not asymmetrically saccate   21

21 Standard glabrous outside   22
Standard pubescent outside   23

22 Corolla over 16 mm long   8. *R. elegans*
Corolla less than 15 mm long
10. *R. ferruginea*

23 Lowest calyx tooth elliptic-lanceolate, longer
and wider than the rest, pod with long
yellow glandular hairs   6. *R. orthobotrya*
Lowest calyx tooth similar to the rest, or, if
longer, then pod with short greyish hairs
24

24 Some pedicels over 3 mm long; standard
pubescent only at apex   3. *R. procurrens*
All pedicels 3 mm long or less; standard
pubescent over all exposed exterior part
25

25 Plant ± viscid   5. *R. pseudoviscosa*
Plant without glandular hairs
11. *R. oblatifoliolata*

1. Rhynchosia hirta (*Andrews*) *Meikle & Verdc.*
(*R. albiflora* (Sims) Alston) (see p. 283)

A robust twiner with broad leaflets and racemes of
dull, white-green flowers; corolla with a crimson
flash inside standard.

This plant is handsome in fruit since the blue
seeds are exposed in the dehisced but persistent
pod. Local but widespread in dry woodland edges
and *Combretum* bushland. HE, HA, HK, MUM,
KIS, NAR, MAC, NBI, KAJ.

Tweedie 2094.

2. Rhynchosia densiflora (*Roth*) *DC.*

A low, prostrate herb from a wiry rootstock with oblong or suborbicular leaflets and subsessile racemes of yellow flowers.

Locally common in stony grassland. HA, MUM, NAR, RV, MAG, MAC.

Bogdan 1659.

3. Rhynchosia procurrens (*Hiern*) *K. Schum.*

A glandular-hairy, trailing herb with broad, often rhomboid leaflets and large, massive racemes of yellow red-streaked flowers; calyx enlarged in fruit.

Rare and only recorded from wooded grassland in KIT.

Bogdan 3575.

4. Rhynchosia resinosa (*A. Rich.*) *Bak.*

A glandular-hairy, woody twiner with ± triangular leaflets and terminal and axillary racemes of yellow red-streaked flowers.

Locally common in dry, rocky bushland. KIT, BAR.

Tweedie 1914.

5. Rhynchosia pseudoviscosa *Harms*

A pubescent, prostrate or ascending twiner with broadly rhomboid leaflets and racemes of few large flowers; standard yellow, streaked with red.

Rare plant found in stony bushland. MAC.

Goodhart in H 271/62.

6. Rhynchosia orthobotrya *Harms* (see p. 283)

A glandular-hairy, woody herb with ovate leaflets and long spikes of numerous smallish, yellow and red subsessile flowers.

Locally common in western Kenya in wooded grassland. HE, KIT, MUM, KIS, BAR.

Tweedie 1140.

7. Rhynchosia nyasica *Bak.*

A glandular-hairy, erect or trailing herb with rhomboid to ovate-elliptic leaflets and axillary racemes of yellow-green flowers.

Uncommon plant found in dry bushland. HA, EMB.

Graham 2402.

8. Rhynchosia elegans *A. Rich.*

A glandular-hairy twiner with ovate to rhombic leaflets and long racemes of large yellow, flushed reddish-pink, flowers; pods reticulated with dark green.

Locally common in the margins of evergreen woodland. HE, HA, NAR, RV, MAC, NBI.

Williams 490.

9. Rhynchosia pulchra (*Vatke*) *Harms*

An erect silky-hairy, hardly glandular herb with lobed, ovate leaflets and long, axillary, subapical racemes of yellow red-streaked flowers; pods reticulated with darker green.

Uncommon plant found in dry rocky country. MAC.

Scheffler 97.

10. Rhynchosia ferruginea *A. Rich.*

A silky-hairy, hardly glandular, twining herb with ovate to suborbicular leaflets and long racemes of pale yellow brown-streaked flowers.

Locally common in wooded grassland. HE, KIT, RV.

Bogdan 3573.

11. Rhynchosia oblatifoliolata *Verdc.*

A trailing, pubescent, eglandular herb with rhomboid to ovate leaflets and long, few-flowered racemes; flowers yellow with orange-pink standard.

Locally common in dry grassland. HT, KIT, RV, MAC, NBI.

Bogdan 936.

12. Rhynchosia usambarensis *Taub.*

A glandular- and spreading-hairy twining herb with ovate, acute leaflets which have paler and darker green areas and long-pedunculate racemes of orange-yellow flowers.

Locally common in upland grassland and forest edges. HE, HM, HA, KIT, MUM, NAR, RV, MAC, NBI.

Glover and Samuel 3120.

13. Rhynchosia totta (*Thunb.*) *DC.*

A small, pubescent, trailing, and twining herb with oblong, stiff leaflets and 1-3-flowered racemes; flowers yellow and brown.

Locally common in dry stony grassland. MUM, KIS, NAR, BAR, RV, MAG.

Tweedie 2899.

14. Rhynchosia alluaudii *Sacleux*

A pubescent or silky-hairy, tuberous-rooted, erect herb with simple, rounded, ovate to orbicular leaves and short racemes of yellow and red flowers.

Uncommon plant found in rocky grassland and forest edges. NAR, EMB, MAC, NBI, KAJ.

Napier 386.

15. Rhynchosia sublobata (*Schum.*) *Meikle*

A pubescent, twining herb with rhomboid leaflets, the lateral leaflets very asymmetric, often shallowly lobed; racemes loose, of yellow red-streaked flowers; pods inflated, minutely pubescent.

Locally common in dry country. MAG, NAN, EMB.

Bogdan 3758.

16. Rhynchosia albissima *Gandoger*

A silky-hairy, erect or spreading, woody herb or shrub with orbicular leaflets and subterminal racemes of yellow and purple flowers.

Locally common at the coast but rare in our area, found in bushland. MAC.

Drummond and Hemsley 3763.

17. Rhynchosia holstii *Harms*

A pubescent trailing or twining herb with ovate to rhomboid, often bullate, leaflets and long racemes of yellow red-streaked flowers.

In rocky grassland, particularly around Nairobi. HA, EMB, MAC, NBI.

Bogdan 1488.

18. Rhynchosia malacophylla (*Spreng.*) *Boj.* (*R. senaarensis* Schweinf.)

A pubescent, minutely glandular, trailing or twining, wiry herb with ± orbicular, rather stiff leaflets and long racemes of yellow red-streaked flowers.

A common plant of dry, stony grasslands. BAR, MAG, EMB, KAJ.

Bally 2569.

19. Rhynchosia minima (*L.*) *DC.* (see p. 283)

Similar to *R. malacophylla* but with more ovate and bullate leaflets and the keyed differences.

A rather variable plant common in some upland grasslands. HE, HT, HA, KIT, MUM, NAR, RV, MAC, NBI, KAJ.

Polhill 80.

20. Rhynchosia kilimandscharica *Harms.*

A minutely pubescent twining or trailing herb with ovate or rhomboid leaflets and long-pedunculate racemes of small yellow red-streaked flowers.

Locally common in montane forest edges. HE, HM, HA, HK, KIT, NBI, KAJ.

Tweedie 721.

35. ERIOSEMA (*DC.*) *Desv.*

Herbs or shrubs, sometimes tuberous, with mostly pinnately trifoliolate or rarely simple leaves gland-dotted below; stipels mostly absent; flowers yellow or brown in axillary (rarely terminal) racemes or spikes; bracts present; bracteoles absent; calyx 5-lobed, the upper pair fused or free; stamens (9) + 1;

anthers all similar; ovary 2-ovuled, hairy; style bent at or below the middle, glabrous above; pods oval or oblong, flat, usually silky-hairy; seeds 2.

1	Flowers present before the leaves	**2**
	Flowers and leaves (even if young) present at the same time	**3**
2	Raceme dense with flowers touching each other	**14. *E. rhodesicum***
	Raceme lax with flowers separated from each other	**13. *E. sparsiflorum***
3	Leaves all simple	**4**
	Leaves 3-foliolate, except sometimes at base	**5**
4	Leaves cordate at base	**17. *E. cordifolium***
	Leaves acute to rounded at base	**14. *E. rhodesicum***
5	Stem flattened; often some leaves more than 3-foliolate	**4. *E. vanderystii***
	Stems not flattened; all leaves 3-foliolate	**6**
6	Leaf petiole longer than 15 mm	**15**
	Leaf petiole shorter than 10 mm	**7**
7	Bracts equalling or longer than the corolla at anthesis	**8. *E. jurionianum***
	Bracts shorter than the corolla at anthesis	**8**
8	Rachis of raceme over 3 cm long	**9**
	Rachis of raceme less than 3 cm long	**12**
9	Leaves oblanceolate, rounded at apex; peduncle less than half the length of the rachis of the raceme	**3. *E. psoraleoides***
	Leaves elliptic to oblanceolate, usually acute; peduncle over half the length of the rachis of the raceme	**10**
10	Flowers and fruits crowded, touching one another; internodes of inflorescence less than 5 mm long	**11**
	Flowers and fruits well spaced, not touching one another; internodes of inflorescence over 5 mm long	**13. *E. sparsiflorum***
11	Stipules over 3 mm wide	**6. *E. buchananii***
	Stipules under 2 mm wide	**5. *E. nutans***
12	Flowers more than 15, crowded in a ± spherical head	**2. *E. glomeratum***
	Flowers fewer than 12, in a short, loose raceme	**13**
13	Plant with a rhizomatous rootstock; leaflets acute at apex	**16. *E. shirense***
	Plant with a woody rootstock; leaflets obtuse at apex	**14**
14	Upper leaf surface with lateral veins prominent or flat	**15. *E. elliotii***
	Upper leaf surface with grooves over the lateral veins	**1. *E. bogdanii***
15	Plant a herb from an underground tuber; stipules green	**12. *E. macrostipulum***
	Plant shrubby; stipules brown	**16**
16	Median floral bracts over 7 mm wide	**11. *E. robustum***
	Median floral bracts under 4 mm wide	**17**

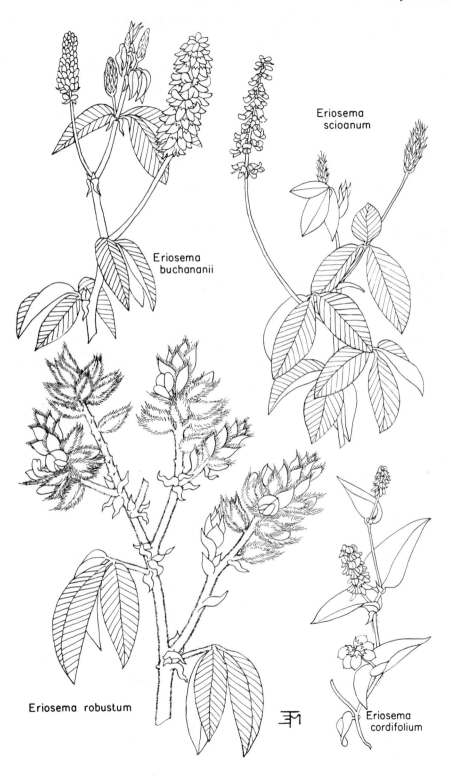

Eriosema
scioanum

Eriosema
buchananii

Eriosema robustum

Eriosema
cordifolium

17 Bracts in two series, the lowest sterile, broad,
± persistent, forming a cone-like base to
the raceme, the upper narrow, caducous
10. *E. flemingioides*
All bracts similar, narrow **18**

18 Claw of keel shorter than the lamina
7. *E. montanum*
Claw of keel equal to or exceeding the lamina
19

19 Spikes ovoid; bracts equalling or longer than
the flowers; corolla scarcely exceeding the
calyx 8. *E. jurionianum*
Inflorescences cylindrical; bracts shorter than
the flowers; corolla much longer than the
calyx 9. *E. scioanum*

1. Eriosema bogdanii *Verdc.*

An erect, tomentose herb from a woody rootstock
with rounded, elliptic leaflets and short axillary
spikes of few yellow flowers.

So far only found in burnt grassland in EMB,
15 miles south of Meru.

Bogdan 3754.

2. Eriosema glomeratum *Hook. f.*

An erect, spreading-hairy, woody herb with mostly
elliptic leaflets and small, shortly pedunculate
heads of yellow flowers.

Plentiful at the coast in bushed grassland but
only recorded by one collection from Thika in our
area. MAC.

Bogdan 2885A.

3. Eriosema psoraleoides (*Lam.*) *G. Don.*

A pubescent, erect, woody herb with rounded,
oblanceolate to cuneate leaflets and long axillary
racemes of yellow flowers.

Locally common in disturbed rocky bushland.
MUM, KIS, EMB, MAC.

Tweedie 1499.

4. Eriosema vanderystii (*de Wild.*) *Hauman*

An erect, velvety-hairy herb from a woody rootstock with linear-lanceolate to oblong leaflets and
a terminal panicle of crowded racemes of yellow
flowers.

Locally common in wet marshy grassland in
western Kenya. MUM.

Tweedie 2882.

5. Eriosema nutans *Schinz.* (see p. 289)

An erect, tomentose herb from a wiry rhizomatous
rootstock with lanceolate to elliptic leaflets and
dense cylindrical racemes of small yellow flowers.

Common in wooded grassland and forest edges.
HT, HA, KIT, RV, MAC.

Bogdan 2102.

6. Eriosema buchananii *Bak. f.* (see p. 287)

Very similar to *E. nutans* but more spreading-hairy
and with larger leaflets.

Uncommon, in upland wooded grassland. HK,
KIT, KAJ.

Napier 1971.

7. Eriosema montanum *Bak. f.*

An erect, sparsely hairy, shrubby herb with ovate,
acute or acuminate leaflets and cylindrical racemes
of small yellow flowers.

Locally common in wooded grassland. HC, HM,
KIT, MUM, KIS.

Symes 203.

8. Eriosema jurionianum *Stan. & De Craene* (see p. 289)

Similar to *E. montanum* but more densely hairy
and with elliptic leaflets and ovoid spikes; flowers
brown and yellow.

Locally common at upland forest edges. HE,
HT, HA, HK, RV.

Irwin 127.

9. Eriosema scioanum *Avetta* (see p. 287)

A sparsely hairy, rhizomatous herb with ascending
stems and elliptic, acute leaflets; spikes cylindrical,
of small orange and brown flowers.

Locally common in montane forest clearings
and upland grassland. HE, HT, HM, HA, KIT, KIS,
MAC, NBI, KAJ.

Tweedie 218.

10. Eriosema flemingioides *Bak.*

A pubescent, woody shrub with broadly elliptic,
apiculate leaflets and a terminal panicle of spikes
of yellow and reddish-brown flowers.

In wet, wooded grassland, only just entering
our area near the Uganda border. MUM.

Tweedie 3582.

11. Eriosema robustum *Bak.* (see p. 287)

A pubescent perennial shrubby herb with elliptic
acute leaflets and a very hairy inflorescence;
corolla yellow.

Locally common and conspicuous, in wooded
grassland especially around Kitale. HA, KIT, KIS,
RV.

Tweedie 2911.

12. Eriosema macrostipulum *Bak. f.* (see p. 289)

An erect pubescent herb from a buried tuber with
lanceolate leaflets and small racemes of yellow
flowers.

Locally common in bushed grassland. HE, HC,
HM, KIT.

Wiltshire 46B.

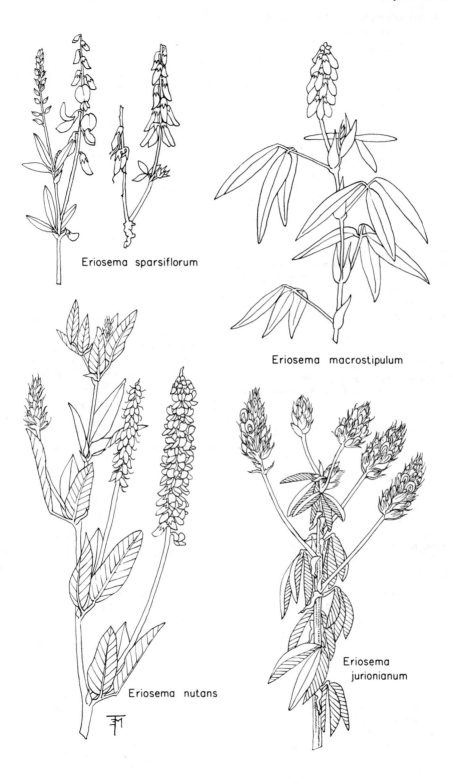

Eriosema sparsiflorum

Eriosema macrostipulum

Eriosema nutans

Eriosema jurionianum

13. Eriosema sparsiflorum *Bak. f.* (see p. 289)

A pubescent herb with erect stems from a woody rootstock and oblong to elliptic leaflets; racemes lax and long-pedunculate; flowers yellow and reddish-brown.

Locally common in western Kenya. HE, KIT, MUM.

Lugard 567.

14. Eriosema rhodesicum *R. E. Fr.*

A pubescent herb with erect stems from a woody rootstock; leaves simple, linear-elliptic to lanceolate; racemes of rather crowded yellow and red flowers appearing before leaves or below them.

Uncommon plant found in short burnt grassland in western Kenya. HC, KIT.

Tweedie 3258.

15. Eriosema elliotii *Bak. f.*

A silky-hairy herb with prostrate or ascending stems from a woody rootstock and obovate to elliptic leaflets; flowers yellow, in inconspicuous few-flowered racemes.

Uncommon plant found in dry upland grassland. HT, KIT.

Bogdan 1706.

16. Eriosema shirense *Bak. f.*

A spreading-hairy rhizomatous herb with erect stems and linear-elliptic leaflets; racemes short, hidden within the leaves; flowers yellow, streaked with red.

Locally common in wooded grassland. EMB, MAC, KAJ.

Bally 8265.

17. Eriosema cordifolium *A. Rich.* (see p. 287)

A pubescent herb with ascending stems from a buried tuber and simple ovate, cordate, subsessile leaves; racemes spike-like, cylindrical, of pink and yellow flowers.

Uncommon plant found in short upland grassland. HE, HT.

Williams 204.

36. FLEMINGIA *Ait. f.*

Herbs or shrubs with digitately trifoliolate glandular leaves without stipels and axillary and terminal, racemose or paniculate inflorescences; calyx 5-lobed, the lobes longer than the tube; corolla small, green or yellow; stamens (9) + 1; anthers all similar; ovary 2-ovuled; style filiform, enlarged above; pods ovoid-oblong, inflated; seeds globose.

Flemingia grahamiana *Wight & Arn.* (*Moghania grahamiana* (Wight & Arn.) O. Ktze)

A stiff herb or shrub, dealt with in KTS p. 371.

Locally common in wooded grassland. HE, KIT, EMB.

Bogdan 3499.

37. LOTONONIS *Eckl. & Zeyh.*

Low herbs, with basifixed or slightly 2-armed hairs; leaves digitately 3-foliolate; stipules solitary or paired; stipels absent; flowers in subsessile or pedunculate terminal and leaf-opposed racemes or clusters, rarely solitary, rather small, yellow; calyx 5-lobed, the 4-upper lobes more united than the narrow lower lobe; keel rounded at the tip; stamens united into a sheath split along the upper side, 4 with long and 6 with short anthers; ovary sessile; pod oblong, usually pointed, only slightly inflated; seeds small, numerous.

1　Annual, covered with long fine spreading hairs
　　　　　　　　　　　　　　1. *L. platycarpos*
　Perennial with the hairs short and appressed or lacking　　　　　　　　　　2
2　Stems creeping, practically glabrous; flowers 6–50 in dense racemes　　2. *L. angolensis*
　Stems erect or spreading, densely silvery-pubescent; flowers 1–5, subumbellate
　　　　　　　　　　　　　　3. *L. laxa*

1. Lotononis platycarpos (*Viv.*) *Pic.-Serm.*

Small creeping hairy annual, with inconspicuous flowers clustered opposite many of the leaves; pod straight, 5 mm long, scarcely exceeding calyx.

Common in dry open places throughout RV.

Bogdan 3048; Verdcourt 1794.

2. Lotononis angolensis *Bak.*

Many-stemmed subglabrous creeping perennial, with numerous small flowers crowded at the top of the ultimately 2–6 cm long ascending peduncles; pods slightly curved, pointed, 1·5–1·8 cm long.

Short grassland, often in disturbed places. MUM, EMB, MAC, NBI.

Bally 7801; Verdcourt 508.

3. Lotononis laxa *Eckl. et Zeyh.*

A low perennial, with many slender spreading-ascending stems, clothed with short appressed slightly biramous hairs; flowers 1–5 at top of a short peduncle, yellow, turning reddish with age, 7–9 mm long; pod straight, pointed, 1·5–2 cm long, pubescent.

Uncommon plant found in dry grassland, usually of mountains and scarps. RV, HA, NBI.

Dowson 269; Verdcourt 3457A.

38. CROTALARIA *L.*

Herbs or shrubs; leaves simple or digitately (1–)3(–7)-foliolate; stipels absent; flowers in terminal, leaf-opposed or rarely axillary racemes, occasionally solitary or in axillary clusters; calyx (3-4-)5-lobed, the lobes generally subequal but occasionally forming 2 lips; petals usually yellow, variously marked, less commonly blue or white, sometimes pubescent particularly on the standard outside; keel generally produced into a prominent beak; stamens all united into a sheath open at least at the base, 5 with basifixed anthers alternating with 5 with smaller dorsifixed anthers; pod inflated (in our area), dehiscent, the seed-bearing part supported within the calyx by a very short to long stalk (stipe); seeds with a distinct hilar sinus, occasionally with a small white aril.

1 Leaves 3–5-foliolate   2
   Leaves simple or 1-foliolate   73
2 Plant spiny   62. *C. spinosa*
   Plant not spiny   3
3 Petals of open flowers blue   4
   Petals yellow or white except for markings 5
4 Keel 1·6–1·8 cm long; pod (3·5–)4–4·5 cm long; plant erect   8. *C. polysperma*
   Keel 1·1–1·4 cm long; pod 2·5–3·2 cm long; plant spreading   9. *C. serengetiana*
5 Bracts fused to pedicel, the free part spreading from just below the calyx, 3-fid; stipules 1–5-fid; flowers in dense heads
                                       21. *C. ononoides*
   Bracts at base of pedicel simple; stipules, if present, not divided   6
6 Stipules resembling small leaflets, very shortly stalked, linear-lanceolate to ovate; keel abruptly rounded to angular, often with white woolly indumentum along upper margin; bracts often soon shed   7
   Stipules linear, narrowly wedge-shaped or lacking   12
7 Stipules heart-shaped, equal-sided, 6–12 mm wide   12. *C. stolzii*
   Stipules linear-lanceolate to curved-oblong, basally narrowed or truncate, very unequal-sided   8
8 Ovary and legume glabrous   9
   Ovary and legume hairy   10
9 Perennial, generally erect, shortly hairy; stipules basally narrowed; standard suborbicular   13. *C. natalitia*
   Annual, spreading, hirsute; stipules basally truncate; standard ovate 16. *C. podocarpa*
10 Keel 1·8–2·5 mm long; pod coarsely furry
                                       17. *C. lachnophora*
   Keel up to 1·5 cm long; pod shortly and finely hairy   11
11 Calyx 6–10 mm long; pod cylindrical, 2·3–3 cm long; petioles mostly 1·5–3·5 cm long
                                       14. *C. cylindrocarpa*
   Calyx 4–5 mm long; pod oblong-ellipsoid, 1·5–2 cm long; petioles mostly 3·5–6·5 cm long   15. *C. goreensis*
12 Flowers clustered in the axils, 1·5–2 cm long
                                                           13
   Flowers, unless much smaller, in terminal and

leaf-opposed racemes   14
13 Pod 8–14 mm across; indumentum usually yellowish, sparse or crisped on the leaflets beneath   51. *C. axillaris*
   Pod 20–26 mm across; indumentum silvery, short, appressed and rather dense on the leaflets beneath   52. *C. scassellatii*
14 Calyx effectively 3-lobed, with upper and lateral lobes joined on either side almost to tips, 1·2–3 cm long   15
   Calyx 5-lobed, with lobes free at maturity, although sometimes slightly adherent at tips in young flowers   17
15 Keel gradually produced into a short projecting beak, 3·5–5·5 cm long; calyx 1·8–3 cm long   1. *C. agatiflora*
   Keel abruptly contracted into an upwardly directed beak, 2·5–3·5 cm long; calyx 1·2–2 cm long   16
16 Leaflets elliptic, mostly 4–9 cm long, shortly hairy beneath   2. *C. lebrunii*
   Leaflets very reduced, narrowly oblong to obovate, less than 1 cm long, glabrous
                                       4. *C. pseudospartium*
17 Keel strongly rounded, ± straight along upper edge, abruptly contracted into an upwardly directed straight ± truncate beak, 2–3 cm long, much exceeding the wings; pod with slender stipe half or more than half as long as the seed-bearing part
                                       3. *C. laburnifolia*
   Keel less abruptly produced into a beak or much smaller; stipe of pod much less than half length of seed-bearing part   18
18 Upper calyx-lobes suboblong, abruptly terminating in an eccentric tip, or lanceolate to ovate, narrowed to the base, about as long as the corolla   19
   Upper calyx-lobes triangular or wedge-shaped, broadest at the base (or just above in Nos. 5, 11)   21
19 Upper calyx-lobes practically oblong, subtruncate, densely covered with short brownish hairs   6. *C. mauensis*
   Upper calyx-lobes lanceolate to ovate, sparsely provided with long whitish hairs
                                                           20
20 Keel abruptly rounded about the middle; standard glabrous outside; pod 3·5–6·5 times as long as broad   7. *C. quartiniana*
   Keel angled in the lower half; standard hairy outside; pod 2–2·5 times as long as broad
                                       10. *C. barkae*
21 Keel rounded about the middle, sometimes rather abruptly so, with a variously developed and orientated beak   22
   Keel angled in the lower half, with a straight rather narrow beak   54

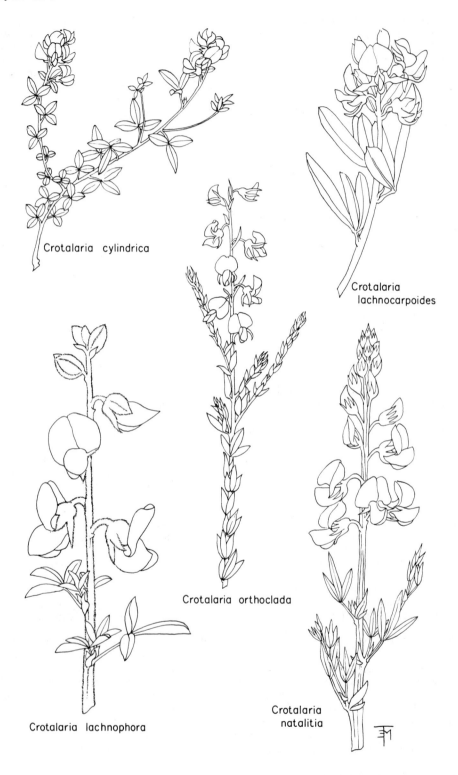

Crotalaria cylindrica

Crotalaria
lachnocarpoides

Crotalaria orthoclada

Crotalaria lachnophora

Crotalaria
natalitia

22   Bracteoles curved up like 2 horns from just below calyx; shrubby, with relatively small membranous elliptic to obovate leaflets and the flowers few on thread-like axes
                        5. *C. goodiiformis*
     Bracteoles not curved up like horns   **23**

23   Keel semi-orbicular, shortly beaked, with a sparse band of hairs on sides towards lower margin; pod shortly cylindrical, 2·5–3 cm long, densely furry; leaflets felty-tomentose   18. *C. lachnocarpoides*
     Keel without a band of hairs on surfaces away from lower margin   **24**

24   Standard extensively pubescent outside (at least medially)   **25**
     Standard glabrous outside, except sometimes for a few hairs along the mid-vein and at the apex   **27**

25   Petioles 2–5(–10) mm long; leaflets oblanceolate; keel about as long as wings
                         19. *C. orthoclada*
     Petioles up to 40–90 mm long; leaflets elliptic to obovate; keel much shorter than wings
                                 26

26   Keel 11–13 mm long; calyx of mature flowers 10–12 mm long; pod 24–36-seeded
                         22. *C. verdcourtii*
     Keel 6–8 mm long; calyx 8–10 mm long; pod 16–20-seeded   23. *C. deflersii*

27   Beak of keel with a spiral twist (look for diagonal course of seam and veins); keel 1–2 cm long; pod oblong-club-shaped, 2·5–6·5 cm long   **28**
     Beak of keel not twisted (discount withered flowers). (In 37. *C. cleomifolia* and 42. *C. ukambensis* the rather long narrow incurved beak of older flowers may become slightly and irregularly twisted as a whole in a corkscrew fashion (at least when dried), but this is quite unlike the integral spiral twist running from base to apex of beak in the other group).   **31**

28   Ovary and pod glabrous; wings enveloping keel; petioles flattened, broadly grooved
                           55. *C. recta*
     Ovary and pod shortly hairy; wings about as long as keel, but not wrapped around it; petioles slender   **29**

29   Leaves (on all but youngest branches) mostly subtending very short lateral shoots bearing clusters of smaller leaves; branches rather persistently tomentose
                         53. *C. fascicularis*
     Leaves not in tufts; branches with a short appressed indumentum, more or less glabrescent   **30**

30   Bracts 3–9 mm long, soon falling; calyx 8–11 mm long, with a conspicuous white fringe of woolly hairs along inside margin of lobes; pod 5–6·5 cm long   49. *C. tabularis*
     Bracts 1–3 mm long, persistent; calyx 5–8 mm long, without a white fringe to lobe-margins; pod 2·5–4 cm long
                         50. *C. keniensis*

31   Bracts falling before flowers open   **32**
     Bracts persistent   **33**

32   Keel shallowly rounded, much exceeding wings, 1·2–1·5 cm long; pod very shortly stipitate, cylindrical, sometimes slightly curved   28. *C. pallida*
     Keel rounded, with a well differentiated practically straight beak, little longer than wings, (1·5–)1·7–2·3 cm long; pod with a 5–7 mm long stipe, oblong-club-shaped
                   24. *C. comanestiana*

33   Stipules present, at least at base of young leaves   **34**
     Stipules absent   **46**

34   Leaflets densely hairy on both surfaces, with 3–5 markedly raised ascending lateral nerves beneath; calyx (5–)6–8 mm long, with narrow lobes 2–3 times as long as tube   45. *C. lotiformis*
     Leaflets with more numerous markedly raised nerves; calyx-lobes less than twice as long as tube.   **35**

35   Keel 10–23 mm long; robust erect well-branched slightly woody herbs mostly 1–4 m tall, with rather uniformly shaped elliptic to obovate leaflets   **36**
     Keel 4–10 mm long; spreading, straggling-ascending or shortly erect, rarely 1 m tall, but if so then leaflets usually variable in shape, longer and proportionally narrower on upper leaves   **38**

36   Keel much exceeding wings, with a narrow slightly incurved beak; leaves 3–5-foliolate; pod narrowly cylindrical, sometimes curved up at tip; bracteoles longer than calyx-tube   37. *C. cleomifolia*
     Keel shorter to a little longer than wings, with a generally straight beak; leaves 3 (exceptionally an odd leaf 4–)-foliolate; pod broadened apically; bracteoles usually shorter than calyx-tube   **37**

37   Keel (1·5–)1·7–2·3 cm long; pod 3·5–5 cm long; bracteoles linear or subulate
                   24. *C. comanestiana*
     Keel 1–1·2 cm long; pod 2–3 cm long; bracteoles narrowly triangular   25. *C. burttii*

38   Racemes dense (slightly laxer with age in 27. *C. bogdaniana*), the flowers and often the fruits more or less obscuring the axis   **39**
     Racemes lax at least on the lower half   **43**

39   Plants hirsute with hairs ± 1 mm long; pods densely covered with brown hairs in 2 storeys   40. *C. vasculosa*

    Plants more shortly hairy; pods white puberulous to pubescent   **40**

40   Petals all strongly lined with purple; pod practically sessile, subcylindrical; stipules less than 1 mm long   **41**

    Petals wholly yellow or faintly lined only on standard; pod shortly stipitate, slightly broadened upwards; stipules 2–7 mm long   **42**

41   Erect or spreading annual, sometimes much branched from the base; calyx coarsely and densely pubescent with irregularly arranged hairs   34. *C. vallicola*

    Trailing perennial, many-stemmed; calyx shortly appressed pubescent

        35. *C. chrysochlora*

42   Calyx glabrous or with few scattered hairs on lobes, 2–2·5 mm long; erect annual, with ribbed branches and oblong-oblanceolate leaflets   26. *C. pycnostachya*

    Calyx pubescent, 2·5–3 mm long; trailing perennial with terete branches and obovate-elliptic leaflets 27. *C. bogdaniana*

43   Bracteoles (at base of calyx) 3–6·5 mm long; calyx becoming basally truncate and deflexed; keel shortly rounded, with a practically straight rather projecting beak exceeding the wings, 8–10 mm long

        38. *C. vatkeana*

    Bracteoles 0·5–3 mm long; calyx not basally truncate and deflexed; beak more incurved or scarcely exceeding wings   **44**

44   Pod 8–11 mm long; racemes with ± 6–18 very laxly arranged flowers; stipules 1–1·5(–2) mm long; keel 4–6(–8) mm long

        44. *C. massaiensis*

    Pod 12–24 mm long; racemes with generally more numerous flowers, more closely arranged on upper part of axis; stipules 3–16 mm long   **45**

45   Keel 9–10 mm long; pod 20–24 mm long

        42. *C. ukambensis*

    Keel 7–8 mm long; pod 12–18 mm long

        43. *C. uguenensis*

46   Perennial, with numerous slender trailing or shortly ascending stems; keel not or little exceeding the wings; pod 1·5–2·2 cm long

        47

    Annual or short-lived perennial, with a single erect stem, variously branched and sometimes with numerous spreading branches from near the base   **48**

47   Leaflets elliptic to obovate; keel very shortly beaked 5–6(–7) mm long

        35. *C. chrysochlora*

    Leaflets narrowly oblong-elliptic to oblanceolate; keel prominently beaked, (7–)8–9 mm long   36. *C. cylindrica*

48   Keel shallowly rounded, 1·7–2·8 times as long as wide, with a distinctly projecting bluntly pointed beak, 1·2–2·4 cm long   **49**

    Keel more strongly rounded, 1·2–1·6 times as long as wide, with an incurved pointed beak or a very short beak, up to 1·3 cm long   **50**

49   Pod 15–20 mm across; calyx glabrous; standard cream or pale yellow

        29. *C. ochroleuca*

    Pod 5–7 mm across; calyx puberulous; standard usually bright yellow

        30. *C. brevidens*

50   Racemes dense, many-flowered, the flowers and fruits more or less obscuring the axis; pods rather shortly and fatly cylindrical; wings longer than keel   **51**

    Racemes laxer at least in lower half or few-flowered; pods narrowly cylindrical   **52**

51   Keel 5–7 mm long, with a very short blunt beak   34. *C. vallicola*

    Keel 10–12 mm long, with a narrow incurved beak   39. *C. petitiana*

52   Keel 10–13 mm long; pod 2·8–4 cm long

        31. *C. dewildemaniana*

    Keel 5–8·5 mm long; pod up to 3·2 cm long (in our area)   **53**

53   Pod 2·4–3·2 cm long; wings exceeding keel (in our area); plants erect, laxly branched; racemes many-flowered

        32. *C. lanceolata*

    Pod 1·8–2·2 cm long; wings shorter than keel; plants with numerous, sometimes rather spreading, branches from near the base; racemes few-flowered   33. *C. balbi*

54   Stipules absent; pods subglobose to oblong-ellipsoid, 3–6 mm long, 2–10-seeded; leaflets narrow, mostly broadest in the upper half   **55**

    Stipules present; pods larger; leaflets various   **59**

55   Flowers, apart from the short terminal racemes, mostly clustered in many of the axils below   67. *C. alexandri*

    Flowers almost all in terminal racemes or heads   **56**

56   Racemes contracted to short dense sessile heads surrounded by longer spreading leaves (bearing leaflets 3–5 cm long)

        63. *C. cephalotes*

    Racemes not surrounded by a false whorl of long leaves   **57**

57   Pod 6–8-seeded; standard puberulous only at apex outside; flowers in heads

        65. *C. jacksonii*

     Pod 1–2-seeded; standard uniformly hairy outside; flowers usually in elongate racemes (unless diseased) **58**

58 Calyx and standard golden-brown tomentose; pod 5–6 mm long
                   64. *C. pseudotenuirama*
     Calyx and standard with short white hairs; pod 3–4(–4·5) mm long
                   66. *C. hyssopifolia*

59 Bracteoles curved up like 2 horns from just below calyx; calyx ± as long as standard; leaflets obovate or suborbicular
                   11. *C. incana*
     Bracteoles not curved up like horns; calyx shorter than standard **60**

60 Leaves (except on youngest branches) mostly subtending very short lateral shoots bearing clusters of smaller leaves; keel 1–1·6 cm long with a spirally twisted beak **61**
     Leaves not in tufts **63**

61 Racemes of 2 sorts, in addition to terminal and leaf-opposed racemes the flowers borne 1–4 on slender axes arising from the leaf-tufts; pod 8–10 mm long (in our area)
                   61. *C. oocarpa*
     Racemes all similar, terminal and leaf-opposed; pod 25–30 mm long **62**

62 Calyx 5–7 mm long, with triangular lobes not much longer than the tube; keel scarcely angled; seeds smooth   53. *C. fascicularis*
     Calyx (6–)7–9 mm long, with narrow lobes mostly 2–3 times as long as tube, becoming reflexed; keel distinctly angular; seeds slightly rough   54. *C. emarginella*

63 Calyx-lobes 2–3 times as long as tube; leaflets densely hairy on both surfaces, with 3–5 markedly raised ascending nerves beneath; spreading perennial   45. *C. lotiformis*
     Calyx-lobes not much longer than tube; leaflets with more numerous, less markedly raised ascending nerves **64**

64 Beak of keel with a spiral twist (look for diagonal course of upper seam and veins); bracteoles inserted on pedicel; calyx-tube protracted on lower side **65**
     Beak of keel not twisted; bracteoles at base of calyx; calyx-lobes arising at ± same level **68**

65 Shrubby, with slender woody puberulous branches; keel 1·1–1·3 cm long; leaflets elliptic-oblanceolate to obovate, often with a clearly visible vein-network
                   50. *C. keniensis*
     Herbaceous; keel smaller or leaflets varying in shape, longer and proportionally narrower above **66**

66 Perennial, with numerous shortly ascending or

prostrate stems; petioles mostly less than 1 cm long; flowers often few, rather crowded at top of a relatively long peduncle
                   59. *C. rhizoclada*
     Annual, sometimes much-branched from near the base; petioles often mostly longer; racemes, except in depauperate plants, generally with numerous flowers **67**

67 Pod, with a 3–9 mm long stipe, (1·5–)2–4 cm long; calyx often glabrous; plants laxly branched, with generally narrow leaflets at least above   57. *C. deserticola*
     Pod, with a 1–2 mm long stipe, 1·4–2·2 cm long; calyx puberulous; plants rather bushy, much branched from base, with rather uniformly shaped oblanceolate to elliptic-obovate leaflets 58. *C. greenwayi*

68 Keel 1·5–2·3 cm long; pod 3·5–5 cm long
                 24. *C. comanestiana*
     Keel up to 1 cm long; pod less than 3 cm long **69**

69 Standard pubescent outside; flowers 4·5–7·5 mm long, in short dense racemes or heads on a relatively long peduncle; pods 6–7·5 x 2–4 mm; small spreading annual
                 46. *C. microcarpa*
     Standard glabrous outside; other characters not combined **70**

70 Racemes shortly pedunculate, dense; pods broadest towards apex **71**
     Racemes lax; pods usually broadest about the middle **72**

71 Calyx glabrous or with a few scattered hairs on lobes, 2–2·5 mm long; erect annual, with ribbed branches and oblong-oblanceolate leaflets   26. *C. pycnostachya*
     Calyx pubescent, 2·5–3 mm long; trailing perennial, with terete branches and obovate-elliptic leaflets
               27. *C. bogdaniana*

72 Pod 23–27 mm long; keel 8–10 mm long, with a projecting beak exceeding the wings; bracteoles 3–6·5 mm long
                 38. *C. vatkeana*
     Pod 8–11 mm long; keel 4–6 mm long, scarcely exceeding wings; bracteoles 0·5–1·5 mm long   44. *C. massaiensis*

73 Keel rounded about the middle, shortly beaked **74**
     Keel angled in the lower half, with a well-developed straight narrow beak **76**

74 Keel 13–14 mm long; pod 45–50 mm long; bracts cordate   56. *C. spectabilis*
     Keel 6–8 mm long; pod 6–32 mm long; bracts narrow **75**

75 Leaves subsessile, simple, narrow, glabrous or practically so; pod stipitate, cylindrical, glabrous, 24–30-seeded   20. *C. glauca*

Leaves with 4-15 mm long petioles; leaflets ovate to oblong-lanceolate, thinly pilose; pod sessile, subglobose, hairy, 1-6-seeded
41. *C. anthyllopsis*

76   Keel 9-11 mm long; pod 2·7-3·5 cm long
60. *C. karagwensis*
Keel 4-6 mm long; pod 1-1·5 cm long   77

77   Leaves with 3-4 mm long petioles, 1-foliolate, pilose beneath; stipules absent
47. *C. bongensis*

Leaves with a petiole less than 1 mm long, simple, thinly puberulous beneath; stipules present   48. *C. shirensis*

1. Crotalaria agatiflora *Schweinf.*

Woody bushy herb, shrub or small tree, with very large lemon- or greenish-yellow flowers. See KTS. p. 358, also as *C. imperialis* Taub., p. 359.

Three races—one a large shrub or small tree, often tomentose, with elliptic-lanceolate leaflets and large caducous bracts, in or near forests, (6500-)7000-10 500 ft, in HE, HT, HM, HL, HA, HK, RV (subsp. *engleri* (Bak. f.) Polhill); another tending to be smaller, hairy, with elliptic-ovate leaflets and much smaller bracts in grassland and bushland, 6000-7000 ft, in HT, ?HM, HL, KIT, KIS, NAR, NAN, (subsp. *imperialis* Taub.) Polhill); the last and typical subsp. *agatiflora* a woody herb, glabrous except sometimes on the leaflets beneath but otherwise as subsp. *imperialis* and occurring in open places, 5000-8000 ft, in HM, HA, RV, MAC, NBI. Intermediates wherever populations of the different races meet.

2. Crotalaria lebrunii *Bak. f.*

Shrub with pointed elliptic leaflets, the flowers like *C. laburnifolia* except for the united upper and lateral calyx-lobes; pods with shorter stipe and much more inflated than in *C. laburnifolia*.
Forest edges, 7000-7700 ft. HA, HK, HN.
Bogdan 2826; Verdcourt and Polhill 2996.

3. Crotalaria laburnifolia *L.*

Robust scarcely woody erect herb, with lax racemes of 2-3 cm long yellow flowers often speckled reddish-brown, free calyx-lobes and slenderly long-stipitate pods. See KTS. p. 359.

Two main races—subsp. *laburnifolia* in bushland and wooded grassland, 3000-5600 ft, almost everywhere, MUM, KIS, NAR, BAR, RV, MAG, EMB, MAC, NBI, KAJ, and subsp. *eldomae* (Bak. f.) Polhill with diffuse habit, short petioles 1-2·5 cm long, small leaflets and few-flowered racemes, in drier places and often on volcanic soils in RV, MAG, KAJ, also a form of subsp. *laburnifolia* approaching subsp. *eldomae* ('Elgon race'), 5000-7400 ft in KIT and MUM.

4. Crotalaria pseudospartium *Bak. f.*

Very similar to *C. laburnifolia* but with very reduced leaflets less than 1 cm long on long petioles, and with the upper and lateral calyx-lobes united. See KTS. p. 359. RV.

5. Crotalaria goodiiformis *Vatke*

Slender-stemmed much-branched shrub, with membranous elliptic to obovate leaflets, the 1-1·2 cm long yellow flowers few on a thread-like rachis, developing thin-valved oblong-club-shaped pods. See KTS. p. 359, under *C. saxatilis* Vatke. HA, EMB, MAC, NBI, KAJ.

6. Crotalaria mauensis *Bak. f.*

Robust bushy herb or shrub, brown tomentellous, with elliptic leaflets and long subdense racemes, the broadly lobed calyx the same length as the chubby yellow corolla, 1·2-1·5 cm long. See KTS. p. 359. HT, HM, HA, HK, MUM, ?BAR, MAC, NBI.

7. Crotalaria quartiniana *A. Rich.*

Laxly branched annual, with spreading hairs and pointed elliptic leaflets, flowering shyly; flowers with ovate-cordate calyx-lobes enveloping the pale yellow wine-marked petals (wings brighter) and further adorned by large ovate bracteoles; standard glabrous; pods thin-valved, oblong-club-shaped, glabrous.

Rare plant found on forest edges or grass and bush nearby, 6700-7900 ft. HE, KIT.
Irwin 133, 133A; Tweedie 1711.

8. Crotalaria polysperma *Kotschy* (see p. 297)

Erect well-branched hairy annual, with elliptic leaflets and 12-20-flowered racemes of large blue flowers, the pilose calyx nearly the same length as the angular keel, 1·6-1·8 cm long; pod broadly oblong-club-shaped, (3·5-)4-4·5 cm long, pilose, c. 70-100-seeded.

Deciduous bushland and grassland, 3000-6200 ft. NAR, RV, MAG, MAC, KAJ.
Bally 10548; Greenway 9199.

9. Crotalaria serengetiana *Polhill*

As *C. polysperma*, but smaller, spreading, generally with narrowly elliptic-lanceolate leaflets, and smaller flowers, blue only when fully open; keel 1·1-1·4 cm long; pod 2·5-2·8 cm long, densely pilose, only c. 20-24-seeded.

Grassland, 5000 ft. KAJ.
Lind 3091.

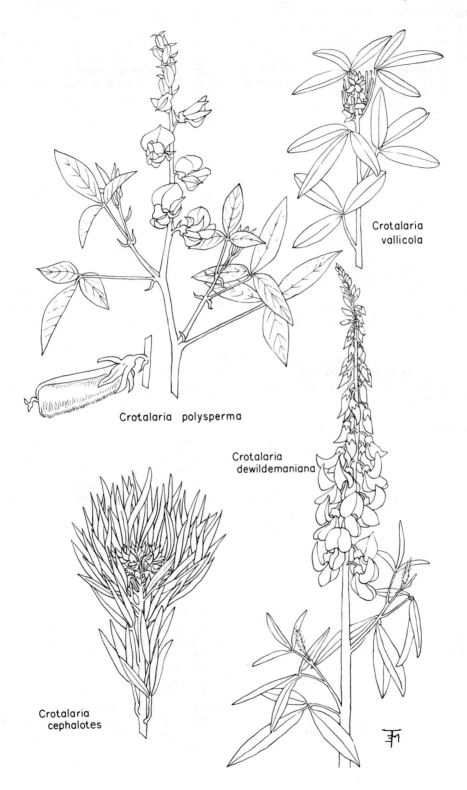

Crotalaria
vallicola

Crotalaria polysperma

Crotalaria
dewildemaniana

Crotalaria
cephalotes

10. Crotalaria barkae *Schweinf.*

Spreading hairy annual (rarely perennial), with lanceolate to elliptic leaflets and few white, cream or greenish-yellow flowers; keel angled, scarcely exceeding the broadly lobed calyx, 1·2–1·6 cm long; pod ellipsoid-club-shaped, 2–3·5 cm long, sparsely pilose or glabrous up to 44-seeded.

   Grassland, 3000–4500 ft. KAJ, MAC.

   Napper 1724; Verdcourt 3970; Agnew 8464.

11. Crotalaria incana *L.*

Erect, well branched, generally annual, with obovate leaflets (drying blackish) and generally long racemes of rather miserable yellow reddish-marked flowers; calyx nearly as long as the 8–12 mm long angular keel, with the linear bracteoles rising like horns from the base; pods somewhat canoe-shaped, 3–4·5 cm long.

   Two races—subsp. *incana*, with shortly pubescent branches, 1–3 mm long bracts and subglabrous calyx-lobes only in deciduous bushland and dry grassland of RV and MAC, the subsp. *purpurascens* (Lam.) Milne-Redh., with long spreading yellow-brown (rarely white) hairs, 4–10 mm long bracts and pilose calyx-lobes, much more catholic, extending into upland grassland and bushland, becoming a weed, 4000–7500 ft. HE, HM, HA, HK, KIT, NAR, RV, MAC, NBI, KAJ.

   Bogdan 3215; Williams 225.

12. Crotalaria stolzii (*Bak. f.*) *Polhill*

Straggling-erect rather stiffly branched subglabrous semi-woody herb, immediately recognizable by the very large equal-sided reticulate-veined heart-shaped stipules; leaflets oblanceolate; flowers bright yellow, 1·1–1·3 cm long; pods oblong, somewhat flattened laterally, 1·6–1·8 cm long.

   Very rare plant found on stream banks, 8000–10 000 ft. HC, HT, HK.

   Bogdan 3858; Thulin and Tidigs 163.

13. Crotalaria natalitia *Meissn.* (see p. 292)

Woody herb or shrub 1–2 m tall, with stiffly ascending densely pubescent branches; leaves clustered, with obliquely lanceolate stipules and oblanceolate to oblanceolate-elliptic leaflets; flowers bright yellow, marked reddish with age, with an ovate-orbicular standard and a somewhat angled 1–1·5 cm long keel woolly along the upper edge; pod broadly cylindrical, stipitate, glabrous, often mottled.

   Forest edges, bushland, wooded or open grasland, 5500–10 000 ft. HE, HC, HT, HM, HA, HK, KIT, BAR, RV, MAC, NBI, KAJ.

   Lucas 211; Napper 637.

14. Crotalaria cylindrocarpa *DC.*

Erect pubescent perennial, with obliquely lanceolate to somewhat crescent-shaped stipules, variably shaped but often oblanceolate to elliptic-obovate leaflets and subdense racemes of reddish-marked yellow flowers; standard ovate; keel subangular, 1–1·5 cm long, woolly along upper edge; pod cylindrical, 2·3–3 cm long, puberulous.

   Wooded grassland. MUM.

   A. Whyte s.n.

15. Crotalaria goreensis *Guill. & Perr.*

Erect much-branched annual, very similar to *C. cylindrocarpa*, but keel less than 1 cm long and pods only 1·5–2 cm long.

   Wooded grassland, only recorded by Lake Victoria. MUM/KIS.

   Tweedie 2835, 2898.

16. Crotalaria podocarpa *DC.*

Spreading hirsute annual, with somewhat curved obliquely oblong-lanceolate stipules, mostly rather narrow leaflets and racemes of few bright yellow flowers; keel angular, 1·2–1·7 cm long, woolly along upper edge; pod fatly cylindrical on a distinct slender stipe, glabrous, pale with darker suture; seeds large, rough, orange.

   Wooded grassland, in dry, open, sandy places, 4000–4700 ft. BAR.

   Bogdan 5173; Tweedie 2272.

17. Crotalaria lachnophora *A. Rich.* (see p. 292)

Robust woody herb 1–3 m tall, with ascending tomentose branches, broad somewhat crescent-shaped stipules, oblanceolate to elliptic-obovate leaflets and handsome yellow flowers fading orange; keel abruptly rounded with a straight beak, 1·8–2·5 cm long, woolly along upper edge; pod cylindrical, furry.

   Open or wooded grassland, bushland, 4500–6700 ft. KIT, KIS, EMB, MAC.

   Bogdan 5479; Napper 1629.

18. Crotalaria lachnocarpoides *Engl.* (see p. 292)

Woody bushy tomentose herb, up to 0·5–2·5 m tall, with linear stipules, short petioles, felty oblong-oblanceolate leaflets and racemes of few yellow flowers which fade reddish; keel shorter than calyx, almost semicircular, shortly beaked, 1·1–1·8 cm long, with a thin band of hairs towards lower margin; pod broadly cylindrical, furry.

   Grassland and bushland, 4500–9000 ft. HE, HC, HT, HM, HA, HK, KIT, MUM, NAR, BAR, RV, MAC, KAJ.

   Greenway 8531; Napper 1623.

19. Crotalaria orthoclada *Bak.* (see p. 292)

Shrubby perennial 1–3 m tall, with many stiffly ascending densely pubescent leafy branches, short petioles, no stipules, rather small oblanceolate leaflets, and lax terminal racemes of few yellow flowers; keel shorter than calyx, strongly rounded, with a twisted beak, 7–9 mm long; pod narrowly cylindrical, with fine spreading hairs.

Wooded grassland and bushland at about 6000 ft, rare. KIT.

Irwin 180; Tweedie 2856.

20. Crotalaria glauca *Willd.*

Slender erect annual, glabrous, glaucous, with narrow subsessile simple leaves and lax few-flowered racemes, the standard pale, the wings brighter yellow; keel as long as calyx, almost semicircular, with a very short circumflexed beak, 6–8 mm long; pod narrowly cylindrical, stipitate.

Locally common in grassland 4500–7600 ft. HE, HT, HM, KIT, MUM, RV, EMB, NBI, KAJ.

Brodhurst-Hill 336; Williams 163.

21. Crotalaria ononoides *Benth.*

Spreading pilose annual, with short petioles, lanceolate, elliptic or obovate leaflets and dense sessile heads of yellow reddish-marked 7–9 mm long flowers, appearing whiskery on account of the long narrow calyx-lobes, the bracteoles and also the 3-fid bracts spreading from just below the calyx; pod ellipsoid, glabrous except at apex.

Only once recorded from dry places in Kavirondo. MUM.

Scott Elliot 7119.

22. Crotalaria verdcourtii *Polhill*

Bushy herb, with tomentellous branches, long-petiolate stipulate leaves, elliptic to obovate leaflets and long racemes; standard broad, bright yellow, usually with a wine-coloured basal zone, turning reddish over-all; keel much shorter than the broad wings and little exceeding the subsequently reflexed calyx-lobes, rounded, with a rather short ultimately twisted beak, 1·1–1·4 cm long; pod oblong-club-shaped, tomentellous, with 24–36 rough seeds.

Wooded grassland, about 5000–5600 ft. NAN, EMB, MAC, KAJ.

Greenway 9540; Verdcourt 2175.

23. Crotalaria deflersii *Schweinf.*

Very similar to *C. verdcourtii*, although often less hairy and with smaller stipules, but the keel very short, 6–8 mm long, and the pod only 16–20-seeded.

Deciduous bushland, often in rocky places, 4000–5000 ft. RV, MAG.

Bogdan 3474; Greenway 9518.

24. Crotalaria comanestiana *Volkens & Schweinf.*

Woody herb, erect to 1·3 m, with tomentellous branches, long petioles and elliptic to obovate leaflets; flowers numerous, bright yellow, turning reddish-brown; keel very much longer than calyx and slightly exceeding the wings, rounded with a long projecting beak, (1·5–)1·7–2·3 cm long; pod oblong-club-shaped, 3·5–5 cm long, pubescent.

Stony ground and lava ridges in deciduous bushland, 3000 ft. MAG.

Bally 8017; Glover and Samuel 2806.

25. Crotalaria burttii *Bak. f.*

Bushy herb, with tomentellous branches, elliptic or obovate leaflets and numerous yellow flowers which fade reddish; calyx much shorter than corolla, with narrowly triangular bracteoles at base; keel slightly shorter than the wings, rounded, with projecting beak, 1–1·2 cm long; pod oblong-club-shaped, 2–3 cm long, densely pubescent.

Clay soils of seasonally inundated depressions in deciduous bushland. MAG.

Verdcourt 3270; Verdcourt *et al.* 2661.

26. Crotalaria pycnostachya *Benth.*

Erect and spreading annual, with ribbed puberulous branches, conspicuous thread-like stipules, oblong-oblanceolate leaflets and dense racemes of small yellow flowers; calyx short, practically glabrous; keel shortly beaked, 4–5 mm long; pod oblong-club-shaped, 1·2–1·5 cm long, puberulous.

Open or wooded grassland and deciduous bushland, generally an opportunist of low rainfall areas, 3800–5600 ft. KIS, BAR, MAC, NBI, KAJ.

Bally 9719; Polhill and Paulo 1018.

27. Crotalaria bogdaniana *Polhill*

Trailing perennial, with shortly petiolate stipulate leaves, obovate-elliptic leaflets and subdense racemes of small pale yellow, sometimes faintly maroon-veined, flowers; calyx short, pubescent; keel scarcely as long as wings, shortly rounded, with a projecting beak, 6–9 mm long; pod oblong-club-shaped, 1·6–2 cm long, pubescent.

Grassland on black clay soils, 3700–5700 ft. EMB, MAC, NBI, KAJ.

Bogdan 3999; Verdcourt 3854.

28. Crotalaria pallida *Ait.*

Erect well-branched puberulous annual or short-lived perennial, 1–2 m tall, with elliptic or obovate leaflets and subdense racemes of many yellow, generally reddish-brown-veined, flowers; bracts caducous; keel shallowly rounded, with a projecting beak much exceeding the calyx and wings, 1·2–1·5 cm long; pod shortly stipitate, rather narrowly cylindrical, often slightly curved, 3·8–4·5 cm long.

Two variants—var. *pallida* with mostly 6–13 cm long elliptic pointed leaflets and var. *obovata* (G. Don) Polhill with smaller obovate leaflets. Bushland near rivers and lakes, 3700–5000 ft. KIT, MUM, KIS, BAR.

Bogdan 2908; Tweedie 2097.

29. Crotalaria ochroleuca *G. Don*

Erect, generally annual, with narrow leaflets and lax racemes of large pale yellow reddish-veined flowers; calyx basally truncate, shortly toothed, glabrous; keel shortly rounded, with a long projecting beak, 1·8–2·2 cm long, conspicuously veined; pods subsessile, broadly cylindrical, 5–7 cm long, 1·5–2 cm across, up to 100-seeded.

Damp riverside grassland, 6000 ft. MUM.

Brodhurst-Hill 385.

30. Crotalaria brevidens *Benth.* (see p. 304)

Erect to spreading annual or short-lived perennial, with variably shaped but mostly narrow leaflets and sublax racemes of yellow, reddish-brown-veined flowers; calyx basally truncate, pubescent; keel shallow, shortly rounded, with a projecting beak, 1·2–2·4 cm long, conspicuously lined; pods subsessile, narrowly cylindrical, often a little curved at ends, (3·5–)4–4·5 cm long, up to 80-seeded.

The common large-flowered form is var. *intermedia* (Kotschy) Polhill, but a smaller flowered var. *parviflora* (Bak. f.) Polhill, with keel only 1·2–1·4 cm long, occurs around Nairobi, east to EMB, also on high ground north to Laikipia and the Mau, and is very similar to the following species except in keel-shape. Grassland and bushland of various types, 4500–9000 ft. HE, HC, HT, HM, HA, HK, KIT, MUM, KIS, NAR, RV, NAN, EMB, MAC, NBI.

Napier 108; Verdcourt 1804.

31. Crotalaria dewildemaniana *Wilczek* (see p. 297)

Very similar to *C. brevidens* var. *parviflora*, but the 1–1·3 cm long keel strongly rounded with a slightly incurved beak and the pods generally smaller; also similar to *C. lanceolata*, but the flowers larger.

Only the subsp. *oxyrhyncha* Polhill, in grassland, (3000–)5000–7200 ft. HE, HT, HM, KIT, RV, MAC, NBI, KAJ.

Leakey in CM 8553; Tweedie 922A.

32. Crotalaria lanceolata *E. Mey.*

Erect laxly branched annual, with mostly narrow leaflets and long racemes of rather small yellow, reddish-purple-veined flowers; calyx basally truncate, shortly lobed, pubescent; keel rounded about the middle, with a slightly incurved conspicuously lined beak shorter than the wings, 8–9 mm long; pod narrowly cylindrical, often curved up at tip, 2·4–3·2 cm long, ± 24–50-seeded.

Only the subsp. *contigua* Polhill, which closely approaches *C. dewildemaniana* subsp. *oxyrhyncha* and may introgress in KIT. Grassland·and forest margins, 5900–7100 ft. HM, KIT, KIS, KAJ.

Kerfoot 3886; van Someren 189.

33. Crotalaria balbi *Chiov.*

Erect to spreading puberulous annual or short-lived perennial, with mostly rather narrow leaflets and long-pedunculate racemes, the often rather few small yellow, reddish- or purplish-veined flowers crowded above; calyx basally truncate; keel rounded about the middle, with a slightly incurved sharp beak exceeding the wings, 5–7 mm long; pod narrowly cylindrical, 1·8–2·2 cm long.

Grassland, 5700–7000 ft. HA, MAC, ?NBI.

Bogdan 3364; Mwangangi 62.

34. Crotalaria vallicola *Bak. f.* (see p. 297)

Erect annual, with many rather spreading densely pubescent branches, minute stipules, oblong-lanceolate to elliptic leaflets and dense shortly pedunculate racemes of small yellow purple-veined flowers; calyx basally truncate; standard obovate; keel rounded, only slightly beaked, shorter than the wings, 5–7 mm long; pod subcylindrical. 1·7–2·2 cm long.

Grassland and bushland, often in rocky or disturbed places, 3800–7500 ft. HE, HC, HT, KIT, MUM, KIS, NAR, RV, MAC.

Bogdan 1826; Verdcourt 4038.

35. Crotalaria chrysochlora *Harms* (see p. 301)

Perennial, with numerous slender creeping or shortly ascending pubescent stems, small elliptic to obovate leaflets and subdense racemes of few yellow purplish-veined flowers similar to those of *C. vallicola*; pod 1·5–1·8 cm long.

Grassland, often in rocky or disturbed places, 5000–8700 ft. HC, HT, HM, HA, HK, KIT, MUM, NAR, KAJ.

Polhill 2414; Williams 235.

36. Crotalaria cylindrica *A. Rich.* (see p. 292)

Similar to *C. chrysochlora*, but with narrower leaflets and rather larger flowers; keel rounded, with a short projecting beak, not or scarcely

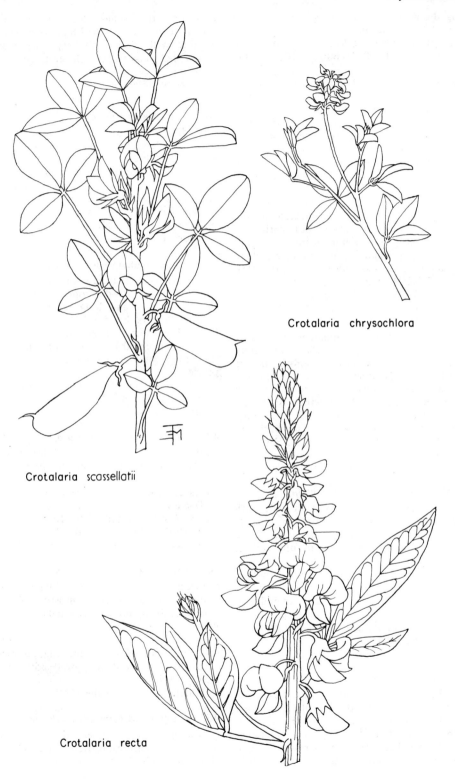

Crotalaria chrysochlora

Crotalaria scassellatii

Crotalaria recta

exceeding the wings, 8–9 mm long; pod narrowly cylindrical, 1·6–2·2 cm long.

Only the subsp. *afrorientalis* Polhill, in montane grassland and moor, 6000–10 600 ft. HE, HC, HT, HM, HK.

Rogers 392; Tweedie 1418.

37. Crotalaria cleomifolia *Bak.*

Shrubby perennial 1–4·5 m tall, with 3–5-foliolate leaves, elliptic leaflets and long racemes of bright yellow faintly reddish-lined flowers; calyx with long bracteoles from the truncate base; standard elliptic; keel rounded, with a narrow slightly incurved beak, much longer than the wings, 1·4–1·7 cm long; pod narrowly cylindrical, 4–5 cm long.

Striking species, generally recognizable by the predominantly 5-foliolate leaves, but with very diversely developed indumentum. Locally common by streams and swamps or in grassland and bushland near forests, 5000–7800 ft. HE, HM, HA, HN, KIT, MUM, MAC.

Bogdan 5478; Polhill and Verdcourt 261.

38. Crotalaria vatkeana *Engl.*

Straggling thinly pubescent annual, with variably shaped leaflets and long-pedunculate ultimately sublax racemes of yellow purplish-veined flowers; calyx with relatively long bracteoles from the truncate base; keel shallow, shortly rounded, with a projecting beak exceeding the wings, 8–10 mm long; pod narrowly cylindrical, 2·3–2·7 cm long.

Openings in forest or grassland and bushland nearby, 6000–10 000 ft. HE, HT, HM, HA, HN, KIT, NBI, KAJ.

Bogdan 924; Verdcourt and Polhill 2961.

39. Crotalaria petitiana (*A. Rich.*) *Walp.*

Erect rather bushy annual 0·5–2 m tall, with tomentellous ribbed branches, no stipules, oblong-lanceolate to elliptic leaflets, and long dense racemes of yellow reddish- or purplish-veined flowers; calyx with relatively long bracteoles from the truncate base; keel strongly rounded, with a narrow slightly incurved beak, shorter than the wings, 1–1·2 cm long; pod shortly cylindrical, 1·5–2·5 cm long.

Grassland and bushland, 3900–6200 ft. KIT, MUM, KIS, NAR, EMB.

Irwin 191, 193, 196.

40. Crotalaria vasculosa *Benth.*

Spreading hirsute annual, with very short petioles, lanceolate to elliptic-obovate leaflets and dense racemes of pale yellow purplish-veined flowers; calyx subglabrous, with relatively long bracteoles from the truncate base; keel shortly rounded, with a narrow slightly projecting sharp beak slightly

exceeding the wings, 6·5–8·5 mm long; pod shortly cylindrical. 1·6–2 cm long, very densely covered with short and very long brown hairs.

Wooded grassland, in old cultivations, 4700 ft. MUM.

Tweedie 3394.

41. Crotalaria anthyllopsis *Bak.*

Spreading hirsute annual, with stipulate 1-foliolate leaves; leaflets oblong-lanceolate to ovate; flowers in dense subsessile racemes, pale yellow with purplish veins, subtended by long bracts and bracteoles; keel strongly rounded, 5–7 mm long; pod subglobose, densely hirsute, 2–6-seeded.

Wooded grassland, sometimes in rocky places, 6000–6700 ft. KIT, MUM, ?BAR.

Brodhurst-Hill 48; Tweedie 1327.

42. Crotalaria ukambensis *Vatke*

Straggling conspicuously pilose short-lived perennial, with well-developed stipules, variably shaped leaflets and long racemes of cream to yellow flowers lined or flushed reddish-purple; bracts 3·5–7 mm long; keel strongly rounded, with a narrow incurved beak exceeding the wings, 9–10 mm long; pod subcylindrical, 2–2·4 cm long, pilose.

Deciduous bushland and wooded grassland, 3000–3500 ft. MAC, KAJ.

Bogdan 3367; Verdcourt 2085.

43. Crotalaria uguenensis *Taub.*

Similar to *C. ukambensis*, but less robust, with shorter hairs and bracts, smaller flowers (keel 7–8 mm long, not much exceeding the wings) and pubescent pods only 1·2–1·8 cm long.

Deciduous bushland, often around rock outcrops, or on clay soils with *Acacia* wooded grassland, 3000–6000 ft. RV, MAG, NAN, MAC, KAJ.

Bogdan 5206; Glover and Samuel 2826.

44. Crotalaria massaiensis *Taub.*

Spreading perennial, with slender pubescent branches, minute stipules, mostly rather small or narrow leaflets, and lax racemes of small cream to yellow purplish-veined flowers; keel strongly rounded, ± as long as the wings, 4–6 mm long; pod shortly cylindrical, 8–11 mm long, pubescent.

Deciduous bushland, 3000–3500 ft. ?BAR, MAG, NAN.

Gillett 16745; Tweedie 1847.

45. Crotalaria lotiformis *Milne-Redh.*

Spreading hairy perennial, with stipules ± as long as the short petioles; leaflets oblanceolate to obovate, apiculate, with few prominent ascending nerves; flowers few on a relatively long peduncle, yellow, veined reddish-purple; keel rather abruptly rounded, with a straight dark-tipped beak scarcely exceeding the wings, 1–1·3 cm long; pod subcylindrical, 1·8–2·4 cm long.

Open and wooded grassland, sometimes in rocky places or on clay soils, 5500–7000 ft. HA (Ngong Hills), NBI, KAJ.

Milne-Redhead and Taylor 11413; Napier in CM 6304.

46. Crotalaria microcarpa *Benth.*

Much-branched spreading pubescent annual, with small stipules, narrow leaflets and clusters of small flowers on relatively long peduncles; standard yellow, marked red, pubescent outside; keel angled, with a narrow beak little exceeding the wings, 4·5–7·5 mm long; pod ± oblong, 6–7·5 mm long.

Wooded grassland and deciduous bushland, often in disturbed places, 3500–5000 ft. BAR, MAC, KAJ.

Bogdan 3418; Verdcourt 4041.

47. Crotalaria bongensis *Bak. f.*

Small erect annual, with many slender spreading coarsely hairy branches, shortly petiolate narrow 1-foliolate leaves, no stipules, and lax racemes of small yellow, maroon-veined flowers; keel angled, with a narrow untwisted beak slightly exceeding the wings, 4–5 mm long; pod ± oblong, 7–10 mm long.

Collected only once in our area near Kisumu. MUM/KIS.

Tweedie 3463.

48. Crotalaria shirensis *(Bak. f.) Milne-Redh.*

Small erect annual, with thread-like sparsely hairy branches, mostly narrow subsessile simple leaves and lax 1–3-flowered racemes; standard pale yellow, marked red; keel angled, with a forward-curved beak exceeding the bright yellow wings, 5–6 mm long; pod narrowly cylindrical, 1–1·3 cm long.

Wooded grassland, in open sandy or damp places, inconspicuous. KIT.

Heriz-Smith and Paulo 900.

49. Crotalaria tabularis *Bak. f.*

Shrub, pubescent, with filiform stipules, elliptic leaflets and rather lax racemes of yellow flowers; keel rounded, with a rather short twisted beak about as long as the wings, 1·5–1·8 cm long; pod oblong-club-shaped, 5–6·5 cm long.

Forest margins and stream banks, 6500–9000 ft. HA, HN.

Napier 2825; Polhill and Verdcourt 294.

50. Crotalaria keniensis *Bak. f.* (see p. 304)

Straggling shrubby pubescent bush, with minute stipules, relatively small elliptic-oblanceolate to obovate leaflets and racemes of bright yellow flowers; keel rather abruptly rounded, with a twisted beak little exceeding the wings, 1·1–1·3 cm long; pod oblong-club-shaped, 2·5–4 cm long, venose.

Forest edges or bushland and streamsides nearby, 6400–9000 ft. HE, HT, HM, HA, HK, KIS, KIJ.

Bogdan 4151; Verdcourt 666.

51. Crotalaria axillaris *Ait.*

Shrub or woody herb, coarsely hairy (in our area), with elliptic leaflets and clusters of yellow flowers in the axils; keel rounded, with a twisted beak ± as long as the wings, 1·5–1·8 cm long; pod oblong-club-shaped, 4·5 cm long, 0·6–1·2 cm across.

Dry evergreen forest and derived communities, persisting in disturbed places, 4400–7500 ft. HT, HA, HK, RV, EMB, MAC, NBI, KAJ.

Bogdan 2422; Verdcourt 2067.

52. Crotalaria scassellatii *Chiov.* (see p. 301)

Similar to *C. axillaris*, but with a silvery tomentum on branches and underside of leaflets and much fatter pods.

Edges of dry forest and in bushland, often in rocky sites, 3000–5000 ft. MUM/KIS, MAC, KAJ.

Tweedie 1550; Verdcourt 3806.

53. Crotalaria fascicularis *Polhill*

Shrubby, coarsely hairy, with stipulate leaves in tufts, oblanceolate to obovate leaflets and subdense racemes of yellow flowers, calyx with short triangular lobes; keel rounded, with a twisted beak, as long as the wings, 1·2–1·6 cm long; pod narrowly subcylindrical, 2·5–3 cm long, puberulous.

Dry evergreen forest, 6700–7000 ft. HA.

Dowson 622; Polhill 20.

54. Crotalaria emarginella *Vatke*

Spreading woody herb, with variably developed indumentum, stipulate leaves in tufts, rather small obovate leaflets and lax racemes of yellow flowers; calyx with long narrow ultimately reflexed lobes; keel subangular, with a narrow twisted beak, slightly exceeding the wings, 1·1–1·4 cm long; pod narrowly cylindrical, 2–2·8 cm long.

Generally in semidesert grassland and deciduous bushland, rarely in less arid situations, 4500–5700 ft. NAN, EMB.

Bogdan 2713; Napier 2444.

Crotalaria
keniensis

Crotalaria
brevidens

Crotalaria   spinosa

55. Crotalaria recta *A. Rich.* (see p. 301)

Robust erect perennial 1-2·7 m tall, with ribbed densely appressed pubescent stems, short stout petioles, linear-lanceolate stipules, generally elliptic to obovate leaflets and long subdense racemes of yellow flowers marked reddish-purple at base of broad standard and wings; calyx glabrous; keel rounded, with a short twisted beak enveloped by the wings, 1·2-1·5 cm long; pod broadly oblong-club-shaped, 5-6 cm long, glabrous.

Grassland or, at lower altitudes, swamp margins, also persisting on cultivated ground, 3000-8400 ft. HE, HT, HM, HA, KIT, MUM, EMB, MAC, KAJ.

Paulo 545; Tweedie 1317.

56. Crotalaria spectabilis *Roth*

Erect annual to 2 m tall, with angular grooved stems, oblong-ovate stipules, shortly petiolate simple oblong-obovate leaves and long lax racemes of yellow flowers; bracts cordate; calyx glabrous; keel rounded, with a short twisted beak enveloped by the broad wings, 1·3-1·4 cm long; pod broadly oblong-club-shaped, 4·5-5 cm long, glabrous.

Introduced species, locally naturalized in wooded grassland on formerly cultivated land, 3900 ft. KIT/MUM.

Tweedie 2891.

57. Crotalaria deserticola *Bak. f.*

Erect or spreading laxly branched inconspicuously hairy annual, with small stipules, generally narrow leaflets and lax racemes of yellow flowers, finely veined reddish-brown on the standard; calyx often glabrous; keel angled, with a narrow twisted beak, 6-18 mm long; pod oblong-club-shaped, (1·5-)2-4 cm long including a 3-9 mm long stipe, puberulous; seeds generally smooth.

Extremely variable, particularly in habit and flower-size; a markedly depauperate form occurs on dry volcanic soils of RV; open and wooded grassland, 3600-8000 ft. HM, HA, HK, KIT, MUM, KIS, NAR, RV, MAC, KAJ.

Bogdan 1857; Napper 1655.

58. Crotalaria greenwayi *Bak. f.*

Similar to *C. deserticola*, but more bushy, with conspicuous short indumentum (always present on calyx), broadly oblanceolate to elliptic-obovate leaflets, constantly small flowers (keel 7-10 mm long) and small legumes, 1·4-2·2 cm long including a 1-2 mm long stipe; seeds rugulose.

Deciduous bushland and semidesert grassland. MAG.

Greenway 8993; Verdcourt 589.

59. Crotalaria rhizoclada *Polhill*

Prostrate or shortly ascending perennial, sending up many slender puberulous stems from a branched rootstock; stipules minute; leaflets small, oblanceolate to obovate; flowers usually few at top of a relatively long peduncle, yellow, finely veined reddish-brown on the standard; keel angled, with a narrow twisted beak, 7-9 mm long; pod very shortly stipitate, oblong-club-shaped, 8-18 mm long; seeds slightly rough.

Grassland, on both red lateritic and black clay soils, 4800-8300 ft. HA, MAC, KAJ.

Bogdan 3458; Pierce in CM 1683.

60. Crotalaria karagwensis *Taub* (*C. lugardiorum* Bullock)

Erect puberulous annual, branched from the base, with simple subsessile linear-lanceolate to oblong-elliptic leaves, and lax racemes of yellow flowers, finely veined reddish-brown on the standard; keel angular, with a narrow twisted beak, 9-11 mm long; pod oblong-club-shaped, 2·7-3·5 cm long.

Open and wooded grassland or bushland, also on cultivated ground, 6000-7600 ft. HE, ?HT, KIT, MUM.

Bogdan 4667; Lugard 197.

61. Crotalaria oocarpa *Bak.*

Bushy annual up to 1 m tall, pilose with fine mostly spreading often yellowish hairs; leaves in tufts, with narrow stipules and oblanceolate to obovate leaflets; racemes both terminal and from the leaf-clusters, the latter with only 1-4 flowers on a slender axis; standard yellow, finely veined reddish-brown; keel angled, with a narrow twisted beak, 1-1·2 cm long; pod ellipsoid, in our area only 8-10 mm long.

Only the subsp. *microcarpa* Milne-Redh., in grassland near Tanzania border. NAR, KAJ.

Bally 1249.

62. Crotalaria spinosa *Benth.* (see p. 304)

Much-branched spiny annual up to 20-70 cm tall, with clustered leaves and small wedge-shaped leaflets; flowers 1-3 on short spine-tipped axes from the leaf-clusters; standard yellow, finely veined reddish; keel angular, with a narrow twisted beak, 4-6 mm long; pod 7·5-9 mm long.

Short grassland, often in disturbed and rather dry places, 5300-7000 ft. HE, HT, KIT, MUM, NAR, RV, MAC, NBI, KAJ.

Bally 5266; Gillett 18315.

63. Crotalaria cephalotes *A. Rich.* (see p. 297)

Small erect coarsely hairy annual, branched from the base, with narrow leaflets and small yellow red-marked flowers in dense terminal heads surrounded by longer spreading leaves; keel angled, with a narrow twisted beak, 4–5·5 mm long; pods globose-ellipsoid, 2-seeded.

Open and wooded grassland, often in disturbed or rocky places, 3000–7600 ft. HE, KIT, MUM, NAR, RV, MAC, KAJ.

Bally 8979; Drummond and Hemsley 4490.

64. Crotalaria pseudotenuirama *Torre*

Erect pubescent annual, with numerous slender ascending branches, mostly rather small narrowly oblanceolate leaflets and sublax racemes of small yellow flowers, the standard lined reddish-brown and golden-brown tomentose outside; calyx 2·5–3·5 mm long, brownish tomentose; keel angled, with a narrow twisted beak, 4–6 mm long; pod subglobose-ovoid, 5–6 mm long, 1–2-seeded.

Open grassland, 7000–8000 ft. HM.

Scott Elliot 6835.

65. Crotalaria jacksonii *Bak. f.*

Similar to *C. pseudotenuirama*, but the flowers in heads, the calyx 4–5 mm long, with short white appressed hairs, the standard puberulous only at the apex outside and the pod 6–8-seeded.

A rare endemic plant of grassland and forest margins, 8000–9000 ft. HM, HA.

Heriz-Smith in EAH 12858; Kerfoot 4590.

66. Crotalaria hyssopifolia *Klotzsch*

Similar to *C. pseudotenuirama*, but leaflets rather more variable in shape, the flowers often rather closely arranged and sometimes smaller, the calyx and standard pubescent with white appressed hairs and the pod 3–4(–4·5) mm long.

Grassland and forest clearings above 5000 ft. ?HE, KIT, MUM.

Brodhurst-Hill 559; Paulo 522.

67. Crotalaria alexandri *Bak. f.*

Small ultimately much-branched coarsely hairy annual, with small oblanceolate leaflets and little yellow red-marked flowers in short dense terminal racemes and clustered in many of the axils below; keel angled, with a narrow twisted beak, 4·5–6 mm long; pod oblong-ellipsoid, 4–5 mm long, 7–10-seeded.

Grassland and scrub, sometimes in rather dry sites, 4700–5200 ft. MUM, KAJ.

Bally 409; Drummond and Hemsley 4488.

39. LUPINUS *L.*

Erect herbs; leaves digitately 5–11-foliolate; stipels absent; stipules basally fused to the petiole; flowers racemose, variously coloured, often variegated; calyx deeply split, the upper lip 2-lobed, the lower shortly 3-fid; standard broad, the sides reflexing; wings broad, enveloping the beaked keel; stamens all joined into a closed tube, with alternately long and short anthers; ovary sessile; pod oblong, only slightly inflated, often with woody valves constricted between the seeds; seeds oblong-elliptic to squarish, with a small hilum near one end.

Lupinus princei *Harms* (see p. 307)

Bushy herb, with racemes of conspicuous blue and white flowers often yellow marked at centre, and thick-valved furry oblong-pointed pods; seeds squarish, hard, papillate, mottled.

Locally common in grassland, (5000–)6000–8500 ft, the distribution possibly associated in part with old pastoral encampments. HT, HK, RV, KAJ.

Battiscombe 928; Williams 297.

Various other species are cultivated for ornament or green manure, including *L. albus* L., *L. angustifolius* L. and *L. luteus* L., and may become locally naturalized in due course.

40. ARGYROLOBIUM *Eckl. & Zeyh.*

Herbs or small shrubs; leaves digitately 3-foliolate; stipules free or united; flowers in terminal or leaf-opposed generally subumbelliform racemes, yellow, medium-sized, sometimes cleistogamous with all parts much reduced; calyx deeply split, the upper lip 2-lobed, the lower 3-fid; keel slightly incurved, obtuse; stamens united into a generally closed tube, with alternately long and short anthers; ovary sessile; pod linear-oblong, compressed to only slightly inflated, not glandular; seeds oblong-ovate, the hilum small with a minute aril.

NOTE. If shrubby and with glandular pods, see *Adenocarpus mannii* (Hook. f.) Hook. f. in KTS, p. 354.

1   Stipules linear-caudate; upper calyx-lobes subulate; valves of the pod constricted between the seeds   4. *A. ramosissimum*
    Stipules lanceolate to ovate, acuminate; upper calyx-lobes oblong-lanceolate; valves of pod continuous over the seeds   **2**
2   Stipules joined along the leaf-opposed margin   2. *A. friesianum*
    Stipules free except at very base   **3**
3   Racemes ± 6–40-flowered; robust woody herb or subshrub, 30–200 cm tall   1. *A. fischeri*
    Racemes ± 1–4-flowered; low diffuse slender-stemmed herbs   3. *A. rupestre*

1. Argyrolobium fischeri *Taub.* (see p. 307)

Bushy often somewhat woody plant, erect to 1–2 m (smaller in burned and grazed places), with

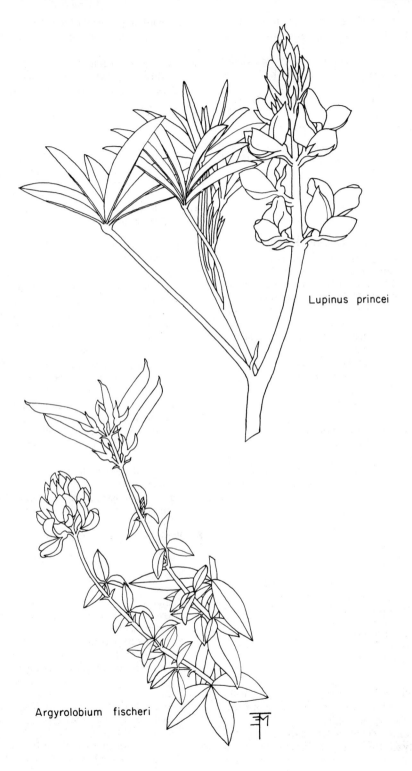

Lupinus princei

Argyrolobium fischeri

generally tomentose elliptic leaflets, free lanceolate or ovate stipules and congested 6–40-flowered racemes.

Forest margins, bushland, and grassland, 5000–8000 ft. HE, HC, HM, HA, HK, KIT, MUM, KIS, RV, MAC, NBI.

Chater-Jack 118; Graham LC 956 in FD 3038.

2. Argyrolobium friesianum *Harms*

Similar to *A. fischeri*, but even more robust and with the stipules united for most of their length along the leaf-opposed margin.

Forest, sometimes at margins, 8000–10 000 ft. HM, HA, HK.

Bally 4568; Gardner in FD 1114.

3. Argyrolobium rupestre (*E. Mey.*) *Walp.*

Creeping or shortly ascending perennial, with many slender stems only up to 1(–2) mm in diameter, ± elliptic hairy leaflets, free lanceolate or ovate stipules and only 1–4 flowers per raceme.

Two races—one with prostrate stems and sparsely hairy calyx on the Aberdare and Mt. Kenya moorlands (subsp. *aberdaricum* (Harms) Polhill), the other with ascending stems and tomentose calyx more widespread in grassland below the forests (subsp. *kilimandscharicum* (Taub.) Polhill). HC, HT, HM, HA, HK, RV.

Chandler 2343; Polhill 234.

4. Argyrolobium ramosissimum *Bak.*

Straggling slender-stemmed perennial, with generally elliptic-obovate sparsely hairy leaflets, very narrow free stipules, and congested 1–12(–16)-flowered racemes; pods distinctly constricted between the seeds.

Forest margins and ericaceous moorland. HC, HM.

Kerfoot 2944; Rawlins 7.

41. TRIFOLIUM *L.*

Herbs with (in ours) digitately trifoliolate, denticulate leaves; stipels absent; flowers often aggregated into umbels or dense racemes; petals persistent after anthesis, adnate to stamen sheath at base; stamens with 9 fused and 1 free, all fertile; pod indehiscent, enclosed by dry remains of calyx and corolla, 1–2 (less often –9)-seeded.

1 Bracts 1- or few-nerved, usually much shorter than the calyx which is not or hardly inflated and usually splits dorsally in fruit; blade of wing auriculate   **2**

   Bracts several-nerved, more than half as long as calyx, forming an involucre; calyx 25–50-nerved, somewhat inflated and

splitting irregularly in fruit; blade of wing not auriculate, tapering gradually into the claw   **16**

2 Petiole of each leaf united with stipules throughout its length; ovules 2   **3**

   Petiole free for most of its length, at least in the lower leaves   **7**

3 Pedicels not conspicuously reflexed in fruit, shorter than the calyx tube; corolla usually purple   **4**

   Pedicels conspicuously reflexed in fruit, those of the upper flowers longer than the calyx tube; corolla white or pinkish
                               5. *T. cheranganiense*

4 Leaflets linear-lanceolate, usually more than 5 times as long as wide, calyx nerves 15–20
                                   1. *T. simense*

   Leaflets rarely more than 5 times as long as wide; calyx nerves 11   **5**

5 Leaflets usually over 9 mm long; inflorescence oblong at least in fruit   **6**

   Leaflets 2–9 mm long, cuneate-obovate, truncate or emarginate, inflorescence hemispherical *c.* 15 mm across; standard *c.* 9 mm long   4. *T. cryptopodium*

6 Leaflets 12–32 mm long, usually acute; standard 7 mm long or more; inflorescence 12 mm or more across and more than twice as long   2. *T. polystachyum*

   Leaflets 6–22 mm long, usually emarginate, truncate or rounded; standard up to 7 mm long; inflorescence, even in fruit, under 18 mm long, 10–12 mm across
                               3. *T. usambarense*

7 Calyx with fewer than 15 nerves (usually 11); ovules 2–9   **8**

   Calyx with 15–25 nerves, somewhat inflated in fruit; 1–6 flowers per inflorescence; ovules 5–9   **15**

8 Pedicels conspicuously reflexed after flowering, those of the upper flowers usually more than 2 mm long and longer than the calyx tube; corolla white or pinkish, perennial   **9**

   Pedicels not reflexed after flowering, rarely over 2 mm long; corolla purple or crimson, rarely white   **10**

9 Free part of petiole absent in the upper leaves, not over 1·5 cm long in the lower leaves, less than twice as long as a leaflet
                               5. *T. cheranganiense*

   Free part of petiole always present, often over 1·5 cm long and often more than twice as long as a leaflet
                                6. *T. semipilosum*

10 Peduncle longer than the inflorescence which nearly always has more than 5 flowers   **11**

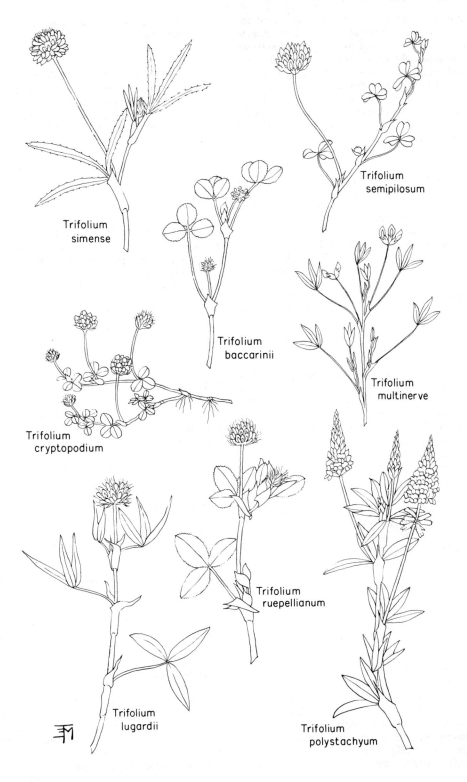

Trifolium
simense

Trifolium
baccarinii

Trifolium
semipilosum

Trifolium
multinerve

Trifolium
cryptopodium

Trifolium
lugardii

Trifolium
ruepellianum

Trifolium
polystachyum

Peduncle shorter than the 1–5-flowered inflorescence; perennial   12. *T. acaule*

11   Calyx teeth 1–1·5 mm wide at base, narrowing gradually with a broad scarious margin; inflorescence 3–15-flowered; standard 8–10 mm long, widest at the middle, then abruptly narrowed to an oblong, downward inflected, truncate tip; ovules 4–8, rarely 2 or 3   11. *T. tembense*

Calyx teeth not over 1 mm wide at base; inflorescence usually more than 1-flowered; standard more or less oblong, straight or bent upwards   **12**

12   Perennial; stem creeping, rooting at the nodes; free part of petiole always well developed; peduncle usually 5–10 times as long as subtending leaflets; standard 7 mm long or more; ovules 2, rarely 3 or 4   7. *T. burchellianum*

Annuals; stem ascending or, if prostrate, rarely rooting at the nodes, free part of petiole often very short in uppermost leaves; peduncle rarely 5 times as long as subtending leaflets   **13**

13   Commissural calyx nerves forking at a wide angle (*c.* 120°) at the base of the sinus; calyx teeth abruptly narrowed at the base; pedicel shorter than the calyx tube; standard 5–8 mm long; leaflets rarely emarginate, usually strongly toothed   **14**

Commissural calyx nerves usually forking at an angle of less than 90° low down the tube; calyx teeth gradually narrowing from the base; pedicel as long as calyx tube; standard 3–4 mm long; leaflets usually emarginate with numerous small teeth; ovules 2   10. *T. baccarinii*

14   Stipules entire; leaflets oval, oblong or obovate, rarely lanceolate, less than 3 times as long as wide, rarely acute; calyx glabrous or with a few hairs on the margin; ovules 2–3, rarely 4 or 5   8. *T. rueppellianum*

Stipules usually somewhat laciniate; leaflets lanceolate, acute, 3 or more times as long as wide; calyx sparsely pilose, the hairs not confined to the margin; ovules 2   9. *T. lanceolatum*

15   Peduncle 1–4 cm long bearing 1–6 flowers; leaflets oblanceolate   13. *T. multinerve*

Peduncle absent, flowers single or 2 together in leaf axils on pedicels 0–1·5 mm long; leaflets obovate   14. *T. elgonense*

16   Corolla shorter than calyx, *c.* 9 mm long; calyx teeth 6–7 mm long; flowers usually more than 20 per head   15. *T. lugardii*

Corolla longer than calyx, 7–8 mm long;

calyx teeth 2–4 mm long; flowers 10–20 per head   16. *T. steudneri*

1. Trifolium simense *Fres.* (see p. 309)

Perennial, often with thick fleshy roots, with stems more or less erect; leaflets narrowly cuneate-oblong or linear-lanceolate; inflorescence many-flowered, hemispherical or ovoid; pedicels erect in fruit; calyx tube 17–20-nerved; corolla reddish purple, or rarely, white; seeds 1–2.

Upland grassland, 6000–9000 ft. HC, HT, HM, HA, KIT.

Knight 56; Bogdan 2009.

2. Trifolium polystachyum *Fres.* (see p. 309)

Perennial, roots fibrous, stems up to 80 cm tall and 3 mm wide, often creeping and rooting at the nodes near the base; leaflets elliptic or oblanceolate, rounded or acute at the apex; inflorescence many-flowered, oblong; pedicels ascending in fruit; calyx 11-nerved; corolla purple; seeds 1–2.

Swampy grassland and forest margins, 5500–7500 ft. HC, ?HT, KIT.

Thulin and Tidigs 153; Symes 637.

3. Trifolium usambarense *Taub.*

Annual or short-lived perennial with fibrous roots; stems ascending, up to 1 m long but usually much less, about 1·5 mm wide, often rooting at the lower nodes; leaflets cuneate-oblanceolate, usually truncate or rounded at the tip; inflorescence more or less oblong, pedicels ascending in fruit; calyx 11-nerved; corolla purple, or rarely white; pod usually 2-seeded.

Marshy places and openings in forest, at the lower altitudes only by streams, 4500–8300 ft. HE, HT, HM, HL, HA, HK, KIT, KIS.

Bogdan 3786; Copley in CM 17261.

4. Trifolium cryptopodium *A. Rich.* (*T. kilimandscharicum* Taub.) (see p. 309)

Perennial, the rootstock sometimes thick and rather woody; stems creeping in their lower portions, rooting at the nodes and often forming mats; leaflets cuneate-obovate; inflorescence hemispherical, pedicels ascending in fruit; calyx 11-nerved; corolla purple; pod 1- or less often 2-seeded.

Often abundant in grassy places above the treeline, especially on rocky ground, also in moist forest openings, 6500–12 000 ft. Intermediates between this species and *T. usambarense* occur. HE, HC, HT, HM, HA, HK.

Bogdan 4968; Napper 754.

5. Trifolium cheranganiense *Gillett*

Perennial with a stout tap-root and prostrate pubescent stems; leaflets cuneate or cuneate-oblong, rounded or emarginate at the apex; inflorescence globose, pedicels reflexed in fruit; calyx pilose, 11-nerved; corolla white or pale pink; pod 1–2-seeded.

Locally abundant in upland grassland, especially where heavily grazed, 6500–9500 ft. HC.

Thulin and Tidigs 267; Thorold 2759.

6. Trifolium semipilosum *Fres.* (*'Kenya wild white Clover'*) (see p. 309)

Perennial with a strong taproot and prostrate pilose stems often rooting at the nodes; leaflets orbicular, elliptic, oblong-elliptic, ovate or cuneate-obovate, rounded truncate or emarginate at the tip, glabrous above but pilose (sometimes very sparsely so) at the margins, on the mid-ribs and usually on the lower but not the upper halves of the two lateral leaflets beneath; inflorescence more or less globose, pedicels reflexed in fruit; calyx 11-nerved; corolla white or pale pink; pod 2–5-seeded.

Often abundant in upland grassland, 4600–9000 ft. HC, HT, HM, HA, HK, KIT, KIS, NAR, RV, NAN, MAC, NBI, KAJ.

The commoner form in moister areas, (var. *glabrescens* Gillett) has cuneate obovate emarginate leaflets with a very sparse indumentum. It has often been confused with the European *T. repens* L. which has been introduced into Kenya as a pasture plant at high altitudes.

Agnew and Humphry 5567.

7. Trifolium burchellianum *Ser.* (*T. johnstonii* Oliv.) (see p. 264)

Perennial with a tap-root, stems glabrous or nearly so, creeping and rooting at the nodes, or, less often, ascending; leaflets glabrous or nearly so, mostly cuneate-obovate, cuneate-oblong, or cuneate-elliptic-emarginate, or, less often, truncate or rounded at the tip; inflorescence many-flowered, more or less globose; pedicels stout, ascending in fruit; calyx 11-nerved, the teeth triangular for 0·5 mm at the base, then subulate; corolla purple; pod 1–2-seeded.

Moist upland grassland, moist forest, or moorland openings, rare in the alpine zone, 5500–10 500 ft. HE, HC, HT, HM, HA, HK, KIS.

Bally 6473; Bogdan 4966.

8. Trifolium rueppellianum *Fres.* (*T. subrotundum* A. Rich., *T. preussii* Bak. f.) (see p. 309)

Annual with glabrous, erect, or less often, prostrate stems, not rooting at the nodes; leaflets glabrous, or nearly so, oval, oblong or obovate, rarely broadly lanceolate, less than 3 times as long as wide, rounded, usually truncate; inflorescence more or less globose, usually 15–30-flowered, (few-flowered and smaller in stunted plants at high altitudes) ascending in fruit; calyx 11-nerved, glabrous except for a few hairs at the margins; teeth abruptly narrowed near the base; corolla purple or rarely white; pod 2–3-, rarely up to 5-seeded.

Upland grassland, moorland, tracks in forest or a weed in cultivated land, usually in rather wet places, 5000–11 000 ft. HE, HC, HT, HM, HA, KIT, KIS, RV, KAJ.

Irwin 305; Mwangangi 218.

9. Trifolium lanceolatum (*Gillett*) *Gillett* (*T. rueppellianum* Fres. var. *lanceolatum* Gillett)

A more or less erect annual resembling *T. rueppellianum* except for the usually toothed stipules, the lanceolate very acute leaflets with prominent whitish nerves and well marked teeth, and the pilose calyx; corolla purple about 5 mm long; pod 1–2-seeded.

Upland grassland and a weed in cultivation, 7300–8500 ft. HM, HA.

Bogdan 3178; Albrechtsen 2749.

10. Trifolium baccarinii *Chiov.* (see p. 309)

Annual, stems often prostrate, sometimes rooting at the nodes; easily confused with *T. rueppellianum* but the leaflets, which are elliptic or obovate, are usually emarginate, the calyx tapers to the base, and has commissural nerves which fork low down, well below the margin, and gradually tapering teeth; corolla purple, 3–4 mm long; pod 1–2-seeded.

Heavily grazed grassland, 5000–5500 ft. MUM, KIS.

Bogdan 4546; Drummond and Hemsley 4749.

11. Trifolium tembense *Fres.* (*T. umbellulatum* A. Rich. *T. goetzenii* Engl.)

Glabrous or subglabrous annual or short-lived perennial, sometimes rooting at the nodes when growing in water; leaflets elliptic or obovate, acute, rounded truncate or slightly emarginate at the apex, the teeth well developed; inflorescence hemispherical 3–16-flowered; pedicels ascending in fruit; calyx sparsely pilose at the margins only, broadly campanulate, strongly 11-nerved, the teeth gradually narrowing from the base; corolla purple about 9 mm long, the standard abruptly narrowed above the middle into an oblong truncate down-curved tip; pod usually 4–6-seeded.

Wet places in upland grassland, forest or moorland openings and in the alpine zone, 6000–11 500 ft. HE, HT, HA, HK, KIT, KIS.

Symes 163; Knight 55.

12. Trifolium acaule *A. Rich.*

Perennial with a tap-root and close-pressed prostrate branches rooting at the nodes; leaflets cuneate-obovate, slightly toothed; inflorescence 1-5-flowered; calyx 11-nerved, with triangular teeth; corolla mauve, about 8 mm long; pod 1-4-seeded.

Locally abundant, in short grass and rock crannies in the alpine zone, 10 000-12 000 ft. HE.

Gillett 18478; Knight 50.

13. Trifolium multinerve *A. Rich.* (see p. 309)

Annual or short-lived perennial, stems erect and up to 20 cm tall, if procumbent not rooting at the nodes; leaflets oblanceolate, acute, or rarely rounded at the tip; inflorescence pedunculate 1-6-flowered; pedicel erect; calyx-tube 3-4 mm long, 15-30-nerved, rather inflated in fruit but splitting dorsally, the teeth triangular-subulate, about as long as the tube; corolla purple, 7-8 mm long; pod up to 9-seeded.

Short upland grassland and moorland, especially in wet places, 5500-11 000 ft. HE, HC, HT, HM, HK.

Gillett 18407; Thulin and Tidigs 83.

14. Trifolium elgonense *Gillett*

Differs from *T. multinerve* in the shorter cuneate-obcordate leaflets, the peduncle under 1 mm long so that the flowers are sessile in the leaf axils, and the calyx teeth 2-2·5 mm long, shorter than the tube which is inflated in fruit and seems not to split dorsally.

Wet open places in the upper forest, moorland, and alpine zones, 8300-10 500 ft. HE.

Gillett 18409; Bogdan 5392.

15. Trifolium lugardii *Bullock* (see p. 309)

Erect sub-glabrous annual up to 60 cm tall; leaflets lanceolate or narrowly oblong, rounded or acute at the tip; inflorescence subglobose, about 30-flowered, outer bracts forming an involucre; calyx-tube about 30-veined, inflated and splitting irregularly in fruit, the teeth narrowly triangular, subulate at the tip, exceeding the purple corolla; pod 4-seeded.

Upland grassland and forest margins, especially in damp places, 5500-7750 ft. HE, KIT.

Irwin 307; Tweedie 81.

16. Trifolium steudneri *Schweinf.* (see p. 264)

Annual herb, differing from *T. lugardii* in the pedicels under 1 mm long and the calyx with triangular teeth shorter than the corolla.

Upland grassland, especially in damp places, 5500-7500 ft. HE, HA, KIT, RV.

Bogdan 3222; Hedberg 37.

42. PAROCHETUS *D. Don*

Monotypic, distinguished from *Trifolium* by the stipules almost free from the petiole, the long pedicels, the caducous corolla and the slightly inflated 10-15-seeded pod, 3-4 times as long as the calyx.

Parochetus communis *D. Don*

Prostrate, glabrous or sparsely pilose herb, rooting at the nodes; leaves digitately trifoliolate on long petioles; stipules oval, acute, scarious, leaflets cuneate-obovate, entire, crenate or 'coarsely toothed; inflorescence a (1-)2(-4)-flowered umbel; bracts brown, scarious, 2-4 mm long; calyx 6-7 mm long, divided to the middle into ovate acute unequal teeth, the upper pair united almost to the tip; corolla glabrous, bright blue, up to 17 mm long; pod glabrous, on deflexed pedicels, thin-walled with numerous fine branching transverse veins, usually not dehiscing until forced open by the germinating seeds.

Forests, especially in moist places, and forest clearings usually on soils of volcanic origin, 6500-10 250 ft. Cleistogamous flowers have been reported for this species in the Himalayas, but seem not yet to have been observed in Kenya. HM, HA, HK, HN, KAJ (Chyulu Hills).

Kerfoot 455; Verdcourt 3265.

43. MELILOTUS *Mill.*

Annual or biennial, more or less fragrant herbs; leaves pinnately trifoliolate; stipules adnate to the petiole; stipels absent; leaflets toothed; flowers small, yellow or white, in elongated spike-like axillary racemes; corolla caducous, glabrous, free from the stamens; pod small, 1-2-, or rarely, 3-4-seeded.

Introduced into East Africa.

1   Style 0·9-1·2 mm long; stipules sometimes
        denticulate at the base   1. *M. indica*
     Style 1·7-2·3 mm long; stipules entire   2
2   Pod strongly transverse-veined, the veins
        rugose; corolla yellow   2. *M. officinalis*
     Pod with a weak irregular vein-network;
        corolla white   3. *M. alba*

M. suaveolens Ledeb., resembling *M. alba* but with yellow flowers, has become common locally in the Serengeti plains (Tanzania) and may be expected from the Kenya side of the border.

1. Melilotus indica (*L.*) *All.*

Weed in cultivated areas, 6000 ft. KIT.

Newton 1144 and EAH253/55.

2. Melilotus officinalis (*L.*) *Pall.*

Weed in cultivated areas, 6500 ft. HA.

Kulkarni in EAH 14116.

3. Melilotus alba *Desr.*

Grassland and abandoned fields, 5000–6000 ft.
KIS, RV.

Bally 6205; Bush in EAH 391/63.

44. MEDICAGO *L.*

Herbs; leaves pinnately trifoliolate; stipules adnate
to the petiole, toothed or laciniate; stipels absent;
leaflets toothed; inflorescence a short, condensed,
often subglobose, pedunculate axillary raceme;
pedicels and bracts short; calyx short with 5
subequal teeth; corolla under 1 cm long, caducous,
glabrous, yellow or, less often, purplish-blue; pod
longer than the calyx, bent through a circle, or
through several spiral coils.

1   Pod 1-seeded, of 1 turn only, without spines;
    racemes 5–20-flowered; leaflets less than
    twice as long as wide; stipules with short
    broad teeth   1. *M. lupulina*
    Pod *c.* 5-seeded, of 3 or 4 turns, with hooked
    spines; racemes 1–2-flowered; leaflets usu-
    ally more than twice as long as wide;
    stipules laciniate   2. *M. laciniata*

M. sativa L., Lucerne or Alfalfa, an erect herb
with blue-purple flowers is commonly grown for
fodder. Several other species have been grown
experimentally.

1. Medicago lupulina *L.*

A more or less pubescent prostrate or ascending
yellow-flowered annual or short-lived perennial.

Probably not native, a weed in cultivation and
in lawns; 6000–6500 ft. HA, RV, NBI.

Bally 1433; Roberts in EAH 181/55.

2. Medicago laciniata (*L.*) *Mill.*

Spreading subglabrous, or sparsely pilose, yellow-
flowered annual. Very likely native in short grassland, especially where seasonally waterlogged,
5000–7650 ft. RV, NAN, MAC, NBI, KAJ.

Gillett 18336; Agnew and Musumba 5334.

45. LOTUS *L.*

Herbs (in our area perennial) or softly woody
subshrubs; leaves imparipinnate, the petiole absent
or very short; leaflets (in our area) 5, the basal pair
usually different in shape from the others and
resembling foliaceous stipules; stipels absent;
inflorescence an axillary or terminal, usually
pedunculate, umbel subtended by a 1–3-foliolate
leafy bract; corolla glabrous, in our species not over
10 mm long; dorsal stamen free; 5 of the 9 united
stamens longer than the others, their filaments
dilated at the tip; pod narrow, subcylindrical,
dehiscing into 2 twisted valves, usually septate

within, in our area glabrous, straight, up to 3 cm
long, 5–25-seeded.

In the following account the 'basal angle' of a
leaflet is that formed between its two edges as
they converge.

1   Peduncle, like the rest of the plant, glabrous,
    or almost so; corolla bright yellow often
    marked with red; umbels 1–2- or rarely
    3-flowered; free parts of shorter filaments
    half as long as those of longer filaments
                                 1. *L. corniculatus*
    Peduncle pubescent; corolla white, cream, or
    pale yellow, marked with pink or crimson;
    umbels 1–8-flowered; free parts of shorter
    filaments more than half as long as those
    of longer filaments   2
2   Leaf rachis 4–7 mm long, more than half as
    long as the basal leaflets which are almost
    as broad as long, usually have a basal angle
    of over 100°, often of nearly 180°, and are
    glabrous or with a few spreading hairs at
    the margins only   2. *L. becquetii*
    Leaf-rachis usually under 4 mm long, less
    than half as long as the basal leaflets which
    are usually much longer than broad, have a
    basal angle of less than 100° and are
    pubescent, at least on the lower surface   3
3   Some of the hairs on most parts of the plant
    usually laxly spreading and up to 1 mm
    long; basal leaflets less than twice as long
    as wide, much less narrowed at the base
    than the 3 terminal leaflets which are
    rarely more than 2·5 times as long as wide
                                     3. *L. goetzei*
    Hairs all appressed, about 0·5 mm long; basal
    leaflets often more than twice as long as
    wide, narrowly wedge-shaped at the base
    like the terminal leaflets which are often 3
    times as long as wide   4. *L. discolor*

1. Lotus corniculatus *L.* (*L. mearnsii* De Wild. non
Britton; *L. friesiorum* Harms)

Glabrous, or almost so; stems weak, slender; leaflets drying a pale yellowish-green without red
flecks, the basal pair distinctly broader at the base
than the others, with a basal angle usually exceeding 100°.

Grassland, especially where seasonally wet,
6000–8000 ft, and common around Lake Naivasha
HA, RV.

Verdcourt 3677; Bogdan 3221.

2. Lotus becquetii *Boutique* ('*L.* sp. near *tigrensis*'
in Jex-Blake 'Some wild flowers of Kenya') (see
p. 264)

Stems slender, weak, straggling; drying a pale
yellowish-green without red flecks.

Grassland and rocky hillsides, 6000–8500 ft. HE, HC, HA, RV.

Thulin and Tidigs 191; Gardner 2014.

3. Lotus goetzei *Harms* (*L. tigrensis* sensu Bak. f. pp. non Bak. *L. oehleri* Harms) (see p. 264)

Stems spreading or ascending or often erect and bushy, stouter than in the other species, up to 3 mm in diameter, drying dark green with numerous reddish flecks which darken with age.

Grassland, open bushland and forest margins, especially on recent volcanic soils, 5250–8250 ft. HE, HM, HA, RV, NAN, NBI.

Verdcourt 694; Greenway 5994.

4. Lotus discolor *E. Mey.* (*L. tigrensis* Bak.)

Dries a less dark green than *L. goetzei*, the leaflets are paler below than above and usually have sparse or numerous reddish flecks which are hardly apparent at first but darken with age.

Fire-swept grassland with scattered *Erythrina*, 5200–6000 ft. KAJ (Chyulu Hills).

Bally 8249; Gillett 18852.

46. ANTOPETITIA *A. Rich.*

Monotypic, distinguished by the remarkable fruits.

Antopetitia abyssinica *A. Rich.* (see p. 262)

Spreading or erect tap-rooted annual, or short-lived perennial, 20–120 cm tall; leaves imparipinnate; stipules reduced to glands, petiole very short or nil; leaflets 5–11, alternate or sub-opposite, linear-lanceolate; inflorescence an axillary pedunculate 2–8-flowered umbel, usually with a foliaceous bract half way up the peduncle, or above; floral bracts and bracteoles minute, caducous; receptacle obconical, calyx teeth acute, subequal, 2–3 mm long; corolla glabrous, yellow or orange, about 4 mm long; style under 1 mm long; pod glabrous, shortly stipitate, curved, 2–5-seeded, up to 1 cm long, composed of spherical 1-seeded segments each splitting into two valves which separate from the persistent upper suture.

Upland grassland, moorland, and open bushland, 5100–10 500 ft. HE, HC, HT, HM, HA, KIT, RV, MAC, NBI, KAJ (Chyulu Hills).

Mwangangi 386; Bogdan 19194.

47. GALEGA *L.*

Erect or ascending herbs; leaves imparipinnate; stipules usually divided, one lobe pointing downwards; leaflets entire; stipels absent; flowers in dense pedunculate racemes; bracts narrow, rather persistent; calyx campanulate with equal subulate-tipped teeth; corolla glabrous, blue; filaments rather persistent, united into a tube; pod ascending, 2–5-seeded, unilocular, dehiscent, not inflated, the sutures not impressed, elliptic or rhombic-lanceolate, curved away from the rhachis near the tip, with a close network of prominent parallel veins sloping upwards towards the style-base.

1 Leaflets up to 20 mm long and 6 mm wide; hairs on the inflorescence-rachis long, weak, not glandular; standard 6 mm long; pod up to 25 mm long   1. *G. lindblomii*
   Leaflets up to 45 mm long and 20 mm wide; hairs on the inflorescence-rachis short, stiff, erect, gland-tipped; standard 9–13 mm long; pod up to 35 mm long
                                        2. *G. battiscombei*

1. Galega lindblomii (*Harms*) *Gillett* (*Astragalus somalensis* Harms var. *lindblomii* Harms; *A. tridens* Jex-Blake (name invalidly published)) (see p. 315)

Annual or short-lived erect perennial up to 1·5 m tall. Mountain grassland, forest margins and bamboo thickets 6500–7000 ft. HE, HC.

Lugard 2900; Gillett 18423.

2. Galega battiscombei (*Bak. f.*) *Gillett* (*Astragalus battiscombei* Bak. f.)

More luxuriant than *G. lindblomii* with weak sprawling stems up to 2 m long. Damp places in forests and at forest margins, 6000–7250 ft. HK.

Battiscombe 709; Rendle 640.

48. ASTRAGALUS *L.*

Herbs (or subshrubs), leaves imparipinnate; stipules entire, rather persistent, often large; flowers in axillary racemes; calyx tubular (or inflated); corolla nearly always glabrous; dorsal filament free; style filiform, glabrous; stigma small, terminal; pod often inflated but hardly so in our species, more or less completely divided into two compartments by a double membrane arising from the lower (abaxial) suture, which is normally impressed (but hardly so in our species); seeds small, kidney shaped, with threadlike funicles.

Astragalus atropilosulus (*Hochst.*) *Bunge* (*A. abyssinicus* A. Rich.; *A. venosus* A. Rich.; *A. bequaertii* De Wild.; *A. elgonensis* Bullock; *A. burkeanus* Harv.) (see p. 315)

Perennial, or perhaps sometimes biennial, subglabrous or pubescent herb up to 1·5 m tall; leaves up to 25 cm long with 11–51 leaflets; stipels absent stipules foliaceous, persistent, cordate at one side at the base, often larger than a leaflet; racemes pedunculate, many-flowered, the pedicels deflexed in fruit; corolla (in our area) purplish and greenish at the base; pod stipitate, lanceolate, with 4–8 seeds in each compartment, up to 4 cm long, up to 7 mm wide (including the stipe).

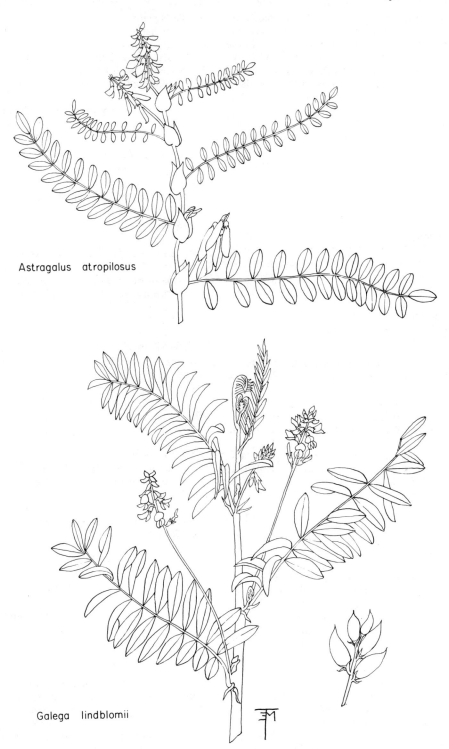

Astragalus   atropilosus

Galega   lindblomii

Grassland, open bushland, forest margins, rarely in moorland, 5300-12 500 ft. A very variable species with several subspecies and varieties in the highlands from Eritrea to the Transvaal. In Kenya the main distinction is between subsp. *bequaertii* (De Wild.) Gillett in the west and on the Aberdares with pods less than 4·5 times as long as wide, whose stipe is usually under 3 mm long, and subsp. *burkeanus* (Harv.) Gillett in central and southern Kenya with pods more than 5 times as long as wide, whose stipe is over 3 mm long. HE, HC, HT, HM, HA, HK, KIT, MUM, NAR, RV, MAC, NBI, KAJ.

Glover *et al.* 249; Gillett 16748.

49. COLUTEA *L.*

Softly woody shrubs; leaves imparipinnate, stipules small; flowers few together in axillary racemes; calyx with 5 subequal teeth much shorter than the tube; corolla over 1 cm long, glabrous, yellow, reddish or brown; style thick, bearded inside near the top and incurved at the tip; pod stipitate, inflated, many-seeded, splitting at the tip only or indehiscent; seeds small with long funicles.

Colutea abyssinica *Kunth & Bouché* (*C. haleppica* Auct. non Lam.; *C. istria* Auct. non Mill.) (see p. 274)
Leaflets 9-15; racemes 2-3-flowered; corolla chocolate-coloured, yellowish at the base, 13-15 mm long; pod papery, 3-8 cm long, including the 5-22 mm long stipe.

Montane grassland, evergreen bushland, and forest margins, 6000-8500 ft. HE, HT, HM, HA, HK, KIT, RV, KAJ.

Lugard 271; Gardner 1466.

50. VICIA *L.*

Annual or perennial climbing (rarely erect) herbs with pinnate leaves usually ending in a tendril; stipules often sagittate; stipels absent; inflorescence axillary, racemose; bracts small; bracteoles absent; calyx 5-lobed, with the tube often oblique; corolla blue, purple or yellow; stamens (10) or (9) + 1; anthers uniform; ovary 2-many-ovuled; style usually hairy, rarely glabrous; pods oblong to linear, compressed.

1 Flowers solitary or few, subsessile in the upper leaf axils   *1. V. sativa*
  Flowers in pedunculate racemes, or, if solitary, then on long peduncles   2
2 Pods about 1 cm long; flowers solitary
                                        2. V. hirsuta
  Pods much longer than 1 cm; flowers in racemes   3

3 Pods glabrous   4
  Pods hairy   5
4 Leaflets in 4-12 pairs   *3. V. villosa*
  Leaflets in 2-3 pairs   *4. V. paucifolia*
5 Racemes as long as or shorter than the subtending leaves; plant densely pubescent
                                      5. V. benghalensis
  Racemes mostly longer than the leaves; plant glabrescent   *3. V. villosa*

1. Vicia sativa *L.* (see p. 317)
A trailing herb with 5-8 pairs of linear leaflets to each leaf and solitary blue flowers.
    Locally common in highland grassland. HE, HC, HM, HA, KIT, RV.
    Bogdan 1983.

2. Vicia hirsuta (*L.*) *S. F. Gray* (see p. 317)
Similar to *V. sativa* but a smaller plant with smaller paler flowers on long peduncles.
    Uncommon plant found in highland grassland. HE, HT, HM, HA.
    Irwin 204.

3. Vicia villosa *Roth*
A pubescent climber with 4-12 pairs of linear leaflets to each leaf and long racemes of bright purple and blue flowers.
    A local escape from upland cultivation. HC, HM.
    Bogdan 3188.

4. Vicia paucifolia *Bak.*
A hairy climber with up to 3 pairs of linear leaflets to each leaf and long pedunculate racemes of pale blue flowers.
    An indigenous species of upland grassland and forest edges. HE, HT, HM, HA, KIT.
    Kerfoot 4711.

5. Vicia benghalensis *L.*
A pubescent climber with 7-12 pairs of elliptic leaflets to each leaf and axillary racemes of purplish flowers.
    An escape from cultivation in upland grassland. HM, HA.
    Bogdan 5015.

51. LATHYRUS *L.*
Annual or perennial herbs with equal-pinnate leaves, usually terminating in a tendril; leaflets 1-few pairs, mostly parallel-veined; stipels absent; flowers solitary or in axillary racemes, bracts small; bracteoles absent; calyx ± equally 5-lobed; stamens (10) or (9) + 1; anthers uniform; ovary few- to many-ovuled; style incurved, often flat and widened

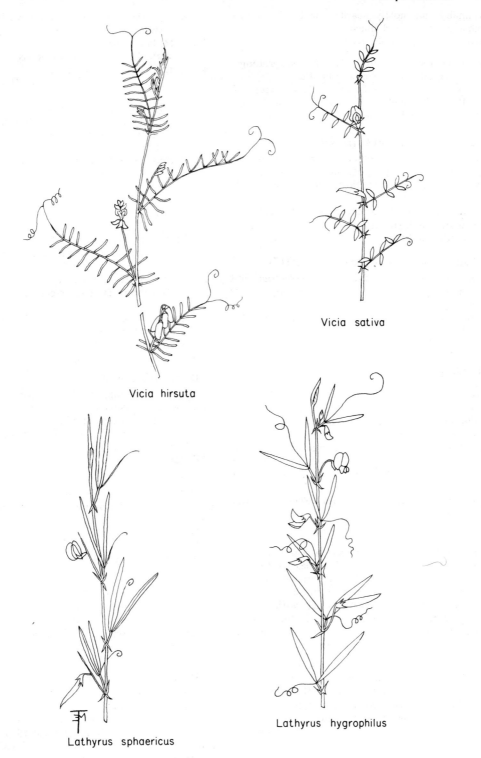

Vicia sativa

Vicia hirsuta

Lathyrus sphaericus

Lathyrus hygrophilus

terminally and mostly bearded on the inner side; stigma capitate; pod linear-oblong, cylindrical or compressed; seeds globose or angular.

1   Racemes 1-flowered, the rachis prolonged beyond the flower as a bristle
                        1. *L. sphaericus*
      Racemes usually 2-flowered, the rachis not prolonged in a bristle   2. *L. hygrophilus*

1. Lathyrus sphaericus *Retz.* (see p. 317)

A glabrescent rhizomatous herb with a few ascending stems and one pair of linear leaflets on each tendrillar leaf; flower solitary, pedunculate, red or pink.

Uncommon plant found in western Kenya in upland grassland. HE, HM.

Tweedie 2050.

2. Lathyrus hygrophilus *Taub.* (see p. 317)

A trailing climber very similar to *L. sphaericus* but with more elliptic leaves and white, cream or very pale blue flowers.

Locally common, in swampy grassland. HC, HT, HA, HK, KIT, KIS.

Napier 710.

58. MORACEAE†

Trees, shrubs or herbs with opposite or alternate, stipulate leaves and with a milky juice; flowers sessile, in spikes or heads, unisexual; male flowers with 1–4 perianth segments and stamens; female flowers with 2–4 perianth segments, and a superior ovary; stigmas 1–2; ovules 1, pendulous; fruit dry or thinly fleshy but often held within a fleshy perianth or receptacle.

All Kenya genera are trees except the one following.

1. DORSTENIA *L.*

Herbs with alternate or opposite stipulate leaves and axillary flat capitula of unisexual flowers; male flowers with a 2–3-lobed perianth and 1–3 stamens; female flowers in deep pits in the receptacle, the ovary completely buried with a single lateral stigma projecting through the 2-lobed perianth; fruit a 1-seeded drupe or achene, ejected from or retained within the receptacle.

1   Leaves borne at intervals along the stem   2
      Leaves in a dense terminal tuft or in a rosette or plants leafless at time of flowering   7
2   Receptacle toothed at margins, the teeth over 8 in number and all ± equal
                        3. *D. brownii*

† By A. D. Q. Agnew.

Receptacle with horns, with or without teeth between them   3
3   Receptacle with only 2 horns   4
      Receptacle with 3 or more horns   5
4   Margin of receptacle entire
                        1. *D. scaphigera*

      Margin of receptacle dentate
                        2. *D. afromontana*
5   Receptacle triangular with 3–4 major horns and smaller teeth between them   6
      Receptacle orbicular in outline with 5 or more major filamentous horns
                        4. *D. denticulata*
6   Leaves dentate; fertile part of receptacle over 1 cm in diameter when ripe
                        5. *D. zanzibarica*
      Leaves crenate or entire; fertile part of receptacle under 1 cm in diameter when ripe
                        6. *D. schlechteri*
7   Leaves ovate to orbicular, often appearing after the receptacles; stem buried, tuberous
                        7. *D. barnimiana*
      Leaves lanceolate to narrow-elliptic, appearing with the receptacles; stems at ground level or above, fleshy   8. *D. foetida*

1. Dorstenia scaphigera *Bur.*

A trailing, ascending, ± scabrid herb or weak shrub with ovate to oblanceolate, entire or coarsely toothed and often variegated leaves.

Rare plant found in riverine forest and recently found at Thika. HK, MAC.

Faden 66242.

2. Dorstenia afromontana *R. E. Fr.*

Similar to *D. scaphigera* but weaker and with ovate leaves.

Only known from wet forests on the Aberdares at 7000 ft. HA.

R. and Th. Fries 1434.

3. Dorstenia brownii *Rendle*

A pubescent ascending herb with elliptic, entire or crenate leaves and small pubescent heads.

Recently discovered in Kakamega forest. MUM.

Faden 69980.

4. Dorstenia denticulata *Peter* (see p. 319)

An erect or ascending, glabrous or pubescent herb with obovate to elliptic, dentate leaves; receptacles pedunculate, with a fringe of long processes.

Our commonest *Dorstenia* found in riverine forest in many areas. HC, HT, NAR, MAC, NBI.

Drummond and Hemsley 1227; Napier 1915.

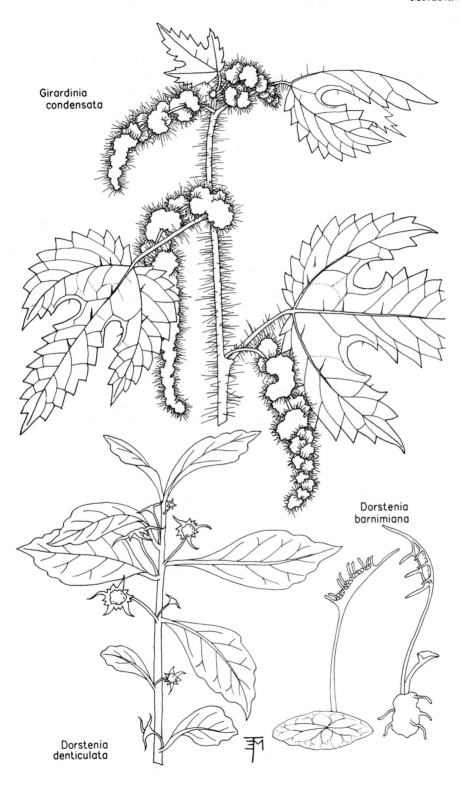

Girardinia
condensata

Dorstenia
barnimiana

Dorstenia
denticulata

5. Dorstenia zanzibarica *Oliv.*

A trailing pubescent herb with ascending stems and elliptic, weakly dentate leaves; receptacles triangular, on short peduncles.

Recorded only from forest in the Chyulu Hills. KAJ.

van Someren 377.

6. Dorstenia schlechteri *Engl.*

A glabrous or minutely pubescent herb with ovate-elliptic leaves and small heads bearing 3–4 horns.

Another recently discovered species of Kakamega forest. MUM.

Faden 692110.

7. Dorstenia barnimiana *Schweinf.* (see p. 319)

A small herb from an underground tuber, with ovate or orbicular, often peltate, leaves; receptacles elongated, with 3 major processes, and often with minor teeth between them.

Locally common in stony upland grassland. Plants from western Kenya have peltate leaves, but those from the Ngong Hills never do. HE, HC, HT, HA, KIT, MUM, MAC.

Napier 6264; Symes 627.

8. Dorstenia foetida (*Forsk.*) *Schweinf.*

An erect glabrescent herb with a thick fleshy stem bearing crowded leaf scars and a terminal rosette of linear to oblanceolate leaves; receptacles pedunculate, orbicular with *c.* 5 long processes.

Rare plant found in dry rocky grassland. MAC.

Verdcourt 3880.

59. URTICACEAE

Mostly herbs (some trees) with well-developed phloem fibres and coarse, often stinging, hairs; leaves usually simple, stipulate; flowers usually in cymes, unisexual (rarely bisexual), without petals; male flower with similar stamen number to the fused or free sepal lobes; female flower with 1–4 sepals, sometimes sheathing the ovary; ovary with a single stigma and one basal ovule.

A well-defined small family, with one tree, *Obetia pinnatifida* Baker in Kenya. Most have crystalline inclusions in their leaves called cystoliths, which may be rod-shaped or spherical, and appear linear or punctate superficially. Useful fibres are obtained from the phloem, and the leaves are frequently used as a vegetable.

1	Leaves alternate	2
	Leaves opposite	11
2	Inflorescences sessile; flowers crowded at nodes	3
	Inflorescences pedunculate	7
3	Leaves asymmetric, held in one plane opposite each other at alternate nodes	
		7. *Elatostema orientale*
	Leaves usually symmetric, spirally arranged all around the stem	4
4	Perennial plant with woody stems, often trailing	9. *Pouzolzia parasitica*
	Annuals or short-lived perennials without woody stems	5
5	Leaves serrate, stipulate; plant trailing or upright	6
	Leaves entire, without stipules; plant trailing	
		10. *Parietaria debilis*
6	Leaves acuminate; flowers subsessile, not held within a bract	12. *Australina acuminata*
	Leaves acute, hardly acuminate; flowers sessile, held within a tubular sheathing bract	11. *Droguetia debilis*
7	Woody shrubs or climbers with no stinging hairs	8
	Herbs, occasionally becoming woody at base, mostly with stinging hairs	9
8	Forest climber (sometimes also trailing over rocks) with a paniculate, loose inflorescence	2. *Urera*
	Forest shrub with flowers in a long interrupted spike of clusters	
		8. *Boehmeria platyphylla*
9	Leaves lobed and/or bullate	5. *Girardinia*
	Leaves entire, surface smooth	10
10	Cystoliths linear, usually lying along the nerves; female flowers on simple, unwinged pedicels	4. *Fleurya*
	Cystoliths dot-like, between the nerves; female flowers on winged pedicels	
		3. *Laportea alatipes*
11	Plant with stinging hairs	1. *Urtica massaica*
	Plant without stinging hairs	12
12	Flowers in pedunculate inflorescences or clustered at nodes; male flowers with 4 stamens and sepals	13
	Flowers always clustered at nodes; male flowers with 1 stamen and tubular, simple perianth	14
13	Flowers in separate, distant clusters along an unbranched spike 8. *Boehmeria platyphylla*	
	Flowers in sessile clusters, or in one pedunculate cluster	6. *Pilea*
14	Inflorescence of small heads, held in undivided involucres	11. *Droguetia iners*
	Inflorescence of pedicellate flowers, not in a head, not surrounded by an involucre	
		12. *Australina flaccida*

1. URTICA *L.*

Erect herbs with opposite simple leaves and stinging hairs; stipules free or connate; flowers monoecious or dioecious in spikes, racemes or panicles; male flower with 4 sepals and stamens; female flower with 4 unequal sepals; achene compressed, enclosed by the two largest sepals.

Urtica massaica *Mildbr.* (see p. 322)

A dioecious erect herb to 2 m, with ovate leaves; inflorescence of axillary groups of spike-like unbranched racemes.

A very irritating plant, often growing in abandoned tracks in the montane forest areas, and particularly associated, in the author's opinion, with the presence of buffaloes. HE, HM, HA, HK, HN, KIT, RV.

Agnew 7265; Mwangangi 74.

2. URERA *Gaud.*

Woody dioecious climbers or shrubs, often (not ours) with stinging hairs, and with alternate, simple, stipulate leaves; flowers in loose cymose panicles; male flower with 4–5 sepals and petals; female flowers with 2 large and 2 small sepals, becoming red and fleshy in fruit, and flattened ovary with a short capitate pubescent stigma.

1 Leaves with 4–6 lateral nerves on each side of the midrib, frequently hairy
1. *U. hypselodendra*
Leaves with not more than 3 lateral nerves on each side of the midrib, glabrous
2. *U. cameroonensis*

1. Urera hypselodendra *Wedd.* (see p. 322)

Heavy woody climber (or trailing over rocks) with ovate to elliptic serrate, pubescent, acuminate leaves with 4–6 major nerves on each side of the midrib; fruits becoming bright red-orange.

Conspicuous when in fruit, this abundant climber is seldom noticed, but is to be found in all wetter montane forest. HE, HM, HA, HK, KIT, MAC, KAJ.

Kerfoot 4691; Agnew 8153.

2. Urera cameroonensis *Wedd.*

Similar to *U. hypselodendra* except for the glabrous leaves which have the basal pair of lateral nerves dominant.

In western Kenya forest, but not, apparently, Kakamega forest. MUM.

Birch 61/201.

3. LAPORTEA *Gaud.*

Erect perennial stinging herbs with alternate, simple leaves and punctate cystoliths; stipules united; flowers monoecious (in ours) or dioecious, in branching, ultimately cymose inflorescences; male flower with 4–5 sepals and stamens; female flower with 4 unequal sepals; achene compressed.

Laportea alatipes *Hook. f.*

Erect herbs with stinging hairs and broad ovate leaves; inflorescences much branched, often exceeding the leaves, the lower male, the upper female; female flowers suspended from horizontal, broadly green-winged pedicels.

Common in disturbed ground in wet montane forest. HM, HA, HK, MUM, KIS, MAC, KAJ.

Lind, Agnew, and Beecher 5481; Kerfoot 3883.

4. FLEURYA *Gaud.*

Annual herbs with or without stinging hairs; cystoliths linear; leaves alternate, simple, with fused stipules; flowers monoecious, in pedunculate panicles or interrupted spikes or cymes; male flower with 4–5 fused sepals and stamens; female flower with 4 sepals; achene compressed.

1 Inflorescence filiform, spike-like, unbranched with glomeruli at intervals
1. *F. interrupta*
Inflorescence branched or the flowers in 1–2 masses
2
2 Inflorescence bisexual, branching
2. *F. aestuans*
Inflorescence unisexual, the flowers usually condensed into masses
3. *F. ovalifolia*

1. Fleurya interrupta *Gaud.*

Erect annual with orbicular-ovate acuminate leaves; inflorescences long, filiform, exceeding the leaves, with glomeruli at intervals.

Rare, and only found once, in Nyeri district, in our area. HA.

Kibui K53.

2. Fleurya aestuans (*L.*) *Mig.*

Erect annual without stinging hairs, and with ovate to suborbicular leaves; inflorescences much branched, often exceeding the leaves.

Rare plant found in lowland eastern Kenya in *Commiphora* woodland after good rains. KAJ.

Agnew 9884.

3. Fleurya ovalifolia (*Schum.*) *Dandy*

An erect, weakly stinging herb with broadly ovate leaves; male inflorescences with flowers crowded into masses, rarely branched; female inflorescences above the male, branched.

Uncommon plant found in western Kenya, rarer in the east. HK, MUM, KIS, MAC.

Jarrett MAK/5; Agnew and Musumba 8557.

5. GIRARDINIA *Gaud.*

Erect herbs, densely covered with large stinging hairs, and with alternate leaves; stipules connate, caducous; flowers dioecious or monoecious in

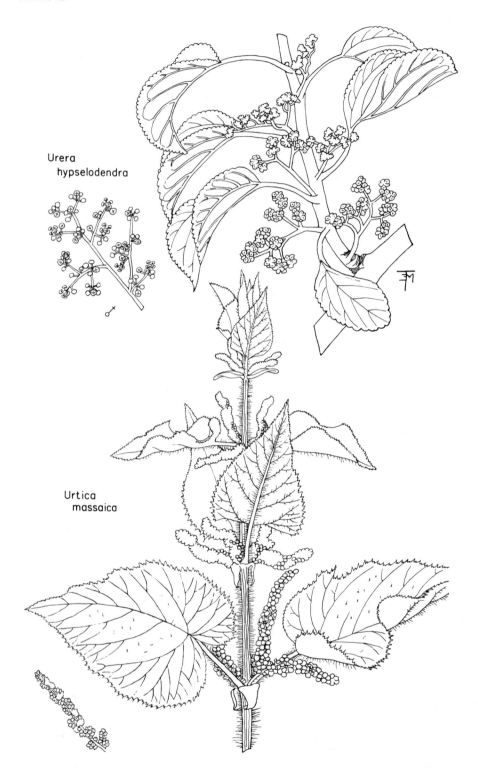

Urera
hypselodendra

Urtica
massaica

dense spike-like inflorescences; male flower with 4-5 sepals and stamens; female flower with a perianth in 2 parts, the posterior part large and enclosing the ovary, the anterior filamentous; achenes compressed.

1   Leaves shallowly acutely lobed (twice dentate) with bullate surface
                             1. *G. bullosa*
    Leaves deeply lobed and denticulate, with a smooth surface   2. *G. condensata*

1. Girardinia bullosa *Wedd.*

A tall, single-stemmed, stinging herb to 2·5 m with large suborbicular leaves; inflorescences to 10 cm long, axillary, often unisexual.

Occasionally found in streamside marshes in wet montane forest. HA, HK.

Agnew 8778; Mathenge 212.

2. Girardinia condensata *Wedd.* (see p. 319)

Similar to the last species but much smaller (seldom more than 75 cm tall) and with deeply lobed leaves.

The commonest stinging-nettle in many places in the wet forest zone, growing in disturbed places and pathsides. HE, HA, HK, RV, KAJ.

Glover 3708; Agnew 7692.

6. PILEA *Lindl.*

Herbs without stinging hairs, often with fleshy stems, with simple, opposite leaves; stipules fused, intrapetiolarly; flowers monoecious or dioecious, often in globose heads; male flower with 3-4 sepals and stamens, the sepals horned; female flower with 3 sepals; achene compressed.

1   Stipules broad, scarious, blunt, persistent   3
    Stipules obsolete, not scarious, or caducous 2
2   Leaves elliptic, with a cuneate base
                         1. *P. usambarensis*
    Leaves ovate, with a rounded base
                         2. *P. veronicifolia*
3   Inflorescences all held at the level of the terminal leaf rosette   3. *P. tetraphylla*
    Inflorescences below the terminal leaf rosette
                                4
4   Inflorescences pedunculate, globose
                         4. *P. johnstonii*
    Inflorescences sessile, often forming an apparent whorl round the nodes
                       5. *P. ceratomera*

1. Pilea usambarensis *Engl.*

Herb with erect fleshy stems from prostrate older stems, with elliptic leaves and pedunculate heads of flowers; peduncles longer than petioles.

Uncommon plants found in clearings in montane rain forest and bamboo. HA.

Agnew 7164.

2. Pilea veronicifolia *Engl.*

Similar to *P. usambarensis* but with ovate leaves, mostly rounded at base.

Common on the forest floor of wet montane forest in the Aberdares and on Mt. Kenya. HA, HK.

Kabuye 80; Agnew and Faden 9982.

3. Pilea tetraphylla *Blume*

A small erect annual with almost triangular leaves, the inflorescences lying within the terminal rosette, horizontally orientated.

Uncommon plant found in montane forest pathsides and riversides. HA, HK, KIT.

Agnew and Coe 8784; Archer 112.

4. Pilea johnstonii *Oliv.* (see p. 324)

Herb with erect fleshy stems from prostrate older ones, and ovate, acuminate, coarsely serrate leaves; stipules broad, brown, scarious; inflorescences of 1-several globose clusters on long, simple or few-branched peduncles.

The commonest *Pilea* in Kenya, occurring particularly by disturbed streamsides in forest. HE, HC, HT, HM, HA, HK, MUM, KAJ.

Tweedie 66/202; Napier 3152.

5. Pilea ceratomera *Wedd.*

Similar to *P. johnstonii* but often smaller and occasionally decumbent, and with sessile clusters of flowers, without a common peduncle, at the nodes.

Uncommon plant found in montane forest streamsides and pathsides. HC, HT, HM, HA, HK, KAJ.

Irwin 378A; Agnew 9004.

7. ELATOSTEMA *Forst*

Herbs with linear cystoliths; leaves simple, opposite or alternate by the abortion of one of an unequal pair (as in ours); flowers held in dense bracteate heads, monoecious or dioecious; male flowers with 4-5 sepals and stamens; female flowers with 3-5 perianth segments, not adhering in fruit.

Elatostema orientale *Engl.* (see p. 324)

Herb with erect stems of limited growth from a perennial stolon; leaves very asymmetric, in two rows, alternate; flower heads sessile.

A common plant of dark, wet places in wet forest. HC, HM, HA, HK.

Agnew 8178; Kerfoot 3899.

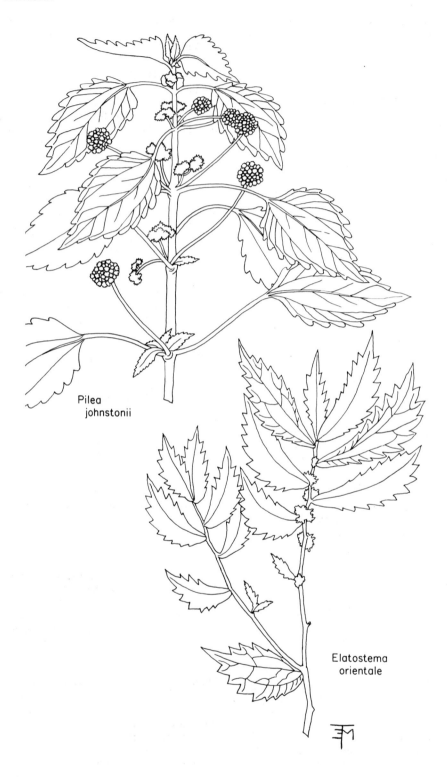

Pilea
johnstonii

Elatostema
orientale

8. BOEHMERIA *Jacq.*

Trees or shrubs with opposite or (in ours) alternate, simple leaves with free stipules; flowers monoecious or dioecious, in globose clusters; male flower with 3–5 sepals (joined at base) and stamens; female flower with a tubular, 2–4-toothed calyx, persistent and enclosing, sometimes adhering to, the fruit.

Boehmeria platyphylla *Don*

Woody herb or shrub with alternate ovate acuminate leaves; flowers in globose clusters on long, slender, unbranched racemes.

Rare plant found in Kakamega forest. MUM.
Dale 3112; Tweedie 69/30.

9. POUZOLZIA *Gaud.*

Herbs or shrubs with alternate leaves, separate stipules, and no stinging hairs; flowers monoecious, clustered in leaf axils; male flowers with 3–5 sepals and stamens; female flower with a tubular perianth which envelops the ripe fruit.

Pouzolzia parasitica (*Forsk.*) *Schweinf.*

A weak trailing shrub with ovate-elliptic leaves; fruit 3-angled, shiny.

Uncommon plant found at the edges of and on rocky areas within dry upland forest. HM, HA, HK, MUM, KIS, MAC, NBI, KAJ.
Agnew and Hanid 8797; Verdcourt 956.

10. PARIETARIA *L.*

Weak herbs with alternate, entire, exstipulate leaves; flowers crowded in axillary cymes, bisexual and unisexual together; bisexual flowers with 4 sepals, 4 stamens and free ovary; unisexual flowers similar but either without stamens or without a functional ovary.

Parietaria debilis *Forsk.*

Annual trailing herb with suborbicular, thin, membranous leaves and very small axillary clusters of flowers.

Rare plant found in disturbed places at the upper forest limits. HE, HA, HK.
Agnew 8879; Hedberg 1964.

11. DROGUETIA *Gaud.*

Herbs with alternate or opposite leaves with free stipules; flowers monoecious, clustered at the nodes in bowl-shaped or cylindrical, toothed involucres; male flower with tubular, 3-lobed calyx and 1 stamen; female flower with no perianth.

1	Leaves alternate	1. *D. debilis*
	Leaves opposite	2. *D. iners*

1. Droguetia debilis *Rendle*

Trailing herb with ascending stems and alternate, ovate-elliptic leaves; involucre ± tubular.

Not uncommon on the floor of highland forest. HE, HM, HA, HK, MAC, KAJ.
Verdcourt 1151; Tweedie 66/278.

2. Droguetia iners (*Forsk.*) *Schweinf.*

Trailing or herbaceous plant (sometimes climbing) with opposite, ovate, subacuminate leaves; involucre usually bowl-shaped.

Often recognizable when sterile by the reddish-chestnut stipules, this plant is fairly common in highland forest, especially near the lower limit of the bamboo. HE, HM, HA, KIS.
Agnew 7111; Glover, Gwynne, and Samuel 1163.

12. AUSTRALINA *Gaud.*

Herbs, usually creeping, with alternate or opposite simple leaves and free stipules; flowers monoecious, clustered in leaf axils, without an involucre; male flower with apparently 1 acute sepal, tubular below enclosing the single stamen; female flower with a sac-like perianth; fruit compressed.

1	Leaves alternate	1. *A. acuminata*
	Leaves opposite	2. *A. flaccida*

1. Australina acuminata *Wedd.*

Annual herb with alternate, ovate acuminate leaves and clusters of flowers at the nodes.

Apparently rare plant found in disturbed places in upland forest. HT, HA.
Agnew 9672 A; Verdcourt and Polhill 3161.

2. Australina flaccida *Wedd.*

Trailing annual very similar to *A. acuminata* except for the opposite leaves without an acumen.

Rare, but probably overlooked, found by streamsides in highland forest. HE, HA.
Agnew 8286; Tweedie 2677.

60. CELASTRACEAE†

Trees, shrubs, or climbers without tendrils, with or without latex; leaves alternate or opposite, simple; stipules inconspicuous; inflorescence cymose or clustered; flowers bisexual, regular; calyx 4–5-lobed, imbricate or valvate; petals usually 5, imbricate or valvate; stamens 3–5, inserted on or below the disc margin; anthers 1–2-celled; ovary superior mostly 3-locular; style short, lobed; seeds few or many, with aril.

† By A. D. Q. Agnew and S. Kibe.

1. HIPPOCRATEA *L.*

Small trees, shrubs or climbers, without latex, climbing by means of twining lateral branches; leaves opposite or subopposite, glabrous; stipules free or ± united interpetiolarly; inflorescence a panicle or cyme, axillary; disc extra-staminal; stamens 3, anthers versatile; carpels 3, fruit of 3 capsular mericarps; seeds winged.

1 Peduncle and pedicel glabrous; flower-buds cylindrical or globular   2
    Peduncle and pedicel puberulous; flower-buds conical   2. *H. africana*
2 Flower-buds cylindrical, leaf apex obtuse
           1. *H. goetzei*
    Flower-buds globular, leaf apex acuminate
           3. *H. indica*

1. Hippocratea goetzei *Loes.*

A woody liane, with elliptic or ovate leaves, and with whitish lenticels which become ± elongated and protuberant; disc cylindrically elongated, united with androgynophore apically; anthers 1-celled; seeds broadly winged.

Occasionally found as a robust climber in upland forest. HM, HA.

Kerfoot 4899; Agnew, Hanid, and Kiniaruh 7916.

2. Hippocratea africana (*Willd.*) *Loes.*

A woody liane with glabrous, brown, lenticellate stem; leaves elliptic-oblong to ovate, apex rounded or obtusely acuminate; bracts pubescent; pedicel and calyx pubescent; anthers 2-celled.

Found in riverine forests. HE, HM, HA, NAR, NBI.

Newbould 7405; Agnew 7243.

3. Hippocratea indica *Wild.*

A woody liane without stem lenticels; leaves big (4–12 x 3–7 cm), elliptic to obovate; inflorescence lax; flower-buds globose; ovary surrounded by the disc.

Found in moist evergreen forests. HM, HK, NAR.

Glover, Gwynne, and Samuel 226.

61. ICACINACEAE†

Trees or shrubs, sometimes climbing; leaves simple, alternate rarely opposite, stipules absent; inflorescence axillary or terminal; flowers bisexual or unisexual by abortion, regular; calyx small, 4–5-lobed, valvate or imbricate; petals 4–5; stamens same number and alternate with petals; anthers 2-celled; ovary superior, 1-celled; style simple or

† By A. D. Q. Agnew.

stigma sessile; fruit drupaceous or a samara, 1-seeded.

1. PYRENACANTHA *Wight*

Climbing shrubs; leaves alternate, petiolate; inflorescence spike-like or racemose; flowers unisexual by abortion; calyx absent; petals valvate, persistent on fruit; vestigial ovary in male flower; vestigial staminode in female flower; fruit a broadly ovoid drupe.

Pyrenacantha malvifolia *Engl.*

Straggling or climbing, ± pubescent perennial shrub with a tuberous rhizome from which the shoots spring; stem with papery, thin, light green bark; leaves suborbicular, cordate, crenate; inflorescence a woolly catkin; fruit pubescent, ovally compressed.

Occasionally found in *Acacia-Commiphora* scrub on sandy or rocky soil. RV, MAG.

Glover and Cooper 3484; Verdcourt 3717 (S).

62. LORANTHACEAE‡

Parasitic shrubs with green photosynthetic, opposite or alternate, entire exstipulate leaves; flowers bisexual or unisexual, regular or zygomorphic; calyx reduced to a tube or rim or obsolete; petals 4–5, valvate in bud; stamens as many as, and opposite to the petals; ovary inferior, the ovules indistinct and the seeds without a clear testa.

All the mistletoes fall in this family. In the following account much material has not been seen and the names and distributions are only tentative.

1 Flowers unisexual, regular; corolla under 5 mm long, with inconspicuous triangular lobes   2. *Viscum*
    Flowers bisexual, often zygomorphic; corolla over 1 cm long, showy, ligulate
           1. *Loranthus*

1. LORANTHUS *L.*

Shrubby parasites growing on branches of trees and shrubs with opposite or alternate, green leaves; flowers bisexual, in cymes, umbels or racemes; calyx tubular or represented by a rim; petals 4–5, free or fused, usually zygomorphic; stamens as many as petals, opposite to the petals and fused to them; style and stigma simple; fruit a berry.

In the following account the old, broad definition of this genus is followed since no comprehensive treatment exists for the group in our area, and it has been found impossible to assign our species

‡ By A. D. Q. Agnew.

Viscum tuberculatum

...eri

Viscum schimperi

to segregate genera as defined for other regions of Africa.

1   Flowers in terminal racemes   1. *L. kirkii*
    Flowers in umbels or fasciculate, usually not terminal   **2**
2   Petals hairy on the outside   **3**
    Petals glabrous on the outside   **8**
3   Corolla lobes much longer than tube   **4**
    Corolla splitting only at the top, the lobes much shorter than the tube (which may be split down one side only)   **6**
4   Bract with a long linear process at one side, exceeding the calyx
                                    2. *L. hildebrandtii*
    Bract truncate, not exceeding the calyx   **5**
5   Calyx long-tubular; stamens breaking in two shortly after anthesis   3. *L. ulugurense*
    Calyx rim-like; stamens with persistent anthers   4. *L. heckmannianus*
6   Flower bud densely reddish-tomentose, with a spherical apical swelling; anthers transversely divided into small chambers   **7**
    Flower bud minutely pubescent, with a cylindrical, 5-angled apical portion; anthers not transversely divided   5. *L. aurantiacus*
7   Leaves ovate/elliptic, mostly rounded at base
                                      6. *L. rufescens*
    Leaves oblong, linear to oblanceolate, cuneate at base   7. *L. dschallensis*
8   Petals fused at least at base   **9**
    Petals free to base   8. *L. curviflorus*
9   Filaments coiled at anthesis   **11**
    Filaments straight or gently curved at anthesis   **10**
10 Leaves crisped at margin; corolla tube straight
                                    9. *L. panganensis*
    Leaves entire at margin; corolla tube curved
                                      10. *L. acaciae*
11 Corolla lobes separating from each other only in the central portion, with a tube, split at one side, above and below it
                                    11. *L. platyphyllus*
    Corolla lobes separating from each other or loosely coherent only at the apex   **12**
12 Corolla tube black within, grey outside with a red tip   16. *L. woodfordioides*
    Corolla tube not black within, except for a black spot sometimes at the filament insertion   **13**
13 Corolla lobes longer than corolla tube (including that part of the corolla tube which may be split at one side)   **14**
    Corolla lobes shorter than corolla tube (including that part of the tube which may be split at one side)   **20**
14 Sepal tube longer than its diameter   **15**

Sepal tube rim-like or shorter than its diameter   **18**
15 Bract pubescent   12. *L. fischeri*
    Bract glabrous   **16**
16 Corolla tube yellow-green; leaves glaucous when young   13. *L. ugogensis*
    Corolla tube red at apex; leaves not glaucous
                                                    17
17 Corolla tube in bud showing 5 indentations and protuberances marking the positions of filament insertion; leaves obovate
                                    14. *L. acacietorum*
    Corolla tube in bud smooth, without showing indentations and protuberances; leaves linear to oblanceolate   15. *L. stuhlmannii*
18 Young stems densely pubescent-tomentose; corolla with a black spot at the insertion of each filament within   17. *L. sp. B*
    Young stems glabrous or glabrescent; corolla unmarked within   **19**
19 Corolla lobes 5, loosely coherent at the apex; corolla tube bulbous at base, split for less than half its length   18. *L. sulphureus*
    Corolla lobes 4, free at apex; corolla tube cylindrical at base, split for more than half its length   19. *L. sp. C*
20 Corolla lobes coiled or bent back at anthesis
                                                    21
    Corolla lobes erect at anthesis   **23**
21 Anthers short, bifid at apex, not toothed at base; petal lobes coiled   20. *L. braunii*
    Anthers long, entire at apex, toothed at base; petal lobes reflexed but not coiled
                                                    22
22 Buds blunt; petals straight but reflexed
                                    21. *L. constrictiflorus*
    Buds acute; petals variously contort and reflexed   22. *L. meridianum*
23 Petal lobes with abruptly demarcated, thickened yellowish shield on inner side of apical lobe; bud 5-ridged at tip
                                      5. *L. aurantiacus*
    Petal lobes without thickened apex, or thickened and gradually weakening below; bud cylindrical to tip   **24**
24 Young twigs densely pubescent to tomentose
                                    23. *L. ziziphifolius*
    Young twigs glabrous   **25**
25 Corolla tube cylindrical throughout
                                        24. *L. sp. D*
    Inflated bulb present at base of corolla tube
                                                    26
26 Sepal tube not split at anthesis by swelling of basal bulb of corolla tube; filament with no apical tooth   25. *L. brunneus*
    Sepal tube split at anthesis by swelling of basal bulb of corolla tube; filament with a small apical tooth   **27**

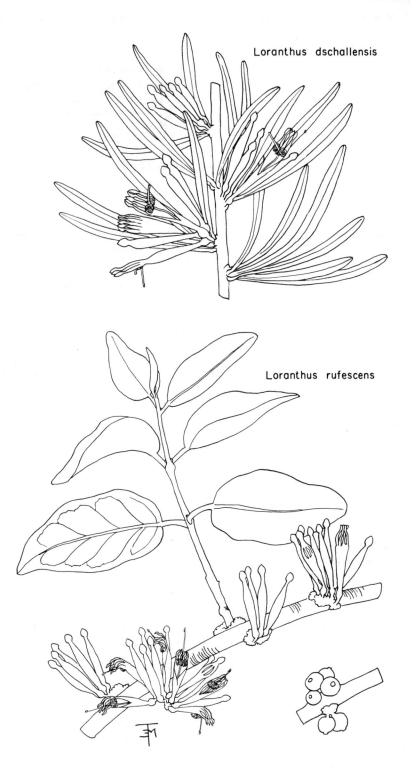

Loranthus dschallensis

Loranthus rufescens

27 Leaves oblanceolate to oblong-elliptic,
    cuneate at base   26. *L. oehleri*
    Leaves ovate to ovate-elliptic, rounded or
    obtuse at base   27. *L. keudelii*

1. Loranthus kirkii *Oliv.*

Plant glabrous with ovate to broad elliptic penninerved leaves; racemes many-flowered; flowers
orange, about 12 mm long.
    Uncommon plant found in dry country and at
the coast. MAG, MAC.
    Lind 5577; EAH 6.

2. Loranthus hildebrandtii *Engl.*

Plant pubescent with ± elliptic, penninerved leaves;
flowers fascicled, with an orange or purple pubescent corolla, split down one side and only
partially split into separate lobes.
    Uncommon plant found in dry country, especi-
ally by riversides. EMB, MAC.
    Archer 462.

3. Loranthus ulugurense *Engl.* (see p. 335)

Plant stellate-pubescent on all parts with broad
ovate ± cordate leaves; petals silky-hairy, greenish
with orange tube.
    Common in dry bushland. HM, HA, NAR, RV,
MAC, NBI.
    Glover 2490; Agnew 5043.

4. Loranthus heckmannianus *Engl.*

Plant tomentose with mostly opposite, ovate
leaves; flowers fasciculate, yellow-green and
orange very hairy outside; filaments toothed at
apex.
    Uncommon plant found in evergreen dry wood-
land and *Combretum* savannah. NAR, RV, MAC.
    Archer 217; Glover 3904.

5. Loranthus aurantiacus *Engl.*

Plant glabrescent or sparsely pubescent with opposite or alternate lanceolate-elliptic leaves; leaves
with 3–5 major veins from near the base; flowers
shortly umbellate, orange, yellow and red, with
abruptly demarcated hard pads under the petal
lobes, and with toothed filaments.
    Rare plant found at the coast and inland in
Commiphora bushland. EMB.
    Archer 518.

6. Loranthus rufescens *DC.* (see p. 329)

Plant stellate-tomentose, especially on the young
parts, with large ovate-elliptic, penninerved leaves;
flowers covered with reddish hairs, the corolla
lobes only free apically; anthers chambered transversely.

Common in highland savannah. HC, HT, HM,
HA, HK, KIT, MUM, NAR, MAC.
    Agnew 9016; Glover 604.

7. Loranthus dschallensis *Engl.* (see p. 329)

Similar to *L. rufescens* but with oblong to linear
leaves, tapering gradually at the base.
    Combretum country and drier bushland. BAR,
NAN, MAC.
    Tweedie 67/353.

8. Loranthus curviflorus *Benth.* (Inc. *L. sagittifolius* Sprague) (see p. 331)

Plant glabrous, creeping over the surface of its host
by means of root-like rhizomes; leaves variable,
suborbicular to oblong, cuneate to sagittate, rarely
both on the same plant; flowers in umbels; petals
yellow and red, curved from the base, free.
    Common on *Acacia* trees in dry bushland,
grassland, and highland savannah. HT, BAR, RV,
MAG, NAN, MAC, KAJ.
    Strid 2695; MacKinnon 2.

9. Loranthus panganensis *Engl.* (see p. 333)

Plant glabrous with alternate, very fleshy, crisped
leaves; flowers subsessile, pink, grey-green and
dark red with 5 prominent ridges below the curved
lobes and stamens.
    Rather uncommon plant found in dry rocky
bushland usually on *Commiphora*. NAR, EMB,
MAC, KAJ.
    Agnew 8746; Archer 465.

10. Loranthus acaciae *Zucc.*

Plant glabrous, creeping over surface of host by
root-like rhizomes; leaves obovate, alternate, thick;
flowers pink and green, straight or slightly curved,
with reflexed green petal lobes at anthesis.
    Rare plant found in dry country, especially on
Acacia and *Commiphora*. MAG.
    Archer 494.

11. Loranthus platyphyllus *A. Rich.*

Plant glabrous, glaucous with alternate lanceolate
or rhomboid leaves; flowers umbellate, pink and
orange, with the petals fused to their tips.
    Rare plant found in the northern part of our
area and in need of further collection. BAR.
    Archer 497.

12. Loranthus fischeri *Engl.* (see p. 327)

Plant finely pubescent when young, with small
alternate elliptic to oblanceolate leaves; flower
with pubescent bract and yellow, much contorted
petals and stamens.

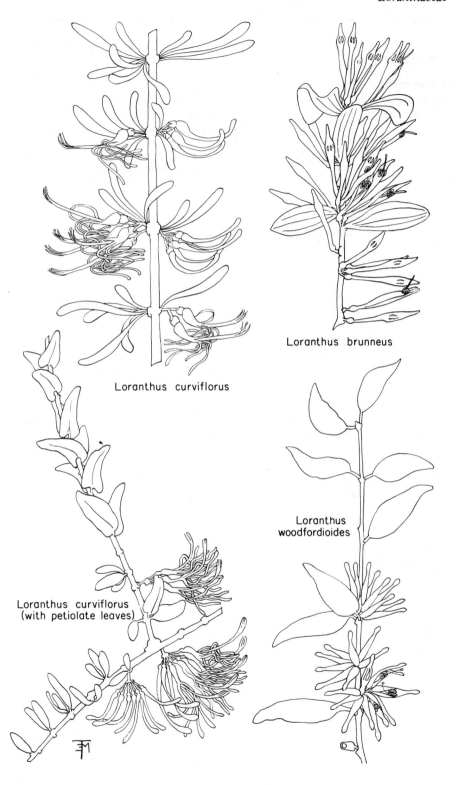

Loranthus brunneus

Loranthus curviflorus

Loranthus curviflorus
(with petiolate leaves)

Loranthus
woodfordioides

Common in dry upland forest and evergreen bushland. HC, HT, HA, NAR, BAR, RV, EMB, MAC, NBI, KAJ.

Agnew 9055; Nattrass 937.

13. **Loranthus ugogensis** *Engl.*

Plant glabrous, with lanceolate-elliptic leaves; flowers in fascicles of 2–3, yellow-green, with much contorted petals and stamens and with 5 pubescent protuberances inside the base of the petal tube.

Locally common in dry *Acacia* bushland. BAR, MAG, MAC, KAJ.

Agnew 9086; Archer 509.

14. **Loranthus acacietorum** *Bullock*

Plant glabrous, with alternate oblanceolate leaves; flowers red and orange, with much contorted petals and stamens.

Rare plant found in dry country and in need of further collection. MAC.

Archer 215.

15. **Loranthus stuhlmannii** *Engl.*

Plant finely pubescent, with narrow, linear to oblanceolate leaves; flowers 1–3 in each fascicle, yellow and red, with a simple, cylindrical corolla tube.

Rare plant found in dry country, only found once by Lake Victoria in western Kenya. MUM.

Agnew, Musumba, and Kiniaruh 8044.

16. **Loranthus woodfordioides** *Schweinf.* (see p. 331)

Plant glabrous with alternate or opposite, penninerved, linear to broad-lanceolate leaves; flowers in dense pedicellate fascicles, grey below, red at tip and with black interior; petals 4 or 5, not reflexed; filaments toothed at apex.

Common in montane rain forest on a wide variety of hosts including many introduced trees. HC, HT, HM, HK, KIS, NAR, MAC, NBI.

Harmsen 6555; Glover 458.

17. **Loranthus** *sp.* B.

Pubescent or tomentose herb with opposite, small blunt broad-ovate leaves; flowers small, in axillary umbels, grey flushed pink above but rather dull; petals 4, with a spot at each filament insertion; filament with a tooth at apex.

Rare plant found in dry bushland in western Kenya. MUM, NAR.

Agnew 8051; Glover 317.

18. **Loranthus sulphureus** *Engl.*

Plant glabrous, with elliptical to obovate, 3-nerved leaves; flowers 3–5 in each fascicled group, yellow with red tip; petals 5, remaining erect, not contort at anthesis.

Uncommon plant found in dry upland forest. HM, HA, NAR, RV, NBI.

Agnew 8951; Archer 272.

19. **Loranthus** *sp.* C.

Plant sparsely pubescent with ovate, subopposite, penninerved leaves; flowers in small pedicellate fascicles, yellow; petals 4, not reflexed; filaments toothed.

Rare plant found in dry bushland. HT, MAC.

Ossent, February 1962; Nattrass 452.

20. **Loranthus braunii** *Engl.* (see p. 333)

Glabrous plant with blunt oblanceolate to elliptical leaves; flowers in pedunculate umbels; corolla pink with green-purple knob at end, red within, the tube with swelling at base and (in bud) at apex, lobes coiling back; anthers short, bifid at apex.

Rare plant found in wet savannah of western Kenya. MUM, KIT.

Archer 240.

21. **Loranthus constrictiflorus** *Engl.* (see p. 335)

Plant glabrous with subopposite, lanceolate, penninerved leaves; flowers in subsessile umbels, reddish-orange; corolla tube with basal bulb, lobes reflexed; filaments toothed at apex.

Uncommon plant found in western Kenya. KIT, MUM.

Archer 237; Dekker 46.

22. **Loranthus meridianum** *Danser*

Glabrous with suborbicular leaves; flowers shortly pedicellate, red with a green tip in bud.

Rare plant found in dry bushland on *Acacia mellifera*. BAR.

Tweedie 2974.

23. **Loranthus ziziphifolius** *Engl.*

Plant pubescent or tomentose, except on the flower and old leaves; leaves oblanceolate, 3-nerved; flowers in subsessile clusters, pink or crimson with bands of green and scarlet; corolla with a bulb at base and erect lobes; filaments entire.

Fairly common in dry (*Combretum*) bushland, especially near Nairobi. HA, RV, EMB, MAC.

Greenway 11180; Agnew 9388.

24. **Loranthus** *sp.* D.

Plant glabrous with ovate-elliptic, 3-nerved, opposite leaves; flowers in subsessile clusters, pink; corolla with no basal bulb and with erect lobes; filaments entire.

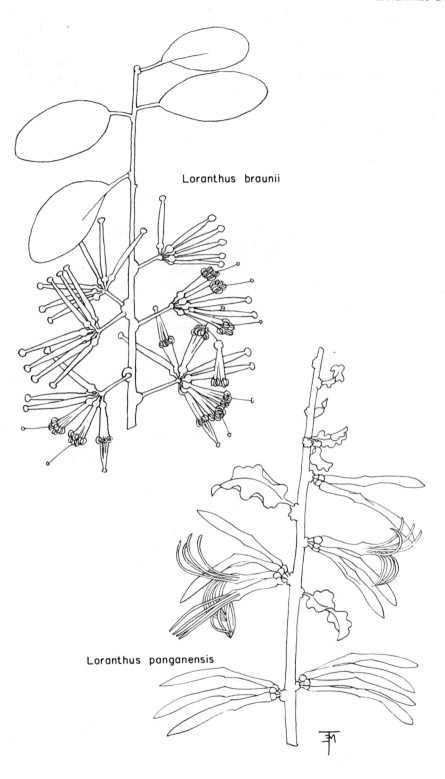

Loranthus braunii

Loranthus panganensis

Only once found and apparently to be looked for in Endau, in MAC.
Archer 264.

25. Loranthus brunneus *Engl.* (see p. 331)

Plant glabrous with broad-elliptic, 3-nerved, sub-opposite leaves; flowes in sessile clusters, yellow-orange with a green band and a red tip; corolla with a basal bulb and apically erect lobes; filaments entire.

Rare plant found in upland forest. HA, HK.
Hanid and Kiniaruh 962; Howard and Verdcourt 3784.

26. Loranthus oehleri *Engl.*

Plant glabrous with alternate, oblanceolate to obovate leaves; flowers in sessile clusters, red and orange; corolla with a basal bulb and erect lobes; filaments toothed.

Rare plant found in dry *Commiphora* bushland. MAG, MAC.
Lind and Agnew 5638; Archer 508.

27. Loranthus keudelii *Engl.*

Similar to *L. oehleri* but with a heavily lenticelled stem, broad-ovate or ovate-elliptic leaves and a shorter flower (*c.* 3 cm compared with *c.* 4 cm).

Rare plant found in riverine forest at lower altitudes. EMB, MAC.
Hanid and Kiniaruh 1032; Faden 66188.

2. VISCUM *L.*

Parasites with opposite green leaves and cymose inflorescences; flowers monoecious or dioecious, regular; calyx obsolete or absent; petals usually 4, with short valvate lobes and a very short tube; fruit a 1-3-seeded berry.

1 Plants with expanded leaves   2
   Plants with scale-leaves only 1. *V. schimperi*
2 Flowers clustered at nodes, sessile; fruit warty   2. *V. tuberculatum*
   Flowers sessile in pedunculate 2-7-flowered heads at the nodes; fruit smooth   3
3 Leaves crisped at margin; disc at apex of fruit of the same size as in the flower and frequently retaining the persistent petals
                                       3. *V. nervosum*
   Leaves entire, hardly undulate at margin; disc at apex of fruit enlarged and rim-like, retaining no trace of petals   4. *V. fischeri*

1. Viscum schimperi *Engl.* (see p. 327)

Plant glabrous, pendulous or erect, with almost sessile flowers and fruit; fruit smooth or slightly warted.

On *Acacia* species, especially in the dry uplands. Most plants collected are female; the male may be a smaller plant to be found on *Juniperus procera*. HM, HK, MUM, MAC, NBI.
Strid 2632B (♂); Agnew 9248 (♀); Faden 66167 (♀).

2. Viscum tuberculatum *A. Rich.* (see p. 327)

Plant glabrous, erect or pendulous, with usually yellowish, obovate to oblanceolate leaves; flowers in ± sessile clusters; fruit tuberculate.

The most widespread mistletoe in Kenya, found in all upland dry woodland. HE, HT, HM, MUM, KIS, NAR, RV, NAN.
Glover 2216A; Tweedie 66/310.

3. Viscum nervosum *A. Rich.*

Plant glabrous, pendulous, with broad- or narrow-elliptic leaves with crisped edges; flowers 1-3 together on short peduncles; fruit smooth, often with persistent perianth.

Uncommon plant, except around Nairobi. HT, NAR, NBI.
Kerfoot 4055; Agnew 8492.

4. Viscum fischeri *Engl.*

Similar to *V. nervosum* except for the oblanceolate to obovate leaves with smooth edges, the longer peduncles (5-7 mm) bearing 4-7 flowers, and the expanded rim at the fruit apex.

Only found in forest near Nairobi. NBI.
Johnstone 63; Harmsen 6553.

63. SANTALACEAE R. Br.†

Trees, shrubs, or herbs, often semi-parasitic; stem ridged; leaves simple, entire, alternate, exstipulate; inflorescence axillary or terminal, perianth in one whorl (sepals), fleshy, often produced above the ovary as a tube, 3-6-lobed, yellow or greenish; stamens the same number as perianth lobes, inserted at or below lobe bases; ovary inferior, one celled, with 1-3 free central ovules; fruit indehiscent, dry or fleshy.

1. Semi-parasitic herbs; leaves linear, filiform or reduced to scales   2. *Thesium*
    Shrub; leaves elliptic to oblanceolate, shortly petiolate   1. *Osyridicarpos*

1. OSYRIDICARPOS *A. DC.*

Non-tendrillate scandent shrub; stem ridged; leaves alternate, simple 1·2-2 cm; flowers in terminal racemes or axillary; bracteoles minute; perianth persistent, adnate to the inferior ovary, tubular; stamens 5; anthers ovoid; fruit a 2-3-seeded drupe.

† By A. D. Q. Agnew and S. Kibe.

Loranthus ulugurense

Loranthus
constrictiflorus

Osyridicarpos scandens *Engl.*

Scandent or straggling undershrub; stem ridged, with rod-like branches, pubescent towards the apex; leaves elliptic to lanceolate; perianth lobes a quarter the length of tube; flowers solitary, axillary, yellowish-green; pedicels pubescent.

Usually found on rocky ground in dry evergreen bushland and dry forest. HC, HM, HA, HK, NAR, RV, NAN, MAC, NBI.

Agnew 8494; Elliot 2383.

2. THESIUM *L.*

Herbaceous plants with woody rootstock, semi-parasitic through root contact, stem wiry; leaves small, usually filiform or broad-linear, alternate, entire; inflorescence racemose; flowers bisexual; bracts often adnate to pedicel; sepals 5, valvate, often hairy within, yellow; fruit 1-seeded, indehiscent.

1	Leaves scale-like, up to 1 cm long	2
	Leaves filiform or linear, over 1 cm long	3
2	Flowers crowded, sessile, in lateral spikes; sepal lobes linear	1. *T. stuhlmanii*
	Flowers 1–3 together usually at apex of a long lateral filiform peduncle, over 1 cm long; sepal lobes oblong, hairy	
		2. *T. unyikense*
3	Leaves terete	4
	Leaves flat	5
4	Inflorescence 6–10-flowered, well defined, terminal, raceme-like; sepals hairy within	
		3. *T. schweinfurthii*
	Inflorescence up to 7-flowered, poorly defined, not raceme-like, without a terminal flower; sepals glabrous	
		4. *T. kilimandscharica*
5	Flowers sessile along lower portion of the long ± unbranched, erect stems; sepal lobes linear	5. *T. ussanguense*
	Flowers pedicellate and pedunculate in branched, well defined inflorescence; sepal lobes oblong	6
6	Fruits dry, reticulate, borne high on plant at apex of most shoots	6. *T. sp. A*
	Fruits fleshy, borne low on plant, and exceeded in height by sterile, leafy shoots	
		7. *T. sp. B*

1. Thesium stuhlmanii *Engl.*

Erect woody annual with leaves reduced to ovate-lanceolate acute scales; flowers sessile, crowded on short compact axillary spikes; sepal-lobes linear, twice as long as the tube.

Occasionally found in grazed or burnt bushland. KIS, RV, MAC.

Archer 545; Kokwaro 1870.

2. Thesium unyikense *Engl.* (see p. 337)

A low wiry herb with flowers solitary or 1–3 together in long-pedunculate lateral groups; peduncle over 1 cm long, filiform, subtended by scale-leaves and with the floral bracts and bracteoles acting as an involucre to the terminal flower; sepal-lobes oblong.

Found only once, in burnt upland grassland at Kitale. In need of further collection. KIT.

Tweedie 68/9.

3. Thesium schweinfurthii *Engl.*

Perennial herb with numerous erect spreading stems (much branched above); leaves flat and tending to be filiform; inflorescence short, 6–10-flowered, well defined, terminal, raceme-like; sepal lobes triangular, with an apical tuft of hairs within, longer than the tube and the short (0·5 mm long) style.

Usually found in burnt upland grassland after rain and (rarely) in forests amongst Kikuyu grass. HA, RV, NAN, EMB, KAJ.

Kabuye 8; Agnew, Kiniaruh, Ngethe, and Wyatt 8913.

4. Thesium kilimandscharica *Engl.*

Similar to *T. schweinfurthii* except in having the inflorescence up to 7-flowered, poorly-defined, not raceme-like, without a terminal flower, sepals glabrous within and hardly fused below, the lobes triangular.

Occasionally found in burnt upland grassland and on shallow rocky soils in *Philippia* woodland. HA, RV, NAN.

Polhill 231; Agnew, Hedberg, and Mmari 9616.

5. Thesium ussanguense *Engl.* (see p. 337)

An erect wiry herb with flat, subulate leaves; flowers sessile along the long, ± scapose spike-like branches; bracts up to 5 mm long; sepal-lobes linear, hairy within.

Found only once, in burnt upland grassland after rain. KIT.

Tweedie 68/12.

6. Thesium sp. A. (see p. 337)

An erect wiry herb with flat, subulate leaves; flowers pedicellate and pedunculate in poorly-defined inflorescences; sepals with a tuft of hairs at the apex of each lobe within, the tube longer than the lobes; style nearly 1 mm long, longer than the sepal tube.

Found in the same habitats as the other species. KIT, NAR, RV.

Kabuye 8B; Tweedie 68/11.

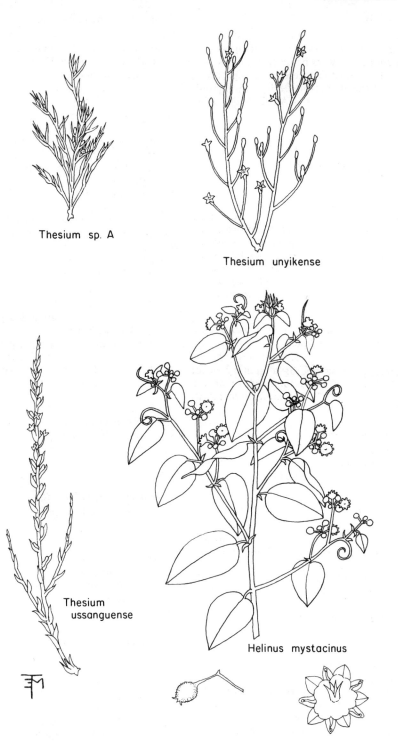

Thesium sp. A

Thesium unyikense

Thesium
ussanguense

Helinus mystacinus

7. Thesium *sp.* **B.**

Perennial herb with spreading stems, branched above; leaves flat; inflorescence overtopped by sterile leafy shoots; flowers pedicellate and pedunculate in poorly defined inflorescences; sepals with a tuft of hairs at the apex; fruit fleshy, turning red.

Found in open grassland. HA, HT, HM, KIT, RV.

Harvey 186.

64. BALANOPHORACEAE L.†

Fleshy annual or perennial herbs parasitic on roots of other plants, without chlorophyll or stomata; stem a thin rhizome or tuberous mass; leaves reduced to scales or absent; inflorescence arising from the ground as a paniculate spike or head with scale leaves, unisexual; petals absent; stamens 1–5; stigma sessile; ovary 1–3-locular, adnate to perianth when present; ovules solitary in each loculus; fruit small, nut- or drupe-like, 1-seeded.

1   Inflorescence branched, often massive and fleshy with obscure bracts
                    1. *Sarcophyte piriei*
    Inflorescence consisting of a solitary head subtended by numerous imbricate bracts on a short peduncle   2. *Thonningia sanguinea*

1. SARCOPHYTE *Sparrm.*

Fleshy parasites with branched unisexual inflorescences; male flowers with 3-valved calyx and one stamen; female flowers with naked ovary.

Sarcophyte piriei *Hutch.*

Fleshy tuberous dioecious plant coloured deep crimson except for the pale bracts; male inflorescence up to 40 cm tall; female inflorescence up to 25 cm or in globular masses at ground level.

Occasionally found parasitizing *Acacia* and *Newtonia* in riverine forests. Smells fruity. HM, MAC, NBI.

Greenway 9833; Beecher 5875.

2. THONNINGIA *Vahl*

Parasites with thin rhizomes and erect, solitary heads of unisexual flowers surrounded by an involucre of acute bracts; flowers unisexual; male flowers with 3–5 sepals and 3–5 united stamens; female flowers with 2–4-lobed perianth and a 1-celled inferior ovary; fruiting head fleshy.

† By A. D. Q. Agnew.

Thonningia sanguinea *Vahl*

Herb with erect, sessile or pedunculate heads subtended by thick, numerous, imbricate, acute, reddish scales; heads unisexual.

Only found once in Kakamega forest. MUM. Dale 3383.

65. RHAMNACEAE‡

Mostly trees or shrubs often climbing by hooks (*Ventilago*), tendrils (*Helinus, Gouania*), or twining; leaves always simple, usually stipulate, alternate or opposite; inflorescence cymose; flowers small hermaphrodite, calyx tubular, 4–5-lobed, lobes valvate; petals 4–5, opposite to and half enclosing the stamens; intrastaminal disc usually present; ovary superior or sunk in the torus (perigynous); carpels 2–4; ovules axile, 1–2 in each loculus, fruit various, often drupaceous, occasionally with wings.

1   Leaves serrate   2
    Leaves entire   4
2   Flowers in paniculate axillary inflorescences; plant with tendrils   3
    Flowers solitary, axillary; plant without tendrils   1. *Rhamnus prinoides*
3   Leaves pubescent on lower surface with reddish hairs on the veins; inflorescence a spike   2. *Gouania*
    Leaves glabrous on both surfaces, inflorescences cymose   4. *Ventilago*
4   Plant with tendrils   3. *Helinus*
    Plant without tendrils   5. *Scutia myrtina*

1. RHAMNUS *L.*

Rhamnus prinoides *L'Hérit.*

Sometimes a woody climber. Dealt with in KTS. p. 391.

2. GOUANIA *Jacq.*

Tendrillate climbing shrubs or lianes; leaves alternate petiolate, entire, or dentate; inflorescence of panicles of spikes; sepals 5; petals 5; ovary inferior; fruit 3-winged, schizocarpic.

Gouania longispicata *Engl.* (see p. 339)

Climber, often woody, with tendrils on the inflorescence branches only; leaves simple, ovate, serrulate, apex acuminate, reddish-hairy on the veins below.

Found growing in riverine forests in the upland area. HA, HK, KIT, MUM, KIS.

Agnew 8739; Heriz-Smith and Paulo 883.

‡ By A. D. Q. Agnew and S. Kibe.

Gouania longispicata

3. HELINUS *Endl.*

Tendrillate shrubs or climbers; leaves alternate, petiolate, entire; inflorescence a 1–several-flowered pedunculate axillary umbel; petals small; ovary inferior, with 3 locules; fruit dry or schizo-carpic.

1   Pedicel and fruit glabrous   1. *H. integrifolius*
    Pedicel and fruit hairy   2. *H. mystacinus*

1. Helinus integrifolius (*Lam.*) *Kuntze*

Perennial climbing shrubs; leaves ovate to broadly obovate, base subcordate, upper surface glabrous and lower one puberulous; pedicel and fruit glabrous.

Found in disturbed dry bushland and in *Commiphora* woodland, HA, HK, RV, MAG, MAC, KAJ.

Agnew 9796; Glover, Gwynne, and Samuel 2927.

2. Helinus mystacinus (*Ait.*) *E. Mey.* (see p. 337)

Similar to *H. integrifolius* except in having glabrous pedicels and fruit, and with leaves broadly ovate to circular.

Found in scrub, grassland, and evergreen woodland. HE, HC, HM, HL, HA, KIS, NAR, RV, EMB, MAC, NBI, KAJ.

Harmsen 64-19; Faden 67174.

4. VENTILAGO *Gaert.*

Trees or climbers; leaves toothed or entire, alternate; inflorescence of loose panicles; floral parts in fives; petals small; style on green central disc; fruit one-seeded, with oblong wing developed from style after fertilization.

Ventilago africana *Exell*

Glabrous trees or woody lianes; leaves ovate, toothed or entire, petiolate, base truncate; inflorescence tomentose, lateral to leaf axil, loosely paniculate; fruit one-seeded, with long wing developed from the style.

Found in relict forest with *Croton* spp. MUM. Drummond and Hemsley 4793.

5. SCUTIA (*DC.*) *Brongn.*

Scutia myrtina (*Burm. f.*) *Kurz*

Sometimes a climbing shrub. Dealt with in KTS p. 391.

66. VITACEAE†

Perennial herbs, shrubs or trees, often climbing by means of branched tendrils; leaves alternate, stipulate, often palmate or palmatifid; flower actino-

† By A. D. Q. Agnew.

morphic, usually bisexual, parts in fours or sixes; calyx often hardly lobed; corolla free or forming a tube below; stamens as many as the petals and opposite to them; ovary superior, usually 2-locular, with 2 ovules in each; fruit a berry with 1–4 (–8 in *Leea*) seeds; seeds with much endosperm.

The family of the grape which many of our wild climbers resemble. The fruit, however, though edible, is not a delicacy.

1   Leaves compound   2
    Leaves simple   5
2   Leaves bipinnate   5. *Leea guineensis*
    Leaves palmately 3–7-foliolate   3
3   Petals 4; leaves 3–7-foliolate   4
    Petals 5–6; leaves trifoliolate   6. *Rhoicissus*
4   Flower buds spherical; fruit with more than 1
    seed   2. *Cayratia*
    Flower buds cylindrical, contracted near or
    above the centre; fruits 1-seeded
                                  4. *Cyphostemma*
5   Flowers subsessile; leaves and stems never
    succulent   1. *Ampelocissus africana*
    Flowers pedicellate, in umbels; leaves and/or
    stems frequently succulent   3. *Cissus*

1. AMPELOCISSUS *Planch.*

Perennial climbers; tendrils usually arising from the peduncle; leaves simple, entire or lobed or 3-foliolate; inflorescences of condensed cymes with flowers ± sessile in capitate heads; calyx entire or ± lobed; petals 5; seeds 4.

Ampelocissus africana (*Lour.*) *Merr.*

A tendrillar ± hairy climber with simple or palmatifid, sub-orbicular, deeply cordate leaves with rounded apex; flowers almost sessile.

Uncommon plant found in hot country and in western Kenya only. KIT, MUM, BAR.

Napier 2000; Bogdan AB4050.

2. CAYRATIA *Juss.*

Climbing tendrillate perennial herbs, very similar to *Cyphostemma* but with a globose flower bud (the petals broad-elliptic), entire disc, short style and 2–4-seeded fruit.

1   Leaves 5-foliolate, the leaf stalk twice divided
                                  1. *C. gracilis*
    Leaves 3-foliolate, palmate   2. *C. ibuensis*

1. Cayratia gracilis (*Guill. & Perr.*) *Suesseng.*

A tendrillate glabrous climber with pedately 5-foliolate leaves; leaflets ovate, serrate.

Uncommon plant found in wet forest areas of western Kenya. KIT, MUM.

Agnew 8551; Bogdan 4221.

2. Cayratia ibuensis *(Hook. f.) Suesseng.*

A tendrillate glabrous to glabrescent climber with 3-foliolate leaves; leaflets ovate to elliptic.

Uncommon plant found along the shore of Lake Victoria. MUM, KIS.

Hanid and Kiniaruh 695; Agnew and Musumba 8006.

3. CISSUS *L.*

Herbs or shrubs with or without tendrils; leaves simple (in ours) or palmate, margins variously toothed (rarely entire); inflorescence leaf-opposed or terminal; flowers in umbels; flowers 4-merous, usually conical in bud; calyx entire or 4-lobed; petals hooded at the apex; anthers 4; disc annular, entire or lobed; fruit usually 1-seeded.

1 Stem heavily succulent and quadrangular **2**
  Stem woody or herbaceous, not succulent **3**
2 Wings on the stem undulating
                          1. *C. cactiformis*
  Wings on the stem straight
                          2. *C. quadrangularis*
3 Leaves fleshy   **4**
  Leaves membranous   **5**
4 Leaves glabrous; pedicel without glands
                          3. *C. rotundifolia*
  Leaves and pedicel with scattered glandular
  hairs   4. *C.* sp. *A*
5 Inflorescences on leafless woody stem; leaves
  rounded or obtuse at apex
                          5. *C. aphyllantha*
  Inflorescence on leafy herbaceous stem;
  leaves acute or acuminate at apex   **6**
6 Pedicel hairy in flower, becoming glabrescent
  in fruit; leaf apex acute or hardly
  acuminate   6. *C. petiolata*
  Pedicel glabrous; leaf with a long, ± parallel-
  sided acumen   7. *C. oliveri*

1. Cissus cactiformis *Gilg.* (see p. 342)

A fleshy, tendrillate plant with 4 broad green undulate wings to its stem and ± orbicular, ephemeral leaves.

Occasional, on stony soils in dry *Acacia-Commiphora* country. BAR, RV, MAC.

Tweedie 67/3; Bally B9488.

2. Cissus quadrangularis *L.*

Similar to *C. cactiformis* but differs in having straight wings on the stem, and smaller flowers.

Similar in habitat but more common than *C. cactiformis*. HT, NAR, MAG, MAC, NBI, KAJ.

Agnew 8224; Harmsen 8.

3. Cissus rotundifolia *(Forsk.) Vahl* (see p. 342)

Climbing tendrillate shrub; stem 4-5-angled, pubescent; leaves fleshy, folded down the midrib where they often split into two, margin toothed.

Common, in dry *Acacia-Commiphora* bushland and on murrum-sand soils. MUM, KIS, NAR, BAR, RV, MAG, MAC.

Agnew, Musumba, and Kiniaruh 7974; Leippert 5258.

4. Cissus sp. A.

Trailing herb; stems ridged; leaves thickly fleshy, toothed; pedicel with scattered glandular hairs; fruit oval, with an indumentum of glandular hairs.

This species needs further investigation. Found only once 2 miles east of Emali along Nairobi-Mombasa road on grey loamy soil. MAC.

Hanid and Kiniaruh 532.

5. Cissus aphyllantha *Gilg.*

Tendrillate woody climber or shrub up to 1-2 m; tendrils and young branches with reddish hairs.

Locally common in *Commiphora-Euphorbia-Acacia* dry scrubland, on rocky outcrops and red sandy loam. MAC.

Verdcourt 2372.

6. Cissus petiolata *Hook. f.*

Perennial climber with ± quadrangular stem developing longitudinal corky wings when old; leaves ± orbicular, cordate, shortly acuminate.

Found in upland forests. HE, HA, NBI.

Perdue and Kibuwa 8091.

7. Cissus oliveri *(Engl.) Gilg*

Perennial climber; similar to *E. petiolata* except for the long-acuminate leaves and glabrous pedicel.

Found in upland forest as a trailer or climber. HA, HN, EMB, MAC.

Agnew 9364; Archer 353.

4. CYPHOSTEMMA *(Planch.) Alston*

Perennial herbs, shrubs or climbers with or without tendrils opposite the palmately divided leaves; inflorescences of pedunculate corymbose cymes, often of fasciculate cymules; flower buds cylindrical, usually constricted about the middle; calyx often entire; petals 4, very caducous; stamens 4; disc of 4 conical or truncate glands; ovary with 1 ovule and a simple subulate style; seed rugose; fruit a berry.

1 Leaves mostly 3-foliolate and never more
  than 4-foliolate   **2**
  At least some leaves with 5 or more leaflets **6**

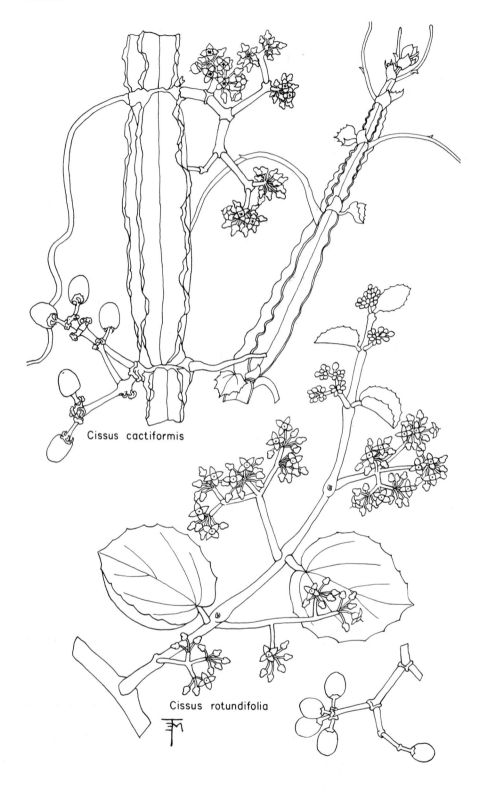

Cissus cactiformis

Cissus rotundifolia

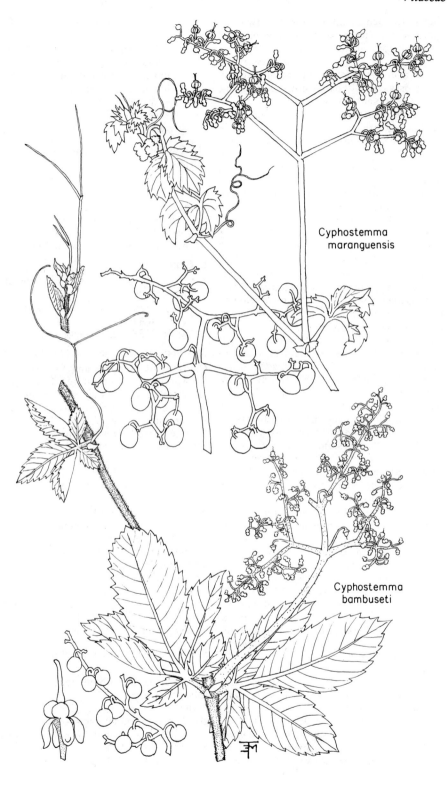

Cyphostemma
maranguensis

Cyphostemma
bambuseti

2 Stipules rounded at apex, glossy brown and glabrescent, sheathing the young leaves at the stem apex; plant never glandular
                           1. *C. kilimandscharicum*
   Stipules acute at apex, green or light brown, not glossy, usually hairy, not sheathing the stem apex; plant often glandular   3

3 Leaflets with an acuminate apex and acute, triangular teeth   2. *C. sp. A*
   Leaflets with rounded or acute apex and obtuse teeth   4

4 Leaflets with conspicuously raised, reticulate venation below, the surface appearing as small ± circular pits; upper leaflet surface glossy, glabrous, dark green   12. *C. sp. B*
   Leaflets without conspicuous reticulation of raised venation below; upper leaflet surface not glossy, usually pubescent, light green 5

5 Leaflets orbicular, becoming glabrous; corolla without glands   13. *C. sp. C*
   Leaflets usually elliptic, hairy; corolla usually with glands   14. *C. maranguense*

6 Climbing plants with tendrils   7
   Erect herbs without tendrils   14

7 The lowermost lateral leaflets borne on a common stalk from the main axis of the leaf   9. *C. adenocaule*
   All leaflets arising from the same point   8

8 Pedicels glandular   10
   Pedicels without glands   9

9 Petioles with long, glandular hairs; bracts of cymules of the inflorescence longer than some pedicels, persistent
                           10. *C. ukerewense*
   Petioles with no long glandular hairs; bracts of cymules of inflorescence shorter than pedicels, caducous
                           11. *C. nodiglandulosum*

10 Flower bud and fruit glandular   11
   Flower bud and fruit without glands   12

11 Leaflets with conspicuously raised, reticulate venation below, the surface appearing as small ± circular pits; upper leaflet surface glossy, glabrous, dark green   12. *C. sp. B*
   Leaflets without conspicuous reticulation of raised venation below; upper leaflet surface not glossy or dark green, often pubescent
                           6. *C. bambuseti*

12 Usually some or all leaves with more than 5 leaflets; leaflets narrow-elliptic
                           7. *C. orondo*
   No leaf with more than 5 leaflets; leaflets oblanceolate to obovate   13

13 Leaflets grey- or white-tomentose below, sparsely pubescent above 8. *C. lentianum*
   Leaflets pubescent not tomentose below, glabrous or pubescent above 3. *C. nierense*

14 Leaflets obovate, crenate, with ± rounded apex   4. *C. sp. D*
   Leaflets elliptic, serrate, with acute or acuminate apex   15

15 Flowers buds glandular   5. *C. heterotrichum*
   Flowers buds without glands   16

16 Leaves sessile, glabrous   15. *C. jatrophoides*
   Leaves petiolate, usually pubescent, rarely glabrous   7. *C. orondo*

1. Cyphostemma kilimandscharicum (*Gilg*) *Wild & Drum.*

A strong trifoliolate climber with ovate-elliptic leaflets and broad brown sheathing stipules; glands totally absent.

Common in montane rain forest. HC, HM, HA, HK, HN, KAJ.

Agnew 7099; Verdcourt and Polhill 2995.

2. Cyphostemma *sp. A.*

A trifoliolate climber with sub-orbicular leaflets, strongly glandular on all parts.

A dry country plant, badly in need of further collecting. KAJ.

Agnew 7338; Gilbert J 8.

3. Cyphostemma nierense (*Th. Fr. jr.*) *Desc.*

Climber with tendrils and 5-foliolate leaves; leaflets orbicular to obovate, finely pubescent to glabrescent, with widely spaced venation; sparsely glandular on pedicels and stem, without glands on flowers and fruit.

A common climber in forest and bushland edges with a wide ecological range from dry *Acacia* bushland to dry upland forest edges. HL, HA, MUM, NAR, RV, EMB, MAC, NBI, KAJ.

Agnew and Kibe 10048; Kokwaro 225.

4. Cyphostemma *sp. D.*

An erect herb without tendrils and with 5–7-foliolate, often very large leaves; leaflets obovate, rounded at apex, densely yellow-pubescent below when young; small glands present on pedicels and fruits, absent from stems and leaves and present or absent on flower buds.

Uncommon plant found in dry bushland in the Machakos district. MAC, KAJ.

Mwangangi 8; Verdcourt 2320

5. Cyphostemma heterotrichum (*Gilg & R. E. Fr.*) *Wild & Drum.*

An erect herb without tendrils and with 5–7-foliolate leaves; leaflets ± elliptical, with mixed indumentum of black glands and white hairs; glands present on all parts.

Locally common in the Kitale area in burnt grassland. HC, HE, KIT.

Tweedie 67/37; Bogdan 4263.

6. Cyphostemma bambuseti (*Gilg & Brandt*) *Wild & Drum.* (see p. 343)

A climber with 3–5-foliolate leaves, the leaflets elliptic to oblong with a pale tomentum below; minutely glandular on all parts.

Not uncommon, found at the edges of dry upland forest. HC, HM, HA, KIT, NAR, MAC.

Agnew 9898; Kirrika 498.

7. Cyphostemma orondo (*Gilg & Bened*) *Desc.* (incl. *C. sesquipedale* of Check List) (see p. 346)

Climbing or trailing, rarely erect, from a swollen tuberous tap-root, with or without tendrils; leaflets 3–7, linear-elliptical, densely pubescent below; glands present on all parts except flowers and fruit.

As defined here this is a species of variable habit, frequently without tendrils. It is common in bushed grassland. HT, KIT, MUM, KIS, NAR, BAR, RV, NAN, MAC, KAJ.

Hanid and Kiniaruh 513; Brown 1122.

8. Cyphostemma lentianum (*Volk. & Gilg*) *Desc.*

Climber with tendrils and 5-foliolate leaves; leaflets obovate-elliptic, grey-tomentose below; glandular on all parts except flowers and fruit.

An uncommon *Cyphostemma* found in rocky places in dry bushland, so far only recorded from a small area of the Rift Valley. RV, MAG.

Glover 4132; Agnew 7154.

9. Cyphostemma adenocaule (*A. Rich.*) *Wild & Drum.*

A 5-foliolate climber with a twice-branched axis to the leaf, with suborbicular, usually glabrous leaflets; glands entirely absent.

A common *Cyphostemma* of dry bushland, from the coast to 5000 ft. KIT, MUM, KIS, MAC, KAJ.

Hanid and Kiniaruh 491; Makin 104.

10. Cyphostemma ukerewense (*Gilg*) *Desc.* (Incl. *C. glandulosissima, C. braunii* of Check List)

A 5-foliolate climber with numerous long glandular hairs on stems, petioles, peduncles and flower buds but none on the pedicel or fruit; leaflets obovate, acute at apex.

An uncommon plant found in western Kenya. HE, HC, KIT, MUM.

Napier 1953; Strid 2865.

11. Cyphostemma nodiglandulosum (*Th. Fr. jr.*) *Desc.* (Incl. *C. cyphopetala p.p.* of Check List)

A climber with 3–5-foliolate leaves, the leaflets elliptic, grey- or white-tomentose below; glands present only at the nodes.

A common plant of dry upland, HE, HC, HT, HM, HA, KIT, KIS, NAR, RV, EMB.

Tweedie 67/64; Jack in EAH 3051.

12. Cyphostemma sp. B.

A trifoliolate climber with elliptic leaflets very prominently reticulate and pubescent below; glands present, but short, on all parts.

Common around Nairobi and in dry bushland and evergreen woodland, especially on shallow, rocky soils. MAC, NBI, KAJ.

Agnew and Hanid 8346; Rogers 2.

13. Cyphostemma sp. C.

A trifoliolate climber with orbicular, fleshy, smooth leaflets; glands present on pedicels but not on corolla.

This is another dry-country species which has been not been collected very satisfactorily. MAG, KAJ.

Bally 7320; Glover, Gwynne, and Samuel 2799.

14. Cyphostemma maranguense (*Gilg*) *Desc.* (see p. 343)

A trifoliolate climber with broad-elliptic leaflets which are often covered with a yellowish tomentum below; usually glandular on all parts.

As defined here a most variable plant grading from pubescent to tomentose leaflets and sparsely to densely glandular vegetative parts. The fruits, however, are always glandular-hairy. Common in dry upland forest edges, particularly between Nairobi and the Kikuyu escarpment. HA, HK, MAC, KAJ.

Agnew 8729; Verdcourt 1027.

15. Cyphostemma jatrophoides (*Bak.*) *Desc.* (*Vitis jatrophoides* Baker) (see p. 346)

An erect herb without tendrils and with 3–6-foliolate leaves; leaflets glabrous, long-elliptic; glands absent.

Rare plant found in the Kitale district in burnt grassland. HE, HC, KIT.

Bogdan 3713; Tweedie 66/26.

5. LEEA *L.*

Trees or shrubs with pinnate, stipular leaves and without tendrils; flowers in dense, compound leaf-opposed pedunculate cymes; flowers bisexual; calyx 5-lobed; corolla tubular, 5-lobed at apex; stamens alternating with truncate staminodes both fused to corolla tube and projecting downwards into it; fruit a berry, lobed, with 3–8 seeds.

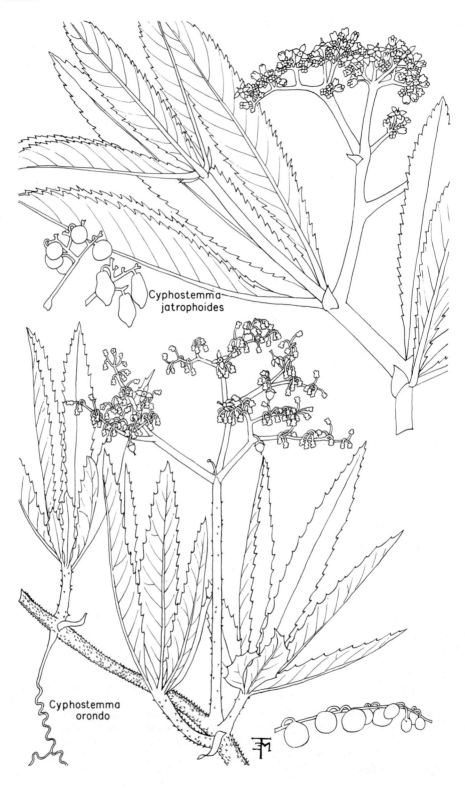

Cyphostemma
jatrophoides

Cyphostemma
orondo

Leea guineensis *G. Don*

A shrub or weak tree to 3 m, with large, glabrous, bipinnate, serrate leaves; flowers orange or red; fruits red, becoming black.

Only found in Kakamega forest, and should be looked for in other wet forests in western Kenya. MUM.

Gillett 16687.

6. RHOICISSUS *Planch.*

Perennial tendrillate shrubs or ± woody climbers; leaves 3-foliolate (in ours), rarely simple or 5-foliolate; inflorescences of leaf-opposed umbellate cymes; petals 5–6; anthers bending over gynoecium; seeds 1–2.

1 Leaflets obovate, dentate or sinuate-dentate, tomentose below   1. *R. tridentata*
Leaflets lanceolate, entire, glabrous below   2. *R. revoilii*

1. Rhoicissus tridentata (*L. f.*) *Wild & Drummond* (see p. 350)

Small tendrillate shrub or climber; leaflets dentate, obovate, often glabrous above, always tomentose below; no tendril on inflorescence branches.

Occasionally found in dry scattered *Combretum* woodland of the uplands. HA, KIT, MUM, KIS, NAR, RV, EMB, MAC, NBI.

Agnew, Musumba, and Kiniaruh 8426; Nattrass 858.

2. Rhoicissus revoilii *Planch.*

Similar to *R. tridentata* except for the leaflets being entire, lanceolate and glabrous.

Found in dry scrubland and *Combretum* woodland and riverine forests. HA, KIS, NAR, MAC, NBI.

Agnew, Musumba, and Kiniaruh 7943; Birch 61/117.

67. SAPINDACEAE†

Trees, shrubs or tendrillate climbers; leaves alternate (rarely opposite), simple or (in ours) divided, petiolate, rarely stipulate; inflorescence usually a raceme or panicle; flowers bisexual (in ours) or unisexual, often zygomorphic; sepals imbricate 4–5, ± connate; petals 3–5, free; stamens 5–12 (often 8), hypogynous; disc extra-staminal; filaments hairy; anthers 2-celled; ovary superior, usually with 3 carpels with 1–2 axile ovules in each; fruits capsular or indehiscent.

A family mainly of trees but with two genera of herbaceous or woody climbers.

1 Plant herbaceous; leaves ternate; fruit a bladder-like membranous capsule
     1. *Cardiospermum*

† By S. Kibe and A. D. Q. Agnew.

     Plant woody; leaves pinnate; fruit a hard bony capsule   2. *Paullinia pinnata*

1. CARDIOSPERMUM *L.*

Annual or perennial climbers; leaves petiolate, biternately compound; inflorescence axillary, corymbose, with a pair of tendrils at the apex of peduncle; flowers pedicellate, zygomorphic; petals 4 in two pairs; stamens 7–8; anther 2-lobed, fruit a bladder-like inflated membranous capsule of 2 cells with 2 black seeds in each.

1 Petals 2–6 mm long; fruit ± spherical or conical   2
Petals 7–10 mm long; fruit ovoid
     1. *C. grandiflorum*
2 Petals 3–4 mm long; primary branches of inflorescence 3   2. *C. halicacabum*
Petals 5–6 mm long; primary branches of inflorescence 4 or more   3. *C. corindum*

1. Cardiospermum grandiflorum *Swartz*

Herbaceous climber, stem hirsute with crisped hairs (2 mm) or glabrous; leaflets deeply crenate, lower surface tomentose with long hairs on the veins; inflorescences with 2 successive whorls of pedunculate racemes; petals 7–10 mm long; fruit ellipsoidal.

Occasionally found in upland forest edges on rocky ground. HC, MUM, KIS, BAR.

Verdcourt 1701; Strid 3388.

2. Cardiospermum halicacabum *L.*

Annual herbaceous climbers with ± woody, sulcate, pubescent or glabrous stem; leaflets incised serrate, ovate; inflorescence an umbel with 3 pedunculate racemes; petals 3–4 mm long; fruit ± spherical.

Found in grassy woodland and *Acacia* forests on rocky or stony ground. HA, KIS, MAG, EMB, MAC, KAJ.

Verdcourt and Napier 2179; Hanid and Kiniaruh 752.

3. Cardiospermum corindum *L.*

Similar to *C. halicacabum* except for the more rounded leaflet-lobes, the petals 5–6 mm long, and 4 or more primary branches of the inflorescence.

Found in *Commiphora* bush on rocky hillsides and riversides. HC, BAR, MAC, KAJ.

Gillett 18216; Agnew, Kibe, and Mathenge 10575.

2. PAULLINIA *L.*

Woody climbing shrubs; stem grooved; leaves 5-foliolate, odd-pinnate, stipulate; tendrils 2, at apex of peduncle; inflorescence axillary, paniculate; flowers irregular; sepals 5, unequal; petals 5, unequal; stamens 8; ovary 3-loculed with 1 seed per locule.

Paullinia pinnata *L.*

A woody climbing shrub with imparipinnate leaves with a broadly winged petiole; leaflets 3-5, obovate-elliptic, widely crenate, hairy only on nerves and their axils; inflorescence a raceme-like panicle.

Uncommon plant found in riverine forests and forest edges. MUM.

Agnew and Musumba 8593; Gillett 16699.

68. UMBELLIFERAE†

Annual or perennial herbs or shrubs with alternate, mostly exstipulate, mostly divided leaves with a sheathing base; all parts of the plant with a resinous smell when crushed owing to the presence of oil in oil ducts; flowers bisexual or unisexual in umbels which are often compound, the primary rays subtended by *bracts,* or bracts absent, and the pedicels subtended by *bracteoles* or bracteoles absent; calyx present as 5 teeth or petaloid lobes or obscure; petals 5, free, often inflexed, pointed or notched; stamens 5, inserted at the edge of the nectiferous disc or *stylopodium*; ovary inferior, with 2 uni-ovulate carpels and 2 styles; fruit a dry schizocarp, variously ridged and ornamented.

A large temperate family, not well-represented here but nevertheless confusing. Two members are woody shrubs and trees and are dealt with in KTS, p. 577. A number are cultivated for their flavouring qualities and are liable to escape. The following account includes only some of these.

1 Lower leaves simple   2
  Lower leaves compound   6
2 Leaves palmately divided, almost to base
                                    3. *Sanicula elata*
  Leaves entire or lobed, but not divided to base   3
3 Leaves circular in outline   4
  Leaves oblong or oblanceolate or ovate in outline   5
4 Leaves crenate at margin, unlobed
                                    2. *Centella asiatica*
  Leaves shallowly lobed and crenate
                                    1. *Hydrocotyle*
5 All leaves simple, ciliate   4. *Alepidea longifolia*
  Upper leaves finely divided into capillary segments   5. *Coriandrum sativum*
6 Lower leaves simply pinnate, the pinnae simple or pinnatisect, the leaf parallel-sided in outline   7

† By A. D. Q. Agnew.

Lower leaves 2-4 times pinnate or ternate, and often with the lower pinnae larger than the upper ones   10
7 Plant with umbels not exceeding the basal rosette of leaves
                    9. *Haplosciadium abyssinicum*
  Plant with umbels much exceeding the basal rosette of leaves, or without a rosette of leaves   8
8 Pinnae lobed; outer flowers of umbels with enlarged, notched, outer petals; fruits flattened   25. *Heracleum*
  Pinnae hardly or not lobed; outer flowers of umbels not differentiated; fruits ± globose   9
9 Umbels with conspicuous reflexed bracts
                                    17. *Berula erecta*
  Umbels without bracts   15. *Pimpinella*
10 All leaves divided into capillary hair-like segments   11
   All leaves with flattened segments   15
11 Bracts present, large, oblong, surrounding the base of the contracted fruiting umbel
                        19. *Diplolophium africanum*
   Bracts absent or few, linear, fruiting umbel not contracted   12
12 Bracteoles absent; flowers yellow   14
   Bracteoles present; flowers white   13
13 Plant annual; fruits roughened with small tubercles, unwinged
                        13. *Trachyspermum copticum*
   Plant perennial; fruits smooth, winged
                                    22. *Peucedanum*
14 Robust plant with typically inflated stem-leaf bases; fruits strongly winged   21. *Ferula*
   Weak erect herb with narrow leaf bases; fruits unwinged   20. *Foeniculum vulgare*
15 Fruits dorsally flattened, the two carpels separating along the widest diameter of the fruit, often winged   16
   Fruits globose or ovoid, separating across the narrowest diameter, never winged   18
16 Plants glabrous; flowers red; fruit glaucous, hardly winged, with thick edges
                    24. *Erythroselinum atropurpureum*
   Plants glabrous or hairy; flowers red or white; fruit strongly winged with paper-thin edges   17
17 Plants glabrous; flowers red or cream; fruit retuse above   23. *Lefebvrea*
   Plants glabrous or hairy; flowers pale-yellow to white; fruit entire above
                                    22. *Peucedanum*
18 Umbels leaf-opposed, sessile with few rays, or apparently simple
                        11. *Apium leptophyllum*
   Umbels pedunculate, terminal, or apparently reduced to a head   19

19 Bracts present, more than 3   **20**
     Bracts absent, or occasionally 1-2 reduced leaf-bases present at the base of the primary umbel   **23**
20 Bracts lobed or divided   12. *Ammi majus*
     Bracts entire   **21**
21 Fruit ovoid, covered with hooked hairs; calyx teeth persistent   8. *Caucalis*
     Fruit ± globose, rough with tiny projections or glabrous; calyx teeth absent   **22**
22 Plant climbing with twining petioles; leaves ternate to trifoliolate, suborbicular in outline; fruits glabrous
         14. *Pseudocarum eminii*
     Plant an erect herb; leaves 2-3 times pinnatisect, lanceolate in outline
         16. *Schimperella aberdarense*
23 Umbels irregular and with less than 5 flowers, without bracteoles; carpels glabrous
         10. *Cryptotaenia africana*
     Umbels regular, with more than 5 rays, or if fewer then the fruits densely hairy; bracteoles present.   **24**
24 Bracteoles much wider than pedicels, oblong, reflexed; fruit ovoid, beaked, glabrous
         6. *Anthriscus sylvestris*
     Bracteoles as wide as, or a little wider than pedicels, erect; fruit globose or hairy   **25**
25 Plant trailing; bracteoles longer than pedicels
         18. *Oenanthe*
     Plant erect; bracteoles shorter than pedicels
         26
26 Rays of primary umbel 2-3; fruit densely covered with white, glochidiate hairs
         7. *Torilis arvensis*
     Rays of primary umbel more than 3; fruit pubescent or glabrous, not densely hairy
         15. *Pimpinella*

1. HYDROCOTYLE *L.*

Creeping perennial herbs with peltate or (in ours) orbicular simple leaves; flowers in whorls, subtended by few bracts; sepals 5, obscure; petals 5, entire; fruit laterally compressed, each carpel with 3 blunt ridges.

1 Plants entirely glabrous   **2**
     Plants hairy at least on the petioles   **3**
2 Usually some leaves more than 2·5 cm in diameter; always some leaves with an apical lobe (opposite the petiole) more deeply cut than the lateral ones
         1. *H. ranunculoides*
     All leaves less than 2·5 cm diameter; all leaves hardly lobed, or if shallowly so then the apical lobe no more deeply cut than the lateral ones   2. *H. monticola*

3 Upper surface of leaf usually hairy; heads with usually more than 12 flowers, on peduncles often longer than petioles
         3. *H. mannii*
     Upper surface of leaf glabrous; heads with less than 10 flowers, on peduncles always much shorter than petioles   **4**
4 Stem with a few hairs, at least at nodes; heads of 6-10 flowers   4. *H. sp. A*
     Stem glabrous; heads of 2-5 flowers
         2. *H. monticola*

1. **Hydrocotyle ranunculoides** *L. f.*

Leaves erect with fleshy petioles, glabrous, with a circular lamina, cut to leave a well marked apical lobe; heads on short peduncles, 5-9-flowered.

Locally common in ponds and marshes, growing in water between the reeds. HE, HT, HA, RV, KAJ.

Tweedie 2584; Strid 3308.

2. **Hydrocotyle monticola** *Hook. f.*

Small, often tiny, creeping plant with glabrous upper leaf surfaces and shallowly lobed and crenate leaves; petioles, stems and lower leaf surfaces glabrous or hairy; flowers less than 4, pink-petalled.

Rather a variable small *Hydrocotyle* found on muddy and peaty stream banks in the upper forest levels into the alpine zone. HE, HA, HK.

Hedberg 396; Agnew 8997.

3. **Hydrocotyle mannii** *Hook. f.*

A tomentose creeper with shallowly lobed leaves and a dense tuft of downward-pointing hairs at the top of the petiole; heads of over 12 green flowers on rather long peduncles.

Quite common on the forest floor in and below the bamboo zone. HM, HA, KIT, KAJ.

Agnew 7126; Glover 1423.

4. **Hydrocotyle** *sp.* **A.** (see p. 350)

Similar to *H. mannii* but usually smaller, with the upper leaf surface glabrous, with hairs on the stem, and with 6-11 green flowers on the shortly peduncled heads.

In grassland at lower altitudes than *H. mannii.* HT, HA, KIT, KIS.

Drummond and Hemsley 4801; Agnew and Beecher 7038.

2. CENTELLA *L.*

Stoloniferous creeping herbs with suborbicular entire leaves; umbels simple, bracteolate; flowers subsessile; fruit laterally flattened, each carpel being semiorbicular, with 5 obscure ridges.

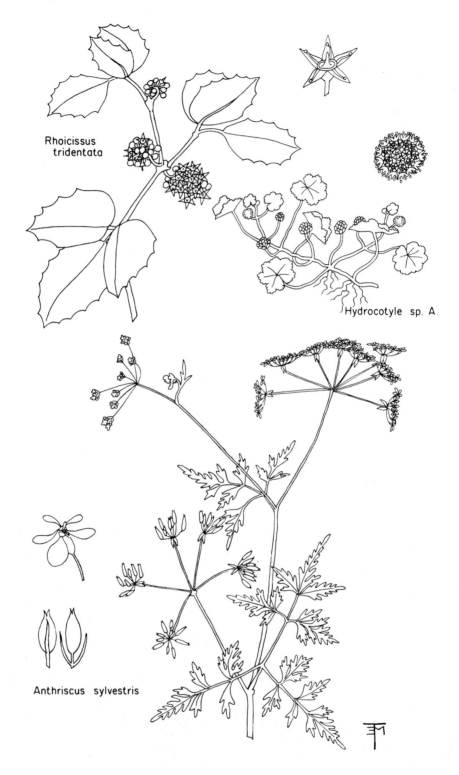

Rhoicissus
tridentata

Hydrocotyle sp. A.

Anthriscus sylvestris

Centella asiatica (*L.*) *Urb.*

Creeping sparsely tomentose perennial with reni-form or suborbicular cordate, crenate leaves.

Common in grassland, especially the artificial grassland of lawns and roadsides, but often over-looked. HT, HM, HK, MUM, KIS, MAC, NBI.

Hanid and Kiniaruh 666; Faden 67263.

3. SANICULA *L.*

Erect perennials with palmately lobed leaves; umbels irregularly compound; bracts and brac-teoles small, few, ± leafy; flowers male and bi-sexual; calyx teeth 5, acute, longer than the inflexed petals; fruit ovoid, covered with hooked bristles, inconspicuously ridged.

Sanicula elata *Don.* (see p. 352)

Stoloniferous subglabrous herb with rosette of long-petioled, deeply 3-7-palmatisect leaves with ± deltoid lobes; flowers few, the male on short pedicels, the bisexual sessile; fruit covered in reddish hooked bristles.

Common in the shady forest floor of the bamboo zone and the forest below this zone. HE, HM, HA, HK, MUM, KAJ.

Gillett 16696; Agnew 8979.

4. ALEPIDEA *Laroch.*

Erect perennial herbs with simple leaves; flowers sessile, in heads, surrounded by an involucre of the fused bracteoles; flowers bisexual, with 5 ovate sepals and white pink petals with an incurved apex; disc annular; fruit obconical, truncate, crowned by the persistent calyx, tubercled.

Alepidea longifolia *E. Mey.* (*A. massaica* Schlecht. & Wolff) (see p. 352)

A glabrous perennial herb with a rosette of lanceo-late ciliate leaves and an erect stem bearing heads in irregular umbels; involucre white, turning pink, persistent.

Locally abundant, in montane grassland, especi-ally on shallow soils and where burnt. HE, HC, HT, HM, HA, HK, MUM

Agnew 7223; Moreau 174.

5. CORIANDRUM *L.*

Annual herbs with entire to tripinnatisect leaves; umbels compound; bracts absent; bracteoles few; flowers male and bisexual, white or pink; sepals well-developed, green; fruit globular, crowned by the persistent calyx, smooth or faintly ribbed.

Coriandrum sativum *L.*

An erect annual with leaves entire at base, divided above, and with pink flowers.

Commonly cultivated for its fruits, coriander occasionally escapes and has been recorded at Nairobi and Kisii as a weed. KIS, NBI.

Verdcourt 1522.

6. ANTHRISCUS *Pers.*

Annual or biennial herbs with 2-3 times pinnate leaves; umbels compound with no bracts but many bracteoles; calyx teeth absent or obscure; petals notched, with an inflexed point, white; fruit ovoid or oblong, each carpel ± terete, smooth and ob-scurely 5-angled.

Anthriscus sylvestris (*L.*) *Hoffm.* (see p. 350)

An erect, glabrous or tomentose, perennial herb with twice pinnate leaves deltoid in outline; leaf segments lobed or serrate; outer flowers of umbels with enlarged petals.

Fairly common in the bamboo and forest zones on our mountains, and often found on disturbed pathsides. HE, HT, HM, HA, HK, RV.

Agnew, Hedberg, and Mmari 9634; Glover 1456.

7. TORILIS *Adans.*

Annual herbs with 1-3 times pinnate leaves; umbels compound; bracts few or absent, brac-teoles present, narrow; calyx teeth 5, triangular; petals pinkish or white, inflexed; fruit ovoid, each carpel with 5 ridges, and covered with spines or hairs.

Torilis arvensis (*Huds.*) *Link* (see p. 353)

An erect, sparsely hairy annual with lanceolate-linear, remotely toothed, leaf-lobes; umbels of few (3-4) rays; flowers pinkish; fruit with glochidiate white hairs.

Locally common along paths in drier upland forest particularly around Nairobi. HE, HC, HT, HM, HA, HK, KIT, MAC, NBI, KAJ.

Tweedie 66/262; Gillett 16136.

8. CAUCALIS *L.*

Annuals or perennials with 2-3 times pinnate leaves; umbels compound, but often condensed; bracts and bracteoles numerous; flowers bisexual and (in ours) unisexual, the outer bisexual, white or pink; calyx teeth 5, acute or capillary; petals inflexed; fruit ovoid, each carpel with primary ridges and secondary ridges usually hairy as well as bearing glochidiate spines.

1 Primary umbels with rays longer than the bract at least in fruit; style and calyx teeth longer than the uppermost glochidiate spines in fruit   1. *C. pedunculata*
  Primary umbels condensed, the rays absent or at least much shorter than the bracts, the

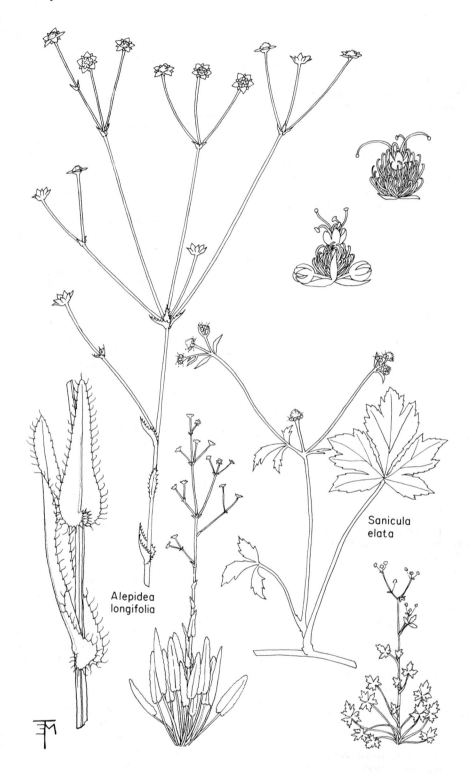

Alepidea
longifolia

Sanicula
elata

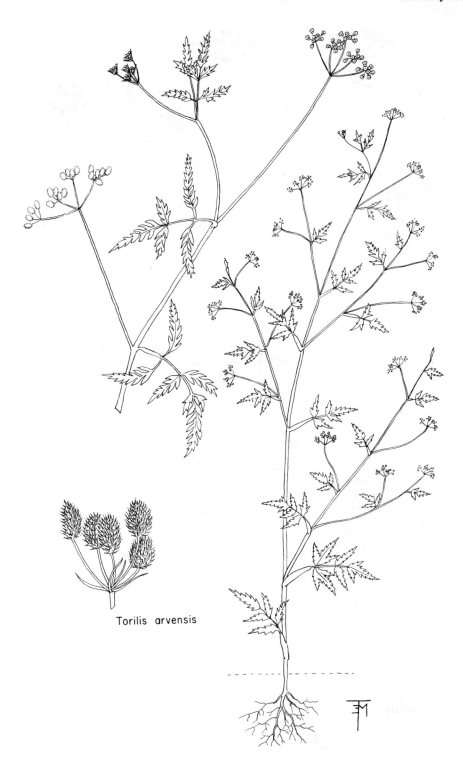

Torilis arvensis

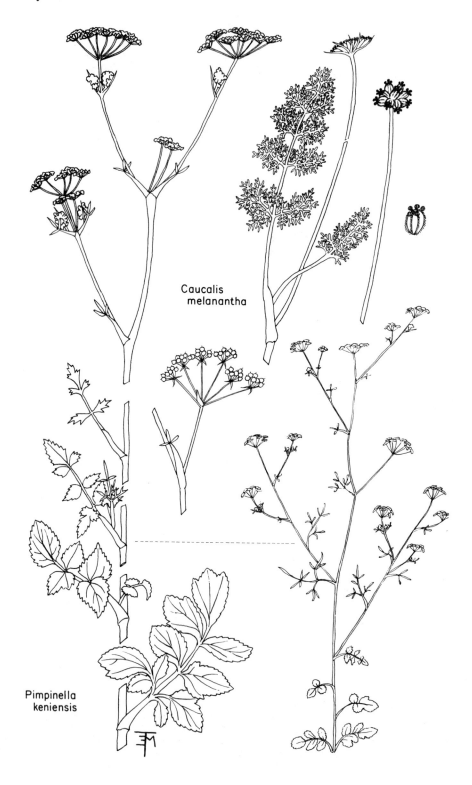

Caucalis
melanantha

Pimpinella
keniensis

inflorescences resembling a head; style and calyx teeth much shorter than the spines   2
2   Ultimate leaf segments linear, entire; petals purple, persistent   2. *C. melanantha*
   Ultimate leaf segments broader than linear, serrate to dentate; petals white or rarely purple, fugaceous   3. *C. incognita*

1. Caucalis pedunculata *Bak. f.*

Weak-stemmed tomentose perennial from fusiform rootstock bearing 3 times pinnate and pinnatifid leaves, ovate in outline, the ultimate segments oblong; umbels and flowers pedunculate and pedicellate respectively; flowers white.

   Uncommon plant found in wooded grassland in western Kenya. HC, KIT, KIS.

   Hanid and Kiniaruh 820; Symes 524.

2. Caucalis melanantha *(Hochst.) Benth. & Hook. f.* (see p. 354)

Tomentose perennial from fusiform rootstock, often forming a rosette, seldom stemmy, with 2–3 times pinnatisect leaves, lanceolate-linear in outline, the ultimate segments linear; flowers purple, sessile in a head.

   Uncommon plant found in high altitude grassland. HE, HC, HM, HA, HK.

   Napier 648; Fleming in EAH 12652.

3. Caucalis incognita *Norman*

A tomentose, weak-stemmed annual herb, often semi-scandent, with 3 times pinnatisect leaves, ovate to deltoid in outline, with ovate to oblong dentate segments; umbels ± sessile in a head; petals white, rarely purple.

   Abundant in all upland areas in forest edges and grassland. The fruits can be a nuisance to one's dog and one's trousers. HE, HC, HT, HM, HA, HK, MAC, KAJ, KIS.

   Agnew 7225; Kokwaro 6.

9. HAPLOSCIADIUM *Hochst.*

Glabrous herbs with pinnate leaves; umbels compound with several bracts and bracteoles; calyx teeth small; petals entire, inflexed, white; fruit ovoid, laterally compressed with 5 blunt ridges on each carpel.

Haplosciadium abyssinicum *Hochst.*

A perennial rosette herb; leaves pinnate with pinnatisect pinnae; peduncle of umbel short and hidden in rosette; flowers numerous; fruit geocarpic on recurved umbel rays.

   Common in disturbed places and solifluction soil in the alpine and highland grasslands of East Africa, this plant usually has its leaves and fruiting umbels so tightly appressed to the ground that they spring downwards when the plant is dug up. HE, HC, HM, HA, HK.

   Hedberg 1786; Lind and Agnew 5155.

10. CRYPTOTAENIA *DC.*

Erect perennial herbs with ternate leaves; umbels compound with neither bracts nor bracteoles; calyx of 5 obtuse teeth; petals white, inflexed; fruit elongate, narrowed and beaked with the persistent styles above, smooth, hardly angled.

Cryptotaenia africana *(Hook. f.) Drude*

A ± tomentose perennial with a rosette of (sometimes incompletely) ternate leaves with suborbicular to lanceolate, dentate leaflets; umbels with few rays, lax.

   Uncommon plant found in the forest floor of wet montane forest. HE, HC, HT, HM, HA, HK, KIT, KAJ.

   Kabuye 79; Strid 3170.

11. APIUM *L.*

Annual (in ours) or perennial glabrous herbs with pinnate or ternate leaves; umbels often leaf-opposed, simple compound, usually without bracts or bracteoles; calyx teeth obscure or absent; petals entire, sometimes inflexed; fruit ovoid, ± laterally compound, each carpel with 5 smooth ridges.

Apium leptophyllum *(Pers.) Benth.*

An erect annual with leaves orbicular in outline, divided into capillary segments; umbels sessile, leaf-opposed, without bracts or bracteoles.

   A recent adventive in the Nairobi district, this little annual with minute white flowers grows in disturbed stony places. NBI.

   Harmsen 6509; Gillett 18345.

12. AMMI *L.*

Annual glabrous herbs with 2–4 times pinnate and pinnatisect leaves; umbels compound terminal; bracts and bracteoles numerous, the bracts often branched; calyx teeth absent; petals inflexed; fruit ovoid or subspherical, each carpel with 5 smooth narrow ridges.

   Weeds of the Middle East, the following species of this genus has been cultivated for its ornamental flowers and has escaped in places. Another species *A. visnaga* (L.) Lam. has capillary leaf segments and may turn up in the future.

Ammi majus *L.*

An erect annual herb with twice pinnate leaves with pinnatisect pinnae, the ultimate segments oblanceolate or elliptic, serrate; bracts divided into linear segments; flowers white, minute, in big showy umbels.

Naturalized. NAN, NBI.

Wood in EAH 10400; Agnew 9910.

13. TRACHYSPERMUM *Link*

Similar to *Ammi*, but with simple bracts and muricate roughened fruits.

Trachyspermum copticum (*L.*) *Link*

An erect annual with leaves oblong in outline, bipinnatisect into linear segments; flowers white.

A weed of arable land, common in Ethiopia and only once recorded from Kenya as a casual in Nairobi. NBI.

Whellan 1848.

14. PSEUDOCARUM *C. Norman*

Trailing herbs with ternate leaves; umbels compound; bracts and bracteoles numerous, broad; calyx teeth absent; petals shortly inflexed, white; fruit ± globose, glabrous, each carpel with 5 narrow wings.

Pseudocarum eminii (*Engl.*) *Wolff*

A ± glabrous climber (by means of petioles) with trifoliolate or ternate leaves with ovate-lanceolate, acute, dentate leaflets; bracts and bracteoles oblong.

Very common in the bamboo zones of mountains, especially where disturbed or where the bamboo has flowered and died. HA, HK.

Agnew 7129; Battiscombe 278.

15. PIMPINELLA *L.*

Annual or perennial herbs often with pinnate leaves; umbels compound with no bracts and few or no bracteoles; flowers white or pinkish with obscure calyx and petals with an inflexed point; fruit ovoid or oblong, laterally compressed, each mericarp with 5 obscure ridges; styles often recurved, with capitate stigmas.

1	Plant annual; fruits pubescent	2
	Plant perennial; fruits pubescent or glabrous	3
2	All leaves ternately divided into linear segments	1. *P.* sp. *A*
	At least the lower leaves pinnate with ovate to orbicular leaflets	2. *P. volkensii*
3	Fruits glabrous	4
	Fruits hairy	3. *P. peregrina*
4	Leaflets sharply serrate; pedicels glabrous	4. *P. keniensis*
	Leaflets crenate or obtusely serrate; pedicels minutely pubescent	5
5	Fruit with the ovary truncate above, and capped by the enlarged disc glands	5. *P. kilimandscharica*

Ovary of fruit narrowing above into the small disc glands   6. *P. friesiorum*

1. Pimpinella *sp.* A.

An erect annual with leaves much dissected into linear segments; fruits turning brown, finely bristly-pubescent but without hooked hairs.

Rare plant found in dry country. MAC.

Bogdan 4371.

2. Pimpinella volkensii *Engl.*

An erect annual with pinnate lower leaves with ovate often cordate leaflets; fruit appressed pubescent on almost glabrous pedicels.

Common in cultivated ground in western Kenya. HE, HC, HA, KIT, MUM.

Symes 759; Tweedie 66/316.

3. Pimpinella peregrina *L.*

An erect perennial (possibly biennial) with pinnate leaves and suborbicular crenate leaflets, the terminal one cordate; ripe fruits with spreading hairs on ± contracted umbels.

Rare plant found in upland grassland and only known from a few specimens. HA, HK.

Kabuye 12; Greenway and Napper 13551.

4. Pimpinella keniensis *Norman* (see p. 354)

An erect perennial or biennial, the branches often opposite above, with pinnate or twice pinnate leaves bearing sharply serrate, ovate to suborbicular cordate leaflets; leaflets becoming narrow and dissected above; fruit and pedicels glabrous.

Common in some areas of upland grassland on well-drained soils. HE, HC, KIT, MUM, NAR, RV, MAC, KAJ.

Agnew, Hanid, and Kiniaruh 9205; Symes 755.

5. Pimpinella kilimandscharica *Engl.*

An erect stoloniferous perennial, with pinnate leaves and crenate leaflets; umbels with glabrous fruits and finely pubescent pedicels; fruits ± cubical with an enlarged disc above.

Rare plant found in alpine grassland and heath. HE, HA, HK.

Taylor 3476; Agnew 7216.

6. Pimpinella friesiorum *Wolff*

Similar to *P. kilimandscharica* but with larger leaflets and the fruit narrowing above.

Found in the upper levels of montane forest and in the heath zones. HA, HK.

Moreau 125; Agnew 7700.

16. SCHIMPERELLA *Wolff*

Erect herbs with 2–3 times pinnate leaves; umbels compound with few linear bracts and several bracteoles; calyx of 1–3 blunt obscure teeth; petals white, shortly incurved; fruit ± globose, each carpel hemispherical, densely roughened with minute protuberances but not grooved or winged.

Schimperella aberdarense *Norman*

An erect glabrous herb, possibly biennial, with 3 times pinnate leaves with lanceolate, serrate acute segments; fruits up to 1·8 mm long.

Rare plant found in disturbed places in montane forest. HE, HM, HA.

Agnew 7264; Napier 605.

17. BERULA *Koch*

Herbs with simply pinnate leaves; umbels compound, leaf-opposed; bracts present, numerous; bracteoles present, numerous; calyx of 5 minute teeth; petals shortly inflexed, greenish; fruit ± sub-spherical, the mericarps ± hemispherical with 5 narrow wings.

Berula erecta (*Huds.*) *Coville*

A trailing glabrous herb with the leaf pinnae lanceolate or ovate, serrate, sometimes the lowermost lobed at base; fruit 2–5 mm long.

Rare, so far only found at the water's edge of Lake Olbolossat in our area. HA.

Lind, March 1964; Meinertzhagen in AN 9382.

18. OENANTHE *L.*

Glabrous trailing herbs with 1–3 times pinnate leaves; umbels compound; bracts 0 (in ours); bracteoles several, well-developed; calyx teeth 5, conspicuous; petals with an inflexed point, white or greenish; fruit ± globose, each mericarp hemispherical with 5 grooves.

1   Leaflet apices round in outline; bracteoles more than twice as long as pedicels
                   1. *Oe. procumbens*
  Leaflet apices acute in outline; bracteoles less than 1·5 times as long as pedicels
                   2. *Oe. palustris*

1. Oenanthe procumbens (*Wolff*) *Norman*

A creeping perennial, rooting at the nodes, with 3 times pinnate or ternate leaves, ± triangular in outline; leaf segments serrate, each serration with a long bristle-like tip, ± rounded at apex; bracteoles more than twice as long as the pedicels; flowers greenish.

A common plant of the shady floor of bamboo-forest. HC, HM, HA, HK.

Agnew 7124; Glover 1494.

2. Oenanthe palustris (*Chiov.*) *Norman*

Similar to *Oe. procumbens* but larger and much more robust, the leaf segments acute in outline, and with short bracteoles.

Locally common around open water and by streamsides above 6000 ft. HE, HT, HM, HA.

Lind, Harris, and Agnew 5102; Glover 1367.

19. DIPLOLOPHIUM *Turcz.*

Erect glabrous herbs with leaves finely divided into linear segments, with inflated sheathing bases; umbels compound; bracts and bracteoles numerous and large; calyx teeth absent or obscure; petals shortly or not at all inflexed; fruit terete or ovoid, each mericarp obscurely 5-ridged and grooved.

Diplolophium africanum *Turcz.*

An erect perennial with long capillary leaf segments, glabrous except for the inflorescences; bracts and bracteoles pubescent, ovate, as long as the umbel rays and pedicels respectively, yellowish; umbel rays pubescent, curved inward in fruit, holding the loose, pubescent mericarps in a cup.

Locally abundant in upland wooded grassland. HC, HM, HA, KIT, MUM, RV, KAJ.

Hanid 192; Verdcourt 1709.

20. FOENICULUM *Mill.*

Glabrous erect herbs with the leaves divided into capillary segments; umbels compound; bracts and bracteoles absent or few; flowers yellowish; calyx teeth absent; petal-tip obtuse, incurved; fruit oblong or ovoid, terete, with 5 ridges and furrows in each carpel

Foeniculum vulgare *Mill.*

An erect, often glaucous biennial with much-divided leaves with capillary segments; bracts and bracteoles absent.

An escape from cultivation, apparently naturalized in waste places locally. HT, NBI.

Brodhurst-Hill 549.

21. FERULA *L.*

Large glabrous herbs with leaves divided into capillary segments and with widely inflated petioles; umbels compound, without bracts or bracteoles; calyx teeth present, small; petals yellow, inflexed; disc flat; fruit dorsally much compressed, broadly winged with 3 well-separated longitudinal ridges in the centre, entire.

1   Umbels on peduncles which are longer than the sheaths of the subtending stem-leaves
                   1. *F. communis*

Umbels on peduncles which are shorter than the inflated leaf bases of the subtending leaves   2. *F. montis-elgonis*

1. Ferula communis *L.*

An erect herb, often very tall (to 3 m), with very large finely divided leaves at base and many yellow umbels subtended by inflated leaf-bases above; fruits nearly 2 cm long, pear-shaped in outline.

Conspicuous where it occurs in disturbed areas of dry evergreen woodland, this plant is never found in large numbers. RV, HM, HA, NAN.

Agnew, Azavedo, and Khatri 9570; Verdcourt 3202.

2. Ferula montis-elgonis *Bak.*

Similar to *F. communis* except for the characters used in the key, this plant is still only known from the type from 12 000 ft on Mt. Elgon. It may eventually turn out to be merely an aberrant form of *F. communis*, and should be searched for. HE.

Lugard 425 (leaf-material only).

22. PEUCEDANUM *L.*

Perennial herbs with (in ours) 2–4 times pinnate or ternate leaves; umbels compound with usually few or no bracts and many bracteoles; 2–3 sepals often present; petals with an inflexed point; fruit flattened dorsally, each mericarp elliptic to orbicular, broadly winged, with 3 raised ridges.

1 Leaves much dissected, the ultimate segments linear or oblong, entire   2
   Leaves 2–4 times pinnatifid, the segments broader than linear, always serrate or crenate   6
2 Stem and leaf rachis tomentose, and densely hairy at nodes and pinna-insertions
         1. *P. kerstenii*
   Stem and leaf rachis glabrous or if minutely pubescent then not more densely hairy at nodes and pinna-insertions   3
3 Stem just below primary umbel with small soft pubescence of minute flaps of tissue; fruit over 9 mm long   2. *P. canaliculatum*
   Stem just below primary umbel glabrous or puberulous only; fruit less than 9 mm long
        5
4 Ultimate leaf segments linear or capillary 5
   Ultimate leaf segments oblong   3. *P. sp. A*
5 Lower leaves with lamina less than 8 cm long
        4. *P. friesiorum*
   Lower leaves with lamina more than 10 cm long   5. *P. aberdarense*
6 Stem roughened by the presence of soft corky flaps   6. *P. aculeolatum*
   Stem smooth   7

7 Stem tomentose or pubescent; fruits entire
        7. *P. elgonense*
   Stem glabrous; fruits strongly cordate below
        8. *P. linderi*

1. Peucedanum kerstenii *Engl.*

A large tomentose herb with an erect stem to 2 m, with big, finely divided leaves which are lanceolate in outline; flowers cream.

Common beside streams in montane situations, at the top of the forest and in the alpine zone. HE, HM, HA, HK.

Agnew 7193; Gillett 18442.

2. Peucedanum canaliculatum *Verde.*

An erect glabrescent herb with leaves ovate in outline, finely divided into channelled, linear segments; flowers white.

Uncommon plant found in dry grassland. HA, NAN, KAJ, MAG.

Verdcourt 3845; Agnew 8897.

3. Peucedanum *sp.* A.

An erect, minutely pubescent herb with leaves lanceolate in outline, 3–4 times pinnate into pinnatisect lobes, the ultimate segments oblong, entire; flowers white.

Only collected once at Eburru, in vlei grassland at 8000 ft. HM.

Agnew, Azavedo, and Khatri 9539.

4. Peucedanum friesiorum *Wolff*

A stoloniferous glabrous herb with an erect stem from a rosette of leaves; leaf lamina ovate to suborbicular in outline, divided into capillary segments; flowers white.

Locally common on stream banks and marshes in alpine grassland. HA, HK.

Hanid 87; Meinertzhagen 9374.

5. Peucedanum aberdarense *Wolff*

Similar to *P. friesiorum* in all respects but bigger and found in the uppermost forest zones, this may turn out to be only a variety of the latter.

Agnew, Hedberg, and Mmari 9624.

6. Peucedanum aculeolatum *Engl.* (see p. 361)

An erect herb, often massive, ± glabrous except for the soft scales on the stem; leaves 2–3 times ternate, triangular in outline, with ovate, crenate, ± lobed leaflets; flowers white.

Locally common in clearings in montane forest, especially around Limuru. HC, HM, HA, KAJ.

Agnew 8296; Kerfoot 5033.

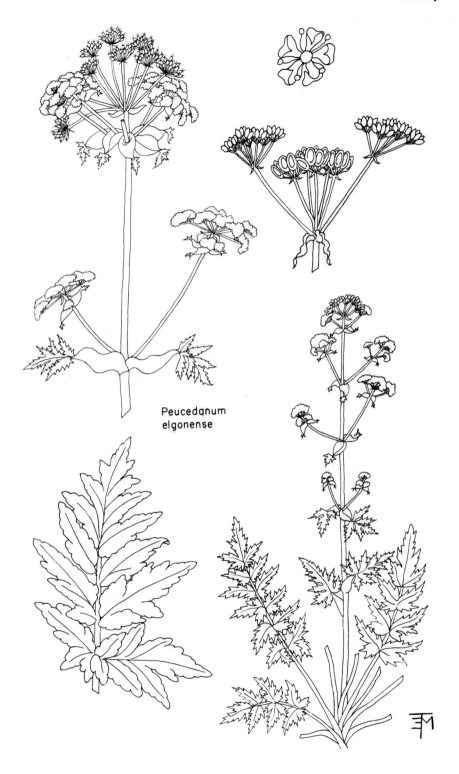

Peucedanum
elgonense

7. Peucedanum elgonense *Wolff* (see p. 359)

An erect tomentose perennial to 1·5 m tall, with 2–3 times pinnatisect leaves ovate-lanceolate in outline; leaf segments lanceolate, crenate; flowers white.

A common plant in streamside marshes in the subalpine zone. HE, HC, HT, HM, HA, HK.

Part II Botany 88; Le Pelleij in EAH 19310.

8. Peucedanum linderi *Norman*

An erect perennial similar to *P. elgonense* but glabrous and with the leaf segments oblong-elliptic and serrate; fruit deeply cordate at base.

The only Kenya *Peucedanum* with a cordate fruit-base, this plant is found in forest clearings and pathsides in lower montane forest. HE, HT, HM, HA.

Kerfoot 4330; Strid 3412.

23. LEFEBVREA *A. Rich.*

Usually a biennial or annual glabrous herb with ternate leaves; umbels compound with 1–3 or no bracts and a few slender bracteoles; calyx absent; petals cream or yellow, inflexed; stylopodia heavy, elongated; fruit dorsally flattened, broadly winged, the wings retuse at apex.

1   Stylopodia (disc-glands) elongated, twice as long as broad, conical, narrowing above
                                    1. *L. abyssinica*
    Stylopodia (disc-glands) short, cylindrical, up to 1·5 times as long as broad, blunt and truncate above   2. *L. brevipes*

1. Lefebvrea abyssinica *A. Rich.*

An erect glaucous herb with ternate or pinnate leaves bearing long lanceolate, remotely serrate leaflets; stylopodium long and conical; petals yellow.

Rare plant found in savannah of western Kenya. KIT.

Bogdan 3432.

2. Lefebvrea brevipes *Engl.*

Similar to *L. abyssinica* but with usually shorter, broader leaflets and cylindrical, truncate stylopodia.

Uncommon plant found in western Kenya savannah. HE, HM, KIT.

Lugard 275.

24. ERYTHROSELINUM *Chiov.*

Erect herbs with 2–4 times ternate or pinnatifid leaves; umbels compound with 0–2 bracts and a few slender bracteoles; calyx teeth absent; petals red, strongly incurved; disc abruptly conical; fruit dorsally flattened, with thick, pithy margins,

hardly ridged on the face and entire at base and apex.

Erythroselinum atropurpureum (*A. Rich.*) *Chiov.*

An erect glabrous annual with very variable leaves, the leaflets often linear, remotely toothed, but sometimes ovate to oblong; fruits pear shaped, glaucous.

Uncommon plant found in upland pastures and disturbed places especially in western Kenya. HA, HM, KIT.

Tweedie 67/272; Drummond and Hemsley 4449.

25. HERACLEUM *L.*

Perennial herbs, hairy (in ours), with 1–3 times pinnate leaves with broad segments; umbels compound with few bracts and many bracteoles; sepals small, unequal; petals often very unequal, the ones on the outside of the umbel enlarged, notched; fruit flattened dorsally, winged, smooth, with 4 incomplete dark lines on the outside and two within.

The genus in Kenya has obviously derived from one stock with specialized groups on every main mountain mass. The status of these plants will be in doubt until experimental work can be undertaken on them, but since one of them at least (*H. elgonensis*) is very distinct, and there is a name available for each, it seems worthwhile at present to recognize them all.

1   Outer petals of the outermost flowers more than 8 mm long; fruit widest below the middle   1. *H. elgonense*
    Outer petals of the outermost flowers less than 6 mm long; fruit, where known, widest above the middle   2
2   Stems branching vegetatively above the ground, often prostrate at base; bracteoles usually shorter than flowering pedicels
                                    2. *H. abyssinicum*
    Stems branching at ground level only, with a rosette of leaves and the aerial stems bearing only inflorescences; at least some bracteoles in each umbel longer than the flowering pedicel.   3
3   Lower surface of leaves uniformly pubescent; outer petals of outermost flowers less than 2·5 mm long   3. *H. taylori*
    Lower surface of leaves pubescent or tomentose on the veins, glabrous between the veins; outer petals of outermost flowers 2–6 mm long   4. *H. inexpectatum*

1. Heracleum elgonense (*Wolff*) *Bullock*

An erect fleshy-stemmed herb from a rosette of pinnate leaves with overlapping crenate pinnae; flowers white with outer petals often over 10 cm long.

Heracleum abyssinicum

Peucedanum
aculeolatum

Common in the alpine zone of Mt. Elgon (to which mountain it is confined) this species grows in marshes. HE.

Hedberg 217; Strid 3557.

2. Heracleum abyssinicum (*Boiss.*) *C. Norman* (see p. 361)

An erect or ± trailing perennial with branching, often ascending stems; leaves pinnate with dentate, often distant segments; flowers white, the outermost petals hardly exceeding 2·5 mm long; fruit broadest above the middle and retuse at apex.

Fairly common in upland grassland, this is probably the closest to the ancestral species from which the alpine ones have developed. HE, HC, HA.

Nattrass 241; Tweedie 67/67.

3. Heracleum taylori *Norman*

An erect herb from a rosette of pinnate leaves with distant, bluntly dentate pinnae; flowers white, fruits not seen.

Rare plant found in the streamsides of the Aberdares above 9500 ft. This plant is represented by only three specimens. HA.

Taylor 1454.

4. Heracleum inexpectatum *Norman*

Similar to *H. taylori* but much bigger in all its parts, and with the pinnae acutely dentate and ± glabrous between the veins below; outermost petals to 6 mm long but usually much less; fruits widest above the middle with a retuse apex.

This is the 'Mt. Kenya version' of the genus; it is abundant in wet screes and streamsides in the alpine zone. HK.

Coe and Kirrika 255; Verdcourt 3729.

69. ERICACEAE†

Wiry evergreen shrubs or small trees; leaves alternate or whorled, simple, needle-like, exstipulate; inflorescence racemose, terminal or lateral, leafy or leafless, bracteate; bracteoles 2 or in whorls of 3; flowers pedicellate; sepals 4–5, ovate, free; corolla-tube 4–5-lobed, bell-shaped; disc present; stamens once or twice sepal number, inserted on the disc, with 2-celled, tailed anthers; ovary superior, 4–5-celled and -loculed with numerous axile ovules; style simple, stigma capitate, fruit mostly capsular.

This family is mainly confined to land above 9000 ft in Kenya, and is better represented in arctic and temperate lands than here. The genus *Philippia* is composed of trees and shrubs which

† By A. D. Q. Agnew.

are dealt with in KTS. It differs from *Erica* in its unequal calyx lobes and large peltate stigma.

1   Wiry low shrubs or herbs, less than 50 cm tall
                                                        2
    Trees or shrubs over 50 cm tall
                                        2. Erica arborea

2   Corolla globose, inflated, narrowed at the lobes   *2. Erica whyteana*
    Corolla cylindrical or funnel-shaped, widest at the lobes   *1. Blaeria*

1. BLAERIA *L.*

Wiry undershrubs with branched or gland-tipped hairs; leaves pubescent; inflorescence paniculate or racemose; flowers 4–5-merous; corolla-tube dilated above; stamens 4–5; ovules indefinite; fruit a capsule.

1   Flowers and most leaves on short lateral branches which have shorter internodes than the main stem; corolla less than 2 mm long, roughly funnel shaped, narrower at base   *1. B. johnstonii*
    Most flowers and leaves usually on the ± numerous erect main stems; corolla more than 2·5 mm long, roughly cylindrical
                                            2. B. filago

1. Blaeria johnstonii *Engl.* (see p. 363)

A low pubescent shrub with monopodial branching often giving it a 'christmas-tree' appearance, the leaves and pink flowers being on short lateral shoots.

This plant is common in disturbed highland and alpine places, especially in peaty soils. HE, HC, HA, (?HK).

Agnew 5870; Kerfoot 1453.

2. Blaeria filago *Almy & Th. Fr. jr.*

A low shrub or wiry annual with numerous erect, usually unbranched stems bearing apical racemes of pink flowers.

A very variable plant of disturbed (often burnt) alpine moorland. Glabrous and heavily glandular and tomentose forms occur. HE, HA, HK.

Hanid 95; Hedberg 874.

2. ERICA *L.*

Wiry shrubs or small trees without gland-tipped hairs; leaves glabrous; inflorescence a paniculate raceme or spike-like; stamens 8, hypogynous; fruit a capsule.

1   Trees or shrubs more than 50 cm tall; inflorescence a paniculate raceme   *1. E. arborea*
    Low woody herbs, less than 50 cm tall; inflorescence spike-like
                                          2. E. whyteana

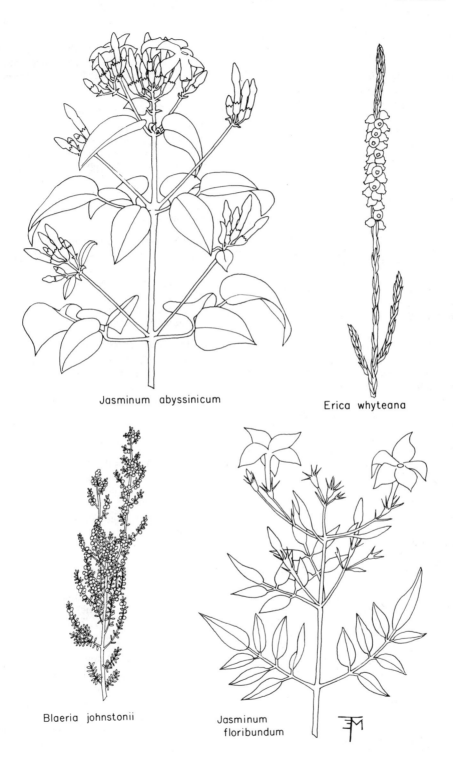

Jasminum abyssinicum

Erica whyteana

Blaeria johnstonii

Jasminum
floribundum

1. Erica arborea *L.*

Dealt with in KTS. p. 179. HE, HC, HA, HK, NAR, RV.

2. Erica whyteana *Britten* (see p. 363)

Small wiry shrubs up to 50 cm; stem ± glabrous; leaves 5–10 mm long, alternate or in whorls of 3, linear; inflorescences spike-like with axillary, globose, pendulous, pinkish flowers.

A very pretty pink heath, found in marshes or along streams above 9000 ft. HC, HA, HK.

Tweedie 66/392; Taylor 1425.

70. OLEACEAE

Trees, shrubs, or climbers; leaves opposite or rarely alternate, or whorled, simple or compound, exstipulate; inflorescence terminal or axillary, racemose or cymose, bracteolate; flowers bisexual, regular; calyx tube 4–6-lobed, corolla tube 4–6-lobed; stamens 2, epipetalous; disc absent; ovary superior, 2-celled; stigma capitate and lobed; fruit capsular, with 2–4 axile seeds.

1. JASMINUM *Dum.*

Climbing shrubs; leaves opposite or alternate, simple or compound, entire; inflorescence cymose or flowers solitary; calyx tube bell-shaped; corolla-tube cylindrical 4–6-lobed, sweetly scented; seeds solitary in each carpel; fruit a berry, often of separate mericarps.

1   Leaves simple, opposite or ternately whorled
         2
   Leaves compound   6
2   Leaves glabrous   3
   Leaves pubescent   4
3   Leaves ternately whorled; corolla lobes oblong
        1. *J. dichotomum*
   Leaves opposite; corolla lobes lanceolate
        2. *J. meyeri-johannis*
4   Corolla lobes shorter than the tube   5
   Corolla lobes as long as the tube
        3. *J. parvifolium*
5   Leaf base cordate; corolla lobes lanceolate; calyx lobes filiform   4. *J. pauciflorum*
   Leaf base rounded; corolla lobes oblong; calyx lobes broad   5. *J. eminii*
6   Leaves pinnate with more than 2 leaflets   7
   Leaves trifoliolate   8
7   Leaves opposite; corolla white, the lobes half as long as the tube   6. *J. floribundum*
   Leaves alternate; corolla yellow, the lobes a quarter as long as the tube   7. *J. sp. A*
8   Leaves with hairy pits (acarodomatia) along the midrib (in the axils of lateral nerves) extending to or above the middle of the

lower surface; calyx lobes 3–4·5 mm long
        8. *J. abyssinicum*
   Leaves with hairy pits only at the base, below the middle of the lower surface; calyx truncate or the lobes 1·5–3 mm long
        9. *J. fluminense*

1. Jasminum dichotomum *Vahl*

A glabrous woody climbing shrub with simple, elliptic-ovate, acute to acuminate, petiolate leaves in whorls of 3; inflorescence terminal or axillary; flowers shortly pedicellate, clustered; corolla white to purplish.

Found in open country and riverine forests with *Albizia*. HE, KIT, MUM, KIS.

Bally B 7465; Agnew and Musumba 8597.

2. Jasminum meyeri-johannis *Engl.*

A glabrous climbing shrub with simple ovate opposite leaves; inflorescence terminal to the main and to small lateral branches, few-flowered; corolla white to pink.

Found in *Acalypha* scrub. KIS.

Napier 3012 and 2967.

3. Jasminum parvifolium *Knobl.*

A twining shrub up to 3 m with densely pubescent young branchlets and glabrous old ones; leaves 10–25 mm long, opposite, simple, puberulous, elliptic-acute; inflorescence 1–4-flowered; corolla white to cream.

Found amongst grazed scrub. MAC.

Shirley Coryndon 1953.

4. Jasminum pauciflorum *Benth.*

Similar to *J. parvifolium* except for the 30–55 mm long elliptic-acuminate, often cordate leaves; corolla white.

Found only once in Kakamega forest. MUM.

Dale 3277.

5. Jasminum eminii *Gilg*

This species is similar to *J. parvifolium* except for the well-developed acarodomatia on the leaves and the keyed characters; corolla white.

Found growing on rocky ground, roadsides, and evergreen thickets. HA, KIS, NAR, MAC, NBI.

Agnew 7652; Verdcourt 2153A.

6. Jasminum floribundum *Fresen.* (see p. 363)

A glabrous perennial climbing or suberect shrub with opposite, typically 5-foliolate leaves; leaflets ovate, acute to acuminate; inflorescence very lax; corolla white.

Found in open hillsides and savannah bush on rocky ground HE, HC, HT, HM, HA, KIT, NAR, RV, MAG, NAN, NBI.

Tweedie 66/232; Archer 92.

7. Jasminum *sp.* **A.**

Similar to *J. floribundum* except in its leaves being alternate, leaflets elliptic, and calyx shortly toothed; corolla yellow.

Found only once in Milimani, Kitale. KIT. Tweedie 66/131 and 67/140.

8. Jasminum abyssinicum *DC.* (see p. 363)

A climbing shrub with glabrous or hardly puberulous young branchlets and inflorescence; leaves 3-foliolate, opposite; leaflets elliptic, acute to acuminate, usually glabrous; acarodomatia present; corolla lobes less than half the tube length.

Common in wet shrubland, shady and riverine forests. HE, HT, HA, HN, KIT, MUM, NAR, RV, MAC, NBI, KAJ.

Glover, Gwynne, Samuel, and Tucker 2295; Agnew and Beecher 8280.

9. Jasminum fluminense *Vell.*

Similar to *J. abyssinicum* except for the keyed characters.

This species is highly variable, and is common in dry *Combretum-Albizia* bushland on shallow soils. HA, HK, KIS, NAR, MAG, NAN, MAC, NBI, KAJ.

Bell 10637.

71. APOCYNACEAE†

Trees, shrubs, or lianes, rarely herbs with latex; leaves mostly opposite or whorled, simple, entire, exstipulate; inflorescence cymose-paniculate, or flowers solitary, terminal or pseudo-lateral; flowers bisexual, usually 5-merous, regular; calyx lobed, often glandular within, imbricate; corolla-tube variously shaped with contorted-imbricate lobes; anthers 2-lobed, convergent on the style; style split at base; disc present, 5-lobed; ovary superior, 2-carpelled, free below but with common style; ovules 2–numerous; fruit of 2 follicles, or a berry or a capsule; seeds winged or with a crown of hairs.

1   Woody climbers; inflorescence a long or short
         panicle   2
     Annual or perennial herbs; flowers solitary or
         paired, axillary   2. *Catharanthus roseus*
2   Panicles terminal; flowers sessile or crowded
         in the panicle; leaves obtuse or acute;
         corolla tube more than 5 mm long   3
     Panicles axillary and terminal; panicle loose,
         with pedicellate flowers; corolla tube less
         than 5 mm long   1. *Baissea alborosea*

† By S. Kibe.

3   Inflorescence of corymbs or cymes, many-
         flowered; flower more than 3·5 cm long
                                            4. *Saba florida*
     Inflorescence paniculate or of few-flowered
         corymbs of cymes; flower less than 3·5 cm
         long   3. *Landolphia buchananii*

1. BAISSEA *A. DC.*

Tall climbing shrubs, leaves opposite, oblong, acuminate; inflorescence leafy, loosely paniculate or of corymbs of few-flowered cymes; calyx herbaceous, eglandular within, imbricate; corolla 5-lobed, funnel- or bell-shaped, lobes overlapping to the right; stigma campanulate; carpels 2, hairy; ovules numerous, pluriseriate; seeds linear-lanceolate.

Baissea alborosea *Gilg & Stapf*

Woody, tall, climbing shrubs, leaf base truncate, inflorescence paniculate, panicles opposite; corolla lobes longer than the tube, lobes linear-lanceolate.

Found once in Kakamega forest. MUM.
Battiscombe K1212.

2. CATHARANTHUS *G. Don*

Much branched undershrubs or herbs up to 1 m; leaves opposite, exstipulate, axillary glands numerous in a fringe; flowers axillary, solitary or paired, white or pink; calyx herbaceous, eglandular; sepals 5, subulate; corolla salver-shaped, lobes overlapping to the left; stamens inserted in the widest part of the corolla tube; anthers free from stigma; disc replaced by 2 long glands alternating with the 2 free carpels; ovules numerous, in rows; fruit a pod.

Catharanthus roseus *(L.) G. Don*

Annual or perennial, much branched undershrubs or herbs; leaves elliptic-oblong, obtuse, fleshy; flowers paired; calyx eglandular, subulate; corolla lobes ovoid; fruit a pod.

An escape from cultivation, found growing in disturbed places, usually near habitation, in drier districts. HA, HK, MUM.

Templer 4; Hanid and Kiniaruh 9717.

3. LANDOLPHIA *Beauv.*

Climbing shrubs; stem lenticellate; tendrils branched or hooked, terminal or pseudo-axillary; leaves elliptic-oblong, often acuminate, rarely obtuse; inflorescence paniculate, terminal; flowers sessile or shortly pedicellate; sepals 5, free or connate below, eglandular; corolla salver-shaped, lobes shorter or longer than the tube, overlapping to the left; ovary entire, 1-celled; ovules numerous, in many rows; fruit a large globose or pear-shaped berry; seeds oblong or ovoid, embedded in juicy pulp.

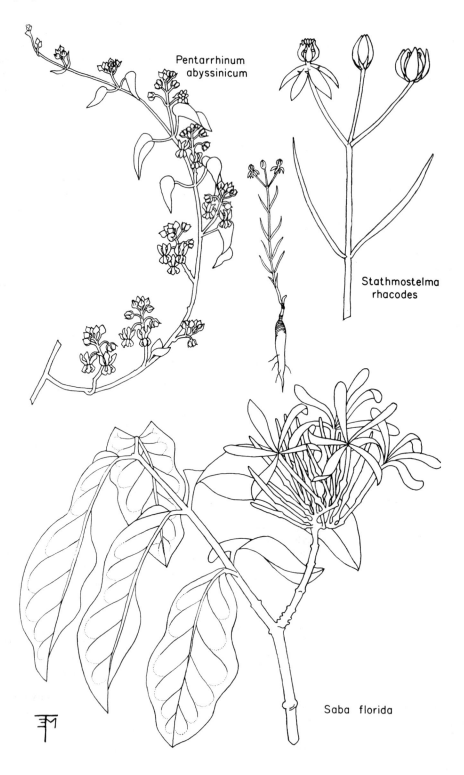

Pentarrhinum
abyssinicum

Stathmostelma
rhacodes

Saba florida

Landolphia buchananii (*Hall. f.*) *Stapf* (*L. kilimandscharica* Stapf, *L. ugandensis* Stapf)

Woody, climbing shrub; tendrils arising from the branch-forks; leaves elliptic-oblong, shortly acuminate; inflorescence a 5- 10-flowered panicle; sepals ovate, obtuse, ± ciliate; corolla lobes ± equal to the tube, yellow or white with touches of red or orange.

Found in riverine forest. HA, HM, HK, KIT, KIS, NAR, MAC, KAJ.

Perdue and Kibuwa 8090; Agnew, Hanid, and Kiniaruh 7917.

4. SABA (*Pichon*) *Pichon*

Woody, climbing or scrambling shrubs; stem glabrous; leaves opposite, large, ovoid-oblong, obtuse, rarely acuminate; inflorescence of corymbs of cymes, overtopped by the two forking branches or pseudo-lateral; flowers sweet-scented, salver-shaped; fruit a large berry.

Saba florida (*Benth.*) *Bullock* (see p. 366)

Climbing or scrambling bush, the stem with numerous dense whitish lenticels; leaves glabrous, leathery; flowers clustered, salver-shaped; corolla lobes as long as the tube or just shorter, oblong; fruit a berry, up to 6 cm in diameter.

Found on stony ground in riverine forests. HA, MUM, KIS, MAC.

Dale 3047; Birch 60/471.

72. ASCLEPIADACEAE†

Herbs, climbers, or shrubs with opposite, entire leaves and usually milky latex; stipules absent or represented by an interpetiolar rim at the nodes; flowers in cymes or umbels, rarely racemes or panicles, regular, bisexual; sepals 5, more or less free; petals 5, connate at base; corona of 5 or more lobes usually present, attached to the corolla or the stamens, sometimes in two whorls, usually acting as nectar dispensers; stamens 5; filaments free or fused; anthers variously and progressively modified from loosely connate, bearing granular pollen, to completely fused to the stigma and each other, bearing pollen in waxy masses (2 per stamen) which are fused to pollen carriers in adjacent pairs (pollinia); carpels 2, free, with a fused capitate stigma; fruit of 2 free follicles, often inflated, dry, bearing very numerous, usually feathery seeds.

A big, biologically successful family, apparently with such an exact pollination apparatus, producing such large quantities of seed from each pollination, that speciation has been rapid. At the same time most species exist in small numbers, being rare or extremely local in occurrence.

† By A. D. Q. Agnew and P. G. Archer (*Ceropegia*).

1   Flowers with a flask-shaped tube, widest at the bottom narrowing above, with the petal lobes apically adherent at anthesis
                                    36. *Ceropegia*
    Flowers with a short tube not narrowing above or without a tube, with the petal lobes mostly free at anthesis   **2**

2   Erect or decumbent fleshy-stemmed (cactus-like) herbs or weak shrubs without leaves, with the nodes and opposite leaf positions usually obscure; stems never twining   **43**
    Leafy herbs, shrubs or climbers, if leafless then with distinct nodes, long internodes and twining stems   **3**

3   Climbers, twining round support   **4**
    Shrubs or decumbent or erect herbs, never twining   **24**

4   Leafless fleshy-stemmed plants   **5**
    Plants with leaves; stems usually not fleshy   **6**

5   Flowers over 5 mm long; corona double; petals erect   25. *Sarcostemma*
    Flowers less than 3 mm long; corona single; petals spreading or reflexed
                        24. *Cynanchum tetrapterum*

6   Plants glabrous except for the corolla   **7**
    Plants hairy or at least pubescent on nodes and inflorescences   **8**

7   Leaves linear; corolla with long hairs within
                            9. *Periploca linearis*
    Leaves broad-ovate or elliptic; corolla glabrous   8. *Parquetina nigrescens*

8   Corona absent or obscure   **9**
    Corona present as conspicuous lobes on the staminal column, or between the petals and the staminal column   **12**

9   Flowers yellow or orange, or combinations of these colours with green   **10**
    Flowers maroon or red, or at least with deep maroon centre to petals and corona
            31. *Tylophora* and 27. *Tylophoropsis*

10 Pedicels over 15 mm long, the flowers in loose cymes; petals over 6 mm long
                            1. *Baseonema gregorii*
    Pedicels less than 10 mm long, the flowers in small tight cymes or subumbellate; petals less than 5 mm long   **11**

11 Leaves hairy, truncate or rounded at base; flowers in crowded, regular, pedunculate axillary umbels   29. *Gymnema silvestre*
    Leaves glabrous or hairy, always cuneate at base, sometimes broadly so; flowers in few-flowered, sometimes terminal cymes, rarely paniculate, rarely apparently umbellate but then leaves not hairy
                                    10. *Secamone*

12 Corona of simple, separate, entire, dorsally flattened lobes or filaments   **19**

Corona of toothed lobes, fused laterally or flattened laterally or toothed below or terete, not dorsally flattened **13**

13 Leaves cordate or hastate at base **14**
Leaves cuneate to truncate at base **17**

14 Corona with an inflexed bristle-like apex
22. *Pentarrhinum*
Corona with erect bristles or teeth at apex, or entire **15**

15 Corona lobes free from each other **16**
Corona lobes fused laterally
24. *Cynanchum*

16 Corolla maroon within, broadly bell-shaped; corona with no basal spur
12. *Oxystelma bornouense*
Corolla green with spreading, hardly fused lobes; corona with a basal spur directed downwards 26. *Pergularia daemia*

17 Flowers over 5 mm long; corona lobes massive, fleshy, terete, truncate above, as long as the staminal column
33. *Dregea abyssinica*
Flowers under 5 mm long; corona lobes laterally compressed, acute or rounded above, seldom as long as the staminal column **18**

18 Leaves and stems uniformly pubescent; flowers fasciculate on short pedicels at nodes 28. *Diplostigma canescens*
Leaves and stems glabrous or glabrescent, pubescent only at nodes and on midrib; flowers in (often small) pedunculate cymes 10. *Secamone*

19 Leaves mostly crowded on lateral short shoots, lanceolate to oblanceolate
3. *Curroria volubilis*
Leaves not crowded on lateral short shoots, mostly ovate to elliptic **20**

20 Corona lobes tomentose at apex
34. *Leptadenia hastata*
Corona lobes glabrous **21**

21 Corona lobes shorter than or equalling the stamens, fused to the staminal column **22**
Corona lobes much longer than the stamens, attached to the corolla **23**

22 Petals pubescent within; corona forming pockets between petal lobes and joined to both staminal column and corolla tube
31. *Tylophora* sp. *B*
Petals glabrous or pubescent; corona attached to staminal column only, not forming pockets between corolla lobes
33. *Dregea* and 30. *Gongronema*

23 Leaves suborbicular in outline; corona lobes reaching only to two-thirds the length of the corolla 7. *Mondia ecornuta*

Leaves oblong to elliptic in outline; corona lobes equalling or exceeding the corolla
5. *Tacazzea*

24 Perennial herbs with annual stems arising from a woody or fleshy rootstock **31**
Perennial shrubs with stems lasting more than one season, or annuals **25**

25 Corolla lobes over 5 mm long **26**
Corolla lobes less than 5 mm long **29**

26 Corolla lobes tomentose along the margin towards the apex within; fruit not inflated **27**
Corolla lobes glabrous within; fruit inflated **28**

27 Leaves attenuate at base; corolla pure white; fruit smooth 19. *Kanahia laniflora*
Leaves truncate or subcordate at base; corolla green and purplish with yellow corona; fruit with soft prickles
13. *Xysmalobium undulatum*

28 Leaves sessile, clasping the stem at base; fruit smooth, rounded 18. *Calotropis procera*
Leaves petiolate, not clasping; fruit with soft prickles or pointed at apex
17. *Gomphocarpus*

29 Leaves pubescent on both surfaces, never more than 2·5 cm long; flowers in sessile fascicles 28. *Diplostigma canescens*
Leaves glabrous, at least above, usually over 2·5 cm long; flowers in pedunculate cymes or racemes **30**

30 Roots with fleshy, globose tubers; leaves lanceolate; flowers apparently in racemes
2. *Sacleuxia tuberosa*
Roots without fleshy tubers; leaves elliptic; flowers in corymbose cymes
4. *Ectadiopsis oblongifolia*

31 Corona bigger than petals, spreading, dentate
23. *Margaretta rosea*
Corona smaller than petals, if spreading then entire **32**

32 Petals linear, over 15 mm long **33**
Petals broader, up to 15 mm long **34**

33 Petal lobes parallel-sided, glabrous
35. *Tenaris rostrata*
Petal lobes narrowing gradually from the base, tomentose 37. *Brachystelma*

34 Corona of filamentous lobes attached to corolla **35**
Corona broader, mostly attached to staminal column **36**

35 Fascicles of flowers sessile; pollinia present; fruit tuberculate
11. *Glossonema revoilii*
Cymes pedunculate; pollen granular; fruit smooth 6. *Raphionacme madiensis*

36 Central staminal column (including stalk if present) ± cylindrical, as long as or longer than broad **37**
Central staminal column sessile, disc-like, much broader than tall **40**
37 Umbels sessile; corona lobes simple, globose or pear-shaped, each with an apical tooth *14. Saxymolbium*
Umbels usually pedunculate; corona dorsally flattened, or with dorsally flattened lobes **38**
38 Corona lobes 5, simple, not divided into secondary lobes, flat not chambered *13. Xysmalobium undulatum*
Corona lobes apparently more than 5 by division, or lobed, or with a dorsal chamber **39**
39 Flowers often bright red, sometimes green with white or yellow; corona lobes each enclosing a chamber *21. Stathmostelma*
Flowers white, green and purple, not red or yellow; corona lobes each 2-lobed, the outer one usually overtopping the staminal column, not chambered *20. Pachycarpus*
40 Flowers in terminal inflorescences *15. Schizoglossum barbatum*
Flowers all axillary **41**
41 Leaves oblong-elliptic, over 10 mm broad; petals maroon *32. Sphaerocodon obtusifolium*
Leaves linear, less than 5 mm broad; petals greenish **42**
42 Stems unbranched, erect *16. Aspidoglossum*
Stems branched, inclined *37. Brachystelma*
43 Stem cylindric, covered by contiguous fleshy truncate leaf bases in 6–10 rows; flowers small, less than 5 mm long *38. Echidnopsis dammiana*
Stem angled, with the swollen leaf bases forming wings or bosses, not truncate, in 4–6 rows; flowers over 5 mm long **44**
44 Stem bearing conical horny knobs; corolla with flat, spreading lobes from a short tube, exceeding 5 cm diameter *39. Edithcolea grandis*
Stem with horny wings or unarmed; corolla with erect or bell-shaped corolla and lobes, always less than 5 cm in diameter **45**
45 Flowers in small lateral umbels; corolla bell-shaped bearing teeth between the lobes; corolla lobes broader than long, with no vibrating hairs *41. Huernia*
Flowers terminal or corolla lobes longer than broad, with vibrating hairs; corolla with no teeth between the lobes *40. Caralluma*

1. BASEONEMA *Schltr. & Rendle*
Woody pubescent climbers with subsucculent stems; flowers in terminal long-pedicellate cymes; petals lobes spreading; corona absent; stamens with free filaments; anthers bearing granular pollen, adnate to the style above.

Baseonema gregorii *Schltr. & Rendle*
A climbing shrub with obovate to elliptic leaves; corolla lobes over 1 cm long, green, reflexed; fruit smooth, of two divergent velvety follicles.
Rare in dry *Commiphora* country. MAC, KAJ. Bally in EAH 7316.

2. SACLEUXIA *Baill.*
Shrubs with axillary, ± racemose inflorescences and tuberous roots; corolla with obconic tube at base, bearing membranous scales between the bases of the filaments; corolla lobes thick, triangular; corona obscure, of small fleshy lobes fused to the free filaments; stamens connate; pollen granular; follicles smooth.

Sacleuxia tuberosa *(Bruce) Bullock*
A pubescent shrub with many, sparsely-branched stems and narrow-lanceolate leaves; peduncles equalling or little longer than petioles, bearing usually 3 racemes of brownish flowers.
Locally common in dry rocky country around Suswa and Naivasha. RV.
Glover and Samuel 3309.

3. CURRORIA *Planch.*
Twiners with flowers in short racemes; corolla with spreading lobes and a glandular pad at the base of each lobe; corona of filiform lobes, inserted on the corolla between corolla lobes; stamens with free filaments; anthers bearing granular pollen, fused to the expanded stigma at their base, and connivent to each other at apex; stigma very obtusely conical, bearing spoon-shaped organs between the anthers.

Curroria volubilis *(Schltr.) Bullock*
A woody, thick-branched climber with most leaves on thick short shoots; leaves lanceolate to linear or oblanceolate, pubescent; flowers in few-flowered racemes, greenish-yellow with a brown centre.
Very rare plant found in dry country. MAG.
Archer 527.

4. ECTADIOPSIS *Benth.*
Erect or twining shrubs with small flowers in cymes; petals shortly campanulate; corona of 5 filiform or fleshy lobes arising from the corolla

tube; stamens with free filaments and granular pollen; follicles smooth.

Ectadiopsis oblongifolia (*Meisn.*) *Schltr.* (see p.372)

An erect loose shrub with puberulent stem and glabrous, oblong-elliptic leaves; flowers pale yellow, in terminal or lateral corymbose cymes.

Common in wooded grassland in western Kenya, rarer in the east. KIT, KIS, EMB, MAC, KAJ.

Hanid and Kiniaruh 811; Faden 66214.

5. TACAZZEA *Decne.*

Similar to *Chlorocodon* except for the simple filiform corona lobes and the oblong petal lobes.

1   Leaves with raised reticulate venation below, cordate (occasionally only just) at base; flowers red; corona lobes twisted together above the stamens; follicles conical
                                     1. *T. apiculata*
     Leaves without a raised venation below, or only the midrib and primary nerves raised, rounded or broadly cuneate at base; flowers green and dull brown; corona lobes free above the stamens; follicles cylindrical
                                     2. *T. galactogoga*

1. Tacazzea apiculata *Oliv.*

A climbing shrub with ovate to oblong leaves and large loose panicles of red flowers.

Common along the Athi river, rare in upland and riverine forests elsewhere. HA, NAR, MAC, NBI.

Verdcourt 1570; Agnew 8230.

2. Tacazzea galactogoga *Bullock*

A climbing shrub with broad-elliptic, glabrous or tomentose leaves and large loose panicles of green flowers.

Locally common in upland rain-forest. HM, HA, HN, KAJ.

Agnew and Haines 8235; Bally 7924.

6. RAPHIONACME *Harv.*

Herbs from a tuberous rootstock with small flowers in pedunculate cymes; petal lobes spreading with a short cylindrical tube at base; corona of 5 entire or divided lobes attached to the corolla tube at the insertion of the filaments; filaments free; stamens with granular pollen; follicles smooth.

1   Leaves elliptic; flowers in axillary cymes
                                     1. *R. madiensis*
     Leaves linear; flowers in terminal cymes or racemes
                                     2. *R. splendens*

1. Raphionacme madiensis *S. Moore* (see p. 371)

An erect branching perennial with elliptic, often undulate leaves overtopping the axillary cymes of numerous green and purple-brown flowers.

Recorded by Mrs E. M. Tweedie from Mt. Elgon. HE.

2. Raphionacme splendens *Schlechter*

An erect herb from a fleshy tuber with ± unbranched stems and linear leaves; flowers few or up to 10 in loose terminal cymes or racemes, white and magenta.

Rare plant found in grassland; recorded once from Langata. NBI.

Archer 127.

7. MONDIA *R. Skeels*

Woody climbing shrubs with well-developed stipular frills at nodes and axillary panicles of flowers; corolla lobes spreading, almost free; corona of broad lobes, each often 3-lobed, the centre one (in ours) filiform; stamens with free filaments and granular pollen; style conical, not exceeding the anthers.

Mondia ecornuta (*N. E. Br.*) *Bullock*

Sparsely pubescent climbing shrub with suborbicular, cordate, abruptly acuminate leaves; flowers red-purple or maroon, to 14 mm long.

Rare plant found in wet western Kenya forests and only collected from Kakamega. MUM.

Dale 3431.

8. PARQUETINA *Baill.*

Similar to *Periploca*, but the corolla lobes auriculate at apex and with the corona usually divided above.

Parquetina nigrescens (*Afz.*) *Bullock*

A glabrous woody climber with elliptic to oblong to suborbicular leaves, rounded or sub-cordate at base and apex; flowers large (over 8 mm long) in few-flowered axillary corymbs, purple-brown.

Rare plant found in riverine forest in hot country and only known from Kibwezi in our area. KAJ.

Verdcourt 3187.

9. PERIPLOCA *L.*

Erect or climbing, glabrous shrubs, with or without leaves; flowers in corymbs; corolla lobes spreading, longer than the tube; corona of 5 filiform lobes arising from the corolla between the petals; stamens with free filaments, anthers bearing granular pollen loosely coherent with style; style shorter than anthers; follicles smooth.

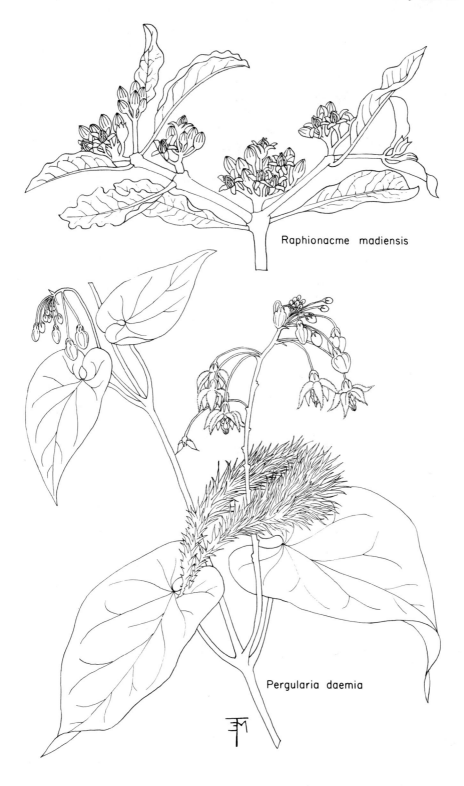

Raphionacme madiensis

Pergularia daemia

Periploca
linearifolia

Ectadiopsis
oblongifolia

Periploca linearifolia *Dill. & Rich.* (see p. 372)

A woody climber with linear leaves and terminal corymbs or purple and white flowers; petals white with a purple line above, hairy; corona lobes connivent at apex, forming a 'lantern' above the stamens.

Common in upland forest edges, but seldom flowering. HE, HC, HT, HM, HA, KIT, KIS, NAR, RV.

Agnew and Beecher 8272; Mwangangi 75.

10. SECAMONE *R. Br.*

Climbing shrubs with rounded or cuneate leaf-bases and rather small, stiff leaves; flowers in few-flowered cymes, which may be isolated, axillary or in branching terminal inflorescences, always (in ours) orange or yellow; petal-lobes spreading or erect, rather thick; corona obscure of 5 laterally-flattened lobes on the staminal column; stamens fused into a column, the pollen in 3-4 minute loose masses in each anther; follicles smooth.

1   Stigma exceeding anthers by more than the diameter of the style, usually visibly expanded above the anthers   2
    Stigma level with the top of the anthers or not exceeding the anthers by more than the diameter of the style, and not expanded above   4
2   Anthers hairy; stigma club-shaped or spherical   *1. S. africana*
    Anthers glabrous   3
3   Leaves softly tomentose, ovate-elliptic; stigma shortly obconical, as long as broad
                         2. S. stuhlmannii
    Leaves glabrous except on midrib and margin, coriaceous, linear-lanceolate; stigma long-obconical, longer than broad
                         3. S. punctulata
4   Apex of corona lobe acute, incurved, reaching nearly to apex of staminal column   5
    Apex of corona lobe held below middle of staminal column, obtuse, rounded
                         4. S. sp. A
5   Leaves lanceolate-linear, abruptly narrowed or rounded at base   *5. S. parvifolia*
    Leaves ovate-elliptic, ± attenuate at base
                         3. S. punctulata

1. Secamone africana (*Oliv.*) *Bullock*

A woody sparsely pubescent climber with elliptic leaves; flowers cream-coloured, rather large (over 4 mm long), in terminal panicles.

Rare plant found in western Kenya. MUM, KIS. Napier 2931: Dekker 3.

2. Secamone stuhlmannii *K. Schum.*

A woody softly tomentose climber with elliptic leaves and yellow flowers in small, lateral cymes.

Rare plant found in the Mara area only. NAR. Verdcourt and Darling 2287.

3. Secamone punctulata *Decne.*

A woody sparsely pubescent climber with narrowly elliptic or linear leaves and flowers in small axillary cymes; corona rounded, below the middle of the staminal column.

Our commonest *Secamone*, found in dry evergreen woodland. HA, NAR, MAC, KAJ.

Gardner 1389; Agnew 8798.

4. Secamone *sp.* A.

Climbing shrub similar to *S. punctulata* except for the linear leaves and terminal cymes; corona with an acute tip held above the centre of the staminal column; stigma not overtopping anthers.

In dry country in rocky soils. Not yet recorded for our area, this species is included as it will probably be found in the future.

Known from East Tsavo. Archer 213.

5. Secamone parvifolia (*Oliv.*) *Bullock*

A woody sparsely pubescent climber with ovate-elliptic leaves and axillary and terminal few-flowered cymes of small flowers.

A rare species of dry bushland, with broad leaves which appear to be undulate at margin when dry, and may be so when fresh. Again, this species is known from only just outside our area at Kiboko and at Mwingi in MAC.

Edwards 85.

11. GLOSSONEMA *Decne.*

Small annual or perennial herbs with flowers in axillary cymes; corolla tube short; corona of 5 lobes arising from the corolla, stamens fused; pollinia pendulous; follicles tuberculate or smooth.

Glossonema revoilii *Franch.*

An erect, pubescent, much-branched perennial herb from a thin woody rootstock, with oblong-elliptic leaves; cymes sessile; flowers cream-yellow with maroon centre, fading to bronze; follicles tuberculate.

Uncommon plant found in dry rocky bushland, MAG, NAN, MAC, KAJ.

Agnew 7300; Archer 532.

12. OXYSTELMA *R. Br.*

Climbers with few-flowered pedunculate cymes or racemes; corolla with a short tube, broadly saucer-shaped and 5-lobed above; corona of 5 erect, fleshy, lanceolate lobes attached to the staminal column; stamens fused; anthers with pendulous pollinia; follicles inflated.

Oxystelma bornouense *R. Br.*
A glabrescent climber with cordate leaves and big maroon and white flowers to 3 cm diameter.

Rare plant found in riverine forest and only recorded from the Athi River in our area. MAC.
Ranwell 3163.

13. XYSMALOBIUM *R. Br.*
Erect herbs with usually unbranched stems and tuberous roots; umbels pedunculate or sessile; corolla lobes divided nearly to base, spreading, ovate-triangular, pubescent or glabrous; corona of 5 lobes, arising from the base of the corolla tube, each lobe flattened, fleshy, ± fused to other lobes laterally at base; pollinia pendulous; staminal appendages conspicuous; fruit softly spiny or smooth.

Xysmalobium undulatum (*L.*) *Ait. f.* (see p. 375)
A robust erect annual or perennial, unbranched, with lanceolate undulate leaves which are truncate or even clasping at the base; flowers brown-purple; fruits densely covered with soft spines.

Common in marshy grassland especially in Western Kenya. KIT, NAN, KAJ.
Rodgers 489; Tweedie 67/216.

14. SAXYMOLBIUM *Bullock* ined.
Similar to *Xysmalobium* but the umbels sessile, petals reflexed and corona lobes attached to the staminal column, each lobe consisting of a ± globose base with a short, papillose point above.

1   Leaves oblong, obtuse   1. *S. heudelotianum*
    Leaves linear, acute   2. *S.* sp. A

1. Saxymolbium heudelotianum (*Decne.*) *Bullock* (*Xysmalobium reticulatum* N. E. Br.) (see p. 375)
Herb with erect unbranched stems bearing oblong, glabrescent leaves and sessile umbels of flowers; petals green, corona brown.

Uncommon plant found in grassland in western Kenya. HT, HA, KIT.
Bickford, April 1948.

2. Saxymolbium *sp.* A.
Similar to *S. heudelotianum* but with very narrow-linear, acute leaves.

Only once collected, on the Chyulu Hills. KAJ.
Archer 543.

15. SCHIZOGLOSSUM *E. Mey.*
Similar to *Xysmalobium* but with an apical or inner horn or points on the corona and with the staminal mass short, disc-like; corolla lobes ovate, glabrous within.

Schizoglossum barbatum *Brit. & Rendle*
An erect pubescent herb with linear leaves and axillary and terminal corymbs of maroon and green flowers; corona hooded, with an apical filamentous point and lateral obtuse lobes.

Rare plant found in highland grassland in Western Kenya. HT, HM.
Polhill 395.

16. ASPIDOGLOSSUM *E. Mey.*
Similar to *Schizoglossum* but having an erect, unbranched stem, axillary (not terminal) inflorescences, linear leaves and narrower, often hairy petals.

1   Petals less than 3 mm long 1. *A. interruptum*
    Petals more than 3 mm long   2
2   Petals connate at tip, glabrous or uniformly
    pubescent within, over 7 mm long; corona
    lobes truncate, usually without an apical
    point   2. *A. connatum*
    Petals free at tip, glabrous or usually
    pubescent, with an apical tuft of long
    hairs; corona lobes truncate, with an apical
    point on the inside   3. *A. angustissimum*

1. Aspidoglossum interruptum (*E. Mey.*) *Bullock*
An erect, unbranched, pubescent herb from a narrow tuber with linear, revolute leaves and small clusters of brownish flowers in the upper axils.

Rare plant found in dry grassland. BAR.
Dale 6960.

2. Aspidoglossum connatum (*N. E. Br.*) *Bullock*
Similar to *A. interruptum* except for the flowers which are larger (to 9 mm long) with connate petals and subentire corona.

Rare plant found in dry grassland in western Kenya. HT, MUM, RV.
Napier 2915.

3. Aspidoglossum angustissimum (*K. Schum.*) *Bullock* (see p. 376)
Similar to the last two species except for the characters given in the key; petals vary in the amount of indumentum they bear.

Fairly common in dry grassland around Nairobi and also found elsewhere. HC, HA, KIT, RV, NAN, NBI.
Agnew and Barnley 10577; Williams in EAH 12335.

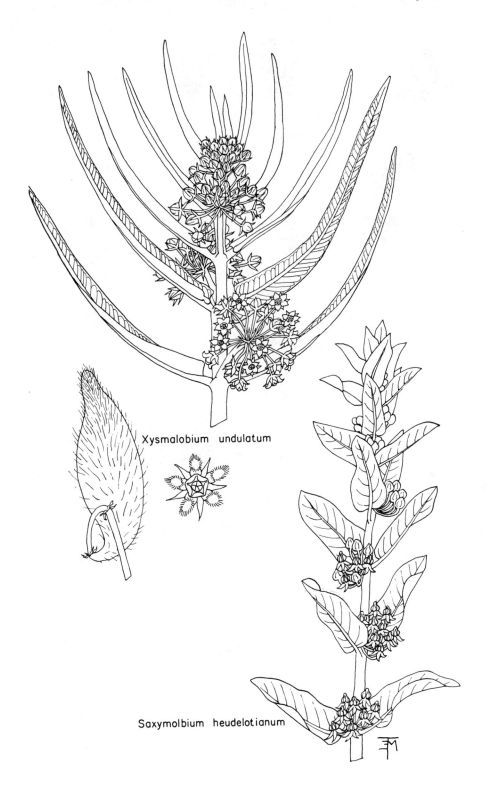

Xysmalobium undulatum

Saxymolbium heudelotianum

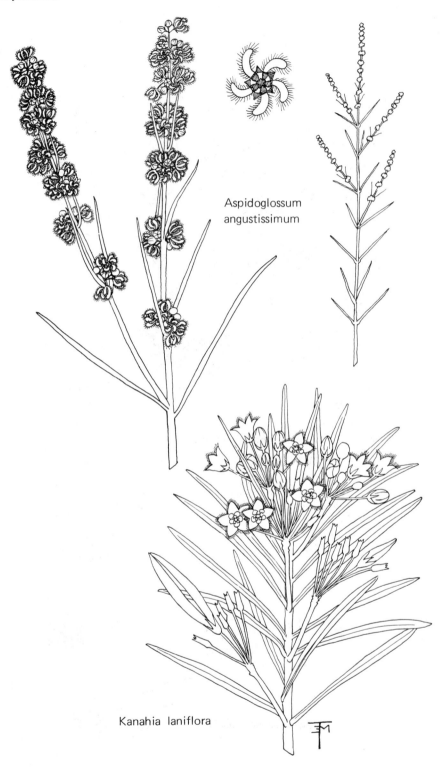

Aspidoglossum
angustissimum

Kanahia laniflora

17. GOMPHOCARPUS *R. Br.*

Erect perennials from a simple, unthickened root, with linear to lanceolate, often whorled or alternate leaves; flowers in pedunculate lateral umbels; corolla spreading or reflexed, lobed nearly to base; corona attached to the base of the stalked staminal column, of infolded lobes usually toothed on the inner angles of the lobes and hollow within; stamens fused; pollinia pendulous; follicles inflated, often bristly.

1 Corona lobes with a tooth on each of the inner angles, the tooth directed outwards and often curved downwards   2
   Corona lobes with erect or obscure teeth on the inner angles   4
2 Leaves with raised lateral veins below; corona overtopped by staminal column; inner angle of corona lobes crenate, the outwardly directed part shorter than the entire tooth   1. *G. semilunatus*
   Leaves with obscure or invisible lateral veins below; corona equalling staminal column; inner angle of corona lobes consisting wholly of the recurved part with or without a minute inner tooth   3
3 Corona with a small erect appendage within the shallow central hollow; fruits obtuse apiculate at apex   2. *G. kaessneri*
   Corona with no appendage within the deeper central hollow; fruits tapering gradually to an acute apex   3. *G. fruticosus*
4 Leaves over 5 mm broad, lanceolate-linear, with visible lateral venation below; corona overtopped by staminal column; fruits with scattered bristles over entire surface   4. *G. physocarpus*
   Leaves less than 5 mm broad, acicular with invisible lateral venation below; corona equalling or overtopping the staminal column; fruits smooth or with a few bristles in 1-2 lines only   5
5 Corona lobes lanceolate in lateral outline, overtopping the staminal column, crenate but not toothed on the inner angle; fruits ovate, acuminate in outline   5. *G. integer*
   Corona lobes suborbicular in lateral outline, equalling the staminal column, with 1-2 small teeth on inner angle; fruits lanceolate, acute in outline   6. *G. stenophyllus*

1. **Gomphocarpus semilunatus** *A. Rich.* (see p. 378)

A large erect perennial with crowded lanceolate leaves and purple-pink flowers; corona mostly with an erect tooth within the central hollow; fruits pubescent, ± semicircular in lateral outline, equally rounded at both ends, thickly covered with minutely scabrid bristles.

One of the commonest species in Kenya, especially in the west, growing in disturbed places and on flooded grassland and roadsides in medium altitude grassland areas. HE, HT, HM, HA, KIT, MUM, KIS, NAR, RV.

Agnew, Kibe, and Mathenge 10610; Lucas 115.

2. **Gomphocarpus kaessneri** *N. E. Br.*

Similar to *G. semilunatus* except for the corona which has a shallow hollow above with a short appendage in it and large recurved lobes on the inner angles; fruit tomentose with spreading-pubescent bristles.

This species replaces *G. semilunatus* in the eastern part of our area. MUM, RV, MAG, MAC, NBI, KAJ.

Greenway 9691; Harmsen 6479; Kaessner 664 (Type).

3. **Gomphocarpus fruticosus** (*L.*) *Ait. f.* (see p. 379)

A branched erect shrub, with acicular to linear-oblong leaves and white and maroon flowers; fruits ovate in outline, covered with almost glabrous purple bristles.

This species has consistently shorter leaves (usually to 8 cm long) than *G. physocarpus*, with which its fruits may be confused. It is our commonest species of *Gomphocarpus* and can be found in dry montane grassland and along watercourses in lowland country. HC, HT, HM, HL, HA, HK, KIT, KIS, BAR, RV, EMB, KAJ.

Moreau 48: Part II Botany 90.

4. **Gomphocarpus physocarpus** *E. Mey.* (see p. 379)

A sparsely branched erect shrub with lanceolate leaves and green and white flowers, occasionally tinged with purple; fruit broadly ovate in outline, rather abruptly constricted into a short ± hooked apex, covered with scattered minutely pubescent bristles.

Uncommon plant found in dry upland grassland. HT, HM, HA, NAR.

Lind, Agnew, and Harris 5101; Napier 5065.

5. **Gomphocarpus integer** (*N. E. Br.*) *Bullock*

A delicate erect sparsely-branched perennial with white woolly hairs on young parts and acicular leaves; flowers yellow, green and pink; fruits ovate-acuminate in outline, with a few glabrous bristles along one side or smooth.

Locally common in grassland at medium altitudes. HA, KIS, NAR, BAR, RV, NAN, MAC, NBI.

Agnew and Gilbert 7808; Turner in EAH 6900.

Gomphocarpus
stenophyllus

Gomphocarpus
semilunatus

Gomphocarpus fruticosus

Gomphocarpus physocarpus

6. Gomphocarpus stenophyllus *Oliv.* (see p. 378)
Similar to *G. integer* but with yellow or reddish flowers and a narrower, usually smooth, fruit.

Locally common in dry grassland at medium altitudes, often on disturbed or rocky soils. HE, HT, HM, HA, KIT, NAR, NAN, MAC, NBI, KAJ.
Strid 2646; Glover 273.

18. CALOTROPIS *R. Br.*

Erect shrubs with clasping leaves and dense axillary umbels of large flowers; corolla shortly saucer-shaped at base, with triangular-ovate lobes; corona of 5 compressed lobes, with 2 apical teeth and an upcurved spur at base arising from the staminal column; anthers fused; pollinia pendulous; follicles inflated, smooth.

Calotropis procera (*Ait.*) *Ait. f.*

A tall, softly woody, sparingly-branched shrub with elliptical or ovate clasping leaves and dense masses of purple, violet and white flowers.

Common in disturbed places, especially where seasonally flooded, in dry country. MUM, KIS, BAR, MAG, EMB, MAC, KAJ.
Greenway 10396; Agnew 10759.

19. KANAHIA *R. Br.*

Shrubs with unbranched stems and linear-lanceolate leaves; flowers in lateral pedunculate cymes; corolla deeply 5-lobed; corona of 5 lobes arising from staminal column, each lobe folded and thus with a central chamber, or fused into a single mass, with two apical teeth; stamens fused; pollinia pendulous; fruits smooth.

Kanahia laniflora (*Forsk.*) *R. Br.* (see p. 376)

A glabrous shrub with many erect stems and linear leaves; flowers large, pure white.

Locally abundant along watercourses in dry country. BAR, NAN, MAC.
Agnew 9948; Ossent 281.

20. PACHYCARPUS *E. Mey.*

Herbs with one (or few) erect, unbranched stems from a perennial, often tuberous, rootstock; leaves often broad, cordate or truncate at base; flowers in pedunculate axillary umbels; corolla lobes broad-ovate, shortly fused at base; corona inserted below the anthers on the stalked staminal column, consisting of 5 free segments each of two parts, an outer often dorsally-flattened lobe joined to two inner often laterally-flattened lobes; stamens fused; pollinia pendulous; fruits smooth, often winged.

1   Outer lobe of each corona segment equal to
      or longer than inner lobes   2
    Outer lobe of each corona segment obscure,
      much shorter than inner lobes 1. *P. fulvus*

2   Inner lobes of corona consisting of erect,
      conical or linear, ± acute projections   3
    Inner lobes of corona consisting of broad
      obtuse lobes   4

3   Leaves mostly lanceolate-ovate without a
      well-marked submarginal vein; inner
      corona lobes filamentous arising near the
      base of the corona   2. *P. grantii*
    Leaves mostly oblong-elliptic, with a well-
      marked submarginal vein; inner corona
      lobes reduced to a pair of teeth arising
      nearly on a level with top of stamens
                                        3. *P. eximius*

4   Leaves linear-lanceolate; outer corona lobe
      twice as long as inner lobes
                                     4. *P. rhinophyllus*
    Leaves oblong-ovate to lanceolate; outer
      corona as long as inner corona   5

5   Corona lobes overtopped by the staminal
      column, and inserted on the stalk of that
      column which is ± as long as the anthers;
      leaves lanceolate-oblong   5. *P. lineolatus*
    Corona lobes equalling the staminal column;
      stalk of staminal column ± half as long as
      anthers; leaves oblong-ovate
                                   6. *P. schweinfurthii*

1. Pachycarpus fulvus (*N. E. Br.*) *Bullock*

An erect pubescent perennial with ovate to oblong ± cordate leaves and striking umbels of cream, orange and brown flowers.

Rare plant found in western Kenya in wooded grassland. HE, KIT.
Tweedie 56.

2. Pachycarpus grantii (*Oliv.*) *Bullock*

An erect pubescent perennial with ovate, lanceolate or oblong leaves which are scabrid along the margin, and with conspicuous (sometimes sessile) umbels of white and maroon or purple flowers.

Uncommon plant found in dry upland grassland. HC, HT, HA, HK.
Strid 2632A; Graham 857.

3. Pachycarpus eximius (*N. E. Br.*) *Bullock* (see p. 383)

Similar to *P. grantii* except for the broader leaves and shorter inner corona teeth.

Uncommon plant found in western Kenya. HE, HC, KIT, MUM, KIS.
Glasgow 46/23; Lugard 570.

4. Pachycarpus rhinophyllus (*K. Schum.*) *N. E. Br.*

An erect pubescent perennial from a tuberous root system with lanceolate-linear leaves which are truncate at base; flowers in (sometimes sessile) umbels, yellow and brown.

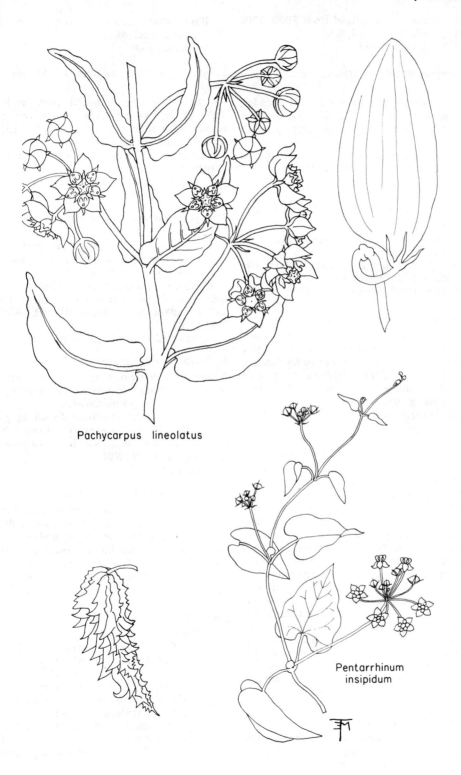

Pachycarpus lineolatus

Pentarrhinum
insipidum

Locally common in grassland from 5000–7000
ft. HA, HK, NAR, MAC, NBI, KAJ.
Agnew 7470; Glover 653.

5. Pachycarpus lineolatus (*Decne.*) Bullock (see
p. 381)
Similar to *P. rhinophyllus* except for the broader,
more oblong leaves with a scabrid edge, and the
key characters; flowers greenish with purplish
corona.
Rare plant found in grassland in western Kenya
and also found at the coast. HE, MUM.
Jack 305.

6. Pachycarpus schweinfurthii (*N. E. Br.*) *Bullock*
(see p. 383)
Similar to the last species in all respects except for
the key characters.
Locally common, in dry wooded grassland. HE,
HC, KIT, MUM, KIS, EMB, KAJ.
Hanid and Kiniaruh 798; Webster 8830.

21. STATHMOSTELMA *K. Schum.*
Perennial herbs from a fusiform tuber, with erect,
dichotomous stems and terminal umbels of showy
flowers; leaves linear; corolla lobes shortly fused at
base, ovate; corona of 5 lobes arising at the base of
the staminal column which is short-stalked, each
lobe folded to enclose a chamber from which a
protuberance usually arises; stamens fused; pollinia
pendulous.

1   Petals white; flowers over 3 cm in diameter
                              1. *S. praetermissa*
    Petals red or olive-green; flowers less than
       3 cm in diameter   2
2   Corona lobes ± truncate above, the inner
       angles held at the same level as the outer
       edge; central protuberance of corona not
       exceeding the top of the corona   3
    Corona lobes lobed above, the inner angles
       produced to greatly overtop the outer edge
       which is also overtopped by the filiform
       central protuberance   2. *S. rhacodes*
3   Corona lobes almost solid, the central pro-
       tuberance acute, lying between the two
       inner edges   3. *S. pedunculata*
    Corona lobes almost completely hollow, with
       the central protuberance arising from the
       back of the hollow and ending obtusely
       between the inner edges   4. *S. propinqua*

1. Stathmostelma praetermissa *Bullock*
A robust erect branched herb with sparsely
pubescent linear leaves and large white, green and
dull purple flowers in many umbels.

Rare plant found in wooded grassland in
Machakos district. MAC.
Verdcourt 844.

2. Stathmostelma rhacodes *K. Schum.* (see p.
366)
An erect, sparsely-branched herb with linear,
glabrous leaves and usually only one terminal
umbel, with some pedicels usually less than 4 cm
long, of red and orange flowers.
Common in seasonally wet or waterlogged
grassland especially on shallow soil. HT, HM, HA,
KIT, KIS, NAR, BAR, RV, MAC, NBI.
Strid 3155; Glover 1643.

3. Stathmostelma pedunculata (*Decne.*) *K.
Schum.*
Very similar to *S. rhacodes* except for the key
characters and the usually longer (over 5 cm)
pedicels and larger flowers.
Common in some areas of sandy grassland as
well as on black-cotton soil, often on shallow soils,
and abundant at the coast. HE, HL, KIT, EMB,
MAC, NBI.
Agnew and Hanid 7520; Napier 3048.

4. Stathmostelma propinqua *N. E. Br.*
A low repeatedly-dichotomous herb with linear
pubescent leaves and several few-flowered umbels
of green and dull purple flowers.
This rare plant has been found in grassland
locally near Nairobi (Langata) and once elsewhere
(Isiolo). It was described from Tanzania, near
Kilimanjaro. NAN, NBI.
Archer 185.

22. PENTARRHINUM *E. Mey.*
Climbing herbs or weak shrubs with cordate leaves
and no stipules; flowers in axillary, pedunculate
racemes, corymbose or almost umbellate; corolla
deeply 5-lobed, the lobes spreading or reflexed;
corona of 5 lobes alternating with the petals,
shortly fused at base, each lobe obconical with an
adaxial groove, expanded at the top and with an
inflexed filamentous apex; stamens united with
pendulous pollinia; follicles usually rugose.

1   Corona-lobes yellow (at anthesis), apparently
       solid, ending in a sharp-edged disc with an
       inflexed central apical appendage
                              1. *P. insipidum*
    Corona-lobes white (at anthesis), hollow,
       folded and rounded at the apex into the
       inflexed apical appendage   2
2   Leaves abruptly acuminate at apex; petals
       with red venation   2. *P.* sp. *A*
    Leaves acute at apex; petals simply green
                              3. *P. abyssinicum*

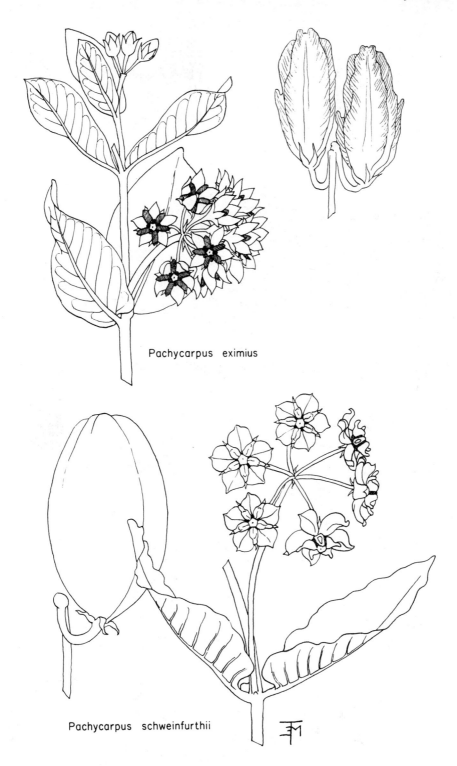

Pachycarpus eximius

Pachycarpus schweinfurthii

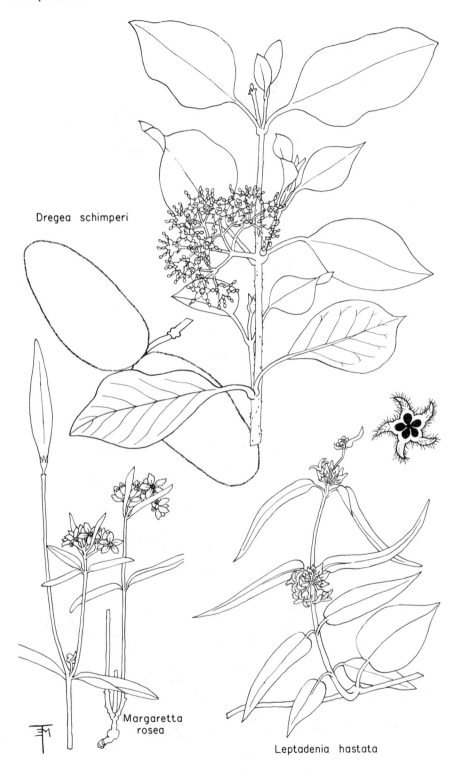

Dregea schimperi

Margaretta
rosea

Leptadenia hastata

1. Pentarrhinum insipidum *E. Mey.* (see p. 381)

Sparsely pubescent climber with glabrescent, sub-orbicular cordate leaves; peduncles of racemes usually longer than petioles; petals green; corona yellow or orange; fruit warty.

Fairly common in dry country and edges of dry evergreen forest. HM, HA, MUM, KIS, RV, MAG, MAC, NBI, KAJ.

Kokwaro 111; Strid 2740.

2. Pentarrhinum *sp.* **A.**

Similar to *P. insipidum* except for the slightly more hairy ovate, cordate and acuminate leaves and the corolla and corona characters mentioned in the key.

Apparently rare plant found in upland forest edges. HC, HA.

Webster 8829; Polhill 457; Agnew and Beecher 8273.

3. Pentarrhinum abyssinicum *Decne.* (see p. 366)

Similar to *P. sp. A.* except for its smaller leaves which are densely tomentose above and below and not acuminate, and the peduncles which are usually shorter than the petioles; corolla and corona characters as in the key.

Locally common in grassland and *Combretum* woodland. MAG, MAC, KAJ.

Archer 91; Tweedie 67/122.

23. MARGARETTA *Oliv.*

Erect herbs from a tuberous rootstock; inflorescences terminal, of corymbose cymes; corolla small, spreading, deeply lobed; corona of 5 lobes arising from staminal column, each lobe with a folded claw at base bearing 2–3 teeth above and an expanded petaloid blade; stamens fused; pollinia pendulous; follicles smooth.

Margaretta rosea *Oliv.* (see p. 384)

An erect pubescent herb with lanceolate to linear leaves and dense terminal masses of pink, orange or yellow flowers.

Common in grasslands of Western Kenya. HE, HA, KIT, KIS.

Tweedie 67/18; Harger 5.

24. CYNANCHUM *L.*

Erect or climbing, glabrous or hairy herbs or shrubs with cordate to cuneate leaf bases; corolla with the tube shorter than the lobes; corona continuous within the corolla, toothed or laciniate, often with secondary lobes and teeth arising within the primary ones; stamens fused, with pendulous pollinia; style shorter or longer than stamens.

1   Leafless fleshy climbers   1. *C. tetrapterum*
    Leafy climbers or fleshy trailing shrubs   **2**

2   At least some leaves hastate or cordate at base   **3**
    All leaves rounded at base   2. *C. altiscandens*

3   Leaves white-tomentose below; petals hairy; corona-lobes longer than the corona tube
                   3. *C. abyssinicum*
    Leaves glabrous or sparsely pubescent below; petals glabrous; corona-lobes shorter than the tube   **4**

4   Inflorescence pedunculate; corona-lobes broad or reduced to teeth   **5**
    Inflorescence sessile, fasciculate; corona-lobes filamentous   4. *C. hastifolium*

5   Leaves suborbicular, as long as broad; inflorescence racemose   5. *C. validum*
    Leaves ovate to elliptic, longer than broad; inflorescence a pedunculate umbel
                   6. *C.* sp. *A*

1. Cynanchum tetrapterum *(Turcz.) R. A. Dyer*

A climbing, glabrous, leafless shrub with fleshy stems and sessile clusters of shortly pedicellate flowers; petals green or brown, often reflexed; corona white, with 5–15 short blunt teeth.

Common in dry *Acacia* bushland, especially where disturbed. KIS, NAR, BAR, RV, MAG, EMB.

Agnew 8750; Glover 3207.

2. Cynanchum altiscandens *K. Schum.*

A climbing sparsely-pubescent shrub with ovate leaves, acute at apex, rounded at base; flowers in shortly pedunculate umbels; petals green; corona white, tubular, toothed; fruit 3-ridged.

Probably the commonest Asclepiad in upland forest edges. HE, HC, HM, HA, NAR, RV, NBI.

Agnew, Kibe and Mathenge 10481; Archer 285.

3. Cynanchum abyssinicum *Decne.* (see p. 386)

A climbing hairy shrub with lanceolate, hastate or cordate leaves which are densely white-tomentose below; flowers in short-pedunculate, very short racemes; petals green and purplish; corona white, with 15 long subulate lobes, 5 within the tube; fruit tuberculate.

Uncommon plant found at the edges of upland rain forest. HE, HT, HM, HA.

Irwin 182; Mathenge 376.

4. Cynanchum hastifolium *N. E. Br.*

A climbing, sparsely-tomentose shrub with ovate to lanceolate, hastate leaves frequently fasciculate; flowers fasciculate in sessile umbels; petals green; corona white with 5 subulate lobes and 5 deltoid teeth all terminal.

Rare plant found in dry country. KAJ.

Rauh Ke 238.

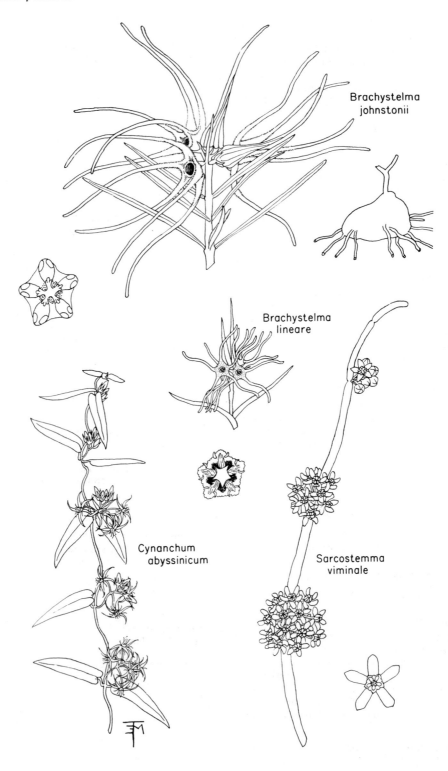

Brachystelma
johnstonii

Brachystelma
lineare

Cynanchum
abyssinicum

Sarcostemma
viminale

5. Cynanchum validum *N. E. Br.*

A semi-succulent, sparsely pubescent, trailing shrub or climber with suborbicular cordate leaves; inflorescences racemose, pedunculate; petals yellow-green with brown spots; corona yellow with 10 short terminal teeth; fruit 3-winged.

Rare plant found in dry rocky country. KAJ, NAR, RV.

Glover 3339.

6. Cynanchum *sp.* A.

A woody, sparsely pubescent climber with ovate-elliptic, bullate, cordate or rounded leaves; flowers in pedunculate umbels; petals green with dull purplish markings; corona green or purple; fruit unknown.

Uncommon plant found in montane rain-forest, especially bamboo. HE, HA.

Agnew 7179, Glover 1492.

25. SARCOSTEMMA *R. Br.*

Twining or decumbent shrubs with green, fleshy stems and reduced, scale-like leaves; flowers in sessile umbels; petals hardly fused at base, with erect lobes; corona-lobes in two series, both fused to staminal column, the outer forming a continuous rim below the stamens, the inner, of lobes one below each stamen; stamens fused with pendulous pollinia; fruit smooth.

Sarcostemma viminale (*L.*) *R. Br.* (see p. 386)

A trailing or twining shrub with pubescent or glabrous green stems; flowers white; petals 5–7 mm long.

A variable plant which has three forms: a prostrate one, rooting at tips of branches, with short internodes and knobbly nodes, a climber with thick (over 8 mm) pubescent internodes, and a climber with thin glabrous internodes. All these forms have similar flowers and fruits, yet they may eventually prove to be distinct.

The plant is found in dry country, often where rocky or disturbed. HE, HT, HA, KIT, MUM, KIS, NAR, BAR, RV, MAG, NAN, MAC, NBI, KAJ.

Bally (11339) 119; Strid 3328.

26. PERGULARIA *L.*

Climbers with cordate leaves and hairy stems; flowers in racemes; corolla with a basal cylindrical tube and erect hairy lobes; corona double, of 5 outer lobes joined in a ring around the base of the staminal column and 5 inner ones fused to the staminal column, each with an erect, bifid apical process and a basal spur; stamens fused; pollinia erect; follicle usually ornamented.

Pergularia daemia (*Forsk.*) *Chiov.* (see p. 371)

A climbing or trailing herb or soft shrub with tomentum of mixed stout and subulate hairs on nearly all parts; racemes very long-pedunculate, often exceeding the leaves; petals green, sometimes with purple tinges; corona pure white; follicles conical, often covered with soft fleshy processes.

Probably our commonest climbing Asclepiad, this species is found in disturbed places in dry country to 6000 ft. The fruits are very variable, some being very woolly and others, principally from drier places, almost glabrous. HE, HC, HA, KIT, MUM, KIS, NAR, BAR, RV, MAG, MAC, NBI, KAJ.

Strid 2738; Napper 846.

27. TYLOPHOROPSIS *N. E. Br.*

Similar to 31. *Tylophora* in all respects except for the pollinia which are pendulous in each anther cell.

Tylophoropsis heterophylla *N. E. Br.*

A tomentose climber with ovate leaves, rounded or very shortly cordate at base; flowers in sparsely branched inflorescences, each fascicle of flowers sometimes appearing umbellate; petals pubescent above, maroon.

Rare plant found in upper forest levels to 11 000 ft altitude at the edges of clearings. HM, HA.

Polhill 248; Agnew 7140.

28. DIPLOSTIGMA *K. Schum.*

Climbers or erect suffrutescent herbs with fascicles of small flowers at nodes; corolla spreading, deeply lobed; corona double, the outer being a ring around the base of the staminal column, the inner consisting of 5 fleshy lobes attached to the stamens above, widening below; follicle smooth; seed with rugosities on one face.

Diplostigma canescens *K. Schum.*

An erect suffrutescent herb with sparsely-branched stems or a weak, woody climber, pubescent, with ovate to linear leaves; flowers minute (to 2·5 mm long), greenish.

Uncommon plant found in dry burnt grassland. MAG.

Greenway 11761.

29. GYMNEMA *R. Br.*

Woody, pubescent climbers; flowers in axillary umbels; corolla with a tube and 5 lobes, bearing the conspicuous corona as fleshy lobes between the petals; stamens fused throughout; pollinia present, minute, erect, solitary in each anther cell.

Gymnema sylvestre *R. Br.*

Softly pubescent climber with ovate leaves; flowers yellow in short-pedunculate umbels; fruit smooth.

Uncommon plant found in evergreen bushland. MUM, KIS.

Agnew, Musumba, and Kiniaruh 7987; Kokwaro 99.

30. GONGRONEMA (*Endl.*) Decne.

Similar in all respects to 33. Dregea except for the constantly cordate leaves, smaller (up to 5 mm long) triangular corolla lobes, and constantly included stigma.

Gongronema angolense (*N. E. Br.*) *Bullock*

A woody tomentose climber with ovate, cordate leaves and pedunculate umbels of green flowers; flowers small, to 6 mm long; stigma not exceeding the stamens.

Rare plant found in western Kenya. KIS.
Bally 7472.

31. TYLOPHORA *R. Br.*

Climbing shrubs; flowers in panicles or umbels; corolla with a short tube and long glabrous or pubescent lobes; corona obscure, adherent to staminal column, free or not at apex; pollinia minute, pollen masses horizontal, often free from the pollen carrier.

1 Leaves deeply cordate, the depth of the sinus equal to more than half the petiole length
                                          1. *Tylophora sylvatica*
   Leaves rounded or cuneate at base, if shallowly cordate then the depth of the sinus much less than half the petiole length
                                          2
2 Petals sparsely tomentose on margins only
                                          2. *Tylophora lugardae*
   Petals densely pubescent on inner surface   3
3 Corona conspicuous, joining the corolla to the staminal column and forming pockets between the corolla lobes
                                          3. *Tylophora* sp. *B*
   Corona inconspicuous, of minute fleshy erect organs adpressed to staminal column
                                          Tylophoropsis heterophylla

1. Tylophora sylvatica *Decne.*

Puberulent climber with ovate cordate leaves and fascicles of maroon flowers in branching panicles; petals glabrous.

Rare plant found in bushland in western Kenya. MUM, NAR.

Archer 269; Agnew and Musumba 8578.

2. Tylophora lugardae *Bullock*

Sparsely pubescent climber with ovate-lanceolate leaves usually rounded at base; flowers in pedunculate rather irregular umbels; petals green with a maroon centre, wrinkled in bud and tomentose on the margin.

Rare plant found in upland dry forest edges and disturbed places. HC, HA, NAR, NBI, KAJ.

Archer 303; Lugard 656 (Type).

3. Tylophora sp. B.

Similar in vegetative parts to 27. *Tylophoropsis heterophylla* and in inflorescence to *Tylophora lugardae* this species has densely pubescent petals and the curious corona characters mentioned in the key.

Only one collection known to this author, from south-west Mau forest, at 7100 ft. HM.

Kerfoot 2886.

32. SPHAEROCODON *Benth.*

Erect herbs or shrubs with flowers in pedunculate lateral cymes; corolla saucer-shaped, with erect lobes; corona of 5 small fleshy tubercles or teeth on the staminal column; stamens fused; pollinia erect.

Sphaerocodon obtusifolium *Benth.*

Usually a many-stemmed herb, or suffrutescent at base, with oblong-elliptic leaves and lateral cymes of maroon flowers.

Rare plant found in western Kenya in burnt grassland and only once recorded, from 7700 ft on Mt. Elgon. HE.

Lugard 618.

33. DREGEA *E. Mey.*

Climbing shrubs, often tomentose, with umbellate or cymose inflorescences; corolla with a short tube and spreading lanceolate lobes over 5 mm long; corona attached to the staminal column, of separate, entire lobes; stamens fused, bearing erect pollinia; style equalling or exceeding the stamens.

1 Stigmas projecting through the staminal disc as a filamentous two-lobed extension   2
   Stigmas not overtopping the staminal disc   3
2 Inflorescences glomerulate, sessile; fruits 4-winged   1. *D. stelostigma*
   Inflorescences pedunculate, loosely cymose; fruits unwinged   2. *D. schimperi*
3 Inflorescence sub-umbelliform, forming a single spherical mass of flowers; corona massive, fleshy, terete   3. *D. abyssinica*
   Inflorescence a branching ± corymbose cyme or umbellate with 2–5 umbels on each peduncle; corona lobes dorsally flattened   4

4   Inflorescence a branching corymbose cyme; corolla lobes longer than tube, hairy within; fruit 4-winged   4. *D. rubicunda*
Inflorescence of umbels; corolla lobes ± equal to the tube, glabrous within; fruit unknown   *Gongronema angolense*

1. Dregea stelostigma (*K. Schum.*) *Bullock*

A pubescent to tomentose climbing herb with suborbicular to broad-ovate leaves, and sessile umbels or fascicles of short-pedicellate flowers; flowers to 4 mm long, yellow-green; fruits 4-winged.

Rare plant found in dry country, and doubtfully recorded for our area. NAN.

Adamson 1.

2. Dregea schimperi (*Decne.*) *Bullock* (see p. 384)

A robust tomentose climber with broad-ovate to orbicular leaves and loose, pedunculate, cymose inflorescences; flowers to 11 mm long, yellow; fruit with numerous wrinkles but not winged.

Common in upland forest edges. HE, HA, HK, HT, NAR, MAC.

Strid 3627; Verdcourt 668.

3. Dregea abyssinica (*Hochst.*) *K. Schum.*

Sparsely pubescent climber similar to *D. schimperi* except for the inflorescences which are umbellate, the fleshy terete corona lobes, and the short stigma; fruit with many undulate ridges.

In rocky places in dry woodland and in riverine forest. NAR, EMB, NBI, KAJ.

Verdcourt 438.

4. Dregea rubicunda *K. Schum.*

A sparsely pubescent climber with suborbicular to ovate-elliptic leaves; flowers in loose, corymbose, pedunculate cymes; corolla pubescent above; corona of flat, lanceolate lobes; fruit strongly 4-winged.

Rare plant found in dry *Acacia-Commiphora* bushland. BAR, MAG.

Bally 2669.

34. LEPTADENIA *R. Br.*

Climbers or shrubs often with reduced leaves and photosynthetic stems; flowers many, in umbel-like lateral cymes; corolla hairy, with spreading or erect lobes and a short, obscure tube; corona of 5 fleshy lobes, hairy at apex, inserted between the corolla lobes; stamens fused, pollinia erect, with a transparent appendage on the pollen-mass.

Leptadenia hastata (*Pers.*) *Decne.* (see p. 384)

A leafy climber, pubescent on all parts, with lanceolate to ovate leaves and dense masses of cream flowers on short lateral peduncles.

Only in dry country in the north of our area. BAR, recorded by Mrs. E. M. Tweedie.

Newbould 6774 (no specimens seen from our area).

35. TENARIS *E. Mey.*

Erect herbs, often leafless in flower, from a tuberous rootstock, with linear leaves, very similar to *Brachystelma* except for the simply 5-lobed outer corona.

Tenaris rostrata *N. E. Br.*

An erect, loosely branched herb with linear leaves and paired flowers on long-pedunculate terminal inflorescences; flowers maroon.

Rare plant found in dry grassland, recorded from Chyulu hills and Narok District. NAR, KAJ.

Bally 510.

36. CEROPEGIA *L.*

Erect or, more usually, climbing herbs, frequently succulent, with flowers in axillary cymes or umbels or, more usually, solitary; leaves entire; calyx with 5 free lobes; corolla tubular, usually inflated at base and with the 5 lobes separating laterally but coherent at tip; corona double, attached to the staminal column, the outer entire or 5–10-toothed ± fused to the 5 inner lobes, or reduced to pouches alternating with the stamens; staminal column almost at the base of the corolla, very short; anthers erect or ascending, without appendages and with solitary, erect pollen masses in each cell; follicles smooth.

1   Corolla lobes with apical club-shaped hairs which are so delicately attached that they wave and vibrate in the gentlest wind   2
Corolla lobes glabrous or with stiffly attached linear hairs   4
2   Stem smooth or obscurely angled; peduncles as long as some pedicels or little shorter   3
Stem rough with small ridges; peduncles much shorter than pedicels or absent
1. *C.* sp. *A*
3   Leaves succulent, often dentate or sinuate at margins, less than 3 cm long
2. *C. denticulata*
Leaves not succulent, entire, usually over 3 mm long   3. *C. batesii*
4   Stems pubescent all over   5
Stems glabrous, or rarely two lines of minute pubescence extending upwards from nodes
9
5   Plant erect   4. *C. abyssinica*
Plant climbing   6
6   Cymes pedunculate   7
Cymes sessile   8

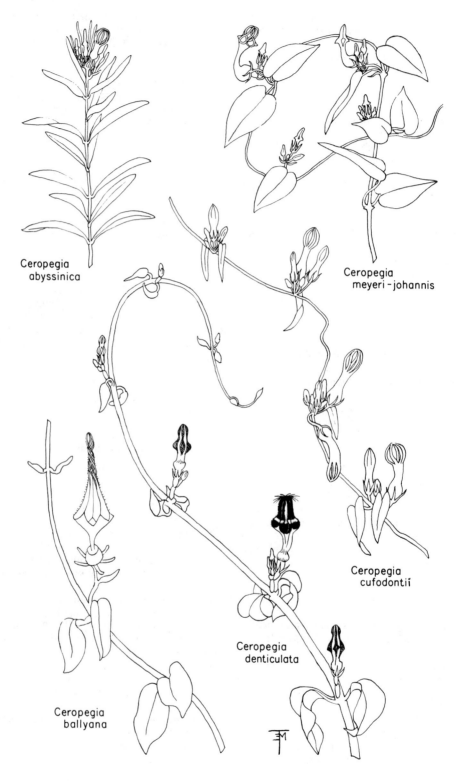

Ceropegia
abyssinica

Ceropegia
meyeri-johannis

Ceropegia
cufodontii

Ceropegia
denticulata

Ceropegia
ballyana

7   Leaves rounded and conspicuously apiculate
　　at apex   5. *C. euryacme*
　　Leaves acute, hardly apiculate at apex
　　　　　　　　　6. *C. meyeri-johannis*
8   Corolla lobes equal to or longer than corolla
　　tube; corolla less than 13 mm long
　　　　　　　　　　7. *C. stenoloba*
　　Corolla lobes much shorter than corolla tube;
　　corolla over 17 mm long   8. *C. cufodontii*
9   Leaves linear, over 6 times as long as wide **10**
　　Leaves ovate to elliptic, less than 4 times as
　　long as wide   **13**
10   Inflorescence elongate, with many flower-
　　bearing nodes; corolla under 11 mm long
　　　　　　　　　　9. *C. crassifolia*
　　Inflorescence of a sessile or pedunculate
　　umbel-like fascicle of flowers   **11**
11   Plant from swollen, spindle-shaped roots;
　　corolla lobes over 1 cm long
　　　　　　　　　10. *C. stenantha*
　　Plant from a globose tuber, with narrow
　　roots; corolla less than 1 cm long   **12**
12   Peduncle over 3·5 mm long   11. *C. brosima*
　　Peduncle less than 2 mm long   12. *C. sp. B*
13   Corolla lobes over 2 cm long, as long as the
　　corolla tube   **14**
　　Corolla lobes less than 1·5 cm long, shorter
　　than the corolla tube   **15**
14   Leaves ovate, cordate at base   13. *C. sp. C*
　　Leaves oblong—elliptic, rounded at base
　　　　　　　　　　17. *C. ballyana*
15   Plant growing from a globose tuber
　　　　　　　　　5. *C. euryacme*
　　Plant with swollen or fibrous roots and
　　without a tuber at base   **16**
16   Plant with fibrous roots   **17**
　　Plant with swollen sausage-shaped roots
　　　　　　　　　　14. *C. sp. D*
17   Leaves ovate, widest at the base, seldom over
　　3 cm long   15. *C. seticorona*
　　Leaves elliptic, widest at the middle, fre-
　　quently over 5 cm long   **18**
18   Calyx lobes over 2 mm long; corolla lobes
　　rounded at apex   16. *C. succulenta*
　　Calyx lobes less than 2 mm long; corolla
　　lobes acute at apex   17. *C. ballyana*

1. Ceropegia *sp.* A.

Roots conspicuously fusiform; stems succulent,
rough, with many small longitudinal ridges, grey-
green; leaves ovate-lanceolate to 8 mm long almost
stem-clasping; flowers sessile; corolla silvery grey,
lobes edged velvety black banded black, white,
green with vibratile clavate hairs at tips.

　　Rocky bushland and grassland. NAR, RV,
MAG.

　　Archer 429.

2. Ceropegia denticulata *K. Schum.* (see p. 390)

Roots hardly swollen; stem succulent sometimes
somewhat angular; green with occasional longitudinal white spots; leaves succulent, ovate, to
3 cm long, sometimes serrate; corolla yellow-green
with varying amounts of brown-maroon streaks and
spots especially towards top of tube, lobes banded
green, white, blackish, with vibratile clavate hairs
at tips.

　　Bushland. HA, KIS, NAR, RV, EMB, MAC,
NBI, KAJ.

　　Gillett 17305.

3. Ceropegia batesii *S. Moore*

Roots fibrous; vegetative parts glabrous; stem
fleshy shiny; leaves large elliptic acuminate somewhat coriaceous; peduncle 1–2 cm; corolla whitish
green, towards lobes brownish maroon, lobes
brown/maroon and yellow with a few vibratile
hairs at tips.

　　Forest. KIS; Archer 433.

4. Ceropegia abyssinica (*A. Rich.*) *Decne.* (see p. 390)

Globose tuber; vegetative parts hairy; stems
straight not twining; leaves ovate to lanceolate
sometimes serrate; flowers sessile, many; corolla
straight, cream with blackish lobes.

　　Grassland. HT, KIT, RV, NBI, KAJ.

　　Harvey 56; Tweedie 97.

5. Ceropegia euryacme *Huber*

Globose tuber; vegetative parts glabrous or sometimes hairy; stem wiry; leaves fleshy, lanceolate-
ovate; peduncle 10 mm; corolla whitish, lobes
maroon with greenish tips, with ciliate hairs on
edges.

　　Under bushes in rocky outcrops. KIS, RV,
MAG, EMB, MAC, NBI.

　　Archer in Bally 8066; Archer 436.

6. Ceropegia meyeri-johannis *Engl.* (see p. 390)

Roots swollen spindle-shaped; vegetative parts
hairy; stem wiry; peduncle 30 mm; corolla
greenish-white with dull maroon spots and streaks,
lobes green or maroon with ciliate hairs on edges.

　　Forest. HT, HA, MUM, KIS, NAR, RV, NAN,
MAC, NBI, KAJ.

　　Napier 3111; Verdcourt 3968(s).

7. Ceropegia stenoloba *Chiov.*

Globose tuber; vegetative parts hairy; stem wiry;
leaves ovate to lanceolate, sometimes doubly
dentate; flowers sessile, corolla 'S' shaped, whitish,
lobes terete, maroon.

　　Rocky grassland. MAC, NBI, KAJ.

　　Archer 422.

8. Ceropegia cufodontii *Chiov.* (see p. 390)

Roots swollen spindle-shaped; vegetative parts hairy; stems wiry; leaves ovate to broadly lanceolate; flowers sessile, corolla whitish, green/yellow more or less streaked maroon, ciliate hairs on inside of lobes.

Rocky grassland and bushland. HE, HC, HT, MUM, RV.

Agnew 10326.

9. Ceropegia crassifolia *Schltr.*

Roots swollen spindle-shaped; vegetative parts glabrous; stem fleshy, short; leaves fleshy linear-lanceolate; peduncle 5 mm; corolla pale cream/green/pink, with ciliate hairs inside lobes.

Grassland. HA, NBI, KAJ.

Armstrong 544.

10. Ceropegia stenantha *K. Schum.*

Roots swollen spindle-shaped; vegetative parts glabrous; stem fleshy, somewhat angular; leaves fleshy linear-lanceolate; flowers sessile, corolla straight, creamy-pink.

Rocky grassed bushland. MAC, KAJ.

Archer 500; Agnew 8825.

11. Ceropegia brosima *Bruce & Bally*

Globose tuber; stem wiry; leaves linear.

Rare plant found in grassland. MUM.

Opiko 697.

12. Ceropegia *sp.* **B.**

Globose tuber; vegetative parts glabrous; stem wiry; leaves linear-lanceolate; peduncle 6 mm; corolla greenish white, lobes dark maroon inside, ciliate hairs on edges.

Grassland. NBI.

Archer 427.

13. Ceropegia *sp.* **C.**

Roots fibrous; stem succulent, blue-grey; leaves ovate, cordate, fleshy; corolla tube yellow with maroon spots, lobes yellow in lower half, upper half maroon, with ciliate hairs on edge.

Thorn-tree bushland. EMB, MAC, KAJ.

Archer 63.

14. Ceropegia *sp.* **D.**

Roots swollen sausage-shaped; vegetative parts glabrous; stem wiry; leaves ovate, elliptic, fleshy; peduncle 30 mm, extending; corolla yellowish, tips of lobes maroon with a few ciliate hairs.

Edge of forest. HA, BAR, RV, NAN, MAC, NBI, KAJ.

van Someren 218; Archer 75.

15. Ceropegia seticorona *E. A. Bruce*

Fibrous roots; stem succulent, blue-grey; leaves ovate, fleshy; calyx lobes 1–2 mm long; corolla yellow with varying amounts of maroon spots and streaks or nearly all maroon, occasional ciliate hairs on lobes.

Thorny bushland. KIS, BAR, MAG, NAN, EMB, MAC, NBI, KAJ.

Milne-Redhead and Taylor 7151.

16. Ceropegia succulenta *E. A. Bruce*

Roots fibrous; stem thick, succulent, leaf nodes prominent or depressed; leaves large oval-elliptic, succulent, dark green with white veins; peduncle 5–10 cm; corolla yellow-green with maroon spots, lobes whitish with green tips, short ciliate hairs on edges.

Dry forest. HA, NAR, RV, NBI.

Agnew 9577.

17. Ceropegia ballyana *Bullock* (see p. 390)

A glabrous succulent climber with broad oblong or elliptic leaves and large solitary flowers; corolla greenish to yellow, with purple spots and long lobes ending acutely.

Dry bushland. BAR, EMB.

Bally 12321; Tweedie 2450.

37. BRACHYSTELMA *R. Br.*

Herb with tubers or fleshy roots, rarely climbers; flowers in lateral or terminal few-flowered umbels; petals spreading, shortly joined at base, usually with linear lobes; corona double, sometimes obscurely so, on staminal column, with an outer corona of bifid lobes or paired teeth, sometimes fused to the inner 5 lobes; pollinia horizontal or ascending with a pellucid margin near the apex; follicles smooth.

1	Petal lobes over 1·5 cm long	2
	Petal lobes under 1 cm long	3
2	Flowers in terminal pedunculate umbels, much overtopping the leaves; petal lobes 2·5–11 cm long	1. *B. Johnstonii*
	Flowers in axillary or terminal sessile umbels, overtopped by linear leaves; petal lobes less than 2·5 cm long	2. *B. lineare*
3	Pedicels longer than flowers	3. *B. keniense*
	Pedicels shorter than flowers	4. *B. sp. A*

1. Brachystelma johnstonii *N. E. Br.* (see p. 386)

Erect small herb from a fleshy tuber, with linear leaves and terminal umbels of short-pedicellate flowers; petals maroon or brown, with masses of white hairs at base.

Rare plant found in short grassland and shallow soils in western Kenya. HE, KIT.

Tweedie, May 1967 (spirit); Irwin 157.

2. Brachystelma lineare *A. Rich.* (see p. 386)

Similar to *B. johnstoni* but with ± subulate leaves overtopping the smaller, greenish-yellow flowers.

Rare plant found in shallow soil grassland near Nairobi. HA, NBI.

Heine in EAH 13765.

3. Brachystelma keniense *Schweinf.*

A dwarf puberulent herb from a globose tuber, with linear-elliptic leaves and 1–3 long-pedicellate flowers at the upper nodes; petals triangular.

Rare plant found in dry grassland. NAN, ?EMB. Hansen 79.

4. Brachystelma *sp.* A.

Similar to *B. keniense* but the flowers almost sessile and the leaves long-linear, pubescent.

Known by 2 collections from grassland near Nairobi, (Langata and Lukenia). MAC, NBI. Archer 287.

38. ECHIDNOPSIS *Hook. f.*

Trailing fleshy-stemmed leafless herbs with leaf-bases enlarged, truncate, covering the stem; flowers lateral, in fascicles or solitary; corolla with 5 spreading lobes and a short, bell-shaped tube; corona arising from the staminal column, often in two series, the outer of 5 short lobes or pouches alternating with the anthers or none, the inner of 5 fleshy lobes bent inwards over the anthers; stamens fused; pollinia horizontal.

Echidnopsis dammiana *Spreng.*

A trailing fleshy herb with 8–10 rows of square outlines on the stem and small, solitary, subsessile dark purple flowers.

Rare plant found around termite mounds in dry bushed grassland. The plant should turn up in the BAR area, and a sight record has been reported from the dry country next the lake in MUM. MAG.

Glover and Samuel 3241.

39. EDITHCOLEA *N. E. Br.*

Succulent with trailing stems and lateral solitary flowers; corolla very large, with a short tube and spreading, flat lobes; corona as in *Echidnopsis*; stamens fused; pollinia erect, large.

Edithcolea grandis *N. E. Br.* (see p. 394)

A trailing succulent with yellow, horny conical knobs on the stems and large (often 12 cm diameter), very conspicuous purple and yellow flowers edged with vibratile, club-shaped hairs.

Rare plant found in dry rocky country. MAC, KAJ.

Jackson 3087.

40. CARALLUMA *R. Br.*

Erect or creeping, fleshy leafless herbs with 4–6 (rarely 3) angles on the stem; flowers in lateral or terminal racemes or heads, or solitary; corolla 5-lobed, sometimes campanulate at base; corona in two series, arising from the staminal column, the outer usually 10-toothed, fused to the inner series of 5 erect or decumbent entire or denticulate lobes; stamens fused; pollinia horizontal or ascending, with a pellucid margin; follicles smooth.

1 Inflorescence a terminal, elongated raceme with a narrow, stiff (not fleshy) rachis   8
  Inflorescence a terminal globose head, or flowers solitary or in pairs on upper part of undifferentiated fleshy stem   2
2 Inflorescence a globose head   3
  Inflorescence of solitary or paired flowers in upper axils   5
3 Corolla lobes with club-shaped, loose (vibratile) hairs along the edges, glabrous or tuberculate within; corona glabrous   4
  Corolla lobes without hairs along the margins but minutely pubescent within; corona hairy on the back   1. *C. russelliana*
4 Corolla lobes glabrous and ± smooth within   2. *C. speciosa*
  Corolla lobes covered with low, minutely pubescent tubercles within   3. *C. foetida*
5 Stems with acute angles or with soft prickles representing leaves   6
  Stems terete, smooth or with rounded obscure ridges   4. *C. socotrana*
6 Corolla with club-shaped, delicate, loosely attached (vibratile) hairs on the basal edges of the pubescent lobes; corona lobes apparently in one whorl   5. *C. vibratilis*
  Corolla lobes glabrous or hairy but never with vibratile hairs at the basal edges of the lobes; corona in two whorls   7
7 Plant rhizomatous; corolla up to 10 mm long, velvety-pubescent above, the hairs without swolled persistent bases; outer coronal lobes erect, denticulate   6. *C. subterranea*
  Plant creeping on the surface of the ground; corolla over 15 mm long, glabrous or hairy above; hairs, if any, long, deciduous, attached to swollen persistent bases; outer corona lobes with spreading points   7. *C. dummeri*
8 Corolla lobes rigidly spreading   9
  Corolla lobes loosely pendulous   8. *C. dicapuae*
9 Corona and gynostemium held on a stalk above the base of the flower   9. *C. gracilipes*
  Corona and gynostemium sessile   10. *C. priogonium*

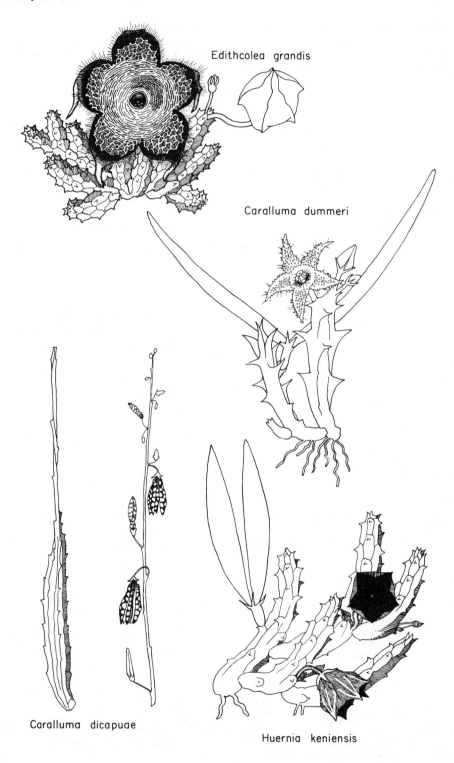

Edithcolea grandis

Caralluma dummeri

Caralluma dicapuae

Huernia keniensis

Caralluma vibratilis

Caralluma
speciosa

Caralluma
russelliana

Caralluma foetida

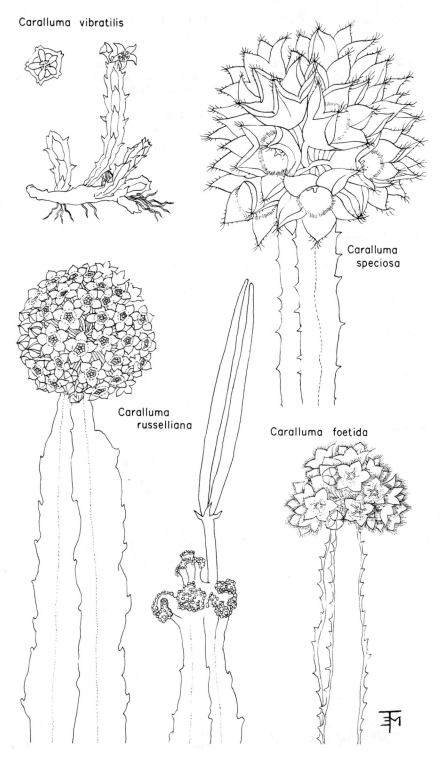

1. Caralluma russelliana (*Brogn.*) *Cufod.* (see p. 395)

A massive erect succulent with 4-angled stem up to 5 cm thick and with a large head of smallish black-purple or dark violet flowers.

Uncommon plant found in dry country. BAR, NAN.

Brown, October 1962.

2. Caralluma speciosa *N. E. Br.* (see p. 395)

Similar in habit to *C. russelliana* but with shorter stems and fewer and much bigger flowers.

Rare plant found in dry alkaline country. MAG. Greenway and White in EAH 12870.

3. Caralluma foetida *E. A. Bruce* (see p. 395)

Similar in habit to *C. speciosa* but with narrower (to 4 cm thick) stems and with hairy flowers.

Uncommon plant found in dry alluvial country. BAR.

Leippert 5278.

4. Caralluma socotrana (*Balf. f.*) *N. E. Br.*

An erect, caespitose, fleshy perennial with cylindrical or obscurely angled stems and terminal groups of 2–3 black-purple flowers.

Rare plant found in alkaline alluvium and stony ground, only recorded from Magadi. MAG.

Greenway 8991.

5. Caralluma vibratilis *Bruce & Bally* (see p. 395)

Perennial with subterranean or superficial then ascending stems bearing linear leaf-scales, and terminal groups of dark flowers.

Rare plant found in rocky grassland. NAN. Bally 2539.

6. Caralluma subterranea *Bruce & Bally*

Similar to *C. vibratilis* but with greenish flowers more scattered along the stem and underground stems.

Rare plant found in dry stony grassland. MUM, RV.

Opiko in EAH 12492.

7. Caralluma dummeri (*N. E. Br.*) *Bruce* (see p. 395)

A decumbent fleshy perennial with ascending, often variegated stems bearing lines of conical projections; flowers ± terminal, pedicellate, glabrous or hairy within, greenish or cream.

Probably the commonest succulent Asclepiad, this is to be found in the *Combretum* woodland and adjacent grassland in rocky places with a sandy soil. HA, KIT, MUM, NAR, RV, MAG, NAN, MAC, NBI, KAJ.

Agnew 7304; Bogdan 77/60.

8. Caralluma dicapuae (*Chiov.*) *Chiov.* (see p. 394)

A caespitose perennial herb with 4 lines of conical projections on the square stems, and with long terminal racemes of grey-green flowers with maroon spots and stripes on the pendulous petals; petals broadest furthest from the flower.

Uncommon plant found in dry rocky bushland. MUM, KIS, BAR, MAG, KAJ.

Verdcourt 30313; Tweedie 66/383.

9. Caralluma gracilipes *K. Schum.*

Similar to *C. dicapuae* but with narrow spotted petals which spread and are widest at the base.

Rare plant found in dry rocky bushland in our area, although it is apparently common in the drier parts of Kenya. MAC.

Record from Bally (1969) in Candollea 24/1:17.

10. Caralluma priogonium *K. Schum*

Similar to *C. gracilipes* except for the keyed characters, also rare in dry areas. BAR.

Record from Bally (1969) in Candollea 24/1:9.

41. HUERNIA *R. Br.*

Trailing, fleshy-stemmed herbs with lateral fascicles or umbels of pedicellate flowers; corolla bell-shaped, the lobes usually shorter than the tube, with accessory teeth between the lobes; corona and stamens as in *Echidnopsis* but with the inner corona often produced into erect horns.

| 1 | Corolla over 15 mm long | 1. *H. keniensis* |
| | Corolla up to 15 mm long | 2. *H. aspera* |

1. Huernia keniensis *R. E. Fries* (see p. 394)

A trailing fleshy herb with 4–6 rows of conical fleshy projections on the stem and lateral, ± pendulous, dark purple-black, rough flowers.

Not uncommon in rocky country and on dry cliff-faces. Like most members of this and neighbouring genera the flowers have an evil smell. HE, HT, HA, KIT, RV, NAN, MAC.

Tweedie 66/385; Bally 11402.

2. Huernia aspera *N. E. Br.*

Similar to the last species except for the smaller flowers.

Recorded from Nairobi Game Park in our area. NAN, NBI, KAJ.

Bally 514.

73. RUBIACEAE†

Trees, shrubs, or herbs, rarely climbers, with opposite or whorled, entire leaves; stipules present, fused between adjacent petioles; inflorescences usually cymose; flowers usually bisexual, with

† By A. D. Q. Agnew.

parts in fours, fives or sixes, regular; calyx tubular or with free teeth; corolla with a tube and free, contort, imbricate or valvate lobes; stamens usually epipetalous; ovary inferior, usually of 2 carpels with axile placentation and few to many seeds.

A family which mostly consists of trees and shrubs. Here no attempt is made to key out these for they are all dealt with in KTS. Amongst the herb genera only *Anthospermum* has shrubby representatives in Kenya.

1   Leaves in whorls of 4 or more, with the interpetiolar sheath obscure   **2**
    Leaves opposite or in whorls of 3 only, with the interpetiolar sheath evident, pointed or fringed   **3**
2   Leaves sessile   20. *Galium*
    Leaves petiolate   21. *Rubia cordifolia*
3   Flowers all axillary, sessile or subsessile with the pedicels and peduncle shorter than the stipular sheath   **4**
    Flowers axillary or terminal, if axillary then the pedicels or peduncles much longer than the stipular sheath   **8**
4   Flowers unisexual
                 14. *Anthospermum herbaceum*
    Flowers bisexual   **5**
5   Perennial herbs
              3. *Conostomium quadrangulare*
    Annual herbs   **6**
6   Fruits indehiscent, globular, free from the stipular sheath and falling entire
                   10. *Paraknoxia parviflora*
    Fruits dehiscent, retained within the stipular sheath   **7**
7   Fruit dehiscent horizontally, the calyx falling entire, attached to a cap which is the top of the ovary   19. *Mitracarpum*
    Fruit dehiscent longitudinally, rarely horizontally as well
            17. *Borreria* and 18. *Arbulocarpus*
8   Climbing woody plant
                 13. *Paederia pospischilli*
    Erect or creeping herbs or shrubs   **9**
9   Flowers pentamerous (parts in fives)   **10**
    Flowers tetramerous (parts in fours)   **18**
10 Trailing or creeping plants   **11**
    Erect shrubs or herbs   **14**
11 Glabrous herb with ± fleshy leaves
                       7. *Pentodon pentandrus*
    Hairy herbs with dry leaves   **12**
12 Flowers solitary; leaves cordate
                         16. *Geophila repens*
    Flowers in spikes; leaves ovate or lanceolate
                                                   13
13 Inflorescences axillary, rarely terminal,

usually paired, peduncles longer than inflorescence   11. *Pentanisia foetida*
    Inflorescences terminal, solitary; peduncles shorter than inflorescence
                          1. *Parapentas battiscombei*
14 Inflorescence terminal, elongating in fruit to look like a long spike   9. *Otomeria*
    Inflorescence terminal or axillary, if terminal then elongating into many spike-like inflorescences or not elongating   **15**
15 Inflorescences terminal   **16**
    Inflorescences axillary   **17**
16 Fruits indehiscent; herbs seldom over 50 cm tall; corolla tube never over 22 mm long
                                     11. *Pentanisia*
    Fruits dehiscent; herbs often over 50 cm tall; corolla tube frequently over 25 mm long
                                         8. *Pentas*
17 Soft trailing herb with paired, axillary, spike-like inflorescences; leaves ± glabrous below   11. *Pentanisia foetida*
    Erect perennial herb with short, axillary, pedicellate cymes; leaves white-woolly below   12. *Fadogia cienkowskii*
18 Inflorescences terminal   **20**
    Inflorescences all axillary or flowers solitary axillary   **19**
19 Corolla tube over 2 cm long
                               3. *Conostomium*
    Corolla tube less than 1 cm long
                                 4. *Oldenlandia*
20 Flowers in a flat- or round-topped head or corymb   **21**
    Flowers solitary or at various levels on the erect elongated flowering branches
                                    2. *Kohautia*
21 Plant entirely glabrous
                6. *Dibrachionostylus kaessneri*
    Plant hairy at least at nodes   **22**
22 Herb with erect ± unbranched stems ending in a solitary head; heads globose, mostly over 2 cm in diameter
                    5. *Agathisanthemum globosum*
    Trailing herbs or erect much branched wiry herbs with heads less than 2 cm in diameter, or flowers corymbose   **23**
23 Heads flat-topped, surrounded by spreading upper leaves; fruit of 2 indehiscent mericarps, each containing one seed
                          15. *Richardia braziliensis*
    Heads rounded or flowers corymbose, not surrounded by uppermost leaves; fruit a many-seeded capsule   4. *Oldenlandia*

1. PARAPENTAS Brem.

Creeping herbs with entire leaves; flowers sessile, few, in terminal or axillary cymes, pentamerous, isostylous or heterostylous; corolla with a long narrow tube and spreading lobes; fruit not beaked, dehiscing within the calyx.

Parapentas battiscombei *Verdc.*

A creeping herb with broad ovate or deltoid leaves and small terminal heads of lilac flowers.

Only known from the shady forest floor of the Mt. Kenya forests. HK, HN.

Polhill and Verdcourt 283.

2. KOHAUTIA *Cham. & Schlecht.*

Herbs with entire leaves and laciniate stipules; flowers in loose terminal monochasial or dichasial cymes; corolla tube cylindrical, 4-lobed, exceeding anthers; stigmas fused or free, shorter than the anthers; fruit ± globose, crowned with the 4 persistent sepals.

1 Plant annual, scabrid on peduncles and fruits

                                           2

   Plants mostly perennial, shrubby at base, not scabrid on peduncles and fruits   **3**

2 Corolla (including the lobes), less than 5 mm long, pale blue or white   1. *K. aspera*

   Corolla (including the lobes) more than 6 mm long, bright red   2. *K. coccinea*

3 Corolla tube usually more than 8 mm long; stigmas 2, filiform, free   3. *K. caespitosa*

   Corolla tube less than 6 mm long; stigmas fused together   4. *K. virgata*

1. Kohautia aspera *(Roth) Brem.*

A small scabrid erect annual, often branched from the base, with linear leaves and minute bluish-white flowers, often in subsessile pairs.

Uncommon plant found in dry country. NAN, EMB, MAC, NBI, KAJ.

Verdcourt 3175; Agnew 7294.

2. Kohautia coccinea *Royle* (see p. 399)

Similar to *K. aspera* but usually unbranched and with larger, red flowers.

In dry grassland. HE, HC, HT, HM, HK, KIT, KIS, RV, MAC, NBI, KAJ.

Verdcourt 530; Strid 3211.

3. Kohautia caespitosa *Schnizl.*

A sparsely pubescent perennial or annual, usually branched below, with linear to elliptic leaves and pink, reddish-brown or orange flowers with long tubes.

Locally common in dry country and at the coast on shallow soils over rock. KIT, BAR, RV, MAG, MAC, KAJ.

Napper 748; Harmsen 645.

4. Kohautia virgata *(Willd.) Brem.*

Similar to *K. caespitosa* but smaller and with shorter flowers with entire stigma.

Rare plant found on shallow soils around Ruiru and Thika and, like *K. caespitosa*, also found at the coast. MAC.

Napier 380; Agnew 10051.

3. CONOSTOMIUM *Cuf.*

Erect perennial herbs with entire leaves and dentate stipular sheaths; flowers solitary axillary, isostylous, tetramerous; calyx teeth ± subulate; corolla with a very long, cylindrical tube; fruit subglobose, with a pronounced beak, dehiscing above, many-seeded.

1 Leaves lanceolate, sessile, clasping at base; flowers sessile   1. *C. quadrangulare*

   Leaves linear, sessile, not clasping at base; flowers pedicellate   **2**

2 Calyx lobes ± as long as the ovary at anthesis; corolla tube to 3·3 cm long

                              2. *C. keniense*

   Calyx lobes twice as long as the ovary at anthesis; corolla tube to 4·5 cm long

                          3. *C. floribundum*

1. Conostomium quadrangulare *(Rendle) Cuf.* (see p. 402)

An erect, sparsely pilose woody herb with sessile lanceolate leaves and sessile cream or white flowers with a very long corolla tube (to 12 cm).

Rare plant found in dry rocky bushland. BAR, NAN.

Adamson 6929.

2. Conostomium keniense *Brem.*

An erect shrub, pubescent except on the stems, with linear leaves and shortly pedicellate white flowers.

Rare plant found in dry rocky country. MAC.

Archer 88; Bally 8374.

3. Conostomium floribundum *Brem.*

Similar to *C. keniense* except for the key characters, and similarly rare, found in dry rocky country. BAR.

Bally 8374.

4. OLDENLANDIA *L. emend Brem.*

Erect or creeping herbs or low shrubs with entire leaves and laciniate interpetiolar sheaths; flowers axillary or terminal in cymes, isostylous or heterostylous, tetramerous; calyx of small teeth; corolla with a ± obconical tube, white, pink, or

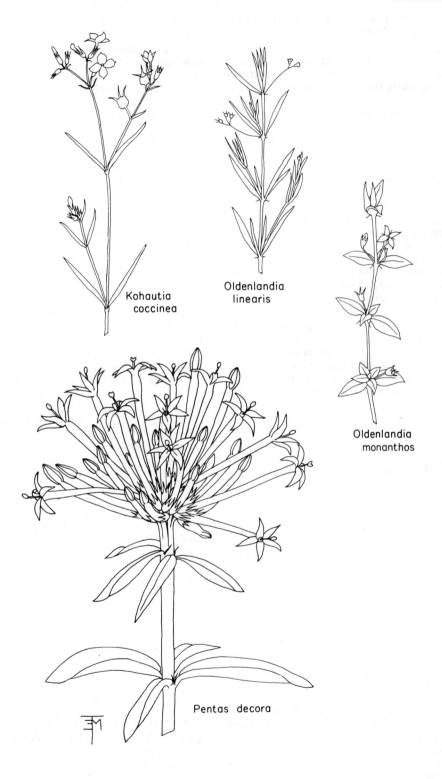

Kohautia
coccinea

Oldenlandia
linearis

Oldenlandia
monanthos

Pentas decora

purple, never red (in ours); style divided into two stigmas, or stigma globose; seeds many.

1 Leaves broad, ovate or oblong, less than 6 times as long as wide, usually abruptly narrowed at the petiole, obtuse or acute at apex   2
  Leaves narrow, linear to linear-elliptic, more than 6 times as long as wide, always gradually narrowed at base, with a very acute apex   6
2 Flowers numerous, whorled, sometimes terminal, exceeded by the leaves; stigma subglobose   3
  Flowers terminal, exceeding the subtending leaves, or, if axillary then only 1-4 together, with long pedicels; stigma elongated   4
3 Some pedicels over 3 mm long; corolla exceeding the calyx   1. *O. bullockii*
  All pedicels under 3 mm long; corolla shorter than or equalling the calyx
                                2. *O. goreensis*
4 Flowers solitary or 1-2 together on long axillary pedicels   3. *O. monanthos*
  Flowers in small cymose inflorescences   5
5 Flowers in few-flowered cymes on long peduncles   4. *O. johnstonii*
  Flowers crowded in cymes with the peduncles suppressed and thus appearing umbellate   5. *O. friesiorum*
6 Flowers subcapitate in dense, terminal, pedunculate inflorescences
                                6. *O. wiedemannii*
  Flowers in axillary cymes or solitary   7
7 Plant creeping and rooting at nodes, with scarcely branched stems   8
  Plant erect, not rooting at nodes   9
8 Flowers solitary   7. *O. lancifolia*
  Flowers in groups of 4 or more
                               11. *O. fastigiata*
9 Corolla over 3 mm long   10
  Corolla less than 2 mm long   11
10 Flowers solitary or in pairs at the nodes with no peduncle and with a long, capillary pedicel   8. *O. herbacea*
   Flowers in small, 3-7-flowered, pedunculate, axillary cymes   9. *O. scopulorum*
11 Fruits held on ± straight pedicels, always reaching beyond half the leaf length, sometimes exceeding the leaves; fruits solitary or in pairs   10. *O. corymbosa*
   Fruits held on recurved pedicels close to the stem, reaching to half way along leaves; fruits in groups of 2-many   12
12 Fruits in groups of 4-many 11. *O. fastigiata*
   Fruits in groups of 2-3   12. *O. acicularis*

1. Oldenlandia bullockii *Brem.* (*O. verticillata* Brem.)

A creeping plant, rooting at the nodes, with rhomboid to almost cordate, shortly petiolate leaves and pale pink flowers.

Very rare and only found once in a marsh in Kipkarren. KIT.

Brodhurst-Hill 349.

2. Oldenlandia goreensis (*DC.*) *Summerhayes*

Procumbent herb with erect stems, very similar to *O. bullockii* except for the key characters.

Rare plant found in swampy ground and only once recorded, from near Kitale. KIT.

Bogdan 4213.

3. Oldenlandia monanthos (*A. Rich.*) *Hiern* (see p. 399)

A creeping, mat-forming herb, rooting at the nodes, with lanceolate to oblong leaves and solitary or paired pink-purple flowers on long pedicels.

Locally common in montane grassland, especially along pathsides and often on shallow soil. HE, HC, HT, HM, HA, HK, KAJ.

Tweedie 67/160; Kerfoot 3918.

4. Oldenlandia johnstonii (*Oliv.*) *Engl.*

A low trailing plant, sometimes shrubby at base, with ascending stems, and ovate to elliptic leaves; flowers pedicellate, white, 3-5 together on a long peduncle.

Locally common in dry forest edges, especially near Nairobi. HA, NBI.

Verdcourt 518; Agnew 7806.

5. Oldenlandia friesiorum *Brem.*

A low trailing herb with ascending stems and broad-ovate leaves; flowers clustered in terminal pseudo-umbels, pale pink.

Rare plant found in montane forest edges. HA, HK.

Lucas, Polhill, and Verdcourt 5.

6. Oldenlandia wiedemannii *K. Schum.*

An erect much-branched pubescent annual or weak perennial herb or wiry shrub with linear leaves and pale flowers in terminal clusters.

One of the commonest *Oldenlandia* species in dry bushland on shallow, rocky soil. RV, MAC, MAG, KAJ.

Verdcourt 3674; Agnew 10087.

7. Oldenlandia lancifolia (*Schum.*) *DC.*

Annual herb with trailing ascending unbranched stems, linear leaves and white, solitary, long-pedicellate flowers.

Rare plant found on shallow sandy soils in wooded grassland. KIT, MAC.

Faden 67/277.

8. Oldenlandia herbacea (*L.*) *Roxb.*

An erect, much-branched, glabrescent annual with linear leaves and solitary white flowers on slightly ascending pedicels.

In stony, open soil of dry grassland country. This plant dries black and is easily recognized. HT, HM, HA, HK, KIT, MUM, RV, EMB, MAC, NBI, KAJ.

Ryan 823; Agnew and Hanid 8369.

9. Oldenlandia scopulorum *Bullock*

An erect, much-branched, glabrescent shrubby short-lived perennial or annual with linear leaves and small cymes of white, lilac, or bluish-pink flowers.

Common in medium-altitude grassland. HT, HM, HL, HA, KIT, NAR, RV, NAN, NBI.

Glover 503: Agnew 10177.

10. Oldenlandia corymbosa *L.* (incl. *O. caespitosa* Hiern. and *O. linearis* DC.) (see p. 399)

An erect, sparsely-branched, annual herb with linear leaves and one or two white flowers on pedicels and peduncles which together often equal the leaves and tend to nod in fruit.

When the flowers are all single, this species resembles *O. herbacea*, but it has smaller flowers and does not dry black. Occasional, on shallow soils and sand in drier areas. HE, HA, KIT, MUM, BAR, RV, EMB.

Verdcourt 2458; Agnew 7480.

11. Oldenlandia fastigiata *Brem.*

An erect, sometimes large, sparsely-branched annual with linear leaves and minute flowers on short pedicels in clusters at the nodes.

Uncommon plant found in dry country and at the coast. MAG, MAC, KAJ.

Verdcourt 1870; Agnew 9853.

12. Oldenlandia acicularis *Brem.*

Very similar to *O. fastigiata* except for the smaller number of flowers.

This species is still known only from the type collected at Kipkarren, and may turn out to be only a form of *O. fastigiata*. KIT.

Brodhurst-Hill 221.

5. AGATHISANTHEMUM *Klotzsch*

Perennial herbs with entire leaves and laciniate stipules; flowers in terminal ± dense corymbs, tetramerous, isostylic or heterostylic; sepals with long lobes; corolla with a tube ± shorter than the lobes; style single; stigmas subglobose; capsule without a beak, loculicidal and septicidal, many-seeded.

Agathisanthemum globosum (*A. Rich.*) *Hiern* (see p. 402)

A tomentose and scabrid perennial herb with many erect unbranched stems bearing lanceolate leaves and a terminal ± globose head; flowers purplish.

A tall herb, rare in wooded grassland in western Kenya. HC, HT, KIT.

Verdcourt 3212; Tweedie 66/116.

6. DIBRACHIONOSTYLUS *Brem.*

Perennial glabrous herbs with entire leaves and toothed stipular sheaths; flowers in dense terminal cymose corymbs; flowers with a short tube, heterostylous; style simple, glabrous dividing at apex into 2 ellipsoid stigmas, linear; capsule loculicidal and septicidal, with many seeds.

Dibrachionostylus kaessneri (*S. Moore*) *Brem.*

An erect glabrous weak shrub or woody herb with linear-elliptic leaves and dense corymbs of pale mauve flowers.

Common in vlei grassland (seasonally water-logged) around Nairobi. EMB, MAC, NBI.

Harmsen 6415; Ward in EAH 5629.

7. PENTODON *Hochst.*

Erect or trailing glabrous herbs with simple leaves and toothed stipular sheaths; flowers in axillary or terminal cymes, pedicellate, isostylous or hetero-stylous, pentamerous with a short tube and lobes; calyx of triangular teeth; corolla blue or white; style single, with 2 filiform stigmas; capsule dehiscing within the calyx, many-seeded.

Pentodon pentandrus (*Schum.*) *Vatke*

A trailing, often large perennial with lanceolate, often glaucous and ± fleshy leaves, and loose axillary cymes of blue flowers.

Locally common along the shore of Lake Victoria, this species is also found at the coast. MUM, KIS, MAC.

Hanid and Kiniaruh 739; Ossent 616.

8. PENTAS *Benth.*

Erect herbs or shrubs with entire leaves and laciniate stipular sheaths; flowers isostylous or heterostylous, cymose in dense terminal corymbs; sepal lobes equal or unequal; corolla with a cylindrical tube, red, purple, or white; fruit a dry capsule, apically and often tardily dehiscent, many-seeded.

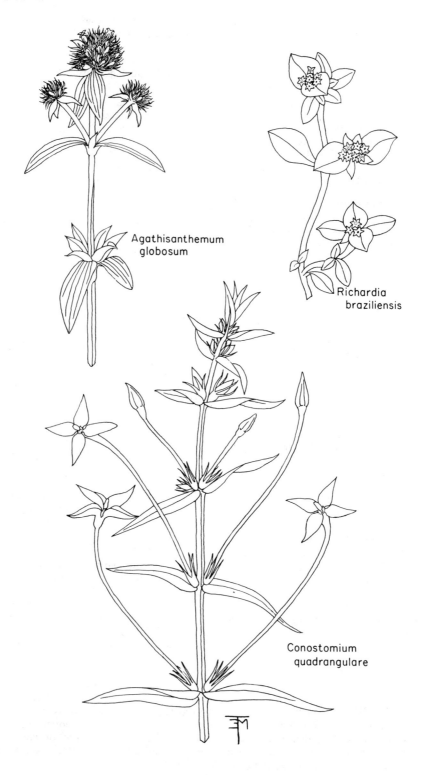

Agathisanthemum
globosum

Richardia
braziliensis

Conostomium
quadrangulare

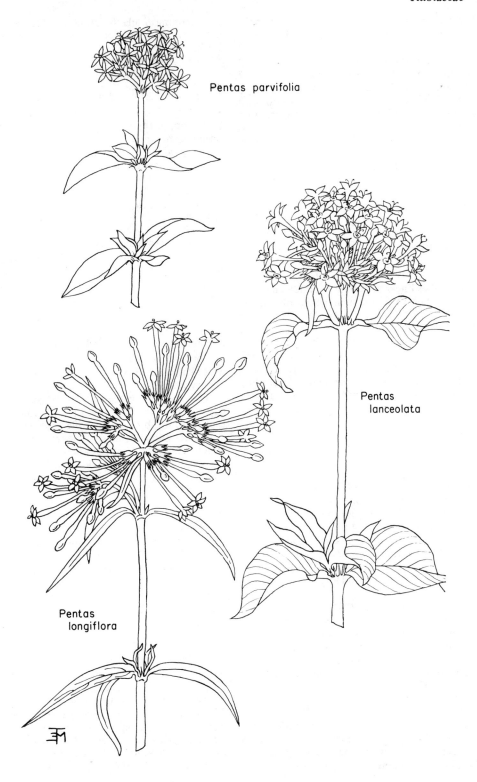

Pentas parvifolia

Pentas lanceolata

Pentas longiflora

1   Flowers bright red   1. *P. parvifolia*
    Flowers white, mauve, or pink, not bright red
                                                                  2
2   Corolla tube more than 1 cm long   **3**
    Corolla tube less than 1 cm long   **7**
3   Inflorescences 3–7-flowered; plant a trailing
        shrub   2. *P. hindsioides*
    Inflorescences of more than 10 flowers; erect
        shrubs or herbs   **4**
4   Calyx lobes linear or subulate, subequal   **5**
    Calyx lobes very unequal, some oblong or
        ovate more than twice the size of others **6**
5   Corolla tube more than 5 cm long at least in
        some flowers   3. *P. decora*
    Corolla tube always less than 4 cm long
                                         4. *P. longiflora*
6   Corolla tube more than 5 cm long at least in
        some flowers   5. *P. suswaensis*
    Corolla tube always less than 5 cm long
                                         6. *P. lanceolata*
7   Calyx lobes linear or subulate, subequal   **8**
    Calyx lobes very unequal, some oblong or
        elliptic twice the length of others   **9**
8   Many-stemmed herb; inflorescence exceeding
        the leaves and without leaf-like bracts
                                          7. *P. arvensis*
    Single- or few-stemmed tall woody herb or
        weak shrub; inflorescence not exceeding
        the leaves and often with leaf-like bracts
                                       8. *P. schimperana*
9   Corolla tube less than 5 mm long
                                          9. *P. pubiflora*
    Corolla tube 6–10 mm long
                                        10. *P. zanzibarica*

1. Pentas parvifolia *Hiern* (see p. 403)

An erect pubescent shrub with elliptic-lanceolate
leaves and dense or lax corymbose heads of bright
red flowers; corolla tube 8–14 mm long.

Common in dry bushland and wooded grassland, especially with *Combretum*. MUM, BAR,
EMB, MAC, NBI, KAJ.

Agnew 9878; Verdcourt 3641.

2. Pentas hindsioides *K. Schum.*

A trailing shrub with ovate to elliptic leaves and
white flowers with the corolla tube 3–4 cm long.

Rare plant found on cliff faces. This species is
found in Northern Tanzania and Teita but has
only been found once in our area, at Nzaui. MAC.

Agnew and Hanid 8356.

3. Pentas decora *S. Moore* (see p. 399)

An erect-stemmed woody herb with often trifoliate lanceolate-elliptic leaves; flowers in a
solitary dense head, white or cream, with the
corolla tube 5–7 cm long.

Uncommon plant found in wooded tall-grass-
land, in western Kenya. HE, HC, KIT, MUM,
BAR.

Strid 2895; Leippert 5172.

4. Pentas longiflora *Oliv.* (see p. 403)

Similar to *P. decora* in general appearance, but
leaves opposite, and with a lax inflorescence of
several separate corymbs; corolla tube 2·5–4 cm
long, cream.

Locally common in dry wooded grassland,
often with *Combretum*. HE, HC, HT, HM, HA,
KIT, MUM, KIS, NAR, RV, KAJ.

Agnew and Hanid 8404; Bally 661.

5. Pentas suswaensis *Verdc.*

Similar to *P. lanceolata* except for the longer,
white flowers.

This endemic species is so far only known from
Mt. Suswa in the Rift Valley. RV.

Verdcourt 710.

6. Pentas lanceolata (*Forsk.*) *Deflers* (see p. 403)

An erect branched shrub or woody herb with
ovate-lanceolate leaves and mauve to white flowers
in corymbs.

This very variable species is widespread in forest
edges. There are two main population types, one
that is dimorphic in its corolla tube length (as well
as in the stamen and style length) and the other
which is not. Occasionally these two may be found
together. HE, HC, HA, HK, HN, KIT, MUM, KIS,
NAR, RV, NAN, MAC, NBI, KAJ.

Hanid and Kiniaruh 979B; Ossent 167.

7. Pentas arvensis *Hiern*

An erect herb with many unbranched stems and
elliptic leaves; flowers in a terminal corymb which
overtops the stem leaves, white to pinkish; corolla
tube 4–5 mm long.

Rare plant found in burnt grassland and only
recorded from Kakamega in our area. MUM.

Carroll H8.

8. Pentas schimperana *Vatke*

An erect woody tomentose herb with unbranched
stems and ovate leaves; inflorescence a dense
terminal corymb, often with leafy bracts or
overtopped by leaves; flowers cream to pink, with
a tube 5–9 mm long.

Uncommon plant found in montane forest
edges in west Kenya. HE, HC, HT, HM, HA.

Tweedie 67/310; Bush 258.

9. Pentas pubiflora *S. Moore* (see p. 406)

An erect herb with elliptic to lanceolate leaves and rather open terminal corymbs, with tiny white and pink flowers; corolla tube 4-5 mm long.

Uncommon, but widespread in montane forest and riverine forest. HE, HC, HT, HM, HA, HN, KIT, MUM, NAR, RV.

Tweedie 67/173; Kerfoot 4339.

10. Pentas zanzibarica (*Klotzsch*) *Vatke*

Similar to *P. lanceolata* except for its occasional rhizomes and shorter blue to purple-pink flowers.

Common in dry grassland especially in the Rift Valley. HT, HM, HL, HA, KIT, NAR, RV, NBI, KAJ.

Agnew, Hanid, and Kiniaruh 7822; Napier 467.

9. OTOMERIA *Benth.*

Very similar to *Pentas* except for the inflorescence which elongates in fruit.

1	Flowers scarlet, not dimorphic; style always exserted	1. *O. elatior*
	Flowers pink or white with a blue or maroon eye in the centre; style dimorphic	2. *O. oculata*

1. Otomeria elatior (*DC.*) *Verdc.*

Herb with many erect unbranched stems and ovate-lanceolate leaves; corolla tube 17-27 mm long.

Rare plant found in swampy places in wooded grassland areas of western Kenya. HT, MUM, KIS.

Napier 5285.

2. Otomeria oculata *S. Moore*

Similar to *O. elatior* but with a dark-centred corolla.

Uncommon plant found in dry rocky grassland. BAR, NAN, EMB, MAC.

Williams in EAH 184162; Strid 2241.

10. PARAKNOXIA *Brem.*

Similar to *Oldenlandia* but with sessile flowers and solitary seeds in each luculus.

Paraknoxia parviflora (*Verdc.*) *Brem.* (see p. 406)

A small, divaricately branched, erect pubescent annual with oblong to linear leaves and axillary groups of sessile, white or blue flowers.

Rare plant found in short grassland in west Kenya. HE, KIT.

Verdcourt 2454; Tweedie 67/240.

11. PENTANISIA *Harvey*

Erect or decumbent annuals or perennials with simple leaves and fimbriate stipular sheaths; flowers in terminal or axillary corymbs or fascicles, dimorphic, pentamerous, often on very short pedicels; calyx with 1-3 lobes enlarged; corolla with a tube and spreading lobes, usually purple; fruit globular, indehiscent (occasionally succulent) with one compressed seed in each loculus.

1	Leaves and calyx glabrous; calyx-lobes up to twice ovary length	1. *P. schweinfurthii*
	Leaves and calyx tomentose; calyx-lobes more than 3 times ovary length	2
2	Inflorescences of paired axillary pseudo-spikes, each up to 12-flowered	2. *P. foetida*
	Inflorescences of solitary, terminal, more than 20-flowered corymbs	3. *P. ouranogyne*

1. Pentanisia schweinfurthii *Hiern* (see p. 406)

An erect subglabrous herb or low shrub, with elliptic leaves and terminal corymbs of blue-violet flowers.

Uncommon plant found in burnt wooded grassland in western Kenya. HC, KIT, MUM.

Bogdan 3719; Tweedie 66/1.

2. Pentanisia foetida *Verdc.*

An erect or trailing tomentose herb with ovate leaves and purple flowers on paired, pedunculate pseudo-spikes.

Common in some areas of montane rain-forest in the Aberdares and Mt. Kenya especially just below and in the bamboo zone. HA, HK, HN.

Rayner 510 A: Agnew 8315.

3. Pentanisia ouranogyne *S. Moore* (see p. 406)

A rhizomatous low tomentose herb with linear to lanceolate leaves and terminal corymbs of bright blue flowers.

This very ornamental plant is abundant in disturbed places in dry country and so is often seen along roadsides. HE, HT, HK, KIS, NAR, BAR, RV, MAG, NAN, MAC, NBI, KAJ.

Lind, Agnew, and Beecher 5718.

12. FADOGIA *Schweinf.*

Herbs, shrubs, or trees with whorled leaves and entire, acute stipules; flowers axillary or in short panicles or clusters, pentamerous, isostylous; calyx with small equal teeth; corolla funnel-shaped or subcylindrical, hairy within; ovary 3-5-celled with 1 ovule in each cell; fruit a drupe of bony sections.

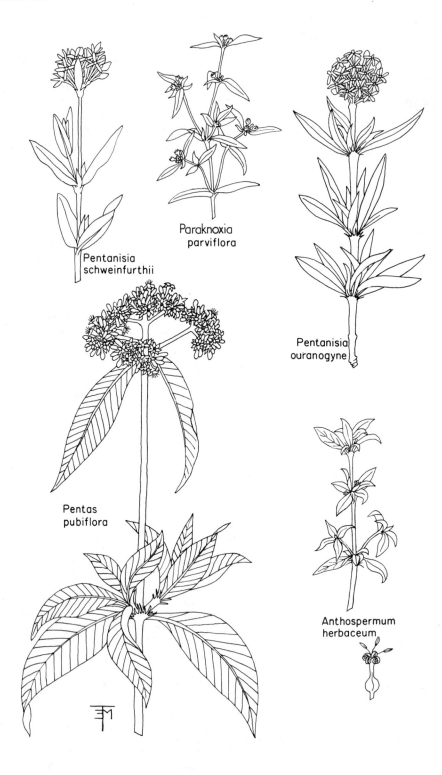

Pentanisia
schweinfurthii

Paraknoxia
parviflora

Pentanisia
ouranogyne

Pentas
pubiflora

Anthospermum
herbaceum

Fadogia cienkowskii *Schweinf.* (see p. 408)

An erect weak shrub or woody herb with trifoliolate leaves densely tomentose below; flowers yellow, axillary, short-pedicellate, solitary or pedunculate in cymes of 3–5.

Uncommon plant found in wooded tall grassland in western Kenya. KIT.

Symes 50; Tweedie 66/75.

13. PAEDERIA *L.*

Climbing, twining woody lianes with opposite (in our plant), or often whorled leaves with minutely bifid stipules; isostylous, pentamerous; calyx of 5 equal teeth; corolla funnel-shaped, with a spreading lobed limb; fruit with one seed in each of the two cells, splitting into 2–3 pyrenes.

Paederia pospischilii *K. Schum.*

A foetid-smelling pubescent twiner with lanceolate to sub-orbicular petiolate leaves and solitary flowers; flowers with a pink tube and white flat limb.

Rare plant found in *Commiphora* bushland. MAC, KAJ.

Agnew 9802; Bally 1342.

14. ANTHOSPERMUM *L.*

Dioecious or monoecious shrubs or herbs with opposite or whorled simple leaves with toothed stipular sheaths; flowers unisexual, mostly tetramerous; calyx of equal or unequal lobes; ovary 2-celled, with one ovule in each cell, and with a style bearing two linear stigmas; fruit of two 1-seeded mericarps.

Other Kenya species are shrubs.

Anthospermum herbaceum *L. f.* (see p. 406)

A low, trailing, dioecious or monecious herb not rooting at the nodes with ovate-lanceolate leaves and minute yellowish flowers.

Found in hedgerows and short grass in the wet forest areas. HE, HC, HT, HM, HA, HK, KIT, KIS, KAJ.

Verdcourt 1046; Hanid 231.

15. RICHARDIA *Adans.*

Trailing perennial herbs with entire leaves; flowers white, sessile in heads subtended by uppermost leaf-pairs; calyx of broad, deltoid lobes of differing sizes; corolla with a short tube; fruit mericarpic into 3, 1-seeded cocci.

Richardia braziliensis *Gomez* (see p. 402)

A trailing pubescent perennial herb with swollen roots; leaves elliptic to spathulate, except those of the involucre which clasp at the base; fruits with a broad face between the mericarps.

Introduced from South America, this weed is found in short grassland such as lawns. HA, KIT, MAC, NBI.

Faden 67214; Strid 2592.

16. GEOPHILA *D. Don*

Creeping herbs, rooting at the nodes, with cordate, entire leaves; flowers small, axillary, in groups of 1–4; corolla with a bearded throat and 5 petal lobes; stamens 5, inserted or included; fruit of 2 1-seeded drupes.

Geophila repens (*L.*) *I. M. Johnst.*

A creeping pubescent herb with orbicular-cordate or reniform leaves and small white flowers; fruit red.

Recorded only recently from Kakamega forest in grassy pathsides. MUM.

Record from Faden *in litt.*

17. BORRERIA *G. F. W. Mey.*

Annual or perennial herbs with entire leaves and fringed stipular sheaths; flowers sessile in axillary clusters in the inflated stipular sheath, tetramerous, isostylic, white or pink; calyx of similar or dissimilar lobes; ovary with a single style and 2-lobed globose stigma; fruit a capsule, dehiscing at the apex to liberate the two seeds.

1	Plant perennial, either creeping or from a woody rootstock	**2**
	Plant annual, erect	**3**
2	Plant creeping; leaves more than 2·5 cm long	*1. B. princei*
	Plant erect from a woody rootstock; leaves less than 2·5 cm long	*2. B.* sp. *A*
3	Calyx lobes more than 2 mm long, overtopping the teeth on the stipular sheath	**5**
	Calyx lobes less than 2 mm long, overtopped by the teeth on the stipular sheath	**4**
4	Leaves hairy below	*3. B. kotschyana*
	Leaves glabrous below	*4. B. stricta*
5	Calyx lobes very unequal, 2 very big and 2 minute, less than one quarter the size of the others; capsule dehiscent at apex, the valves persistent	*5. B. scabra*
	Calyx lobes ± equal; capsule dehiscent at base, the valves falling entire leaving the conspicuous white placenta	*Arbulocarpus sphaerostigma*

1. **Borreria princei** *K. Schum.*

A trailing, pubescent perennial, rooting at the nodes, with elliptic leaves; leaves deeply impressed with ± parallel nerves on the upper side; flowers few, white.

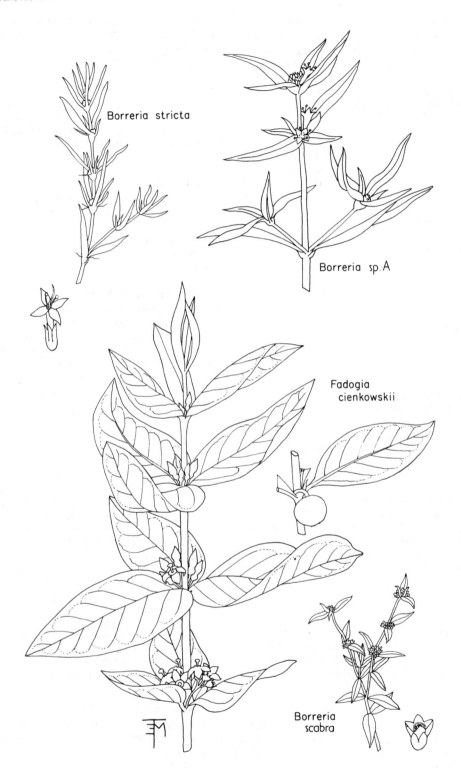

Borreria stricta

Borreria sp. A

Fadogia
cienkowskii

Borreria
scabra

Common in hedgerows and forest edges in wet country below 8000 ft. HC, HT, HA, HK, KIT, KIS, NAR, MAC.

Agnew 8205; Verdcourt 2465.

2. Borreria *sp.* **A.** (see p. 408)

An erect, branching, wiry, almost glabrous herb from a woody rootstock, with elliptic leaves and dense clusters of white flowers.

Uncommon plant found in short grass in wooded grassland in western Kenya. HE, HC, HM, HT, KIT.

Tweedie 66/15; Symes 38.

3. Borreria kotschyana (*Oliv.*) *K. Schum.*

An erect pubescent annual, branched below, with linear-elliptic leaves and dense ± globose clusters of small cream flowers, amongst which filiform bracts are evident.

Rare plant found in disturbed places in dry country. BAR.

Bogdan 5605.

4. Borreria stricta (*L. f.*) *G. F. W. Mey.* (see p. 408)

Similar to *B. kotschyana* but more slender, glabrous except for the stipular sheaths, and with the filiform bracts not reaching to the flowers.

Common as a field weed in western Kenya and in dry country. HE, KIT, MUM, MAC, KAJ.

Agnew and Musumba 8586; Tweedie 67/230.

5. Borreria scabra (*Schumach. & Thonn.*) *K. Schum.* (see p. 408)

An erect pubescent annual, branched below, with linear-elliptic leaves and semiglobose heads of white flowers in the stipular sheaths; calyx with 2 very long sepals (to 6 mm) and 2 less than 1 mm long.

Rare plant found in dry country, recorded from East Tsavo and by one specimen from Thika District. MAC.

Hanid and Kiniaruh 471; Greenway 9772.

18. ARBULOCARPUS *Tennant*

Similar in all respects to 17. *Borreria* except for the dehiscence of the capsule which is from the base, so that the valves fall, exposing the placenta.

Arbulocarpus sphaerostigma (*A. Rich.*) *Tennant*

An erect, often scabrid-pubescent, annual, branching from the base, with elliptic leaves and hemispherical clusters of white flowers in the stipular sheaths; calyx lobes subequal.

A field weed in grassland, particularly in western Kenya. HE, HC, HT, KIT, KIS, MAC.

Nattrass 987; Strid 2496.

19. MITRACARPUM Zucc.

Erect herbs with entire leaves and laciniate stipular sheaths; flowers clustered at the nodes, isostylous, bisexual tetramerous; calyx with 4 teeth, alternately long and short; corolla bell-shaped; ovary with a single style and two slender stigmas; fruit a capsule of 2 cells with one seed in each, dehiscing transversely with the top and stiff persistent calyx lobes lifting off like a cap.

Mitracarpum verticillatum (*Schum. and Thonn.*) *Vatke* (*M. scaber* Zucc.)

An erect annual with oblong to elliptic leaves and hemispherical clusters of untidy-looking white flowers at the nodes.

Rare plant found in waste places in warmer, wetter districts. This plant is common in Tanzania and Uganda but curiously little-known in Kenya. MUM.

Drummond and Hemsley 4486.

20. GALIUM *L.*

Annual or perennial herbs with whorls of 4–10 entire leaves and often retrorse barbs; inflorescence cymose; flowers bisexual, isostylous, tetramerous; calyx obsolete; corolla of 4 valvate deltoid segments and a very short tube; styles 2, joined below; fruit of 2 dry, 1-seeded mericarps, or a berry with the seed adherent to the ovary wall.

1   Leaves always only 4 at each node, orbicular to broad-elliptic, 3-nerved
                    1. *G. thunbergianum*
    Leaves more than 4 at each node, narrow-elliptic to linear, 1-nerved   2
2   Retrorse prickles present on the stem and frequently but not always also on the leaf edges (these may be discovered by the 'sticky' feel of the stem when rubbed upwards); fruits glabrous or hairy   3
    Retrorse prickles absent from the glabrous or hairy stem (and leaves) which feel smooth; fruits always glabrous   9
3   Fruit glabrous   4
    Fruit hairy   6
4   Flowers in corymbose terminal cymes which overtop the leaves; fruit dry when ripe
                    11. *G. scioanum*
    Flowers in small irregular cymes which are not corymbose, mostly lateral, and hardly overtop the leaves; fruits fleshy   5
5   Leaves up to 15 mm long, each with a tuft of hairs at the base; stem usually minutely pubescent under the prickles
                    2. *G. ruwenzoriense*

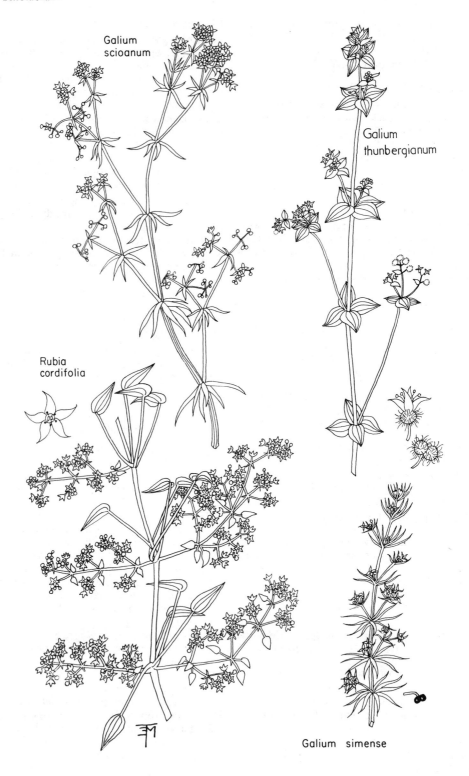

Galium
scioanum

Galium
thunbergianum

Rubia
cordifolia

Galium simense

Some leaves more than 15 mm long, with a tuft of pale brown to colourless hairs at the base; stem glabrous under the prickles
3. *G. simense*

6 Fruits covered with yellow hooked bristles, each fruit often ± sessile and subtended by a small leafy bract   7
   Fruits covered with white hooked or straight bristles, each fruit pedicellate   8

7 Prickles on leaf-margin retrorse, pointing towards the base of the leaf
4. *G. chloroionanthum*
   Prickles on leaf margin not retrorse but pointing towards the leaf-apex 5. *G.* sp. *A*

8 Most fruits solitary, or 2-3 together, axillary, on long pedicels   6. *G. spurium*
   Most fruits in small terminal inflorescences, held on short pedicels   7. *G. aparinoides*

9 Leaves with a terminal acute tip ending in a bristle   10
   Leaf obtuse or acute at tip but without a terminal bristle   11

10 Creeping herb with scattered flowers and ± spathulate leaves less than 5 mm long
8. *G. glaciale*
    Erect-stemmed herb with terminal inflorescences and linear leaves often over 5 mm long   9. *G. ossirwaense*

11 Leaves less than 5 mm long; flowers scattered
10. *G. kenyanum*
    At least some leaves over 10 mm long; flowers mostly terminal   11. *G. scioanum*

1. Galium thunbergianum *Eckl. and Zeyh.* (see p. 410)

A creeping tomentose herb with quadrifoliate suborbicular leaves and loose cymes of pale yellow flowers; fruit covered with straight glossy hairs.

Rare plant found in wet montane forest. HE, HM, HK.

Agnew and Coe 8754.

2. Galium ruwenzoriense (*Cort.*) *Chiov.*

'Sticky' climber with linear leaves and small axillary inflorescences; fruits glabrous, becoming black and fleshy.

Common above 7500 ft on all our three great mountains, on forest edges and bushland. HE, HA, HK.

Hedberg 1025; Hanid 123.

3. Galium simense Fres. (see p. 410)

Similar to *G. ruwenzoriense*, but larger in all its parts and differing in the key characters. These two species may turn out to be altitudinal forms of the same.

Rather rare plant found in bushland edges between 5000 and 6500 ft. NAR, RV, HA.

Agnew, Hanid, and Kiniaruh 7885; Verdcourt 634.

4. Galium chloroionanthum *K. Schum.*

'Sticky' climber or scrambler with elliptic leaves rounded at apex, and axillary cymes of sessile, bracteate flowers; fruits covered with brown hooks.

Apparently very rare and only found in HM.

Bally 4891.

5. Galium *sp.* **A.**

Similar to *G. chloroionanthum* but often creeping and without the retrorse bristles on the leaf margin.

This species may be but a form of *G. chloroionanthum* since it is found in the same areas, in deep, wet montane forest and bamboo where it creeps on the forest floor. HM, HA.

Kerfoot 665; Agnew 7132.

6. Galium spurium *L.*

A 'sticky' climber or scrambler with narrowly oblanceolate, acute leaves and usually solitary axillary flowers on long pedicels; pedicels sharply bent below the hairy fruit.

A rather uncommon weed of cultivation. HC, HT, HM, HA, NBI.

Bogdan 1931; Agnew 8991.

7. Galium aparinoides *Forsk.*

Similar to *G. spurium* but the leaves broader, rounded, apiculate at tip, and flowers mostly in terminal inflorescences.

Locally common in montane forest edges. HC, HM, HA, HK, KIT, KAJ.

Glover 1471; Agnew 8881.

8. Galium glaciale *K. Krause*

Prostrate glabrous creeper from central rootstock with spathulate, acuminate leaves and scattered flowers; fruits glabrous, dry.

Uncommon plant found in disturbed places along river banks etc, in the alpine zone. HE, HK.

Hanid 93; Hedberg 1733.

9. Galium ossirwaense *K. Krause*

A rhizomatous, sparsely pubescent herb with tufted ascending stems and linear leaves; flowers yellow, crowded towards the stem apex; fruits glabrous, dry.

Uncommon plant found in dry grassland. HT, HA, HK.

Napper 536; Strid 2132.

10. Galium kenyanum *Verdc.*

A trailing herb, glabrous except for sparse hairs on young parts, with linear-oblong leaves and scattered flowers; fruits glabrous, dry.

Uncommon plant found in alpine grassland. HA, HK.

Coe 364; Polhill 239.

11. Galium scioanum *Chiov.* (see p. 410)

A trailing herb with narrow-elliptic leaves and flowers in ± terminal corymbose cymes; fruits glabrous, dry.

Found in swamps and moist woodland mostly in Western Kenya, this species exists in two forms, one almost glabrous except for the nodes, the other sparsely tomentose on stems and below the leaves. HC, HM, HT, HA, KIT.

Tweedie 67/166; Symes 108.

21. RUBIA *L.*

Perennial climbing herbs, sometimes woody below with 4–6 entire leaves in each whorl; flowers as in *Galium* but pentamerous; fruit a berry, usually derived from only 1 carpel; seed fused to the ovary wall.

Rubia cordifolia *L.* (*R. longipetiolata* Bullock) (see p. 410)

A climbing herb covered with prickly, recurved hairs and with long-petiolate, cordate, ovate or lanceolate-acuminate leaves; flowers in short axillary cymes, which are produced terminally, greenish-yellow.

A variable plant, examples from western Kenya having narrower leaves and longer petioles, grading into short petioles and cordate-ovate leaves in the east. Common in the margins and clearings of dry woodland as well as in riverine bushland in drier climates. HE, HT, HM, HL, HA, HK, KIT, KIS, NAR, RV, MAC, NBI, KAJ.

Lugard 204; Harmsen 6498.

74. CAPRIFOLIACEAE†

Shrubs or small trees, rarely herbs; leaves opposite, simple or compound; stipules absent or interpetiolar; inflorescence cymose; flowers bisexual, regular or irregular, 4–5-merous; calyx imbricate or open; corolla imbricate with a short or long tube; stamens epipetalous, alternating with petals; ovary inferior with 1–numerous ovules per loculus; fruit a fleshy berry or drupe, or achene.

1. SAMBUCUS *L.*

Shrubs or herbs, stem with thick pith or hollow; leaves pinnate, leaflets serrate; inflorescence cymose; flowers small with a tube shorter than the

† By S. Kibe.

lobes; ovary 3–5-celled, 1 pendulous ovule per cell; fruit a berry with compressed seeds.

Sambucus africana *Standley* (see p. 413)

Fleshy herb up to 5 m; leaflets obovate, large, sharply serrate, acute-acuminate, asymmetric or irregularly adhering to the petiole, puberulous; calyx minutely lobed; petals white; fruit black, edible.

Found along elephant/buffalo paths in the bamboo zone and montane forest. Dominant where bamboo has flowered and died.

Mathenge 211; Clapham, Greenway, Lind, and Agnew s.n., January 1962.

75. VALERIANACEAE‡

Annual herbs, rarely shrubs; leaves opposite, entire, dentate or pinnatifid, exstipulate; inflorescence paniculate, cymose, flowers bisexual, occasionally unisexual, regular or (mostly) zygomorphic; calyx lobes often rolled up in flower, unrolling to form a feathery pappus in fruit; corolla 3–5-lobed, funnel-shaped, lobes imbricate; stamens 1–4, anthers 2-celled; ovary inferior, 3-celled, 2 cells sterile, the solitary ovule pendulous; stigmas 2–3, free or connate; fruit an achene.

1   Annual; corolla not spurred at base; calyx not forming a feathery pappus in fruit
                                        2. *Valerianella*
     Perennial; corolla spurred at base; calyx forming a feathery pappus in fruit
                                        1. *Valeriana*

1. VALERIANA *L.*

Perennial herbs with bitter and peculiar smell; leaves entire, pinnatifid or pinnate; inflorescence cymose, terminal, subcapitate; flowers protandrous, bisexual or unisexual, bracteolate; calyx inrolled in flower, forming a feathery pappus in fruit; corolla 5-lobed, lobes unequal; stamens 3.

1   Leaves compound   2
     Leaves simple   1. *V. kilimandscharica*
2   Leaves 3–5-foliolate; leaflets entire; inflorescence a very lax cyme   2. *V. volkensii*
     Leaves more than 7-foliolate; leaflets dentate or undulate; inflorescence of clustered flowers or subcapitate   3. *V. capensis*

1. Valeriana kilimandscharica *Engl.*

Perennial herb with suffrutescent decumbent and shortly ascending stem, often rooting at the nodes; leaves simple, spathulate, connate at base, crenate or entire; inflorescence racemose; fruit ovoid.

‡ By S. Kibe.

Valeriana volkensii

Sambucus africana

Found in the alpine region in tussock grassland of sloping moist ground amongst other herbs and bryophytes. HE, HA, HK.

Hedberg 1699; Hanid 94.

2. Valeriana volkensii *Engl.* (see p. 413)

Perennial pubescent herb with sparsely branched erect or ascending suffrutescent stem; leaves 3–7-foliolate; with elliptic entire leaflets, the terminal one largest; inflorescence a lax raceme.

Found only on Mt. Elgon on moist ground along streamsides in the bamboo zone. HE.

Gillett 18414.

3. Valeriana capensis *Thunb.*

Erect, delicate perennial herb; stem fleshy, glabrous; leaves more than 7-foliolate; leaflets elliptic, dentate or undulate-crenate; inflorescence terminal, of dense hairy heads.

Found with tussock grasses in stony ground along well-drained streamsides in the ericaceous zone of the Aberdares only. HA.

Coe 757.

2. VALERIANELLA *Mill.*

Annual dichotomously branched herbs; leaves entire, cleft or toothed; flowers in terminal bracteate cymose heads or solitary; calyx persistent, dentate or crown-like, divided into 10–14 subulate lobes; corolla 5-lobed, not spurred or saccate at base; stamens 3, epipetalous; stigma 3-fid; fruit ovoid, glabrous.

Valerianella microcarpa *Lois.*

Erect or spreading, dichotomously branched annual with lower leaves entire, oblong, and upper ones dentate at base; inflorescence very lax cymose with white flowers in forks of the branches and in terminal bracteate heads.

Rare plant found in short alpine vegetation. HK.

Verdcourt 3504 and 3529.

76. DIPSACACEAE†

Annual or perennial herbs; leaves opposite or verticillate, exstipulate; inflorescence a head; flowers bisexual, zygomorphic, protandrous; epicalyx often present; corolla tube 4–5 lobed; stamens usually 4, epipetalous; anthers 2-celled; ovary 1-loculed, ± inferior, sessile with one solitary pendulous ovule; fruit an achene, often enclosed in the epicalyx, 1-seeded; seeds thinly membranous.

† By S. Kibe.

1   Flowering head flat-topped; flowers purple, pinkish or blue   2
     Flowering head spherical or flat-topped, flowers white or yellowish   3
2   Plant a weak, prostrate shrub with woody stem; hairs on the fruit branched
                              3. Pterocephalus frutescens
     Plant a herb without a woody stem; hairs on the fruit not branched
                              4. Scabiosa columbaria
3   Stem with spines; bracts lanceolate, narrowing gradually to a sharp tip
                              1. Dipsacus pinnatifidus
     Stem without spines; bracts oblong, apically rounded, sharply mucronate
                              2. Cephalaria pungens

1. DIPSACUS *L.*

Erect stout biennial herbs; leaves often connate at base, dentate; capitulum subglobose; flowers subtended by stiff, spiny bracts; epicalyx obscure, 4-grooved; corolla tube 4-lobed; stamens 4; ovary inferior; stigma dilated.

Dipsacus pinnatifidus *A. Rich.* (see p. 415)

Erect herb to 2 m; leaves connate at base, ovate to lanceolate, serrate; involucral bracts linear-lanceolate, spiny; flowers white.

Found in the upper forest and lower alpine zones, commonly by streamsides in *Erica* woodland. HE, HM, HA, HK.

Glover *et al.* 1519; Agnew 7279.

2. CEPHALARIA *Schrad.*

Perennial herbs without prickles; leaves entire, dentate or pinnatifid; heads involucrate with imbricating scales shorter than the bracts of the receptacle; epicalyx with 4 small teeth; calyx tube adnate to the inferior ovary; corolla funnel-shaped, 4-lobed; stigma obliquely dilated.

Cephalaria pungens *Szabo* (see p. 415)

Erect pubescent herb; leaves at base long-spathulate, entire, upper leaves variously toothed or dentate; capitulum flat-topped when in flower; flowers subtended by oblong, mucronate, brown bracts; fruit with a crown of hairs.

Found in montane and subalpine grassland in western Kenya. HE, HC, HM, KIT.

Bally B4782; Agnew, Kibe, and Mathenge 10523.

3. PTEROCEPHALUS *Adans.*

Herbs or shrubs; leaves entire or variously divided (in ours); heads flat or globose; receptacle hairy; calyx enlarged into 12–24 plumose awns in fruit; epicalyx present, hardly expanded, 8-grooved; corolla-tube 5-lobed.

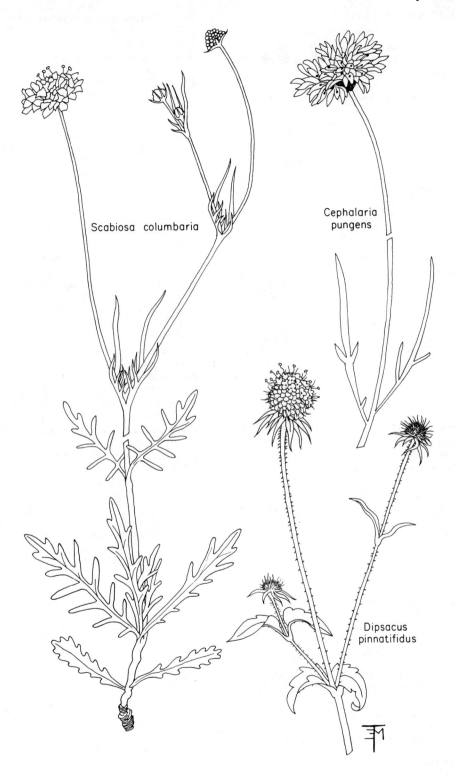

Scabiosa columbaria

Cephalaria
pungens

Dipsacus
pinnatifidus

Pterocephalus frutescens *Hochst.*

Trailing shrub; leaves linear-lanceolate, entire or variously dentate or divided; involucral bracts ovate, acute, pubescent; flower pinkish-red, pubescent outside.

Found amongst grasses on eroded ground and on stony soils on dry exposed hillsides. HA, HM, NAR, RV, KAJ.

Glover, Gwynne, and Samuel 1310; Hanid 259.

4. SCABIOSA *L.*

Erect or ascending perennial or annual herbs; stem puberulous or glabrous; leaves entire, or variously divided (in ·ours); heads terminal, flat or globose; receptacle hairy; calyx of 5 bristles in fruit; epicalyx present, 8-grooved, winged in fruit; corolla tube 5-lobed.

Scabiosa columbaria *L.* (see p. 415)

Erect herb from a thick rootstock with a rosette of spathulate, entire or divided leaves; involucral bracts linear-lanceolate, pubescent; corolla pinkish mauve, 5-lobed, velvety.

Found in *Erica* scrub on rocky slopes, streamsides, *Tarchonanthus* and *Philippia* bushland and in forest clearings. HE, HC, HM, HA, HK, KIT, RV, NAN.

Hedberg 129; Isaac A. 31.

77. COMPOSITAE†

Mostly herbs, with alternate or opposite, entire or divided exstipulate leaves; flowers bisexual, monoecious, polygamous or dioecious, sessile in heads or capitula, surrounded by a series of bracts called *phyllaries* and sometimes subtended by bracts or scales on the receptacle; sepals variously reduced, frequently to scales or bristles (*pappus*); corolla of florets (flowers) of three types: (1) zygomorphic with a spreading 3-toothed ligule, with or without two upright teeth at the apex of the corolla tube, (2) zygomorphic with a spreading 5-toothed ligule at the apex of the tube, (3) regular with 4–5 lobes at the apex of the tube; stamens 5, fused in a ring round the style, the filaments free and joined to the corolla tube; ovary inferior, with one erect ovule and an erect style and bifid stigma; fruit a dry, indehiscent achene, often winged or dispersed by the calyx hairs, rarely fleshy.

1 Tubular florets present; no milky latex   2
  Only ligulate florets present; milky latex usually present   104
2 Plants armed with spines on stems and leaves   3
  Plants without spines on stems and leaves   8

† By A. D. Q. Agnew.

3 Heads 1-flowered, aggregated into globose 'heads of heads'   72. *Echinops*
  Heads each with many flowers   4
4 Ray florets present 71. *Berkheya spekeana*
  No ray florets present   5
5 Central florets yellow
              26. *Helichrysum citrispinum*
  All florets purple or white   6
6 Pappus plumose   74. *Cirsium*
  Pappus hairs simple or scabrid only   7
7 Leaves marbled or veined with pale green or white   75. *Silybum marianum*
  Leaves uniformly green   73. *Carduus*
8 Leaves opposite, at least the basal ones   9
  Leaves alternate or plants stemless   36
9 Achenes each completely enclosed by a hard woody bract, making a disseminule 8–10 mm long; ray florets sterile
              40. *Sclerocarpus africanus*
  Achenes not so enclosed; disseminule usually smaller; ray florets, where present, mostly fertile   10
10 Rays with a spreading limb present   11
   Rays absent, or, if marginal zygomorphic florets present, then without a spreading limb   21
11 Pappus present   12
   Pappus absent   17
12 Inner phyllaries fused along their entire length, forming a tube or cone; leaves pinnate   53. *Tagetes minuta*
   Inner phyllaries free or fused to half-way or less; leaves entire   13
13 Pappus coroniform or of scales, sometimes with bristles   14
   Pappus of bristles or hairs only   15
14 Rays white; annual herb
              50. *Galinsoga parviflora*
   Rays yellow; shrubs   42. *Aspilia*
15 Pappus plumose; prostrate herb
              49. *Tridax procumbens*
   Pappus simple or scabrid; erect herbs, shrubs, or climbers   16
16 Pappus of 4–10 caducous bristles, scabrid but not with retrorse barbs; heads more or less spherical in fruit; leaves entire; achenes not compressed
                            44. *Melanthera*
   Pappus of 2–4 persistent bristles often with retrorse barbs; heads hemispherical in fruit; leaves mostly divided; achenes compressed   48. *Bidens*
17 Ray florets white   39. *Eclipta alba*
   Rays yellow   18
18 Receptacle conical
              45. *Spilanthes mauritiana*
   Receptacle flat   19

19 Inner florets sterile; achenes from ligulate florets only 67. *Osteospermum vaillantii*
Inner florets fertile; outer florets sterile   20
20 Rays small, their length less than half the diameter of the involucre
37. *Sigesbeckia*
Rays large, their length more than the diameter of the involucre   46. *Guizotia*
21 Pappus present   22
Pappus absent   31
22 Pappus of scales   23
Pappus of bristles   24
23 Leaves capillary or divided into capillary (thread-like) segments, glabrous; florets yellow   52. *Schkuhria pinnata*
Leaves ovate or elliptic, hairy; florets blue
8. *Ageratum conyzoides*
24 Pappus of 2–4 gland-tipped bristles
7. *Adenostemma*
Pappus not glandular   25
25 Stem winged with decurrent leaf bases; heads sessile   31. *Geigeria alata*
Stem unwinged; heads pedunculate   26
26 Receptacle with scales subtending the florets   27
Receptacle naked   29
27 Leaves pinnate; mostly trifoliolate
48. *Bidens pilosa*
Leaves simple   28
28 Creeping herb; receptacle conical
45. *Spilanthes oleracea*
Erect herb; receptacle flat
41. *Blainvillea rhomboidea*
29 Florets bright purple   4. *Erlangea*
Florets cream or white   30
30 Plant a climber with cordate leaf bases
10. *Mikania cordata*
Plant an erect herb with cuneate leaf bases
9. *Eupatorium adenophorum*
31 Florets purple, conspicuous, overtopping the involucre   3. *Gutenbergia*
Florets white, yellow or inconspicuous   32
32 Achenes over 5 mm long when ripe, with hooked or simple spines
34. *Acanthospermum*
Achenes less than 5 mm long, never spiny 33
33 Leaves 3-nerved; florets bright yellow
51. *Flaveria australasica*
Leaves with a prominent midrib; florets white or very pale yellow   34
34 Leaves pinnately lobed into oblong-linear segments   56. *Cotula cryptocephala*
Leaves simple   35
35 Heads sessile; florets overtopped by phyllaries   38. *Enydra fluctuans*
Heads pedunculate; florets equalling phyllaries   39. *Eclipta alba*

36 Heads with conspicuous spreading ray (ligulate) florets all around the head in one row   38
Heads without conspicuously spreading rays, the rays absent or not spreading or in many rows   37
37 Heads aggregated into uniform 'heads of heads'   99
Heads not aggregated, usually free from one another, if tightly grouped then the groups not uniform in composition   57
38 Pappus present   39
Pappus absent   52
39 Pappus of bristles with or without scales 40
Pappus of scales alone   50
40 Stemless herbs with a rosette of leaves and solitary heads on long unbranched peduncles   41
Herbs or shrubs with leafy stems, or heads more than 3, in branched inflorescences
42
41 Leaves oblong, rounded at the petiole; peduncles not inflated below the head; ligulate florets exceeding the phyllaries by 5 mm or more
81. *Gerbera viridifolia*
Leaves oblanceolate to elliptical, narrowing gradually into the petiole; peduncles inflated below the head; ligulate florets hardly exceeding the phyllaries
82. *Piloselloides hirsuta*
42 Inner row or all of the phyllaries equal in length, parallel-sided, fused or coherent at their edges forming a cylinder round the head   43
Phyllaries not as above, not parallel-sided and coherent, often the inner not of equal length   44
43 Achenes flattened, with a minute wing along each side; lower leaves petiolate with a roughly circular lamina
61. *Cineraria grandiflora*
Achenes cylindrical, not flattened or winged; lower leaves usually of other shapes   62. *Senecio*
44 Rays purple, pink, blue or mauve, sometimes very pale   45
Rays yellow, or, if pale, with a yellow tinge
47
45 Phyllaries in 3–4 rows or all more or less the same length, appressed to head   46
Phyllaries of all lengths, numerous, recurved at tip   28. *Athrixia rosmarinifolia*
46 Heads solitary   13. *Felicia*
Heads in corymbs of 3–7   14. *Erigeron*
47 Leaves linear, simple   48
Leaves of other shapes   49

48 Perennial shrubs; phyllaries in one row, fused laterally   66. *Euryops*
    Annuals; phyllaries free, in many rows
                            18. *Chrysocoma* sp. A
49 Heads over 4 cm diameter; receptacle with scales subtending the florets
                            43. *Tithonia diversifolia*
    Heads under 2 cm diameter; receptacle naked   17. *Conyza*
50 Receptacle paleate   32. *Anisopappus*
    Receptacle naked   51
51 Stemless, rosette-leaved, scapose plant; phyllaries unarmed   69. *Haplocarpha*
    Stemmed, branching plant; phyllaries softly spine-tipped   70. *Hirpicium diffusum*
52 Receptacle paleate   53
    Receptacle naked   56
53 Rays white   54
    Rays yellow   55
54 Heads solitary, more than 2 cm in diameter
                            54. *Anthemis tigrensis*
    Heads corymbose, less than 1 cm in diameter   55. *Achillea millefolium*
55 Inner achenes winged
                    47. *Chrysanthellum americanum*
    Inner achenes terete
                            32. *Anisopappus holstii*
56 Achenes fleshy
            68. *Chrysanthemoides monilifera*
    Achenes winged
            67. *Osteospermum vaillantii*
57 Pappus present   58
    Pappus absent   91
58 Pappus of bristles with or without paleae   59
    Pappus of paleae or coroniform only   85
59 Phyllaries equal in length, parallel-sided, fused or coherent or appressed at their edges forming a cylinder around the head at anthesis, with or without a few outer shorter phyllaries   60
    Phyllaries not as above, not parallel-sided or coherent, often in very many rows, and the inner usually not all the same length
                                                67
60 Succulents with fleshy, mostly entire or reduced leaves and fleshy stems   61
    Not succulent, or if semi-succulent then the plants climbers with lobed or dentate leaves   62
61 Herbs; extremities of style branches continuous, not interrupted, papillose; heads solitary or in diffuse panicles
                                    65. *Notonia*
    Shrubs; extremities of style branches penicilliate, interrupted with a short hairy terminal appendage; heads crowded, corymbose   64. *Kleinia*

62 Phyllaries in only one row   63
    At least a few, sometimes small, phyllaries outside the inner cylindrical part of the involucre   64
63 Style branches terminating in an acute appendage; plants annual; florets mostly purple, orange or white   63. *Emilia*
    Style branches abruptly truncate; florets yellow, or if of other colours, then plants perennial   62. *Senecio*
64 Climbers with twining petioles; leaves heart-shaped; outer florets female
                            58. *Mikaniopsis*
    Trees, shrubs or herbs, if climbing then without twining petioles; leaves never perfectly heart-shaped; outer florets bisexual   65
65 Style branches truncate, papillose, without appendages; florets yellow or white
                                    62. *Senecio*
    Style branches always tapering to a narrow point; florets yellow, orange or red   66
66 Style branches long, pubescent, uninterrupted, gradually tapering to a narrow point, undulate but not recurved after anthesis   59. *Gynura*
    Style branches with a short thin and pointed appendage after a more or less conspicuous papillose interruption, short and recurved after anthesis
                            60. *Crassocephalum*
67 Corolla of tube florets exceeding both the involucre and pappus by at least one quarter of their length at anthesis   68
    Corolla of tube florets ± equalling or shorter than either the involucre or the pappus at anthesis   72
68 Receptacle scaly or hairy   69
    Receptacle naked and glabrous, sometimes pitted   70
69 Phyllaries with a spiny appendage
                                77. *Centaurea*
    Phyllaries apically serrate but not spiny
            80. *Erythrocephalum microcephalum*
70 Florets purple or white   71
    Florets yellow   17. *Conyza*
71 Pappus of 5–10 caducous bristles which do not exceed the pappus at maturity
                                    4. *Erlangea*
    Pappus of more than 20 usually persistent bristles which exceed or equal the pappus at maturity   5. *Vernonia*
72 Plants glabrous; leaves gummed together before opening   16. *Psiadia punctulata*
    Plants hairy at least on the peduncles, or, if glabrous, then leaves not gummed together when young   73

73 The greater part of at least the inner phyllaries scarious, often attractive and often exceeding the florets
                26. *Helichrysum* and *Gnaphalium*
    Phyllaries mainly herbaceous, sometimes with a scarious margin, but if so, not attractive   **74**
74 Outer florets female, usually filiform or ligulate, often in many rows   **75**
    All florets bisexual and similar   **80**
75 Central florets purple, red, pink or white   **76**
    Central florets yellow or cream   **79**
76 Leaves decurrent on the stem, with wings covering more than half the length of the internode   **77**
    Leaves not decurrent, stems unwinged or with only 2–3 lobes below the node **78**
77 Plant a shrub; phyllaries less than 5 mm long
                            21. *Pluchea ovalis*
    Plant a robust herb; phyllaries more than 5 mm long   20. *Laggera*
78 Annual herbs   19. *Blumea*
    Perennial shrubs   21. *Pluchea*
79 Mature pappus 1–1·5 times the length of the outer phyllaries; heads in dense ± sub-globose corymbs; stigmas included in the ray florets   15. *Nidorella*
    Mature pappus 2–3 times the length of the outer phyllaries; heads in flat-topped corymbs; stigmas exserted in ray florets
                            17. *Conyza*
80 Annual plants   **81**
    Perennial plants   **82**
81 Phyllaries spine-tipped; pappus in two series, the inner of blunt scales
                    78. *Dicoma tomentosa*
    Phyllaries not spine-tipped; pappus in two series, the inner of bristles
                30. *Pegolettia senegalensis*
82 Perennial herbs with a woody rootstock from which arise yearly the erect flowering shoots   **83**
    Perennial rhizomatous or monocarpic herbs, with flowering shoots arising singly   **84**
83 Florets bright yellow; stigmas inconspicuous, not or hardly exceeding the corolla   15. *Nidorella spartioides*
    Florets pale yellow to off-white; stigmas long, exceeding the corolla
                9. *Eupatorium africanum*
84 Plant a rhizomatous herb; heads solitary
                    4. *Erlangea calycina*
    Plant an erect monocarpic herb; heads densely crowded   29. *Inula*
85 Receptacle long-hairy or scaly   **86**
    Receptacle glabrous and naked   **88**

86 Heads pedunculate; leaves toothed or lobed   **87**
    Heads sessile; leaves entire
                    31. *Geigeria acaulis*
87 Phyllaries appendaged, the appendages palmately or pinnately spiny or toothed
                    77. *Centaurea*
    Phyllaries not appendaged, entire
                    76. *Volutaria*
88 Florets purple to pale mauve   **89**
    Florets yellow   **90**
89 Plant glabrous   1. *Hoehnelia vernonioides*
    Plant hairy or at least peduncles hairy below the heads   2. *Ethulia*
90 Leaf lobes oblong; heads hemispherical
                11. *Grangea maderaspatana*
    Leaf lobes linear, filiform; heads obconical
                52. *Schkuhria pinnata*
91 Heads unisexual, with but one floret type **92**
    Heads bisexual, with bisexual florets or both female and bisexual florets   **93**
92 Leaves finely divided with linear-oblong segments   35. *Ambrosia maritima*
    Leaves dentate or shallowly lobed only
                    36. *Xanthium*
93 Heads conspicuously heterogamous, with the outer florets female   **94**
    Heads homogamous, all florets similar **95**
94 Heads hemispherical; leaves pinnatipartite
                    56. *Cotula*
    Heads globular; leaves mostly simple
                12. *Dichrocephala*
95 Florets yellow or green   **96**
    Florets purple or red   **97**
96 Leaves twice pinnatisect, aromatic
                57. *Artemisia afra*
    Leaves entire, toothed, not aromatic
            79. *Achyrothalamus marginatus*
97 Plant entirely glabrous
            1. *Hoehnelia vernonioides*
    Plant hairy at least on peduncles   **98**
98 Petal lobes hairy; each achene rounded at apex   4. *Erlangea* and *Gutenbergia*
    Petal lobes glabrous, each achene with a raised ring at tip   2. *Ethulia*
99 Styles all divided into 2 stigmas   **100**
    Styles of at least the central florets undivided, with solitary stigma   **102**
100 Heads of heads subtended by several bracts which appear to act as an involucre, but which are many times larger than the true involucre   **101**
    Heads of heads naked below
                    25. *Athroisma*
101 Phyllaries of individual heads acuminate, with a long, bristle-like, plumose apex
                    33. *Lagascea mollis*

Phyllaries of individual heads acute, not
    acuminate   6. *Elephantopus scaber*
102 Florets white or yellow; dry land shrubs
        24. *Blepharispermum*
    Florets purple or pink; mostly herbs of wet
    places   **103**
103 Heads of heads subtended by broad woolly
    bracts; stems unwinged
        23. *Triplocephalum holstii*
    Heads of heads without subtending bracts;
    stems mostly winged with decurrent leaf
    bases   22. *Sphaeranthus*
104 At least the inner achenes beaked, with a
    stalk below the pappus   **105**
    Pappus sessile on the achenes, beak absent
        108
105 Outer phyllaries reflexed or spreading;
    peduncle simple and naked
        85. *Taraxacum officinale*
    Outer phyllaries appressed to head; peduncle
    usually branched and with scale-leaves
        106
106 Pappus plumose; receptacle paleate
        84. *Hypochoeris glabra*
    Pappus simple; receptacle naked   **107**
107 Achenes cylindrical, gradually tapering into
    the beak; florets yellow   91. *Crepis*
    Achenes flattened, abruptly tapering into
    the beak; florets blue or yellow
        88. *Lactuca*
108 Alpine rosette plant with sessile heads
        90. *Dianthoseris schimperi*
    Mainly lowland plants (some montane),
    with leafy stems or pedunculate heads
        109
109 Phyllaries glabrous, at least the outer ones
    with broad white or hyaline margins **110**
    Phyllaries papillose or hairy, often white-
    hairy at the base, with no white or
    hyaline margins   **111**
110 Heads cylindrical, not markedly inflated and
    not naked at the base   86. *Launea*
    Heads almost spherical, inflated and (at least
    in fruit) naked at base
        89. *Reichardia tingitana*
111 Achenes more or less cylindrical; scapose
    herb   83. *Tolpis capensis*
    Achenes flattened; plants with leafy stems
        87. *Sonchus*

1. HOEHNELIA *Schweinf.*

Similar to *Ethulia* except for the produced 'crown'
at the apex of the achenes, which is tubular, longer
than wide, and usually elongated at one side.

Hoehnelia vernonioides *Schweinf.* (see p. 421)
An erect, weak, sparsely branched, glabrescent
shrub with oblong to narrow-elliptic serrate leaves

and terminal corymbs of purple heads; phyllaries
with a broad, undulate, scarious, rounded apex.
    Locally abundant in grassland at higher alti-
tudes. HE, HC, HT, HM, HA, HK, KIT.
    Glover 1364; Lind 5125.

2. ETHULIA *L.*

Herbs with alternate leaves and corymbs of purple
heads; involucre ± bell-shaped, of many rows of
bracts; receptacle naked; florets all tubular, bisexual, purple; achenes narrowly. 2–5-winged,
glabrous, ± cylindrical with a narrow rim at the
apex; pappus absent.

1 Inflorescences mostly sessile, of a ± spherical
    mass of crowded heads   1. *E.* sp. *A*
    Inflorescences pedunculate, of corymbose
    heads   2
2 Phyllaries with a scarious border at apex
        2. *E. scheffleri*
    Phyllaries green at apex, without a scarious
    border   3. *E. conyzoides*

1. Ethulia *sp.* A.

An erect woody herb (mostly annual), pubescent
or tomentose, with oblanceolate, linear, serrate
leaves and linear phyllaries to the crowded heads;
inner achenes often 2-winged.
    Apparently endemic to central Kenya, near
Nairobi, this species is found in swamp grassland.
HA, RV, MAC, NBI, KAJ.
    Agnew 8497; Glover 3905A.

2. Ethulia scheffleri *S. Moore*

Similar to the last species but with larger heads
and broader blunt phyllaries and 3–4-winged
achenes.
    Common in swampy grasslands near Nairobi
from 5000–8000 ft. NA, RV, NBI.
    Agnew 8119; Bally 1012.

3. Ethulia conyzoides *L.*

Similar to *E. scheffleri*, but with smaller heads and
achenes.
    Locally common in swamp grassland in western
Kenya. HE, MUM.
    Dekker 24; Webster 9656.

3. GUTENBERGIA *Sch. Bip.*

Similar to *Erlangea* in all respects except for the
more hairy corolla and 8–10-ribbed achenes with
no pappus.
    For Key see 4. *Erlangea*

1. Gutenbergia rueppellii *Sch. Bip.* (see p. 421)
A small erect annual, white-felty below the
oblong-linear sessile leaves; heads purple, in small
terminal corymbs.

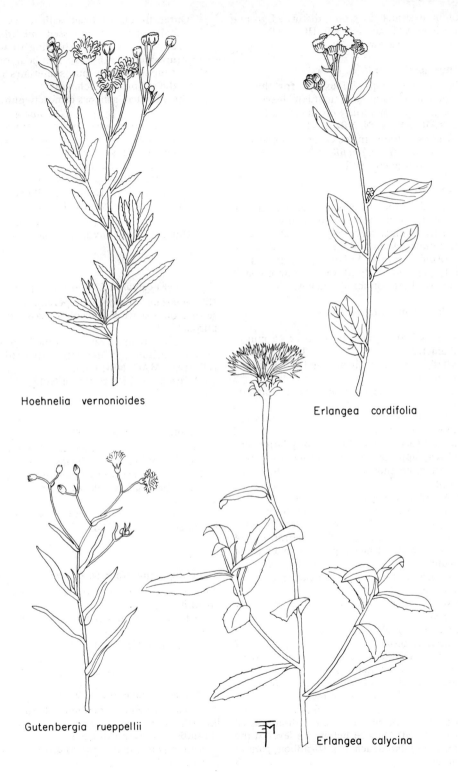

Hoehnelia vernonioides

Erlangea cordifolia

Gutenbergia rueppellii

Erlangea calycina

A common annual of stony, disturbed ground in the north-west of our area. HE, HC, BAR.
Bogdan 3853; Agnew 10250.

2. Gutenbergia fischeri *R. E. Fries*

Very similar to *G. ruppellii* except for the frequently perennial habit and undulate leaves and slightly larger (to 6 mm long) involucres. HM, HL, HA, HK, NAR, RV, NAN, NBI, KAJ.

This species is found in rocky, eroded grassland further south than *G. rueppellii.*
Glover 4016; Agnew 8912.

4. ERLANGEA *Sch. Bip.*

Herbs or shrubs with opposite or alternate simple leaves, usually white-tomentose below; heads solitary or in terminal corymbs; florets all tubular, bisexual, purple, with oblong-linear petal lobes, achenes ovoid, bluntly 4–5-angled, glabrous or pubescent; pappus of 2–20 very caducous stiff bristles, rarely absent on some achenes.

Key to *Erlangea* and *Gutenbergia*

1 Phyllaries leafy, green; heads over 15 mm in
    diameter   1. *E. calycina*
   Phyllaries not leafy; heads under 15 mm in
    diameter   2
2 Leaves white- or pale-tomentose of felty on
    underside   5
   Leaves similar above and below, pubescent
    never tomentose   3
3 Leaves broad ovate-elliptic; phyllaries not
    closely appressed to each other, the outer-
    most more than half as long as the inner-
    most   3. *E. amplifolia*
   Leaves oblong-linear or narrow-ovate; phyl-
    laries closely appressed to each other, very
    regularly ranked, with the outermost much
    less than half as long as the innermost   4
4 Plant herbaceous; heads globose in bud and
    fruit   4. *E. somalensis*
   Plant shrubby; heads cylindrical or ovoid in
    bud and fruit   2. *E. duemmeri*
5 Leaves mostly opposite, conspicuously
    serrate   6
   Leaves mostly alternate, entire or obscurely
    minutely toothed   7
6 Leaves glabrescent above, bright green,
    densely white-felted below   5. *E. fusca*
   Leaves sparsely tomentose above, pale green,
    with a woolly tomentum below
                                      6. *E. tomentosa*
7 Outer florets of head covered with appressed
    (medifixed) hairs to below the level of the
    inner phyllaries; achenes 10-ribbed; pappus
    absent   8

   Outer florets of head with a few spreading
    hairs or rarely appressed (medifixed) hairs
    at tip only, not extending to within the
    involucre; achenes 5-ribbed or angled;
    pappus present but sometimes absent on
    the majority of achenes   9
8 Erect annual, achenes minutely pubescent
                                      3. *Gutenbergia rueppellii*
   Decumbent or erect weak perennial; achenes
    glabrous   3. *Gutenbergia fischeri*
9 Phyllaries densely tomentose all over includ-
    ing the scarious margin   7. *E.* sp. *A*
   Phyllaries with a broad glabrous scarious
    margin, never tomentose all over   10
10 Outer row of phyllaries ovate
                                      8. *E. boranensis*
   Outer row of phyllaries lanceolate to linear
                                      9. *E. cordifolia*

1. Erlangea calycina *S. Moore* (see p. 421)

Rhizomatous tomentose perennial herb with sessile, oblong to oblanceolate leaves and solitary purple heads.

Locally common in disturbed grassland at medium altitudes in the eastern part of our area. HT, MAG, MAC, NBI, KAJ.
Battiscombe 989; Harmsen 6443.

2. Erlangea duemmeri *S. Moore*

An erect, branched, pubescent shrub with dense terminal corymbs of blue heads.

Rare in western Kenya, where it is to be found in disturbed sandy places near Lake Victoria. MUM, KIS.
Agnew, Musumba, and Kiniaruh 8033; Rammell in EAH 15010.

3. Erlangea amplifolia *O. Hoffm. & Muschl.*

Similar to *E. fusca* but with glabrescent leaves and larger heads.

Rare plant found in montane rain-forest. HA, HK.
Polhill and Verdcourt 308.

4. Erlangea somalensis *O. Hoffm.*

An erect pubescent perennial herb with sessile linear-oblong leaves and scattered terminal corymbs of a few heads each.

Rare plant found in dry country. NAN.
Kirrika 27.

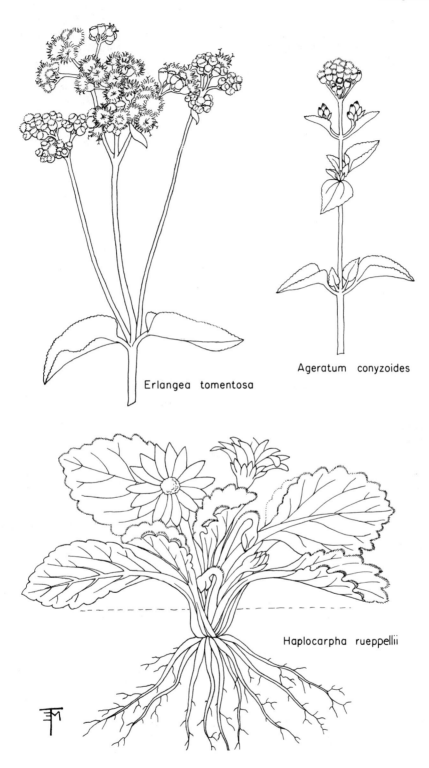

Erlangea tomentosa

Ageratum conyzoides

Haplocarpha rueppellii

5. Erlangea fusca *S. Moore*

An erect shrub with lanceolate-elliptic serrate leaves which are white-hairy below, and terminal corymbs of purple to violet heads.

Abundant on roadsides and disturbed places in the upper forest zones, seldom below 8500 ft. HE, HC, HT, HM, HA, HK, RV.

Strid 2282; Bie 319.

6. Erlangea tomentosa *S. Moore* (see p. 423)

Similar to *E. fusca* but with looser, spreading tomentum and paler florets.

Common at forest margins at medium altitudes, seldom above 8000 ft. HE, HT, HM, HA, HK, HN, KIT, MUM, KIS, NAR, KAJ.

Bally 896; Agnew and Musumba 8533.

7. Erlangea *sp.* **A.**

An erect shrubby annual or perennial with the aspect of *E. cordifolia* but with the phyllaries tomentose and more numerous, and the achenes not rugose between the broad ribs.

Rare, found near Olorgesailie. MAG.

Harmsen 6408; Bally 18.

8. Erlangea boranensis *S. Moore*

Short-lived perennial herb or weak shrub with erect stems and petiolate, lanceolate lower leaves which are white below; heads 2–7 in each of many small terminal corymbs; achenes subglobose, glabrous on the broad ribs.

Locally common in dry sandy disturbed grassland. Some forms may closely resemble *E. cordifolia*. BAR, RV, MAG, MAC.

Lind and Agnew 5690; Ward 2574.

9. Erlangea cordifolia (*Benth.*) *S. Moore* (inc. *E. marginata* (Oliv. and Hiern) S. Moore of Check List) (see p. 421)

An erect annual with subsessile opposite to alternate, obovate to ovate and oblong leaves which are white-woolly below; heads in loose but conspicuous terminal corymbs; achenes minutely pubescent on the ribs, mostly rugose between them.

A rather variable, common weedy annual of disturbed places in grassland below 6000 ft. The phyllaries can vary from acute to obtuse, with a broad to narrow scarious margin, green or purple. Specimens are known with fewer than 5 and over 8 pappus bristles. A dry-land form exists with most of the achenes lacking a pappus. HL, HA, KIT, MUM, KIS, NAR, RV, NAN, EMB, MAC, NBI, KAJ.

Agnew and Musumba 5427; Verdcourt 596.

5. VERNONIA *Schreb.*

Herbs, shrubs or trees with alternate simple leaves and usually terminal corymbs of heads; involucre various, of many rows of phyllaries; receptacle naked; florets all bisexual, blue, white or purple, very rarely yellow or orange, exceeding the involucre at anthesis; achenes columnar, often angled or ribbed; pappus usually of two series, outer scales and inner bristles, sometimes of many rows of bristles, rarely of one row.

1	Leaves (at least the median ones) expanded at the node into a pair of lobes which clasp the stem	2
	Leaves petiolate or sessile but not clasping at the base	7
2	Outer phyllaries with a large white petaloid appendage	19. *V. hymenolepis*
	Outer phyllaries without a petaloid appendage	3
3	Involucre tubular; inner phyllaries falling with the achenes	5
	Involucre bell-shaped; inner phyllaries persistent	4
4	Heads solitary; phyllaries over 10 mm long	1. *V.* sp. *B*
	Heads corymbose; phyllaries up to 7 mm long	2. *V.* sp. *C*
5	Heads 1-flowered	3. *V. auriculifera*
	Heads more than 1-flowered	6
6	Heads 10-flowered	4. *V. seretii*
	Heads 5-flowered	5. *V. subuligera*
7	Scapose or subscapose herbs with a nearly leafless flowering stem and few heads, with or without a basal rosette of leaves	8
	Shrubs or herbs with leafy stems and no basal rosette of leaves	11
8	Involucre less than 1 cm long; pappus bright purple	6. *V. violacea*
	Involucre over 1 cm long; pappus white	9
9	Leaves in a basal rosette; heads mostly solitary	10
	Upright leafy stems present or absent but the heads borne separately before leafy stems appear; heads numerous	7. *V. pumila*
10	Heads borne above rosette of foliage	8. *V. gerberiformis*
	Perennial herb with a basal rosette of leaves; heads borne singly on a short scape, at a different season from the leaves	9. *V. chthonocephala*
11	Annuals, sometimes large but then with one generation of heads only	12
	Perennial herbs or shrubs, if short-lived perennial shrubs, then with more than one generation of heads	17

12   Involucre less than 8 mm long   **13**
       Involucre 10 mm or more long   **14**

13   Stem smooth with appressed hairs; achenes without longitudinal ridges or angles
                              10. *V. cinerea*
       Stem rough with spreading hairs; achenes 4-angled   11. *V. aemulans*

14   Outer phyllaries with a linear-oblong, green appendage which is rounded at the apex
                            12. *V. stenolepis*
       All phyllaries without appendage, or if with one, then the appendage acute at apex   **15**

15   Leaves linear, less than 5 cm long; phyllaries tightly appressed forming a smooth involucre   13. *V. perottetii*
       Leaves broader, always some over 5 cm long, phyllaries loose   **16**

16   Outer phyllaries recurved at tip; phyllaries numerous, in many rows, the innermost over 20 in number   14. *V. pauciflora*
       Outer phyllaries not recurved at tip; phyllaries few, in few rows, the innermost less than 12 in number   15. *V.* sp. *D*

17   Shrubs or scramblers   **18**
       Erect perennial herbs with annual stems   **34**

18   Pappus purple during flowering, turning brown later   16. *V. brachycalyx*
       Pappus white or brown during flowering   **19**

19   Involucre 1 cm or more long   **20**
       Involucre less than 1 cm long   **24**

20   Phyllaries flat, without any appendage   **21**
       Outer phyllaries spreading, with a terminal, expanded or keeled, glabrous or pubescent appendage   **23**

21   Phyllaries rounded at apex, closely appressed to each other, with white-woolly edges
                          17. *V. wakefieldii*
       Phyllaries acute, not closely appressed to each other, without white margins   **22**

22   Intermediate phyllaries acuminate, with a long narrow green acumen   15. *V.* sp. *D*
       Intermediate phyllaries acute, not acuminate
                              41. *V. glabra*

23   Appendage of phyllaries green, keeled, densely pubescent, usually twisted
                            18. *V. adoensis*
       Appendage of phyllaries white, pink or violet, flat, straight and ± glabrous
                          19. *V. hymenolepis*

24   Some phyllaries (usually the innermost) or all of them rounded at apex, sometimes with a minute apical mucro, never subulate   **25**
       All phyllaries acute or acuminate at apex, sometimes subulate   **31**

25   Leaves obovate, rounded at apex
                       20. *V. cinerascens*
       Leaves elliptic to ovate, acute at apex   **26**

26   Involucre spherical in bud, saucer-shaped in fruit   **27**
       Involucre cylindrical in bud and early flowering, bell-shaped later   **28**

27   Leaves ovate, widest below the middle; involucre over 4 mm long; achenes glabrous
                         25. *V. colorata*
       Leaves elliptic, widest about the middle; involucre less than 4 mm long; achenes hairy   26. *V. amygdalina*

28   Leaves white- or pale-tomentose below; phyllaries with a weakly demarcated appendage   23. *V. lasiopus*
       Leaves green, glabrescent below; phyllaries with no appendage   **29**

29   Leaves ovate, widest at base, often crenate on the margin   21. *V. tufnellii*
       Leaves elliptic, widest about the middle, serrate or entire   **30**

30   Plant often scrambling; outermost phyllaries ovate, more or less pointed at tip; achenes glabrous   22. *V. urticifolia*
       Plant seldom scrambling; outermost phyllaries broad-elliptic, rounded at tip; achenes sparsely and minutely hairy
                         24. *V. pteropoda*

31   Climbing or trailing shrubs   **32**
       Erect shrubs   **33**

32   Petioles winged; achenes hairy   27. *V.* sp. *E*
       Petioles unwinged; achenes glabrous
                       28. *V. syringifolia*

33   Peduncles and often outermost phyllaries woolly   29. *V. holstii*
       Peduncles tomentose but not woolly; outermost phyllaries pubescent   30. *V. jugalis*

34   Leaves silky-hairy below   **35**
       Leaves tomentose, pubescent or scabrid below   **36**

35   Phyllaries lanceolate-linear, gradually narrowing above to a long, subulate point
                        31. *V. kraussii*
       Phyllaries oblong, abruptly narrowed or obtuse at apex with a small mucro
                     32. *V. smithiana*

36   Inflorescence with branches underneath the heads so that the heads appear subsessile at divaricate dichotomies or in monochasia
                                     37
       Inflorescence branching well below the heads; heads all pedunculate   **38**

37   Involucres over 10 mm long
                       33. *V. turbinata*
       Involucres 5-6 mm long   34. *V. karaguensis*

38   Heads solitary   35. *V. schweinfurthii*
       Heads corymbose   **39**

39   Leaves linear-oblong   36. *V.* sp. *F*
       Leaves broader   **40**

40   Leaves acute at apex, narrowing to a point **41**
      Leaves rounded or obtuse at apex   **43**
41   Stems unbranched except at the terminal
      corymb; phyllaries mucronate or with a
      terminal bristle   **42**
      Stems branched into the terminal corymb
      and also often below; phyllaries entire at
      apex   41. *V. glabra*
42   Involucres more than 7 mm long; all phyl-
      laries acute or acuminate at apex
                                    37. *V. dummeri*
      Involucres less than 6 mm long; inner phyl-
      laries obtuse-mucronate   38. *V. undulata*
43   Involucres 10–13 mm long   39. *V.* sp. *G*
      Involucres 5–7 mm long   40. *V. hindii*

1. Vernonia *sp.* **B.**

A scabrid-pubescent trailing scrambler with
amplexicaul lanceolate-elliptic leaves and solitary
heads of mauve florets; achenes glabrous, 4–6-
ridged; pappus with outer scales.

This species has heads very similar to those of
V. pauciflora. It is apparently rare in dry country,
having been collected only twice, both times from
MAC.

Gardner in EAH 11416.

2. Vernonia *sp.* **C.**

A pilose weak perennial shrub with oblanceolate
leaves of which the median are amplexicaul at
base; heads in loose terminal corymbs, purple;
achenes hairy, 4-angled; outer pappus of short
scales.

This species closely resembles *V. aemulans*
except for the amplexicaul leaves, perennial habit
and smaller heads. It is uncommon in dry country.
BAR, RV, MAC.

Lind and Agnew 5654; Leippert 5046.

3. Vernonia auriculifera *Hiern*

A large erect woody herb, grey-tomentose under
the ovate, auriculate, petiolate leaves, with a very
large terminal corymb of minute purple heads;
achenes sparsely pubescent.

Locally abundant in disturbed bushland in the
area of wet montane forest. The uppermost leaves
sometimes lack the auricles, but lower leaves
always have them. HE, HC, HT, HM, HA, HK,
KIT, KIS, NAR, RV, MAC.

Agnew 7604; Glover 843.

4. Vernonia seretii *de Wild.*

Similar to the last species but with elliptic, almost
glabrous, sessile leaves and a more lax corymb, as
well as bigger heads; achenes hairy, obscurely
10-ridged.

Uncommon plant found in west Kenya. KIT,
MUM.

Tweedie 66/375; Brodhurst-Hill 831.

5. Vernonia subuligera *O. Hoffm.*

A loose erect branched tree or shrub with large,
sessile, elliptic, auriculate leaves which are grey-
tomentose below; heads pale mauve or white, in
loose terminal corymbs; achenes almost glabrous,
smooth or 10-ridged.

Locally common in the Chyulu Hills at the edge
of forest patches. KAJ.

Agnew 10620; Bally 8170.

6. Vernonia violacea *Oliv. & Hiern*

A perennial with a rosette of oblanceolate,
sparsely hairy leaves and an erect tomentose stem
bearing few leaves and branching into a loose
corymb of very few heads; heads with purple
florets; achenes pubescent, 4-angled, with an outer
pappus of broad scales.

Uncommon plant found in wooded grassland in
western Kenya. KIT, MUM.

Tweedie 68/13; Bogdan 3695.

7. Vernonia pumila *Kotschy & Peyr.* (see p. 430)

Inflorescences produced before the leafy stems, to
11·5 cm tall with one to several heads paniculately
arranged; mature achenes of this species have never
been collected.

A species of openings and burnt grassland
where it is probably frequently overlooked. KIT,
MUM.

Archer 246; Tweedie 357.

8. Vernonia gerberiformis *Oliv. & Hiern*

A plant with large leaves in a basal rosette and
single, blue heads, often to 2·5 cm high and 3·0 cm
in diameter, borne on a scape to 0·5 m tall.

These grow among obscuring grasses and other
plants during the rainy season. Along with the
next two species, they are seldom seen unless they
are encountered immediately underfoot. Uncommon in wooded grassland in western Kenya.
HT, HM, KIT.

Bogdan 3721; Elliot 7032.

9. Vernonia chthonocephala *O. Hoffm.*

Scapes to 4·0 cm tall, each bearing a single head,
produced before the rosette of leaves.

A rare plant of openings and plains. KIT.
Mainwaring 25.

10. Vernonia cinerea *(L.) Less.*

An erect pubescent annual with lanceolate-elliptic
(occasionally broader) leaves and a terminal
panicle of purple heads; achenes without angles,
pubescent; outer pappus of broad scales.

This annual is rather variable, especially in the pubescence. It is locally common in disturbed dry sandy bushland. MUM, MAC, KAJ.

Agnew 10681; Napier 2980.

11. Vernonia aemulans *Vatke*

An erect pubescent to tomentose annual (sometimes becoming woody with further growth in one season) with oblanceolate to oblong leaves and ± solitary or loosely corymbose terminal purple heads; achenes pubescent, 4-angled, rugose; outer pappus of short scales.

This plant is also found in dry, but not necessarily disturbed, bushland. The heads are bigger than in *V. cinerea*. EMB, MAC, NBI, KAJ.

Thomas 656; Hanid and Kiniaruh 466.

12. Vernonia stenolepis *Oliv.*

An erect, sparsely and minutely pubescent annual with oblanceolate leaves and solitary heads of purple florets; achenes pubescent, cylindrical, obscurely 10-grooved; outer pappus of a few short bristles.

Locally common in dry country. MAC, KAJ.

Agnew 5663; Bally 1699.

13. Vernonia perottetii *Sch. Bip.*

A small erect pubescent annual with crowded linear leaves and terminal, solitary, ± globose heads of purple florets; achenes bristly with about 8 ridges and a short scaly outer pappus.

An uncommon *Vernonia* of shallow soils in western Kenya. MUM, KIS.

Agnew and Musumba 8583; Drummond and Hemsley 4476.

14. Vernonia pauciflora *Less.* (inc. *V. afromontana* R. E. Fries) (see p. 428)

A large erect, usually unbranched, annual with elliptic to linear leaves and large terminal (sometimes solitary) scattered heads of blue florets; phyllaries with narrow to broad, recurved or spreading, apical green appendage; achenes densely pubescent, 10-ridged; outer pappus of very short, broad bristles.

A very variable robust annual with a wide ecological range, growing in cleared dry woodland or forest. The montane forest type has broad heads and broad recurved appendages on the phyllaries, while the dry bushland type has bristle-like phyllaries and narrow heads and leaves. There are intermediates between these forms, including the Nairobi plants. The high altitude plant has been given a separate name, *V. afromontana*, HE, HC, HT, HM, HL, HA, HK, HN, NAR, BAR, MAG, EMB, MAC, NBI, KAJ.

Agnew and Musumba 5450; van Someren 368.

15. Vernonia *sp.* D.

A big erect woody herb or shrub with scabrid elliptic serrate leaves and terminal corymbs of blue flowers; achenes long, hairy, 10-ridged; outer pappus of short bristles.

A plant for which more information is needed. It is found in montane forest edges in the Uplands-Kinangop area only. HA.

Agnew 8982; Verdcourt 3267.

16. Vernonia brachycalyx *O. Hoffm.* (see p. 435)

A trailing pubescent scrambler with thin wiry stems and ovate to elliptic entire leaves; corymbs terminal, of many small purple heads; achenes sparsely pubescent, obscurely 4-angled; outer pappus of a few bristles.

A showy climber with its purple pappus and florets protruding from the phyllaries long before flowering. This plant is abundant in all dry forest edges. HE, HC, HM, HK, NAR, RV, NAN, EMB, MAC, NBI.

Glover and Samuel 3200; Agnew, Kibe, and Mathenge 10301.

17. Vernonia wakefieldii *O. Hoffm.*

An erect bushy shrub with rather fleshy oblanceolate-elliptic glabrous entire leaves and woolly peduncles; heads large in small terminal corymbs; florets grey or 'livid' blue; achenes silky-hairy, 10-ribbed; outer pappus of medium-length bristles.

A rare plant of dry bushland, and only recorded from near Kibwezi and Kitui. MAC, KAJ.

Napper 1663.

18. Vernonia adoensis *Walp.*

An erect pubescent shrub with ovate crenate leaves which are densely tomentose below; heads large solitary or in small groups of 2–3, with hairy, often twisted phyllaries and pale mauve florets; achenes pubescent, 10-ribbed; outer pappus obscure.

A common shrub of abandoned cultivation and disturbed places in west Kenya. The above name is only tentative for this species. HE, HC, HT, MUM, KIS, NAR, RV.

Lugard 32; Irwin 365.

19. Vernonia hymenolepis *A. Rich.*

A tall erect shrub with lanceolate-elliptic serrate leaves which are grey-tomentose below; heads with white, pink, or purple phyllaries, in terminal corymbs; achenes short, 10–15-ridge, glabrous; outer pappus obscure.

Common in upland bushland. HE, HC, HT, KIT, MUM.

Agnew, Kibe, and Mathenge 10490; Symes 87.

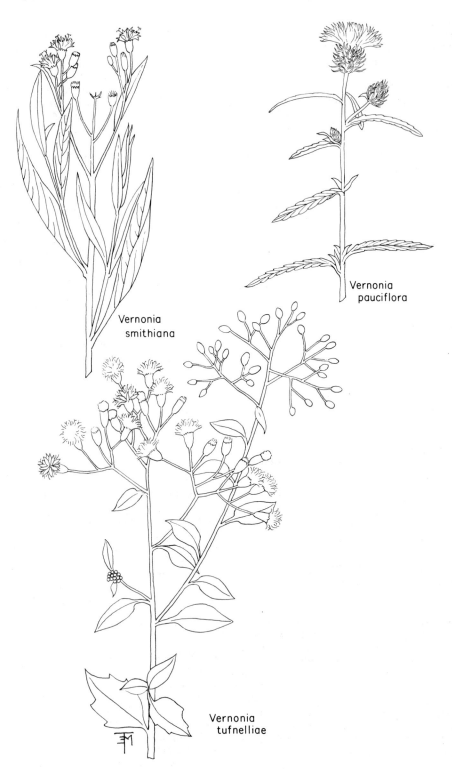

Vernonia
smithiana

Vernonia
pauciflora

Vernonia
tufnelliae

20. Vernonia cinerascens *Sch. Bip.*

A bushy shrub, densely pubescent when young becoming glabrous later, with spathulate leaves and loose round-topped terminal corymbs of often subsessile, pale purple heads; achenes pubescent, 8-10-ribbed; outer pappus of small bristles.

Common in some areas of dry bushland. MAG, MAC.

Harmsen 6482; Hanid and Kiniaruh 514.

21. Vernonia tufnellii *S. Moore* (see p. 428)

A pubescent scrambling or low erect shrub with ovate, often coarsely crenate leaves and large terminal corymbose panicles of purple heads; achenes pubescent, 6-7-ridged; outer pappus of very short bristles.

Locally common in bushland in western Kenya and rare in the east. HT, HA, HK, MUM, KIS, RV.

Dale 1012; Hanid and Kiniaruh 950.

22. Vernonia urticifolia *A. Rich.* (see p. 430)

A scabrid-pubescent trailing, scrambling shrub with elliptic, minutely crenate leaves and large terminal paniculate corymbs of pale purple heads; achenes glabrous, 10-ribbed; outer pappus obscure.

Uncommon plant found in montane forest edges, HE, HM, HA.

Agnew 7117; Kerfoot 4694.

23. Vernonia lasiopus *O. Hoffm.* (*V. dumicola* S. Moore)

An erect, weakly shrubby perennial with ovate, coarsely serrate leaves which are pale-tomentose below, and terminal corymbs of cylindrical heads; florets pale purple; achenes pubescent, 10-ribbed; outer pappus obscure.

Abundant, in abandoned cultivation at medium altitudes. HE, HC, HM, HA, HK, KIT, NAR, RV, EMB, MAC, NBI, KAJ.

Agnew 9449; Verdcourt 2345.

24. Vernonia pteropoda *Oliv. & Hiern*

An erect weak sparsely pubescent shrub with long-elliptic serrate leaves and terminal paniculate corymbs of cylindrical heads with pale purple or white florets; achenes sparsely, minutely pubescent; outer pappus of minute bristles.

A rare plant of the undergrowth in montane rain-forest. HA, HK.

Agnew 7761; Verdcourt 2311.

25. Vernonia colorata *Drake*

An erect loose shrub with ovate-lanceolate ± entire leaves which are grey- or pale-tomentose below; heads in terminal corymbs with white florets; achenes glabrous, 10-ribbed; outer pappus absent.

An uncommon riverine shrub of dry country. KAJ.

Verdcourt 2375.

26. Vernonia amygdalina *Del.*

An erect single-stemmed shrub or small tree with glabrescent, ovate-elliptic ± entire leaves and terminal corymbs of small heads; florets white; achenes minutely pubescent, obscurely 10-ribbed; outer pappus absent.

Locally common in western Kenya in disturbed forest and cultivation. MUM, KIS, NAR.

Napier 2921; Agnew and Musumba 8523.

27. Vernonia sp. E.

Very similar to *V. syringifolia* but differing in the constantly deeply cordate leaves which are white-tomentose below, and the pale green (not purple-edged) phyllaries, as well as in the key characters.

This species is found in eastern Kenya in dry forest edges. HA, HK, NBI.

Hanid and Kiniaruh 951; Verdcourt 3706B.

28. Vernonia syringifolia *O. Hoffm.* (see p. 432)

A scrambling shrub with cordate or truncate, ovate leaves which are variously hairy below; heads with purplish phyllaries, in terminal round-topped corymbs; florets pale purple; achenes glabrous, 4-angled, very glandular; outer pappus obscure.

Uncommon, at edges of montane rain forest. HE, HC, HT, HM, HA, KIT.

Agnew 7262; Napier 660.

29. Vernonia holstii *O. Hoffm.*

An erect weak shrub with ovate serrate leaves which are white-woolly below; heads pale, woolly at base, in small terminal corymbs; florets white tinged purple; achenes pubescent, 10-ribbed; outer pappus of short bristles.

Abundant in the shrub-layer of the Nairobi forest and apparently nowhere else. HA, MAC, NBI.

Agnew 8476; Verdcourt 1839.

30. Vernonia jugalis *Oliv. & Hiern* (inc. *V. hochstetteri* of Check List)

An erect, tall, often single-stemmed shrub with elliptic, minutely dentate leaves which are pale-tomentose below; heads in dense terminal corymbs; florets blue; achenes pubescent between the 10 ridges; outer pappus of blunt oblong-linear scales.

A big *Vernonia* of the shrub layer in dry forest as well as the forest edge which resembles *V. lasiopus* in its habit. HE, HA, HK, MUM, MAC, NBI, KAJ.

Harmsen 6455; Verdcourt 3710.

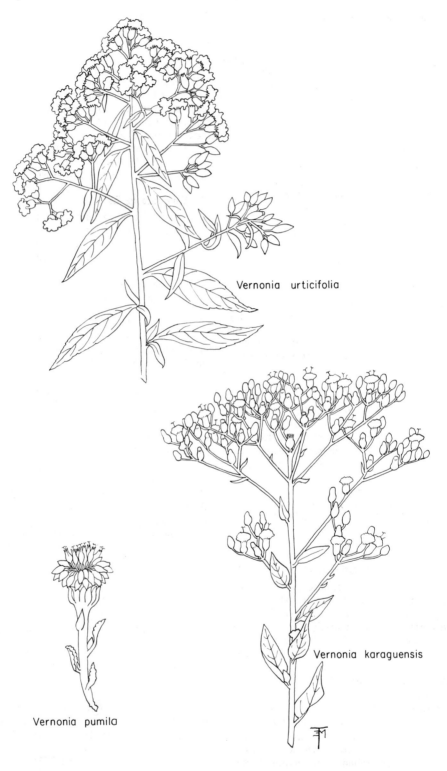

Vernonia urticifolia

Vernonia karaguensis

Vernonia pumila

31. Vernonia kraussii *Sch. Bip.*

An erect herb from a woody rootstock with narrow-elliptic to oblanceolate, silky-hairy leaves and a terminal corymb of purple heads; achenes silky, without ridges; outer pappus of soft bristles.

An uncommon herb of wooded grassland in eastern Kenya. HM, MAC.

Ivens 2072; Agnew 7686.

32. Vernonia smithiana (*DC.*) *Less.* (see p. 428)

Similar to *V. kraussii* except for the key characters and with the upper leaf surface not silky, this species is found in western Kenya in wooded grassland. HE, HC, HT, HA, KIT, MUM, KIS.

Hanid and Kiniaruh 800; Bogdan 3670.

33. Vernonia turbinata *Oliv. & Hiern* (see p. 432)

A tomentose herb from a woody rootstock with simple stems and ovate to elliptic leaves; heads broadly spreading, with very numerous phyllaries usually branched below each head so that these appear to be in dichasia or monochasia, the whole forming a flat-topped inflorescence; florets purple; achenes sparsely pubescent between the 4 angles; outer pappus of short broad scales.

A most distinctive species from wooded grassland in western Kenya. KIT.

Tweedie 66/257; Knight in Bogdan 4401.

34. Vernonia karaguensis *Oliv. & Hiern* (inc. *V. cistifolia* and *V. elliottii* of the Check List) (see p. 430)

Similar to *V. turbinata,* but scabrid-pubescent with smaller heads and phyllaries in few rows; inflorescence often paniculate.

This common herb of wooded grassland is found all over Kenya. It is a beautiful, conspicuous plant with its mass of purple/blue and grey heads. HE, HC, HT, HM, HA, KIT, MUM, KIS, NAR, RV, EMB, MAC, NBI, KAJ.

Agnew 7683; Drummond and Hemsley 4763

35. Vernonia schweinfurthii *Oliv. & Hiern* (see p. 432)

Erect glabrescent herb from a woody rootstock, with blunt linear leaves and solitary long-pedunculate heads of purple flowers; achenes silky-hairy, obscurely 10-ribbed; outer pappus of long bristles.

Uncommon plant found in grassland around Eldoret. HT.

Williams 2000.

36. Vernonia *sp.* F.

An erect pubescent branched herb from a woody rootstock, with linear blunt leaves and loose terminal corymbs of a few purple heads; achenes densely pubescent, 4-angled; outer pappus of short broad scales.

Apparently rare and only found twice in rocky soil in Mara. NAR.

Glover 2204.

37. Vernonia dummeri *S. Moore* (see p. 435)

An erect, scabrid-pubescent unbranched herb from a woody rootstock, with ovate to lanceolate, serrate leaves and dense terminal corymbs of brownish heads with purple florets; achenes pubescent between the 10 ridges; outer pappus of bristles, obscure.

This conspicuous *Vernonia* is found in wooded grassland particularly on shallow soils. HC, HT, HM, KIT, MUM, KIS, NAR, MAC, KAJ.

Agnew 7310; Nattrass 993.

38. Vernonia undulata *Oliv. & Hiern*

Similar to *V. dummeri* but the leaves inclined to be lanceolate, undulate on the margin, and the heads small, in an open corymb, with long peduncles; achenes pubescent, without ribs; outer pappus of short bristles.

Rare, found in wooded grassland in western Kenya. KIT.

Irwin 380.

39. Vernonia *sp.* G.

Erect woody sparsely pubescent herb with oblanceolate, coarsely-serrate sessile leaves and loose terminal corymbs of cylindrical heads; florets blue or becoming blue; achenes densely silky-hairy, hardly ridged; outer pappus of shorter bristles.

An uncommon plant of disturbed grassland in western Kenya. KIS.

Verdcourt 2912; Hanid and Kiniaruh 677.

40. Vernonia hindii *S. Moore*

Similar to *V* sp. *G.* and differing only in the narrower, hardly serrate leaves and smaller heads. this species is found on shallow and impermeable soils in eastern Kenya, particularly near Thika. EMB, MAC.

Hanid and Agnew 26; Nattrass 1272.

41. Vernonia glabra (*Steetz*) *Vatke*

An erect sparsely pubescent shrub or woody herb, with elliptic, shallowly serrate leaves and terminal corymbs of cylindrical heads; florets blue to purple; achenes pubescent between the 10 ribs; outer pappus of thin narrow scales.

Uncommon, found in wet forest edges in western Kenya. HE, HM, MUM, KIS.

Strid 3375; Copley in EAH 18906.

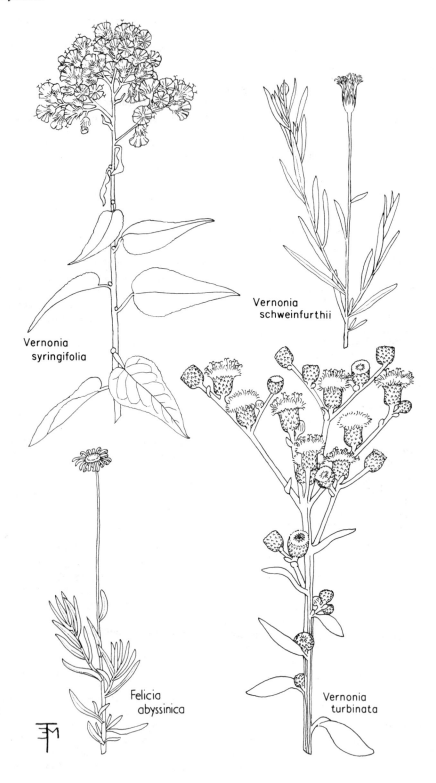

Vernonia
syringifolia

Vernonia
schweinfurthii

Felicia
abyssinica

Vernonia
turbinata

6. ELEPHANTOPUS *L.*

Erect rigid herbs with alternate simple leaves; inflorescences of few or many, tightly clustered sessile heads (heads of heads); involucre cylindrical of two series of bracts; receptacle naked; florets 2–5, tubular, bisexual; achenes columnar, angled; pappus of 5–6 or many bristles in 1–2 rows.

Elephantopus scaber *L.*

An erect tomentose herb from a rosette of petiolate oblanceolate basal leaves; stem leaves clasping, entire; inflorescence a terminal corymb of hemispherical, greyish 'heads of heads' with white florets.

　　Rare in our area and only recorded from Kisii, but common in wooded grassland in southern Kenya. KIS.
　　Napier 2890.

7. ADENOSTEMMA *Forst.*

Soft glandular herbs with opposite leaves and loose corymbose inflorescences; involucre saucer- or bell-shaped, of one row of equal bracts, sometimes partially fused laterally; receptacle naked; florets all tubular, bisexual, white, adhering to each other by dense interwoven hairs on the corolla; achenes flattened, not ribbed; pappus of 4–5 glandular bristles.

1　Achenes glandular on both faces; leaves lanceolate-rhombic, subsessile
　　　　　　　　　　　　　　1. *A. caffrum*
　　Achenes not glandular on the face; leaves ovate, then attenuate into the petiole　　2
2　Phyllaries up to 3 mm long in fruit; achenes rough on both faces　2. *A. perottetii*
　　Phyllaries over 4 mm long in fruit; achenes entirely smooth　　3. *A. mauritianum*

1. **Adenostemma caffrum** *DC.* (see p. 434)

A spreading annual or short-lived perennial with lanceolate-rhombic leaves and very loose corymbs of white heads on long peduncles; phyllaries over 4 mm long in fruit.
　　Uncommon, found in shady marshes in western Kenya. HE, KIT, MUM.
　　Lugard 183; Brodhurst-Hill 151.

2. **Adenostemma perottetii** *DC.*

Similar to *A. caffrum* but with broader, petiolate leaves and smaller heads in loose panicles.
　　Uncommon, found in shady streamsides in wet forest. KIT, MUM.
　　Agnew and Musumba 8555; Bogdan 3806.

3. **Adenostemma mauritianum** *DC.*

Similar to *A. caffrum* but with broad-ovate or rhombic leaves and corymbose heads.
　　This is the commonest species of *Adenostemma* but is local, turning up on wet forest floors from time to time throughout montane forest areas. HE, HM, HA, HK, MUM, KAJ.
　　Tweedie 68/4; Bally 1075.

8. AGERATUM *L.*

Erect herbs with opposite leaves and heads in corymbs; involucre bell-shaped, of many rows of bracts; receptacle naked; florets all similar, bisexual, tubular, white, purple or blue, with elongated stigmas; achenes columnar, 4–5-angled; pappus of ± 5 awned scales.

Ageratum conyzoides *L.* (see p. 423)

Erect branching tomentose annual with ovate serrate leaves and terminal corymbs of blue-purple heads.
　　A common weed in disturbed ground, introduced from America. One form exists with large florets which may prove to be distinct. HE, HC, HM, HA, HN, KIT, MUM, KIS, NAR, BAR, RV, EMB, MAC, NBI.
　　Leippert 5125; Harmsen 6506.

9. EUPATORIUM *L.*

Erect herbs or shrubs with opposite or alternate leaves and terminal corymbs of white or purplish flowers; involucre ± cylindrical of few, equal bracts; receptacle naked; florets all similar, tubular, bisexual, with elongated filiform stigmas; achenes columnar, 5-angled; pappus of very many bristles in 2–3 rows

1　Erect herbs from a woody rootstock, with alternate, lanceolate leaves
　　　　　　　　　　　　　　1. *E. africanum*
　　Erect herb or shrub, with opposite, ovate-elliptic leaves　　2. *E. adenophorum*

1. **Eupatorium africanum** *Oliv. & Hiern* (see p. 435)

An erect sparsely pubescent herb from a woody rootstock with lanceolate-elliptic, dentate or entire leaves and a terminal lobed corymb of white heads.
　　Uncommon, found in wooded grassland in western Kenya. HC, HA, KIT, MUM.
　　Symes 282; Tweedie 66/21.

2. **Eupatorium adenophorum** *Spreng.*

An erect pubescent herb or shrub with opposite, ovate-elliptic leaves and a terminal corymb of pale yellow or cream heads.

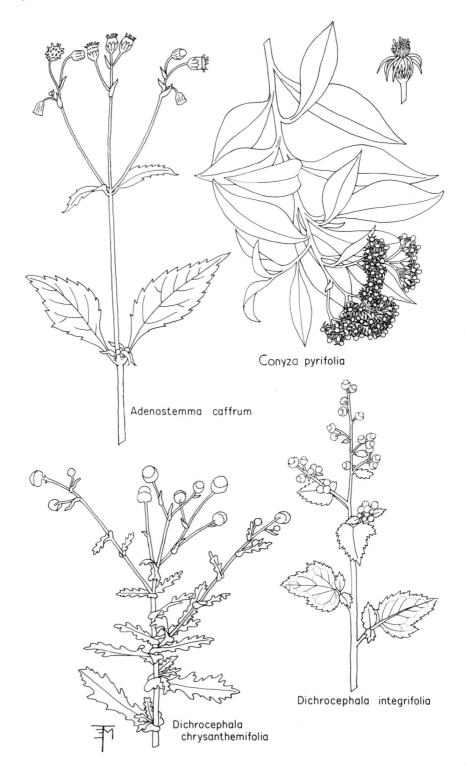

Conyza pyrifolia

Adenostemma caffrum

Dichrocephala integrifolia

Dichrocephala
chrysanthemifolia

Vernonia brachycalyx

Eupatorium
africanum

Vernonia
dummeri

Rare, found in forest edges in western Kenya.
KIT.
Tweedie 68/145.

10. MIKANIA *Willd.*

Climbing plants with opposite leaves and axillary
corymbs of white heads; involucre tubular, of few,
equal bracts; receptacle small, naked; florets few,
all bisexual, white; achenes columnar, 5-ribbed;
pappus of 1 row of bristles.

Mikania cordata (*Burm. f.*) *B. L. Robinson*

Sparsely pubescent climber with long-petiolate
ovate cordate leaves and corymbs of white heads.
   This plant is found particularly climbing over
riverine forest trees. It is commoner in western
than in eastern Kenya, but is found in Karura
forest and along the Athi River near Nairobi. HE,
HM, HA, HK, HN, KIT, MUM, NAR, MAC, NBI,
KAJ.
   Agnew and Musumba 8550; Pegg in EAH
13870.

11. GRANGEA *Adans.*

Herbs with alternate pinnatifid leaves; heads
globose, ± solitary; involucre hemispherical or flat,
of 2 rows of equal bracts; receptacle conical,
naked; outer florets in many rows, tubular-
filiform, female; inner florets many, tubular, bisexual; achenes columnar, ribbed; pappus a corky
crown on the achene, minutely ciliate.

Grangea maderaspatana *Poir.*

Much-branched, tomentose, low herb with oblong
pinnatifid leaves; heads yellow.
   Rare, found in river sands and muds in hot, dry
country. MAC.
   Bogdan 4092.

12. DICHROCEPHALA *DC.*

Herbs with alternate dentate and often pinnatifid
leaves; heads globose, solitary or in loose terminal
racemes; involucre small, inconspicuous, of 1 row
of bracts; recptacle semiglobose, naked; outer
florets in many rows, female, tubular, pale green in
colour; inner florets tubular, bisexual, darker
green; achenes compressed, glabrous; pappus
absent.

1   Heads solitary; plant perennial, creeping
                                        1. *D. alpina*
     Heads in loose racemes; plant annual   2
2   Leaves sessile, clasping the stem at base;
        peduncles over 1 cm long; heads over 5
        mm diameter   2. *D. chrysanthemifolia*
     Leaves petiolate, not clasping at base;
        peduncles less than 1 cm long; heads less
        than 4 mm diameter   3. *D. integrifolia*

1. Dichrocephala alpina *R. E. Fries*

A low, pubescent, creeping perennial with
spathulate dentate leaves and solitary heads on
ascending stems; heads over 5 mm in diameter.
   Uncommon, found in the alpine zone on
shallow wet soils. HE, HA, HK.
   Coe and Kirrika 423; Bie 292.

2. Dichrocephala chrysanthemifolia *DC.* (see p. 434)

An erect pubescent annual with oblanceolate or
obovate sessile leaves, often pinnatifid and always
coarsely dentate; heads in loose open racemes;
bisexual florets often dull reddish.
   A common herb of disturbed wet montane
forest. HE, HC, HT, HM, HA, HK, MAC, NBI.
   Lind, Napper and Beecher 5495; Rauh 400;

3. Dichrocephala integrifolia *O. Kuntze* (see p. 434)

An erect pubescent herb with rhomboid-ovate
petiolate leaves sometimes pinnate at base; heads in
terminal, ± conical panicles, reddish.
   In similar places as *D. chrysanthemifolia*, but a
little less common. HE, HC, HT, HM, HA, HK,
HN, KIT, MUM, KIS, RV, MAC, NBI.
   Hanid and Kiniaruh 990; Glover 1392.

13. FELICIA *Cass.*

Perennial herbs with alternate simple (often entire)
leaves; involucre of many rows of bracts;
receptacle naked; outer florets ligulate, blue, white
or purple, female, in one row, rarely absent; inner
florets bisexual, yellow; achenes flat, not ribbed;
pappus of 1 row of bristles.

1   Heads solitary   2
     Heads in small corymbs of 5 or more
                                        1. *F. grantii*
2   Leaves needle-like; older stems with tufts of
        short leaves in leaf axils   2. *F. muricata*
     Leaves broader than needle-like; older stems
        without tufts of leaves in leaf axils
                                        3. *F. abyssinica*

1. Felicia grantii (*Oliv. & Hiern*) *Grau* (*Erigeron grantii* Oliv. & Hiern.)

An erect annual or perennial herb usually from a
woody rootstock bearing linear-oblong, pubescent
leaves and small terminal corymbs of whitish
heads.
   Rare in western Kenya in wooded grassland and
much commoner across the border in Uganda.
MUM.
   Webster in EAH 8861.

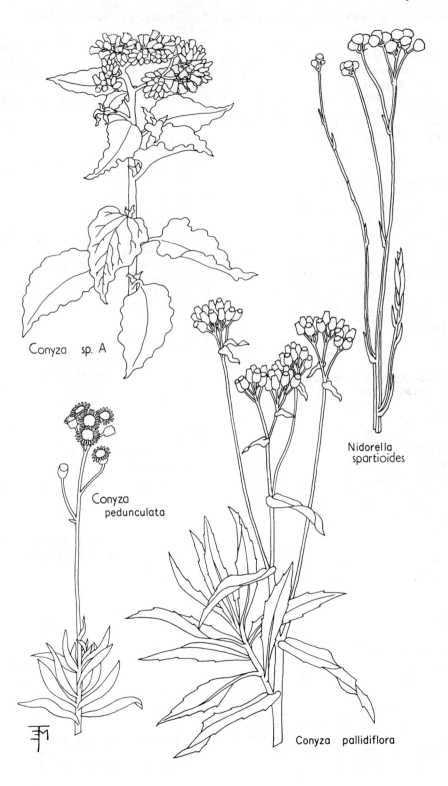

Conyza sp. A

Conyza
pedunculata

Nidorella
spartioides

Conyza pallidiflora

2. Felicia muricata (*Thunb.*) *Nees* (*Aster muricatus* Less)

A low erect or trailing weakly woody shrub, sometimes rhizomatous, glabrous or bristly-hairy, with linear leaves; heads solitary with spreading blue to mauve rays and a yellow centre.

A low shrub of dry grassland on clay soils in the upland region. It is very common in parts of the rift valley and is also found in the Nairobi National Park. HM, HA, NAR, RV, NBI.

Agnew 7076.

3. Felicia abyssinica *A. Rich.* (see p. 432)

Similar to *F. muricata* but with broader, oblanceolate leaves and sometimes with stalked glands on the peduncle below the heads.

This plant is found in burnt grassland on clay soils, particularly in the west of our area. Intermediates occur between this and the last species. HC, HM, HA, HK, NAR, RV, NAN, MAG, MAC, NBI, KAJ.

Bogdan 3685.

14. ERIGERON *L.*

Similar to *Felicia* but with the ray florets in 2 or more rows.

1   Phyllaries ± 5 mm long; ray florets white, turning yellow with age 13. *Felicia grantii*
    Phyllaries ± 9 mm long; ray florets purple to pink   *E. alpinus*

Erigeron alpinus *L.*

A tufted perennial pubescent herb with thick creeping stems and oblinear leaves; heads 3–7 together on short scapes, purplish-pink or mauve.

A rare alpine, so far only recorded from the northern side of Mt. Kenya. HK.

Hanid 74.

15. NIDORELLA *Cass.*

Similar to 17. *Conyza* except for the keyed characters,

1   Plant annual   1. *N. resedifolia*
    Plant perennial   2. *N. spartioides*

1. Nidorella resedifolia *DC.*

An erect tomentose annual herb with oblanceolate to oblong leaves and a few small apical corymbs of yellow heads.

This species is only known from waste places near Nairobi. It much resembles entire-leaves forms of *Conyza aegyptiaca*, but has smaller heads and ligulate female florets. NBI. KAJ.

Natrass 845A; Agnew 5448.

2. Nidorella spartioides (*O. Hoffm.*) *Cronq.* (see p. 437)

An erect pubescent-scabrid herb from a woody rootstock, with rather few sessile linear-oblong leaves and a loose terminal corymb of a few, rather large heads.

In wooded grassland of western Kenya. HC, HT.

Tweedie 67/124.

16. PSIADIA *Jacq.*

Similar to *Conyza* but with columnar, ribbed achenes and toothed anther-base.

Psiadia punctulata (*DC.*) *Vatke* (*P. arabica* J. & S.)

An erect, round-topped, glabrous shrub with entire lanceolate-elliptic leaves which are glossy with a gum-like secretion when young; heads bright yellow, in terminal corymbs.

Very abundant at edges of disturbed bushland in evergreen woodland and dry forest areas. HC, HT, HA, MUM, NAR, RV, NBI.

Agnew, Kibe, and Mathenge 10266; Glover and Samuel 3177.

17. CONYZA *Less.*

Herbs or shrubs with alternate, simple leaves and heads usually in terminal corymbs; involucre bell-shaped and often contracted at the mouth, of many rows of phyllaries; outer florets in many rows, filiform (narrowly tubular) or ligulate, female; inner florets few or many, bisexual; achenes slightly flattened or cylindrical, ribbed, glabrous or, more often, hairy; pappus of one row of minutely scabrid bristles.

1   Phyllaries less than 1 mm wide, always linear-lanceolate, acute at apex   2
    At least some phyllaries over 1·5 mm wide, frequently rounded at apex   21
2   Outer florets ligulate, the ligules spreading   3
    Outer florets without a ligule, or the ligules erect   10
3   Plants annual   4
    Plants perennial   5
4   Bisexual florets more than 10
                             Nidorella resedifolia
    Bisexual florets fewer than 5
                             6. *Conyza stricta*
5   Plant a herb with ascending stems   6
    Plant a shrub   7
6   Leaves white-woolly below
                             1. *Conyza pedunculata*
    Leaves green-pubescent below
                             Nidorella spartioides
7   Upper leaves clasping the stem at base
                             5. *Conyza vernonioides*
    Upper leaves shortly petiolate at base   8

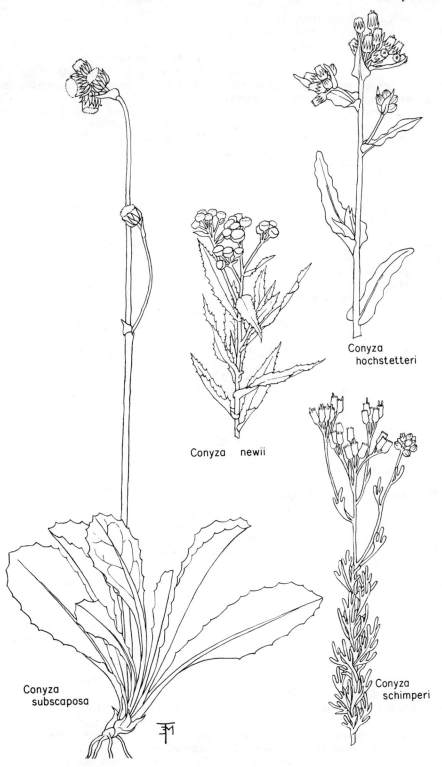

Conyza
hochstetteri

Conyza   newii

Conyza
subscaposa

Conyza
schimperi

8 Leaves deeply reticulated below by virtue of the prominent second and third order nervelets which are frequently conspicuously white-hairy.
2. *Conyza hypoleuca*
Leaves not deeply reticulated below, with only the second order nervelets slightly raised and never white-hairy 9

9 Some leaves abruptly narrowed into the petiole; ligules yellow, spreading
4. *Conyza pyrifolia*
All leaves narrowing gradually into the indistinct petiole; ligules cream or white, mostly erect 7. *Conyza pyrrhopappa*

10 Plants perennial, often shrubby 11
Plants annual 17

11 Leaves pinnatifid 8. *Conyza schimperi*
Leaves simple 12

12 Leaves clasping at base 13
Leaves not clasping at base 15

13 Leaves oblong to narrow elliptic, sessile; peduncles and often leaves and stems with cobwebby hairs 14
Leaves ovate, with a winged petiole; cobwebby hairs absent 12. *Conyza steudelii*

14 Leaves over 2 cm wide, narrowly elliptic, widest above the middle
5. *Conyza vernonioides*
Leaves under 1 cm wide, linear-oblong, widest at the clasping base
9. *Conyza welwitschii*

15 Leaves glabrous above, less than 1 cm wide
10. *Conyza* sp. *B*
Leaves hairy above, more than 1 cm wide 16

16 Leaves narrowing gradually to base
7. *Conyza pyrrhopappa*
Leaves abruptly narrowed into the petiole
3. *Conyza* sp. *A*

17 Stem leaves clasping the stem at base 18
Stem leaves gradually narrowing, not clasping at base 20

18 Phyllaries densely pubescent
11. *Conyza aegyptiaca*
Phyllaries glabrous or with a few hairs, not densely pubescent 19

19 Stem leaves mostly cuneate at base; branches of inflorescence straight, divaricating; phyllaries always lanceolate
12. *Conyza steudelii*
Stem leaves mostly rounded, truncate or subcordate at base; branches of inflorescence ascending and ± parallel after their initial divergence; phyllaries often ovate
13. *Conyza volkensii*

20 Leaves often undulate; pappus of mature heads, much exceeding the longest phyllaries 14. *Conyza bonariensis*

Leaves always flat; pappus of mature heads equalling or only just exceeding the longest phyllaries 15. *Conyza floribunda*

21 Perennial shrub 22
Perennial or annual herbs 24

22 Leaves entire; phyllaries oblong, glabrous
16. *Conyza* sp. *C*
Leaves serrate; some phyllaries suborbicular to broad elliptic, sparsely hairy 23

23 Bisexual (central) florets less than 10
17. *Conyza pallidiflora*
Bisexual (central) florets more than 20
18. *Conyza newii*

24 Plant a creeping stoloniferous herb with leafy stems 25
Herbs with erect stems, not creeping, or with a rosette of leaves at base 26

25 Phyllaries purple, with a median line of long hairs above the centre
19. *Conyza theodori*
Phyllaries green, glabrous or minutely puberulent at base 20. *Conyza* sp. *D*

26 Phyllaries glabrous 21. *Conyza tigrensis*
Phyllaries hairy 27

27 Stems leafy 28
Stems bearing leaves only at branches of the inflorescence or heads sessile in the centre of a rosette of leaves
22. *Conyza subscaposa*

28 Involucre over 9 mm long 23. *Conyza* sp. *E*
Involucre less than 6 mm long
24. *Conyza hochstetteri*

1. Conyza pedunculata (*Oliv.*) *Wild* (*Nidorella pedunculata* Oliv. & Hiern) (see p. 437)
A trailing, white-hairy weak shrub from a woody rhizome, with oblanceolate-obovate leaves and clusters of yellow heads on long erect peduncles.
Locally common in medium altitude grasslands. HA, NAR, RV, NAN, MAC.
Agnew 9187.

2. Conyza hypoleuca *A. Rich.*
An erect shrub, often white-woolly on stems and under leaves, with oblanceolate cobwebby leaves and small terminal groups of yellow heads.
Locally common in dry montane bushland. HT, HM, HA, NAR.
Agnew, Azavedo and Khatri 9568; Verdcourt 2761; Glover, Gwynne, and Samuel 467.

3. Conyza sp. A. (see p. 437)
An erect bushy (or rarely scrambling) shrub with broad-ovate, acuminate, petiolate leaves and terminal erect corymbs of pale cream heads; outer florets in many rows; bisexual florets 0–3.

Common in disturbed forest country at medium altitudes. HT, HM, MUM, KIS, BAR, EMB, MAC, NBI.

Agnew and Musumba 8521; Williams 115.

4. Conyza pyrifolia *Lam.* (see p. 434)

Very similar to the last species but usually scrambling, with narrower, longer leaves and often hanging corymbs of yellow heads; outer florets in ± one row; bisexual florets 4-6.

Abundant in disturbed dry forest. HE, HC, HT, HM, HA, KIT, NAR, EMB, MAC, NBI, KAJ.

Agnew and Beecher 9593; Bally 1205.

5. Conyza vernonioides (*A. Rich.*) *Wild*

An erect bushy shrub or weak tree with lanceolate, sessile leaves and flat-topped corymbs of yellow heads.

At the upper levels of forest on the wetter mountain slopes. HE, HM, HA, HK.

Agnew 7061.

6. Conyza stricta *Willd.*

An erect pubescent annual with linear to oblanceolate, entire to pinnatifid leaves and a terminal, many-flowered corymb of small heads.

Common in disturbed places in dry grassland. HE, HC, HT, HA, KIT, NAR, BAR, RV, NAN, EMB, MAC, NBI, KAJ.

Williams 437; Agnew 5551.

7. Conyza pyrrhopappa *Sch. Bip.* (*Microglossa oblongifolia* O. Hoffm.)

An erect pubescent woody or shrubby herb or shrub with oblanceolate, usually remotely dentate leaves and dense terminal corymbs of pale heads.

A large shrub of dry rocky hills is the ssp. *oblongifolia*, but the more common herb is to be found in disturbed upland bushland. HC, HT, MUM, NAR, BAR, MAC, NBI, KAJ.

Verdcourt 1016; Agnew 10043.

8. Conyza schimperi *Sch. Bip.* (see p. 439)

An erect pubescent annual or weakly shrubby perennial with pinnatifid revolute leaves and smallish terminal corymbs of pale heads.

A common plant of upland grassland especially on soils with impeded drainage. HC, HT, HM, HA, KIT, NAR, RV, NAN, EMB, MAC.

Lind 5486; Glover 4631.

9. Conyza welwitschii (*S. Moore*) *Wild* (*C. ruwenzoriensis* (S. Moore) R. E. Fries)

An erect, scabrid and woolly short-lived low perennial shrub with linear-oblong, entire or serrate, clasping leaves and small terminal corymbs.

A common herb of grassland clearings within the highland forest and alpine zones. HE, HM, HA, HK.

Agnew and Armstrong 8138A; G. Taylor 5321.

10. Conyza *sp.* B.

An erect glabrescent branching shrub with oblanceolate entire leaves and loose terminal corymbs of long-pedunculate heads.

Uncommon plant found in grasslands on soils with impeded drainage within upland forest. HM, HA.

Agnew 9164; Glover, Gwynne, and Samuel 1461.

11. Conyza aegyptiaca (*L.*) *Ait.*

An erect pubescent annual with oblong to oblanceolate, simple or pinnatifid leaves and terminal racemes or weak corymbs of rather large, pale heads.

Common in disturbed places in dry country. HE, HT, HA, KIT, KIS, MAG, NAN, EMB, NBI, KAJ.

Symes 350; Lind, Agnew, and Beecher 5721.

12. Conyza steudelii *Sch. Bip.*

A stiff, erect, often very big, coarse herb with broad-ovate, sharply serrate lower leaves connected by a winged petiole to a sheathing leaf-base; leaves glabrous or sparsely tomentose; heads in terminal loose corymbs.

Common in disturbed places at medium altitudes, often in dry country. In Nairobi it flowers during the dry season, while the next species is found principally during the rains. HC, HA, KIT, MUM, BAR, RV, EMB, NBI.

Hanid and Kiniaruh 955; Verdcourt 646.

13. Conyza volkensii *O. Hoffm.*

Very similar to *C. steudelii* but often decumbent, with soft stems and tomentose, bluntly-dentate leaves; inflorescence of a series of spherical masses of heads, hardly corymbose.

Abundant in disturbed grassland, often where wet, along ditches etc, and generally in more moist situations than *C. steudelii.* HE, HT, HM, HA, HK, NAR, BAR, RV, MAC, NBI, KAJ.

Agnew 7252; Nattrass 1443.

14. Conyza bonariensis (*L.*) *Cronq.* (*Erigeron bonariensis* L.)

An erect herb from an ephemeral rosette of oblanceolate, distantly serrate leaves; stem leaves linear, usually undulate on margins; heads in a loose corymb or panicle of corymbs.

A rather uncommon introduction (except around Nairobi), growing in cultivated ground. KIT, RV, NBI, KAJ.

Agnew and Humphry 5565; Bally 9013.

15. Conyza floribunda *H. B. K.* (*Erigeron floribundum* (H. B. K.) Sch. Bip.)

Similar to *C. bonariensis* but with flat leaves and more numerous, smaller flowers in a pyramidal terminal panicle.

Very common in disturbed soil at medium altitudes and in wetter districts. HC, HT, HM, HA, KIT, MUM, KIS, NAR, BAR, RV, NAN, EMB, NBI, KAJ.

William 131; Agnew and Kibe 10294.

16. Conyza *sp.* C.

A branched glabrous shrub with linear-elliptic leaves and long-pedunculate dense corymbs of pale flowers.

This curious *Conyza* has only been collected twice, in montane rain forest. HE, HA, HK.

Agnew, Kiniaruh, and Wyatt 8890; Kerfoot 632.

17. Conyza pallidiflora *R. E. Fries* (see p. 437)

A branched shrub (sometimes annual) sparsely tomentose on the stem and glabrous on the elliptic, serrate leaves; leaves clasping the stem at base; heads pale yellow, in terminal corymbs.

Common in disturbed places in montane forest. HE, HM, HA, HK, NAR, KAJ.

Glover 2601; Agnew, Beals, and Modha 7074.

18. Conyza newii *Oliv. & Hiern* (see p. 439)

Similar to *C. pallidiflora* but with leaves seldom clasping the stem at base and more sharply serrate, and with bright yellow heads.

Common in rocky shallow soils within the montane forest area, especially on escarpment slopes. HC, HT, HM, HA, KIS, RV, MAC, KAJ.

Agnew, Azavedo, and Khatri 9562; Verdcourt 1480.

19. Conyza theodori *R. E. Fr.*

A trailing, stoloniferous, pubescent perennial with oblanceolate to linear, distantly dentate leaves and ascending stems bearing few, large, purple-phyllaried heads.

Uncommon, found in subalpine marshes. HE, HA, HK.

Strid 2288; Hedberg 2014.

20. Conyza *sp.* D.

Similar to *C. theodori* but glabrous and with smaller heads with pale-green phyllaries.

Rare plant found in lowland marshes in western Kenya. HM, KIT.

Tweedie 68/48; Symes 93.

21. Conyza tigrensis *Oliv. & Hiern*

Woody annual herb or soft shrub, pubescent, with few branches and leaves similar to those of *C. steudelii*; heads in dense terminal corymbs, mostly with purple-edged phyllaries.

An distinctive species of disturbed places in upland forest. HC, HT, HM, HA, HK.

Polhill, Verdcourt, and Lucas 320; Agnew, Kiniaruh, and Ngethe 8891.

22. Conyza subscaposa *O. Hoffm.* (see p. 439)

A perennial, pubescent or subglabrous, rosette herb with oblanceolate leaves; heads solitary, sessile, or 2–5 together shortly pedunculate on a scape; phyllaries green or purple-edged.

Common in alpine and subalpine grassland. HE, HC, HT, HM, HA, HK.

Hanid 78; Hedberg 122.

23. Conyza *sp.* E.

An ascending or erect scabrid pubescent perennial herb, with oblong to oblanceolate leaves clasping at base and terminal clusters of shortly pedunculate, large heads; phyllaries narrowly acute, green at apex.

An uncommon plant of wooded grassland in the Kitale region. KIT.

Bogdan 3703; Agnew 10859.

24. Conyza hochstetteri *Sch. Bip.* (see p. 439)

Similar to *C. sp. E.* but with broader, more coarsely dentate leaves and tighter clusters of more numerous, smaller heads; phyllaries often obtuse, tinged purple at apex.

Very common in disturbed grassland in upland Kenya. HE, HC, HT, HM, HA, KIT, KIS, NAR, RV, MAC, NBI, KAJ.

Hanid and Kiniaruh 602; William 191.

18. CHRYSOCOMA *L.*

Similar to *Felicia* but with yellow ray florets and with many rows of bristles in the pappus.

Chrysocoma *sp.* A.

An erect, branching annual with linear pubescent leaves and hemispherical, solitary, long-pedunculate heads.

A curious unnamed plant (even the genus is uncertain) which is found in disturbed places on sandy soil in dry country. It is particularly common on the Mua Hills. MAC.

Verdcourt and Napper 2165; Agnew 9391.

19. BLUMEA *DC.*

Erect annual herbs with alternate, sessile, simple or pinnatifid leaves and terminal, corymbose, purple heads; involucre bell-shaped or tubular, of many rows of usually soft, linear, hairy phyllaries; receptacle naked; outer florets in many rows, tubular-filiform, female; inner florets fewer than the outer, bisexual; anthers tailed at base; achenes cylindrical or ovoid with a white basal ring; pappus of one row of scabrid bristles.

1   Phyllaries distinctly smaller towards the outside, with only one row of the longest within, and many rows of decreasing sizes towards the outside, the latter ovate
                                         1. *B. aurita*
     Phyllaries mostly of the longest, innermost length, very few outside, all linear, none ovate   2
2   Heads shortly pedunculate in clusters near the stem, so that the upper part of the plant becomes a ± cylindrical mass of heads   2. *B. perottetiana*
     Heads with long peduncles, in a loose but flat-topped terminal corymb   3. *B. caffra*

1. Blumea aurita *DC.*

An annual glandular-pubescent herb with erect or ascending branches and obovate, sessile, often shortly decurrent leaves; heads long-pedunculate, loosely arranged all round the stems, purple.

Uncommon, found in dry country, especially where disturbed by cattle. BAR, MAC.

Agnew and Allen 9946; Verdcourt 1802.

2. Blumea perottetiana *DC.*

An erect tomentose annual herb with obovate to oblanceolate, sessile or alternate leaves; heads in dense masses on upper part of stem, with many linear purple phyllaries.

Locally common, found by streamsides and in the more naturally disturbed places at altitudes from 5500 to 8000 ft. HA, HT, KIT, KIS, NAR, RV, NBI.

Mendes 45; Bogdan 5566.

3. Blumea caffra (*DC.*) *O. Hoffm.*

An erect annual with oblong-lanceolate leaves which clasp the stem at base; heads with wide-spreading involucre, in a terminal open corymb, purple.

Uncommon, found in dry areas (e.g. Voi) and only once recorded from our area as an introduced casual at Machakos. MAC.

Napper 1234.

20. LAGGERA *Sch. Bip.*

Similar to *Blumea* but with stems always winged by the decurrent leaf-bases, and without the tailed anther base of that genus.

1   Leaves glabrescent except on the nerves below; stem wings serrate or dentate
                                         1. *L. pterodonta*
     Leaves usually tomentose, at least scabrid-pubescent below; stem wings entire   2
2   All phyllaries except the innermost row with a stiff, leathery, pubescent, reflexed tip which is wider than the innermost phyllaries   2. *L. brevipes*
     Few (on the outside), or no phyllaries with a reflexed leathery herbaceous tip; phyllaries mostly erect, thin, with or without pubescent tips   3
3   Outer phyllaries spreading; heads wider than long   4. *L. elatior*
     Outer phyllaries appressed to the head; heads longer than wide   3. *L. alata*

1. Laggera pterodonta *Sch. Bip.* (see p. 444)

A large erect single-stemmed glabrescent annual herb with oblanceolate leaves and toothed stem wings; heads long-pedunculate, about as wide as long in loose terminal corymbs.

Uncommon, found in wetter forest margins. HK, KIT, MUM, KAJ.

Verdcourt 2925.

2. Laggera brevipes *Oliv. & Hiern* (see p. 444)

A large, erect, densely pubescent or tomentose, single-stemmed annual with oblong-ovate leaves and entire stem wings; heads often subsessile, in dense terminal cylindrical panicles, mostly as wide as long.

Common in upland grassland particularly where disturbed, and at forest edges. HE, HA, HM, KIT, MUM, KIS, NAR, BAR, EMB, MAC, NBI.

Knight 497; Brodhurst-Hill 84.

3. Laggera alata *Sch. Bip.*

Similar to *L. brevipes* but with narrower leaves, usually a looser inflorescence and heads longer than wide. The last two species are no doubt closely related, and some intermediate specimens may be hybrids, for many plants show the outermost few phyllaries reflexed and leathery like those of *L. brevipes*.

This species is found in moist grassland. HA, HK, KIT, NAR, EMB, KAJ.

Agnew, Hanid, and Kiniaruh 7848; Napier in EAH 10168.

4. Laggera elatior *R. E. Fries* (see p. 444)

A robust erect pubescent or tomentose annual with lanceolate leaves and entire stem-wings; heads in loose terminal corymbs, wider than long, purplish.

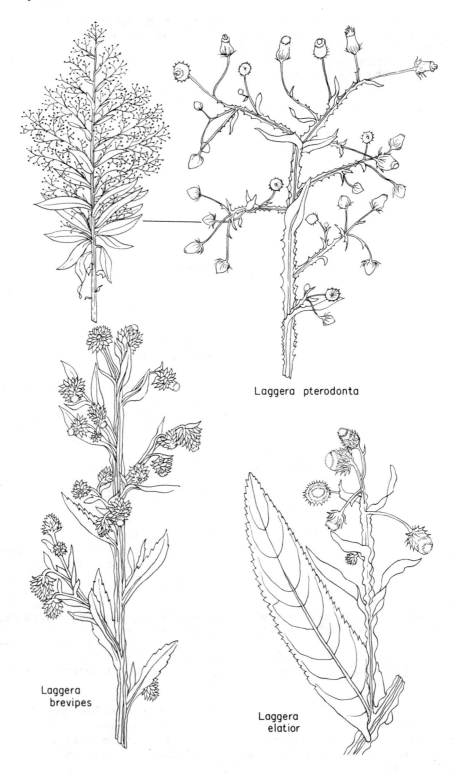

Laggera pterodonta

Laggera
brevipes

Laggera
elatior

Locally common and mainly in wet montane forest clearings. HE, HC, HT, HM, HA, KIS, RV. Lind, Agnew, and Kettle 5897; Glover 1001.

21. PLUCHEA *Cass.*

This genus is similar to *Blumea* in all respects except habit, all the present species being shrubby.

1 Leaves linear   1. *P. nitens*
  Leaves broader   2
2 Leaves decurrent along the stem as continuous wings   2. *P. ovalis*
  Leaves not decurrent, or at most up to 2 pairs of small lobes present on the stem below the node   3
3 Involucre 8-11 mm long   3. *P. bequaertii*
  Involucre less than 5 mm long
                                  4. *P. dioscoridis*

1. Pluchea nitens *O. Hoffm.* (*Nicolasia nitens* (O. Hoffm.) Leins)

A short-lived wiry shrub, silky-hairy on young parts, with linear leaves and purplish heads in loose terminal corymbs; involucre to 10 mm long.

Locally abundant in dry, rocky, eroded grassland. This plant should properly be placed in the genus *Nicolasia* S. Moore. RV, MAG.
Agnew 7775; Glover 3846.

2. Pluchea ovalis *DC.*

An erect pubescent shrub with winged stem and dentate elliptic leaves; heads to 6 mm long in dense terminal corymbs.

Uncommon, where ground water occurs near the surface in dry country. HA, KIS, NAR, RV, NAN, MAC, KAJ.
Mwangangi 72.

3. Pluchea bequaertii *Robyns*

An erect pubescent weak shrub with shortly decurrent or sessile, obovate dentate leaves and loose terminal corymbs of purple heads.

This species is also found in wet places within dry country and is confined, in our area, to ground-water forest mainly in the Rift Valley. HA, RV, KAJ.
Agnew and Allen 9940; Bally 9861.

4. Pluchea dioscoridis *DC.*

An erect, much-branched, pubescent or glabrescent shrub with oblanceolate to obovate, sessile but not decurrent leaves; heads mauve, in dense terminal corymbs.

This species is again confined to ground-water areas in dry country, especially in riverine alluvium. BAR, NAR, MAG.
Rodgers 5; Glover 3237.

22. SPHAERANTHUS *L.*

Erect or trailing herbs or weak shrubs with sessile, usually simple leaves; stems usually winged with decurrent leaf-bases; heads sessile, on a common receptacle, forming a 'head of heads'; involucre tubular, of 1-2 rows of usually spathulate bracts; receptacle (of the individual heads) naked; florets purple in two series; the outer florets narrow-tubular, female, few or many, with an included, bifid stigma; inner florets male, or bisexual, but usually not setting seed, with an expanded corolla and long-exserted, single stigma; achenes smooth, ovoid; pappus absent.

1 Inflorescences cylindrical, longer than broad
                                  1. *S. ukambensis*
  Inflorescences ovoid, conical or spherical   2
2 Florets exceeded by and partially concealed behind large overlapping bracts at anthesis; basal bracts of the inflorescence clearly visible and erect, not deflexed or pushed downwards by the lowest heads   3
  Florets much longer than the bracts of the inflorescence; basal bracts of the inflorescence concealed or pushed downwards by the lowest heads   4
3 Stems unwinged; inflorescences conical, pointed at apex; bracts of the inflorescence narrowed gradually at apex into a fine point   2. *S. cyathuloides*
  Stems winged; inflorescences rounded at apex; bracts of the inflorescence rounded or obtuse at apex with a short apical bristle
                                  3. *S. gomphrenoides*
4 Leaves hairy; stem wings untoothed; heads many-flowered, forming easily distinguished separate knobs on the young inflorescence   4. *S. confertifolius*
  Leaves glabrous or hairy, if hairy then stem wings toothed; heads few-flowered, never distinguishable as separate knobs on the outside of the young inflorescence   5
5 Leaves glabrous when fully expanded; inflorescence bracts glabrous, with an obtuse apex and a terminal bristle, always clearly visible   5. *S. suaveolens*
  Leaves hairy, sometimes sparsely so with age; inflorescence bracts strongly hairy and ciliate, narrowing gradually to the terminal bristle, difficult to distinguish individually
                                              6
6 Inflorescences longer than broad or circular, the basal bracts never visible
                                       6. *S. bullatus*
  Inflorescences broader than long, the basal bracts usually clearly visible
                                       7. *S. napierae*

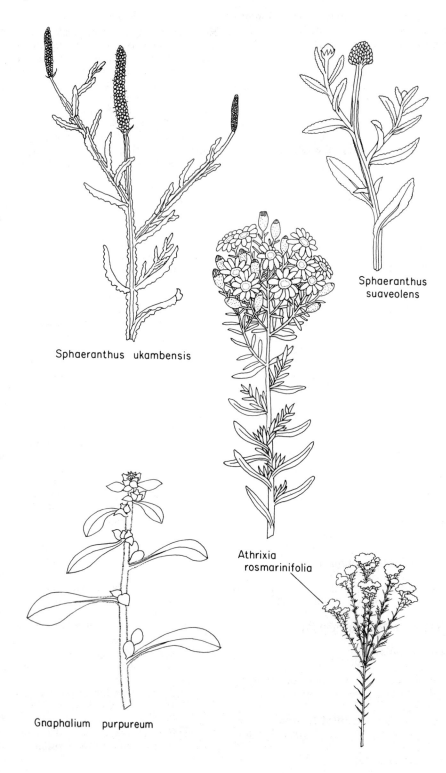

Sphaeranthus ukambensis

Sphaeranthus
suaveolens

Athrixia
rosmarinifolia

Gnaphalium   purpureum

1. Sphaeranthus ukambensis *Vatke & O. Hoffm.* (see p. 446)

An erect, scabrid-pubescent woody herb with lanceolate, acute, serrate leaves and ± entire, continuous stem wings; inflorescences cylindrical.

Uncommon, in wet places within dry country. KIS, BAR, RV, MAG, MAC.

Hanid and Kiniaruh 527; Glover 4059.

2. Sphaeranthus cyathuloides *O. Hoffm.*

An erect glabrous woody herb with narrow lanceolate-linear, minutely serrate leaves and unwinged stems; inflorescences conical.

Fairly common in wet places within grassland around Nairobi. MAC, NBI, KAJ.

Hanid and Kiniaruh 559; Ossent 288.

3. Sphaeranthus gomphrenoides *O. Hoffm.*

A glabrous weak ascending herb with lanceolate leaves and interrupted stem wings; inflorescences smaller than *S. cyathuloides*, paler in colour and rounded at apex.

Locally common along watercourses and ephemeral pools in hotter country. MUM, KIS, NAR, BAR, MAG, MAC, KAJ.

Agnew, Musumba, and Kiniaruh 8022; Ossent 506.

4. Sphaeranthus confertifolius *Robyns*

A scabrid-pubescent loose shrub with narrow-elliptic serrate leaves and entire-winged stem; heads with over 30 florets.

Locally common in disturbed ground in upland forest and grassland areas. Unlike other species of *Sphaeranthus* this is not always found near water. HT, HA, NAR, RV, NBI.

Agnew 9070; Glover 3966.

5. Sphaeranthus suaveolens *(Forsk.) DC.* (see p. 446)

A glabrous trailing herb with ascending stem bearing elliptic, serrate leaves and subentire, continuous wings; inflorescences globose, purple, terminal.

This is our commonest (and most variable) member of the genus, being found in fresh water, 4000–8000 ft. The smell of the leaves resembles apples. HE, HC, HT, HM, HL, HA, HK, KIT, KIS, NAR, MAC, NBI.

Hanid and Kiniaruh 626; Symes 106.

6. Sphaeranthus bullatus *Mattf.*

A weak pubescent shrub with deeply serrate oblong leaves and continuous stem-wings; heads globose, small, hairy.

Locally common in wooded grassland, not found by water. RV, MAG, MAC, NBI, KAJ.

Agnew and Tweedie 9296; Perdue and Kibuwa 8069.

7. Sphaeranthus napierae *Ross-Craig*

Similar to *S. suaveolens* except for the pubescence, the shape of the inflorescence, and the hairy, gradually narrowing bracts.

A common endemic in freshwater in central Kenya. MUM, RV, EMB, MAC, NBI.

Hanid and Kiniaruh 431; Napier 425 (Type).

23. TRIPLOCEPHALUM *O. Hoffm.*

Erect shrubs with alternate sessile leaves; inflorescences terminal, of groups of usually 3 'masses', each consisting of broad bracts subtending heads which themselves consist of groups of the sessile, ultimate heads, thus the whole is a 'head of heads'; the ultimate heads have one row of scarious phyllaries and 3–4 female, filiform, fertile florets or 2–3 male florets; achenes columnar; pappus represented by a crown of minute scales.

Triplocephalum holstii *O. Hoffm.*

An erect, silky-hairy shrub with oblong leaves which clasp the stem at base; heads in loose terminal corymbs, pinkish purple.

A strange plant, only thus far recorded from the Amboseli subsaline marshes in Kenya, but more common further south. KAJ.

Foster in EAH 13034.

24. BLEPHARISPERMUM *Wight*

Shrubs, erect or scrambling, with alternate simple petiolate leaves; inflorescences of masses of sessile heads ('heads of heads'); involucre of 1 row of scarious bracts; receptacle bearing boat-shaped scales which subtend the flowers; outer florets few, female; inner florets few, bisexual, often not setting seed; outer achenes two-winged, with a median angle within, the wings ciliate; inner achenes columnar, grooved; pappus of 4–7 scales.

1   Leaves ovate, truncate at base, coarsely dentate; outer achenes linear   1. *B.* sp. *A*
    Leaves oblanceolate or ovate-elliptic, entire; outer achenes broader   2
2   Leaves oblanceolate; outer achenes suborbicular   2. *B. fruticosum*
    Leaves ovate-elliptic; outer achenes obovate   3. *B. zanguebaricum*

1. Blepharispermum *sp.* A.

A trailing or erect, minutely pubescent shrub; leaves ovate, truncate at base, acute at apex, coarsely dentate; inflorescences solitary, terminal, white.

Rare in western Kenya, and only once found amongst granite rocks near Kisumu. MUM.
Agnew, Musumba, and Kiniaruh 804.

2. Blepharispermum fruticosum *Klatt*

An erect glabrous shrub with many sparsely branched stems from ground level; leaves entire, oblanceolate, rounded at apex; inflorescences solitary, terminal, white.

Uncommon, found in dry *Combretum-Acacia* woodland. MAC.
Greenway 8856.

3. Blepharispermum zanguebaricum *Oliv. & Hiern*

An erect (sometimes scrambling) glabrescent shrub with large entire ovate-elliptic leaves, and a projection below the petiole insertion at the node; inflorescences few, in loose terminal cymes or solitary, white.

Uncommon, in *Combretum* woodland and riverine alluvium in dry country. MAC, KAJ.
Agnew 9880; Ibrahim 667.

25. ATHROISMA *DC.*

Annual or perennial herbs with alternate, simple leaves; inflorescences of crowded sessile many-flowered heads, uniform in size ('heads of heads'); involucre of one row of bracts; receptacle elongated, stem-like, bearing scales which subtend the florets; florets many to few, all bisexual, white; achenes ovoid, slightly flattened, 2-angled, glabrous or hairy; pappus absent.

1 Leaves linear or lanceolate, usually entire   2
   Leaves ovate to orbicular, coarsely toothed
                            1. *A. hastifolium*
2 Annual; heads subsessile   2. *A. stuhlmannii*
   Rhizomatous perennials; heads on long
      peduncles exceeding the leaves   3
3 Usually some leaves over 10 cm long; achenes
      heart-shaped, square, or suborbicular in
      outline, flat and 2-winged   3. *A. sp. A*
   Never any leaves more than 10 cm long;
      achenes oblong, hardly flattened   4
4 Involucral bracts conspicuously fringed at
      apex; achenes 1·25–1·50 mm long, tuber-
      culate   4. *A. psyllioides*
   Involucral bracts hardly fringed at margin;
      achenes less than 1 mm long, smooth
                               5. *A. gracile*

1. Athroisma hastifolium *Mattf.*

A perennial pubescent stoloniferous herb with ovate to suborbicular, coarsely-toothed leaves and terminal, long-pedunculate pinkish inflorescences.

Uncommon, in dry, seasonally waterlogged grassland. MAG, KAJ.
Verdcourt 3664.

2. Athroisma stuhlmannii (*O. Hoffm.*) *Mattf.*

A trailing glabrous annual with serrate lanceolate leaves and subsessile white inflorescences.

Rare, as a weed of arable land in west Kenya. MUM.
Bradley K 30.

3. Athroisma *sp.* A.

A perennial glabrous rhizomatous herb with erect tufts of linear-leaved stems; inflorescences white, solitary on very long peduncles; achenes smooth, winged, up to 1 mm long.

Uncommon, found on forest pathsides near Nairobi. HA, NBI.
Mainwaring 2099; Agnew 8473.

4. Athroisma psyllioides (*Oliv.*) *Mattf.*

Similar to *A. gracile* except for the shorter linear to lanceolate, entire or toothed leaves, shorter-peduncled more corymbose heads, and longer tuberculate achenes.

This is the commonest species of *Athroisma* in our area, occurring in grassland, particularly along roadsides leading through black-cotton soil. The inflorescences may be either pink or white. NAR, RV, MAG, MAC, NBI, KAJ.
Mainwaring 2154; Agnew 10214A.

5. Athroisma gracile (*Oliv.*) *Mattf.*

Similar to the last species but with a tendency to produce thread-like leaves and with the differences mentioned in the key.

This species has nearly the same habitat as the last, but is often found in rocky soils, and occurs further north. NAR, RV, MAG, NAN, MAC, NBI.
Agnew 7423; Kerfoot 3369.

26. HELICHRYSUM *Mill.*

Annual or perennial herbs or shrubs with alternate, often glandular, entire leaves; heads solitary or in terminal corymbs; involucre tubular or hemispherical, of many rows of scarious bracts, often brightly coloured; receptacle naked or with fleshy outgrowths; floret composition of the head variable, but never with spreading ligulate florets; outer florets filiform, tubular, female, in one to many rows or absent; inner florets one to numerous, bisexual; achenes ovoid, glabrous or pubescent; pappus of one row of scabrous bristles.

Key to 26. *Helichrysum* and 27. *Gnaphalium*

1 Involucre up to 6 mm long, always broader
      than long, more or less tubular   2
   Involucre over 6 mm long, sometimes broader
      than long, tubular or spreading   17
2 Annuals, or low herbs with decumbent stems,
      rooting at the nodes
                        (27. *Gnaphalium*)   3

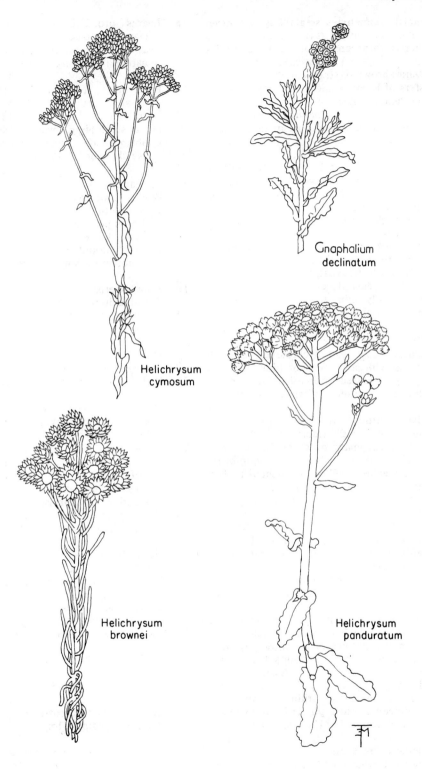

Gnaphalium
declinatum

Helichrysum
cymosum

Helichrysum
brownei

Helichrysum
panduratum

Perennials, sometimes scrambling but never trailing and rooting at the nodes **6**

3 Phyllaries with conspicuous white spreading tips   1. *Gnaphalium declinatum*
Phyllaries brown or straw-coloured   **4**

4 Clusters of heads sessile in the upper part of the stem, forming a spike-like raceme
                          2. *Gnaphalium purpureum*
Clusters of heads corymbose or in a globose terminal mass   **5**

5 Leaves woolly on both surfaces
                          3. *Gnaphalium luteo-album*
Leaves rough-hairy, not woolly, on upper side
                          4. *Gnaphalium undulatum*

6 Plant a herb with 1–2 erect, unbranched, annual flowering stems from a woody rootstock   **7**
Plant a herb or shrub, with some perennial sterile stems, sometimes scrambling   **11**

7 Florets mostly bisexual, with few or no thin female marginal florets   **8**
Florets mostly thin, female, with only 1–2 larger central bisexual ones
                          1. *H. globosum*

8 Phyllaries white or pink   **9**
Phyllaries yellow or straw-coloured   **10**

9 Phyllaries with stiff green or pink base and slightly expanded, spoon-shaped, rounded, white apex; outer phyllaries not wrinkled
                          2. *H. rhodolepis*
Phyllaries without stiff base, entirely white and usually with transversely wrinkled, acute apex; many outer phyllaries transversely wrinkled   3. *H. albiflorum*

10 Phyllaries golden yellow, boat-shaped, stiff, unwrinkled and rounded at apex
                          4. *H. nudifolium*
Phyllaries straw-coloured, flat but wrinkled, acute at apex   5. *H. gerberifolium*

11 Stem winged with the narrow decurrent leaf-bases   6. *H. odoratissimum*
Stem unwinged   **12**

12 Leaves petiolate, ovate-elliptic   **13**
Leaves sessile, usually clasping the stem, or linear   **14**

13 Heads white or pale yellow, narrowing gradually to the base, sessile in tight groups within the inflorescence; outer phyllaries smooth, not wrinkled; florets 4–7 in each head   7. *H. schimperi*
Heads bright golden yellow, cylindrical, shortly pedunculate within the corymbose inflorescence; outer phyllaries transversely wrinkled; florets 11–13 in each head
                          8. *H.* sp. *A*

14 Phyllaries white or pink   **15**
Phyllaries straw-coloured or yellow   **16**

15 Leaves broad-obovate, rounded at apex, clasping at base   9. *H. panduratum*
Leaves narrow-linear, acute at apex, attenuate, not clasping at base
                          10. *H. glumaceum*

16 Plant erect, herbaceous or shrubby; leaves usually widest at base, not more than 3·5 cm long   11. *H. cymosum*
Plant scrambling, weakly shrubby; leaves oblanceolate widest above the middle, usually over 5 cm long
                          12. *H. maranguense*

17 Phyllaries yellow   **18**
Phyllaries white pink or red   **22**

18 Leaves with underside (and sometimes also the upperside) covered with white, cobwebby hairs   **19**
Leaves without cobwebby hairy covering, glandular on both surfaces
                          13. *H. setosum*

19 Annual herbs   **20**
Perennial herbs or shrubs   **21**

20 Heads saucer-shaped; inner phyllaries exceeding the florets by only one quarter of their length.   14. *H. foetidum*
Involucre globose; inner phyllaries twice as long as the florets   15. *H. kilimanjari*

21 High altitude shrub; heads over 15 mm long
                          16. *H. gloria-dei*
Medium altitude herb with annual stems from a woody rootstock; heads less than 11 mm long   17. *H. kirkii*

22 Leaves with a leaf-base lying along the stem below the spreading (lamina) part of the leaf   **23**
Leaves sessile on the stem, without a distinct sheathing or appressed leaf base   **27**

23 Heads solitary, commonly some heads on each plant approaching 2 cm long
                          18. *H. newii*
Heads in corymbs, or rarely solitary, never more than 1·5 cm long   **24**

24 Leaves linear, the same whitish colour on both surfaces   **25**
Leaves narrow elliptic to broader, always much whiter on the lower surface   **26**

25 Leaf with a small glabrous point at apex
                          19. *H. brownei*
Leaf with hairs over entire apex
                          20. *H. amblyphyllum*

26 Low weak shrub to 50 cm tall; leaves elliptic, grey above   21. *H. ellipticifolium*
Erect woody shrub often over 1 m tall; leaves linear to elliptic, bright green above
                          22. *H. chionoides*

27 Plant frequently spiny; leaves less than 1 cm long   23. *H. citrispinum*

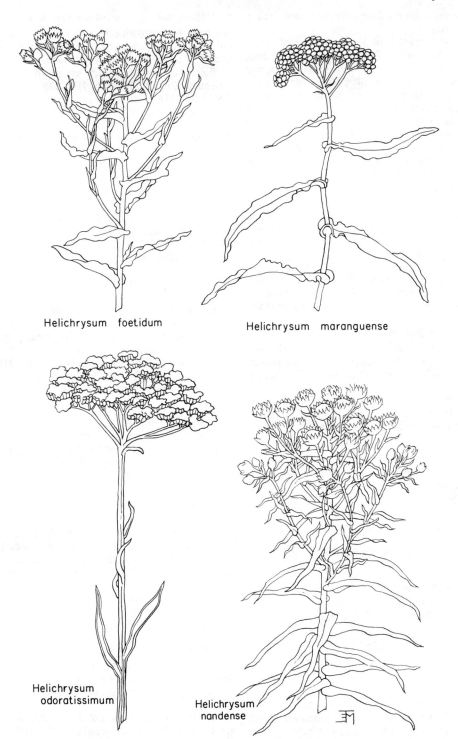

Helichrysum foetidum

Helichrysum maranguense

Helichrysum
odoratissimum

Helichrysum
nandense

Plant never spiny; leaves always more than 1 cm long **28**

28 Herb with rosette of leaves at ground level, and an erect flowering shoot bearing appressed leaves *24. H. meyeri-johannis*
Shrub with erect or decumbent stems with neither leaf rosette nor appressed leaves on flowering stems **29**

29 Most leaves over 5 mm broad **30**
Most leaves less than 5 mm broad **31**

30 Leaves with numerous coarse glandular hairs with or without a thin cobwebby layer of hairs on upper surface
25. H. formosissimum
Leaves with few or no glandular or coarse hairs but always with a cobwebby layer of hairs on upper surface *26. H. guilelmi*

31 Leaves broadest at the base; receptacles usually less than 4 mm in diameter
27. H. nandense
At least some leaves broadest about the middle; receptacles 4 mm or more in diameter *28. H. argyranthum*

1. Helichrysum globosum *Sch.Bip.* (see p. 453)
An erect perennial herb from a rosette of long-petiolate, often broadly elliptical, 3-nerved leaves, with a terminal umbel of clusters of brownish heads.
Fairly common, in upland grassland from 6000–10 000 ft. HE, HC, HT, HM, HA, HK, MAC.
Lind and Napper 5491; Kerfoot 3756.

2. Helichrysum rhodolepis *Baker*
Similar to *H. globosum* except for the capitula which are white and pink and contain mostly bisexual flowers; also, like the last species, the receptacle has fleshy protuberances.
Rather uncommon, in dry rocky country. HE, HT, KIT, KIS, MAC.
Symes 362; Hanid and Kiniaruh 822.

3. Helichrysum albiflorum *O. Hoffm.*
Similar to *H. rhodolepis* but smaller in all parts and with the inflorescence differences noted in the key.
Rare, and only represented by specimens from Kapenguria area. HC.
Symes 30.

4. Helichrysum nudifolium (*L.*) *Less.*
Similar to *H. rhodolepis* but with narrower leaves and compact umbels of golden-yellow heads.
Rare, in highland dry grassland. KAJ.
Bally 8172; Ables 26.

5. Helichrysum gerberifolium *Sch. Bip.*
An erect herb growing from a rosette of narrowly elliptical leaves, bearing a fairly loose terminal umbel of clusters of brownish heads.
Fairly common, in dry grassland at medium altitudes. HE, HC, HT, HA, HK, KIT, MUM, NAR, RV, NAN, MAC, NBI.
Agnew 8695; Glover 1903.

6. Helichrysum odoratissimum (*L.*) *Less.* (see p. 451)
A weak straggling shrub, silvery-hairy all over, with decurrent linear-lanceolate leaves and dense corymbs of yellow heads terminating naked peduncles.
Very common throughout our area except in the driest localities. HE, HC, HT, HM, HA, HK, KIT, MUM, KIS, NAR, RV, MAC, NBI, KAJ.
Brodhurst-Hill 180; Agnew and Kibe 10328.

7. Helichrysum schimperi (*Sch. Bip.*) *Moeser* (see p. 453)
A trailing soft shrub, white-hairy except on the upper side of the petiolate, broad-elliptic leaves; inflorescences rather diffuse, of tightly packed, sessile, yellowish or white heads.
Common in the edges of upland forest. HE, HC, HT, HM, HA, NAR, RV, MAC, NBI, KAJ.
Agnew 10631; Nattrass 1112.

8. Helichrysum *sp.* **A.**
Similar to *H. schimperi* except for the key characters, this beautiful scrambler has only been found in the north-west of Kenya. HE, HC.
Irwin 142; Agnew, Kibe, and Mathenge 10307.

9. Helichrysum panduratum *O. Hoffm.* (see p. 449)
A soft erect (often supported) shrub, covered with long white hairs except on the upper side of the obovate, sessile, clasping leaves; heads white, rather large, the clusters borne corymbosely on long naked peduncles.
A showy uncommon plant in western Kenya. HE, HC, HA, KIT, MUM, KIS.
Napier 5801; Tweedie 66/48.

10. Helichrysum glumaceum *DC.*
A weakly shrubby low perennial, grey-hairy with linear acute leaves; heads white or pink in tight clusters, the clusters racemosely borne on naked peduncles.
A plant variable in colour, common in dry grassland and wooded grassland. HA, HK, NAR, BAR, RV, NAN, MAG, MAC, KAJ.
Gilbert C4; Lind 5289.

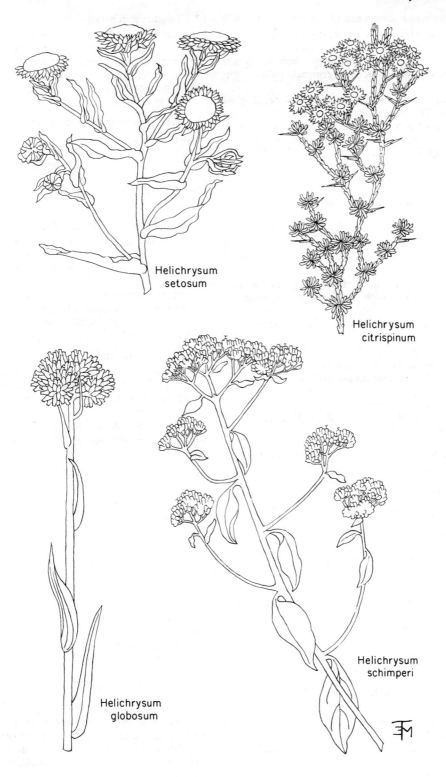

Helichrysum
setosum

Helichrysum
citrispinum

Helichrysum
globosum

Helichrysum
schimperi

11. Helichrysum cymosum (*L.*) *Less.* (see p. 449)

A weak or wiry, erect or straggling herb or low shrub with yellowish-woolly, linear, oblong or lanceolate, erect or reflexed leaves; heads brownish-yellow in dense terminal balls or in corymbs.

A very variable plant with a wide ecological tolerance. The florets are also variable, there being a majority of either bisexual or female florets. It is found in stony grassland from the alpine zone down to 6000 ft. HE, HC, HT, HM, HA, HK, KIT, MUM, NAR, RV, NAN, MAC.

Glover 3545; Agnew 10405.

12. Helichrysum maranguense *O. Hoffm.* (see p. 451)

A trailing scrambling shrub with white undersides to the sessile oblanceolate undulate leaves, and with shortly peduncled masses of brownish-yellow heads.

Uncommon, in the edges of montane rain forest, especially with *Podocarpus milanjianus*. HE, HM, HA.

Agnew, Beals, and Modha 7056; Kerfoot 757.

13. Helichrysum setosum *Harv.* (see p. 453)

An erect glandular-hairy annual, branching above into the diffusely corymbose golden-yellow heads; leaves lanceolate to oblong, clasping at base.

Locally common in grassy clearings in montane rain forest. HE, HM, HA, MUM, MAC, KAJ.

Kerfoot 2708; Strid 2044.

14. Helichrysum foetidum (*L.*) *Cass.* (see p. 451)

Similar to *H. setosum* except for the key characters and the smaller, more numerous heads.

Locally common in disturbed places in the dry upland forest area. HC, HT, HM, HA, HK, KIT, KIS, NBI.

Agnew 5857; Gillett 16635.

15. Helichrysum kilimanjari *Oliv.*

A small wiry erect annual with oblanceolate or oblinear pale-backed leaves and reddish stems; heads in a terminal loose corymb, brownish-yellow on the outside.

Rather uncommon, found in disturbed, burnt places at the lower end of the alpine zone. HE, HC, HA, HK, KAJ.

Agnew 7205; Verdcourt 3498.

16. Helichrysum gloria-dei *Chiov.*

An erect branching shrub with white-woolly linear crowded leaves and large solitary pale golden-yellow heads.

Endemic on the Aberdares moorlands. HA.

Fox 32.

17. Helichrysum kirkii *Oliv.*

An erect perennial herb from a woody rootstock, bearing crowded, sessile, lanceolate-linear leaves and terminal clusters of bright yellow heads.

Very rare and only collected once from Thika district in wooded grassland. MAC.

Rayner 209.

18. Helichrysum newii *Oliv. & Hiern*

A small bushy shrub, grey-silver with matted hairs, bearing narrow-elliptic, sessile, crowded leaves and large solitary terminal white heads.

Uncommon plant found in alpine stony heathland. HE, HA, HK.

Lugard 386; Kokwaro 23.

19. Helichrysum brownei *S. Moore* (see p. 449)

A low bushy shrub, similar to *H. newii* but with short linear leaves each with a glabrous apical mucro and with solitary or clustered smaller heads at the stem apex.

Locally common, in high altitude shrubby vegetation on the drier sides of the Aberdares and Mt. Kenya above the heath zone. HA, HK.

Hanid 69; Salt 72.

20. Helichrysum amblyphyllum *Mattf.*

A stiff shrub up to 1 m tall with a loose cobwebby covering all over the linear leaves, including the apex; heads pink or white, in terminal rounded crowded corymbs.

Only found in the alpine zone of Mt. Elgon where it grows amongst shrubs on stony soils.

Strid 3549; Bickford 37.

21. Helichrysum ellipticifolium *Moeser*

A weak, semi-trailing shrub with a grey-green hairy covering; leaves elliptic; heads in clusters terminating leafy ascending branches, white or red.

Common in alpine grassland on the Mau, Aberdares, and Mt. Kenya. HM, HA, HK.

Glover 1060; Agnew 8137.

22. Helichrysum chionoides *Philipson*

An erect loose shrub to 2 m tall, with crowded linear to narrow-elliptic leaves; leaves green on the upper side, white-woolly below; heads white, in dense terminal corymbs.

Locally common, in bogs and wet streamsides in the Aberdares and Mt. Kenya alpine zones. HA, HK.

Coe 306; Hedberg 1889.

23. Helichrysum citrispinum *Del.* (see p. 453)

A dense low shrub, covered with greyish wool, often spiny, with small linear leaves often in small fascicles terminating short branches; heads sessile, few, in terminal groups, rather small, white.

Locally common in rocky scree and moraine soils of the middle and upper alpine zones. HE, HA, HK.

Strid 3560; Coe 253.

24. Helichrysum meyeri-johannis *Engl.*

A rhizomatous perennial, white-woolly (especially on the stems and undersides of the leaves) with erect stems from a leaf-rosette; stems with appressed leaves and bearing a dense terminal corymb of pink or white heads.

Fairly common in some damp alpine grasslands. HE, HC, HK.

Verdcourt 3512; Lind 5227.

25. Helichrysum formosissimum (*Sch. Bip.*) *A. Rich.*

A weak loose shrub to 1 m tall, with a loose cobwebby covering over the leaves and stem, or only glandular hairs; leaves oblong-lanceolate; heads pink or white, in dense or loose terminal corymbs.

The commonest of the conspicuous 'everlasting flowers' of the alpine zone, this species is often found in tussock and burnt grassland on all high mountain masses. Sometimes it may appear in forest roadsides in the bamboo zone.

HE, HC, HT, HM, HA, HK.

Strid 3550; Moreau 145.

26. Helichrysum guilelmi *Engl.*

A large weak shrub to 2 m tall, covered (loosely on the upper leaf surfaces) with cobwebby hairs, with lanceolate-oblong sessile leaves and large white or red heads in terminal loose corymbs.

Rare, in the upper forest and lower alpine zones. HA, HK.

Winmill 36.

27. Helichrysum nandense *S. Moore* (see p. 451)

A large loose shrub to 3 m tall (with support) with linear leaves which are auriculate at base; heads white or pink, smallish, in loose terminal corymbs.

This is a common plant at the upper forest edges and in streamside heathland of the lower alpine zones. HE, HC, HT, HM, HA, HK.

Kerfoot 5035; Strid 3198.

28. Helichrysum argyranthum *O. Hoffm.*

This species is very similar to *H. nandense* except for the key characters, and is much rarer. It is not confirmed for our area, but is common on Mt. Kilimanjaro, and recorded from the Kenya track to the top. The ecology of the species also appears to be similar to that of *H. nandense*.

Coe, August 1957.

27. GNAPHALIUM *L.*

Similar to *Helichrysum* in all respects and only retained here for convenience. All our species tend to have spathulate leaves.

1 Phyllaries with conspicuous opaque white scarious tips   1. *G. declinatum*
   Phyllaries brown or straw-coloured   2
2 Heads in a terminal spike-like raceme
                   2. *G. purpureum*
   Heads in a terminal globose or corymbose mass   3
3 Leaves woolly on both surfaces
                3. *G. luteo-album*
   Leaves rough, not woolly, on upper side
                4. *G. undulatum*

1. Gnaphalium declinatum *L. f.* (see p. 449)

A trailing annual or rhizomatous perennial with oblong-spathulate or linear, white-woolly, often crisped leaves and ascending stems bearing terminal corymbs of small white heads.

A common plant of disturbed places, with a very big ecological range, from the alpine zone to black cotton soil in the dry lowlands. HE, HC, HT, HM, HL, HA, HK, KIT, MUM, RV, NAN, MAC, NBI, KAJ.

Agnew 7237; Kokwaro 308.

2. Gnaphalium purpureum *L.* (see p. 446)

A small annual weed with erect stems and ascending branches from the base; leaves spathulate and covered with loose wool; heads straw-coloured, in axillary masses.

Apparently introduced, and found at medium altitudes in gardens and arable cultivation. KIT, NBI.

Bogdan 5591; Harmsen 6547.

3. Gnaphalium luteo-album *L.*

An erect white-woolly annual with spathulate-oblong leaves and terminal ± globose masses of straw-coloured or yellow heads.

Common, in disturbed places in highland grassland. HE, HC, HM, HA, HK, HN, KIT, RV, NBI.

Hanid and Kiniaruh 1019; Glover 800.

4. Gnaphalium undulatum *L.*

Similar to *G. luteo-album* except for the leaves (see key) and the white or pale straw-coloured heads in corymbs.

Less common than *G. luteo-album* in the same type of locality but not found as high as that species. HT, HA, RV.

Agnew and Humphry 5566; Agnew 7041.

28. ATHRIXIA *Ker.*

Erect herbs or shrubs with alternate linear leaves and numerous heads in terminal corymbs; involucre obconical, of very many rows of imbricate bracts; receptacle naked; outer florets (in ours) rayed, in one row, female; inner florets tubular, bisexual, numerous; achenes columnar; pappus of one row of long, alternating with short, bristles; achenes cylindrical, hairy.

Athrixia rosmarinifolia (*Walp.*) *Oliv. & Hiern* (see p. 446)

An erect, much branched (possibly annual) shrub with linear leaves and dense corymbs of purple-rayed, yellow-centred heads.

This most attractive plant is often cobwebby-hairy, and can be found in dry highland shrubland. HE, HC, HT, HM, HA, KIT.

Tweedie 67/312; Glover 3923.

29. INULA *L.*

Erect hairy herbs from a rosette of large simple basal leaves (in ours); stem leaves alternate, simple, ± sessile; involucre bell-shaped of many rows of entire phyllaries; receptacle naked; outer florets tubular, female, inner bisexual, or all bisexual; achenes cylindrical; pappus of one row of bristles, fused obscurely at base.

1 Florets pink or purple   1. *I. mannii*
   Florets yellow   2
2 Heads in one or two flat-topped corymbose groups, at least some on peduncles over 4 mm long   2. *I. decipiens*
   Heads in numerous spherical or flat-topped clusters, all subsessile or on short peduncles to 2·5 mm long   3. *I. glomerata*

1. Inula mannii (*Hook. f.*) *Oliv. & Hiern*

An erect-stemmed herb from a rosette of large obovate leaves, with dense terminal corymbs of small pubescent heads; phyllaries acute; achenes glabrous.

Rare plant found in wet montane forest edges. HE, HM.

Kerfoot 2699.

2. Inula decipiens E. A. Bruce (see p. 457)

Similar to *I. mannii* but with yellow florets, linear obtuse inner phyllaries, and achenes with a few hairs towards the apex.

Locally common, in wooded grassland. HE, HT, HM, KIT, KIS, MAC.

Agnew 7311; Lugard 293.

3. Inula glomerata Oliv. & Hiern

Similar to *I. decipiens* except for the given key characters.

Rare, in lowland wet forest in western Kenya. MUM.

Drummond and Hemsley 4762.

30. PEGOLETTIA *Cass.*

Annual herbs or shrubs with alternate entire leaves and loose terminal corymbs of yellow heads; involucre ± tubular, of few rows of narrow, acute bracts; receptacle naked; florets all tubular, bisexual; achenes columnar, grooved, pubescent; pappus in two series, the inner of long, plumose bristles, the outer of short, toothed scales.

Pegolettia senegalensis *Cass.*

An erect annual to 50 cm, with oblinear, sometimes remotely toothed, leaves and small yellow heads.

Uncommon, in dry country. NAR, RV, MAG, NAN, KAJ.

Harmsen 641; Glover and Samuel 3148.

31. GEIGERIA *Griessel.*

Herbs with opposite or alternate leaves and usually sessile, axillary yellow heads; involucre ovoid or bell-shaped of many rows of stiff bracts; receptacle bearing narrow hair-like scales; outer florets in one row, rayed, female; tubular florets many, bisexual; achenes angled, hairy; pappus of 2 rows, one of acute, the other of awned scales.

1 Stemless herb with linear woolly leaves
                                    1. *G. acaulis*
   Stemmed herb with glabrous leaves
                                    2. *G. alata*

1. Geigeria acaulis Oliv. & Hiern

An annual grey-woolly herb with a sessile cluster of yellow heads half hidden by the rosette of linear leaves.

Rare, in dry subdesert country after good rains. BAR, MAG.

Tweedie 67/142; Polhill and Greenway 452.

2. Geigeria alata (*Hochst. & Steud.*) *Oliv. & Hiern*

An erect glabrous annual with a winged stem and elliptic leaves, bearing axillary clusters of small yellow heads.

Rare, in subdesert country and only doubtfully recorded for our area at Isiolo. NAN.

Kirrika 39.

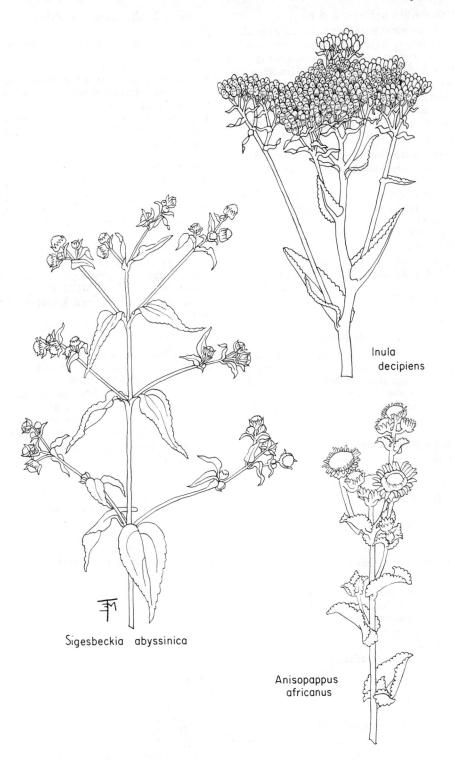

Inula
decipiens

Sigesbeckia abyssinica

Anisopappus
africanus

32. ANISOPAPPUS *Hook. & Arn.*

Annual or perennial herbs with alternate simple or pinnatisect leaves; heads yellow, in loose terminal dichasia or corymbs; involucre shallowly bell-shaped of 3-5 rows of stiff linear bracts; receptacle bearing scales; marginal florets in one row, rayed, female; central florets numerous, bisexual; achenes usually cylindrical, ribbed, often pubescent; pappus present or absent, of scales with or without a few bristles.

1 Annual herb with heads less than 11 mm. diameter including rays; pappus absent
　　　　　　　　　　　　　　1. *A. holstii*
　Perennial herbs with heads over 15 mm diameter including rays; pappus present or absent　　　　　　　　　　　　　2
2 Pappus absent　　　　　2. *A. oliveranus*
　Pappus present　　　　　　　　　　　3
3 Pappus of the ray florets of short scales and bristles at least twice as long as the scales
　　　　　　　　　　　　3. *A. africanus*
　Pappus of all florets of subequal short scales only　　　　　　4. *A. buchwaldii*

1. Anisopappus holstii (*O. Hoffm.*) *Wild*

A slender erect branching glandular annual with ovate dentate leaves and scattered terminal yellow heads; receptacular scales with two lateral teeth.

Locally common, in dry rocky grassland in the southern end of the Rift Valley. NAR, RV, MAG.
Glover 4165; Agnew 9582.

2. Anisopappus oliveranus *Wild*

Rhizomatous glandular perennial with ascending stems, broadly ovate crenate leaves, and long-pedunculate yellow heads; receptacular scales very narrow, almost bristle-like.

Uncommon, on rocky high ground and only recorded from Meru within our area. HK.
van Someren 1717.

3. Anisopappus africanus (*Hook. f.*) *Oliv. & Hiern* (see p. 457)

A rhizomatous glandular perennial with erect stems and broadly ovate crenate leaves which are often white-tomentose below; peduncles often shorter than the upper leaves, occasionally longer; heads yellow; receptacular scales simple, lanceolate-linear, minutely ciliate.

Locally common in dry upland areas. HE, HM, KIT, KIS, NBI, KAJ.
Hanid and Kiniaruh 815; Napier 165.

4. Anisopappus buchwaldii (*O. Hoffm.*) *Wild*

Similar to *A. africanus* except for the keyed characters and the long-pedunculate heads.

Rare, in dry upland basement complex hills. MAC.
Agnew and Hanid 8368; Copley in Bally 565.

33. LAGASCEA *Cav.*

Herbs with opposite or alternate leaves; heads 1-flowered, aggregated into a compound head subtended by upper stem leaves; involucre tubular of 4-6 fused bracts; floret solitary, bisexual; achenes smooth, slightly flattened, oblanceolate in outline; pappus absent.

Lagascea mollis *Cav.*

Much branched, tomentose, wiry small annual with ovate-elliptic leaves and compound heads of pale purple to white florets on long stalks; compound heads sessile in an involucre of broad suborbicular mucronate bracts.

Common around Kisumu town, but apparently hardly known elsewhere, this small annual resembles a *Scabiosa* on first sight. It is an introduction from Central America. MUM, KIS.
Agnew, Musumba, and Kiniaruh 8072; Boardman 6.

34. ACANTHOSPERMUM *Schrank*

Annual herbs with opposite leaves and subsessile heads in pairs at apex of branches; involucre poorly developed, of 2 rows of free bracts; receptacle scaly; outer florets 5-8 in one row, female, shortly rayed, completely enclosed in a glandular bract which becomes enlarged, hard and spiny in fruit; inner florets many or few, male, subtended by soft, open bracts; achenes smooth, enclosed within the enlarged bract; pappus absent.

1 Disseminules (enlarged bracts enclosing the achenes) covered with hooked spines which are all of ± equal length　　　2
　Disseminules with straight spines, of which the apical pair are 2-3 times larger than the others　　　　　　1. *A. hispidum*
2 Disseminules 4-5 in each head, each ± 10 mm long　　　　　　　2. *A. glabratum*
　Disseminules 7-9 in each head, 7-8 mm long
　　　　　　　　　　　　3. *A. australe*

1. Acanthospermum hispidum *DC.*

An erect, much-branched, tomentose and minutely glandular annual with rhomboid-elliptic leaves and subsessile heads of small yellow florets; disseminules boldly spiny with two apical diverging spines larger than the rest.

A common weed of cultivation in the hotter parts of our area, and introduced from America as are all other members of this genus. MUM, KIS, MAC, KAJ.
Hanid and Kiniaruh 515; Faden 67292.

2. Acanthospermum glabratum (*DC.*) *Wild*

A trailing annual, tomentose or glabrous on the stems, with ovate to sub-orbicular glabrous leaves and shortly-pedunculate heads of small yellow florets; disseminules bluntly ellipsoid, yellowish, with hooked spines and a wide apical mouth.

Uncommon, in disturbed grassland at medium altitudes, especially near Nairobi. HA, NBI.

Agnew and Ossent 7436; Verdcourt 3670A.

3. Acanthospermum australe (*L.*) *Kuntze*

A creeping glandular herb, very similar to *A. glabratum* but tomentose on all parts and with more and smaller disseminules which have a narrow apical mouth.

Uncommon, in disturbed grassland at medium altitudes, this plant is often found in Nairobi. HA, NBI.

Strid 2536.

35. AMBROSIA *L.*

Erect shrubs or herbs with alternate or opposite, pinnatisect, aromatic leaves; heads unisexual, in racemes or spikes; male heads with a cup-shaped involucre in one row with 3–6 yellow male florets subtended by narrow glandular bracts; female heads with one row of bracts enclosing 2 florets, each without corolla and enclosed in a bract which enlarges with the fruit to yield a disseminule with 5 small radial protuberances or spines; achenes smooth, obovate in outline; pappus absent.

Ambrosia maritima *L.*

An erect branched shrub to 1·5 m tall bearing female capitula along the main stem and yellow male terminal spikes; leaves twice pinnatifid, ovate in outline.

Uncommon, in cultivated land in western Kenya; this plant is used medicinally and may not be truly indigenous. MUM, KIS.

Agnew and Musumba 8570; Napier 2955.

36. XANTHIUM *L.*

Erect annual herbs with alternate leaves and unisexual monoecious heads; male heads with hemispherical involucre of 1 row of free bracts and a scaly receptacle bearing numerous tubular florets; female heads with 2 florets completely enclosed by the two fused bracts which become woody and spiny in fruit; achenes smooth; pappus absent.

Xanthium pungens *Wallroth*

An erect branching woody annual with shallowly palmately lobed, suborbicular, roughly scabrid leaves; disseminules subsessile in groups at the nodes, ovoid, minutely pubescent, covered with hooked spines and with two apical hooked horns.

Uncommon, as a weed of river beds and cultivation in warmer parts of our region. MUM, KIS, RV, MAC, NBI.

Tweedie 68/56; Mwangangi 37.

37. SIGESBECKIA *L.*

Erect herbs with opposite simple leaves and heads solitary or in loose terminal corymbs; involucre of 1–2 rows of free bracts; receptacle with scales subtending and enclosing the florets; outer florets in one row, very shortly rayed, female; inner florets numerous, bisexual; achenes smooth, ± obconical, sometimes curved; pappus absent.

1   Leaves narrowing gradually to the petiole; involucral bracts in two series, the outer linear-spathulate, much longer than the florets   1. *S. orientalis*

     Leaves truncate at base; outer involucral bracts equal to the inner ones, and both much shorter than the florets

                                          2. *S. abyssinica*

1. Sigesbeckia orientalis *L.*

An erect, woody, glandular-pubescent, aromatic annual herb, with rhombic to elliptic leaves and a lax panicle of yellow heads.

Uncommon, in disturbed places in dry woodland country. HK, KIS, MAC, NBI.

Agnew 8245; Napier 2420.

2. Sigesbeckia abyssinica (*Sch. Bip.*) *Oliv. & Hiern* (see p. 457)

An erect, often tall, annual herb, branched above, with ovate-lanceolate leaves and yellow heads in a loose terminal panicle.

Locally common, along disturbed streamsides from 5000–8000 ft. HE, HT, HM, HA, HK, HN.

Agnew, Hanid, and Kiniaruh 7921; Verdcourt 3988.

38. ENYDRA *Lour.*

Trailing herbs with opposite leaves and axillary sessile heads; involucral bracts in ± 1 row, of hardly modified leafy bracts; receptacle conical, covered with scales which sheathe the florets; outer florets in one row, inconspicuously rayed, female; inner florets bisexual; achenes oblong, angled; pappus absent.

Enydra fluctuans *Lour.*

A trailing marsh plant with sessile clasping oblong leaves and axillary subterminal sessile heads of whitish flowers.

Uncommon, in marshes in warmer districts. MUM, KAJ.

Agnew, Musumba, and Kiniaruh 7997; Verdcourt 3285.

39. ECLIPTA *L.*

Trailing or erect herbs with opposite leaves and ±
solitary pedunculate heads; involucre hemispherical, of one row of bracts; receptacle bearing
folded scales; outer florets inconspicuously rayed,
in one row, female; inner florets bisexual; achenes
columnar, angled, tubercled; pappus absent or of
two bristles.

Eclipta alba (*L.*) *Hassk.*

A low trailing tomentose annual with sessile elliptic leaves and shortly pedunculate heads of white
flowers.

Locally common, along the shores of Lake
Victoria. MUM, KIS, NAR, MAG.

Hanid and Kiniaruh 730; Glover 3497.

40. SCLEROCARPUS *Jacq.*

Erect herbs with opposite leaves and loose terminal corymbs of yellow heads; involucre of a few
leafy bracts; receptacle bearing conspicuous scales
which enclose the florets and become hardened in
fruit; florets few, all tubular, bisexual; achene
enclosed by the hardened bract; pappus absent.

Sclerocarpus africanus *Jacq.*

An erect scabrid annual with elliptic leaves and
small heads of yellow flowers; disseminule
narrowed below, rugose on the back and asymmetrically beaked above.

Uncommon, in disturbed bushland in dry
Commiphora country. MAG, EMB, NAN, MAC.

Lind and Agnew 5670; Adamson 611.

41. BLAINVILLEA *Cass.*

Erect herbs with opposite leaves and terminal
corymbs or cymes of heads; involucre ± tubular, of
one row of herbaceous bracts; receptacle scaly, the
scales folded around the florets; outer florets in
one row, inconspicuously ligulate, female; inner
florets few, bisexual; achenes columnar, sharply
3-angled; pappus of 2-3 stiff bristles.

Blainvillea rhomboidea *Cass.*

An erect, scabrid or pubescent annual (often large)
with rhomboid leaves and ± hemispherical heads in
terminal dichotomous cymes.

Locally common in disturbed areas in dry
country. MAG, KAJ.

Agnew 9888; Greenway 9022.

42. ASPILIA *Thouars*

Rough scabrid herbs or shrubs with opposite,
mostly 3-nerved leaves and solitary heads; involucre in 1-2 rows of herbaceous bracts, often
exceeding the florets; receptacle scaly; outer
florets in one row, conspicuously rayed, female or
neuter; inner florets numerous, bisexual, tubular;
achenes ± oblanceolate in outline, with 2 ridges,
pubescent; pappus of a cup of small scales, with or
without 2-3 erect bristles.

1   Flowers maroon to black-purple
                                  1. *A. kotschyi*
    Flowers yellow   2
2   Receptacular bracts usually ± obtuse at apex;
      pappus often with 2-3 bristles and always
      with a ring of acuminate scales
                                  2. *A. pluriseta*
    Receptacular bracts linear, acuminate at
      apex; pappus with no bristles, composed of
      truncate scales   3. *A. mossambicensis*

1. Aspilia kotschyi (*Sch. Bip.*) *Oliv.* (see p. 461)

An annual or weak perennial, scabrid-tomentose
herb with lanceolate-linear leaves and shortly
pedunculate heads of deep black-purple or maroon
flowers.

Locally common, in west Kenya in wooded
grassland. HE, HT, KIT, MUM, KIS, BAR.

Mendes 89; Symes 144.

2. Aspilia pluriseta *Schweinf.* (see p. 461)

A woody herb or shrub, usually much-branched,
with scabrid elliptic-lanceolate to ovate leaves and
yellow heads in loose terminal cymes or solitary.

A variable plant in habit which grows to a large
size when unburnt and may even scramble over
bushes.

Abundant, in black-cotton and dry bushed
grassland, mostly in eastern Kenya. HE, HA, RV,
MAG, NAN, MAC, NBI, KAJ.

Harmsen 64/21; Williams 167.

3. Aspilia mossambicensis (*Oliv.*) *Wild* (see p. 461)

Similar to *A. pluriseta* in all respects except in the
key characters and slightly larger heads, this plant
is just as abundant and shows little ecological
differentiation from the former but is found a
little more commonly in west Kenya. HE, HC,
KIT, MUM, KIS, MAC.

Agnew and Musumba 8524; Glover, Gwynne,
and Samuel 1707.

43. TITHONIA *Juss.*

Shrubs with opposite or alternate lobed leaves and
big solitary heads; involucre saucer-shaped, of
many rows of broad bracts; receptacle with scales;
outer florets neuter, with a well-developed ray;
inner florets many, tubular, bisexual; achene
smooth, pubescent, half enclosed by the 2-keeled
receptacle scales; pappus a short ciliate scaly
crown, with two longer scales above the two blunt
ridges on the achene.

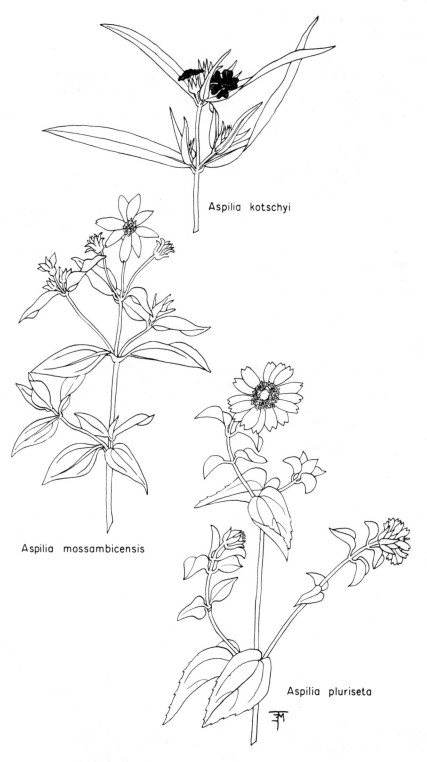

Aspilia kotschyi

Aspilia mossambicensis

Aspilia pluriseta

Tithonia diversifolia (*Hemsl.*) *Gray*

A branched soft shrub with simple to 5-lobed, opposite or alternate leaves; peduncle expanded below the large head of orange-yellow florets.

Introduced from Central America, this plant is common in west Kenya and on the western slopes of the Aberdares, as a hedgerow and waste-ground plant. HA, KIT, MUM, KIS, NBI.

Hanid and Kiniaruh 615; Trapnell 2194.

44. MELANTHERA *Rohr*

Trailing or erect herbs or shrubs with the aspect of *Aspilia* and similar to that genus but with the receptacular bracts flat, not keeled, with many longitudinal nerves; achenes glabrous below, naked above; pappus absent or of 1-15 very stiff and caducous bristles.

1 Trailing scrambling shrub; ligulate florets with stigma; pappus of 8-15 bristles
                                    1. *M. scandens*
   Erect herb from woody rootstock; ligulate florets without style and stigma; pappus absent or of 1-2 bristles   2. *M. albinervia*

1. Melanthera scandens (*Schumach. & Thonn.*) *Roberty* (see p. 463)

A trailing shrub, often 2-3 m tall, with ovate-lanceolate sometimes lobed leaves and terminal sprays of conspicuous yellow heads.

Common (but only occasionally flowering) in the dry upland forest area. HM, HA, MUM, KIS, NAR, MAC, NBI.

Kokwaro 105; Agnew and Faden 9986.

2. Melanthera albinervia *O. Hoffm.*

An erect herb to 1 m, with ovate, regularly serrate leaves which are rounded at base, not serrate as in *M. scandens*; heads large, yellow, often solitary.

Found in wooded grassland in the western part of our area. HE, HC, KIT.

Tweedie 68/35; Napier 4953.

45. SPILANTHES *L.*

Trailing herbs with simple opposite leaves and solitary heads; involucre of broad spreading bracts in 1-2 rows, the outer as long as or longer than the inner; receptacle usually markedly conical, with scales around the florets; outer florets in one row, with inconspicuous rays, or absent; inner florets numerous, tubular, bisexual; achenes compressed, lens-shaped; pappus absent or of 2-3 bristles.

1 Florets white or pale purple; involucral bracts over half as long as head   1. *S. oleracea*
   Florets orange or yellow; involucral bracts less than half as long as head
                                    2. *S. mauritiana*

1. Spilanthes oleracea *L.*

A trailing herb with shortly petiolate, broad-elliptic leaves, and terminal heads of pale inconspicuous florets.

Uncommon, in lakeside marshes in western Kenya. This plant is an introduction from Central America. MUM, KIS.

Agnew, Musumba, and Kiniaruh 7996.

2. Spilanthes mauritiana (*Pers.*) *DC.* (see p. 463)

A trailing herb with ovate dentate leaves and small heads of rather bright orange-yellow flowers, with noticeable ray florets.

Common, in riverside grassland and lawns in the upland districts of Kenya. HE, HC, HA, HN, KIT, KIS, NBI.

Hanid and Kiniaruh 590; Bally 1008.

46. GUIZOTIA *Cass.*

Perennial or annual herbs with opposite, sessile, often scabrid leaves; heads solitary or in loose terminal cymes; involucral bracts free to the base, in ± one row, herbaceous; receptacle bearing oblong, 3-5-nerved, persistent scales; outer florets in one row, female, with a conspicuous 3-lobed ligule; inner florets bisexual, numerous; achenes smooth, glabrous, columnar, truncate above, ± 4 angled; pappus absent.

1 Plant creeping; heads solitary   1. *G. reptans*
   Plant erect; heads in loose cymes   2
2 Plant perennial, usually scabrid   2. *G. scabra*
   Plant annual, never scabrid   3. *G. abyssinica*

1. Guizotia reptans *Hutch.*

A creeping herb with elliptic, obscurely dentate leaves and shortly pedunculate, bright yellow heads.

Found in disturbed ground and short grass in the bamboo and heath zones. HE, HM, HA, HK.

Lind, Agnew, and Woodley 5750; Glover 1465.

2. Guizotia scabra (*Vis.*) *Chiov.* (see p. 463)

An erect, usually scabrid herb from a wiry perennial rootstock, bearing oblong, dentate or entire leaves and many yellow heads in a loose terminal corymb.

Common in upland grassland except around Nairobi. This plant is very variable and may appear to grow as an annual, so that its separation from the next species may be difficult. HE, HC, HT, HA, HK, KIT, MUM, KIS, RV, NAN.

Lind, Harris, and Agnew 5098; Nattrass 1308.

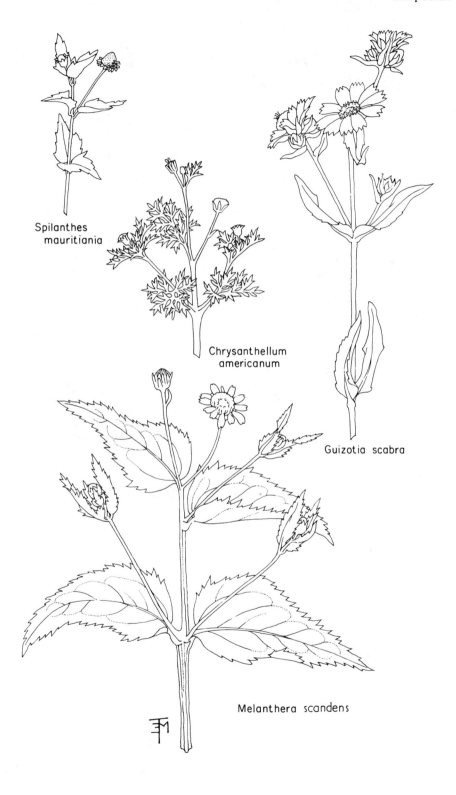

Spilanthes
mauritiania

Chrysanthellum
americanum

Guizotia scabra

Melanthera scandens

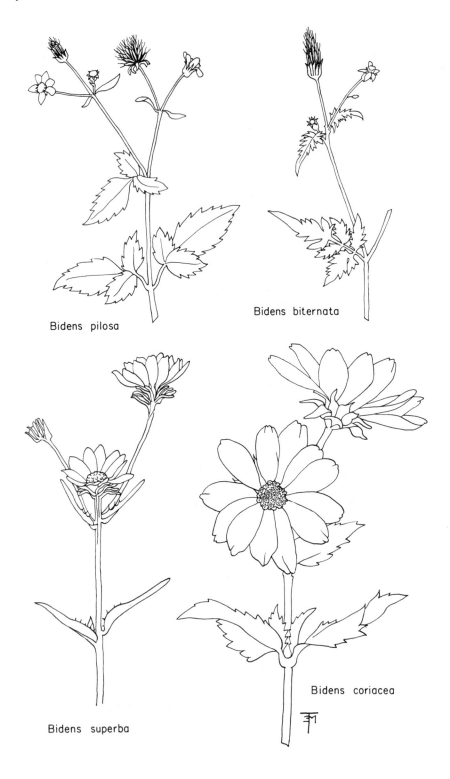

Bidens pilosa

Bidens biternata

Bidens superba

Bidens coriacea

3. Guizotia abyssinica *Cass.*

Similar to *G. scabra* but an annual with smaller heads.

This is grown as an oil-seed crop plant in Ethiopia, from where it has occasionally been introduced. KIT.

Bogdan 5584.

47. CHRYSANTHELLUM *Rich.*

Annual herbs with alternate, much divided leaves and pedunculate yellow heads; involucre ± tubular in flower, of 1–2 rows of equal bracts; receptacle scaly, the scales flat, not enclosing the florets; outer florets in one row, ligulate, inconspicuously rayed, with the tube very short, female; inner florets tubular, bisexual, with a long tapering papillose stigma; achenes ± flat, with corky margins, oblong in outline; pappus reduced to 2 minute teeth.

Chrysanthellum americanum (*L.*) *Vatke* (see p. 463)

A small annual herb with ascending or erect branches and suborbicular leaves divided into linear segments.

Common along roadsides in the warmer country in the west of our area, especially by Lake Victoria. MUM, KIS.

Hanid and Kiniaruh 665; Bradley 27.

48. BIDENS *L.*

Erect herbs or shrubs with opposite, divided, lobed or simple leaves; heads terminal, solitary or corymbose, usually yellow, rarely white, pink or purple; involucre bell-shaped or tubular, the bracts in ± two rows all shortly fused basally, the outer herbaceous, the inner often scarious; receptacle bearing entire scales; outer florets usually neuter, ligulate; inner florets bisexual, tubular, glabrous above the achene; achene winged or transversely flattened or columnar, 4-angled, glabrous or scabrous; pappus absent or of a crown of short hairs and 1–5 long bristles.

1 Leaves subsessile, with an enlarged basal pair of diverging leaflets at least three-quarters as long as entire leaf, thus appearing whorled; pappus entirely absent; achenes glabrous **2**

Leaves usually petiolate, if subsessile then the outline of the leaf ovate, with the basal pair of leaflets not half as long as the entire leaf, never appearing whorled; pappus of bristles (sometimes rather short) always present; achenes bristly at apex **3**

2 Heads on long peduncles, greatly overtopping the leaves, solitary or 1–3 together
1. B. elgonensis

Heads on shorter peduncles, overtopped by or at most equalling the uppermost leaves, usually more than 3 at the apex of each stem *2. B. morotonensis*

3 Pappus with 2 or more erect bristles bearing retrorse barbs which are strongly adherent to clothing **4**

Pappus with 2 awns with erect barbs or without barbs but in any case not adherent to clothing **9**

4 Achenes becoming longer than the involucre; the innermost achenes narrowed above, black in colour **5**

Achenes never longer than the involucre, never narrowed above, usually brownish in colour **6**

5 Lower leaves with 3 (rarely 5) leaflets; rays white; inner achenes up to 1·5 times as long as involucre *3. B. pilosa*

Lower leaves pinnate with 5–7 leaflets; rays yellow; inner achenes twice as long as involucre *4. B. biternata*

6 Perennial shrub; heads corymbose
5. B. incumbens

Annual or perennial; heads solitary **7**

7 Annual *6. B. schimperi*

Perennial **8**

8 Leaf lobes linear to lanceolate; achenes with tuberculate hairs when mature
7. B. lineata

Leaf lobes ovate to suborbicular; achenes pubescent but not tuberculate
8. B. sp. A

9 Bristles of pappus glabrous or rarely with 1–2 weak downward-pointing hairs **13**

Bristles of pappus pubescent with upward-pointing hairs **10**

10 Leaves with a long hair at apex of each lobe and serration **12**

Leaves with no long hair at apex of each lobe and serration **11**

11 Perennials; leaves glabrous, divided into capillary to linear segments *9. B. kirkii*

Annuals or weak perennials; leaves ± pubescent, divided into lanceolate to oblong segments *15. B. grantii*

12 Lower leaves simple, attenuate at base
10. B. superba

Lower leaves pinnatisect, ovate in outline with a truncate base *11. B. rueppellii*

13 Leaf-segments linear; heads solitary
12. B. ugandensis

Leaf segments broader; heads in corymbs **14**

14 Leaves sessile, simple, glabrous
13. B. coriacea

Leaves petiolate, pinnatisect, if entire then strongly dentate and hairy **15**

15   Involucre more than 1 cm diameter during
      flowering   14. *B. kilimandscharica*
      Involucre less than 1 cm diameter during
      flowering   15. *B. grantii*

1. Bidens elgonensis (*Sherff*) Agnew *nov. comb.*
(*Coreopsis elgonensis* Sherff in Bot. Gaz. **80**, 374
(1925))

A weak shrub with long straggling branches bearing trifoliolate leaves with cuneate-dentate leaflets,
and with yellow terminal solitary heads.

Uncommon, in the forest edge and heath zone
at the upper levels of Mt. Elgon only. HE.

Tweedie 2338; Lugard 32/a.

2. Bidens morotonensis (*Sherff*) Agnew *nov.
comb.* (*Coreopsis morotonensis* Sherff in Amer. J.
Bot. **34**, 157 (1947))

An erect shrub with the lateral leaflets of the
trifoliolate leaves oblanceolate-cuneate and with
loose terminal corymbs of yellow flowers.

Like other groups of species in this genus, it is
not clear quite how distinct this species is from *B.
elgonensis*, for every isolated mountain mass in
northern Kenya seems to have its own form. This
species is found on Cherangani and Sekerr. HC.

Tweedie 68/342; Agnew, Kibe, and Mathenge
10540.

3. Bidens pilosa *L.* (see p. 464)

An erect annual, often branching above, with
pinnate mostly trifoliolate leaves and white-rayed
or rayless flowers.

The common 'black-jack' weed of gardens and
disturbed places all over the highland area of
Kenya. HE, HC, HT, HM, HA, KIT, MUM, KIS,
NAR, RV, EMB, MAC, NBI, KAJ.

Harmsen 6516; Faden 67187.

4. Bidens biternata *(Lour.) Merr.* (see p. 464)

Very similar to *B. pilosa*, but more hairy, and with
yellow rays and longer achenes.

Fairly common in western Kenya as a weed of
disturbed places, rare in eastern districts. HE, HC,
KIT, NAR, BAR, RV, MAC, NBI.

Nattrass 556; Tweedie 67/278.

5. Bidens incumbens *Sherff*

A shrub with long-petiolate, deeply twice pinnatisect leaves which are ovate in outline and have
oblong segments; heads bright yellow, in large
terminal corymbs.

Uncommon, in dry country, this plant may
occasionally flower in its first year. RV, MAC.

Glover 4527.

6. Bidens schimperi *Sch. Bip.*

An erect or straggling annual with pinnatifid leaves
with usually oblong obtuse segments; heads
yellow, terminal in loose dichasia.

Locally common, in dry grassland. HM, HL,
MAG, MAC, NBI, KAJ.

Strid 2732; Verdcourt 3261.

7. Bidens lineata *Sherff* (*B. palustris* Sherff; *B.
cinereoides* Sherff; *B. angustata* Sherff)

A straggling woody perennial, very similar to *B.
schimperi* but with linear to oblong-ovate leaf
segments and a tendency towards solitary heads.

This species and *B. schimperi* form a complex
series which is difficult to evaluate. I have taken
the view that there is only one, widespread and
variable, perennial species, found in bushed grassland. HT, HA, KIT, MAG, NAN, MAC, NBI, KAJ.

Agnew 9406; Williams 247.

8. Bidens *sp.* **A.**

A weak straggling shrub with spreading branches
and deeply or shallowly 3-lobed leaves; leaf lobes
suborbicular; heads solitary, orange-yellow.

This species has been found recently along the
new road alignment at Kibwezi. KAJ.

Agnew 10698.

9. Bidens kirkii (*Oliv. & Hiern*) *Sherff*

An erect glabrescent perennial from a woody
rootstock, bearing leaves divided into linear or
filamentous segments, and loose terminal corymbs
of yellow heads.

Common in higher altitude grasslands from
5000–10 000 ft especially on thin soils. HC, HT,
HM, HA, HK, KIT, RV, MAC.

Coe 453; Verdcourt 1044.

10. Bidens superba *Sherff* (see p. 464)

An erect, sparsely branched perennial from a
woody rootstock, with simple serrate leaves, or
occasionally the uppermost leaves with two short
basal lobes; heads yellow, in a loose terminal
dichasium.

Uncommon, in wooded grassland in western
Kenya. HE, HC, HT, KIT, MUM.

Tweedie 67/309.

11. Bidens rueppellii (*Sch. Bip.*) *Sherff* (*B.
rueppellioides* Sherff)

Similar to the last species except for the much-
divided leaves. Some intermediates between the
two species exist and it may be that they should
be combined in future.

Uncommon, in wooded grassland further south
than *B. superba*. HT, HA, RV.

Strid 3111; Kerfoot 2988.

12. Bidens ugandensis *Sherff* (see p. 468)

Perennial with ascending, sparsely branched stems from a woody rootstock; leaves pinnate, leaflets linear; heads solitary, yellow.

Uncommon, in short burnt grassland in the west of Kenya. KIT.

Tweedie 66/34; Bogdan 3694.

13. Bidens coriacea (*O. Hoffm.*) *Sherff* (see p. 464)

Perennial with erect, sparsely-branched stems bearing simple, glabrescent, serrate leaves and a terminal corymb of large yellow heads.

Uncommon, in wooded grassland in western Kenya, especially amongst rocks. HE, KIT, MUM, KIS.

Agnew, Kibe, and Mathenge 10583; Steel in EAH 3387.

14. Bidens kilimandscharica (*O. Hoffm.*) *Sherff* (*B. napierae* Sherff; *B. insignis* Sherff; *B. meruensis* Sherff; *B. ukambensis* Sherff)

An erect, short-lived perennial shrub, glabrous or hairy, much-branched above; leaves once or twice pinnatisect, rarely ± simple, with ovate, serrate lobes; heads in loose terminal dichasia.

A very variable plant (as shown by the list of synonyms), which can flower in its first year. Simple-leaved plants may be mistaken for *B. coriacea* except that the habit of the two species is rather different and *B. coriacea* has glabrescent leaves. It is found in upland forest edges, especially in drier districts and on stony soils. HC, HT, HM, HA, HK, RV, MAC.

Lind, Harris, and Agnew 5097; Verdcourt 1615.

15. Bidens grantii (*Oliv.*) *Sherff*

An erect annual or short-lived perennial with twice pinnatisect leaves terminating in lanceolate to oblong segments; heads yellow, in loose terminal dichasia.

Rare in Kenya, in highland grasslands and only found twice, on the Ngong Hills and near Molo. This species is rather variable, for the pappus bristles may be present and long or virtually absent. HT, HA.

Ryan 1064.

49. TRIDAX *L.*

Herbs with opposite dentate leaves and solitary terminal capitula; involucral bracts numerous, ± all the same length, free; receptacle scaly; outer florets rayed, female; inner florets tubular, bisexual; achenes hairy with a pappus of about 20 plumose hairs.

Tridax procumbens *L.* (see p. 468)

A trailing plant with ascending flowering stems and ovate dentate leaves; rays short, white; tubular florets yellow.

An abundant weed in roadsides and waste places at altitudes below 7000 ft. This plant is an introduction from Central America. MUM, KIS, MAG, EMB, NBI.

Hanid and Kiniaruh 657; Faden 67188.

50. GALINSOGA *Ruiz & Pav.*

Erect herbs with opposite, crenate or entire leaves and heads mostly in loose terminal corymbs; involucre bell-shaped, of 1 row of ovate bracts; outer florets female, usually 5, shortly rayed; inner florets tubular, bisexual; achenes ± cylindrical, those of the ray florets with no pappus, those of the bisexual florets with a pappus of *c.* 20 ciliate scales.

1   Receptacular scales divided into 3 teeth, the two outer ending much lower than the central one; pappus scales all similar in length, obtuse   1. *G. parviflora*
     Receptacular scales entire; pappus scales differing in length, at least some elongated into a long point   2. *G. ciliata*

1. Galinsoga parviflora *Cav.* (see p. 468)

A soft erect annual with ± glabrous or spreading-hairy stems and leaves and small groups of terminal, minutely white-rayed heads.

A common weed of cultivated land in the moist uplands. HE, HC, HT, HM, HA, HK, HN, KIT, MUM, KIS, NAR, RV, EMB, MAC, NBI, KAJ.

Hanid 218; Kerfoot 4606.

2. Galinsoga ciliata (*Rafn.*) *Blake*

Similar to *G. parviflora* except for the key characters and also more hairy and more densely glandular-hairy below the rather smaller heads.

Apparently a rare and recently introduced weed of disturbed places in the highlands. HE, HA, KIT, NBI.

van Someren 162; Agnew, Kibe, and Zamierowski 10148.

51. FLAVERIA *Juss.*

Annual or perennial herbs with opposite, entire or dentate leaves and sessile terminal clusters of minute yellow heads; heads small, 2-4-flowered, 1 female and the rest bisexual subtended by a minute cylindrical involucre of 3-4 bracts in one row; female floret with a small erect or spreading ray; achenes glabrous, ± cylindrical, minutely ribbed; pappus none.

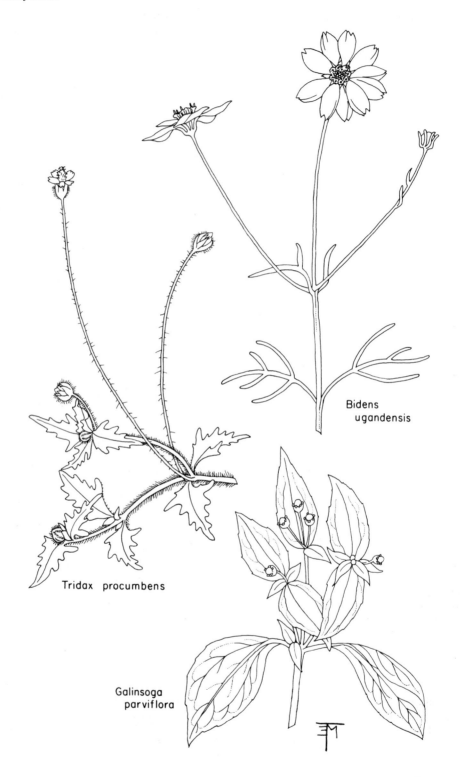

Bidens
ugandensis

Tridax procumbens

Galinsoga
parviflora

Flaveria australasica *Hook.*

An erect, often robust annual with divergent branches and elliptical, dentate, 3-nerved leaves; heads yellow, sessile in clusters in the axils of a false involucre of terminal leaves.

Uncommon, in cultivated land in the warmer parts of Kenya. Introduced from subtropical America. MUM, KIS, MAC.

Agnew 7322; Tweedie 2358.

52. SCHKUHRIA *Roth.*

Erect annual glabrous herbs with alternate or opposite, usually finely dissected leaves; heads small; involucre narrowly bell-shaped, of 1 row of free bracts; receptacle naked; florets all bisexual; achenes hairy, 4-angled; pappus of 8 scales, 4 of them shortly awned.

Schkuhria pinnata *(Lam.) O. Ktze.*

A small erect annual with capillary leaf segments, forming a 'bush-shape' covered with small yellow obconical heads.

Locally abundant in cultivation at medium altitudes; introduced from South America. HA, KIT, MUM, KIS, MAC, NBI.

Agnew 9172; Kokwaro 115.

53. TAGETES *L.*

Erect herbs with pinnate or pinnatisect opposite leaves with a strong, almost foetid odour when crushed; heads 3–5-flowered; involucre campanulate or cylindrical of fused bracts; flowers all tubular, bisexual or with 1–2 small, female, shortly rayed florets; receptacle naked; achenes glabrous, cylindrical; pappus of 4–5 scales.

Tagetes minuta *L.*

An erect strong-smelling annual, often very robust but variable in habit, with pinnate leaves with elliptic, serrate leaflets; heads creamy-yellow, in terminal corymbs.

An abundant and troublesome weed in upland arable farming which has been introduced from tropical America. HE, HC, HT, HA, HK, KIT, NAR, RV, NBI.

Hanid and Kiniaruh 975; Leippert 5006.

54. ANTHEMIS *L.*

Annual or perennial, often prostrate herb with alternate, pinnatisect scented leaves and solitary terminal heads with white rays; involucre saucer-shaped, of many rows of numerous bracts; receptacle (at least towards the centre) scaly; outer florets female, with a white, spreading ray; inner florets tubular, bisexual; achenes obconical or ± cylindrical, 4-angled and ribbed; pappus absent.

Anthemis tigrensis *A. Rich.*

An annual or short-lived perennial with spreading branches and pubescent, twice pinnatisect leaves; leaves oblong in outline, the ultimate segments minute; involucral bracts black-edged.

Fairly common along roadsides and in disturbed places at the upper forest limits and in the lower alpine zone. HE, HM, HA, HK.

Coe 495; Glover, Gwynne, and Samuel 1460.

55. ACHILLEA *L.*

Perennial herbs with alternate, usually pinnate leaves and terminal corymbs of heads, always scented when crushed; involucre bell-shaped, or cylindrical of many rows of bracts; receptacle with narrow scales; outer florets female, yellow or white, rayed; inner florets tubular, bisexual; achenes strongly compressed, truncate above; pappus absent.

Achillea millefolium *L.*

An erect herb with twice pinnate leaves, and small white rayed, yellow-centred heads in a dense terminal corymb.

Once recorded from Mt. Elgon, this plant is possibly introduced. HE.

Jack 163.

56. COTULA *L.*

Annual or perennial aromatic herbs with opposite or alternate, usually pinnate leaves and terminal heads of inconspicuous flowers; involucre saucer-shaped, of many rows of ovate bracts; receptacle often conical, naked; outer florets in 1 row, female, with practically no corolla, sometimes pedicellate; inner florets tubular, bisexual; achenes compressed, ± winged; pappus absent.

1   Leaves opposite; heads greatly overtopped by leaves   1. *C. cryptocephala*
    Leaves alternate; heads exceeding or equalling the leaves   2
2   Peduncles many times longer than leaves; pedicels of marginal florets longer than those of central florets   2. *C. abyssinica*
    Peduncles at most 1·5 times the leaf-length; pedicels of marginal florets not longer than those of central florets
                           3. *C. anthemoides*

1. Cotula cryptocephala *A. Rich.*

A small perennial decumbent herb with the leaves opposite and once to twice pinnatisect into linear segments; heads almost sessile, terminal, green.

Rare, in the alpine zone of Mt. Elgon in short grass along paths. HE.

Hedberg 996.

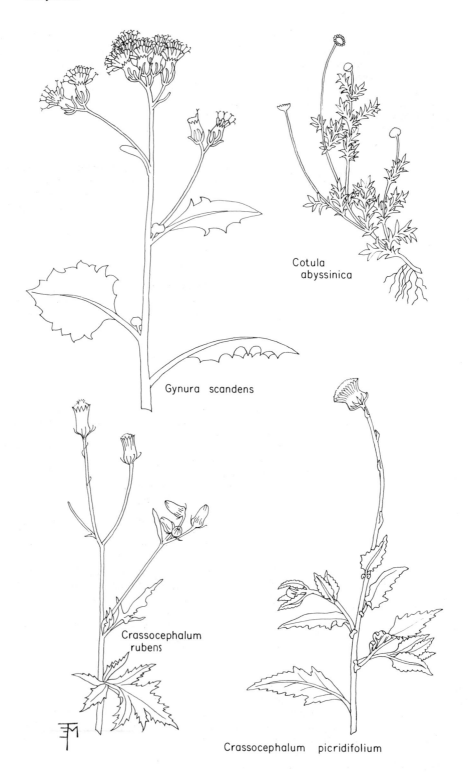

Gynura scandens

Cotula
abyssinica

Crassocephalum
rubens

Crassocephalum picridifolium

2. Cotula abyssinica *A. Rich.* (see p. 470)

Similar to *C. cryptocephala* but with smaller, alternate leaves and long-pedunculate heads of whitish florets; outer florets with elongated pedicels.

Fairly common in short alpine grassland and along pathsides in the bamboo zone. HE, HC, HM, HA, HK.

Coe 466; Symes 643.

3. Cotula anthemoides *L.*

A low annual herb from a central taproot and with spreading branches; leaves alternate, pinnatisect into linear-oblong segments; heads shortly pedunculate, hardly overtopping the leaves, greenish.

A weed of disturbed and trodden ground in the moist uplands, especially near Nairobi. HM, HA, MAC, NBI.

Agnew and Hodges 9661; Bogdan 4754.

57. ARTEMISIA *L.*

Herbs or shrubs with aromatic, pinnatisect, alternate leaves and small heads usually in panicles; involucre cylindrical or globular, of many rows of ovate bracts; receptacle flat, naked; outer florets tubular, female or absent; inner florets tubular, bisexual; achenes cylindrical or a little compressed, not ribbed; pappus absent.

Artemisia afra *Willd.*

An erect loose shrub to 2 m, with grey-green aromatic foliage of twice pinnate leaves; leaves ± ovate in outline, the ultimate segments linear; heads in an elongated, racemose panicle, yellow, each with very few outer female florets.

Common in dry shrubby montane grassland. HE, HC, HT, HA, HK, KIT, RV, MAC, KAJ.

Agnew, Hanid, and Kiniaruh 7839; Kerfoot 3501.

58. MIKANIOPSIS *M.-R.*

Similar to *Senecio*, but petiolar climbers with cordate simple leaves and paniculate inflorescences of rayless heads; outer florets female, in one row; achenes glabrous.

1 Leaves white-woolly below, green above
                                    1. *M. clematoides*
  Leaves glabrescent below and above
                                    2. *M. usambarensis*

1. Mikaniopsis clematoides (*A. Rich.*) *M.-R.*

A strong woody climber with ovate dentate leaves and panicles of clusters of shortly pedunculate heads; florets cream to white.

A common climber of montane rain forest, but curiously has been found flowering only on the Aberdares and Mt. Elgon. HE, HC, HM, HA, HK.

Polhill 240; Mwangangi 340.

2. Mikaniopsis usambarensis (*Muschl.*) *M.-R.*

Similar to *M. clematoides* but glabrescent; florets orange-yellow.

This rare climber has only been recorded from the wet forests around Kericho. HM.

Kerfoot 2978.

59. GYNURA *Cass.*

Similar to *Senecio* except for the absence of ray florets and the presence of a long pubescent tip to the style which is equal to or longer than the free glabrous part of the stigmas.

1 Climbers   1. *G. scandens*
  Erect herbs   2
2 Leaves simple but dentate
                                    2. *G. amplexicaulis*
  Leaves pinnatifid   3
3 Stems erect from a buried tuber; phyllaries
    pubescent   3. *G. miniata*
  Stems ascending, without a basal tuber;
    phyllaries glabrous   4. *G. valeriana*

1. Gynura scandens *O. Hoffm.* (see p. 470)

A glandular-pubescent, weak scrambler with auriculate, ovate, fleshy, serrate leaves and terminal corymbs of orange-yellow heads.

Locally common, in wetter situations within the drier zones. HE, HT, HM, HA, HK, KIT, NAR, RV.

Strid 2947; Polhill 80.

2. Gynura amplexicaulis *Oliv.*

An erect-stemmed pubescent herb from a creeping rootstock, with oblanceolate leaves and a few orange heads in a long-pedunculate terminal corymb.

Locally common, in disturbed places in western Kenya. HE, KIT, KIS.

Lugard 240; Knight 4405.

3. Gynura miniata *Welw.*

A sparsely tomentose erect perennial herb with oblanceolate, usually pinnatifid leaves and rather few (3-7) orange-yellow heads in a terminal corymb.

Locally common in black-cotton soil grassland. NBI, KAJ.

Agnew 8203; Verdcourt 2596.

4. Gynura valeriana *Oliv.*

A glabrescent weak juicy herb with oblanceolate, deeply pinnatifid leaves and a loose terminal corymb of orange heads.

Only known from within the wettest forest on the Chyulu hills where it is uncommon. KAJ.

Agnew 9813; Bally 955.

60. CRASSOCEPHALUM *Moench.*

Similar to *Senecio* but with no ray florets, more orange or red tube-florets and with a short, abruptly narrowing, pubescent apex on the stigma.

1 Plant a climber; leaves glabrous, fleshy, pin-
       natifid   1. *C. bojeri*
     Plant an erect herb or shrub; leaves simple or,
       if pinnatifid, then hairy at least on the
       midribs   2
2 Plant a tall shrub or small tree with simple,
       glabrous or glabrescent leaves
                                          2. *C. mannii*
     Plant a herb (sometimes softly woody) with
       hairy or lobed leaves   3
3 Trailing herbs   4
     Erect herbs   5
4 Leaves petiolate, ovate, truncate at base;
       heads solitary   3. *C. vitellinum*
     Leaves often sessile, elliptic to lanceolate,
       narrowing gradually at base; heads often
       2–5 together   4. *C. picridifolium*
5 Heads in tight clusters, usually with some
       peduncles less than 5 mm long; florets
       yellow   5. *C. montuosum*
     Heads solitary or in loose clusters, with most
       pedicels over 5 mm long; florets orange,
       red or purple   6
6 Heads nodding in bud; phyllaries usually
       pubescent; florets usually red to orange
                                       6. *C. crepidioides*
     Heads erect in bud; phyllaries usually
       glabrous; florets reddish-purple
                                            7. *C. rubens*

1. Crassocephalum bojeri (*DC.*) *Robyns* (see p. 473)

A glabrous, thinly succulent climber with deeply pinnatifid, oblong leaves and terminal panicles of yellow heads in crowded umbels. HE, HC, HM, HA, KIT, MUM, RV, MAC, NBI, KAJ.

Common in all upland forest and woodland edges.

Symes 276; Strid 2009.

2. Crassocephalum mannii (*Hook. f.*) *Milne-Redh.* (see p. 474)

A glabrous tree dealt with in KTS p. 157. HE, HC, HA, HK, HN, MAC.

3. Crassocephalum vitellinum (*Benth.*) *S. Moore*

A tomentose to glabrescent trailing perennial herb with petiolate, ovate, often auriculate leaves and solitary, long-pedunculate, orange-yellow heads.

Common in grassy clearings in upland forest and woodland. West Kenya forms frequently have no auricles at the nodes, whereas plants from eastern Kenya have them; there are also considerable differences in hairiness. HE, HT, HM, HA, HK, HN, KIT, MUM, KIS, NAR, RV, EMB, MAC, NBI.

Hanid 603; Bally 999.

4. Crassocephalum picridifolium (*DC.*) *S. Moore* (see p. 470)

A trailing annual or perennial similar to *C. vitellinum* except for the key characters. This species and the last are rather unsatisfactory and difficulty may be experienced in identifying some specimens particularly solitary-headed plants (common on the Aberdares) of *C. picridifolium*. There appears to be no difference in the ecology or distribution of the two species, a fact which suggests that further work is required here. HE, HC, HT, HM, HL, HA, KIT, RV, MAC, NBI.

Agnew 10050; Symes 76.

5. Crassocephalum montuosum (*S. Moore*) *Milne-Redh.* (see p. 473)

An erect woody annual or weak perennial with ovate to elliptic, simple to basally pinnatifid, glabrescent leaves and tight terminal clusters of pale yellow heads.

Common in clearings in montane forest. HE, HC, HT, HM, HA, HK, MUM, NAR, RV, KAJ.

Hanid 20; Greenway 13536.

6. Crassocephalum crepidioides (*Benth.*) *S. Moore*

An erect pubescent annual with ovate, pinnatifid or entire leaves and drooping clusters of heads; florets orange to brick red, rarely purple.

A common weed in disturbed arable land. HE, HT, HA, HK, KIT, MUM, NAR, RV, EMB, MAC, NBI, KAJ.

Lugard 108; Agnew 8103.

7. Crassocephalum rubens (*Jacq.*) *S. Moore* (see p. 470)

A pubescent to glabrescent annual with ovate to elliptic, entire or pinnatifid leaves and long-pedunculate purple or red heads.

This species is rather variable and may have solitary to corymbose heads. It is found in disturbed, often cultivated ground, and is most common in the west of Kenya at higher altitudes. HE, HC, HT, HM, HA, HK, KIT, MUM, NBI, KAJ.

Lind 5091; Lugard 439.

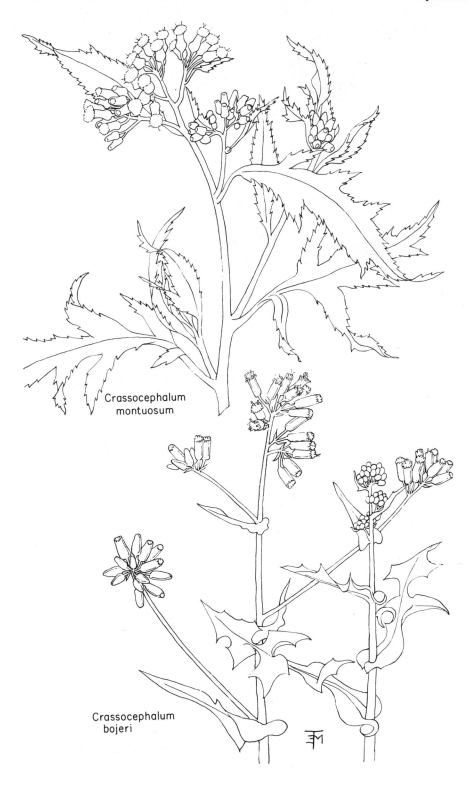

Crassocephalum
montuosum

Crassocephalum
bojeri

Crassocephalum mannii

61. CINERARIA *L.*

Similar to *Senecio* but with flattened achenes.

Cineraria grandiflora *Vatke*

A pubescent, erect or sometimes supported herb with petiolate, auriculate, suborbicular to triangular, serrate leaves and a terminal corymb of rayed, yellow heads.

A common species of roadsides, forest edges and cliffs from 6500 ft to 11 000 ft which shows considerable variation in size of head and achene. In general those from higher altitudes tend to be larger with broader, blacker achenes. HE, HC, HT, HM, HA, HK, KIT, KAJ.

Hedberg 1947; Strid 2034.

62. SENECIO *L.*

Herbs, trees, shrubs or climbers with alternate, usually simple leaves and corymbose or solitary heads; involucre cylindrical to globose, of an inner row of equal, parallel-sided, ± coherent phyllaries with or without outer shorter, narrower, unequal phyllaries; receptacle naked or with weak 'honeycomb' between the florets; female florets each with a spreading ligule present in one row or absent, most florets tubular bisexual; achenes cylindrical, usually 10-ribbed, pubescent or glabrous; pappus of many rows of simple hairs.

A very big genus which is badly in need of revision in Africa, so that we have many species at present without a name. The large-leaved mountain forms are put in a separate subgenus (*Dendrosenecio*) and are all keyed out here (after KTS p. 158) although many of them are trees. When attempting an identification it should be remembered that in many species ray florets may be present or absent.

1	Leaves large, simple, at least some more than 30 cm long, all in a terminal rosette (*Dendrosenecio*)	**35**
	Leaves smaller, seldom in a terminal rosette, sometimes lobed (*Eusenecio*)	**2**
2	Climbers or scramblers with weak, trailing stems	**3**
	Erect herbs or shrubs, some with prostrate stems but then rooting at the nodes	**7**
3	Leaves glabrous	**4**
	Leaves, at least when young, hairy	**5**
4	Leaves elliptic, narrowing gradually at base; heads with spreading ray florets	
	1. *S. petitianus*	
	Leaves triangular, truncate or cordate at base; heads with no ray florets	
	2. *S. syringifolius*	
5	Stems ± 5 mm thick, fleshy; heads touching each other in a dense terminal corymb	**6**

	Stems less than 3 mm thick, not fleshy; heads not touching each other, in a loose terminal panicle	5. *S. lyratipartitus*
6	Leaves entire except for obscure low marginal teeth, white-cobwebby on both sides	
	3. *S. stuhlmannii*	
	Leaves coarsely dentate and lobed, pubescent but not woolly on both sides	
	4. *S. nandensis*	
7	Florets yellow, cream or white	**9**
	Florets purple or pink	**8**
8	Ray florets present; involucre semiglobose	
	6. *S. roseiflorus*	
	Ray florets absent; involucre tubular	
	7. *S. cyanus*	
9	Peduncles of individual heads bearing a few scale-like bracts; phyllaries usually in two series, with some outer shorter or narrower members	**14**
	Peduncles naked; phyllaries in one row only	**10**
10	Leaves linear, mostly entire, acute at apex	
	8. *S. ukambensis*	
	Leaves broader, mostly toothed, rounded at apex	**11**
11	Plant annual; involucres tubular, less than 3 mm wide	9. *S. abyssinicus*
	Plant annual or perennial; involucres tubular or hemispherical, always over 3 mm wide	**12**
12	Heads grouped in apparent umbels; ray florets absent	10. *S. sp. A*
	Heads solitary; ray florets present	**13**
13	Plant perennial, glabrous	11. *S. sp. B*
	Plant annual or perennial, pubescent at least on young leaves	12. *S. discifolius*
14	Sticky glandular hairs present on the plant, especially at top of peduncles and base of involucre (a ×10 lens is necessary to see these, but also try dusting the involucre with dry soil — if it adheres when shaken then sticky glandular hairs are present)	**15**
	Sticky glandular hairs absent	**20**
15	Herbs with lateral inflorescences from a creeping or ascending woody stem bearing an apical tuft of leaves	**16**
	Herbs or shrubs with terminal inflorescences	**17**
16	Florets bright yellow	20. *S. schweinfurthii*
	Florets white to cream-coloured	
	13. *S. hochstetteri*	
17	Leaves regularly pinnatifid to over half the width of the leaf	14. *S. sotikensis*
	Leaves dentate or dentate-serrate	**18**
18	Erect herbs	**19**
	Creeping herbs with prostrate stems rooting at the nodes	21. *S. keniophytum*

19 Ligule of ray florets over 10 mm long, always present; leaves obscurely dentate, usually with recurved margins   15. *S. snowdenii*

Ligule of ray florets less than 10 mm long, often absent or very much shorter in some plants of each population; leaves coarsely dentate, without recurved margins
16. *S. purtschelleri*

20 Shrubs with erect, branched, perennial stems **21**

Herbs with erect or creeping stems, if erect then the stems annual, often unbranched **23**

21 Involucre less than 5 mm long; leaves lanceolate to ovate, widest below the middle   17. *S. maranguensis*

Involucre 5 mm or longer; leaves linear or narrow-elliptical, widest above the middle **22**

22 Leaf bases bearing expanded dentate auricles on each side of the stem   18. *S. moorei*

Leaf bases without auricles
19. *S. rhammatophyllus*

23 Stems at base creeping and rooting at the nodes **24**

Stems erect from woody, succulent or annual rootstocks **27**

24 Inflorescences lateral or or separate from the rosettes of leaves   20. *S. schweinfurthii*

Inflorescences terminal **25**

25 Heads equalled by the upper leaves; leaves white-cobwebby below
21. *S. keniophytum*

Heads on long peduncles held well above the upper leaves; leaves not white-cobwebby below **26**

26 Leaves entire or rarely with a few distant acute teeth, glabrescent   22. *S. jacksonii*

Leaves lobed, pubescent to tomentose
23. *S. transmarinus*

27 Leaves entire, elliptic, sessile, blunt at both ends   24. *S. ruwenzoriensis*

Leaves not entire, or if entire then not elliptic and sessile **28**

28 Heads solitary but often numerous
25. *S. sp. C*

Heads in terminal corymbs **29**

29 Plant annual; leaves lobed   26. *S. vulgaris*

Plant perennial; leaves simple, rarely the uppermost lobed **30**

30 Rootstock a fleshy tuber   27. *S. goetzei*

Rootstock woody, not fleshy **31**

31 Stem leaves reduced, linear **32**

Stem leaves well-developed, broader than linear **33**

32 Lower leaves ± entire; ray florets absent; achenes glabrous   28. *S. sp. D*

Lower leaves dentate; ray florets usually present; achenes pubescent   29. *S. sp. E*

33 Lower leaves gradually narrowed at base stem leaves sessile; phyllaries less than 15 **34**

Lower leaves cordate at base; at least the lower stem-leaves petiolate; phyllaries more than 18   30. *S. trichopterygius*

34 Leaves glabrescent, green below
31. *S. subsessilis*

Leaves white-cobwebby below   32. *S. sp. F*

35 Plants with prostrate stems and rosettes of leaves at ground level **36**

Plant tree-like, with erect stems **37**

36 Leaves thickly woolly below
33. *S. brassica*

Leaves glabrous below   34. *S. brassiciformis*

37 Base of adult leaf cordate or rounded **38**

Base of adult leaf gradually narrowed **40**

38 Ray florets absent or hardly exceeding the phyllaries   35. *S. barbatipes*

Ray florets exceeding the phyllaries by 10 mm or more **39**

39 Petiole winged towards the rounded leaf-base
36. *S. elgonensis*

Petiole unwinged towards the usually cordate leaf-base   37. *S. amblyphyllus*

40 Lower side of leaf-blades (not midribs) glabrous to thinly hairy **41**

Lower side of leaf-blades densely woolly
38. *S. battiscombe*

41 Ray florets present   39. *S. cheranganiensis*

Ray florets absent   40. *S. keniodendron*

Subgenus EUSENECIO

1. Senecio petitianus *A. Rich.* (see p. 477)

A robust, glabrous, semi-succulent trailing climber with elliptic, ± entire or minutely toothed leaves and large terminal corymbs of yellow, rayed or unrayed heads.

Common in all upland drier forest edges and sometimes flowering in masses over large tracts of country. HT, HM, HA, NAR, RV, NAN, MAC.

Agnew 9379; Glover 3205.

2. Senecio syringifolius *O. Hoffm.* (see p. 477)

A glabrous, semi-succulent climber with twining stems and ovate or triangular leaves often with lateral lobes at base; flowers in a loose corymb, without rays.

Common, in montane rain forest and the bamboo zone. HE, HM, HA, HK, KAJ, MAC.

Lind 5616; Hedberg 58.

Senecio petitianus

Senecio
discifolius

Senecio
syringifolius

3. Senecio stuhlmannii *Klatt*

A succulent-stemmed, white-woolly trailing climber with large, petiolate, ovate, subentire leaves and dense spherical masses of yellow, rayless heads in a conical panicle.

Locally common in dry evergreen upland woodland. HA, NAR, MAC, NBI.
Verdcourt and Polhill 2921; Agnew 7859.

4. Senecio nandensis *S. Moore*

A pubescent, semi-succulent trailing climber with ovate, coarsely dentate and shallowly lobed leaves; inflorescence a terminal crowded corymb of rayless yellow heads.

Uncommon, at the edges of dry upland forest, this plant has rather a foetid smell. HM, HA, RV.
Agnew 9574; Polhill 6.

5. Senecio lyratipartitus *A. Rich.* (*Cineraria schimperi* Sch. Bip.; *Senecio sarmentosus* O. Hoffm.)

A wiry trailing climber, tomentose on young parts, with triangular or ovate dentate leaves which are often lobed at base; inflorescence a loose panicle of rayed or rayless yellow heads; achenes cylindrical, pubescent, except those of the ray florets which are narrowly winged and glabrous.

Locally common in dry upland forest and woodland. HC, HA, HM, HK, KIT, KIS, NAR, RV, EMB, NBI.
Glover 3279; Agnew 8480.

6. Senecio roseiflorus *R. E. Fr.*

An erect, densely glandular herb or weak shrub with sessile, oblong-lanceolate, lobed leaves and a terminal corymb of a few purple, rayed heads.

Locally common, in the lower and drier alpine zone of Mt. Kenya and the Aberdares. HA, HK.
Hedberg 1884; Coe 430.

7. Senecio cyanus *O. Hoffm.*

An erect, glandular-pubescent herb with oblong, ± pinnatifid or toothed, sessile leaves and a terminal panicle of cylindrical, rayless, purple heads.

Recorded from Tanzania and only known in Kenya from the Loitokitok side of Mt. Kilimanjaro, in the heath-zone. KAJ.
Nattrass 1224.

8. Senecio ukambensis *O. Hoffm.*

A low, trailing or caespitose, wiry perennial shrub with linear, rarely toothed, glabrous to cobwebby leaves and solitary, yellow-rayed heads on long peduncles.

Common in loose volcanic soils of the Chyulu Hills but not recorded from elsewhere. KAJ.
Hanid 276; Bally 731.

9. Senecio abyssinicus *Sch. Bip.* (see p. 488)

A small erect annual with tomentose or glabrescent, spathulate to oblong leaves and narrow, short-rayed yellow heads in small umbel-like groups.

Rare, in warmer country in western Kenya MUM, BAR.
Tweedie 67/246.

10. Senecio sp. A.

Similar to *S. abyssinicus* but a perennial herb with a woody rootstock, and campanulate, not tubular rayless heads.

Rare, in grassland of western Kenya. KIT.
Brodhurst-Hill 748.

11. Senecio sp. B.

A weak, woody, glabrous perennial with spathulate to oblanceolate leaves which have 2–3 pairs of terminal blunt teeth; heads large, yellow-rayed, solitary, on long peduncles.

Only known from the *Acacia* grassland on the slopes of Mt. Longonot in RV.
Verdcourt 3586.

12. Senecio discifolius *Oliv.* (see p. 477)

An annual to weak perennial with spathulate to obovate to oblong crenate leaves and solitary, long-pedunculate, orange-yellow rayed heads.

As defined here this is a variable plant which may have a rosette of leaves at the base or can be upright with a leafy stem. The heads are very variable in size. It is a common weed of all lowland districts, frequently found in stony soils and on cliffs. HE, HC, HT, HM, HA, KIT, MUM, KIS, NAR, RV, MAG, NAN, EMB, MAC, NBI, KAJ.
Lind and Agnew 5645; Glover 4051.

13. Senecio hochstetteri *Sch. Bip.* (*S. lugardae* Bullock) (see p. 482)

A glandular-pubescent herb with a base of woody, ascending stems bearing crowded terminal rosettes of oblanceolate, doubly dentate leaves; inflorescences from axillary branches, of loose corymbs of cream or white rayless heads; achenes pubescent.

Fairly common, at the edges of dry upland forest, this species does not occur near Nairobi. HE, HC, HT, HM, HK, KIT, RV, KAJ.
Agnew 10721; Lugard 541.

14. Senecio sotikensis *S. Moore*

A glandular-pubescent woody herb or soft shrub bearing sessile, oblong, pinnatifid leaves and showy terminal corymbs of large yellow-rayed heads.

On Mt. Elgon only, in heathland and woodland edges above 10 000 ft. HE.
Tweedie 68/19; Hedberg 871.

15. Senecio snowdenii *Hutch.*

A glandular-pubescent shrub with sessile linear leaves and a few yellow-rayed heads in each small terminal corymb.

Above 9000 ft on the moorland of Mt. Elgon only. HE.

Lind 5225.

16. Senecio purtschelleri *Engl.*

A glandular-pubescent erect or ascending herb with sessile, oblanceolate, deeply dentate leaves and loose terminal panicles of rayed or rayless heads.

This herb appears to be annual in places; in others it creeps by means of a decumbent stem. Forms with and without rays, and with short or long rays are common. It is found in marshy streamsides in the alpine zone of Mt. Kenya. HK.

Hanid 130; Bally 3370.

17. Senecio maranguensis *O. Hoffm. (S. hageniae R. E. Fries)*

An erect pubescent branching shrub with petiolate, oblong-ovate, dentate leaves which are often auriculate at base, and dense terminal corymbs of small campanulate yellow-rayed heads.

Rare, in the upper forest zones of the Aberdares. HA.

Agnew 9059.

18. Senecio moorei *R. E. Fr.*

An erect shrub or woody herb, cobwebby-hairy to glabrescent, with oblanceolate, minutely dentate leaves which are auriculate at the gradually narrowed base; heads campanulate, conspicuously yellow-rayed, in large corymbs.

Common in grassland at higher altitudes, especially in forest clearings above 8000 ft. HT, HM, HA, HK, KIT, RV.

Coe 497; Polhill 25.

19. Senecio rhammatophyllus *Mattf.*

A pubescent or glabrescent, erect branching wiry shrub with linear, entire to conspicuously dentate leaves and terminal corymbs of rather few, broad-campanulate yellow-rayed heads.

As defined here this includes a much hairier form that grows on Sekerr Mt. HE, HC.

Lugard 306; Agnew, Kibe, and Mathenge 10526;

20. Senecio schweinfurthii *O. Hoffm.*

A glandular-pubescent to pubescent perennial with trailing woody stems and terminal rosettes of sessile, linear-oblong leaves; inflorescences axillary or separate from terminal leaf rosette, erect with a loose corymb of rayless yellow heads.

Locally common in disturbed places in montane and alpine grassland, especially at higher altitudes. HC, HT, HM, HA, HK, KIT, KAJ.

Hedberg 1881; Tweedie 67/315.

21. Senecio keniophytum *R. E. Fr.*

A creeping perennial, white-tomentose below and often above the ± crowded oblanceolate serrate leaves, with 1-5 terminal yellow-rayed heads on short peduncles; achenes glabrous.

This plant is often white-woolly on all parts and is confined to the alpine zone of Mt. Kenya where it is one of the first to colonise stony disturbed soils beside glaciers and streamsides. HK.

Coe and Kirrika 264; Hedberg 1749.

22. Senecio jacksonii *S. Moore (S. aequinoctialis R. E. Fr.)*

Similar to *S. keniophytum* but with entire, often linear leaves and long peduncles to the solitary heads; achenes hairy.

This species is found in rocky streamsides and wet solifluction soils in the alpine zone. HE, HA, HK.

Hedberg 1880; Agnew, Hedberg, and Mmari 9615.

23. Senecio transmarinus *S. Moore*

A pubescent herb, often with a rosette of leaves and trailing or weak stems; leaves oblong, pinnatifid or simple, often auriculate at base; heads with large yellow rays, in a loose terminal corymb.

A rare plant of the alpine and subalpine region represented by only one collection from Kenya. HA.

Polhill in EAH 12021.

24. Senecio ruwenzoriensis *S. Moore* (see p. 482)

An erect glabrous herb from a woody rootstock, with sessile, entire elliptic leaves and a loose terminal corymb of yellow-rayed heads.

Locally common in western Kenya in wooded grassland. HE, HC, HT, HA, KIT.

Tweedie 66/96; Bally 4563.

25. Senecio sp. **C.** (*S. coronopifolius* of Check List)

A glabrescent annual or perennial with entire or toothed linear leaves and loose yellow-rayed heads on long peduncles.

This plant appears to be sometimes a rhizomatous perennial, and sometimes (in the Nairobi National Park for example) an annual. It is found in drier grassland, often where disturbed. HT, NAR, RV, MAC, NBI.

Hanid and Kiniaruh 884; Glover 1577.

26. Senecio vulgaris *L.*

An erect pubescent annual with sessile, oblong, pinnatifid and dentate leaves and dense terminal clusters of rayless (rarely rayed) heads of yellow florets.

A rare introduced weed in upland arable country. HT, HA.

Kerfoot 2875.

27. Senecio goetzei *O. Hoffm.*

An erect glabrescent herb from a fleshy tuberous base with oblanceolate dentate to pinnately-lobed leaves and a large corymb of small yellow rayless heads.

This rare plant has been found only once in a marsh by the Athi River. MAC.

Ossent 528.

28. Senecio *sp.* D.

An erect pubescent perennial from a woody rootstock with linear to oblanceolate leaves and a corymb of a few, yellow, rayless heads; achenes glabrous.

Only two examples of this plant have been seen, which, except for the achenes and floret colour, resembles *S. hochstetteri*. In wooded grassland of western Kenya. KIT.

Tweedie 66/46; Brodhurst-Hill 65.

29. Senecio *sp.* E.

Similar to *S. hochstetteri* but with no glands, bright yellow heads and mostly with ray florets.

This species is found in upland grassland on the western side of the Aberdares. HA.

Bally 7427.

30. Senecio trichopterygius *Muschl.*

A large erect rhizomatous herb from a large basal rosette of petiolate ovate cordate leaves which are often white-tomentose below; heads with yellow rays in a large corymb, each with 18-25 inner phyllaries.

Locally common in montane forest edges. The form on Mt. Kenya and the Aberdares lacks the tomentose lower leaf surface. HM, HA, HK.

Agnew, Azavedo, and Khatri 9527; Coe 754.

31. Senecio subsessilis *Oliv. & Hiern*

Similar to *S. trichopterygius* but with sessile ovate to elliptic leaves and fewer (up to 15) inner phyllaries.

Locally common, at the edge of montane rain forest. HC, HM, HA, HK.

Tweedie 67/162; Lucas, Polhill, and Verdcourt 4.

32. Senecio *sp.* F.

Apparently similar to *D. subsessilis* but with softer hairy leaves, and weak loose corymbs.

This species is represented by inadequate material from the Kenya side of Mt. Kilimanjaro in the forest zone. KAJ.

Coe 238; Ibrahim 688.

Subgenus DENDROSENECIO

All these species have been dealt with by Dale and Greenway in KTS pp. 158-160, and so only distributions are given here. They all occur at or above 9000 ft, often near water. Recently they have been united into two species, 33 and 34 in our enumeration become *S. brassica* R. E. Fries and 35-40 become *S. johnstonii* Oliv. according to A. Mabberley in *Kew Bulletin* 28: 61 (1973). But this group of giant plants is so attractive that this key and enumeration is retained for general interest.

33. Senecio brassica *R. E. Fries*—HK.
34. Senecio brassiciformis *R. E. Fries*—HA.
35. Senecio barbatipes *Hedb.*—HE.
36. Senecio elgonensis *Th. Fr. jr.*—HE.
37. Senecio amblyphyllus *Cotton*—HE.
38. Senecio battiscombei *R. E. & Th. Fries*—HA, HK.
39. Senecio cheranganiensis *Cotton & Blacklock*—HC. (see p. 481).
40. Senecio keniodendron *R. E. & Th. Fries*—HA, HK.

63. EMILIA *Cass.*

A genus very close to *Crassocephalum* and *Senecio* but differing from them in the lack of short outer phyllaries and in the short terminal appendage to the stigma.

1   Leaves clasping the stem; florets orange
                                    1. *E. javanica*
    Leaves sessile but not clasping the stem; flowers white or purple   2
2   Florets white, as long as the involucre
                                    2. *E. kikuyorum*
    Florets purple, much longer than the involucre   3. *E. integrifolia*

1. Emilia javanica (*Burm. f*) *Merr.* (*E. coccinea* (Sims) Sweet) (see p. 488)

An erect glabrescent annual with oblong or lanceolate amplexicaul leaves and loosely arranged, terminal, bright orange heads; florets almost twice as long as the involucre; achenes minutely pubescent.

Senecio cheranganiensis

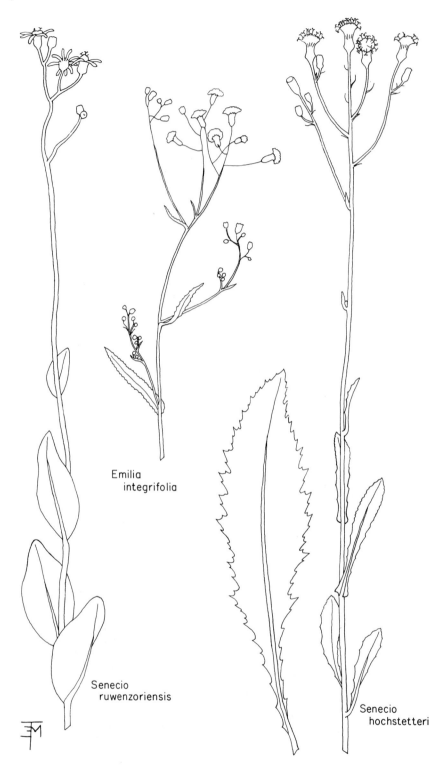

Emilia
integrifolia

Senecio
ruwenzoriensis

Senecio
hochstetteri

A conspicuous annual weed of roadsides and waste places, often in dry country, often at lower altitudes. HE, HL, KIT, MUM, NAR, BAR, RV, MAC, NBI, KAJ.

Tweedie 66/196; Johnstone 144.

2. Emilia kikuyorum *R. E. Fries* (see p. 488)

An erect pubescent annual with usually linear leaves and a loose terminal corymb of cream to whitish heads; achenes glabrous.

Uncommon, in disturbed marshes and roadsides in higher altitude grassland. HC, HT, HA, HK, KIT, KIS.

Strid 3156; Drummond and Hemsley 4465.

3. Emilia integrifolia *Bak.* (see p. 482)

Similar to *E. kikuyorum* but glabrescent and with the keyed differences.

Local, especially in western Kenya upland grassland where disturbed. HE, HT, HM, HA, KIT.

Lugard 101; Agnew, Kibe and Mathenge 10600.

64. KLEINIA *Mill.*

Similar to *Senecio* but succulent-stemmed, without ray florets and with more or less umbellate inflorescences.

1	Florets yellow	2
	Florets purple or red	4
2	Leaves spindle shaped, persistent	
	1. *K. barbertonicus*	
	Leaves flat, or early deciduous	3
3	Leaves flat, orbicular	5. *K.* sp. *C*
	Leaves minute, scale-like	2. *K.* sp. *A*
4	Phyllaries up to 11 mm long; buds cylindrical, truncate or open at the apex	
	4. *K.* sp. *B*	
	Phyllaries over 12 mm long; buds narrowing to an acute apex	3. *K. kleinioides*

1. Kleinia barbertonicus (*Klatt*) *Burtt-Davy*

A glabrous, glaucus, bushy shrub with narrow cylindrical fleshy leaves and stem and terminal umbelliform corymbs of bright yellow heads.

Only recorded from Mt. Margaret in the Rift Valley and reported from near Kajiado. RV, KAJ.

Bally 1013.

2. Kleinia *sp.* **A.**

A tortuous-branched bushy glabrous shrub with reduced scale-leaves and umbels of pale yellow to cream heads.

Locally common in dry *Commiphora* bushland. MAG.

Agnew 7002; Lieppert 5209.

3. Kleinia kleinioides (*Sch. Bip.*) *M. R. F. Taylor*

A glabrous loose shrub or climber with fleshy stems and obovate or oblong deciduous leaves; inflorescences much as in *K.* sp. *A* but with more numerous pink or mauve florets.

Locally common in dry bushland. KIS, BAR, MAC, KAJ.

Agnew 5734; Lucas 12.

4. Kleinia *sp.* **B.**

Similar to *K. kleinioides* except for the key characters, this species appears to be commoner in the Rift Valley. NAR, RV, MAG.

Verdcourt 3561.

5. Kleinia *sp.* **C.**

Similar to *K.* sp. *B* but with yellow flowers and orbicular leaves.

Uncommon in dry country. BAR.

Tweedie 2965.

65. NOTONIA *DC.*

Similar to *Senecio* but herbaceous, fleshy, without outer small phyllaries and with gradually tapering, uninterrupted stigmas.

1	Creeping herbs with trailing stems on the surface of the ground	2
	Erect herbs with or without rhizomes or tubers	3
2	Leaves and young stems glabrous	
	1. *N. petraea*	
	Leaves and young stems pubescent	
	2. *N. implexa*	
3	Leaves absent, represented only by short deciduous scales less than 1 cm long	
	3. *N. gregorii*	
	Leaves present, persistent	4
4	Phyllaries longitudinally ridged and grooved on their lower halves	5
	Phyllaries smooth	6
5	Stems perennial, with thickened leaf-scars	
	4. *N. picticaulis*	
	Stems annual, without thickened leaf-scars	
	5. *N. coccinea*	
6	Rhizomatous or tuberous herbs with annual erect stems; heads solitary; pappus ± equalling or exceeding florets	7
	Herbs with perennial (often short-lived) stems; heads usually in groups; florets exceeding pappus by 2–4 mm	8
7	Flowering stems leafy; pappus seldom longer than 15 mm	6. *N.* sp. *A*
	Flowers on leafless stems; pappus over 20 mm long	7. *N. schweinfurthii*

8   Heads more than 7, in large terminal
     corymbose inflorescences
                        9. *N. abyssinica*
     Heads fewer than 7, in loose terminal cymes
                        8. *N. hildebrandtii*

1. Notonia petraea *R. E. Fries* (see p. 485)

A glabrous trailing succulent herb with obovate to
suborbicular leaves and 1-4 orange heads on erect,
naked peduncles; pappus exceeding the florets.

    Locally common in dry bushed grassland. HT,
HA, NAR, RV, NAN, MAC, NBI.

    Glover 2263; Agnew 8974.

2. Notonia implexa (*Bally*) *Agnew* comb. nov.
(*Senecio implexus* Bally in *Candollea* **18**, 18
(1962))

Similar to *N. petraea* but pubescent, with elliptic,
acute leaves, and constantly solitary heads.

    Rare plant found in dry bushland. KAJ.

    Bally 8496.

3. Notonia gregorii *S. Moore* (see p. 485)

A glabrous rhizomatous herb with erect, cylindrical, mottled, leafless stems and solitary terminal
red heads; phyllaries ridged towards the base.

    Locally common in dry rocky grassland,
especially where disturbed. KIS, NAR, RV, MAC.

    Verdcourt 2361; Agnew 7825.

4. Notonia picticaulis (*Bally*) *Agnew* comb. nov.
(*Senecio picticaulis* Bally in *Candollea* **19**, 163
(1964))

A small erect glabrous herb from short rhizomes or
tubers, with linear cylindrical fleshy leaves and
solitary or few pedunculate heads; pappus almost
equalling the red florets.

    Rare plant found in dry country. NAN.

    Bally Aug. 1963.

5. Notonia coccinea *Oliv. & Hiern*

Very similar to *N. picticaulis* (which may ultimately prove to be the same) except for the
usually broader, elliptic leaves.

    Uncommon in dry country. BAR, RV, MAC,
KAJ.

    Fitzgibbon 1635.

6. Notonia *sp.* **A.**

A glabrous rhizomatous perennial with elliptic to
oblanceolate, frequently dentate leaves and solitary or paired heads; pappus ± equalling the red
florets; stigmas flat, triangular.

    Rare plant found in dry stony grassland. NAR,
KAJ.

    Tweedie 67/98; Glover 2295.

7. Notonia schweinfurthii *Oliv. & Hiern*

Similar to *N.* sp. *A* but with frequently dentate-
serrate leaves and the keyed characteristics.

    Rare plant found in dry country. KAJ.

    Bally 747.

8. Notonia hildebrandtii *Vatke* (*N. grantii* of
Check List)

A glabrous herb with ascending stems and oblanceolate to obovate, usually entire, acute leaves;
heads bright red, 1-7 together in loose terminal
cymes; stigmas filiform.

    The commonest species of *Notonia*, especially
round Nairobi, found frequently in rocky soils
along bushed stream banks. HE, HT, HA, MUM,
NAR, RV, NAN, MAC, NBI, KAJ.

    Bally 11566; Strid 2807.

9. Notonia abyssinica *A. Rich.* (see p. 485)

Very similar to *N. hildebrandtii* but larger and
found in the west of Kenya. Further study may
reveal that these two species are but forms of the
same plant. HE, HA, HT, KIT, RV.

    Lind 5070; Brodhurst-Hill 546.

66. EURYOPS *Cass.*

Erect or prostrate shrubs, with simple, crowded
and (in ours) linear, glabrous leaves; heads solitary;
involucre hemispherical of one row of bracts
which are ± laterally fused at base; receptacle
naked; outer florets ligulate, yellow, female, in one
row; inner florets tubular, bisexual; achenes
cylindrical, ribbed, glabrous; pappus of 1 row of
short, caducous bristles.

1   Peduncles and the base of the involucre
     tomentose or woolly   1. *E. brownei*
     Peduncles and base of the involucre glabrous
                                             2
2   Peduncles shorter than the leaves
                        2. *E. elgonensis*
     Peduncles at least twice as long as leaves
                        3. *E. jacksonii*

1. Euryops brownei *S. Moore*

An erect, much-branched shrub with short leaves
and dense masses of axillary yellow heads at
branch apices.

    A common shrub at the upper forest levels and
lower heath zone on the drier sides of the
Aberdares and Mt. Kenya. HA, HK.

    Agnew, Hedberg, and Mmari 9620; Coe and
Kirrika 367.

2. Euryops elgonensis *Mattf.*

Similar to *E. brownei* but with wider leaves and
shorter, glabrous peduncles.

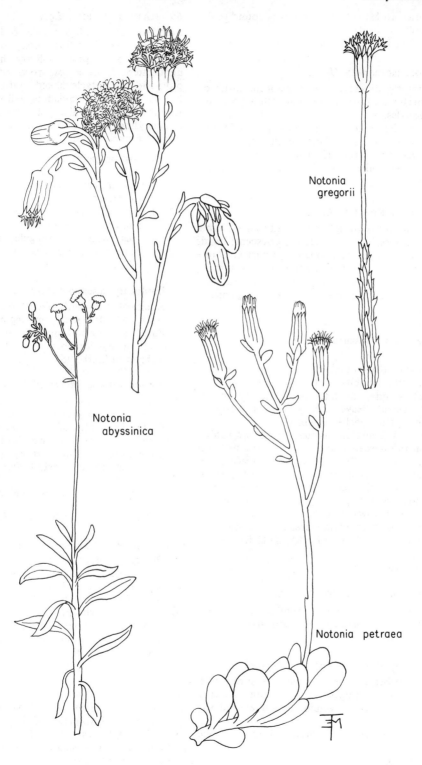

Notonia
gregorii

Notonia
abyssinica

Notonia petraea

Confined to Mt. Elgon where it is found in the lower heath-zone. HE.

Lugard 368; Tweedie 3213.

3. Euryops jacksonii *S. Moore*

A low trailing, or shortly erect, glabrous shrub or woody herb with linear leaves and yellow heads on long peduncles.

This species is found in rocky places in dry upland grassland, particularly in the Rift Valley and western Aberdares. HT, HM, HA, RV.

Glover, Gwynne, and Samuel 1073; KSTC June 1967.

67. OSTEOSPERMUM *L.*

Herbs or shrubs with opposite or alternate, simple or lobed leaves, often glandular-pubescent; heads solitary or in corymbs; involucre cylindrical of one row of ± equal phyllaries; outer florets female, ligulate, in one row; inner florets male, tubular, numerous; achenes winged or smooth, ± glabrous; pappus absent.

Osteospermum vaillantii *(Decne.) T. Norl.* (see p. 487)

An erect glandular-pubescent annual, or sometimes perennial and shrubby, with alternate (or rarely opposite) simple, dentate or pinnately lobed, elliptic-lanceolate leaves; heads in a loose raceme or corymb, yellow; achenes winged.

Usually a common annual weed with long racemose inflorescence and large (± 10 mm long) achenes, but in the Rift Valley (Suswa to Menengai) there is a shrubby plant with corymbose heads and shorter (*c.* 7 mm) achenes. These two appear to intergrade (e.g. through Kerfoot 4025 quoted below) so no specific distinction has been made between them here, but the situation needs review. HE, HM, HT, HA, KIT, RV, MAC, NBI, KAJ.

Kerfoot 4025; Agnew 5355.

68. CHRYSANTHEMOIDES *Medik.*

Shrubs, sometimes spiny, similar to *Osteospermum* but the phyllaries in many rows and the fruit fleshy, of drupes.

Chrysanthemoides monilifera *(L.) T. Norl.*

An erect, pubescent, much-branched shrub with alternate, broad-elliptic leaves and solitary terminal yellow heads which do not exceed the leaves.

Only known from the Chyulu Hills in Kenya. KAJ.

Bally 1170.

69. HAPLOCARPHA *Less.*

Stemless herbs with a rosette of leaves which (in ours) are densely white-woolly below, and with subsessile or scapose, solitary heads; involucre hemispherical, of a few rows of thin, scarious phyllaries; receptacle naked; outer florets female, in one row, with spreading yellow ligules; inner florets bisexual, tubular, yellow; achenes obconical or subcylindrical, glabrous, angled; pappus of 5–10 minute fimbriate scales.

1   Heads on peduncles at least as long as the
     leaves   1. *H. scaposa*
     Heads almost sessile in the centre of the
     rosette of leaves   2
2   Leaves oblong in outline, pinnatifid into
     numerous blunt lobes   2. *H. schimperi*
     Leaves ovate to triangular to orbicular in
     outline, entire or coarsely toothed but not
     lobed   3. *H. rueppellii*

1. Haplocarpha scaposa *Harv.*

A perennial herb with oblanceolate entire leaves and solitary yellow heads on long peduncles.

Rare in western Kenya, in wooded grassland and only once recorded.

Webster in EAH 9967.

2. Haplocarpha schimperi *(Sch. Bip.) Beauv.*

A flat rosette-leaved plant, with the leaves appressed to the ground and small pale yellow heads in the centre of the rosette; peduncles of fruiting heads bent down into the soil.

Uncommon, in short grassy clearings within dry, cold montane forest, 8000–10 000 ft. HM, HK.

Glover, Gwynne, and Samuel 945; Strid 3277.

3. Haplocarpha rueppellii *(Sch. Bip.) Beauv.* (see p. 423)

Similar to *H. schimperi* but with simple leaves and much larger, deeper yellow heads.

This species is an alpine, growing in frosty places where the soil is unstable. The strongly recurved peduncles allow the seeds to germinate even in this environment. Most specimens have glabrous glossy upper leaf surfaces but in some (especially from western Kenya) they are dull and loosely tomentose. HE, HC, HA, HK.

Hanid 76; Mwangangi 310.

70. HIRPICIUM *Cass.*

Herbs with alternate, lobed leaves and solitary yellow heads; involucre bell-shaped, of 1–2 rows of entire phyllaries; receptacle naked; outer florets ligulate, in one row, neuter; central florets bisexual tubular, numerous; achenes obconical, hairy;

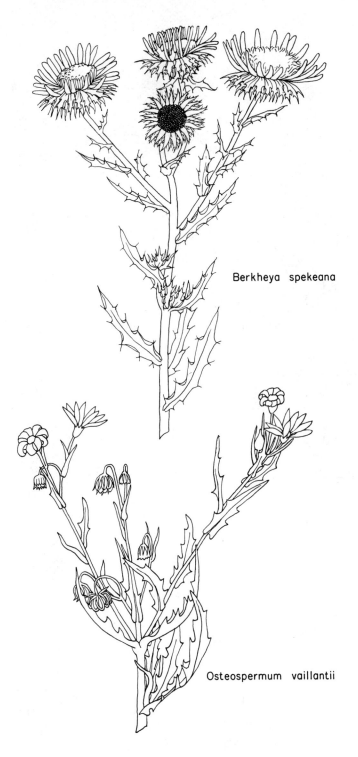

Berkheya spekeana

Osteospermum vaillantii

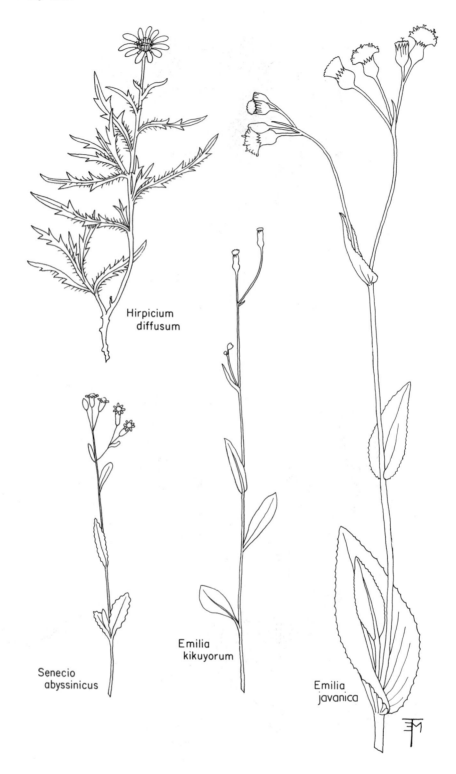

Hirpicium
diffusum

Senecio
abyssinicus

Emilia
kikuyorum

Emilia
javanica

pappus in two rows, the outer of long delicate scales, the inner of short scales.

Hirpicium diffusum (*O. Hoffm.*) *Roess.* (see p. 488)

A spreading-bristly annual with oblong to linear or oblanceolate, entire to pinnatilobed leaves and solitary yellow heads.

A common plant of disturbed places in dry grassland. HT, HM, HA, NAR, BAR, RV, NAN, MAC, NBI, KAJ.

Glover, Gwynne, and Samuel 819; Agnew 8340.

71. BERKHEYA *Ehrh.*

Erect spiny herbs with pinnatifid or simple leaves and solitary or corymbose heads; involucre hemispherical, of many rows of pinnately spiny bracts; receptacle deeply pitted, the pits containing the achenes; outer florets in one row, ligulate, neuter; inner florets tubular; achenes obconical, 10-ribbed, pubescent; pappus of a single row of oblong blunt scales.

Berkheya spekeana *Oliv.* (see p. 487)

An erect annual herb with lanceolate to oblong, simple or pinnatifid spiny leaves which are white-woolly below; heads solitary or weakly corymbose, bright yellow.

Common in wooded grassland at medium altitudes, especially in western Kenya. HE, HC, HT, HM, HA, HK, KIT, MUM, RV, NAN, MAC.

Mwangangi 470; Hanid 829.

72. ECHINOPS *L.*

Herbs, usually with a woody rootstock and alternate, often pinnately divided and spiny, leaves; heads 1-flowered, aggregated into globose inflorescences (heads of heads); phyllaries in many rows, fused or free, forming a cylindrical involucre; florets tubular, bisexual; achene hairy, cylindrical; pappus of a ring of fused or free, short narrow scales.

1 Florets red   1. *E. amplexicaulis*
   Florets blue to white   2
2 Leaves simple, with parallel venation
                                        2. *E. eryngiifolius*
   Leaves lobed, with reticulate venation   3
3 Phyllaries tipped with brushes of plumose feathery bristles, closely packed on the outside of the inflorescence so that the individual heads can hardly be distinguished   3. *E. aberdaricus*
   Phyllaries ciliate at apex, the spines or bristles not feathery; individual heads distinguishable   4

4 Leaves divided into triangular segments; upper surface of leaf loosely woolly when young, becoming glabrous, never glandular
                                                                5
   Leaves divided into linear segments; upper surface of leaf bristly or glandular   6
5 Most lower nodes with thick red or brown bristly hairs as well as the white cobwebby covering; phyllaries with hooked terminal bristles   4. *E. hoehnelii*
   Stem with cobwebby covering only; phyllaries simple, spiny at apex, without hooked bristles   5. *E. longifolius*
6 Stem and upper side of leaves with stiff bristles; phyllaries narrowed below the terminal (often small) bristly appendage
                                          6. *E. hispidus*
   Stem and upperside of leaves glandular-hairy and cobwebby only; phyllaries ciliate above but not appendaged.
                                    7. *E. angustilobus*

1. Echinops amplexicaulis *Oliv.* (see p. 490)

A robust erect herb with usually sessile, shallowly lobed ovate-elliptic leaves and large coarse spherical inflorescences.

Common and conspicuous in wooded grassland and cultivation edges in north-western Kenya. HE, HC, HT, HM, HA, KIT, MUM, BAR, RV.

Vercourt 2204A.

2. Echinops eryngiifolius *O. Hoffm.*

An erect herb with long-linear, coarsely ciliate, sessile leaves and solitary ovoid inflorescences with white florets.

Rare, in wet savannah. KIT.

Greenway 8525.

3. Echinops aberdaricus *R. E. Fr.*

An erect herb, sometimes branched above, with sessile, doubly pinnatifid, oblong leaves with lanceolate segments; inflorescences large, globose, whitish.

Locally common in subalpine grassland just above the bamboo zones of the Aberdare and Mau ranges. HM, HA.

Agnew, Beals, and Modha 7070; Glover, Gwynne, and Samuel 950.

4. Echinops hoehnelii *Schweinf.* (see p. 490)

An erect branched herb with pinnatifid oblong leaves and a few smallish spherical inflorescences with white, pale blue or purple-pink florets.

This species is common in forest edges and open high altitude woodland and heathland of the Aberdares and Mt. Kenya. HA, HK.

Mathenge 380; Verdcourt 1031.

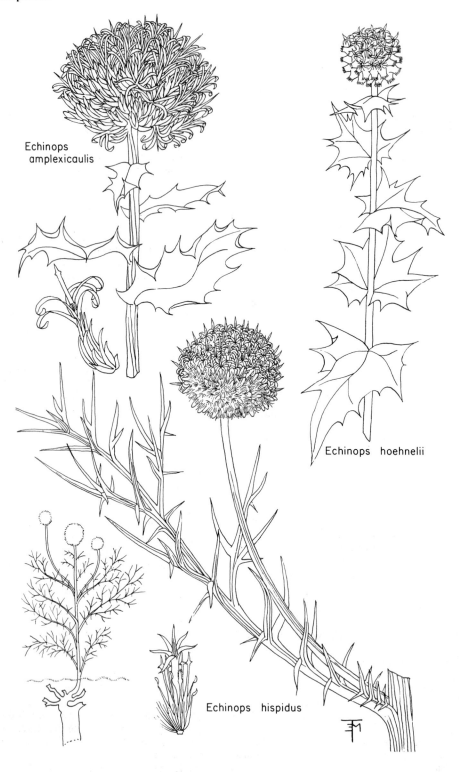

Echinops
amplexicaulis

Echinops hoehnelii

Echinops hispidus

5. Echinops longifolius *A. Rich.*

Similar to *E. hoehnelii* but with narrower leaves (oblong to linear in outline) and the keyed differences.

Uncommon, in highland grassland. HT.

Williams 178.

6. Echinops hispidus *Fresen.* (see p. 490)

A robust erect herb with petiolate, much pinnatifid leaves and a few large globose inflorescences with whitish florets.

Locally common in upland grassland in western Kenya. HE, HC, HT, KIT, NAR, RV.

Tweedie 65/22; Jack 83.

7. Echinops angustilobus *S. Moore*

Similar to *E. hispidus* except for the rather smaller inflorescences and absence of bristly hairs.

This species is also found in grassland and forest edges, but mostly at higher altitudes than the last species. HE, HC, HT, HM, HA.

Bogdan 5008; Hanid and Agnew 39.

73. CARDUUS *L.*

Herbs with alternate spiny-lobed leaves, the leaf bases decurrent as spiny wings on the stems; heads often subsessile, in terminal panicles; involucre bell-shaped, of many rows of acute bracts; receptacle densely hairy; florets all tubular, bisexual; achenes obliquely inserted, ovoid, smooth; pappus of a few rows of simple bristles, caducous as a whole by means of minutely coherent bases.

1   Stemless rosette plants with sessile heads
                                  1. *C. chamaecephalus*
    Plants with erect stems   2
2   Involucral bracts pinnate at margins   3
    Involucral bracts entire, ciliate or minutely
        serrate but not pinnate   4
3   Heads embedded in a dense straw-coloured
        spiny mass, in which some spines are over
        2 cm long   2. *C. keniensis*
    Heads not embedded in a spiny mass, no
        spines over 1 cm long   3. *C. millefolius*
4   Heads as broad as or broader than long
        (disregarding any spreading spines); phyl-
        laries ovate, acute but not spine-tipped
                                      4. *C. sylvarum*
    Heads longer than broad (disregarding any
        spreading spines); phyllaries mostly spine-
        tipped, linear to lanceolate, rarely ovate   5
5   Outer phyllaries over half as long as inner-
        most and obscuring the median series;
        innermost phyllaries with an oblong-linear
        apex, all others with a long (usually more
        than 5 mm) apical spine   5. *C. nyassanus*

Outer phyllaries mostly less than half as long as innermost and not obscuring the bases of the median series; innermost phyllaries mostly with a lanceolate or linear but not oblong apex, and all others with a short (less than 5 mm long) apical spine   6
6   Leaves more or less oblong, parallel-sided;
        pappus over 15 mm long
                                      6. *C. kikuyorum*
    Leaves ± elliptical, widest at the middle;
        pappus less than 14 mm long
                                    7. *C. afromontanus*

1. Carduus chamaecephalus (*Vatke*) *Oliv. & Hiern* (*C. platyphyllus* R. E. Fries; *C. theodori* R. E. Fries) (see p. 492)

A prostrate spiny rosette plant with thick fleshy roots and the pinnatifid leaves tightly appressed to the ground; heads 1-2, sessile, in the centre of the rosette, purple.

Common in short alpine and subalpine grassland. HE, HC, HT, HM, HA, HK, KIS, RV, NAN.

Hanid 77; Greenway 7857.

2. Carduus keniensis *R. E. Fries*

A spiny rosette plant with large, pinnate oblong leaves and an occasional central stem bearing a crowded, spiny apical panicle of ± sessile heads.

A very conspicuous plant in tussock grassland on the Aberdare and Mt. Kenya moorlands. HA, HK.

Lind 5762; Hedberg 1837.

3. Carduus millefolius *R. E. Fries*

Similar to the last species but with very narrow, linear leaves with crowded, imbricate segments and much shorter, finer, often purplish, spines.

This plant is also to be found on the Aberdares and Mt. Kenya moorlands but usually in wet soil by streamsides. HA, HK.

Polhill 228.

4. Carduus sylvarum *R. E. Fries*

An erect herb with elliptic glabrescent leaves and a loose terminal panicle of broad, pedunculate heads.

Only known from the forests of Mt. Kenya and the Aberdares where it grows in deep shade. HA, HK.

Verdcourt 3039.

5. Carduus nyassanus (*S. Moore*) *R. E. Fries* (see p. 492)

An erect tall pubescent herb with sessile, elliptic to oblong, pinnatifid leaves and clusters of sessile terminal spiny heads with white to pale purple flowers.

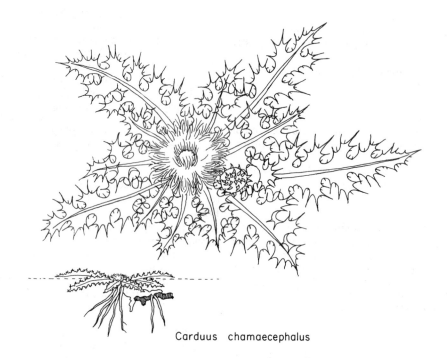

Carduus chamaecephalus

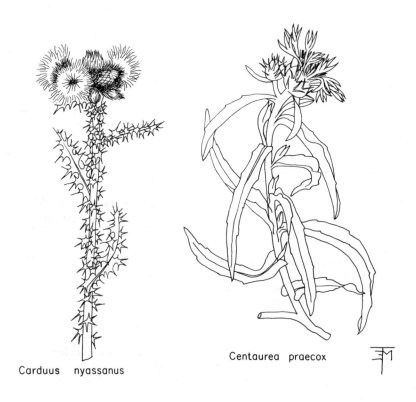

Carduus nyassanus

Centaurea praecox

This species is found in the montane forest area mostly in western Kenya, where it often grows in disturbed places. Occasional specimens grade into the next species. HE, HC, HM, HA, HK, KAJ.

Strid 3116; Tweedie 48.

6. Carduus kikuyorum *R. E. Fries*

Similar to *C. nyassanus* except for the key differences, this species is found in similar situations, especially in eastern Kenya. HT, HM, HA, HK, KIS.

Agnew, Azavedo, and Khatri 9501; Glover, Gwynne, and Samuel 1599.

7. Carduus afromontanus *R. E. Fries*

Similar to the last two species except for the keyed characteristics; this plant is found in forest clearings especially in the bamboo zone. HA, HK.

Hedberg 1938; Agnew and Lind 5623.

74. CIRSIUM *Mill.*

Similar to *Carduus* but with a plumose feathery pappus.

1 Leaves bristly-hairy on upper surface; phyllaries entire   1. *C. vulgare*
   Leaves pubescent on upper surface, smooth; phyllaries with a short, pinnately spiny appendage   2. *C. buchwaldii*

1. Cirsium vulgare *(Savi) Ten.*

An erect, often robust annual with sessile, oblong to elliptic, deeply pinnatifid leaves and large solitary heads with spreading phyllaries.

A weed of arable land, especially wheat, introduced from Europe and persisting. HA, RV.

Polhill 40.

2. Cirsium buchwaldii *O. Hoffm.*

An erect herb, possibly perennial, similar to *C. vulgare* but less richly branched and with much smaller (to 2 cm long) involucres.

This species is mainly found in swamps in western Kenya but has occurred at Uplands. HE, HA, KIT.

Bogdan 4303; Tweedie 66/295.

75. SILYBUM *Adans.*

Similar to *Carduus* but the leaves variegated and not decurrent on the stem, and the filaments united below the anthers.

Silybum marianum *(L.) Gaertn.*

An erect annual from a basal rosette of obovate, spiny, white-veined leaves; heads large (over 5 cm diameter) with a very strong spreading apical spine on each phyllary.

An introduced weed in wheat from southern Europe. HT.

Peers D2.

76. VOLUTARIA *Cass.*

Herbs or shrubs with alternate, simple or pinnatifid leaves; heads mostly solitary; involucre bell-shaped or hemispherical of many rows of closely appressed entire, spine-tipped bracts; receptacle densely hairy; all florets bisexual, tubular, with rather long corolla lobes; achenes ovoid, with an oblique base, often glossy; pappus of many rows of blunt, oblong, persistent scales.

1 Phyllaries with a recurved apical bristle; leaves simple   1. *V. muricata*
   Phyllaries acute, without an apical bristle; leaves pinnatifid   2. *V. lippii*

1. Volutaria muricata *(L.) Maire*

An erect pubescent annual with simple, oblong-elliptic, sessile leaves and globose, purple heads.

Introduced from the Mediterranean, this is a weed of arable land so far only recorded from Eldoret. HT.

van Someren 224.

2. Volutaria lippii *(L.) Maire*

An erect pubescent annual or weak perennial with oblong, pinnatifid, ± petiolate leaves and ovoid purple heads in loose terminal corymbs.

This plant is also found in the Mediterranean but appears to be more at home in Kenya. It often occurs as a roadside plant in dry upland grassland. NAR, RV, MAG, NAN, MAC, KAJ.

Lind 5376; Verdcourt and Napper 2178.

77. CENTAUREA *L.*

Similar to *Volutaria* but with a spiny appendage on the phyllaries.

1 Plant annual; stem winged with the decurrent leaf bases; florets yellow   1. *C. melitensis*
   Plant perennial; stem unwinged; florets purple   2. *C. praecox*

1. Centaurea melitensis *L.*

An erect scabrid pubescent annual with sessile, oblong-lanceolate, simple leaves and solitary yellow heads which are sessile in the uppermost 2-4 leaves.

An introduced weed which is a pest of wheat in highland arable land. HT, HM, KIT, RV.

Bogdan 5717.

2. Centaurea praecox *Oliv. & Hiern* (see p. 492)

A pubescent perennial with ascending branches from a woody rootstock and narrow, simple, oblanceolate leaves; heads solitary, large, with purple florets.

Locally common in wooded grassland in western Kenya. HC, KIT.

Tweedie 66/27; Symes 523.

78. DICOMA *Cass.*

Erect or stemless herbs with simple alternate leaves and solitary heads; involucre tubular or bell-shaped of many rows of entire phyllaries; receptacle naked; florets all tubular, bisexual, rarely the outermost female; achenes cylindrical, silky-hairy; pappus of plumose bristles with or without an inner row of scales.

Dicoma tomentosa *Cass.*

An erect wiry annual, ± white woolly on all parts, with linear leaves and subsessile heads bearing spine-tipped phyllaries and yellow florets.

Locally common in dry bushland. MAG, MAC, KAJ.

Tweedie 67/261; Bally 10564.

79. ACHYROTHALAMUS *O. Hoffm.*

Herbs with alternate simple leaves and solitary heads; involucre bell-shaped of many rows of entire bracts; receptacle with large scales subtending the florets; florets all bisexual, tubular; achenes ovoid, 5-ribbed, glabrous; pappus absent.

Achyrothalamus marginatus *O. Hoffm.*

An erect rhizomatous herb or weak shrub with white-woolly stems and undersides of leaves; leaves elliptic, subentire; heads solitary; florets often green.

An uncommon plant of stony places in dry bushland. EMB, MAC.

Agnew and Hanid 8457; Williams in EAH 12338.

80. ERYTHROCEPHALUM *Benth.*

Rhizomatous or tuberous-rooted perennial herbs, often white-woolly, with alternate, simple, often entire leaves and solitary heads; involucre saucer- or bell-shaped, of many rows of toothed bracts; receptacle with scales subtending the florets; outer florets bisexual, with a 2-lipped corolla, in one row or absent; inner florets tubular, bisexual; achenes ovoid, 5-angled; pappus of 4–5 caducous scales.

Erythrocephalum microcephalum *Dandy*

An erect annual, white-cobwebby on all parts, but less so on the upper side of the sessile, oblong leaves; heads solitary, pedunculate, with a cup-shaped involucre and yellowish florets.

A rare plant of dry country. MAC.

Bogdan 4375.

81. GERBERA *Cass.*

Mostly rosette-leaved, perennial herbs with entire leaves and solitary, scapose heads; involucre bell-shaped, of many rows of entire phyllaries; receptacle naked; outer florets ligulate, with an inner, 2-pointed lip, usually female; achenes compressed and ± beaked, hairy; pappus of 1–many rows of soft bristles.

Gebera viridifolia (*DC.*) *Sch. Bip.* (see p. 495)

A tomentose, rosette herb with petiolate oblong-elliptic leaves and solitary heads of pinkish flowers.

Locally common in wooded grassland in western Kenya. HE, HT, HM, HL, HK, KIT.

Tweedie 66/5; Bogdan 3718.

82. PILOSELLOIDES (*Less.*) *C. Jeffrey*

Similar to *Gerbera* but with expanded scapes below the heads, staminodes not present in ray florets and achene-hairs inflated.

Piloselloides hirsuta (*Forsk.*) *C. Jeffrey* (*Gerbera piloselloides* (L.) Cass.) (see p. 495)

Very similar to *Gerbera viridifolia* but with leaves which narrow gradually at base and outer florets which hardly exceed the involucre.

Common in upland and highland grassland. HE, HC, HT, HM, HA, HK, MAC, KAJ.

Agnew 7285; Polhill 396.

83. TOLPIS *Adans.*

Annual or perennial herbs with dentate leaves, scapose or with a branching stem; involucre in many rows, of lanceolate bracts; florets all ligulate, bisexual, yellow, on a naked receptacle; achenes obconic, truncate above with a pappus of coarse scabrid bristles.

Tolpis capensis (*L.*) *Sch. Bip.*

Subscapose perennial herb with a rosette of oblanceolate dentate leaves and a branched or simple scape.

Common in short subalpine grassland in forest clearings and in short wet grassland at lower altitudes. HC, HT, HA, HK.

Kirrika 420.

84. HYPOCHOERIS *L.*

Scapose herbs with dentate leaves and yellow ligulate florets subtended by receptacle scales;

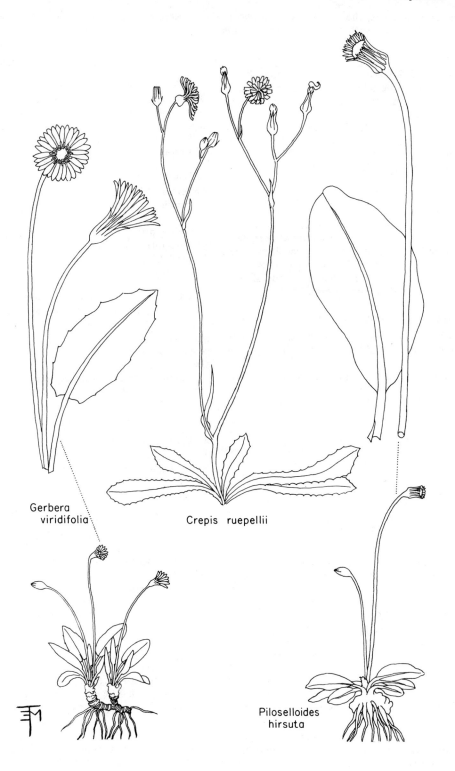

Gerbera
viridifolia

Crepis ruepellii

Piloselloides
hirsuta

achenes in two series, the outer truncate above, the inner beaked, all with some feathery pappus hairs.

Hypochoeris glabra *L.*

A scapose annual herb with a rosette of oblanceolate dentate leaves and a branched scape bearing a few yellow heads.

This introduced plant thrives in disturbed palces in highland grassland up to 9500 ft. HT, HM, HA.

Agnew, Beals, and Modha 7051.

85. TARAXACUM *Weber*

Herbs with a rosette of pinnatifid leaves and solitary heads on simple, hollow scapes; phyllaries in many rows, simple or bifid at apex; receptacle naked; florets all ligulate, bisexual, usually yellow; achenes flattened, coarsely toothed above and abruptly joined to a long beak; pappus simple; ovules usually (and in ours) apomictic.

Taraxacum officinale *Wiggers*

A glabrous to sparsely pubescent scapose herb with oblong, pinnatifid leaves and solitary yellow heads.

Introduced from Europe and only recently recorded from Limuru. HA.

Aleljung March, 1969.

86. LAUNEA *Cass.*

Herbs or shrubs with dentate or pinnatifid leaves and usually yellow flowers; involucral bracts usually grading into scales on the peduncles; heads often corymbose; receptacle naked; achenes angled, cylindrical or obconical, ridged, glabrous or spreading-hairy, with a pappus of very numerous simple (often caducous) both stiff and soft hairs.

1   Plant stemless, of leaves and a cluster of inflorescences at ground level, the leaves overtopping the heads   1. *L. nana*
     Plants with well-developed stems carrying the heads well above the leaves   2
2   Heads subsessile, clustered at the nodes of primary inflorescence branches   3
     Heads pedunculate, distant, not clustered   4
3   Plant perennial, with a rhizome; pappus 8–10 mm long; anthers over 4 mm long
                                       2. *L. nigricola*
     Plant annual; pappus 6–8 mm long; anthers less than 3 mm long   3. *L. intybacea*
4   Stems divaricately branching so that no single stem is dominant; heads held at periphery of bush-shaped plant   4. *L. hafunensis*

Stems not divaricately branching, with always one axis dominant; heads held at various levels, close to and distant from the centre of the plant   5. *L. cornuta*

1. Launea nana (*Bak.*) *Chiov.*

Dwarf perennial from a woody rootstock, with oblanceolate denticulate leaves and numerous heads in a cushion-shaped inflorescence.

Rare, in burnt wooded grassland. HE, MAC.
Verdcourt 423; Lugard 518.

2. Launea nigricola *C. Jeffrey*

An erect rhizomatous perennial or biennial with pinnatifid to entire, lanceolate-elliptic leaves and clusters of large yellow-flowered heads along the ascending primary branches of the stem.

Uncommon, in wooded grassland from 4500–7500 ft. MAC.
Greenway in EAH 11192.

3. Launea intybacea (*Jacq.*) *Beauverd*

Very similar to the last species but an annual and smaller in all its parts. The achene character mentioned by Jeffrey (in *Kew Bulletin* **18**, 471) as separating these two species has not been seen by this author.

Uncommon, in disturbed places within grassland areas at low altitudes and also found at the coast. MAG.
Verdcourt 3281.

4. Launea hafunensis *Chiov.*

An erect, many-stemmed, divaricately branched bushy herb from a woody rootstock; leaves linear-lanceolate in outline, pinnatifid; heads terminal to each branchlet.

Common in some areas of dry alluvial soils at low altitudes. MAG, KAJ.
Agnew 7301; Verdcourt 1435.

5. Launea cornuta (*Oliv. & Hiern*) *C. Jeffrey* (see p. 497)

A rhizomatous perennial with erect stems from a rosette of leaves at ground level, stems branching above into the diffuse inflorescence; leaves linear-lanceolate or elliptic in outline, entire or pinnatifid into linear segments.

This is the commonest species of *Launea*, especially around Nairobi, growing along roadsides and in disturbed grassland from the coast to 7500 ft. HM, NAR, RV, NAN, MAC, NBI.
Thomas 807; Agnew 5352.

87. SONCHUS *L.*

Annual or perennial herbs with sessile clasping leaves and cymose terminal aggregations of heads

Launea
cornuta

Sonchus
asper

Sonchus
schweinfurthii

which may resemble an umbel; involucre ± tubular, white-woolly at base, glabrous above, of more or less glabrous bracts in many rows; receptacle naked; flowers ligulate, bisexual; achenes compressed, elliptic to oblong in outline and strongly 3–5-ribbed on each face; pappus of thin undulate hairs and stiff straight bristles.

1   Annuals   2
    Perennials   3
2   Auricles at leaf base rounded in outline;
        achenes smooth   1. *S. asper*
    Auricles at leaf base pointed, ± triangular in
        outline; achenes minutely roughened on
        the ribs   2. *S. oleraceus*
3   Dwarf herbs less than 50 cm tall, with a
        rosette of leaves or with leaves on very
        short stems   4
    Erect or trailing herbs with leafy stems, over
        50 cm tall   5
4   Wool at base of involucre brown-purple;
        achenes less than 4 mm long
                                    3. *S. afromontanus*
    Wool at base of involucre white; achenes over
        4 mm long   4. *S. camporum*
5   Involucral bracts over 15 mm long
                                    5. *S. stenophyllus*
    Involucral bracts less than 15 mm long   6
6   Leaves pinnately lobed; heads subsessile
                                    6. *S. luxurians*
    Leaves sharply toothed but not pinnately
        lobed; at least some heads pedunculate   7
7   Wool below heads brownish
                                    7. *S. schweinfurthii*
    Wool below heads white   8. *S. bipontini*

1. Sonchus asper (*L.*) *Hill* (see p. 497)

An erect unbranched annual with glaucous, sharply toothed and often pinnatifid leaves; flowers yellow in a terminal umbel-like cyme.
    A rare field weed. HT, HA, MUM, KIS, MAC.
    Agnew and Musumba 8564; Peers 2.

2. Sonchus oleraceus *L.*

Similar to *S. asper* except for the key characters.
    A common weed of cultivation and gardens at medium altitudes during the rains. HE, HM, HA, RV, MAC, NBI, KAJ.
    Mathenge 401; Kerfoot 3491.

3. Sonchus afromontanus *R. E. Fr.*

A rhizomatous perennial with short leafy stems or rosettes of oblanceolate, coarsely dentate or entire leaves, and with erect scape-like stems bearing 2–5 heads; involucre blackish, glabrous except for the patch of purple wool at base.

In highland wet grassland, often along streamsides in forest clearings in the subalpine zone, but rare. HE, HM, HA, HK.
    Hanid, Agnew, and Mendes 142.

4. Sonchus camporum (*R. E. Fr.*) *C. Jeffrey*

A dwarf herb from a perennial rootstock, with coarsely dentate or pinnatilobed leaves and greenish involucre; achenes over 4 mm long.
    Rare, apparently a plant of upland burnt grassland. HE, HT, HA, HK.
    Bickford in Bally 6265.

5. Sonchus stenophyllus *R. E. Fr.*

A robust plant, erect to over 75 cm, with sharply dentate and pinnately lobed leaves and large, mostly pedunculate heads with a green involucre.
    Rare, in scattered localities in highland Kenya. HA.
    Record from FTEA.

6. Sonchus luxurians (*R. E. Fr.*) *C. Jeffrey*

A robust erect or trailing herb, often woody below, with pinnately divided leaves, the pinnae usually curved away from the leaf apex; heads usually ± sessile, in tight terminal clusters, with a dark involucre and white wool below each.
    The commonest species of indigenous *Sonchus*, found in roadsides and grassland edges throughout the area of montane forest mostly in eastern Kenya. HE, HT, HM, HA, HK, HN, RV, MAC, NBI.
    Lind 5497; Polhill 29.

7. Sonchus schweinfurthii *Oliv. & Hiern* (see p. 497)

Similar to *S. luxurians* except for the key characters and a tendency for the wool below the heads to be brownish.
    This species is found replacing *S. luxurians* in western Kenya. HE, HC, KIT, MUM, MAC.
    Agnew and Musumba 8536; Lugard 195.

8. Sonchus bipontini *Aschers.*

With linear unlobed leaves and white wool below the orange-yellow heads this species is similar to the last two. HE, HM, NAR, RV.
    Record from FTEA.

88. LACTUCA *L.*

Annual or perennial with clasping alternate leaves and panicles of cylindrical heads; involucre cylindrical, of many rows of blunt glabrous bracts; receptacle naked; florets all ligulate, bisexual; achenes with an elliptic, flat, ribbed body and a thin beak above; pappus of simple hairs.

Lactuca
capensis

Lactuca
glandulifera

1   Erect herbs with blue flowers   1. *L. capensis*
     Trailing herbs with yellow-cream flowers   2
2   Lower leaves pinnately divided, with at least
        some pinnae on short petiolules; achenes
        with blunt, corky ribs   2. *L. paradoxa*
     Lower leaves pinnatifid only, no pinnae on
        petiolules; achenes with narrow, sharp ribs
                              3. *L. glandulifera*

1. Lactuca capensis *Thunb.* (see p. 499)

An erect herb, usually branched only above, with
pinnatifid entire leaves and a diffuse terminal mass
of blue heads.

Common in disturbed ground in the medium-
altitude grasslands of our area, especially along
roadsides. HE, HC, HT, HM, HL, HA, HK, KIT,
KIS, NAR, RV, NAN, MAC, NBI, KAJ.

Verdcourt 1565; Agnew 9502.

2. Lactuca paradoxa *Sch. Bip.*

A scrambling pubescent herb with pinnate or
pinnatifid leaves with 3–5 pinnae, the lowermost
with a narrowed petiolule.

Very rare, in montane rain forest and only
recorded from Gatamayu. HA.

Verdcourt 2299.

3. Lactuca glandulifera *Hook. f.* (see p. 499)

Similar to *L. paradoxa* except for the key characters, this species is also found in the montane rain
forest but is locally common. MUM, HE, HA, HK,
HN.

Agnew 8738; Graham 35.

89. REICHARDIA *Roth*

Annual herbs with denticulate and lobed leaves;
involucre broadly cup-shaped, of many rows of
orbicular, glabrous, white-edged bracts; receptacle
naked; florets many, ligulate, yellow; achenes of
two forms, the outer columnar, grooved, the inner
obconical, smooth; pappus of soft woolly hairs
and stiff bristles.

Reichardia tingitana (*L.*) *Roth*

An erect glabrous annual with oblanceolate dentate leaves and terminal solitary heads borne on
swollen peduncles, which become hardened and
corky in fruit.

An uncommon weed of disturbed and rocky
places in the Rift Valley and near Nairobi. BAR,
RV, NBI.

Verdcourt 3231.

90. DIANTHOSERIS *Sch. Bip.*

Herbs similar to *Sonchus* but without a stem, with
the (usually) single head sessile in the leaf rosette,
and with a pappus of coarse bristles only.

Dianthoseris schimperi *A. Rich.*

A small glabrous rosette herb with entire spathulate leaves and a solitary sessile head.

An alpine of short herbage by streams, found
above 11 000 ft. HE, HK.

Hanid 79A.

91. CREPIS *L.*

Herbs with spirally arranged dentate leaves and
usually branched flowering stems; heads in
panicles or corymbs or solitary; involucre ± tubular, of one row of ± equal bracts and a few outer
small ones; florets all ligulate, yellow, bisexual;
achenes cylindrical, narrowed into a beak above,
ribbed; pappus of simple hairs.

1   Heads solitary or in pairs on leafless stems
                              1. *C. carbonaria*
     At least some stems bearing a loose corymb
        of more than 3 heads   2
2   Involucre over 13 mm long   2. *C. oliverana*
     Involucre less than 11 mm long   3
3   Inner involucral bracts less than 11, at least
        some over 2 mm broad   3. *C. rueppellii*
     Inner involucral bracts more than 10, none
        over 1·5 mm broad   4. *C. newii*

1. Crepis carbonaria *Sch. Bip.*

A scapose perennial herb with a rosette of oblanceolate obtuse leaves and 1–2 heads on the leafless
scape; 1–15 inner involucral bracts 10–12 mm
long.

Common in highland short grassland, this plant
is rather variable in its involucre with may be
green, whitish or black. HE, HC, HT, HM, HA,
HK, KIS.

Hedberg 848; Agnew 10001.

2. Crepis oliverana (*Kuntze*) *C. Jeffrey*

A scapose perennial with a rosette of oblanceolate
acute leaves and a central ± leafless stem bearing a
corymb of 4–8 heads; involucre blackish with
tentacular hairs.

Locally common in grassland beside streams in
the subalpine (heath) zones of the mountains. HA,
HK.

Coe and Kirrika 422; Hedberg 1693.

3. Crepis rueppellii *Sch. Bip.* (see p. 495)

Similar to *C. oliverana* except for the less regular
corymb and the shorter, fewer, grey-green involucral bracts.

Uncommon, in highland grassland and mainly
found in western Kenya. HE, HC, HT, HK.

Tweedie 66/343; Brodhurst-Hill 418.

4. Crepis newii *Oliv. & Hiern.*

Similar to *C. oliveriana* but with obtuse leaf apices and a less regular corymb of smaller heads with narrow ± glabrous bracts.

Recorded only once from Kaimosi by Jeffrey in *Kew Bull.* **18**, 460. MUM.

78. GENTIANACEAE †

Herbs, rarely shrubs with usually opposite entire leaves and flowers in cymes; calyx of 4–5 free or fused lobes; corolla of 4–5 fused petals mostly contorted in the bud; stamens 4–5 often with apical glands to the anthers and the filaments fused to the corolla tube; ovary with 2 carpels, with or without a style; fruit a capsule, rarely fleshy, with incompletely axile or more often parietal placentation; seeds with endosperm.

1 Aquatic plant with floating leaves
　　　　　　　　　　　5. Nymphoides indica
　Terrestrial plants　　　　　　　　　　　2
2 Flowers white or blue or purple　　　　　3
　Flowers yellow or red　　　　　　　　　4
3 Flowers in axillary cymes
　　　　　　　　　　　2. Enicostema axillare
　Flowers in terminal cymes　　*4. Swertia*
4 Flowers red　　*3. Chironia elgonensis*
　Flowers yellow　　　　　　　*1. Sebaea*

1. SEBAEA *R. Br.*

Annual or perennial herbs with opposite or entire leaves and flowers in terminal cymes; calyx of 4–5 free lobes; corolla with a cylindrical tube and 4–5 lobes; stamens 4–5, included or exserted, each anther with a small terminal appendage; style thin, with a capitate stigma; capsule globose, 2-celled, septicidally 2-valved.

1 Plants annual; leaves rounded at apex
　　　　　　　　　　1. S. brachyphylla
　Plants perennial, rhizomatous; leaves acute at
　apex　　　　　　　　　　　　　　2
2 Calyx in fruit cuneate at base; leaves scale-
　like, stiff　　　　　*2. S. microphylla*
　Calyx in fruit rounded at base; leaves small
　but not scale-like　　*3. S. grandis*

1. Sebaea brachyphylla *Griseb*

An erect, often branched, annual with sessile orbicular leaves and a terminal corymb of crowded yellow flowers.

Here are lumped together all the yellow annual **Sebaeas** and although forms are separable it seems that a complete treatment must await detailed study.

† By A. D. Q. Agnew.

A common plant on wet pathsides and streamsides in the montane forest regions; also found but uncommonly in disturbed shallow-soil grassland at lower altitudes. HE, HC, HT, HM, HA, HK, KIT, BAR, RV, MAC, NBI.

Harmsen and Agnew 6530; Kerfoot 1390; Tweedie 68/127.

2. Sebaea microphylla *(Edgw.) Knobl.* (see p. 502)

A small rhizomatous perennial with erect, almost leafless stems bearing rather conspicuous yellow flowers.

Uncommon plant found in seasonally wet, shallow soils in western Kenya. KIT. Tweedie 67/235; Jack 321.

3. Sebaea grandis *(E. Mey.) Steud.* (*Exochaenium macranthum* A. W. Hill) (see p. 502)

A small erect herb from a rhizomatous rootstock with lanceolate oblong leaves and conspicuous yellow flowers in a loose terminal cyme.

Uncommon plant found in wooded grassland. HE, HC, HT, HM, KIT, NAR, KAJ.

Symes 218.

2. ENICOSTEMA *Blume*

Erect glabrous herbs with opposite entire leaves and flowers in dense axillary cymes; calyx tube bell-shaped with 5 lobes; corolla tube long, cylindrical, with 5 small lobes; stamens 5, with a scale at the base of each filament and the anthers held in the mouth of the corolla tube; style short, with a capitate stigma; capsule oblong, 1-celled, septicidal.

Enicostema axillare *(Lam.) A. Raynal*

A rhizomatous perennial with erect stems bearing linear to lanceolate-elliptic leaves and axillary clusters of white flowers.

Uncommon plant found in dry stony grassland especially where water is temporarily available. RV, NAR, MAG, KAJ.

Verdcourt 4162.

3. CHIRONIA *L.*

Erect glabrous annual or perennial herbs with flowers in cymes; calyx of 5 nearly free lobes; corolla tube short, with 5 large lobes; stamens overtopping the corolla tube; style long, stigma capitate; capsule 1-celled, septicidally 2-valved.

Chironia elgonensis *Bullock* (see p. 502)

An erect annual with elliptic lower and narrow-lanceolate upper leaves; flowers in very loose cymes, dark red.

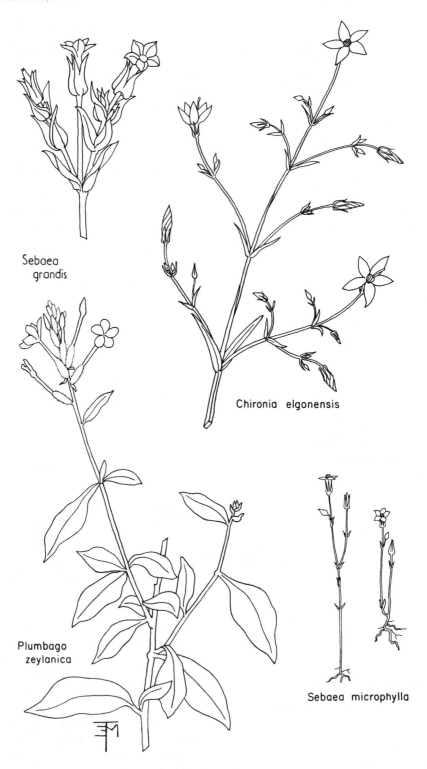

Sebaea
grandis

Chironia elgonensis

Plumbago
zeylanica

Sebaea microphylla

Locally common in swamps in western Kenya. HE, HC, KIT.

Tweedie 67/276; Lugard 21.

4. SWERTIA *L.*

Glabrous herbs with opposite, entire leaves and flowers in corymbose cymes; sepals 5, free; petals 5, shortly joined at base, each with one or two, often fringed glands towards the base within; stamens 5, free; capsule oblong or ovoid, dehiscent at the sessile stigma.

1	Plants perennial	2
	Plants annual	9
2	Basal leaves present, always spathulate	3
	Basal leaves often absent and only stem-leaves present, never spathulate	6
3	Flowers exceeded by the leaves	
	1. *S. subnivalis*	
	Flowers exceeding the leaves	4
4	Sepals spathulate, rounded at apex	
	2. *S. crassiuscula*	
	Sepals lanceolate-elliptic, acute at apex	5
5	Flowers solitary	3. *S. uniflora*
	Flowers more than 3 together	
	4. *S. volkensii*	
6	Plant trailing or weakly ascending	8
	Plant erect	7
7	Flowers in corymbs; petals with two glands at the base of each, bluish	5. *S. quartiniana*
	Flowers in loose racemes, petals with one gland at the base of each, white	
	6. *S. kilimandscharica*	
8	Leaves acute at apex; sepals erect, lanceolate, acute	7. *S. scandens*
	Leaves rounded at apex; sepals spreading, spathulate, rounded	8. *S. calycina*
9	Sepals spathulate and rounded at apex	
	9. *S. lugardae*	
	Sepals lanceolate-elliptic, acute at apex	10
10	Sepals ± as long as petals, usually 4	
	10. *S. tetrandra*	
	Sepals longer than petals, usually 5	11
11	Corolla up to 6 mm long; inflorescence conical in outline	11. *S. eminii*
	Corolla over 7 mm long; inflorescence corymbose, even if loosely so	12
12	Stems unbranched except into the inflorescence above; stem-leaves sessile, clasping	12. *S. welwitschii*
	Stems branched below; stem-leaves petiolate	13. *S. usambarensis*

1. Swertia subnivalis *Th. Fr. jr.*

A creeping stoloniferous herb with spathulate leaves and subsessile white flowers.

Rare plant found in wet mossy communities of the alpine zone. HE, HK.

Hedberg 1783.

2. Swertia crassiuscula *Gilg* (*S. parnassiflora* Th. Fr. jr.; *S. sattimae* Th. Fr. jr.) (see p. 504)

A stoloniferous (sometimes weakly so) herb with thick roots and spathulate leaves; flowers in a short raceme, white to bluish

A very variable species which has two distinct forms (with large and small petals respectively) on the Aberdares, these forms grading into one another on Mt. Elgon. Local on wet, shallow and stony soils in the heath zone and the lower part of the alpine zone. HE, HC, HA, HK.

Coe 381; Agnew, Hedberg, and Mmari 9612.

3. Swertia uniflora *Mildbr.*

A trailing herb with woody stems and dense terminal tufts of oblanceolate to linear leaves; flowers solitary, on an erect pedicel, white to blue.

Rare plant found in moist short grass in the alpine zone. HE.

Lugard 377; Hedberg 926.

4. Swertia volkensii *Gilg*

Similar to *S. crassiuscula* except for the smaller bracts on the raceme and usually nodding flowers (erect in *S. crassiuscula*).

Local in wet mossy grassland along streambanks in the alpine zone. HA, HK.

Hanid 90; Verdcourt 3522.

5. Swertia quartiniana *A. Rich.*

An erect, simple-stemmed herb from a ± woody rootstock bearing lanceolate-oblong to obovate, rounded leaves and a dense terminal corymb of purplish or bluish flowers.

Uncommon plant found in montane grassland. HT.

Jex-Blake 2123.

6. Swertia kilimandscharica *Engl.* (see p. 504)

An erect, usually unbranched, possibly short-lived perennial with sessile, lanceolate to oblong, acute leaves, and irregular terminal racemes or corymbs of large white to pale blue flowers.

Conspicuous but often local, in montane grassland from the bamboo to the alpine zone. HE, HC, HA, HK.

Strid 3417; Kirrika 419.

7. Swertia scandens *Th. Fr. jr.*

A trailing woody herb, frequently ciliate below the nodes, with ovate, acute leaves and white flowers, solitary or 2–3 together.

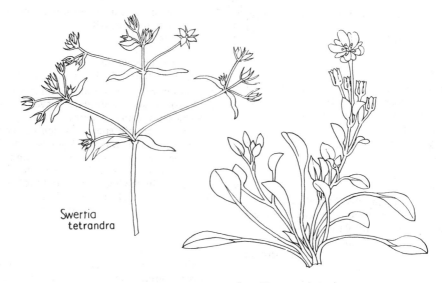

Swertia
tetrandra

Swertia crassiuscula

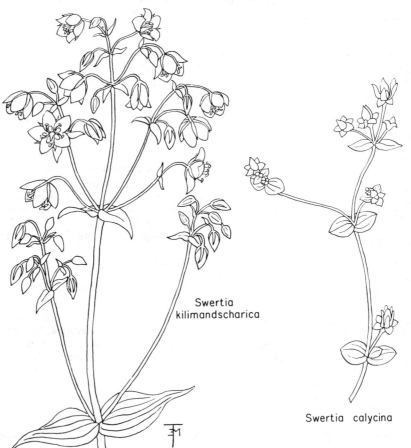

Swertia
kilimandscharica

Swertia calycina

Abundant in one or two places in the upper forest levels of Mt. Kenya and unknown elsewhere. HK.

Coe 312; Agnew 8671.

8. Swertia calycina *N. E. Br.* (see p. 504)

A trailing, much-branched herb from a weakly woody rootstock with oblong to elliptic, rounded leaves and plentiful terminal cymes of white flowers.

Uncommon plant found on swampy riversides in wooded grassland. HT, KIT, MAC.

Tweedie 66/185; Hedberg 1079.

9. Swertia lugardae *Bullock*

An erect, branched annual with orbicular to broad-elliptic to spathulate, rounded leaves and numerous white to dull purple flowers in loose terminal corymbose cymes.

Locally common in wet stony grassland and even wooded country at the upper forest levels and the alpine zone. HE, HM, HA, HK.

Strid 3291; Lugard 409.

10. Swertia tetrandra *Hochst.* (see p. 504)

An erect, little-branched annual with narrow oblong to linear, acute leaves and small scattered white flowers.

Uncommon plant found in disturbed upland grassland. HC, HT, KIT, MUM.

Tweedie 67/181; Ossent in EAH 12464.

11. Swertia eminii *Engl.*

An erect, much-branched annual with linear-elliptic, obtuse or rounded leaves and a conical inflorescence of very numerous small white to greenish flowers.

Local in shallow soils in western Kenya. HC, HM, KIT, KIS.

Napier 2855; Agnew, Kibe, and Mathenge 10310.

12. Swertia welwitschii *Engl.*

An erect, wiry, unbranched annual with linear-lanceolate sessile leaves and dense terminal corymbs of white flowers.

Locally common in marshes in western Kenya. HE, KIT.

Bogdan 3812; Tweedie 66/292.

13. Swertia usambarensis *Engl.* (inc. *S. stellarioides* of Check List)

An erect herb with obovate basal leaves and linear to oblong stem leaves, branching above into a loose corymb of white flowers.

This species, as defined here, is very variable, with short or long petals. It is common in shallow soils and short montane grassland. HE, HC, HT, HM, HA, HK, KIT, KAJ.

Tweedie 67/332; Verdcourt 2443.

5. NYMPHOIDES *Hill*

Aquatic glabrous herbs with creeping rhizome and simple, alternate, entire, orbicular leaves; flowers in an umbel-like cluster on the stem apex (which deceptively resembles a petiole); calyx lobes 5, free; corolla with a short tube and 5 valvate lobes; stamens 5, with anthers at the mouth of the corolla tube; capsule 1-celled, opening irregularly.

Nymphoides indica (*L.*) *Kuntze*

An aquatic with floating, kidney-shaped leaves and pale yellow flowers in clusters below them; seeds weakly tubercled or glabrous.

Rare plant found in permanent ponds. MUM, MAC.

Lind in UCNH 10; McMahon 12.

79. PRIMULACEAE †

Annual or perennial herbs with usually opposite leaves and racemose inflorescences; sepals 5, fused; petals 5, fused at base; stamens 5, often joined at base, always inserted on the corolla opposite the lobes (alternate with the sepals), each with 2 simple anthers; ovary superior, 1-celled, with few to many ovules on a free-central placenta; fruit a capsule, valvate or circumscissile in dehiscence.

1 Pubescent herbs; leaves crenate and dentate
                                   1. *Ardisiandra*
  Glabrous herb; leaves entire   2
2 Flowers in terminal spike-like racemes; bracts
     very reduced   2. *Lysimachia*
  Flowers axillary; bracts leaf-like   3
3 Corolla pink, blue or white; capsule circum-
     scissile   4. *Anagallis*
  Corolla yellow or cream; capsule dehiscing
     longitudinally   3. *Asterolinon adoense*

1. ARDISIANDRA *Hook. f.*

Pubescent creeping herbs with alternate, petiolate, ovate leaves and short racemes of flowers; corolla bell-shaped with the lobes shorter than the tube; capsule globose, dehiscing by 5 valves or indehiscent.

1 Calyx only half as long as corolla; fruit
     indehiscent   1. *A. wettsteinii*
  Calyx ± equal to corolla; fruit dehiscent
                            2. *A. sibthorpioides*

† By R. Griffiths and A. D. Q. Agnew.

1. Ardisiandra wettsteinii *R. Wagner*

A hairy prostrate herb with orbicular crenate leaves and 1–6-flowered racemes; flowers pendulous, white.

An uncommon plant found in subalpine bushland. HA, HK.

Agnew 7062.

2. Ardisiandra sibthorpioides *Hook. f.*

Similar to *A. wettsteinii* except for the key characters, this species is found in dry forest and bushland clearings. It appears to be rare and more collections are required to prove its distinctness in our area. HA.

Record from FTEA.

2. LYSIMACHIA *L.*

Herbs or shrubs with opposite or alternate entire leaves and racemose inflorescences; calyx 5–6-lobed; corolla 5–6-lobed, white, yellow, pink or purple; stamens often alternating with staminodes; capsule dehiscing by 5 valves.

1 Leaves petiolate; style never more than 1·5 mm long   1. *L. ruhmeriana*
   Leaves subsessile; style more than 2 mm long   2. *L. volkensii*

1. Lysimachia ruhmeriana *Vatke* (see p. 507)

A glabrous herb with trailing and ascending stems which often root at the nodes, and petiolate, elliptic to lanceolate leaves with superficial punctate glands; flowers pinkish in spike-like racemes.

Locally common in wet upland grassland. HE, HT, HM, HA, HK, KIT.

Agnew 5855; Kokwaro and Kabuye 332.

2. Lysimachia volkensii *Engl.*

Similar to *L. ruhmeriana* but the trailing stems never rooting, and with lanceolate sessile leaves without punctate glands.

Very locally abundant in upland wet grassland. HA, HK, KIS, NAR, NAN, MAC.

Agnew 10129; Paulo 502.

3. ASTEROLINON *Hoffmg. & Link*

Similar to *Anagallis* except for the capsule which has valvate dehiscence.

Asterolinon adoense *Kunze* (see p. 507)

An erect herb with sessile, ovate leaves and solitary flowers on long pedicels which bend downwards in fruit.

This plant can be mistaken for *Anagallis pumila* but it is larger, with broader leaves and cream, not pink, corolla. It is locally common on shallow soils. HC, HT, HA, KIT, MUM.

Symes 769; Agnew, Kibe, and Mathenge 10311.

4. ANAGALLIS *L.*

Glabrous annual or perennial herbs with entire leaves and axillary or racemose flowers; petals shortly fused at base; capsule circumscissile or indehiscent.

1 Corolla white; plant perennial
                                1. *A. tenuicaulis*
   Corolla pink or blue, or plant annual   2
2 Stems prostrate, rooting at the nodes   3
   Stems erect   5
3 Corolla less than 3 mm long; leaves orbicular to obovate   2. *A. brevipes*
   Corolla over 3 mm long; leaves ovate   4
4 Leaves broadest above the middle; pedicels shorter than leaves; petals 5; filaments glabrous   3. *A. serpens*
   Leaves broadest at the middle; pedicels longer than the leaves; petals usually 6; filaments usually bearded   4. *A. hexamera*
5 Sepals less than 2 mm long; corolla pink
                                5. *A. pumila*
   Sepals over 3 mm long; corolla pink or blue
                                6. *A. arvensis*

1. Anagallis tenuicaulis *Baker*

A trailing perennial herb with subsessile ovate acute leaves and small, star-shaped white flowers with bearded filaments.

Uncommon plant found in grassy marshes in western Kenya. HT, KIT, MUM.

Brodhurst-Hill 285; Agnew, Kibe, and Mathenge 10595.

2. Anagallis brevipes *P. Tayl.*

A trailing annual with obovate to orbicular leaves and small pink flowers.

A rare weed found in upland grassland. HM. Whitehead 9.

3. Anagallis serpens *DC.* (see p. 507)

A trailing plant with obovate leaves and conspicuous pink flowers.

Common in alpine and subalpine streamside marshes. HE, HC, HM, HA, HK.

Part II Botany 78; Moreau 160.

4. Anagallis hexamera *P. Tayl.*

Similar to *A. serpens* but the stems longer before roots develop and with larger flowers.

Uncommon plant found in some streamside marshes at upper forest levels. HC, HT, HK.

Hedberg 1085.

5. Anagallis pumila *Sw.*

A small erect sparsely-branched annual with elliptic, acute leaves and pinkish flowers.

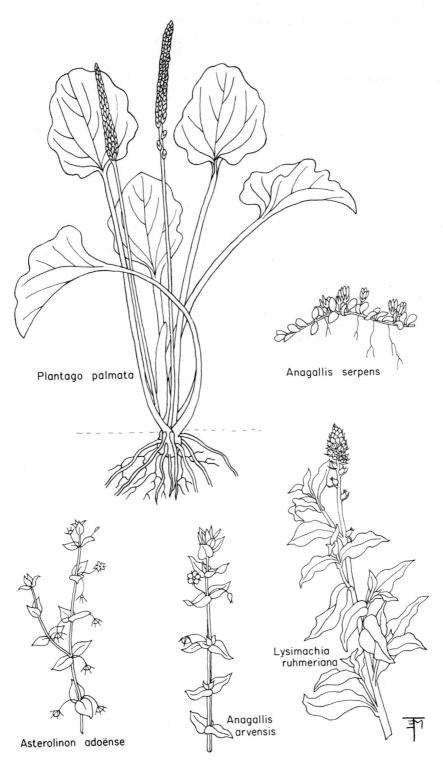

Plantago palmata

Anagallis serpens

Lysimachia
ruhmeriana

Asterolinon adoënse

Anagallis
arvensis

Locally common in shallow-soil grassland, HT, HM, HA, KIT, MAC, NBI.

Agnew 9415; Tallantire 126.

6. Anagallis arvensis *L.* (see p. 507)

An erect, much branched annual with ovate to lanceolate leaves and blue or reddish-pink flowers on long pedicels which curve downwards in fruit.

This introduced plant (the scarlet pimpernel of Europe) is locally common in shallow soils and disturbed places. HE, HT, HM, HA, KIT, RV, MAC, NBI.

Ables 76; Nattrass 1088.

80. PLUMBAGINACEAE†

Annual or perennial herbs or shrubs with alternate exstipulate entire leaves and flowers in terminal cymose panicles or spikes; flowers bisexual, regular; calyx tubular, 5-lobed, persistent; petals 5, free or slightly joined at base or tubular; stamens 5, inserted in the corolla tube or free, always opposite the petals; ovary superior, 1-celled with 1 basal ovule; styles 5 or 1 with 5 stigmas; fruit a dry capsule.

1 Flowers in spikes; calyx glandular, much longer than the bracts   1. *Plumbago*
  Flowers in heads; calyx not glandular, as long as the bracts
                      2. *Ceratostigma abyssinicum*

1. PLUMBAGO L.

Herbs or climbing shrubs with often fascicled leaves; flowers in terminal spikes, with reduced bracts; calyx tubular, with stalked glands; corolla with a long tube and spreading lobes; style single, with 5 apical stigmas; capsule membranous, included in the persistent calyx.

1 Peduncles with stalked glands; calyx with scattered glands towards the apex only
                      1. *P. montis-elgonis*
  Peduncles with sessile glands; calyx densely covered all over with glands
                      2. *P. zeylanica*

1. Plumbago montis-elgonis *Bullock*

A herb with ovate leaves with winged petioles and spikes of magenta flowers.

Rare plant found on Mt. Elgon and only once collected. HE.

Lugard 657.

† By A. D. Q. Agnew.

2. Plumbago zeylanica *L.* (see p. 502)

A trailing glabrous shrub with ovate leaves and white flowers.

Common throughout dry bushland. KIT, MUM, NAR, BAR, RV, NAN, MAC, KAJ.

Agnew, Hanid, and Musumba 8348; Polhill 12.

2. CERATOSTIGMA *Bunge*

Low woody shrubs with simple leaves; flowers sessile, in crowded cymes; bracts and bracteoles enlarged, stiff; calyx tubular, without glands, stiff; corolla with a long tube and spreading lobes; stamens fused to the corolla for half the length of the tube; capsule membranous inside the persistent calyx.

Ceratostigma abyssinicum *Asch.*

A low scabrid shrub, with stiff, elliptic, sharply pointed leaves and heads of blue and crimson flowers.

Rare plant found in dry rocky bushland. NAN. Joy Bally 29.

81. PLANTAGINACEAE‡

Herbs with opposite or alternate simple or lobed leaves and flowers in dense spikes; flowers bisexual, wind-pollinated; calyx of 4 free lobes; corolla tubular below, with 4 spreading lobes; stamens 4, inserted in the corolla tube, anthers exserted on long filaments; ovary superior 2-celled, axile, with 1–few ovules in each cell; fruit a capsule.

1. PLANTAGO L.

The only genus, having the characters of the family; capsule circumscissile; seeds with a mucilaginous testa when wet.

1 Leaves lobed or toothed   1. *P. palmata*
  Leaves entire   2
2 Leaves ovate; lowest flowers distant from each other on the spike; seeds over 4 per capsule   2. *P. major*
  Leaves lanceolate to linear; all flowers crowded and contiguous; seeds 2 per capsule   3. *P. lanceolata*

1. Plantago palmata *Hook. f.* (see p. 507)

A pubescent perennial herb with a rosette of ovate, coarsely crenate leaves and axillary spikes; flowers rather distant from each other towards the base of the spike, whitish; seeds 2 per capsule.

Common on pathsides in montane rain-forest. HE, HM, HA, HK, KIS, RV.

Agnew 7247; Glover *et al.* 1147.

‡ By A. D. Q. Agnew.

2. Plantago major *L.*

Similar to *P. palmata* but annual and with entire leaves and more seeds to the capsule.

An uncommon introduction from Europe, growing in disturbed stream banks. NBI.

Harmsen 6549; Verdcourt 3046.

3. Plantago lanceolata *L.*

Similar to *P. palmata* but with simple linear-lanceolate leaves and dense, cylindrical spikes.

This is another, more recent, introduction from Europe, found on pathsides above 6000 ft. HT, KIT.

Tweedie 68/70; Nattrass 513A.

82. CAMPANULACEAE†

Herbs or shrubs with alternate or opposite, usually simple, leaves and solitary or racemose flowers; flowers bisexual, regular or zygomorphic; sepals 5, fused or free; petals 5, usually fused at least at base; stamens 5, loosely fused or coherent round the stigma and dehiscent in the bud, often with broad filaments; ovary inferior, or at least partially so, of 2–5 carpels; style single; stigmas 2–5; fruit a dry capsule, dehiscent by apical or basal valves or pores.

1	Flowers regular	2
	Flowers zygomorphic	5
2	Petals free nearly to base	3. *Lightfootia*
	Petals fused for at least half of their length	3
3	Sepals with a deflexed margin between the lobes	2. *Campanula*
	Sepals entire, simple between the lobes	4
4	Leaves opposite; flowers orange, more than 3 cm long	1. *Canarina*
	Leaves alternate; flowers blue or white, less than 1·5 cm long	4. *Wahlenbergia*
5	Leaves opposite	7. *Monopsis stellarioides*
	Leaves alternate or in rosettes	6
6	Plant growing from an underground tuber; anthers not fused around the style	5. *Cyphia glandulifera*
	Plant without an underground tuber; anthers strongly fused around the style	6. *Lobelia*

1. CANARINA *L.*

Climbing or trailing glabrous herbs with opposite simple leaves and solitary flowers; calyx with 5 lobes; corolla large, tubular or bell-shaped, orange, shortly lobed; ovary inferior, 5-carpellate; style thickened above, with 5 stigmas; capsule dehiscing as in *Campanula*.

† By A. D. Q. Agnew.

1	Climbing plant, with peduncles and petioles often coiled; sepals united in bud	1. *C. abyssinica*
	Epiphytic or erect herb, without twining peduncles or petioles; sepals free in bud	2. *C. eminii*

1. Canarina abyssinica *Engl.* (see p. 510)

A glaucous climber from a fleshy rootstock, with triangular-ovate leaves and pendulous orange flowers; ovary cup-shaped.

Uncommon plant found in wet forest at medium altitudes in western Kenya. HE, HC, HM, HA, KIT.

Tweedie 66/183; Dowson 543.

2. Canarina eminii *Schweinf.* (see p. 510)

Erect or pendulous (epiphytic or not) herb similar to *C. abyssinica* except for the key characters and the obconical ovary. HE, HC, HT, HM, HA, HK.

Agnew 7256; Williams 584.

2. CAMPANULA *L.*

Herbs or low shrubs with simple or lobed leaves and flowers in racemes or solitary; calyx entire or with reflexed appendages between the lobes; petals fused over half way, usually bell-shaped, mostly blue; stamens hardly coherent around the style; ovary inferior, stigmas mostly 3; capsule pendulous, dehiscing by pores which open below the sepals.

1	Plant annual; corolla densely pubescent over outer surface	1. *C. sp. A*
	Plant perennial; corolla pubescent only on midribs of lobes	2. *C. rigidipila*

1. Campanula *sp.* A.

An erect bristly-hairy annual with sessile oblong leaves and a few terminal heads of blue flowers; corolla hardly exceeding the calyx.

Known only from the Ngong Hills. HA.

Archer 528; Agnew 9681.

2. Campanula rigidipila *A. Rich.*

A perennial with ascending, trailing stems and sessile oblong leaves; heads solitary; corolla blue or white or mauve, often pale, hardly exceeding the calyx.

In dry upland grassland. HA, KAJ.

Bally 221.

3. LIGHTFOOTIA *L'Hérit.*

Perennial or annual herbs or weak shrubs with simple, entire or toothed leaves; flowers solitary or in terminal racemes or corymbs; calyx of 5 free, entire lobes; petals 5, almost free or partially fused

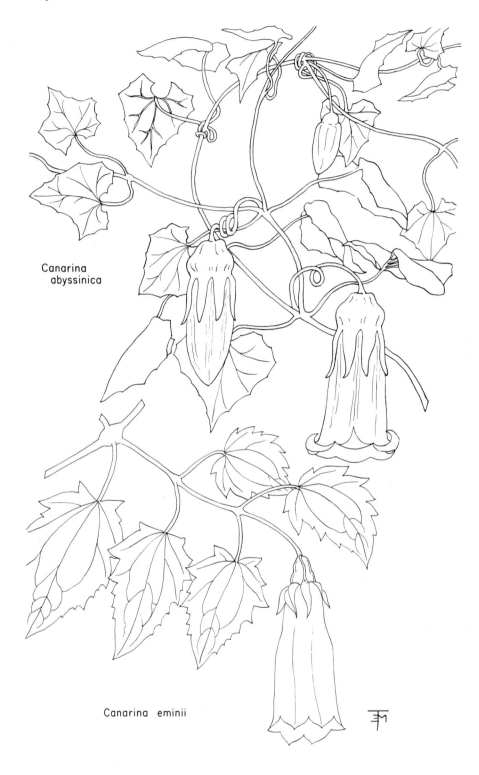

Canarina
abyssinica

Canarina eminii

at base; stamens 5, hardly coherent; ovary inferior, of 3 carpels, beaked above the insertion of the sepals and capsule eventually dehiscent through valves on this beak.

1 Plant annual; leaves elliptic; flowers scattered over the whole plant **2**
   Annual or perennial plant; leaves lanceolate to linear; flowers in definite inflorescences **3**
2 Seeds flat, 2-sided   1. *L. perotifolia*
   Seeds 3-sided, triangular in crossection
                                          2. *L. hirsuta*
3 Plant creeping; flowers solitary on leafy branches   3. *L. cartilaginea*
   Plant erect or with ascending stems; flowers in corymbs or racemes **4**
4 Flowers subsessile in spike-like inflorescences **5**
   Flowers long-pedicellate, in panicles or corymbs **6**
5 Calyx stiffly pubescent; seeds flat, rounded
                                          4. *L. glomerata*
   Calyx glabrous; seeds sharply 3-angled
                                          5. *L.* sp. *A*
6 Flowers in panicles **7**
   Flowers in corymbs **8**
7 Leaves glabrous with rarely a few marginal hairs; stems glabrous   6. *L.* sp. *B*
   Leaves coarsely pubescent; stem hairy below
                                          7. *L. abyssinica*
8 Leaves glabrous, linear, regularly dentate throughout their length   8. *L. denticulata*
   Leaves with a few stiff hairs, often entire for most of their length   9. *L. tanneri*

1. Lightfootia perotifolia (*Willd.*) *E. Wimm.* (*Cephalostigma erectum* (Roth.) Vatke)

A small pubescent annual, divaricately branched above, with elliptic, often undulate leaves and minute white flowers.
   Locally common in shallow-soil grassland. HC, MAC, RV.
   Agnew, Kibe, and Mathenge 10316.

2. Lightfootia hirsuta (*Edgw.*) *E. Wimm.*

Similar to *L. perotifolia* but often more divaricately branched below.
   This plant is also found on shallow soils which are wet for only short periods of the year. KIT.
   Tweedie 67/311, 3508.

3. Lightfootia cartilaginea *Scott* (see p. 512)

A creeping wiry herb with sessile, lanceolate, subentire leaves which have a pale thickened margin; flowers lilac and blue.

Uncommon plant found in wooded grassland. KIT.
   Tweedie 66/357.

4. Lightfootia glomerata *Engl.*

A stiffly pubescent perennial, woody below, with lanceolate leaves and terminal spike-like racemes of groups of subsessile blue flowers.
   Locally common in dry rocky grassland. HE, KIT, MAC.
   Agnew 9399; Napper 1907.

5. Lightfootia *sp.* **A.**

Similar to *L. glomerata* except for the key characters and mostly with solitary flowers at the nodes.
   Locally common at the edges of shallow-soil grassland. KIT, MAC.
   Faden 67226; Agnew 8323.

6. Lightfootia *sp.* **B.**

A straggling glabrescent perennial herb with ascending stems from a woody base and linear leaves; flowers blue, in a very loose panicle.
   Common in dry grassland on well-drained mineral soils especially in the Rift Valley. RV, KAJ.
   Verdcourt 3573; Agnew 10632.

7. Lightfootia abyssinica *A. Rich.* (see p. 512)

Similar to *L.* sp. *B* but often annual, with very hairy, dentate, lanceolate leaves.
   Locally common in dry grassland. KAJ.
   Hanid 195.

8. Lightfootia denticulata *Sond.*

A straggling glabrescent herb with linear, serrate leaves and terminal corymbs of bright blue flowers which have a white throat.
   Rare plant found in wooded grassland. MAC.
   Tweedie 67/114; Verdcourt 2170.

9. Lightfootia tanneri *E. Wimm.*

An erect herb, often annual, with hairy, lanceolate leaves and pale flowers in terminal corymbs; seeds 3-angled.
   A plant of disturbed soils in dry grassland. KAJ.
   Gilbert M9.

4. WAHLENBERGIA *Schrad.*

Erect herbs or weak shrubs with alternate simple leaves and flowers solitary or in racemes or corymbs; calyx 5-lobed; corolla fused over one-third of its length, bell-shaped; stamens with expanded filaments; ovary inferior, 2–3-carpellate; style bearing 3 stigmas; capsule dehiscent at apex above the insertion of the sepals.

1 Flowers solitary **2**
   Flowers in long-pedunculate inflorescences **3**

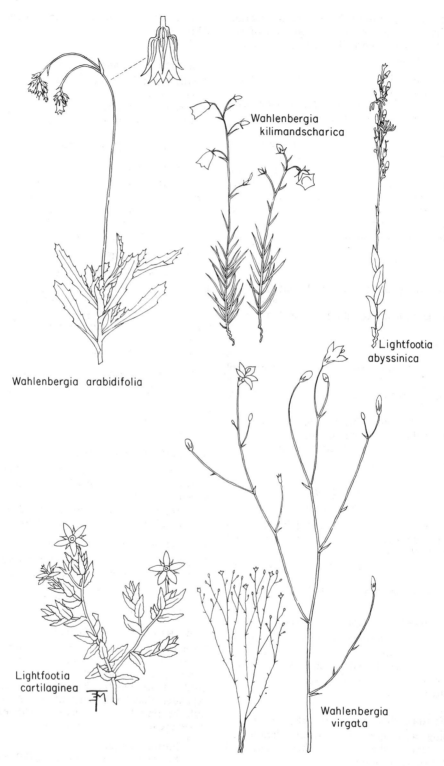

Wahlenbergia kilimandscharica

Wahlenbergia arabidifolia

Lightfootia abyssinica

Lightfootia cartilaginea

Wahlenbergia virgata

2   Stems leafy; flowers white; capsules cylindric
                              1. *W. silenoides*
    Leaves in rosettes; flowers blue; capsules sub-
      globose   2. *W. pusilla*
3   Leaves lanceolate to broad-elliptic   4
    Leaves linear or scale-like   5
4   Plant annual   4. *W. sp. A*
    Plant perennial   3. *W. arabidifolia*
5   Flowers white; leaves scale-like 5. *W. virgata*
    Flowers blue; leaves linear
                              6. *W. kilimandscharica*

1. Wahlenbergia silenoides *Hochst.*
A trailing and ascending perennial herb with small,
narrowly lanceolate to elliptic leaves and white or
pale blue flowers; capsules cylindric.
    Locally common in montane grassland. HC,
HM.
    Tweedie 3020.

2. Wahlenbergia pusilla *A. Rich.*
A pubescent, trailing perennial herb with leafless
stolons or rhizomes bearing a terminal rosette of
oblanceolate leaves; flowers clear blue.
    Locally common in disturbed peaty or soli-
fluction soils in alpine zone. HE, HA, HK.
    Lind 5755; Agnew 7211.

3. Wahlenbergia arabidifolia *(Engl.) Brehm.* (see p. 512)
A glabrescent to pubescent trailing herb with
oblanceolate, coarsely dentate leaves and a few
pale blue flowers on an erect leafless peduncle.
    Locally common in grassland in the lower
alpine and heath zones and upper forest levels. HE,
HC, HM, HA, HK.
    Lind 5027; Verdcourt 606.

4. Wahlenbergia *sp.* A.
An erect annual with elliptic leaves crowded at the
base of the stem, and white flowers on long erect
pedicels.
    In dry rocky shallow-soil areas. MAC.
    Agnew 10099.

5. Wahlenbergia virgata *Engl.* (see p. 512)
An erect, branching, glabrous perennial herb from
deep rhizomes, with leaves reduced to short scales,
and solitary white flowers.
    This plant looks as if it is partially parasitic, but
it is probably not. The main phytosynthetic area is
the stem, many branches of which end blindly
without flowering. It is locally common in disturbed dry, cold upland grassland. HE, HC, HT,
HM, HA, HK, KAJ.
    Agnew, Kibe, and Mathenge 10377; Glover
4207.

6. Wahlenbergia kilimandscharica *Engl.* (see p. 512)
An erect glabrous perennial herb from a woody,
rhizomatous rootstock, with linear leaves and
bright blue flowers in a terminal corymb.
    Locally common in rocky soils within the
bamboo zone. The KAJ record comes from Kilimanjaro. HC, HA, HK, KAJ.
    Coe and Kirrika 375; Agnew, Kibe, and
Mathenge 10522.

5. CYPHIA *Berg.*
Erect or twining herbs usually with a buried tuber;
leaves alternate, simple; flowers in terminal or
axillary racemes; sepals 5, free; petals 5, free, with
three curving upwards and two sharply bent downwards; stamens free; ovary inferior, of 2 carpels;
stigma and style continuous, unlobed, with a
central, apparently nectiferous pit.

Cyphia glandulifera *A. Rich.* (see p. 514)
A pubescent perennial herb with obovate or elliptic leaves ± in a rosette at base, and an erect,
sometimes twining raceme of pink flowers.
    This pretty plant of shallow soils flowers im-
mediately after the first rains. As the above description shows, it is very variable (as defined here)
and the form with twining stems (found mostly
near Kedong and the Rift Valley escarpment) as
well as the elliptic-leaved, much branched form
(found principally in dry bushland) may both
prove to be distinct from the obovate-leaved one.
HA, BAR, RV, MAC, NBI, KAJ.
    Faden 67247; Agnew and Hanid 7487.

6. LOBELIA *L.*
Herbs or shrubs with alternate, simple leaves;
flowers solitary or in racemes, bisexual, zygomorphic; corolla split along the upper side, with 2,
usually filiform, upper teeth, and 3 broader ones;
anthers fused around the style; ovary inferior, with
or without an apical part above the insertion of
the sepals and thus sometimes appearing superior,
dehiscing by an apical slit above the sepals or by
irregular ruptures.

1   Large herbs with crowded nodes and a
      terminal rosette of sessile, simple, linear to
      lanceolate leaves and sessile flowers   2
    Small herbs with well-spaced leaves and long
      internodes   8
2   Bracts ovate or elliptic   3
    Bracts linear   6
3   Stamens much longer than bracts
                                 1. *L. aberdarica*
    Bracts much longer than stamens   4

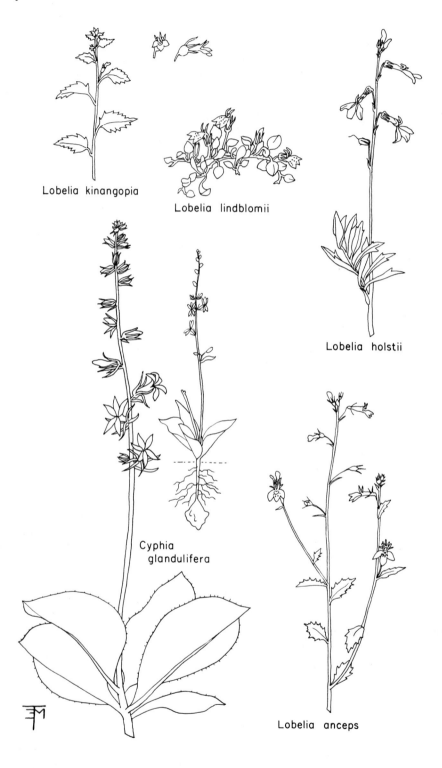

Lobelia kinangopia

Lobelia lindblomii

Lobelia holstii

Cyphia
glandulifera

Lobelia anceps

4 Anthers hairy at base   2. *L. keniensis*
   Anthers glabrous at base   5
5 Bracts pubescent on both sides; corolla with
   two oblong lateral holes   3. *L. sattimae*
   Bracts glabrous on both sides; corolla without
   holes   4. *L. elgonensis*
6 Bracts at least 4 times as long as flowers
                                    5. *L. telekii*
   Bracts less than twice as long as flowers   7
7 Calyx and corolla pubescent externally
                                    6. *L. gibberoa*
   Calyx and corolla glabrous, the calyx ciliate
   at margin only   7. *L. bambuseti*
8 Creeping plants with solitary or paired axillary flowers   9
   Erect or creeping plants with flowers in an
   erect raceme   12
9 Flowers white with purple markings
                                    8. *L. baumanii*
   Flowers blue or purple   10
10 Ovary below the sepal lobes pubescent (use
   10 x lens)   9. *L. minutula*
   Ovary below the sepal lobes glabrous   11
11 Leaves elliptic, narrowing gradually at base
   and apex   10. *L. duripratii*
   Leaves suborbicular, ± cordate at base,
   rounded at apex   11. *L. lindblomii*
12 Perennial from woody rootstock; flowers
   purple to pinkish-mauve   12. *L. holstii*
   Annuals or perennials from creeping rootstock; flowers blue   13
13 Anthers glabrous on the dorsal (upper) surface   13. *L. molleri*
   Anthers pubescent on the dorsal surface   14
14 Erect annuals, stems sometimes ascending
   from the base, but not rooting at the nodes;
   leaves orbicular to lanceolate-elliptic   15
   Annual or perennial with creeping stems,
   rooting at the nodes, the flowering stems
   ascending; leaves linear to linear-lanceolate
                                  14. *L. welwitschii*
15 Bracts of the lowest flowers linear to oblanceolate, sessile   15. *L. anceps*
   Bracts of the lowest flowers orbicular to
   broad ovate, narrowed into a short, winged
   petiole   16. *L. kinangopia*

1. Lobelia aberdarica *R. E. Fr. & Th. Fr. jr.* (see
p. 516)
A large, densely to sparsely pubescent, soft perennial shrub with ovate-elliptic bracts and pale
greenish corolla.

This species is found in swamps, 7000–10 500
ft, except on Mt. Kenya. HE, HC, HT, HM, HA,
KIT.

Tweedie 67/267; Piers in EAH 17868.

2. Lobelia keniensis *R. E. Fr. & Th. Fr. jr.*
A stemless, glabrous rosette plant with a pool of
water in the rosette and an erect spike of blue-
purple flowers.

Only found on Mt. Kenya above 10 000 ft in
marshes, where it is common. HK.

Dyson 530; Coe 652.

3. Lobelia sattimae *R. E. Fr. & Th. Fr. jr.*
Similar to *L. keniensis* except for the keyed
characters, and with the curious 'window' in the
side of the corolla. This species is confined to
swamps in the Aberdares above 9500 ft. HA.

Hedberg 1608.

4. Lobelia elgonensis *R. E. Fr. & Th. Fr. jr.*
Similar to the preceding species but with a longer
entire corolla.

This is the Mt. Elgon vicariad of the last two
species and is found in swamp situations above
10 000 ft. HE.

Synge 911.

5. Lobelia telekii *Schweinf.*
Similar to *L. keniensis* but with narrower,
pubescent leaves and long, hairy (almost feathery)
bracts which completely hide the small white and
purple flowers.

In wet stony ground on the three highest
mountains, above 10 000 ft. HE, HA, HK.

Dale 6956; Coe 499.

6. Lobelia gibberoa *Hemsl.* (see p. 516)
A pubescent soft shrub, with sparsely-branched
stems which terminate in large rosettes of oblanceolate, serrate leaves; inflorescences long (whole
plant reaching 10 m on occasion) with green
flowers bearing conspicuous blue-mauve stamens.

Common in disturbed places in wet montane
forest above 6000 ft. HE, HC, HT, HM, HA, HK,
KAJ.

Bally 7986; Agnew 7457.

7. Lobelia bambuseti *R. E. Fries*
Similar to *L. gibberoa* but a smaller, more richly
branched shrub.

Locally common in bamboo forest edges above
8500 ft in the Aberdares and Mt. Kenya. HA, HK.

Agnew, Hedberg, and Mmari 9628; Verdcourt
2062.

8. Lobelia baumanii *Engl.*
A trailing herb with ovate coarsely-toothed leaves
and 1–2 axillary, white and purple flowers.

An uncommon forest floor plant of wetter
montane forest, often found on pathsides. HA,
HK, HN.

Agnew 5844; Nattrass 700.

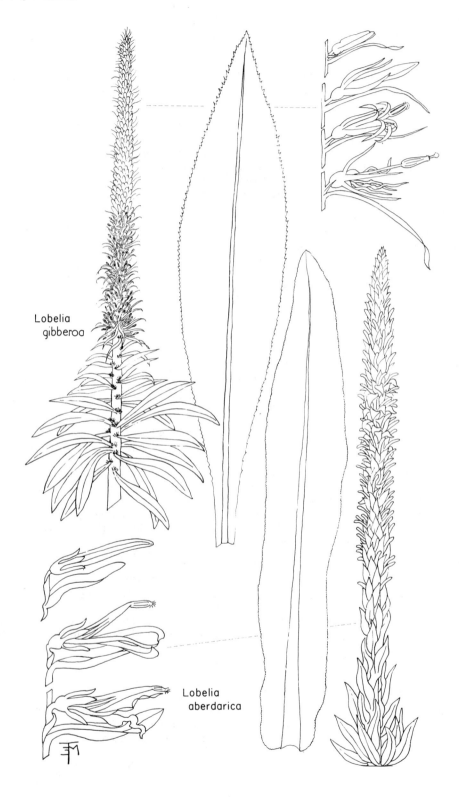

Lobelia
gibberoa

Lobelia
aberdarica

9. Lobelia minutula *Engl.*

A mat-forming, creeping herb with small orbicular leaves and blue flowers on short pedicels.

Common in disturbed alpine and subalpine soils of the Aberdares and Mt. Kenya. HA, HK.

Strid 2318; Napier 3161.

10. Lobelia duripratii *Th. Fr. jr.*

Similar to *L. minutula* but with elliptic leaves and forming looser mats, with flowers raised above leaf level on longer peduncles.

Uncommon plant found in wet montane short grassland. HM, HA, HK, KIT.

Agnew 5861; Glover, Gwynne, and Samuel 1047.

11. Lobelia lindblomii *Mildbr.* (see p. 514)

A creeping herb with orbicular, often cordate leaves and shortly pedicelled blue flowers.

Only known from alpine and subalpine grassland on Mt. Elgon. HE.

Hedberg 123; Strid 3435.

12. Lobelia holstii *Engl.* (see p. 514)

A stiff perennial with ascending stems and oblanceolate sessile leaves; flowers rather few, at top of leafless flowering stem, reddish, purple or mauve, not blue.

Our commonest *Lobelia*, found in rocky places in dry grassland from 6000–11 000 ft. HC, HT, HM, HA, HK, KIT, RV, NAN, MAC, NBI, KAJ.

Hedberg 1083; Lind 5123.

13. Lobelia molleri *Henriques*

An ascending annual or weak perennial, rooting at the nodes, with ovate-elliptic leaves and small blue flowers, the corolla often shorter than the calyx.

Rare plant found in short grassland and only once recorded in Kenya, from Sekerr. HE.

Agnew, Kibe, and Mathenge 10315.

14. Lobelia welwitschii *Engl. & Diels*

A trailing perennial with leaves linear-elliptic or reduced to short linear scales; flowers blue.

Uncommon plant found in grassy marshes in western Kenya. KIT.

Rogers and Gardner 375.

15. Lobelia anceps *L.f.* (*L. melleri* Hemsl. var. *grossidens* E. Win.) (see p. 514)

An erect annual with leaves varying from orbicular at the base to linear above, but mostly elliptic; flowers conspicuous and bright blue.

This is the showy *Lobelia* of shallow soils especially near Nairobi and at the coast. HE, HT, HM, HA, KIT, KIS, EMB, MAC, NBI.

Lugard 149; Agnew 9414.

16. Lobelia kinangopia *Wimmer* (see p. 514)

An erect or ascending annual with mostly orbicular leaves and a fruit which often protrudes as much as half its length above the insertion of the sepals.

This plant is similar to *L. anceps* but is much smaller and has broader leaves. It is rare on higher altitude shallow soils. HE, HC, HA.

Agnew, Kibe, and Mathenge 10317; Verdcourt 604 (type).

7. MONOPSIS *Salisb.*

Herbs similar to *Lobelia* except for the opposite leaves.

Monopsis stellarioides (*Presl.*) *Urb.* (see p. 519)

A trailing herb from a central fibrous rootstock, with backwardly directed bristles on stems similar to those of *Galium*; leaves linear-elliptic; flowers solitary, violet-orange or dull pink or liver-coloured.

Locally common in dry upland grassland. HE, HC, HM, HA, KIT.

Agnew 9511; Kerfoot 1387.

83. BORAGINACEAE†

Herbs, shrubs, or trees with alternate, exstipulate, usually simple leaves and cymose inflorescences; flowers regular or rarely zygomorphic, bisexual; sepals 4–5, shortly joined at base; corolla with a short or long tube and 4–5 imbricate or contort lobes; stamens 5, inserted on the corolla tube; ovary of 2 carpels which are each subdivided into 2 chambers each with one ovule, the style terminal or basal; fruit of 4 nutlets or splitting into 4 nutlets or rarely drupes.

1 Calyx zygomorphic, with reduced upper lobe; corolla zygomorphic, 2-lipped
         8. *Echiochilon lithospermoides*
   Calyx and corolla regular, 4–5-lobed   2
2 Flowers and fruits sessile   3
   Flowers and fruits pedicellate   4
3 Flowers solitary; styles 2
         1. *Coldenia procumbens*
   Flowers in elongating scorpioid cymes; style 1   2. *Heliotropium*
4 Flowers in panicles; stamens, especially the connective, exserted from the corolla tube
                           5
   Flowers in raceme-like inflorescences; stamens included within the corolla tube   6
5 Calyx enlarging in fruit; stamen connective very hairy   4. *Trichodesma*
   Calyx not enlarging in fruit; stamen connective glabrous   3. *Vaupelia hispida*

† By C. H. S. Kabuye and A. D. Q. Agnew.

6   Nutlets covered with hooked ('sticky') spines
                                    5. *Cynoglossum*
    Nutlets smooth and glossy   7
7   Flowers blue; nutlets brown, loosely held
        within the calyx   6. *Myosotis*
    Flowers white; nutlets white, persistent on
        the pedicel
                    7. *Lithospermum afromontanum*

1. COLDENIA *L.*

Trailing herbs with entire or dentate leaves and
solitary axillary flowers; calyx deeply 4–5-lobed,
but enlarging in fruit; corolla with a short tube and
4–5 spreading lobes; stamens 4–5 included in the
corolla tube; styles 2, from the top of the ovary;
fruit separating into 4 nutlets.

Coldenia procumbens *L.*

A low spreading annual with obovate to orbicular
crenate leaves which are silky-hairy above except
on the channelled nerves; flowers minute, white.
    Rare plant found in hot subsaline alluvial
seasonally flooded land. BAR.
    Bally 7739.

2. HELIOTROPIUM *L.*

Erect, hairy herbs with alternate, entire or toothed
leaves and terminal scorpioid cymes of subsessile
flowers; calyx bell-shaped, deeply 5-lobed; corolla
with a cylindrical tube and 5 spreading lobes;
stamens 5, included; ovary 4-celled, with a simple
terminal style, fruit schizocarpic into 2 or 4 dry,
hairy or glabrous portions.

1   Spikes sessile; bracts present, scattered along
        spike or only a few at base of spike   2
    Spikes often pedunculate; bracts absent   5
2   Stigma sessile or subsessile on the ovary (best
        seen in fruit)   3
    Stigma borne on a style at least half as long as
        the fruit   4
3   Plant a perennial shrub; leaves crowded,
        lanceolate-elliptic, less than 5 times as long
        as broad; stigma globose
                            1. *H. sessilistigma*
    Plant a woody annual; leaves well-spaced,
        lanceolate to linear-oblong, usually over 6
        times as long as wide; stigma conical with a
        small central protuberance
                            2. *H. strigosum*
4   Corolla lobes hairy above the tube; stigma
        globose   3. *H. albohispidum*
    Corolla lobes glabrous except for the mouth
        of the tube; stigma minutely conical
                            4. *H. rariflorum*
5   One sepal, outermost on the developing
        spike, twice as wide as the rest; flowers
        subsessile   5. *H. ovalifolium*

    All sepals similar; flowers sessile   6
6   Plant prostrate   6. *H. supinum*
    Plant erect   7
7   Leaves linear; corolla lobes triangular, obtuse,
        acute or acuminate at apex   8
    Leaves lanceolate to ovate; corolla lobes
        oblong to orbicular, rounded at apex   10
8   Corolla lobes with a long filiform tip
                            7. *H. subulatum*
    Corolla lobes acute or obtuse, without a long
        filiform tip   9
9   Leaves usually undulate; corolla lobes acute
                            8. *H. undulatifolium*
    Leaves flat; corolla lobes obtuse
                            9. *H. somalense*
10 Plants mostly scabrid-hairy; spikes mostly in
        pairs, occasionally solitary or in threes at
        stem apices   11
    Plants softly hairy; spikes more than 4, in a
        terminal panicle   10. *H.* sp. *A*
11 Plant trailing; leaves ovate, entire
                            12. *H. scotteae*
    Plant erect; leaves lanceolate to ovate,
        minutely crisped or serrate at margin
                            11. *H. steudneri*

1. Heliotropium sessilistigma *Hutch. & E. A. Bruce*

An erect, bristly-hairy, much branched low wiry
shrub or woody herb with elliptic leaves and
short sessile spikes of white flowers.
    Rare plant found in dry stony country. MAG.
Greenway 9569.

2. Heliotropium strigosum *Willd.*

An erect, wiry, stiffly-hairy annual with elliptic to
linear leaves and short spikes of dirty white
flowers.
    Locally common in dry stony country especi-
ally where disturbed. MUM, MAG, EMB, MAC,
NBI, KAJ.
    Hanid and Kiniaruh 457; Napper 1647.

3. Heliotropium albohispidum *Bak.*

Similar to *H. strigosum* but usually perennial and
more straggling.
    Locally common in dry stony bushland. MAG,
KAJ.
    Agnew 5393; Verdcourt 2565.

4. Heliotropium rariflorum *Stocks*

Similar to *H. albohispidum* except for the keyed
characters.
    Rare plant in dry country. MAC.
    Greenway 9570.

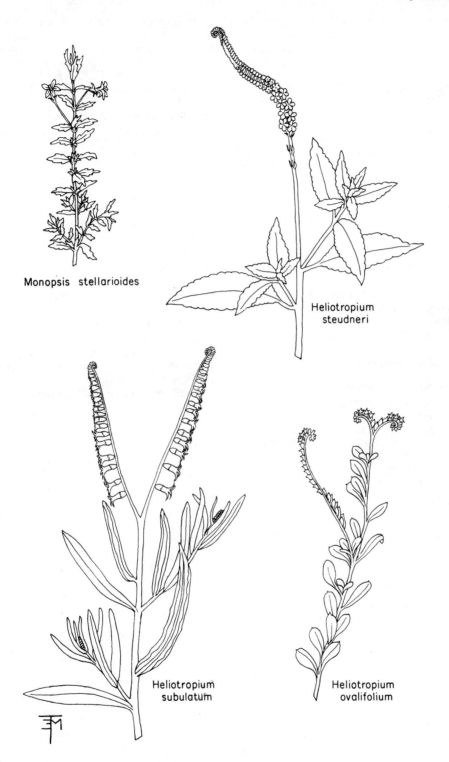

Monopsis stellarioides

Heliotropium
steudneri

Heliotropium
subulatum

Heliotropium
ovalifolium

5. Heliotropium ovalifolium *Forsk.* (see p. 519).

A white-hairy, woody, prostrate or ascending, annual or perennial shrub with petiolate spathulate to elliptic leaves and subsessile spikes of white flowers.

Locally common in disturbed *Combretum* woodland. MAG, MAC, KAJ.

Agnew and Tweedie 9291.

6. Heliotropium supinum *L.*

A prostrate, annual, white-hairy herb with petiolate, spathulate to elliptic, usually impressed-nerved leaves; spikes conspicuously elongating in fruit; calyx almost concealing the white corolla, and enclosing the fruit.

Rare plant found in seasonally flooded river sands in hot country. MAG, MAC.

Polhill and Greenway 447.

7. Heliotropium subulatum *(DC.) Martelli* (see p. 519)

A spreading-hairy, erect perennial herb from a woody rootstock with elliptic to linear leaves and long spikes of yellow flowers.

Locally common in dry bushland. BAR, MAC, KAJ.

Agnew 9861; Napper 522.

8. Heliotropium undulatifolium *Turrill*

An erect pubescent perennial herb with linear undulate leaves and short spikes of crowded conspicuous white to cream flowers.

An attractive species of dry upland grassland. HT, HA, NAR, RV, MAG.

Glover, Gwynne and Samuel 820; Agnew 9306.

9. Heliotropium somalense *Vatke*

An erect, minutely hairy herb with linear leaves and elongating spikes of white flowers; nutlets winged and ridged.

Locally common in disturbed dry country. BAR, MAG.

Agnew 5392; Leippert 5177.

10. Heliotropium *sp.* **A.**

An erect, densely pubescent herb from a creeping rootstock with lanceolate-elliptic leaves and a terminal panicle of rather dense spikes; corolla white.

Locally common in disturbed places in dry grassland. RV, MAG, KAJ.

Verdcourt 3759; Agnew 7621.

11. Heliotropium steudneri *Vatke* (see p. 519)

An erect, scabrid-pubescent herb from a perennial rootstock, with ovate to lanceolate leaves and elongating spikes of white or cream flowers.

A common and variable species, the form from more arid areas (which may prove to be distinct) having smaller, more pointed and often entire leaves. It is a plant of disturbed dry grassland. NAR, RV, MAG, MAC, NBI, KAJ.

Kerfoot 1870; Agnew and Hanid 7565.

12. Heliotropium scotteae *Rendle*

A minutely scabrid robust trailing perennial herb with large ovate leaves and long spikes of white flowers.

Locally common and often forming large masses in montane forest edges. HA, HK, HN, KIT, MAC, NBI.

Napper, Lind, Agnew, and Beecher 1715; Hanid and Kiniaruh 993.

3. VAUPELIA *Brand.*

Herbs similar to *Trichodesma* but the calyx not enlarging in fruit and the connectives of the stamens glabrous, stiff, straight.

Vaupelia hispida *(Bak. & Wright) Brand.*

An erect strigose annual with elliptic leaves and blue flowers in raceme-like monochasial cymes.

Locally common in grassland, especially in the Rift Valley. RV, KAJ.

Pohill and Paulo 1008; Agnew and Azavedo 9312.

4. TRICHODESMA *R. Br.*

Erect herbs or shrubs with entire leaves and large flowers in panicles; calyx deeply 5-lobed, enlarging in fruit; corolla with a short tube and 5 broad or narrow spreading lobes; stamens with short filaments and linear, connivent anthers; connective of anthers produced beyond them and often twisted and hairy; nutlets smooth or tubercled.

1   Plant annual; pedicels and sepals with long spreading hairs   1. *T. zeylanicum*
     Plant perennial; peduncles and sepals glabrous or with a few stiff bristles only   2
2   Plant shrubby; leaves narrowing gradually at base into a short petiole   2. *T. schimperi*
     Plant herbaceous; leaves rounded at base, subsessile   3. *T. physaloides*

1. Trichodesma zeylanicum *(L.) R. Br.*

An erect hispid annual with lanceolate-elliptic subsessile leaves and an open panicle of pale blue to white flowers.

Locally common in disturbed dry bushland. MUM, KIS, EMB, MAC, KAJ.

Agnew and Musumba 8619; Gillett 18354.

2. Trichodesma schimperi *Baker*

A small strigose shrub with elliptic-linear leaves and small flowers with heart-shaped sepals.

Rare plant found on stony hillsides in the Machakos area. MAC.

Katumani 49.

3. Trichodesma physaloides *A. DC.* (see p. 522)

An erect glabrescent herb from a woody or tuberous rootstock with subsessile ovate-lanceolate leaves and rather few to many large white flowers in a terminal panicle.

Locally common in wooded grassland in western Kenya. HE, HC, HT, KIT, MUM.

Mainwaring 2508; Tweedie 68/149.

5. CYNOGLOSSUM *L.*

Erect herbs with entire leaves and blue flowers in raceme-like scorpioid cymes; calyx 5-lobed, not enlarging in fruit; corolla with short tube and 5 spreading lobes, each with an erect protuberance at base which may close the throat; stamens 5 with short filaments; ovary 4-lobed; fruit of 4 nutlets each bearing barbed, glochidiate spines.

1 Stem leaves ovate, with more than 3 pairs of veins parallel to the midrib at apex   2
   Stem leaves ovate-lanceolate to lanceolate, with only 2 submarginal veins parallel to the midrib at apex   3
2 Nutlets glabrous above except for a central row of spines; leaves softly pubescent beneath   1. *C. lancifolium*
   Nutlets uniformly spiny all over; leaves scabrid beneath (when rubbed towards the apex)   2. *C. amplifolium*
3 Racemes in pairs usually divergent from each other at 90° or more; fruits less than 5 mm in diameter   3. *C. lanceolatum*
   Raceme pairs divergent at less than 90°; fruits 5·5 mm or more in diameter   4
4 Lower leaves ± oblanceolate, rounded at apex; flowers white   6. *C.* sp. *A*
   All leaves lanceolate, acute; flowers mostly blue   5
5 Face of nutlets usually with a strong central row of spines and either glabrous on each side of this or sparsely covered with shorter spines   4. *C. geometricum*
   Nutlets uniformly spiny all over   6
6 Lower leaves in a rosette arising from woody rootstock; mature fruits up to more than 10 mm in diameter   5. *C* sp. *B*
   Leaves not in a rosette, well distributed along the stem; mature fruits 5·5–8 mm in diameter   7. *C. coeruleum*

1. Cynoglossum lancifolium *Hook. f.*

An erect perennial pubescent herb with petiolate, ovate-elliptic lower leaves and sessile upper ones; flowers blue, rather large; fruiting pedicels often over 1 cm long; nutlets over 5 mm wide.

Locally common in disturbed montane forest clearings. HE, HC, HM, HA, HK.

Agnew 9068; Glover, Gwynne, and Samuel 1491.

2. Cynoglossum amplifolium *DC.*

Similar to *C. lancifolium* except for the key characters, this species is rarer, being principally found near Uplands. HM, HA.

Agnew 9436; Verdcourt 1158.

3. Cynoglossum lanceolatum *Forsk.*

An erect annual with lanceolate to ovate-lanceolate leaves and very small white or pale blue flowers; fruits densely bristly.

Locally common as a weed of disturbed places and arable land. HC, HM, HA, MAC, NBI.

Verdcourt 383; Agnew, Kibe, and Mathenge 10258.

4. Cynoglossum geometricum *Baker & Wright* (see p. 522)

A hispid annual or perennial with ovate-lanceolate to lanceolate, acute leaves and simple or branched stems; cymes in panicles or racemes; flowers bright blue; fruits usually with two glabrous areas on the upper side.

A very variable plant, as defined here, which shows intergrading variation in plant habit, fruit size and fruit spines. It is generally distributed in montane forest clearings and pathsides and as a field weed at higher altitudes. HE, HC, HM, HA, HK, KIT, MUM, KIS, NAR, MAC, NBI, KAJ.

Agnew, Azavedo, and Khatri 9535; Nattrass 652.

5. Cynoglossum *sp.* **B.**

A very scabrid perennial herb with a rosette of linear-elliptic leaves from a woody rootstock and blue flowers on long pedicels; fruits spiny all over.

Rare plant found in montane grassland. HM, NBI.

van Someren 363; Agnew, Azavedo, and Khatri 9536.

6. Cynoglossum *sp.* **A.**

A scabrid perennial herb with linear leaves, a woody rootstock and white flowers; fruits not seen.

Rare plant found in the Elgon area in wooded grassland. HE, KIT.

Hedberg 19; Tweedie 67/135.

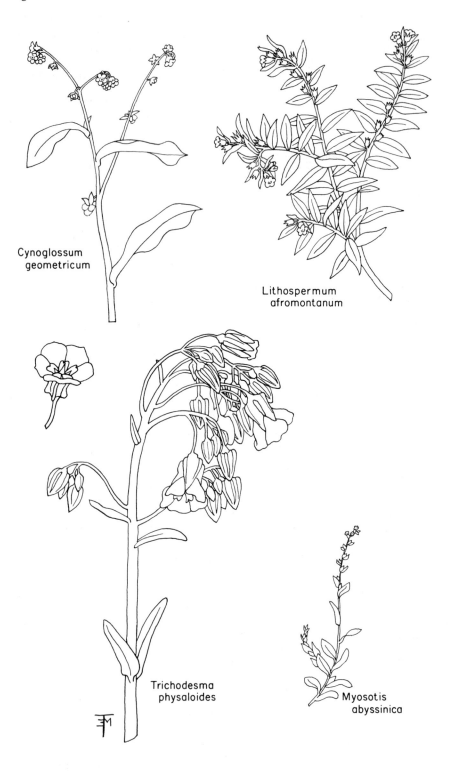

Cynoglossum
geometricum

Lithospermum
afromontanum

Trichodesma
physaloides

Myosotis
abyssinica

7. Cynoglossum coeruleum *DC.*

A trailing, sometimes shrubby, scabrid perennial with linear leaves in sterile and fertile rosettes, and small blue flowers; fruits usually spiny all over.

Common in upland grassland. HE, HC, HT, HM, HA, KIT, NAR, RV, NAN, MAC, NBI, KAJ.

Glover 4549; Harmsen 6494.

6. MYOSOTIS *L.*

Annual or perennial herbs with entire leaves and small blue flowers in raceme-like monochasial cymes with no or few bracts; calyx deeply 5-lobed; corolla with a short tube, hairy at the throat, and with 5, contort, spreading half-rounded lobes; stamens 5, included in the tube; nutlets ovoid, 3-angled, smooth and glossy.

1 Cushion-forming plant; inflorescences shorter than the leaves   1. *M. keniensis*
   Erect plant, not cushion-forming; inflorescences longer than the leaves   2
2 Plant annual; calyx over 3 mm long, and longer than the pedicel in fruit
           2. *M. abyssinica*
   Plant perennial; calyx less than 2·5 mm long, and shorter than the pedicel in fruit
           3. *M. vestergrenii*

1. Myosotis keniensis *Th. Fr. jr.*

A low cushion-forming plant with obovate or spathulate leaves overtopping the few, blue flowers.

Rare plant found in the alpine zone of Mt. Kenya. HK.

Coe and Kirrika 291.

2. Myosotis abyssinica *Boiss & Reut.* (see p. 522)

An erect pubescent annual, often only sparsely branched, with oblong-elliptic leaves and long raceme-like inflorescences of small blue flowers.

Locally common on Mt. Kenya only in disturbed soil in the alpine and subalpine zone. HE, HC, HM, HA, HK.

Hedberg 187; Agnew, Kibe, and Mathenge 10545

3. Myosotis vestergrenii *Stroh.*

Similar to *M. abyssinica* but a trailing perennial with a larger corolla and smaller calyx.

Locally abundant along watercourses and marshes in the heath zone. HE, HA.

Agnew 7278; Rauh 527.

7. LITHOSPERMUM *L.*

Similar to *Myosotis* but sometimes woody, always with a bract subtending the flowers, and the corolla imbricate, without hairs at the mouth of the tube.

Lithospermum afromontanum *Weim.* (see p. 522)

A weak, trailing silky-hairy shrub with sessile ovate to lanceolate leaves and white flowers with a yellow centre; nutlets ovoid, white, persistent.

Locally common in clearings in montane forest and heath woodland. HE, HC, HA, HM, HK, KAJ.

Lind and Agnew 5628; Thulin and Tidigs 239.

8. ECHIOCHILON *Desf.*

Erect woody herbs with entire leaves and bracteate flowers scattered in raceme-like inflorescences; calyx deeply 4–5-lobed; corolla zygomorphic, with a curved tube and bilabiate limb; stamens 5, included in the corolla tube; nutlets ovoid.

Echiochilon lithospermoides (*S. Moore*) *Johnston*

An erect, scabrid woody annual with small sessile ovate leaves and pink-mauve flowers.

Locally common in dry bushland. NAN, KAJ.

Napper 1723.

84. SOLANACEAE†

Herbs, shrubs, or rarely trees with alternate, exstipulate leaves and racemose or cymose inflorescences or flowers solitary; flowers regular, rarely zygomorphic, bisexual; calyx of 5 fused lobes; corolla of 5 fused petals, contort or imbricate in the bud; stamens 5, with filaments fused to corolla tube; ovary usually with two carpels and a simple style and stigma; ovules numerous, on intrusive axile placentas; fruit a berry or capsule.

1 Calyx loose, inflated and papery in fruit   2
   Calyx not enlarged in fruit, of if so then closely appressed to the fruit   4
2 Corolla blue; carpels 5   6. *Nicandra*
   Corolla yellow to orange; carpels 2   3
3 Flowers solitary at each node   3. *Physalis*
   Flowers many at each node
         4. *Withania somnifera*
4 Corolla tube saucer-shaped or bell-shaped, never more than 1 cm long   5
   Corolla tube cylindrical, over 1 cm long   6
5 Calyx lobes longer than the calyx tube; corolla saucer-shaped   1. *Solanum*
   Calyx lobes shorter than the calyx tube; corolla bell-shaped   2. *Discopodium*
6 Capsule spiny   8. *Datura*
   Capsule smooth, or fruit a berry   7
7 Thorns present at nodes
         5. *Lycium europaeum*
   Unarmed shrubs or herbs   8
8 Corolla pubescent   9. *Nicotiana*
   Corolla glabrous   7. *Cestrum*

† By A. D. Q. Agnew.

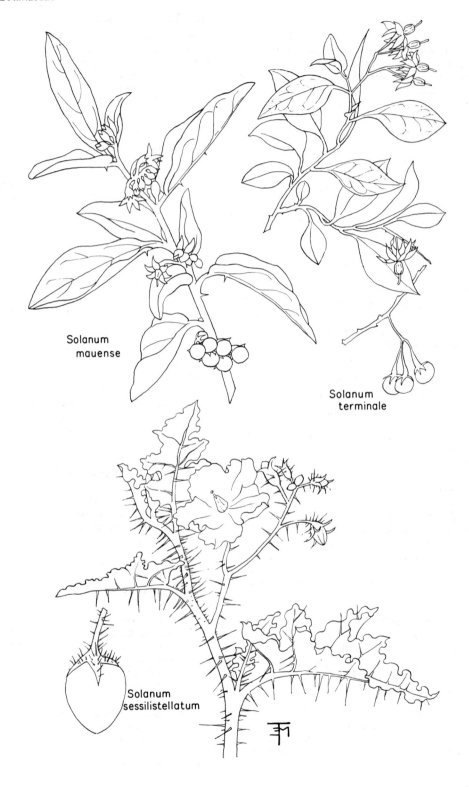

Solanum
mauense

Solanum
terminale

Solanum
sessilistellatum

1. SOLANUM *L.*

Trees, shrubs, herbs or climbers, often stellate-hairy, with alternate, simple or pinnately lobed leaves and racemose or cymose inflorescences of ± regular flowers; calyx shortly fused at base, 5-lobed; corolla contort, with 5 spreading lobes, and a saucer-shaped tube; stamens 5, shortly fused to the corolla at base, the anthers erect, loosely held round the style; anthers often with porose dehiscence; fruit a berry.

In the following enumeration the order of species, the lettering of the unnamed species and much of the key follows an excellent unpublished account by R. Polhill in EAH.

1 Plant annual, herbaceous, unarmed
                       1. *S. nigrum*
   Plants perennial, woody and/or armed   2
2 Climbers, unarmed   3
   Erect herbs or shrubs, if climbers then prickly
                               4
3 Leaves often woolly below; inflorescence with at least 4 dichotomies below the cymose flowers   4. *S. benderianum*
   Leaves pubescent, not woolly, below; inflorescence with only 1–2 branches below the umbellate flowers   3. *S. terminale*
4 Fruits less than 1·5 cm diameter   5
   Fruits mostly over 2 cm diameter, always over 1·5 cm diameter   16
5 One filament larger than the others; calyx enlarged, spiny and enclosing the fruit when mature; fruit 10–15 mm diameter seeds black   18. *S. dubium*
   All filaments ± equal; calyx not enlarged in fruit; fruit less than 10 mm diameter; seeds brown   6
6 Flowers in dichotomous cymose corymbs 7
   Flowers in racemes or few in subsessile inflorescences   11
7 Stems covered with soft prickly hairs; leaves glabrous below   7. *S. schumannianum*
   Stems unarmed or with few, remote spines; leaves woolly to sparsely pubescent below
                               8
8 Leaves auriculate at base of petiole; fruits pubescent   5. *S. mauritianum*
   Leaves without basal auricles; fruits glabrous
                               9
9 Leaves densely white-felted below
                 6. *S. giganteum*
   Leaves densely to sparsely pubescent below but never white   10
10 Hairs simple; stem unarmed 2. *S. nakurense*
   Hairs stellate; stem with scattered prickles
                   8. *S. renschii*
11 Inflorescence with peduncle and rachis together less than 5 mm long, so that the

flowers are apparently in a sessile umbel 12
   Inflorescence with peduncle and rachis together more than 5 mm, and usually over 10 mm long   13
12 Twigs with many crowded very fine bristle-like prickles   13. *S. setaceum*
   Twigs with scattered woody prickles
                   14. *S. taitense*
13 Leaves over 4 times as long as broad, entire
                 12. *S. sp. A*
   Leaves broader, frequently with sinuate-lobed margins   14
14 Anthers over 5 mm long
               11. *S. hastifolium*
   Anthers less than 5 mm long   15
15 Leaves entire; hairs on upper side of leaf with a long stalk and equally-rayed stellate top
              10. *S. mauense*
   Leaves shallowly to deeply lobed or sinuate; hairs on upper leaf surface with a short stalk, and long central ray so that they appear almost simple 9. *S. indicum*
16 Leaves lobed or dentate and/or glabrescent and glossy on the upper surface   20
   Leaves entire or sinuate on the margin, always densely pubescent on the upper surface   17
17 Leaves cordate at base; flowers mostly solitary or in pairs   18
   Leaves mostly cuneate to rounded at base; flowers in racemes of more than 3 19
18 Stem prickles hooked 16. *S. dennekense*
   Stem prickles straight   17. *S. sp. G*
19 Scrambler or weak shrub over 1·5 m tall
               22. *S. richardii*
   Erect woody herb or shrub up to 1 m tall
               25. *S. incanum*
20 Leaves glabrescent on the upper surface 21
   Leaves coarsely pubescent on the upper surface   22
21 Leaves glabrescent on both sides; fruit globose   15. *S. arundo*
   Leaves white-hairy on the lower side; fruit ovoid   23. *S. aculeastrum*
22 Hairs on twigs simple
             19. *S. aculeatissimum*
   Hairs on the twigs mostly stellate   23
23 Fruits red when ripe   24. *S. sp. J*
   Fruits yellow when ripe   24
24 Stellate hairs of upper leaf surface with central ray much longer than the others 25
   Stellate hairs of upper leaf surface with ± equal rays   26
25 Leaves narrowing gradually to the base
            20. *S. dasyphyllum*
   Leaves truncate at base 21. *S. sessilistellatum*
26 Plant a scrambler to 1·5 m 22. *S. richardii*
   Plant an erect woody herb 25. *S. incanum*

1. Solanum nigrum *L.* (see p. 527)

A soft, erect, pubescent or glabrous, unarmed annual with elliptic, entire or crenate leaves; inflorescences extra-axillary, umbellate; flowers white; fruits black or orange.

A very variable plant which is a common weed in cultivated land below 7000 ft. HE, HT, HM, HA, HK, KIT, MUM, KIS, NAR, RV, NAN, EMB, MAC, NBI, KAJ.

Hanid and Kiniaruh 453; Thomas 1063.

2. Solanum nakurense *C.H. Wright*

An erect, unarmed herb or shrub from a trailing woody rootstock, with broad-elliptic, entire leaves and subterminal corymbs of white to pale blue flowers.

Locally common in evergreen upland bushland. HE, HC, HT, HM, HA, KIT, KIS, NAR, RV.

Strid 3113; Greenway 9700.

3. Solanum terminale *Forsk.* (see p. 524)

A glabrescent unarmed climber with elliptic leaves and terminal corymbs of pale violet flowers.

Very similar to *S. nakurense* and locally common in wet lowland forest edges. HC, HT, HM, HA, HN, MUM, KIS, EMB, MAC, KAJ.

Strid 2835; Nattrass 345.

4. Solanum benderianum *Engl.*

A densely tomentose climber with ovate-elliptic leaves and terminal panicles of blue-purple flowers.

Uncommon plant found in montane forest. HA.

Agnew 7171; Polhill 250.

5. Solanum mauritianum *Scop.*

A densely tomentose unarmed tree or shrub with elliptic leaves and dense terminal corymbs of blue flowers; ripe fruits yellow.

Introduced from South America and escaped in the Nairobi region. NBI.

Bally 8645.

6. Solanum giganteum *Jacq.*

A loose shrub with remotely spiny stems and oblanceolate entire leaves and dense subterminal corymbs of white flowers.

Uncommon plant found in wet montane forest. HA, HK, HN.

Polhill and Verdcourt 267.

7. Solanum schumannianum *Dammer*

An erect loose shrub, glabrescent except for the bristly stem, with narrowly elliptic leaves and subterminal corymbs of pale blue flowers.

Locally common in dry montane forest. HA, HK.

Polhill 258; Agnew 8984.

8. Solanum renschii *Vatke*

An erect prickly-stemmed shrub, stellate pubescent on all parts, with narrowly elliptic leaves and ± dense terminal corymbs of blue to mauve flowers.

Common in dry bushland. EMB, MAC, KAJ.

Verdcourt 1494; Hanid and Kiniaruh 550.

9. Solanum indicum *L.*

An erect pubescent woody herb or shrub with ovate leaves which are sinuate to pinnately lobed; prickles usually on stems and leaves; flowers pale mauve, in small extra-axillary racemes.

Variable and widespread, this plant is sometimes cultivated for its fruits. HE, HC, HM, HA, HN, KIT, MUM, KIS, RV, MAC, NBI, KAJ.

Polhill 172; Tweedie 66/152.

10. Solanum mauense *Bitter* (see p. 524)

Similar to *S. indicum* except for the keyed characters, this species is a low woody herb found in dry montane forest clearings. HE, HT, HM, HA, HK, HN, KIT, KIS, NAR.

Agnew 10730; Polhill in EAH 12426.

11. Solanum hastifolium *Dunal* (see p. 524)

An erect, prickly-stemmed pubescent woody herb or shrub with pinnately lobed ovate leaves and racemes of pale lilac flowers.

Uncommon plant found in dry rocky *Commiphora* bushland. MAG.

Heriz-Smith January, 1962; Verdcourt 2666.

12. Solanum sp. A.

An erect herb very like *S. hastifolium* but with linear-oblong entire leaves and fewer, rather smaller flowers.

Uncommon plant found in dry, impeded-drainage grassland. KIT, NAR, RV.

Bogdan 382.

13. Solanum setaceum *Dammer*

Similar to *S. hastifolium* but with a bristly stem, entire lanceolate-oblong leaves and 2-3 purple flowers in each sessile umbel.

Rare plant found in dry *Commiphora* bushland. KAJ.

Verdcourt 3851.

14. Solanum taitense *Vatke*

A pubescent, prickly-stemmed, weak, often supported, shrub with ovate, pinnately-lobed leaves and small lateral sessile umbels of 1-2 white or mauve flowers.

Locally common in dry *Acacia* bushland. RV, MAG, KAJ.

Lind 5711; Gilbert M12.

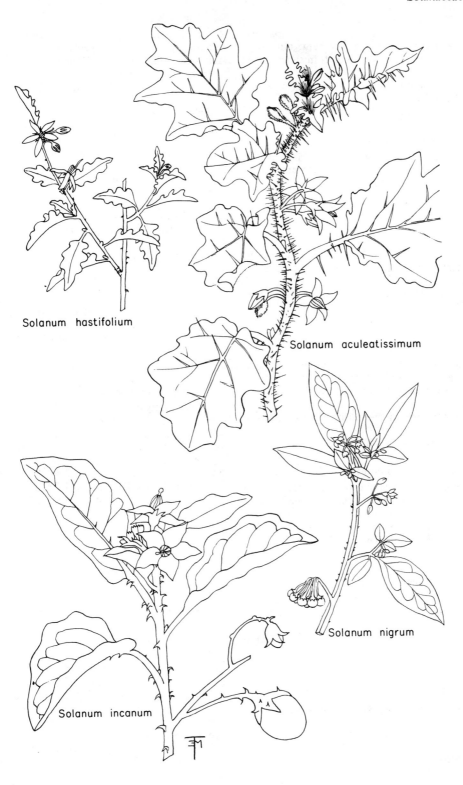

Solanum hastifolium

Solanum aculeatissimum

Solanum incanum

Solanum nigrum

15. Solanum arundo *Mattei*

A shrub with pubescent, prickly, sparsely-branched stems and ovate, glabrescent, pinnately-lobed prickly leaves; flowers violet, in short lateral racemes.

Locally common in dry sandy *Acacia* woodland. NAN, MAC, NBI, KAJ.

Nattrass 1034; Strid 2135.

16. Solanum dennekense *Dammer*

A grey-pubescent shrub with recurved hooks on the stems and ovate, entire leaves; flowers 1–3 together, axillary.

Rare plant found in dry rocky bushland. RV.

Glover, Gwynne, and Samuel 724.

17. Solanum *sp.* G.

Similar to *S. dennekense* but with small straight stem spines and larger flowers with corolla over 12 mm long.

Uncommon plant found in dry grassland. HA, NAR, RV, KAJ.

Glover 3854.

18. Solanum dubium *Fres.*

A low, pubescent, branched perennial herb with prickly stem and midribs to the ovate, sinuate leaves; flowers bright purple, in leaf-opposed racemes.

Locally common in dry bushland. BAR, MAG, MAC, KAJ.

Lind, Agnew, and Beecher 5716; Pratt 318.

19. Solanum aculeatissimum *Jacq.* (see p. 527)

A soft, tomentose perennial with prickles as well as soft hairs on stem and leaves, and lateral, sessile umbels of pale purple flowers.

Locally common in clearings in montane forest. HE, HC, HM, HA, KIT, MAC, KAJ.

Agnew 9998.

20. Solanum dasyphyllum *Thonn.*

Similar to *S. aculeatissimum* except for the attenuate leaf bases, the hairs and the pedunculate inflorescences.

Uncommon plant found in lowland riverine grassland. KIS, NAR, NBI, KAJ.

Glover, Gwynne, and Samuel 1877.

21. Solanum sessilistellatum *Bitter* (see p. 524)

Similar to *S. aculeatissimum* except for the hairs and the stalked inflorescence.

Locally common in clearings in montane rain forest. HE, HC, HM, HA.

Verdcourt 2424; Agnew 8300.

22. Solanum richardii *Dunal.*

A weakly scrambling pubescent shrub with sparse prickles on stems and midribs and broadly elliptic, sinuate or pinnately-lobed leaves; flowers lilac, in extra-axillary racemes.

Uncommon plant found in dry forest types and recorded from Karura. NBI.

Polhill 251.

23. Solanum aculeastrum *Dunal.*

A large shrub or small tree, white-tomentose and coarsely prickly on stems and underside of leaves; leaves elliptic, pinnately-lobed or entire, glabrescent above; flowers in lateral umbel-like cymes.

Uncommon plant found in upland forest clearings. HE, HC, HT, HM, HA, HK, MUM, KIS, EMB.

Strid 3542; Glover, Gwynne, and Samuel 935.

24. Solanum *sp.* J.

A weak shrub similar to *S. aculeastrum* but with pubescent upper leaf surfaces and short, weak, curved stem-prickles.

Uncommon plant found in clearings in montane forest. HA, HK.

Verdcourt and Polhill 2993.

25. Solanum incanum *L.* (see p. 527)

An erect, felty-pubescent woody herb or shrub with prickles present or absent from stem and petioles; leaves ovate to lanceolate, entire to sinuate; flowers in racemes, blue to mauve.

This is the common 'sodom-apple', everywhere abundant in waste ground, and very variable in its prickles. HE, HC, HL, HA, KIT, MUM, KIS, NAR, BAR, RV, MAG, EMB, MAC, NBI, KAJ.

Polhill 37; Harmsen 6451.

2. DISCOPODIUM *Hochst.*
Dealt with in KTS p. 537.

1. Discopodium eremanthum *Chiov.* (*Discopodium* sp. = Rammell 1060 in KTS) HE, HA, HK.

2. Discopodium penninervum *Hochst.*
HE, HT, HA.

3. PHYSALIS *L.*

Erect or trailing soft herbs with entire or dentate simple leaves and solitary flowers in axils or at branches; calyx bell-shaped, shortly 5-lobed, inflated and loose in fruit; corolla widely bell-shaped, with very short and blunt lobes; berry globose, 2-celled.

These are the Cape-gooseberries which are frequently cultivated and as frequently escape from cultivation to become harmless weeds of upland arable land. They are all American in origin.

1   Corolla more than 15 mm in diameter   2
     Corolla less than 10 mm in diameter   3
2   Leaves glabrous, cuneate at base; berry purple
                                    1. *P. ixocarpa*
     Leaves pubescent, cordate at base; berry
        yellow to orange   2. *P. peruviana*
3   Inflated fruiting calyx over 2 cm long
                                    3. *P. angulata*
     Inflated fruiting calyx less than 2 cm long
                                    4. *P. minima*

1. Physalis ixocarpa *Brot.*

A trailing herb with ovate dentate leaves and pale yellow, dark-centred flowers.
    Locally common. HT, HM, HA, RV, MAC.
    Nattrass 298; Agnew 10754.

2. Physalis peruviana *L.*

A trailing pubescent herb with ovate, cordate, ± entire leaves and yellow, brown-centred flowers.
    Commonly cultivated and escaped. HE, HT, HM, HN, KIT, KIS, NAR, MAC, NBI.
    Hanid and Kiniaruh 795; Mwangangi 21.

3. Physalis angulata *L.*

An erect glabrous herb with ovate, dentate leaves, cuneate at base, and small yellow flowers.
    Locally common. MAC.
    Strid 2220; van Someren in EAH 11983.

4. Physalis minima *L.* (inc. *P. divaricata* of the Check List)

Similar to *P. angulata* but often pubescent, with smaller fruits.
    This may be but a variety of the last species. HM, KIT, MUM, BAR, MAC.
    Kokwaro 1750; Bogdan 4248.

4. WITHANIA *Pauq.*

Shrubs with alternate, simple, entire leaves and fascicles of axillary flowers; calyx with a short tube and 5 lobes inflated in fruit; corolla bell-shaped, with 3–6 valvate lobes; stamens inserted near the base of the corolla; berry globose.

Withania somnifera (*L.*) *Dunal*

An erect pubescent woody herb or soft shrub with ovate leaves and greenish flowers.
    Locally common in disturbed places in dry country. HC, HA, NAR, BAR, RV, MAG, MAC, NBI, KAJ.
    Strid 2813; Glover and Samuel 3093.

5. LYCIUM *L.*

Lycium europaeum *L.*

Deslt with in KTS p. 573. RV, MAG, NAN, MAC, KAJ.

6. NICANDRA *Adans.*

Herbs with simple leaves and solitary flowers; calyx with a short spreading tube, winged and recurved-auricled between the ovate lobes; corolla funnel-shaped, shortly lobed; filaments with a tuft of hairs at base; ovary 5-locular; dry berry included within the stiffly papery enlarged calyx.

Nicandra physalodes *Scop.*

An erect glabrous annual with elliptic dentate leaves and blue flowers.
    An introduced weed from South America in arable land from 5000–8000 ft. HM, KIT, RV, NBI.
    Mathenge 339; Nattrass 255.

7. CESTRUM *L.*

Similar to *Nicotiana* but without spreading corolla lobes and with a berry, not capsule for the fruit. Many American species are cultivated of which the following often escapes.

Cestrum aurantiacum *Lindl.*

An erect pubescent shrub with ovate leaves and terminal panicles of orange flowers.
    Local in disturbed montane forest areas. HA.
    Ndirito in EAH 13811; Agnew and Harris 5052.

8. DATURA *L.*

Erect herbs or soft, woody shrubs, usually foetid and with poisonous alkaloids, with entire or lobed alternate leaves; flowers solitary, often at branches; calyx tubular, with 5 lobes or split on one side; corolla tubular at base, funnel-shaped above with 5 short lobes; stamens 5; capsule loculicidal and septicidal, usually armed.

1   Young leaves glabrous; corolla less than 10
        cm long; fruit with spiny prickles
                                    1. *D. stramonium*
     Young leaves softly pubescent; corolla over
        12 cm long; fruit with blunt protuberances
                                    2. *D. metel*

1. Datura stramonium *L.*

An erect glabrous annual with ovate, dentate leaves, dichotomously branched with a white flower at each fork.
    This introduced weed is common in disturbed places, 5000–8000 ft. HT, HA, KIT, KIS, NAR, RV, EMB, MAC, NBI.
    Nattrass 219; Harmsen 6459.

2. Datura metel *L.*

Similar to *D. stramonium* but usually larger, with cream-coloured flowers.

Common at the coast but only once recorded from our area at Thomson's Falls. HA.

Veterinary Officer H149/61.

9. NICOTIANA *L.*

Shrubs or herbs with usually entire leaves and flowers in terminal cymose panicles; calyx bell-shaped, with 5 short teeth; corolla with a long tube and short or long spreading lobes; stamens 5, inserted below the middle of the corolla tube; capsule 2–4-celled.

1   Plant a shrub; leaves glaucous and glabrous
                                    1. *N. glauca*
     Plant a herb; leaves glandular-pubescent
                                    2. *N. tabacum*

1. Nicotiana glauca *R. Grah.*

An erect, loose shrub with ovate, long-petiolate leaves and yellow-orange flowers.

Locally escaped from cultivation and found in rocky disturbed soils, old walls, etc. RV, NBI.

Verdcourt 594; Hanid 6.

2. Nicotiana tabacum *L.*

An erect glandular-pubescent annual with elliptic to ovate leaves and a terminal panicle of white to pink flowers.

The cultivated tobacco plant which has been used as an ornamental and escaped locally. HC, MAC, NBI, KAJ.

Mwangangi 581; Mathenge 343.

85. CONVOLVULACEAE†

Herbs, shrubs, or leafless parasites, rarely small trees, mostly twining or prostrate, less often erect; hairs when present simple or sometimes stellate; leaves alternate, mostly simple, entire or frequently lobed; flowers solitary or in various inflorescences, axillary or terminal, almost always regular, bisexual or rarely unisexual; sepals 4–5, imbricate, free or joined at the base, often enlarging in fruit; petals joined to form a variable but often funnel-shaped or salver-shaped corolla, entire or 4–5-lobed, induplicate-valvate or contorted; stamens (3–)4–5, inserted on the corolla tube; pollen smooth or minutely spiny; ovary superior of 2–3 carpels, 1–4 (rarely 3 or 5)-locular, entire or sometimes lobed; styles 1–2(–3), simple or forked; stigmas 1–4, linear to globose or rarely

† By B. Verdcourt.

irregular; fruit usually dry and capsular, less often indehiscent; seeds 1–4 (rarely 6 or 10).

1   Plants leafless parasites   1. *Cuscuta*
     Plants not parasites, green and leafy   2
2   Ovary very distinctly lobed; flowers small; prostrate plants with rather small oblong or reniform leaves   3
     Ovary not distinctly lobed   4
3   Ovary 2-lobed   2. *Dichondra*
     Ovary 4-lobed   3. *Falkia*
4   Styles 2, quite or almost separate   5
     Style 1   6
5   Each style forked for about half its length i.e. stigmas 4   4. *Evolvulus*
     Styles not forked i.e. stigmas 2   5. *Seddera*
6   Stigmas linear, or if somewhat oblong then flowers pink   7. *Convolvulus*
     Stigmas oblong to globose   7
7   Whole plant covered with conspicuously stellate hairs   13. *Astripomoea*
     Plant with simple hairs (in our area)   8
8   Corolla small, bright blue, about 1 cm long; a prostrate plant of lake edges with obtuse elliptic leaves; stigmas elliptic, flattened
                                6. *Jacquemontia*
     Without the above characters combined   9
9   Corolla 2–2·5 cm long, cream to yellow with a maroon centre; flowers in bracteate inflorescences; twining or prostrate plant of bushland, woodland or grassland; stigmas ovate-oblong   8. *Hewittia*
     Corolla variously coloured but if of similar size and colour to the above, then bracts not so conspicuous; stigmas globose   10
10   Corolla urceolate, constricted at the apex of the tube; basal part of filaments dilated into concave scales which arch over the ovary   10. *Lepistemon*
     Corolla not urceolate   11
11   Pollen grains smooth; flowers usually yellow or white with a dark eye; leaves pinnately or palmately lobed or entire
                                    9. *Merremia*
     Pollen grains minutely spiny; flowers variously coloured but yellow only in species 21, 22 and 34 of *Ipomoea* (note: the pollen grain character is easily visible under a ×15 lens)   12
12   Fruit indehiscent or pericarp breaking irregularly   13
     Fruit a capsule splitting by valves
                                    14. *Ipomoea*
13   Corolla campanulate, under 2 cm long, white or yellowish; flowers in axillary pedunculate cymes   11. *Lepistemonopsis*
     Corolla funnel-shaped or salver-shaped, over 3 cm long   14

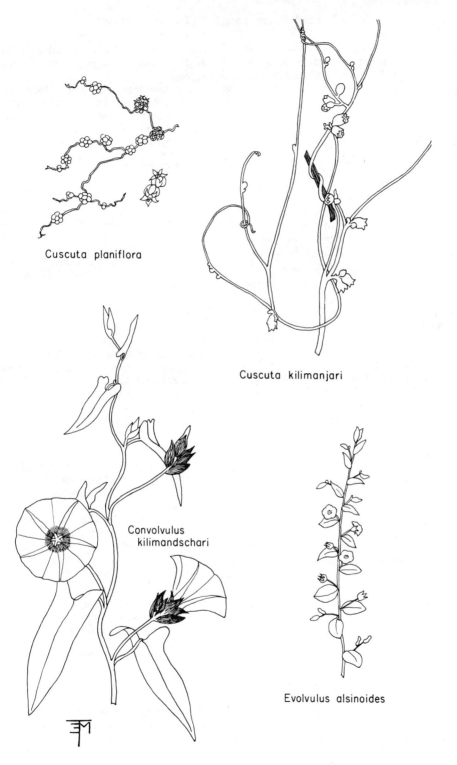

Cuscuta planiflora

Cuscuta kilimanjari

Convolvulus
kilimandschari

Evolvulus alsinoides

14 Corolla funnel-shaped, 4·5-5·5 cm long,
    bright crimson
                    12. *Stictocardia beraviensis*
    Corolla salver-shaped with a long narrow
    tube, 11-13 cm long, white (in our area)
                                    15. *Turbina*

1. CUSCUTA *L.*

Twining leafless parasites, free-living only in seedling stage; flowers small, in lax or compact
clusters; sepals 4-5, united at the base; petals 4-5,
united into a tube at the base; stamens 4-5, attached
to the corolla and nearly always with a whorl of
fringed scales at their base; ovary 2-locular, 4-
ovuled; styles 2, free or united completely; stigmas
linear or globose; fruit a capsule or indehiscent;
embryo thread-like, without cotyledons.

1 Styles united into a single column
                                    6. *C. cassytoides*
   Styles free   2
2 Stigmas capitate   3
   Stigmas linear   7
3 Mature flowers larger, 4-6 mm long, 4-9 mm
     wide; capsule at length circumscissile;
     corolla-lobes obtuse   4. *C. kilimanjari*
   Mature flowers smaller, 2-4 mm long, 2-3·5
     mm broad; capsule not circumscissile or if
     so then corolla lobes very acute   4
4 Corolla lobes obtuse; marshy places
                                    1. *C. australis*
   Corolla lobes acute   5
5 Scales absent; calyx lobes acute
                                    5. *C. hyalina*
   Scales present   6
6 Inflorescence a compact spherical cluster;
     calyx lobes obtuse   2. *C. campestris*
   Inflorescence a very loose cluster; calyx lobes
     obtuse or abruptly acute
                                    3. *C. suaveolens*
7 Stigmas slender, about 0·1 mm diameter;
     seeds separate   7. *C. planiflora*
   Stigmas thick, about 0·2-0·25 mm diameter;
     seeds joined in pairs, at least sometimes; an
     introduced parasite on flax
                                    8. *C. epilinum*

1. Cuscuta australis *R. Br.*

Flowers in loose to compact cymes, shortly
pedicellate; calyx and corolla lobes obtuse or
blunt; stamens up to 1 mm long; capsule drying a
reddish-brown.

Parasitic on swamp vegetation. HM, HA, EMB,
NBI.

Fries 2160; van Someren 699.

2. Cuscuta campestris *Yuncker*

Flowers in rather compact cymes, shortly pedicellate; calyx lobes obtuse or subacute; corolla lobes
acute; capsule drying pale brownish straw-
coloured.

An American species now widely naturalized in
the Old World and parasitizing a wide variety of
hosts in bushy and waste places. HT, HM, HA, HK,
KIT, KIS, RV, MAC, NBI.

Verdcourt 407, 924; Gillett 15174.

3. Cuscuta suaveolens *Seringe*

Flowers in loose clusters, the pedicels usually
exceeding the flowers; calyx lobes usually considerably shorter than the calyx tube, usually
acute with reflexed edges (but not in single Kenya
specimen seen); corolla lobes acute; styles slender,
up to 2 mm long.

A South American species mostly parasitic on
lucerne, now cosmopolitan. KIT, RV.

Nattrass 209.

4. Cuscuta kilimanjari *Oliv.* (see p. 531)

Stems coarser than in other species and flowers
bigger in compact clusters, cream, waxy in texture;
pedicels shorter than the flowers; calyx and corolla
lobes obtuse; stamens and styles short and thick.

A common species nearly always on herbaceous
Acanthaceae in forest areas. HE, HC, HT, HA, HK,
KIT, MUM, KIS, NAN, MAC, NBI, KAJ.

Verdcourt 355, 726, 1673.

5. Cuscuta hyalina *Roth*

Stems very slender; flowers pedicellate, white and
rather shining in loose umbellate clusters; calyx
and corolla lobes very acute; scales absent in East
African specimens.

A species of the arid belt, mostly on *Portulaca*,
Trianthema, and *Tribulus*. BAR.

Bogdan 4744.

6. Cuscuta cassytoides *Engelm.*

Stems rather coarse; flowers subsessile, yellowish,
in few-flowered cymes arranged in lax spike-like
inflorescences; calyx and corolla lobes very obtuse;
easily recognized by the styles being united into a
single column.

Apparently only known in Kenya from the
Karura forest. NBI.

Verdcourt 659.

7. Cuscuta planiflora *Tenore* (see p. 531)

Stems slender, yellowish or crimson; flowers small,
subsessile, in very dense globose clusters; calyx and
corolla lobes often rather fleshy at the tips, obtuse
or acute.

A very variable species often divided into numerous ill-defined species by botanists with narrow specific concepts. The following gives some idea of varieties to be found.

1 Flowers densely papillate var. *A*
Flowers almost smooth or sparsely papillate 2
2 Flowers small; calyx 1·5–3·5 mm in diameter; corolla 1·5–2·5 mm long; style and stigmas together 0·5–1 mm long
var. *planiflora*
Flowers larger; calyx 3–5 mm in diameter; corolla 2–3·5 mm long; style and stigmas together 1–2·2 mm long; lobes of calyx and corolla more or less obtuse
var. *madagascarensis*

Widespread; occurring on various hosts. HE, HT, HM, HA, HK, RV, MAC, NBI, KAJ.
Bogdan 1039, 3065; Ossent s.n.; Verdcourt 3570.

8. Cuscuta epilinum *Weihe*
Stems slender; flowers in dense globose clusters; calyx and corolla lobes acute; styles and stigmas very short.
An introduced species parasitic on flax wherever the latter is grown, but rare in East Africa. HC, KIT.
Schouten H348/58.

2. DICHONDRA *J. R. & G. Forst.*
Prostrate perennial herbs with petiolate cordate-reniform leaves; flowers small, solitary, axillary; sepals ovate-spathulate, almost free; corolla very small, deeply 5-fid, rather shorter than the calyx; ovary deeply 2-lobed, 4-ovuled; styles 2; stigmas capitate.

Dichondra repens *J. R. & G. Forst.*
Leaves 0·6–2·2 cm long, 0·8–2·6 cm wide, glabrescent to pilose; corolla white or greenish, about 2·5 mm long; lobes of capsule subglobose, 1·5–2 mm long.
A pantropical weed in irrigated grasslands, lawns and roadsides in wetter districts. HM, HA, KIT, MUM, NBI.
Napier 147; Bogdan 1066.

3. FALKIA *L. f.*
Prostrate perennial herbs with petiolate oblong, round or reniform leaves, sometimes cordate; flowers small, axillary; sepals ovate, joined at the base; corolla funnel-shaped, folded, more or less lobed, exceeding the calyx; ovary 4-lobed, 4-ovuled; styles 2; stigmas capitate.

Falkia canescens *C. H. Wright*
Somewhat similar to *Dichondra* but with oblong-reniform leaves about 8 x 9 mm; calyx silky-pilose, often enlarging in fruit; corolla white, pink or pale bluish-mauve, much exceeding the calyx, about 5 mm long; lobes of fruit subglobose, up to 1·5 mm in diameter.
An uncommon but often overlooked plant of upland grasslands and roadsides. HT, HA, NBI.
Napier 159; Powell 10.

4. EVOLVULUS *L.*
Annual or perennial herbs or subshrubs; leaves simple, variously shaped; flowers small, in axillary cymes or terminal spike-like inflorescences; sepals small, subequal; corolla funnel-shaped, rotate or salver-shaped; ovary 1–2-celled, 2–4-ovuled; styles 2, filiform, united at the base or free, each bifid; stigmas 4, filiform or slightly clavate; capsule ovoid or globose, not lobed, 1–4-seeded.

1 Corolla white, deeply lobed; capsule 1-locular
1. *E. nummularius*
Corolla blue, rarely white, shallowly lobed; capsule 2-locular 2. *E. alsinoides*

1. Evolvulus nummularius (*L.*) *L.*
Perennial prostrate herb rooting at the nodes; leaves rounded or rounded obovate or oblong, glabrous or sparingly pubescent; flowers solitary or rarely paired, axillary; peduncles short; corolla 4·5 mm long.
A pantropical weed of warm wet sandy grassland. MUM, KIS.
Turner 3527; Padwa 462.

2. Evolvulus alsinoides (*L.*) *L.* (see p. 531)
Extremely variable annual or perennial herb, erect or trailing and mostly covered with long silky hairs; leaves elliptic to linear-oblong; peduncles 1–5-flowered, slender; corolla 6 mm long.
Another pantropical weed of grasslands in warmer country. HA, KIS, NAR, BAR, RV, NAN, EMB, MAC, NBI, KAJ.
Verdcourt 373; Bally 11559.

5. SEDDERA *Hochst.*
Small intricately branched herbs or subshrubs, prostrate or erect; leaves mostly small; flowers axillary or in terminal spikes or dense few-flowered cymes; corolla funnel-shaped, mostly small; ovary 2-locular, 4-ovuled; style bifid usually to the base; stigmas more or less peltate, often bilobed; capsule 4-valved.

1 Plant densely covered with appressed, velvety indumentum; leaves elliptic or broadly elliptic 1. *S. latifolia*

Plant fairly densely covered with appressed hairs but not velvety; leaves oblong-elliptic, oblanceolate or linear-oblong

2. *S. hirsuta*

1. Seddera latifolia *Hochst. & Steud.*

Small woody subshrub about 30 cm tall covered with greyish or silvery velvety indumentum; leaves elliptic, 1·3–2·7 cm long, 0·6–1·8 cm wide; flowers subsessile, solitary; sepals unequal, ovate, acute or acuminate, 4–5 mm long, 1·5 mm wide, silvery-pubescent; corolla 4–5 mm long.

An uncommon plant of rather arid bushland. MAG, NAN.

Bally 10555; Verdcourt 2759.

2. Seddera hirsuta *Hall. f.*

Woody subshrub with long prostrate branches, the shoots ascending to 15 cm, glabrescent to fairly densely covered with appressed hairs; leaves oblong-elliptic, oblanceolate or linear-oblong, 0·4–1·5 cm long, 1–7·5 mm wide; flowers usually solitary or in 1–3-flowered cymes, more or less subsessile; sepals 5–9 mm long with apical foliaceous parts 1·5–4 mm long, 1–2 mm wide; corolla about 5 mm long.

Locally common in *Commiphora-Acacia* bushland. KAJ.

Verdcourt 2582.

6. JACQUEMONTIA *Choisy*

Twining and prostrate herbs or shrubs, rarely erect, mostly hairy (often with stellate hairs in extra-African forms); flowers in axillary mostly stalked cymes or solitary or in compact heads; sepals equal or unequal; corolla funnel-shaped, predominantly blue; ovary 2-celled, 4-ovuled; style simple, filiform; stigmas predominantly elliptic or oblong, rarely globose or filiform; capsule 4-seeded.

Very close to *Convolvulus* but universally upheld as being a separate genus and having a distinctive appearance.

Jacquemontia ovalifolia *(Vahl) Hall. f.*

Annual or biennial prostrate herb with slender glabrous branches; leaves oblong, oblong-lanceolate or elliptic, up to 8 cm long, 4·5 cm wide, obtuse or emarginate at the apex, cuneate, glabrous; inflorescences few-flowered; corolla blue, about 1 cm long.

Found on bare mud of seasonal and permanent lakes only at Lake Baringo in our area. BAR.

Bickford in EAH 11062; Verdcourt 3579.

7. CONVOLVULUS *L.*

Annual or perennial erect, prostrate or twining herbs; leaves very variable but often hastate; flowers axillary, in one- to few-flowered cymes or dense heads; sepals equal or unequal; corolla mostly funnel-shaped, variously coloured, practically entire; ovary 2-celled, 4-ovuled; style simple, filiform; stigmas 2, nearly always filiform; capsule mostly 4-seeded.

1   Corolla large, 2·5–3 cm long
                                            1. *C. kilimandschari*
    Corolla smaller, under 2 cm long   2
2   Annual plant with erect or prostrate stems; leaves more or less cuneate at the base; corolla small, about 6 mm long
                                            2. *C. siculus*
    Perennial plants; stems twining or prostrate 3
3   Corolla large, 1·5–2·0 cm long; leaves oblong, sagittate or hastate, glabrescent
                                            3. *C. arvensis*
    Corolla smaller, 0·8–1·3 cm long, rarely more and then, if so, leaves ovate-cordate and/or hairy   4
4   Twining plant with leaves ovate or triangular, pubescent   4. *C. farinosus*
    Usually prostrate plants with leaves oblong or linear, more or less sagittate, or if tending to be ovate then densely sericeous
                                            5. *C. sagittatus*

1. Convolvulus kilimandschari *Engl.* (see p. 531)

Perennial climber up to 2 m long; leaves triangular-oblong or oblong-ovate, rarely narrow, 3–8·5 cm long, 2·3–6 cm wide, glabrescent or rarely very hairy; inflorescence capitate, densely bracteate; bracts ovate up to 10 mm long, 7·5 mm wide; corolla white, often with purple streaks or pink with dark centre (2·1–)2·5–3 cm long.

Upland evergreen forest and bamboo thicket, 6000–12 500 ft; HE, HM, HA, HK, NBI.

Tweedie 1737; Gillett 16641.

2. Convolvulus siculus *L.*

Annual herb to 60 cm; leaves oblong-lanceolate, up to 5 cm long and 2 cm wide, sparsely pilose; inflorescence 1–3-flowered; bracts narrow, linear, up to 11 mm long, 1 mm wide; sepals ovate-lanceolate; corolla white or tinged bluish-lilac, about 6 mm long.

Grassland, particularly where disturbed, and common in the Rift Valley. HE, HA, HK, RV, NAN, NBI.

Bogdan 3041; Verdcourt 1525.

3. Convolvulus arvensis *L.*

Perennial herb with twining or prostrate stems and mostly glabrescent ovate-oblong to lanceolate leaves, 1·5–7·5 cm long, 1–3 cm wide, hastate or sagittate; peduncle 1(–2–3)-flowered; bracts 3 mm long; sepals elliptic-orbicular or oblong; corolla white or pink or both, about 2 cm long.

A very widely distributed weed in the temperate regions of both hemispheres, now introduced in many parts of the world. HM, HA, MAC. Fries 169; Bogdan 3463.

4. Convolvulus farinosus *L.*

Perennial herb with twining or prostrate stems and pubescent ovate or triangular-ovate leaves, 6–7·5 cm long, 3·8–4·5 cm wide, subsagittate or cordate, mostly shallowly crenate; inflorescences 1–6-flowered; bracts minute; sepals ovate-orbicular, ovate or elliptic; corolla white or tinged pinkish-purple, 1·1–1·6 cm long.

A widespread plant of upland grassland. HA, HK, KIT, NAR, RV, NBI.
Verdcourt 987; Napier 456.

5. Convolvulus sagittatus *Thunb.*

Perennial herb with twining or prostrate stems; leaves narrowly linear to oblong, more or less sagittate at the base, undulate or entire, pubescent of glabrescent; inflorescences 1–3(–several)-flowered; bracts minute, linear; inner sepals round and hyaline, outer oblong, the edges sometimes crisped; corolla white to pink with a purple centre, about 9 mm long.

Grassland and bushland, particularly where disturbed. HT, KIT, NAN, EMB, NBI.
Brodhurst-Hill 625; Verdcourt 368.

8. HEWITTIA *Wight & Arn.*

Perennial twining or prostrate herbs; leaves variable, mostly cordate; flowers in 1–several-flowered bracteate axillary cymes; sepals herbaceous, acute, the 3 outer large, ovate and accrescent in fruit; inner smaller; corolla funnel-shaped; ovary hairy, 1-celled or almost 2-celled, 4-ovuled; style simple, filiform; stigmas 2, ovate-oblong, flattened; capsule 1-celled, 2–4-seeded, pilose.

Hewittia sublobata (*L. f.*) *O. Kuntze*

Stems 1–2 m long; leaves 2·5–16 cm long, 1·4–13 cm wide; bracts oblong-lanceolate, 0·5–1·7 cm long; corolla yellow or white, usually with a purple or claret centre, 2–2·5 cm long.

In warm bushland especially where disturbed, and also in grassland where it is commonest at the coast. HA, KIT, MUM, KIS, EMB, MAC.
Graham 2175; Brodhurst-Hill 433.

9. MERREMIA *Hall. f.*

Perennial or annual herbs or shrubby, mostly with twining or prostrate stems; flowers solitary or in few- to many-flowered axillary inflorescences; sepals usually subequal, elliptic or rounded, obtuse or acute, sometimes enlarging in fruit; corolla funnel-shaped or campanulate, entire or somewhat lobed, white or often yellow, mostly with a darker centre; ovary 2–4-celled, 4-ovuled; style simple, filiform; stigma biglobular. Very similar to *Ipomoea* but with smooth pollen.

1   Leaves not prominently lobed, but sometimes with small lobes near the base, linear-lanceolate to oblong   1. *M. tridentata*
     Leaves conspicuously pinnately or palmately lobed   2
2   Leaves pinnately lobed, the lobes being narrow and linear   2. *M. pinnata*
     Leaves palmately lobed   3
3   Leaf-lobes lobed and toothed; corolla 3 cm long, acutely lobed   3. *M. ampelophylla*
     Leaf-lobes practically entire   4
4   Stems distinctly winged; leaf-lobes mostly ovate; sepals about 1 cm long; corolla about 3·5 cm long   4. *M. pterygocaulos*
     Stems less distinctly winged; leaf-lobes linear to lanceolate; sepals 0·8–1 cm long; corolla 1·5–3 cm long   5. *M. palmata*

1. Merremia tridentata (*L.*) *Hall. f.*

A very variable perennial with prostrate or twining stems up to 2 m long, glabrous or hairy; leaves 2·5–10 cm long, 0·2–2 cm wide; inflorescences 1–few-flowered; corolla pale yellow, cream, green or white, often with a maroon eye, 1–2 cm long.

A grassland plant of the coast which just enters our area. KAJ (Garabani Hill).
van Someren 286.

2. Merremia pinnata (*Choisy*) *Hall. f.*

Annual prostrate or trailing herb about 60 cm long; leaves sessile, deeply pinnatifid with 8–12 pairs of narrow lobes extending almost to the mid-rib, about 8 mm long, 0·5 mm wide; inflorescence 1–3(-few)-flowered; corolla white to yellow, up to 7 mm long.

A widespread species in rocky grassland, and bushland. HT, MAC.
Napper 1648; Harvey 157.

3. Merremia ampelophylla *Hall. f.*

Perennial prostrate herb with radiating stems to about 1 m; leaves palmately 5–7-lobed, 2–8 cm long, 3–14 cm wide, usually undulate at margins; flowers 1–3 in loose cymes; corolla primrose-yellow with brownish claret centre.

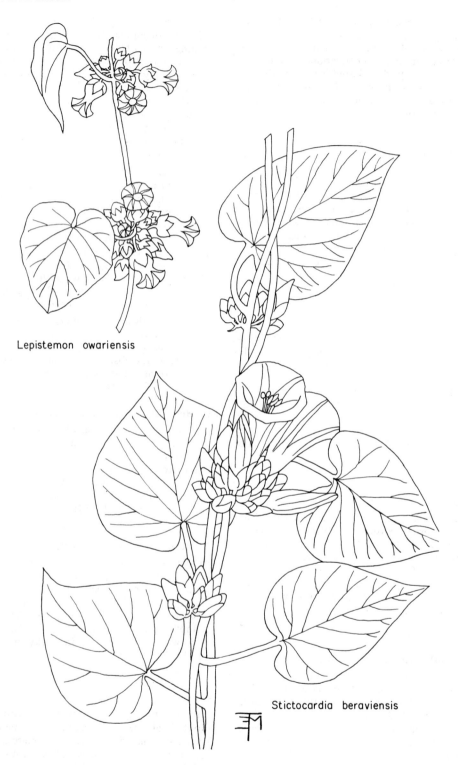

Lepistemon owariensis

Stictocardia beraviensis

Mostly in bare places in dry bushland. NAN?, MAC, KAJ.

Kirrika 152; Verdcourt 3858.

4. Merremia pterygocaulos (*Choisy*) Hall. f.

Perennial twining herb with mostly conspicuously 4-winged stems; leaves palmately 3–5-lobed to the middle or beyond, up to 9 cm long, 12 cm wide; peduncle winged, mostly 4-flowered; corolla white or cream with red or purple throat, more rarely yellow; mid-petaline areas pilose above outside.

A widespread African species in grassland often by streams or in swampy places, but rare in Kenya. KIT.

Brodhurst-Hill 448.

5. Merremia palmata Hall. f.

Perennial twining herb with stems very slightly or not winged; leaves deeply palmately 5-lobed, 1–7 cm long, 1–6 cm wide; peduncles mostly 1-flowered; corolla lemon-yellow or greenish-cream, usually with a brown to purple centre; midpetaline areas glabrous or pilose above outside.

Uncommon in wooded grassland and bushland. MAC.

Irwin 405; Napper 1624.

10. LEPISTEMON *Blume*

Herbaceous or woody twiners; flowers in dense axillary sessile or stalked clusters; sepals subequal, obtuse or acute; corolla urceolate with the tube distinctly narrowing upwards; filaments dilated at the base into large scales; ovary 2-celled, 4-ovuled; style short; stigma capitate, bilobed or 2 separate stigmas; capsule 4-valved or almost indehiscent, 4-seeded; pollen grains with spinules.

Lepistemon owariensis (*Beauv.*) Hall. f. (see p. 536)

Perennial climber; stems covered with yellow-brown bristly hairs; leaves ovate, up to 16 cm long and wide, cordate, entire, shallowly lobed or coarsely dentate; inflorescences many-flowered, subsessile or shortly stalked; sepals glabrescent or, more usually, bristly-hairy; corolla white, up to 1·4 cm long; capsule about 1·5 cm long, covered with long yellow bristles.

Rare in lowland and riverine forest BAR.

Tweedie 2909.

11. LEPISTEMONOPSIS *Dammer*

Perennial twiner with hairy stems; flowers in stalked cymes; sepals somewhat unequal, ovate, acute; corolla campanulate, the tube not constricted, limb 5-lobed; filaments with fleshy scales at the base; ovary 2-celled, 4-ovuled; style simple,

slender; stigma biglobular; fruit indehiscent or perhaps ultimately splitting (?), 4-seeded; pollen grains with spinules.

Lepistemonopsis volkensii *Dammer*

Leaves ovate, up to 10 cm long, 9 cm wide, cordate, usually 3 lobed, pilose; outer sepals pilose on back, slightly enlarging in fruit; corolla white, yellow, pale orange or sometimes greenish-striped; fruit globose, fleshy, about 1·4 cm long, green with pinkish tinge, glabrous.

Locally common in upland forest, upland grassland, and secondary bushland. HM, RV, MAC, NBI, KAJ.

Verdcourt, Baring and Williams 2184; Bally 7363.

12. STICTOCARDIA Hall. f.

Woody lianes or herbaceous twiners; leaves ovate, cordate at the base, typically densely covered with minute dark glands beneath; flowers in axillary, short- to long-stalked, 1–many-flowered cymes; sepals subequal, typically blunt, truncate or emarginate, enlarging in fruit; corolla large, crimson, purple or pink, funnel-shaped; ovary 4-celled, 4-ovuled; style simple; stigma biglobular; fruit globular, with thin pericarp which breaks irregularly, 4-seeded; pollen grains with spinules.

Stictocardia beraviensis (*Vatke*) Hall. f. (see p. 536)

Woody liane; leaves ovate, up to 23 cm long and 20 cm wide; inflorescences shortly stalked, peduncles 0·8–1(–2·5) cm long; sepals elliptic or rounded, 0·7–1·3 cm long, 0·5–1·2 cm wide, blunt or emarginate; corolla very bright crimson with base of tube orange-yellow, 4·5–5·5 cm long.

Uncommon in wet submontane forest, riverine forest and grassland with scattered trees. HK, MUM, KIS, BAR.

Tweedie 358; Gardner 3150.

13. ASTRIPOMOEA *Meeuse* (*Astrochlaena* Hall. f.)

Perennial woody or annual, erect or trailing herbs covered with very obviously stellate hairs; flowers solitary or in dense to lax cymes; sepals subequal, ovate to lanceolate; corolla funnel-shaped with short or long tube, purple or white with a purple centre; ovary 2-locular, 4-ovuled; style simple; stigmas oblong or capitate; capsule 4-valved, 4-seeded.

1   Perennial herb with several to many separate stems arising from a woody rootstock; corolla entirely rose or mauve (rarely white)   1. *A. malvacea*

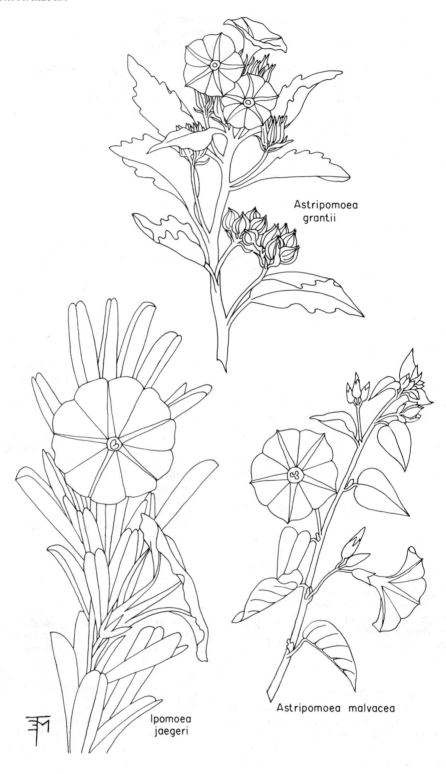

Astripomoea
grantii

Ipomoea
jaegeri

Astripomoea malvacea

Annual or short-lived perennial; stems single, often considerably branched above the base; corolla white with a mauve centre or less often entirely mauve 2

2 Corolla shorter, about 1–1·5 cm long
2. *A. lachnosperma*
Corolla longer, over 2 cm long 3

3 Leaves elliptic to obovate, coarsely crenate or lobed, rarely entire; peduncle and petiole always free 3. *A. grantii*
Leaves usually elliptic-lanceolate, entire or slightly repand, rarely crenate, sometimes borne on the peduncle
4. *A. hyoscyamoides*

1. Astripomoea malvacea (*Klotzsch*) *Meeuse* (see p. 538)

An extremely variable subshrubby perennial with prostrate or erect stems; leaves elliptic to broadly ovate, 1·7–12 cm long, 0·8–9 cm wide, acute to rounded at the apex, cuneate to subcordate at the base; sepals round to lanceolate, 5–10 mm long, 2·5–2·8 mm wide; corolla 2·5–5 cm long.

Widespread in dry grassland and wooded grassland at medium altitudes and divisible into very poorly defined varieties, extremes of which are, however, distinctive enough to have been considered distinct species in the past. HA, HK, KIT, MUM, KIS, BAR, MAG, NAN, EMB, MAC, NBI, KAJ.
Verdcourt 1125, 1495; Hanid 445.

2. Astripomoea lachnosperma (*Choisy*) *Meeuse*

Annual herb with simple erect stems 20–120 cm tall; leaves ovate or rhomboid, 3·5–12 cm long, 1·8–10 cm wide, acute to rounded at the apex, cuneate or truncate at the base; margin wavy above the middle, entire below; corolla white with a purple centre, 1–1·5(–2) cm long.

Common in disturbed bushland, often in rather dry, rocky places. BAR, MAG, NAN, MAC.
Verdcourt 1470; Tweedie 3312.

3. Astripomoea grantii (*Rendle*) *Verdc.* (see p. 538)

Short-lived perennial up to 1·2 m tall with erect or rarely decumbent stems; leaves broadly elliptic or obovate, 6·3–10 cm long, 3·8–6 cm wide, blunt and mucronate at the apex, narrowly cuneate at the base, mostly rather coarsely tomentose; corolla purple with paler limb or white with a purple eye, (2–)2·5–3·5 cm long.

Restricted to western Kenya in grassland, bushland or rocky places, often on poor soils. HE, HT, KIT, MUM, KIS, RV, NBI.
Napier 3420; Irwin 145.

4. Astripomoea hyoscyamoides (*Vatke*) *Verdc.*

Shrubby short-lived perennial or annual with erect stems 0·5–2·4 m tall; leaves elliptic or elliptic-lanceolate (rarely obovate-rhomboid), either borne normally on the stem or high up on the peduncles, 2–16 cm long, 1·1–6·3 cm wide, acute and apiculate at the apex, cuneate at the base, entire or wavy above the middle, rather finely tomentose; corolla white with a purple tube, (1·8–)2·5–3·8 cm long.

Restricted to lower altitudes, 170–4000 ft, in desert grassland, bushland, and disturbed areas. EMB, MAC, KAJ.
Verdcourt 1251A; Livingstone and Weigle 64–1.

14. IPOMOEA *L.*

Annual or perennial herbs or shrubs; stems prostrate, twining or erect; leaves very variable nearly always simple but entire to variously lobed; flowers solitary or in few- to many-flowered stalked or sessile inflorescences; bracts and bracteoles minute to very conspicuous; sepals 5, very variable; corolla mostly funnel-shaped, less often salver-shaped or trumpet-shaped, predominantly white or purple with a darker centre but other colours including yellow occur; pollen grains spinulose; ovary 2–5-celled, 4–(6–10)-ovuled; style filiform; stigma biglobular; capsule ovoid or globose, 3–10-valved, (3–)4(–10)-seeded; seeds glabrous to densely silky with long hairs.

1 Sepals very distinctly awned 2
Sepals not awned but often acute or mucronate 3

2 Flowers scarlet 29. *I hederifolia*
Flowers white or almost so, very large
28. *I. alba*

3 Flowers in heads subtended by a boat-shaped involucre 12. *I. involucrata*
Flowers if in heads then not subtended by a boat-shaped involucre 4

4 Leaves conspicuously bilobed at the apex
25. *I. pes-caprae*
Leaves not bilobed at the apex or scarcely so 5

5 Plant erect or suberect or if prostrate then a cultivated plant grown for its edible tubers (note: *I. longituba* is sometimes decumbent) 6
Plant with prostrate or twining stems, not cultivated as a food plant 18

6 Subshrubs with stout, more or less woody, stems 7
Annual or perennial herbs including those

which flower as first year rosette plants or when young and suberect but later send out short trailing or ascending shoots   **11**

7   Sepals linear to narrowly lanceolate, 5–18 × 2–2·5 mm   **8**

Sepals oblong to orbicular, 1–2·7 × 0·4–1·6 cm; corolla large 4·5–11·5 cm   **9**

8   Leaves oblanceolate to linear-oblong; seeds with appressed golden-brown hairs   38. *I. jaegeri*

Leaves ovate or ovate-elliptic; seeds not known but may prove to have long silky hairs   37. *I. sp. near cicatricosa*

9   Calyx subtended by two conspicuous opposed bracts; corolla funnel-shaped, yellow to purple   **10**

Calyx not subtended by two conspicuous opposed bracts; corolla with tube long and narrow, whitish, opening at night   32. *I. longituba*

10   Sepals and bracts elliptic to ovate, 1·4–2·5 × 0·5–1·1 cm; seeds with dark appressed hairs   33. *I. hildebrandtii*

Sepals oblong-spathulate, 1–1·8 × 0·3–0·5 (–0·9) cm; bracts ovate-spathulate, 1–1·8 × 1 cm; seeds with long spreading golden hairs   34. *I. spathulata*

11   Leaves all lobed or lobed and entire on the same plant   **12**

Leaves all entire   **14**

12   Annual or biennial; leaves ovate-oblong, coarsely lobed; corolla white or pink, 1·4–1·6 cm long   4. *I. polymorpha*

Perennials with tuberous roots   **13**

13   Pilose herb with funnel-shaped corolla 2–4 cm long   5. *I. oenotherae*

Glabrous herb with bell-shaped corolla about 3 cm long; cultivated for its edible tubers   20. *I. batatas*

14   Leaves with dense silvery-silky appressed hairs beneath; flowers in terminal bracteate heads   13. *I. crepidiformis*

Leaves hairy or glabrescent but not densely silvery beneath; plants which start erect but then trail or climb   **15**

15   Bracts paired, ovate, 1·5–0·7 cm, flowers solitary or in lax cymes; corolla 2·5–3·5(–5) cm long   7. *I. fulvicaulis* (variants)

Bracts minute, linear   **16**

16   Sepals hastate or cordate at the base with narrow apical part; annual with corolla about 1·3 cm long   10. *I. sinensis* (variants)

Sepals not hastate nor cordate at the base   **17**

17   Leaves linear-lanceolate, subsessile; flowers solitary or more usually several in compact stalked umbellate heads; perennial herb

with fusiform rootstock; corolla 2–2·5 cm long   23. *I. lapathifolia* (variant)

Leaves oblong-ovate, cordate or subcordate, petiolate; flowers solitary or paired with long peduncles and pedicels; corolla 2·7 cm long   11. *I. tenuirostris* (variant)

18   Strong woody climber with many flowers in shortly stalked axillary inflorescences; calyx lobes blunt or emarginate; corolla bright crimson with base of tube orange, funnel-shaped, 4·5–5·5 cm long; seeds without long hairs

see *Stictocardia beraviensis*

Not as above   **19**

19   Bracts and sepals ovate or elliptic, spathulate above; woody subshrubby climber with flowers in many-flowered cymes; seeds with long silky hairs   34. *I. spathulata*

Bracts small, linear, scattered or absent or, if larger, paired and ovate, then plant herbaceous   **20**

20   Woody liane up to 9 m long with the leaves soon deciduous; corolla salver-shaped, white, opening at night with tube 5·5–7·5 cm long, 6–9 mm diameter, limb 9 cm in diameter; seeds with hairs about 3 cm long   31. *I. lapidosa*

Not as above   **21**

21   Woody liane up to 9 m; corolla salver-shaped with tube 11–13 cm long, 2–3 mm in diameter; limb 4–5·5 cm wide; stamens and style exserted; seeds shortly velvety

see *Turbina*

Not as above   **22**

22   Leaves with sparse to dense matted white indumentum beneath; sepals with mixed indumentum of cottony tomentum, yellow bristles and sessile glands (one sort may be absent)   **23**

Leaves hairy, tomentose or glabrous but without matted white indumentum beneath; sepals with different indumentum   **25**

23   Annual; corolla 1·2–2 cm long   17. *I. arachnosperma*

Perennial; corolla 2–5·3 cm long   **24**

24   Flowers in small to large dense heads   15. *I. wightii*

Flowers in lax cymes   16. *I. ficifolia*

25   Sepals ovate to lanceolate, usually long and narrow at the apex, widened to a cordate or subhastate base   **26**

Sepals if widened at the base then not cordate or subhastate   **27**

26   Corolla 1·3(–2·2) cm long   10. *I. sinensis*

Corolla exceeding 3 cm   9. *I. mombassana*

27   Corolla small, 0·5–1·7 cm long   **28**

Corolla usually over 2 cm long   **34**

28 Corolla mostly bright yellow with a crimson-purple eye; flowers mostly solitary
                                                      22. *I. obscura*
    Corolla differently coloured   **29**
29 Leaves lobed   **30**
    Leaves entire   **31**
30 Annual or biennial erect or prostrate plant; leaves subentire to coarsely lobed; corolla narrowly funnel-shaped, white or pink often with darker centre, 1·4–1·6 cm long; no scales at base of filaments
                                                      4. *I. polymorpha*
    Perennial twiner; leaves 3-lobed, cordate at the base; corolla campanulate, white, yellow, pale orange or greenish-striped, 1·6–1·8 cm long; fleshy scales present at base of filaments
                                see *Lepistemonopsis volkensii*
31 Leaves cuneate, rounded or scarcely cordate at the base   **32**
    Leaves ovate, hastate or cordate at the base
                                                      33
32 Leaves linear or linear-lanceolate, cuneate; flowers several in stalked subumbellate cymes; perennial with rootstock fusiform; corolla mostly white   23. *I. lapathifolia*
    Leaves elliptic, rounded or scarcely cordate at the base; inflorescences small, axillary, sessile, 1–3-flowered; plant annual; corolla red or white   2. *I. coscinosperma*
33 Sepals hairy; corolla pink, rarely white; capsule pubescent   1. *I. eriocarpa*
    Sepals glabrous or pubescent; corolla white; capsule glabrous   3. *I. plebeia*
34 Leaf-blades all lobed or lobed and entire on the same plant   **35**
    Leaf-blades all entire or margins rarely sinuate below or sometimes somewhat rounded-lobed at the base (subhastate)
                                                      40
35 Leaves all palmately deeply to shallowly lobed or lobed and entire on the same plant; lobes broad, 1·7–4·2 cm wide or if narrow then only 3-lobed   **36**
    Leaves palmately deeply 5–9-lobed; lobes narrow, 0·2–2·8 cm wide   **38**
36 Sepals ovate, somewhat obtuse; leaves mostly entire but rarely lobed; seeds with long hairs; usually near water   30. *I. rubens*
    Sepals lanceolate or elliptic with attenuate linear tips; seeds glabrescent or pubescent
                                                      37
37 Sepals regularly lanceolate, softly pubescent or glabrescent; corolla 6–7·5 cm long
                                                      18. *I. acuminata*
    Sepals lanceolate, narrowed above the basal part which alone is bristly; corolla 4–5 cm long   19. *I. purpurea*

38 Corolla under 2·5 cm long
                                                      27. *I. hochstetteri*
    Corolla 3–6 cm long   **39**
39 Plant with spreading bristly hairs on the stem; leaves pilose; bracts leafy, oblong to oblong-lanceolate surrounding a head-like inflorescence; corolla 3·5–5 cm long
                                                      14. *I. pes-tigridis*
    Plant more or less glabrous but main stems often warty; bracts minute; flowers solitary or inflorescence lax; corolla (3–)4·5–6 cm long   26. *I. cairica*
40 Glabrous swamp plant usually with thick semi-succulent stems trailing in the water or at least on seasonally flooded ground; peduncle 1-few-flowered; corolla (2·5–)4·5–7·5 cm long, mostly pink or purple   24. *I. aquatica*
    Not as above   **41**
41 Shrubby climbers or woody-stemmed lianes; seeds with long woolly hairs or glabrous with a short tuft of hairs near the hilum
                                                      42
    Annual or perennial twiners or trailers; seeds glabrous or shortly hairy all over   **44**
42 Leaves ovate, acuminate; sepals ovate 6–8 x 5–8 mm; seeds with long hairs; usually near water   30. *I. rubens*
    Leaves reniform or ovate, mostly rounded at the apex, less often acute or acuminate and, if so, sepals lanceolate or linear, 1–2 x 0·15–0·4 cm; not usually near water   **43**
43 Indumentum of very fine silky appressed hairs; sepals linear-lanceolate; seeds with long hairs all over   35. *I. kituiensis*
    Indumentum of bristly hairs; sepals oblong; seeds glabrous save for a short but conspicuous tuft of golden hairs near the hilum   36. *I. hartmannii*
44 Peduncles bearing paired oblong or ovate bracts mostly just below the inflorescence
                                                      45
    Bracts minute or linear   **46**
45 Indumentum typically short and dense; flowers solitary or few in small heads; corolla 2·5–3 cm long; leaves emarginate or subcordate at the base   7. *I. fulvicaulis*
    Indumentum typically longer; flowers usually solitary; corolla (2·7–)4–5 cm long; leaves cuneate or subhastate at the base
                                                      8. *I. crassipes*
46 Leaves oblong to lanceolate, rounded at the base; sepals lanceolate, about 1·8 x 0·4 cm; corolla 4–5·5 cm long with tube markedly narrowed at the base
                                                      6. *I. blepharophylla*
    Leaves ovate to triangular, cordate, sagittate or hastate at the base   **47**

47 Corolla yellow or whitish mostly with a crimson purple centre; flowers mostly solitary **48**

Corolla blue or purple, rarely white, mostly with a darker throat; flowers solitary or in few- to several-flowered inflorescences **49**

48 Corolla 2·7–4 cm long 21. *I. ochracea*

Corolla 1·4–2·5 cm long 22. *I. obscura*

49 Sepals narrowed at apex with broader distinctly bristly basal part (naturalized) 19. *I. purpurea*

Sepals more uniformly pubescent though sometimes also marginally ciliate **50**

50 Sepals 1·4–2·2 x 0·3–0·5 cm; corolla 5–8·5 cm long (naturalized) 18. *I. acuminata*

Sepals 0·7–1·3 x 0·05–0·3cm; corolla 2–4 cm long **51**

51 Leaves more regularly ovate-cordate; sepals mostly wider; mostly a plant of rather higher altitudes, 1350–2250 m. 11. *I. tenuirostris*

Leaves mostly more elongate, subhastate-cordate at the base; sepals very finely drawn out at the tips; mostly a plant of lower altitudes in Masailand, 900–1500 m 9. *I. mombassana*

1. Ipomoea eriocarpa *R. Br.*

Annual twiner with hairy stems; leaves ovate-cordate to linear-oblong, often subhastate, pilose or glabrescent, 2·5–8 cm long; flowers in (1–)3–many-flowered usually almost sessile axillary inflorescences; corolla mauve or white or pink or white with a mauve centre, 6–9 mm long; capsule pubescent.

A widespread plant of disturbed places in bushland. HK, KIS, EMB, KAJ.

Verdcourt 2915; Bally 103.

2. Ipomoea coscinosperma *Choisy*

Spreading glabrescent or hairy annual; leaves narrowly elliptic-lanceolate or oblong, mostly rounded or cuneate at the base, glabrescent or hairy, 4–11 cm long; flowers in 1–3-flowered sessile axillary inflorescences; corolla red or white, 5–8 mm long; capsule glabrous.

Rare in Kenya in disturbed grassland and cultivated ground. NBI.

Bogdan 3077.

3. Ipomoea plebeia *R. Br.*

Annual with twining or prostrate pubescent stems; leaves triangular-ovate, cordate at the base; flowers solitary or in 2–5-flowered cymes; sepals ovate-triangular; corolla white, often with a purple centre, 6–7 mm long; capsule glabrous.

Locally common in dry bushland. MAC.

Ossent EAH 11834; Napper 1592.

4. Ipomoea polymorpha *Roem. & Schultes* (see p. 543)

Annual or biennial with erect or prostrate hairy stems; leaves ovate, oblong or elliptic, subentire or shallowly to deeply and coarsely lobed, 2–4(–5) cm long; flowers axillary, solitary; outer sepals with partly subhyaline ovate-orbicular basal part and narrow attenuate foliaceous apical part; corolla white or pink, often with a dark centre, 1·4–1·6 cm long.

Widespread but local in moister bushland on shallow soils and in grassland, HT, HA, KIT, MUM, RV, MAC, NBI.

Tweedie 519; Verdcourt 517.

5. Ipomoea oenotherae (*Vatke*) *Hall. f.* (see p. 543)

Perennial with a tuberous rootstock and prostrate or ascending pilose stems; leaves very variable, mostly 2–5–9-lobed but rarely entire or undulate, up to 8 cm long; flowers axillary, solitary, subsessile or pedicellate; calyx similar to last species; corolla mauve or white, almost salver-shaped, 1·4–3·2(–4) cm long.

Both var. *oenotherae* with corolla 2–3·2(4) cm long and var. *angustifolia* (Oliv.) Verdc. with narrower leaves and a corolla mostly 1·4–1·6 cm long occur in our area.

Locally common in seasonally moist grassland. HE, HT, HL, HA, KIT, NAR, RV, MAC, NBI, KAJ.

Irwin 153; Verdcourt 510.

6. Ipomoea blepharophylla *Hall. f.* (see p. 543)

Perennial with several prostrate pubescent stems from a woody rootstock; leaves lanceolate to narrowly oblong, rounded or subcordate at the base, glabrescent, up to 8(–12) cm long; flowers solitary, shortly stalked; sepals long and narrow, up to 1·8 cm long; corolla mauve with darker centre, narrowly funnel-shaped with the tube distinctly narrowed at the base, up to 6 cm long.

Typically a plant of burnt *Combretum* woodland where it is fairly common. HA, KIT, MUM, KIS, EMB, NBI, KAJ.

Tweedie 1697; Verdcourt 1126.

7. Ipomoea fulvicaulis (*Choisy*) *Hall. f.* (see p. 543)

Perennial with woody rootstock and yellow-brown pubescent twining stems; leaves oblong or ovate, cordate, long-stalked; flowers in few-flowered

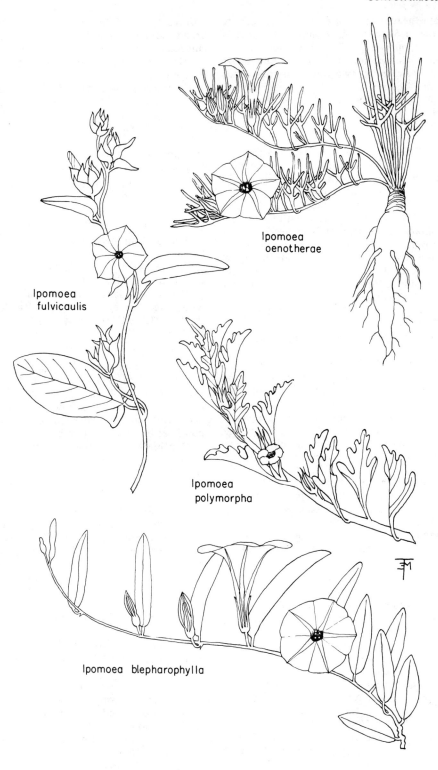

Ipomoea
oenotherae

Ipomoea
fulvicaulis

Ipomoea
polymorpha

Ipomoea blepharophylla

pedunculate heads with large ovate, acuminate bracts about 1·5 cm long, 7 mm wide; corolla funnel-shaped, mauve, 2·5–3·5(–5) cm long.

The above description and distribution refers only to var. *fulvicaulis*; two other varieties occur elsewhere in East Africa.

Local in short grassland, often on shallow soils. KIT, NAN.

Tweedie 583 and 672.

8. Ipomoea crassipes *Hook.*

An excessively variable perennial erect or creeping herb with a woody rootstock and densely softly hairy stems; leaves ovate, elliptic, oblong or lanceolate, mostly truncate or rounded at the base, less often slightly hastate, covered with long hairs; flowers solitary or in small stalked heads; bracts linear to ovate, 0·4–2 cm long, 1–9 mm wide; sepals ovate, acute or drawn out at the apex, rounded or subcordate at the base, 1–2·2 cm long, 0·7–1·1 cm wide; corolla white, red or purple and white, 2·7–5 cm long.

In shallow soil or black-cotton soil grassland. EMB, MAC, KAJ.

Graham 2169; van Someren 251 and 287.

9. Ipomoea mombassana *Vatke*

Annual or perennial twiner with hairy stems; leaves ovate or ovate-oblong, or elongate-oblong, cordate, cordate-sagittate or subhastate-cordate, glabrous or hairy; inflorescences 1–several-flowered; corolla funnel-shaped, white or purple with a purple centre, with a narrow tube 3–5 cm long and limb 5·5–6·5 cm in diameter.

Two subspecies occur in the area:

Subsp. **mombassana** Annual; sepals with a distinctly hastate base; corolla usually white with a purple centre.

A lowland plant, often very common in dry bushland, and *Commiphora* and *Combretum* woodland. MAC.

Napper 1591.

Subsp. **massaica** *Verdc.* Perennial; sepals slightly widened at the base but not hastate; corolla purple with a darker centre; very similar to *I. tenuirostris* but with differently shaped leaves and much more slender sepals.

Found in bare ground in desert bushland, and dry wooded grassland, etc. RV, MAG, KAJ.

Verdcourt 588; Greenway 8831.

10. Ipomoea sinensis (*Desr.*) *Choisy*

Annual with prostrate or twining pilose stems; leaves ovate or ovate-oblong, cordate or subhastate at the base, 2–10 cm long, glabrous to pubescent;

inflorescence 1–3-flowered, stalked; sepals with a broad cordate or subhastate base and narrow lanceolate apex; corolla pale mauve, white with purple centre, pink or purple white, funnel-shaped, 1·3 cm long.

Common in seasonally flooded grassland, and dry bushland, and sometimes a weed. HM, KIS, NAR, BAR, RV, MAG, EMB, MAC, NBI, KAJ.

Verdcourt and Polhill 3167; Bogdan 3085.

11. Ipomoea tenuirostris *Choisy* (see p. 543)

Perennial herb with twining or prostrate stems; leaves ovate to oblong, cordate, hairy; inflorescences 2–5-flowered, stalked; corolla 2–3·8 cm long.

Two subspecies occur in the area:

Subsp. **tenuirostris** Mostly an extensive twiner; leaves mostly densely pilose; inflorescences mostly several-flowered with rather stout peduncle; corolla usually all purple.

Often abundant especially in cleared upland woodland, but extending into dry bushland and thicket. HE, HC, HT, HA, HK, KIT, MUM, EMB, KAJ.

Napier 2117; Verdcourt 2505.

Subsp. **hindeana** (*Rendle*) *Verdc.* Often flowering when only 7 cm tall but later developing prostrate stems; leaves usually sparsely pubescent; inflorescences 1–2-flowered with slender peduncles; corolla white, sometimes with a little purple at the base of the tube.

Confined to southern Kenya and northern Tanzania in upland grassland, often on black-cotton soil. KAJ.

Napier 574; Verdcourt 2507.

12. Ipomoea involucrata *Beauv.*

Very variable annual or perennial mostly hairy twiner; leaves ovate-cordate; inflorescence a dense head enclosed in a large leafy boat-shaped involucre; corolla purple, pink, white or white with a pink throat, funnel-shaped, 2–5·5 cm long.

Locally common in western Kenya in forest clearings and by Lake Victoria. MUM, ?KIS.

Mainwaring in Napier 2664; Lyne Watt 1415.

13. Ipomoea crepidiformis *Hall. f.*

Annual or perennial herb with erect or prostrate stems; leaves discolourous, oblong or linear-lanceolate, densely to sparsely white-pilose beneath; flowers congested in small densely pilose heads; corolla red or mauve, funnel-shaped, 1·7–3·3 cm long.

A variable plant of dry and wooded grassland. HA, BAR, EMB, MAC, KAJ, NBI.

Napper 1651; Bally 11528.

14. Ipomoea pes-tigridis *L.*

Annual with trailing stems covered with long spreading yellow bristly hairs; leaves palmately 7–9-lobed often to near the base, lobes narrowly elliptic to obovate; flowers in long-stalked few-flowered bracteate heads; bracts leafy; corolla white, pink or purple with a darker throat, funnel-shaped, 3·5–5 cm long.

This, the type of the genus, is widely distributed in tropical Africa but in Kenya is found along the coastal strip. It is doubtfully present from our area at Murka. KAJ.

No specimen seen.

15. Ipomoea wightii (*Wall.*) *Choisy* (see p. 546)

Variable perennial prostrate or twining hairy herb; leaves ovate-cordate, either entire or shallowly to deeply 3-lobed, with characteristic white cottony tomentum beneath; flowers in few- to many-flowered dense or somewhat lax heads; sepals linear to ovate-lanceolate, with white cottony tomentum, appressed or spreading bristly hairs and sessile or stalked marginal glands; corolla mostly mauve, 2–3(–5) cm long.

Common in upland grassland and montane forest edges. HE, HC, HT, HM, HA, HK, KIT, MUM, NAR, NBI, KAJ.

Lugard 290; Irwin 150.

16. Ipomoea ficifolia *Lindl.*

Perennial prostrate or twining hairy herb; leaves entire or 3-lobed with similar indumentum to the last species but sometimes very sparse; flowers in much laxer heads; sepals glandular and with bristly hairs; corolla pink or mauve, (2·5–)4·5–5·3 cm long.

A coastal bushland plant which just enters our area in MAC.

Napper 1538.

17. Ipomoea arachnosperma *Welw.*

Annual prostrate or twining hairy herb; leaves usually 3-lobed, rarely entire, with dense cottony white tomentum beneath; flowers several in dense or lax cymes; sepals bristly and glandular; corolla pink or mauve, 1·2–1·7(–2) cm long.

An uncommon plant of disturbed places in dry bushland. KIS, BAR.

Napier in CM 6648.

18. Ipomoea acuminata (*Vahl*) *Roem & Schultes*
(*I. congesta* R. Br.; *I. learii* Paxton)

Perennial pubescent twiner or trailer; leaves entire or sometimes 3-lobed, pilose on both surfaces, sometimes densely so beneath; flowers few to several in fairly dense cymes; sepals lanceolate, 1·4–2·2 cm long, 3–5 mm wide, glabrescent or

softly pubescent but not bristly; corolla blue or bluish-purple, often · tinged red, funnel-shaped, 5–8·5 cm long.

Now pantropical and cultivated widely as an ornamental Morning Glory† and sometimes occurs as an escape in waste places. HA, KIT, NBI (fide Check List).

Napier 1841.

19. Ipomoea purpurea (*L.*) *Roth*

Annual pubescent twiner or trailer; leaves entire or 3-lobed, glabrous or pubescent; flowers solitary or in few-flowered cymes; sepals lanceolate, 1·3–1·6 cm long, 1·5–4·5 mm wide, somewhat attenuated above; basal part bristly; corolla white, pink, or magenta with tube white below, funnel-shaped, 4–5 cm long.

Native of South America now widely naturalized in the tropics on waste and cultivated ground. HA, KIT, NBI.

Napier 1517; Kirrika 254.

20. Ipomoea batatas (*L.*) *Lam.*

Herb with underground fusiform edible tubers; stems mostly prostrate; leaves triangular in outline, truncate or cordate, entire to palmately shallowly to very deeply 3–5-lobed; inflorescences 1–several-flowered; corolla lilac or violet, white above, bell-shaped, 3–4·7 cm long.

The sweet potato is probably South American in origin but is now very widely cultivated in the tropics, and can occur as an escape. MUM, NBI.

Williams 719; Whyte s.n.

21. Ipomoea ochracea (*Lindl.*) *G. Don* (see p. 546)

Perennial herb with slender prostrate or twining pubescent or hairy stems; leaves ovate; inflorescences 1–several-flowered lax; corolla yellow or white with a dark purple or brown centre, 2·7–4 cm long.

Frequently in riverine forest edges in hot dry country but also in *Commiphora* and *Combretum* dry bushland. KIT, MUM, KIS, NAR, NBI.

Bally 5268; Verdcourt 1508.

22. Ipomoea obscura (*L.*) *Ker-Gawl.*

Very similar indeed to the last but with smaller flowers: the two are really scarcely distinct; corolla bright yellow, orange, cream, or white and in our area always with a purple, crimson, or chocolate-brown centre, 1·4–2·3(–2·5) cm long.

---

†*I. tricolor* Cav. is perhaps the most commonly cultivated Morning Glory with a pale tube and usually blue limb and much smaller sepals, e.g. Ol Tukai (Verdcourt 3973); Nairobi (Verdcourt 2272).

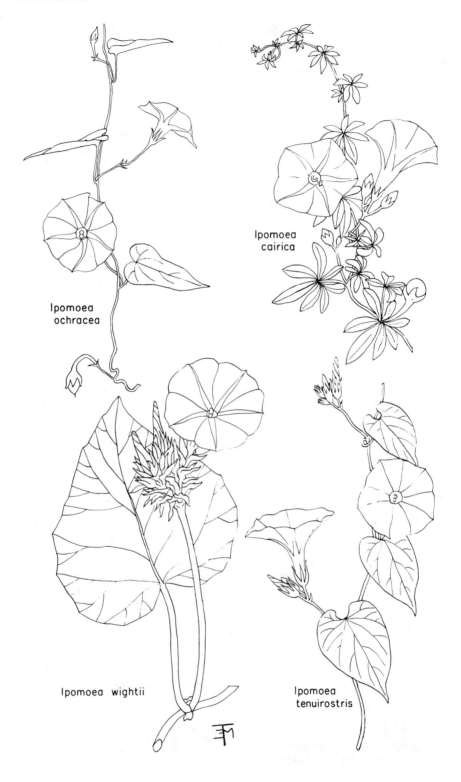

Ipomoea
ochracea

Ipomoea
cairica

Ipomoea wightii

Ipomoea
tenuirostris

Widespread in stony bushed-grassland and dry woodland. HT, HA, KIT, NAR, RV, MAG, NAN, EMB, MAC, NBI, KAJ.

Napper 1587; Williams 306.

23. Ipomoea lapathifolia *Hall. f.*

Perennial herb with fusiform rootstock, typically twining or prostrate but in our plants often more or less erect; leaves linear; flowers several in close umbellate stalked heads; corolla much smaller than in typical variety, white, tube 1 cm long, limb 2·5 cm wide. The above description refers to var. *parviflora* Verdc.

Uncommon in grassland on black cotton soil. MAC, KAJ.

Irwin in EAH 11427; Ossent 452.

24. Ipomoea aquatica *Forsk.*

Annual or perennial herb with prostrate or floating, often thick semi-succulent glabrous stems; leaves very variable, narrowly to broadly triangular or linear-oblong, truncate, cordate or somewhat hastate at the base; inflorescences 1-few-flowered; corolla purple, pink or white with deeper purple centre, funnel-shaped with a narrow tube, (2·5–)4–7·5 cm long.

A pantropical plant mostly in swamps, ponds, seasonal water in semidesert country, rice-fields, etc. KIS (recorded from K5 and 6 in FTEA).

Much used as a vegetable in the orient where many varieties have been developed but not or scarcely used in Africa.

25. Ipomoea pes-caprae *(L.) R. Br.*

Glabrous perennial with thick hollow creeping stems; leaves almost round, quadrangular or elliptic, emarginate or slightly to conspicuously bilobed at the apex; inflorescences 1-many-flowered; corolla pink or red-purple with a darker centre, funnel-shaped, 3–5·5 cm long.

A pantropical plant almost restricted to sandy sea shores just above hightide mark, more rarely on inland lake shores e.g. Lake Tanganyika. The record from MAC (Sultan Hamud) seems almost impossible to believe and confirmation is required.

Irwin 165.

26. Ipomoea cairica *(L.) Sweet* (see p. 546)

Practically or quite glabrous, perennial twining herb with smooth or warty stems; leaves ovate to round in outline, palmately divided to the base into 5–7 ovate to lanceolate or elliptic lobes up to 4 cm long and 1·6 cm wide; inflorescences lax, 1-many-flowered; corolla purple, red or white with a purple centre, funnel-shaped, (3–)4·5–6 cm long; seeds with short tomentum and some long silky hairs.

This is the common 'railway creeper' which occurs in forest clearings, lake shores, swampy grassland, hedges, waste, and cultivated ground at medium altitudes. HE, KIT, MUM, KIS, NAR, RV, EMB, NBI.

Polhill 4A; Williams 715.

27. Ipomoea hochstetteri *House*

Glabrous annual with twining prostrate stems; leaves rounded in outline, palmately divided to the base into 5 lobes; lobes elliptic, 2·5–7 cm long, 0·7–2·8 cm wide; inflorescences 1-several-flowered; corolla white or mauve, funnel-shaped, 1·9–2·4 cm long; seeds densely tomentose and often with long cottony hairs as well. The seeds are usually black but a vermillion-seeded variant occurs on the Nairobi-Magadi road about which much more information is required.

On black-cotton soil and in dry bushland at medium altitudes. MAG, MAC, NBI, KAJ.

Williams in EAH 12340; Bogdan 3078.

28. Ipomoea alba *L.*

A usually glabrous annual or perennial with prostrate or twining stems; leaves ovate or round in outline, entire or 3-lobed, often large; inflorescences 1-several-flowered; outer sepals with a long awn-like appendage; corolla white with greenish-cream tube, scented, opening at night, salver-shaped with tube cylindrical, 7–12 cm long, 5 mm wide and limb 11–16 cm in diameter; stamens and style exserted.

American in origin but now pantropical as an escape, and also cultivated for its large but short-lived flowers; often found on rubbish heaps, waste places, forest edges in dry country. MAC.

van Someren 178.

29. Ipomoea hederifolia *L.*

Annual with glabrous or sparsely hairy twining stems; leaves ovate or rounded in outline, entire or 3-lobed, with margins entire, angular or toothed; inflorescences few to several-flowered, often long; sepals shortly awned; corolla scarlet, salver-shaped, tube 2·8–4 cm long, limb 2–2·5 cm in diameter; stamens and style exserted.

Native of tropical America now widely naturalized and cultivated throughout the tropics; found in waste places, thickets, cliffs, and forest edges. MUM, MAC, NBI.

Williams 12545; Meinertzhagen in EAH 11364.

30. Ipomoea rubens *Choisy* (*I. riparia* G. Don; *I. lilacina* Blume)

Perennial hairy twiner; leaves entire or rarely 3-lobed; inflorescences few- to many-flowered; corolla purple, funnel-shaped, 3–4·5 cm long.

Practically pantropical in papyrus and *Echinochloa* swamps by rivers, lakes, and on seasonally inundated clays and silts. KIS, KAJ.

Verdcourt 3974.

31. Ipomoea lapidosa *Vatke*

A woody liane with perennial branches often ascending trees for a distance of 9 m from possibly a tuberous rootstock; leaves ovate, cordate, densely tomentose on nerves below when young, bullate, soon deciduous and often not present during flowering and fruiting stages; flowers solitary, clustered at the apices of the shoots; corolla white and greenish-cream, sweetly scented, opening at night, salver-shaped, tube cylindrical, slender, 5·5–7·5 cm long, (4–)6–9 mm wide, limb 9 cm in diameter with a lobed frilly edge; seeds with long white or pale brown hairs.

Known only from Kenya, on rocky soil in dry deciduous (mainly *Commiphora*) bushland. MAC, KAJ.

Verdcourt 3691; Napper 1334.

32. Ipomoea longituba *Hall. f.*

Perennial shrub with erect or straggling stems which usually die back annually, up to 1 m long; rootstock tuberous; leaves ovate, cuneate or truncate at the base, entire or in recent years very often deeply lobed; flowers solitary, clustered at the apices of the shoots; corolla white and greenish-cream, sweetly scented, opening at night, salver-shaped, tube cylindrical, very slender, (7·5–)9–11 cm long, 3·5–4 mm in diameter, limb 7–9 cm in diameter, distinctly lobed with the lobes square in outline but bifid at the apex and with a thin crinkly margin; seeds with long very pale purplish brown hairs.

On the Serengeti Plains this species was found to be slightly trimorphic with regard to the arrangement of the stamens and style; specimens with lobed leaves are now very abundant in the field but are not known from herbarium collections before 1960. These two problems would repay study as also would the relationships between this and *I. lapidosa*.

In grassland with or without scattered trees, and in crevices of rocky outcrops in deciduous bushland etc. HM, HA, NAR, RV, MAG, NAN, MAC, KAJ.

Verdcourt 3004; Bally 754.

33. Ipomoea hildebrandtii *Vatke*

Variable subwoody pubescent shrublet up to 2–5 m tall; leaves round to elliptic-oblong, often large, very finely pubescent beneath; flowers few to many in dense to lax branched cymes; bracts and sepals large, 1·4–2·6 x 0·5–1·4 cm; corolla purple, white or white with a purple tube, funnel-shaped, 4·5–11·5 cm long; seeds with dark appressed hairs.

Two main subspecies occur in the area, the typical one in the east and the other in the west.

Subsp. **hildebrandtii** Bracts and sepals broad, hairy or villous, ratio of length to breadth 1·6–2·8; corolla (5·7–)7–11·5 cm long.

Common in grassland with scattered *Acacia* and *Acacia-Commiphora* deciduous bushland particularly along the Namanga road. NAR, KAJ.

Verdcourt 3648; Hedberg 1440.

Subsp. **grantii** (*Bak.*) *Verdc.* Bracts and sepals narrow, pubescent, ratio of length to breadth (2·25–)2·9–4·16; corolla 4–8·5 cm long.

In grassland with scattered trees. MUM, KIS.

Tweedie 2145; Verdcourt 1628.

Apart from these two subspp., subsp. *megaensis* Verdc. with more silky sepals and corolla entirely purple, 4–5·5 cm long is known from NAN (Rumuruti) e.g. (Bogdan 472). Subsp. *grantii* var. mahonii (C. H. Wright) Verdc. with very narrow elliptic-oblong leaves occurs on Mt. Elgon, Trans-Nzoia, East Sudan, 6400 ft. (Irwin 143).

34. Ipomoea spathulata *Hall. f.*

Shrub with suberect, partly twining or scrambling branches up to 2·5 m long, covered with grey or yellowish pubescence; leaves round, very obtuse at the apex, cordate, finely appressed silky-pubescent beneath; flowers several to many in stalked branched cymes; bracts broadly ovate-spathulate to round, 1–1·8 x 0·4–1·3 cm; sepals oblong-spathulate or elliptic, broadest near the apex, 1–1·8 x 0·3–0·9 cm, the inner linear or lanceolate; corolla white, cream or distinctly yellow, with a purple centre, funnel-shaped, 5–7·5 cm long; seeds with long pale golden hairs.

Found generally in Uganda, Kenya, and Ethiopia in *Acacia-Commiphora* bushland. HC, HT, KIT, BAR.

Leippert 5249; Hemming 1871.

35. Ipomoea kituiensis *Vatke*

Similar to *I. spathulata* but with apiculate, acuminate or even slightly bilobed leaves, and looser inflorescences; sepals and bracts linear-lanceolate. Merges with last species where the ranges meet.

Another large species of dry bushland, particularly where it is regenerating after disturbance. KIT, MUM, KIS, NAR, BAR, MAC, NBI, KAJ.

Verdcourt 1482; Tweedie 2576.

36. Ipomoea hartmannii *Vatke*

Similar to *I. spathulata* except for the narrower bracts and sepals (up to 1 and 4 mm wide respectively) and bristly yellow hairs; seeds glabrous save for a short but conspicuous tuft of golden hairs near the hilum.

Uncommon in *Acacia-Commiphora* deciduous bushland often on rock outcrops. MAC, KAJ.

van Someren 225; Verdcourt 3122.

37. Ipomoea *sp. nov. near* **cicatricosa** *Bak.*

Perennial shrub about 60 cm tall with stems covered with short dense pubescence; leaves ovate or ovate-elliptic, about 7 cm long, 4 cm wide, glabrous above, appressed silky-pilose beneath especially when young, petiole up to about 4 cm long; cymes 2–3-flowered, axillary, shorter than the petioles; peduncles about 1 cm long; bracts 3, linear-lanceolate, about 1·3 cm long situated just below the calyx; calyx lobes similar to the bracts, up to 1·5 cm long; corolla purple, probably funnel-shaped, at least 3·5 cm long, pilose outside; fruit not seen but seeds probably with long hairs.

Appears to be a new species; found in thorny bushland by roadsides. MAC.

Hanid, Hanid, and Kiniaruh 481.

38. Ipomoea jaegeri *Pilger* (*I. argyrophylla auctt. non Vatke*) (see p. 538)

Erect subsucculent shrub to 0·75 m with many stems; leaves linear-oblong to oblong-oblanceolate, obtuse at the apex, cuneate, green and glabrous above, silvery pubescent, woolly or glabrescent beneath; flowers solitary, very shortly stalked; bracts linear; sepals lanceolate, acuminate, 0·6–1·8 cm long, 2–2·5 mm wide, silvery pubescent; corolla white or pink with a darker centre, funnel-shaped, 2·7–5(–6·3) cm long; seeds densely appressed silky golden hairy.

A beautiful and common plant of stony soils in grassland and bushland at medium altitudes. NAR, RV, MAG, MAC, NBI, KAJ.

Glover, Gwynne, and Samwell 759; Verdcourt 2357.

15. TURBINA *Raf.*

Similar in habit and most characters to *Ipomoea* but differing in having an indehiscent ovoid-oblong or ellipsoid fruit, mostly with a single puberulous seed.

A rather artificial genus which perhaps should not be separated from *Ipomoea*.

Turbina stenosiphon (*Hall. f.*) *Meeuse*

Woody climbing shrub to 9 m; leaves ovate, usually glabrous but sometimes pubescent; flowers fascicled on short shoots, opening at night and said to be evil-smelling; corolla white; tube very slender, 11–13 cm long; limb about 5·5 cm wide; stamens and style exserted from the mouth of the tube.

Uncommon in bushland, often in rocky country, sometimes on termite mounds. MAC, KAJ.

Napper 1632; Bally in CM 7746.

86. SCROPHULARIACEAE†

Herbs or shrubs with usually opposite exstipulate leaves and racemose inflorescences; bracts and bracteoles usually present; calyx with a short or long tube and 4–5 lobes; corolla lobes fused at base into a short or long, often zygomorphic tube and with 5, variously zygomorphic lobes; stamens 2–5, usually 4, fused to the corolla tube; ovary of two carpels with axile placentation; style long; stigma simple or 2-lobed; fruit a capsule; seeds usually numerous, minute.

1	Corolla 2-lipped, with an erect, not spreading, upper lip	2
	Corolla with spreading lobes, not 2-lipped	15
2	Corolla tube spurred at base	3
	Corolla tube entire at base	4
3	Leaves ovate, dentate	5. *Diclis*
	Leaves linear, entire	6. *Misopates orontium*
4	All leaves in the basal rosette	5
	All leaves on elongated stems	6
5	Leaves linear or with a long petiole and expanded blade; fruiting pedicels recurved downwards	11. *Limosella*
	Leaves ovate to elliptic, sessile; fruiting pedicels not recurved	12. *Craterostigma*
6	Leaves entire	7
	Leaves dentate or serrate on the margin	12
7	Stamens 2	8
	Stamens 4	9
8	Leaves reduced to scales at and just below the inflorescence	10. *Dopatrium*
	All leaves similar	15. *Ilysanthes*
9	Flowers sessile	11
	Flowers long-pedicelled	10
10	Plant an erect annual; corolla white, with a curved upper lip	9. *Mimulus gracilis*
	Plant a trailing perennial; corolla blue with a straight upper lip	14. *Lindernia oliverana*
11	Flowers in globose spikes; corolla less than 5 mm long	31. *Selago thomsonii*
	Flowers in elongated spikes; corolla over 5 mm long	27. *Striga*
12	Plant an erect shrub; flowers yellow	29. *Bartsia*
	Plant herbaceous, often trailing; flowers blue, white or cream	13
13	Calyx over 5 mm long, zygomorphic	13. *Torenia thouarsii*
	Calyx under 5 mm long, regular	14

† By A. D. Q. Agnew.

14   Plant woody at base; upper lip of corolla curved outwards   8. *Stemodiopsis*
      Plant herbaceous throughout; upper lip of corolla straight and in line with the corolla tube   14. *Lindernia*
15   Tree or woody shrub over 1 m tall; flowers mostly solitary on old woody stems
                                  7. *Halleria lucida*
      Herbs or shrubs smaller than 50 cm tall; flowers mostly in racemes, never on old woody stems   16
16   Corolla yellow   17
      Corolla white, blue or purplish, never yellow   19
17   Stamens 5   1. *Verbascum*
      Stamens 4   18
18   Pedicels longer than the calyx; plant from a basal rosette of leaves   2. *Celsia floccosa*
      Pedicels shorter than the calyx; plant without a basal rosette of leaves   18. *Alectra*
19   Corolla tube split below so that all the corolla lobes form together one upper lip
                                  30. *Hebenstretia dentata*
      Corolla tube entire, not split, corolla lobes spreading more or less equally all round   20
20   Corolla tube cylindrical, sometimes with small bulges above the middle; corolla tube longer than or equal to the lobes; stamens hidden within the tube   21
      Corolla tube funnel-shaped below the mouth; corolla tube often shorter than the lobes; stamens usually visible in the corolla mouth   25
21   Corolla tube sharply bent above the middle   22
      Corolla tube straight or evenly curved   23
22   Plant prostrate   25. *Cycniopsis*
      Plant erect   27. *Striga*
23   Corolla lobes less than 8 mm in diameter
                                  23. *Buchnera*
      Corolla lobes over 1 cm in diameter   24
24   Corolla tube over 5 cm long; leaves elliptic, regularly serrate   24. *Cycnium*
      Corolla tube under 4 cm long, or, if more, then the leaves irregularly dentate and not elliptic   26. *Rhamphicarpa*
25   Plant stemless; all leaves in a basal rosette
                                  11. *Limosella*
      Plant with a leafy stem   26
26   Creeping herbs with orbicular leaves set at 90° to the erect petiole
                                  16. *Sibthorpia europaea*
      Erect herbs, or, if creeping then the leaves not orbicular and not in a different plane to the petiole   27
27   Stamens 2   28
      Stamens 4   29

28   Leaves opposite; sepals and petals 4
                                  17. *Veronica*
      Leaves alternate; sepals and petals 5
                                  3. *Anticharis linearis*
29   Leaves simple, dentate to crenate   30
      Leaves entire or trifoliolate   31
30   Plant a climber   19. *Buttonia hildebrandtii*
      Plant an erect herb   29. *Bartsia*
31   Flowers subsessile axillary
                                  4. *Aptosimum pumilum*
      Flowers in terminal spikes or racemes   32
32   Spikes globose   31. *Selago thomsonii*
      Spikes or racemes elongate   33
33   Corolla tube over 2 cm long
                                  28. *Harveya obtusifolia*
      Corolla tube less than 2 cm long   34
34   Each anther with two fertile cells
                                  21. *Micrargeria filiformis*
      Each anther with one fertile and one sterile cell   35
35   Corolla tube ± as long as the calyx; sterile cell of anthers cylindrical   20. *Sopubia*
      Corolla tube usually twice as long as calyx; sterile cell of lower pair of anthers disc-shaped   22. *Pseudosopubia hildebrandtii*

1. VERBASCUM *L.*

Usually monocarpic herbs with a rosette of simple alternate leaves and a simple or compound raceme of flowers in fascicles; calyx 5-lobed; corolla with scarcely any tube, almost regular, of 5 spreading lobes; stamens 5; capsule septicidally 2-valved, the valves 2-lobed.

Verbascum sinaiticum *Benth.*

An erect woolly herb from a rosette of large ovate to oblong leaves, bearing simple or branched terminal racemes of yellow flowers.

Locally common in disturbed upland country, this showy introduction is commonest in regions of dry wheat cultivation. HT, HM, HA, RV, NAN. Verdcourt 1137.

2. CELSIA *L.*

Similar to *Verbascum* but with only 4 stamens.

Celsia floccosa *Benth.* (inc. *C. scrophulariaefolia* & *C. brevipedicellata* of the Check List) (see p. 552)
An erect, often woody, woolly to glabrescent herb with ovate to lanceolate to oblong leaves and glandular-hairy pedicels and calyx; flowers attractive and yellow.

This pretty plant is found in upland grassland especially on shallow soil. HE, HC, HT, HM, HA, HK, KIT, KIS, NAR, RV, NBI, KAJ.
Drummond and Hemsley 4808; Hanid 229.

3. ANTICHARIS *Endl.*

Small herbs with alternate entire leaves and glandular pubescence; flowers in terminal leafy racemes, almost regular, on long pedicels; sepals 5; petals with a dilated tube and 5 spreading lobes; stamens 2, without staminodes; capsule ovoid, loculicidal and septicidal, with numerous seeds.

Anticharis linearis *Aschers.*

An erect, glandular annual with linear leaves and small blue flowers.

Locally common in hot dry country. BAR, MAG.

Polhill and Greenway 448.

4. APTOSIMUM *Burch.*

Small wiry herbs or shrubs with alternate entire leaves and axillary solitary subsessile flowers; sepals 5; corolla with a rapidly widening tube and 5 obliquely spreading lobes; stamens 4; capsule septicidally 2-valved; seeds numerous.

Aptosimum pumilum *Benth.*

A woody, sparsely hairy annual with linear leaves long-exceeding the crowded axillary pale lilac flowers.

This plant appears to belong to the *Acanthaceae* at first sight. It is rare in desert conditions and has only been recorded once, near Magadi in our area. MAG.

Greenway and Polhill in EAH 12409.

5. DICLIS *Benth.*

Weak herbs with opposite dentate leaves and solitary axillary flowers; calyx 5-lobed; corolla with a short tube with an anterior spur, and 2-lipped; stamens 4; capsule ± globose, loculicidal.

1 Plant an erect annual; sepals shorter than the capsule   1. *D. ovata*
  Plant a creeping perennial; sepals as long as the capsule   2. *D. bambuseti*

1. Diclis ovata *Benth.*

A minute, erect, sparsely glandular-pubescent annual with suborbicular to broad-ovate leaves and white to cream flowers.

Uncommon plant found in disturbed grassland. HA, KIT, KIS, RV, MAC, NBI.

Polhill 430; Faden 67366.

2. Diclis bambuseti *R. E. Fries* (see p. 552)

A sparsely pubescent creeping herb, similar to *D. ovata* except that the flowers are larger and frequently pink.

Locally common on bamboo and *Podocarpus* forest floor. HE, HA, HK.

Kabuye 57; Tweedie 67/10.

6. MISOPATES *Rafin.*

Similar to *Diclis* but with linear entire leaves, the throat of the corolla tube closed by the palate of the lower corolla lip, and the capsule dehiscent by apical pores.

Misopates orontium (*L.*) *Rafin.* (*Antirrhinum orontium* L.) (see p. 552)

An erect glabrous annual with linear leaves and subsessile flowers in a loose terminal raceme; corolla pale purple or pink or cream with purple guide-lines.

Uncommon plant found as a wheat weed and in disturbed shallow soils at medium altitudes. HM, KIT, RV, MAC, KAJ.

Agnew and Waithaka 9893; Drummond and Hemsley 4296.

7. HALLERIA *L.*

Glabrous shrubs with entire or dentate, opposite leaves and solitary or fasciculate axillary flowers; calyx bell-shaped with 5 short lobes; corolla with a long curved or straight tube and 2-lipped oblique mouth; stamens 4, usually exserted; fruit a berry.

Halleria lucida *L.*

A trailing or erect shrub with ovate-elliptic entire leaves and red and yellow flowers.

Locally common in the undergrowth of montane forest and bushland. HE, HC, HT, HM, HA, HK, HN, KAJ.

Nattrass 1424; Lind, Agnew, and Harris 5076.

8. STEMODIOPSIS *Engl.*

Herbs or low shrubs with opposite, petiolate, orbicular to ovate leaves and small axillary flowers; calyx with 5 lobes; corolla bell-shaped, not spurred, 2-lipped, with a palate on the lower lip; stamens 4; capsule septicidal.

1 Leaves densely pubescent   1. *S. humilis*
  Leaves glabrous   2. *S. buchananii*

1. Stemodiopsis humilis *Skan.*

A pubescent, trailing perennial with ovate dentate leaves and tiny white or cream flowers; calyx up to 2·5 cm long in fruit.

Rare plant found in rock crevices in dry country. MAC.

Edwards 103.

2. Stemodiopsis buchananii *Skan*

Similar to *S. humilis* but with longer calyx segments (over 3 mm long in fruit) and almost glabrous.

Rare plant found in rock crevices in dry country. KAJ.

Gilbert 69.

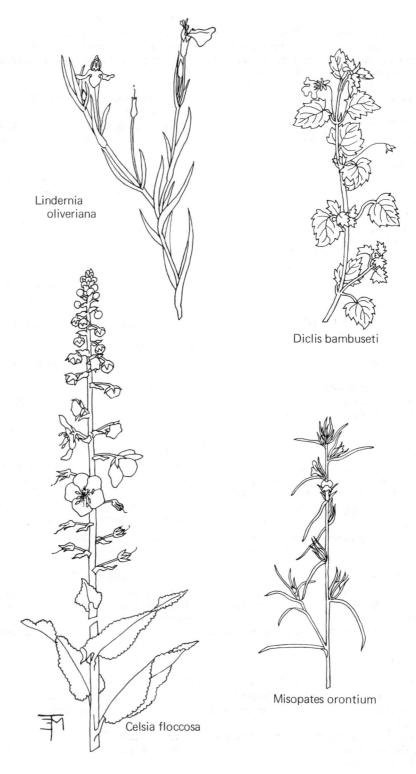

Lindernia
oliveriana

Diclis bambuseti

Celsia floccosa

Misopates orontium

9. MIMULUS *L.*

Similar to *Stemodiopsis* but the calyx lobes fused for over half their length and the pedicels without bracteoles.

Mimulus gracilis *R. Br.*

An erect glabrous annual with oblong-lanceolate, clasping leaves and small white flowers on long pedicels in the upper axils.

Rare and probably introduced, this species has been found only twice in marshes and wet shallow soils. KIT, MAC.

Irwin 486; Faden 68307.

10. DOPATRIUM *Benth.*

Erect and (in ours) glabrous herbs with simple, opposite leaves and a terminal raceme of pedicellate flowers without bracteoles; calyx bell-shaped and 5-lobed; corolla with a long or short tube, 2-lipped, the upper lip erect; stamens 2, posterior, included; staminodes minute or obscure; capsule globose, loculicidal; seeds tuberculate.

1   Basal leaves oblong; corolla up to 9 mm long
                                    1. *D. junceum*
    Basal leaves scale-like; corolla over 12 mm
    long   2. *D. dortmanna*

1. Dopatrium junceum *Benth.*

An erect annual with oblong, linear, ± fleshy lower leaves and a square stem; flowers small, blue.

Rare plant found in seasonally wet shallow soils. MAC.

Faden 68215.

2. Dopatrium dortmanna *S. Moore*

An aquatic, probably perennial, with erect ± leafless square stems and rather large purple flowers.

Rare plant found in pools in western Kenya. KIT.

Brodhurst-Hill 33.

11. LIMOSELLA *L.*

Small glabrous rosette herbs with entire leaves and solitary flowers; calyx bell-shaped, the 5 lobes shorter than the tube; corolla with a short tube and 5 spreading lobes, almost regular or 2-lipped; stamens 4; capsule breaking irregularly or 2-valved, geocarpic (in ours), i.e. the pedicel recurved in fruit so that the capsule is pressed into the soil.

1   Leaves with an expanded blade; corolla ±
    regular, the tube as long as the calyx   2
    Leaves linear, bristle-like throughout; corolla
    2-lipped, the tube longer than the calyx
                                    1. *L. macrantha*

2   Calyx over 4 mm long, bell-shaped in fruit
    and minutely glandular; fruit shorter than
    calyx   2. *L. major*
    Calyx less than 3·5 mm long, semiglobose in
    fruit, not glandular; fruit as long as or
    more commonly longer than calyx
                                    3. *L. aquatica*

1. Limosella macrantha *R. E. Fries*

A tiny rosette annual, with filiform leaves and small pinkish flowers; fruits, enclosed by the globose calyx, reflexed and pressed into the soil.

Rare plant found on the moorlands in eroded peaty patches. HE, HA.

Gillett 18480; Agnew and Menezes 7143.

2. Limosella major *Gluck*

A stoloniferous annual with narrowly spathulate leaves and rather long-pedicellate pale blue or white flowers.

Rare plant found in temporary pools in grassland. KIT, RV.

Greenway and Hemming 8768.

3. Limosella aquatica *L.* (*L. africana* Gluck)

A small herb with (if submerged) floating cordate to ovate leaves or (if on dry land) erect elliptic leaves and tiny pinkish flowers on short pedicels among the leaf bases.

Locally common in ephemeral pools on shallow soils, or in the alpine zone on peaty soils. HE, HA, HK, RV, NBI.

Hedberg 1021; Agnew 10023.

12. CRATEROSTIGMA *Hochst.*

Small, rosette, poikilohydric herbs (in ours) with entire or serrate leaves and flowers in a terminal raceme or spike; calyx fused for most of its length, often winged, 5-lobed; corolla with a small upper lip and wide spreading lower lip; stamens 4, the anterior two bent back at an inflated portion which is fused to the lower lip and forms two (often yellow) protuberances closing the palate of the corolla, capsule septicidal.

1   Peduncle shorter than pedicels   2
    Peduncle longer than or equal to pedicels   3
2   Upper leaf surface glossy, glabrous; leaf with
    5–8 veins   1. *C. pumilum*
    Upper leaf surface dull, often hairy; leaf with
    usually over 10 parallel veins   2. *C.* sp. *A*
3   Leaves erect, oblanceolate, over 4 times
    longer than broad   4
    Leaves spreading, elliptic, less than 3 times
    longer than broad   5
4   Flowers in a corymb; pedicel often over
    twice as long as its bract; calyx winged
    in fruit   3. *C.* sp. *B*

Ilysanthes pusilla

Ilysanthes parviflora

Lindernia abyssinica

Craterostigma plantagineum

Craterostigma hirsutum

Craterostigma pumilum

Flowers in a spike-like raceme with pedicels
 seldom longer than the bract; calyx not
 winged in fruit   4. *C. lanceolatum*
5 Leaf bases with persistent fibres, forming a
 fibrous covering to the rhizome; leaves
 rough, with a pustule at the base of each
 hair   5. *C. hirsutum*
 Leaf bases not persistent; leaves smooth   6
6 Leaves less than 2·5 cm long; peduncles more
 than twice the length of the leaves
                              6. *C. sp. C*
 Leaves over 3 cm long; peduncles never more
 than twice the leaf length
                        7. *C. plantagineum*

1. Craterostigma pumilum *Hochst.* (see p. 554)

A rosette herb with a thick creeping rhizome and
very long-pedicellate blue to pinkish flowers.

Common in shallow, frequently waterlogged
soils in dry highland grassland areas. HC, HT, HM,
HA, HK, KIT, NAN.
    Strid 2383; Bogdan 534.

2. Craterostigma *sp.* **A.**

Similar to *C. pumilum* except for the key charac-
ters but with a thin rhizome and smaller flowers.
    Locally common on shallow soils around
Nairobi and at similar altitudes. HA, RV, MAC,
NBI.
    Lind and Agnew 5134; Archer 321.

3. Craterostigma *sp.* **B.**

A rosette herb with a thick rhizome and erect
glabrescent, oblanceolate to linear leaves: flowers
large, violet to purple, in a corymb.
    Rare plant found on rock domes in dry
country. MAC.
    Edwards 24.

4. Craterostigma lanceolatum *Skan.*

Similar to *C.* sp. *B* but with broader, more hairy
leaves and cylindrical racemes of white flowers.
    Locally common in shallow soils, often on
basement-complex rocks. MAC, KAJ.
    Bally 12778; Agnew 7499.

5. Craterostigma hirsutum *S. Moore* (see p. 554)

A small silky-hairy rosette herb forming mats from
thickish rhizomes with erect elliptic to obovate
leaves and long-pedunculate racemes of usually
white flowers.
    Abundant in shallow soils and seasonally
flooded or wet short grassland. HE, HC, HT, HA,
NAR, RV, NAN, MAC, NBI, KAJ.
    Faden 67236; Agnew 9191.

6. Craterostigma *sp.* **C.**

A minute rosette perennial usually with a thin
rhizome and obovate, rounded leaves; flowers
crowded but distinctly pedicellate, purple to
violet.
    An attractive plant known from a few localities
in Central Province. As usual, it grows on shallow
soils. HA, NBI.
    Agnew 8786; Mainwaring 2633.

7. Craterostigma   plantagineum   *Hochst.*   (see
p. 544)

A rosette herb with a thick or thin rhizome and
spreading, broad-elliptic, often serrate leaves;
flowers often blue to violet.
    Locally common on shallow soils in dry grass-
land. HE, HT, MUM, NAR, RV, MAG, NAN, KAJ.
    Williams 109; Agnew, Musumba, and Kiniaruh
7972.

13. TORENIA *L.*

Trailing or erect herbs with opposite, entire or
dentate leaves and solitary flowers; calyx tubular,
often ridged, 2-lipped, with 5 short lobes; corolla
with a cylindrical tube, 2-lipped at apex; stamens 4,
with entire filaments arched under the upper lip;
stigmas orbicular; capsule cylindrical, septicidal.

Torenia thouarsii (*Cham. & Schlecht.*) *Kuntze*

A trailing sparsely pubescent herb with petiolate,
ovate serrate leaves and solitary bright blue flowers
on long pedicels.
    An uncommon creeper found in marshy grass-
land in western Kenya and at the coast. KIT,
MUM.
    Agnew and Musumba 8615; Bogdan 4283.

14. LINDERNIA *Allioni*

Similar to *Craterostigma* but (in ours) herbs with
stems and the anterior stamens with a definite
appendage on the filaments.

1 Leaves linear   1. *L. oliverana*
 Leaves ovate to oblong   2
2 Leaves clasping the stem at base   3
 Leaves either narrowed to the base or shortly
   petiolate   4
3 Plant an erect annual; bracts becoming much
   smaller than foliage leaves at apex; pedicels
   less than 3 mm long   2. *L. whytei*
 Plant a creeping perennial; bracts similar to
   foliage leaves; pedicels over 3 mm long
                                3. *L. sp. A*
4 Leaves narrowed to the base, oblong
                               4. *L. abyssinica*
 Leaves round or cordate at the base, ovate
                                5. *L. diffusa*

1. Lindernia oliverana *Dandy* (*L. lobelioides* (Oliv.) Engl.) (see p. 552)

A trailing glabrous perennial herb with linear entire leaves and solitary, axillary blue or rarely white flowers.

Locally common in marshes in western Kenya. HE, KIT.

Lugard 148; Symes 10.

2. Lindernia whytei *Skan*

An erect or decumbent glabrous or pubescent annual with sessile, orbicular to ovate, serrate leaves and a weak terminal raceme of purple and white flowers.

Uncommon plant found in disturbed marshes at the coast and in western Kenya. HE, KIT.

Webster in EAH 8934.

3. Lindernia *sp.* A.

Similar to *L. whytei* but a trailing perennial with larger solitary, axillary flowers.

Known from two collections from marshes south of Mt. Kenya. HK.

Battiscombe 1175.

4. Lindernia abyssinica *Engl.* (see p. 554)

An erect or trailing pubescent annual with crowded sessile oblong dentate leaves and axillary pink to purple flowers.

Rare plant found on shallow soils of Mt. Elgon and only once collected.

Gardner 2258.

5. Lindernia diffusa (*L.*) *Wettst.*

A trailing pubescent or glabrescent annual or possibly perennial with shortly petiolate ovate leaves and 2–5 pedunculate flowers at the terminal dichotomous forks; flowers purple or violet.

Rare plant found in western Kenya marshes. KIT, MUM.

Graham 12.

15. ILYSANTHES *Rafin.*

Herbs with entire opposite, sessile, or subsessile leaves and solitary axillary flowers; calyx with a long or short tube, 5-lobed; corolla 2-lipped, with a cylindrical tube and a hairy palate; stamens 2, with entire filaments, and 2 staminodes on the anterior lip; capsule septicidal.

1 Calyx fused for half its length or more   2
   Calyx lobes ± free   3
2 Leaves linear-elliptic, glabrous; flowers scattered   1. *I. pusilla*
   Leaves rhomboid to ovate-elliptic, minutely pubescent; flowers in a loose corymb
        2. *I. pulchella*

3 Calyx less than 3 mm long at anthesis; leaves acute at apex   4
   Calyx over 4 mm long at anthesis; leaves rounded at apex   3. *I. rotundifolia*
4 Fruiting pedicels deflexed   4. *I. parviflora*
   Fruiting pedicels erect   5. *I. sp. A*

1. Ilysanthes pusilla *Urban* (see p. 554)

An erect perennial from a small soft rootstock, or creeping, with glabrous narrow elliptic leaves and small pink flowers.

Locally common in shallow soil areas, this species appears to be poikilohydric, HE, HC, HT, KIT, MAC, NBI.

Greenway 8536; Agnew 10064.

2. Ilysanthes pulchella *Skan*

A tiny erect pubescent annual or perennial with ovate-elliptic leaves; corolla white, tipped purplish.

Rare plant found in short grassland, seasonally flooded. KIS, NAR, BAR.

Glover, Gwynne, and Samuel 2676.

3. Ilysanthes rotundifolia *Benth.*

A glabrous, trailing perennial herb with orbicular leaves and large (for the genus) purple and blue flowers.

Only known from grassy marshes near Limuru. HA.

Agnew 7081.

4. Ilysanthes parviflora *Benth.* (see p. 554)

A small erect weak glabrous annual with elliptic leaves and tiny white and pink flowers.

Rare plant found on shallow soils. KIT, HA, NBI.

Tweedie 67/284; Verdcourt 3241.

5. Ilysanthes *sp.* A.

An ascending, possibly perennial-stemmed glabrous herb with broad-elliptic leaves and tiny flowers.

Rare plant found in marshes in Western Kenya and only once collected. MUM.

McMahon 313.

16. SIBTHORPIA *L.*

Creeping herbs with kidney-shaped or orbicular alternate leaves and small axillary flowers; calyx 4–8-lobed; corolla nearly regular, with usually 5 spreading lobes and a very short tube; stamens 5 or fewer; capsule loculicidal.

Sibthorpia europaea *L.*

A creeping pubescent perennial with crenate orbicular leaves and minute pale pinkish flowers hidden at the leaf-bases.

This plant is often mistaken for a *Hydrocotyle* which it much resembles. It is locally common in open places in montane bushland and streamsides, up to the alpine zone. HE, HA, HK.

Hedberg 270; Agnew, Beals, and Modha 8882.

17. VERONICA *L.*

Annual or perennial herbs or shrubs with opposite leaves and flowers solitary or in racemes; calyx 4-lobed; corolla with a short tube and 4 spreading, almost regular lobes; stamens 2; capsule laterally compressed; seeds few.

1   Flowers in racemes   2
     Flowers solitary axillary   4
2   Leaves sessile, clasping the stem at base,
        oblong   1. *V. anagallis-aquatica*
     Leaves petiolate, ovate   3
3   Plant an erect annual; corolla shorter than or
        equal to calyx length   2. *V. javanica*
     Plant a creeping perennial, rooting at the
        nodes; corolla much longer than calyx
                                       3. *V. abyssinica*
4   All stems prostrate and rooting at the nodes
                                          4. *V. gunae*
     At least the flowering stems erect
                                       5. *V. glandulosa*

1. Veronica anagallis-aquatica *L.* (see p. 558)

An erect glabrous annual with oblong leaves and lax axillary racemes of small blue flowers.

An introduction from Europe, this species is locally common by streamsides. HA, NAN, KAJ.

Hanid and Kiniaruh 428; Napper 853.

2. Veronica javanica *Bl.* (see p. 558)

An erect pubescent annual, often branching from the base, with ovate, deeply crenate leaves; flowers pale blue or violet, small, over 5 in each raceme.

Uncommon plant found in disturbed short grassland. HM, KIT.

Agnew 10000.

3. Veronica abyssinica *Fres.* (see p. 558)

A trailing pubescent herb with ovate, cordate, serrate leaves and 2–5-flowered racemes; flowers large, blue.

Common in upland grassland and forest edges. HE, HC, HT, HM, HL, HA, KIT, MUM, KIS, RV, NBI.

Harmsen 6536; Symes 516.

4. Veronica gunae *Engl.*

A trailing glabrescent herb with small, subsessile, broad-elliptic, remotely crenate leaves and solitary blue or pink flowers.

Uncommon plant found in rocky alpine soils. HE, HK.

Hanid, Agnew, and Mendes 120; Hedberg 941.

5. Veronica glandulosa *Benth.*

A trailing pubescent herb with shortly petiolate, ovate, rounded, minutely crenate leaves and solitary blue flowers.

Locally common in forest and bushland edges in the upper forest zones and the alpine zone. HE, HC, HA, HK.

Agnew, Hedberg, and Mmari 9632; Hedberg 857.

18. ALECTRA *Thunb.*

Erect parasitic herbs with opposite or alternate leaves and yellow-orange flowers in terminal racemes; calyx bell-shaped, 10-nerved, 5-lobed; corolla with a short tube hardly longer than the calyx and 5, almost regular lobes; stamens 4, in two pairs, included with corolla; anthers often apiculate; ovary glabrous; stigma club-shaped; capsule globose, loculicidal; seeds with a very small embryo loose within the cylindrical expanded testa.

1   Plants semi-parasitic with green leaves longer
        than the bracts   2
     Plants almost totally parasitic with leaves
        reduced to scales, shorter than the bracts
                                       1. *A. parasitica*
2   Calyx lobes linear-lanceolate, longer than the
        calyx tube   2. *A. sp. A*
     Calyx lobes triangular, shorter than the calyx
        tube   3
3   Leaves lanceolate to ovate; one pair of
        filaments hairy   3. *A. sessiliflora*
     Leaves linear to lanceolate; all filaments
        glabrous   4. *A. vogelii*

1. Alectra parasitica *A. Rich.*

An erect pubescent parasite with scale-like yellowish leaves and yellow flowers with oblong petal lobes; filaments glabrous or sparsely hairy.

An uncommon species found in dry country. NAR, RV, MAG, NAN.

Greenway 9728.

2. Alectra *sp.* A.

A scabrid erect herb with lanceolate leaves and sessile flowers.

Known only from one specimen from the Mara area. NAR.

Glover, Gwynne, and Samuel 1869.

Veronica javanica

Veronica anagallis - aquatica

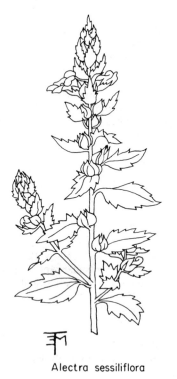

Alectra sessiliflora

Veronica abyssinica

3. Alectra sessiliflora (*Vahl*) *Kuntze* (inc. *A. asperrima* of Check List) (see p. 558)

An erect, scabrid-pubescent annual semiparasite with ovate to lanceolate, dentate leaves and sub-sessile flowers; corolla lobes as broad as long, yellow to orange.

Rather variable in leaf shape and locally common in upland forest areas. HE, HC, HT, HM, HA, KIT, MUM, KIS, NAR, MAC.
Kerfoot 2932; Strid 3352.

4. Alectra vogelii *Benth.*

An erect scabrid-pubescent annual parasitic herb similar to *A. sessiliflora* except for the key characters.

Rare plant found in dry country crops and annual vegetation. RV, MAG, EMB.
Archer 96.

19. BUTTONIA *McKen*

Climbing, twining, glabrous herbs with opposite, pinnatisect leaves and terminal racemes of showy flowers; calyx bell-shaped with 5 short valvate lobes; corolla tube funnel-shaped, broad at the top with 5 spreading oblique lobes; stamens 4, in two pairs, with anthers joined in pairs, one cell of the shorter pair reduced to an awn, and one cell of the longer pair virtually absent; capsule globular, included in the calyx, loculicidal; seeds with a loose netted testa.

Buttonia hildebrandtii *Engl.*

A glabrous climber with simple, long-petiolate, ovate, dentate leaves and loose leafy racemes of purple-lined white flowers.

Uncommon plant found in dry bushland. MUM, RV, MAC, KAJ.
Agnew, Musumba, and Kiniaruh 8056; Archer 453.

20. SOPUBIA *Buch.-Ham.*

Annual herbs to low perennial shrubs with oppo-site or alternate, often linear leaves and flowers in terminal racemes; calyx bell-shaped with a short tube and valvate lobes; corolla with a tube shorter than the calyx and 5 spreading lobes; stamens 4, each pair of anthers joined and consisting of one perfect cell and one sterile cell; capsule ellipsoid to subglobose, loculicidal; seeds oblong, numerous, with a loose testa.

1　Calyx densely woolly on the outside
　　　　　　　　　　　　　1. *S. welwitschii*
　　Calyx scabrid or glabrous on the outside　2
2　Plants usually branched above; all pedicels
　　　shorter than the calyx　　　2. *S. ramosa*

Plants usually simple above; at least the
　　lowest pedicels longer than the calyx　3
3　Plant perennial; stem glabrous, deeply
　　grooved and sharply ridged　3. *S. simplex*
　　Plant annual; stem minutely pubescent, not
　　sharply ridged　　　　　　　4. *S. trifida*

1. Sopubia welwitschii *Engl.*

An erect pubescent herb with simple linear leaves and terminal woolly spike-like racemes of pink flowers.

Locally common in well drained montane grassland. HM, HT, HA, HK, KAJ.
Nattrass 961.

2. Sopubia ramosa (*Hochst.*) *Hochst.* (see p. 561)

An erect scabrid (possibly annual) woody herb with simple linear or rarely pinnatifid leaves and terminal spike-like racemes of purple flowers.

Locally common in wooded grassland. HE, HC, HT, HM, HA, KIT, MUM, KIS, RV, KAJ.
Tweedie 67/291; Verdcourt 1699.

3. Sopubia simplex *Hochst.* (see p. 561)

An erect glabrous herb from a woody rootstock with linear leaves and longer terminal racemes of pink to purple flowers.

Rare plant found in swamps in western Kenya. KIT, NAR.
Napier 5344.

4. Sopubia trifida *D. Don.* (see p. 561)

An erect scabrid annual with trifoliolate, linear-lobed or entire linear leaves and a loose terminal raceme of yellow to white flowers with maroon centres.

Locally common in shallow-soil grassland. HE, HT, HA, KIT, MAC.
Hanid and Kiniaruh 878; Drummond and Hemsley 4462.

21. MICRARGERIA *Benth.*

Erect scabrid herbs with linear, entire or trifid, opposite or alternate leaves, and flowers in simple terminal racemes; calyx bell-shaped, 5-toothed; corolla with a funnel-shaped tube with 5 ± equal spreading lobes; stamens 4, each with a 2-celled entire anther; capsule loculicidal or septicidal; seeds with a ± loose testa.

Micrargeria filiformis (*Schumach.*) *Hutch. & Dalziel*

An erect, minutely scabrid annual with simple linear leaves and pink flowers.

Uncommon plant found on shallow soils in western Kenya. MUM.
Tweedie 67/283.

22. PSEUDOSOPUBIA *Engl.*

Erect herbs with opposite or alternate often linear leaves, and flowers in terminal racemes or spikes. Similar to 20. *Sopubia* except for the corolla which has an inflated tube longer than the calyx, the stamens which have a disc-shaped appendage to the single-celled anthers of the lower pair, and the seeds which are larger and pitted, without a loose testa.

Pseudosopubia hildebrandtii (*Vatke*) *Engl.* (inc. *P. kituiensis* of Check List) (see p. 561)

An erect or prostrate pubescent woody herb with linear, acute or obtuse leaves and loose terminal racemes of purple-pink flowers.

Uncommon plant found in dry bushland. BAR, MAC.

Williams in EAH 12547.

23. BUCHNERA *L.*

Erect, pubescent annual herbs, often semi-parasitic, with alternate or opposite ± entire leaves and flowers in terminal spikes; calyx tubular, fused for over half its length; corolla with a narrow cylindrical tube and 5 spreading lobes; stamens 4, included, each with a 1-celled anther; capsule loculicidal; seeds many, with a reticulate testa.

1 Spikes axillary, forming a terminal panicle
                  1. *B. nuttii*
  Spikes terminal, not paniculate   2
2 Flowers all touching one another, forming a
    dense ovoid head   2. *B. capitata*
  Flowers in an open elongated spike with at
    least the lower nodes longer than the calyx
                      3
3 All bracts longer than the subtended calyx;
    calyx over 8 mm long   3. *B. scabridula*
  Most bracts shorter than the subtended calyx;
    calyx less than 6 mm long   4. *B. hispida*

1. Buchnera nuttii *Skan*

An erect scabrid-pubescent herb with sessile oblong leaves and a terminal panicle of mauve flowers.

Rare plant found in wooded grassland in Elgon and Cherangani. HE, HC.

Gardner 3723.

2. Buchnera capitata *Benth.* (see p. 561)

An erect, scabrid to glabrescent herb with a rosette of oblong leaves at base and a terminal head-like spike of mauve flowers.

Locally common on shallow-soil grassland in western Kenya. HE, HT, KIT.

Tweedie 67/270; Irwin 245.

3. Buchnera scabridula *E. A. Bruce*

An erect or scrambling scabrid herb with oblong-elliptic leaves and terminal spikes of blue-mauve flowers.

Rare plant found in the Cherangani Hills. HE. Dale 3428.

4. Buchnera hispida *Buch.-Ham.* (see p. 561)

An erect scabrid pubescent annual from a rosette of obovate to oblong leaves, with a terminal lax spike of blue to purple flowers.

Locally common on shallow soils and short grassland especially near Nairobi and in the Rift Valley. KIT, RV, MAC, NBI, KAJ.

Agnew 10059; Glover 4626.

24. CYCNIUM *E. Mey.*

Pubescent, erect or trailing herbs with opposite or alternate leaves and large, racemose or solitary, axillary flowers; calyx tubular, with spreading lobes; corolla with a long straight or little curved tube and 5 spreading lobes, the upper pair joined for more than half their length; stamens 4, included in the tube, each with only 1 anther cell; capsule included in the calyx, ovoid or ellipsoid, loculicidal or indehiscent; seeds small with a reticulate testa.

1 Calyx slit on one side   1. *C. tomentosum*
  Calyx equally 5-toothed   2. *C. adonense*

1. Cycnium tomentosum *Engl.*

An erect or trailing pubescent woody herb with sessile oblanceolate serrate leaves and terminal loose racemes of large white flowers.

Uncommon plant found in wooded grassland in western Kenya. HE, MUM.

Irwin 449.

2. Cycnium adonense *Benth.* (see p. 566)

A perennial scabrid pubescent herb with fibrous roots and ascending stems bearing sessile elliptic serrate leaves; flowers white, with a long hairy tube.

In wooded grassland, where it is locally common at the coast and in western Kenya, but rare elsewhere. HE, HC, HT, KIT, MUM, EMB, KAJ.

Symes 32; Lugard 568.

25. CYCNIOPSIS *Engl.*

Similar to *Cycnium* but small prostrate plants with the corolla tube rather abruptly curved and widened below the lobes.

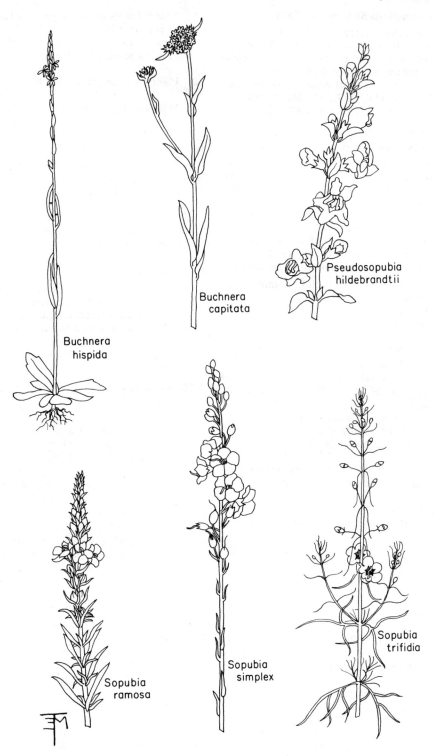

Buchnera
hispida

Buchnera
capitata

Pseudosopubia
hildebrandtii

Sopubia
ramosa

Sopubia
simplex

Sopubia
trifidia

Cycniopsis obtusifolia *Skan* (see p. 566)

A small pubescent prostrate herb from a fibrous root system with sessile entire elliptic leaves and solitary long-tubed flowers; calyx with 5 oblong blunt lobes; corolla pink with a yellow throat.

Locally common in short grassland on fine soil. HE, HT, HM, HA, KIT, NAR, RV, MAC, NBI.

Hanid and Agnew 37; Kerfoot 840.

26. RHAMPHICARPA *Benth.*

Herbs or weak shrubs with opposite or alternate, simple or compound leaves and flowers solitary or in racemes; calyx with a short bell-shaped tube and 5 lobes; corolla with a long curved tube, often abruptly inflated for a short distance above the middle, and with 5 spreading lobes of which the upper two are fused, white or pinkish; stamens 4, each anther with 1 cell and with hairy filaments; capsule zygomorphic with an asymmetric beak; seeds conical or cylindrical, smooth or tuberculate.

1	Leaves deeply pinnately lobed into linear segments	2
	Leaves simple	6
2	Plant annual	3
	Plant perennial	5
3	Corolla tube over 3 cm long　1. *R. fistulosa*	
	Corolla tube less than 2 cm long	4
4	Leaf segments flat; corolla tube over 12 mm long; beak of fruit cylindrical, spreading laterally　　2. *R.* sp. *A*	
	Leaf segments triangular in crossection; corolla tube usually less than 12 mm long; beak of fruit conical, lateral but erect　3. *R. recurva*	
5	Leaf segments flat　4. *R. meyeri-johannis*	
	Leaf segments triangular in crossection　5. *R. tenuisecta*	
6	Pedicels shorter than calyx	7
	At least the lower pedicels longer than the calyx	11
7	Corolla tube with an abrupt bulge on the upper side above the middle	8
	Corolla tube curved but cylindrical throughout	9
8	Upper leaves linear, entire　6. *R. jamesii*	
	Upper leaves elliptic, serrate　7. *R. veronicifolia*	
9	Plant with ascending stems; calyx zygomorphic with the posterior lobe smaller than the others and held below them　8. *R. ajugifolia*	
	Plant with erect stems; calyx regular with all lobes equal	10
10	Corolla tube less then 2 cm long　9. *R. asperrima*	
	Corolla tube over 2 cm long　11. *R. tubulosa*	

11	Lower leaves ovate; calyx over half as long as corolla tube　　10. *R. herzfeldiana*	
	Lower leaves lanceolate to elliptic linear; calyx less than half as long as corolla tube　12	
12	Plant prostrate; flowers solitary　12. *R. montana*	
	Plant erect; flowers in weak racemes　11. *R. tubulosa*	

1. Rhamphicarpa fistulosa *Benth.*

An erect glabrescent annual with deeply pinnatifid leaves and solitary white or pale pink flowers; capsule almost regular, with an erect, slightly lateral, beak.

Rare in our area, found in marshes in western Kenya and only once collected. KIT.

Brodhurst-Hill 29.

2. Rhamphicarpa sp. A.

An erect pubescent annual with the leaves deeply once or twice pinnatifid into linear lobes; flowers subsessile in terminal racemes, white.

In disturbed grassland in western Kenya. MUM, NAR.

Padwa 460; Agnew and Mussumba 8058.

3. Rhamphicarpa recurva *Oliv.* (see p. 563)

Similar to *R.* sp. *A* but less hairy, with smaller flowers.

Locally common on shallow soils in western Kenya. HE, HC, KIT, MUM.

Tweedie 67/279; Jack 339.

4. Rhamphicarpa meyeri-johannis *Engl.*

An erect pubescent perennial herb or weak shrub with leaves pinnatisect into linear segments and with short terminal racemes (2-4 consecutive nodes only) of subsessile pink flowers.

Common in upland Tanzania and only recorded from our area above Loitokitok in KAJ.

Ibrahim 672.

5. Rhamphicarpa tenuisecta *Standley*

Similar to *R. meyeri-johannis* but usually glabrescent and with the keyed differences.

Locally common in grassy marshes above 6000 ft. HE, HC, HT, HM, HA, HK, KIT, RV.

Agnew, Kibe, and Mathenge 10536; Bally 4163.

6. Rhamphicarpa jamesii *Skan* (see p. 563)

An erect, usually glabrescent annual or weak perennial with linear, remotely toothed lower leaves and entire upper leaves; flowers white, in a terminal raceme.

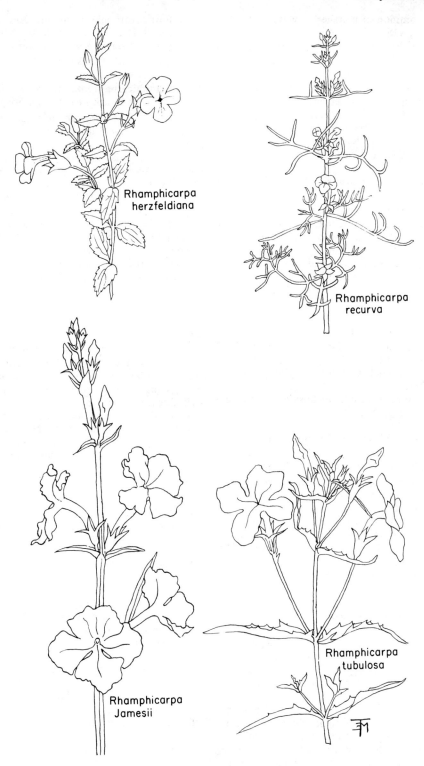

Rhamphicarpa
herzfeldiana

Rhamphicarpa
recurva

Rhamphicarpa
Jamesii

Rhamphicarpa
tubulosa

Locally common in marshes in western Kenya. HE, HT, KIT, KIS.

Agnew, Kibe, and Mathenge 10591; Jack 10849.

7. Rhamphicarpa veronicifolia *Vatke*

An erect annual, with pubescent stems and deeply serrate leaves; flowers bright pink.

Often abundant after rains in dry *Commiphora* bushland. MAG, MAC, KAJ.

Agnew 10683; Verdcourt 3271.

8. Rhamphicarpa ajugifolia *(Gilg) Skan* (see p. 566)

A pubescent to tomentose perennial herb from a woody rootstock, with ascending stems and small ovate-elliptic, coarsely 2–5-toothed leaves; flowers subsessile, pale pink or white.

An easily identified plant which is found in dry stony *Combretum* woodland soils. HA, RV, MAG, MAC.

Greenway 13546; Lind 5368.

9. Rhamphicarpa asperrima *Skan*

A pubescent, weak erect (sometimes scrambling) shrub with elliptic to oblong, coarsely toothed leaves and terminal racemes of pink or white subsessile flowers.

Locally common in upland bushland especially in the Rift Valley. HA, RV, KIS, NAR, EMB, NBI, KAJ.

Agnew 5474; Glover and Gwynne 2480.

10. Rhamphicarpa herzfeldiana *Vatke* (see p. 563)

A pubescent trailing perennial herb with ovate serrate leaves and solitary, axillary, long-pedicellate flowers; calyx lobes longer than the tube, lanceolate; corolla white with a maroon throat.

Locally common in well-drained upland grassland. HE, HC, HA, HK, KIT, KIS, NAR, EMB, MAC, NBI, KAJ.

Agnew, Hanid, and Kiniaruh 7869; Kokwaro 331.

11. Rhamphicarpa tubulosa *(L. f.) Benth.* (see p. 563)

A frequently glabrous erect or ascending perennial herb from a fibrous rootstock, with linear-lanceolate, often sparsely toothed leaves and often few large pink or white pedicellate flowers in a loose raceme.

This species as defined here is very variable, with some tall erect forms with many-flowered racemes found principally in western Kenya, while the Nairobi form, with few flowers and ascending stems often appears to grade into the next species.

It is found throughout upland Kenya on black-cotton soils. HA, MUM, KIS, MAC, NBI, KAJ.

Agnew and Hanid 7545; Kokwaro 1816.

12. Rhamphicarpa montana *N. E. Br.* (inc. *R. heuglini* of the Check List) (see p. 566)

Similar to *R. tubulosa* but more often pubescent, with elliptic leaves, larger calyx lobes, and white flowers.

This species is again very variable, some forms having a calyx over 2 cm long, and others, growing with them, much smaller. Occasional semi-erect plants may be found which are difficult to place with certainty in this or the last species.

This plant is often referred to as the 'waste-paper plant', because it looks just like blown white scraps of paper scattered over black-cotton soil grasslands. HE, HT, HL, HA, HK, KIT, MUM, KIS, NAR, RV, NAN, MAC, NBI, KAJ.

Verdcourt 2601; Ables 10.

27. STRIGA *Lour.*

Erect, mostly partially parasitic herbs with opposite or alternate simple leaves and flowers in terminal spikes; sepals with a cylindrical tube and 5 ± equal linear lobes; corolla with a long cylindrical tube, sharply bent and often inflated at the middle or above, hairy within and glandular-hairy without; corolla lobes spreading, the 3 lower free from each other, and the two smaller upper ones partially fused; stamens included, with glabrous filaments, each with one anther cell; capsule loculicidal; seeds small, numerous, with a striate testa.

1	Plants glabrous, smooth	2
	Plants pubescent and usually scabrid	3
2	Calyx tube finely striate; corolla usually maroon	1. *S. baumannii*
	Calyx tube smooth; corolla mauve to pink	2. *S. gesnerioides*
3	Leaves linear to scale-like; corolla tube less than 18 mm long	4
	Leaves broader than linear; corolla tube usually over 2 cm long	5
4	Leaves linear; flowers vivid scarlet	3. *S. asiatica*
	Leaves scale-like; flowers white, tinged mauve	4. *S. linearifolia*
5	Calyx scabrid and ridged	6
	Calyx smooth	5. *S. hermonthica*
6	Leaves ± entire; calyx tube cylindrical in fruit	6. *S. latericea*
	Leaves usually dentate; calyx tube inflated and papery in fruit	7. *S. forbesii*

1. Striga baumannii *Engl.*

An erect, densely pubescent parasitic herb with scale-like leaves and small maroon flowers.

Rare plant found in western Kenya and only once recorded. KIT.

Brodhurst-Hill 755.

2. Striga gesnerioides (*Willd.*) *Engl.*

An erect parasite usually unbranched and without chlorophyll, with scale-like leaves and a spike of mauve to pale purple flowers.

Locally common in dry grassland. MUM, KIS, RV, MAG, MAC, KAJ.

Harmsen 6469; van Someren 767.

3. Striga asiatica (*L.*) *Ktze* (see p. 568)

An erect, scabrid-pubescent, green annual parasite with linear to filamentous leaves and bright crimson flowers in a terminal spike.

This conspicuous plant is found in upland and dry lowland grassland at the coast and inland. HE, HT, KIS, NAR, RV, EMB, MAC, NBI, KAJ.

Agnew 10222; Nattrass 438.

4. Striga linearifolia (*Schum. & Thonn.*) *Hepper* (*S. canescens* Engl.)

An erect, grey-pubescent annual parasite with scale leaves and white to pale mauve flowers with linear corolla lobes.

Locally common in dry grassland. RV, EMB, MAC, NBI, KAJ.

Strid 2527; Verdcourt 3200.

5. Striga hermonthica (*Del.*) *Benth.*

An erect, often robust, sparsely scabrid annual parasite with narrow-oblanceolate, ± entire leaves and rather large pinkish flowers in branching spikes.

Locally common in western Kenya where it can be a severe weed in some crops. MUM, KIS.

Agnew and Musumba 8629; Nattrass 216.

6. Striga latericea *Vatke*

An erect, densely scabrid pubescent annual parasite with lanceolate, mostly entire leaves, and large pink to salmon flowers.

Locally common in dry grassland. NAN, MAC, KAJ.

Verdcourt 3690; Strid 4276.

7. Striga forbesii *Benth.* (see p. 568)

Similar to *S. latericea* but often smaller and with the sepal lobes often over 1·5 times the length of the sepal tube, as well as with the keyed differences.

Locally common as a field weed in dry country. HE, HT, KIT, MUM, KIS, NAR, KAJ.

Bogdan 4827; Tweedie 66/122.

28. HARVEYA *Hook.*

Erect, glabrous or hairy semi-parasitic herbs often with reduced leaves and sessile axillary flowers; calyx bell-shaped or tubular, 5-lobed; corolla tube inflated in the upper part, with 5, ± spreading lobes round an oblique mouth; stamens 4, in two pairs, ± included, with 2 cells to each anther; one cell perfect, sharply pointed, the other cell sterile; capsule loculicidal; seeds small with a loose reticulate testa.

Harveya obtusifolia (*Benth.*) *Vatke*

An erect, glandular-pubescent herb with scale-leaves at base and elliptic bracts above; flowers pale pink.

Locally occasional plant found in upland grassland. HA, RV, MAC, NBI, KAJ.

Lind 5743; Bally 716.

29. BARTSIA *L.*

Erect, often glandular-pubescent herbs or shrubs with opposite simple crenate leaves and terminal racemes of shortly pedicelled flowers; calyx 4-lobed; corolla with a long or short tube, widening above into either a 2-lipped or a ± equally 5-lobed limb; stamens 4, each with two pointed or awned anther cells; capsule septicidal; seeds minute, winged.

1 Corolla yellow, with the cylindrical part of the tube longer than the calyx; shrubs   **2**
  Corolla pinkish to white, with the cylindrical part of the tube shorter than the calyx; herbs   **4**

2 Corolla tube straight; each anther with a minute point on lower apex
            1. *B. longiflora*
  Corolla tube ± curved; each anther with a long spine (to 0·5 mm) on lower apex   **3**

3 Leaves erect and appressed to stem; corolla not as long as twice the calyx length
           2. *B. macrocalyx*
  Leaves spreading; corolla more than twice the length of the calyx
         3. *B. kilimandscharica*

4 Plant annual, densely glandular hairy on all parts   4. *B. trixago*
  Plant perennial, pubescent but not glandular
            5

5 Stems ascending, unbranched above ground level, with longer internodes and appressed leaves below the raceme   5. *B. petitiana*
  Stems erect or ascending, branched above, internodes below the raceme similar to others   6. *B. abyssinica*

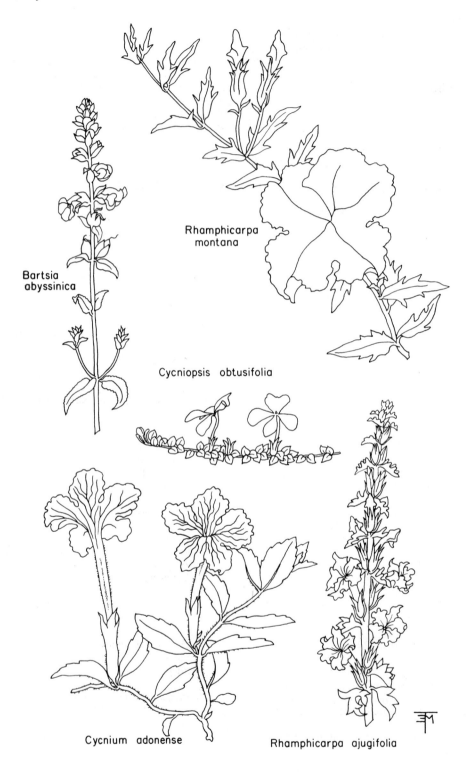

Rhamphicarpa
montana

Bartsia
abyssinica

Cycniopsis obtusifolia

Cycnium adonense

Rhamphicarpa ajugifolia

1. Bartsia longiflora *Benth.*

An erect, sparsely glandular-pubescent, loose shrub, with oblong to oblanceolate spreading leaves and yellow and brown flowers.

Locally common in the edges of the upper forest zones and heath zones of all our mountains. HE, HA, HK.

Agnew 7235; Verdcourt 3543.

2. Bartsia macrocalyx *R. E. Fr.*

Similar to *B. longiflora* but with rather broader, appressed leaves and smaller flowers.

Endemic on rocky soils in the moorland of Mt. Elgon. HE.

Hedberg 868.

3. Bartsia kilimandscharica *Engl.*

Similar to *B. longiflora* but with small linear-oblong leaves (to 2·5 cm long) and a smaller corolla.

Locally common in the alpine belt of all our mountains, on rocky soils amongst heaths or giant Senecios. HE, HA, HK.

Hedberg 1659; Hanid, Agnew, and Mendes 138.

4. Bartsia trixago *L.*

An erect, glandular-hairy annual with oblong dentate leaves clasping the stem at base; flowers crowded, pink and white.

Uncommon plant found in the northern highland part of our area, particularly Cherangani. HE, HC, HA.

Tweedie 67/322; Ward in EAH 6729.

5. Bartsia petitiana (*A. Rich.*) *Hemsl.*

A glabrescent perennial with ascending, rooting stems from a woody rootstock; leaves elliptic, rounded, crenate; flowers in an open spike-like raceme, pink.

Common on rocky ground in the alpine zone. HE, HC, HA, HK.

Hanid 169; Hedberg 1646.

6. Bartsia abyssinica (*A. Rich.*) *Benth.* (see p. 566)

A trailing or ascending scabrid-pubescent herb with lanceolate-elliptic leaves and white to pinkish flowers.

Locally common in rocky montane grassland. HE, HC, HT, HA, HK.

Lind and Agnew 5168; Irwin 368.

30. HEBENSTRETIA *L.*

Shrubs or herbs with alternate or opposite simple leaves and terminal spikes of flowers each subtended by a stiff bract; calyx represented by a bract-like organ opposite the bract; corolla tubular below, split on the lower side, with a ± flat, 4-lobed limb; stamens 4, included in the corolla tube; ovary 2-celled, with one pendulous ovule in each cell.

Hebenstretia dentata *L.* (see p. 612)

A small erect glabrous wiry shrub with alternate, linear, entire or toothed leaves and terminal spikes of white and orange flowers.

This plant is rather variable as regards leaf-toothing and flower size. It is common in rocky heathland at high altitudes and occasional below 5500–8000 ft, in dry grassland. HE, HC, HA, HK, RV, KAJ.

Hanid 158.

31. SELAGO *L.*

Annual herbs or small shrubs with opposite, entire leaves and flowers in terminal cymes, racemes or spikes; calyx bell-shaped, 2–5-lobed; corolla funnel-shaped with 5 spreading lobes, ± bilabiate; stamens 4, each with a 1-celled anther; ovary 2-celled with one pendulous ovule within each; fruit of dry schizocarps.

Selago thomsonii *Rolfe*

A low tufted wiry shrub with ascending branches bearing fascicles of linear-elliptic leaves and corymbs of small terminal spikes of small mauve or pale purple (rarely white) flowers.

Locally common on dry subalpine heathland especially on thin soil. HE, HA, HK.

Coe 380; Ivens 2078.

87. OROBANCHACEAE†

Herbs without chlorophyll, parasitic on roots, with alternate scale leaves and zygomorphic bisexual flowers in spikes or racemes; bracts and bracteoles often present; calyx 5-lobed; corolla zygomorphic, tubular at base, ± 2-lipped above; stamens 4, in two pairs, the filaments arising from the corolla tube; anthers 2-celled; ovary superior, of 2 carpels and with a 2-lobed stigma; ovules very numerous, on parietal placentas; seeds small, rounded.

1 Calyx tubular with obtuse or rounded lobes; corolla yellow   1. *Cistanche tubulosa*
  Calyx bell-shaped with acute lobes; corolla off-white or purplish   2. *Orobanche*

1. CISTANCHE *Hoffmgg. & Link.*

Fleshy parasites with large showy flowers; bracts

† By A. D. Q. Agnew.

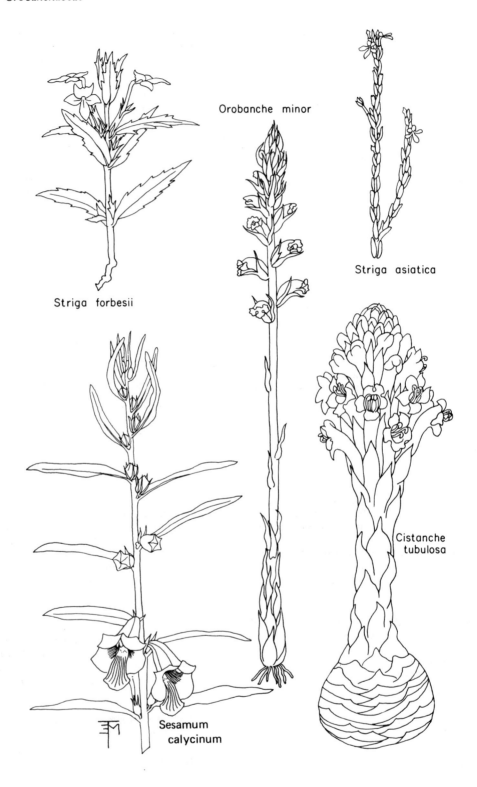

Striga forbesii

Orobanche minor

Striga asiatica

Sesamum
calycinum

Cistanche
tubulosa

and bracteoles present; calyx with 5 rounded lobes; corolla tubular at base, widening above into a funnel-shaped mouth; anthers glabrous to hairy; style curved back at apex; stigma orbicular.

Cistanche tubulosa (*Schenk*) *Hook. f.* (see p. 568)
An erect, unbranched perennial parasite of shrubs and trees, with bright yellow flowers.
　　Locally common in dry bushland. NAR, RV, MAG, KAJ.
　　Agnew 7638; Napier 3500.

2. OROBANCHE *L.*

Similar to *Cistanche* but with the keyed differences, the corolla 2-lipped and the stigma bilobed, peltate or funnel-shaped.

1	Bracteoles present	1. *O. ramosa*
	Bracteoles absent	2. *O. minor*

1. Orobanche ramosa *L.*
An erect, sparsely branched parasite with bright blue flowers; calyx split only on upper side.
　　Uncommon plant found in upland grassland. HA, NBI.
　　Lind and Agnew 5744; Verdcourt 2275.

2. Orobanche minor *Smith* (inc. *O. cernua* of FTEA) (see p. 568)
Similar to *O. ramosa* but with pale dirty white to purple flowers, and the calyx split above and below the flower.
　　Common in cultivation, upland grassland, and forest edges. HE, HC, HT, HM, HA, HK, HN, KIT, MUM, RV, MAG, MAC, NBI.
　　Brodhurst-Hill 367; Lind and Agnew 5745.

88. LENTIBULARIACEAE†

Insectivorous herbs with alternate, simple or entire, exstipulate leaves and zygomorphic flowers in racemes or spikes; calyx 5-lobed or 2-lipped; corolla 2-lipped, spurred; stamens 2, (the lower pair) and 1–2-celled; ovary of 2 carpels with numerous ovules on a free-central placenta; fruit a capsule.

1	Calyx 5-lobed	1. *Genlisea hispidula*
	Calyx 2-lipped	2. *Utricularia*

1. GENLISEA *St. Hil.*

Erect herbs with a rosette of spathulate leaves and pitchers arising from the short stem; pitchers with an ovoid chamber and long cylindrical neck terminating in two ribbon-like appendages, both

† By A. D. Q. Agnew.

chamber and neck with bands of hairs and digestive glands; calyx of 5 sepals shortly fused at base; other characters as for the family.

Genlisea hispidula *Stapf.*
A small rosette herb with an open raceme or loose panicle of blue or purple flowers; ovary hairy.
　　Rare plant recently discovered in mud beside montane grassland in the Cherangani Hills. HE. Thulin and Tidigs 182.

2. UTRICULARIA *L.*

Insectivorous herbs with trailing stems and whorls of leaf-like organs, both of which may bear bladder-like traps triggered by small hairs to suck in minute copepods and the like; leaves entire to much divided; flowers in spikes or racemes, blue, purple or yellow; calyx 2-lobed; flowers as in the family.

1	Plants anchored in mud, or terrestrial; bracteoles present	2
	Plants free-floating; bracteoles absent	7
2	Bracts 4 times as broad as the bracteoles; pedicels longer than fruiting calyx	3
	Bracts and bracteoles similar; pedicels shorter than the fruiting calyx	4
3	Flowers yellow	2. *U. prehensilis*
	Flowers purple	1. *U. spiralis*
4	Lower lip of corolla 5-lobed.	3. *U. pentadactyla*
	Lower lip of the corolla entire or 2-lobed	5
5	Corolla pubescent; palate of lower lip without wrinkles	4. *U. firmula*
	Corolla glabrous; palate of lower lip wrinkled	6
6	Lower lip of corolla up to half as long as spur	5. *U. arenaria*
	Lower lip of corolla more than half as long as spur	6. *U. livida*
7	Traps often over 4 mm long, inserted in the angle between dichotomies and the leaf	7. *U. reflexa*
	Traps never over 2 mm long, inserted laterally on leaf segments	8
8	Plant with a definite stem and whorls of trap-bearing leaves; bladder floats present on the inflorescence	8. *U. inflexa*
	Plant with no easily defined stem and leaves, and scattered traps; bladder-floats absent	9. *U. gibba*

1. Utricularia spiralis *Smith*
Similar to *U. prehensilis* but with purple and white flowers.
　　Rare plant found in western marshes. MUM. Tweedie 3487.

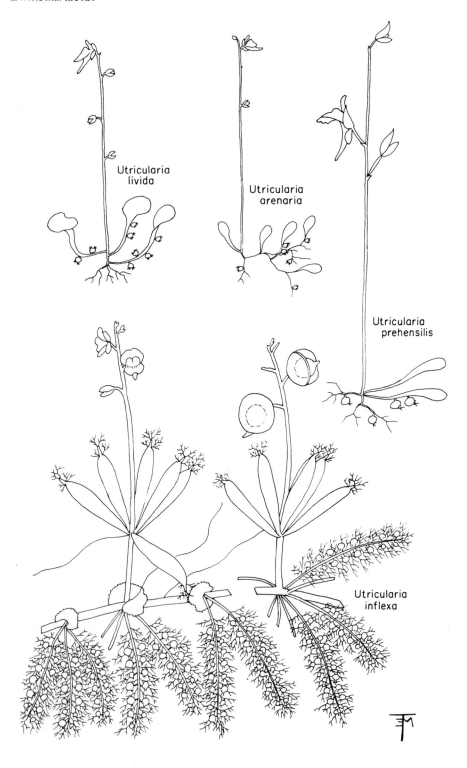

Utricularia
livida

Utricularia
arenaria

Utricularia
prehensilis

Utricularia
inflexa

2. Utricularia prehensilis *E. Mey.* (see p. 570)

An erect herb with a few simple, many-nerved, spathulate basal leaves and an erect, twining raceme of bright yellow flowers.

A local plant of grassy upland marshes, especially common around Eldoret. HT, KIT.

Heriz-Smith and Paulo 889; Agnew, Kibe, and Mathenge 10601.

3. Utricularia pentadactyla *P. Tayl.*

An erect herb with minute linear 1-nerved leaves and a straight spike of mauve to whitish flowers.

Wet shallow soils in western Kenya. KIT.

Recorded from Taylor in *Kew Bull.* **18**, 133 (1964).

4. Utricularia firmula *Oliv.*

Similar to *U. pentadactyla* but with smaller, yellow flowers.

Rare plant found in western Kenya in open marshes. KIT.

Brodhurst-Hill 715.

5. Utricularia arenaria *A. DC.* (see p. 570)

An erect herb with a few linear-spathulate 1-nerved leaves at base and an erect raceme of mauve flowers with yellow markings.

Rare plant found in shallow-soil seasonal swamps. HE, HT, HM, KIT, NBI.

Verdcourt 3245.

6. Utricularia livida *E. Mey.* (see p. 570)

Similar to *U. arenaria* except for the key characters.

Locally common in peaty mud at edges of seasonal pools. HC, HA, HK, KIT.

Archer 376; Agnew 7159.

7. Utricularia reflexa *Oliv.*

A trailing aquatic with long stems and short, much divided leaves bearing large traps and terminating in bristly points; flowers rare, solitary or 2 in a short raceme, yellow.

Locally common in pools. HE, RV.

Chater Jack 52; Mendes 35.

8. Utricularia inflexa *Forsk.* (see p. 570)

A trailing aquatic with cylindrical, often auricled, leaves which are much divided and end in minutely bristly segments; bladder-like float-leaves are present below the raceme of yellow, white or mauve flowers; calyx enlarging in fruit.

Common in warmer fresh water. MUM, KIS, BAR, RV, MAG, MAC.

Hanid and Kiniaruh 723; McMahon 22.

9. Utricularia gibba *L.*

A very loosely organised trailing aquatic with lateral bladders on stems and leaves and short erect racemes of few yellow flowers.

Locally common in slow-moving streams and freshwater pools at medium altitudes. HE, HA, KIT, RV.

Mendes 36; Williams in EAH 12347.

89. GESNERIACEAE†

Herbs with opposite (rarely alternate) leaves, often unequal at each node; leaves simple, exstipulate; inflorescence of open cymes in axillary panicles; flowers bisexual, usually zygomorphic; sepals 5; petals 5, fused into a tube below and often 2-lipped above; stamens 2–4 with free or connate 2-celled anthers; ovary superior, of 2 carpels with parietal placentation; fruit a capsule (or berry) with numerous small seeds; seeds without endosperm.

1. STREPTOCARPUS *Lindl.*

Herbs with or without leafy stems and normally leafy to unifoliate, with axillary cymose inflorescences; calyx 5-lobed; corolla tubular or 2-lipped; stamens 2, the anthers loosely adherent; stigma capitate; fruit a narrow capsule in which the 2 valves twist spirally after dehiscence.

1 Plants with leafy stems   2
  Plants with all leaves in a basal rosette
                   3. *S. montanus*
2 Capsule (and ovary) glabrous
                   1. *S. caulescens*
  Capsule (and ovary) pubescent
              2. *S. glandulosissimus*

1. Streptocarpus caulescens *Vatke*

A soft, trailing, pubescent herb with ascending fleshy stems bearing ovate-elliptic entire petiolate leaves and loose panicles of richly violet and purple flowers with a conspicuous lower lip.

Locally common in shady wet forest especially along streamsides, but only found in the Chyulu Hills in our area. KAJ.

Bally 1155.

2. Streptocarpus glandulosissimus *Engl.*

Similar to *S. caulescens* except for the keyed characters, and more hairy, especially on the pedicels.

In similar situations to *S. caulescens* but this is a more northerly species, reaching the Ruwenzori. HA, HK, MAC.

Faden 62298.

† By A. D. Q. Agnew.

3. Streptocarpus montanus *Oliv.*

A pubescent rosette herb with a short rhizome and subsessile oblanceolate to elliptic serrate leaves; inflorescence a loose panicle of pale mauve bell-shaped flowers, borne on a leafless scape.

Locally common, often epiphytic, in shady wet forests. HK.

Kabuye 42.

90. PEDALIACEAE†

Annual or perennial herbs, or shrubs or trees, covered at least on the young parts with 4-celled mucilage glands (easily recognized as white dots), which become slimy when wetted; leaves exstipulate, opposite (upper ones sometimes alternate) or fasciculate on short branches (then plant a shrub or tree); flowers usually solitary in the axil of leaves or bracts that are similar to leaves; pedicels generally with 2 nectarial glands at the base; flowers bisexual, zygomorphic, sometimes spurred; corolla sub-bilabiate or subequally 5-lobed; stamens 4, the fifth often represented by a staminode; anther-cells 2, parallel or divergent; ovary superior, of two carpels, 2-celled or divided completely into four cells by two false septa; placenta axile; style filiform, very long, exceeding the anthers; stigma 2-lobed; fruit very variable (very important for determination of genera and species), dehiscent or indehiscent, often provided with emergences such as wings or apical horns; seeds winged or not (sometimes with prominent double margins).

Most species of this family live in the arid zones of Africa; many species behave under suitable conditions as weeds. *Sesamum indicum* L. is a well-known cultivated plant (for oil of the seeds).

1   Shrubs or small trees, 2–6 m high; leaves of the long branches generally transformed into spines; flowers in few-flowered racemes   1. *Sesamothamnus rivae*
    Annual or perennial herbs, less than 2 m tall; leaves not spiny; flowers solitary in the axils of the leaves or bracts that are similar to leaves   2
2   Fruit with four membranous wings, 2-celled, indehiscent; perennial herb with thickened root; flowers yellow to orange; anther-cells kidney-shaped, divergent
       2. *Pterodiscus ruspolii*
    Fruit without membranous wings, 4-celled, dehiscent; usually annual herbs, sometimes perennial, then a little woody at the base; root not thickened; flowers not yellow; anther-cells oblong, parallel   3

† By H. D. Ihlenfeldt.

3   Fruit with two lateral horns at the apex (which open into four horns), but horns sometimes rather short
       3. *Ceratotheca sesamoides*
    Fruit at the apex without lateral horns, but with a single acute (sometimes bipartite at the top) terminal beak   4. *Sesamum*

1. SESAMOTHAMNUS *Welw.*

Branched spiny shrubs or small trees, trunks smooth, usually swollen at the base; leaves deciduous, leafless when flowering; flowers white (at the base sometimes reddish), tube 5–7 cm long, about 3–6 mm wide; spur 3–6 cm long; fruit a woody, 4-celled, compressed capsule, apiculate to emarginate at the apex, 2–2·5 cm broad, 3·5–6·5 cm long; seeds obovate, more or less winged all-round, 4–5 mm broad, 5–6 mm long excluding the 1·5–2·5 mm broad wing.

Sesamothamnus rivae *Engl.*, dealt with in KTS p. 380.

BAR.

Bally 7738.

2. PTERODISCUS *Hook.*

Small perennial herb, up to 20 cm, with a swollen tuberous root and swollen stem base from which the suberect simple or basally branched annual stems arise.

Pterodiscus ruspolii *Engl.*

Leaves entire, ovate, 1·5–5·5 cm long, 0·5–3 cm broad; flowers yellow to orange, often with a red or purple centre spot; corolla (including limb) 3–5 cm long; fruit more or less orbicular, 1·7–3 cm in diameter.

All specimens belong to a narrow-leaved variety which differs conspicuously from the variety that is represented by the type-specimen.

Locally common, found in degraded *Acacia* bush on black soil, up to 3700 ft. NAN.

Adamson 3; Bally 3709.

3. CERATOTHECA *Endl.*

Small suberect herbs, annual and perennial (then woody at the base); leaves polymorphic, lower ones lanceolate to deltoid, usually coarsely dentate towards the base, 1·5–8 cm long, 0·4–4·5 cm broad, upper ones narrower and subentire.

Ceratotheca sesamoides *Endl.*

Flowers pink to purple, lowest lobe of the limb enlarged and often cream with darker lines; apical horns of the fruit 1–3·5 mm long (sometimes nearly suppressed).

Found as a weed on wasteland in sandy soil, 2700–5300 ft. MAG.

Bally 3813.

4. SESAMUM *L.*

Annual or perennial, erect or suberect herbs; leaves very variable and often polymorphic; corolla conspicuously sub-bilabiate; capsule dehiscent, with an apical beak; form of beak and capsule and structure of seeds are important for the delimination of the species.

1 Corolla 3·5–7 cm long, 2–3 cm in diameter at the throat   1. *S. angolense*
   Corolla 2–3·5 cm long, 0·9–1·8 cm in diameter at the throat   2
2 Capsule 14–25 mm long, 2–4 mm broad, straight, gradually narrowed into a flattened *concave*-triangular beak; seeds clearly rugose   2. *S. calycinum*
   Capsule 27–35 mm long, 5–6 mm broad, slightly curved, gradually narrowed into a flattened *convex*-triangular beak; seeds foveolate-reticulate   3. *S. latifolium*

1. Sesamum angolense *Welw.*

Shrubby annual or sometimes perennial herb, 0·8–3 m high; leaves subsessile or shortly petiolate, very polymorphic (elliptic to narrowly oblong), margins entire, more or less inrolled, upper surface glabrescent, lower surface tomentose; flowers pink to purple with deeper markings.

Found in grassland, by roadsides, and in abandoned cultivation, 1200–7700 ft. HT, MUM, KIS, EMB, NBI.

Bally 9224; Bogdan 4620.

2. Sesamum calycinum *Welw.* (see p. 568)

Erect herb, generally simple (only strong specimens branched and then sometimes woody at the base), 30–90 cm high; leaves sessile or subsessile, narrowly linear to linear-lanceolate, 2–12 cm long, 0·1–1 cm broad, margins entire sometimes lower leaves coarsely and irregularly toothed; flowers pink to purple, often spotted within; corolla 2–3·5 cm long, 0·9–1·8 cm in diameter at the throat.

Found in grassland and waste areas, also cultivated, 2000–6700 ft. Our specimens belong to var. *angustifolium* (Oliv.) Ihlenf. & Seidenst. HA, KIT, MUM, NAN, EMB, MAC.

Battiscombe 258; Lind and Agnew 5646.

3. Sesamum latifolium *Gillett*

Erect herb, 40–120 cm high; lower leaves long petiolate, ovate-cordate or 3-lobed, 8–13 cm long, 9–18 cm broad, serrate at the margin, upper leaves

(bracts) much smaller, ovate to ovate-lanceolate, subtruncate or cuneate at the base, often only inconspicuously serrate, pubescent on both sides, mucilage glands present, but not conspicuous; flowers pink to mauve, 2·5–2·8 cm long, about 1 cm broad at the throat.

Found among rocks, 1000–4300 ft, also cultivated. NAN, BAR, MAG.

Glover and Samuel 3258; Bickford 11063.

91. ACANTHACEAE†

Mostly herbs, rarely shrubs or small trees, with opposite exstipulate leaves usually bearing cystoliths; inflorescences various but often spike-like with conspicuous bracts; bracteoles often present; flowers bisexual, zygomorphic; sepals 4–5, free or connate (rarely reduced); petals 5, fused below and 5-lobed or 2-lipped above; stamens 2–4 fused to the corolla tube with anther sacs (thecae) normal, or solitary and sometimes held at different levels or tailed; ovary superior, with 2 loculi bearing mostly 1–2 ovules per loculus; seeds usually arranged one above the other with a thickened funicle which aids dispersal, without endosperm.

1 Fertile stamens 4   2
   Fertile stamens 2, reduced or partially developed staminodes sometimes present also 17
2 Corolla with 1 lip only   3
   Corolla with 2 conspicuous lips or an almost regular limb; anthers usually 2-celled   5
3 Anthers 1-celled; capsule ellipsoid, 2–4-seeded   4
   Anthers 2-celled; capsule cylindric, 6–10-seeded   8. *Eremomastax polysperma*
4 Calyx-segments 4   2. *Blepharis*
   Calyx-segments 5   3. *Crossandra*
5 Flowers mostly solitary, sheathed below by 2 large broad green bracts fused on 1 side; calyx a narrow rim; corolla limb almost regular; capsule globose with a more or less sharply defined woody beak, colaterally 4-seeded, lacking retinacula; seeds subglobose, variously ornamented
                            1. *Thunbergia*
   Flowers variously arranged but lacking the large paired bracts; calyx cupular to cylindric, 4- or 5-toothed or divided almost to the base; capsule 2–many-seeded, usually chartaceous, retinacula usually present; seeds compressed, usually with hygroscopic hairs   6
6 Capsule cylindric, 6–many-seeded   7
   Capsule ellipsoid, clavate or subcylindric, 2–4-seeded   10

† By D. Napper and A. D. Q. Agnew.

7	Corolla limb almost regularly 5-lobed	8
	Corolla conspicuously 2-lipped	
	4. *Hygrophila*	
8	Herbs or shrubs; stamens with all anthers muticous	9
	Shrubs; anterior stamens with 1 long-spurred anther, the others muticous	
	9. *Mimulopsis*	
9	Flowers solitary or paired in the leaf axils	
	11. *Ruellia*	
	Flowers in a globose head 2–3 cm diam. of dense scorpioid cymes surrounded by spiny bracts 15. *Crabbea velutina*	
10	Calyx with 5 white lobes free almost to the base; corolla tube 2·5–5 cm long; seeds discoid, glabrous	
	13. *Whitfieldia elongata*	
	Calyx lobes green, free to the base or in the upper half only; corolla tube up to 2 cm long; seeds discoid with hygroscopic hairs, or compressed with an irregular margin and glabrous	11
11	Calyx segments united into 2 distinct lips; corolla limb rhomboidal with the upper segment notched 16. *Neuracanthus*	
	Calyx segments free to the base or united in a tube but never 2-lipped	12
12	Corolla limb distinctly 2-lipped	
	17. *Lepidagathis*	
	Corolla limb more or less regularly 5-lobed	13
13	Corolla tube campanulate with a spreading almost flat limb; anthers tailed or muticous	14
	Corolla broadly funnel-shaped; anthers muticous; seeds with hygroscopic hairs	
	12. *Acanthopale pubescens*	
14	Seeds discoid with hygroscopic hairs; flowers axillary, sessile or subsessile	15
	Seeds compressed, irregular in outline, glabrous; flowers distant in racemes or spikes; bracts never foliaceous	
	18. *Asystasia*	
15	Flowers in a dense terminal strobilate inflorescence with subreniform to broadly ovate obtuse foliaceous bracts; calyx lobes free to the base; corolla white	
	10. *Phaulopsis imbricata*	
	Flowers sessile, 1–several in distant leaf-axils, not contracted into a strobilate spike; corolla blue-mauve or lurid greenish yellow	16
16	Anthers tailed or mucronate at the base; capsule subcylindric to elliptic, 4-seeded	
	6. *Dyschoriste*	
	Anthers muticous below; capsule ovoid, flattened, 2-seeded 7. *Duosperma*	

17	Corolla limb more or less regularly 5-lobed	18
	Corolla limb conspicuously 2-lipped	19
18	Calyx 4-lobed 14. *Barleria*	
	Calyx 5-lobed	
	19. *Pseuderanthemum ludovicianum*	
19	Capsule cylindric with numerous seeds; corolla very large, deep purple blue	
	5. *Brillantaisia*	
	Capsule obovoid to ellipsoid with 2–4 seeds	20
20	Flowers appearing from between paired opposite free or connate bracts; anthers not tailed	30
	Flower ebracteate or with 1 bract and with or without 2 bracteoles but not appearing from between 2 simple equal or unequal bracts	21
21	Anthers 1-celled	22
	Anthers 2-celled	23
22	Flowers large solitary or in few-flowered cymes; corolla red and black about 3 cm long; shrub 21. *Ruttya fruticosa*	
	Flowers small in dense terminal spikes; corolla white, about 1·5 cm long; herb	
	20. *Monothecium glandulosum*	
23	Anther cells at equal height, muticous; corolla tube funnel-shaped 23. *Ecbolium*	
	Anther cells inserted with 1 completely or partly above the other, acute, mucronate or shortly tailed	24
24	Corolla large with a short broad tube and lips of equal length; seeds large; shrubs	25
	Corolla slender or small; seeds small and rugose, rarely smooth	27
25	Inflorescence strobilate with bracts over 10 mm broad; stigma 2-lobed	
	25. *Adhatoda englerana*	
	Inflorescence without large foliaceous bracts; stigma entire or minutely 2-fid	26
26	Flowers in short spikes, red; seeds shed by the explosive action of the placenta-base springing free from the capsule valves	
	29. *Macrorungia pubinervia*	
	Flowers in short spikes, yellow; seeds shed by normal capsule dehiscence	
	28. *Anisotes ukambensis*	
27	Anther cells not tailed	28
	Anther cells, or at least the lower one, tailed	29
28	Corolla tube linear 22. *Rhinacanthus*	
	Corolla tube inflated above and much broader in the throat 24. *Isoglossa*	
29	Capsule 4-seeded; seeds rough or tubercled	
	26. *Justicia*	
	Capsule 2-seeded; seeds smooth, shining, or with scabrid hairs 27. *Monechma*	

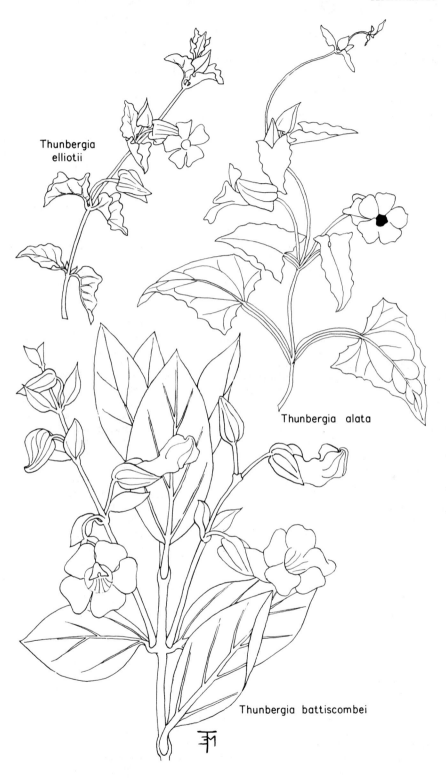

Thunbergia
elliotii

Thunbergia alata

Thunbergia battiscombei

30 Anthers 1-celled;   32. *Hypoestes*
   Anthers 2-celled, 1 much above the other   **31**
31 Inflorescence of dense axillary clusters or
   shortly pedicellate more or less contracted
   umbels; seeds shed by the explosive action
   of the placenta-base springing free from
   the capsule valves   30. *Dicliptera*
   Inflorescence paniculate, spreading; seeds
   shed by normal capsule dehiscence
                          31. *Peristrophe bicalyculata*

1. THUNBERGIA *Retz.*

Annual or perennial herbs with erect or trailing
stems, or shrubs or lianes; leaves without cystoliths, pinnate or palmately veined; flowers enclosed at the base between 2 large partially
connate bracteoles, axillary, solitary or racemose;
calyx cupular, a narrow rim or with 10–20
unequal linear lobes; corolla tubular, widening at
the insertion of the stamens with a subequally
5-lobed spreading orange, yellow, white or blue-
purple limb; stamens 4, included, equal or didyna-
mous with 2-thecous anthers spurred or ornamented at the base; stigma funnel-shaped or
unequally 2-lobed; capsule broadly triangular,
obscurely beaked or subglobose with a sharply
differentiated woody beak; seeds 4, hemispherical
or somewhat narrower, smooth, lamellate or
reticulate on the back.

1 Shrub   1. *T. holstii*
   Erect or climbing or trailing herbs   **2**
2 Corolla limb blue or mauve, rarely white,
   throat always yellow   **3**
   Corolla limb orange, yellow or white, throat
   purple-black or like the limb   **6**
3 Flowers more than 3 together, sessile between toothed bracts   2. *T. fasciculata*
   Flowers pedicellate, not clustered between
   bracts   **4**
4 Flowers in axillary racemes
                          3. *T. battiscombei*
   Flowers solitary or in pairs   **5**
5 Leaves ovate, 10 cm long or more; petioles
   very short or up to one third of the lamina
   length; corolla limb deep blue-purple,
   rarely white   4. *T. natalensis*
   Leaves ovate, 4–8 cm long; petiole at least
   one third of the lamina length; corolla limb
   white or pale lilac   5. *T. usambarensis*
6 Corolla cream to orange throughout, sometimes the throat slightly darker   **7**
   Corolla white to orange (rarely red) with a
   contrasting black or purple throat   **11**
7 Leaves sessile or subsessile; flowers white or
   lemon yellow, sessile or shortly pedunculate   **8**

Leaves petiolate, the petiole sometimes
   narrowly winged; flowers orange, less commonly lemon yellow, with peduncles usually longer than the leaves   **9**
8 Erect annual herb; flowers subsessile, white
                                6. *T. annua*
   Creeping or erect herb, often densely white-
   haired; flowers pedunculate, lemon yellow
                                7. *T. fischeri*
9 Corolla tube straight or slightly curved, not
   over 2 cm long   8. *T. elliotii*
   Corolla tube sharply curved in the middle,
   1·5–4 cm long   **10**
10 Petioles conspicuously winged; stems and
   peduncles with setose orange bristles
                                9. *T. gregorii*
   Petioles not winged; stems, petioles, and
   peduncles pubescent to densely pilose
                                10. *T. gibsonii*
11 Corolla tube straight or slightly curved;
   petioles usually conspicuously winged, but
   wings sometimes obscure   **12**
   Corolla tube sharply bent; petioles not
   winged   11. *T.* sp. *E*
12 Leaf-base decurrent into the cuneate petiolar
   wing; corolla limb yellow; seeds echinate
                                12. *T.* sp. *C*
   Leaf-base cordate or truncate, not decurrent,
   petiolar wing linear   **13**
13 Base of lamina cordate; corolla limb orange
   or golden yellow, rarely red, lemon yellow
   or white; seeds reticulate   14. *T. alata*
   Base of lamina truncate; corolla limb white,
   cream or yellow; seeds echinate or
   lamellate   **14**
14 Petiole from two fifths to as long as the
   lamina; corolla lemon yellow to cream;
   seeds lamellate   13. *T.* sp. *D*
   Petiole short, rarely exceeding two fifths of
   the length of the lamina; corolla limb
   white, rarely cream; seeds echinate
                                15. *T.* sp. *F*

1. Thunbergia holstii *Lindau* (see p. 577)

Erect much branched shrub with elliptic-lanceolate
shortly petiolate leaves and large bluish-purple
solitary flowers.
   Scattered in wooded grassland and bushland
from sea-level to 5000 ft. MAG, EMB, MAC, KAJ.
Napier 2403; Agnew and Tweedie 9290.

2. Thunbergia fasciculata *Lindau*

A woody glabrescent climber with ovate, dentate
leaves and axillary pedunculate inflorescences of
sessile, blue, trumpet-shaped flowers with yellow
throats.
   Rare plant found in wet lowland forest. MUM.
Faden and Evans 69/2056.

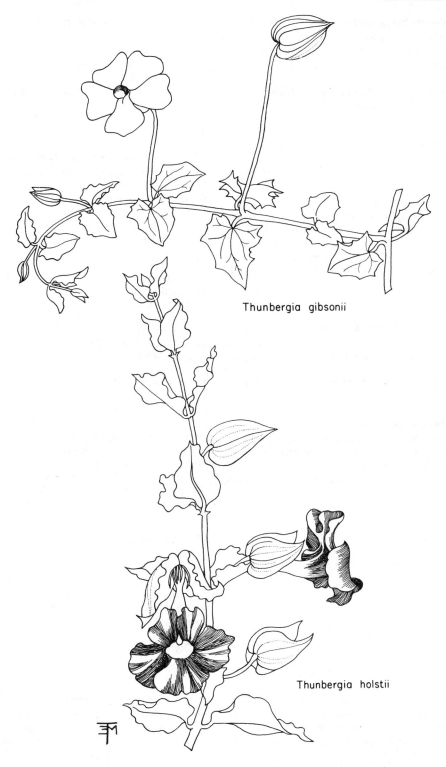

Thunbergia gibsonii

Thunbergia holstii

3. Thunbergia battiscombei *Turrill* (see p. 575)

Erect herb, rarely with long climbing stems, with lanceolate-oblong petiolate leaves and racemes of large lilac-blue flowers with orange or yellow throat.

In savannah and grassland with frequent burning as an erect herb; in the semishade of thicket or woodland it frequently appears to have a more slender-stemmed, twining habit; burning many be instrumental in maintaining the erect habit in the former, 3000–7500 ft. HE, KIS, KIT.

Mainwaring 2661 in CM 5058; Tweedie 67/13.

4. Thunbergia natalensis *Hook.*

Erect or climbing herb with ovate petiolate leaves, cordate or cordate-hastate at the base and solitary or paired purple-blue flowers, rarely white.

Shady places in forest margins and undergrowth, rarely in grassland, 4000–8000 ft. HK, EMB.

Napier 2440.

5. Thunbergia usambarensis *Lindau*

Erect or climbing herb with ovate to lanceolate leaves rounded or hastate at the base, and solitary white or pale lilac flowers.

In forest undergrowth, 5000–8000 ft. MUM.
Dale 3278.

6. Thunbergia annua *Nees*

Erect annual herb with sessile or subsessile oblong-elliptic leaves and solitary, subsessile or very shortly pedicellate white flowers.

Seasonal swamps and grassland on clay soils, 4000–5500 ft. KIS.

Napier 3456 in CM 6615.

7. Thunbergia fischeri *Engl.* (see p. 590)

Procumbent or erect white-tomentose herb with elliptic to obovate or oblong subsessile or shortly petiolate leaves and solitary or paired pedicellate pale lemon yellow flowers.

Upland grasslands 4000–8500 ft. HT, HA, HK, KIT, KIS, NAR, NAN, NBI.

Napier 1314 in CM 2006; Tweedie 66/180.

8. Thunbergia elliotii *S. Moore* (see p. 575)

Trailing pubescent or densely hairy herb with oblong-triangular petiolate leaves narrowing abruptly into a petiole broadly winged in the upper half and naked below; flowers solitary on long peduncles, golden-yellow to orange.

Upland grassland, usually appearing after burning, 5000–9500 ft. HC, HT, KIT, MUM, NAR.

Glover *et al.* 1216; Tweedie 67/175.

9. Thunbergia gregorii *S. Moore*

Trailing herb having orange setose stems and peduncles and broadly lanceolate-triangular, petiolate leaves and solitary long-pedunculate deep-orange flowers.

Upland grasslands, 4500–7500 ft. HA, KIS, MAC, NBI, KAJ.

Agnew and Musumba 5329; Steele in CM 10733.

10. Thunbergia gibsonii *S. Moore* (see p. 577)

Trailing tomentose or pubescent herb with broadly lanceolate to ovate petiolate leaves and solitary deep-orange flowers.

Upland grassland and forest edges, 5000–10 000 ft. HT, HA, MUM, KIS, RV.

Drummond and Hemsley 4443; Tweedie 3245.

11. Thunbergia *sp.* E.

Trailing pubescent to tomentose herb with ovate or broadly lanceolate densely tomentose petiolate leaves; similar to *T. gibsoni* but with solitary orange flowers with a blackish purple throat.

Stony ridges and rocky places in grassland, 6000–8000 ft. HA, RV, KAJ.

Bally B750; Agnew 7469.

12. Thunbergia *sp.* C.

Suberect or trailing herb with narrowly oblong petiolate leaves having winged petioles, the wing up to half the width of the lamina at the top and gradually widening into it, tapering below; flowers solitary, cream or lemon yellow with a deep-purple throat; seeds echinate.

Roadsides and in open bushland, usually in rocky places, 4500–6000 ft. MAC, KAJ.

van Someren in CM 5712; Agnew and Hanid 7552.

13. Thunbergia *sp.* D.

Small woody herb with erect or ascending stems, the triangular-lanceolate petiolate leaves having a broad truncate subhastate base and narrowly winged petiole usually less than two fifths of the length of the lamina; flowers solitary, white or cream, rarely yellow, with a purple throat; seeds echinate.

Dry bushland, especially *Acacia-Commiphora* thicket and dry grassland, 1000–4000 ft. KAJ.

van Someren in CM 8037.

14. Thunbergia alata *Sims* (see p. 575)

Twining perennial herb with triangular to lanceolate or ovate petiolate leaves having a cordate base with hastate or rounded lobes and broadly or very narrowly winged petiole from two fifths of the length of the lamina to equalling it; flowers usually orange but local forms with white, yellow or red corolla limb and purple tube do occur; seeds reticulate at maturity.

Bushland and thicket, usually in partial shade, also in secondary grassland, up to 9000 ft. HE, HC, HT, HM, HA, HK, KIT, MUM, KIS, NAR, RV, EMB, MAC, NBI.

Kokwaro 57; Harmsen 6505.

15. Thunbergia *sp.* F.

Climbing or trailing herb with truncate-based, triangular, often tomentose leaves having a winged petiole over two fifths of the lamina length and a lemon yellow to cream corolla limb.

Grassland and rocky hilltops, more open and drier than for *T. alata*. 2500–6000 ft. MAC, KAJ.

Bally 3609; Hanid and Kiniaruh 476.

2. BLEPHARIS *Juss.*

Erect or prostrate, annual or perennial herbs with leaves in whorls of 4, the alternate leaf-pair in each whorl being smaller than the other, sessile or shortly petiolate, cystoliths absent; flowers in an indefinite bracteate spike, or solitary terminal on a spike of up to 4 bract-pairs, such a spike solitary or in contracted inflorescences with foliaceous subtending bracts (floral leaves) often differing markedly from the ordinary leaves; calyx 4-cleft, the upper segment much exceeding the rest; corolla with a short tube and 3–5-lobed lip, upper lip absent; stamens 4 with 1-celled anthers, the anterior pair with a broad filament bifurcating to give a large tooth and a short branch bearing the anther; capsule ellipsoid, woody, 2-seeded; seeds discoid with long hairs.

1 Spike with several flowers; corolla 5-lobed
  1. *B. linariifolia*
  Spike with a solitary terminal flower; corolla 3-lobed 2
2 Spikes solitary; or several clustered in the axils of ordinary leaves 3
  Spikes clustered on short axillary branches, each subtended by leaves which usually differ conspicuously from the foliage leaves 5. *B. stuhlmannii*
3 Upper calyx segment exserted 4
  Upper calyx segment included
  4. *B. maderaspatensis*
4 Upper calyx segment with a truncate mucronate tip; spikes up to 1·2 cm long
  2. *B. integrifolia*
  Upper calyx segment with a tapering, subacute tip; spikes 1·7–2·2 cm long
  3. *B. fruticulosa*

1. Blepharis linariifolia *Pers.* (see p. 580)

Prostrate or suberect annual plants with sessile, unequal, sinuate, spine-toothed leaves and elongated terminal spikes, short at first, bearing bright blue flowers.

Open spaces in dry thornbush and grassland, 1500–4500 ft. BAR, RV, MAG, MAC, KAJ.

Bogdan 2213; Agnew 7634.

2. Blepharis integrifolia (*L. f.*) *Schinz* (see p. 580)

Prostrate herb forming dense mats, with sessile unequal leaves and axillary flower spikes each bearing a single terminal blue flower; bracts of the spike each with a recurved tip and 8–10 marginal glochidiate bristles; lower stamen filaments with a short rounded tooth.

Grassland and open spaces in thicket, 2500–6500 ft. HA, BAR, RV, MAC.

Fauna Research Unit 360; Agnew 9172.

3. Blepharis fruticulosa *C. B. Cl.*

Dense sub-shrub or woody herb with leathery unequal sessile leaves and axillary flower spikes bearing a single terminal blue flower; bracts of the spike with a stout, recurved terminal spine and scabrid marginal bristles; lower stamen filaments with a short rounded tooth.

Rocky places in dry bush and grassland, 1000–7000 ft. RV, MAG, NBI, MAC, KAJ.

Greenway 9567; Agnew and Musumba 5301.

4. Blepharis maderaspatensis (*L.*) *Roth* (see p. 580)

Erect or prostrate plants with unequal, elliptic, usually entire-margined leaves and axillary solitary or clustered flower spikes each bearing a single terminal pale blue-mauve flower; upper bracts of the spike rounded above with recurved tips and retrorsely scabrid bristles; lower stamen filaments with a slender tooth almost as long as the anther.

A common weed of grassland and bushland, 1500–9000 ft. KIT, KIS, RV, MAC, NBI.

Verdcourt 520; Hanid and Kiniaruh 567.

The plants from the area treated in this Flora are of the subspecies *rubiifolia* (Schumach.) Napper. Subspecies *maderaspatensis*, with a protruding upper calyx segment, occurs along the coast.

5. Blepharis stuhlmannii *Lindau*

A much-branched prostrate or erect, pubescent or velutinous plant with sessile unequal leaves and dense lateral leafy inflorescences of flower spikes each bearing a single terminal off-white to lilac flower; bracts spine-tipped; lower stamen filaments with a subacute tooth.

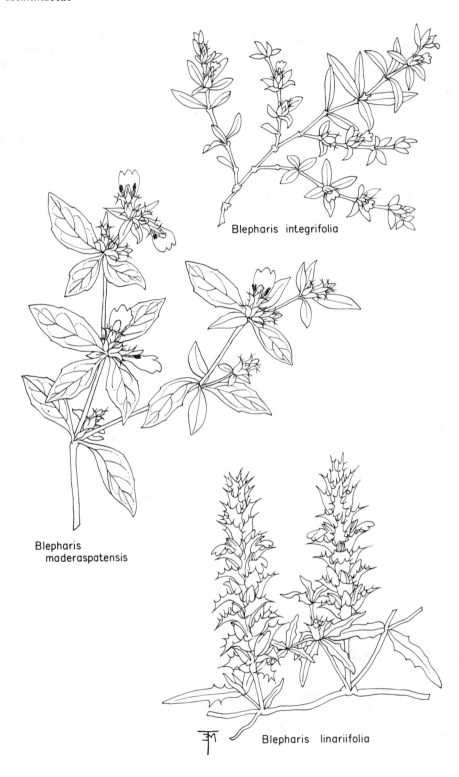

Blepharis integrifolia

Blepharis
maderaspatensis

Blepharis linariifolia

Grassland and dry bushland, 3000–6600 ft. NAR, MAC.

Glover 2106; Strid 2697.

3. CROSSANDRA *Salisb.*

Subshrubs or perennial herbs with opposite or whorled leaves lacking cystoliths; flowers in dense strobilate sessile or pedunculate spikes; bracteoles 2, linear or narrow; calyx 5-cleft, segments unequal; corolla with a long linear tube and limb split posteriorly to give a single 3–5-lobed lip; stamens 4 with 1-celled anthers; capsule oblong ellipsoid, woody 4–2-seeded; seeds flat, covered by appressed laciniate-margined scales

1   Bract margins spiny; stems unbranched, naked, with an apical rosette of leaves and a terminal inflorescence
                          1. *C. stenostachya*
  Bract margins ciliate, setose-ciliate or entire 2
2   Bracts entire   3
  Bracts 3-toothed or 3-lobed to the middle   5
3   Tip of each bract a straight or recurving short spine   4
  Tip of each bract shortly mucronate or acute
                          2. *C. nilotica*
4   Stems over 15 cm high excluding the flowering scape; bracts broadly elliptic, the width being more than half the length
                     3. *C. mucronata*
  Stems contracted, plant reduced almost to a rosette; bracts oblong-lanceolate, width less than half the length   4. *C. subacaulis*
5   Leaves 8–10 cm long, cuneate below, petiole not winged   5. *C. tridentata*
  Leaves 4–8 cm long, abruptly truncate below the middle, with lyrate or tapering petiolar wing   6. *C. friesiorum*

1. Crossandra stenostachya (*Lindau*) C. B. Cl.

Erect herb with simple unbranched stem crowned by a rosette of subsessile narrowly obovate leaves, with 1–2 sessile dense bracteate spikes with yellow flowers; bracts broadly obovate with numerous marginal spines.

Grassland and seasonally wet places in arid areas, up to 3000 ft. MAC.

Bogdan 4378.

2. Crossandra nilotica *Oliv.*

Erect or straggling branched herb with petiolate elliptic-lanceolate leaves and pedunculate spikes of apricot or red flowers; bracts obovate to oblanceolate, acute, mucronate.

Partial shade in wooded grassland and dry bushland, occasionally in *Euclea-Olea* forest, 3500–8000 ft. HT, KIS, RV, NAR, BAR.

Kirrika in Bally 7750; Agnew 10776.

Only the subspecies *massaica* (Mildbr.) Napper occurs in the area of this flora; it is distinguished by the shape of the bracts and the absence of glandular hairs on them.

3. Crossandra mucronata *Lindau* (see p. 582)

Erect branching or semiclimbing herb with petiolate or subsessile ovate-elliptic leaves and pedunculate bracteate spikes of pale orange to red flowers; bracts obovate-elliptic, obtuse with a recurved short terminal spine.

In dry thicket, rarely in forest or woodland, up to 6000 ft. RV, MAG, EMB.

Napper 1637.

4. Crossandra subacaulis C. B. Cl. (see p. 582)

Low, almost stemless herb with sessile oblanceolate leaves crowded almost into a rosette, and pedunculate bracteate spikes of apricot to red flowers; bracts similar to *C. mucronata* but slightly narrower.

Savannah after grassfires, short grassland or waste ground, up to 5500 ft. NAR, MAC, NBI, KAJ.

Napier 106; Kokwaro and Waithaka 1596.

5. Crossandra tridentata *Lindau*

Straggling or erect herbs with petiolate or subsessile obovate leaves and pedunculate spikes of small white flowers; bracts broadly elliptic, 3-lobed except for the lower ones.

Dense shade in undergrowth of wet forest, up to 8000 ft. HA, KAJ.

Napier 2711.

6. Crossandra friesiorum *Mildbr.*

Straggling herb differing from *C. tridentata* in the lyrate, petiolate leaves with undulating petiolar wings; spikes pedunculate, white-flowered with bracts similar to *C. tridentata*.

Damp places in forest undergrowth, 4000–5000 ft. HK, MAC.

Bally in CM 7462; Agnew and Faden 9984.

4. HYGROPHILA *R. Br.*

Annual or perennial herbs having simple or branched stems and entire leaves; flowers in axillary sessile or subsessile clusters, these sometimes with reduced floral leaves and contracted into a spike-like head; bracteoles in some species modified into long simple spines, otherwise foliaceous, but small; calyx-segments 4 or 5, equal or unequal; corolla markedly 2-lipped, the upper lip hooded, the lower 3-lobed and usually plicate in the throat, tube cylindric or campanulate above; stamens 4, the upper pair slightly smaller, filaments united in

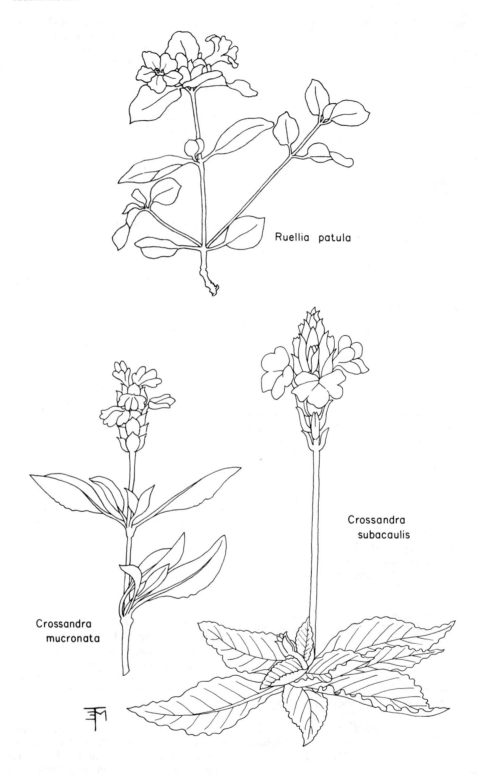

Ruellia patula

Crossandra
subacaulis

Crossandra
mucronata

lateral pairs at the base, anthers 2-locular, muticous; stigma 2-lobed, the upper lobe minute, the lower one linear; capsule 2-celled, linear-oblong or linear, with numerous discoid seeds with a marginal fringe of appressed hygroscopic hairs.

1   Stems sparingly branched, erect; flowers in distinct axillary clusters with up to 10 spines per node   1. *H. auriculata*
     Stems branched, erect or procumbent; axillary clusters of flowers forming a terminal interrupted spike or uninterrupted spike, always without spines   2
2   Flowers small 1–1·5 cm long, almost glabrous; leaves linear-oblanceolate
                 3. *H. pobeguinii*
     Flowers 2–2·5 cm long; plant sparingly hairy to shortly pilose   3
3   Inflorescence interrupted, the lower cymes shortly pedunculate; calyx glabrous; capsule more than 15 mm long   4. *H. sp. A*
     Inflorescence continuous or interrupted at the base only, all cymes subsessile; calyx pilose; capsule 10 mm long
                 2. *H. spiciformis*

1. Hygrophila auriculata (*Schumach.*) *Heine* (see p. 584)

Erect sparingly branched annual herb with square stems and shortly petiolate elliptic leaves; flowers in axillary sessile clusters, each with a few stout spines and oblong-elliptic bracts, corolla blueymauve, pinkish or white.

    Vlei, swamps, and open bushland, up to 7000 ft. KIT, MUM, KIS, RV, MAC.

    Bogdan 5735; Lugard 182.

2. Hygrophila spiciformis *Lindau*

Large straggling or bushy herb with shortly petiolate or sessile elliptic leaves and spiciform or interrupted terminal leafy inflorescences of mauve or purple flowers. Occasional plants occur with very narrow leaves, but these do not seem distinct.

    Woodland, thicket, forest, and damp grassland, up to 7000 ft. HT, HA, KIT, NAR, MAC, NBI.

    Verdcourt 716; Lind 5110; Irwin 148.

3. Hygrophila pobeguinii *R. Benoist*

Erect branched glabrous annual with narrowly oblanceolate sessile leaves and small mauvish flowers in sessile axillary clusters.

    Damp grassland and ditches, up to 6000 ft. MUM, KIS.

    McMahon 117; Tweedie 3583.

4. Hygrophila *sp.* **A.**

Erect branching herb to 1·5 m high, with softly pubescent elliptic subsessile leaves much reducing in size in the inflorescence and large pale-mauve or purple flowers.

    Wet grassland and swamps, also wet places in forest, up to 4500 ft. MUM.

    Kokwaro 1770.

5. BRILLANTAISIA *P. Beauv.*

Mostly large shrubby perennial herbs, to 3 m high with large, often highly characteristic leaves; flowers in terminal panicles; bracts foliaceous; bracteoles paired, similar to the calyx but longer; calyx with 5 long linear to spathulate segments, the upper one usually much larger than the other four; corolla conspicuously 2-lipped with a very short cylindric tube; stamens 4, the lower 2 reduced to staminodes, the upper 2 perfect, 2-celled, muticous; stigma exserted, the upper lobe reduced to a very small tooth; capsule linear, 2-celled with numerous flat round seeds with hygroscopic hairs on the margins.

1   Inflorescence a dense bracteate spike
             1. *B. madagascariensis*
     Inflorescence an elongated panicle   2
2   Leaf margins very coarsely and irregularly toothed, large teeth alternating with fine ones; calyx glabrous or almost so, the upper segment up.to twice as broad as the others, 10–14 mm long   3. *B. nitens*
     Leaf margins evenly serrate or evenly crenate or subentire; calyx segments subsimilar, the upper one slightly larger than the others, glandular pubescent
               2. *B. nyanzarum*

1. Brillantaisia madagascariensis *Lindau*

Erect branched sparsely hairy perennial herb to 2 m high with broadly ovate, acuminate, finely crenate-serrate-margined leaves narrowing sharply below into the winged petiole; flowers in terminal spikes with broad cordate bracts and large purple corollas.

    Forest undergrowth, up to 5500 ft. MUM.

    Verdcourt 1656.

2. Brillantaisia nyanzarum *Burkill* (see p. 584)

Erect much branched perennial herb to 2 m high, with broadly ovate acuminate evenly serrate leaves narrowing sharply below into the winged petiole, rarely cordate; flowers in a long narrow panicle, with the upper bracts elliptic to oblanceolate and large purple corollas.

    Forest undergrowth, up to 6000 ft. KIT, MUM.

    Dale 3208; Tweedie 3413.

Hygrophila auriculata

Brillantaisia nyanzarum

3. Brillantaisia nitens *Lindau*

Erect branching perennial herb to 4 m high with broadly ovate very irregularly toothed leaves truncate or cordate below, usually abruptly narrowed into the winged petiole; flowers in a long narrow panicle with the upper bracts ovate cordate and large purple corollas.

Forest undergrowth, up to 7200 ft. HM, MUM, KIS.

HM Gardner K3731; Strid 2916.

6. DYSCHORISTE *Nees*

Herbs or (more often) shrubs with entire or obscurely crenate leaves and axillary cymes of flowers; bracts and bracteoles linear, much smaller than the calyx; calyx tubular, the 5 lobes free for about half the calyx length; corolla lobes 5, contort in bud, hardly 2-lipped; stamens 4, in two groups of two, the filaments usually joined for a short distance, each with 2 shortly tailed anthers; capsule ± cylindrical, 4-seeded; seeds orbicular, flat, densely pubescent.

1 Corolla over 2 cm long   2
  Corolla under 2 cm long   4
2 Plant glandular on the young stems and calyx tube   3
  Plant without glands or minutely glandular only on the calyx lobes 1. *D. procumbens*
3 Corolla usually less than 4·0 cm long; anther tails minute, less than 0·25 mm long and difficult to see   2. *D. hildebrandtii*
  Corolla usually more than 4·5 cm long; anther tails conspicuous, about 0·5 mm long   3. *D. thunbergiflora*
4 Capsule longer than calyx   4. *D. perrottetii*
  Capsule shorter than or equal to calyx in length   5
5 Plant an erect herb or shrub   6
  Plant a prostrate or trailing herb
               5. *D. radicans*
6 Plant a wiry shrub; leaves obovate, rounded at apex; flowers rarely more than 6 at each node   6. *D. sp. A*
  Plant an erect herb; leaves ovate-elliptic, acute at apex; flowers usually over 20 at each node   7. *D. trichocalyx*

1. Dyschoriste procumbens *E. A. Bruce*

A spreading or erect, finely pubescent wiry shrub or woody herb with small obovate leaves and scattered 3-flowered cymes; corolla a strange green-yellow colour.

Locally common in dry rocky grassland, in the Rift Valley. RV, MAG.

Napier 413 (type); Lind and Agnew 5383.

2. Dyschoriste hildebrandtii *S. Moore*

An erect, densely glandular pubescent herb or low shrub with ovate to obovate, slightly crenate leaves and rather loose, pedunculate cymes of mauve to greenish-purple flowers.

Locally common in dry wooded grassland. BAR, EMB, MAC, KAJ.

Blencowe 18; Nattrass 1276.

3. Dyschoriste thunbergiflora (*S. Moore*) *Lindau*

Similar to *D. mollis* but less hairy and with larger flowers.

Uncommon plant found in dry country. RV, EMB, MAC, KAJ.

Strid 2523; Verdcourt 1789.

4. Dyschoriste perrottetii *S. Moore*

An erect glabrescent herb with trailing basal stems and elliptic leaves; flowers smaller than in any other species of *Dyschoriste*, sessile in axillary groups, pale lilac.

Locally common in artificial grassland and swamp edges at medium altitudes. KIT, KIS, MAC, NBI.

Verdcourt 349; Hanid and Kiniaruh 599.

5. Dyschoriste radicans *Nees* (see p. 595)

A pubescent or glabrescent trailing herb with elliptic to obovate leaves and few to many sessile flowers in distant axils; corolla pale purple to mauve.

Common in disturbed grassland at medium altitudes. HE, HC, HT, HM, HA, HK, HN, KIT, MUM, NAR, BAR, RV, NAN, NBI, KAJ.

Drummond and Hemsley 1235; Hanid 272.

6. Dyschoriste sp. A.

Similar to *D. radicans* but an erect shrub with blue-purple flowers.

Local, in wooded grassland, especially near Thika. EMB, MAC, NBI.

Bogdan 230; Strid 2230.

7. Dyschoriste trichocalyx *Lindau*

An erect pubescent herb from a woody rootstock with elliptic, acute leaves and dense masses of sessile pale mauve flowers in the upper axils.

Rare, and only recorded once from the Kisii area. KIS.

Napier 2905.

7. DUOSPERMA *Dayton* (*DISPERMA* C.B.Cl.)

Erect or climbing shrubs with serrate leaves and condensed axillary cymes of flowers; bract and bracteoles often as long as the calyx; calyx tubular, the 5 lobes fused for half their length or

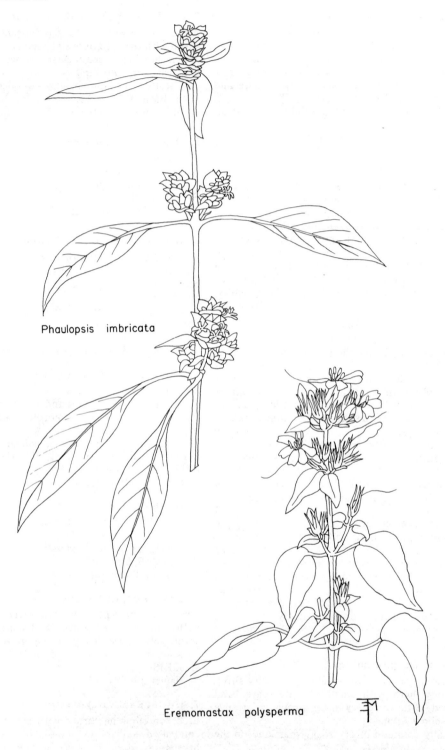

Phaulopsis   imbricata

Eremomastax   polysperma

more; corolla as in *Dyschoriste* but often small and ± 2-lipped; stamens 4, free from each other, each with 2 anthers without appendages; capsule 2-seeded, flattened, obovate; seeds orbicular, with hygroscopic hairs on the margin.

1 Corolla large, trumpet shaped, over 2·5 cm long   1. *D.* sp. *A*
   Corolla small, bilabiate, less than 1 cm long 2
2 Leaves with stellate pubescence especially on the underside, truncate at apex
                                   2. *D. eremophilum*
   Leaves glabrous or with simple pubescence, rounded at apex 3. *D. kilimandscharicum*

1. Duosperma *sp.* A.

A sparsely pubescent low shrub or woody herb with elliptic, acute leaves and large, pale mauve flowers.

This species can be mistaken for *Dyschoriste thunbergiflora*, but the large bracts and bracteoles distinguish it. Uncommon, in disturbed dry bushland. EMB, MAC.

Trapnell 2408.

2. Duosperma   eremophilum   (*Milne-Redh.*) *Napper*

An erect, often white-pubescent shrub with suborbicular to obovate leaves and axillary masses of small white flowers.

This plant is found in dry stony grassland and appears to be poikilohydric, since it remains alive even when dry. Since it absorbs atmospheric water at night, and loses it by day, it forms an important dietary source of water for night-feeding browsing animals in the dry country of northern Kenya. KAJ.

Lind, Agnew, and Beecher 5698.

3. Duosperma kilimandscharicum (*Lindau*) *Dayton*

Similar to *D. eremophilum* but with glabrous or simply pubescent leaves and the corolla yellowish with a purple throat.

Locally common in dry sandy bushland, especially where disturbed. MAG, MAC, KAJ.

Edwards 3133; Agnew 10684.

8. EREMOMASTAX *Lindau*

Herbs or shrubs with entire leaves; inflorescences as in *Mimulopsis*; bracts small, linear, falling early; bracteoles linear, small; calyx of 5, equal almost free lobes; corolla with a curved tube and 5 contorted lobes which all form the lower and only lip; stamens 4, each with 2 anthers which bear a small protuberance at base; capsule cylindrical, with 6–16 seeds; seeds hairy on the margin.

Eremomastax   polysperma (*Benth.*) Dandy (see p. 586)

An erect, sparsely pubescent weak shrub or herb with ovate, long-petiolate leaves and a terminal panicle of blue purple flowers.

Rare plant found in riverine forest in western Kenya. KIT.

Tweedie 66/302.

9. MIMULOPSIS *Schweinf.*

Trees, shrubs or herbs with serrate or crenate, ovate leaves which are rounded or cordate at the base; flowers in open or contracted racemes of cymes; bracts and bracteoles present, similar to the calyx or larger; calyx of 5, almost free, linear lobes; corolla tube broadly funnel-shaped from the base, with 5 nearly equal lobes; stamens 4, each with 2 anthers, one anther of each anterior stamen produced below into a tail; capsule 6–8-seeded; seeds orbicular, glabrous except for the margin.

1 Plant a tree; calyx in fruit over 3 cm long
                                   1. *M. arborescens*
   Plant a herb or weak shrub; calyx in fruit less than 2·5 cm long 2
2 Lateral cymes of the inflorescence with long peduncles so that the whole resembles a panicle and the flowers do not touch each other; sepals rarely over 1·5 mm wide
                                   2. *M. solmsii*
   Lateral cymes of the inflorescence condensed, with short peduncles so that the whole resembles a spike and the flowers touch each other; sepals often over 1·5 mm wide   3. *M. alpina*

1. Mimulopsis arborescens *C. B. Cl.*

Dealt with in KTS p. 17. HE, HM, HA.

2. Mimulopsis solmsii *Schweinf.* (see p. 588)

A trailing woody herb often covered with long reddish hairs and with ovate, crenate or serrate leaves; corolla pale blue to yellowish with purple guide-lines within.

An abundant herb of the forest floor in some areas, and showing the phenomenon of mass-flowering every 5–9 years after which it may be difficult to find until it increases again. HA, HM, HT, HE.

Irwin 470.

3. Mimulopsis alpina *Chiov.* (see p. 588)

Similar to *M. solmsii* but without the reddish hairs and with a condensed, spike-like raceme of mauve flowers; corolla usually mauve with yellow guide lines and an orange patch on the lower side.

Distribution and habitat similar to *M. solmsii.* HE, HC, HT, HM, HA, HK, MUM.

Tweedie 3512; Verdcourt 1036.

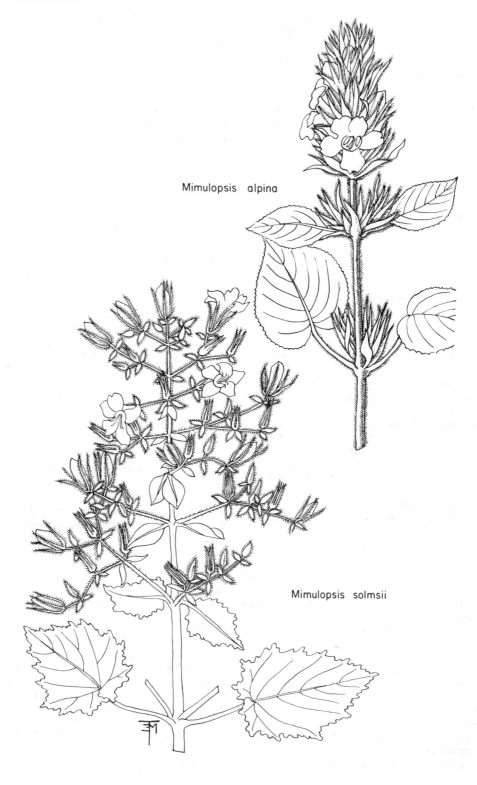

Mimulopsis alpina

Mimulopsis solmsii

10. PHAULOPSIS *Willd.*

Herbs with entire leaves and axillary fascicles of flowers forming terminal or axillary spikes with the floral leaf subtending each fascicle bract-like; bracts and bracteoles obsolete or absent; calyx of 5 unequal lobes, the posterior enlarged; corolla as in *Dyschoriste*; stamens 4, each with 2 untailed anthers; capsule elliptic, flattened, 4-seeded; seeds flat, orbicular, with marginal hygroscopic hairs.

Phaulopsis imbricata (*Forsk.*) *Sweet* (see p. 586)

A pubescent trailing herb with ascending stems bearing elliptic leaves; leaves gradually narrowed at base and apex; flowers small, in one-sided lateral or terminal dense spikes; corolla over 8 mm long, white.

Common on the forest floor of drier forest and evergreen woodland. HE, HT, HA, HK, KIT, MUM, KIS, NAR, EMB, MAC, NBI, KAJ.

Drummond and Hemsley 1233; Agnew, Musumba, and Kiniaruh 8073.

11. RUELLIA *L.*

Much branched erect or creeping herbs or shrubs with entire elliptic leaves; flowers pinkish-lilac to blue-mauve or white borne in subsessile axillary clusters of 1–3, or 2–3 distant in axillary one-sided cymes; bracts foliaceous; bracteoles ovate-petiolate to linear-spathulate and cuneate below, much exceeding the calyx in length; calyx deeply 5-fid in most species but sometimes united nearly to half way; corolla with the tube cylindric below, campanulate above and the limb subequally 5-fid; stamens 4, all fertile, subsimilar, anther-cells 2, not spurred; stigma with 1 oblong compressed branch, the other reduced to a small tooth; capsule ovoid-stipitate or linear-cylindric, glabrous or pubescent, with numerous discoid seeds with long appressed hygroscopic hairs on the margins.

All the species listed here are night flowering, i.e. the corollas open around dusk or in the night and fall before noon the following day.

1 Shrub to 2 m high; cylindric portion of the corolla tube very long, the total length of the tube 8–11 cm **1. *R. megachlamys***
  Creeping or erect woody herbs up to 1·2 m high; corolla tube not over 3 cm long **2**
2 Erect branched woody herb 30–120 cm high, with mauve or white flowers; calyx 8–11 mm long, with linear subulate lobes; capsule 16–20 mm long, stipitate, shortly pubescent all over **2. *R. prostrata***
  Creeping or semierect branched herb to 100 cm high, with pinkish-lilac or white flowers; calyx 5–8 mm long, with linear acute lobes; capsule 10–18 mm long, glabrous **3. *R. patula***

1. Ruellia megachlamys *S. Moore* (see p. 590)

Tall woody much branched perennial with broadly ovate petiolate leaves; flowers solitary, axillary, sessile, white, with a very long corolla tube expanding to the throat only, and small limb.

Dry bushland with *Acacia*, *Commiphora*, *Grewia*, etc. NAR, MAG, KAJ.

Napier 2389 in CM 5719; Agnew 9773.

2. Ruellia prostrata (*Nees*) *T. Anders.*

Much branched woody herb with petiolate, sparingly pubescent, ovate-elliptic leaves with obtuse to acuminate tips and acuminate bases; flowers in sessile axillary clusters of 1–3 with petiolate elliptic obtuse bracteoles and calyx with 5 subequal long linear lobes; corolla pinkish-mauve to white with a campanulate tube, linear at the base, and a subequally 5-lobed limb; capsule stipitate, ovoid, acute.

In open bushland or forest. MAC.

Edwards E 159; Agnew 9137.

3. Ruellia patula *Jacq.* (see p. 582)

Much branched semi-erect or erect herb with petiolate, ovate-spathulate, obtuse or acute leaves and pinkish-lilac flowers in subsessile axillary clusters of 1–3; calyx small with linear-lanceolate lobes; capsule ovoid, acute, stipitate, glabrous.

In bushland, grassland, and open places in forest, up to 7600 ft. HC, HT, KIT, MUM, NAR, BAR, MAG, MAC, NBI, KAJ.

This is a very variable species and two forms can be recognised among the plants from Upland Kenya. One form has short strigose hairs usually intermixed with glandular ones and occurs chiefly in the semi-arid areas and dry bushland of BAR, MAG, and KAJ.

Verdcourt 3578; Lind, Agnew, and Beecher 5704.

The other form is a more bushy, often creeping plant with numerous long fine multicellular hairs mixed with the short strigose ones on the young shoots and petioles; glandular hairs frequently present as well. This form is found throughout central and western Kenya.

Polhill 402; Agnew, Kibe, and Mathenge 10254.

12. ACANTHOPALE *C. B. Cl.*

Weak shrubs similar to *Dyschoriste* but with flowers in bracteate racemes, the corolla trumpet-shaped from the base, the stamens not joined in pairs, and the anthers not tailed.

Acanthopale pubescens (*Engl.*) *C. B. Cl.* (see p. 590)

An erect, pubescent or glabrescent, branched shrub, with elliptic leaves gradually narrowed at base and apex; racemes small, lateral and terminal

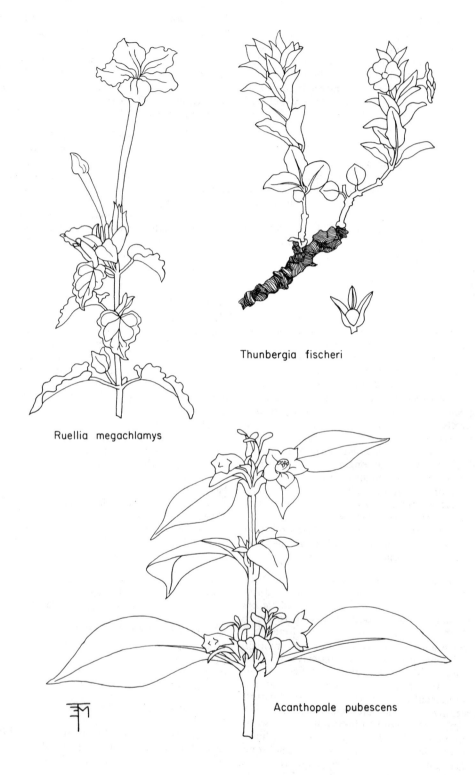

Ruellia megachlamys

Thunbergia fischeri

Acanthopale pubescens

of large white flowers (spotted and lined pink-purple within) which mostly open one at a time.

Locally common in wet forest. HE, HC, HM, HA, HK, MUM.

Drummond and Hemsley 4773; Agnew and Hanid 7465.

13. WHITFIELDIA *Hook.*

Shrubs with entire leaves and flowers in terminal or axillary racemes; bracts and bracteoles present, ovate to elliptic, usually white or cream; calyx of 5 broad, delicate, white lobes; corolla as in *Dyschoriste*; stamens 4, each with 2 anthers without tails; capsule 4-seeded; seeds orbicular, glabrous.

Whitfieldia elongata (*Beauv.*) *C. B. Cl.*

An erect or climbing shrub with large glabrous elliptic leaves gradually narrowed at both ends; racemes yellowish-white, glandular on all parts; corolla with a long (2·5–4·0 cm) tube, white.

A rare plant of wet lowland forest in western Kenya (Bukura). MUM.

Graham 5.

14. BARLERIA *L.*

Herbs or shrubs, often very spiny, with entire leaves having cystoliths, glabrous or simply pubescent, rarely with stellate or medifixed T-shaped hairs; flowers solitary axillary or in axillary few-flowered cymes, these sometimes condensed into terminal heads; bracts and bracteoles simple or of toothed spines or leaflike; calyx of 4 segments free almost to the base, the 2 outer ones, (upper and lower) large, both entire or the upper entire and the lower 2-toothed, lateral segments linear or linear-lanceolate; corolla orange or mauve to blue or white, tube cylindric throughout or cylindric below and funnel-shaped above, limb subequally 5-fid or more or less 2-lipped; fertile stamens 2 with exserted 2-celled muticous anthers, the cells parallel; staminodes 2, very small; stigmas linear, subequal; capsule oblong-ellipsoid or ovoid 2–4-seeded, or globose with a linear beak (like *Thunbergia*) and 2-seeded; seeds long-pilose, the hairs more or less elastic on application of water.

1 Interpetiolar spines present; small spiny much branched shrubs 2
   Spines absent from the vegatative shoots, though the calyx is sometimes spiny-margined 8
2 Flowers yellow or orange 3
   Flowers bluish-mauve or white 6
3 Corolla with one lobe free to as much as half-way down the tube 4
   Corolla tube cylindric, limb subequally 5-lobed 5

4 Leaves elliptic, obtuse, 5–6 cm long; calyx 1·5–2 cm long 1. *B. sp. A*
   Leaves obovate, rounded above, 1·5–4 cm long; calyx 1 cm long 2. *B. proxima*
5 Calyx with a spinous tip about one third of the total length; bracts foliaceous with sparingly ciliate margins; bracteole narrowly lanceolate; leaves about twice as long as wide 3. *B. eranthemoides*
   Calyx with a spinous tip half or more of the total length; bracts linear, not ciliate; bracteole a linear spine; leaves about 3 times as long as wide 4. *B. sp. Q*
6 Corolla white with a cylindric tube, 7–9 cm long when fully expanded; bracteole a toothed spine or toothed leaf 5. *B. acanthoides*
   Corolla blue with a campanulate tube, not over 5 cm long; bracteole a simple spine 7
7 Outer calyx segments narrowly elliptic, deeply toothed; leaves 1·5–2·5 cm long 6. *B. spinisepala*
   Outer calyx segments ovate, cordate below, with toothed margins; leaves at least 2·5 cm long 7. *B. grandicalyx*
8 Capsule globose, 2-seeded, with a long linear beak; calyx segments narrow; corolla blue-mauve or white 9
   Capsule with a short conic beak or not beaked, 2–4-seeded; upper and lower calyx segments broadly elliptic to ovate; corolla blue-mauve 11
9 Corolla 1–1·8 cm long; calyx small, up to 7 mm long, lower segment shortly 2-toothed, or rarely entire 8. *B. diffusa*
   Corolla 2–2·8 cm long, lilac-blue or white with purple markings; calyx 9–15 mm long, with linear-ovate entire segments, or the lower one 2-toothed 10
10 Lower calyx segment lanceolate acuminate, entire, venation not conspicuous 9. *B. sp. G*
   Lower calyx segment narrowly oblong, 2-toothed, conspicuously parallel-veined 10. *B. sp. K*
11 Calyx segments broadly ovate, about 20 mm long; calyx 4–6 cm long 11. *B. volkensii*
   Calyx segments broadly elliptic to lanceolate, 7–15 mm long; corolla 1·5–5 cm long 12
12 Corolla large, 3·5–5 cm long; leaf bases rounded 14. *B. submollis*
   Corolla small to medium, up to 3·5 cm long; leaf bases narrowing into the petiole 13
13 Flowers solitary or 2–3 in each axil; calyx segments broadly elliptic, toothed, glabrous or almost so 12. *B. micrantha*
   Flowers in heads but some axillary ones also

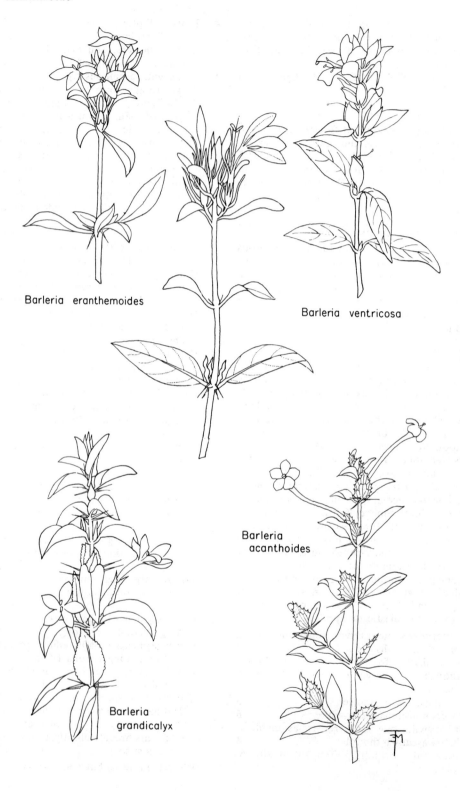

Barleria eranthemoides

Barleria ventricosa

Barleria grandicalyx

Barleria acanthoides

present; bracts and calyx densely covered with yellow hairs; calyx segments entire

13. *B. ventricosa*

1. Barleria *sp.* A.

Small, much branched spiny shrub with subsessile elliptic obtuse leaves and 4-fid subsessile interpetiolar spines; flowers orange in dense spiny heads; bracts narrowly obovate with a long apical spine; outer calyx segments broadly elliptic with a very long apical spine; corolla with 1 lobe free for one third of the length of the tube; stamens almost as long as the corolla with 3–4 mm long anthers; capsule conic, 1·5 cm.

In dry bushland and rocky places, up to 3500 ft. MAG.

Bogdan 400; Lind 5578.

2. Barleria proxima *Lindau*

Small, much branched spiny shrub differing from the above in the more leaf-like bracts and larger calyx with straight, stiff spiny tips.

One record only of which the locality may be mistaken as this is normally a species of the hot dry bushland below 3000 ft in the northern and coastal provinces. HA.

Jex-Blake in CM 3262.

3. Barleria eranthemoides *C. B. Cl.* (see p. 592)

Small, much branched spiny shrub with subsessile broadly elliptic leaves and sessile 3–4-fid interpetiolar spines; flowers orange in dense spiny heads; bracts elliptic-lanceolate to oblanceolate, spine-tipped, yellow-green; corolla tube cylindric, narrow, with a subequally 5-lobed limb; anthers 2–3 mm long and partially or wholly emergent from the throat of the corolla.

Dry grassland and bushland, up to 5500 ft. NAR, BAR, MAG, MAC, KAJ.

Napper 1542; Agnew 5664.

4. Barleria *sp.* Q.

Small spiny shrub differing from *B. eranthemoides* in the usually slightly larger flowers, the linear, spinescent grey-green bracts and bracteoles and the calyx segments with a longer spine tip.

Grassland and bushland. RV, MAC, NBI, KAJ.

Drummond and Hemsley 1245; Agnew and Beecher 5346.

5. Barleria acanthoides *Vahl* (see p. 592)

Small shrub with subsessile, broadly elliptic to oblong spathulate leaves with toothed interpetiolar spines often as long as the leaves; flowers solitary or on short 1-sided racemes; outer calyx segments ovate-cordate to broadly lanceolate, cordate, mucronate becoming papery and heavily veined;

corolla white with a long cylindric tube and small flat limb; capsule ellipsoidal, 4-seeded, black. A night-flowering species.

In dry scrub, bushland, and semi-arid grassland, often in rocky places. NAR, BAR, MAG, MAC, KAJ.

Glover and Samuel 2950; Lind and Agnew 5650.

6. Barleria spinisepala *E. A. Bruce*

Low-growing, much branched woody perennial herb with subsessile elliptic mucronate leaves and pinnatisect interpetiolar spines; flowers solitary axillary with spiny-margined calyx and blue corolla; capsule ellipsoid, 4-seeded.

A common herb of *Acacia* savannah especially in the Rift Valley. Like many of the genus, this is night-flowering and the corollas drop around mid-day. NAR, BAR, RV, MAG, NAN, MAC, KAJ.

Strid 3647; Napper 1223.

7. Barleria grandicalyx *Lindau* (see p. 592)

Erect or straggling, much branched herb with simple inter-petiolar spines and subsessile or shortly petiolate ovate mucronate leaves; outer calyx segments oblong-ovate, densely pilose with toothed margins; corolla white or blue with a long cylindric tube, capsule ellipsoid, 4-seeded.

In dry savannah, wooded grassland, or *Combretum-Acacia* bushland. HA, KIT, MUM, KIS, NAR, MAG, MAC, KAJ.

Kabuye 37; Kokwaro 1659.

8. Barleria diffusa (*Oliv.*) *Lindau*

Small woody perennial herb with subsessile or shortly petiolate oblong leaves with strigose medifixed hairs; calyx segments narrowly lanceolate, with medifixed hairs and minute glands; corolla pinkish-mauve, pale lilac or almost white; capsule conspicuously beaked.

In dry grassland and savannah. NAR, BAR, EMB, MAC.

Agnew 5410; Leippert 5181.

9. Barleria *sp.* G.

Much branched woody perennial herb 20–80 cm high with petiolate, elliptic, coarsely strigose glandular pubescent leaves and axillary cymes of large mauve flowers; bract, bracteoles and calyx linear, densely pubescent; corolla lilac with purple markings in the throat; capsule beaked, 2-seeded.

In *Acacia-Commiphora* or *Cordia* thicket grassland community, usually in shade of trees and shrubs, up to 4000 ft. MAG.

Verdcourt 1829; Harmsen 6465.

10. Barleria *sp.* K.

Much branched decumbent shrubby herb with petiolate lanceolate-elliptic obtuse pubescent leaves and axillary cymes of large, pale blue, pale lilac, or white flowers with purple marks in the throat; calyx lobes linear acute with the lower one 2-toothed or notched and conspicuously 2-veined; capsule beaked, 2-seeded.

Scrambling among rocks on granite outcrops in dry *Acacia* thicket-grassland community, up to 5500 ft. MAG, KAJ.

Glover *et al.* 2911; 3883; 4022.

11. Barleria volkensii *Lindau*

Creeping, erect, or semiscandent herbs with ovate-elliptic petiolate leaves and flowers in terminal leafy inflorescences or 1–3 axillary; outer calyx segments large, broadly elliptic, toothed; corolla large, blue; capsule ellipsoid, apiculate.

In thicket and montane forest. EMB, MAC.

Bally 1486.

12. Barleria micrantha *C. B. Cl.*

Erect or semiscandent herb with shortly petiolate rather small elliptic obtuse leaves; flowers 1–3 in the leaf axils, not in terminal heads; outer calyx segments broadly elliptic with toothed margins; inner segments linear, spreading; corolla variable in size, pale blue or lavender, rarely white; capsule ellipsoid, light brown, 2-seeded.

In woodland or thicket, rarely in grassland. BAR, NAR, RV, NAN, EMB, MAC.

Bally 8261; Agnew 10772.

A form with exceptionally large flowers occurs in the forests and woodland of the Nairobi and eastern upland areas. HA, EMB, NBI.

Verdcourt 487; Agnew and Musumba 5444.

13. Barleria ventricosa *Nees* (see p. 592)

Scandent herb with subsessile elliptic subacute leaves attenuate below; flowers in the axils of the upper leaves congested into a head but axillary cymes usually present also; outer calyx segments elliptic, entire, yellow-haired; corolla medium to large, blue; capsule ellipsoid, 2-seeded.

In forest undergrowth. HE, HT, HM, HA, HK, KIT, MUM, NAR, RV, NAN, EMB, MAC, KAJ.

Verdcourt 2149; Lugard 130.

14. Barleria submollis *Lindau*

Erect or semiprostrate herb sometimes rooting at the nodes, with broadly-ovate petiolate obtuse leaves rounded at the base; flowers in axillary clusters of 1–3, shortly pedicellate, bracts ovate-elliptic, toothed, corolla blue, large; capsule 2-seeded.

In savannah and bushland. BAR, RV, MAG, MAC.

Lind and Agnew 5651; Verdcourt 1788.

15. CRABBEA *Harvey*

Small perennial herbs often almost stemless having a compact tuft of slightly toothed leaves; flowers in dense round bracteate subsessile or pedunculate axillary heads; bracts leafy, more or less spiny-margined; calyx-segments 5, more or less unequal; corolla small with a slightly funnel-shaped tube and subequally 5-lobed limb; stamens 4, subsimilar; anthers 2-celled, muticous, usually one slightly lower and often smaller than the other; stigma 1, the other reduced to a minute ledge; capsule small, narrowly oblong, 8–4-seeded with conspicuous retinacula; seeds discoid covered with fine hygroscopic hairs.

Crabbea velutina *S. Moore* (see p. 595)

Low tufted herb with shortly petiolate oblong-elliptic leaves; flowers white to pale lilac with a yellow patch on lower lip, opening in the early evening and dying the following morning.

Bush and grassland. KIS, BAR, RV, MAC, NBI, KAJ.

Napper 1674; Kokwaro 1804.

16. NEURACANTHUS *Nees*

Perennial herbs or small shrubs with elliptic to ovate entire leaves; flowers in dense sessile one-sided spikes, often several together in a leaf axil; bracts ovate or linear, sometimes spinous; bracteoles absent; calyx deeply 2-partite, the upper segment 3-lobed, the lower segment 2-lobed or both segments almost entire; corolla funnel-shaped, the lip shallowly 4-lobed, the lobes subacute triangular with the upper one shortly 2-fid; stamens 4, the lower pair with 2-celled anthers, the upper pair with 1-celled anthers, the anther cells oblong, muticous; stigma lobe solitary, oblong; capsule ovoid, compressed, beaked with 2 or 4 discoid seeds covered with tufts of hygroscopic hairs.

1   Bracts acuminate 9–12 mm long; leaves glabrous beneath, or shortly hispid on the veins   1. *N.* sp. *A*
     Bracts subacute or shortly acuminate 10–16 mm long; leaves white-tomentose beneath   2. *N.* sp. *C*

1. Neuracanthus *sp.* A.

Woody much branched perennial with subsessile broadly elliptic almost glabrous leaves; spikes axillary, 8–10 mm wide with scarious, long acuminate bracts enlarging in fruit and white square-limbed flowers.

Bushland and scattered-tree grassland; 3000–5000 ft. NAR.

Glover *et al.* 3454.

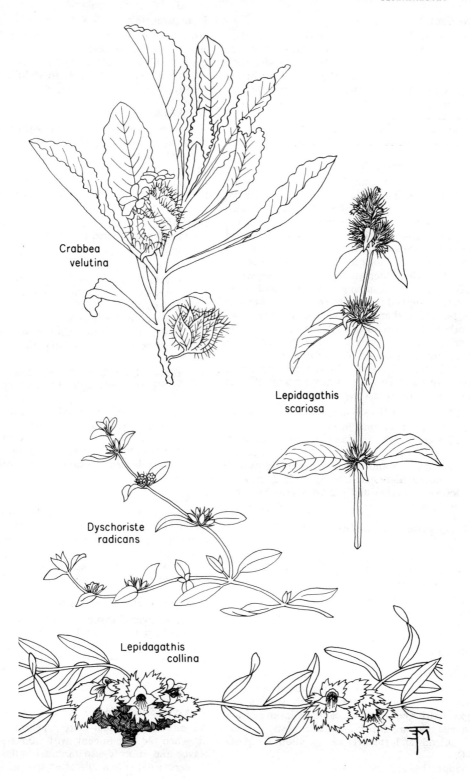

Crabbea
velutina

Lepidagathis
scariosa

Dyschoriste
radicans

Lepidagathis
collina

2. Neuracanthus *sp.* C.

Much branched small shrub with shortly petiolate broadly elliptic leaves, white-tomentose beneath, and subovoid spikes up to 16 mm wide, with leathery, acute or very shortly acuminate bracts enlarging in fruit and white or pale mauve square-limbed flowers.

Grassland, *Acacia* savannah, and on rocky outcrops, 2000–5000 ft. MAG, KAJ.

Polhill and Greenway 444; Lind 5713.

17. LEPIDAGATHIS *Willd.*

Perennial herbs or small shrubs with much branched stems and entire elliptic or linear leaves; flowers in short or long uniseriate cymes, solitary or several together and sometimes so congested as to make dense ovoid often tomentose and spinescent heads; bracts foliaceous; bracteoles absent; calyx of 5 unequal sepals, the upper one larger than the others and often subspinescent; corolla with a campanulate tube and con-spicuously 2-lipped limb; stamens 4, the lower pair with 2-celled anthers, one cell a little lower than the other, acute or mucronate below, the upper pair with 2-celled anthers (section *Lepidagathis*) or 1-celled anthers (section *Neuracanthopsis*); stigma lobe solitary, oblong or elliptic; capsule small, ellipsoid to ovoid with 2 or 4 densely hairy discoid seeds, hairs more or less hygroscopic.

1 Flowers pale blue-mauve in one-sided lateral spikes or terminal heads   2
  Flowers yellow in dense rounded lateral or basal heads   1. *L. collina*
2 Flowers in round, terminal heads; leaves with some stellate hairs   2. *L. scariosa*
  Flowers in one-sided axillary spikes; hairs not stellate   3. *L. scabra*

1. Lepidagathis collina (*Endl.*) Milne-Redh. (see p. 595)

Perennial herb with dense heads at the base of the stems with yellow flowers often spotted with brown or purple, occasionally producing sessile lateral inflorescences also; leaves oblong to oblong-elliptic, subsessile.

Savannah herb growing up quickly after burning, 5000–6500 ft. KIT.

Bogdan 548.

2. Lepidagathis scariosa *Nees* (see p. 595)

Much branched shrubby herb with elliptic-ovate leaves densely hairy beneath with stellate and simple hairs and terminal capitate inflorescences with pale lilac or whitish 2-lipped flowers.

Bushland and thicket, up to 4000 ft. MAG, MAC.

Napper 1882; Agnew 10846.

3. Lepidagathis scabra *S. Moore*

Prostrate or erect much branched herb with elliptic subsessile leaves and axillary one-sided spikes of blue or whitish flowers.

Thicket and bushland, up to 4000 ft. MAC.

Napper 1545.

18. ASYSTASIA *Blume*

Herbs or weak shrubs with entire leaves and terminal or rarely axillary spikes or racemes of flowers; bracts and bracteoles large or small; calyx of 5 nearly free, minutely glandular segments; corolla ± funnel-shaped, with a wrinkled palate at the mouth of the tube, and 5 nearly equal lobes; stamens 4, all 2-celled, with an often minute projection at base; capsule with 4 seeds; seeds rough and ornamented but glabrous.

1 Bracts and bracteoles wider than the sepals; flowers sessile   2
  Bracts and bracteoles narrower than the sepals; flowers shortly pedicellate   4
2 Leaves linear   1. *A. sp. A*
  Leaves broader than linear   3
3 Bracts ovate, mostly obtuse, shorter than the calyx; corolla over 2 cm long
                                        2. *A. charmian*
  Bracts lanceolate, acute; longer than the calyx; corolla under 14 mm long
                                        3. *A. schimperi*
4 Leaves ovate, rounded or cordate at base; sepals less than 4·5 mm long
                                        4. *A. gangetica*
  Leaves oblong, narrowed to the very short petiole; sepals 5 mm or more long
                                        5. *A. laticapsula*

1. Asystasia *sp.* A.

A trailing herb or weak shrub with glabrous, ridged stems and linear, scabrid leaves; inflorescence a terminal dense spike of yellow-green flowers.

An uncommon plant of the Rift Valley grass-land between Kedong and Olorgesailie. RV, MAG.

Agnew 5416; Verdcourt 1457.

2. Asystasia charmian *S. Moore*

An erect weak shrub or herb from a woody rootstock, with scabrid 4-angled stems and ovate-lanceolate leaves; flowers white with mauve or purple spots in loose terminal spikes.

Uncommon, found in dry bushland. MAC.

Blencowe 1; Verdcourt 849.

3. Asystasia schimperi *T. Anders.* (see p. 597)

An pubescent annual (rarely perennating), erect or, when old, decumbent, with obovate to elliptic leaves and short dense terminal spikes of white flowers; palate of corolla often spotted with green.

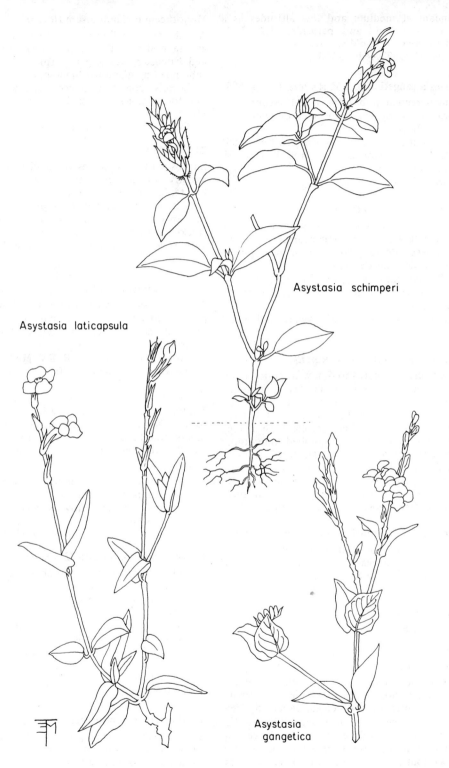

Asystasia schimperi

Asystasia laticapsula

Asystasia
gangetica

Abundant at medium and low altitudes as a weed of arable land and pathsides. HA, KIT, MUM, KIS, BAR, RV, EMB, MAC, NBI.
Nattrass 1301; Tweedie 3270.

4. Asystasia gangetica (*L.*) *T. Anders.* (see p. 597)
A trailing perennial, pubescent or glabrescent, with ovate leaves and one-sided racemes of white and pale purple flowers.
Common at the coast and in western Kenya but rare elsewhere, in secondary grassland. KIT, MUM, KIS, RV, EMB.
Kokwaro 95; Tweedie 66/322.

5. Asystasia laticapsula *C. B. Cl.* (see p. 597)
A pubescent to tomentose perennial from a woody rootstock with ascending stems bearing subsessile, oblong leaves; flowers white with pale purple markings, in very loose racemes.
Locally common in grassland, especially in black cotton soil in Central Province. HA, MAG, EMB, MAC, NBI, KAJ.
Verdcourt and Polhill 3163; Agnew and Hanid 7517.

19. PSEUDERANTHEMUM *Randlk.*
Shrubs or perennial herbs to 4 m with entire leaves having cystoliths; flowers in axillary or terminal pedunculate spike-like panicles; bracts small, bracteoles absent; calyx small, 5-lobed to the base, with linear-lanceolate lobes; corolla with a long cylindric tube and subequally 5-lobed limb; upper stamens represented by staminodes; fertile stamens 2, with 2 oblong muticous or minutely mucronate cells; ovary glabrous with 2 ovules in each cell; stigmas 2, linear; capsule stalked, 4-seeded; seeds discoid, one face rugose, the other reticulate.

Pseuderanthemum ludovicianum (*Buettn.*) *Lindau*
Scandent woody herb with oblanceolate, shortly petiolate acuminate leaves and terminal spikes of white or pale lilac flowers; corolla tube long and narrow, limb irregularly 5-lobed, spotted with purple.
Forests. MUM.
Battiscombe in FD K1210.

20. MONOTHECIUM *Hochst.*
Shrubs or herbs with entire leaves and numerous flowers at each node of dense terminal spikes; bracts erect, enclosing the bracteoles and sepals; bracteoles similar to the sepals; sepals 5, free; corolla with a long tube and strongly 2-lipped, the upper lip linear, bifid at apex, the lower lip without a palate at base; stamens 2, each with 1 anther without a tail; capsule with 4 rugose seeds.

Monothecium glandulosum *Hochst.*
A pubescent trailing herb or weak shrub, rooting at the nodes, with petiolate ovate-elliptic leaves and ± dense spikes of pale purple to mauve flowers subtended by glandular bracteoles.
Locally common in evergreen woodland and low forest edges, especially where disturbed. HT, MUM, NAR.
Tweedie 3385; Hume 116.

21. RUTTYA *Harvey*
Shrubs with entire leaves and pedicellate flowers in axillary or terminal short cymes; bracts and bracteoles minute; calyx with 5, ± free lanceolate sepals; corolla 2-lipped, the upper erect, 2-lobed, the lower sharply deflexed from a glossy black, thickened throat, 3-lobed; stamens 2, each with 1 anther, without a tail; capsule 4-seeded; seeds ± smooth.

Ruttya fruticosa *Lindau*
An erect shrub with ovate to obovate-elliptic glabrescent leaves and small lateral cymes of black and red, rarely black and yellow flowers; sepals glabrous.
Local, in bushland. NAR, RV, MAC, KAJ.
Agnew 10077; Bally 8870.

22. RHINACANTHUS *Nees*
Trailing or erect perennial herbs or shrubs similar to 26. *Justicia* but with constantly small, linear bracts and bracteoles, a very narrow cylindrical corolla tube and without soft appendages to the anthers.

1   Stems erect or ascending; flowers white in
        pedunculate panicles   1. *R. nasutus*
     Stems creeping; flowers mauve in axillary
        clusters   2. *R. ndorensis*

1. Rhinacanthus nasutus (*L.*) *Kurz*
A trailing or erect, sparsely pubescent woody herb with narrow elliptic leaves and a terminal, glandular-hairy, diffuse panicle of pure white flowers.
This species does not look like any other member of the family with its loose leafless and apparently bractless panicle. It is locally common in dry sandy bushland especially on river banks. MAC, KAJ.
Napper 1255.

2. Rhinacanthus ndorensis *Schweinf.*
A glabrous low creeping wiry herb from a woody rootstock with obovate to orbicular leaves and sessile mauve or purple flowers.

This plant is easily mistaken for *Dyschoriste radicans*; rare, in grassland in the Nanyuki region. NAN.

Moreau 34.

23. ECBOLIUM *Kurz*

Shrubs with entire leaves and terminal and axillary cone-like spikes; bracts large, green, often imbricate; bracteoles minute; calyx of 5 ± free lanceolate lobes; corolla 2-lipped but often appearing 4-lobed, the upper lip entire, the lower lip often deeply 3-lobed; stamens 2, each with 2 elliptic anthers divergent at base but equal in height, not tailed; capsule with 2-seeds; seeds smooth, often hairy.

1 Stems with spreading pubescence which is more dense between the leaf bases than under the leaf bases; spikes markedly tapering towards the tip; bracts in fruit curved around the spike, each hardly overlapping the petiole of the subsequent one above it   1. *E. hamatum*
   Stems uniformly densely or sparsely minutely crisped-pubescent; spikes hardly tapering at apex; bracts in fruit flat, each overlapping the subsequent one above it
                     2. *E. revolutum*

1. Ecbolium hamatum (*Klotzsch*) C. B. Cl.

A small shrub with ovate to elliptic, acute or rounded glabrescent leaves and spikes to 12 cm long of blue (rarely white) flowers; bracts with spreading and glandular hairs.

Locally common in dry sandy bushland. BAR, MAC, KAJ.

Napper 1241; Agnew, Kibe, and Mathenge 10571.

2. Ecbolium revolutum (*Lindau*) C. B. Cl.

Similar to *E. hamatum* but with minute pubescence (glabrescent on the leaves) on all parts and shorter (up to 8 cm long) spikes.

Locally common on fine soils in dry bushland, to the west of the area of *E. hamatum*, but the two species grow together in Tsavo National Park East. MAG, MAC, KAJ.

Milne-Redhead and Taylor 7143; Harmsen 6472.

24. ISOGLOSSA *Oerst.*

Herbs with entire leaves and terminal panicles or spikes of pale flowers; bracts small or large; bracteoles present, similar to the sepals; corolla 2-lipped, often with a prominent wrinkled palate; stamens two, each with two divergent anthers,

without tails; capsule with two papillate seeds in each cell.

1 Inflorescence a diffuse panicle with the second order (and often third order) branches well-developed; flowers white   2
   Inflorescence a spike-like raceme, with sessile flower glomerules or only first order branches shortly developed; flowers seldom white, often with mauve spots, or pale purple   3
2 Calyx glandular-hairy; corolla pubescent
                     2. *I. laxa*
   Calyx glabrous; corolla glabrous   1. *I. lactea*
3 Bracts of flower whorls linear-lanceolate, less than 5 mm long   3. *I. oerstediana*
   Bracts of flower whorls ovate, over 7 mm long   4
4 Corolla white, often with pink spots, with a broad, ridged and grooved palate on the lower lip   5. *I. substrobilina*
   Corolla pink, rarely white, without a ridged and grooved palate on the lower lip
                   4. *I. gregorii*

1. Isoglossa lactea *Lindau*

A trailing glabrous herb with ascending stems bearing petiolate, ovate-elliptic, acuminate leaves and terminal panicles of pure white flowers; corolla funnel-shaped, broad.

Local, in the Aberdares montane rain forest at Uplands. HA.

Agnew 8310; Dale 1861.

2. Isoglossa laxa *Oliv.* (see p. 600)

Similar to *L. lactea* but with ovate pubescent leaves, often subsessile below the inflorescence which is glandular-hairy.

Locally common in dry evergreen woodland, and lowland forest. HT, HA, MUM, RV, MAC, NBI, KAJ.

Verdcourt and Newbould 2276; Agnew 10769.

3. Isoglossa oerstediana *Lindau* (see p. 600)

A trailing pubescent herb with petiolate ovate-elliptic leaves which are subsessile below the inflorescence; inflorescence simple or more usually branched, of spike-like racemes of white, pink-spotted flowers.

Locally common in montane rain forest undergrowth. HE, HT, HM, MUM, MAC.

Tweedie 66/165; Lucas 96.

4. Isoglossa gregorii (*S. Moore*) *Lindau* (see p. 608)

Similar in habit to *I. oerstediana,* this species differs in its inflorescence and more delicate, pink flowers.

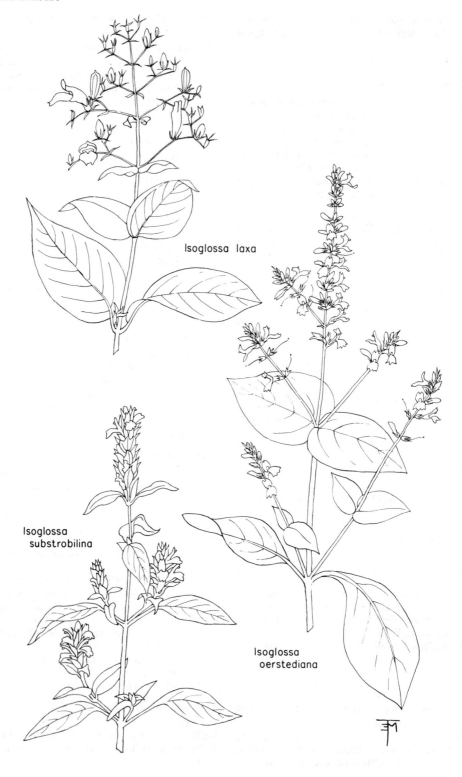

Isoglossa laxa

Isoglossa
substrobilina

Isoglossa
oerstediana

Locally common in the higher montane forest and bamboo zone. HE, HC, HT, HM, HA, HK, KAJ.

Part II Botany 37; Verdcourt 3269.

5. Isoglossa substrobilina *C. B. Cl.* (see p. 600)

A trailing pubescent herb with ascending stems bearing ovate-elliptic acuminate leaves and short terminal and lateral spike-like racemes of glandular-hairy flowers; corolla broader than in *I. gregorii*, spotted-pink within.

Rare, in montane rain forest and suspected of periodic mass-flowering. HE, HC, HT, HM, HA, MUM.

Tweedie 68/177; Verdcourt 1840.

25. ADHATODA *Nees*

Similar to *Justicia* but shrubs and with the lower anther sac apiculate and not tailed with a soft white appendage as in that genus.

Adhatoda englerana *C. B. Cl.*

An erect, much-branched, pubescent shrub with large, petiolate, elliptic leaves and groups of wide-cylindrical terminal and subterminal spikes; bracts ovate or rhomboid; corolla similar in shape to a *Monechma* but greenish-white.

Rare plant found in rich sandy bushland and only recorded from Kibwezi in our area. It is also found nearer the coast. MAC.

Bally 8038.

26. JUSTICIA *L.*

Herbs or shrubs with entire leaves and flowers in axillary or terminal clusters; bracts and bracteoles present, sometimes enlarged; sepals 4–5, shortly fused at base, linear to lanceolate; corolla 2-lipped, pubescent on the outside with a 2-lobed posterior hood-like lip which covers the stamens, and a 3-lobed spreading anterior lip; anterior part of mouth of corolla tube wrinkled and grooved; stamens 2, each with 2 anther cells, one above the other and the lowest one tailed; capsule with 2 seeds, one above the other, in each cell; seeds with a raised reticulate, or roughly ornamented surface.

1 Flowers in a single row on one-sided axillary leafless spikes   2
  Flowers 1 or more at each node, axillary to foliage leaves, or in terminal spikes or racemes   7
2 Stems entirely glabrous except for a small fringe of hairs at the nodes and scabrid leaf-margins; peduncles sharply reflexed in fruit   1. *J. anselliana*
  Stems with two lines of pubescence on each

internode; peduncles rarely reflexed in fruit   3
3 Leaves narrowly linear with white hairs along the margin when young   2. *J.* sp. *A*
  Leaves broader and usually lacking the marginal hairs   4
4 Some leaves over 4 cm long, elliptic-lanceolate; sepals minutely pubescent on margins and back   3. *J.* sp. *C*
  Leaves less than 4 cm long, oblong to elliptic; sepals glabrous   5
5 Largest sepal over 6 mm long
                                  4. *J. uncinulata*
  Largest sepal under 5·5 mm long   6
6 Capsule glabrous or sparsely bristly on its upper half only   5. *J. exigua*
  Capsule finely pubescent all over
                                  6. *J. matammensis*
7 Flowers sessile in terminal, crowded spikes, with bracts not leaf-like   8
  Flowers solitary or in inflorescences in the axils of leaf-like bracts, or in loose pedunculate panicles   15
8 Flowers white or yellow   9
  Flowers blue, pink, purple or mauve, not white or yellow   13
9 Flowers 2 at each node of the inflorescence, each subtended by one bract and one bracteole   10
  Flowers more than 2 at each node of the inflorescence, subtended by one bract and numerous bracteoles   10. *J. flava*
10 Bracts with a narrow or yellow margin   11
   Bracts with a uniformly green margin   12
11 Leaves rounded at apex, subsessile; bracts with more green than pale yellow or white areas   8. *J. betonicoides*
   Leaves acute or acuminate at apex, petiolate or subsessile; bracts with more white than green areas   7. *J. betonica*
12 Bracts less than 9 mm long, with prominent lateral nerves   9. *J. ruwenzoriensis*
   Bracts more than 12 mm long, with three ± parallel nerves from the base and no lateral nerves   (Genus 27) *Monechma subsessilis*
13 Corolla blue   11. *J. caerulea*
   Corolla pink to purple   14
14 Bracts and bracteoles linear-lanceolate, all similar   12. *J. nyassana*
   Bracts ovate to oblong-ovate
                    (Genus 27) *Monechma debile*
15 Flowers sessile axillary, solitary or in clusters   19
   Flowers in panicles or pedunculate, axillary cymes   16
16 Flowers in a loose terminal and axillary panicle   13. *J. extensa*
   Flowers in axillary cymes   17

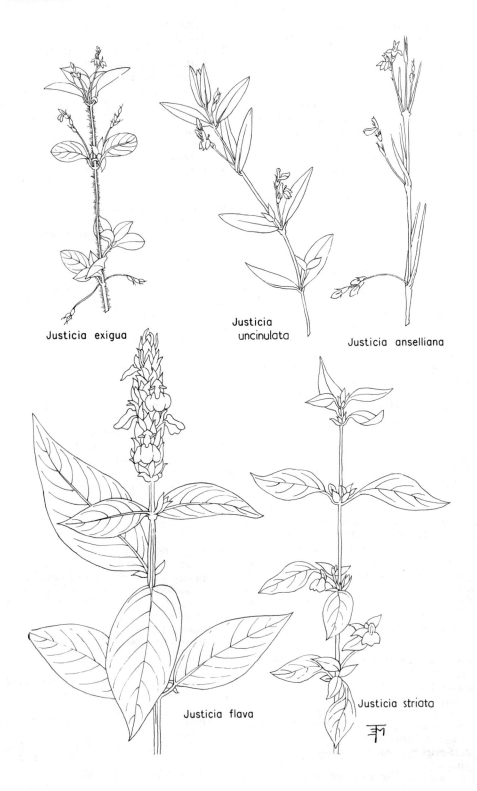

Justicia exigua

Justicia
uncinulata

Justicia anselliana

Justicia flava

Justicia striata

17 Leaves acute at apex; peduncles with 3 or
    more long slender branches at apex
                                    14. *J. glabra*
    Leaves rounded or obtuse at apex; peduncle
    unbranched, bearing a cluster of subsessile
    flowers at apex   **18**
18 Leaves rounded at base; sepals linear-lanceo-
    late, glandular-pubescent   15. *J.* sp. *D*
    At least some leaves cordate at base; sepals
    lanceolate-ovate, glabrous   16. *J. cordata*
19 Flowers yellow; plant shrubby   17. *J. odora*
    Flowers purple, pink or white; plants mostly
    herbaceous   **20**
20 Leaves subtending the flowers oblong-linear
    less than 4 mm wide   **21**
    All leaves elliptic-ovate to lanceolate, rarely
    broadly oblong, never linear, over 5 mm
    wide   **22**
21 Stems white-pubescent; sepal lobes 2-3 mm
    long   18. *J. elliotii*
    Stems glabrescent; sepal lobes over 4 mm
    long   19. *J. leikipiensis*
22 Corolla over 17·5 mm long   **23**
    Corolla up to 15 mm long   **24**
23 Flowers at anthesis usually at the terminal
    node as well as below; upper leaves oblong;
    lower lip of corolla held at 45° to the tube
                                    20. *J. pinguior*
    Flowers at anthesis never at the terminal
    node, always at lower nodes; upper leaves
    ovate to elliptic; lower lip of corolla held
    at nearly 90° to the tube   21. *J.* sp. *E*
24 Sepals over 0·75 mm wide, broad lanceolate
    to ovate; flowers white with red streaks on
    palate   22. *J. striata*
    Sepals less than 0·5 mm wide; flowers white,
    pink or purple   **25**
25 Plant annual   23. *J. heterocarpa*
    Plant perennial   **26**
26 Underside of leaves with long, soft hairs
    which have expanded bases
                                  25. *J. keniensis*
    Underside of leaves with stiff erect hairs
    without expanded bases
                              24. *J. diclipteroides*
    Species 1-6 inclusive belong to section
Anselliana, which all have white corollas faintly
streaked with pale pink on the throat. The colour
of these has not been given in each species
description.

1. Justicia anselliana (*Nees*) *T. Anders.* (see
p. 602)
An almost glabrous perennial herb from a rhizome,
with ascending stems and linear to narrowly
elliptic leaves; flowers 2-5 on a spike.

Common in marshy grasslands in western
Kenya. HE, HT, KIT, MUM, KIS.
    Gosnell 691; Agnew, Kibe, and Mathenge
10589.

2. Justicia *sp.* **A.**
A perennial herb often tufted from a woody
rootstock, with ascending stems often rooting at
the nodes; leaves linear; flowers seldom more than
3 to the spike; sepals less than 5 mm long.
    Locally common in rocky grassland in the
southern end of the Rift Valley. RV, NAR, KAJ.
    Bogdan 1026; Agnew 5605.

3. Justicia *sp.* **C.**
A trailing herb with ascending stems and oblanceolate to linear leaves.
    Rare, and only recorded from sandy bushland
in the Kajiado area. KAJ.

4. Justicia uncinulata *Oliv.* (see p. 602)
A herb from a woody rootstock, with trailing
stems and elliptic to almost orbicular leaves.
    This species, as defined here, is very variable in
its leaf size and shape and its pubescence. Most
forms have elliptic leaves and some long spreading
stem-hairs outside the two lines of pubescence. It
is found in grassland mainly on black cotton soil.
HE, HC, HT, HM, KIT, NAR, RV, NAN, MAC,
NBI, KAJ.
    Agnew 9902; Polhill and Paulo 1020; Lugard
206; Agnew, Kibe, and Mathenge 10251.

5. Justica exigua *S. Moore* (see p. 602)
A creeping annual or perennial, rarely erect, with
pubescent to spreading-hairy stems, elliptic to
obovate leaves and usually 4-flowered spikes.
    Common in damper grassland below 7000 ft,
especially in lawns. This species is here separated
from the next (*J. matammensis*) by an artificial
character which leaves some erect, hairy annual
plants in *J. exigua*; experimental work is required
here. HE, HC, HT, KIT, MUM, KIS, NAR, RV,
MAC, NBI.
    Hanid and Kiniaruh 659; Verdcourt 1523.

6. Justicia matammensis *Oliv.*
A hairy annual with ascending or erect stems and
elliptic to oblanceolate leaves; spikes usually 4-
flowered.
    Locally common in sandy soils in disturbed
bushland. EMB, MAC, KAJ.
    Kirrika 137; Lind and Agnew 5652.

7. Justicia betonica *L.* (see p. 606)
A weakly erect or trailing glabrous to pubescent
herb from a woody rootstock; leaves elliptic, often

with undulate margins; flowers white with red guide-lines.

A variable and widespread plant. Forms from wet forest have large pubescent leaves and pale green bracts while those from riversides in drier areas have conspicuously white and green bracts, and smaller, glabrous or pubescent leaves. HE, HT, HM, KIT, MUM, NAR, BAR, MAC, NBI, KAJ.
Strid 3358; Tweedie 2958.

8. Justicia betonicoides *C. B. Cl.*

Similar to *J. betonica* except for the smaller bracts and keyed characters, this species can also be pubescent or glabrous.
Rare, in dry bushland. BAR.
Tweedie 67/35.

9. Justicia ruwenzoriensis *C. B. Cl.*

A pubescent trailing perennial herb with ovate to suborbicular, subsessile leaves and short terminal spikes of whitish flowers; bracts slightly mottled with paler green.
Rare, found in the Narok area in rocky grassland. NAR.
Fauna Research Unit 324.

10. Justicia flava *Vahl* (see p. 602)

A trailing or erect, pubescent woody herb, with ovate acute leaves and crowded terminal spikes of yellow flowers subtended by oblong to lanceolate bracts.
Common in a variety of open habitats, this species appears to have a very wide ecological range. HE, HC, HT, KIT, MUM, KIS, NAR, RV, MAG, MAC, NBI, KAJ.
Williams 300; Lind, Agnew, and Kettle 5880.

11. Justicia caerulea *Forsk.* (see p. 606)

An erect, pubescent woody herb with lanceolate to ovate leaves which continue into the bases of the loose weak terminal spikes of blue flowers; bracts and bracteoles linear.
Locally common in disturbed dry country. KIS, BAR, MAG, NAN, EMB, MAC, KAJ.
Hanid and Kiniaruh 509; Makin 88.

12. Justicia nyassana *Lindau*

A pubescent trailing herb with ascending branches bearing ovate petiolate leaves and dense terminal spikes of mauve or purple flowers.
Locally common in damp places within dry forest. HC, HM, HA, HN, EMB, MAC.
Glover, Gwynne, and Samuel 2129; Hanid and Kiniaruh 1048.

13. Justicia extensa *T. Anders.*

An erect, much-branched glabrescent shrub, with petiolate ovate leaves and loose terminal or axillary panicles of pedunculate cymes; flowers greenish-cream or white.
Rare, found in warm wet forest and only recorded from Kakamega. MUM.
Drummond and Hemsley 4784.

14. Justicia glabra *Roxb.*

A loose glabrescent to pubescent spreading herb or weak shrub, with petiolate ovate leaves and pedunculate axillary cymes of white or yellowish flowers.
Uncommon, found in riverine forest in hot dry country. MUM.
Jack 146.

15. Justicia *sp.* D.

An erect pubescent shrub, white-hairy on the stems, with ovate to oblong, rounded leaves and shortly peduncled axillary groups of cymes; flowers mauve to off-white.
Uncommon, found in dry country in the north of our area. BAR, NAN.
Adamson 610.

16. Justicia cordata *(Nees) T. Anders.*

An erect, sparsely branched, glabrescent shrub with subsessile, usually oblong leaves with shortly clasping or cordate bases; flowers dirty white with translucent areas in the upper corolla lip.
Common in dry bushland especially in the Rift Valley. RV, MAG, MAC, KAJ.
Napier 2464; Strid 3631.

17. Justicia odora *(Forsk.) Vahl* (inc. *J. fischeri* Lindau of Check List)

An erect shrub, pubescent or glabrous, with subsessile suborbicular to oblong to obovate leaves and sessile yellow flowers in groups of 1–3 in the upper axils.
A common and very variable shrub of dry stony bushland. BAR, RV, MAG, NAN, EMB, MAC, KAJ.
Strid 2242; Lind 5379.

18. Justicia elliotii *S. Moore*

A low wiry shrub, usually densely canescent on all parts with ovate young leaves and sessile linear-oblong older ones; flowers purple, solitary, scattered.
Locally common in rocky places in medium altitude grassland. NAR, RV, NBI.
Agnew 10213; Paulo 697.

19. Justicia leikipiensis *S. Moore*

A glabrescent wiry herb with erect branches from a woody rootstock, bearing linear leaves and purple flowers in upper axils.

Rare plant found in grassland in the north of our area. HC, NAN.

Symes 522.

20. Justicia pinguior *C. B. Cl.* (see p. 606)

An erect or spreading, densely pubescent herb from a woody rootstock with ovate to oblong leaves and terminal and subterminal axillary large red/purple flowers.

A common attractive plant of wooded grassland in western Kenya. HE, HT, KIT, MUM.

Strid 2844; Leippert 5130.

21. Justicia *sp.* E.

A trailing, pubescent woody herb with spreading-hairy stems and ovate-lanceolate leaves; flowers large, numerous in upper axils, purple.

Locally common in forest edges and the lower levels of rain-forest. HT, HM, HA, NAR, MAC, KAJ.

Agnew 9385; Gower 16.

22. Justicia striata *(Kl.) Bullock* (see p.602)

A pubescent herb, with ascending stems rooting at the lower nodes, and often with ascending or spreading hairs on the upper internodes; leaves ovate with cuneate base, rarely elliptic; flowers with broad sepals and white corolla.

Common in evergreen woodland edges and in bushed grassland. HM, HA, KIT, MUM, KIS, NAR, EMB, MAC, NBI, KAJ.

Agnew and Musumba 5429; Drummond and Hemsley 1231.

23. Justicia heterocarpa *T. Anders.* (inc. *J. leptocarpa* Lindau of Check List)

An erect pubescent annual, branching from the base or simple, with ovate to elliptic leaves and pale purple flowers; fruits often heterocarpic, some indehiscent, with glochidiate spines on the wings, mixed with others, normally dehiscent.

Locally common in dry grassland. KIS, RV, MAC, KAJ.

Hanid and Kiniaruh 655; Kerfoot 3405.

24. Justicia diclipteroides *Lindau*

A sparsely pubescent trailing herb, rooting at the nodes, with ovate leaves and scattered purple to pink flowers in the upper axils; fruit sometimes heterocarpic.

A common species in evergreen forest edges in the east of our area. The common upland form around Nairobi has tightly downward curved stem-hairs, while a dry bushland form (in EMB, MAC, and KAJ) which has spreading straight mixed glandular and eglandular stem hairs, may ultimately prove to be distinct. HM, HA, NAR, NAN, EMB, MAC, NBI, KAJ.

(Upland form) Drummond and Hemsley 1244; Agnew and Musumba 5447, 8560; (dry country form) Hanid and Kiniaruh 1022; Gilbert C25.

25. Justicia keniensis *Rendle*

A trailing herb with ascending stems and a sparse pubescence of spreading hairs; leaves ovate-elliptic, rounded at apex, often subsessile; flowers often rather regular in the upper axils and apparently spicate, pink or pale mauve, rarely white or deep purple.

Locally common within and at the edge of montane rain-forest. HE, HC, HM, HA, RV, MUM.

Verdcourt 1668; Tweedie 67/177.

27. MONECHMA *Hochst.*

Similar to *Justicia* except for the seeds which are constantly only 1 in each loculus and smooth, flattened and orbicular.

1   Leaves orbicular; flowers white or yellow
                        1. *M. subsessilis*
   Leaves oblanceolate to elliptic; flowers purple
     or mauve   2. *M. debile*

1. Monechma subsessilis *(Oliv.) C. B. Cl.*

An erect pubescent herb from a woody rootstock with subsessile orbicular leaves and a terminal spike of cream flowers partially hidden by the lanceolate-ovate bracts.

An uncommon herb, found in wooded grassland. EMB, MAC.

Hanid and Kiniaruh 447; Bally 9804.

2. Monechma debile *(Forsk.) Nees* (see p. 606)

An erect pubescent often woody annual with petiolate, elliptic to oblanceolate leaves and terminal and axillary spikes of purplish flowers subtended by broad oblong-elliptic bracts.

Common in disturbed places in dry country. A perennial form can be found outside our area in dry *Commiphora* bushland, which may prove to be a distinct species. HE, HM, NAR, RV, NAN, MAC, NBI, KAJ.

Gilbert C35; Hanid and Kiniaruh 478.

28. ANISOTES *Nees*

Shrubs with entire leaves and sessile clusters of long flowers; bracts and bracteoles small, not exceeding the calyx, linear; calyx of 5 ± free small

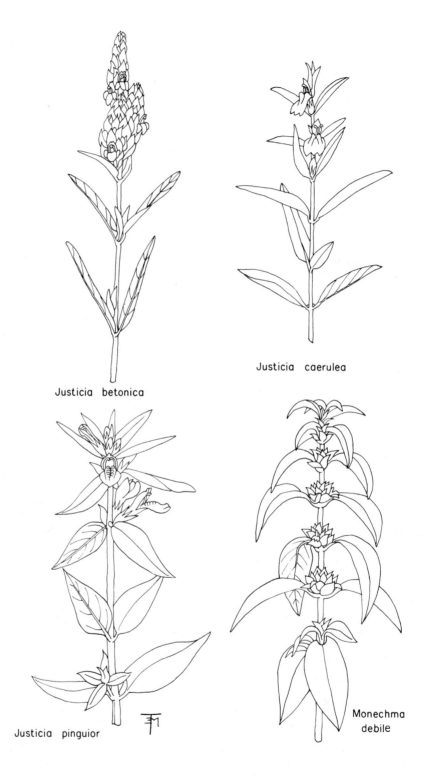

Justicia betonica

Justicia caerulea

Justicia pinguior

Monechma
debile

lobes, 3-nerved; corolla strongly 2-lipped, the upper lip continuing the corolla tube and slightly arched, the lower lip soft, often crumpled, linear, ± entire; stamens 2, each with 2 anthers one above the other, without tails; capsule 4-seeded; seeds rough.

A genus of dry country plants of which only one has been found in our area. This species differs from others in Kenya in its calyx, the others having densely pubescent sepals.

Anisotes ukambensis *Lindau*

An erect shrub with narrow lanceolate leaves and dense clusters of yellow or brownish flowers; calyx lobes lanceolate, sparsely glandular-pubescent.

Rare, found in dry bushland and only recorded from Kibwezi. MAC, KAJ.

Polhill and Paulo 465.

29. MACRORUNGIA *C. B. Cl.*

In KTS p. 17.

Macrorungia pubinervia (*Benth.*) *C. B. Cl.*

Shrub to 4 m high with axillary secund pendulous spikes of red (rarely white) flowers.

In forest undergrowth. MUM, HK.

Verdcourt 1702.

30. DICLIPTERA *Juss.*

Erect or straggling herbs with opposite leaves having cystoliths; inflorescence (in ours) of axillary bracteate umbels borne singly or 2–3 in each leaf axil; flowers usually paired between a pair of large sessile appressed bracts, the bract pair being shortly or conspicuously pedicellate; bracteoles paired linear-lanceolate; calyx subequally 5-fid; corolla with a tube widening slightly upwards and a conspicuously 2-lipped limb with a reflexed upper lip and broader spreading lower lip; stamens 2, exserted, with 2 D-shaped cells one above the other; capsule ovoid, shortly stipitate, 4-seeded, compressed, with the base of the valves separating from the elastically reflexing placenta; seeds discoid, finely papillose.

1 Bracts of the umbel narrowly linear-lanceolate 2

   Bracts of the umbel ovate to broadly oblanceolate 5

2 Flower bracts acuminate 1. *D. verticillata*
   Flower bracts subacute to rounded 3

3 Small perennial herb with erect or creeping stems; flower bracts oblanceolate, the larger 7–8 mm long, densely glandular, obscurely veined 2. *D.* sp. *A*
   Straggling perennial herbs; flower bracts elliptic, the larger 8–15 mm long, glabrous or sparingly glandular with a conspicuous

submarginal pair of lateral veins arising near the base 4

4 Bracts acute, thin, glabrous, green throughout; flowers white with purple markings, rarely pink 3. *D. laxata*
   Bracts subacute, mucronate, pubescent and glandular, usually suffused with red or purple or white in the lower half; flowers magenta with white markings 4. *D. colorata*

5 Flowers magenta or mauve with white streaks in the throat 6
   Flowers white or cream occasionally flushed with pale mauve, with dark streaks in the throat 7

6 Erect herb; bracts elliptic-ovate, glabrous, with fine perpendicular veining 5. *D. napieri*
   Straggling herb; bracts broadly oblanceolate with evenly spaced veins at an obtuse angle to the midrib 6. *D.* sp. *B*

7 Bracts oblanceolate, densely glandular, inconspicuously veined 7. *D. albicaulis*
   Bracts ovate, glandular pubescent, 3-veined from near the base 8. *D.* sp. *C*

1. Dicliptera verticillata (*Forsk.*) *C. Chr.*

Erect, much branched herb with petiolate ovate-elliptic leaves and axillary sessile umbels of small magenta flowers; flower bracts oblanceolate acute with a long rigid mucro and short spinose hairs on the prominent midrib.

In *Acacia* thicket and roadsides. MAC.

Napper 1889.

2. Dicliptera *sp.* A.

Creeping or suberect perennial herb, usually flowering before the leaves develop fully, with erect spike-like inflorescences of magenta flowers.

Short open or wooded grassland, usually appearing shortly after burning or rain; 5000–6500 ft. KIT, KIS.

Bogdan 3693; Tweedie 67/48.

3. Dicliptera laxata *C. B. Cl.* (see p. 608)

Straggling perennial herb with lanceolate petiolate leaves and subsessile axillary umbels of white or cream flowers streaked with purple.

Forest undergrowth, 5000–9000 ft. HC, HA, MUM, KIS, NBI.

Verdcourt 1642; Lind, Harris, and Agnew 5085.

4. Dicliptera colorata *C. B. Cl.* (see p. 608)

Straggling perennial herb with lanceolate petiolate leaves and subsessile axillary umbels, very rarely pedunculate, of bright magenta flowers streaked with white.

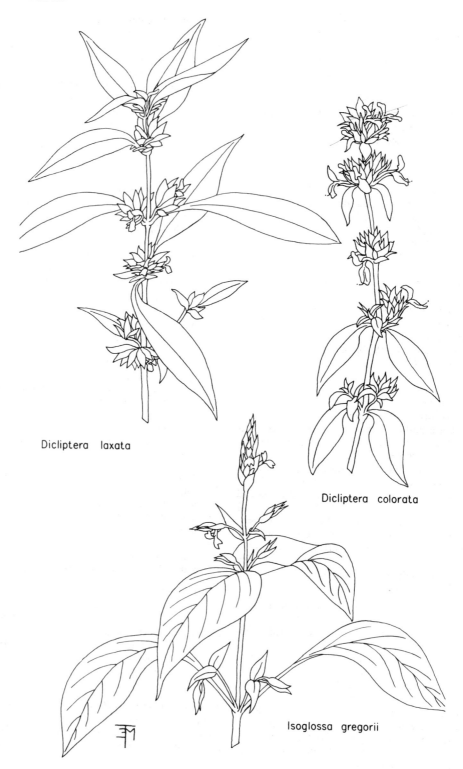

Dicliptera laxata

Dicliptera colorata

Isoglossa gregorii

Undergrowth in forest or bushland, or procumbent in grassland near forest remnants growing in the shade of taller herbage, 5000–8000 ft. HT, HM, HA, NAR, MAC.

Bally B8414; Agnew, Kibe, and Mathenge 10535.

5. Dicliptera napierae *E. A. Bruce*

Suberect herb with shortly petiolate ovate or elliptic leaves and pedunculate axillary umbels of 2–3 pedicellate bract-pairs only, with white or pale mauvish flowers.

Grassland, or grassland with shrubs or thorn trees, 5000–8000 ft. HA, NAN, EMB.

Verdcourt and Polhill 2924; Strid 2146.

6. Dicliptera *sp.* B.

Straggling herb with petiolate lanceolate or elliptic leaves and long-pedunculate axillary umbels of 3–7 subsessile bract pairs, with magenta corolla.

In forest undergrowth and in thicket, rarely in grassland, 6500–9000 ft. HT, HA.

Brodhurst-Hill 666 in CM 3615.

7. Dicliptera albicaulis (*S. Moore*) *S. Moore*

Woody, much branched herb with ovate or elliptic leaves rounded or narrowing below, and pedunculate umbels of white or cream or pale lilac flowers.

In *Acacia* woodland, often in riverine thicket in dry country up to 4500 ft. KAJ.

Bally B9869.

8. Dicliptera *sp.* C.

Erect shrub with subsessile ovate leaves and white stems like *D. albicaulis* but with sessile axillary umbels shorter than the leaves and white flowers.

In *Acacia-Commiphora* or *Acacia* bushland, 4000–5000 ft. MAC.

Greenway 8835; Agnew 7001.

31. PERISTROPHE *Nees*

Herbs with petiolate lanceolate leaves having cystoliths; flowers solitary or 2(–3) in pedunculate heads; bracts of each flower-pair subopposite, very unequal, enclosing the 4 linear bracteoles looking like a four-lobed calyx within which are 2 small calyces of linear-lanceolate segments free for three quarters of their length, usually only one perfecting a flower; calyx of 5 subequal linear-lanceolate segments free almost to the base, shorter than the bracteoles; corolla with a long curved tube, with 2 conspicuous entire lobes, the lower erect, the upper reflexed; stamens 2, anthers with 2 D-shaped muticous cells one above the other; stigma bifid; capsule stalked, oblong-lanceolate, acuminate, constricted in the middle,

4-seeded; seeds discoid, smooth or finely papillose. *Dicliptera* scarcely differs except in the capsule dehiscence.

Peristrophe bicalyculata (*Vahl*) *Nees*

Much branched herb to 2 m with shortly petiolate elliptic-lanceolate leaves and a large much-branched panicle of magenta flowers resembling those of *Dicliptera*.

Open bushland up to 4500 ft. MAG, MAC.

Lind and Agnew 5644; Verdcourt 1830.

32. HYPOESTES *R. Br.*

Erect or straggling herbs with opposite leaves having cystoliths; inflorescences of pedunculate axillary bracteate umbels, of sessile axillary clusters or whorls, or of whorled axillary spikes; flowers borne singly between a pair of bracts free almost to the base or connate for half their length; bracteoles present; calyx subequally 5-fid; corolla tube widening slightly upwards, corolla limb 2-lipped with upper lip reflexed, the lower lip broader and spreading; stamens 2, exserted with 1 D-shaped cell; capsule ellipsoid, 4-seeded; seeds discoid, smooth or finely papillose.

1 Flowers in crowded axillary spikes; bracts of the flowers connate for one third to half their length   3. *H. verticillaris*
   Flowers in axillary whorls, not spikes, bracts of the flowers free to the base or almost so
                                                              2
2 Small weak-stemmed annual herb with pedunculate clusters of usually 3 white or pale mauve flowers   2. *H. triflora*
   Stout-stemmed erect herb with sessile whorls of numerous pale mauve or white flowers
                                                1. *H. aristata*

1. Hypoestes aristata (*Vahl*) *Roem. & Schult.*
(see p. 610)

Erect perennial herb with petiolate lanceolate leaves and axillary whorls of pale mauve, pink or white flowers; calyx segments long-aristate.

Forest, thicket and near margins of relict forest patches, 4000–9000 ft. HE, HT, HM, HA, HK, RV, NAR, NAN, MAC, KAJ.

Tweedie 66/168; Agnew 10689.

2. Hypoestes triflora (*Forsk.*) *Roem. & Schult.*
(see p. 610)

Straggling annual herb very variable in size with petiolate elliptic leaves and white or pale mauve flowers in pedunculate axillary umbels or solitary; calyx segments subacute.

Forest undergrowth or on forest edges, 5500–10 000 ft. HE, HM, HA, HK, MUM, EMB.

Irwin 242; Agnew 8110.

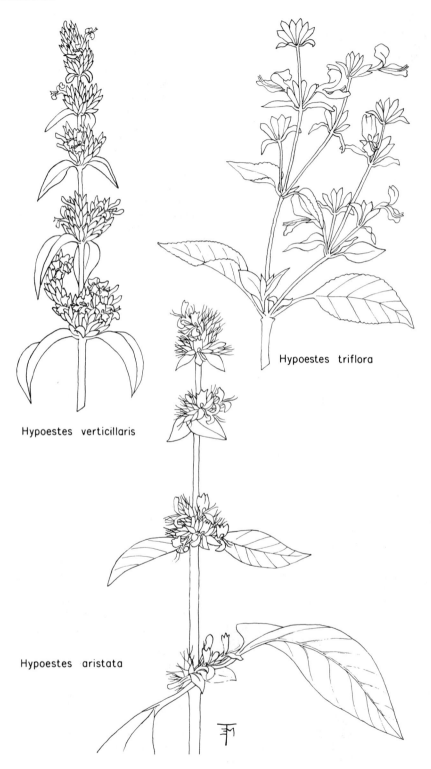

Hypoestes triflora

Hypoestes verticillaris

Hypoestes aristata

3. Hypoestes verticillaris (*Linn. f.*) *Roem. & Schult.* (see p. 610)

Straggling or erect perennial herb, very variable in habit and indumentum, with elliptic petiolate leaves and axillary, pubescent to pilose, frequently glandular inflorescence of white or very pale mauve flowers streaked with pink or purple.

Found in a very wide range of habitats and correspondingly variable in habit. In dry grassland, bushland, or forest edges or clearings, up to 9000 ft. HE, HT, HM, HA, KIT, MUM, KIS, NAR, RV, MAG, NAN, EMB, MAC, NBI, KAJ.

Agnew 10812; Lugard 78.

Several forms are recognizable in this very variable species but there is so much introgression that only var. *hildebrandtii* (Lindau) Benoist seems to be sufficiently distinct to maintain. This is a grey pubescent plant of dry bushland, rare in Upland Kenya, up to 4000 ft. MAC.

92. VERBENACEAE†

Plants of every habit, with opposite, exstipulate leaves and racemose, cymose or solitary bisexual flowers; calyx of 5 fused sepals, usually regular; corolla of 5 fused petals, forming a tube below and a spreading 4–5-lobed limb above, zygomorphic (often obscurely so) by the curved tube or the almost 2-lipped limb; stamens 4, fused to the corolla tube; ovary of 2 fused carpels, with a terminal style, each carpel dividing by 1–many false septa in fruit; fruit fleshy drupaceous, or dry schizocarpic.

A family comprised mostly of trees and shrubs which are dealt with in KTS. However, the key below is to all genera.

1 Leaves palmately compound 10. *Vitex*
  Leaves simple or pinnately lobed 2
2 Flowers solitary
          6. *Cyclocheilon eriantherum*
  Flowers in inflorescences 3
3 Flowers in compound cymose inflorescences, sometimes forming globose, head-like masses 4
  Flowers in racemes or spikes 5
4 Corolla funnel-shaped, widening gradually into the lobes; stamens and style shorter than or ± equalling corolla lobes
          8. *Premna*
  Corolla tubular with abruptly spreading, often reflexed lobes; stamens and style overtopping corolla lobes
          9. *Clerodendrum*
5 Flowers shortly pedicelled, in racemes 6
  Flowers sessile in spikes 7

† By A. D. Q. Agnew.

6 Herbs with an inflated sticky calyx around the dry fruit 2. *Priva*
  Trees or shrubs with an obscure calyx at the base of the fleshy fruit
          11. *Duranta repens*
7 Corolla white or cream 8
  Corolla coloured violet, purple or even yellow and orange but not white or cream 10
8 Spike elongating in fruit; bracts much smaller than the calyx
          7. *Chascanum hildebrandtii*
  Spike dense, hardly elongating in fruit; bracts much larger than fruiting calyx 9
9 Erect herbs or shrubs 5. *Lippia*
  Creeping herbs, rooting at the nodes
          4. *Phyla nodiflora*
10 Erect shrubs; fruits fleshy 3. *Lantana*
  Annual or perennial herbs; fruits dry
          1. *Verbenu*

1. VERBENA *L*

Annual to perennial herbs or shrubs with simple or divided leaves and sessile flowers in terminal spikes; calyx tubular, 5-toothed; corolla tube straight or curved, ± 2-lipped, with 5 lobes; stamens 4, included within the tube; ovary 4-celled with 1 ovule in each cell; fruit of 4 1-seeded schizocarps.

1 Leaves simple; spikes in corymbs
          1. *V. bonariensis*
  Leaves lobed; spikes solitary or paniculate 2
2 Spikes in panicles; calyx 2–2·5 mm long
          2. *V. officinalis*
  Spikes solitary; calyx 7–9 mm long
          3. *V. tenera*

1. Verbena bonariensis *L.*

An erect, often robust, pubescent annual with sessile, oblong, serrate leaves and large terminal corymbs of short spikelets; flowers violet.

A common introduced weed in Upland Kenya. HT, HA, RV, NBI.

Mathenge 336; Verdcourt 1006.

2. Verbena officinalis *L.* (see p. 612)

An erect, branching, pubescent annual with pinnately or ternately lobed subsessile leaves and long thin spikes of pale mauve flowers.

Locally common in disturbed ground, this species is also introduced. HC, HA, HA, KIT, RV.

Agnew 9173; Napier 1853.

3. Verbena tenera *Spreng*

A prostrate annual or short-lived perennial bearing much-dissected leaves with linear segments and solitary, purple-flowered spikes on ascending stems.

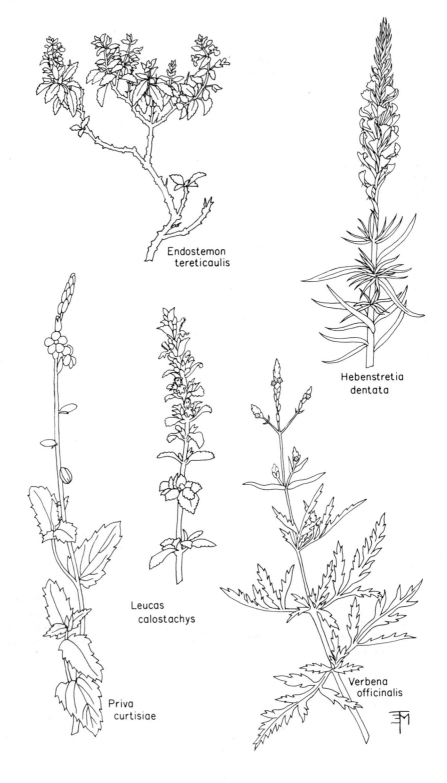

Endostemon
tereticaulis

Hebenstretia
dentata

Leucas
calostachys

Priva
curtisiae

Verbena
officinalis

This is a cultivated plant from America, which has escaped in a few places and persists. HT, NBI. Heriz-Smith and Paulo 932.

2. PRIVA *Adans*

Herbs with simple leaves and simple racemes of shortly pedicelled flowers; calyx tubular in flower, densely covered with hooked hairs and inflated in fruit; corolla hardly bilabiate, with 5 ± equal lobes and a bent tube; stamens 4, included in the corolla tube; fruit of 2 hard spiny mericarps, each 2-seeded.

1   Leaves subsessile, the petiole less than quarter the length of the lamina; corolla pink to purplish   1. *P. curtisiae*
    Leaves petiolate, the petiole over half as long as the lamina; corolla white
                       2. *P. cordifolia*

1. **Priva curtisiae** *Kobuski* (see p. 612)

An erect pubescent herb from a woody rootstock, with oblong to ovate leaves and long, unbranched racemes of pink flowers; calyx in fruit globose, hardly beaked above.

    Locally common, in dry country. KIS, NAR, BAR, RV, MAG, MAC, NBI, KAJ.

    Hanid and Kiniaruh 556; Glover, Gwynne, and Samuel 822.

2. **Priva cordifolia** (*L.*) *Druce*

Similar to *P. curtisiae* but a looser plant, with the fruiting calyx wider than long and with an apical beak.

    Local, in dry sandy *Commiphora* bushland. MAC, KAJ.

    Agnew 9865; Bally 787.

3. LANTANA *L.*

All species are keyed in KTS p. 586.

4. PHYLA *Lour.*

Similar to *Lippia* but trailing herbs, rooting at the nodes.

Phyla nodiflora (*L.*) *Greene*

A trailing, glabrous herb with obovate leaves and dense purplish spikes of cream flowers.

    Locally common in disturbed watersides in hot country. MUM, BAR.

    Agnew, Musumba, and Kiniaruh 8009; Bogdan 4898.

5. LIPPIA *L.*

Shrubs with simple pubescent leaves, and flowers in pedunculate crowded spikes; calyx small, 2–4-lobed, 2-keeled; corolla obscurely bilabiate, with 4 rounded lobes, white or cream in ours; stamens 4, included in the corolla tube; fruit of 2 hard mericarps, each 1-seeded.

1   Erect shrub   2
    Herb from a woody rootstock   1. *L. wilmsii*
2   Leaves never more than 3 cm long, the petiole up to half as long as the lamina
                  2. *L. somalensis*
    Some leaves over 3 cm long; all leaves subsessile   3
3   Bracts at base of spike over twice as wide as upper bracts   3. *L. ukambensis*
    Bracts at base of spike similar to upper bracts
                             4
4   Spikes 6 mm wide or less, with erect bracts; terminal leaves of flowering branches not reduced   4. *L. javanica*
    Spikes 6 mm wide or more, with spreading bracts; terminal leaves of flowering branches reduced   5. *L. grandifolia*

1. **Lippia wilmsii** *H. H. W. Pears*

A perennial herb from a woody rootstock, with elliptic to ovate, pubescent but not scabrid leaves, and paired spikes with spreading ovate bracts.

    Local in grassland above 5000 ft. HC, HT, KIT, NAR, RV, MAC, NBI.

    Hanid and Kiniaruh 810; Faden 67234.

2. **Lippia somalensis** *Vatke*

An erect pubescent shrub with petiolate, ovate leaves and paired spikes with oblong, erect bracts.

    Rare, found on dry mountains, and only recorded from Mt. Suswa. RV.

    Glover and Samuel 3371.

3. **Lippia ukambensis** *Vatke*

An erect pubescent shrub with lanceolate to oblong leaves and 2 (or uncommonly 4) long-pedunculate spikes at each upper node; lowest bracts enlarged, the upper ones lanceolate, spreading in fruit.

    A common and abundant colonizer of disturbed land at the margins of evergreen woodland. HL, HA, HN, KIS, NAR, RV, EMB, MAC, NBI.

    Graham 2141; Agnew 5243.

4. **Lippia javanica** (*Burm. f.*) *Spreng*

Similar to *L. ukambensis* but with a dense white, not scabrid, pubescence below the leaves and usually more than 4 narrow spikes at each node.

    Abundant, in disturbed places and rocky soils in dry woodland. HE, HC, HT, HA, KIT, KIS, NAR, RV, MAC, NBI, KAJ.

    Verdcourt 973; Agnew, Hanid, and Kiniaruh 7856.

5. Lippia grandifolia *A. Rich.*

An erect pubescent shrub with oblong to lanceolate, subsessile leaves and terminal racemes of
short-peduncled spikes; spikes often more than 4
at each node.

Common in disturbed forest and woodland on
rocky soils in western Kenya. HE, HC, KIT, MUM.
Lind, Harris, and Agnew 5096; Lugard 109.

6. CYCLOCHEILON *Oliv.*

Cyclocheilon eriantherum (*Vatke*) *Engl.*
In KTS p. 586. MAC.

7. CHASCANUM *E. Mey.*

Herbs or low shrubs with simple leaves and flowers
in dense terminal spikes; calyx narrow, cylindrical,
splitting on the anterior side in fruit; corolla with a
long tube, 2-lipped; stamens 4, included in the
corolla tube; fruit of 2 cylindrical dry mericarps
which are rugose but not winged above.

Chascanum hildebrandtii (*Vatke*) *Gillett*

A perennial herb from a woody rootstock, with
long-petiolate obovate to elliptic leaves and spikes
of white flowers.

This plant seems to belong to the *Acanthaceae*
at first sight. It is common in some areas of dry
Commiphora or *Combretum* woodland, especially
where sandy and disturbed. BAR, MAG, NAN,
EMB, MAC, KAJ.
Leippert 5059; Hanid 489.

8. PREMNA *L.*

All species are keyed in KTS p. 588.

9. CLERODENDRUM *L.*

Trees, shrubs or climbers, rarely herbs, with
opposite or whorled simple leaves; flowers mostly
in cymose inflorescences; calyx usually tubular,
5-toothed; corolla zygomorphic with an enlarged
anterior lobe, or ± regular with 5 equal lobes;
stamens 4, with long filaments; ovary 4-celled,
with 1 ovule in each cell; fruit a drupe with 4 hard
'stones' containing the seeds.

Many of these species are dealt with in KTS but
all from our area are keyed our here.

1 Flowers crowded in dense globose heads,
    apparently capitulate   2
   Flowers in loose panicles or cymes or
    corymbs   3
2 Corolla tube less than 1·5 cm long; leaves
    cuneate at base   1. *C. eriophyllum*
   Corolla tube over 5 cm long; leaves cordate at
    base   2. *C. capitatum*
3 Calyx over 7 mm long, with the lobes ± as
    long as the tube   4

Calyx less than 5 mm long, or if up to 8 mm
    long then the lobes much shorter than the
    tube   5
4 Corolla tube over 5 cm long
                               3. *C. rotundifolium*
   Corolla tube less than 2 cm long
                               4. *C. cordifolium*
5 Corolla lobes as long as or longer than the
    corolla tube; corolla blue or lilac   6
   Corolla lobes much shorter than the corolla
    tube; corolla yellow or white   7
6 Peduncles of axillary cymes over half as long
    as the subtending leaves; calyx cup-shaped
    with broad rounded lobes
                               5. *C. myricoides*
   Peduncles of axillary cymes much less than
    half as long as subtending leaves; calyx
    tubular or bell-shaped with linear acute
    lobes   6. *C. sp. A*
7 Some leaves with the basal pair of lateral
    nerves stronger than all the rest
                               7. *C. triplinerve*
   All leaves with the lowest pair of lateral
    nerves weaker than the median lateral
    nerves   8
8 Inflorescence a strictly flat-topped corymb
                               8. *C. johnstonii*
   Inflorescence a conical or cylindrical panicle
                                                   9
9 Calyx lobes ± as long as the cup-shaped tube;
    leaves drying black; corolla pale yellow
                               9. *C. melanocrater*
   Calyx lobes shorter than the cylindrical tube;
    leaves drying green; corolla white
                               10. *C. buchholzii*

1. Clerodendrum eriophyllum *Guerke*
In KTS p. 584. MAC, KAJ.

2. Clerodendrum capitatum *Schum. & Thonn.*
(inc. *C. cephalanthum Oliv.* of Check List)

An erect shrub or weak climber with glabrous to
stiffly hairy, ovate, cordate leaves, and terminal or
lateral heads of long white flowers with reddish or
green calyces.

Uncommon, found in lowland wet forest at the
coast and in western Kenya. MUM.
Trapnell 2291; Strid 3392B.

3. Clerodendrum rotundifolium *Oliv.*
In KTS p. 585. HE, HK, HL, MUM, KIS, NAR,
EMB.

4. Clerodendrum cordifolium *A. Rich.* (see
p. 615)

A weakly erect or twining scrambling woody herb
with ovate acuminate leaves and loose panicles of
greenish-yellow and red flowers.

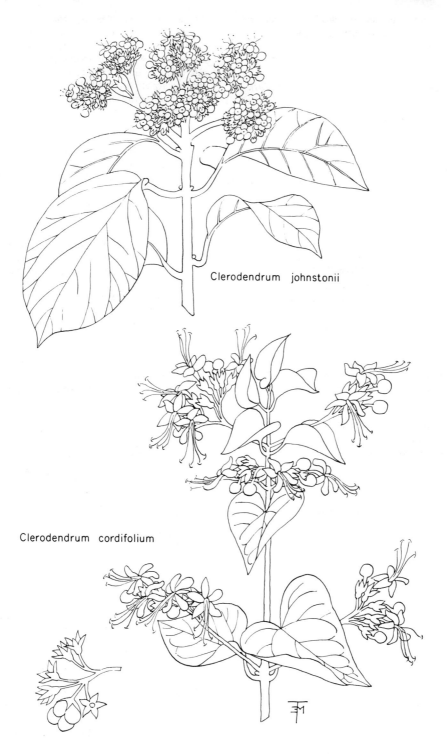

Clerodendrum johnstonii

Clerodendrum cordifolium

Uncommon, found in wooded grassland in western Kenya, and only known from the Kacheliba escarpment. KIT.

Napier 2007; Tweedie 66/386.

5. Clerodendrum myricoides (*Hochst.*) *Vatke* (*C. ugandensis* Prain, *C. discolor* (Klotzsch) Vatke)

In KTS p. 585. HC, HT, HA, HK, KIT, MUM, KIS, NAR, BAR, RV, MAG, NAN, EMB, MAC, NBI, KAJ.

6. Clerodendrum *sp.* **A.**

A woody herb or weak shrub with petiolate, opposite, lanceolate leaves and small dense axillary cymes of lilac flowers.

This species is represented by only one specimen from Kitale. KIT.

Tweedie 68/91.

7. Clerodendrum triplinerve *Rolfe*

Shrub or climber with elliptic leaves and loose, almost umbellate terminal panicles of white flowers.

Uncommon, found in lowland forest in western Kenya. MUM.

Paulo 537.

8. Clerodendrum johnstonii *Oliv.* (see p. 615)

A climber dealt with in KTS p. 584. HC, HT, HM, HA, MUM, KIS, EMB, MAC, KAJ.

9. Clerodendrum melanocrater *Guerke*

A woody climber with ovate leaves and terminal panicles of long-pedicelled, pale yellow flowers.

Uncommon, found in lowland wet forest and only recorded from Kakamega forest. MUM.

Strid 2917; Verdcourt 1668.

10. Clerodendrum buchholzii *Guerke*

A trailing or scrambling shrub with alternate or opposite, elliptic leaves, and loose racemes of white flowers which mostly come from old wood.

Rare plant found in Kakamega forest. MUM.

Verdcourt 1669.

10. VITEX *L.*

All species are keyed in KTS, p. 592.

11. DURANTA *L.*
Duranta repens *L.*

In KTS p. 586. KIS, NAR.

93. LABIATAE†

Herbs or shrubs with opposite, often aromatic leaves, and inflorescences which usually consist of racemes of axillary dichasia which may be con-

† By A. D. Q. Agnew.

densed to fascicles or spikes; flowers usually bisexual; calyx of 5 fused lobes, often zygomorphic; corolla zygomorphic, usually 2-lipped; stamens 2–4, *arched* to lie under the upper lip or *declinate* to lie next the lower lip or straight; ovary of 2 carpels divided into 4, 1-seeded portions which surround the base of the style; fruit of 4 indehiscent nutlets.

1	Calyx with the posterior lobe flat, ovate or oblong, blunt or rounded at apex, often laterally decurrent on the calyx. tube, much bigger than the rest of the lobes which may or may not be equal	2
	Calyx equally 4–10-lobed with the posterior lobe acute or spine-tipped or the upper 3 lobes and the lower 2 forming two lips	10
2	Stamens included in the corolla tube	3
	Stamens longer than the corolla tube	4
3	Flowers reddish, mostly 4–6 at each node	14. *Endostemon*
	Flowers white, 2 at each node (sometimes apparently 4 at a node through the absence or shortening of one internode)	32. *Fuerstia africana*
4	Corolla tube straight	6
	Corolla tube curved or bent at the mouth of the calyx	5
5	Lateral calyx lobes rounded at apex; anterior calyx lobes fused for most of their length	19. *Solenostemon*
	Lateral calyx lobes acute; anterior calyx lobes hardly fused at base	18. *Plectranthus*
6	Upper calyx lobe enlarging to become bright red and to enclose the rest of the fruiting calyx	25. *Erythrochlamys spectabilis*
	Upper calyx lobe remaining the same size relative to the other lobes in fruit as in flower	7
7	Stamens exceeding the corolla lobes	8
	Stamens shorter than the lower corolla lip	31. *Orthosiphon*
8	Bracts of floral whorls caducous, each with an enlarged fleshy base which becomes glandular as the raceme elongates; lateral calyx lobes obscure, represented by an oblique, ciliate-toothed margin	30. *Becium*
	Bracts of floral whorls persistent or caducous, without a glandular base; lateral calyx lobes each consisting of an entire tooth	9
9	Lower bracts of racemes similar to foliage leaves but white and attractive; flowers over 15 in each whorl	28. *Geniosporum paludosum*
	Lower bracts of racemes minute, often caducous; flowers 6 in each whorl	29. *Ocimum*

10   Calyx 2-lipped or truncate and without teeth (easiest to observe in fruit)   **11**
      Calyx 4-10-lobed   **16**

11   Plants fleshy; calyx dehiscent around the base, falling off like a cap   13. *Aeolanthus*
      Plants not fleshy; calyx not dehiscent   **12**

12   Flowers in head-like terminal spikes
                    27. *Haumaniastrum*
      Flowers in open racemes or solitary   **13**

13   Calyx with a dorsal flat appendage
                    2. *Scutellaria*
      Calyx with no dorsal appendage   **14**

14   Flowers solitary; corolla black
                  4. *Tinnea aethiopica*
      Flowers in racemes; corolla white or coloured   **15**

15   Corolla white; stamens 4
               26. *Platostoma africanum*
      Corolla blue or purple or red; stamens 2
                    9. *Salvia*

16   Flowers unisexual   24. *Iboza multiflora*
      Flowers bisexual   **17**

17   Calyx enlarging in fruit to over 3 times its size at anthesis   **18**
      Calyx not enlarging in fruit, or enlarging to less than 3 times its size at anthesis   **20**

18   Calyx inflated in fruit, with broad, dry lobes
            16. *Capitanya otostegioides*
      Calyx without broad dry lobes in fruit   **19**

19   Calyx tube dry, inflated
        21. *Homalocheilos ramosissimum*
      Calyx tube fleshy, orange in colour
            23. *Hoslundia opposita*

20   Lower corolla lip deeply concave (boat-shaped) with the stamens curved downwards into it   **21**
      Lower corolla lip flat, or concave only at the apex; stamens straight, or arching upwards to lie under the upper lip   **26**

21   Posterior (upper) calyx lobe spine-like, not flat   **22**
      Posterior (upper) calyx lobe flat   **23**

22   Flowers subsessile in crowded spikes
               15. *Pycnostachys*
      Flowers pedicellate in open panicles
         20. *Isodictyophorus defoliatus*

23   Upper calyx lobe larger than the rest
               18. *Plectranthus*
      Upper calyx lobe as wide as the rest   **24**

24   Flowers in dichasial cymes
        21. *Homalocheilos ramosissimus*
      Flowers in racemes or paired at the nodes   **25**

25   Inflorescence of terminal spike-like racemes
            22. *Neohyptis paniculata*
      Inflorescence of lateral racemes
               17. *Englerastrum*

26   Calyx lobes or teeth 8-10   **27**
      Calyx lobes or teeth 4-5   **28**

27   Flowers over 3 cm long, white or red or orange; calyx with 8 spiny teeth
                  5. *Leonotis*
      Flowers less than 3 cm long, white; calyx with 8-10 soft teeth   6. *Leucas*

28   Calyx flat at the mouth; calyx teeth bristle-like   12. *Hyptis*
      Calyx lobed at the mouth; calyx teeth lanceolate or wider   **29**

29   Upper lip of the corolla in more or less the same line as the corolla tube, not bent back at right angles to it; stamens hidden under or appressed to the upper lip of the corolla   **31**
      Upper lip of the corolla bent upwards at right angles to the corolla tube; stamens straight, not held under upper lip of corolla   **30**

30   Racemes with white leaf-like bracts at the base   28. *Geniosporum*
      Racemes with normal green leaf-like bracts at the base   11. *Mentha*

31   Flowers sessile at nodes, not in terminal inflorescences; stamens long-exceeding upper lip of corolla   3. *Ajuga remota*
      Flowers in terminal inflorescences or at least pedicellate at nodes; stamens shorter than upper corolla lip   **32**

32   Stamens 2   9. *Salvia*
      Stamens 4   **33**

33   Calyx with 10 nerves or ridges on the tube **34**
      Calyx with 13-15 nerves or ridges on the tube   **35**

34   Flowers in spike-like inflorescences
            8. *Achyrospermum*
      Flowers solitary or in open racemes
                7. *Stachys*

35   Flowers numerous, blue to mauve, crowded in open pedunculate branching cymes at each node; calyx 15-ribbed
             1. *Nepeta azurea*
      Flowers solitary to numerous, pink to purplish-pink in sessile or shortly pedunculate fascicles at each node; calyx 13-ridged
              10. *Satureia*

1. NEPETA *L.*

Herbs with a characteristic scent, entire leaves, and flowers crowded in regular dichasia at each upper node; calyx tubular, zygomorphic, with 15 ribs and 5 teeth; corolla tube 2-lipped, dilated at the throat; stamens 4, the inner pair the longest, arching dorsally, each with 2 divergent anther cells; nutlets ovoid, small.

Nepeta azurea *Benth.* (see p. 618)

An erect pubescent perennial with lanceolate, cordate leaves and terminal spike-like inflorescences of purple-blue flowers.

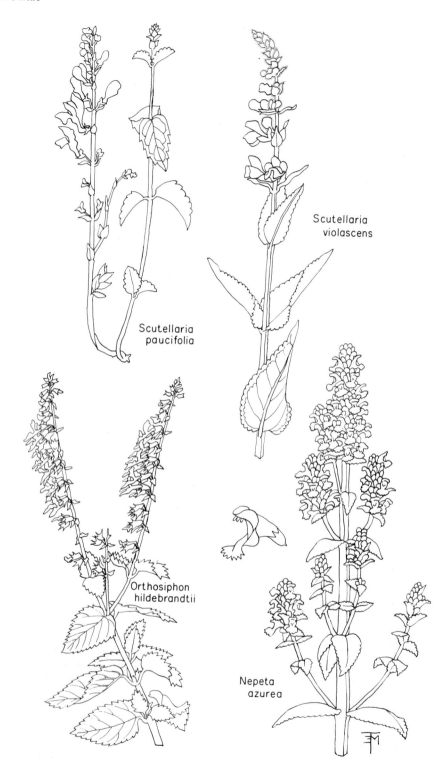

Scutellaria
paucifolia

Scutellaria
violascens

Orthosiphon
hildebrandtii

Nepeta
azurea

A conspicuous and common herb in bushed grassland. HE, HC, HM, HA, HK, KIS.

Agnew 10733; Verdcourt 1039.

2. SCUTELLARIA *L.*

Erect shrubs or herbs with simple leaves and terminal racemes of paired flowers; calyx zygomorphic, with two lips and a dorsal flat appendage, closed after flowering; corolla tube exserted, two-lipped; stamens 4, arching dorsally, outermost with 1 anther cell sterile or obsolete; nutlets often tubercled or hispid.

1   A tall herb usually over 50 cm high; calyx with very conspicuous long spreading hairs and dense shorter glandular hairs below the long ones   1. *S. violascens*

    A shorter herb usually less than 50 cm tall; calyx with but one kind of short pubescence and no glandular hairs   2. *S. paucifolia*

1. Scutellaria violascens *Guerke* (see p. 618)

An erect herb, pubescent or tomentose on all parts, with ovate cordate leaves and purple and white flowers.

Rare plant found in tall wooded grassland in western Kenya. KIT.

Irwin 150.

2. Scutellaria paucifolia *Bak.* (see p. 618)

An erect pubescent herb from a woody rootstock with the ovate leaves on separate shoots, not numerous on flowering branches; flowers purple, mauve, or (rarely) white.

Locally common in short grassland in western Kenya. I doubt the record from Nairobi. HE, KIT, MUM, KIS, ?NBI.

Tweedie 67/49; Symes 33.

3. AJUGA *L.*

Erect or trailing herbs with simple or lobed leaves much exceeding the axillary flower-clusters; calyx bell-shaped, 5-toothed; corolla often short, with very small upper lip and much larger lower lip, usually blue; stamens 4, the lower pair longest, with 2 anther cells each; nutlets reticulated, obliquely attached.

Ajuga remota *Benth.* (see p. 621)

An erect, often rhizomatous, pubescent herb with oblanceolate, coarsely toothed leaves and small subsessile axillary pale blue flowers.

Common in disturbed areas in grassland. A mountain form, more strictly rhizomatous with a rosette of leaves at ground level, also occurs, and may merit specific status when it has been carefully studied. It is found on HA and HK. The species as a whole is known from HE, HC, HT, HM, HA, HK, KIT, MUM, NAR, NAN, MAC, NBI, KAJ.

Lind 5500; Glover, Gwynne, and Samuel 1628.

4. TINNEA *Kotschy & Peyr.*

Shrubs with simple leaves; calyx bell-shaped with 2 entire lips, inflated in fruit; corolla hardly exceeding the calyx, 2-lipped; stamens 4, the uppermost the longest, arching above, each with 2-celled anthers; nutlets winged.

Tinnea aethiopica *Kotschy & Peyr.* (see p. 621)

An erect or straggling pubescent shrub with elliptic, coarsely toothed leaves and paired flowers; flowers with red calyx and black corolla.

Common in all upland forest edges and also known from the coast. HE, HC, HM, HA, HK, KIT, MUM, KIS, NAR, BAR, RV, MAC, NBI, KAJ.

Lugard 452; Verdcourt 1474.

5. LEONOTIS *(Pers.) R.Br.*

Erect herbs or shrubs with coarsely dentate, simple leaves and flowers in few dense globular masses at upper nodes; calyx tubular or funnel-shaped, 8-spined, the uppermost usually largest; corolla long-exceeding the calyx, with a densely hairy tube and upper lip and glabrous, marcescent lower lip; stamens 4, the uppermost longest, arching under the upper lip of the corolla, on the bristly terminal hairs of which the pollen is deposited, ready for brushing off on to bird pollinators; nutlets glabrous, smooth, long and thin.

1   Leaves ovate, acute at apex   2
    Leaves orbicular to suborbicular, rounded at apex   3

2   Plant annual; leaves with petiole over half as long as lamina, finely pubescent but not white-hairy below   1. *L. nepetifolia*
    Plant perennial; leaves with petiole less than half as long as lamina, white-hairy below   2. *L. mollissima*

3   Leaves never wider than 4 cm; flowers orange   3. *L. leonitis*
    Leaves often wider than 4 cm; flowers white, cream, or pale yellow   4. *L. africana*

1. Leonotis nepetifolia *R. Br.*

A finely pubescent erect woody annual with long-petiolate ovate leaves and orange flowers.

This is the common weed species of cultivation in Kenya. HE, HC, HT, HM, HA, HK, MUM, KIS, NAR, RV, NAN, NBI, KAJ.

Harmsen 6533; Glover, Gwynne, and Samuel 1706.

2. Leonotis mollissima *Guerke* (*L. velutina* of Check List, *L. elliottii* Bak.) (see p. 621)

An erect woody herb or shrub (sometimes reaching tree-like proportions) with woolly, ovate cordate leaves and orange (occasionally white) flowers in 1–3 terminal spherical masses.

This is the common species by roadsides and in disturbed places above 6500 ft, often in montane forest. HA, HE, HC, HT, HM, HA, HK, KIT, KIS, RV, KAJ.

Part II Botany 53; Lugard 113.

3. Leonotis leonitis *R. Br.*

A pubescent or woolly, erect woody herb, with long-petiolate, suborbicular, coarsely crenate leaves and orange flowers.

Locally common on dry hillsides. HA, HM, RV, MAC, KAJ.

Glover 4324; Harmsen 6429.

4. Leonotis africana (*P. Beauv.*) *Briq.*

An erect, pubescent or woolly annual or short-lived perennial herb with suborbicular leaves, truncate at base, and pale white to yellow flowers.

Uncommon plant found in disturbed grassland in south-western Kenya. KIS, NAR.

Hanid and Kiniaruh 802.

6. LEUCAS *R. Br.*

Herbs or shrubs with simple leaves and flowers in dense or loose clusters in the upper axils, bracteate or not; calyx bell-shaped or conical, actinomorphic or zygomorphic by production of one side, 10-toothed, the alternate teeth rather smaller; corolla as in *Leonotis* but always white (in ours); stamens as in *Leonotis*, orange; nutlets oblong, glabrous, truncate and minutely glandular at apex.

1	Plants annual, erect	2
	Plants perennial, erect or trailing	8
2	Spine on upper side of calyx overtopping all the others	1. *L. martinicensis*
	Spine on upper side of calyx shorter than all the others, or all calyx spines equal	3
3	All calyx spines ± equal	2. *L. concinna*
	Lower calyx spines produced into a lip	4
4	Flower clusters globular, distant from each other	5
	Flowers few, in small clusters which coalesce towards the top of the stem	14. *L. neuflizeana*
5	Bracts of flowers broad, oblanceolate to obovate, transparent and papery with thickened nerves	3. *L. bracteosa*
	Bracts of flowers narrow-linear, thick, opaque and green	6

6	Mouth of calyx very oblique, with a spreading but hardly recurved lower lip	7
	Mouth of calyx oblique but without a definite lower lip, the whole tube recurved downwards at apex	7. *L. micrantha*
7	Underside of leaves finely pubescent or sparsely hairy	6. *L. urticifolia*
	Underside of leaves densely woolly	4. *L. mollis*
8	Whorls of flowers solitary at branch apex or sometimes with one whorl above	9
	Whorls of flowers more than 2 at stem apex	12
9	Bracts of flowers oblanceolate, widening markedly above	17. *L. masaiensis*
	Bracts of flowers bristle-like, not widening above	10
10	Leaves glabrous between the veins below; calyx zygomorphic with a small, spreading portion below the anterior (outermost) 3 teeth	18. *L. tricrenata*
	Leaves usually pubescent between the veins below; calyx not spreading anteriorly	11
11	Calyx with a straight mouth, or almost so	16. *L. venulosa*
	Calyx with an oblique mouth	15. *L. oligocephala*
12	Bracts of flowers (not the opposite, leaf-like bracts of the flower cluster) absent or shorter than half the length of lowermost calyces	13
	Bracts of flowers (not the opposite, leaf-like bracts of the flower cluster) present and longer than half the length of lowermost calyces	19
13	Calyx mouth straight, not oblique; calyx teeth obtuse or very soft, not ending in a bristle	14
	Calyx mouth oblique, sometimes obscurely so; calyx teeth always ending in a bristle	15
14	Calyx papery, woolly, with acute teeth, falling early	8. *L. pododiskos*
	Calyx hard, minutely pubescent, with obtuse teeth, persistent	9. *L. jamesii*
15	Leaves white-woolly below; upper whorls of flowers exceeding their subtending leaves and confluent into a cylindrical mass	12. *L. calostachys*
	Leaves not woolly below; upper whorls of flowers not confluent, or if confluent, then always exceeded by their subtending leaves	16
16	Calyx teeth all, or only the anterior (outermost) ones, triangular, about twice as long as broad	17
	Calyx teeth all, even the anterior ones, linear-lanceolate or bristle-like, much more than 4 times as long as broad	18

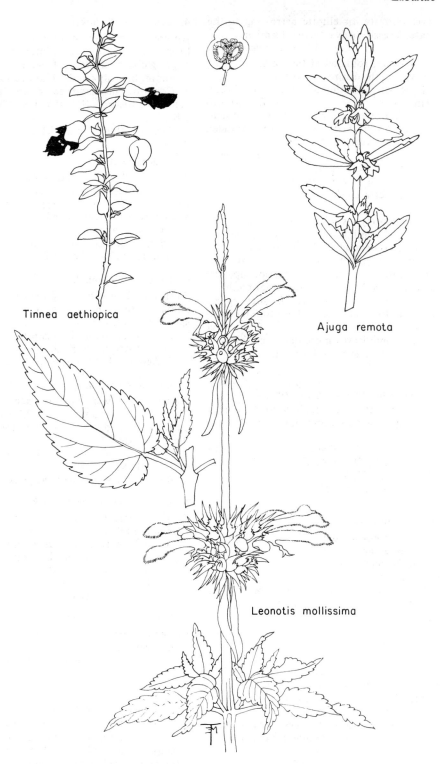

Tinnea aethiopica

Ajuga remota

Leonotis mollissima

17 Leaves obovate, or elliptic narrowing to the base, ± sessile; calyx teeth all similar
13. *L. schweinfurthii*
Leaves ovate, rounded at the base, petiolate; calyx teeth dissimilar, the anterior ones triangular with the posterior ones linear-lanceolate
10. *L. pratensis*

18 Bracts of flowers green and soft, or absent; calyx teeth bristle-like, with rounded sinuses between the teeth
15. *L. oligocephala*
Bracts of flowers short, yellow and spiny; calyx teeth linear-lanceolate, with acute sinuses between the teeth
11. *L. glabrata*

19 Leaves densely woolly-silky below; calyx with 2–3 teeth on an anterior lip which is produced beyond all the other teeth   20
Leaves pubescent below; calyx oblique but not produced into an anterior lip, the anterior teeth similar to the other teeth
15. *L. oligocephala*

20 Leaves up to 3 cm long, with up to 5 teeth on each side   5. *L.* sp. *A*
At least some leaves more than 5 cm long, all with more than 8 teeth on each
4. *L. mollis*

1. Leucas martinicensis *(Jacq.) R. Br.*

An erect pubescent annual with ovate to elliptic leaves and tight balls of white flowers with spiny calyces.

A common weed of disturbed soil, especially farmland. HE, HC, HT, HA, HK, HN, KIT, KIS, NAR, RV, MAC, NBI, KAJ.

Hanid 668; Mwangangi 215.

2. Leucas concinna *Baker*

An erect pubescent annual with ovate, elliptic or lanceolate leaves and small axillary clusters of up to 12 white flowers with almost regular calyces.

This species has only been recorded in our area from black cotton soil in the Nairobi National Park, but it is also found at the coast. NBI.

Verdcourt 3177B.

3. Leucas bracteosa *Guerke*

An erect branched pubescent annual with elliptic-lanceolate leaves and rather few semiglobose flower-clusters subtended by numerous very broad papery bracts; calyx zygomorphic with 3–5 enlarged scarious teeth on the anterior side.

A rare weed of disturbed places, only recorded from the Mara region. It is common further south. NAR.

Glover, Gwynne, and Samuel 2236.

4. Leucas mollis *Baker*

An erect, tomentose-woolly, woody herb or short-lived shrub with ovate-elliptic leaves and rather large globose clusters of white flowers with a zygomorphic calyx and ± blunt calyx teeth.

Common in disturbed ground particularly in Machakos district. HM, HA, HK, RV, EMB, MAC, NBI, KAJ.

Agnew, Hanid, and Kiniaruh 9210; Perdue 8408.

5. Leucas *sp.* A.

An erect silky-tomentose shrub with small, orbicular to ovate-elliptic leaves and globose clusters of white flowers; calyx zygomorphic, produced anteriorly, with acuminate lobes.

Locally common on Mt. Elgon and the Cherangani Hills in disturbed bushland. HE, HC.

Dale 1595; Tweedie 66/355.

6. Leucas urticifolia *R. Br.*

Similar to *L. mollis*, but pubescent and always an annual, with acuminate calyx teeth and the dorsal side of the calyx green, not at all papery.

Locally common in disturbed places in dry country. NAN, EMB, KAJ.

S. Agnew, May 1968; Bally 1192.

7. Leucas micrantha *Guerke*

Similar to *L. martinicensis* except for the calyx which is zygomorphic but tubular and curved outwards and downwards with the anterior side slightly produced.

Locally common, as a ruderal weed in western Kenya. HT, KIT, MUM, KIS.

Agnew and Musumba 8543; Baker 1279.

8. Leucas pododiskos *Bullock*

A white-tomentose, erect or ascending shrub or perennial herb with obovate to cuneate, subsessile leaves and up to 5 flowers at most nodes; calyx regular, with ovate-triangular teeth.

Locally common in dry bushland, especially where disturbed and along river banks. BAR, KAJ.

Tweedie 2307; Agnew 7622.

9. Leucas jamesii *Baker*

An erect pubescent shrub with oblanceolate to linear leaves and clusters of white flowers in most upper axils; calyx regular, with short blunt teeth.

Uncommon, found in dry bushland. NAN.

Kirrika 20.

10. Leucas pratensis *Vatke*

A pubescent to tomentose perennial herb or weak shrub with petiolate, elliptic to ovate leaves and clusters of up to 12 flowers at many upper nodes; calyx zygomorphic, with triangular anterior teeth.

Locally common in upland grassland. HC, MUM, NAR, BAR, RV, NBI, KAJ.

Agnew and Azavedo 9784; Verdcourt 1152.

11. Leucas glabrata *R. Br.*

Very similar to *L. pratensis* but with the calyx differences mentioned in the key.

This plant is only known from Magadi and the adjacent Rift Valley in our area and may well be but a local form of *L. pratensis.* RV, MAG.

Harmsen 646; Glover 3578.

12. Leucas calostachys *Oliv.* (see p. 612)

A tomentose, erect, sparsely branched shrub with elliptic to obovate, subsessile leaves and terminal spike-like masses of white flowers; calyx oblique, with short, ± equal teeth.

Common in disturbed bushland in western Kenya at higher altitudes. HE, HC, HT, HM, HA, KIT, MUM, KIS.

Lind 5073; Verdcourt 2914.

13. Leucas schweinfurthii *Guerke*

An erect, tomentose to pubescent shrub with sessile, cuneate to obovate leaves and clusters of few (2-5) flowers at most of the upper nodes; calyx as in *L. calostachys.*

Locally common in dry bushland. MAC, KAJ.

Heriz-Smith, June 1962; Rauh 278.

14. Leucas neuflizeana *Courb.*

An erect pubescent annual, similar to *L. schweinfurthii* except for the much smaller calyx (to 7 mm long) and corolla (to 10 mm long), and the oblong-elliptic leaves.

Common in disturbed sandy or alluvial soils in dry grassland. KIS, RV, MAC, NBI, KAJ.

Mendes 69; Verdcourt 3245A.

15. Leucas oligocephala *Hook. f.*

A hirsute, ± trailing or erect shrub or herb from a woody rootstock, with leaves often oblong and parallel-nerved; flowers numerous, in clusters at 2-many of the upper nodes, with or without bracts; calyx oblique at mouth, with fine soft teeth.

As defined here this is very variable plant which is often found at forest edges and in wooded grassland. HM, HA, KIT, MUM, MAC.

Verdcourt 1023; Hanid and Kiniaruh 828.

16. Leucas venulosa *Baker*

A loosely hirsute herb with many trailing and ascending stems from a woody rootstock, and obovate to elliptic leaves; flowers in 1-2 dense hemispherical clusters at stem apex; calyx ± regular, with short mucronate teeth.

Common in black-cotton soils, especially near Nairobi. HK, NAN, MAC, NBI, KAJ.

Agnew and Musumba 5461; Verdcourt 1127.

17. Leucas masaiensis *Baker*

A low, tufted, pubescent herb, trailing from a woody rootstock, with obovate to elliptic, small leaves and a single terminal cluster of crowded flowers; calyx as in *L. venulosa.*

Locally common in highland grassland. HC, HT, HM, HA.

Nattrass 1003.

18. Leucas tricrenata *Bullock*

Similar to *L. masaiensis* but with hairier oblong elliptic leaves and the keyed differences.

This species has only been found in highland grassland in Elgon and Cherangani. HE, HC.

Irwin 221; Tweedie 66/356; Lugard 471.

7. STACHYS *L.*

Erect or trailing herbs or shrubs with (usually) cordate, simple leaves and flowers in terminal racemes of verticillasters; calyx almost regular, funnel-shaped, with 5 ± equal teeth, 10-nerved; corolla bilabiate, the two lips more or less equal in ours, white, pink or purple; stamens 4, arching; nutlets ovoid, smooth, rounded.

1	Stems rough with prickle-hairs	3
	Stems smooth, not prickly or rough	2
2	Erect herb with oblong leaves	
	1. *S. hildebrandtii*	
	Creeping herb with orbicular leaves	
	2. *S. alpigena*	
3	Petioles more than half as long as leaves	4
	Petioles less than half as long as leaves	
	3. *S. lindblomiana*	
4	Leaves rounded at apex, with up to 10 coarse rounded teeth on each side	
	4. *S. subrenifolia*	
	Leaves acute or acuminate at apex, with more than 12 smaller crenations on each side	5
5	Leaves mostly acute, softly hairy on both surfaces; calyx tomentose and minutely glandular　　　5. *S. bambuseti*	
	Leaves mostly acuminate, with stiff hairs on upper surface and ± glabrous below; calyx minutely glandular only　　6. *S. aculeolata*	

1. Stachys hildebrandtii *Vatke*

A low shrub or herb from a woody rootstock, densely woolly with stellate hairs on all parts; leaves oblong, sessile, entire or crenate; flowers in terminal leafless racemes of verticillasters, pale mauve or purple.

Common in some grasslands at medium and low altitudes, particularly where adjacent to black cotton soils. HM, HL, HA, MAG, NAN, NBI, KAJ.
Hansen 44; Harmsen 6444.

2. Stachys alpigena *Th. Fr. jr.*

A creeping, sparsely tomentose herb with petiolate orbicular leaves, and groups of white flowers in subterminal leaf axils, occasionally in short erect racemes.

This plant is only known from frosted, disturbed grassland in the lower alpine zone of the Aberdares. HA.
Lind, Agnew, and Woodley 5756; Battiscombe 539.

3. Stachys lindblomiana *Th. Fr. jr.* (see p. 625)

An ascending or trailing tomentose herb with recurved prickles on the stem and short-petiolate, triangular, cordate leaves; flowers white or pink, in ± dense terminal racemes.

An uncommon *Stachys* in the edges of high altitude forest, known only from Mt. Elgon. HE.
Irwin 244.

4. Stachys subrenifolia *Th. Fr. jr.*

A trailing or creeping, sparsely tomentose herb with ascending stems and suborbicular, cordate, long-petiolate leaves; flowers white or pale pink with purple markings.

Locally common in the bamboo zone, at forest edges. HE, HA, HK.
Tweedie 67/316; Hedberg 1992.

5. Stachys bambuseti *Th. Fr. jr.*

Similar to *S. subrenifolia* but with triangular cordate leaves, acute, rarely rounded at apex, and with darker purple or pink flowers, and also differing in the key characters given.

This the commonest prickly-stemmed *Stachys* of the Aberdares and Mt. Kenya found in forest edges below and throughout the bamboo zone. HA, HK.
Hedberg 1524; Strid 2190.

6. Stachys aculeolata *Hook. f.*

Similar to *S. bambuseti* but with heart-shaped, cordate, acuminate leaves and more glabrous stem and calyx.

This plant is found in wet montane forest edges, but is rather local. HE, HM, HA, HK, MAC.
Lind 5482; Kerfoot 3734.

8. ACHYROSPERMUM *Blume*

Low shrubs with simple leaves and flowers in spike-like inflorescences; calyx tubular, 10-nerved, 5-toothed, slightly zygomorphic; corolla bilabiate;

stamens 4, arching, the lower pair the longest; nutlets ovoid, scaly at apex.

1   Inflorescences produced laterally on leafless parts of the branches   1. *A. carvalhi*
    Inflorescences terminal   2
2   Stems with appressed crisped hairs; bracts of racemes acute; calyx tube with a straight mouth   2. *A. parviflorum*
    Stems with spreading hairs; bracts of racemes rounded, mucronate; calyx tube curved, with oblique mouth   3. *A. schimperi*

1. Achyrospermum carvalhi *Guerke* (inc. *A radicans* of the Check List)

An erect soft shrub, tomentose below the elliptic, acute and attenuate leaves, with short racemes of bright red, long-tubed flowers.

A rare plant of the wettest montane forests which has not been recorded for some time. HK.
Gardner 339.

2. Achyrospermum parviflorum *S. Moore*

A crisped-pubescent herb or weak shrub with elliptic, acute leaves and small pink flowers in dense racemes borne terminally on lateral branches.

Locally common in the shade of wet lowland forest, and only recorded from Kakamega forest. MUM.
Lind 5883; Jack 148.

3. Achyrospermum schimperi *(Hochst.) Perkins* (see p. 625)

A stiff erect tomentose herb with broad-elliptic, acute leaves and dense terminal spikes of flowers, the pink corolla hardly exceeding the large calyx.

Locally common in wet streamsides in partial shade within the montane forest. HE, HC, HM, HA, MAC.
Strid 2183; Nattrass 695.

9. SALVIA *L.*

Herbs or shrubs with simple or lobed leaves and flowers in terminal racemes of verticillasters; calyx funnel-shaped, 10-nerved, 5-toothed, usually 2-lipped; corolla 2-lipped; stamens 2, arching, each with a sterile and fertile anther joined by a long connective; nutlets ovoid, smooth.

1   Flowers bright red   1. *S. coccinea*
    Flowers purple   2
2   Upper calyx teeth less than 1 mm long; corolla more than twice as long as calyx   2. *S. merjamie*
    Upper calyx teeth more than 1 mm long; corolla less than twice as long as calyx   3. *S. nilotica*

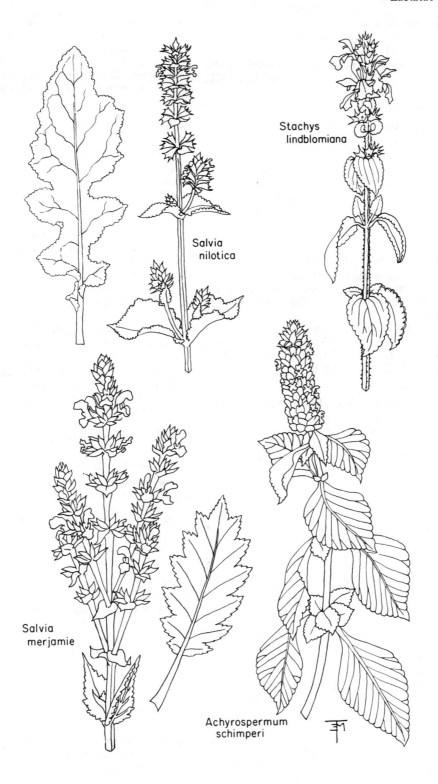

Salvia
nilotica

Stachys
lindblomiana

Salvia
merjamie

Achyrospermum
schimperi

1. Salvia coccinea *L.*

An erect annual with ovate cordate leaves and conspicuous red flowers.

An escape from cultivation, growing in disturbed places in the Nairobi and Elgon areas. HE, NBI.

Kirrika 217.

2. Salvia merjamie *Forsk.* (see p. 625)

An erect, loosely tomentose perennial from a rosette of leaves on a thick woody taproot; leaves oblong, often lobed; flowers in dense racemes, pale purple, the calyx often bluish at anthesis.

Locally common in grassland from 8000–11 000 ft, especially where burning takes place. HE, HC, HT, HM, HA, HK.

Kokwaro 28; Strid 2353.

3. Salvia nilotica *Jacq.* (see p. 625)

A rhizomatous hirsute perennial herb with pinnatifid obovate lower leaves and ovate amplexicaul stem-leaves; flowers white, pink or purple, in branching, open racemes.

This is our commonest species of *Salvia*, found in grassland from 6000–10 000 ft. HE, HC, HT, HM, HA, HK, KIT, KIS, RV, KAJ.

Tweedie 66/114; Moreau 114.

10. SATUREIA *L.*

Herbs or sometimes low shrubs, with entire or serrate leaves and axillary or terminal inflorescences; calyx tubular or bell-shaped, with 13 ridges or nerves, mostly zygomorphic, with 2 anterior, longer teeth; corolla bilabiate, pink or purplish; stamens 4, arching posteriorly; nutlets smooth, ovoid.

1   Leaves with entire, distinctly thickened margin   1. *S. biflora*
     Leaves serrate (sometimes obscurely) at margin, not thickened   2
2   Flowers all axillary to well developed leaves; calyx zygomorphic   3
     Flowers mostly in a terminal raceme-like inflorescence, without leaf-like bracts; calyx regular   2. *S. abyssinica*
3   Leaves with petiole usually half to quarter the length of the lamina; calyx tubes mostly green   4
     Leaves subsessile, with petiole less than quarter the length of the lamina; calyx tubes mostly purple   5
4   Leaves orbicular, ± cordate at base; upper calyx teeth lanceolate
                3. *S. kilimandschari*
     Leaves broad-ovate, truncate to cuneate at base; upper calyx teeth ± triangular
                4. *S. simensis*

5   Leaves sparsely tomentose, between the veins above, and only on the veins below; corolla less than 12 mm long
                5. *S. pseudosimensis*
     Leaves densely tomentose between the veins on both surfaces, corolla over 12 mm long
                6. *S. uhligii*

1. Satureia biflora (*D. Don*) Benth. (*S. punctata* (Benth.) Briq.) (see p. 627)

An erect woody herb, glabrous to tomentose, with elliptic to orbicular entire leaves and axillary clusters (2–20) of pink flowers.

This is a common species of upland dry grassland. The alpine form with the lower calyx teeth twice as long as the upper has been known by this name, while the lowland form has been called *S. punctata*, but there appear to be so many intermediates that we unite them in this account. HE, HC, HT, HM, HA, HK, HN, KIT, NAR, RV, NAN, EMB, NBI, KAJ.

Glover 4281; Hanid 164.

2. Satureia abyssinica (*Benth.*) Briq. (see p. 627)

A pubescent herb with many ascending unbranched stems from a woody rootstock, bearing broad-ovate, elliptic, petiolate leaves and terminal racemes of pale purple flowers.

Not uncommon in woodland from 7000–9000 ft. HE, HC, HT, HM, HA, HK, KIT, MUM, MAC, KAJ.

Agnew 8441; Lugard 125.

3. Satureia kilimandschari (*Guerke*) Hedb.

A low trailing wiry tomentose herb with orbicular, cordate, petiolate leaves and pink flowers in 2s or 4s in the upper leaf axils.

Uncommon, found in the alpine zones of the larger mountains. HE, HA, HK.

Hedberg 1815; Coe and Kirrika 270.

4. Satureia simensis (*Benth.*) Briq.

Similar to *S. kilimandschari* but with smaller, more densely clustered flowers which hardly exceed the petioles, as well as the keyed differences.

Recorded from marshy ground in bamboo forest edges. HE, HA, HK.

Record from Hedberg *Symb. bot. Uppsal.* **15**, 163 (1957).

5. Satureia pseudosimensis *Brenan* (see p. 627)

A tomentose herb with weakly branching, ascending stems from a woody base; leaves ovate to orbicular, subsessile; flowers in dense axillary fascicles, purple.

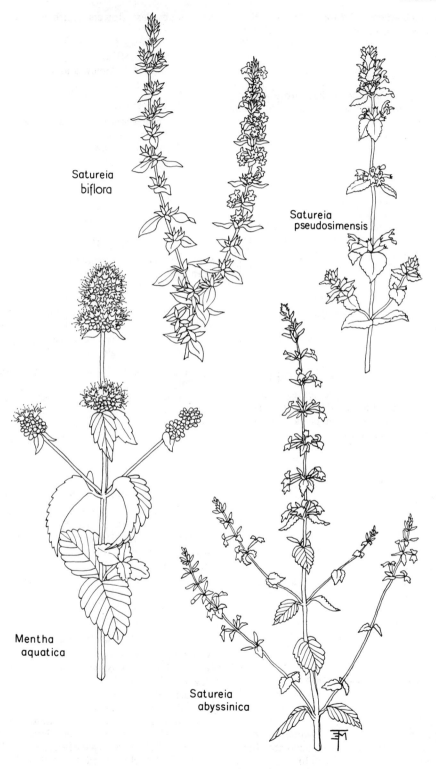

Satureia
biflora

Satureia
pseudosimensis

Mentha
aquatica

Satureia
abyssinica

Common in clearings and forest edges mostly at the upper limits of montane rain-forest and within the heath zone. HE, HC, HT, HM, HA, HK, KIS.
Lugard 40; Lind 5630.

6. Satureia uhligii *Guerke*

Similar to *S. pseudosimensis* but more densely tomentose and more robust, with large pink and pale purple flowers.
Uncommon, found in the heath zone on Mt. Elgon. HE.
Tweedie 27.

11. MENTHA *L.*

Perennial rhizomatous herbs with simple, serrate leaves; flowers often forming a terminal spike or head, small, purple, pink or white; calyx tubular or bell-shaped, 10–13-nerved, with 5 ± equal teeth; corolla with a short tube and 4 ± equal lobes; stamens 4, diverging, ± equal; nutlets ovoid, rounded, smooth.

1 Leaves sessile, glabrous above, white-woolly below; racemes elongated
                        1. *M. longifolia*
   Leaves shortly petiolate, pubescent above and below; racemes ± globose   2. *M. aquatica*

1. Mentha longifolia (*L.*) *L.* (*M. sylvestris* L.)

An erect herb with lanceolate leaves and long, tapering terminal racemes of pale pink flowers.
This plant is found in marshes within the upland forest. HA, HK, NAR.
Kibui 20.

2. Mentha aquatica *L.* (see p. 627)

Similar to *M. longifolia* but with the keyed differences and bright mauve flowers.
Locally common in marshes, mostly in western Kenya. HE, HA, KIT.
Tweedie, January 1966; Symes 213.

12. HYPTIS *Jacq.*

Erect herbs with simple leaves and flowers crowded in spike-like racemes of dichasia; calyx bell-shaped, 10-nerved, with 5 ± equal teeth; corolla small, hardly bilabiate, the lower lip sharply deflexed; stamens 4, declinate, with free filaments; nutlets ovoid, usually smooth.

1 Inflorescence a globose 'head' 1. *H. brevipes*
   Inflorescence an elongated raceme
                        2. *H. pectinata*

1. Hyptis brevipes *Poit.*

An erect pubescent unbranched annual or short-lived perennial herb, with oblanceolate-elliptic leaves and globose, spiny flower clusters on axil-lary peduncles; flowers white with purple upper lip.
Only recorded from swamp grassland in western Kenya. MUM.
McMahon 147; Agnew and Musumba 8612.

2. Hyptis pectinata *Poit.*

An erect, pubescent to tomentose, sometimes large and straggling annual herb, with ovate leaves and dense terminal racemes of small flowers which are reminiscent of *Nepeta*; flowers pale cream and purple.
Locally common, in dry bushland at lower altitudes. MUM, EMB, MAC, NBI, KAJ.
Nattrass 909; Harmsen 6512.

13. AEOLANTHUS *Mart.*

Very aromatic, subsucculent herbs or shrubs with simple or divided leaves and flowers mostly in spikes of cymes or capitate; calyx truncate, hardly lobed, the two lips coming together in a horizontal line and circumscissile at the base in fruit; corolla with a bent tube and two lips, pink to white or pale purple; stamens 4, declinate; nutlets ovoid, ± flattened, smooth, glossy.

1 Plant annual   1. *A. heliotropoides*
   Plant perennial   2
2 Plant a trailing shrub; bracts with a con-spicuous (often purple) gland at apex
                        2. *A. repens*
   Plant an erect, rarely trailing shrub; bracts with no gland at apex   3. *A. stormsii*

1. Aeolanthus heliotropoides *Oliv.* (see p. 629)

A pubescent, erect, branched or simple annual, with hardly fleshy, usually sessile, oblong to obovate distantly dentate leaves; inflorescence of spike-like branches; bracts rounded, with a small subterminal gland.
Locally common on shallow soil in western Kenya. HE, KIT, MUM.
Tweedie 67/287; Tweedie 11.

2. Aeolanthus repens *Oliv.* (see p. 629)

A trailing, pubescent, soft fleshy shrub with sessile, oblong or oblanceolate, distantly dentate leaves and ascending leafless peduncles; inflor-escence of a group of spikes; bracts with a conspicuous raised gland at apex.
Common on shallow soils in the lower forest and wooded grassland zones. HE, HT, HM, HL, HA, HK, KIT, KIS, NAR, EMB, MAC, NBI, KAJ.
Dale 2424; Hanid and Kiniaruh 185.

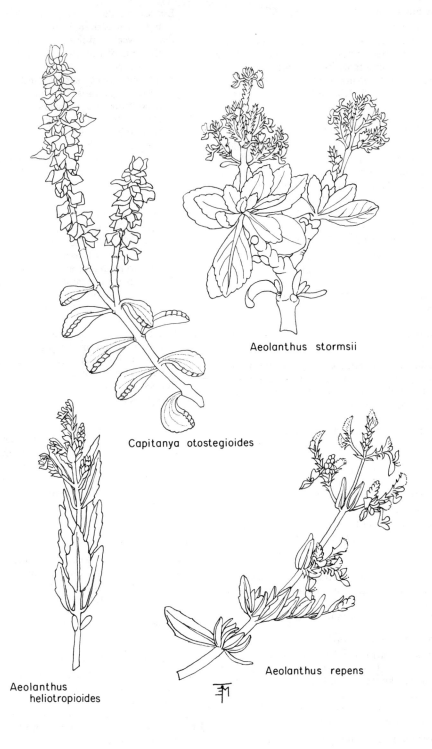

Aeolanthus stormsii

Capitanya otostegioides

Aeolanthus
heliotropioides

Aeolanthus repens

3. Aeolanthus stormsii *Guerke* (see p. 629)

An erect or trailing pubescent soft shrub with petiolate, obovate, minutely serrate or entire leaves and short peduncles; inflorescences shorter than in *A. repens*; bracts without glands.

Common on wet or misty cliff-faces in shallow soil. HE, HC, HA, BAR, RV, MAC.

Harmsen 6424; Tweedie 27.

14. ENDOSTEMON *N. E. Br.*

Low shrubs or herbs with subsessile, simple leaves and terminal racemes of few-flowered whorls; calyx zygomorphic, with an expanded, ± orbicular upper lobe overlapping the 4 linear to oblong lower lobes, all becoming stiff in fruit; corolla longest below, hardly two-lipped; stamens 4, included in corolla tube, declinate; nutlets smooth or irregularly minutely pitted, ovoid, rounded.

1 Bracts longer than flowers at anthesis; corolla less than twice calyx length
  1. *E. tereticaulis*
  Bracts shorter than flowers at anthesis; corolla about twice calyx length 2. *E. camporum*

1. Endostemon tereticaulis (*Poir.*) *Ashby* (see p. 612)

An erect, loosely tomentose, wiry annual herb or short-lived perennial shrub, with oblanceolate leaves and small inconspicuous purple flowers; lateral calyx lobes truncate at apex, as long as the anterior ones.

Common in dry bushland and wooded grassland especially on rocky, shallow soils. BAR, RV, MAC, NBI, KAJ.

Hanid and Kiniaruh 500; Bally 9745.

2. Endostemon camporum (*Guerke*) *Ashby*

A perennial low woody tomentose herb from a woody rootstock, with elliptic to oblanceolate leaves and conspicuous terminal racemes of purple and white flowers; calyx very similar to *E. tereticaulis*.

An uncommon plant of stony soils known only from Machakos district and neighbouring areas. EMB, MAC.

Mwangangi 48; Agnew and Kiniaruh 8832.

15. PYCNOSTACHYS *Hook.*

Erect herbs or shrubs with simple leaves and terminal spikes of sessile flowers; calyx with 5 equal spine-like teeth and a regular or zygomorphic tube; corolla similar to *Plectranthus* with a bent tube, blue (in ours); stamens 4, declinate; nutlets ovoid, smooth, glabrous.

1 Leaves petiolate, the petiole more than 15 mm long 2

Leaves sessile or very shortly petiolate, the petiole less than 5 mm long 4

2 Plant a weak trailing climber; spikes elongate, the axis of the spike clearly visible between the flowers 1. *P. umbrosa*
  Plant an erect shrub, spikes very short, appearing almost like heads, the axis of the spike hidden by flowers 3

3 Leaves pubescent below; calyx with tomentose hairs at the inside of the mouth and at the bases of the teeth 2. *P. eminii*
  Leaves glabrous below, sometimes with pubescence on the nerves only; calyx glabrous at mouth and at bases of teeth
  3. *P. meyeri*

4 Flowers less than 8 mm long 5
  Flowers more than 8 mm long 6

5 Bracts of spike and bases of calyx teeth ciliate with white hairs; fruiting spikes over 15 mm in diameter 4. *P. deflexifolia*
  Bracts of spike and bases of calyx teeth glabrous or pubescent only; fruiting spikes less than 15 mm in diameter
  5. *P. coerulea*

6 Leaves attenuate at base 7
  Leaves rounded or abruptly cuneate at base 8

7 Spikes solitary at ends of branches; leaves lanceolate-oblong 6. *P. speciosa*
  Spikes in loose terminal corymbs; leaves ovate-elliptic to oblanceolate to linear
  7. *P. stuhlmannii*

8 Calyx teeth 5 mm or more long; calyx mouth open, not closed by lateral ingrowths
  8. *P. niamniamensis*
  Calyx teeth less than 3 mm long; calyx mouth completely closed at maturity by lateral ingrowths from between the calyx teeth 9. *P. sp. A*

1. Pycnostachys umbrosa (*Vatke*) *Perkins*

An erect shrub or weak scrambler with ovate-elliptic acute leaves and terminal, solitary or branched diffuse spikes of blue flowers.

Uncommon, in riverine forest in dry country. HA, MAC.

Verdcourt and Polhill 2683.

2. Pycnostachys eminii *Guerke*

An erect woody herb with ovate acute leaves often truncate or shortly attenuate at base; spikes dense, terminal, with blue flowers.

Apparently rare, in riverine forest in western Kenya, since it has been found in only one locality, Sotik. KIS.

Bally 7832.

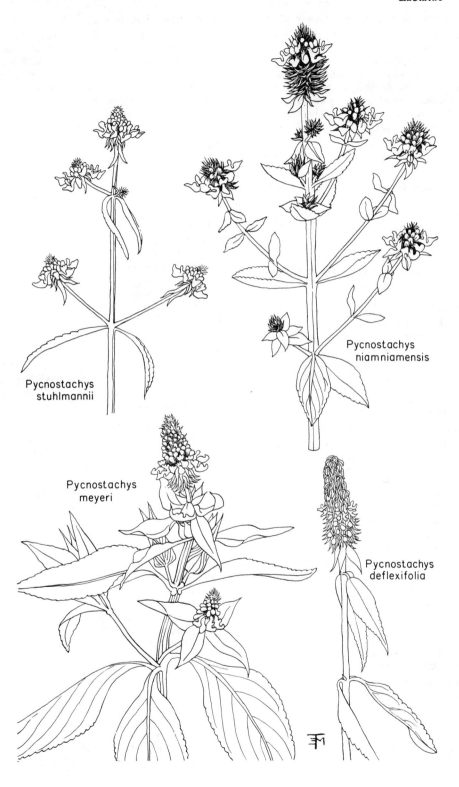

Pycnostachys
stuhlmannii

Pycnostachys
niamniamensis

Pycnostachys
meyeri

Pycnostachys
deflexifolia

3. Pycnostachys meyeri *Guerke* (see p. 631)

An erect woody herb or shrub, sometimes large, with lanceolate acute leaves and numerous dense terminal spikes of blue flowers.

Locally common in wet montane forest especially at streamsides. As defined here, this is a very variable species, pubescent or glabrous, and with thick, or narrow and sharply-tapering, or cylindrical spikes. HE, HC, HM, HA, HK, HN, KAJ.

Agnew, Hanid, and Kiniaruh 7920; Verdcourt and Polhill 2972.

4. Pycnostachys deflexifolia *Bak.* (see p. 631)

An erect glabrescent annual or short-lived perennial herb with lanceolate-elliptic leaves and terminal, usually solitary, long-tapering spikes of blue flowers.

Locally common as a weed in disturbed ground, principally in western Kenya. HE, HM, KIT, RV.

Bogdan 5596; Strid 3127.

5. Pycnostachys coerulea *Hook.*

Similar to *P. deflexifolia* except for the frequently drooping leaves and the key characters as given.

Locally common in swampy places particularly around Lake Naivasha, rare elsewhere. MUM, RV.

Agnew and Humphrey 5571; Poland in EAH 5492.

6. Pycnostachys speciosa *Guerke*

An annual, glabrescent, frequently tall herb with oblong or narrow-lanceolate leaves and large terminal spikes of blue flowers.

Rare, in wooded grassland in west Kenya in disturbed places. NAR.

Glover, Gwynne, and Samuel 599.

7. Pycnostachys stuhlmannii *Guerke* (see p. 631)

An erect pubescent annual or short-lived perennial herb with linear to narrow-lanceolate to narrow-elliptic leaves and short heads in a loose terminal corymb; flowers powder-blue.

Locally common in marshes in western Kenya. HE, HC, KIT, MUM.

Heriz-Smith and Paulo 854; Agnew, Kibe, and Mathenge 10584.

8. Pycnostachys niamniamensis *Guerke* (inc. *P. nepetifolia Bak.* of Check List) (see p. 631)

An erect pubescent woody herb with sessile, oblong to ovate-elliptic or even obovate leaves, and a terminal corymbose cluster of tapered spikes of powder-blue flowers.

Uncommon, in upland marshes in western Kenya. HT, HM, KIT, MUM, NAR.

Tweedie 67/301; Gosnell 736.

9. Pycnostachys *sp.* **A.**

Similar to *P. niamniamensis* except for the leaves which tend to clasp the stem at base and are rounded at apex, and the bracts which are nearly always smaller, and the key characters as given.

This plant has been found in the wet forest of eastern Mt. Kenya on one occasion. HK.

Gardner in EAH 15734.

16. CAPITANYA *Guerke*

Fleshy herbs or shrubs similar to *Plectranthus* except for the calyx which has very blunt subequal lobes which enlarge in fruit.

Capitanya otostegioides *Guerke* (see p. 629)

A spreading or trailing shrub with pubescent elliptic to obovate leaves, and terminal racemes of purple or white or cream flowers.

Common in bushland in dry country. BAR, MAG, NAN, MAC.

Glover and Samuel 2937; Lind, Agnew, and Isaac 5412.

17. ENGLERASTRUM *Briq.*

A genus similar to *Plectranthus* except for the axillary inflorescences which have but 1–2 often secund flowers at each node, and the calyx which has five almost equal teeth.

1   Plant erect, shrubby   1. *E.* sp. *A*
    Plant trailing, herbaceous or fleshy-stemmed 2
2   Plant annual, trailing not fleshy; flowers in
       loose axillary panicles
                                   2. *E. schweinfurthii*
    Plant perennial, trailing or climbing, fleshy,
       with flowers in spike-like axillary secund
       racemes   3. *E. scandens*

1. Englerastrum *sp.* **A.**

An erect pubescent shrub with shortly petiolate orbicular leaves and axillary or terminal racemes or panicles of pedicellate blue flowers; nutlets pubescent.

This plant has only been recorded from rough rocky ground on Mt. Suswa. RV.

Glover 4291.

2. Englerastrum schweinfurthii *Briq.*

A partially erect or trailing annual with almost simple glabrescent ovate-elliptic leaves and minute blue flowers in small panicles.

An uncommon plant of marshy grassland in western Kenya. KIT, MUM.

Agnew and Musumba 8609; Brodhurst-Hill 509.

3. Englerastrum scandens *Alston*

A trailing fleshy soft woody herb or soft shrub with square stems and petiolate, ovate, often deflexed leaves; flowers in secund spike-like racemes and panicles, deep purple.

An uncommon plant of riverine edges and rocky places in *Combretum* bushland. EMB, MAC, NBI.

Hanid and Kiniaruh 1050, Napier 378.

18. PLECTRANTHUS *L'Hérit.*

Erect or trailing shrubs or herbs with simple leaves and terminal racemes or panicles of whorled flowers; flowers usually more than two in each whorl; calyx zygomorphic with an enlarged upper lobe and 4, often equal lower teeth; corolla with a sharply bent tube and 2 lips, the upper often flat, the lower jointed to the tube and deeply concave; stamens 4, free or fused around the style; style bifid at apex; nutlets orbicular, ± flattened, smooth, glabrous.

1 Flowers more than 20 at each node of the inflorescence, densely crowded so that the pedicels are completely hidden 2
  Flowers less than 20, often fewer than 10 at each node; pedicels clearly visible 6
2 Plant hardly succulent; calyx erect in fruit, over 5 mm long 1. *P. lactiflorus*
  Plant succulent; calyx pendulous in fruit, less than 5 mm long 3
3 Leaves cordate or truncate at base 4
  Leaves cuneate at base 5
4 Two short lateral spikes as well as whorled flowers present at each node of the inflorescence; upper lobe of calyx as long as the lower lobes 27. *P. cyanus*
  Only whorled flowers present at each node of the inflorescence; upper lobe of calyx much longer than the lower lobes.
    2. *P.* sp. *A*
5 Corolla 7-10 mm long 3. *P. marrubioides*
  Corolla less than 6 mm long
    4. *P. cylindraceus*
6 Mature calyx closed at mouth by a dense tuft of white hairs 7
  Mature calyx glabrous within or with only a few loose woolly hairs 11
7 Inflorescence of crowded whorls which touch one another and thus appear spike-like 8
  Inflorescence of distant whorls of flowers which are separated by long internodes 10
8 Bracts of inflorescence white-translucent, falling before anthesis, blunt but with a small acute mucro at apex 9
  Bracts of inflorescence green, opaque, fleshy,

persistent at anthesis, rounded at apex without a mucro 7. *P. tetensis*
9 Plant perennial; leaves broadly cuneate at base, rounded at apex, corolla over 2 cm long 5. *P. comosus*
  Plant annual or short-lived perennial; leaves cuneate at base, obtuse or acute but not rounded at apex; corolla less than 1·5 cm long 6. *P. caninus*
10 Plant an erect shrub from a single rootstock
    8. *P. barbatus*
  Plant an erect herb from a woody perennial rootstock 9. *P.* sp. *B*
11 Plant bearing axillary cylindrical brown-hairy bulbils; flowers yellow 10. *P. luteus*
  Plant without bulbils; flowers blue or purple or white 12
12 Bracts of the flowering whorls small, shorter than pedicels, persistent to fruiting 13
  Bracts of the flowering whorls large, longer than pedicels, or falling early and not present in the fruiting stage 25
13 Upper lip of corolla much shorter than lower lip 14
  Upper lip of corolla as long as lower lip but erect 16
14 Plant not succulent; whorls of flowers without long hairs at the node 15
  Plant succulent; whorls of flowers with tufts of lanate hairs at the node
    11. *P. tenuiflorus*
15 Superficial glands on leaves, calyx and corolla bright red; inflorescences seldom branched
    13. *P. assurgens*
  Superficial glands on leaves, calyx and corolla yellow; inflorescences mostly branched
    12. *P. sylvestris*
16 An erect herb with a few tufted stems from a woody rootstock 14. *P. pubescens*
  An erect or trailing herb or shrub without a woody rootstock 17
17 Flowers in whorls of 2-3 at the nodes 18
  Flowers in 3-flowered pedunculate cymes at the nodes 15. *P. albus*
18 Flowers 2 in each whorl 19
  Flowers more than 2 in each whorl 20
19 Pedicels jointed about half way along their length 17. *P. pauciflorus*
  Pedicels unjointed 16. *P. masukensis*
20 Leaf apex acute 21
  Leaf apex rounded 18. *P. longipes*
21 Plant annual 22
  Plant perennial 23
22 Plant densely glandular; the 3 flowers subtended by each bract of the raceme sessile, without a short common peduncle
    19. *P.* sp. *G*

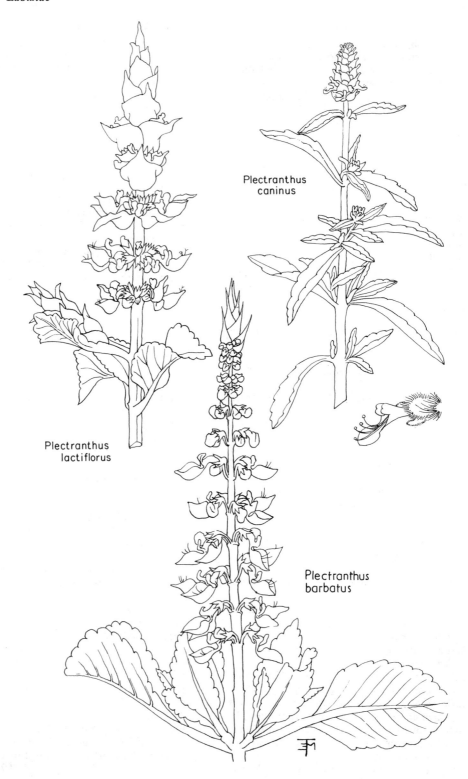

Plectranthus
caninus

Plectranthus
lactiflorus

Plectranthus
barbatus

Plant glandular but not densely so; the 3 flowers subtended by each bract of the raceme borne on a short common peduncle
20. *P. parvus*

23 Leaf lamina strictly truncate or cordate at the base   **24**
Leaf lamina shortly narrowing into the petiole   21. *P. alboviolaceus*

24 Leaves cordate at base, pubescent or almost tomentose on lower surface
22. *P. kamerunensis*
Leaves truncate at base, glabrous below
23. *P. laxiflorus*

25 Bracts of flower whorls present at anthesis **26**
Bracts of flower whorls deciduous, absent at anthesis   **27**

26 Bracts of flower whorls similar to the leaves, leaves ± entire; corolla less than 4 mm long
24. *P. prostratus*
Bracts of flower whorls very distinct from the leaves; leaves sharply serrate; corolla over 1 cm long   25. *P. coeruleus*

27 Plant an erect shrub   **28**
Plant a trailing or erect herb   **30**

28 Calyx with a few woolly hairs inside the mouth in fruit; plant usually without leaves at flowering   26. *P. igniarius*
Calyx glabrous within; plant leafy at flowering   **29**

29 Raceme paniculate; corolla 1 cm long or less
27. *P. cyaneus*
Racemes unbranched; flowers only in whorls; corolla over 1 cm long   28. *P. sp. H*

30 Lower lip of corolla concave, 2 mm or more deep from the margin to the keel   **31**
Lower lip of the corolla flat or slightly concave, less than 2 mm deep   **33**

31 Leaves thinly succulent   **32**
Leaves not succulent   30. *P. edulis*

32 Hairs on axis of inflorescence glandular; filaments fused for ± half their length
29. *P. lanuginosus*
Hairs on axis of inflorescence not glandular; filaments free from one another
3. *P. marrubioides*

33 All pedicels equal to or longer than the calyx
31. *P. zatarhendi*
Some pedicels shorter than the calyx
32. *P. sp. F*

1. Plectranthus lactiflorus (*Vatke*) *Agnew* comb. nov. (*Coleus lactiflorus* Vatke in *Linnaea* **43**, 89 (1880–1882)) (see p. 634)
A somewhat succulent woody herb from a perennial rootstock, with ovate petiolate leaves and dense terminal racemes; leaves usually absent at flowering time; whorls subtended by large ovate acuminate bracts; flowers lilac or purple.
Rather uncommon, found in rocky wooded grassland. HE, HC, KIT, RV, KAJ.
Tweedie 66/239; Glover 4176.

2. Plectranthus sp. A.
A fleshy trailing pubescent shrub with ovate to orbicular cordate leaves and simple terminal spike-like racemes of densely crowded flowers; flowers white to pale mauve.
Uncommon, found in rocky bushed dry country. BAR.
Agnew 10431; Bogdan 3839.

3. Plectranthus marrubioides *Benth.* (see p. 637)
A low pubescent trailing fleshy herb or soft shrub with ovate leaves and sparsely branched, very hairy terminal spike-like racemes of blue or lilac flowers.
Locally common in dry rocky grassland in the Rift Valley. RV.
Verdcourt 1019S; Agnew 9046.

4. Plectranthus cylindraceus *Benth.* (see p. 637)
A pubescent fleshy scrambling shrub with elliptic to obovate leaves and sparsely branched, densely hairy spike-like racemes of small powder-blue flowers.
Locally common in dry rocky bushland. KIT, BAR, RV, NAN, MAC, NBI, KAJ.
Agnew 10425; Mwangangi 41.

5. Plectranthus comosus *Roth*
A decumbent or erect perennial herb or weak shrub with suborbicular to obovate leaves; inflorescence as in *P. caninus* but larger and frequently interrupted at base.
Rare plant found in dry country. MAG.
Rauh 92.

6. Plectranthus caninus *Roth* (see p. 634)
A low fleshy annual with ascending stems bearing elliptic to cuneate leaves and dense uninterrupted terminal spike-like racemes of bright blue or violet flowers; bracts much longer than the flowers, apiculate.
Locally common in disturbed dry rocky country. It is remarkable for its very nasty smell. HC, HM, MUM, NAR, RV, MAC, NBI, KAJ.
Rauh 83; Agnew, Azavedo, and Khatri 9479.

7. Plectranthus tetensis (*Bak.*) *Agnew* comb. nov. (*Coleus tetensis* Baker in Dyer, *Flora of Tropical Africa* **5**, 431 (1900); *Coleus decumbens* Guerke)
A fleshy prostrate pubescent herb with narrow-elliptic to oblanceolate leaves and uninterrupted simple terminal spikes of blue and/or white flowers; bracts elliptic, entire, rounded at apex.

Occasional, in dry rocky grassland. NAR, RV, KAJ.

Bally 3540; Williams in EAH 12354.

8. Plectranthus barbatus *Andr.* (see p. 634)

An erect soft pubescent shrub, sometimes tree-like, with ovate or ovate-elliptic leaves and terminal racemes of large bright blue flowers.

Occasional in upland bushland and frequently cultivated. This large species is used as a quick-growing hedge plant in Kikuyu country. HC, HA, HK, KIT, BAR, MAC, EMB, NBI, KAJ.

Stone 7938; Agnew 10105.

9. Plectranthus *sp.* B. (see p.641)

An erect herb from a woody rootstock with tufted stems and oblanceolate-elliptic leaves and with a long terminal raceme of dense whorls of pale mauve or even white flowers.

Locally common in dry grassland especially amongst rocks. HC, HT, HA, KIT, KIS.

Tweedie 66/35; Symes 655.

10. Plectranthus luteus *Guerke*

An erect branched shrub, sparsely pubescent on upper parts, with elliptic leaves and cylindrical brown-hairy bulbils in the axils of the upper leaves; flowering infrequent; racemes short, axillary or terminal; flowers yellow.

This species is found as undergrowth at the edges of the wettest upland rain-forest. HM, HA, HK.

Agnew 9009; Battiscombe 1171.

11. Plectranthus tenuiflorus (*Vatke*) *Agnew* comb. nov. (*Coleus tenuiflorus* Vatke in *Linnaea* **43**, 92 (1880–1882))

A fleshy soft shrub or herb with trailing and ascending stems and ovate to elliptic leaves; racemes terminal, unbranched, rather loose; flowers white or pale mauve.

Locally common in dry rocky bushland. BAR, MAC.

Agnew 10421; Bally 8391.

12. Plectranthus sylvestris *Guerke* (see p. 637)

A glabrescent erect sparsely branched shrub with ovate acuminate leaves and a usually branched inflorescence of bright blue flowers with white spots on the upper lip.

This species is common in disturbed places in the higher levels of montane forest especially amongst bamboo forest. HE, HT, HM, HA, HK.

Nattrass 701; Strid 2289.

13. Plectranthus assurgens (*Bak.*) *J. K. Morton*

Similar to *P. sylvestris* but frequently trailing, with broad-ovate, almost suborbicular leaves and usually unbranched simple racemes.

This species also is found in shady montane forest edges. HC, HT, HM, HA, HK, KIT.

Part II Botany 29; Napper 657.

14. Plectranthus pubescens *Bak.*

An erect glandular pubescent herb from a fleshy or woody rootstock, with ovate-elliptic leaves and terminal inflorescences of white or pale mauve flowers.

This species looks very similar to an *Orthosiphon* at first sight but has the bifid stigma and bent (although only slightly) corolla of *Plectranthus*. It is found in wooded grassland, particularly where rocky. HE, HC, RV, MAG, KAJ.

Verdcourt 3811; Tweedie 67/69.

15. Plectranthus albus *Guerke*

An erect or decumbent pubescent herb with ovate cordate leaves and a very loose inflorescence of paired triflorate cymes of pink or pale purple flowers.

Common in disturbed ground in wet montane forest areas. HA, HK.

Agnew 7190; Verdcourt 2997.

16. Plectranthus masukensis *Bak.*

An erect annual with ovate triangular leaves and rather small white or mauve flowers.

A rare weed of roadsides and waste places in western Kenya. KIT.

Tweedie 3075.

17. Plectranthus pauciflorus *Bak.*

A trailing subsucculent pubescent herb, frequently annual, with orbicular leaves, often auriculate at the insertion of the petiole; inflorescence terminal, branched, of loose racemes of blue flowers.

This species is unique in its jointed pedicels. It is found in disturbed soils, frequently near cultivation, principally in western Kenya. HK, KIT, MUM, NAR.

Agnew, Musumba, and Kiniaruh 7995; Glover, Gwynne, and Samuel 585.

18. Plectranthus longipes *Bak.*

A subsucculent pubescent herb with ascending stems and orbicular crenate leaves and terminal racemes of bright blue flowers.

This species is frequently found in disturbed places in evergreen dry woodland country. HA, HK, MUM, NAR, RV, MAC, NBI, KAJ.

Harmsen 6492; Greenway 9539.

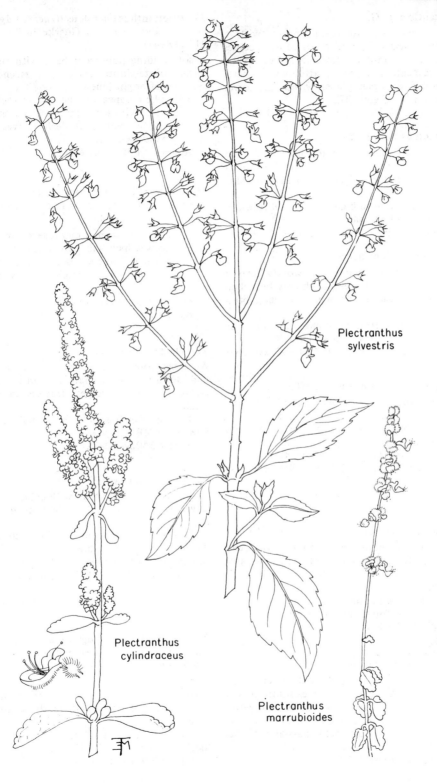

Plectranthus
sylvestris

Plectranthus
cylindraceus

Plectranthus
marrubioides

19. Plectranthus *sp.* **G.**

An erect, glandular, pubescent annual with a terminal branched inflorescence of loose racemes bearing blue or mauve flowers; leaves ovate, petiolate, truncate and shortly attenuate at base.

Recorded from open places within the lower forest zone on Mt. Elgon. HE.

Verdcourt 3234; Mendes and Sequeira 14.

20. Plectranthus parvus *Oliv.*

An erect annual with ovate to rhomboid long-petiolate leaves and a branched terminal group of racemes of rather small white to mauve or blue flowers.

Uncommon, found in highland cleared forest in western Kenya and Kilimanjaro. HE, KAJ.

Trelawny in Bogdan 4411; Coe, August 1957.

21. Plectranthus alboviolaceus *Guerke*

An erect or decumbent glabrescent woody herb or weak shrub with ovate leaves and shortly branched racemes of pale purple or white flowers; both corolla lips very short.

Found in the wettest montane rain forest as undergrowth and at forest edges. HA, HK.

Agnew, Kibe, and Zamierowski 10142; Gardner 1395.

22. Plectranthus kamerunensis *Guerke*

A tomentose or pubescent, weak erect shrub or scrambler with ovate leaves and branched or simple inflorescences of pink to pale purple and white flowers.

Found throughout the montane forest area, occasionally common. HE, HC, HT, HM, HA, HK, HN.

Agnew, Kibe, and Mathenge, 10529; Polhill 218.

23. Plectranthus laxiflorus *Benth.* (see p. 639)

A weak shrub or herb similar to *P. pubescens* except for the frequently unbranched racemes and the flowers which have a broader, not cylindrical corolla tube and are blue or violet at the edges with usually some white markings.

This species is found in wet montane forest. HT, HM, HA, HK, KAJ.

Strid 2948; Kabuye 78.

24. Plectranthus prostratus *Guerke*

A low trailing succulent herb with erect stems bearing opposite succulent obovate-elliptic leaves which grade into the bracts of the few-flowered racemes; flowers very small, inconspicuous.

Locally common in dry rocky grassland. MUM, NAR, RV, MAC.

Agnew 8228; Glover 3722.

25. Plectranthus coeruleus *(Guerke) Agnew* comb. nov. (*Coleus coeruleus* Guerke in *Bot. Jahrb.* **19**, 217 (1894))

A soft trailing pubescent herb with fleshy sessile serrate ovate-elliptic leaves and ascending inflorescences of bright blue flowers.

This plant appears to be rare in rocky areas in the region of Kibwezi. Apparently accessory reproduction is by bulbils of fleshy leaves which fall from the old stems. KAJ.

Agnew 10696; Bally 8972.

26. Plectranthus igniarius *(Schweinf.)* *Agnew* comb. nov. (*Coleus ignarius* Schweinfurth in *Beitr. Fl. Aethiop.* 121 (1867))

An erect shrub with tomentose obovate or orbicular leaves which fall before the production of the terminal inflorescences of unbranched, rather long racemes; flowers bright blue with a white upper lip.

Found in dry rocky country. MUM, MAC.

Agnew 10688.

27. Plectranthus cyaneus *Guerke*

An erect tomentose shrub with orbicular leaves and terminal much-branched inflorescences of tightly whorled racemes; flowers mauve, rather small.

This species has only been collected once at Utembe. EMB.

Napier 5402.

28. Plectranthus *sp.* **H.**

An erect tomentose shrub with orbicular to elliptic leaves and terminal unbranched racemes of bright blue flowers.

This species resembles *P. barbatus* except for the less conspicuous bracts of the inflorescence and the lack of hairs within the calyx mouth. It is only found in the Rift Valley and adjacent regions. NAR, RV.

Glover, Gwynne, Samuel, and Tucker 2580.

29. Plectranthus lanuginosus *(Benth.)* *Agnew* comb. nov. (*Coleus lanuginosus* Bentham in DC. *Prodromus* **12**, 79 (1848))

A pubescent trailing subsucculent herb with orbicular to wide-elliptic to ovate leaves and terminal simple racemes of rather tightly whorled bright blue flowers.

Found in dry upland grassland where it is very local in occurrence. HE, HA, KAJ.

Lind 5749; Hedberg 39.

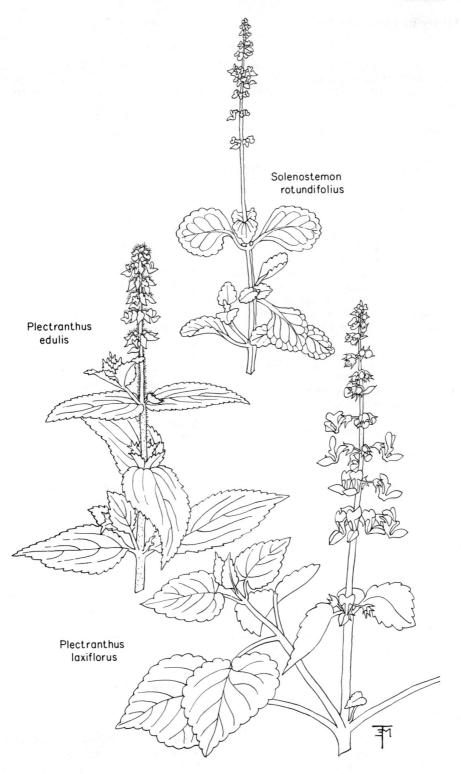

Solenostemon
rotundifolius

Plectranthus
edulis

Plectranthus
laxiflorus

30. Plectranthus edulis (*Vatke*) *Agnew* comb. nov.
(*Coleus edulis* Vatke in *Linnaea* **37**, 319 (1871–
1873)) (see p. 639)
A pubescent annual or short-lived perennial with
trailing stems rooting at the nodes and ascending
inflorescences; leaves elliptic to broad-ovate,
serrate; flowers in crowded whorls, bright blue
with dark blue hair bases.

Frequent, in the upland forest region especially
in the bamboo zone, where disturbed. It exists in
two forms with large and small flowers respectively and is also variable in leaf shape. HE, HC,
HT, HM, HA, HK, KIT.

Agnew, Hedberg, and Mmari 9652; Verdcourt
and Tweedie 2479.

31. Plectranthus zatarhendi (*Forsk.*) *E. A. Bruce*
A trailing pubescent subsucculent perennial herb
with ascending stems and long-petiolate, coarsely
serrate, orbicular, leaves; flowers in terminal
sparsely branched racemes, lilac or purple-blue.

Local, in disturbed rocky places in dry evergreen woodland. HA, NAR, BAR, RV, NBI.

Verdcourt 2765; Agnew 10180.

32. Plectranthus *sp.* **F.**
A pubescent trailing fleshy shrub with orbicular
leaves and a branched inflorescence of blue and
purple flowers in crowded whorls.

This plant has only been collected once in the
Sekerr range on cliff sides. HC.

Agnew, Kibe and Mathenge 10389.

19. SOLENOSTEMON *Schum.*
Herbs or shrubs similar to *Plectranthus* except for
the inflorescence whorls which have the flowers on
short raceme-like cymes, the calyx which has fused
anterior segments and obscure or blunt lateral
segments, and the corolla which has a very much
expanded lower lip with a reduced upper lip.

1	Plants annual	3.	*S. latifolius*
	Plants perennial		2
2	Leaves rounded at apex	4.	*S. rotundifolius*
	Leaves acute or acuminate at apex		3
3	Leaves narrowing into the petiole, densely tomentose beneath	1.	*S. zambesiacus*
	Leaves truncate at base, hardly narrowing into the petiole, glabrous below	2.	*S. sylvaticus*

1. Solenostemon zambesiacus *Bak.*
An erect shrub with ovate acuminate leaves,
tomentose below, bearing solitary terminal somewhat dense racemes of lilac to purple flowers.

Rather rare, found in wet places in montane
forest in western Kenya. HE, KIS.

Tweedie 68/112; Rauh 597.

2. Solenostemon sylvaticus (*Guerke*) *Agnew*
comb. nov. (*Coleus sylvaticus* Guerke in *Bot.
Jahrb.* **19**, 213 (1894))
Similar to *S. zambesiacus* but sometimes scrambling
and frequently almost glabrous; the inflorescences
are less dense than in *S. zambesiacus.*

This species is found in wet forest by streamsides in the eastern half of our area. HK.

Agnew 7736; Copley 603.

3. Solenostemon latifolius (*Benth.*) *J. K. Morton*
(see p. 641)
An erect annual, branching from the base, sparsely
pubescent on all parts, with ovate-orbicular serrate
leaves and terminal racemes of rich purple or blue
flowers.

An uncommon annual of shallow soils and
rocky places in western Kenya. HC, HT, KIT,
MUM, EMB.

Agnew and Musumba 8580; Williams 249.

4. Solenostemon rotundifolius (*Poir.*) *J. K.
Morton* (see p. 639)
An erect herb, sometimes large, from a woody or
tuberous rootstock, with obovate to spathulate to
orbicular leaves and a long branched inflorescence
of numerous narrow racemes of blue or pale
purple flowers.

An uncommon plant of grasslands principally
found in western Kenya. HE, HC, HT, HA, KIT,
KIS, NAR.

Hanid and Kiniaruh 821; Napier 5398.

20. ISODICTYOPHORUS *Briq.*
A genus similar to *Plectranthus* except for the
calyx teeth which are all equal and the inflorescence which is a large terminal panicle.

Isodictyophorus defoliatus (*Benth.*) *Agnew* comb.
nov. (*Plectranthus defoliatus* Bentham in DC.
Prodromus **12**, 60 (1848)) (see p. 641)
An erect herb from a perennial rootstock, bearing
ovate-elliptic leaves which fall before the production of the massive terminal panicle of deep blue
and maroon flowers.

Uncommon, found in wooded grassland in
western Kenya. HE, KIT.

Tweedie 67/359; Graham 1107.

21. HOMALOCHEILOS *J. K. Morton*
Similar to *Plectranthus* but with a hardly concave
lower lip to the corolla and equal triangular calyx
teeth.

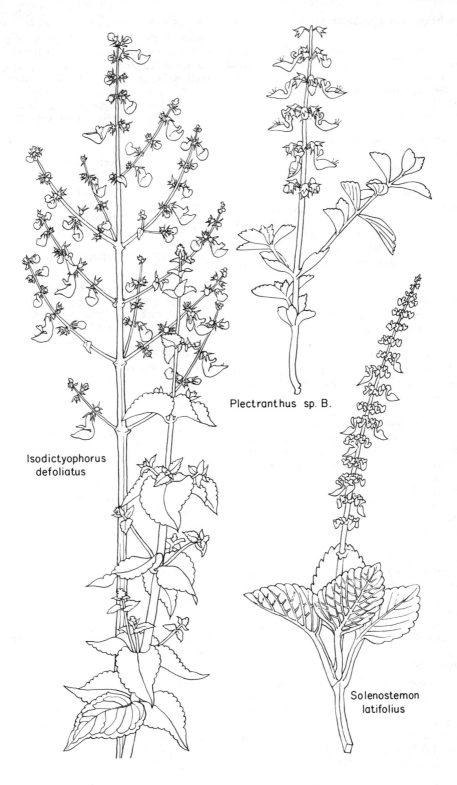

Isodictyophorus
defoliatus

Plectranthus sp. B.

Solenostemon
latifolius

Homalocheilos ramosissimum (*Hook. f.*) *J. K. Morton*

An erect herb with ovate leaves and loose terminal panicles of small white (and sometimes spotted purple) flowers.

Locally common in western Kenya grasslands. KIT, MUM.

Verdcourt 1664.

22. NEOHYPTIS *J. K. Morton*

Similar to *Plectranthus* but with a hardly concave lower corolla lip and regularly 5-toothed calyx.

Neohyptis paniculata (*Bak.*) *J. K. Morton*

An erect minutely pubescent annual with small obovate-elliptic leaves and short lateral and terminal spike-like racemes of crowded flowers, flowers mauve and white.

Local, in swamps in western Kenya. HT, KIT.

Bogdan 3813.

23. HOSLUNDIA *Vahl*

Herbs or shrubs with opposite simple leaves and flowers in terminal panicles; calyx almost regular, 5-toothed, enlarged, fleshy and closed around the nutlets in fruit; corolla obscurely bilabiate, the upper lip small, the lower lip large, concave; stamens 2, declinate; nutlets ovoid, slightly roughened.

Hoslundia opposita *Vahl* (see p. 647)

An erect or rarely decumbent pubescent shrub with elliptic-lanceolate leaves and terminal racemes of small white flowers; calyx in fruit orange.

A common plant of disturbed places and roadsides in the warmer areas of Upland Kenya. HE, HC, HA, KIT, MUM, KIS, NAR, BAR, EMB, MAC, KAJ.

Agnew 9123; Kokwaro 84.

24. IBOZA *N. E. Br.*

Erect shrubs with entire leaves and terminal panicles of small flowers; flowers unisexual, calyx almost regular, 5-toothed; corolla slightly zygomorphic with spreading, suborbicular lobes; stamens 4, free, declinate, stigmas 2, filiform; nutlets smooth, ovoid.

Iboza multiflora (*Benth.*) *E. A. Bruce*

An erect, subsucculent dioecious shrub with ovate, cordate, crenate leaves, densely pubescent on the lower surface, and large terminal panicles of white or pale blue flowers.

Locally common in dry rocky evergreen bushland. HC, NAR, RV, MAC, KAJ.

Lind 12; Greenway 13096.

25. ERYTHROCHLAMYS *Guerke*

Shrub or herbs with simple leaves, and flowers in terminal racemes; calyx zygomorphic, the upper lip much larger than the lower and enlarging in fruit to wrap around the sub-equal lower teeth, corolla tube slightly exserted, corolla bilabiate, the upper lip much larger than the lower; stamens 4, filaments free; nutlets ovoid, smooth, included in the persistent calyx.

Erythrochlamys spectabilis *Guerke*

An erect pubescent shrub with oblong-lanceolate subsessile leaves and simple terminal racemes of purple flowers, calyx becoming very enlarged and conspicuous and bright red in fruit.

Common in disturbed, dry, sandy bushland. EMB, MAC.

Strid 2519; Greenway 8851.

26. PLATOSTOMA *P. Beauv.*

Herbs or shrubs with opposite entire leaves and terminal racemose inflorescences; calyx 2-lipped, the lips entire; corolla short, 2-lipped, the upper lip 4-toothed, the lower concave, entire; stamens 4, declinate, filaments free; nutlets ovoid, minutely reticulated.

Platostoma africanum *P. Beauv.*

An erect or decumbent trailing annual or short-lived perennial with ovate-elliptic petiolate leaves and rather narrow terminal inflorescence; flowers white, subtended by small, often whitish bracts along the raceme.

Found in all the wet forest regions of Kenya, often in partial shade at forest edges. HM, HA, HK, KIT, MUM, KIS.

Kerfoot 4885; Hanid and Kiniaruh 623.

27. HAUMANIASTRUM *Duvign. & Planke*

Erect herbs or shrubs with simple, often narrow leaves and the flowers in 12-flowered whorls contracted at the apex of the branches to appear capitate or spike-like; calyx bilabiate with 2 entire lips, or the upper lip 3-toothed, the lower lip 2-toothed; the corolla with an expanding tube, bilabiate above, stamens 4, declinate; nutlets smooth, glabrous.

1	Woody annuals or perennials; spikes all in a dense terminal corymb	2
	Weak erect annuals; spikes scattered at ends of every branch	1. *H. galeopsifolius*
2	Spikes each subtended by broad white bracts, the bracts as long as or longer than the spike; calyx lips entire	2. *H. caeruleum*

Spikes subtended by narrow, frequently un-
coloured bracts which are never as long as
the spike; lower calyx lip with 2 apical
teeth   3. *H. venosum*

1. Haumaniastrum galeopsifolius (*Bak.*) *Duvign. & Planke* (inc. *Acrocephalus cylindraceus Oliv.* of Check List)

An erect pubescent annual with oblong to lanceolate, serrate, shortly petiolate leaves and small
terminal globose or cylindrical heads of blue
flowers.

This species is uncommon in disturbed places,
especially in shallow soils, in western Kenya. HE,
HM, KIT, MUM, KIS.

Tweedie 67/285; Verdcourt 1634.

2. Haumaniastrum caeruleum (*Oliv.*) *J. K. Morton*

An erect woody annual or short-lived perennial,
tomentose to pubescent on all parts with linear to
oblanceolate leaves, and a dense terminal corymb
of white-flowered spikes subtended by broad
white bracts.

Uncommon, found in western Kenya. HE, KIT.

Tweedie 68/148; Lugard 91.

3. Haumaniastrum venosum (*Bak.*) *Agnew*
comb. nov. (*Acrocephalus venosus* Baker in *Kew
Bull.* (1898) 160)

An erect shrubby pubescent perennial with linear
leaves and a dense terminal corymb of small
mauve- or blue-flowered heads.

Rare, found in western Kenya. KIS.

Irwin 198.

28. GENIOSPORUM *Wall*

Erect shrubs or herbs similar to *Ocimum* but with
c. 20 flowers in each whorl, the calyx 5-toothed,
the upper tooth largest (sometimes obscurely so)
sometimes decurrent on the tube, and the lower
raceme bracts whitish or coloured, enlarged.

1   Leaves with raised reticulate venation below;
    calyx almost equally 5-toothed, not in-
    flated above   1. *G. paludosum*
    Leaves smooth, hardly with raised venation
    below; calyx with 2 prominent inflated
    raised areas on the tube on the upper side,
    and an enlarged upper lobe
                              2. *G. hildebrandtii*

1. Geniosporum paludosum *Bak.* (see p. 647)

An erect herb from a woody rootstock, branching
above, with shortly petiolate, ovate to oblong
leaves and terminal racemes of small pinkish
flowers subtended by large white bracts at the base
of the racemes.

Not uncommon in marshes in western Kenya.
HE, HC, HT, HM, KIT, MUM, KIS.

Lind 5164; Lugard 30.

2. Geniosporum hildebrandtii (*Vatke*) *Ashby*

An erect herb from a woody rootstock, similar to
G. paludosum but less hairy on all parts and with
more constantly ovate-elliptic leaves and with the
bracts of the racemes rather less conspicuous.

Uncommon, found in disturbed places in dry
shady bushland. MAC, KAJ.   .

Lind and Agnew 5684; Napper 1727.

29. OCIMUM *L.*

Herbs or shrubs with simple leaves and terminal
racemes of rather short-pedicelled flowers; calyx
zygomorphic, with a large upper lobe which is
decurrent upon the tube, and 4 lower teeth;
corolla bilabiate with a cylindric or obconic tube
and a flat upper lip and a concave lower lip;
stamens 4, declinate, the 2 uppermost with a tooth
or tuft of hairs near the base of the filaments;
nutlets rough, ovoid.

1   Calyx in fruit open at the mouth, with a tuft
    of stiff hairs within which serve to retain
    the nutlets inside the calyx   2
    Calyx in fruit closed by the lower lip which is
    curved upwards and pressed against the
    bottom of the upper calyx tooth, without
    stiff hairs within the.tube   5
2   Corolla over 8 mm long   4. *O. hadiense*
    Corolla less than 5 mm long   3
3   Plant annual, sometimes woody; at least some
    leaves with petiole longer than half lamina
    length   5. *O. basilicum*
    Plant perennial, herb or shrub; all leaves with
    petiole less than half lamina length   4
4   Plant an erect shrub; leaves smelling only of
    peppermint when crushed; upper calyx
    tooth sparsely pubescent above
                              6. *O. kilimandscharicum*
    Plant a rhizomatous herb or apparently
    annual; leaves smelling of peppermint
    mixed with aniseed when crushed; upper
    calyx tooth glabrous above   1. *O.* sp. *A*
5   Corolla tube cylindrical   6
    Corolla tube obconical, widening markedly to
    the mouth of the tube   7
6   Axis of inflorescence and base of calyx
    cream- to white-woolly
                              2. *O. lamiifolium*
    Axis of inflorescence and base of calyx
    pubescent only, not woolly   3. *O.* sp. *B*
7   Leaves rounded at apex; racemes mostly
    solitary, without accessory racemes and
    not in panicles   7. *O.* sp. *C*

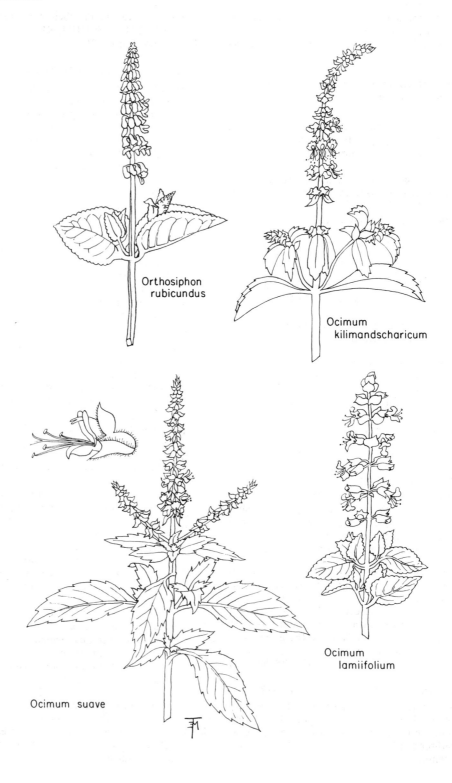

Orthosiphon
rubicundus

Ocimum
kilimandscharicum

Ocimum suave

Ocimum
lamiifolium

Leaves acuminate or acute at apex; racemes usually paniculate or with accessory racemes at the base **8**

8　Whorls of racemes crowded, touching one another; lower lip of calyx densely white-tomentose　　　　**8. *O. tomentosum***

Whorls of racemes not continuous, not touching one another; lower lip of calyx pubescent, not tomentose　　**9. *O. suave***

1. Ocimum *sp.* A.

A rhizomatous herb with ascending stems and subsessile ovate-elliptic leaves, racemes simple, terminal, similar to those of *O. kilimandscharicum* but more slender.

Locally abundant, in black-cotton and water-logged vlei soils, but found only around Nairobi and in one place in north Mt. Kenya. HA, HK, MAC, NBI.

Bogdan 137; Agnew 9677.

2. Ocimum lamiifolium *Benth.* (see p. 644)

An erect robust branching shrub, with pubescent to tomentose ovate acute leaves, and white or very pale purple flowers in compound or simple terminal racemes.

Locally common in montane forest edges, and where disturbed. HC, HT, HM, HA, HK, KIT, KIS.

Agnew, Azavedo, and Khatri 9558, Irwin 213.

3. Ocimum *sp.* B.

An erect branched shrub with pubescent ovate bluntly crenate leaves and loose terminal racemes of white, tinged purple flowers.

Uncommon, on the Rift Valley side of the Ngong hills and in the dry bushland between there and Magadi, on stony ground. HA, MAG.

Glover, Gwynne, and Samuel 2917; Agnew 9584.

4. Ocimum hadiense *Forsk.*

An erect shrub with sparsely pubescent or glabrous, shortly petiolate, lanceolate to elliptic leaves, and large pale purple flowers in terminal, usually simple racemes of rather distant whorls; hairs of the inflorescence and calyx often tinged with purple.

Locally common in dry *Commiphora* bushland. NAN, MAC.

Adamson 690.

5. Ocimum basilicum *L.* (*O. americanum* L.)

An erect branching annual, pubescent and with long hairs, and with long-petiolate, lanceolate to ovate leaves; racemes rather dense, of minute flowers.

Locally common in disturbed, dry country. MUM, KIS, MAG, EMB, MAC, KAJ.

Agnew 5395, Glover and Samuel 2774.

6. Ocimum kilimandscharicum *Guerke* (see p. 644)

An erect branching pubescent shrub, with ovate to elliptic leaves and simple terminal racemes of rather distant whorls of small white to pinkish flowers.

A common plant of rocky ground in the evergreen wooded area of Upland Kenya. HE, HM, HA, HK, KIT, MUM, NAR, BAR, RV, NAN, EMB, MAC, NBI.

Agnew and Musumba 5333; Glover, Gwynne, and Samuel 1291.

7. Ocimum *sp.* C.

A pubescent erect woody herb or shrub with suborbicular leaves and simple terminal racemes of inconspicuous dirty-white flowers.

Uncommon, in dry *Acacia-Commiphora* bush-land. RV, KAJ.

Agnew 7624.

8. Ocimum tomentosum *Oliv.*

An erect shrub with pubescent ovate leaves and thick dense terminal racemes of rather woolly calyces; corolla whitish-green.

Uncommon, in the Kitale area this species appears to hybridise with the next, *O. suave*. KIT.

Tweedie 67/300; Symes 156 (hybrid); Brodhurst-Hill 430.

9. Ocimum suave *Willd.* (see p. 644)

An erect shrub with long-petiolate ovate serrate leaves and terminal paniculate racemes of small dirty white flowers; buds often with reddish-purple hairs.

Common in the upland forest areas where disturbed. HE, HC, HT, HM, HA, HK, KIT, MUM, KIS, NAR, BAR, RV, MAC, NBI, KAJ.

Faden 66196; Tweedie 68/61.

30. BECIUM *Lindl.*

Shrubs or herbs with entire leaves, similar to *Ocimum* except for the enlarged glandular bases to the caducous bracts of the floral whorls, and the lateral calyx lobes which are obsolete and represented by an oblique minutely toothed and ciliate margin to the calyx.

1　Plant an erect annual; leaves clearly petiolate, the petiole of at least some leaves up to half the length of the lamina; bracts of the floral whorls linear-spathulate, erect

　　　　　　　　　　　　　　　1. *B.* sp. *A*

Plants perennial, shrubs or herbs; leaves sessile or with shorter petioles; bracts of the floral whorls ovate-lanceolate, often inconspicuous and recurved   2

2   Corolla less than 5 mm long; leaves linear or oblinear   2. *B. angustifolium*
Corolla over 6 mm long; leaves broader than linear   3

3   Midrib of leaf curved downwards at base or apex with the two lateral halves of the leaf folding upwards when young and when drying; leaves ovate to orbicular, rounded at base and/or apex   3. *B. capitatum*
Leaves flat, not folded upwards when young or drying; leaves oblong to lanceolate-elliptic   4

4   Leaves oblong to oblanceolate to ovate-oblong with an obtuse or rounded apex; flowers opening before the elongation of the internodes of the raceme so that they appear to be in heads   4. *B. obovatum*
Leaves lanceolate to elliptic to oblanceolate, acute at apex, attenuate at base; flowers opening after the elongation of the internodes of the raceme and thus appearing strictly racemose   5. *B.* sp. *C*

1. Becium *sp.* A.

An erect often woody annual with elliptic to lanceolate, acute, pubescent leaves and long interrupted racemes of white to pale pink flowers.

Locally common in dry rocky country. KIS, MAG, EMB, MAC, KAJ.

Glover and Samuel 2793; Agnew 9138.

2. Becium angustifolium (*Benth.*) *N. E. Br.*

A woody herb from a thick woody rootstock with fascicled linear to oblinear leaves and simple racemes of rather small mauve flowers.

Uncommon plant found in dry grassland. NAR. Ossent in EAH 13674.

3. Becium capitatum (*Bak.*) *Agnew* comb. nov.
(*Ocimum capitatum* Baker in *Flora of Tropical Africa* 5, 348 (1900)

An erect or trailing shrub with pubescent to glabrescent, shortly petiolate, ovate to orbicular leaves and apparent heads of flowers which elongate only in fruit.

This plant is rather variable in habit, being either prostrate or a tall woody shrub. It is locally common in dry upland bushland in the north of our area. HC, HK.

Rauh 467; Agnew, Kibe, and Mathenge 10366.

4. Becium obovatum (*E. Mey.*) *N. E. Br.* (p. 647)

An erect or trailing pubescent or glabrescent herb or wiry shrub, from a woody rootstock or rhizomatous, with oblong, ovate or obovate leaves, rounded at base or apex, and with head-like inflorescences, elongating only in fruit, with white or pale pink flowers.

Common in upland grassland and very variable. This plant appears to grow where drainage is rather poor. HM, HA, NAR, RV, NAN, MAC, NBI, KAJ.

Verdcourt 3822; Agnew and Musumba 5309.

5. Becium *sp.* C.

An erect often glabrous herb from a woody rootstock, sparsely branched, with linear to oblanceolate acute leaves and purple stems; inflorescence rather elongate of white and pink flowers.

Locally common in wooded grassland. Plants from the West of Kenya have a tuft of hairs within the calyx at the lower side, but otherwise they appear identical with plants from elsewhere. HL, KIT, KAJ.

Tweedie 66/32, Lucas 196.

31. ORTHOSIPHON *Benth.*

Erect or scrambling herbs or weak shrubs with entire leaves and terminal racemes of whorled flowers; flowers in whorls of 6 (in ours); calyx bell-shaped, 5-lobed with an enlarged upper lobe decurrent on the tube at its edges, and a small accessory blunt lobe between each anterior tooth and the posterior lobe; corolla bilabiate with a long or short tube which is hardly bent, or straight; stamens 4, declinate; stigma entire; nutlets ovoid or globose, rather rough when mature.

1   Plant an (often woody) annual; flowers less than 5 mm long at anthesis   3. *O. somalensis*
Plant perennial; flowers over 7 mm long at anthesis   2

2   Leaves uniformly pubescent on both surfaces when mature; axis of inflorescence with a dense covering of short white downward-curved hairs and without glands   1. *O. parvifolius*
Leaves glabrous below between the nerves or with a more dense covering of hairs on the lower side than on the upper; axis of inflorescence with long spreading hairs and usually with dense glandular hairs beneath the spreading indumentum   3

3   Leaves tomentose below, densely pubescent above   2. *O. hildebrandtii*
Leaves glabrous below between the nerves   4

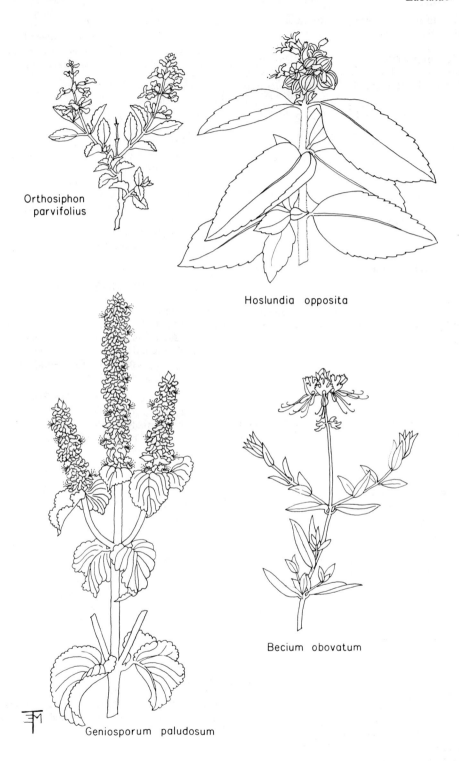

Orthosiphon
parvifolius

Hoslundia opposita

Geniosporum paludosum

Becium obovatum

4   Calyx purple above, green below; corolla tube at least twice as long as the calyx at anthesis   4. *O. suffrutescens*
    Calyx uniformly red or reddish-purple; corolla tube less than twice as long as the calyx tube at anthesis   5. *O. rubicundus*

1. Orthosiphon parvifolius *Vatke* (see p. 647)

A pubescent herb with a tuft of erect stems from a small woody rootstock, bearing subsessile petiolate oblong to elliptic to linear leaves and terminal inflorescences of pinkish flowers; corolla tube about twice as long as calyx at anthesis.

A common plant of shallow soil and seasonally flooded grassland in the upland dry forest region. NAR, NAN, EMB, MAC, NBI, KAJ.

Verdcourt 2508; Agnew 5310.

2. Orthosiphon hildebrandtii *Bak.* (see p. 618)

A tomentose erect or trailing weak shrub with petiolate ovate rounded leaves and simple terminal racemes of pale mauve or pinkish-white flowers.

Rather uncommon, found in dry forest edges in the north of our area. HE, HC.

Agnew, Kibe, and Mathenge 10492; Newbould 7113.

3. Orthosiphon somalensis *Vatke*

An erect woody annual with scattered long white hairs and petiolate, ovate leaves; flowers minute, whitish.

Uncommon, found in dry country. KIS.

Hanid and Kiniaruh 776.

4. Orthosiphon suffrutescens (*Thonning*) *J. K. Morton* (*O. australis* Vatke)

A sparsely pubescent erect herb or weak shrub with obovate to ovate leaves which tend to be attenuate into the petiole at base; flowers pale mauve or pinkish in rather loose terminal racemes.

A rather variable plant of grassland and wooded grassland especially in drier regions, extending to the coast. MUM, NAR, MAC, KAJ.

Agnew, Hanid, and Kiniaruh 9227; Ivens 2098.

5. Orthosiphon rubicundus *Benth.* (see p. 644)

An erect pubescent herb from a woody or fleshy rootstock with obovate to oblong-ovate leaves which are frequently attenuate at base into the short petiole; flowers in conspicuous terminal reddish racemes; corolla mauve.

A fairly common plant of wooded grassland, mostly in western Kenya. HE, HC, HT, KIT, MUM, MAC.

Napier 5494; Tweedie 67/28.

32. FUERSTIA *T. C. E. Fr.*

Shrubs similar to *Orthosiphon* except for the calyx which is smaller in flower and the flowers which are but 2 in each whorl and have only 2 included stamens.

Fuerstia africana *T. C. E. Fr.*

An erect shrub or herb, pubescent to loosely tomentose, with ovate serrate leaves and loose terminal racemes of small white flowers.

This species is common in shallow-soil grassland at medium altitudes. It is easy to recognize by the small white flowers with 2 stamens, and moreover, the crushed leaves usually stain the fingers red due to the presence of numerous superficial glands containing a red dye. HC, HT, HM, HA, HK, MUM, KIS, NAR, RV, NAN, MAC, NBI.

Agnew and Musumba 5268; Glover and Napper 4273.

94. HYDROCHARITACEAE†

Aquatic herb with alternate or opposite, usually stipulate, simple leaves, and flowers in clusters within usually bifid spathes; flowers bisexual or unisexual, regular; sepals 3, free; petals 0–3, free; stamens 3–12, with short filaments; ovary inferior 1-celled, with parietal, diffuse placentation.

1   Leaves on elongated trailing stems   2
    Leaves in a rosette on a short stem   4
2   Plant strongly rooted in mud with a swollen corm at base; leaves stiff, often recurved, ovate or elliptic   2. *Hydrilla verticillata*
    Plant with roots trailing in water, unfixed, sometimes also fixed; leaves oblong to linear, soft, never recurved   3
3   Stipules present, minute, intra-axillary; male flowers free-floating, pink; female flowers with 6 stigmas   3. *Lagarosiphon*
    Stipules absent; male flowers attached to plant, white; female flowers (rare) with 3, lobed stigmas   1. *Elodea densa*
4   Leaves petiolate, elliptic; peduncle of female flowers remaining straight   4. *Ottelia*
    Leaves strap-shaped, sessile; peduncle of female flowers coiling after pollination
        5. *Vallisneria spiralis*

1. ELODEA *Michx.*

Submerged dioecious herbs with sessile whorled exstipulate leaves and sessile, tubular spathes; flowers solitary, with sepals 3 and petals 3; male flowers with 3–9 stamens; female flowers with a long axis and 3 notched styles.

† By A. D. Q. Agnew.

Elodea densa (*Planch.*) *Casp.*

A trailing aquatic with oblong-linear entire or ciliate leaves and white to pale yellow flowers; male flowers attached to plant, with 9 stamens; female flowers not seen.

An introduced plant (from America) which is used in aquaria. HA, NBI.

Verdcourt 3044.

2. HYDRILLA *L. C. Rich.*

Submerged dioecious herbs with whorled exstipulate leaves; spathes sessile, axillary; male flower solitary with 3 petals, 3 sepals and 3 stamens; female flowers 1–2 together with sepals 3, petals 3 and 3 undivided styles.

Hydrilla verticillata *Casp.*

A strongly rooted submerged herb with elliptic to ovate, minutely serrate leaves and small pinkish axillary flowers; pollination of the long-stalked female flower is effected by the free-floating male flowers.

Uncommon, found in Lake Victoria. MUM.

Glasgow 50/2.

3. LAGAROSIPHON *Harv.*

Similar to *Hydrilla* but stipulate and with the leaves sometimes alternate, and with many male flowers in each spathe; stigmas 6.

1 Leaves minutely serrate with over 50 minute teeth on each side or entire, ciliate; stipules lanceolate   1. *L. hydrilloides*
  Leaves coarsely serrate with 25–40 teeth on each side; stipules filamentous or rounded
         2

2 Leaves oblong; stipules obovate or oblong
         2. *L.* sp. *A*
  Leaves very narrow and ± tapering from their base; stipules minute, hair-like
         3. *L. tenuis*

1. Lagarosiphon hydrilloides Rendle

A trailing, free-floating aquatic with whorled oblong-linear leaves and small pinkish flowers.

Locally common in lakes and reservoirs above 6000 ft. HE, HT, HA, NBI.

Lugard 534; Lind, Agnew, and Kettle 5895.

2. Lagarosiphon *sp.* A.

Similar to *L. hydrilloides* but with the keyed differences, this species is recorded on the basis of one specimen from Nairobi. NB1.

Mother Cyril in EAH 13883.

3. Lagarosiphon tenuis *Rendle*

A free-floating or anchored submerged aquatic with subulate leaves and small pink flowers.

Locally common in ephemeral pools in drier, warmer country. MUM, MAG.

McMahon 1.

4. OTTELIA *Pers.*

Rooted aquatic herbs with a rosette of petiolate, floating or submerged leaves and white or yellow flowers in a bifid, pedunculate spathe; flowers bisexual or unisexual; sepals 3, smaller than the 3 petals; stamens 6–12; ovary ovoid, with ovules scattered over the 6 intrusive placentas, styles 6.

1 Spathe with two lateral wings; flower axis hardly elongated, and the flowers borne one at a time in the mouth of the spathe
         1. *O. ulvifolia*
  Spathe without two lateral wings; flower axis elongated, the flowers borne well above the opening of the spathe   2. *O.* sp. *A*

1. Ottelia ulvifolia *Walp.*

An aquatic perennial with submerged or floating elliptic leaves and conspicuous yellow flowers held above the water surface.

Locally common in pools. HE, HT, KIT, MUM, EMB, NBI.

Wood 749.

2. Ottelia *sp.* A.

Similar to *O. ulvifolia* except for the keyed characters, this species has only been found in western Kenya. MUM.

Whitehead H220.

5. VALLISNERIA *L.*

Submerged stoloniferous perennial herb with rosettes of linear leaves and unisexual flowers; male flowers numerous in a 2-toothed shortly peduncled spathe, floating to the surface at anthesis, with 3 sepals, petals 0 and 3 stamens; female flower solitary in a long-pedunculate spathe which coils to submerge the fruit after pollination with 3 sepals, 3 minute petals and 3 bifid stigmas; capsule cylindrical.

Vallisneria spiralis *L.*

A submerged herb with strap-shaped, blunt leaves and pinkish flowers.

Known from Lake Victoria, but needs confirmation for the Kenya side on which it almost certainly occurs.

95. ALISMATACEAE†

Perennial aquatic herbs with rosettes of erect simple leaves and flowers in whorls; flowers bisexual, regular; sepals 3, smaller than the 3 petals; stamens 3–9; carpels free, superior, 3–many, whorled or spiral, with 1–many ovules.

1   Achenes in one whorl
            1. *Alisma plantago-aquatica*
    Achenes spiral   2. *Burnatia enneandra*

1. ALISMA *L.*

Herbs with submerged or floating leaves and erect panicles of whorled branches bearing pinkish flowers; stamens 6; carpels many, in one whorl, free.

Alisma plantago-aquatica *L.* (see p. 651)

An erect aquatic herb with long-petiolate ovate leaves; inflorescence of about 6 whorls of branches and flowers.

Locally common in wet places, especially by streamsides. HE, HT, HA, EMB, NBI.
Verdcourt 914; Lugard 532.

2. BURNATIA *Mich.*

Similar to *Alisma* but dioecious with 3 branches of the inflorescence in each whorl (in *Alisma* often 4 or more) and flowers racemose on each branch; flowers unisexual; male flowers with sepals and petals 3, and stamens 9; female flowers with no petals and numerous spiral carpels.

Burnatia enneandra *Mich.*

Similar to *Alisma plantago-aquatica* in habit but with the generic differences as described.
Uncommon, found in marshes. MUM, NBI.
Bogdan 1637.

96. APONOGETONACEAE‡

Aquatic herbs (rarely growing on wet soil) with tuberous rhizome; leaves all basal, simple or with long petioles; leaf-blades oblong to linear, sometimes almost indistinguishable from the petiole; inflorescence a simple or bifid spike, at first enclosed in a thin caducous spathe; flowers bisexual or more rarely unisexual; tepals 1–6 or absent, petal-like, often persistent in fruit; stamens 1–6, rarely more; ovaries 3–8, each with 2–10 ovules; fruit a 2–10-seeded follicle.

1. APONOGETON *L. f.*

The only genus with the characters of the family.

1   Spikes bifid   2
    Spikes simple   5

† By A. D. Q. Agnew.
‡ By K. Lye.

2   Leaves thick and narrow; tepals whitish
            1. *A. junceus*
    Leaves with distinct floating leaf-blade   3
3   Tepals absent in female flowers (spikes)
            4. *A. nudiflorus*
    Tepals present in all flowers   4
4   Tepals purple   2. *A. abyssinicus*
    Tepals cream or yellow   3. *A. subconjugatus*
5   Leaves without distinct leaf-blade
            7. *A. vallisnerioides*
    Leaves with distinct leaf-blade   6
6   Tepals white; plant very slender
            6. *A. stuhlmannii*
    Tepals purple, plant more robust
            5. *A. violaceus*

1. Aponogeton junceus *Schlechtd.*

Leaves with linear, thick and fleshy leaf-blade 5–7·5 cm long and 5–8 mm wide; tepals 1–2.
Rare plant found in temporary pools near Thika. MAC.
Lye 6375.

2. Aponogeton abyssinicus *A. Rich.* (see p. 651)

Leaves with usually long petiole and oblong-lanceolate to ovate leaf-blade, more rarely narrow oblong-linear; base cuneate or rounded only rarely cordate; tepals 2–3, lilac to pink, stamens usually 6.
A variable species with several different leaf-forms; some of these taxa may deserve varietal status. In temporary pools, water-filled ditches and dams, usually in 5–30 cm deep water. RV, MAC, NBI, KAJ.
Lye 2454; Polhill 421; Verdcourt and Polhill 3156; Verdcourt and Fraser Darling 2294.

3. Aponogeton subconjugatus *Schum. & Thonn.*

Similar to *A. abyssinicus*, but differs in its cream or yellow flowers and constantly cordate leaves.
In seasonal pools. Specimens seen from Karamoja district in Uganda only, but the plant is likely to occur in western Kenya.

4. Aponogeton nudiflorus *A. Peter*

Leaves with long petiole and 2–13 cm long and 0·3–4·5 cm wide leaf-blade; tepals 2 in male spikes, absent in female, white or cream; stamens usually 6.
Rare plant found in shallow water at Lake Kamar. BAR.
Edmonson 26.10.61.

5. Aponogeton violaceus *K. Lye*

Similar to *A. abyssinicus* in leaf-form, but differs in its solitary spikes; stamens 1 or (in most flowers) absent.

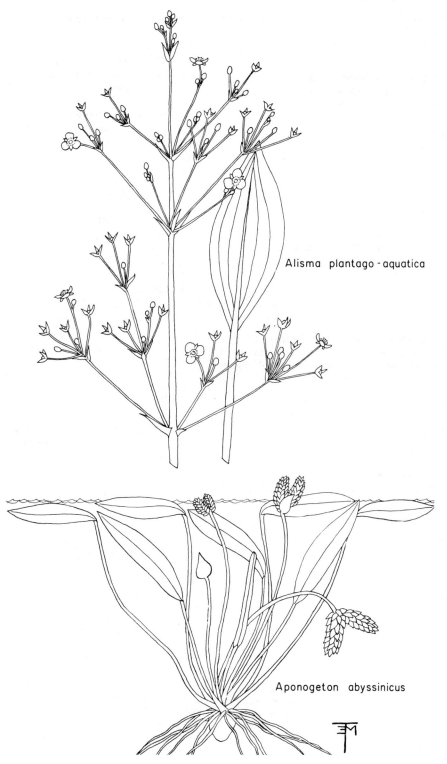

Alisma plantago-aquatica

Aponogeton abyssinicus

Rare plant found in seasonal pools or ditches, in and near Thika. MAC.

Faden 67/312; Lye 6348.

6. Aponogeton stuhlmannii *Engl.*

Leaves with slender petioles and 2-5 cm long and 3-9 mm wide leaf-blades; tepals 2, white and shiny, but often with a lilac tinge especially near the margin; stamens 6.

Rare plant found in seasonal pools near Thika. MAC.

Lye 6376.

7. Aponogeton vallisnerioides *Bak.*

A densely tufted aquatic with narrow (4-8 mm wide) leaves; tepals 2, white and shiny, set on one side of the flattened inflorescence-axis.

Rare plant found in seasonal pools or ditches, Kipkarren. KIT.

Brodhurst-Hill 32.

97. POTAMOGETONACEAE†

Submerged aquatic herbs with alternate or opposite, distichous, stipulate leaves and flowers in spikes without bracts or spathes, bisexual, regular; sepals 4; petals 0; stamens 4, sessile on the perianth segments; carpels usually 4, superior, free, each with one ovule; fruit a small drupe or achene.

1. POTAMOGETON *L.*

1	Floating leaves present	2
	Floating leaves absent	4
2	Submerged leaves present, persistent	3
	Submerged leaves disappearing early and not present in the mature plant 1. *P. richardii*	
3	Submerged leaves less than 3 mm broad 2. *P. octandrus*	
	Submerged leaves more than 15 mm broad 3. *P. schweinfurthii*	
4	Leaves over 15 mm broad 3. *P. schweinfurthii*	
	Leaves less than 5 mm broad	5
5	Stipules present as a winged and 2-pointed leaf base 4. *P. pectinatus*	
	Stipules present as a sheath round the stem and/or axillary bud; leaf base entire	6
6	Carpels 3-4 in each flower; leaves with a distinct band of air-filled cells each side of the midrib, and apparently 1-nerved 2. *P. octandrus*	
	Carpels 1-2 in each flower; leaves without a distinct band of air-filled cells, 3-nerved 5. *P. trichoides*	

† By A. D. Q. Agnew.

1. Potamogeton richardii *Solms*

An anchored trailing aquatic with floating leaves and erect emergent spikes.

Locally common in streams and moving water as well as in lakes. HT, HM, HA, KIT, NBI.

Lind, Agnew, and Kettle 5891; Nattrass 1289.

2. Potamogeton octandrus *Poir.*

A remotely anchored or free submerged perennial with linear 1-nerved submerged leaves and elliptic petiolate floating ones; spikes to 1·5 cm long, hardly interrupted.

Locally common in artificial ponds. HT, NBI.

Agnew 9920; Lind 5892.

3. Potamogeton schweinfurthii *A. Bennett*

A robust, anchored aquatic with sessile or petiolate, occasionally floating, elliptic leaves; spikes to 8 cm long.

Locally common in lakes. HT, HA, MUM, RV. Macpherson 4.

4. Potamogeton pectinatus *L.*

A loose trailing anchored aquatic with linear leaves and a short spike which becomes very interrupted in fruit.

Locally common, especially in subsaline and brackish water. HT, RV, NBI.

Bally 241.

5. Potamogeton trichoides *Cham. & Schlecht.*

Similar to *P. pectinatus* except for the stipules and the shorter (to 1·5 cm long) uninterrupted fruiting spike.

Locally common in lakes and slow-moving streams especially in warmer districts. HA, NAN, MAC.

Nattrass 1316.

98. NAJADACEAE‡

Submerged annual or perennial, monoecious, or rarely dioecious herbs with adventitious roots; stems slender, forked repeatedly; leaves sessile, subopposite or in whorls of 3 or more, linear-dentate, with an open folded basal sheath and 2 axillary scales; flowers mostly solitary and axillary, unisexual, small; male flower a single stamen enclosed in an outer spathe and an apically bilobed inner envelope; female flower a single ovoid carpel, naked or surrounded by a very thin spathe; ovule solitary; style filiform, with (in ours) 2 stigmatic branches; fruit a small nut, ovoid, with reticulated epicarp; seed exendospermous.

‡ By A. D. Q. Agnew.

1. NAJAS *L.*

The only genus with characters of the family.

1 Leaves with conspicuous, triangular, spine-tipped teeth mostly exceeding leaf width in length   1. *N. pectinata*
   Leaves filiform, obscurely toothed
                                           2. *N. graminea*

1. Najas pectinata (*Parl.*) *Magnus*

A submerged dioecious perennial much branched herb with narrow-linear dentate leaves; fruit about 2·5 mm long, cylindrical, apiculate, pitted.

The common 'sawgrass' which forms dense brownish-green masses in fresh-water lakes. HT, BAR, RV, MAC.

Greenway 9468; Lind, Agnew, and Kettle 5893.

2. Najas graminea *Del.*

A submerged monoecious aquatic herb with obscurely spinulose filiform leaves; male flowers pedicellate, in upper axils; female flowers sessile, mostly in lower axils; fruits about 1·5 mm long, narrow-oblong.

An important weed of irrigation often found in irrigation furrows, especially in rice-fields, so far recorded from only two of our areas. KIS, EMB.

McMahon 31; Wood 752.

99. COMMELINACEAE†

Succulent perennial or annual herbs; leaves simple, alternate, entire, parallel-veined, the base (petiole) sheathing the stem, the blade sometimes narrowed into a false petiole (pseudopetiolate), inflorescence a simple or compound helicoid cyme (cincinnus), terminal, terminal and axillary, or axillary, sometimes subtended by, or partially enclosed in, a spatheaceous bract; individual flowers usually subtended by bracteoles; flowers pedicellate or sessile, regular or irregular; sepals 3, free or united; petals 3, deliquescent, distinct from the sepals, free or united, equal in size or 1 smaller than the other 2; stamens 6, or 1–4 reduced to staminodes; filaments often with moniliform hairs, anthers 2-celled; ovary superior, 2–3-loculed with 1–several ovules per cell, placentation axile; style simple, stigma capitate; fruit mostly a loculicidal capsule, rarely indehiscent.

The species are found at low and medium altitudes where they occur in dry or wet habitats, in shade or full sun. Several species of *Commelina* are important weeds. *Zebrina* is a tropical American plant which has become naturalised in a few places.

† By R. B. Faden.

1 Inflorescence piercing the leaf sheath
                                           1. *Ballya zebrina*
   Inflorescence not piercing the leaf sheath   2
2 Inflorescence enclosed in, or closely subtended by, a spatheaceous bract   3
   Inflorescence neither enclosed in, nor closely subtended by, a spatheacous bract   5
3 Fertile stamens 3, filaments glabrous; petals free, 2 large and 1 small   2. *Commelina*
   Fertile stamens 6 or 5, filaments hairy; petals united into a tube, all equal in size   4
4 Inflorescences axillary or terminal and axillary; stems usually tufted, not long trailing; leaves not variegated   3. *Cyanotis*
   Inflorescence terminal; stems long trailing, not tufted; leaves variegated
                                           4. *Zebrina pendula*
5 Fruit indehiscent, hard, shiny metallic blue; flowers white; plants of wet forests
                                           5. *Pollia condensata*
   Fruit capsular, green to brown or grey; flowers yellow or pink to bluish-purple, rarely white; plants of various habitats   6
6 Fertile stamens 6, filaments glabrous; sepals pink, densely long pilose
                                           6. *Floscopa glomerata*
   Fertile stamens 3 or 2, filaments glabrous or hairy; sepals green, sometimes tinged with red or purple, glabrous or sparsely pubescent   7
7 Upper 2 petals larger than the lower one; the 2–3 stamens below the three staminodes; bracts and/or bracteoles glandular; capsules 2-valved   7. *Aneilema*
   Petals equal; stamens alternating with the staminodes; bracts and bracteoles not glandular; capsules 3-valved   8
8 Inflorescence of 1–few terminal false umbels; anthers ± equal in length to their filaments, filaments never hairy; leaves lanceolate, (10–)15–30 mm wide; root tubers present
                                   8. *Anthericopsis sepalosa*
   Inflorescence a terminal panicle; anthers shorter than their filaments, filaments sometimes hairy; leaves linear, 2–11 mm wide; root tubers absent   9. *Murdannia*

1. BALLYA *Brenan*

Perennial herbs; stems creeping; inflorescence axillary; cincinni branched near the base, or unbranched, piercing the leaf sheath; sepals 3, free, the lower 2 larger than the upper one; petals 3, free, the lower one cup-shaped, hooded, the upper 2 larger and clawed; androecium with the 3 upper stamens reduced to staminodes, the antherodes bilobed; lower 3 stamens functional; filaments of all stamens and staminodes joined at the base, the middle staminode nearly free; ovary 3-celled, densely hairy; capsule 2-valved, 5-seeded (or less because of abortion); seeds reniform to triangular-reniform, reticulate.

Ballya zebrina (*Chiov.*) *Brenan*

A small, succulent herb with small ovate, variegated leaves which are not pseudopetiolate; flowers pale mauve.

This species occurs in dry bushland and in light forest. It has been collected only twice in our area. BAR.

Faden and Evans 70/888; Bally 12348.

2. COMMELINA *L.*

Perennials or annuals; stems erect or trailing; roots fibrous, thin or variously thickened; inflorescence of (1–)2 cincinni included within, or partly within, a folded spathe; upper cincinnus frequently absent or reduced to 1-several staminate flowers; sepals 3, free usually glabrous; petals 3, free, the upper 2 large and long-clawed, the lower one small; androecium with the upper 3 stamens reduced to staminodes, rarely the middle one absent, antherodes yellow and usually cruciform; lower 3 stamens fertile or sometimes the middle one reduced to a staminode; middle stamen always different in shape and size from the outer 2; ovary 3-celled, 2 cells equal, 1–2-ovuled, dehiscent in fruit, third cell 1-ovuled or empty or suppressed, sometimes dehiscent in fruit; capsule 2-valved, 1–5-seeded.

1	Spathes free to the base	2
	Spathes fused, at least near the base	8
2	Flowers blue to white	1. *C. diffusa*
	Flowers yellow or pinkish-buff to salmon	3
3	Flowers yellow	4
	Flowers pinkish-buff to salmon	5

4   Spathes single, glabrous or pubescent with white or grey hairs; stems usually decumbent; plants of sunny situations, rarely of forests   2. *C. africana*
Spathes clustered at the ends of the shoots, pilose with long red hairs; stems erect to ascending; plants of shady places in forests   3. *C. capitata*

5   Roots fusiform or with root tubers; leaves lanceolate to linear-lanceolate, usually twisted and with undulate margins; spathes 16–27 mm long on stalks 1–3.5(–7.5) cm long (rarely nearly sessile on young plants); flowers 2–2.5 cm wide; stems usually looping along the ground and rooting at the nodes   4. *C. reptans*
Roots fibrous, sometimes uniformly thickened; leaves usually linear, not twisted; margins seldom undulate; spathes 7–18 mm long, or if longer, then the veins

purple, on stalks 0.2–1.0 cm long; flowers up to 2 cm wide; stems rarely looping along the ground   6

6   Spathe partially surrounded by the conspicuously broadened base of the subtending leaf; seeds flat, 3-lobed   5. *C. trilobosperma*
Spathe fully exserted from the subtending leaf, the base of which is not conspicuously broadened; seeds ellipsoid or ovoid, unlobed   7

7   Spathes 10–17 mm long or rarely longer, mostly 12–15 mm long; upper petal 8–9 mm wide; anthers of lateral stamens blue   6. *C. purpurea*
Spathes 7–12 mm long, mostly 8–10 mm long; upper petal 3–4.5 mm wide; anthers of lateral stamens yellow   7. *C. subulata*

8   Spathes 3.5–9.5 cm long, the two halves spreading at maturity; paired sepals fused laterally   8. *C. foliacea*
Spathes less than 3 cm long, the two halves appressed; sepals free or fused   9

9   Flowers pinkish-buff to salmon; leaf base cordate; capsule square, 4-seeded; paired sepals fused laterally; middle petal filiform; plants of seasonally swampy grassland   9. *C. velutina*
Flowers white, yellow, blue or mauve; leaf base cordate or not; capsule variously shaped, 2–5 seeded; sepals fused or free; middle petal variously shaped; plants of various habitats, but rarely of seasonally swampy grassland   10

10   Flowers white or yellow; leaf base asymmetric; plants of wet forests   11
Flowers blue or mauve†; leaf base various; plants of various habitats, but rarely of forests   12

11   Flowers white; spathes single, dark green, glabrous; stems decumbent   10. *C.* sp. *E*
Flowers yellow; spathes clustered at the ends of the shoots, pale green, pilose with long red hairs; stems erect to ascending   3. *C. capitata*

12   Spathes on stalks up to 1.5 cm long, or occasionally to 2 cm long; leaf base never cordate or auriculate   13
Spathes on stalks 1.5–8 cm long, or if less, than the leaf base cordate or auriculate   18

13   Roots fusiform; spathes long-exserted from the sheaths; capsule 4-seeded; petals subequal; antherodes unlobed   11. *C.* sp. *B*

† White-flowered forms of several normally blue-flowered species occur rarely, but these species seldom occur in forests, and their flowers have yellow anthers (cf. white anthers in *C.* sp. *E*).

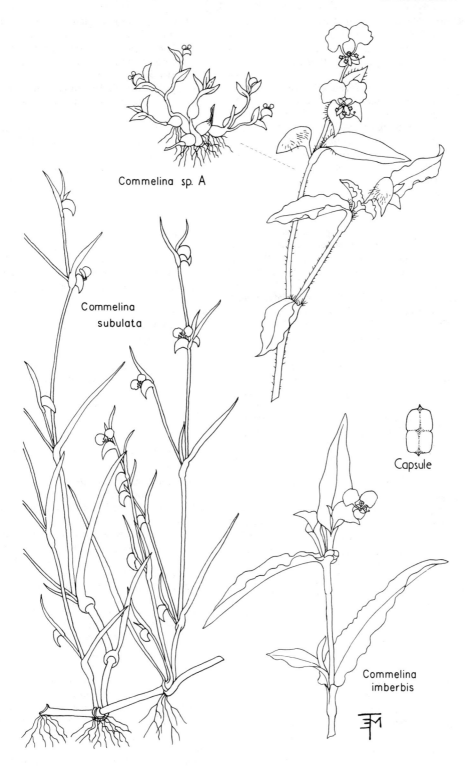

Commelina sp. A

Commelina
subulata

Capsule

Commelina
imberbis

Roots fibrous or fusiform; spathes long exserted to not exserted from the sheaths; capsule 1-3- or 5-seeded; lower petal much smaller than upper 2; antherodes cruciform
14

14 Angle between the fused edge of the spathe and the folded edge more than 90°; spathes never crowded at the ends of the shoots; margin of spathe sometimes purple; filaments of lateral stamens winged; subterranean cleistogamous flowers usually present; stems creeping and rooting at the nodes   12. *C. forskalaei*

Angle between the fused edge of the spathe and the folded edge less than 90°; spathes usually crowded at the ends of the shoots; margin of spathe never purple; filaments of lateral stamens not winged; cleistogamous flowers rarely present; stems usually erect or scrambling, rarely creeping and rooting at the nodes   **15**

15 Leaves lanceolate to linear-lanceolate, length more than 6 times the width   **16**

Leaves ovate to elliptic or lanceolate, length less than 6 times the width   **17**

16 Folded edge of spathe straight to slightly curved; flowers blue   13. *C. erecta*

Folded edge of spathe strongly curved; flowers usually pinkish-purple, rarely (never?) blue   14. *C. albescens*

17 Roots fusiform; apex of sheath with white hairs less than 3 mm long, capsule 2-3 seeded; seeds spherical   15. *C. sp. C*

Roots fibrous; apex of sheath with white, or more commonly, purple or orange hairs more than 3 mm long; capsule 5-seeded; seeds slightly elongate 16. *C. benghalensis*

18 Leaf base cordate or auriculate, sometimes clasping the stem and the leaf appearing peltate; leaves never pseudopetiolate   **19**

Leaf base not cordate or auriculate, never clasping the stem; leaves pseudopetiolate or not   **22**

19 Plants erect; leaves and stems usually densely pubescent; paired sepals fused; middle petal filiform; flowers mauve, rarely (never?) blue; antherodes blue and yellow   17. *C. elgonensis*

Plants scrambling, erect only when young; leaves and stems glabrous or sparsely pubescent; paired sepals separate; middle petal lanceolate to ovate; flowers blue; antherodes entirely yellow   **20**

20 Upper cincinnus present and 1-3-flowered, exserted from spathe for more than 1 cm; middle petal blue; capsule elongate
18. *C. sp. D*

Upper cincinnus usually absent, or if present, then 1-flowered and exserted less than 1 cm; middle petal hyaline white, rarely tinged with blue; capsule square or elongate   **21**

21 Capsule distinctly longer than wide; seeds elongate; anther of middle stamen yellow
19. *C. imberbis*

Capsule almost square; seeds globose; anther of middle stamen blue and yellow
20. *C. latifolia*

22 Roots fusiform; petals subequal; antherodes unlobed   11. *C. sp. B*

Roots fibrous, sometimes uniformly thickened; lower petal much smaller than upper 2; antherodes cruciform   **23**

23 Stem bases swollen, moniliform; plants of seasonally swampy grassland and ditches
21. *C. sp. A*

Stem bases cylindrical, not swollen; plants of forests, forest edges, dry grassland or thickets   **24**

24 Spathes glabrous or nearly so; capsule square; seeds round, spiny; anthers of stamens blue or blue and yellow; plants of dry forests
22. *C. eckloniana*

Spathes hairy; capsule elongate; seeds elongate, transversely wrinkled; anthers of stamens entirely yellow; plants of dry grassland, wooded grassland, thickets or forest edges   23. *C. petersii*

1. Commelina diffusa *Burm. f.* (*C. nudiflora* L. of Check List)

A glabrous herb with weakly ascending or prostrate stems rooting at the nodes, bearing spathes with both cincinni well-developed and several-flowered.

Common in wet situations such as edges of swamps and drainage ditches, river banks, and occasionally in wet forests. HM, HK, HN, KIT, MUM, KIS, MAC.

Faden 68/890; Lind, Harris and Agnew 5108.

2. Commelina africana *L.* (inc. *C. kirkii* C. B. Cl. *C. mannii* C. B. Cl., and *C.* sp. aff. *C. obscura* K. Schum. in Engl. of Check List) (see pp. 658 and 663)

A small herb with usually prostrate branches and thickened fibrous roots.

A very variable plant of grassland, disturbed areas, and cultivated land. A common weed. The densely hairy, narrow-leaved form occurs on vlei soils. HE, HC, HT, HM, HA, HK, KIT, MUM, KIS, NAR, BAR, RV, MAG, NAN, EMB, MAC, NBI, KAJ.

Faden 68/858; A. and S. Agnew 9165.

3. Commelina capitata *Benth.*

This yellow-flowered species is vegetatively similar to *C.* sp. *E*, differing chiefly in the more erect habit, larger leaves and in the presence of red hairs at the apex of the sheath.

This West African species occurs in shaded situations in wet forest. In Kenya it is known only from the Kakamega forest. MUM.

Faden 70/31.

4. Commelina reptans *Brenan*

A herb with erect branches when young, with twisted lanceolate leaves and flowers at least 2 cm wide.

A plant of seasonally swampy grassland and vlei soils. HA, HK, KIT, NAR, RV, MAG, NAN, MAC, NBI, KAJ.

Faden 67/251; Agnew 9194.

5. Commelina trilobosperma *K. Schum.*

A decumbent herb up to 60 cm tall.

This species occurs in grassland, occasionally along roadsides, or as a weed in cultivated land. KIS.

Kokwaro 1643; Evans and Maikweki 13.

6. Commelina purpurea *Rendle* (*C. lugardii* Bullock)

A tufted herb with purple internodes and erect or sometimes decumbent stems, seldom rooting at the nodes.

Common in shallow soil in rocky areas and in grassland. HE, HM, HA, HK, KIT, MUM, KIS, MAC, NBI.

Faden 68/947; Ossent 625.

7. Commelina subulata *Roth* (see p. 655)

A small herb with single or tufted, erect, or rarely decumbent stems 5–25 cm tall and flowers about 1 cm wide.

Common in vlei soils. HC, HM, HA, HK, KIT, KIS, BAR, MAC, NBI.

Faden 68/031; Agnew, Kibe, and Mathenge 10409.

8. Commelina foliacea *Chiov.*

A small herb with prostrate to weakly ascending branches and small blue flowers.

The plant has been collected in wet montane forest, riverine forest, dry bushland and as a lawn weed. HA, HK, HN, EMB, MAC, NBI, KAJ.

Faden and Evans 69/282; McCarthy 1.

9. Commelina velutina *Mildbr.* (see p. 659)

An erect plant with thick roots, dense grey pubescence and small, somewhat inflated spathes.

A species of seasonally swampy grassland, associated with *Cyanotis paludosa*. KIT.

Faden, Evans, and Tweedie 69/711; Irwin 146.

10. Commelina *sp.* E.

A decumbent perennial with very dark green foliage often suffused with maroon, and white flowers with white anthers.

This species grows in shaded situations, often along streams in wet forests. It is known only from the Kakamega forest. MUM.

Faden 69/2115; 70/20.

11. Commelina *sp.* B. (see p. 665)

A small herb with prostrate or erect stems with the stalks of the spathes frequently standing out at right angles to the stem.

The plant has been collected on or near rocky outcrops and along roadsides. KIT, KIS.

Tweedie 67/208; Hanid and Kiniaruh 646.

12. Commelina forskalaei *Vahl*

A small trailing herb rooting at the nodes with very narrow leaves usually having undulate margins.

A plant of grassland and bushland, most common below 3000 ft. (?HK), HN, MUM, BAR, MAC.

Mwangangi and Fosberg 598; Heriz-Smith s.n.

13. Commelina erecta *L.* (see p. 659)

A herb with tufted, erect or ascending stems and flowers with the paired sepals fused, the paired petals with very short claws and the middle petal filiform.

Fairly common in grassland and bushland. KIS, NAR, RV, MAG, EMB, MAC, KAJ.

Faden 68/101; Tweedie 67/93.

14. Commelina albescens *Hassk.*

A small herb with erect or ascending branches and strongly falcate spathes.

A plant of dry grassland and bushland. The species usually occurs in drier situations than *C. erecta*, but the two may occasionally be encountered together. MAG, MAC, KAJ.

Rauh Ke/137; Verdcourt 2632.

15. Commelina *sp.* C.

A small herb with prostrate branches and small sessile, elliptic to lanceolate-elliptic leaves.

This plant is known from cultivated bushland and sandy slopes. MAC, KAJ.

Agnew 9872; Gillett 16961.

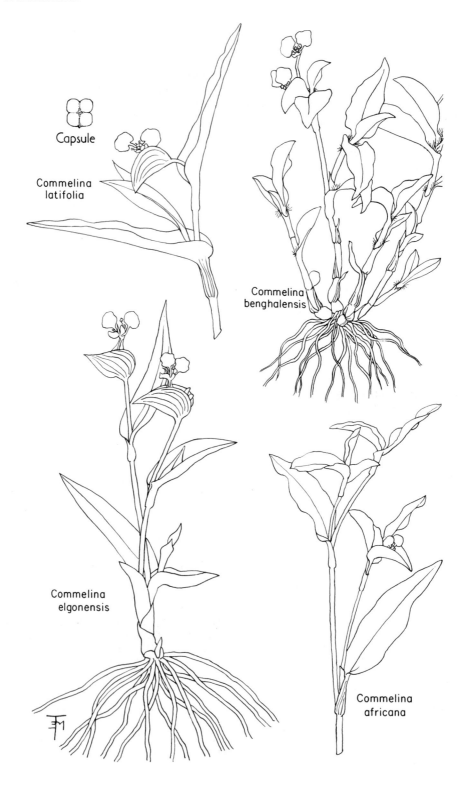

Capsule

Commelina
latifolia

Commelina
benghalensis

Commelina
elgonensis

Commelina
africana

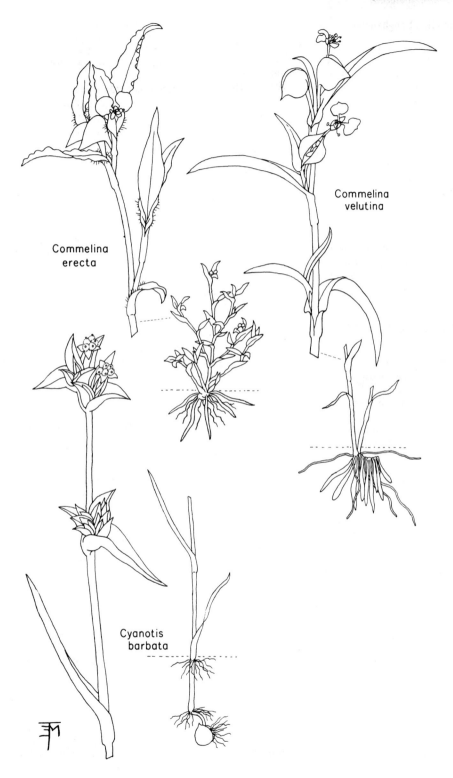

Commelina
velutina

Commelina
erecta

Cyanotis
barbata

16. Commelina benghalensis *L.* (see p. 658)

A herb with ascending or erect branches with usually petiolate and oblique based leaves. Two forms occur: one with narrow leaves and white hairs on the sheath margins; the other with broad leaves and purple or orange hairs on the sheath margins. Hanid 207 and Bally 1112 from the Chyulu Hills with purplish, densely hirsute leaves and spathes may represent a distinct form.

A common species of cultivated land and other disturbed habitats. HE, HC, HM, HA, HN, KIT, MUM, KIS, NAR, BAR, RV, MAG, NAN, EMB, MAC, NBI, KAJ.

Faden 68/008; Mendes 67.

17. Commelina elgonensis *Bullock* (see p. 658)

An erect herb with large spathes usually marked with purple and with mauve to lavender flowers.

A species of grassland, rocky areas, swamps, forest edges, roadsides, and cultivated areas. HE, HC, KIT, MUM, KIS.

Tweedie 67/184; Lucas 197.

18. Commelina *sp.* **D.**

A straggling species with large blue flowers and elongate smooth seeds.

This common coastal species is known in our area only along the edge of Lake Victoria (Sindo, Homa Point, Waturi Point). KIS.

Faden and Evans 69/1966; Napier 3434.

19. Commelina imberbis *Hassk.* (see p. 655)

A herb with erect to scandent branches and pale blue flowers.

This species is fairly common in cultivated ground and other disturbed habitats. HM, HA, KIS, NAR, BAR, RV, MAG, EMB, MAC, NBI, KAJ.

Faden 68/891; Tweedie 67/84.

20. Commelina latifolia *A. Rich.* (see p. 658)

A herb with ascending, erect or scandent stems to two metres long. Flowers darker blue than in *C. imberbis.*

A common plant of cultivated ground, other disturbed habitats, bushland, and forest edges. HA, HN, KIT, MUM, KIS, NAR, MAG, NAN, MAC, NBI, KAJ.

Faden 68/100; Tweedie 66/151.

21. Commelina *sp.* **A.** (see p. 655)

An erect herb with dark blue flowers and hairy leaves and spathes.

This plant occurs in seasonally swampy grassland; very common along the Thika-Nairobi Road. HA, HK, MAG, MAC, NBI.

Faden 68/896; Tweedie 67/87.

22. Commelina eckloniana *Kunth*

A glabrous herb with trailing stems (except when young) and pseudopetiolate, lanceolate leaves.

The plant has been noted only in dry forests. MAC.

Faden 68/905; Faden, Napper, and Evans 69/255.

23. Commelina petersii *Hassk.*

An erect or scrambling herb with large acuminate spathes.

A plant of dry grassland, bushland and savannah or occasionally at forest edges (Kibwezi). BAR, EMB, MAC, KAJ.

Faden, Evans, and Siggins 69/310; Faden, Evans, and Rathbun 69/392.

3. CYANOTIS *D. Don*

Perennial or annual herbs; stems erect to decumbent; rhizomes and corms sometimes present; roots fusiform or fibrous, sometimes with root tubers; inflorescence of sessile or sessile and stalked cincinni (flower clusters), each enclosed in, or partially exserted from, a spatheaceous bract; cincinni bracteolate; flowers regular, subsessile; sepals 3, equal, fused into a tube; petals 3, equal, fused into a tube; stamens 6, all fertile and equal, filaments with few to many beaded hairs; ovary 3-celled, style with or without beaded hairs, with a swelling below the stigma; capsule 3-celled, 3-valved, normally 5–6 seeded; seeds superposed, with a large round scar at the top of the upper one and at the bottom of the lower one.

1   Branches erect to ascending; plants with rhizomes, corms, root tubers or fusiform roots; stalked flower clusters usually present   2

Branches decumbent to ascending or sometimes weakly erect and many-noded; plants with fibrous roots only; stalked flower clusters present or absent   5

2   Plants with rhizomes; roots fibrous; internodes with long spreading hairs 3–5 mm long; plants often 1 m tall or taller; plants of swamps   1. *C. paludosa*

Plants with corms, root tubers or fusiform roots; internodes woolly or glabrous, or if long spreading hairs present, then these mixed with appressed hairs; plants to 60 cm tall, rarely taller; plants of grassland or rocky places   3

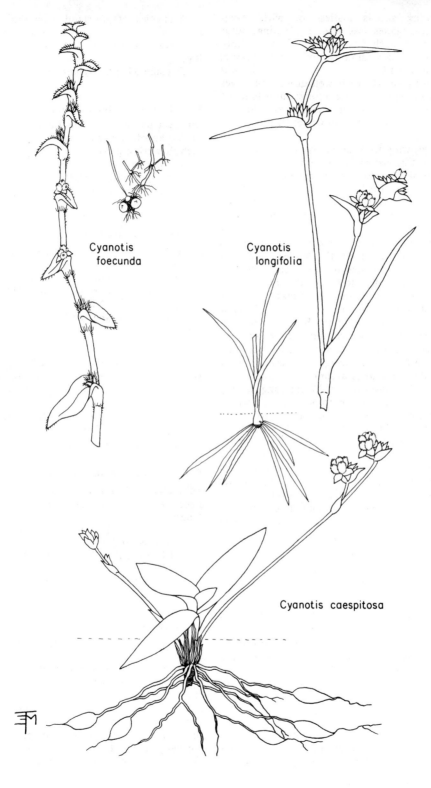

Cyanotis
foecunda

Cyanotis
longifolia

Cyanotis caespitosa

3   Flowering shoots leafless or with leaves having blades less than 1 cm long; outer bract of each flower cluster not, or only slightly, exceeding it; roots with tubers; corm absent   2. *C. caespitosa*
Flowering shoots with well developed leaves having blades 2–20 cm long; outer bract of each flower cluster clearly exceeding it; roots fusiform or fibrous; corm present or absent   4

4   Plant growing from an easily detached corm; roots fibrous; basal leaves absent; indumentum of appressed or appressed and spreading pilose hairs   3. *C. barbata*
Plant not growing from a corm; roots fusiform; basal leaves present; indumentum woolly   4. *C. longifolia*

5   Leaves not clasping the stem; bracts usually 2 at some or all of the nodes, not conspicuously reduced in size towards the end of the shoot; flower clusters borne at 1–3(–4) nodes/shoot; stalked flower clusters never present   5. *C. lanata*
Leaves clasping the stem; bracts 1 at each node, conspicuously reduced in size towards the end of the shoot; flower clusters borne at 3–15 nodes/shoot; stalked flower clusters present or absent   6

6   Flowering shoots up to 25 cm long, arising from a creeping perennial stem of which the internodes are completely covered by the leaf sheaths; flower clusters borne at 3–5 nodes/shoot; stalked flower clusters usually present in addition to the sessile ones   6. *C. arachnoidea*
Flowering shoots up to 40 cm long, arising from annual stems; flower clusters borne at 5–15 nodes/shoot; stalked flower clusters absent   7. *C. foecunda*

1. Cyanotis paludosa *Brenan*

A rhizomatous herb with erect or ascending stems to 1 m tall.

This species grows in swampy places. KIT.
Tweedie 67/223; Napper 805.

2. Cyanotis caespitosa *Kotschy & Peyr.* (see p. 661)

A small erect herb, either leafless when flowering or with a basal rosette of leaves, the stem base covered by fibrous leaf sheaths.

This species occurs in grassland, often in shallow soil over rocks. HE, KIT.
Tweedie 67/36; Thorold 3245.

3. Cyanotis barbata *D. Don* (see p. 659)

A herb with erect to ascending few-noded stems and flower clusters often in dense spherical heads.

A species of grassland, sometimes in shallow soil over rocks, occurring from medium to high altitudes. HE, HC, HT, HM, HA, KIT, MUM, KIS, RV.
Tweedie 67/202; Symes 617.

4. Cyanotis longifolia *Benth.* (see p. 661)

An erect or rarely scandent herb with usually long leaves, and flower clusters borne at 1–2 nodes on each flowering shoot.

A species of grassland or occasionally of swampy spots. KIT, MUM, KIS, NAR, MAC, NBI.
Glover, Gwynne, Samuel, and Napier Bax 2662; Kokwaro 1648.

5. Cyanotis lanata *Benth.*

An annual or short-lived perennial usually with a woolly indumentum.

This species occurs in rocky places in grassland at low and medium elevations. HT, KIT, KIS, NAR, BAR, MAC, NBI.
Agnew, Musumba, and Kiniaruh 7966; Faden 68/177.

6. Cyanotis arachnoidea *C. B. Cl.*

A perennial herb with decumbent branches, a woolly indumentum and often reddish leaves.

This species is common on rocky outcrops at medium to high elevations. HT, HA, HK, KIT, NAR, NAN, MAC, NBI, KAJ.
Agnew 10108; Faden and Evans 69/166.

7. Cyanotis foecunda *Hassk.* (see p. 661)

An annual or short-lived perennial with weakly erect, many-noded flowering shoots becoming decument with age.

A common species usually growing among rocks in grassland, bushland or at forest edges. HC, HM, HK, KIT, KIS, NAR, BAR, RV, NAN, MAC, NBI, KAJ.
Agnew and Braun 10197; Faden and Evans 69/298.

4. ZEBRINA *Schnizl.*

Perennial herbs; stems trailing, often rooting at the nodes, roots fibrous; inflorescence terminal, composed of a fused pair of cincinni enclosed in a pair of spatheaceous bracts; flowers regular; sepals 3, equal, united into a tube; petals 3, equal, united into a tube; stamens 6, epipetalous, all equal and fertile; anthers with connectives much wider than the anther sacs; filaments with beaded hairs; ovary 3-celled, with 2 ovules in each cell; capsule 3-celled, 3-valved; cells 1–2 seeded.

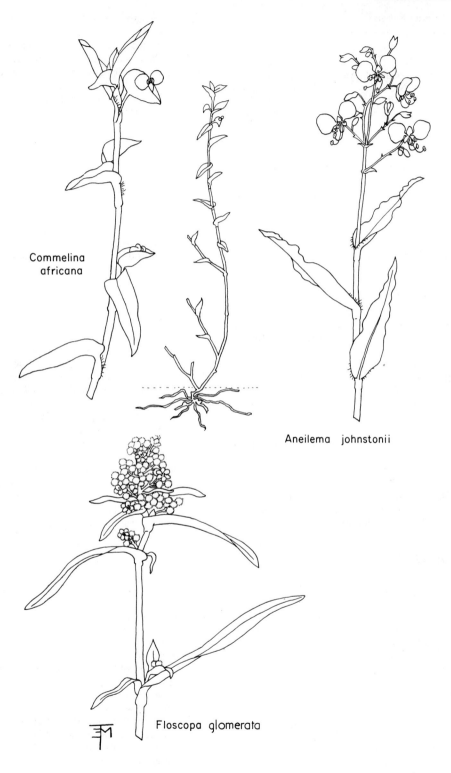

Commelina
africana

Aneilema johnstonii

Floscopa glomerata

Zebrina pendula *Schnizl.*

A cultivated plant with leaves purple beneath, green and white striped above and with pink to magenta flowers.

A native of tropical America, this species is naturalized in Nairobi and Thika and perhaps elsewhere. MAC, NBI.

Faden and Evans 69/548; Faden and Evans 69/550.

5. POLLIA *Thunb.*

Perennial herbs; stems rooting at the lower nodes; inflorescence a dense (in our species) or loose terminal thyrse of cincinni; sepals 3, free, equal; petals 3, free, equal, white; stamens 3 plus 3 staminodes (in our species), filaments glabrous; ovary 3-celled, the cells equal; ovules 5-10 per cell; fruit indehiscent, hard, dry, spherical and metallic blue (in our species); seeds 5-10 in each cell, flattened trapezoidal in shape.

Pollia condensata *C. B. Cl.*

A herb with erect flowering stems and large (10-25 cm long), dark green, pseudopetiolate, elliptic leaves clustered at the ends of the flowering shoots.

This West African species occurs only in wet forest. It is known in our area from a single collection from the Kakamega forest. MUM.

Faden 69/2107.

6. FLOSCOPA *Lour.*

Perennial herbs; stems erect to ascending; roots fibrous; inflorescence a terminal, more or less leafy, panicle or thyrse; sepals 3, free, equal; petals 3, free, equal or unequal; stamens 6 (rarely 5), all fertile; filaments glabrous; ovary 2-celled, each cell with 1 ovule; capsule 2-celled, 2-valved, 2-seeded, seeds hemispherical or depressed conical.

Floscopa glomerata (*J. A. & J. H. Schult.*) *Hassk.* (*F. rivularis* (A. Rich.) C. B. Cl. of Check List) (see p. 663)

A herb with decumbent stems, clasping leaves and a dense terminal thyrse of small, bluish-white or purple flowers with pink to purple sepals.

This species occurs along watercourses and standing water in forests or in full sun. HC, HT, HL, HA, KIT, MAC, NBI.

Agnew 8966; Faden 68/148.

7. ANEILEMA *R. Br.*

Perennials or annuals; stems erect or trailing, rarely rhizomatous; inflorescence a terminal thyrse of cincinni or rarely consisting of short separate nearly sessile cincinni; sepals 3, free, glandular; petals 3, free, the upper 2 large and clawed, the lower one usually smaller; androecium with the 3 upper stamens reduced to staminodes, the middle one sometimes absent, antherodes yellow and bilobed; lower 3 stamens functional or, more commonly, the middle one reduced to a staminode; ovary 2-3-celled, ovules 1-several in each cell; capsule 2-valved, 2-3-loculed, 2-several-seeded; seeds coarsely wrinkled, with a narrow longitudinal scar across the back and a small sunken apicule on one side.

1 Inflorescence a thyrse or consisting of short, separate, nearly sessile cincinni clustered in the axils of the upper leaves; flowers less than 5 mm wide, white to pale mauve; staminodes 2; plant an annual 11. *A.* sp. *B*
   Inflorescence a terminal thyrse of cincinni; flowers 8-25 mm wide, variously coloured; staminodes 3; plants perennial or annual 2
2 Flowers yellow or orange; inflorescence always lax 3
   Flowers blue to white or mauve; inflorescence lax or dense 4
3 Stems erect, not rooting at the nodes; root tubers present; leaves less than 2 cm wide; inflorescence branches whorled, rarely opposite or alternate; capsule 4·5-6 mm long, rounded at apex; style yellow to golden brown; filaments of lateral stamens glabrous 1. *A. johnstonii*
   Stems decumbent, rooting at the nodes; only thin fibrous roots present; leaves more than 2 cm wide; inflorescence branches alternate or opposite, rarely whorled; capsule 7-10 mm long, truncate with 2 acute corners; style purple; filaments of lateral stamens hairy 2. *A. aequinoctiale*
4 Inflorescence lax, 3-10 cm long; some or all of the internodes along the inflorescence axis 10 mm long or longer; sepals 7-9 mm long 3. *A. hockii*
   Inflorescence dense or occasionally lax, 1-5(-7) cm long; internodes up to 5 mm long, or occasionally longer; sepals 3-5 mm long 5
5 Plant rhizomatous; roots 3-5 mm thick; leaf blades lanceolate to linear-lanceolate, finely pubescent on both surfaces; leaf sheaths becoming grey and papery, covering the older parts of the stem; axis of inflorescence purple; flowers white or very pale mauve 4. *A.* sp. *A*
   Plant not rhizomatous; roots less than 1·5 mm thick; leaf blades lanceolate to lanceolate-elliptic or lanceolate-ovate, glabrous or with long pilose hairs often mixed with finer hairs, the former rarely absent; leaf

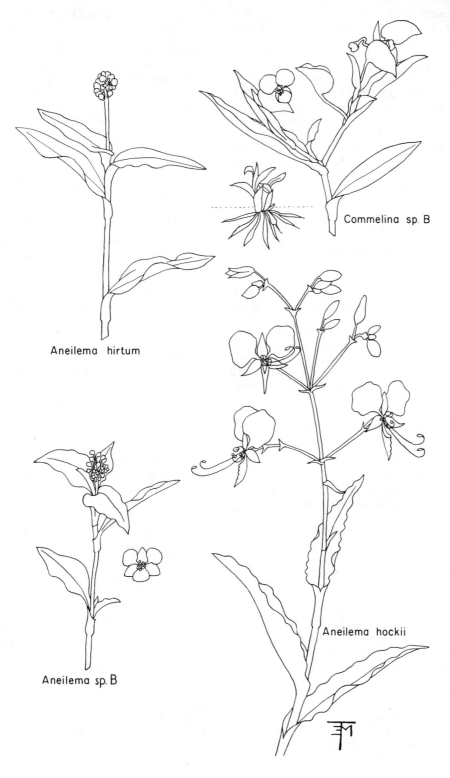

Commelina sp. B

Aneilema hirtum

Aneilema sp. B

Aneilema hockii

sheaths not becoming grey or papery; axis
of inflorescence green to white; flowers
pink to bluish purple, rarely white   **6**

6 Inflorescence lax; pedicels strongly recurved
in fruit; capsule obconical, 3-locular, 2-
valved; petals subequal, the middle cucullate
and conspicuous; filaments glabrous   **7**

Inflorescence dense or lax; pedicels ± erect in
fruit; capsule oblong to ovoid, 2-locular,
2-valved; middle petal much smaller than
other 2, usually inconspicuous; filaments
hairy (except in *A. rendlei*)   **8**

7 Bracteoles scarious, eccentrically perfoliate or
not perfoliate, pubescent; flowers white to
pale mauve in our area   *5. A. petersii*

Bracteoles herbaceous, ± symmetrically
perfoliate, glabrous; flowers lilac
12. A. sp. *C*

8 Axis of inflorescence glabrous; bracteoles
cup-shaped; axes of cincinni 2-5 cm long
when mature; leaves pseudopetiolate; filaments of lateral stamens glabrous or with
minute inconspicuous hairs on the lower
surface only   **9**

Axis of inflorescence hairy; bracteoles not
cup-shaped; axes of cincinni up to 1 cm
long; leaves pseudopetiolate or not; filaments densely and conspicuously hairy   **10**

9 Leaves glabrous; sheaths glabrous at apex;
cincinni 28–55 per inflorescence; filaments
of lateral stamens minutely hairy; style
arcuate and decurved; capsule 4–6-seeded;
plants of forests   *6. A. beniniense*

Leaves pilose on both surfaces; sheaths
ciliate at apex; cincinni 12-23 per inflorescence; filaments glabrous; style S-shaped
and recurved at apex; capsule (4-)6-10-
seeded; plants of dry bushland
7. A. rendlei

10 Leaves pseudopetiolate; decumbent perennials of upland forests
8. A. pedunculosum

Leaves not pseudopetiolate; annuals or short-
lived perennials of various habitats but
rarely (never ?) of forests   **11**

11 Bladeless sheath present ± halfway up
peduncle; axis of inflorescence with short
hairs only; bracts ovate to ovate-lanceolate,
with a gland on the lower surface near the
apex; capsule usually 4-seeded; filament
hairs bluish-purple   *9. A. spekei*

Bladeless sheath barely exserted from the
sheath of the uppermost leaf; axis of inflorescence with some hairs at least 3 mm long
as well as with shorter hairs; bracts mostly
linear to linear-lanceolate, their apices
drawn out and glandular; capsule usually

2-seeded, filament hairs maroon to reddish-
purple   *10. A. hirtum*

1. Aneilema johnstonii *K. Schum.* (see p. 663)
A herb with tufted, erect to ascending stems to
1 m tall, and with large orange-yellow flowers.

A locally common species of grassland and
bushland in sandy or black cotton soil. MAC, KAJ.

Agnew, Hanid, and Kiniaruh 9213; Ivens 2097.

2. Aneilema aequinoctiale (*P. Beauv.*) *Kunth*
A herb with trailing stems with hooked hairs and
large yellow flowers.

A species of forests and forest edges or
occasionally along roadsides (Nairobi). HA, HK,
HN, EMB, MAC, NBI, KAJ.

Hanid and Kiniaruh 933; Faden 67/554.

3. Aneilema hockii *De Wild.* (see p. 663)
A herb with tufted, ascending to decumbent stems
with hooked hairs and large mauve to blue flowers.

This species is common in grassland, but also
occurs in bushland and on rocky hills at lower
altitudes. HA, NAR, MAG, EMB, MAC, NBI, KAJ.

Agnew and Haines 8242; Faden and Napper
69/237.

4. Aneilema *sp.* **A.**
A herb with erect branches and large 6-8-seeded
capsules.

The species occurs among rocks in *Acacia*
bushland. MAG.

Faden and Napper 69/251; Verdcourt,
Hemming and Polhill 2667.

5. Aneilema petersii (*Hassk.*) *C. B. Cl.*
Annual with erect stems or perennial with long
decumbent stems, with a small, hairy, few-
branched inflorescence and white to pale mauve
flowers.

A species of bushland. MAC, KAJ.

Gillett and Mathew 19073; Faden, Evans and
Rathbun 69/395.

6. Aneilema beniniense (*P. Beauv.*) *Kunth*
A straggling herb with a very dense inflorescence
and lilac flowers (in our area).

A forest species known in Kenya only from the
Kabras (Malava) forest and at Yala. MUM.

Horsfall s.n.; Faden and Evans 69/2060.

7. Aneilema rendlei *C. B. Cl.*
A perennial with erect to decumbent stems with
pink to mauve flowers and conspicuously glandular sepals.

This species occurs in dry bushland at low
altitudes and is known in our area from only one
collection. MAC.

Katumaini Experimental Farm 1061B.

8. Aneilema pedunculosum *C. B. Cl.*

A small herb with a small dense inflorescence often with long hairs on the axis, and with violet-margined sepals.

A fairly common plant of upland forests. HM, HL, HA, HK, KIS, NAN, MAC, KAJ.

Kabuye 54; Bally 7792.

9. Aneilema spekei *C. B. Cl.*

A short lived perennial with erect to scandent stems and a dense, usually elongate inflorescence.

A rarely collected species in Kenya known from wet savannah and as a weed of cultivation. KIT, MUM, KIS, BAR.

Tweedie 66/190; Templer H5.

10. Aneilema hirtum *A. Rich.* (see p. 665)

A small annual with erect to decumbent stems and a small dense inflorescence.

A species of grassland, roadsides and cultivation. KIT.

Tweedie 76B; Heriz-Smith and Paulo 857.

11. Aneilema *sp.* **B.** (see p. 665)

A herb with pseudopetiolate, ovate–elliptic leaves similar to those of *A. pedunculosum,* and minute flowers with the lateral filaments sparsely hairy.

A plant of montane and riverine forests which differs from *A. pedunculosum* in its 2-seeded capsules, smaller, paler flowers and annual habit. HE, HC, HT, HA, KIT, NAN.

Faden and Evans 70/899; Tweedie 759.

12. Aneilema *sp.* **C.**

A decumbent perennial herb with the upper petals narrower and more pointed and the antherodes less bilobed than in *A. petersii.*

This is a species of bushland thickets. KIS, BAR.

Faden and Evans 70/894; Napier and Fox 3431.

8. ANTHERICOPSIS *Engl.*

Perennial herbs; main stem very short or almost none, the leaves mostly basal; roots fibrous with root tubers; inflorescence of 1–few false umbels each composed of a pair of sessile cincinni subtended by 1–several bracts; sepals 3, free, equal; petals 3, free, equal; androecium with 3 stamens opposite the sepals and 3 staminodes opposite the petals, filaments glabrous; ovary 3-celled; capsule 3-celled, 3-valved; seeds cylindrical, smooth, with a sunken apicule on one side, up to about 8 per cell.

Anthericopsis sepalosa (*C. B. Cl.*) *Engl.* (see p. 668)

A small herb with a basal rosette of leaves and large white to pale pink or blue flowers.

The species occurs in grassland or less commonly in woodland or bushland. EMB, MAC, KAJ.

Faden 67/331; Tweedie 67/75.

9. MURDANNIA *Royle*

Perennial herbs; stems erect or ascending; roots fibrous, usually thick; inflorescence a terminal panicle of cincinni (in our species); flowers regular; sepals 3, free, equal; petals 3, free, equal or subequal; androecium composed of 3 stamens opposite the sepals (sometimes one transformed into a staminode) alternating with 3 (rarely 0, 1 or 2) staminodes opposite the petals; antherodes 3-lobed; filaments sometimes with beaded hairs, sometimes fused near the base; ovary 3-celled; capsule 3-valved; seeds 2-several per cell.

1   Leaves 3·5–11 mm wide; fertile stamens 2; filaments of stamens hairy; filaments of stamens and staminodes free to the base
                                  1. *M. simplex*
     Leaves 2 mm wide or less; fertile stamens 3, filaments of stamens glabrous; filaments of the 3 stamens and 2 staminodes united near the base, 1 staminode free   2
2   Pedicels 2·5–5 mm long; petals about 2 mm long; plants flowering in the morning
                                  2. *M. semiteres*
     Pedicels 4–13 mm long; petals 4–7 mm long; plants flowering in the afternoon
                                  3. *M. clarkeana*

1. Murdannia simplex (*Vahl*) *Brenan* (see p. 668)

A glabrous herb with erect to ascending stems and lavender to bluish-mauve flowers.

This species grows in swamps, grassland, or rocky places. HC, HA, KIT, MUM, KIS, NAR, MAC, NBI.

Faden 67/311; Tweedie 67/219.

2. Murdannia semiteres (*Dalz.*) *Santapau* (see p. 668)

A small herb with tufted, erect stems and tiny, blue to mauve flowers.

A species which grows at the edge of temporary pools in rocky areas. KIT, MUM.

Agnew and Musumba 8588; Tweedie 76.

3. Murdannia clarkeana *Brenan*

A small herb with erect to ascending branches, pointed, blue to lavender petals, and reddish-purple sepals.

A species of seasonally waterlogged, usually thin soil over rocks in grassland. HA, HK, MAC, NBI.

Faden and Evans 69/304; Agnew 8935.

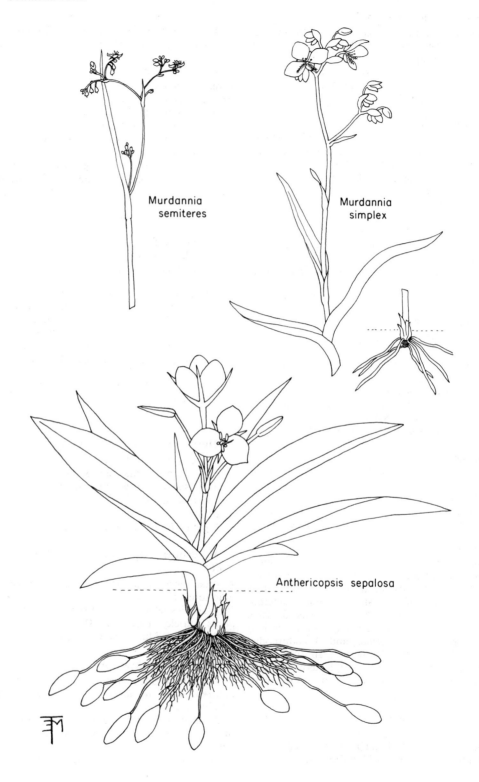

Murdannia
semiteres

Murdannia
simplex

Anthericopsis sepalosa

100. XYRIDACEAE†

Erect perennial or annual herbs with a rosette of linear or filamentous leaves and a leafless scape bearing a terminal spike or head of sessile, regular, bisexual flowers; flowers subtended by a bract; sepals 2–3, the two lateral ones scarious; corolla tube cylindrical, often split at base, expanded above into 3 yellow lobes; stamens in two whorls, the outer between the corolla lobes reduced to feathery staminodes, the inner inserted in the mouth of the corolla tube and exserted; ovary superior, with 3 parietal placentas and numerous ovules; style simple; stigmas 3.

1. XYRIS *L.*

Characters of the family.

1   Bracts entire at apex; lateral calyx lobes
     glabrous on the keel   1. *X. capensis*
     Bracts with an apical twisted awn; lateral
     calyx lobes minutely pubescent on the keel
                                  2. *X. rehmannii*

1. Xyris capensis *Thunb.* (see p. 670)

An erect glabrous rhizomatous herb with tufts of stiff linear leaves from the base and a globose head of yellow flowers.

Locally common in shallow-soil grassland where seasonally flooded. HE, HM, HA, KIT.

Tweedie 66/387; Verdcourt 2650.

2. Xyris rehmannii *Nils* (see p. 670)

Similar to *X. capensis* but a bigger plant of swampy grassland, and with the keyed differences.

Locally common around Kitale. KIT.

Tweedie 67/186; Napper 785.

101. ERIOCAULACEAE‡

Herbs of wet places with simple linear leaves and unisexual flowers in pedunculate bracteate heads; flowers very small, monoecious, regular; sepals and petals 3, in separate whorls; stamens up to 6; ovary of 3 carpels, with 3 linear stigmas and axile placentation; fruit a 3-seeded capsule.

1. ERIOCAULON *L.*

A genus with the characters of the family, the petals free (or absent), and stamens 6.

1   Plants annual; heads black or straw-coloured,
     not white-pubescent   2
     Plants perennial; heads white-pubescent   3
2   Leaves over one third as long as the scapes,
     and equal to the scapes in number
                                      1. *E.* sp. A

Leaves less than one third as long as the scapes, and much fewer than them in number (do not confuse the tubular prophyll at the lower end of the scape with a leaf)   2. *E. abyssinicum*

3   Scapes longer than the leaves 3. *E. schimperi*
     Scapes shorter than the leaves   4. *E. volkensii*

1. Eriocaulon *sp.* A.

A small tufted annual with narrowly tapering leaves and brown heads on scapes 4–7 cm long.

Collected twice from bare, wet mud in the Kitale area. KIT.

Symes 8.

2. Eriocaulon abyssinicum *Hochst.*

A small almost leafless annual with small brown heads on scapes 2–4 cm tall.

Locally common but often overlooked on wet shallow soils. HE, HA, MAC, NBI.

Tweedie 67/236; Verdcourt 535.

3. Eriocaulon schimperi *Engl.*

A densely tufted perennial herb with numerous bluntly tipped, linear-tapering leaves and white heads on long scapes.

Locally common in marshes in the upper bamboo and heath zones. HE, HC, HA, HK.

Wood 773; Agnew and Armstrong 8157.

4. Eriocaulon volkensii *Engl.*

Similar to *E. schimperi* in all respects except for the short scape, this species often forms dense cushions in peaty pools in the heath and lower alpine zones. HC, HA, HK.

Verdcourt 2001; Agnew 7226.

102. ZINGIBERACEAE§

Herbs with aromatic roots and fruits, with alternate, distichous, ligulate, pinnate-veined, entire leaves and terminal racemes or spikes of cymes of flowers; flowers zygomorphic, bisexual, bracteate; sepals 3, usually stiff and scarious; petals 3, larger than the sepals, the posterior often the largest, an anterior enlarged petaloid lip present within the petals; stamen 1, with or without 2 staminodes; ovary inferior, with 3 axile placentas and mostly numerous ovules.

1   Plant with erect, herbaceous (but apparently
     perennial) leafy stems over 1 m in height
                             1. *Afromomum keniense*
     Plant with annually produced leaves or low
     leafy stems, less than 50 cm in height   2

† By A. D. Q. Agnew.
‡ By A. D. Q. Agnew.

§ By A. D. Q. Agnew.

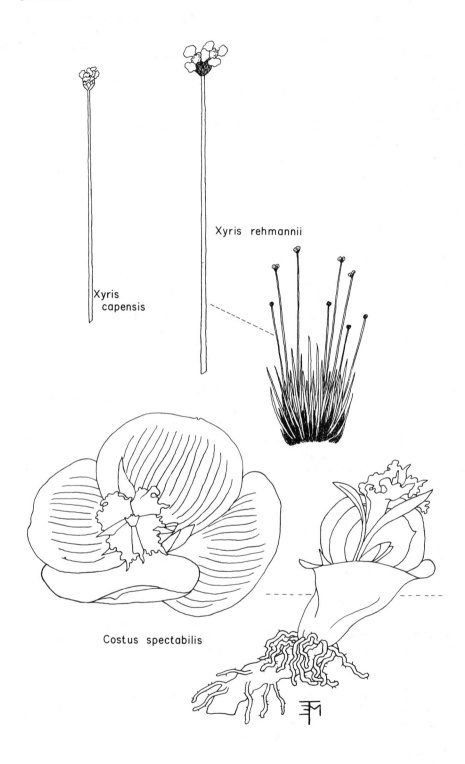

Xyris
capensis

Xyris rehmannii

Costus spectabilis

2 Plant with stems and leaves in two ranks   3
   Plant with spiral leaves in a sessile rosette
                          3. *Costus spectabilis*
3 Flowers appearing from below the ground, on
   a buried stem, up to 6 together
                       4. *Kaempferia aethiopica*
   Flowers on an erect pedunculate inflorescence, more than 10 on the raceme
                            2. *Renealmia* sp. A

1. AFROMOMUM *K. Schum.*

Herbs from tuberous, aromatic rhizomes bearing
erect vegetative shoots of elliptic, distichous
leaves and short leafless flowering shoots; flowers
in heads; petals with the posterior one enlarged;
stamen bearing 2 tiny lateral teeth as staminodes
and 2 horns on the connective; fruit a red, ovoid
berry.

Afromomum keniense *R. E. Fr.*

Herb with robust stems and elliptic leaves; leaves
densely silky-hairy on the margin at least towards
the apex; flowers less than 2 cm long, white to
pink.
    Locally common along pathsides in the wettest
forest. HK, HN, MUM, EMB.
    Polhill and Verdcourt 277.

2. RENEALMIA *L. f.*

Herbs with fleshy rhizomes and mostly distinct
leafy and flowering stems; inforescence an
elongate raceme or panicle; calyx 3-toothed;
corolla tube as long as the calyx with 3 ± equal
lobes; lateral staminodes small, anterior staminode
longer than the corolla, fertile anthers 2-celled;
ovules many; fruit a globose, fleshy capsule.

Renealmia *sp.* **A.**

A glabrous herb with oblanceolate leaves and
reddish flowers on a separate stem.
    Recently discovered in Kakamega forest. MUM.
    Record from R. B. Faden *in litt.*

3. COSTUS *L.*

Herbs with spirally arranged leaves in which the
veins are often almost parallel; flowers in heads or
spikes; lip large, often orbicular in outline on the
flower; lateral staminodes absent; stamen fused to
a ligulate petaloid organ; stigma dilated; fruit a
capsule.

Costus spectabilis (*Fenzl*) *K. Schum.* (see p. 670)
A rosette herb with sub-orbicular crimson-edged
leaves and sessile orange to yellow flowers.
    Locally common at Broderick Falls, on shallow
soil, where it is said to be decreasing, and rare in
wooded grassland in western Kenya. KIT, MUM.
    Tweedie 67/34; Webster 8997.

4. KAEMPFERIA *L.*

Tuberous rooted herbs with distichous leaves and
sessile flowers; petals all similar; lateral staminodes
large and petaloid; fertile stamen with 2 diverging
cells and a crested connective; fruit a berry.

Kaempferia aethiopica (*Schweinf.*) *Solms-Laub.*

An erect herb with 3–7 large elliptic to oblanceolate leaves produced after the tuft of large delicate
yellow and purple flowers; fruit red.
    Locally common in dry sandy bushland,
especially near Kibwezi. KAJ.
    Agnew 9857; Rauh 12440.

103. LILIACEAE†

Perennial herbs or rarely shrubby or arborescent;
roots fleshy or fibrous and often with tubers from
an aerial stem, rhizome, corm, bulb, or tuber;
aerial stem erect, climbing, or scrambling, with or
without leaves; flowers regular or nearly so,
bisexual or rarely unisexual, sometimes large
and showy, mostly in racemes, rarely in pseudo-
umbels or solitary; perianth segments or lobes 6
(in ours) in two series of 3, white or coloured;
stamens usually 6, hypogynous or adnate to the
perianth segments; filaments free or rarely united
at the base; anthers 2-celled, introrse or extrorse,
usually opening lengthwise; ovary superior, sessile,
or rarely stipitate, mostly 3-celled with axile
placentas, or rarely 1-celled with parietal placentas, usually with numerous and mostly biseriate
ovules in each cell; style entire or divided, rarely
styles free; stigma mostly small, capitate; fruit a
capsule or berry; seeds globose, discoid, or angled
by pressure, rarely hairy; embryo small; endosperm copious.

1 Leaves thick, succulent, with marginal prickles
                                      12. *Aloe*
   Leaves thin, not succulent, without marginal
   prickles   2
2 Leaves tendrillous at the apex; underground
   organ V-shaped   1. *Gloriosa simplex*
   Leaves not tendrillous at apex; underground
   organ not V-shaped   3
3 Plant with climbing or scrambling aerial stems
                                              4
   Plant not with climbing or scrambling aerial
   stems   5
4 Aerial stem mostly spiny, scrambling, woody,
   sparsely branched, from tuberous or
   fibrous roots; assimilatory organs
   (cladodes) filiform or needle-like and
   fascicled or ovate to lanceolate and sessile
                                  20. *Asparagus*

† By M. A. Hanid and A. D. Q. Agnew (Genus 12).

Arial stem unarmed, climbing, fleshy and green, intricately branched, from a bulb; without cladodes　　　　　9. *Bowiea*

5　Flowers trumpet-shaped; perianth tube much longer than the very short free lobes
　　　　　　　　　　　　11. *Kniphofia*
　Flowers not trumpet-shaped; perianth tube much shorter than the free lobes or perianth segments free to the base　　6

6　Filaments covered with yellow hairs
　　　　　　　　　　　5. *Bulbine abyssinica*
　Filaments glabrous　　　　　　　7

7　Flowers with 3 styles　　　　　　8
　Flowers with 1 style　　　　　　9

8　Inflorescence with large showy bracts, veined dark-green to brown, sheathing the pseudo-umbel; perianth segments inconspicuous
　　　　　　2. *Androcymbium melanthioides*
　Inflorescence with small bracts not sheathing the raceme; perianth segments with a pair of purple spots at base　3. *Wurmbea tenuis*

9　Plants from a tuber; flowers yellow; seeds hairy　　　　　　10. *Eriospermum*
　Plants from bulbs, corms or rhizomes; flowers never entirely yellow; seeds glabrous　10

10　Plants from a small ovoid corm; flowers inconspicuous, solitary, in the upper leaf axils　　　　　4. *Iphigenia oliveri*
　Plant from a bulb or rhizome; flowering stem without leaves; flowers in racemes　11

11　Plant from a bulb　　　　　　12
　Plant from a rhizome　　　　　18

12　Flowers blue to mauve or purple ·　17. *Scilla*
　Flower white, yellowish, brownish, or greenish, rarely with purple tinged edge to perianth segments　　　　　13

13　Outer perianth segments with a short appendage at tip　　　　16. *Dipcadi*
　Outer perianth segments entire at tip　14

14　Bracts obsolete; flowers small, subglobular; leaves often spotted dark green or purple
　　　　　　　19. *Drimiopsis botryoides*
　Bracts conspicuous; flowers elongated; leaves not spotted　　　　　　15

15　Inner perianth segments cohering at anthesis often with a yellowish papillate gland at apex; outer segments spreading
　　　　　　　　　　　13. *Albuca*
　Inner and outer perianth segments erect, spreading or reflexed at anthesis, without a yellowish gland at apex　　　16

16　Perianth segments free to the base; stamens inserted at the base of segments; bracts not spurred　　　　18. *Ornithogalum*
　Perianth segments united into a short tube at the base; stamens inserted on top of the perianth tube; bracts pouched or spurred on the back　　　　　17

17　Perianth segments united for lower third or quarter, free parts linear-spathulate, 1–2 cm long　　　　　　15. *Drimia*
　Perianth segments united for lower fifth, free parts elliptic, less than 1 cm long
　　　　　　　　　　　14. *Urginea*

18　Flowers solitary, subtended by one bract; pedicels not articulated; leafbase tubular
　　　　　　　7. *Trachyandra saltii*
　Flowers fascicled, or, if solitary, subtended by bracts; pedicels usually articulated; leafbase folded, not tubular　　19

19　Seeds small, angled, with many folds
　　　　　　　　　　　6. *Anthericum*
　Seeds large, round and flat with a pointed hilum　　　　8. *Chlorophytum*

1. GLORIOSA *L.*

Erect or climbing herbs with tuberous roots and slender leafy stems; leaves sessile, apex tendriliform; flowers few, large, showy, pendulous, corymbose; perianth segments free, equal, spreading or reflexed, persistent; stamens hypogynous, shorter than the perianth, spreading; filaments filiform; anthers versatile; ovary sessile, oblong; ovules many in each cell; style sharply deflexed at the base, three-branched; capsule septicidally 3-valved, seeds globose, bright red; endosperm firm.

A small genus of Africa and Madagascar (and tropical Asia).

Gloriosa simplex *L.* (*Gloriosa virescens* Lindl.) (see p. 673)

Erect or climbing plant from a V-shaped tuber; leaves mostly alternate but with at least one pair opposite, lanceolate; pedicels up to 15 cm long, recurved at the top; flowers yellow or yellow and scarlet to dark red with segments broadening towards the middle, narrowed towards the base, curving inwards away from the ovary in the upper half; capsule up to 8 cm long, usually smaller.

Widespread below 8300 ft. The brightly coloured perianth segments are characteristically reflexed into the shape commonly called the 'Turk's Cap' among the lilies. This is a very variable complex with a number of distinctive local forms. It has been reported as climbing to 5 m or more in some upland forests.

Verdcourt 954; Hanid and Kiniaruh 669.

2. ANDROCYMBIUM *Willd.*

Underground stem an ovoid, tunicate corm; leaves few, borne on an aerial stem; peduncle in ours short and simple; inflorescence in ours an irregular umbel with an involucre of broad exterior bracts much exceeding the sessile or pedicellate flowers;

Gloriosa simplex

perianth segments free, subequal; stamens exserted in ours, inserted at the base of perianth segments; filaments filiform, thickened towards the base; anthers slightly versatile, dehiscing laterally; ovary sessile, 3-celled, with many ovules in each cell; styles 3, free, filiform, persistent; stigma minute; capsule ellipsoid, septicidal; seeds subglobose, brown; embryo minute.

Androcymbium melanthioides *Willd.* (see p. 675)

A small, erect herb up to about 30 cm high from a dark brown corm with 2–3 stem leaves and an involucre of white, conspicuously green- to mauve-veined, ovate bracts around the inconspicuous flowers.

Rocky soils and evergreen bushland or woodland. HE, HC, HT, HA, HK, KIT, RV, NAN, KAJ. Polhill 12314.

3. WURMBEA *Thunb.*

Underground stem a tunicated corm with simple aerial stem; stem leaves narrow, few; inflorescence an ebracteate spike; perianth persistent; tube short, campanulate or cylindric; segments equal, spreading with two glands above the base; stamens inserted at the base of perianth segments, filiform; anthers oblong, versatile; ovary sessile, 3-celled; ovules many; styles 3, free, stigmatose at the apex, persistent; capsule septicidally 3-valved; seeds subglobose, brown; endosperm firm.

Wurmbea tenuis *Bak.* (see p. 675)

A small erect herb from a bulb-like corm, 4–10 mm across, with the basal linear leaf arising from within a tubular sheath and usually exceeding the aerial stem which bears two spathe-like sheathing upper leaves and a few white sessile flowers, each perianth segment with two contiguous purple spots towards the base.

An uncommon but ± gregarious pretty little lily of upland grasslands, forest floors, and shallow soils overlying rocks; above 7100 ft. HE, HM, HA, HK, RV.

Coe 657; Polhill 431.

4. IPHIGENIA *Kunth*

Underground stem a small tunicated corm with few–many distant, narrow, stem leaves; flowers inconspicuous, usually solitary in upper leaf axils; perianth segments free, equal, linear to lanceolate, spreading, caducuous; stamens shorter than perianth-segments; filaments thickened; anthers versatile; ovary sessile, 3-celled; ovules many; styles 3, short, free, falcate, capsule oblong to obovoid, loculicidally 3-valved; seed subglobose, brown, with a small appendage; albumen fleshy.

Iphigenia oliveri *Engl.*

An erect, slender, grass-like herb from a dark brown corm, up to 30 cm high, with flexuous aerial stem bearing ascending narrowly linear leaves which become gradually shorter towards the top; pedicels lengthening after anthesis, up to 3·5 cm long, ascending or recurved in fruit.

An inconspicuous rare herb of grasslands and shallow soils over rocks; above 2500 ft. MAC.

Lucas and Williams in EAH 12358A; Faden 68047.

5. BULBINE *Willd.*

Shortly rhizomatous herbs; leaves fleshy, sub-terete, linear, or lanceolate; inflorescence a raceme; pedicels articulated at the apex; bracts membranous, persistent; flowers usually bright yellow; perianth segments free, subequal, 1-nerved, spreading or reflexed; stamens shorter than the perianth; filaments densely hairy; anthers dorsi-fixed, versatile; ovary globose, with 4 to many ovules per cell; style filiform; stigma minute, capitate; capsule globose or turbinate, loculicidally 3-valved; seeds black, angular; endosperm fleshy.

Bulbine abyssinica *A. Rich.* (see p. 675)

Erect herb from a vertical rhizome with many fleshy roots; leaves in a basal rosette, erect, filiform to linear, flat or rolled; inflorescence a many-flowered, simple raceme, dense upwards; pedicels ascending to spreading; capsule globose, constricted at the base.

A widespread lily of grasslands with very attractive bright yellow or sulphur-yellow flowers that look puffy because of tufts of long yellow hairs on the filaments; in our area above 4000 ft. HE, HT, HL, HA, HK, KIT, NAR, RV, NAN, MAC, NBI.

Bally 7718; Agnew and Hanid 7521.

6. ANTHERICUM *L.*

Herbaceous perennials with ephemeral aerial shoots; roots many, long, thin, fibrous, often with scattered watery tubers near the tips, or fairly short, swollen and cylindrical, or tapering from thickened base; rhizome usually underground, creeping, knobby, woody, often covered with fibrous remains of old leaf bases, rarely aerial; leaves distichous or rosulate, flat or folded, rolled or terete, glabrous or hairy; inflorescence a raceme, central or rarely in axil of outer leaves, simple or branched; scape flattened or terete; fertile bracts small; pedicels articulated or not so, lengthening at anthesis; flowers in fascicles surrounded by bracts or sometimes solitary and subtended by a bract and bracteole; perianth rotate, usually white, shiny, the dark median stripe

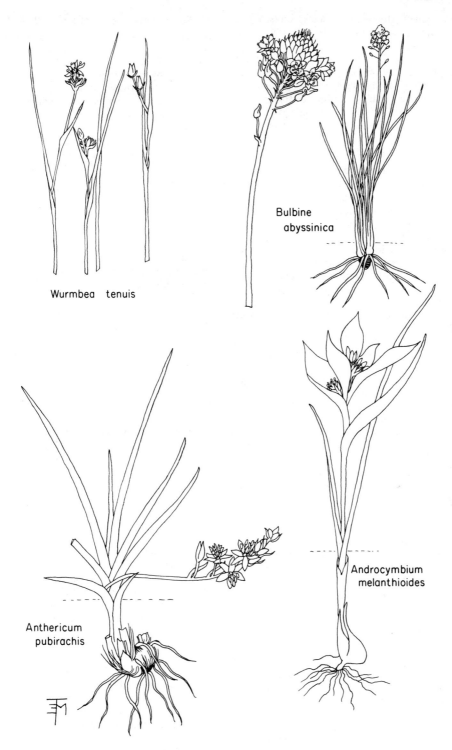

Wurmbea   tenuis

Bulbine
abyssinica

Anthericum
pubirachis

Androcymbium
melanthioides

appearing when the flower fades, covering the ripening capsule; stamens adnate to the very base, and slightly shorter than the perianth; filaments glabrous or papillate in upper half, usually flattened below; anthers basifixed; anthers curling backwards when fading; ovary sessile, globose with 10–30 biseriate ovules; style filiform, often declinate; stigma minutely penicillate or capitate; capsule, globose, obtuse smooth or transversely ridged; seeds small, irregularly angled, minutely granular, black; embryo cylindric; endosperm firm.

1   Rhizome aerial, prostrate or erect; leaves in apical tufts, not basal 8. *A. suffruticosum*
    Rhizome underground, usually creeping; leaves in a basal rosette   2
2   Flowers single to a bract, not fascicled; pedicels long, not articulated   3
    Flowers fascicled, 2–4-nate, rarely solitary; pedicels short, articulated   4
3   Peduncle short, hidden in leaf rosette; pedicels much longer than peduncle; leaf margins smooth   1. *A. angustifolium*
    Peduncle long, not hidden in leaf rosette; pedicels shorter than peduncle; leaf margins ciliated   4. *A. gregorianum*
4   Roots thick, fleshy, short, without tubers; peduncle terete   5
    Roots stringy, long, with tubers; peduncle compressed or terete
5   Peduncle with closely spaced sheathing bracts from base upwards   6. *A. nubicum*
    Peduncle naked at the base   6
6   Lamina of innermost leaf forming a tubular sheath for most of its length around the peduncle; rhizome corm-like globose, subsequent rhizomes forming a vertical series   5. *A. monophyllum*
    Lamina of inner leaf usually narrowed and subpetiolate in its lower half; rhizome moniliform, horizontal
                       7. *A. subpetiolatum*
7   Rachis pubescent; flowers, except lower ones, solitary to a bract   10. *A. pubirachis*
    Rachis glabrous or papillate; flowers mostly fascicled, 2–4-nate   8
8   Inflorescence congested, pseudocapitate, seldom somewhat elongate, rachis very short, sometimes zigzagging; leaves minutely ciliated at margins 3. *A. cooperi*
    Inflorescence elongated, fairly lax; rachis long, zigzagging; leaves smooth or distinctly hairy at margins   9
9   Leaf bases with irregular purple markings; leaves with smooth margins 2. *A. cameronii*
    Leaf bases without any markings, leaves distinctly hairy at margins
                        9. *A. venulosum*

1. Anthericum angustifolium *A. Rich.* (see p. 677)
A small plant from a scarcely distinguishable, fibrous rhizome, with thick, short, fleshy roots tapering from the swollen base; the shoot surrounded by a membranous, tubular sheath at the base; leaves narrowly linear, glabrous, longer than the pedicels; flowers few, white, star-like on pedicels much longer than the peduncle which is often hidden in the leaf rosette; capsule about 8 mm long, slightly indented at the apex.
A gregarious lily of highland grasslands, often on shallow soils overlying rocks, flowering at first rains. HE, HC, HT, HA, KIT.
Williams 209; Tweedie 67/58.

2. Anthericum cameronii *Bak.* (*A. uyuiense* Bak.) (see p. 677)
A glabrous herb with a horizontal fibrous, knobby rhizome and thin wiry roots with distant tubers; leaves distichous, linear to linear-lanceolate, folded or flat, bases sheathing with irregular purple markings just above ground level; scape flattened, narrowly winged, rachis usually zigzagging between axils; flowers in groups of 1–3, white, with a very faint broad median stripe per segment; pedicels articulated near the base, up to 6 mm long in fruit, angular; capsule about 6 mm long.
A pretty lily of highland grasslands often on rocky slopes, flowering after first rains. HE, HC, HT, KIT, KIS, NAR, BAR.
Symes 373; Tweedie 66/99.

3. Anthericum cooperi *Bak.* (*A. subpapillosum* Poelln.) (see p. 680)
Small plant, from a horizontal, knobby rhizome covered with fibrous remains of old leaf bases and producing many, thin, stringy roots with some scattered tubers near their tips; leaves distichous, erect or falcate, linear to lanceolate, variable in length and breadth, usually folded, glabrous or papillate on the prominent ribs with entire margins; inflorescence usually simple and congested near the apex, scape compressed, narrowly winged, bracts dark or white and membranous; pedicels short, up to 10 mm in fruit, articulated below the middle, angular or flattened; flowers 1–3-nate, white, with a green to red-brown median stripe per segment; capsule globose, bluntly 3-angled, about 8 mm in diam., slightly indented at the apex, with many transverse ridges.
A common lily of grasslands, black cotton soil or shallow soils overlying rocks, flowering after first rains, often preceded by fires. HC, HA, KIT, MAG, NAN, MAC, NBI, KAJ.
Verdcourt 461; Hanid 29.

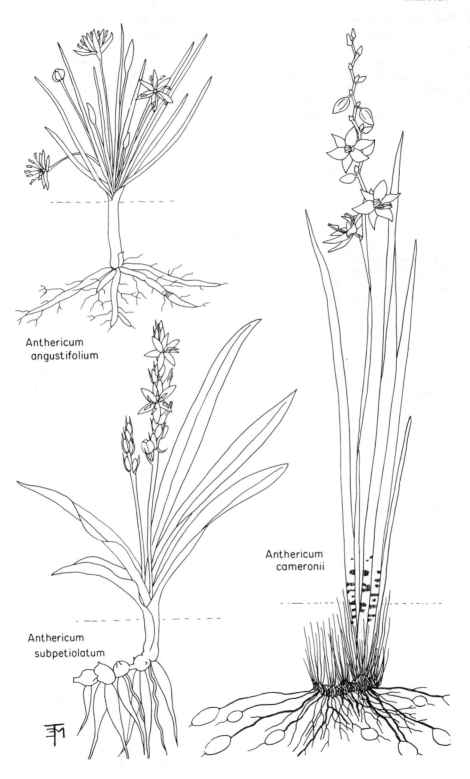

Anthericum
angustifolium

Anthericum
subpetiolatum

Anthericum
cameronii

4. Anthericum gregorianum *Rendle*

Plant similar to *A. angustifolium*, but more robust, with canaliculate, fleshy linear-lanceolate leaves ciliated at margins and a distinct 5–15 cm long, peduncle bearing stiffly erect spreading pedicels up to 4 cm long; flowers white, with a 3-veined green median stripe per segment; bracts white membranous; capsule indented at the apex, transversely ridged.

A pretty little lily of highland grasslands and shallow soils overlying rocks, appearing soon after first rains. HA, HK, NAN, MAC, NBI, KAJ.

Polhill 372; Hanid 385.

5. Anthericum monophyllum *Bak.*

Small plant originally from a single corm-like, globose rhizome covered with fibres from old leaves, later growth giving rise to new rhizomes which are superimposed on older ones; roots thickened at the base; leaves usually three, dimorphic, closely-ribbed; two outer ones short and ciliated at margins in upper half; innermost leaf large, lanceolate, glabrous, with thickened margins and lamina forming a tubular sheath for most of its length around the pubescent peduncle; raceme moderately dense; bracts ciliated at margins; flowers mostly 3-nate with 3–5-nerved brown median stripe per segment; pedicel short, up to 6·5 mm in fruit, articulated at or below the middle; capsule typical.

A rare plant so far recorded from HC, but possibly also occurring in KIT. HC, ?KIT.

Symes 284.

6. Anthericum nubicum *Bak.*

Plant from an erect rhizome copiously covered with fibrous remains of old leaf bases; roots thick, fleshy without tubers, leaves much shorter than the scape, usually membranous or brownish; scape terete, slender, with closely spaced sheathing bracts from base upwards, many of the lower bracts sterile; raceme lax, simple or branched; pedicel up to 14 mm in fruit, articulated below the middle, angular; perianth segments with a 3-nerved median stripe.

Herb of upland grasslands, often flowering leafless during the dry season and after first rains. So far it has been recorded from Kipkarren only. KIT.

Brodhurst-Hill 692.

7. Anthericum subpetiolatum *Bak.* (see p. 677)

Small plant from a horizontal, moniliform rhizome with short fleshy roots tapering from a thickened base, without tubers; outermost 2–3 leaves small, often curved; inner leaves up to 30 cm long, much narrowed and petiole-like in their lower half, flat or usually folded, margin minutely ciliate; peduncle 6–25 cm long, shortly hairy; inflorescence somewhat lax usually congested near the apex; bracts membranous, with ciliate margins; perianth segments white, not conspicuously striped in fresh material; pedicels short, rarely exceeding 6 mm, angular; capsule 3-angled 5–7 mm long, slightly indented at the apex.

A delicate lily of grasslands and woodlands above 2800 ft.

Polhill 398; Hanid and Kiniaruh 391.

8. Anthericum suffruticosum (*Bak.*) *Milne-Redhead*

Plant with erect or prostrate, eventually branched, aerial rhizome usually about 2·5 cm thick or more and covered with stiff fibres from old leaf bases; leaves distichous, grass-like, borne at the apices of branches; peduncle axillary with flattened upper surface; inflorescence simple or branched; flowers white with a greenish or brown median stripe.

This remarkable lily is quite unlike any other species of the genus and is easily identified from its thick aerial rhizome. It is found on rocky outcrops and is predominantly coastal where it is also found on coral outcrops. It is recorded in our area only from Ulu Hills which is so far the farthest inland record for Kenya. MAC.

Ossent 252.

9. Anthericum venulosum *Bak.*

Similar to *A. cooperi* but more robust and leaves with conspicuously ciliate, often undulate and raised margins; scape glabrous but for the ciliate wings; inflorescence more lax and rachis often visible between fascicles of flowers, fruits without transverse wrinkles when fresh, slightly indented at the apex.

A plant of grasslands and open woodlands mostly recorded along Thika–Kangode and Thika–Sagana roads.

van Someren 1588; Nasim, Hanid, and Kiniaruh 390.

10. Anthericum pubirachis *Bak.* (see p. 675)

Small plant from a woody, knobby, shortly and sparsely fibrous rhizome with stringy roots bearing scattered distant tubers; leaves linear folded, erect to arcuate, minutely crisped-ciliate; inflorescence not central but in axil of one of the outer leaves, shorter than the inner leaves; rachis pubescent; flowers mostly solitary; pedicels articulated at or below the middle.

A rare herb of dry bushland, appearing in moist depressions after first rains, often with the scape arcuate at the base and protruding away from the laterally flattened base of aerial shoot. Well collected fruiting specimens needed to ascertain whether it should be retained under *Anthericum* or transferred to *Chlorophytum*. MUM, BAR.

Symes 389.

7. TRACHYANDRA *Kunth*

In ours, herbaceous perennials with underground, vertical rhizome; leaves in a basal rosette, base tubular; lamina in ours terete or canaliculate, hairy or glabrous or glandular-pubescent; inflorescence axillary, in ours a simple, many-flowered raceme; scape terete; bracts one per flower; pedicel single, not articulated, changing position during anthesis, erect, patent or recurved in ripe capsule; flowers single, usually opening in the afternoon; perianth in ours rotate, white with a greenish to dark brown median stripe per segment; perianth base forming a small rim or cup below the fruit, stamens adnate to the very base of the perianth, slightly shorter than the segments; filaments retrorsely scabrid; anthers versatile; ovary sessile, globose, with 2-16 biseriate ovules per cell, with septal glands; style filiform, ultimately exserted, stigma small; capsule loculicidally 3-valved in ours glabrous, globose, coriaceous and constricted at the base; seeds angled, usually brown or grey, in ours smooth.

Trachyandra saltii (*Bak.*) Oberm. (*Anthericum kassneri* Poellm.; *Anthericum saltii* Bak.; *Anthericum oatesii* Bak.) (see p. 680)
Grasslike plants with many thin, but fairly stout roots; leaves filiform to linear, gradually dilated into a tubular membranous base, glabrous or pubescent; scape usually arcuate near the base protruding outside the leaf-rosette; pedicels ascending or recurved in fruit, capsule about 5 mm in diam.

A very variable and adaptable species remaining small in dry surroundings and becoming fairly robust in wetter conditions. It has three forms. HA, NAR, NAN, MAC, NBI, KAJ.

Polhill 371.

8. CHLOROPHYTUM *Ker Gawl.*

Herbaceous perennials with persistent or ephemeral aerial shoots; rhizome creeping or erect, sometimes covered with fibres from old leaf bases, with many, long, swollen roots or rarely wiry and with watery tubers; leaves in a basal rosette or rarely subdistichous, a few or many; lamina flat or sometimes folded, glabrous or pubescent, often petiole-like at base, margin usually fimbriate; inflorescence a central, simple or branched raceme; scape terete, bracteate; bracts large or small, often foliaceous; pedicels articulated near or below the middle, rarely at the apex; flowers 1-6-nate, opening consecutively; perianth rotate or reflexed, white, translucent, keel becoming dark with age, marcescent, covering capsule; stamens hypogynous; filaments glabrous or papillate, shorter or sometimes longer than the segments; anthers basifixed, usually large; ovary sessile or shortly stipitate, trigonous with 6-30 biseriate ovules; style simple; stigma minute, penicillate; capsule trigonous, oblong, obcordate, or globose in suttine, smooth or transversely ridged or tuberculate; seeds large, flat, round in outline with a notch where the pointed hilum is situated, shiny black, minutely granulate.

1 Flowers very shortly pedicellate, with exserted stamens; pedicels not articulated; inflorescence spike-like   2. *C. bakeri*
  Flowers long-pedicellate, not bell-shaped, stamens not exserted; pedicels nearly always articulated; inflorescence spike-like or lax   2
2 Rhizome irregular, woody, knobby, with stringy roots bearing tubers; leaves distichous or subdistichous, ciliated at margins   3
  Rhizome horizontal or erect, not knobby; roots fleshy without tubers; leaves in a basal rosette, margins ciliated or not   4
3 Sheathing leaf bases brown above ground level followed by a white band before the green; lamina without raised midrib on lower surface, very narrow   10. *C. tordense*
  Sheathing leaf bases without any pattern; lamina with raised midrib on lower surface, linear-lanceolate   13. *C. sp. B*
4 Flowers large, showy, white; perianth segments 1·3-2·5 cm long; median stripe not conspicuous in living flowers   5
  Flowers not showy, yellowish to greenish or white; perianth segments less than 1·3 cm long, with or without median stripe   8
5 Perianth segments strongly reflexed from base at anthesis, narrow; inflorescence lax; bracts minute   9. *C. tenuifolium*
  Perianth segments erect to spreading at anthesis, ovate or narrow; inflorescence dense; bracts long   6
6 Perianth segments broadly ovate, overlapping; bracts membranous   11. *C. tuberosum*
  Perianth segments narrow, not overlapping; bracts withering blackish   7
7 Leaves broadly lanceolate, flat or folded   6. *C. macrophyllum*
  Leaves linear-lanceolate, U-shaped in cross-section   12. *C. sp. A*

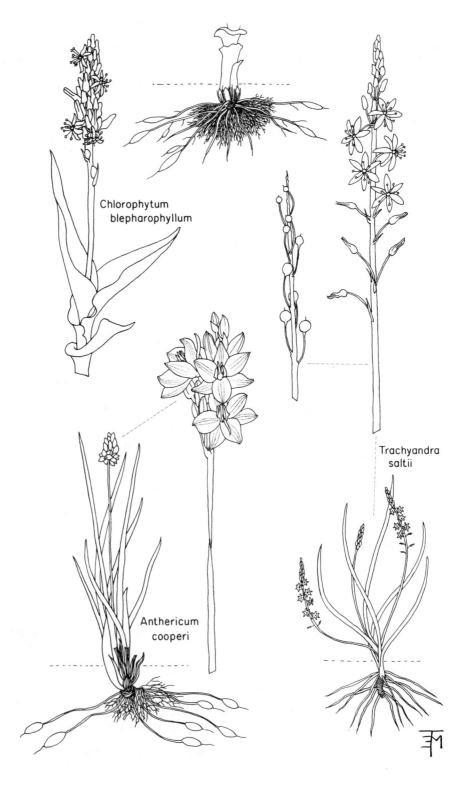

Chlorophytum
blepharophyllum

Trachyandra
saltii

Anthericum
cooperi

Chlorophytum
macrophyllum

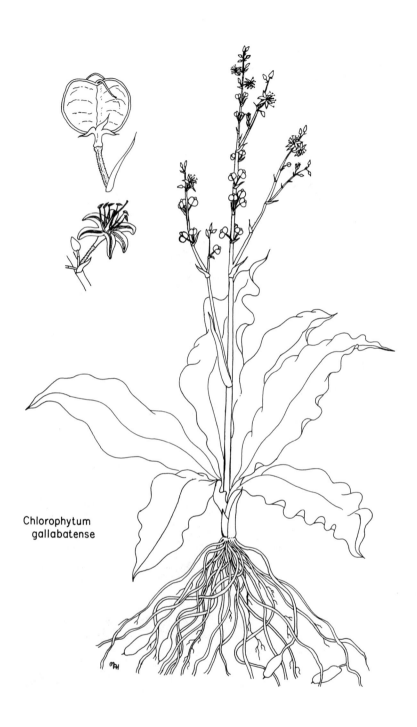

Chlorophytum
gallabatense

8   Inflorescence with well-developed branches, subtended by large bracts   **9**

Inflorescence simple or with 1–2 short ascending, basal branches; bracts large or small   **10**

9   Perianth segments connate and cup-shaped at the base; ovary stipitate, protruding from cup; pedicels not papillate, articulated at or below the middle   1. *C. andongense*

Periatnh segments free almost to the base; ovary not stipitate; pedicels frequently papillate, articulated above the middle or immediately below the perianth   4. *C. gallabatense*

10   Leaves distinctly ciliated at margins, with sheathing bases usually purple-tinged   3. *C. blepharophyllum*

Leaves smooth or not distinctly ciliated at margins, bases not purple-tinged   **11**

11   Peduncle slender; leaves linear-lanceolate folded, short; roots thin   7. *C. micranthum*

Peduncle stout; leaves lanceolate, flat or half folded, long; roots thick   **12**

12   Leaves usually petiole-like in lower half; capsule deeply 3-sided, lobes rounded, deeply indented at apex, broader than long   8. *C. sparsiflorum*

Leaves gradually narrowed in lower half, not petiole-like; capsule shallowly 3-sided, lobes somewhat elongated, slightly indented at apex, longer or as long as broad   5. *C. elgonense*

1. Chlorophytum andongense *Bak.* (*C. viridescens* Engl. of Check List)

Glabrous plant, from a compact, woody rhizome, with numerous thick finely furry roots; leaves in an ascending basal rosette, sword-shaped, tapering towards base and apex, half-folded, somewhat glaucous, with wavy margin; inflorescence tall, with a number of erect to ascending branches; raceme many-flowered, bracts lanceolate-acuminate, upper fertile bracts deltoid, acute; pedicels 6–12 mm long in flower, up to 2·5 cm in fruit, articulated at or below the middle; flowers 3–8-nate; free part of segments narrowed at the base, ligulate, reflexed in open flower and in fruit, greenish to white, with a dark green median stripe; capsule oblong, 10–15 mm long; seeds 3–4 mm in diameter.

A robust plant of river or stream banks, in grasslands or woodlands. The cup-shaped base of the perianth and the stipitate ovary are rather unusual for this genus. HE, HT, HA, KIT, MAC, KAJ.

Brodhurst-Hill 671.

2. Chlorophytum bakeri *Poelln.* (*Dasystachys debilis* Bak.; *Dasystachys gracilis* Bak.)

A small plant from an erect, shortly fibrous rhizome, with roots swollen, fleshy, and often shortly furry; leaves in an ascending rosette, progressively larger, narrow, glabrous, half-folded and wavy at margins; inflorescence a dense, sub-spicate raceme, usually simple and short but up to 30 cm tall; bracts usually projecting beyond the very shortly pedicellate, white, small, bell-shaped flowers with exserted stamens; fruit broader than long, about 3·5 mm long, winged, deeply indented at the apex.

A fairly common graceful little herb of grasslands and open woodlands, appearing after first rains. HM, HA, NAR, BAR, RV, NAN, MAC, NBI, KAJ.

Polhill 386; Hanid 386.

3. Chlorophytum blepharophyllum *Bak.* (see p. 680)

Plant from a short, erect rhizome, with narrow roots bearing distant elongate tubers; leaves in an ascending rosette, very short and broad to long, folded, narrowed in their lower half and clasping the peduncle, the sheathing bases and veins of outer leaves purple-tinged, margins crisped-ciliate; inflorescence usually with one to three short branches and with a crowded raceme of 2–4-nate flowers; fruits oblong, 6–9·5 mm long, winged, with persistent perianth segments.

Locally common in burnt grassland, especially in Elgon area. HE, HC, HT, KIT, MUM, NAR, BAR.

Polhill 413; Tweedie 67/55.

4. Chlorophytum gallabatense *Bak.* (see p. 682)

Plant from a short compact rhizome with many long narrow roots bearing distant small tubers; leaves progressively larger, membranous, often undulate at margins and petiole-like in lower half, bases dilated, very shortly clasping, drying yellowish; inflorescence laxly branched, up to 60 cm or more tall; pedicels articulated above the middle or below the perianth, usually papillate (under a lens) below the articulation; flowers white or greenish, with segments reflexed when fully open in the afternoon; fruits conspicuously winged, small, broader than long.

A fairly frequent plant of grasslands, open woodlands, and shallow soils, appearing after first rains. HE, HM, HA, KIT, KIS, BAR, NAN, MAC.

Bogdan 3724; Hanid and Agnew 28.

5. Chlorophytum elgonense *Bullock* (*C. limurense* Rendle of Check List)

Plant similar to *C. sparsiflorum* but slightly more robust and leaves more succulent and broader, not petiole-like in lower half.

A locally common forest species. HA, KIT, NBI.

Napier 321; Agnew 7812.

6. Chlorophytum macrophyllum *Aschers.* (see p. 681)

Small or robust, glabrous herb from a vertical or horizontal underground rhizome, with many, somewhat thick and fleshy roots bearing ovoid tubers; leaves broadly lanceolate, wavy and crisped at margins, narrowed above the shortly clasping, dilated base; inflorescence up to 30 cm tall; raceme dense, usually simple; flowers white, up to 1·5 cm long, in fascicles of up to 5; lower bracts long, projecting beyond flowers, drying off blackish; pedicels up to 1·5 cm in fruit, shorter in flower, articulation above the middle if present; capsules usually blackish when dehiscing, 5–12 mm long, winged, indented at apex.

A handsome plant of grasslands or open bushland on black cotton soil, with flowers opening a few at a time; common in Ngong area and on Athi Plains near Nairobi. HA, NAR, MAC, NBI, KAJ.

Polhill 102; Hanid and Kiniaruh 401.

7. Chlorophytum micranthum *Bak.*

Small glabrous plants from a small rhizome which is crowned with copious fibres from old leafbases and bears thinly fleshy roots with small tubers; leaves usually very small, linear-lanceolate, folded, margin often wavy, base clasping the slender peduncle which bears one or two short branches; flowers small, about 6 mm long, usually paired greenish to white with a narrow green median stripe; pedicel slender, recurved in bud; fruits about 4 mm long, 3-winged.

Locally common in Trans-Nzoia in burnt grassland, appearing after first showers. KIT.

Symes 295; Tweedie 2797.

8. Chlorophytum sparsiflorum *Bak.* (*C. limurense* Rendle)

Glabrous plant up to 30 cm or more tall, from a compact vertical rhizome with many, long, swollen roots bearing scattered tubers and thin rootlets; leaves in a basal rosette, linear-lanceolate, semi-folded or flat, usually narrowed and petiole-like above the dilated, shortly clasping base; inflorescence simple, sometimes with a short, basal lateral branch, few-flowered; lowest bract lanceolate or linear-acuminate, pedicels up to 1 cm long in fruit,

articulated at or above the middle; flowers white or greenish, 1–4-nate, segments reflexed in open flowers; capsule deeply 3-lobed, broader than long, deeply indented at apex.

A shade-loving plant of wet places in forest; sometimes viviparous. HA, HK, HN, KIS, MAC, NBI.

Polhill 359; Hanid 1055.

9. Chlorophytum tenuifolium *Bak.*

Fairly large plant from a densely fibrous rhizome with thick, fairly short, fleshy roots bearing ellipsoid tubers; leaves in a basal, ascending rosette, glabrous, delicate, lanceolate, half-folded, margins undulate and sometimes inrolled; inflorescence usually simple, lax; flowers solitary or rarely paired, segments narrow, constricted above the base, strongly reflexed at anthesis; stamens 3 long and 3 short; capsule oblong, sutures prominent, 1·1–2·2 cm long.

A locally common plant of black cotton soils and seasonally wet dry grasslands. MAG, NAN, MAC, NBI, KAJ.

Verdcourt 2643; Hanid 564.

10. Chlorophytum tordense *Chiov.*

Small plants from an irregularly branched, woody, knobby, fibrous rhizome with stringy roots bearing tubers; leaves somewhat distichous, outer basal sheaths characteristically marked brown above ground-level, followed by a white band before the green; inflorescence simple or branched, rachis often zigzagging; perianth segments white, with greenish brown median stripe; fruits deeply 3-winged.

Rather an unusual species of *Chlorophytum* with distichous, linear folded leaves with ciliated margins and dilated bases; occurring in dry grasslands, often on black cotton soil. NAR, MAG, MAC, NBI, KAJ.

Polhill 383; Hanid 318.

11. Chlorophytum tuberosum *Bak.*

Plants from a fibrous rhizome with short, fleshy roots the majority of which bear a well-developed ellipsoid tuber; leaves in an ascending basal rosette, broad, with sparsely hairy margins; inflorescence usually simple, dense, with large, often paired, cup-shaped white flowers; segments broad, ovate, overlapping towards the base, sweet scented; capsule oblong, 3-winged, slightly indented at the apex.

A handsome plant of dry grasslands on black cotton soils. NAN, MAC, NBI, KAJ.

Polhill 370.

12. Chlorophytum *sp.* A.

Plant similar to *C. macrophyllum* but with linear-lanceolate, half-folded leaves, usually with undulate margins.

A rare plant, so far collected in a stony marsh near Tala River, at Kisukioni on Thika–Tana road. MAC.

Hanid and Agnew 48.

13. Chlorophytum *sp.* B.

Small plant from an irregularly branched, woody, knobby, sparsely fibrous rhizome with stringy roots bearing scattered distant tubers; leaves sub-distichous to distichous, shiny, folded, often broader in upper half, distinctly ciliate at margins, midrib keeled on lower surface; inflorescence simple; raceme short, few-flowered; capsule usually broader than long, deeply 3-lobed.

A rare plant, so far collected at Kithimani on Thika–Kangonde road and in Embu area. EMB, MAC.

Stone 7940; Hanid 399.

9. BOWIEA *Hook. f.*

Underground stem a large bulb; basal leaves 1–2, perishing early; stem long, much branched, climbing, herbaceous, with inconspicuous, scale-like stem leaves; flowers solitary, pedicellate, bisexual; perianth segments free, persistent; stamens perigynous, much shorter than the perianth; filaments gradually narrowing from base upwards, slightly flattened; anthers basifixed; ovary sessile, conical, with many ovules in each cell; style persistent; stigma obscurely 3-lobed; fruit thickly membranous, dehiscing loculicidally; seeds shining black, striate-granular, elongate, compressed; endosperm fleshy.

1   Capsule ellipsoid, widest below the middle, apex gradually narrowing to the tip; seeds up to 1 cm long or more
                  1. *B. kilimandscharica*
    Capsule conical, apex obtusely or narrowly emarginate and shortly apiculate; seeds 6 mm long or shorter   2. *B. volubilis*

1. Bowiea kilimandscharica *Mildbr.* (see p. 686)

Herbaceous climber with long, profusely branched, slender, twining, green stems bearing narrow, fleshy ultimate branchlets and solitary flowers on pedicels 2–5 cm long; branchlets and pedicels growing downwards to keep the plant securely draped over its support, perianth segments narrow, greenish, horizontally spreading to deflexed.

A poisonous plant of evergreen bushland and woodland on rocky soils; it profusely covers the plants and rocks in its neighbourhood; below 7500 ft. HA, NAR, MAC, NBI, KAJ.

Bally 5293; Agnew 10205.

2. Bowiea volubilis *Harv.*

Plant similar to *B. kilimandscharica* except for differences in the key characters.

A rare plant, so far recorded only from Endebess at about 7700 ft. More flowering and fruiting material needed. HE.

Webster in EAH 9943.

10. ERIOSPERMUM *Jacq.*

Underground organ a large tuber with a fibrous neck, leaves usually solitary or few, often appearing after the flowers, in ours simple and glabrous; inflorescence racemose; bracts minute, membranous; flowers small, in ours yellow; perianth campanulate, persistent; segments free or shortly united at the base, subequal, 1-nerved; stamens shorter than the segments, attached to the base of the segments; filaments linear; anthers dorsifixed; ovary sessile or subsessile, globose, 3-celled, with 2 to few ovules in each cell; style short, subulate; stigma entire, capitate; capsule top-shaped, with emarginate apex and rounded lobes; seeds densely covered with long white hairs; embryo long, cylindrical.

1   Leaves absent or usually 1, rarely 2, prominently veined, the lower half very much narrowed, petiole-like; pedicels 2·5–7 cm long   1. *E. abyssinicum*
    Leaves usually 2–3 or more, without prominent veins, slightly narrowed towards the base, pedicels less than 2·5 cm long
                  2. *E. triphyllum*

1. Eriospermum abyssinicum *Bak.* (see p. 686)

Erect herb from a depressed globose tuber often with a solitary leathery leaf much narrowed in the lower half and appearing petiole-like; inflorescence with well spaced flowers on long ascending pedicels and rachis often flexuous.

An infrequent plant of seasonally wet, rocky soils above 5800 ft. HE, HT, KIT.

Williams 171; Irwin in cm 20921.

2. Eriospermum triphyllum *Bak.* (see p. 686)

Erect herb similar to *E. abyssinicum* but for the differences in the key characters and the tuber which is discoid to subglobose and red when cut.

A locally frequent plant on shallow soils overlying rocks. HE, HA, KIT, MAC, NBI.

Edwards 55; Hanid and Agnew 47.

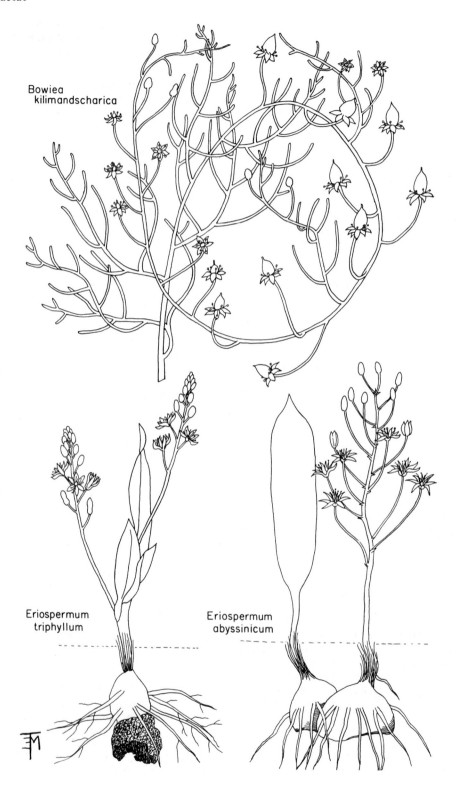

Bowiea
kilimandscharica

Eriospermum
triphyllum

Eriospermum
abyssinicum

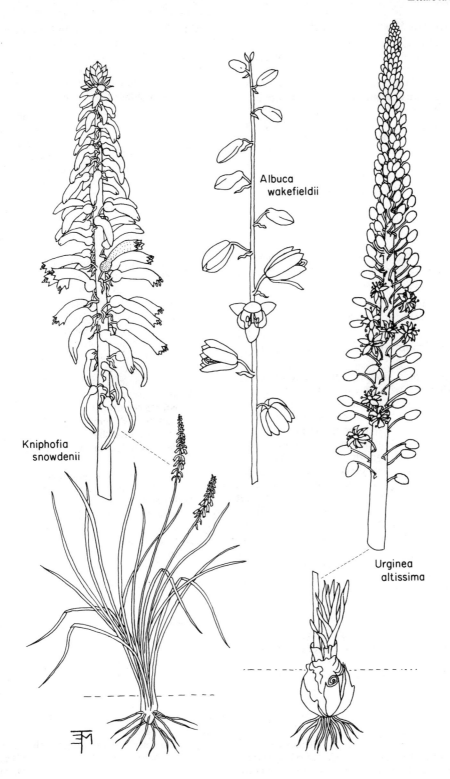

Albuca
wakefieldii

Kniphofia
snowdenii

Urginea
altissima

11. KNIPHOFIA *Moench.*

Underground organ a rhizome; leaves basal, long, narrowing gradually to the apex; inflorescence a terminal, many-flowered, dense raceme, lengthening in fruit; peduncle erect, long, naked; flowers pendulous, bright yellow or red; pedicels short; bracts persistent, scarious; perianth-tube long, cylindric or narrowly funnel-shaped; segments subequal, small, much shorter than the tube; stamens united to the disc at the base of the ovary, as long as the perianth or exserted; filaments filiform; anthers dorsifixed, versatile, ovary sessile, ovoid, 3-celled, with many ovules in each cell; style long, filiform, usually exserted in old flowers; stigma minute, capitate; capsule globose to ovoid, loculicidally 3-valved; seed 3-angled, black.

This genus is confined to the continent of Africa, except for one species in Madagascar, and extends from Abyssinia to the Cape.

1   Flowers hairy outside   2. *K. snowdenii*
      Flowers glabrous outside   1. *K. thomsonii*

1. Kniphofia thomsonii *Bak.* (*K. rogersii* E. A. Bruce)

Erect herb from a fibrous, sometimes branched, irregular rhizome with leaves up to 100 cm long, and a dense to lax raceme; flowers elongate, trumpet-shaped, up to 3 cm long, or longer, yellow to flame red, constricted above the inflated base, with lobes about 2 mm long, spreading, ovate, obtuse and subequal; capsule pointed ovoid.

There is a dry area form which has shorter racemes and distinctly keeled leaves, the apices of which are sometimes triangular in section. The wet area form (described formerly as *K. rogersii* E. A. Bruce) is robust with longer racemes and flat leaves and is found along streams and in marshy places, and is not sufficiently distinct to be regarded as a separate species. HE, HM, HC, HT, HA, KIT, BAR, RV.

Wood 738; Hanid, Agnew, and Mendes 140.

2. Kniphofia snowdenii *C. H. Wright* (see p. 687)

Erect herb similar to *K. thomsoni* Bak. except for differences in the key characters and long, linear leaves.

Plant of marshy places above 5800 ft. HE, HM, HC, HT.

Lugard 83; Strid 3570.

12. ALOE *L.*

Fleshy-leaved herbs or shrubs, sometimes tuberous at base, with distichous or (in ours) rosetted, serrate leaves and lateral racemes of red or yellow flowers; bracts present, bracteoles absent; perianth ± zygomorphic, with a cylindrical tube and free, ± equal lobes; stamens 6, each group of 3 elongating and exserted, and then retracted in turn during anthesis; style and stigma simple; fruit a capsule with many angular or flattened black seeds.

1   Racemes solitary or inflorescence a simple panicle with only one order of branching, if occasional lower inflorescence branches compound then plant shrubby   3
      Racemes in a large panicle, with lower branches themselves branched and thus second order branches present; plants with a large rosette of big leaves and very short stem   2
2   Most flowers erect or horizontal or ascending racemes   1. *A. secundiflora*
      Flowers arranged horizontally or nodding all round the erect racemes   2. *A. tweediae*
3   Plants without an erect stem, all the leaves being in a basal rosette   4
      Plants with erect or trailing leafy stems   11
4   Perianth with a distinct globose basal swelling; more than 3 sterile bracts usually present below each raceme   5
      Perianth ± cylindrical at base; sterile bracts 0–3 at base of racemes   8
5   Leaves less than 30 cm long, inflorescence with 5 or fewer branches   7
      Leaves over 30 cm long; inflorescence with 6 or more branches   6
6   Racemes conical in early anthesis   3. *A. lateritia*
      Racemes round-topped in early anthesis   5. *A. graminicola*
7   Inflorescence simple or rarely with 1–2 branches; perianth less than 3 cm long   4. *A. amudatensis*
      Inflorescence branched, rarely simple; perianth over 30 cm long   5. *A. graminicola*
8   Leaves less than 1 cm wide; inflorescence simple; plant with a tuberous rootstock   6. *A. myriacantha*
      Leaves over 2 cm wide; inflorescence mostly branched; plant with no swollen rootstock   9
9   Bracts acuminate, linear to lanceolate   7. *A. ukambensis*
      Bracts acute or obtuse, broad-ovate to oblong, not acuminate   10
10   Young racemes erect   8. *A. macrosiphon*
      Young racemes nodding   9. *A. deserti*
11   Young racemes nodding, with buds covered by the oblong, obtuse or acute bracts   9. *A. deserti*

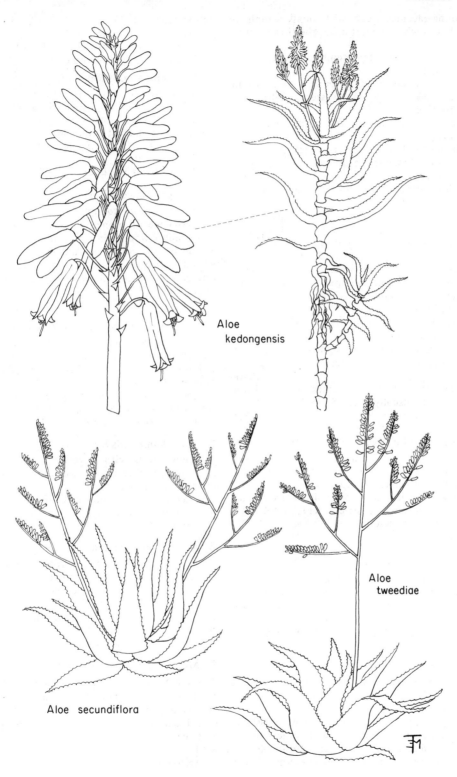

Aloe
kedongensis

Aloe
tweediae

Aloe secundiflora

Young racemes erect, with small, acuminate bracts which do not cover the flower buds   **12**

12   Plant a tall single-stemmed tree to over 3 m in height   **13**
      Plant a low shrub, or if over 2 m then forming a thicket, with many stems falling and rooting   **14**

13   Stems naked below; bracts more than half as long as the pedicel   **10. *A. ballyi***
      Stems covered with persistent dead leaves below; bract less than half as long as the pedicel   **11. *A. volkensii***

14   Inflorescences 0–2 branched, rarely an odd one with branches   **15**
      Inflorescences with 3 and more branches   **16**

15   Leaves less than 4 cm wide at base; racemes becoming rounded in outline at apex
                                          12. *A. kedongensis*
      Leaves over 5 cm wide at base; racemes remaining conical at apex   **13. *A. elgonica***

16   Racemes round-topped even at the start of anthesis   **14. *A. rabaiensis***
      Racemes acutely conical at the start of anthesis   **17**

17   Peduncles of the racemes purple to red; lower pedicels usually less than 14 mm long
                                               15. *A. dawei*
      Peduncles of the racemes green; lower pedicels usually over 15 mm long
                                          16. *A. nyeriensis*

1. Aloe secundiflora *Engl.* (see p. 689)

A large fleshy herb with a rosette of green, unspotted, ± glossy leaves at ground level and a much-branched panicle of red flowers.

Common in alluvial sandy soils in drier areas, especially Machakos District. KIT, BAR, RV, MAG, NAN, MAC, KAJ.

Napier 1869.

2. Aloe tweediae *Christian* (see p. 689)

Similar to *A. secundiflora* but with the keyed differences and shorter, more orange flowers.

Known only from Karamoja and adjacent parts of Kenya in dry, sandy bushland. BAR.

Record based on observation by Mrs E. M. Tweedie.

3. Aloe lateritia *Engl.* (see p. 691)

A medium-sized *Aloe* with a sessile rosette of white-spotted and streaked leaves and a simple panicle of green and orange or red flowers.

Locally common in upland wooded grassland. Two varieties exist. The one with bracts longer than the pedicels and green- and flesh-coloured flowers is known as var. *kitaliensis* (Reynl.) Reynl.

and is found in HT and KIT. The type variety has bracts shorter than the pedicels and red flowers. HE, HT, HM, HA, KIT, KIS, BAR, NAN, MAC.

Tweedie 68/116; Napier 6594.

4. Aloe amudatensis *Reynolds*

A small stoloniferous *Aloe* with a rosette of conspicuously white-spotted triangular leaves and solitary or paired racemes of pink to coral-red flowers on long erect peduncles.

Uncommon, found in the north of our area in dry bushland. BAR.

Record from Mrs E. M. Tweedie.

5. Aloe graminicola *Reynolds* (see p. 691)

Similar to *A. amudatensis* but with a branching inflorescence of orange, almost capitate racemes.

Locally common in dry sandy grassland, in the north-east of our area, and especially common around Naro Moru. Some specimens seem to intergrade with *A. lateritia*. HM, HA, RV, NAN, MAC.

Agnew 9911; Tweedie 2459.

6. Aloe myriacantha *(Harv.) R. & S.* (see p. 691)

A small herb from a tuberous, and sometimes bulbous base, with linear-subulate leaves and a solitary erect raceme of flesh-coloured to whitish or green flowers.

Locally common in rocky grassland. HC, HM, HA, NAR, RV, NAN, MAC, NBI, KAJ.

Agnew 9148; Napier Bax 2629.

7. Aloe ukambensis *Reynolds*

A robust herb with a rosette of large, usually unspotted, dull leaves at base and 1–3 racemes of red flowers to each scape.

Uncommon and confined to rock faces and rocky slopes in MAC.

Napper 1619.

8. Aloe macrosiphon *Bak.*

A stemless herb with a large rosette of long, glossy spotted leaves and a 4–6-branched erect panicle of red flowers subtended by rather large bracts.

Locally common in Serengeti in rocky bushland, from whence it extends northwards into Southern Mara. NAR.

Agnew 10184; Bally 5426.

9. Aloe deserti *Berger* (see p. 691)

A low herb or shrub with short-stemmed or sessile rosettes of spotted leaves and erect, 2–5-branched panicles of pink flowers subtended by large bracts which are often reflexed in age.

Locally common in dry country. RV, MAC, KAJ.

Archer 410.

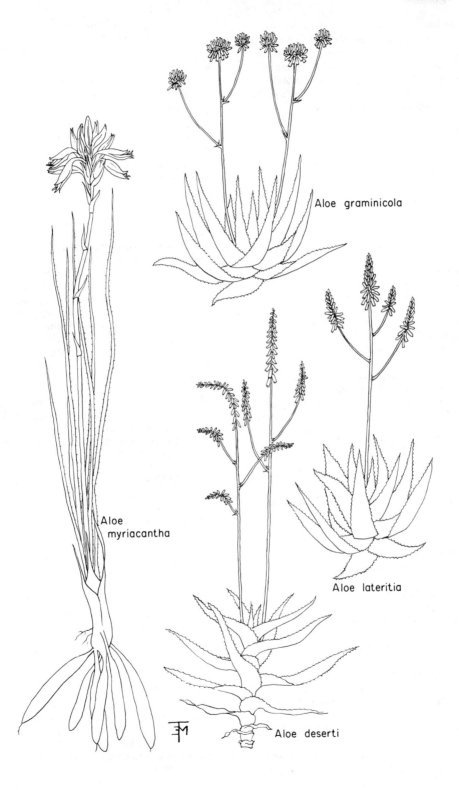

Aloe graminicola

Aloe lateritia

Aloe myriacantha

Aloe deserti

10. Aloe ballyi *Reynl.*

A tall single-stemmed tree (to 8 m) with a solitary terminal rosette of dull, grey-green leaves and much-branched panicles of reddish-orange flowers.

Rare, found in riverine bushland. MAC.

Record from Reynolds' *The Aloes of Tropical Africa and Madagascar* p. 325 (1966).

11. Aloe volkensii *Engl.*

A tall single-stemmed or occasionally branched tree (to 6 m) with dull, grey-green leaves in a terminal rosette and much-branched panicles of red flowers.

Common in rocky bushland in the Narok area. NAR, KAJ.

van Someren in Bally 11448; Agnew 10196.

12. Aloe kedongensis *Reynl.* (see p. 689)

A thicket-forming shrub (branches occasionally falling and rooting) with narrow, bright green, hardly crowded leaves and 1-2-branched inflorescences of red flowers.

Common in riverine bushland in the Rift Valley, rare elsewhere, HA, NAR, RV, KAJ.

Agnew and Waithaka 9890; Polhill 173.

13. Aloe elgonica *Bullock*

A thicket-forming shrub with broad, dull-green, coarsely toothed leaves in a rosette and 1-2-branched panicles of bright red-orange flowers.

Locally common on the slopes of Mt. Elgon on shallow soils. HE, KIT.

Tweedie 68/136; 2406.

14. Aloe rabaiensis *Rendle*

A thicket-forming shrub with dull green, hardly crowded leaves and 4-7-branched terminal panicles of bright orange-red flowers.

Locally common in rocky ground near Nairobi. HT, HA, RV, MAC, NBI, KAJ.

Agnew 10697; Bally 47.

15. Aloe dawei *Berger*

A thicket-forming shrub with deep green, rather narrow leaves and branched panicles of red flowers.

This species and the next form a puzzling complex which requires further work in our area. It is mostly found in rocky bushland in western Kenya. HC, HT, HM, KIT, MUM, KIS.

Tweedie 66/382; van Someren in Bally 736.

16. Aloe nyeriensis *Christian* (*A. ngobitensis* Reynl.)

Similar to *A. dawei* but differing in the keyed characters. *A. ngobitensis* is a plant which differs apparently only in flower-colour and therefore it seems best to regard them as both the same here, for both grow in similar localities near Nyeri and Laikipia. HA, NAN.

Agnew 9170; Napier 2625.

13. ALBUCA L.

Plants with tunicated bulbs; leaves basal flat or U-shaped in section or terete, tapering to a point; inflorescence a dense or lax raceme; bracts persistent, membranous; pedicels not articulated, sometimes lengthening considerably in fruit; flowers yellow or white, rarely entirely green; perianth persistent; segments unequal, free almost to the base, usually broadly keeled with green or reddish-brown, the 3 outer oblong, ± spreading, the 3 inner shorter, hooded at the apex and cohering to enclose the reproductive structures; the stamens fertile or the anthers of the 3 outer small and imperfect or absent; filaments flattened, often winged and dilated at the base, or filiform; ovary, oblong-sessile, 3-celled, with many ovules in each cell; style usually obconic, 3-angled, rarely cylindric; stigma usually 3-lobed; capsule ovoid, slightly 3-lobed, pointed at the apex, loculicidally 3-valved; seeds black, compressed; endosperm fleshy.

1 Leaves narrowly linear or broad, not terete   2
  Leaves filiform almost terete, with a longitudinal groove   1. *A.* sp. *A*
2 Flowers long-pedicelled, erect at anthesis; pedicels up to 8 cm or more in mature flowers   3
  Flowers short-pedicelled, generally nodding at anthesis; pedicels up to 2·2 cm in mature flowers   4
3 Peduncle long, much taller than 20 cm; usually flowering with the leaves
                                         2. *A.* sp. *B*
  Peduncles short, less than 20 cm tall; flowering before the leaves (KAJ area only)   3. *A. pachychlamys*
4 Leaves narrowly linear, canaliculate, margin smooth and often involute   4. *A.* sp. *C*
  Leaves generally broad, flatter, folded margin smooth or ciliated and often undulate
                                      5. *A. wakefieldii*

1. Albuca *sp.* A.

Slender plant up to 35 cm or more tall, from a small bulb up to about 2 cm across and drawn into a long fibrous neck with horizontal striations; leaves often ciliate at margins towards the base; raceme few-flowered; flowers crowded towards the top, 6-10 mm long.

A rare but locally common herb in seasonally water-logged soils; more material desirable. MAC, NBI.

Archer 541; Hanid and Agnew 51.

2. Albuca *sp.* B.

Glabrous plant from globose to ovoid bulb; leaves linear, with upper surface canaliculate and margins often involute; raceme eventually lax, generally 5-7-flowered; pedicels lengthening at anthesis, long, ascending to erect.

A rare herb of upland grasslands. It is much in need of further collecting and may eventually prove to be a robust form of *A. pachchlamys*. RV, MAC.

Polhill 138; Faden 67/885.

3. Albuca pachychlamys *Bak.*

A small plant up to 20 cm high, from a large bulb covered with tough old leaf sheaths and drawn into a short, transversely striate, fibrous neck; leaves not contemporary with flowers; raceme moderately lax, with long, ascending pedicels; rachis somewhat zigzagging.

A rare plant so far recorded only once from between Kibwezi and Chyulu Hills; further material needed to ascertain the variation within the species. KAJ.

Teophilo in Bally 7592.

4. Albuca *sp.* C.

Glabrous plant from a yellowish globose-ovoid bulb which is drawn into a long, transversely striate neck; leaves contemporary with flowers; raceme moderately lax, generally up to 10-flowered; flowers small, usually 9-12 mm long.

A rare herb of wooded grasslands and shallow soils overlying rocks; more material desirable. KIT, MAC, NBI.

Bogan 3714; Agnew and Hanid 8939.

5. Albuca wakefieldii *Bak.* (see p. 687)

Plants generally robust, up to 1 m or more tall, from an ovoid bulb produced into a neck which is sometimes fibrous; leaves variable, folded, often twisted, with margins ciliated and often undulate in smaller forms; flowers bell-shaped, never opening fully; segments up to 2·7 cm long or more; bracts generally longer than pedicels in flower.

This is our commonest but very variable species of *Albuca* found below 8300 ft. HE, HC, HT, HA, HK, KIT, KIS, NAR, RV, MAC, NBI, KAJ.

Symes 291; Hanid, Hanid, and Kiniaruh 540.

14. URGINEA *Steinh.*

Underground stem a tunicated bulb often produced into a neck; leaves several, basal, usually appearing after the flowers; inflorescence a simple, central raceme; scape terete, naked; bracts membranous, the lower, or all, prolonged backwards into a spur at the base or the middle; flowers whitish; perianth deciduous, the segments free or slightly united at the base, subequal, with a green to purple-brown median stripe; stamens inserted at the base of the perianth-segments; filaments in ours filiform or tapering from a broadened base; anthers versatile, introrse, elongate in ours; ovary sessile, ovoid; ovules few to many in each cell; style ending in a capitate stigma; capsule membranous, globose to ellipsoid, loculicidally 3-valved; seed discoid, black, shiny, often winged.

1 Leaves broadly lanceolate, lamina flat; raceme dense, many flowered; capsule globose, winged, apex emarginate, shortly apiculate   1. *U. altissima*
    Leaves linear, upper surface canaliculate; raceme lax, rather few-flowered; capsule ovoid, not winged, apex pointed not apiculate   2. *U. indica*

1. Urginea altissima (*L. f.*) *Bak.* (see p. 687)

Erect, robust herb from a large, ovoid bulb drawn into a neck which is often covered with cotton-wool-like remains of old leaf bases; inflorescence 0·6-1·8 m tall; perianth segments 6-9 mm long.

A common plant of rocky and sandy soils below 8000 ft. HE, HT, HA, KIT, MUM, KIS, BAR, RV.

Williams 128; Agnew 10753.

2. Urginea indica *Kunth* (see p. 696)

Small herb from a bulb with thin outer tunic; outer leaves and capsule-walls often purple-spotted; inflorescence 10-45 cm tall; scape 2-3 mm in diameter.

An infrequent plant of rocky soils and evergreen bushland. BAR, MAC, KAJ.

Napper 567.

15. DRIMIA *Jacq.*

Bulbous herbs, flowering before the leaves; flowers whitish to greenish, sometimes marked reddish-brown to purplish; bracts pouched or spurred on the back; perianth-segments all similar, united for lower third or quarter, the free parts linear-spathulate, slightly hooded at tip; stamens inserted at top of perianth-tube; capsule oblong-ovoid, 3-valved; seeds papery, black, papillose.

All species imperfectly known and require study.

1   Flowers 16–20 mm long, in dense racemes; bracts 16–24 mm long   1. *D. congesta*
Flowers smaller, in lax racemes; bracts 4–15 mm long   2
2   Pedicels of open flowers 7–12(–15) mm long; flowers whitish, often marked red or maroon, 14–16 mm long   2. *D. elgonica*
Pedicels of open flowers 2–5 mm long (a little longer in fruit); flowers greenish-brown, 10–14 mm long; anthers less than 1·2 mm long   3. *D. zombensis*

1. Drimia congesta *Bullock*

Bulb 10 + cm across; leaves unknown; scape 60–90 cm tall, the flowers densely crowded on upper part, whitish, lined pinkish or purplish-brown, 16–20 mm long; bracts as long as flowers; pedicels 3–5(–6 in fruit) mm long; anthers 1·5–3 mm long.

Highland grassland or moorland. HE.
Lugard 474.

2. Drimia elgonica *Bullock* (see p. 696)

Bulb large, red; leaves hairy (according to Chater Jack); scape 40–120 cm tall, with numerous flowers laxly arranged on upper part (crowded only at tip); flowers whitish, often with red maroon markings, 14–16 mm long; bracts 6–15 mm long; pedicels 7–12(–15) mm long; anthers 1·5–3 mm long.

Possibly only a high altitude robust variant of the widespread *D. zombensis*. Highland grassland, flowering at first rains. KIT, possibly also HE.
Lugard 563; Tweedie 277.

3. Drimia zombensis *Bak.*

Bulbs 3–6 cm across, reddish-purple; leaves narrowly oblong-lanceolate, developed after flowering; scape slender, 20–70 cm tall, with rather few to numerous laxly arranged flowers above; flowers greenish-brown, 10–12(–14) mm long; bracts 3–7 mm long; pedicels 2–7 mm long; pedicels 2–5(–7 in fruit) mm long; anthers not more than 1(–1·2) mm long.

Wet savannah, after fires, flowering at first rains. KIT.
Mainwaring K10; Tweedie 2988.

16. DIPCADI *Medik.*

Herbs from small, ovoid bulb, with thin outer tunics, sometimes produced into a neck; leaves basal, narrow to wide, flat or folded, straight or spirally twisted, glabrous or hairy dorsally; margin smooth, rarely undulate ciliate or papillate, free or clasping at base; inflorescence a simple central raceme, with few to many flowers; scape terete, rachis drooping in bud, becoming erect during anthesis; bracts small, caducous or persistent; pecicels very short to long, lengthening in fruit; flowers green or brown; perianth deciduous; segments dissimilar, forming a tube, fused at the base, the 3 outer spreading from the middle or erect with recurved tips and in ours extended into a caudate, terete appendage; the 3 inner shorter, often connivent with only the tip curved outwards; stamens 6, included, filaments flat and fused to the tube below; ovary turbinate, sessile or stipitate, 3-celled, with many biseriate ovules per cell; style shorter than stamens, papillate; stigma with 3 papillate lobes or rarely capitate; capsule rounded, oblong, or trigonous in cross-section, seeds flat, round, black, shiny, papillose.

Predominantly an African genus, but also found in the Mediterranean region, Madagascar, Socotra and India.

1   Mature leaves 6–16 mm wide, flat or folded, not inrolled   2
Mature leaves filiform or narrow, less than 3·5 mm wide, frequently inrolled   1. *D. arenarium*
2   Leaf-margins smooth; outer perianth segments of mature flowers with caudate appendages more than 5 mm long   2. *D. viride*
Leaf-margins distinctly ciliate; outer perianth segments with very short caudate appendages, about 3–5 mm long   3. *D. sp. A*

1. Dipcadi arenarium *Bak.*

Slender plants 10–55 cm tall with very narrow leaves, often dilated and clasping at the base and rarely more than 25 cm long; inner segments of the perianth narrow and conspicuously pointed.

A small graceful lily of grasslands, often on seasonally wet shallow soils overlying rocks and black cotton soil. KIT, NAR, RV, MAC, NBI.
Lucas and Williams in EAH 12358; Agnew and Hanid 7492.

2. Dipcadi viride (*L.*) *Moench* (see p. 696)

Glabrous plants 10–60 cm or more high with linear to linear-lanceolate, shiny, flaccid, indistinctly veined leaves which are variable in size; scape terete, shiny, sometimes arcuate at the base; flowers green with khaki to yellowish tinge; tips of inner segments curved outwards; capsule oblong in outline, trigonous, about 1 cm long.

Our commonest but variable species of *Dipcadi* often found in wetter areas of grasslands and in bushland. KIT, BAR, RV, EMB, MAC, NBI.
Napier 2370; Hanid, Hanid, and Kiniaruh 501.

3. Dipcadi *sp.* A..

Slender plant from a small, globose bulb, with leaves linear-lanceolate, ciliated at margins, clasping at the base, and progressively larger; caudate appendages of outer segments of flowers very short.

A rare plant much in need of further collecting. RV, MAC.

Bally 7662.

17. SCILLA *L.*

Plants from a tunicated bulb; leaves fleshy, flat, in a basal rosette, often spotted dark green or purple; inflorescence a raceme; pedicels not articulated; bracts small, scarious; flowers generally blue or mauve-purple; perianth persistent; segments subequal, spreading to strongly reflexed, 1-nerved; stamens attached to the base of segments; filaments filiform or slightly flattened; ovary sessile or stipitate, 3-celled, with 2–several ovules per cell; style subulate; stigma capitate; capsule loculicidally 3-valved; seeds black, globose or angled by pressure; endosperm firm.

A widely spread genus through the Old World.

1　Leaves thick, fleshy, often spotted dark green or purple; mature raceme much longer than 2·7 cm, elongate; peduncle not hollow　　　　　　　　　　　　　　　　　2

　　Leaves scarcely fleshy, not spotted; mature raceme up to 2·7 cm long, globose in outline; peduncle hollow (only HT)
　　　　　　　　　　　　　　　　　3. *S.* sp. *A*

2　Plants robust; flowers 9–13 mm long; pedicels somewhat thick, 5–10 mm long
　　　　　　　　　　　　　　　　　1. *S. kirkii*

　　Plants smaller; flowers less than 6 mm long; pedicels slender, generally up to 5 mm long
　　　　　　　　　　　　　　　　　2. *S. indica*

1. Scilla kirkii *Bak.*

Bulbs large, up to 8 cm or more across, covered with brownish papery tunics; leaves ovate to sword-shaped, sessile; peduncle plano-convex in section towards the base, capsule with three, rounded lobes, usually 1-seeded.

A pretty lily of seasonally wet soils, appearing after first rains. It may eventually prove to be a robust form of *S. indica* as intermediates between the two species do exist. MAG, MAC, NBI, KAJ.

Verdcourt 2570; Lind 5740.

2. Scilla indica *Bak.* (see p. 696)

Similar to *S. kirkii* but for differences in the key characters; leaves often with a chanelled petiole-like base.

Widespread in Upland Kenya, appearing after first rains. HE, HT, HK, KIT, RV, NBI.

3. Scilla *sp.* A.

Rosette herb from a globose bulb with erect or arching, flat or folded leaves up to 2 cm × 15 cm; peduncle terete, hollow, purplish, short, up to 10 cm long; raceme dense, globose in outline; pedicels ± horizontally spreading; flowers not inflated around the ovary; perianth segments not broadened at the base, ± uniform in width; filaments flattened, tapering from a broadened base.

A rare plant, so far recorded only from halfway along Lumbwa–Londiani road. More material desirable. HT.

Stewart 947.

18. ORNITHOGALUM *L.*

Plants with tunicated bulbs; leaves basal; inflorescence a raceme or corymb; pedicels not articulated; scape naked; bracts membranous, persistent, not spurred; flowers white or yellow; perianth persistent, segments subequal, free, or very shortly joined at the base, usually spreading, with or without a median stripe; stamens hypogynous, shorter than the perianth; filaments often flattened and unequal; anthers dorsifixed; ovary sessile, globose, 3-celled, with many ovules in each cell; style short or elongated; stigma capitate, minute; capsule thickly membranous, loculicidal, not deeply lobed; seeds black, globose or angled by pressure; endosperm firm.

A widely distributed genus of temperate, sub-temperate and tropical areas of the Old World.

1　Plants small; leaves filiform; peduncle thread-like; flowers few, small; bracts small, 1–4 mm long　　　　　　　　1. *O. gracillimum*

　　Plants robust; leaves broadly lanceolate to linear-lanceolate, flat or folded; peduncle stout, terete; flowers many; bracts large, much longer than 4 mm　　　　　　2

2　Pedicels 1·8–5 cm in flower, up to 7 cm in fruit; perianth segments up to 1·9(–2·2) cm at anthesis　　　　　　　2. *O.* sp. *A*

　　Pedicels less than 1·5 cm in flower, up to 1·7 cm in fruit; perianth segments up to 1·4 cm long at anthesis　　　　　　　　　　3

3　Pedicels 1·5–3(–5) mm long; bracts 3–12 mm long; perianth segments 4·7–6 mm long
　　　　　　　　　　　　　　　　　3. *O. ecklonii*

　　Pedicels 6–12 mm long; bracts 1·2–5 cm long; perianth segments up to 1·4 cm long
　　　　　　　　　　　　　　4. *O. longibracteatum*

1. Ornithogalum gracillimum *R. E. Fries* (see p. 696)

Plant 5–20 cm tall from a small bulb up to 1 cm across, with a few, small, 3–7 mm long, laxly

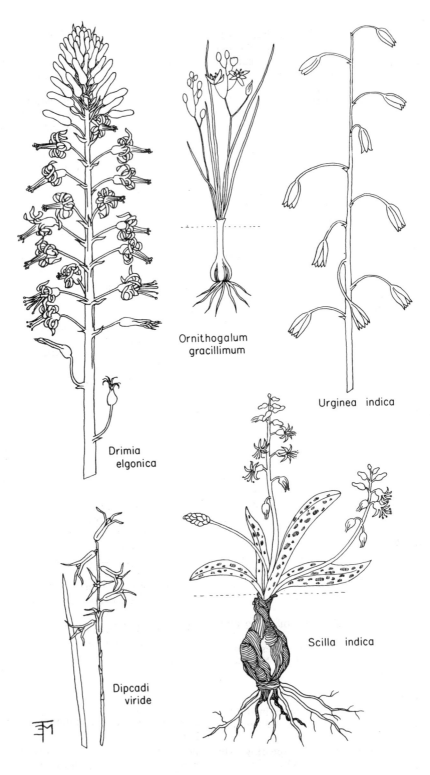

Ornithogalum
gracillimum

Urginea indica

Drimia
elgonica

Dipcadi
viride

Scilla indica

arranged white flowers; capsule small, up to about 4 mm long.

A graceful little plant of grasslands and shallow soils overlying rocks, appearing after first rains; below 10 000 ft HE, HC, HT, HM, HA, HK, KIT, NAR, RV, NAN.

Polhill 406; Tweedie 67/133.

2. Ornithogalum *sp.* A. (*Albuca donaldsonii* Rendle)

Robust plant up to 1 m or more tall from a large bulb about 8 cm across; flowers large, white to cream, outer segments with a green median stripe; pedicels long, erect to ascending.

A frequent plant in grassland and bushland along Mombasa road at Ulu and beyond. MAC.

Verdcourt 3860; Ossent 560.

3. Ornithogalum ecklonii *Schlecht.*

Similar to *O. longibracteatum*, but with shorter pedicels, bracts and flowers.

A fairly frequent plant appearing after first rains in open grasslands and shallow soils overlying rocks. It seems to hybridise with *O. longibracteatum* and may eventually prove to be conspecific with it, as intermediates do occur. HE, HC, HA, KIT, NAR, RV, NAN, NBI.

Polhill 415; Tweedie 66/17.

4. Ornithogalum longibracteatum *Jacq.*

Glabrous plant from a globose bulb; leaves long, linear-lanceolate, lamina usually folded or canaliculate, clasping at the base, margins often inrolled in upper half; young raceme conical, dense, with bracts projecting beyond the buds and also the flowers as they open and the raceme becomes rather lax; perianth segments with a broad green median stripe and white margins.

A widespread but locally common herb of open woodlands and grasslands on seasonally wet soils. HA, RV, MAC, NBI.

Verdcourt 1715; Agnew 9393.

19. DRIMIOPSIS *Lindl.*

Underground stem a tunicated bulb; leaves flat in a basal rosette, usually fleshy, in ours mottled dark green or purple and petiole-like at the base; inflorescence a dense subspicate raceme, upper flowers minute, abortive; bracts not apparent; flowers small, cup-shaped, white to greenish-white; perianth segments subequal, ovate to oblong, 1-nerved, incurved at apices, very shortly connate at the base; stamens shorter than the perianth, attached to the base of segments, filaments very short, flattened, attenuate triangular; anthers ovoid, versatile; ovary sessile, globose, 3-celled, with 2 ovules in each cell; style short, subulate; stigma minute, capitate; capsule globose, loculicidally 3-valved; seeds turgid, shining black.

An African genus; only one species represented in Upland Kenya.

Drimiopsis botryoides *Bak.*

Small, glabrous, bulbous plant with thick, fleshy, ovate to oblanceolate, small, spotted leaves of up to 30 cm or more long and drawn into a petiole-like base; raceme dense; flowers small, whitish-green, remaining almost closed at anthesis, without bracts; pedicels very short, about 1 mm long, not articulated; filaments united into a very short tube at the base.

A rare but locally common lily of seasonally wet or moist places in upland woodlands or grasslands and on shallow soils overlying rocks; more material desirable. HK, MAC.

Faden 68/824; Agnew 9807.

20. ASPARAGUS *L.*

Annual or, more often, perennial and woody, much-branched, often armed with spines, erect or climbing herbs with tuberous or less frequently fibrous roots; true leaves greatly reduced, scarious, often produced into spines; assimilating organs (called cladodes) linear, or flat, leaflike and with one or more veins, solitary or clustered; flowers solitary, paired or numerous, small, terminal or axillary or sometimes terminal and axillary, with articulated pedicels; flowering shoots with or without cladodes; perianth segments free or nearly so, ± similar, ascending or spreading, white or nearly so; stamens fused to perianth segments towards the base; ovary 3-celled, with several axile ovules per cell; fruit a 1–several-seeded berry, globose, or rarely ovoid, usually red, less often black or brown.

Predominantly an African genus but also distributed in Europe, Asia, and Australia. Although seven species are described here there is at least one more species for which herbarium material is scanty and inadequate. It is therefore excluded until well-collected and properly annotated specimens are at hand.

1	Cladodes conspicuously flattened	2
	Cladodes terete, angled, or absent during flowering	3
2	Cladodes more than 1-veined	
		1. *A. asparagoides*
	Cladodes 1-veined	2. *A. falcatus*
3	Cladodes and ultimate branchlets in different planes	4
	Cladodes and ultimate branchlets all in one plane	4. *A. setaceus*
4	Spines not flattened dorsally at the base, not stout; pedicels mostly paired or fascicled	5

Asparagus racemosus

Spines flattened dorsally at the base, stout (especially on stems and large branches); pedicels mostly solitary   5. *A. buchananii*
5   Spurs in axils of spines conspicuous, white; flowers all lateral, paired; pedicels articulated very near the base   6. *A. flagellaris*
Spurs in axils of spines not pure white; flowers both lateral and terminal, solitary and paired or fascicled; pedicels articulated below the flower or below the middle   6
6   Stems yellowish; young branches glabrous; cladodes spreading, arcuate, generally more than 10 mm long; flowers solitary and paired laterally, fascicled terminally
7. *A. racemosus*
Stems greenish to grey-brown; young branches pubescent; cladodes rigid, erect, generally up to 10 mm long; flowers 2-many together   3. *A. africanus*

1. Asparagus asparagoides (*L.*) *Wight*

Climbing or straggling or under exceptional circumstances erect, glabrous, unarmed herb with fusiform, sessile or sometimes distant tubers and tortuous, terete or angled stems and branches; cladodes alternate sessile, broadly ovate to lanceolate, base obtuse, acute to subacuminate; several longitudinal and prominent veins; leaves scarious, not forming spines; flowers axillary, solitary or in pairs, with slender stalk up to 2·5 cm long and articulated near the apex; filaments with 2 basal spurs; berry globose, up to 8-seeded, red.

A shade-loving plant of upland forests and woodlands sometimes climbing to 3 m. It is easily recognised by its flattened leaf-like cladodes which are very variable in shape and size. HA, KIT, NAN, MAC, NBI.
Verdcourt and Greenway 445; Agnew and Ossent 7089.

2. Asparagus falcatus *L.*

A much-branched, glabrous climber or scrambler with tortuous, smooth, pale stems and spreading branches which are usually solitary; cladodes flattened, linear, straight or falcate, dark-green, fascicled; flowers cream to white; berry fleshy, usually 1-seeded, red.

A plant of upland forests and woodlands, but sometimes found scrambling on bushes in drier areas. HM, HA, HK, KIS, NAR, RV, MAC, NBI.
Paulo 700; Agnew and Hanid 7482.

3. Asparagus africanus *Lam.* (*A. asiaticus* L. of Check List)

Glabrous to pubescent, much-branched armed, woody climber with fibrous roots and smooth or slightly grooved, somewhat zigzagging, grey-brown to greenish stems; branches usually solitary at each node, with a tendency to pubescence, usually spreading but often reflexed in pubescent forms; cladodes fascicled, ascending to spreading, needle-like, straight or slightly arcuate; spines present on the stem and larger branches, generally absent on branches, spreading to reflexed; flowers white, axillary and terminal, frequently 2-3-nate, but up to 20-nate, stalks articulated below the middle; berry globose, fleshy, red, single-seeded.

A frequent plant of forest edges and bushy wooded areas where it climbs to about 3 m, but also occurs in open vegetation where it forms low bushes up to 1 m high or scrambles among rocks. Also found in drier areas. HE, HC, HM, HA, KIT, NAR, RV, EMB, NBI, KAJ.
Symes 281; Tweedie 67/44.

4. Asparagus setaceus (*Kunth*) *Jessop* (*A. plumosus* L.)

Glabrous plant with fibrous roots and twining, smooth or grooved, greenish to reddish-brown stems; branches solitary at nodes, copiously pinnate, branchlets and needle-like, fine, arcuate cladodes all in the same (horizontal) plane, giving the plant a fern-like appearance; spines small, reflexed, usually absent; flowers usually solitary, cream-white, with pendent stalk articulated near the middle; berry red, fleshy, up to 3-seeded.

Predominantly a forest species, but also found in open country provided there is sufficient support; also cultivated as an ornamental plant. HL, HA, RV, MAC, NBI, KAJ.
Verdcourt 3628; Agnew 7788.

5. Asparagus buchananii *Bak.*

Glabrous, much-branched, armed, woody climber with tortuous and often strongly zigzagging, smooth stem and branches which are very variable in colour; branchlets lacking spines, spreading to ascending; cladodes in fascicles of 6-8, angled, terete or grooved, needle-like, slightly arcuate; spines well-developed, up to 4 cm long or more on the main stems, dorsally flattened towards the base, usually reflexed; flowers solitary, white; pedicel with variable articulation; ovary stalked; berries fleshy, red, 1-2-seeded.

A frequent forest climber, but also found scrambling over bushes in open country where it often appears after early rains. It is easily recognized by its stout, extremely pungent, strongly reflexed spines which are characteristically flattened at the base. HT, HA, KIT, NAR, BAR, RV, MAG, EMB, MAC, NBI, KAJ.
Greenway 9687; Tweedie 66/78.

6. Asparagus flagellaris (*Kunth*) *Bak.* (*A. pauli-guilelmi* Solms.; *A. nudicaulis* Bak. of Check List)
Erect to climbing, glabrous, armed, woody perennial with tortuous, grooved often greenish stems and terete solitary branches; branchlets often well-defined, mostly solitary; cladodes fascicled, needle-like, terete, numerous, stiffly erect and mostly longer than internodes on vegetative branches; conspicuous white spurs at the base of fascicles of cladodes which lie in axils of spines; cladodes very few or absent on flowering shoots but numerous in fruiting and vegetative shoots; flowers white, in axillary pairs, sometimes single or fascicled; pedicel articulated very near the base; berry fleshy, orange, 1-seeded.

A plant of dry areas, sometimes scrambling over rocks. It is easily recognized by the conspicuous white spurs and by cladodes which lie close to the axis. HE, KIT, MUM, KIS, BAR, MAC.

Verdcourt 2368; Agnew, Musumba and Kiniaruh 7969.

7. Asparagus racemosus *Willd.* (see p. 698)
Glabrous, woody climber or scrambler with twining, usually grooved and yellowish stem; branches and branchlets spreading to ascending, solitary at nodes, or branchlets up to 3-nate and grooved; cladodes fascicled, numerous, angled, straight, up to 1 mm broad, green at first but turning greyish; spines pungent short, 3–6 mm long, brownish to greyish; peduncles paired; flowers white; pedicels solitary or 2-nate laterally, more numerous terminally, 2–3 mm long, articulated near or below the middle; berry globose, red, with wrinkled pericarp, 1-seeded.

A widespread plant of drier parts and forest margins. HE, HM, HA, NAR, BAR, RV, MAC.

Kerfoot 4057; Agnew, Azavedo, and Khatri 9515.

104. PONTEDERIACEAE†

Aquatic herbs with floating or aerial leaf blades; flowers bisexual in racemose inflorescences, surrounded by a leaf sheath or solitary; perianth of 6 lobes in 2 series; stamens 1, 3, or 6, fused to the perianth at base; ovary superior with 3 axile or parietal placentas; style entire or lobed; fruit a capsule or achene; seeds ribbed.

1. HETERANTHERA *Ruiz & Pav.*
Rooted aquatic herbs with emergent or submerged leaves; leaves entire, often ovate or cordate; flowering stems with an apical leaf; perianth regular, tubular below; stamens 3; ovary with 3 parietal placentas; fruit a capsule.

† By M. A. Hanid.

Heteranthera callifolia *Kunth*
A glabrous rooted aquatic with ovate-cordate emergent leaves and white, blue or purple flowers in short terminal spikes.

Rare, found in ponds in western Kenya. MUM. McMahon 37.

105. SMILACACEAE‡

Climbing or straggling, dioecious, rhizomatous shrubs, often with prickly stems and branches; leaves alternate or opposite, 3–5-nerved, ± coriaceous, with stipular or leaf-sheath tendrils; flowers regular, mostly unisexual, rarely bisexual, in axillary umbels, racemes or spikes; perianth segments 6, free or rarely united; stamens 6, free or united; anthers introrse; ovary superior, 3-celled, with 3 recurved stigmas and 1–2 ovules per cell; staminodes present in male flower; fruit a 1–3-seeded globose berry; endosperm hard.

1. SMILAX *L.*
Shrubs armed with recurved prickles which aid in climbing; leaves net-veined; base of petiole with two spiral tendrils, one on either side; flowers small, greenish, in small, axillary, simple or racemose umbels.

1 Leaves ovate-elliptic to broadly-elliptic; inflorescence a simple umbel
1. *S. kraussiana*
Leaves broadly- or narrowly-ovate; inflorescence a racemose umbel 2. *S. goetzeana*

1. Smilax kraussiana *Meisn.*
Glabrous climbing plant with shortly petiolate, ovate-elliptic to broadly-elliptic or ovate-orbicular leaves; peduncle with a pair of bracts, usually half-way up; berry 0·5–1 cm in diam., red, ripening purple.

A widespread climber in wet evergreen forests and woodlands, but not well-collected in our area. HA, MAC.

Kirrika 451; Bally 11139.

2. Smilax goetzeana *Engl.*
Glabrous, prickly, climbing shrub similar to *S. kraussiana* but with ovate to subcordate leaves and racemes of umbels in the leaf axils.

A rare climber of evergreen upland forest, which, in our area, is represented by a single collection from Nanyuki River, 6600 ft. NAN.

Moreau and Moreau 49.

‡ By M. A. Hanid.

106. ARACEAE†

Rhizomatous or cormous herbs with distichous or spiral, reticulately veined, often cordate leaves; flowers small, unisexual or bisexual, regular, sessile on a spike and enclosed in a spathe which is often attractive; perianth of 6 parts present or absent; stamens 2–8; ovary superior or immersed in the spike, usually with few, basal or apical ovules, but sometimes with axile placentation; fruit usually a berry.

1	Leaves divided into more than 3 lobes	2
	Leaves entire or hastate with 3 lobes	4
2	Leaves palmately lobed or divided	3
	Leaves ternate into pinnately lobed portions	2. *Amorphophallus*
3	All leaflets ± equal	1. *Arisaema*
	Terminal leaflets ± twice the size of basal leaflets	5. *Sauromatum venosum*
4	Plant floating with blunt leaves in a rosette	4. *Pistia stratiotes*
	Plant not floating with acute, ± smooth leaves	5
5	Plant climbing; leaves entire at base	3. *Culcasia scandens*
	Plant erect from a corm; leaves hastate at base	6. *Stylochiton*

1. ARISAEMA *Mart.*

Herbs with erect palmate leaves; spathe tubular throughout, with a ± nodding apex; spike unisexual or bisexual, with or without neuter flowers above; flowers without perianth; male flowers of 2–4 stamens above the female in bisexual spikes; anthers opening by pores or slits; female flowers densely crowded in a spike; ovary 1-celled, with 1–10 ovules.

1	Leaflets all arising from the same place	1. *A. schimperanum*
	Lateral leaflets borne on branching lateral petiolules	2. *A. mildbraedii*

1. Arisaema schimperanum *Schott* (see p. 702)

A cormous dioecious herb with 2–3 erect, 5–11-foliolate leaves and a central peduncle bearing a tubular green and white spathe; appendage of spike cylindrical, green, just exceeding the tube of the spathe.

Rather uncommon, found in montane forest edges in the west of our area. HE, HT, HM.

Tweedie 68/18; Glover, Gwynne, and Samuel 1182.

†By A. D. Q. Agnew.

2. Arisaema mildbraedii *Engl.* (see p. 702)

Similar to *A. schimperianum* except for the keyed characters and the entire leaflets; the spathe tends to be less white than in that species.

Locally common in wet montane forest edges. HE, HA, HN, KIT.

Agnew 8211; Gillett 16646.

2. AMORPHOPHALLUS *Blume*

Herbs producing a solitary ternate and pinnate leaf from a flattened corm; spathe solitary, long-pedunculate, not produced with the leaves, overlapping and tubular at base, spreading above, often blackish-purple within; spike bearing female flowers below, male flowers above, with no neuter flowers; perianth absent; ovaries with or without a style, with 1–4 ovules; stamens crowded, dehiscing by apical pores.

1	Appendix to the spike exceeding the spathe, very long and tapering; style almost as long as ovary	1. *A gallaensis*
	Appendix to the spike shorter than the spathe, club-shaped; stigma sessile on the ovary	2. *A. abyssinicus*

1. Amorphophallus gallaensis *(Engl.) N. E. Br.*

Leaf erect, large with decurrent lobes; spathe bell-shaped below, with a suborbicular acuminate spreading portion, purple, smooth within.

Uncommon, found in dry bushland. KAJ.

Agnew 9883.

2. Amorphophallus abyssinicus *(A. Rich.) N. E. Br.* (see p. 702)

Similar to *A. gallaensis* except for the keyed characters, this species is uncommon in the wooded grassland of western Kenya. HE, KIT.

Bally 8194.

3. CULCASIA *Beauv.*

Climbing or erect herbs on stilt roots, with distichous entire leaves on elongated stems and axillary pedunculate bisexual spathes; spathes leathery, not coloured, falling early; spike with female (below) and male flowers contiguous, without an appendix; perianth absent; anthers sessile, 2-celled, opening by a pore; ovaries crowded, 1–2-celled, with a sessile circular stigma; fruit a red berry.

Culcasia scandens *Beauv.* (see p. 702)

A trailing epiphytic glabrous herb, climbing by means of adventitious roots, with elliptic to lanceolate, acute leaves and small pale green or almost white spathes.

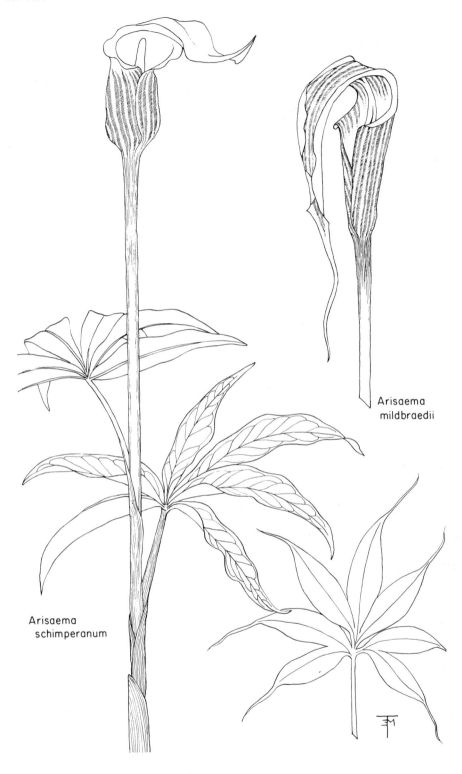

Arisaema
mildbraedii

Arisaema
schimperanum

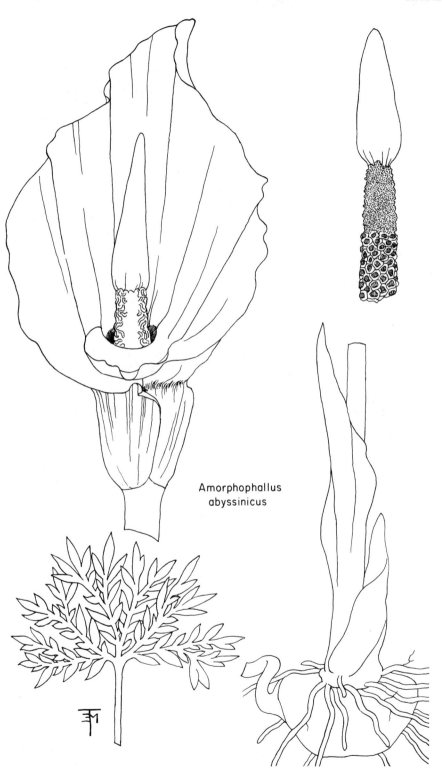

Amorphophallus
abyssinicus

Culcasia scandens

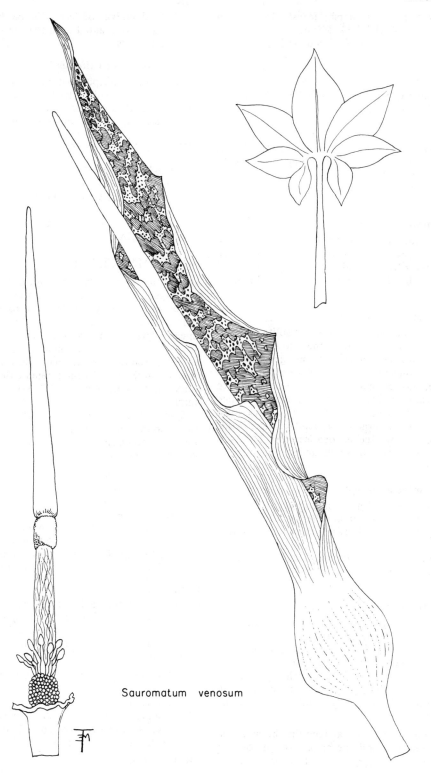

Sauromatum venosum

Locally common in marshy forest edges in high rainfall areas. HM, HN, KIT, MUM.

Agnew, Hanid and Kiniaruh 7914; Williams 593.

4. PISTIA *L.*

Floating aquatic with a rosette of parallel-veined, air-filled leaves; spathes axillary, shortly pedunculate, bisexual; spike short with female part adnate to back of spathe and the male part free with two neuter organs at base; perianth absent; female inflorescence of a single oblique ovary with numerous basal ovules; male inflorescence of 6-8 flowers, each of 2 anthers; fruit capsular, manyseeded.

Pistia stratiotes *L.*

The 'nile cabbage' needs no description. It is an occasional weed on all low-lying perennial fresh water. MUM, KIS, BAR, MAC.

Agnew, Hanid and Kiniaruh 8001; Leippert 5224.

5. SAUROMATUM *Schott.*

Herbs with a disc-shaped corm and solitary leaves appearing separately from the flowers; leaves palmatifid; spathe tubular with margins fused at base, very elongate above, purple-spotted within; spike free, shorter than the spathe, bisexual, with female flowers lowest, then elongated club-shaped neuter flowers, then, very distantly, a dense mass of male flowers; terminal appendage narrowing; female flowers of 1-celled ovaries with 2-4 basal ovules; male flowers of single anthers opening by apical pores.

Sauromatum venosum *(Ait.) Kunth.* (see p. 705)

A glabrous herb with erect solitary palmatifid (7-lobed) leaves and, at another season, a large spear-shaped spathe, brown and purple spotted within.

Uncommon, found in wooded grassland in western Kenya. HE, KIT.

Tweedie 67/199.

6. STYLOCHITON *Lepr.*

Rhizomatous herbs with a rosette of cordate or sagittate leaves appearing with the flowers; spathe connate into a tube below, later falling; spike bisexual; female florets in few rows below, separated from males; perianth cup-shaped; female flowers with superior or inferior ovary; male flowers with 3-4 stamens longitudinally dehiscent; fruit a berry.

1   Lateral margin of leaf (the line between the basal lobe and the apex) straight or concave   1. *S. angustifolius*

Lateral margin of leaf (the line between the basal lobe and the apex) convex, bulging outwards   2. *S. salaamicus*

1. Stylochiton angustifolius *Peter*

Leaves 2-many, purple-spotted at the basal sheath, narrowly or broadly triangular-hastate above; flowering spathes not seen but at least 3 cm long.

Uncommon, found in dry sandy bushland. MAC, KAJ.

Hanid and Kiniaruh 565.

2. Stylochiton salaamicus *N. E. Br.*

Similar to *S. angustifolius* but leaves broader, often densely black-dotted below; flowers or fruit not seen.

Rare, found in dry bushland. KAJ.

Glover in EAH 11740.

107. LEMNACEAE†

Aquatic herbs, usually floating on the surface, or submerged; whole plant reduced to a small 'leaf' or thallus with simple capped root or roots or lacking them entirely; reproduction usually vegetative by repeated lateral budding; flowers infrequent, monoecious, enclosed in a membranous sheath or naked; perianth absent; male flowers with 1-2 stamens, anthers 1-2 celled; female flowers sessile, ovary unilocular, ovules 1-7, style and stigma simple.

So-called duck-weeds, characteristic of fresh water ponds and still water surfaces throughout the world, some species being cosmopolitan except on high mountains.

1   Thallus toothed   1. *Lemna trisulca*
     Thallus entire   2
2   Roots present   1. *Lemna*
     Roots absent   3
3   Thallus thin, foliaceous about 4 mm long
         2. *Pseudowolffia hyalina*
     Thallus thick, more or less globular, 1·5 mm long   3. *Wolffia arrhiza*

1. LEMNA *L.*

Floating or submerged aquatics with small flat or inflated thalli; lateral pocket bearing minute inflorescence with 1 female flower and 2 male flowers enclosed in a sheath; reproduction generally by lateral budding.

1   Submerged, only fertile thalli floating
         1. *L. trisulca*
     Surface-floating   2
2   Thallus ± hemispherical, with large inflated cells beneath; root-cap obtuse 2. *L. gibba*
     Thallus thin; root-cap acute   3. *L. perpusilla*

† By F. N. Hepper.

1. Lemna trisulca *L.*

Thalli thin, oblong, about 1 cm long, 3 mm wide, distinctly stalked at one end, toothed towards the other end; daughter thallus budding off usually simultaneously on either side, several to many thalli remaining together as chains.

Submerged in shallow permanent water. RV, KAJ.

Rayner 559; Suttie EA H241/62/2; Verdcourt 3975.

2. Lemna gibba *L.*

Thalli inflated, convex on lower side; daughter thalli soon separating.

Floating on still permanent water. KAJ.

Brown s.n.; Greenway 8795.

3. Lemna perpusilla *Torrey*

Thallus more or less 3-nerved; root sheath winged at junction of root with thallus.

Floating on still water. KAJ, MAC, MUM.

McMahon 216; Verdcourt 3117.

Note: This species may be separable as *L. paucicostata* Hegelm., if this can be reliably distinguished from true *L. perpusilla.*

2. PSEUDOWOLFFIA *den Hartog & van der Plas*

Floating or partially submerged aquatics, lacking roots; thallus thin, flat or curved, daughter thallus budding from linear transverse slit.

Pseudowolffia hyalina *(Del.) den Hartog & van der Plas*

Thallus in two parts; nearly opaque green floating portion, broadly elliptic, about 2 mm long, 1·5 mm broad, and a hyaline oblong appendage 2-4 mm long, 1 mm broad at a right angle to the other and suspended in the water; budding pouch between the two parts arising from the thicker portion.

Found floating on still water. Probably commoner in Africa than would appear from its scattered records. KAJ.

Verdcourt 3116.

3. WOLFFIA *Schleid.*

Floating aquatic with minute rootless thallus.

Wolffia arrhiza *(L.) Wimm.*

Thallus minute 1-1·5 mm long, rather less in breadth and depth, upper surface flattened and dark green, paler elsewhere; flowers opening on to upper surface from a single median pit; style short, stigma concave; stamen solitary with filament 0·5 mm long.

Although each individual is minute, the species occurs in great abundance on certain areas of open water. KAJ.

Verdcourt 3107.

108. TYPHACEAE†

Rhizomatous herbs with unbranched stems and broadly linear leaves with long slit sheathing bases; inflorescence a continuous or interrupted dense spike, the upper part male, the lower part broader, often darker and female; flowers reduced to stamens or ovary and interspersed with linear or laciniate bracteoles; fruit a dry 1-seeded follicle surrounded by long fine hairs.

1. TYPHA *L.*

Stout glabrous herbs like giant grasses; male inflorescences apical, dense, with the flowers reduced to a pedicellate group of 2-4 stamens with the filaments fused below and paired oblong anthers; bracteoles filiform, spathulate or spathulate-laciniate; female inflorescences below the male and remote from them or contiguous, rarely with 1 or 2 additional female spikes remote from each other below the first, the flowers with perigynous hairs and bracteoles of similar length, both shorter than the stigmas; bracteoles, when present, filiform and broadening into an expanded ovate or spathulate lamina, carpodia (sterile modified flowers) about as long as the bracteoles.

1 Spikes remote, approximately equally long or the male longer; bracteoles present in the female spike; stigma linear, bracteoles of the male spike red-brown, forked; leaf-sheath with sloping shoulder, purple-spotted within and on the base of the blade   1. *T. domingensis*

  Spikes contiguous, the male usually much shorter than the female; bracteoles absent from the female spike; stigma lanceolate; bracteoles of the male spike whitish, filiform; leaf-sheath with auriculate or rounded shoulders, sometimes spotted within but not on the base of the blade

2. *T. latifolia*

1. Typha domingensis *Pers.*

Stout grasslike herb with sloping scarious-margined shoulders to the leaf-sheaths and linear leaf-blades narrowing at the base; male and female spikes separated by a 1-3 cm long internode, the male spike light brown with yellow anthers, the female spike wider and bright chestnut or reddish brown at maturity with lighter patches where the carpodia show in clusters.

Swamps, dams, lakes, and rivers; sea-level to 7000 ft and usually mixed with *T. latifolia* at the

† By D. Napper.

higher altitudes but rare above 5000 ft. HT, HM, RV, MAC, NBI, KAJ.

Verdcourt 912; University College Nairobi 5103B.

2. Typha latifolia *L.*

Grasslike herb similar to the above, but usually less tall when growing together, with abruptly rounded or auriculate scarious-margined shoulders to the leaf-sheaths; male and female spikes contiguous, the male spike greenish-brown with yellow anthers, the female becoming very much wider and yellow-green, turning dark sepia-brown or almost black at maturity.

In swamps, dams, and rivers with a permanent flow; rarely found below 4500 ft. HE, HT, HM, HA, KIT, KIS, RV, MAC, NBI, KAJ.

Napper 1680; University College Nairobi 5103A.

109. AMARYLLIDACEAE†

Herbs with swollen bulbs below ground and all leaves from the base; flowers bisexual, regular, in umbels at the apex of a leafless stem, subtended by 2 or more membranous bracts, sometimes reduced to solitary flowers subtended by the same bracts; perianth of 6 equal segments, with or without a tube; stamens 6; ovary inferior or superior of 3 carpels with axile placentation; seeds few or numerous, often angular or winged.

1   Flowers solitary or up to 3 together   2
    Flowers more than 3 in each umbel   4
2   Filaments of stamens webbed with a corona
                            7. *Pancratium trianthum*
    Filaments of stamens free; corona absent   3
3   Bracts free to base; flowers 1–3 in each
    umbel   6. *Cyrtanthus*
    Bracts fused to form a tube at base; flowers
    always solitary
                        3. *Zephyranthes grandiflora*
4   Leaf sheaths purple- to red-spotted; leaves
    elliptic, narrowing at base
                        1. *Haemanthus multiflorus*
    Leaf sheaths unspotted; leaves strap-shaped,
    not narrowed to the base   5
5   Pedicels longer than the perianth tube
                            2. *Boöphone disticha*
    Pedicels shorter than the perianth tube   6
6   Leaves annual, green to the tip, spiral or in
    two rows but if the latter then never
    fan-like   4. *Crinum*
    Leaves perennial, dying back at the tips, in
    two fan-like rows   5. *Ammocharis*

† By A. D. Q. Agnew.

1. HAEMANTHUS *L.*

Herbs with a short corm below the bulb and oblong to elliptic leaves with a distinct lamina and spotted sheathing base; flowers crowded in a ± globose umbel, pedicellate; perianth with a tube shorter than the lobes; stamens long; ovules 1–2 in each cell; fruit a berry.

Haemanthus multiflorus *Martyn* (*H. filiflorus* of Check List) (see p. 709)

Bulbous scapose herb with leaves and inflorescences appearing at different times; leaves elliptic with purple-spotted sheaths; inflorescence of *c.* 150 densely packed red to pink flowers.

A showy plant of rocky places in forest edges, riverine forest, or open bushland. Forms with wide perianth segments intergrade with those with narrow segments. HE, HT, HM, HA, KIT, MUM, NAR, RV, NAN, EMB, MAC, NBI.

Agnew 8216; Bally 110.

2. BOÖPHONE *Herb.*

Bulbous scapose herbs with distichous strap-shaped leaves and very numerous pedicellate flowers in a terminal umbel; perianth with the tube shorter than the lobes; stamens long; ovule solitary in each cell; fruit a capsule.

Boöphone disticha *Herb.* (see p. 710)

A herb with an annually-produced fan of leaves and a dense umbel of dull red flowers; pedicels lengthening and spreading in fruit, becoming stiff and straight, so that the entire fruiting inflorescence can break away and roll over the ground, distributing seeds.

A good example of a tumble-weed, this species is locally common in rocky grassland, 5000–8000 ft. HE, HC, HT, NAR, BAR, RV, NBI, KAJ.

Bally 1126.

3. ZEPHYRANTHES *Herb.*

Similar to 6. *Cyrtanthus* except for the keyed differences.

Zephyranthes grandiflora *Herb.*

A bulbous scapose herb with narrow strap-shaped leaves and large, solitary, pink or pale red flowers.

This species is commonly cultivated and apparently has escaped on Mt. Elgon. HE.

Padwa 14.

4. CRINUM *L.*

Scapose herbs with bulbs and usually spiral leaves; leaves linear to ovate; scape simple bearing a terminal umbel with 2 to many bracts; perianth bell-shaped, with a long tube which may be

Haemanthus multiflorus

Boöphone disticha

Crinum kirkii

pubescent within; stamens declinate, with semi-circular, medifixed anthers; seeds few in each cell; fruit a berry or irregularly dehiscent capsule.

1   Anthers yellow; perianth segments linear-oblong   1. *C.* sp. *A*
    Anthers purple or dark brown; perianth segments elliptic   2. *C. kirkii*

1. Crinum *sp.* **A.**

A herb with a spreading rosette of broad to narrow strap-shaped leaves and an umbel of 6–9 large white and pink flowers.

Uncommon, found in sand in dry country. MAG.

Greenway 9573.

2. Crinum kirkii *Bak.* (see p. 711)

Similar to *C.* sp. *A* but with larger nodding flowers.

This is the common 'pyjama lily' found all over Kenya in upland grassland. It is rather variable, having long or short pedicels and deep or shallow bulbs but the forms intergrade. HE, HT, HA, KIS, NAR, MAC.

Graham 850; Agnew and Musumba 5347.

5. AMMOCHARIS *Herb.*

Similar to *Crinum* but the leaves in two fan-like series and perennial, and the flowers not zygomorphic, not bell-shaped.

1   Stamens more than half the length of the perianth segments   1. *A. tinneana*
    Stamens less than half the length of the perianth segments   2. *A. heterostyla*

1. Ammocharis tinneana (*Kotschy & Peyr.*) *Milne-Redhead & Sch.* (see p. 713)

A bulbous herb with opposite spreading fans of perennial leaves and over 20 long-tubed, short-pedicelled flowers, pink changing to red later.

Locally common in dry bushland or wooded grassland. NAR, BAR, MAG, EMB, KAJ.

Glover, Gwynne, and Samuel 229.

2. Ammocharis heterostyla (*Bullock*) *Milne-Redhead & Sch.* (see p. 713)

Similar to *A. tinneana* but with fewer flowers turning pink, not red.

Locally common in western Kenya in rocky bushland. HE, HT.

Lugard 421; Jex Blake in Bally 1372.

6. CYRTANTHUS *Ait.*

Bulbous, scapose herbs with strap-shaped leaves in a basal rosette and few-flowered umbels; flowers sessile or pedicellate, 1–3 (in ours) together, with a short perianth tube; stamens free from their insertion at the throat of the tube; style with 3 stigmas; ovules many to a cell; fruit a capsule.

1   Perianth less than 3·5 cm long, funnel-shaped from the base, without a cylindrical tube, yellow to orange   1. *C.* sp. *A*
    Perianth over 4 cm long, with a distinct cylindrical tube below the funnel-shaped part, orange, pink or red   2
2   Perianth orange to salmon-coloured
                              2. *C. salmonoides*
    Perianth bright red   3. *C. sanguineus*

1. Cyrtanthus *sp.* **A.**

A small herb with an elongated bulb and 1–3 yellow flowers in each umbel.

Known only from the Rift Valley highlands about Gilgil and Nakuru. HA, RV.

Byng-Hall in EAH 10288.

2. Cyrtanthus salmonoides *Bally & Carter*

An erect herb with linear, strap-shaped leaves and a funnel-shaped pink to orange perianth; flowers mostly solitary, rarely 2 together.

Uncommon, in rocky grassland, but occasionally found near the Ngong Hills. HA, RV, KAJ.

Beecher 2/59.

3. Cyrtanthus sanguineus (*Lindl.*) *Walp.*

Similar to *C. salmonoides* but the flowers 1–3 together and bright red.

Locally common in stony grasslands, and sometimes abundant in the Nairobi Game Park. NBI, KAJ.

Bally 5135; Agnew 10229.

7. PANCRATIUM L.

Scapose bulbous herbs with a basal rosette of strap-shaped leaves and 1–many-flowered scapes; flowers with a long tube and spreading or funnel-shaped lobes; stamens united with a conspicuous coronal cup above their insertion at the mouth of the tube; ovules many in each cell; fruit a capsule.

Pancratium trianthum *Herb.* (see p. 717)

A small herb with (in ours) solitary white flowers with a very long perianth tube.

This plant is known as the spider lily. It occurs locally in dry bushland. MUM, BAR, MAC.

Tweedie 67/33; Gillett 16366.

110. IRIDACEAE†

Herbs with rhizomatous or cormous rootstocks and linear, often laterally flattened, parallel-veined leaves; flowers bisexual, regular or zygomorphic in

† By A. D. Q. Agnew.

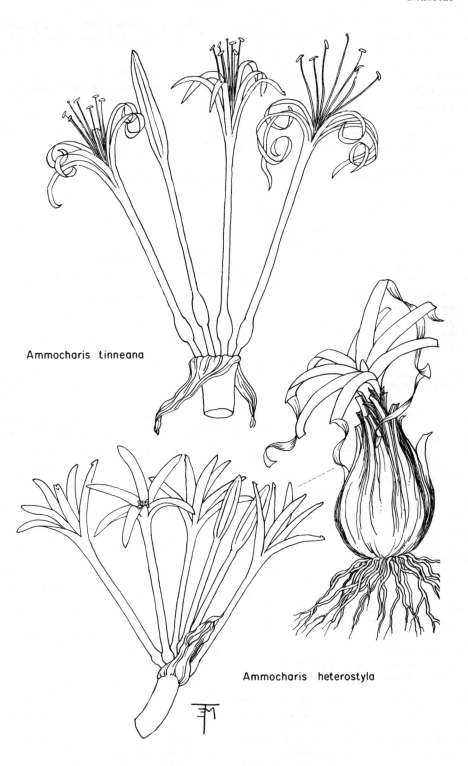

Ammocharis tinneana

Ammocharis heterostyla

panicles or spikes, subtended usually by a bract and bracteole; perianth of 3 + 3 similar petaloid organs; stamens 3, opposite or alternate with the stigmas; ovary inferior of 3 carpels with axile placentation; stigmas 3-6; seeds few or numerous, flattened or globose.

1 Flowers regular; style central, petaloid, 3-branched   **2**
  Flowers more or less zygomorphic or regular; style entire, not petaloid, bearing 3-6 stigma arms apically   **3**
2 Plant rhizomatous; leaves flattened laterally   10. *Dietes*
  Plant cormous; leaves channelled dorsiventrally, not flattened laterally   11. *Moraea*
3 Flowers in clusters at the nodes   2. *Aristea*
  Flowers always solitary at the nodes   **4**
4 Bracts of flower less than 2 cm long; flowers regular, held erect or pendulous   **5**
  Bracts of flower over 3 cm long; flowers zygomorphic, held laterally   **9**
5 Flowers solitary   **6**
  Flowers in spikes   **7**
6 Upper floral bract (bracteole) notched at apex, lower floral bract obtuse; styles 3   3. *Hesperantha petitiana*
  Both floral bracts obtuse or acute, neither notched; styles apparently 6   1. *Romulea*
7 Inflorescence branched; flowers pendulous   4. *Dierama pendulum*
  Inflorescence simple; flowers erect   **8**
8 Bracts acute; corolla tube twice as long as corolla lobes   5. *Lapeyrousia laxa*
  Bracts obtuse; corolla tube not longer than corolla lobes   3. *Hesperantha petitiana*
9 Bracts large, coloured and enclosing the flower   8. *Oenostachys dichroa*
  Bracts smaller than the flower   **10**
10 Flowers white   6. *Acidanthera*
  Flowers red or orange   **11**
11 Stamens and stigma arched together to lie under the upper perianth lobe   7. *Gladiolus*
  Stamens and stigma straight, not held under upper corolla lobe   9. *Pentamenes*

1. ROMULEA *Maratti*

Similar to *Hesperantha* but the flowers always solitary, and the stigmas divided into 6 branches.

1 Bracts and bracteoles both obtuse, often rounded   1. *R. keniensis*
  Bracts and also often bracteoles acute   **2**
2 Bracteole with narrow, unspotted scarious margin; style overtopped by anthers   2. *R. campanuloides*

Bracteole with broad, brown-flecked scarious margin; anthers overtopped by style   3. *R. fischeri*

1. Romulea keniensis *Hedb.*

A small herb with subulate leaves and solitary mauve or pale purple-pink flowers.

In stony wet soils, especially streamsides, in the alpine zone of the Aberdares and Mt. Kenya. HA, HK.

Hedberg 1784; Strid 3285.

2. Romulea campanuloides *Harms*

Similar to *R. keniensis* but for the key characters.

Rare, found in subalpine stony soils. HC, HA.

Agnew, Kibe, and Mathenge 10542; Napier 2108.

3. Romulea fischeri *Pax* (see p. 715)

Similar to *R. keniensis* but with bigger flowers and bracts as well as the keyed differences.

This is the commonest *Romulea* species, found in wet upland and alpine stony grassland. HE, HC, HT, HM, HA, HK.

Verdcourt 2469; Tweedie 69/43.

2. ARISTEA *Ait.*

Rhizomatous herbs with laterally flattened linear leaves and clusters of sessile or pedicellate flowers; bracts leaf-like; perianth without a tube, ± regular, of 6 equal segments; stamens 3, alternate with the stigmas; fruit many-seeded; seeds globose.

1 Flower clusters sessile or pedunculate, on a raceme or spike; flowers sessile   1. *A. angolensis*
  Flower clusters solitary, cymose or corymbose, not racemose; flowers often pedicellate   2. *A. alata*

1. Aristea angolensis *Bak.* (see p. 715)

An erect herb with rather few, very long leaves at base, bearing a leafy, erect stem with sessile clusters of blue flowers; stem flattened but not winged.

Locally common on wet grassland in western Kenya. HE, HT, HA, KIT.

Agnew, Kibe, and Mathenge 10590; Godden 20U.

2. Aristea alata *Bak.* (see p. 715)

An erect, tufted herb, with numerous fans of short, stiff leaves at base and an erect, branching inflorescence of clusters of blue flowers; stem flattened, with narrow wings.

Locally common in highland wet grassland. HE, HC, HT, HM, HA, KIT, KIS.

Strid 3199; Kerfoot 4368.

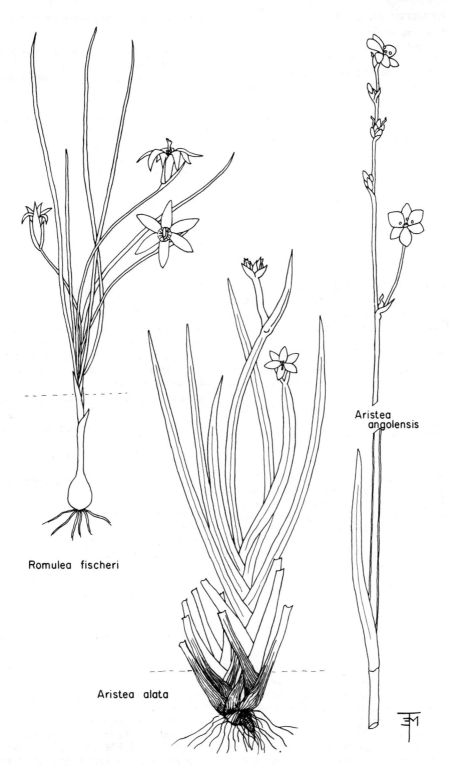

Romulea fischeri

Aristea alata

Aristea
angolensis

3. HESPERANTHA *Ker-Gawl.*

Herbs with corms covered with scales, and narrow bristle-like leaves; flowers solitary or in spikes; bracts and bracteoles well developed; perianth regular with a tube and of 6 equal segments; stamens 3, alternate with the 3 stigmas; seeds globose.

Hesperantha petitiana (*A. Rich.*) *Bak.*

A small herb with subulate leaves and single or spiked pink to pale mauve flowers; perianth with a yellow spot in the throat.

Locally common in subalpine and alpine stony grassland. HE, HA, HK.

Gillett 18473; Agnew, Hedberg, and Mmari 9611.

4. DIERAMA *K. Koch*

Erect cormous or shortly rhizomatous herbs with laterally flattened linear leaves and branched panicles of racemes; bracts and bracteoles scarious; perianth regular, with a short tube and 6 equal segments; stamens alternate with the stigmas; stigmas 3, entire; seeds small, angled.

Dierama pendulum (*L. f.*) *Bak.*

A robust, densely tufted perennial with large panicles of delicate, nodding, purple or mauve flowers.

Common in high altitude grassland. HE, HC, HM, HA, HK.

Agnew 7202; Gillett 18481.

5. LAPEYROUSIA *Pourr.*

Herbs with corms bearing fibrous coverings; leaves laterally flattened, linear; flowers in unbranched spikes or panicles; perianth with a long tube, and almost equal segments, ± zygomorphic; stamens alternate with the bifid stigmas; seeds small, angular.

Lapeyrousia laxa *N. E. Br.* (see p. 718)

A small erect herb with a tuft of leaves at base and long pink flowers in a terminal spike on the almost leafless scape.

Uncommon, found in rocky grassland. KIT.
Brodhurst-Hill 2.

6. ACIDANTHERA *Hochst.*

Erect herbs with a fibrous covering to the globose corms, and laterally flattened leaves; inflorescence a simple spike; bracts and bracteoles lanceolate, acute; perianth zygomorphic, with a long curved tube and almost equal lobes; stamens inserted in the throat of the perianth tube, convergent above to lie together with the stigma, anthers sagittate at base; ovary with many ovules and 3-lobed stigma; seeds flattened.

1   Cylindrical part of perianth tube more than twice as long as bracts   1. *A. candida*
    Cylindrical part of perianth tube less than twice as long as bracts   2. *A. ukambanensis*

1. Acidanthera candida *Rendle* (see p. 717)

An erect herb with long, white, beautifully scented flowers.

Common in grasslands on soils with impeded drainage at medium altitudes. HA, NAR, RV, NAN, MAC, NBI, KAJ.

Agnew 9196; Faden 67239.

2. Acidanthera ukambanensis *Bak.*

Similar to *A. candida* but with more robust, thicker flowers.

Uncommon, found in Machakos district in stony grassland. MAC.

Churcher in EAH 13784.

7. GLADIOLUS *L.*

Similar to *Acidanthera* except for the key characters and the very zygomorphic perianth lobes, with the uppermost forming a hood over the stamens and stigma and usually smaller than the two adjacent perianth lobes.

1   Perianth uniformly bright red in colour
             1. *G. watsonioides*
    Perianth yellow or orange, usually streaked with darker colour   2
2   Plant with leafy flowering stem
             2. *G. natalensis*
    Plant with separate leafy and flowering stems
             3. *G.* sp. A

1. Gladiolus watsonioides *Bak.*

A conspicuous erect herb with leafy stems bearing a single spike of bright red flowers, with a long, curved perianth tube.

One of the most arresting wild flowers in Kenya, growing in wet stony soils of the alpine and subalpine zones. HA, HK.

Strid 2207; Verdcourt 2037.

2. Gladiolus natalensis (*Eckl.*) *Lodd.* (*G. psittacinus* Hook.) (see p. 718)

An erect herb, glabrous or the basal sheathing leaves pubescent, with large orange or yellow, often streaked and flecked flowers with a short perianth tube.

Common in upland grassland to 10 000 ft, rarely higher. HE, HC, HT, HM, KIT, MUM, KIS, NAR, RV, NAN, EMB, MAC, NBI, KAJ.

Agnew, Kibe, and Mathenge 10612; Kirrika 190.

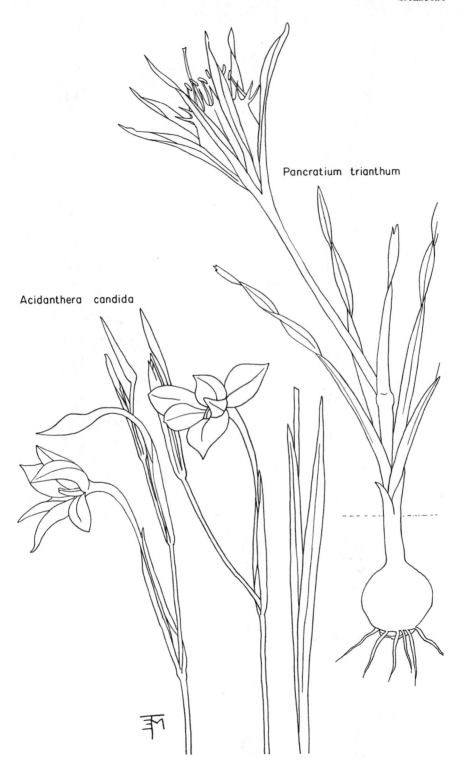

Pancratium trianthum

Acidanthera candida

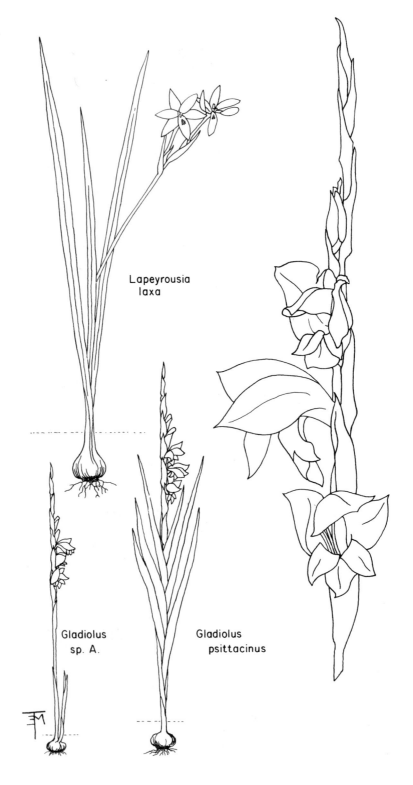

Lapeyrousia
laxa

Gladiolus
sp. A.

Gladiolus
psittacinus

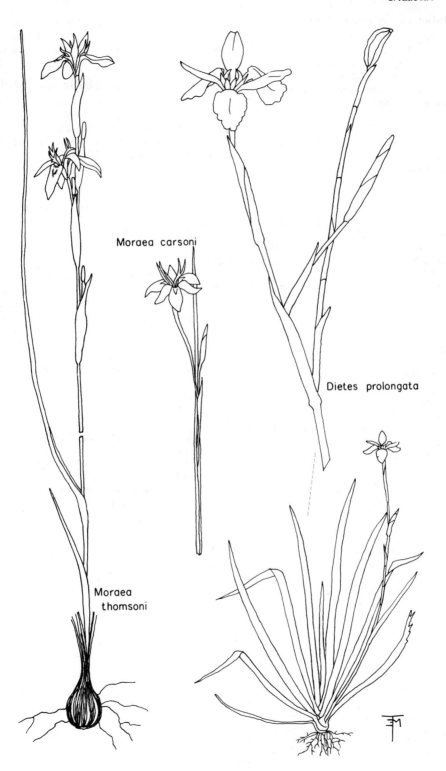

Moraea carsoni

Dietes prolongata

Moraea
thomsoni

3. Gladiolus *sp.* **A.** (see p. 718)

An erect herb, often ± leafless on the vegetative shoots, and with pubescent sheathing leaves; flowers yellow, streaked orange.

Locally common in rocky wooded grassland, principally in western Kenya. HE, HK, KIT, MUM.
Battiscombe 658.

8. OENOSTACHYS *Bullock*

Erect herbs similar to *Gladiolus* but with entire scaly coverings to the corm and large petaloid bracts almost concealing the flowers.

Oenostachys dichroa *Bullock*

An erect herb with rather broad-linear stem and basal leaves and a very conspicuous spike of rich red-purple flowers and bracts.

Recorded from stony highland grassland, and known in our area only from one collection on Mt. Elgon. HE.
Record from Bullock in *Kew Bull.* (1930) p. 465.

9. PENTAMENES *Salisb.*

Similar to *Gladiolus* but with straight stamens.

Pentamenes *sp.* **A.**

An erect herb from a fibrous corm, with 2–4 linear leaves and a short spike of rather small, pink or red, gladiolus-like flowers.

Uncommon, found in montane grassland. HC, HA, KIT.
Gardner 3232.

10. DIETES *Salisb.*

Similar to *Moraea* except for the rhizome and laterally flattened leaves.

Dietes prolongata (*Bak.*) *N. E. Br.* (see p. 719)

A creeping, tufted, rhizomatous herb with a fan of stiff linear leaves and a very diffuse panicle of white and yellow flowers.

Locally common in thickets and riparian forest in dry country. HC, KIT, NAR, MAC, NBI, KAJ.
Hanid 304; Faden 67181.

11. MORAEA *L.*

Erect herbs from a corm bearing reticulated coverings; leaves not flattened laterally; flowers in panicles or spikes; perianth of 6 equal segments; stamens 3, opposite the 3 enlarged petaloid styles, each of which bears a small stigmatic lip on its lower surface just overtopping the anther.

1   Bracts of the flowers all similar; flowers sessile on a spike   1. *M. thomsonii*

Bracts differing in size, the outer, often subtending a pedicel, smaller; flowers mostly pedicellate, in a panicle
                              2. *M. carsonii*

1. Moraea thomsonii *Bak.* (see p. 719)

An erect herb with narrow leaves and spikes of white-spotted blue flowers.

This pretty iris-like plant is found locally, in stony grassland at medium altitudes. HC, HT, HA, HK, KIT, MUM, NAN, NBI.
Verdcourt 2148; Strid 3126.

2. Moraea carsonii *Bak.* (see p. 719)

Similar to *M. thomsoni* except for the keyed characters, this species is commoner further west. HE, KIT, MUM.
Agnew 10848A; Polhill 411.

111. DIOSCOREACEAE†

Climbers from a swollen rootstock with alternate or opposite, simple or palmate, usually cordate, net-veined leaves; flowers small, in spikes or racemes, unisexual and regular; perianth of 6 free, equal lobes; male flowers with 3–6 stamens; female flowers often with staminodes and with inferior, 3-styled ovary; ovary with 2 axile ovules in each cell; fruit a 3-valved capsule (in ours) or a berry.

1. DIOSCOREA *L.*

Characters as for the family, with the stem not swollen immediately above the ground and the fruit a 3-winged dehiscent capsule bearing winged seeds.

The yams form important crop plants in some parts of the world.

1   Leaves entire cordate   2
    Leaves palmately divided into 3–5 leaflets   3
2   Leaves white felty-hairy below
                              1. *D. schimperana*
    Leaves glabrous below   2. *D. praehensilis*
3   Leaflets 3; male inflorescence a branched panicle of spikes; female inflorescence usually over 13 cm long   3. *D. dumetorum*
    Leaflets 3–5; male inflorescence of ± umbellate unbranched spikes or spikes solitary; female inflorescence less than 13 cm long
                              4. *D. quartiniana*

1. Dioscorea schimperana *Kunth* (see p. 721)

A robust climber with usually opposite, ± orbicular, cordate and acuminate leaves; male spikes ± umbellate at nodes; female spikes solitary; fruit heart-shaped.

† By A. D. Q. Agnew.

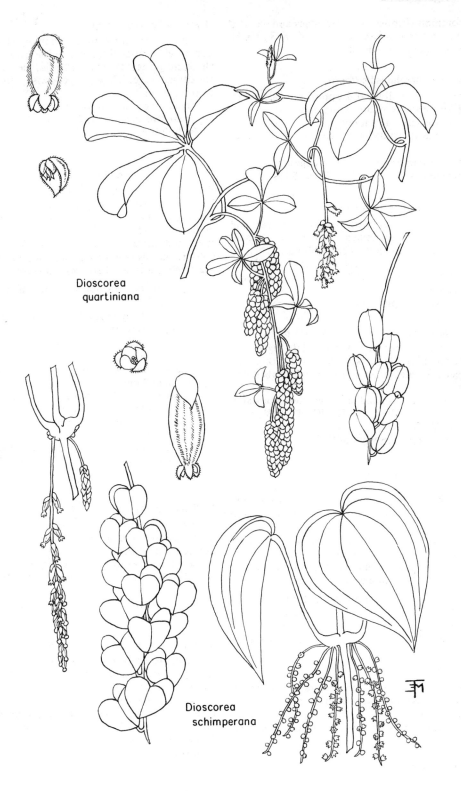

Dioscorea
quartiniana

Dioscorea
schimperana

A common climber in forest edges and wooded grassland in western Kenya. HE, HM, KIT, MUM.
Tweedie 68/45; Irwin 185.

2. Dioscorea praehensilis *Benth*

A climber with bulbils and opposite or alternate, oblong to ovate, cordate acuminate leaves; male spikes umbellate at nodes; female flowers in solitary spikes; fruits with almost semicircular valves.

Locally common in wet forest edges. MUM.
Agnew and Musumba 8552; Paulo 533.

3. Dioscorea dumetorum *Pax*

A pubescent climber with trifoliate leaves and ovate leaflets; male spikes in panicles; female spikes solitary; fruits pubescent, oblong.

Recorded from the coast and from one specimen from Nairobi in 1930. This record needs confirmation. NBI.
Jex-Blake in Napier 330.

4. Dioscorea quartiniana *A. Rich.* (see p. 721)

A pubescent climber with 3–5-foliolate leaves and obovate to elliptic leaflets; male spikes catkin-like, in umbels; female spikes solitary; fruit pubescent, oblong.

Common in bushland and wooded grassland, mainly in western Kenya. HE, HC, HT, HM, KIT, MAG, MAC, NBI.
Lugard 674; Greenway 8540.

112. AGAVACEAE†

Rhizomatous herbs, shrubs or trees with woody stems and spiral or distichous linear to ovate-elliptic leaves; flowers in racemes, bisexual or rarely unisexual, regular; perianth with a cylindrical tube and 6 spreading lobes; stamens 6; ovary superior or inferior, with a few axile ovules in each of the three cells; fruit a capsule or berry.

1 An erect trailing shrub with distant, elliptic
   leaves   1. *Dracaena laxissima*
   Herbs with crowded flat or ± cylindrical
   linear leaves   2. *Sansevieria*

1. DRACAENA *L.*

Shrubs or trees with the characters of the family and flowers bisexual, with a fused perianth tube and fruit a berry.

The other woody species are dealt with in KTS p. 8.

† By A. D. Q. Agnew.

Dracaena laxissima *Engl.*

An erect or trailing shrub, with many stems from a perennial rootstock; stems with little secondary thickening; leaves ovate-elliptic, sessile on the sheathing base; flowers yellowish, in an open terminal panicle.

Locally common in dry montane forest, especially near streams. HA, EMB, MAC, KAJ.
Bally 7464; Agnew 7929.

2. SANSEVIERIA *Thunb.*

Woody or fibrous, succulent, usually scapose herbs with distichous or spiral leaves; flowers bisexual, usually fascicled on a terminal raceme; pedicels usually articulated; perianth with a fused tube and spreading, often coiled lobes, dull in colour, but sweet-scented especially at dusk; fruit a scarcely succulent berry with 3 seeds.

1 Leaves flat throughout, much wider than
   thick   2
   Leaves ± cylindrical, at least in the upper
   part, as wide as thick   4
2 Leaves with a sharp red edge; flowers over
   2·5 cm long   3
   Leaves with a blunt green edge; flowers less
   than 2 cm long   1. *S. parva*
3 Flowers over 4·5 cm long   2. *S. conspicua*
   Flowers less than 3·5 cm long 3. *S. raffillii*
4 Leaves cylindrical, smooth; raceme unbranched   5. *S. intermedia*
   Leaves angular, ± D-shaped in cross-section;
   raceme branched   4. *S. ehrenbergii*

1. Sansevieria parva *N. E. Br.*

A rhizomatous succulent with linear-elliptic leaves in a rosette, and a erect raceme of whitish to dull-reddish flowers.

Locally common in the herb layer of dry woodland or bushed grassland. HM, MUM, RV, NBI.
Verdcourt and Brown 2919; Agnew 7978.

2. Sansevieria conspicua *N. E. Br.* (see p. 723)

A rhizomatous herb with 3–6 erect, strap-shaped, variegated leaves and a central spike of fasciculated dull whitish flowers.

This species has only been collected in flower from Chiperaria, BAR. All the sansevierias need more collection since they are so seldom seen in flower. *S. conspicua* may prove to be conspecific with the next species, *S. raffillii*.
Napier 2030.

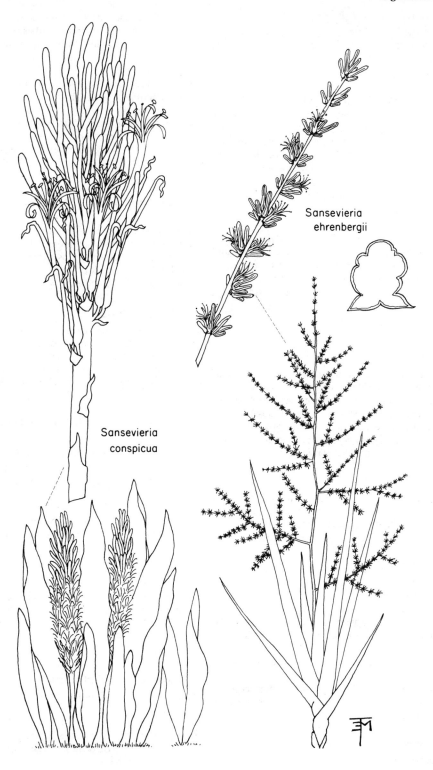

Sansevieria
conspicua

Sansevieria
ehrenbergii

3. Sansevieria raffillii *N. E. Br.*

Similar to the last species but with smaller flowers.

Locally common in dry bushland but seldom flowering. MUM, MAG.

Bally 5.

4. Sansevieria ehrenbergii *Bak.* (see p. 723)

An erect rhizomatous herb with vegetative shoots bearing 3–6 pairs of opposite crowded, spear-like channelled leaves; flowering rarely, the flowers up to 15 mm long on a much-branched panicle.

Common in many areas of dry bushland. NAR, BAR, RV, MAG, KAJ.

Tweedie 3522; van Someren 8505.

5. Sansevieria intermedia *N. E. Br.*

A stoloniferous perennial with stiff, usually straight, cylindrical, scarcely variegated leaves and a terminal unbranched raceme of white and dirty reddish flowers; flowers to 3·5 cm long.

Locally common in dry rocky bushland. NAR, RV, MAC.

Agnew 8198; Polhill 12312.

113. HYPOXIDACEAE†

Herbs from a perennial corm with a rosette of hairy leaves and axillary flowering scapes; hairs frequently stellate; inflorescence cymose or of whorled cymes on a raceme; perianth segments 6, the outer enclosing the inner in bud but otherwise similar; stamens 6; ovary inferior, with 3 carpels and axile placentation; ovules few; seeds globose.

1. HYPOXIS *L.*

Plants with characters of the family and with stellate hairs, open racemose or cymose inflorescences and flowers without a perianth tube.

In the following account names follow those of Baker (1898) in FTA Vol. 4.

1 Perianth segments obtuse; leaves more than 5 mm wide   2
  Perianth segments acute; leaves less than 5 mm wide   4
2 Inflorescence appearing slightly before the leaves, of a raceme of whorled cymes
                                                    1. *H. multiflora*
  Inflorescence appearing after the leaves, of paired flowers or cymes   3
3 Outermost leaves often glabrous between the midrib and margin below; upper leaves ± as hairy above as below, less than 1 cm wide; stigma up to 2·5 mm long, usually less than half as long as anthers   2. *H. villosa*

† By A. D. Q. Agnew.

Outermost leaves pubescent below; upper leaves much more pubescent below than above, usually over 1 cm wide; stigma over 3 mm long, more than half as long as anthers   3. *H. obtusa*
4 Flowers solitary with glabrous ovary and pedicel; fruits burying themselves; seeds smooth   4. *H. kilimanjarica*
  Flowers in pairs, rarely solitary, with silky-hairy ovary and pubescent pedicel; fruits not burying themselves; seeds rough with projections   5. *H. angustifolia*

1. Hypoxis multiflora *Nel* (see p. 725)

A perennial herb with a rosette of broad linear-lanceolate ± glabrous leaves from an ovoid corm, and dense or loose racemes of big yellow flowers.

Locally common in western Kenya in burnt grassland. HE, HC, KIT.

Symes 286; Tweedie 66/43.

2. Hypoxis villosa *L. f.*

A perennial herb with narrow strap-shaped leaves from an ovoid corm and 2–4 long-pedicellate yellow flowers on a slender scape.

Common in burnt grassland on shallow or rocky soil and occasionally in black cotton soil especially near Nairobi. HE, HC, HT, KIT, NAR, RV, NBI, KAJ.

Agnew and Musumba 5321; Gosnell 683.

3. Hypoxis obtusa *Burch.* (see p. 725)

Similar to *H. villosa* except for the key characters and with more and bigger flowers and more recurved leaves.

Common in burnt grassland and shallow soils. HE, HC, HA, KIT, NAR, NAN, MAC, NBI, KAJ.

Agnew and Kiniaruh 8821; Napier 169.

4. Hypoxis kilimanjarica *Bak.*

A small perennial with a rosette of glabrescent linear leaves from a 15 mm diameter corm, and solitary yellow flowers.

Recorded from one specimen on shallow soil by a stream near Thomson's Falls. HA.

Bogdan 536.

5. Hypoxis angustifolia *Lam.* (see p. 725)

Similar to *H. kilimanjarica* but more hairy and usually with more flowers.

This plant is rather variable in habit and size, having perianth segments from 4–10 mm long. Some of the 1-flowered, large forms may prove ultimately to be separable when more material is

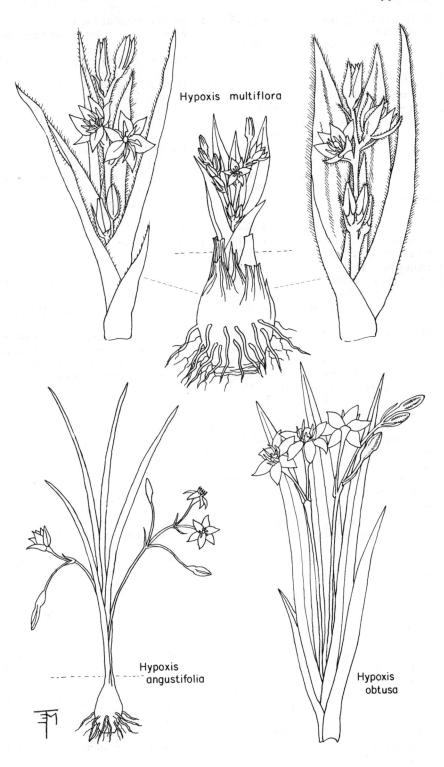

Hypoxis multiflora

Hypoxis
angustifolia

Hypoxis
obtusa

gathered. HE, HC, HM, HT, HA, KIT, MUM, KIS, NAR, NAN, EMB, MAC.

Glover, Gwynne, and Samuel 1846; Hanid 651.

114. ORCHIDACEAE†

Perennial, terrestrial, epiphytic or saprophytic herbs with rhizomes or tuberous roots, stem leafy or scapose, frequently swollen at the base into a pseudobulb and bearing aerial assimilating roots. Leaves entire, alternate and often distichous, sometimes reduced to scales, often fleshy, sheathing at the base; inflorescence spicate, racemose, paniculate, or flowers solitary. Flowers bracteate, hermaphrodite, zygomorphic. Perianth epigynous, composed of 6 tepals in 2 whorls, free or variously adnate, the middle segment of each whorl often different in size and colour from the lateral ones, especially the middle petal which is called the lip (*labellum*); frequently the lip or the dorsal sepal is prolonged in a sac-like outgrowth or spur. The ovary may be twisted through 180° (resupinate), placing the labellum in an abaxial position. Stamens 1 or 2, united with the style to form a special structure, the column; pollen granular or agglutinated into mealy, waxy, or horny masses (*pollinia*). Ovary inferior, 1-locular with 3 parietal placentas, or very rarely 3-locular with axile placentas; stigmas 3 fertile, or more frequently 2 fertile, the other sterile and transformed into a small outgrowth (*rostellum*) which lies between the anther and the stigmas; a portion of the rostellum is sometimes modified into a viscid disk or disks (*viscidia*) to which the pollinia are attached, often by a stalk (*stipes*). Ovules minute, very numerous. Fruit a capsule opening by 3 or 6 longitudinal slits. Seeds very numerous, minute, without endosperm.

1   Terrestrial herbs or, if epiphytic, plants with tuberous roots but no pseudobulbs   2
    Epiphytic herbs or lianes, rarely terrestrial and if so usually scrambling through the basal growths of bushes and scrub   24
2   Plants with tuberous or slender roots but without a perennial pseudobulbous base to the leafy stem   3
    Plants with a row or group of perennial pseudobulbs standing on a basal rhizome, at or below the surface of the ground   20
3   No leaves present at time of flowering, or saprophytic plants   4
    Leafy plants   5
4   Leafless saprophyte; lip shortly spurred
                                                    11. *Epipogium*
    Single leaf appearing after the inflorescence; lip without a spur   14. *Nervilia*

† by Joyce Stewart.

5   Flowers without a spur   6
    Flowers with a spur on the lip or dorsal sepal
                                                         7
6   Flowers pink or purple, not or only slightly hairy   2. *Brachycorythis*
    Flowers greenish or yellowish brown, very hairy   12. *Epipactis*
7   Spur present on the dorsal sepal   8. *Disa*
    Spur or spurs or sacs present on the lip or formed by the lateral sepals   8
8   Lip with one or two distinct but sometimes short spurs   9
    Lip not spurred, but sometimes boat-shaped at the base   18
9   Spurs 2, flowers not resupinate; (lip uppermost)   9. *Satyrium*
    Spur 1   10
10 Flowers green, white or yellow   11
    Flowers pink or mauve, or if white then flushed with mauve or pink   15
11 Lateral sepals and front lobe of petals joined to lip and to stigmatic arms in their lower parts; tooth present in the mouth of the spur   5. *Bonatea*
    All these parts not united at the same time; no tooth in the mouth of the spur   12
12 Stigmas 2-lobed, the lobes projecting in different directions, upwards and downwards
                                                    7. *Roeperocharis*
    Stigmas sessile, or each on a simple projection, not branched   13
13 Flowers bright yellow   6. *Platycoryne*
    Flowers white or green   14
14 Flowers secund on the scape, stigma sessile
                                                    1. *Holothrix*
    Flowers arranged on all sides of the inflorescence, stigmas located on distinct processes   4. *Habenaria*
15 Leaves 1 or 2, radical   16
    Leaves borne on the stem   17
16 Petals free, longer than the sepals and usually divided into several lobes in the upper part
                                                    1. *Holothrix*
    Petals adnate to the column at the base, as long as or shorter than the sepals and usually held inside the hooded dorsal sepal
                                                    3. *Cynorkis*
17 Stigma sessile or hollowed out of the surface of the column; stem and flower surfaces glabrous, or with velvety indumentum but not glandular   2. *Brachycorythis*
    Stigmatic surfaces projecting, partly united to lateral lobes of the rostellum; stem and outer surfaces of the flowers bearing pedicellate glands   3. *Cynorkis*
18 Flowers not resupinate (lip uppermost)
                                                    9. *Satyrium*

Flowers resupinate (dorsal sepal uppermost) **19**

19 Lateral sepals spurred or saccate
10. *Disperis*
Lateral sepals not spurred or saccate
2. *Brachycorythis*

20 Column united to the lip for most of its length 15. *Calanthe*
Column free from the lip **21**

21 Flowers with a distinct spur between base of column and base of lip **22**
Flowers not spurred **23**

22 Lip 3-lobed, the side lobes usually upright on either side of the column 23. *Eulophia*
Lip 4-lobed 24. *Eulophidium*

23 Plants of grassland, flattened pseudobulbs underground 25. *Pteroglossaspis*
Plants of shady forests; conical pseudobulbs above the ground 17. *Liparis*

24 Leaves laterally compressed, overlapping at the base and forming a small fan **25**
Plants with flat, keeled or cylindrical leaves not laterally compressed, or leafless **26**

25 Racemes of white flowers arising from the old leaf axils 29. *Bolusiella*
Racemes of pale brown flowers produced at the apex of the growth 16. *Oberonia*

26 Plants with pseudobulbs, growth sympodial **27**
Plants without pseudobulbs, growth monopodial **31**

27 Inflorescence terminal, arising from the apex of the recently formed pseudobulb **29**
Inflorescence lateral, arising from the base of a recently formed pseudobulb **28**

28 Pseudobulbs bearing 1–3 leaves at the apex 18. *Bulbophyllum*
Pseudobulbs bearing 6–11 leaves at the apex 19. *Chaseella*

29 Flowers resupinate (dorsal sepal uppermost) **30**
Flowers not resupinate (lip uppermost)
21. *Polystachya*

30 Flowers solitary 22. *Stolzia*
Flowers in racemes, small, greenish or purplish 17. *Liparis*
Flowers in racemes or panicles, large, yellowish with slight to dense brown markings
20. *Ansellia*

31 Plants leafless 27. *Microcoelia*
Plants lianes (climbers) with large ovate leaves
13. *Vanilla*
Plants epiphytic but not lianes, leaves ligulate, strap shaped **32**

32 Rostellum deeply indented, not elongated
26. *Angraecum*
Rostellum distinctly elongated **33**

33 Labellum distinctly 3-lobed **34**
Labellum not, or only indistinctly lobed **35**

34 Plants stemless or almost so
36. *Angraecopsis*
Plants with distinctly elongated stems
37. *Tridactyle*

35 Flowers white **36**
Flowers yellowish or greenish, never pure white **39**

36 Pollinia on a single stipes and viscidium; sometimes the stipes lobed or divided in the upper part and bearing one pollinium on each lobe **37**
Pollinia with separate stipites, and either a common viscidium or 2 separate viscidia **38**

37 Plants pendent; leaves grass-like, longer than the inflorescence 33. *Ypsilopus*
Plants usually upright; leaves ligulate or obovate, not grass-like, inflorescence often longer than the leaves 31. *Aerangis*

38 All tepals similar in shape and size
34. *Cyrtorchis*
Lip broader at the base than sepals and petals
32. *Rangaeris*

39 Minute plant, almost stemless; leaves less than 3 mm wide 35. *Triceratorhynchus*
Larger plants with distinct stems; leaves more than 5 mm wide **40**

40 Viscidia 2, each with its own pollinium and stipes **41**
Viscidium 1, common to 2 stipites and pollinia **42**
Viscidium 1, bearing a single long stipes with 2 pollinia 37. *Tridactyle*

41 Lip broader than long 28. *Diaphananthe*
Lip lanceolate 32. *Rangaeris brachyceras*

42 Flowers in whorls along the inflorescence **43**
Flowers alternating along the inflorescence
28. *Diaphananthe*

43 Lip fimbriate
28. *Diaphananthe fragrantissima*
Lip entire 30. *Chamaeangis*

1. HOLOTHRIX *Lindley*

Terrestrial herbs with small ovoid or ellipsoid underground tubers and one or two sessile ovate or orbicular radical leaves; inflorescence erect, unbranched, flowers often secund; sepals subequal, free from each other, often hairy, petals longer than sepals, entire, or divided in the upper part into 3 or more finger-like lobes, lip similar to petals but broader with more lobes, spurred at the base, adnate to the column which is very short.

1 Flowering stem without sheaths **2**
Flowering stem bearing a number of acute sheaths **4**

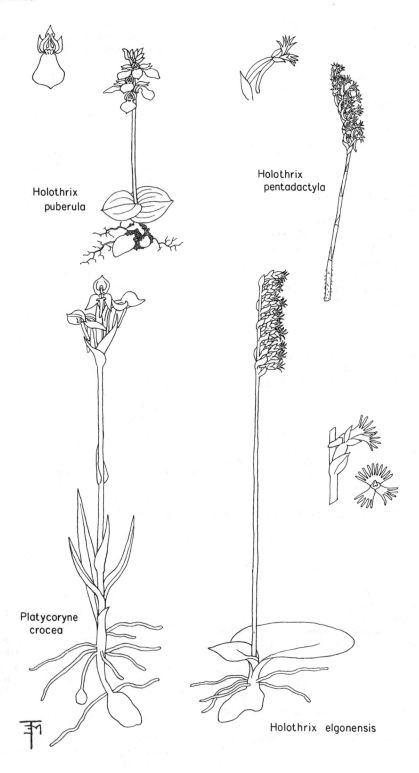

Holothrix
puberula

Holothrix
pentadactyla

Platycoryne
crocea

Holothrix elgonensis

2   Petals entire, narrowed towards the apex   3
    Petals 4–6-lobed in the upper part, widened
        from the base upwards   1. *H. elgonensis*
3   Lip entire or very shortly 2-lobed at the apex,
        bracts almost glabrous   2. *H. puberula*
    Lip 3-lobed in the upper half, bracts hairy
                                3. *H. arachnoidea*
4   Lip 3-lobed, petals 3-lobed at apex
                                4. *H. aphylla*
    Lip 5–7 lobed, petals 5-lobed
                                5. *H. pentadactyla*

1. Holothrix elgonensis *Summerhayes* (see p. 728)
Leaves 2, unequal, elliptic to orbicular-reniform, inflorescence 25–40 cm high, hairy; flowers white or cream sometimes flushed pink, sepals thin, hairy, petals glabrous, lip 9–13 lobed in upper third, glabrous.
    Known only from the upland grassland of Mt. Elgon; 10 000–11 000 ft. HE.
    Mwangangi 349.

2. Holothrix puberula *Rendle* (see p. 728)
Leaves 2, reniform-orbicular, inflorescence to 20 cm high, hairy; flowers lilac or mauve, sepals almost glabrous, lip much longer than other perianth parts.
    Short upland grassland, often among rocks; 7000–9500 ft. HC, HT, HM, HA, MAC.
    Irwin in EAH 11621.

3. Holothrix arachnoidea *(A. Rich.) Reichb. f.*
Leaves 2, lanceolate to orbicular, hairy, inflorescence to 27 cm high, hairy; flowers white or greenish, sepals ovate, glabrous, petals ligulate, lip ovate, 3-lobed in the upper third.
    Upland grassland, *c.* 6500 ft. NAN.
    Copley 120.

4. Holothrix aphylla *(Forsk.) Reichb. f.*
Leaves 2, orbicular or reniform, usually shrivelled at flowering time, inflorescence 6–27 cm high, glabrous; flowers white, tinged purple or bluish, petals and lip ± papillose.
    Upland grassland, 7000–7800 ft. HE, HT, HA.
    Beecher in EAH 29/58.

5. Holothrix pentadactyla *(Summerhayes) Summerhayes* (see p. 728)
Leaf 1, reniform, cordate at base, withering before time of flowering; inflorescence 14–37 cm high, markedly secund; flowers white, petals and lip papillose.
    Upland grassland and open rocky ground, 7500–9500 ft. HC, HM, HA, HK.
    Gardner 1488.

Note: Tweedie 2774 from Kaisungor, Cherangani Hills, has been identified as *H. nyasae* Rolfe at Kew but we have not seen this specimen. It is a species with sheathless flowering stems and differs from the others in this group by the long cilia on the lobes of the petals and lip.

2. BRACHYCORYTHIS *Lindley*
Terrestrial or rarely epiphytic herbs with tuberous roots and leafy stems; flowers few to numerous in a terminal inflorescence with leaf-like bracts, pink or mauve, often spotted darker or with some white or yellow in the throat; sepals free, petals usually adnate to the side of the column at the base, lip projecting forward, basal part (hypochile) boat-shaped or spurred, upper part (epichile) flattened, entire or 2–3 lobed; column erect, rather slender.

1   Leaves glabrous   2
    Leaves densely but shortly hairy
                                1. *B. pubescens*
2   Lip hypochile forming a distinct spur, 5–
        10 mm long   2. *B. tenuior*
    Lip hypochile very shortly saccate or boat-
        shaped but not projecting as a spur   3
3   Epichile of lip with a conical callus just in
        front of the hypochile; dorsal sepal 4–
        5 mm long   3. *B. buchananii*
    Epichile of lip without a conical basal callus
        but with a median longitudinal ridge;
        dorsal sepal 5–14 mm long   4
4   Leaves terminating in a very fine point, lip
        hypochile 1·5–2·5 mm long from back to
        front   4. *B. pleistophylla*
    Leaves acuminate but not very finely
        pointed; lip hypochile 3·5–6 mm long
        from back to front   5
5   Flowers in a dense spike of 20–100, lip
        12–16 mm long   5. *B. ovata*
    Flowers in a lax spike, up to 22, lip 1·5–
        2·5 cm long   6. *B. kalbreyeri*

1. Brachycorythis pubescens *Harv.* (see p. 730)
Leaves, bracts and flowers minutely, velvety hairy; inflorescence densely many-flowered, flowers small, lip hypochile 2–3 mm long and epichile 5–10 mm long, bent downward in a knee-like manner from its attachment, 3-lobed at the apex.
    In upland grassland and open woodland, 6000–8000 ft. HE, HM, HA, RV.
    Piers in B 9451.

2. Brachycorythis tenuior *Reichb. f.*
Leafy stems to 55 cm high, inflorescence densely many-flowered; flowers spreading, purple or violet

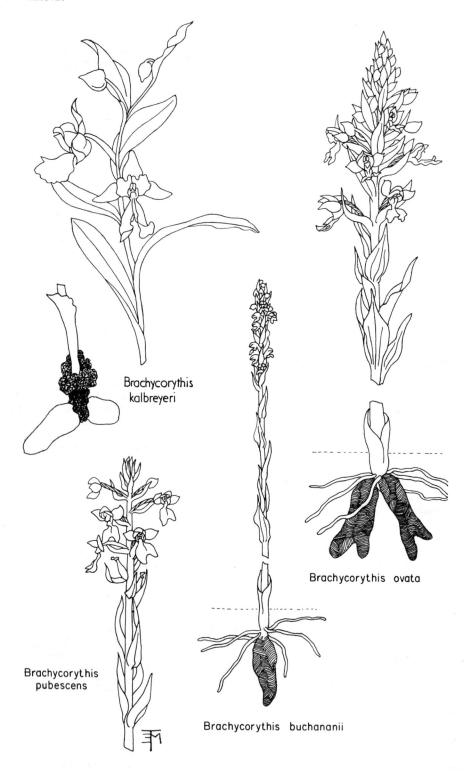

Brachycorythis
kalbreyeri

Brachycorythis ovata

Brachycorythis
pubescens

Brachycorythis buchananii

with darker spots or white areas, lip epichile projecting forward, 3-lobed.

Grassy swamps and cleared woodland, 4000–5000 ft. MUM, MAC.

Archer 16.

3. Brachycorythis buchananii (*Schltr.*) *Rolfe* (see p. 730)

Slender leafy herb 20–55 cm high, inflorescence densely many-flowered; flowers pink, mauve or purple, small, lip hypochile boat-shaped 1·5–2·5 mm long, epichile reniform, 3-lobed with the side lobes longer than the middle lobe.

Grassland and swamps, 5000–6500 ft. KIT, MUM.

Tweedie 99.

4. Brachycorythis pleistophylla *Reichb. f.*

Very leafy herb 25–100 cm high, inflorescence many-flowered; flowers lilac or purple with a white or yellow centre, petals semi-orbicular, lip epichile elliptic, 3-lobed with the middle lobe tooth-like and much smaller than the rounded side lobes, or lacking.

Grassland, and edges of deciduous woodland, 6000–8000 ft. HE.

Jack 247.

5. Brachycorythis ovata *Lindl.* (see p. 730)

Very leafy herbs 40–100 cm, inflorescence rather laxly flowered; flowers purple or mauve with an admixture of white, relatively large, the lip epichile 3-lobed in the upper part and with a raised keel running along the centre of the middle lobe.

Grassland, 6000–7600 ft. Our plants belong to subspecies *schweinfurthii* (Reichb. f.) Summerhayes. HE, HC, KIT, MUM.

Barnley in EAH 12370.

6. Brachycorythis kalbreyeri *Reichb. f.* (see p. 730)

Epiphytic or rarely terrestrial leafy herb 15–40 cm high, inflorescence laxly 3–10 flowered or rarely more; flowers large, pink, mauve or rarely whitish, lip epichile 3-lobed in the upper part, the middle lobe triangular and curved upwards, much smaller than the broadly incurved side lobes.

Riverine forest and upland rain forest, on mossy forest trees and decomposing logs and trunks, 6000–7000 ft. HE, HC, HM, MUM, KIS.

Copley s.n.; Royston H 63/52.

3. CYNORKIS *Thou.*

Terrestrial herbs with elongated fleshy or tuberous roots, stems glandular pubescent, leaves almost all radical, few or solitary; flowers few or numerous in a terminal raceme, ovary and outer surface of perianth usually bearing glandular hairs, pink or mauve, dorsal sepal forming a helmet with the two petals arching over the column and smaller than the lip which is often 3–5-lobed, spurred at the base; column short and broad; capsules oblong or fusiform.

1　Leaves 2–6; lip quite entire
　　　　　　　　　　　1. *C. anacamptoides*
　Leaves 1 or rarely 2; lip 3-lobed
　　　　　　　　　　　2. *C. kassnerana*

1. Cynorkis anacamptoides *Kraenzl.* (see p. 732)

Stems slender 10–60 cm high with 2–6 lanceolate leaves at the base and several sheath-like ones above; flowers small pink, mauve or purple, lip 3–5 mm long with spur of same length.

Upland moorland and grassland, bogs, swamps, and by streams in upland rain-forest, 6500–10 000 ft. HE, HC, HA.

Irwin 247.

2. Cynorkis kassnerana *Kraenzl.* (see p. 732)

Terrestrial or epiphytic herb with woolly ellipsoid tubers, stems slender, erect and glandular, 15–50 cm high, the single leaf at the base lanceolate or oblanceolate, often tessellated; flowers 4–22, pinkish-purple or mauve.

Upland rain forest, on mossy banks, among rocks of the forest floor, or epiphytic on moss-covered tree-trunks and branches, 5000–8500 ft. HC, HM, HK.

Archer 459.

4. HABENARIA *Willd.*

Terrestrial, or rarely epiphytic herbs with fleshy or tuberous roots; leaves sometimes 1 or 2 radical and closely appressed to the ground, or arranged along the stem with the lowest 2–3 often smaller and funnel-shaped and the upper ones much larger, then gradually tapering off in size; inflorescence terminal, 1–many-flowered; flowers resupinate, green and/or white; sepals free, the laterals spreading, the dorsal erect and forming a helm with the two petals or the posterior lobe of the divided petals, or reflexed; lip entire or 3-lobed, spurred at the base; column tall or short, bearing an upright or reclinate anther with 2 loculi, sometimes with auricles (staminodes), stigmatic processes which vary from shortly club shaped to very long and capitate, and a 3-lobed rostellum between the anther and stigma; capsules oblong or fusiform.

1　Leaves several, borne along the stem　　　　2
　Leaves 1 or 2, basal, orbicular, appressed to
　　the ground　　　　　　　　　　　　　34
2　Petals entire　　　　　　　　　　　　　3
　Petals deeply 2-lobed　　　　　　　　　18

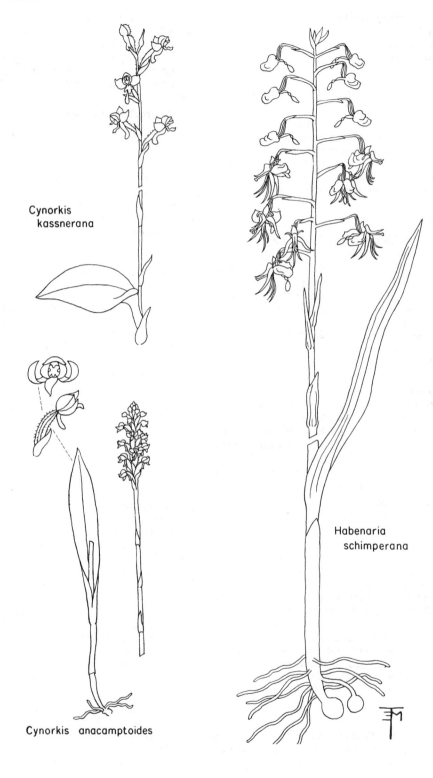

Cynorkis
kassnerana

Cynorkis anacamptoides

Habenaria
schimperana

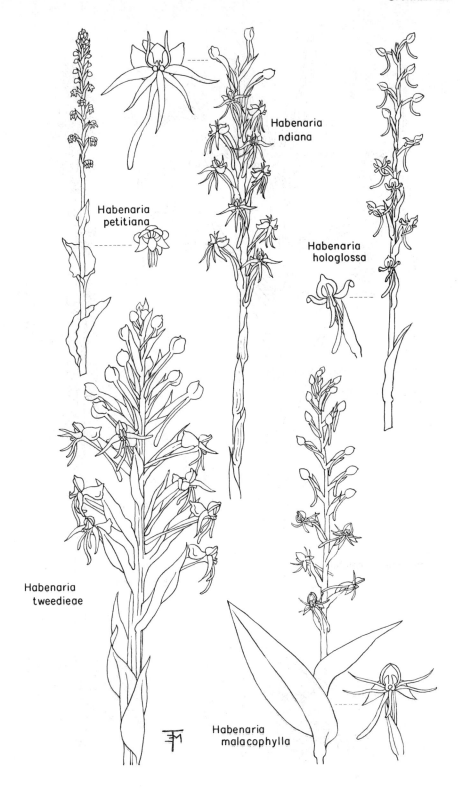

Habenaria
petitiana

Habenaria
ndiana

Habenaria
hologlossa

Habenaria
tweedieae

Habenaria
malacophylla

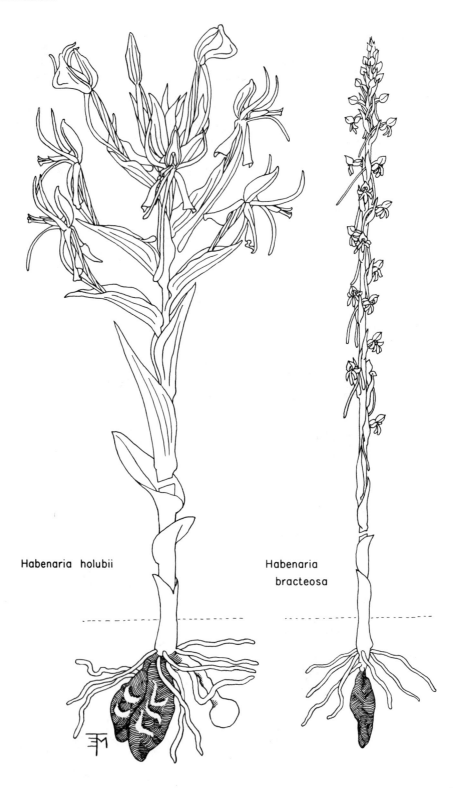

Habenaria holubii

Habenaria
bracteosa

3 Flowers entirely green or yellowish-green   4
   Flowers white or greenish-white; or partly green and partly white   10
4 Spur 1 cm or more long   5
   Spur less than 1 cm long   8
5 Spur 10–15 mm long   6
   Spur 15–30 mm long   7
6 Petals broadly lanceolate, back margin infolded   1. *H. attenuata*
   Petals ovate or oblong-ovate   2. *H. hologlossa*
7 Petals triangular to ovate, equalling the dorsal sepal   3. *H. bracteosa*
   Petals falcately lanceolate, acute, adherent to dorsal sepal to form a hood   4. *H. chlorotica*
8 Spur 5–6·5 mm long   5. *H. eggelingii*
   Spur 3 mm long or shorter   9
9 Spur scarcely 1 mm long, pedicel with ovary 4–6 mm long   6. *H. petitiana*
   Spur 1·5–3 mm long, pedicel with ovary 7–10 mm long   7. *H. peristyloides*
10 Flowers entirely white   8. *H. zambesina*
   Flowers greenish-white, or with some of the perianth parts green   11
11 Side lobes of lip entire   9. *H. epipactidea*
   Side lobes of lip divided into a number of narrow segments in a comb-like manner   12
12 Spur 10 cm or more long   13
   Spur less than 5 cm long   14
13 Dorsal sepal 1–2 cm long, obtuse   10. *H. cavatibrachia*
   Dorsal sepal 3–4 cm long, acute   11. *H. egregia*
14 Anther connective between the 2 loculi up to 6 mm broad   15
   Anther connective between the 2 loculi over 10 mm broad   17
15 Stigmatic arms 2–4 mm long, slightly swollen in the upper part   16
   Stigmatic arms 9–21 mm long, upper receptive part very much thickened   12. *H. keniensis*
16 Dorsal sepal only slightly smaller than laterals; middle lobe of lip tapering from base   13. *H. decorata*
   Dorsal sepal much smaller than laterals; middle lobe of lip parallel sided   14. *H. quartiniana*
17 Basal part of lip glabrous; staminodes not stalked   15. *H. macrantha*
   Basal part of lip pubescent; staminodes stalked   16. *H. splendens*
18 Spur less than 3 cm long   19
   Spur more than 4 cm long   30
19 Dorsal sepal erect, arching over the column   20
   Dorsal sepal reflexed, exposing the column   23

20 Stigmatic arms projecting forwards or upwards, slender nearly to the tips, the tips suddenly widened and truncate   21
   Stigmatic arms projecting downwards, often ± appressed to the lip, not much thickened towards the tips, with tapering, obtuse or acute tips   22
21 Lateral sepals rolled up lengthwise in opened flowers   17. *H. cornuta*
   Lateral sepals not rolled up lengthwise   18. *H. tweedieae*
22 Bracts leafy, as long as or longer than the flowers   19. *H. njamnjamica*
   Bracts distinctly shorter than the flowers   20. *H. malacophylla*
23 Column narrowed towards the base, with a sterile stalk 1·5–3 mm long between ovary and anther   21. *H. ndiana*
   Column widest at the base, sterile stalk very short or absent   24
24 Anterior petal lobe densely pubescent with ciliate margins   22. *H. altior*
   Anterior petal lobe glabrous or papillose but not pubescent, sometimes with ciliate margins   25
25 Bracts, at least the lower ones, as long as or longer than the pedicel plus ovary   23. *H. huillensis*
   Bracts distinctly shorter than the pedicel plus ovary   26
26 Petals divided almost to the base   27
   Petals divided to within 2·5 mm of the base   24. *H. linderi*
27 Spur narrowly cylindrical, equal in diameter throughout, only the extreme apex ± truncate and very slightly broader; auricles (staminodes) large, stalked, 2-lobed, white   25. *H. chirensis*
   Spur ± widened in the distal part, sometimes markedly so; auricles small, sessile   28
28 Spur 10–16 mm long   29
   Spur 17–24 mm long   26. *H. humilior*
29 Spur parallel to the ovary, not twisted   27. *H. thomsonii*
   Spur straight or incurved beneath the flower and spirally twisted more than once in the middle   28. *H. schimperana*
30 Spur 4–8 cm long   31
   Spur more than 8 cm long   32
31 Side lobes of lip lanceolate, much shorter than middle lobe   29. *H. holubii*
   Side lobes of lip linear, as long as or longer than the middle lobe   30. *H. laurentii*
32 Anterior lobe of petals and side lobes of lip broadly lanceolate or oblong-elliptic, obtuse, 2–6·5 mm broad   33
   Anterior lobe of petals and side lobes of lip

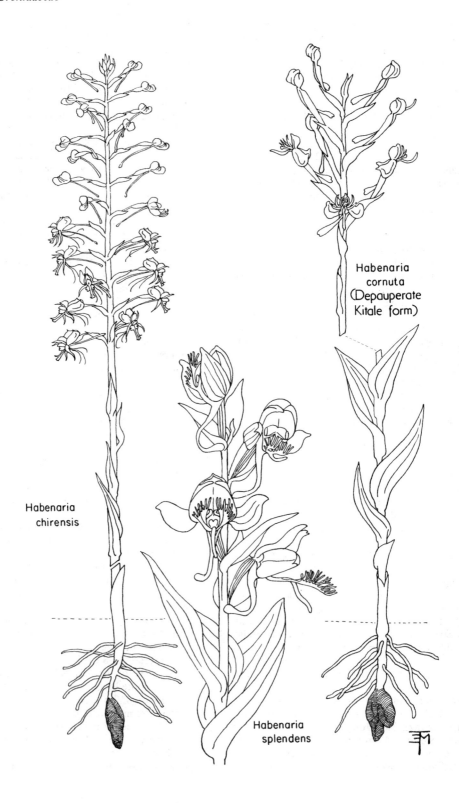

Habenaria
cornuta
(Depauperate
Kitale form)

Habenaria
chirensis

Habenaria
splendens

about 1 mm broad, petal lobe fleshy and curving forwards and upwards like a horn
31. *H. cirrhata*

33 Stigmas narrowly club shaped 8-12 mm long; lobes of lip 1·5-3 cm long   32. *H. walleri*
Stigmas broadly club shaped 3-4 mm long; lobes of lip 1-1·5 cm long
33. *H. macruroides*

34 Petals entire   34. *H. vaginata*
Petals distinctly 2-lobed   35

35 Spur 10-17 cm long   35. *H. macrura*
Spur less than 4 cm long   36

36 Side lobes of lip much longer than middle lobe, almost filiform and curved
36. *H. helicoplectrum*
Side lobes of lip slightly shorter than the middle lobe   37. *H. lindblomii*

1. Habenaria attenuata *Hook. f.*

Stem 15-50 cm high bearing 4-7 lanceolate-oblong leaves; flowers green, up to 20 in a single spiral row; lip 3-lobed nearly to the base, 3·5-4·5 mm long, the middle lobe longer and broader than the spreading side-lobes; spur slender 10-16 mm long.

Upland grassland among bracken and in conifer plantations, 7000-8500 ft. HM.

FTEA (1968).

2. Habenaria hologlossa *Summerhayes* (see p. 733)

Stem 30-80 cm high bearing 6-9 linear or ligulate-linear, acute, leaves; flowers green, many; lip undivided, ligulate, 6 mm long; spur 10-12 mm long.

Among grass in damp places in open bushland, *c.* 6500 ft. HE, KIT.

FTEA (1968).

3. Habenaria bracteosa *A. Rich.* (see p. 734)

Stem 15-95 cm high bearing 5-10 lanceolate or oblong-lanceolate, acute, leaves; flowers green or yellowish-green, many; lip 3-lobed from near the base, side-lobes a little longer than the middle lobe; spur slender 15-28 mm long.

Grassy glades in mountain forest and heath zones, 7500-12 000 ft. HE, HC, HM, HK.

Kerfoot 648.

4. Habenaria chlorotica *Reichb. f.* (see p. 738)

Stem 20-80 cm high bearing 5-11 linear or linear-lanceolate leaves; flowers green, 7-many; lip deeply 3-lobed from near the base, lobes incurved, fleshy, linear, the middle lobe longer and broader than the side-lobes; spur slender, ± incurved 2-3 cm long.

Damp grassland, especially badly drained areas over rock, 3500-8500 ft. HE, HT, HM, KIT.

Heriz-Smith 930; Dyson 375.

5. Habenaria eggelingii *Summerhayes*

Stem reaching 120 cm high, bearing 6-12 lanceolate, acute leaves; flowers green, many; lip 3-lobed from the middle, middle lobe longer and broader than side-lobes, spur swollen in apical part, 5-6·5 mm long.

In damp shady places in upland rain forest and moor, often in gullies, 8000-12 000 ft. HE, HA, HK.

FTEA (1968).

6. Habenaria petitiana (*A. Rich.*) *Dur. & Schinz* (see p. 733)

Stem 10-100 cm high, bearing 7-14 ovate or broadly lanceolate leaves, base clasping the stem; flowers very small, green, many; lip almost as broad as long and 3-lobed in the apical half, side lobes usually longer than the middle lobe; spur almost globose.

Short grassland and forest edges, 5000-10 000 ft. HE, HC, HT, HM, HA, HK, HN.

Stewart 879.

7. Habenaria peristyloides *A. Rich.* (see p. 742)

Stem 10-80 cm high, bearing 4-9 lanceolate, oblanceolate or linear-lanceolate leaves; flowers green, many; lip with broad, cordate base, 3-lobed in the apical two thirds, the middle lobe about twice as long as the side lobes; spur cylindrical.

Short upland grassland, marshes and open scrub, 6000-8500 ft. HE, HT, HM, HA, KIT, KIS.

Heriz-Smith 904; Lucas 149.

8. Habenaria zambesina *Reichb. f.* (see p. 742)

Stem 40-120 cm high, bearing 9-14 broadly lanceolate or elliptic-ovate, acute leaves; flowers white, many; sepals and petals ovate; lip entire, ligulate or with 2 minute lobes at the base; spur slender 3-6·5 cm long.

Grassy swamps, 3000-5000 ft. KIT.

FTEA (1968).

9. Habenaria epipactidea *Reichb. f.*

Stem 15-55 cm high, bearing 8-15 lanceolate or broadly lanceolate, overlapping leaves; flowers greenish white, rather thick and opaque, 7-many; dorsal sepal ovate, laterals much narrower; petals ovate or round; lip 3-lobed almost from the base, side lobes much shorter and narrower than the middle lobe.

Short grassland, especially where seasonally damp, 3800-6000 ft. MAC, NBI.

Archer 537.

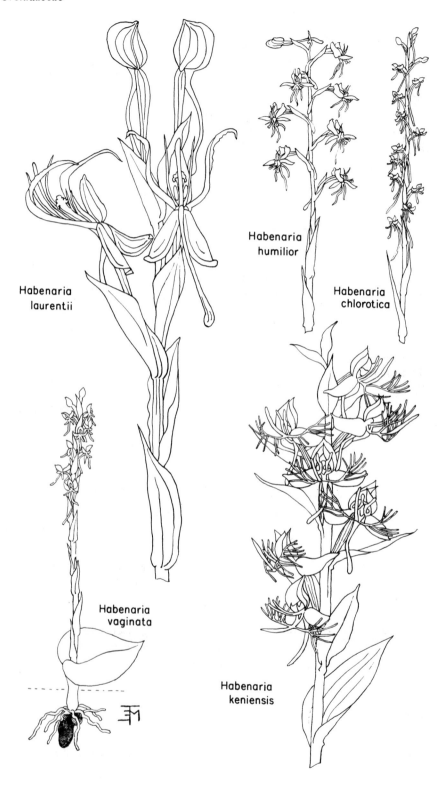

Habenaria
laurentii

Habenaria
humilior

Habenaria
chlorotica

Habenaria
vaginata

Habenaria
keniensis

10. Habenaria cavatibrachia *Summerhayes*

Stem 15-50 cm high, bearing 4-7 lanceolate or broadly lanceolate leaves; flowers 2-6, curving outwards, green, side lobes of the lip whitish, column brown; lip 3-lobed just below the middle, 2·5-3 cm long, side lobes longer than the middle lobe, and divided on the outer margin into 3-8 threads which are up to 12 mm long.

Upland grassland, 7000-9000 ft. HC, HT, HM, HA

Polhill 418.

11. Habenaria egregia *Summerhayes*

Stem up to 100 cm high bearing about 8 lanceolate or broadly lanceolate leaves; flowers 4, sepals green petals and lip white; lip 4-5·5 cm long, 3-lobed, middle lobe slightly longer than side lobes which are divided on their outer margin into about 14 threads 1-2 cm long.

Grassland, 5000 ft. MUM.

Carroll H32.

12. Habenaria keniensis *Summerhayes* (see p. 738)

Stem 20-60 cm high, bearing 5-7 lanceolate or elliptic lanceolate leaves; flowers 6-32, green and white; dorsal sepal 13-19 mm long, erect; lip 18-25 mm long, 3-lobed, side lobes widely divergent, 15-20 mm long, and bearing 6-10 narrow threads on their outer margin.

Terrestrial and/or rarely epiphytic in open woodland and upland rain forest edges, 6500-8800 ft. HE, HT, HM, HA.

Irwin 448; Glover 1375.

13. Habenaria decorata *A. Rich.*

Stem 10-45 cm high, bearing 3-7 lanceolate or oblong-lanceolate leaves; flowers 1-11, sepals pale green, petals and lip white; dorsal sepal erect 8-12 mm long; lip 3-lobed, 13-22 mm long, side lobes divergent, longer than triangular middle lobe, and divided into 4-6 narrow threads on their outer margin.

Rocky places in upland moor, with *Erica arborea*, 7500-11 000 ft. HA.

Dale K2841.

14. Habenaria quartiniana *A. Rich.* (see p. 743)

Stem 25-70 cm high, bearing 5-7 lanceolate or ovate-lanceolate leaves; flowers 6-20, sepals green, petals and lip white; dorsal sepal erect 4·5-9 mm long; lip 3-lobed 10-18 mm long, side lobes diverging, longer than middle lobe with 6-11 slender threads on outer margins.

Upland grassland, often among rocks, thick bush and forest edges, 7000-8500 ft. HE.

Tweedie 2627.

15. Habenaria macrantha *A. Rich.*

Stem 20-50 cm high, bearing 5-7 lanceolate to ovate-lanceolate leaves; flowers 2-9, green or whitish green; dorsal sepal erect 2-2·6 cm long, sepals and petals papillose and ciliolate; lip glabrous, 3-lobed, about 3 cm long, side lobes longer than middle lobe, diverging but ± incurved with 6-10 narrow threads on the outer margin.

Upland grassland and moor among *Erica arborea*, 8500-10 000 ft. HA.

Dale in K2842.

16. Habenaria splendens *Rendle* (see p. 736)

Stem 30-75 cm high, bearing 6-8 lanceolate to ovate leaves; flowers 4-17, sepals green, petals and lip white, often fragrant; dorsal sepal erect, 2-3 cm long; lip deeply 3-lobed, 2·7-4·5 cm long and densely hairy, side lobes a little longer than middle lobe, diverging, and with 6-12 threads on the outer margin.

Upland grassland, often near forest margins, 5000-8000 ft. HE, KAJ.

Symes 628.

17. Habenaria cornuta *Lindl.* (see p. 736)

Stem 20-80 cm high, bearing 9-15 linear-lanceolate to ovate leaves; flowers 4-many, green or yellowish green; anterior lobe of petal 3-4 times as long as posterior and curving upwards like a long horn, linear below, subulate above; lip deflexed, 3-lobed from very near the base, side lobes shorter than middle lobe and often pectinate on their outer margins.

Open, often badly drained grassland, 5000-8000 ft. HE, HM, HA, KAJ.

Piers in Bally B9447.

18. Habenaria tweedieae *Summerhayes* (see p. 733)

Stem 40-100 cm high, bearing 9-15 lanceolate to elliptic leaves; rachis and bracts hairy; flowers 15 to many, green and white; sepals hairy on outer surface; anterior lobe of petal slightly longer than posterior, both very shortly hairy; lip 3-lobed almost from base, side lobes half the length of the middle lobe and narrower.

In grass on rocky hills, 6500-7800 ft. HE, HT, HA.

Irwin 524.

19. Habenaria njamnjamica *Kraenzl.*

Stem 30-55 cm high, bearing 11-17 lanceolate, overlapping leaves; flowers 8-18 green and white; dorsal sepal ovate, laterals lanceolate, petal lobes linear, the posterior shorter and wider than the anterior which is almost filiform; lip 3-lobed from near the base, lobes equal in length but side lobes

half the width of the middle lobe; spur 1-2 cm
long, swollen in the distal half.

Grassland, 4500-6000 ft. KIT.
Brodhurst-Hill 25.

20. Habenaria malacophylla *Reichb. f.* (see
p. 733)

Stem 30-100 cm high, bearing 10-19 oblanceolate
rather soft leaves; flowers green, many; dorsal
sepal elliptical-ovate, laterals lanceolate; anterior
lobe of petal longer and narrower than posterior,
curving upwards; lip 3-lobed almost from the base,
lobes linear, side-lobes longer than middle lobe;
spur 9-18 mm long, thicker in the middle that at
either end.

Upland rain forest, and grassland in forest,
4000-8000 ft. HE, HM, MUM, KAJ.
Tweedie 66/261.

21. Habenaria ndiana *Rendle* (see p. 733)

Stem 30-90 cm high, bearing 10-16 linear or
lanceolate-linear leaves; flowers 10-many, green;
dorsal sepal elliptic, laterals slightly longer, semi-
orbicular or obovate; posterior petal lobe linear
and shorter than lanceolate anterior lobe; lip
3-lobed almost from the base, all lobes linear,
about 1 mm broad and of almost equal length;
spur twisted in the middle and swollen in the
apical half, 1·8-2·5 cm long.

Grassland, 5000-9000 ft. HE, HM, KIT, KAJ.
Greenway 8527.

22. Habenaria altior *Rendle*

Stem 20-95 cm high, bearing 9-13 linear or
lanceolate leaves; flowers 7-many, suberect, green
and white; dorsal sepal elliptic, laterals larger,
obliquely obovate; petal lobes lanceolate, the
anterior slightly longer and broader than the
posterior; lip 3-lobed almost from the base, side
lobes about two-thirds the length of the middle
lobe and a little broader; spur swollen in the apical
half, 15-22 mm long.

Grassland, especially near streams, and in forest
glades, 6000-11 000 ft. HE, HC, HT, HM, HA.
Greenway in EAH 13567.

23. Habenaria huillensis *Reichb. f.*

Stem 30-110 cm high, bearing 8-16 linear leaves;
flowers 20-many, green or yellowish-green with
whitish centre; dorsal sepal narrowly elliptic,
laterals larger, oblong elliptic or semi-orbicular;
anterior petal lobe elongate-lanceolate, twice as
long and wide as linear posterior lobe; lip 3-lobed
almost from the base, all lobes 1 mm broad, linear,
the side lobes slightly shorter than the middle
lobe; spur 1·5-3 cm, swollen in the apical half.

Grassland, 7500 ft. HE, KIT.
Irwin 224.

24. Habenaria linderi *Summerhayes*

Stem 30-55 cm high, bearing 7-13 lanceolate or
linear-lanceolate leaves; flowers 10-35, suberect,
green; dorsal sepal elongate-elliptical, laterals
larger, obliquely obovate or semi-orbicular; petal
lobes linear, equal in length, about 1 mm broad;
lip 3-lobed from a short undivided base, lobes
linear, side lobes a little shorter than middle lobe;
spur 10-14 mm long, scarcely swollen towards the
apex.

Upland grassland and forest glades, 7000-
9000 ft. HE, HM, HA.
Baker K337.

25. Habenaria chirensis *Reichb. f.* (see p. 736)

Stem 20-100 cm high, bearing 7-13 linear or
lanceolate-linear leaves; flowers 12-many,
spreading, white or greenish white with an unpleasant smell; dorsal sepal narrowly elliptic,
laterals larger, obovate; anterior petal lobe slightly
longer and twice the width of the posterior lobe;
lip 3-lobed almost from the base, side lobes two
thirds the length of the middle lobe and narrower;
spur 1-2 cm long, almost cylindrical.

Damp grassland, swamps and wet places among
rocks, 5500-7000 ft. HE, HA, KIT, MUM, NBI.
Wood 852; Symes 395.

26. Habenaria humilior *Reichb. f.* (see p 738)

Stem 15-70 cm high, bearing 7-13 lanceolate or
almost linear leaves; flowers 6 to many, spreading,
green or greenish white; dorsal sepal narrowly
elliptic, laterals larger, obliquely obovate; anterior
petal lobe twice as long and 3-6 times as broad as
linear posterior lobe; lip 3-lobed almost from base,
side lobes as broad as middle lobe but shorter; spur
1·5-2·5 cm long, slightly twisted, swollen in the
apical half.

Short grassland, often on shallow wet soil over
rocks, 4000-8000 ft. HE, HC, HT, HM, HA, HK,
KIT.
Tweedie 2671; Symes 164.

27. Habenaria thomsonii *Reichb. f.*

Stem 30-55 cm high, bearing 7-10 lanceolate or
broadly lanceolate leaves; flowers 12-35, curving
outwards, green with white centre; dorsal sepal
elliptic, laterals only slightly longer, obovate; petal
lobes papillose or minutely hairy, linear, the
anterior twice the width of the posterior; lip
3-lobed almost from the base, lobes 1 mm wide
and middle lobe twice the length of the side lobes,
spur 10-12 mm long, swollen in the distal half.

Damp or swampy grassland, 6000-8000 ft. HM,
RV.
Polhill 40.

28. Habenaria schimperana *A. Rich.* (see p. 732)

Stem 30-100 cm high, bearing 6-10 linear or linear-lanceolate leaves; flowers 4-many, spreading, green with white centre, with an unpleasant smell; dorsal sepal narrowly elliptic, laterals larger, obliquely obovate, twisted; petal lobes ciliate, anterior lobe much longer and twice the width of the linear posterior lobe; lip 3-lobed from an undivided base 2-3 mm long, all lobes linear, 0·5 mm wide, middle lobe longer than side lobes; spur 10-16 mm long, twisted several times in the middle and much swollen in the apical half.

Swamps or wet grassland on badly drained soil, 7500-8500 ft. HT, HM, HA, KIT.

Dyson 374.

29. Habenaria holubii *Rolfe* (see p. 734)

Stem 25-80 cm high, bearing 7-11 ovate to narrowly lanceolate leaves; flowers 3-19, curved upwards, pale green or greenish white; posterior petal lobe erect, linear 1·5-2 cm long, anterior lobe 2-4 cm long, tapering, curving upwards and outwards like a horn; lip 3-lobed from near the base, middle lobe linear, 2·5-3 cm long, side lobes shorter, projecting forward but upright on each side of the column.

Swampy grassland, often by streams, 3500-7000 ft. HE, HC, KIT.

Tweedie s.n.; Agnew 10580.

30. Habenaria laurentii *De Wild.* (see p. 738)

Stem 25-75 cm high, bearing 6-11 ovate to oblong-lanceolate leaves; flowers 3-15, curved upwards, white or greenish with white centre; posterior petal lobe erect, linear, anterior lobe at least twice as long, curving upwards and outwards like a horn, fleshy; lip 3-lobed, 2·5-3·5 cm long; spur 5·5-8 cm long curving backwards like a bow.

Grassland, often among rocks or scattered bushes, 6000-7000 ft. HE, HT, KIT, MUM.

Jack 301B.

31. Habenaria cirrhata (*Lindl.*) *Reichb. f.*

Stem 50-130 cm high, bearing 9-13 lanceolate to orbicular leaves; flowers 3-11, green with white central parts; petal lobes ± linear, posterior 2-2·5 cm long, anterior 5-9 cm long; lip 3-lobed from an undivided basal part 2-4 mm long, middle lobe longer and wider than side lobes; spur 13-22 cm long, often caught in the bracts and coiled.

Grassland with scattered bushes, 8000 ft. HC, HT.

Lindsay 157.

32. Habenaria walleri *Reichb. f.* (see p. 742)

Stem 40-80 cm high, bearing 7-10 lanceolate or broadly lanceolate leaves; flowers 2-14, green and white, fragrant at night; anterior petal lobe 2-3 times as long and wider than posterior lobe; lip 3-lobed from an undivided base, 3-6 mm long, lobes diverging, side lobes longer and wider than the middle lobe; spur 13-17 cm long, swollen in apical third.

Swampy grassland, 3500-7000 ft. HE, HC, KIT, RV.

Tweedie s.n.

33. Habenaria macruroides *Summerhayes* (see p. 743)

Stem 35-50 cm high, bearing 8-10 lanceolate leaves; flowers 3-8 suberect, white, fragrant; petal lobes same length but posterior slightly broader than anterior lobe; lip 3-lobed from an undivided base 2-5 mm long, side lobes slightly shorter and narrower than middle lobe; spur slender, 10-14 cm long, hidden among the bracts.

Grassland or near swamps, 5500-6500 ft. KIT.

Webster 9026.

34. Habenaria vaginata *A. Rich.* (see p. 738)

Stem 10-50 cm high, with 1 or 2 ovate or orbicular leaves at or near the base and a few sheaths on the upper part; flowers 6 to many, curving outwards, green; lip 3-lobed from near the base, side lobes a little shorter and narrower than the middle lobe; spur 1·7-2·7 cm long, slightly swollen in the apical half.

Short damp grassland, forest edges, 5000-9000 ft. HE, HT, HM, HA, NAR, NBI.

Kabuye 18; Tweedie 2672.

35. Habenaria macrura *Kraenzl.*

Stem 20-65 cm with 2 ovate or rounded, acute or apiculate basal leaves and a number of appressed sheaths throughout its length; flowers large, few-11, white or cream with sepals green outside; petal lobes broad, curved-lanceolate to semi-ovate; lip 3-lobed, the lobes broad; spur slender 9-17 cm long, often caught up in the stem sheaths.

Grassland, 4500-6500 ft. KIT.

Tweedie 3817.

36. Habenaria helicoplectrum *Summerhayes*

Stem 25-55 cm high, with 2 large basal, ovate to orbicular leaves and several smaller ones along the stem; flowers many, white to greenish-cream; anterior petal lobes filiform, curving forwards and crossing over each other in front of the flower, 2-3 times as long as upright posterior lobes; lip 3-lobed, side lobes filiform and longer than middle lobe; spur 4·5 cm long, curved in a complete loop.

Grassland and scrub, sometimes in rocky places, 3150-5200 ft. KIS, MAC, KAJ.

Archer 440.

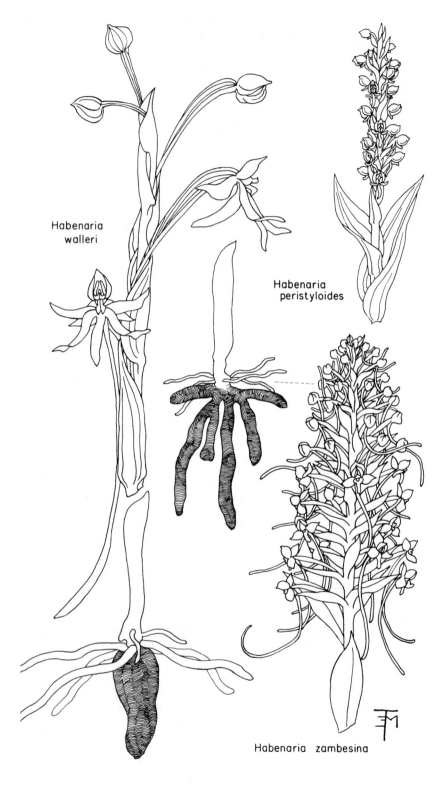

Habenaria
walleri

Habenaria
peristyloides

Habenaria zambesina

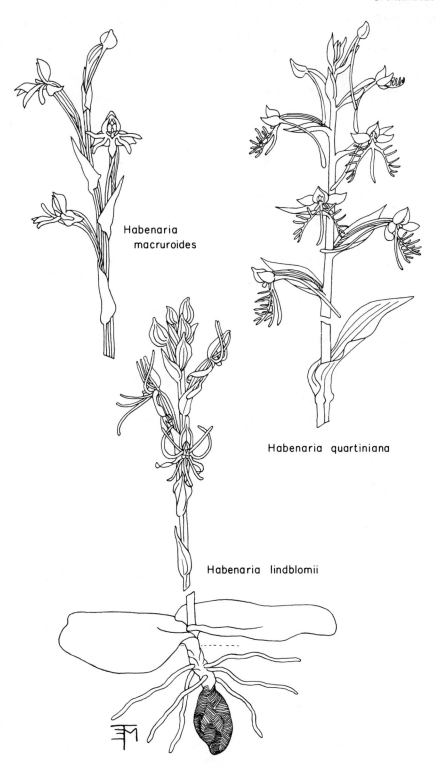

Habenaria
macruroides

Habenaria quartiniana

Habenaria lindblomii

37. Habenaria lindblomii *Schltr.*(see p. 743)

Stem 20-65 cm with 2 ovate or transversely elliptic basal leaves and 5-10 small lanceolate leaves higher up; flowers 7-21, green with a white centre, strongly fragrant; posterior petal lobe linear, erect, anterior lobe a little longer, curving upwards, rather horn-like; lip 3-lobed; spur 1·4-2·3 cm long, hanging ± parallel to the ovary and much swollen in the apical half.

Grassland, 5500–6500 ft. HE, KIT.

Lucas 148.

5. BONATEA *Willd.*

Terrestrial herbs with elongated tuberous roots and very leafy unbranched stems; flowers resupinate, green and white, in a terminal inflorescence; dorsal sepal free but usually forming a helm with the upper petal lobes, the lateral sepals united for some distance to the base of the lip, as also are the lower petal lobe and the basal part of the stigmatic arms, the free part of the lip 3-lobed, the lip spurred at the base and with a small tooth on its surface just in front of the spur opening; the 3-lobed rostellum stands out conspicuously between the anther and the stigmatic arms of the column.

1	Spur more than 7 cm long	1. *B. steudneri*
	Spur less than 7 cm long	2
2	Side-lobes of rostellum slender, much longer than the hooded middle lobe, pedicel with ovary 3-4 cm long	2. *B. volkensiana*
	Side-lobes of rostellum equalling or shorter than the middle lobe, pedicel with ovary 2·5 cm long	3. *B. tentaculifera*

1. Bonatea steudneri (*Reichb. f.*) *Dur. & Schinz* (see p. 745)

Robust herb 25-125 cm high, bearing 10-20 leaves and 6-30 green and white flowers; bracts leafy, shorter than the pedicel with ovary; lip claw 1·5-3 cm long, then divided, middle lobe linear, 2-3·5 cm long, usually sharply bent backwards from the middle, side lobes much longer, 2·5-8·5 cm long; spur usually 10-20 cm long and slightly twisted.

In bush, scrub and grassland, at the edge of thickets, roadsides, and in rocky places, 5000-8000 ft. HE, HA, KIS, NAR, RV, NAN, MAC, NBI, KAJ.

Williams 737; Copley 69.

2. Bonatea volkensiana (*Krzl.*) *Rolfe*

Leafy herb 20-70 cm high, bearing 3-25 green and white flowers; bracts leafy, usually much shorter than the pedicel with ovary; lip claw 1-1·5 cm long, then divided, middle lobe linear 1·5-3 cm long, side lobes diverging, 2-4·5 cm long; spur 3-4·5 cm long.

Bush or rocky grassland, 5000-7200 ft. HA, HK, NAN, NBI, KAJ.

Greenway in EAH 13568.

3. Bonatea tentaculifera *Summerhayes*

Leafy herb more than 60 cm high, many-flowered; bracts leafy, equalling or longer than the pedicel with ovary; lip claw 4 mm long, then divided, middle lobe 2 cm long, 2·5 mm broad, side lobes 6·5 cm long, 1 mm broad, resembling the anterior petal lobes; spur 2·5-3 cm long.

Known only from one collection in Nairobi City Park, 5400 ft. NBI.

FTEA (1968).

6. PLATYCORYNE *Reichb. f.*

Terrestrial herbs with tuberous roots, a tuft of leaves at the base and others scattered along the stem; inflorescence terminal, 1-many-flowered, flowers usually yellow; sepals free, the dorsal forming a hood with the two petals which are often adnate to it; lip free, with short side lobes at its base and a cylindrical spur; column erect; capsules oblong or fusiform.

Platycoryne crocea (*Reichb. f.*) *Rolfe* (see p. 728)

Basal leaves 3-6, to 1 cm broad and longer than the 1-3 cauline ones; flowers few, bright yellow, lip deflexed, or upcurved in its apical part, side-lobes 1 mm long, spur dependent, slightly swollen in the apical part.

Grassy areas in shallow soil over rocks, 4000-7800 ft. Our plants belong to subspecies *montis-elgon* (Schltr.) Summerhayes. HE, HC, HT, KIT.

Greenway 8512; Tweedie s.n.

7. ROEPEROCHARIS *Reichb. f.*

Terrestrial herbs with tuberous roots and leaves scattered along the flowering stem; inflorescence many flowered, flowers green; sepals free, ± equal in size, the laterals spreading; petals free, rather fleshy, lip dependent, 3-lobed with cylindrical spur; column erect with distinctively bilobed stigmatic processes, one lobe of each projecting downwards in front of the lip base, the other upright in front of the anther connective.

Roeperocharis bennettiana *Reichb. f.*

Flowering stems 35-95 cm high, glabrous, bearing 5-10 leaves and a narrow but densely flowered inflorescence of 15-many fleshy green flowers, each about 2·5 cm long from tip of dorsal sepal to apex of lip.

Bonatea steudneri

Swamps and damp grassland, 6800–8500 ft.
HC.
Dale R3445.

8. DISA *Berg.*

Terrestrial herbs with tuberous roots and leafy stems, some flowering and some sterile; inflorescence terminal 1–many-flowered; flowers resupinate, variously coloured; sepals free, the dorsal erect, hooded, spurred; petals adnate to column at the base, often inside the dorsal sepal, lip small and narrow, not spurred; column short, ovary twisted; capsule cylindric, club-shaped or narrowly ellipsoid.

1	Dorsal sepal measured from base to apex of spur more than 1·5 cm long	2
	Dorsal sepal measured from base to apex of spur less than 1·5 cm long	3
2	Flowers 2–12, deep orange, scarlet or deep red, tips of petals orange or yellow with reddish spots	1. *D. erubescens*
	Flowers 10–many, pink to wine red or purple	2. *D. stairsii*
3	Petals entire	4
	Petals 2-lobed	6
4	Petals lanceolate or oblanceolate, widest at the middle or towards the base	5
	Petals ± rectangular, widest in the upper part	3. *D. hircicornis*
5	Flowers pink or rose coloured, rarely mauve; dorsal sepal suddenly narrowed below the middle to a pendent, cylindrical spur	4. *D. deckenii*
	Flowers whitish to purple with darker purple spots and markings; spur erect, rounded and blunt, gradually narrowed from base of dorsal sepal	5. *D. concinna*
6	Flowers orange or yellow	6. *D. ochrostachya*
	Flowers pink, scarlet, crimson or magenta	7
7	Dorsal sepal and lip usually spotted or marked with darker colour; back (upper) lobe of petal as long as or shorter than front lobe	7. *D. scutellifera*
	Flowers not usually marked with deeper colour; back (upper) lobe of petal as long as or longer than front lobe	8. *D. welwitschii*

1. Disa erubescens *Rendle* (see p. 748)

Flowering stems 30–90 cm high, bracts shorter than the very distinctive, large flowers; dorsal sepal slightly incurved but not really hooded, spurred at about the middle, the spur projecting backwards or slightly upwards; petals 2-lobed, lip narrowly linear, 1 mm broad.

In short upland grassland, particularly where drainage is poor, and in swamps, 4500–8500 ft. HE, HC, HT, HM, KIT, KIS.
Glover 3223; Lucas 161.

2. Disa stairsii *Kraenzl.* (see p. 750)

Terrestrial, or rarely epiphytic herb with slender hairy roots but no tubers; inflorescence cylindrical often rather dense, bracts, at least the lower ones, longer than the flowers; dorsal sepal erect, convex and hooded, spurred below the middle, spur pendent and cylindrical; petals entire, lip ligulate, 2–3 mm broad.

Always above 9000 ft in grassland, moorland and rocky areas, 9000–12 000 ft. HE, HC, HA, HK.
Lucas 164; Kerfoot 1518.

3. Disa hircicornis *Reichb. f.* (see p. 747)

Flowering stems 30–85 cm high, inflorescence densely 16–many-flowered; lowermost bracts often overtopping the pale pink to purple flowers; dorsal sepal curved forward, narrowly conical, narrowed into a short slender spur which is usually curved round like a goat's horn; petals entire, erect, lip linear-spathulate.

Wet grassland and swamps, often near streams, 5000–8500 ft. HC, HT, KIT.
Napper 806.

4. Disa deckenii *Reichb. f.*

Flowering stems 5–50 cm high, inflorescence very densely 10–many-flowered; bracts as long as or shorter than the flowers; dorsal sepal incurved, very convex, with short cylindrical, pendent spur arising below the middle; petals entire, erect, lip ligulate, scarcely 1 mm broad.

Grassy glades at upper edges of forest and among *Erica arborea*, stony and rocky places on hilltops, 7000–11 000 ft. HC, HM, HA, HK.
Dale K3251.

5. Disa concinna *N. E. Br.* (see p. 747)

Flowering stems 20–60 cm high, inflorescence 10–many-flowered; bracts thin and usually shorter than the flowers; dorsal sepal inclined forwards, narrowing gradually into the short erect spur; petals entire, erect, lip projecting forwards, narrowly oblong or elliptical, ± 1·5 mm broad.

In grassland, often amongst scattered bushes, 6800–7600 ft. HE, HC, HM, KIT.
Napier 1898; Smart 96.

6. Disa ochrostachya *Reichb. f.* (see p. 747)

Flowering stems slender or robust, 35–100 cm high, inflorescence long and slender, densely many-flowered, lowermost bracts only over-

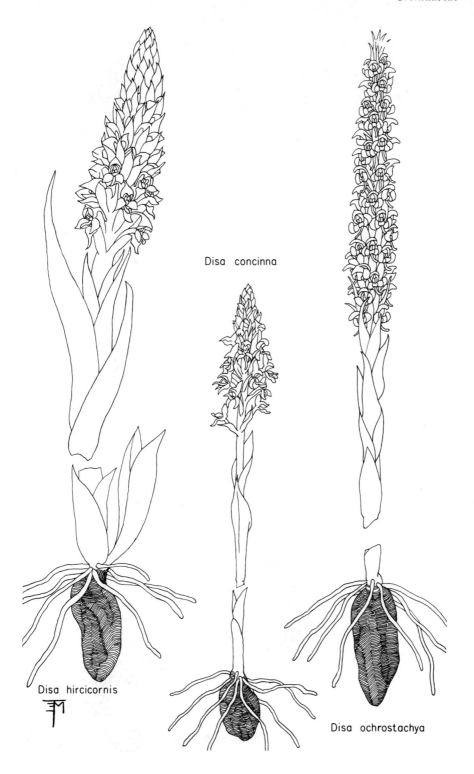

Disa concinna

Disa hircicornis

Disa ochrostachya

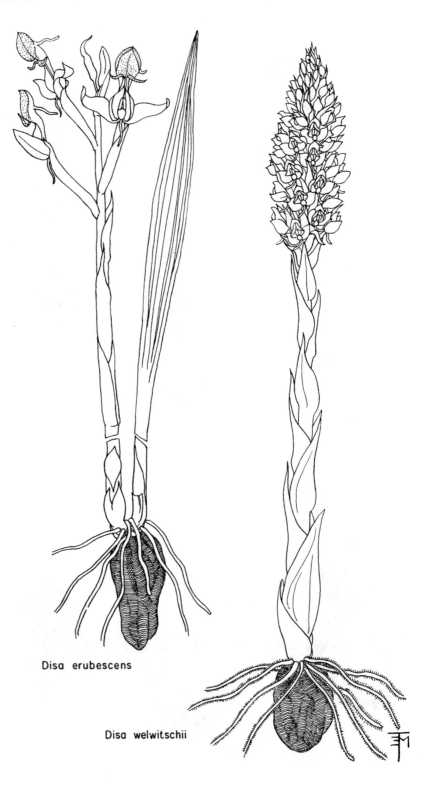

Disa erubescens

Disa welwitschii

topping the flowers; dorsal sepal erect, very convex, with a pendent, somewhat club-shaped spur arising below the middle; petals erect, unequally 2-lobed at or above the middle, lip pendent, linear, 0·5-2 mm broad.

Upland grassland and grassy glades in forest, 4800-8800 ft. HT, HM.

Tweedie 664; Smart G31.

7. **Disa scutellifera** *A. Rich.* (see p. 750)

Flowering stems 25-75 cm high, inflorescence densely 14-many-flowered, the lowermost bracts overtopping the flowers; dorsal sepal erect, convex, spurred below the middle; petals erect, 2-lobed in the upper part, lip pendent, linear.

Damp grassland, and grassy rocky slopes, 6000-8000 ft. HE, HT, HM, HA, HK.

Dyson 414.

8. **Disa welwitschii** *Reichb. f.* (see p. 748)

This species is extremely variable and very similar to the above with which it may be conspecific. It seems to occur at slightly lower altitudes but within the same area as the above. See FTEA for a detailed description.

Damp grassland, 5000-6000 ft. HE, HM, KIS, KIT.

Harvey 202.

9. SATYRIUM *Sw.*

Terrestrial herbs with tubers, leaves near the base of the flowering stem or on separate sterile shoots; flowers not resupinate, variously coloured, in dense terminal inflorescences; sepals ± united to the petals and lip, lip erect, ± hooded, with 2 spurs at the base, sometimes with 2 extra ones; column erect and incurved, included in the lip; ovary not twisted, often 6-ribbed; capsule ellipsoid.

1	Spurs more than 2 cm long	2
	Spurs less than 2 cm long	3
2	Flowering stem with 2 broad, basal leaves appressed to the ground 1. *S. fimbriatum*	
	Flowering stem with sheathing leaves only, the foliage leaves on separate sterile shoots 2. *S. volkensii*	
3	Lip equalling or longer than the spurs	4
	Lip shorter than the spurs	5
4	Leaves 2, basal, orbicular, appressed to the ground; lip 9-14 mm long 3. *S. carsonii*	
	Leaves along the stem; lip 5·5-8 mm long 4. *S. paludosum*	
5	Foliage leaves borne on the lower part of the flowering stems	6
	Foliage leaves on separate sterile shoots, the leaves on flowering stems sheath-like	9

6	Flowers green, or yellowish green, sometimes tinged purple 5. *S. schimperi*	
	Flowers red or pink	7
7	Flowering stem with 2 almost equal broad leaves near the base, the remainder sheath-like; sepals and petals narrowly oblong, much longer than the lip 6. *S. cheirophorum*	
	Flowering stem with a number of leaves, either along or towards the base of the stem; sepals oblong, only slightly longer than the lip	8
8	Lip 7-10 mm long, adnate to sepals for one third of its length; leaves bunched at base of stem, usually ovate or broadly lanceolate 7. *S. robustum*	
	Lip 5-6·5 mm long, adnate to sepals for about half its length; leaves spaced out along stem, narrowly lanceolate or ligulate 8. *S. crassicaule*	
9	Flowers green or yellowish green 2. *S. volkensii*	
	Flowers, white, orange, red or flame-coloured 10	
10	Lip usually with 2 additional short spurs at its base 9. *S. sacculatum*	
	Lip never with additional spurs at the base 11	
11	Lip thin in texture with a rather wide mouth, column long and slender, the stalk much longer than the fertile portion 10. *S. sceptrum*	
	Lip fleshy with a narrow mouth, column short and thick 11. *S. coriophoroides*	

1. **Satyrium fimbriatum** *Summerhayes* (see p. 751)

Flowering stem 15-40 cm high with few thin sheathing leaves; inflorescence with 6-12 rose-pink or deep pink, rarely white flowers; petals and lip with fimbriate margins; spurs very slender, 2·5-6·5 cm long.

Open grassland, near streams or forest edges and on stony slopes and rock ledges, 6000-10 000 ft. HC, HT, HM, HA, RV.

Polhill 416.

2. **Satyrium volkensii** *Schltr.* (see p. 753)

Flowering stem 20-110 cm high, with few sheathing leaves, sterile shoots to 5 cm high with 3-4 lanceolate to oblong-elliptic leaves; inflorescence narrow, with many green or yellowish-green flowers sometimes tinged purplish or brownish; lateral sepals twisted; petals pubescent and ciliolate; spurs very slender, 11-23 mm long, often with 2 additional very short spurs.

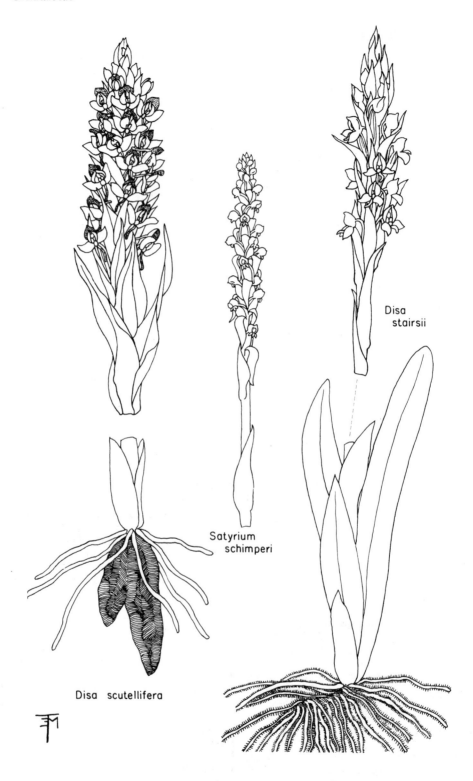

Disa stairsii

Satyrium
schimperi

Disa scutellifera

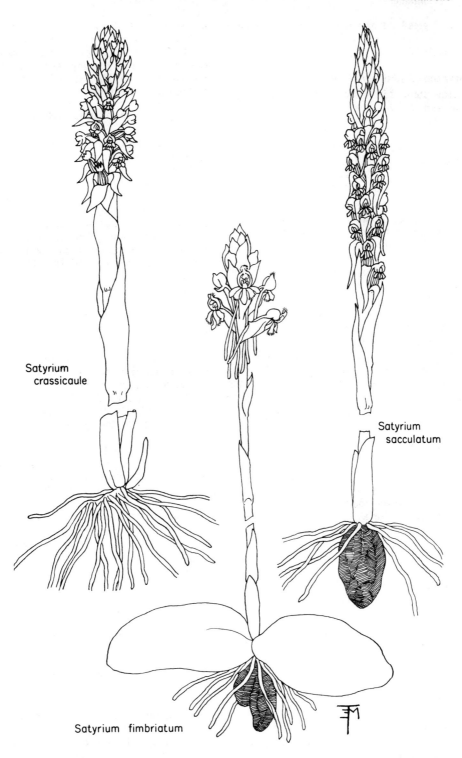

Satyrium
crassicaule

Satyrium
sacculatum

Satyrium fimbriatum

Upland grassland and open woodland or bushland, 6700-8000 ft. HE, HC, HA.

Napier 1940.

3. Satyrium carsonii *Rolfe* (see p. 753)

Flowering stem 25-90 cm high bearing distant sheaths and 2 ovate basal leaves; inflorescence dense bearing 3-18 white flowers; spurs 6-14 mm long.

Open grassland, 6000-7000 ft. HE, HC.

Tweedie 2666; Lucas 150.

4. Satyrium paludosum *Reichb. f.*

Flowering stem 30-80 cm high bearing 5-11 leaves and a densely-flowered, pyramidal inflorescence; flowers white, sometimes with pink markings; spurs up to 2·5 mm long but sometimes scarcely developed.

Damp grassland or swamps, 8000-8500 ft. HA, RV.

FTEA (1968).

5. Satyrium schimperi *A. Rich.* (see p. 750)

Flowering stem 15-60 cm high bearing 5-7 leaves and a narrowly cylindrical inflorescence of 9-many flowers; flowers green or yellowish green, all tepals with papillose margins; spurs slender 5-8 mm long.

Upland grassland, often among rocks, 7000-9500 ft. HC, HT, HM, HA.

Irwin 426.

6. Satyrium cheirophorum *Rolfe*

Flowering stem 15-80 cm high bearing 6-10 leaves, the 2 or 3 near the base much larger than the others, and a cylindrical 10-many-flowered inflorescence; flowers pale to bright pink; spurs slender 10-18 mm long.

Damp or poorly drained upland grassland, 5000-8500 ft. HM, HA, KIS, NBI.

Glover 1760; Dyson 360.

7. Satyrium robustum *Schltr.*

Flowering stem 25-70 cm high bearing 7-11 leaves, mostly in a bunch at its base, upper ones sheathing; inflorescence cylindrical, densely many-flowered; flowers deep pink to crimson; spurs slender 12-18 mm long.

Swampy grassland or bogs, especially near streams 8000-9000 ft. HE, HC, HK.

Bickford 14.

8. Satyrium crassicaule *Rendle* (see p. 751)

Flowering stem 30-120 cm high with a tuft of broadly lanceolate leaves at the base and other smaller ones along the stem; inflorescence densely many-flowered; flowers pink to mauve, rarely white; spurs slender, 8-13 mm long.

Damp grassland or swamps especially by streams, often in running water, 5500-10 000 ft. HE, HC, HT, HM, HA, HK, KIT, RV.

Symes 94; Irwin 181.

9. Satyrium sacculatum (*Rendle*) *Rolfe* (see p. 751)

Flowering stem 30-120 cm high with 13-17 sheathing leaves, sterile shoot to 7 cm high bearing 3-6 leaves; inflorescence narrowly cylindrical, many flowered; flowers· red to orange-brown, rarely white, margins of petals ciliolate; spurs 8·5-10·5 mm long, usually with a pair of additional very short spurs in front.

Short grassland, often on rocky slopes or in badly drained grassland and amongst scattered bushes, 5000-8300 ft. HE, HC, HT, HM, HA, KIT, MUM.

Dyson 541.

10. Satyrium sceptrum *Schltr.* (see p. 753)

Flowering stem 30-100 cm high with 7-11 sheaths, sterile shoot to 12 cm high, 2-5 leaved; inflorescence cylindrical, densely many-flowered; flowers orange-yellow to flame-coloured, rarely white; spurs slender 10-15 mm long.

Upland grassland, often in damp places, 6400-9000 ft. HE, HT, HM, HA, HK, RV.

Smart G4; Verdcourt 696.

11. Satyrium coriophoroides *A. Rich.*

Flowering stem 40-100 cm high with 6-10 sheaths, sterile shoot to 5 cm high, 4-5 leaved; inflorescence narrowly cylindrical, many-flowered; flowers white, or greenish, sometimes crimson-red, petal margins ± ciliolate; spurs slender, 11-17 mm long.

Damp places in upland grassland and rocky slopes, 6500-7000 ft. HC, HT, KIT, MUM, KIS.

Barnley in EAH 12372.

10. DISPERIS *Sw.*

Terrestrial or epiphytic herbs with tuberous roots; stems short, bearing 1-2 sheathing scale leaves, 1-2 leaves and leaf-like bracts supporting the flowers; flowers white, yellow, pink, mauve or magenta; dorsal (intermediate) sepal united with the petals, lateral sepals each with a conspicuous spur near the inner margin; petals variously shaped, often falcate, lip claw joined to the face of the column and ascending above it, often dilated into a straight or reflexed limb, which has an appendage at its apex which varies greatly in shape from species to species; column erect, stout; capsule cylindrical or ovoid.

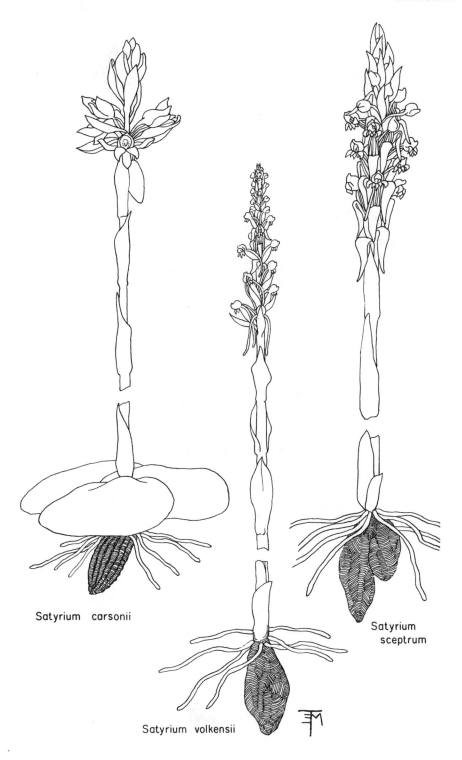

Satyrium carsonii

Satyrium volkensii

Satyrium sceptrum

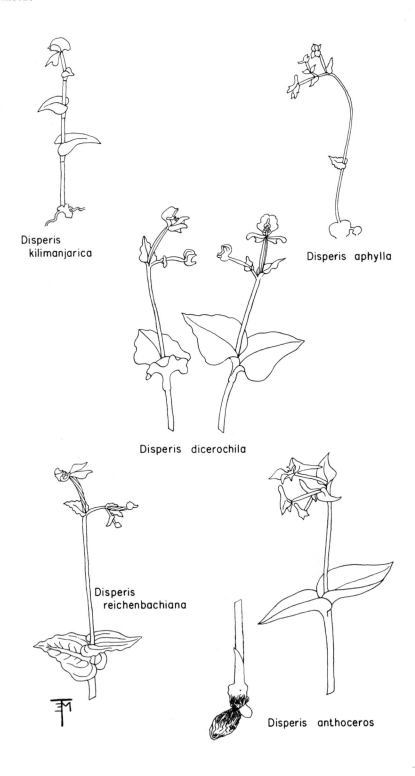

Disperis
kilimanjarica

Disperis aphylla

Disperis dicerochila

Disperis
reichenbachiana

Disperis anthoceros

1   Intermediate sepal fused with petals to form
    an open or boat-shaped hood but never a
    distinct spur   2
    Intermediate sepal and petals joined to form
    a distinctly spur-like structure   4
2   Leaves single or alternate   3
    Leaves opposite   1. *D. dicerochila*
3   Plant glabrous, leaves alternate
                                2. *D. reichenbachiana*
    Plant hairy, leaf single   3. *D. pusilla*
4   Leaves absent or alternate   5
    Leaves opposite or almost so   6
5   Lip appendage entire   4. *D. kilimanjarica*
    Lip appendage deeply divided into 2 narrow
    lobes, much longer than the short limb
                                    5. *D. aphylla*
6   Lip elongated, reaching end of spur where it
    is recurved, and terminating in a flattened
    appendage 9 mm long, nearly reaching
    mouth of the spur   6. *D. nemorosa*
    Lip limb 1·5 mm long, not reaching end of
    spur; appendage reduced to fimbriate
    vestiges   7. *D. anthoceros*

1. Disperis dicerochila *Summerhayes* (see p. 754)
Stem 6-26 cm high bearing 2 opposite, ovate
leaves; flowers 1-3, white, tinged rose or purple,
or entirely magenta; lip 7-9 mm long with a long
claw bearing two 2-lobed appendages at its apex.
    Leaf-litter, mossy branches and on rocks in
upland rain forest, 6000-8500 ft. HE, HC, HM,
HA, RV.
    Smart G25; Napier 635.

2. Disperis reichenbachiana *Reichb. f.* (see p. 754)
Stem 7·5-25 cm high bearing 2-4 alternate ovate
to ovate-lanceolate sessile leaves; flowers 2-5,
mostly mauve but with some yellow markings; lip
white or yellowish 6·5-8 mm long, with claw
sharply bent back on itself near the base and
bearing a stout 2-lobed appendage at the bend.
    Leaf-mould of forest floor and in rock crevices
in grassland and bush, 4500-7000 ft. HE, HT, HA,
KIT, MUM, RV.
    Tweedie 9.

3. Disperis pusilla *Verdc.*
Stem 2·5-3·5 cm high bearing one sessile ovate
leaf; flowers solitary, yellow, yellowish-brown or
reddish; lip with bent claw expanded at the tip
into a papillate triangular limb.
    Grassland, *c.* 8000 ft. HC.
    FTEA (1968).

4. Disperis kilimanjarica *Rendle* (see p. 754)
Stem 7·5-12 cm high bearing 2 sessile ovate leaves;
flowers solitary, white, tinged green and pink, or
distinctly green and mauve; lip 6 mm long with

linear claw expanded above into a narrowly
triangular blade with a reflexed tip.
    Dense shade of evergreen forest, on branches
covered with mosses and liverworts or in leaf-litter,
7000-9000 ft. HE, HA, HK, HN.
    Verdcourt 2948.

5. Disperis aphylla *Kraenzl.* (see p. 754)
Stem 7·5-16 cm high, leafless or bearing 1 tiny
ovate leaf; flowers 3-4, white sometimes tinged
pink or green; lip claw 2-4·5 mm long, reflexed
near the apex and the short limb bearing 2 linear
or anther-shaped appendages.
    Leaf-litter in dense evergreen forest, 1000-
5000 ft. MUM, also in the Shimba Hills.
    Tweedie 169.

6. Disperis nemorosa *Rendle*
Stem 8-28 cm high bearing 2-4 opposite ovate
leaves; flowers 1-4, white or white and mauve.
    Mossy places and leaf-litter on floor of cool
forests, 6500-8500 ft. HC, HA, HK, KAJ.
    Dyson 396; Dale K3443.

7. Disperis anthoceros *Reichb. f.* (see p. 754)
Stem 8-30 cm high bearing 2 opposite, ovate
leaves; flowers 1-4, white, tinged green or partly
pinkish, sometimes spotted.
    On ground-litter in evergreen and bamboo
forest, 8000-9000 ft. HE, HM, KIT.
    Smart G24.

11. EPIPOGIUM *R. Br.*
Leafless saprophytic herbs with tuberous
rhizomes, inflorescences erect, fleshy, simple, with
a few basal sheaths; raceme up to 25-flowered,
flowers usually pendulous, sepals and petals
similar, lip sessile at the base of the column,
shortly spurred; column short, much thickened at
the apex, and with swollen stigmatic lobes at its
base.

Epipogium roseum (*Don*) *Lindley* (see p. 757)
Saprophytic leafless herb with a small ovoid tuber;
flowers white or cream with small pink or purplish
spots, lip entire with a cordate base and two lines
of short hairs running from base to apex.
    Growing in leaf-mould in forests. HE.
    Tweedie (1964).

12. EPIPACTIS *R. Br.*
Terrestrial herbs with creeping rhizomes and
simple, erect, leafy stems; leaves ovate or lanceolate, plicately veined; flowers medium-sized, green
or purplish, drooping, bracts leafy, often longer
than the flowers; sepals and petals similar, lip
sessile at the base of the column with a narrow,

concave hypochile, a broadly ovate epichile, and 2 large membranous staminodes at its base; column short.

Epipactis africana *Rendle* (see p. 757)

Leafy herb to 3 m high with ovate leaves and a terminal inflorescence; flowers greenish, brownish or purplish, covered with a brown tomentum on the outer surface; pedicellate ovaries long so that the flowers are usually pendulous.

Forest, often on river banks, 7000-8500 ft. HE, HC, HM, HA, HK.

Irwin 149; Verdcourt 3022.

13. VANILLA *Swartz*

Climbing, liane-like plants attaining several metres in extent, often branched, bearing shiny succulent leaves at the nodes, or leafless, also roots which may become twining, attaching the plant to other vegetation, or penetrate the earth and develop a thick covering of root hairs; flowers conspicuous, in large axillary corymbs; sepals and petals free, ± spreading, similar to each other, lip ± adnate by its margins to the column forming a tube which broadens towards the apex, the limb broad and smooth, the disc bearing various scales or hairs; column elongated and curved.

Vanilla polylepis *Summerhayes*

Climbing herb, stems often reaching several metres in length, about 2 cm thick; leaves succulent, elliptic-lanceolate, and a bright shiny green colour, 6-20 cm long, 2·5-8 cm wide; flowers opening one at a time, pale green or whitish-green with mauve coloration in the lip; lip to 5 cm long, tubular and surrounding the column in its lower half, dilated apically and with a row of variously shaped scales and hairs forming a central crest along it.

Gorges of Thika, Chania, and Muthaiga rivers, 5000-6000 ft. HA, MAC, NBI.

Faden 66/165; Stewart 934.

14. NERVILIA *Gaud.*

Terrestrial herbs with tuberous rhizomes, bearing a single large, reniform or orbicular, petiolate leaf, after the inflorescence has died; inflorescence racemose, 2-12-flowered; sepals free, spreading, petals similar, lip 3-lobed in the basal part, without a spur, disc variously crested or lamellate; column elongated.

Nervilia kotschyi (*Reichb. f.*) *Schltr.* (see p.757)

A slender terrestrial herb 10-30 cm high, with a short raceme of 2-5 pale olive green flowers with purple veins on the lip; leaf broadly ovate, short-petioled, lamina 7-16 cm long.

Short grassland, 1000-6000 ft. KIT, MUM, also in the Shimba Hills.

Tweedie (1964).

15. CALANTHE *R.Br.*

Terrestrial herbs with short leafy stems, arising from small pseudobulbs borne in rows; leaves petiolate, broadly lanceolate, rather thin and often plicate; flowers showy in dense racemes usually held above the leaves; sepals and petals similar, free, spreading, lip usually ± adnate to the column, 3- or 4-lobed, disc callous or lamellate, base extended into a short spur.

Calanthe volkensii *Rolfe* (see p. 758)

Leaves to 55 cm long with petiole about 15 cm long; inflorescence 30-50 cm long bearing 10-30 pale-mauve flowers; lip fading to salmon-pink or orange colour as the flower matures except for the white warty crest near the base; spurs 2-4 cm long.

Plant of the forest floor, usually near rivers, 6000-9000 ft. HM, HA, HK, HN, KAJ.

Smart in EAH 12376; van Someren 2706.

16. OBERONIA *Lindl.*

Epiphytic herb with leafy stems, leaves laterally compressed, distichous and equitant; inflorescence terminal with whorls of minute flowers; sepals free, spreading, larger than the petals, lip 2-4-lobed, column very short.

Oberonia disticha (*Lam.*) *Schltr.*

Leafy stems up to 10 cm long; whole plant looks as if it has been in a press; flowers yellowish-green or ochre-coloured, to 2 mm in diam., lip bilobed and fimbriate at the apex.

Epiphyte of shady humid forests, 4000-5500 ft. KIS, MUM: also known from the Teita Hills.

Piers (1968).

17. LIPARIS *L. C. Richard*

Terrestrial or epiphytic herbs with conical pseudobulbs bearing 2-4 lanceolate to ovate, plicate, rather soft leaves and a terminal raceme of flowers; flowers usually rather few, greenish or purplish, resupinate; dorsal sepal much narrower than the two lateral sepals which are nearly connate; petals very narrow, lip continuous with the base of the column, broader than long and often apparently 2-lobed; column long and slender, incurved, anther terminal, pollinia 4.

1   Petals slightly longer than the lip; lip at least
         8 mm wide, margin smooth 1. *L. neglecta*
      Petals much longer than the lip; lip 6 mm
         wide or less, margin toothed   2. *L. deistelii*

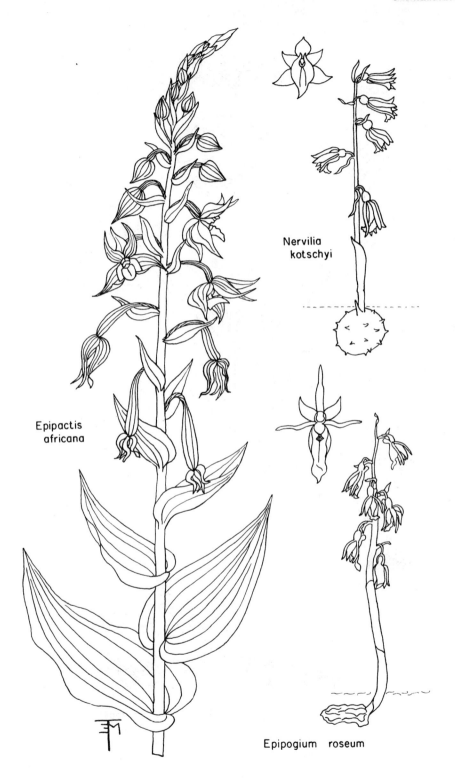

Nervilia
kotschyi

Epipactis
africana

Epipogium   roseum

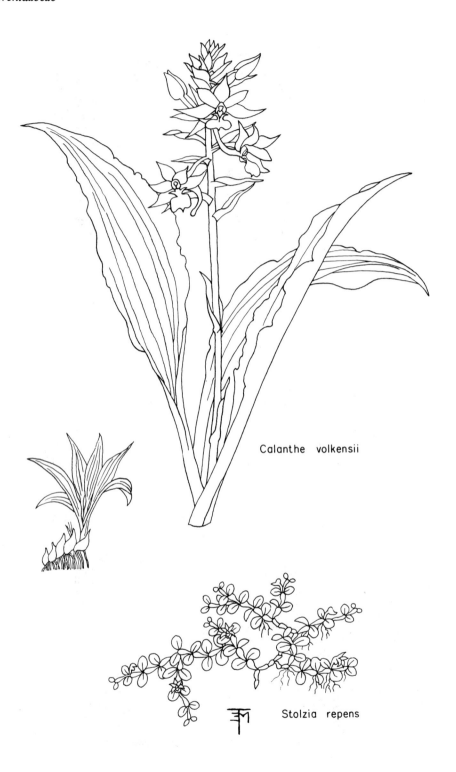

Calanthe volkensii

Stolzia repens

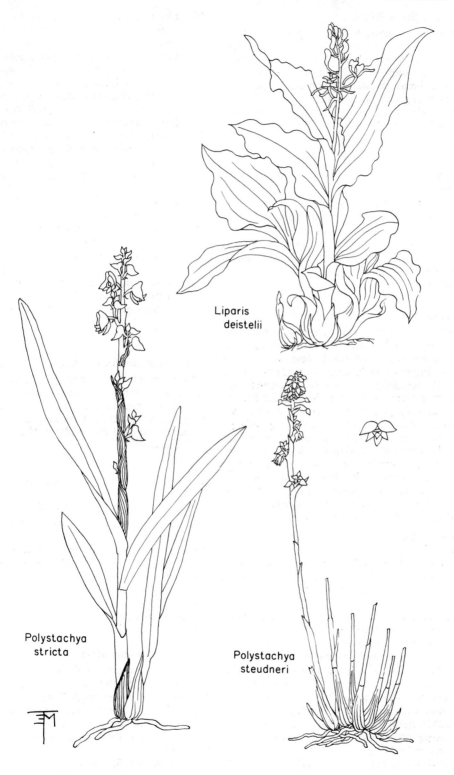

Liparis
deistelii

Polystachya
stricta

Polystachya
steudneri

1. Liparis neglecta *Schltr.*

Terrestrial or epiphytic herb to 20 cm high, stems swollen to form a pseudobulb at the base and bearing 2 (rarely 4) oblanceolate or ovate leaves; flowers green, sometimes tinged with purple, lip at least 8 mm broad, ± bilobed with a metallic green shiny patch or groove along its centre.

Mossy banks and amongst moss on forest trees, 6000–8000 ft. HE, HC, HM, HA, KAJ.

Hanid 311.

2. Liparis deistelii *Schltr.* (inc. *L. odontochilus* Summerhayes) (see p. 759)

Terrestrial or epiphytic herb to 20 cm high; pseudobulbs 3–4-leaved; inflorescence 2–12-flowered; flowers yellow, green or purplish.

Mossy banks and amongst moss on the trunks of tree-ferns and other forest trees, 6000–8000 ft. HE, HC, HM.

Stewart 994; 1009.

18. BULBOPHYLLUM *Thouars*

Epiphytic herbs with stout creeping rhizomes, bearing sessile, 3–5-angled pseudobulbs at intervals; pseudobulbs 1- or 2-leaved at apex and with scapes arising from the base, often more than one from each pseudobulb; inflorescence simple, upright or pendulous, bearing rather small flowers which are usually green, red, purplish or brownish in colour; dorsal sepal free, erect or spreading, lateral ones oblique at the base and adnate to the foot of the column forming a chin, usually free; petals usually smaller and narrower than the sepals, lip contracted at the base and articulated to the foot of the erect column; column apex bearing 2–4 variously-shaped teeth, pollinia normally 4 in the terminal anther; capsule ovoid or oblong.

1	Pseudobulbs 1-leaved	2
	Pseudobulbs 2-leaved	4
2	Pseudobulbs 1 cm long or less; scape very slender, usually less than 10 cm long; flowers 2–7, rarely up to 12
		1. B. intertextum
	Pseudobulbs 1·5 cm long or more; scape stout, more than 10 cm long and bearing more than 12 flowers	3
3	Rachis thickened laterally and bearing flowers along its edges; bracts 2·5–5 mm long	*2. B. encephalodes*
	Rachis not thickened, often pendulous; bracts 6–9 mm long	*3. B. schlechteri*
4	Rachis fleshy and swollen, flattened into a wing-like growth on each side of the central vein	5
	Rachis slender and unthickened	7

5	Lip pectinate in the lower half; petals triangular, maroon and white striped on the inner surface	*4. B. oxypterum*
	Lip not pectinate; petals linear or oblong, usually yellow at least at the apex	6
6	Dorsal sepal lanceolate-linear; petals filiform with a thickened club-shaped apex	*5. B. tentaculigerum*
	Dorsal sepal spathulate, the sides of the wider part thickened and fleshy, often yellow; petals linear or oblong, much shorter than the dorsal sepal	*6. B. falcatum*
7	Lip bearing long slender hairs along its entire margin	*7. B. cochleatum*
	Lip without hairs, or with a few short ones near the base only	8
8	Flowers in two rows but all facing towards one side; bracts 6–7 mm long, black or reddish; flowers reddish-brown or deep red	*8. B. bequaertii*
	Flowers in two rows on opposite sides of the rachis; bracts 9–12 mm long, straw-coloured; flowers whitish or rose-pink	*9. B.* sp. A

1. Bulbophyllum intertextum *Lindl.* (see p. 761)

Small epiphyte with numerous yellowish pseudobulbs borne close together in a mat, each bearing one linear-lanceolate leaf apically; flowers usually few, pale green with red markings, or reddish.

Warm forests, 5000–6000 ft. MUM, KIS.

Tweedie 623.

2. Bulbophyllum encephalodes *Summerhayes* (see p. 762)

Yellow pseudobulbs, each bearing one leaf, borne 2–8 cm apart on tough woody rhizome; inflorescence reddish-brown, 10–30 cm long, bearing flowers in the apical third; lip very fleshy and sculptured so that it resembles the surface of the brain.

Epiphyte of tropical rain forest, *c.* 5000 ft. MUM, KIS.

Verdcourt 1711.

3. Bulbophyllum schlechteri *De Wild.* (see p. 761)

Pseudobulbs conical, yellow or red, *c.* 2 cm high, borne close together on a woody rhizome; inflorescence erect or pendulous with numerous brownish bracts 6–9 mm long; flowers greenish-white or yellowish-green.

Epiphyte of tropical rain forest, 5000–7500 ft. MUM, KIS.

Tweedie 98; Stewart 995.

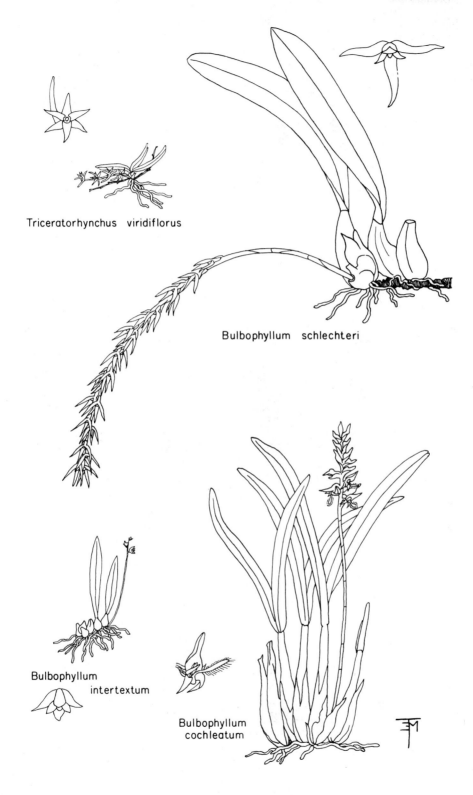

Triceratorhynchus viridiflorus

Bulbophyllum schlechteri

Bulbophyllum
intertextum

Bulbophyllum
cochleatum

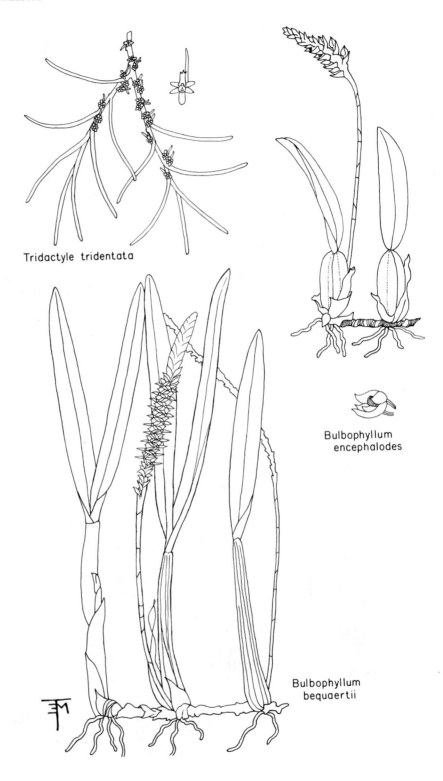

Tridactyle tridentata

Bulbophyllum
encephalodes

Bulbophyllum
bequaertii

4. Bulbophyllum oxypterum (*Lindl.*) *Reichb. f.*
Pseudobulbs yellow, with 4–6 distinct angles, borne at intervals of 3–10 cm on a thick woody rhizome; inflorescence 15–50 cm long bearing numerous flowers along the centre of the enlarged, ribbon-like rachis; flowers dark reddish-purple on the outside, the inside of the sepals and petals greyish-yellow with purplish-black longitudinal streaks.

An epiphyte of hotter areas, common at the coast and Thika, up to 5000 ft. HA, MAC.

Stewart in cultivation.

5. Bulbophyllum tentaculigerum *Reichb. f.*
Pseudobulbs ovoid, 4-angled, 3–3·5 cm long, 1·5–2 cm in diameter; flowers dark red, broad sepals velvety on inner surface, lip small.

Epiphyte of shady forests, 7500–8000 ft. HA. Ombler s.n. in cultivation.

6. Bulbophyllum falcatum (*Lindl.*) *Reichb. f.*
Pseudobulbs elongate-ovoid, 3–4 angled, 2–6 cm long; inflorescence up to 30 cm long (usually only 10–15 cm) bearing red and yellow flowers along the centre of the wing-like rachis.

Epiphyte of warm, shady forests. MUM. Evans 33.

7. Bulbophyllum cochleatum *Lindl.* (see p. 761)
Pseudobulbs narrowly cylindrical, sometimes slightly flattened, 2·5–10 cm long, 3–15 mm in diameter; flowers yellowish-green with a dark purple spoon-shaped lip with very hairy margins.

Epiphyte of shady forests, 4300–6000 ft. HE, KIT, MUM, KIS.

Carroll 663; Irwin 433.

8. Bulbophyllum bequaertii *De Wild.* (see p. 762)
Pseudobulbs narrowly conical or cylindrical, 4–12 cm long and 3–8 mm in diameter, bearing 2 linear-lanceolate leaves; flowers reddish-purple or reddish-brown.

Epiphyte of shady forests, 5000–6500 ft. MUM, KIS.

Verdcourt 1705.

9. Bulbophyllum *sp.* **A.** (near *B. bifarium* Summerhayes)
Pseudobulbs 3–6 cm long, 5–6-angled, narrowly conical; inflorescence as long as or longer than the leaves, covered with boat-shaped, straw-coloured bracts; bracts distinctly longer than the fleshy rose-pink flowers.

Epiphyte of shady forest, 6000–7000 ft. KIS. Stewart 1193.

19. CHASEELLA *Summerhayes*
Epiphytic herb with long creeping rhizome bearing sessile heteroblastic pseudobulbs at intervals with 6–11 closely-placed apical leaves; inflorescence arising from the base of the pseudobulb, bearing 1–2 resupinate flowers; sepals free, larger than the free petals, lip mobile, attached to the column foot; column winged with distinct stelidia at its apex, pollinia 2.

Chaseella *sp.* **A.** (possibly *C. pseudohydra* Summerhayes)
Rhizome long and slender bearing pseudobulbs at intervals of 2–5 cm; pseudobulbs oblong-ovoid, 8–10 mm high, bearing 6–11 linear leaves 8–12 mm long, 1–1·5 mm wide; inflorescence arising from the base of the pseudobulbs; flowers not yet seen.

Only known from one sterile gathering so far. Epiphyte in tree canopy, 6500–7000 ft. KIS. Stewart 1194.

20. ANSELLIA *Lindl.*
Epiphytic or occasionally terrestrial herbs with thick bamboo-like stems, 10–100 cm long, bearing 4–10 alternate, plicately-veined leaves terminally; inflorescence terminal, usually branched; flowers rather large, yellow or green, more or less blotched with brown; sepals and petals subequal, spreading, lip 3-lobed, articulated to the foot of the column, disc keeled; column erect, slightly curved, anther terminal, capsule oblong.

1 Petals usually broader than the sepals; lip usually broader than long, front-lobe more or less orbicular with two raised keels; spots on the flowers very large and dark, sometimes blackish and coalescing
1. *A. africana*

Petals usually the same width as the sepals; lip usually longer than broad, front-lobe elliptical or almost oblong with three raised keels, the central one often less well-developed; spots on flowers varying in size but always brown and usually small and distinct
2. *A. gigantea*

1. Ansellia africana *Lindl.*
A robust plant usually 50–100 cm high; inflorescence a large branching panicle of dull yellowish green, heavily spotted flowers.

Found in deep shade, 5000–7300 ft. HE, HC, KIT, MUM, NAR, RV.

Glover 3381; Tweedie 129/62.

Ansellia gigantea

2. Ansellia gigantea *Reichb. f.* (see p. 764)

A robust plant of variable height; inflorescence usually but not always branching; flowers yellow and mostly lightly spotted with brown.

    Epiphytic, or occasionally found on rocks or amongst tree roots, usually in sunny positions or in light shade. Common at the coast, 0–7000 ft. Our plants are of variety *nilotica* (Bak.) Summerhayes. HE, HC, MUM, KIS, NAR, BAR, RV, KAJ.

    Webster 9023.

21. POLYSTACHYA *Hook.*

Epiphytic herbs, stems often short and sometimes thickened into pseudobulbs at the base, with one or several nodes and therefore bearing 1–several leaves; leaves distichous, oblong or narrow; inflorescence terminal, spicate or paniculate, flowers not resupinate therefore dorsal sepal on lower side and lip uppermost; dorsal sepal free, laterals united to each other and to the foot of the column and slightly hooded at their apex to form a distinct *mentum* from inside which the labellum emerges; petals small, labellum entire or 3-lobed, articulated at its base to the base of the foot and sometimes bearing a callus or disc on its surface.

1 Pseudobulbs or stems narrowly cylindrical, or rarely swollen at the apex, each one arising about half way along the length of the preceding one   2

    Pseudobulbs or stems close together on a basal rhizome, often in dense tufts, sometimes swollen at the base, or narrowly cylindrical   6

2 Leaves less than 6 mm wide   3

    Leaves more than 10 mm wide   4

3 Pedicellate ovary hairy   1. *P. lindblomii*

    Pedicellate ovary glabrous   2. *P. spatella*

4 Flowers small, sepals 3 mm long or less   3. *P. fusiformis*

    Flowers larger, sepals 5 mm long or more   5

5 Perianth parts yellow or brown, acuminate   4. *P. simplex*

    Perianth parts lime-green, rounded, or minutely mucronate   5. *P. eurygnatha*

6 Plants with one leaf surmounting each pseudobulb, at least when flowering   7

    Plants with no leaves, or with more than one leaf at time of flowering   10

7 Leaves less than 1 cm wide   8

    Leaves more than 1 cm wide   9

8 Flowers white with mauve anther cap   6. *P. latilabris*

    Flowers greenish yellow with mauve anther cap   7. *P. inconspicua*

9 Flowers more than 1 cm in diameter, pink   8. *P. bicarinata*

    Flowers less than 8 mm in diameter, pink white or yellow   9. *P. cultriformis*

10 Stems short and thickened into a more or less rounded pseudobulb, or if elongated with a rounded pseudobulb at the base only   11

    Stems elongated, gradually tapering from the base to apex   19

11 Stems leafless or almost so at the time of flowering   12

    Stems bearing leaves at the time of flowering   14

12 Flowers white, pink or lilac   13

    Flowers greenish-yellow   10. *P. steudneri*

13 Flowers flat and open, more than 8 mm in diameter   11. *P. tayloriana*

    Flowers partly closed, less than 6 mm in diameter   12. *P. eurychila*

14 Pseudobulbs oval and laterally compressed, flowers bright yellow-orange   13. *P. bella*

    Pseudobulbs rounded, flowers not yellow-orange   15

15 Flowering stems less than 10 cm high   16

    Flowering stems 10–50 cm high   18

16 Flowers large, more than 10 mm in diameter; lip white   14. *P. campyloglossa*

    Flowers 6–8 mm in diameter; lip the same as perianth but with a yellow or orange central patch   17

17 Flowers pink with bright orange central puberulous patch on lip   15. *P. confusa*

    Flowers dull reddish-brown with yellow hairy patch on lip   16. *P. holstii*

18 Stems leafless for some distance above the slightly swollen base; flowers white or cream   17. *P. isochiloides*

    Stems leafy from the base; flowers dull yellowish-green or brownish   18. *P. shega*

19 Flowers small, 3–8 mm from tip of mentum to apex of lip   20

    Flowers large, 8–12 mm from tip of mentum to apex of lip   22

20 Inflorescence a simple raceme   19. *P. adansoniae*

    Inflorescence branched   21

21 Leaves fleshy, 0·5–1·5 cm broad, V-shaped in cross-section   20. *P. golungensis*

    Leaves thin, 1–6 cm broad, flat   21. *P. tessellata*

22 Flowers hairy; basal sheaths of stems green   22. *P. stricta*

    Flowers glabrous; basal sheaths of stems black   23

23 Sepals yellowish-green or reddish-green; lip white; flowers 1–8   23. *P. transvaalensis*

    All parts of perianth yellowish-green but with red markings on the lip; flowers usually more than 10, but opening successively   24. *P. albescens*

1. Polystachya lindblomii *Schltr.* (see p. 770)

Pseudobulbs very slender and of even width; leaves linear, grass-like; flowers yellowish-green sometimes reddish, sepals and petals acuminate, lip orange or bright yellow, recurved, anther cap mauve.

Forest edge, *c.* 5000–7000 ft. HE, KIT, MUM. Smart E10.

2. Polystachya spatella *Kraenzl.* (see p. 771)

Pseudobulbs slender, slightly enlarged at the middle; leaves lanceolate; flowers yellowish-green, sepals and petals rounded at their tips, or mucronate, lip brighter yellow than other parts, column mauve.

Common in highland forests, 6000–8500 ft. HE, HT, HM, HA, HK, KIT, MUM, RV.

Stewart 945; Moreau 577.

3. Polystachya fusiformis (*Thou.*) *Lindl.* (see p. 767)

Plants usually pendulous; pseudobulbs spindle-shaped, leaves lanceolate; flowers minute, brownish-purple, in large panicles.

Forests and isolated trees, 5000–7000 ft. MUM. Tweedie s.n.

4. Polystachya simplex *Rendle* (see p. 769)

Plants upright or pendulous, sometimes on rocks; pseudobulbs spindle-shaped; leaves broadly lanceolate; flowers in large panicles, greenish-yellow with reddish markings, sepals and petals acuminate, mentum narrow.

Dry highland forests, 6000–7000 ft. HE, HM, HT, HA.

Tweedie 81.

5. Polystachya eurygnatha *Summerhayes* (see p. 771)

Plants usually pendulous; pseudobulbs spindle-shaped; leaves broadly lanceolate; flowers in large panicles, lime-green with bright mauve anther cap, mentum very broad.

Upland rain forest, only known in Kericho District, 6000–7000 ft. KIS.

Copley 58 (type); Stewart 1266.

6. Polystachya latilabris *Summerhayes* (see p. 767)

Pseudobulbs thin and upright to 5 cm high in a dense tuft; leaves coriaceous, linear; inflorescence simple, 5–8-flowered usually shorter than the leaves; flowers white with yellow and mauve markings on the lip and mauve anther cap.

Forest, 7000–8000 ft. HE, HC, HK, HA, HM, KIS.

Archer 455; Stewart 1315.

7. Polystachya inconspicua *Rendle* (see p. 767)

Pseudobulbs slender, horizontal or upright; leaves coriaceous, linear; inflorescence simple or paniculate, usually longer than the leaves; flowers greenish-yellow, suffused with purple, lateral sepals up to 8 mm long and often each produced at the apex into a spur about 1 mm long.

Highland forests, 5000–7500 ft. HE, HT, MUM. Tweedie 2634.

8. Polystachya bicarinata *Rendle* (see p. 770)

Pseudobulbs robust and upright, conical, to 20 cm high; leaves thin, oblanceolate; inflorescence paniculate, drooping, bracts conspicuous, 5–8 mm long; flowers pale pink, lip white.

Highland forest often near rivers, 7000–8500 ft. HE, HC, HM, HA, KIS.

Napier 3145; Stewart 1271.

9. Polystachya cultriformis (*Thou.*) *Spreng.* (see p. 769)

Pseudobulbs conical, very variable in size, 2–20 cm long; leaves oblanceolate, margins often undulate; inflorescence paniculate, bracts small, flowers white, yellow, pink, mauve, or purple.

Forests, often near rivers, very common, 1000–8000 ft. HE, HC, HT, HM, HA, HK, MUM, KIS, KAJ, NAR.

Tweedie 7; Bally 7860.

10. Polystachya steudneri *Reichb. f.* (see p. 759)

Pseudobulbs short and swollen at the base, bearing several pairs of linear leaves; inflorescence paniculate bearing overlapping papery sheaths, and very small flowers; sepals green, petals yellow, lip green with purplish markings.

On *Acacia* spp. and other large trees offering light shade, 5500–7500 ft. HE, HC, KIT, MUM, KIS.

Tweedie 54; Stewart 1329.

11. Polystachya tayloriana *Rendle*

Pseudobulbs in tufts or ascending rows, short, conical, bearing several pairs or linear leaves which sometimes fall before the flowers appear; inflorescence covered with greyish sheaths, flowers pale pink with darker markings, borne on slender pedicels in several small groups along the peduncle.

On rocks and epiphytic on *Vellozia* stems, in very dry areas, 2000–5000 ft. KAJ.

Bally 1087.

12. Polystachya eurychila *Summerhayes* (see p. 770)

Pseudobulbs short and swollen at the base, bearing several pairs of narrowly elliptic leaves; inflorescence simple or paniculate, flowers mostly

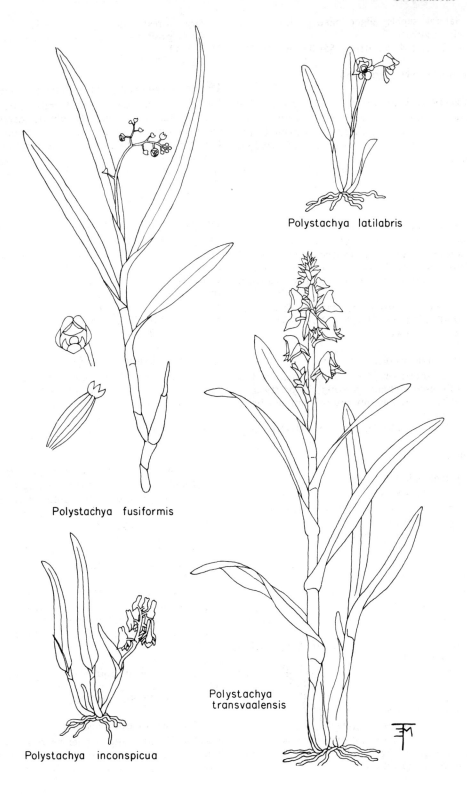

Polystachya latilabris

Polystachya fusiformis

Polystachya inconspicua

Polystachya transvaalensis

white, lateral sepals edged mauve, lip yellow, edged with mauve.

On rocks and *Acacia* trees, 5500–7000 ft. HE, HC.

Tweedie (1964); Piers 1968.

13. Polystachya bella *Summerhayes* (see p. 769)

Pseudobulbs oval in shape and laterally compressed, bearing 2–6 ligulate, dark green leaves; inflorescence simple bearing large orange-yellow pubescent flowers.

High up in forest trees, 6000–7000 ft. HE, HC, HM, KIS.

Jex-Blake 3195; Stewart 1369.

14. Polystachya campyloglossa *Rolfe* (see p. 769)

Pseudobulbs short, almost spherical, bearing 2–3 oblanceolate leaves; inflorescence bearing 2–5 large flowers, variable in colour from greenish-yellow to reddish-brown sepals, each with a white lip.

Cool forests, often in rather dry areas, 5000–9000 ft. HE, HC, HM, HA, MAC, KAJ.

Smart E 15; Stewart 1318.

15. Polystachya confusa *Rolfe*

Pseudobulbs short, ovoid or globose, bearing 1–3 leaves; inflorescence hairy, bearing 1–5 pretty pink flowers with an orange, puberulous but not hairy streak on the lip.

Cool forest, 8000–9000 ft. KAJ. (Namanga Hill).

Archer s.n.

16. Polystachya holstii *Kraenzl.*

Pseudobulbs short, ovoid or globose, bearing 2–3 lanceolate leaves; inflorescence hairy bearing 3–8 dull red, hairy flowers.

Cool forest edges, 5000 ft. KAJ (Chyulu Hills). Stewart 1348.

17. Polystachya isochiloides *Summerhayes*

Pseudobulbs very slightly swollen at the base and bearing 3–4 linear leaves on an elongated, narrow stem; inflorescence simple with few cream-coloured hairy flowers.

Dry open forests, 3000–5000 ft. Only known from the Chyulu Hills.

Hooker's Icones Plantarum tab. 3443; Stewart 1338.

18. Polystachya shega *Kraenzl.* (see p. 771)

Pseudobulbs short and swollen usually in rows bearing 2–4 linear leaves; inflorescence paniculate, sepals olive-green with mauve lines, petals yellowish-green, lip yellow.

Dry forest and open woodland, often in exposed positions, 5000–6000 ft. HA, HK, NAN, NBI, KAJ.

Piers H27/53.

19. Polystachya adansoniae *Reichb. f.* (see p. 770)

Pseudobulbs narrow and uniformly swollen, bearing 2–4 linear or narrowly elliptic leaves; inflorescence simple, flowers white or greenish-white, tepals with acuminate, sometimes purplish tips.

Common in relatively dry situations, on *Acacia* spp. etc. 5000–7000 ft. HE, HM, KIT, MUM, KIS, NAR, RV.

Tweedie 2598; Rhead EAH 10100.

20. Polystachya golungensis *Reichb. f.* (see p. 771)

Pseudobulbs slightly swollen basally, bearing 2–3 ligulate, coriaceous, sometimes almost succulent leaves; inflorescence paniculate, flowers very small and shiny yellow, cream, or lime-green, borne on the young pseudobulbs.

On small and large trees in light shade, 3000–4000 ft. KIT, MUM.

Saunders 2.

21. Polystachya tessellata *Lindl.*

Pseudobulbs 8–30 cm long, slightly swollen towards the base; leaves elliptic or elliptic-oblong; inflorescence paniculate with many small greenish or yellowish, sometimes mauve-streaked flowers.

Riverine forest, *c.* 4300 ft. KIS.

Faden 69/1310.

22. Polystachya stricta *Rolfe* (see p. 759)

Pseudobulbs long and slender bearing 4–6 elliptic or lanceolate, pointed leaves; inflorescence paniculate, flowers yellowish-green or whitish-green, with some purple streaks on the lip.

In light shade in the drier forests, 5000–7000 ft. HE, HC, HM, HT, KIT, MUM, KIS, RV.

Archer H 45/60; Stewart 944.

23. Polystachya transvaalensis *Schltr.* (see p. 767)

Pseudobulbs long and slender bearing 4–6 elliptic, thickened leaves with rounded tips; inflorescence paniculate; sepals yellowish-green or reddish-green, petals spathulate, paler, lip nearly white with purplish spots.

Highland forests, 5000–10 000 ft. HE, HC, HM, HA, HK, KAJ.

Glover 1170; Stewart 1303.

24. Polystachya albescens *Ridl.*

Pseudobulbs long and slender bearing 4–6 lanceolate, pointed leaves; inflorescence paniculate, flowers borne close together so that bracts overlap;

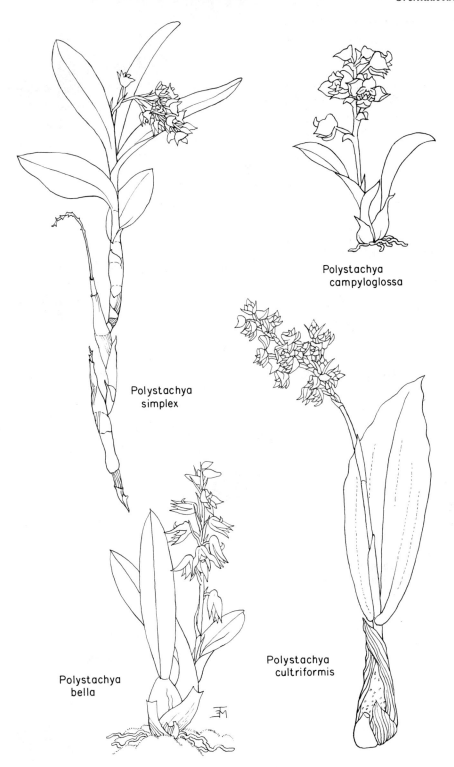

Polystachya
campyloglossa

Polystachya
simplex

Polystachya
bella

Polystachya
cultriformis

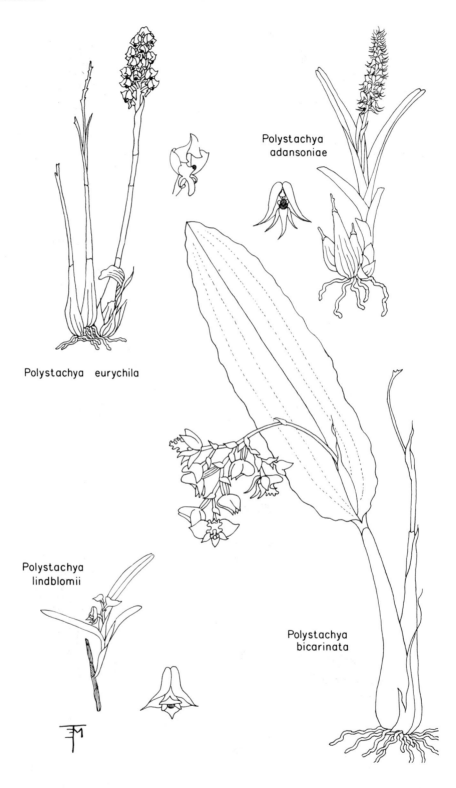

Polystachya adansoniae

Polystachya eurychila

Polystachya lindblomii

Polystachya bicarinata

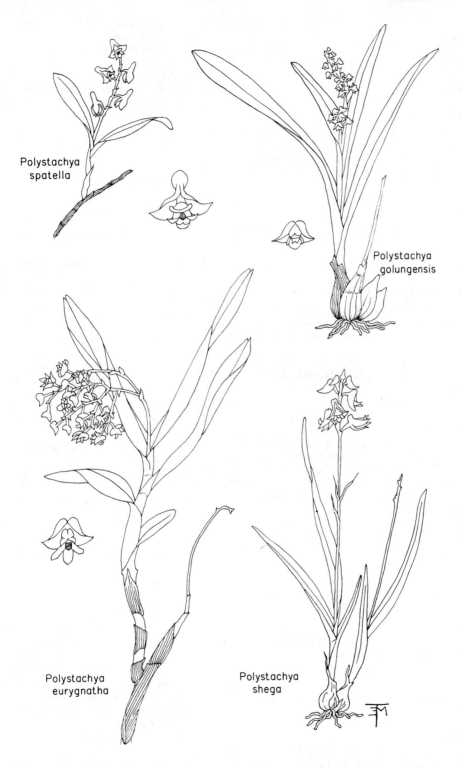

Polystachya
spatella

Polystachya
golungensis

Polystachya
eurygnatha

Polystachya
shega

sepals greenish with faint mauve lines, petals white, pointed, lip greenish with purple streaks.

Dry forest, *c.* 5000 ft. Our plants belong to subspecies *kraenzlinii* (Rolfe) Summerhayes. Only recorded in Kenya from the Chyulu Hills.

Piers (1968).

22. STOLZIA *Schlechter*

Small epiphytic herbs with spreading growth, pseudobulbs long and narrow, thickened at the apex just below the leathery leaves, always parallel to the surface of the substratum, a new pseudobulb arising just below the apex of each preceding one; leaves 2 or 3 at the apex of the pseudobulb, ovate or orbicular, leathery; flowers solitary or in few-flowered inflorescences arising from the apex of the pseudobulb, resupinate, red or orange-brown, sepals partly fused at the base, lip undifferentiated, column short, bearing 8 pollinia.

Stolzia repens (*Rolfe*) *Summerhayes* (see p. 758)
Pseudobulbs 2–4·5 cm long, growing horizontally and forming a mat or chains of growth, bearing 2–3 leathery leaves and a single small red flower at each apex.

Riverine forest, usually in shady places, 5800–8500 ft. HE, HC, HT, HM, HA, HK, MUM, KIS, RV, NBI.

Lucas 117; Archer 67.

23. EULOPHIA *Lindl.*

Terrestrial herbs, rarely saprophytic, with creeping underground stems, either thickened into rhizomes or tubers or with aerial pseudobulbs developing within the base of the leaves of each year's growth; leaves distichous, usually linear or linear-lanceolate and plicate; inflorescence lateral, often arising before the leaves, a raceme or panicle; bracts usually small; sepals subequal, spreading or reflexed, the lateral sepals sometimes adnate to the foot of the column; petals similar to the sepals or much larger and more brightly coloured; lip continuous with the foot of the column, saccate or spurred at the base, 3-lobed, disc smooth, lamellate or cristate; column erect with a distinct foot on which the sepals are borne, anther terminal, pollinia 4, united in pairs, affixed to a broad stipes and gland; capsule ovoid or oblong.

1	Sepals reflexed along the ovary, or spreading away from the petals	2
	Sepals not reflexed, usually held close to the petals	17
2	Petals yellow or green	3
	Petals pink or mauve	11
3	Sepals about half as long as the petals	4
	Sepals nearly as long as, or longer than the petals	5

4	Inner surface of petals streaked with red, or entirely red	1. *E. orthoplectra*
	Petals entirely yellow	2. *E. wakefieldii*
5	Lip yellow	6
	Lip white and pink	3. *E. petersii*
6	Sepals less than twice as long as broad	7
	Sepals more than 3 times as long as broad	9
7	Peduncle less than 30 cm high; flowers less than 3 cm in diameter	8
	Peduncle 60–100 cm high; flowers more than 3 cm in diameter	4. *E. grantii*
8	Petals more than 1 cm long	5. *E. pyrophila*
	Petals less than 1 cm long	6. *E. parvula*
9	Sepals longer than the petals; plant of swampy ground	7. *E. angolensis*
	Sepals nearly or quite as long as the petals; plant of bush and forest, often in rocky ground	10
10	Leaves never more than 2 cm wide	8. *E. stenophylla*
	Leaves 4–10 cm wide	9. *E. paivaeana*
11	Sepals and petals very similar	12
	Petals much broader than the sepals	14
12	Lip deep mauve with reflexed sides	13
	Lip pale mauve, orbicular, flat	10. *E. quartiniana*
13	Lip with numerous longitudinal lamellae which are divided like teeth	11. *E. cristata*
	Lip with thickened veins but no distinct lamellae	12. *E. livingstoniana*
14	Robust plants, flowering stem more than 1 m high	15
	Smaller plants, flowering stems 30–90 cm high	16
15	Lip distinctly 3-lobed, petals longer than broad	13. *E. horsfallii*
	Lip indistinctly 3-lobed, petals orbicular or broader than long	14. *E. latilabris*
16	Lip bearing 3–several low keels on the middle lobe	15. *E. calantha*
	Lip bearing 2 quadrate calli in the throat	16. *E. cucullata*
17	Plant a leafless saprophyte	17. *E. galeoloides*
	Terrestrial plants containing chlorophyll	18
18	Flowers predominantly mauve or white	19
	Flowers yellowish, greenish or brownish	20
19	Sepals longer and wider than petals; lip hairy	18. *E. montis-elgonis*
	Sepals and petals similar; lip with raised veins but no hairs	10. *E. quartiniana*
20	Sepals and petals pure yellow	21
	Sepals and petals of different colours, or not clear yellow	23
21	Flowers small, in a lax raceme	19. *E. warneckeana*
	Flowers large, borne close together at the tip of the peduncle	22

Eulophia
porphyroglossa

Eulophia
orthoplectra

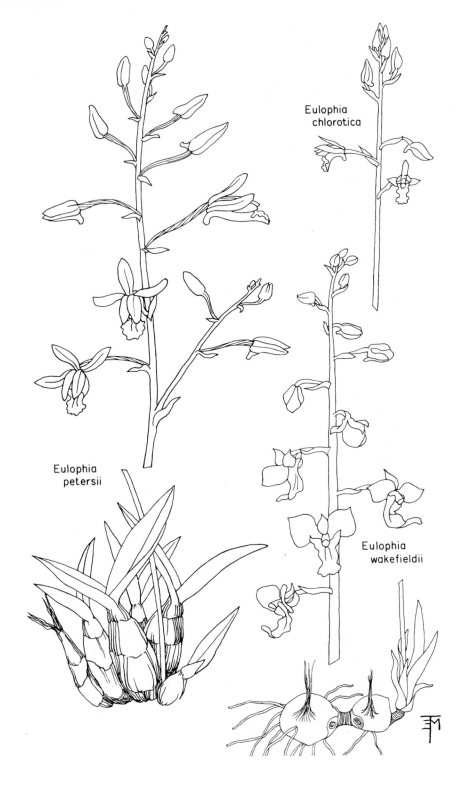

Eulophia
chlorotica

Eulophia
petersii

Eulophia
wakefieldii

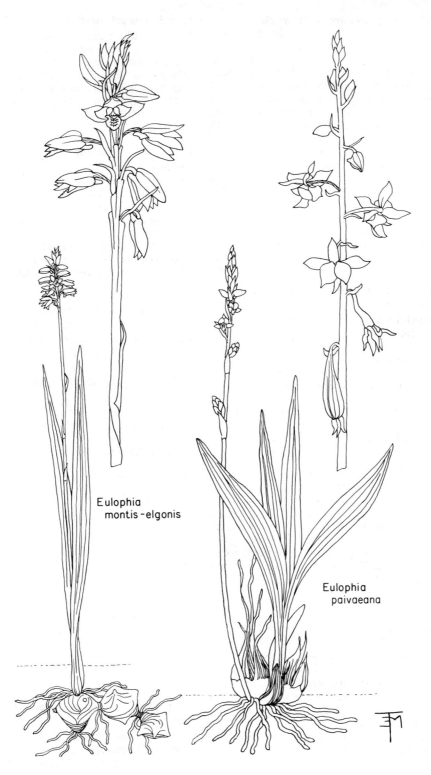

Eulophia
montis-elgonis

Eulophia
paivaeana

22 Papillae on lip deep red or brownish
                                    20. *E. zeyheri*
    Papillae on lip yellow or orange
                                    21. *E. subulata*
23 Petals white   22. *E. stachyodes*
    Petals greenish, yellowish or brownish   24
24 Sepals and petals greenish, lip mauve   25
    Sepals brown or brownish, petals yellow or
        yellow with brown overlay   26
25 Lip bearing numerous hairs 2–4 mm long
                                    23. *E. chlorotica*
    Lip with mauve papillae but no hairs
                                    24. *E. adenoglossa*
26 Petals less than 1 cm long   6. *E. parvula*
    Petals more than 1 cm long   27
27 Peduncle entirely covered with overlapping
        chaffy sheaths   25. *E. shupangae*
    Peduncle not covered with sheaths
                                    5. *E. pyrophila*

1. Eulophia orthoplectra (*Reichb. f.*) *Summerhayes* (see p. 773)

Rhizome subterranean, moniliform, leaves lanceolate, sometimes developed at time of flowering; inflorescence laxly flowered; sepals reflexed yellowish-brown; petals yellow on outer, red or veined in red on inner surface, larger than the sepals, lip yellowish with several keels, spur 11–19 mm.
Grassland, 3500–7000 ft. HE, HT, KIT, MUM, KIS, KAJ.
Verdcourt 1697.

2. Eulophia wakefieldii (*Reichb. f. & S. Moore*) *Summerhayes* (see p. 774)

Rhizome subterranean, moniliform, leaves developing after flowering; inflorescence to 1 m high, many flowered; sepals reflexed, small, green, petals orbicular, bright yellow, with reddish veins.
Grassland, seasonally wet, and on poor, rocky soil, 0–7000 ft. KIT, KIS, MAC. (Also common near the coast.)
Napier 2917; Napper 1594.

3. Eulophia petersii *Reichb. f.* (inc. *E. schimperana* A. Rich.) (see p. 774)

Rhizome subterranean, linking aerial pseudobulbs which are spindle-shaped and bear a group of thick, leathery leaves with serrate margins at the apex; inflorescence a panicle; sepals and petals greenish with brown markings, circinate, lip white tinged with pink.
Grassland and among rocks in dry localities, 0–6000 ft. HC, NAR, RV, MAC, KAJ.
Archer 490; Napper 1532.

4. Eulophia grantii (*Reichb. f.*) *Summerhayes*

Rhizome subterranean, leaves linear; inflorescence many flowered; sepals broadly elliptic, green, spotted with brown, petals smaller and narrower, pale yellow, lip yellow, suffused with purple and with 3 distinct keels on its middle lobe.
Uncommon, found in grassland, 3000–7000 ft. HE, KIT, MUM, KAJ.
Piers (1968).

5. Eulophia pyrophila (*Reichb. f.*) *Summerhayes* (see p. 777)

Rhizome subterranean, moniliform, leaves fleshy, absent at time of flowering; inflorescence simple; flowers small; sepals brown, as long as, or shorter than the elliptic or orbicular yellow petals, lip with basal spreading side lobes and a group of irregular calli in front of the spur opening.
Grassland, usually appearing after a burn, 3000–8200 ft. HT, HM, RV, KAJ.
Smart G12.

6. Eulophia parvula (*Rendle*) *Summerhayes*

Very similar to *E. pyrophila* but said to be smaller, and to have a short mauve column.
Summerhayes *Kew Bull.* (1957) p. 125–6.

7. Eulophia angolensis (*Lindl.*) *Reichb. f.* (see p. 778)

Rhizome subterranean, cylindrical, sometimes branched; leaves narrowly lanceolate; inflorescence laxly 4–20 flowered, to 1 m high; sepals reflexed, yellowish-brown, slightly longer than the much broader bright yellow petals, lip yellow with 3–5 lamellae and greyish purple markings.
Swampy ground, 0–7500 ft. HT, HA, KIT, KIS, MUM, NBI.
Gosnell 702; Williams and Parsons in EAH 12375.

8. Eulophia stenophylla *Summerhayes*

Herb with ovoid pseudobulbs at or above ground level, leaves well developed at time of flowering, usually less than 2 cm wide; flowers 2·5 cm or less in diameter, sepals green overlaid with brown, petals yellow, inner surface grey, lip yellow with purplish veins.
Usually in bush or among rocks with some shade, 2000–6000 ft. NAR, NBI.
Napier 384.

9. Eulophia paivaeana (*Reichb. f.*) *Summerhayes* (see p. 775)

Herb with ovoid pseudobulbs above the ground, leaves well developed at time of flowering; inflorescence a raceme; sepals greenish heavily overlaid

Eulophia quartiniana

Eulophia
pyrophila

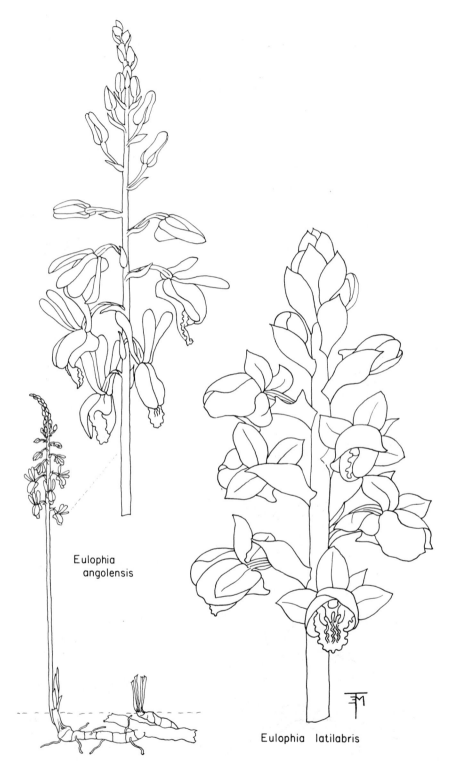

Eulophia
angolensis

Eulophia latilabris

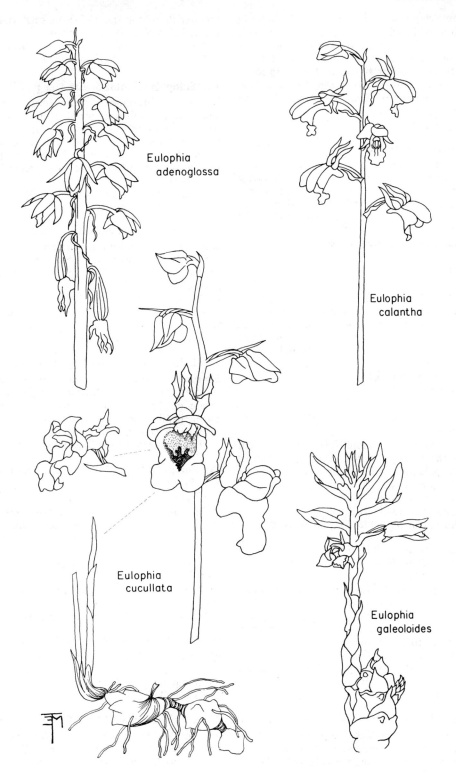

Eulophia
adenoglossa

Eulophia
calantha

Eulophia
cucullata

Eulophia
galeoloides

with brownish-purple, reflexed; petals yellow, lip pale yellow with side lobes heavily streaked with purple, central lobe with reflexed sides and bright yellow lamellae in the centre; spur 1·5 mm long.

Forests, bush and grassland, often among rocks, 4000–7000 ft. Our plants belong to subspecies *borealis* Summerhayes. HE, HM, HA, KIT, KIS, NAR, NBI, KAJ.

Kerfoot 2990.

10. Eulophia quartiniana *A. Rich.* (See p. 777)

Rhizome at soil level connecting aerial pseudo-bulbs which are ovoid, dark green, and bear a tuft of lanceolate leaves which develop after the flowers; sepals and petals brownish-mauve, similar, re-flexed, lip obovate or orbicular, pale mauve with darker veins.

Among lightly shaded rocks, 5000–7000 ft. HE, KIT, KIS.

Tweedie 1.

11. Eulophia cristata *(Sw.) Steud.*

Rhizome subterranean, moniliform, leaves not present at time of flowering or just developing; inflorescence many flowered; sepals and petals pale mauve, lip deep mauve with several rows of crests on the middle lobe.

Grassland, 5500 ft. KIT.

Brodhurst-Hill 723.

12. Eulophia livingstoniana *(Reichb. f.) Schltr.* (see p. 781)

Rhizome subterranean, moniliform, leaves appearing after the many flowered inflorescence; sepals and petals pale lilac, reflexed, lip and column deep mauve, lip 3-lobed, middle lobe with raised central keels and reflexed sides.

Grassland, 0–7000 ft. HE, KIT.

Brodhurst-Hill 699; Bickford in Bally B 5727.

13. Eulophia horsfallii *(Batem.) Summerhayes* (inc. *E. porphyroglossa* (Reichb. f.) Bolus) (see p. 773)

Rhizome subterranean, rhizomatous; leaves plicate to 1 m tall and 15 cm wide; peduncle 1–3 m, flowers large; sepals reflexed, bronze-purple, petals longer than broad, mauve, often white on inner surface, lip distinctly 3-lobed with several rows of tall lamellae on the middle lobe.

Robust orchid of swamps and at river edges, 0–8000 ft. HE, HL, HA, HK, KIT, KIS.

Gillett 18055; Symes 525.

14. Eulophia latilabris *Summerhayes* (see p. 778)

Rhizome subterranean; leaves large to 60 cm long, 15 cm wide, plicate; peduncle to 2 m high; sepals dark mauve, reflexed, petals mauve orbicular, or broader than long and hiding the small indistinctly 3-lobed lip which bears 3–5 keels.

Swampy grassland, 4500–6500 ft. KIT.

Tweedie (1964); FWTA (1968).

15. Eulophia calantha *Schltr.* (see p. 779)

Rhizome subterranean, moniliform; leaves thin and plicate; inflorescence 4–12-flowered; sepals narrow, reflexed, pink and green; petals longer than and more than twice as wide as sepals, white or pale pink, lip deep pink 3-lobed, with several low keels on mid lobe, side lobes greenish yellow, spur short.

Seasonally moist grassland. KIT, MUM.

FWTA (1968) for Kenya.

16. Eulophia cucullata *(Sw.) Steud.* (see p. 779)

Rhizome subterranean, moniliform, leaves appearing after the flowers; inflorescence 3–8-flowered; sepals greyish-mauve, reflexed, petals bright pink-mauve, very broad, lip broad with two quadrate calli in the centre near the base.

Grassland, 0–7000 ft. HE, HT, KIT, MUM, KIS, KAJ.

Symes 60; Bally B 6196.

17. Eulophia galeoloides *Kraenzl.* (see p. 779)

Saprophyte with brown scales on a paler stem; inflorescence up to 5-flowered; sepals and petals cream or pale yellow, lip 3-lobed with numerous purple papillae on the middle lobe.

Tropical forest, 5500 ft. MUM.

Tweedie (1964); FWTA (1968).

18. Eulophia montis-elgonis *Summerhayes* (see p. 775)

Rhizome subterranean; leaves plicate, 2–5 cm broad, appearing with the many-flowered inflorescence; flowers not opening fully, pinky-mauve, sometimes rather pale; sepals longer and wider than petals, lip darker mauve, often with a white edge and bearing numerous coarse hairs on the centre lobe.

Grassland, among rocks and in damp areas, 6000–7000 ft. HE, KIT.

Barnley in EAH 12364; Tweedie 91.

19. Eulophia warneckeana *Kraenzl.* (see p. 781)

Rhizome subterranean, leaves and peduncle slender to 45 cm high; flowers pale yellow, crests on the lip a deeper yellow, middle lobe hairy.

FWTA (1968) for Kenya.

20. Eulophia zeyheri *Hook. f.* (see p. 781)

Rhizome subterranean, moniliform, leaves partly developed at flowering time; scape 30–90 cm high bearing flowers in a dense cluster at its apex; sepals

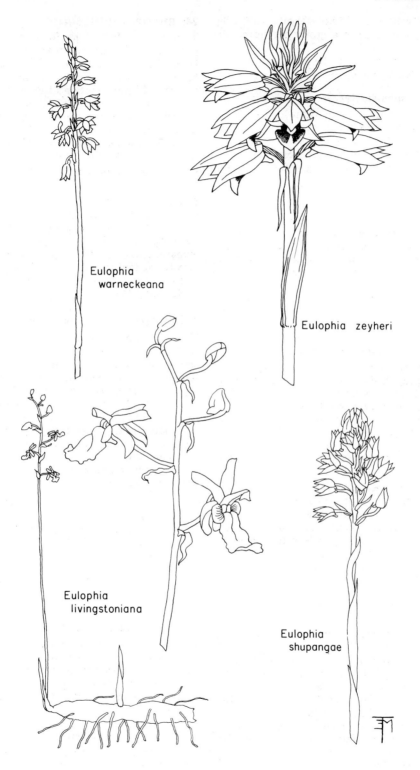

Eulophia
warneckeana

Eulophia zeyheri

Eulophia
livingstoniana

Eulophia
shupangae

and petals pale yellow, lip yellow with deep reddish-purple papillae in a group on the middle lobe.

Grassland, 6000–7000 ft. HE, KIT, MUM.
Webster in EAH 9676.

21. Eulophia subulata *Rendle*

Rhizome subterranean, moniliform, leaves partly developed at flowering time; scape 30–45 cm high bearing 5–12 flowers; sepals and petals pale yellow, lip brighter yellow sometimes orange.

Grassland, often appearing after a burn, 4000–6000 ft. KIS.
Napier 2914B.

22. Eulophia stachyodes *Reichb. f.*

Rhizome subterranean, leaves present at time of flowering, up to 6 cm wide; inflorescence many flowered; sepals dark purplish-brown; petals white, lip brownish-purple with white margin and white on lower surface.

Highland grassland and scrub, 5500–7000 ft MUM.
Carroll H 31.

23. Eulophia chlorotica *Kraenzl.* (see p. 774)

Leaves narrow and plicate to 1 m high, inflorescence slightly taller, many-flowered; sepals and paired petals green with brown veins, lip pinkish-mauve with copious hairs on the middle lobe.

In damp grassland, 5000–6500 ft. KIT, MUM.
Carroll in Bally 11919; Tweedie 131.

24. Eulophia adenoglossa *(Lindl.) Reichb. f.* (see p. 779)

Rhizome subterranean, moniliform, leaves absent or developing at time of flowering; inflorescence simple, lax 30–80 cm high; sepals yellow-green or olive-green, slightly longer than the paler and narrower petals, lip pale purple with nerves and distal crest papillae dark purple.

Grassland, 4000–5000 ft. KIT.
FWTA (1968) for Kenya.

25. Eulophia shupangae *(Reichb. f.) Kraenzl.* (see p. 781)

Rhizome subterranean, moniliform, leaves partly of fully developed at flowering; peduncle covered with chaffy overlapping bracts, flowers close together; sepals slightly larger than petals, both basically yellow and overlaid with maroon and brown coloration, lip brownish, 3-lobed with 2 basal lamellae in the lower half and numerous papillae or hairs on the middle lobe.

Grassland, 5000–7000 ft. HE, HT, HM, KIS, MUM.
Harvey 198; Carroll 130.

24. EULOPHIDIUM *Pfitzer*

Terrestrial herbs of the forest floor with aerial pseudobulbs bearing one or two petiolate, leathery leaves; inflorescence a lax spike, arising from the base of the pseudobulbs bearing numerous resupinate flowers; petals often shorter than the sepals, lip distinctly 4-lobed, or 3-lobed with a clearly retuse middle lobe, with a distinct spur; column thick, pollinia 2, ovoid, stipes very short or absent, viscidium semi-orbicular or oblong.

Eulophidium saundersianum *(Reichb. f.) Summerhayes*

Pseudobulbs narrowly conical to 20 cm high bearing 2 petiolate dark green leaves which become disarticulated some distance above the pseudobulbs; inflorescence to 1 m high bearing numerous large yellowish-green flowers which are heavily overlaid with dark purplish-black.

By rivers in warm forests, 5000–6000 ft. HK.
Stewart 1449.

25. PTEROGLOSSASPIS *Reichb. f.*

Terrestrial herbs with underground stem composed of fleshy tubers; leaves 1 or 2 on a very short aerial stem, surrounded by sheaths at the base, narrowly lanceolate, long petiolate, plicate; scape arising separately and covered with overlapping, chaffy bracts, 30–90 cm tall bearing a number of flowers in a short terminal raceme; bracts long and slender, overtopping the flowers; flowers resupinate, perianth parts all rather similar but lip shorter, 3-lobed in lower part, spur absent; column without a foot, pollinia attached to the transversely rhomboid viscidium by a stipes.

1   Flowers white, sometimes tinged with mauve, lip with dark maroon spot   2
    Flowers maroon or purplish, lip deeper in colour   *1. P. eustachya*
2   Lip velvety-hairy, 3–5-nerved   *2. P. englerana*
    Lip verrucose, but not hairy, nerves indistinct   *3. P. ruwenzoriensis*

1. Pteroglossaspis eustachya *Reichb. f.*

Herb with 2–3 narrow plicate leaves on a separate growth from flowering scape; flowers deep purple in a dense terminal cluster, shorter than pale straw-coloured bracts.

Wet grassland, 5000–6000 ft. HE, KIT, MUM.
Brodhurst-Hill 306.

2. Pteroglossaspis englerana *Kraenzl.*

Herb with 2–3 narrow, plicate leaves; flowering scape 30–45 cm; flowers white with a dark maroon spot on the lip, lip bearing 3-5 elevated tuberculate veins, and a pair of calli at the base.

Wet grassland, 6000 ft. KIS.

Bally B6208.

3. Pteroglossaspis ruwenzoriensis *Rolfe*

Herb with 2-3 narrow plicate leaves; flowering scape 30-90 cm; flowers white or tinged with mauve with maroon blotch on lip, lip only slightly verrucose with a pair of calli in the throat.

Grassland, seasonally wet and in rocky places, 5000-7600 ft. HE, HT, HM, HA, KIT, MUM, KIS, RV, NBI.

Parsons in EAH 12319; Smart G14.

26. ANGRAECUM *Bory*

Epiphytic, leafy herbs, stemless with a tuft of closely set leaves, or with an elongated stem a few-100 cm long bearing sessile, alternate leaves; inflorescences axillary with single flowers or few- to many-flowered racemes; flowers white, green or yellowish-green; sepals and petals very similar to each other in shape and size but the lip different, sometimes markedly so, and usually distinctly concave, produced at the base into a spur; column broad, the apex and the rostellum divided deeply into two broad, rounded, ± quadrate lobes.

1 Plant stemless or almost so, with a tuft of 3-8 linear-lanceolate leaves up to 2·5 cm long; inflorescence slender, bearing 3-15 flowers   2
   Plant with erect, pendulous or horizontal stem bearing alternate leaves; inflorescence axillary, flowers solitary or in a raceme   4
2 Flowers white, ± secund on the raceme
                                      1. *A. chamaeanthus*
   Flowers green or yellowish-green, not secund
                                                      3
3 Flowers 1-6, green; ovary curved and twisted round the short, thick spur
                          2. *A. sacciferum*
   Flowers 5-15, green or yellowish-green; spur carried parallel to ovary   3. *A. decipiens*
4 Stem less than 15 cm long; flowers 3-7   5
   Stem more than 15 cm long; flowers single or (rarely) in pairs   7
5 Leaves very thickened and flattened, almost triangular in cross section, apex pointed, the upper surface restricted to a narrow groove   6. *A. humile*
   Leaves rigid, linear-lanceolate and distinctly bilobed at apex   6
6 Labellum orbicular and terminating in a distinct acumen 4-6 mm long; plant of Kakamega district   4. *A. firthii*

Labellum boat-shaped, without an acumen; plant found above 7000 ft
                                  5. *A. montanum*
7 Labellum orbicular or ovate, sometimes with a small acumen at its apex   8
   Labellum similar in shape to sepals and petals
                                  7. *A. erectum*
8 Leaves more than 5 cm long and 2 cm wide; perianth parts more than 5 cm long
                                  8. *A. infundibulare*
   Leaves up to 5 cm long and less than 1 cm wide; perianth parts less than 4 cm long
                                  9. *A. conchiferum*

1. Angraecum chamaeanthus *Schltr.*

Very small epiphyte with 3-4 lanceolate leaves to 1·5 cm long, 4-5·5 mm wide; raceme erect, secund, bearing 10-15 white flowers each barely 2 mm in diameter.

Only recorded in Kenya from Kikuyu forest, c. 7000-8000 ft. HA.

Smart E27.

2. Angraecum sacciferum *Lindl.* (see p. 784)

Small plant with stem to 3 cm long or absent, bearing a tuft of narrow, ligulate leaves, 2-4 cm x 2·5-5 mm; inflorescence slender, erect, with 1-6 green flowers each 5 mm in diameter and of thin texture.

Widely distributed in shady forests, 5000-8000 ft. HE, HM, HA, HK, KIT, MUM, NBI.

Williams 618; Irwin 178.

3. Angraecum decipiens *Summerh.*

Very small stemless plant bearing 4-8 curved linear-lanceolate leaves, 1·5-3·5 cm long, 2·5-3·5 mm; inflorescence to 5 cm long bearing 5-15 yellowish-green flowers each 4 mm in diameter.

Forest, in deep shade, usually growing on thin branches and twigs, 5000-7000 ft. HA, NBI.

Powis EAH348/62.

4. Angraecum firthii *Summerhayes*

Flexuose stems to 15 cm long bearing alternate ligulate leaves 5-11 cm long and 1-3 cm wide with unequally bilobed tips; inflorescence as long as, or longer than the leaves, bearing 3-7 yellowish-green flowers each 3-4 cm in diameter.

Warm forest, 4500-5000 ft. MUM.

Stewart 1483.

5. Angraecum montanum *Piers*

Small epiphyte with short stems to 10 cm long bearing closely set linear-lanceolate leaves 3-3·5 cm long with unequally bilobed tip; inflorescence to 3 cm long bearing 5-7 yellowish flowers each 1 cm in diameter.

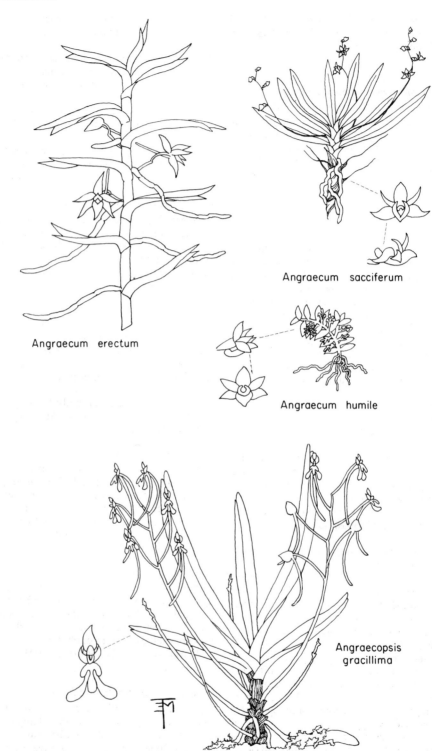

Angraecum erectum

Angraecum sacciferum

Angraecum humile

Angraecopsis gracillima

On bushes and small trees with its roots amongst moss and lichens, above 7000 ft. HC, HA, HK, KAJ.

Stewart 827, 1010.

6. Angraecum humile *Summerhayes* (see p. 784)

Most distinctive small plant with stems usually less than 5 cm long, bearing closely set, thickened leaves flattened all in one plane; inflorescence minute, axillary to 7 mm long and bearing 2–4 greenish-white flowers each 2·5–4 mm in diameter.

On mossy twigs in forests, usually near streams, 5500–7500 ft. HC, HA, MUM, KIS, MAC.

Carroll 413; Stewart 1197.

7. Angraecum erectum *Summerhayes* (see p. 784)

Epiphyte with erect stems 10–100 cm long bearing rigid lanceolate leaves 2–8 cm long and 4–10 mm wide; flowers borne singly, rarely 2 in one leaf axil, usually white or with salmon pink tints, 2–3 cm in diameter.

A very common species in the drier forests of Kenya, often rooting at the base of shrubs or trees and ascending stiffly through the host, 4000–6000 ft. HE, HC, HT, HM, HA, HK, KIS, NAR, RV, NAN, MAC, NBI.

Polhill 216; Bally 7532.

8. Angraecum infundibulare *Lindl.*

Erect or pendent stems to 60 cm long, somewhat flattened and bearing 2 rows of alternate, elliptic leaves 5–10 cm long and 2–5 cm wide, unequally bilobed at the apex; inflorescences arising opposite a leaf bearing a large single flower; sepals and petals green, lip white, spur S-shaped, broad at the mouth.

Rain-forest, *c.* 4000 ft. MUM.

Evans 31.

9. Angraecum conchiferum *Lindl.*

Erect stems to 25 cm bearing alternate linear-ligulate leaves, 4 cm long and up to 6 mm wide with slightly unequally lobed tips; inflorescence axillary, 1–2 flowered; sepals and petals yellowish or greenish, lip white, orbicular and with an acumen to 5 mm long at its tip.

Forests, 7000–7500 ft. HA, HK, MAC, KAJ.

Archer 501; Archer 549.

27. MICROCOELIA *Lindley*

Leafless epiphytes with a short woody stem, plant mainly composed of a tangled mass of silvery-grey roots; inflorescences usually many, simple racemes bearing small white flowers which are variously tinted with pink or green; column short and stout, androclinium usually sloping, 2 pollinia with a common stipes and a single viscidium.

1 Lip of flower over 5 mm long, much narrowed at the base   1. *M. koehleri*
   Lip of flower less than 3·5 mm long, only slightly or not at all narrowed at the base 2
2 Roots very fine, less than 1 mm in diameter
                                        2. *M. smithii*
   Roots fine, 1–3 mm in diameter
                                       3. *M. guyoniana*

1. Microcoelia koehleri *(Schltr.) Summerhayes* (inc. *M. pachystemma* Summerhayes) (see p. 786)

Attached roots often somewhat flattened on the substrate; flowers relatively large with a bright yellow anther cap, spur longer than the lip.

Bush and forest, 5000–5500 ft. MUM, KIS.

Tweedie 138.

2. Microcoelia smithii *(Rolfe) Summerhayes*

Minute plants with very thin roots; flowers white, spur about the same length as the lip and often tinged with green or pink at its tip, perianth parts rather narrow.

Dry forest and bush, 1000–6000 ft. NBI. Also occurs in coastal forests.

Stewart, in cultivation.

3. Microcoelia guyoniana *(Reichb. f.) Summerhayes* (see p. 786)

Small to robust plants with thicker roots and larger flowers than the above; perianth parts wider, anther cap yellow or brown, apical part of conical spur yellowish, greenish or brownish.

Dry forest and bush, 5000–6500 ft. KIT, MUM, KIS, NAR, BAR, RV, NBI.

Verdcourt 408; Archer 652.

28. DIAPHANANTHE *Schltr.*

Epiphytic herbs with woody stems bearing thin or thickened leaves either apically in tufts or evenly spaced throughout their length, leaves very unequally bilobed at the tip; inflorescences usually plentiful, below the apical tuft or spaced out along the stem, flowers usually whitish-green, yellow or yellowish-green and easily recognizable by their semi-transparent, diaphanous substance; sepals and petals similar, spreading, the lip broader than long, frequently with a small tooth at the base in the mouth of the spur.

1 Leaves curved and thickened, leathery or fleshy and more than 10 cm long, hanging down on either side of the horizontally held woody stem   2
   Leaves thin and straight or if thickened less than 10 cm long, variously held on a long or short stem   3

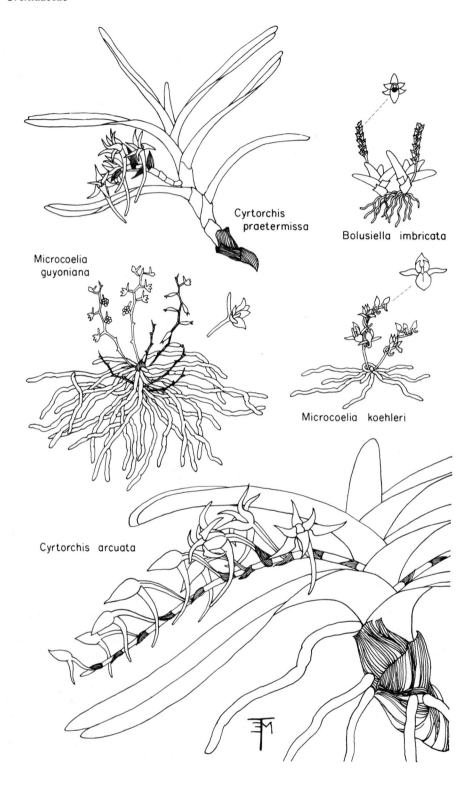

Cyrtorchis
praetermissa

Bolusiella   imbricata

Microcoelia
guyoniana

Microcoelia   koehleri

Cyrtorchis   arcuata

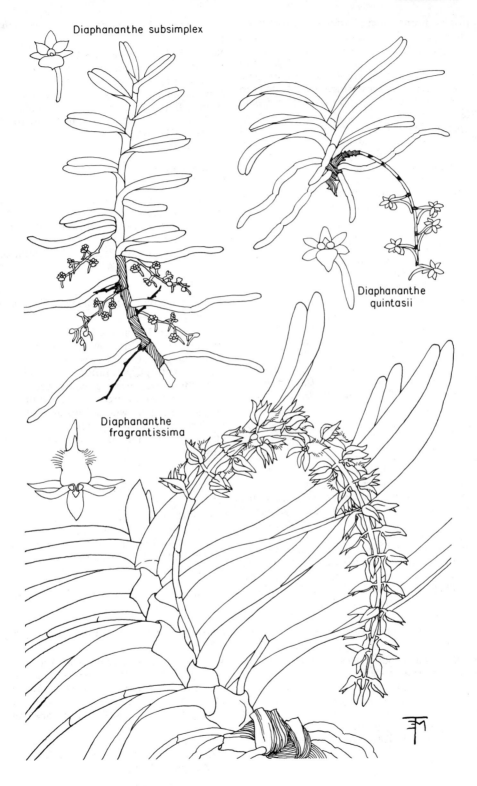

Diaphananthe subsimplex

Diaphananthe
quintasii

Diaphananthe
fragrantissima

2   Flowers borne singly, arranged spirally on
      pendent inflorescences which may be
      longer or shorter than the leaves
                                  1. *D. lorifolia*
      Flowers arranged in groups of 2-4 on pen-
      dent inflorescences which usually exceed
      leaves in length   2. *D. fragrantissima*
3   Stems woody but short, aerial roots mostly
      protruding below the apical tuft of leaves **4**
      Stems woody and usually more than 15 cm
      long, with aerial roots spaced out among
      leaves along the stem   **5**
4   Flowers pale yellowish green, 10-15 mm in
      diameter; lip sub-orbicular; spur as long as
      or slightly longer than the lip
                                       4. *D. pulchella*
      Flowers usually green, 6-7 mm in diameter;
      lip spade-shaped and pointed; spur 2-3
      times the length of the lip   3. *D. quintasii*
5   Leaves all green   **6**
      Leaves with purplish coloration, at least on
      lower surface   5. *D. rutila*
6   Flowers greenish-yellow; lip with a small
      upright tooth in the mouth of the spur   **7**
      Flowers yellow; lip smooth, without a tooth
      in the mouth of the spur
                                  6. *D. xanthopollinia*
7   Spur less than 1 cm long   7. *D. subsimplex*
      Spur more than 2 cm long   8. *D. tenuicalcar*

1. Diaphananthe lorifolia *Summerhayes* (see
p. 789)

Woody stems pendulous, becoming horizontal and
bearing two rows of leathery pale green or
yellowish leaves which are strap-shaped, curved,
and hang downwards, frequently with their tips
touching; inflorescence pendulous, usually shorter
than the leaves and laxly 10-16-flowered; flowers
pinkish or yellowish-white with the lip broader
than long and the spur slightly longer than the lip.

Epiphyte on trees at forest edges and on small
groups of trees near rivers and swamps,
5500-7000 ft. HE, HC, HM, KIT, MUM, KIS.

Williams 617; Gardner 3625 (Type).

2. Diaphananthe fragrantissima (*Reichb. f.*)
Schltr. (see p. 787)

Stems thick and woody, often branched so that
several plants grow together in a clump; leaves
thick, curved, 20-30 cm long and 2-3 cm wide;
2-4 inflorescences often arising together from the
leafless stem or from leaf axils, up to 35 cm long;
flowers greenish-white, lip fimbriate.

Epiphyte of tall forest trees, 3500-5500 ft.
MUM, KIS.

Tweedie 1964.

3. Diaphananthe quintasii (*Rolfe*) *Schltr.* (see
p. 787)

Stems short and covered with old leaf bases, leaves
at apex up to 8 cm long, 15 mm wide; inflorescences longer than the leaves, 8-12-flowered;
flowers small, darker green than any other species
of the genus and not always diaphanous.

Epiphyte of rather dry highland forests, over
8000 ft. HE, HC, HM, HA.

Stewart 1314.

4. Diaphananthe pulchella *Summerhayes* (see
p. 800)

Similar to the above but the flowers much larger
and the inflorescences very freely produced, often
6-8 at each flowering; flowers much larger and
always semi-transparent.

Epiphyte of dry forests of medium altitudes,
4500-7000 ft. HE, HA, MAC.

Tweedie 2603.

5. Diaphananthe rutila (*Reichb. f.*) *Summerhayes*
(see p. 789)

Stems rather thin at the base and often insecurely
attached to host tree by small aerial roots, larger
roots hanging free; leaves rather leathery and
suffused with purple; inflorescences usually longer
than the leaves bearing many densely arranged
flowers of a dingy greenish-mauve; lip wider than
long and the spur twice as long as the lip.

Very widely distributed in forested areas,
300-7000 ft. HM, HA, HK, MUM, KIS, MAC,
NBI.

Williams s.n.; Ivens 602.

6. Diaphananthe xanthopollinia (*Reichb. f.*)
Summerhayes

Rather similar to the above but differing in its
distribution and also by the usually longer and
narrower leaves and longer inflorescences; flowers
yellow with a bright yellow anther cap, lip much
broader than long and obscurely 3-lobed at its
apex.

Riverine forest, 3500-5500 ft. KIS, MUM.

Piers (1968).

7. Diaphananthe subsimplex *Summerhayes* (see
p. 787)

A straggling and untidy plant with long aerial roots
entangled among the many branching, pendent
stems; inflorescences as long as or shorter than the
leaves, 5-13-flowered; flowers semi-transparent,
the lip ± quadrate, wider at the apex than at the
base.

Common in forests at higher altitudes,
5500-8800 ft. HE, HM, HA, HK, KAJ.

Moreau 578 (type); Smart E4.

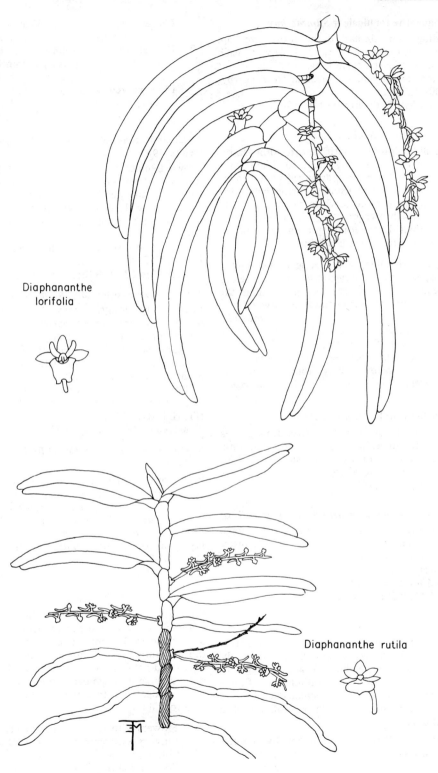

Diaphananthe
lorifolia

Diaphananthe rutila

8. Diaphananthe tenuicalcar *Summerhayes*

A straggling plant similar to the above two spp. but inflorescences with only 3-4 flowers each having a spur at least 2·5 cm long.

Montane forests and on savanna trees nearby, 7000-8000 ft. HT.

Hooker's Icones Plantarum tab. 3567.

29. BOLUSIELLA *Schltr.*

Very small epiphytes with short, thin roots; stemless, or with a woody stem to 5 cm long; leaves fleshy, 1-4 cm long, arranged in the shape of a fan; inflorescences usually arising below the leaves, with many minute white flowers partially hidden by dark brown bracts, pedicels very short; sepals less than 4 mm long, spur shorter than or equal to limb of lip which is 3-lobed.

1 Leaves with a deep V-shaped groove along the upper surface, very fleshy, often slightly recurved; inflorescences longer than the leaves, bracts shorter than the flowers
                              1. *B. iridifolia*
Leaves not grooved along the upper surface or margin, fleshy, flattened in a vertical plane; inflorescences longer than the leaves, bracts usually longer than the flowers   2. *B. imbricata*

1. Bolusiella iridifolia (*Rolfe*) *Schltr.*

Minute plant of cool, exposed situations; leaves only 1·5-4 cm long; inflorescences to 6 cm long.

Usually epiphytic on twigs and small branches, 5300-8000 ft. HC, HA, KAJ.

Archer 69; Bally 1103.

2. Bolusiella imbricata (*Rolfe*) *Schltr.* (see p. 786)

Minute epiphyte of warm and humid situations; leaves 1-3·5 cm long, rather fleshy with convex surfaces; inflorescences to 7 cm long, densely many-flowered.

Below 6000 ft. HA, MUM, KIS.

Smart E11; Williams 615.

30. CHAMAEANGIS *Schltr.*

Robust epiphytes with rather succulent leaves borne alternately in two rows on elongated woody stems; flowers small, yellow, orange, or green, borne in pairs or whorls on rather lax inflorescences; sepals and petals very small and thick in texture, lip also small but with a relatively long spur at its base.

1 Leaves flat, ligulate, with unequally bilobed tips, somewhat leathery but not fleshy
                              1. *C. odoratissima*

Leaves very fleshy, often V-shaped in section, ± linear with acute apices, often curved   2
2 Flowers orange or salmon pink; spurs slender 15-20 mm long usually pointing upwards
                              2. *C. orientalis*
Flowers yellow or green; spurs 4·5-10 mm long, swollen and almost bulbous at the tip
                              3. *C. vesicata*

1. Chamaeangis odoratissima (*Reichb. f.*) *Schltr.* (see p. 798)

Leaves ligulate, up to 15 cm long and 2·5 cm wide, well-spaced on the pendent woody stems; inflorescences usually pendulous below the leaves, bearing small yellow flowers in whorls of 3-6; spurs 7-12 mm long, not, or only slightly swollen in the apical half.

Usually on trunks of forest trees, 4600-7300 ft. HE, KIT, MUM, KIS.

Carroll in CM 11920; Saunders 6.

2. Chamaeangis orientalis *Summerhayes* (see p. 791)

Leaves very fleshy, usually pendulous from the woody stem and curved inwards so that their tips touch, often dull brownish-green; inflorescences upright bearing salmon-pink or orange flowers in whorls of 2-4 which are held so that the spurs point upwards.

Epiphyte of dry forests on mountains and on trees just below the forest belt, 4500-7500 ft. HE, HT, HM, HK, KAJ.

Moreau 676; Stewart 1437.

3. Chamaeangis vesicata (*Lindl.*) *Schltr.* (see p. 791)

Plant very similar to *C. orientalis*; leaves less curved but often rather shrivelled and droopy; inflorescences usually in same plane as leaves, with yellowish-green flowers in whorls of 1-3.

Growing on small trees in bush or the drier types of forest, 5000-6500 ft. HK, KIS, NAR, MAC, NBI.

Ivens 605; Smart E25.

31. AERANGIS *Reichb. f.*

Epiphytic herbs with tough, leathery green leaves borne alternately on a short woody stem; inflorescences racemose, one or more axillary or below the lowermost leaves; flowers white, conspicuous, sepals and petals similar, lip usually wider and with a tubular spur dependent from its base; column often elongated with a conspicuous slender, elongated rostellum.

1 Flowers with spurs less than 10 cm long   2
  Flowers with spurs more than 10 cm long   4
2 Column white   3
  Column red or yellow   1. *A. rhodosticta*

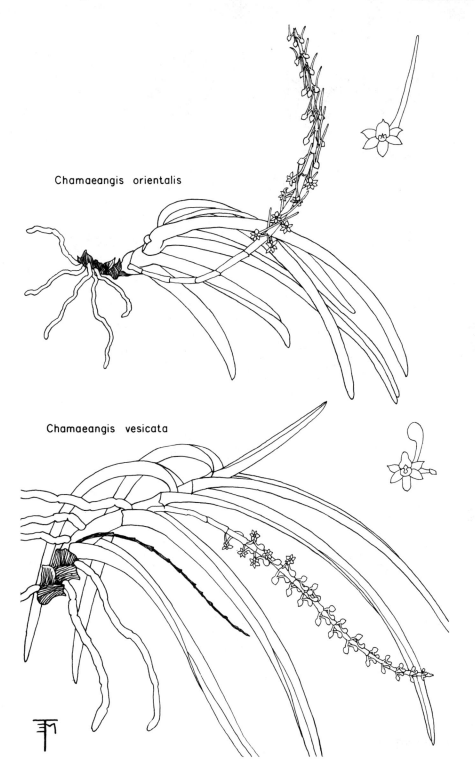

Chamaeangis orientalis

Chamaeangis vesicata

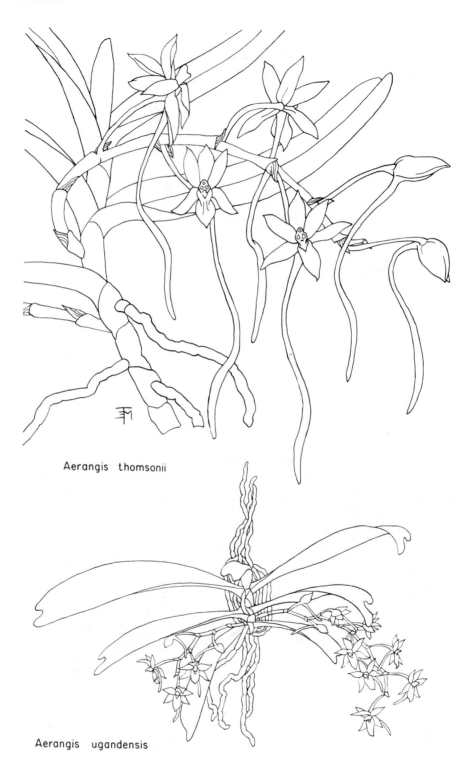

Aerangis thomsonii

Aerangis ugandensis

3 Leaves fleshy or leathery with no clearly
defined midrib and usually rather curved;
flowers with spurs less than 3 cm long
                                    2. *A. ugandensis*
Leaves thick and leathery with distinct midrib, wider in the upper half and unequally
bilobed at the tip; spurs 4–6 cm long
                                    4. *A. brachycarpa*

4 Perianth parts all narrow and gradually
pointed, strongly reflexed within a few
days of opening   5
Perianth parts, at least the lip, distinctly
rounded or suddenly pointed at the tip,
the lip broader than the other parts   6

5 Woody stem usually less than 15 cm; leaves
wider in the upper half, tip unequally
bilobed and rounded   3. *A. flabellifolia*
Woody stem usually more than 15 cm long;
leaves ± parallel-sided, tip unequally
bilobed and rounded   5. *A. thomsonii*

6 Leaves with wavy margins, slightly wider
towards the tip than at the base; spurs
10–20 cm long, only slightly twisted or
curved   7
Leaves with wavy margins, at least twice as
wide at the tip as at the base; spurs 20–25
cm long, slightly thickened and with a
distinct corkscrew twist in the lower half
                                    7. *A. kotschyana*

7 Leaves deep green; usually flowering March–
May; spurs 15–20 cm long   6. *A. coriacea*
Leaves grey green; usually flowering Septem-
ber–October; spurs 10–15 cm long
                                    8. *A. verdickii*

1. Aerangis rhodosticta (*Kraenzl.*) *Schltr.* (see
p. 797)
Small almost stemless plant with 6–12 thick green
leaves up to 12 cm long, usually less than 1 cm
wide; inflorescence with 4–20 creamy white
flowers, rather flat and up to 3 cm in diameter with
a bright red or occasionally yellow column at the
centre.
   Plant restricted to shady position, usually near
water, in warm moist localities, usually attached to
branches and twigs of shrubs, 4500–7000 ft. HE,
HK, HN, MUM, KIS, NAR, EMB, MAC.
   Archer 307; Lucas 112; van Someren 8606.

2. Aerangis ugandensis *Summerhayes* (see p. 792)
Stem woody, 20–25 cm long, bearing 4–10 leaves
which usually lack midribs; racemes pendulous,
bearing 10–15 white flowers usually less than 2 cm
in diameter.
   Plant of dense shade, usually on forest trees
near water, 4000–7000 ft. HE, KIT, MUM, KIS.
   Tweedie 2631; Stewart 991.

3. Aerangis flabellifolia *Reichb. f.*
Stem woody, usually short; leaves dark green,
borne close together in a fan; flowers 4–6 cm in
diameter and pale green in colour when first
opening, becoming white or with pink tinges and all
perianth parts reflexed after a few days; spurs
12–15 cm long.
   Found in bush and forest in dense shade,
usually rather near the ground, 5000–7500 ft. HA,
HK, RV, EMB, MAC, NBI.
   Kanure s.n.; Stewart 1188.

4. Aerangis brachycarpa (*A. Rich.*) *Reichb. f.* (see
p. 794)
Similar to the above except that the spurs are
always only 4–6 cm long, and only the petals are
reflexed.
   Found in rather dry highland forest and bush,
usually in deep shade, 5500–7500 ft. HM, HA,
HK, RV, MAC, NBI.
   Glover 2200; Smart E24.

5. Aerangis thomsonii (*Rolfe*) *Schltr.* (see p. 792)
Stem stout, woody, 15–60 cm long with very
thick aerial roots; leaves deep green, hard and
leathery; flowers pure white, 6–12 per raceme, all
perianth parts strongly reflexed, spur distinctly
thickened towards the tip.
   Common in highland forests, usually above
7000 ft on the trunks of tall trees. HE, HC, HT,
HM, HA, HK, KAJ.
   Lucas 79; Glover 1374.

6. Aerangis coriacea *Summerhayes*
Stem stout, woody, 10–40 cm long bearing
greyish-green or dark green leaves in which the
venation shows up as darker lines in a reticulate
pattern; flowers 6–22 per raceme usually tinged
with salmon-pink especially in the spur.
   Not common, found in warmer forests near
streams, 4500–7500 ft. HA, HK, HN, EMB.
   None in EAH.

7. Aerangis kotschyana (*Reichb. f.*) *Schltr.*
Stemless or with a very short woody stem bearing
a fan of 4–10 leaves; racemes with 10–20 con-
spicuous flowers each 5 cm in diam.
   In light shade, sometimes high in the tree
canopy, below 4000 ft. MUM, KIS, also in the
Shimba Hills.
   None in EAH.

8. Aerangis verdickii (*De Wild.*) *Schltr.*
Stemless or with a short woody stem bearing 2–6
dull greyish-green leaves with darker reticulate
venation, wider at the apex than near the base and

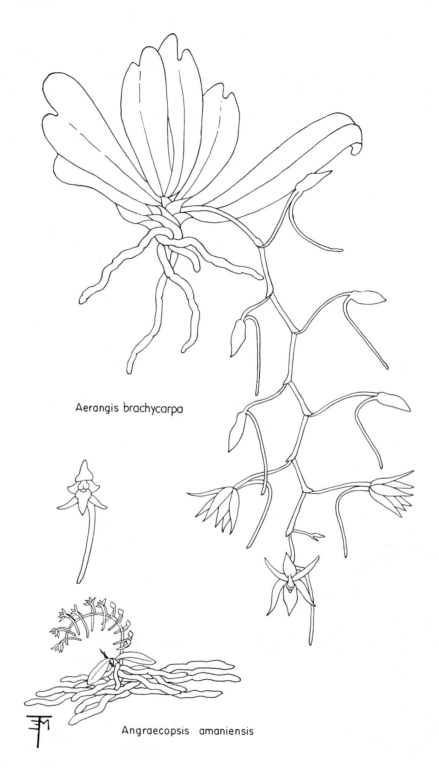

Aerangis brachycarpa

Angraecopsis amaniensis

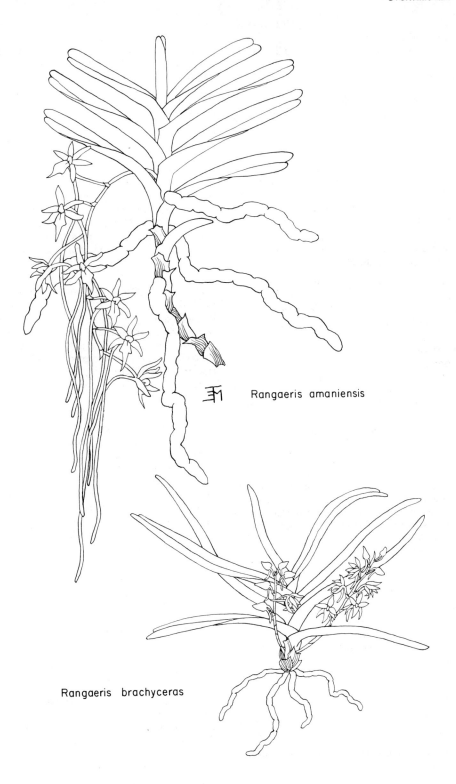

Rangaeris amaniensis

Rangaeris brachyceras

with undulate margins; inflorescence 4–10-flowered, flowers pure white or slightly greenish.

In light shade amongst bush and small trees in dry localities, below 5000 ft. MAC, KAJ.

Stewart 990.

32. RANGAERIS (*Schltr.*) *Summerhayes*

Epiphytic herbs with short or elongated woody stems and tough leathery green leaves which are bilobed at the tip; inflorescence a simple raceme, 2–15-flowered, usually several racemes produced at each flowering, arising below or among the lowermost leaves; flowers white or yellowish, the sepals and petals similar and joined at the base, the lip broader than the other petals, sometimes indistinctly lobed near the base, the spur straight and usually longer than the lip; column long or short, rostellum 2- or 3-lobed, viscidia one or two, pollinia with separate stipites.

1   Flowers white with spurs at least twice as
    long as the lip   2
    Flowers yellowish-white or green, spurs
    scarcely longer than the lip
                                   1. *R. brachyceras*
2   Lip broadly ovate, not lobed, spur 5–9 cm
    long   2. *R. muscicola*
    Lip lanceolate, with obscurely rounded or
    quadrate lobes in the lower part, spur 8–15
    cm long   3. *R. amaniensis*

1. Rangaeris brachyceras (*Summerhayes*) *Summerhayes* (see p. 795)

Small plants with or without a short woody stem bearing 2–6 pairs of linear-ligulate leaves; inflorescences as long as or longer than the leaves, with thin peduncles, bearing 6–15 yellow or greenish-white flowers which always appear partly closed.

Near rivers in warm forests, 5000–6000 ft. HE, HC, KIT, MUM, KIS.

Williams 586; Carroll 792.

2. Rangaeris muscicola (*Reichb. f.*) *Summerhayes* (see p. 797)

Small plants, usually without a woody stem, bearing 4–12 linear leaves, V-shaped in cross section, usually more than 10 cm long; inflorescence usually shorter than the leaves, bearing large ovate bracts and 5–15 white flowers.

Forests, 5000–7000 ft. HE, HM, HA, KIS, MUM, NBI.

van Someren 9205; Stewart 1226.

3. Rangaeris amaniensis (*Kraenzl.*) *Summerhayes* (see p. 795)

Stems elongated and often branched, bearing two rows of short leathery leaves near the tip and very

thick, robust roots; inflorescence usually longer than the leaves, bearing 5–12 flowers.

Dry forests, 4500–7000 ft. HK, HA, KIT, KIS, NAR, RV, NAN, MAC, NBI, KAJ.

Moreau 164; Hemming 1337.

33. YPSILOPUS *Summerhayes*

Epiphytic herbs with short pendent woody stems; leaves few, grass-like, very long and narrow, the lamina disarticulating at an oblique angle from the sheath; inflorescences simple and horizontal or erect, arising below the leaves, 2–8-flowered; flowers white, sepals and petals lanceolate, petals slightly smaller than the sepals, lip rhomboid-lanceolate, spur curved; column short, rostellum truncate, dilated at the apex and bearing a single reniform viscidium, stipes single in the lower two thirds and forked above into two divergent arms which each bear a pollinium.

Ypsilopus longifolia (*Kraenzl.*) *Summerhayes* (see p. 798)

Pendent epiphyte, leaves 5–23 cm long, 1·5–4 mm wide, arising from the short woody stem; flowers white 1·5 cm in diam., spur 4 cm long.

Widespread in dry forest, 4000–7600 ft. HM, HA, HK, NAN, NBI.

Copley 115; Smart in EAH 12785.

34. CYRTORCHIS *Schlechter*

Robust epiphytes with elongated woody stems, sometimes branched, usually upright; leaves leathery, or thickened and succulent, distichous, ligulate with unequally bilobed tips; inflorescences axillary, bearing few–many white flowers; bracts large, turning black; perianth parts lanceolate and recurved, spur somewhat widened towards the mouth, at least twice as long as the lip; column short, rostellum long and beak-like, bifid for two thirds of its length.

1   Leaves 1 cm wide or more   2
    Leaves less than 1 cm wide
                                   1. *C. praetermissa*
2   Flowers small, spur 2–3 cm long
                                   2. *C. brownii*
    Flowers large, spur (3–)4–6 cm long
                                   3. *C. arcuata*

1. Cyrtorchis praetermissa *Summerhayes* (see p. 786)

Upright plant with dark green linear leaves; inflorescences rather short and dense, bearing 5–15 small flowers with spurs 2–3 cm long.

Upper branches of shady trees near rivers, 4500–7000 ft. KIS, NAR, MAC.

Saunders 8; Coryndon K2.

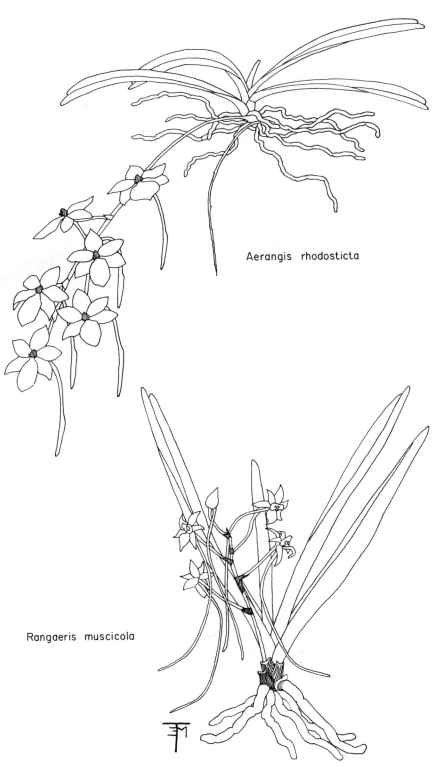

Aerangis rhodosticta

Rangaeris muscicola

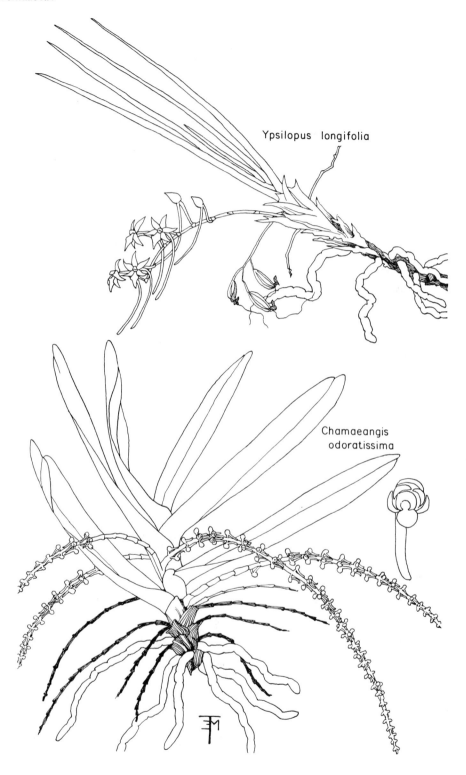

Ypsilopus longifolia

Chamaeangis
odoratissima

2. Cyrtorchis brownii (*Rolfe*) *Schltr.*

Small plant with thick succulent leaves; inflorescence short and dense with large bracts; flowers closely arranged, less than 2 cm in diam.

Riverside forest, 5600 ft. MUM, also in the Teita Hills.

Archer 383.

3. Cyrtorchis arcuata (*Lindl.*) *Schltr.* (see p. 786)

Large plant with green root tips; leaves rather leathery; flowers white 4–6 cm in diameter, scented at night.

Very common, usually found in rather open forest and bush, near rivers, and in dry places, 0–10 000 ft. All districts.

Symes 356; Williams 227.

35. TRICERATORHYNCHUS *Summerhayes*

Very small epiphyte with linear, curved leaves; inflorescences axillary bearing one to several green to yellow flowers; distinguished from small species of *Angraecum* by the trident-shaped rostellum, and the relatively large flowers for the size of the plant.

Triceratorhynchus viridiflorus *Summerhayes* (see p. 761)

Leaves 3–5, 1–5 cm long, 1–3·5 mm wide; inflorescences axillary, bearing 1–9 green to yellow flowers; flowers 1 cm in diameter with a curved spur 5–8 mm long.

Warm forests, *c.* 5000 ft. MUM.

Summerhayes, V.S.; *Harvard Bot. Mus.* (1951) 14, 234.

36. ANGRAECOPSIS *Kraenzl.*

Epiphytic herbs with short stems bearing 2–6 leaves which are frequently obliquely curved; inflorescences usually longer than the leaves with 4–many white or greenish flowers; flowers distinguished by the 3-lobed lip, the lateral sepals being longer than the dorsal and held in a forward position parallel to the lip, and by the small triangular petals which are strongly reflexed.

1   Leaves at least 4 cm, usually 7–20 cm long; spur more than 2 cm long   1. *A. gracillima*

     Leaves small, usually less than 2·5 cm long; spur less than 2 cm long   **2**

2   Spur not inflated towards the tip, 10–20 mm long   2. *A. amaniensis*

     Spur markedly inflated towards the tip, about 4·5 mm long   3. *A. breviloba*

1. Angraecopsis gracillima (*Rolfe*) *Summerhayes* (see p. 784)

Stem short, woody, bearing a tuft of dark green leaves; inflorescence of 4–8 orange-tinged white flowers.

In shady forests, 4000–6000 ft. HC, KIT, MUM, KIS.

Ivens 601; Smart E12.

2. Angraecopsis amaniensis *Summerhayes* (see p. 794)

A very small epiphyte with 2–4 leaves and a large mat of aerial roots; inflorescence pendent, to 8 cm long, with green flowers opening from the tip of the raceme first.

In shady forests, 5300–7000 ft. HE, KIT, MUM, NBI.

Stewart s.n. in cultivation.

3. Angraecopsis breviloba *Summerhayes*

A very small plant with few leaves and a mass of aerial roots; very similar to the preceding species and differing from it by the short bulbous spur.

Forest trees, usually in rather shady but not particularly humid places, 5000–7500 ft. HT, HM, MAC, NBI.

Stewart 989.

37. TRIDACTYLE *Schlechter*

Epiphytes with long straggling woody stems, often many together in an untidy clump; leaves linear or ligulate, unequally bilobed at the apex, often thick and fleshy; inflorescences very short or elongated; racemes bearing 1–many white, green, yellowish, or brownish flowers; sepals and petals oblong, ovate or lanceolate, often slightly recurved, the sepals longer than the petals, lip nearly always 3-lobed and with 2 additional auricles at its base on each side of the mouth of the spur, the side lobes often fimbriate at their tips, spur as long as or longer than the lip; column short and thick, viscidium small with a single rather long stipes sometimes forked in the upper half and bearing 2 pollinia, rostellum elongated.

1   Inflorescences of 2–4 flowers or flowers borne singly on main woody stem   **2**

     Inflorescences of axillary peduncles bearing 4–20 flowers   **5**

2   Lip entire, or with a very short tooth on each side of the central lobe

                 1. *T. anthomaniaca*

     Lip 3-lobed   **3**

3   Leaves terete or subulate   2. *T. tridentata*

     Leaves ligulate or linear   **4**

4   Leaves short and stiff; inflorescences very short, 1–3-flowered   3. *T. scottellii*

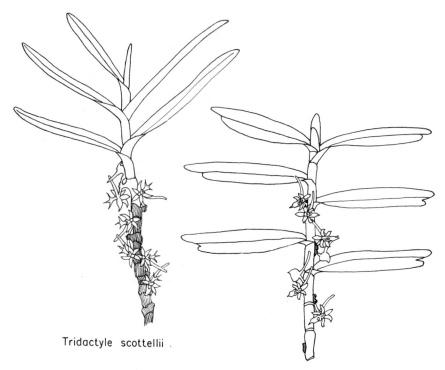

Tridactyle scottellii .

Tridactyle anthomaniaca

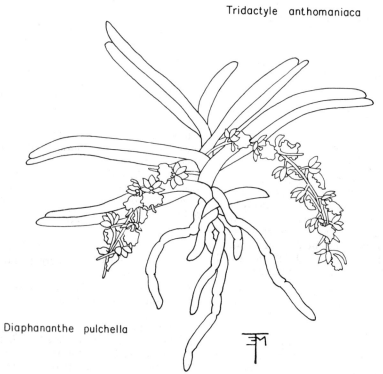

Diaphananthe pulchella

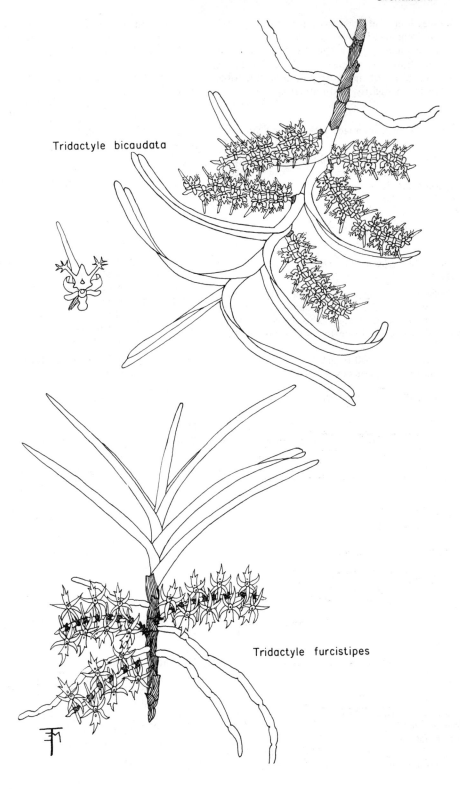

Tridactyle bicaudata

Tridactyle furcistipes

Leaves long and grass-like; inflorescences 2–5 cm long, 4–13-flowered   4. *T. cruciformis*

5   Lateral lobes of lip longer than middle lobe, very fimbriate at apex   5. *T. bicaudata*

Lateral lobes of lip shorter than middle lobe, entire or slightly fimbriate at apex
6. *T. furcistipes*

1. Tridactyle anthomaniaca (*Reichb. f.*) *Summerhayes* (see p. 800)

Stems elongated bearing fleshy ligulate alternate leaves; inflorescences bearing 2–3 flowers below and among the leaves, flowers yellow, green or brownish; lip lamina usually entire but basal auricles well developed.

Warm forests, *c.* 5000 ft. MUM.
Verdcourt 1704.

2. Tridactyle tridentata (*Harv.*) *Schltr.* (see p. 762)

Stems slender, elongated, bearing very narrow, terete leaves near the tips; inflorescences of 1–3 flowers below and among the leaves, flowers cream; side lobes of lip entire, much shorter than the middle lobe.

Warm forest, *c.* 5000 ft. MUM.
Drummond and Hemsley 4794.

3. Tridactyle scottellii (*Rendle*) *Schltr.* (see p. 800)

Stems woody elongated, often blackish, bearing thin linear-lanceolate leaves in their upper parts; inflorescences 1–3-flowered, below and among the leaves; flowers green, fading to ochre; side lobes of lip entire, as long as or longer than the middle lobe.

Highland forests, 6700–9000 ft. HE, HC, HM, HT, HK, HA.
Smart E8; Tweedie 88.

4. Tridactyle cruciformis *Summerhayes*

Stems woody, elongated, with few very narrow linear leaves near their tips; inflorescences 4–13-flowered on old part of stems; flowers small, pale green.

Forest, *c.* 6500 ft. KAJ, in the Chyulu Hills.
Bally 7856.

5. Tridactyle bicaudata (*Lindl.*) *Schltr.* (see p. 801)

Stems woody, elongated, bearing ligulate-linear leaves near the tips; inflorescences many-flowered, below and among the leaves; flowers yellowish or greenish fading to brown, side-lobes of the lip as long as or longer than the middle lobe and divided into many narrow hair-like lobes at their tips.

Common in drier forests throughout Kenya, 0–7000 ft. HE, HA, HL, NAR, RV, KAJ.
Glover 358; Bally 7876.

6. Tridactyle furcistipes *Summerhayes* (see p. 801)

Stems woody, elongated, usually erect, bearing linear-ligulate leaves and many-flowered inflorescences; flowers greenish-white or creamy, fading to ochre; lateral lobes of lip triangular, entire, or slightly fimbriate at apex, much shorter than middle lobe.

Highland forest, *c.* 7000–8500 ft. HC, HT, HM, HA.
Smart 14; Stewart 1332.

115. JUNCACEAE†

Annual or perenial rhizomatous or stoloniferous herbs with usually leafy stems; leaves flat or cylindrical; flowers bisexual and regular, usually in compound panicles of cymes; perianth segments of 6 equal brown or green segments; stamens 6; ovary superior, with 3 stigmas and 3 carpels; ovules axile, few to many; fruit a capsule.

1   Leaves and bracts glabrous; capsule with many seeds   1. *Juncus*

Leaves and bracts hairy on the margins; capsule with 3 seeds   2. *Luzula*

1. JUNCUS *L.*

Glabrous annual or perennial rhizomatous herbs with leaves cylindrical or flat or reduced; inflorescence a bracteate compound panicle of cymes; flowers bisexual, as in the family; capsule with numerous parietal or axile seeds.

1   Plant annual, usually less than 15 cm tall
1. *J. bufonius*

Plant perennial, usually over 15 cm tall   2

2   Leaves or stem-like leaves cylindrical   3

Leaves flat   2. *J. dregeanus*

3   Stems leafy; leaves hollow except for regularly spaced transverse bars of tissue
3. *J. oxycarpus*

All leaves basal, stem-like, solid and pithy within   4. *J. effusus*

1. Juncus bufonius *L.*

A small erect branched annual with greenish flowers crowded at first, often later in apparently 1-sided spikes.

Locally common in muddy pool margins in highland grassland. HT, HA.
Agnew 7201; Sherwood 36.

† By A. D. Q. Agnew.

2. Juncus dregeanus *Kunth*

An erect tufted perennial with most of the leaves basal, and flowers in subsessile or pedunculate, ± globose heads.

Common in alpine and subalpine wet flushes. HE, HC, HT, HM, HA, HK.

Lind and Agnew 5765; Taylor 3594.

3. Juncus oxycarpus *Kunth*

A stoloniferous perennial with most of the septate leaves borne on the ascending stems; flowers in ± spherical clusters.

Locally common on stream banks at lower altitudes than *J. dregeanus*. HC, HT, HM, HA, HK, KIT, NBI.

Lind and Agnew 5625; Verdcourt 2649.

4. Juncus effusus *L.*

A robust, tufted perennial with stem-like erect cylindrical leaves and flowering stems arising directly from the rhizome; inflorescence apparently lateral, a compound panicle of cymes of small brownish flowers.

Locally common on pathsides in the wet montane forest. HE, HM, HA, HK.

Agnew 10832; Kabuye 75.

2. LUZULA *L.*

Similar to *Juncus* but with constantly flat leaves and cells of the fruit 1-seeded.

1   Flowers separate from each other, each distinctly pedicellate   1. *L. johnstonii*

Flowers crowded, toughing one another, not distinctly pedicellate   2

2   Heads of flowers pedunculate, the peduncles radiating from ± the same place and thus umbellate, the whole inflorescence wider than tall   2. *L. campestris*

Heads of flowers arranged in a raceme, on short erect peduncles, the whole inflorescence taller than wide   3. *L. abyssinica*

1. Luzula johnstonii *Buchen.*

A perennial, stoloniferous herb with strap-shaped, mostly basal, leaves and a diffuse, almost corymbose inflorescence of brown flowers.

This species is locally common in the undergrowth of subalpine heathland and wet montane forest. HE, HA, HK.

Agnew 7088; Wood 743.

2. Luzula campestris *(L.) DC.*

Similar to *L. johnstonii* except for the narrower leaves and the key characters as given.

Confined in our area to the alpine and subalpine heathland and wet grassland of Mt. Elgon. HE.

Strid 3554; Hedberg 186.

3. Luzula abyssinica *Parl.*

Similar to *L. johnstonii* but usually more hairy, and with a condensed, elongate inflorescence.

Locally common in alpine and montane wet heathland and rocky grassland. HE, HC, HA, HK.

Coe and Kirrika 281; Hedberg 1766.

INDEX

In this index the species names in italics are synonyms, numbers in roman type refer to the page on which the family, genus, or species is described or mentioned, while numbers in bold type refer to plates.

Abrus, 241
  canescens, 241
  precatorius, **240**, 241
  schimperi, 241
Abutilon, 203
  figaranum, 205
  fruticosum, 205
  grandiflorum, 205
  guineense, 205
  hirtum, 205
  longicuspe, **204**, 205
  mauritianum, **204**, 205
  ramosum, 205
  sp. A, 205
Acalypha, 213
  bipartita, 215
  brachystachva, 215
  ciliata, 215
  crenata, 215
  fruticosa, 215
  glomerata, 215
  lanceolata, 215
  indica, 215
  neptunica, **214**, 216
  ornata, **214**, 216
  racemosa, **214**, 216
  paniculata, 216
  psilostachya, 215
  senenis, 216
  sp. A, 215
  stuhlmannii, 215
  subsessilis, 216
  villacaulis, 216
  volkensii, **214**, 215
Acanthaceae, 573
Acanthopale, 589
  pubescens, 589, **590**
Acanthospermum, 458
  australe, 459
  glabratum, 459
  hispidum, 458
Acetosella vulgaris, 123
Achillea, 469
  millefolium, 469
Achyranthes, 137
  aspera, 137, **138**
  schinzii, 137
Achyropsis, 137
  greenwayii, 137
Achyrospermum, 624
  carvalhi, 624
  parviflorum, 624
  radicans, 624

  schimperi, 624, **625**
Achyrothalamus, 494
  marginatus, 494
Acidanthera, 716
  candida, 716, **717**
  ukambensis, 716
Acrocephalus
  cylindraceus, 643
  venosus, 643
Actiniopteris, 40
  dimorpha, 43
  radiata, 43
  semiflabellata, **42**, 43
Adenia, 163
  bequaertii, 164
  cissampeloides, 164
  ellenbeckii, 166
  globosa, 165
  gummifera, 164
  keramanthus, 165
  lanceolata, 165
  metriosiphon, 165
  rumicifolia, 165
  schweinfurthii, 165
  stolzii, 164
  venenata, 165
  volkensii, 165
  wightiana, 166
Adenostemma, 433
  caffrum, 433, **434**
  mauritianum, 433
  perottetii, 433
Adhatoda, 601
  englerana, 601
Adiantum, 32
  capillus-veneris, 33, **42**
  hispidulum, 32
  incisum, 32, **42**
  raddianum, 33, **42**
  thalictroides, 32, **42**
Aeolanthus, 628
  heliotropoides, 628, **629**
  repens, 628, **629**
  stormsii, **629**, 630
Aerangis, 790
  brachycarpa, 793, **794**
  coriacea, 793
  flabellifolia, 793
  kotschyana, 793
  rhodosticta, 793, **797**
  thomsonii, **792**, 793
  ugandensis, **792**, 793
  verdickii, 793

Aerva, 136
  lanata, 136
  persica, 136
Aeschynomene, 261
  abyssinica, **262**, 263
  cristata, 261
  elaphroxylon, 261
  gracilipes, 261
  indica, 261
  mimosifolia, 261
  pfundii, 261
  schimperi, 261
  uniflora, 261
Afromomum, 671
  keniense, 671
Agathisanthemum, 401
  globosum, 401, **402**
Agavaceae, 722
Ageratum, 433
  conyzoides, **423**, 433
Aizoaceae, 115
Ajuga, 619
  remota, 619, **621**
Albuca, 692
  donaldsonii, 697
  pachychlamys, 693
  sp. A, 692
  sp. B, 693
  sp. C, 693
  wakefieldii, **687**, 693
Alchemilla, 225
  argyrophylla, 226
  cryptantha, 227
  cyclophylla, 227
  elgonensis, 226, **228**
  ellenbeckii, 226
  fischeri, 227
  gracilipes, 227
  hageniae, 226
  johnstonii, 226
  kiwuensis, 226
  microbetula, 227
  rothii, 227
Alectra, 557
  asperrima, 559
  parasitica, 557
  sessiliflora, **558**, 559
  sp. A, 557
  vogelii, 559
Alepidea, 351
  longifolia, 351, **352**
  massaica, 351
Alisma, 650

Alisma–*continued*
  plantago-aquatica, 650, **651**
Alismataceae, 650
Aloe, 688
  amudatensis, 690
  ballyi, 692
  dawei, 692
  deserti, 690, **691**
  elgonica, 692
  graminicola, 690, **691**
  kedongensis, **689**, 692
  lateritia, 690, **691**
  macrosiphon, 690
  myriacantha, 690, **691**
  ngobitensis, 692
  nyeriensis, 692
  rabaiensis, 692
  secundiflora, **689**, 690
  tweediae, **689**, 690
  ukambensis, 690
  volkensii, 692
Alternanthera, 137
  peploides, 137
  pungens, 137
  sessilis, 137
Alysicarpus, 267
  glumaceus, **265**, 268
  rugosus, 268
  sp. A, 268
  vaginalis, 268
  zeyheri, 268
Amaranthaceae, 130
Amaranthus, 132
  acutilobus, 133
  caudatus, 133
  graecizans, 133
  hybridus, 133
  hypochondriacus, 133
  lividus, 132
  sp. A, 133
  sparganiocephalus, 133
  spinosus, 132
Amaryllidaceae, 708
Ambrosia, 459
  maritima, 459
Ammannia, 153
  aegyptiaca, **152**, 154
  auriculata, 154
  baccifera, 154
  prieureana, 154
  sarcophylla, 154
Ammi, 355
  majus, 355
Ammocharis, 712
  heterostyla, 712, **713**
  tinneana, 712, **713**
Amorphophallus, 701
  abyssinicus, 701, **702**
  gallaensis, 701
Ampelocissus, 340
  africana, 340
Ampelopteris prolifera, 54
Amphicarpa, 268
  africana, 268, **269**

Anagallis, 506
  arvensis, **507**, 508
  brevipes, 506
  hexamera, 506
  pumila, 506
  serpens, 506, **507**
  tenuicaulis, 506
Androcymbium, 672
  melanthioides, 674, **675**
Aneilema, 664
  aequinoctiale, 666
  beniniense, 666
  hirtum, **665**, 667
  hockii, **663**, 666
  johnstonii, **663**, 666
  pedunculosum, 667
  petersii, 666
  rendlei, 666
  sp. A, 666
  sp. B, **665**, 667
  sp. C, 667
  spekei, 667
Anemia, 27
  schimperana, 27
Anemone, 76
  thomsonii, 76
Angraecopsis, 799
  amaniensis, **794**, 799
  breviloba, 799
  gracillima, **784**, 799
Angraecum, 783
  chamaeanthus, 783
  conchiferum, 785
  decipiens, 783
  erectum, **784**, 785
  firthii, 783
  humile, **784**, 785
  infundibulare, 785
  montanum, 783
  sacciferum, 783, **784**
Anisopappus, 458
  africanus, **457**, 458
  buchwaldii, 458
  holstii, 458
  oliveranus, 458
Anisotes, 605
  ukambensis, 607
Anogramma, 32
  leptophylla, 32
Ansellia, 763
  africana, 763
  gigantea, **764**, 765
Anthemis, 469
  tigrensis, 469
Anthericopsis, 667
  sepalosa, 667, **668**
Anthericum, 674
  angustifolium, 676, **677**
  cameronii, 676, **677**
  cooperi, 676, **680**
  gregorianum, 678
  kassneri, 679
  monophyllum, 678
  nubicum, 678

  oatesii, 679
  pubirachis, **675**, 678
  saltii, 679
  subpapillosum, 676
  subpetiolatum, **677**, 678
  suffruticosum, 678
  uyuiense, 676
  venulosum, 678
Antherotoma, 181
  naudinii, 181, **189**
Anthospermum, 407
  herbaceum, **406**, 407
Anthriscus, 351
  sylvestris, **350**, 351
Anticharis, 551
  linearis, 551
Antirrhinum orontium, 551
Antopetitia, 314
  abyssinica, **262**, 314
Antrophyum, 72
  mannianum, 72
Apium, 355
  leptophyllum, 355
Apocynaceae, 365
Aponogeton, 650
  abyssinicus, 650, **651**
  junceus, 650
  nudiflorus, 650
  stuhlmannii, 652
  subconjugatus, 650
  vallisnerioides, 652
  violaceus, 650
Aponogetonaceae, 650
Aptosimum, 551
  pumilum, 551
Arabidopsis, 99
  thaliana, 99
Arabis, 97
  alpina, 97
  glabra, 97
Araceae, 701
Arachniodes, 48
  foliosa, 48
Arbulocarpus, 409
  sphaerostigma, 409
Ardisiandra, 505
  sibthorpioides, 506
  wettsteinii, 506
Arenaria, 114
  foliacea, 114
Argemone, 88
  mexicana, 88
Argyrolobium 306
  fischeri, 306, **307**
  friesianum, 308
  ramosissimum, 308
  rupestre, 308
Arisaema, 701
  mildbraedii, 701, **702**
  schimperanum, 701, **702**
Aristea, 714
  alata, 714, **715**
  angolensis, 714, **715**

Aristolochia, 84
  bracteata, 84
  densivenia, 84
Aristolochiaceae, 84
Artemisia, 471
  afra, 471
Arthropteris, 43
  monocarpa, 44
  orientalis, 44
Asclepiadaceae, 367
Asparagus, 697
  africanus, 699
  asiaticus, 699
  asparagoides, 699
  buchananii, 699
  falcatus, 699
  flagellaris, 700
  nudicaulis, 700
  pauliguilelmi, 700
  plumosus, 699
  racemosus, **698**, 700
  setaceus, 699
Aspidoglossum, 374
  angustissimum, 374, **376**
  connatum, 374
  interruptum, 374
Aspidotis, 40
  schimperi, 40
Aspilia, 460
  kotschyi, 460, **461**
  mossambicensis, 460, **461**
  pluriseta, 460, **461**
Asplenium, 58
  abyssinicum, **59**, 68
  actiniopteroides, 69
  adamsii, 64
  adiantum-nigrum, 68
  aethiopicum, **59**, 68
  angolense, 62
  atroviride, 64
  blastophorum, 68
  boltonii, 64
  buettneri, 69
  bugoiense, **63**, 67
  ceii, **63**, 64
  christii, 64
  dregeanum, **63**, 67
  elliottii, **63**, 64
  erectum, **59**, 65
  formosum, 65
  friesiorum, **59**, 65
  gemmiferum, 62, **63**
  hypomelas, 67
  inaequilaterale, **63**, 65
  kassneri, 69
  linckii, **59**, 68
  lividum, **59**, 69
  loxoscaphoides, **63**, 68
  macrophlebium, **63**, 64
  mannii, **63**, 67
  megalura, 64
  monanthes, 65, **66**
  normale, 64
  praegracile, 68
  protensum, **59**, 64

  pseudoauriculatum, 67
  rutifolium, **63**, 68
  sandersonii, 62, **66**
  sp. A, 62
  sp. B, **63**, 65
  sp. C, 67
  sp. D, 67
  sp. E, 69
  stuhlmannii, **66**, 68
  suppositum, 65
  theciferum, **66**, 67
  trichomanes, 65
  uhligii, 69
  unilaterale, **63**, 65
  varians, 68
Aster muricatus, 438
Asterolinon, 506
  adoense, 506, **507**
Astragalus, 314
  abyssinicus, 314
  atropilosulus, 314, **315**
  battiscombei, 314
  bequaertii, 314
  burkeanus, 314
  elgonensis, 314
  somalensis, 314
  tridens, 314
  venosus, 314
Astripomoea, 537
  grantii, **538**, 539
  hyoscyamoides, 539
  lachnosperma, 539
  malvacea, **538**, 539
Asystasia, 596
  charmian, 596
  gangetica, **597**, 598
  laticapsula, **597**, 598
  schimperi, 596, **597**
  sp. A, 596
Athrixia, 456
  rosmarinifolia, **446**, 456
Athroisma, 448
  gracile, 448
  hastifolium, 448
  psyllioides, 448
  sp. A, 448
  stuhlmannii, 448
Athyrium, 57
  scandicinum, 57, **59**
  schimperi, 57
Atriplex, 129
  halimus, 130
  muelleri, 130
  semibaccata, 129
Australina, 325
  acuminata, 325
  flaccida, 325
Azolla, 73
  nilotica, 74
  pinnata, 74

Baissea, 365
  alborosea, 365
Balanophoraceae, 338

Ballya, 653
  zebrina, 654
Balsaminaceae, 149
Barbarea, 97
  intermedia, 97
Barleria, 591
  acanthoides, **592**, 593
  diffusa, 593
  eremanthoides, **592**, 593
  grandicalyx, **592**, 593
  micrantha, 594
  proxima, 593
  sp. A, 593
  sp. G, 593
  sp. K, 594
  sp. Q, 593
  spinisepala, 593
  submollis, 594
  ventricosa, **592**, 594
  volkensii, 594
Bartsia, 565
  abyssinica, **566**, 567
  kilimandscharica, 567
  longiflora, 567
  macrocalyx, 567
  petitiana, 567
  trixago, 567
Basella, 139
  alba, 139, **148**
Basellaceae, 139
Baseonema, 369
  gregorii, 369
Becium, 645
  angustifolium, 646
  capitatum, 646
  obovatum, 646, **647**
  sp. A, 646
  sp. C, 646
Begonia, 178
  eminii, 180
  johnstonii, 180
  keniensis, **179**, 180
  meyeri-johannis, 180
  oxyloba, 180
Begoniaceae, 178
Bergia, 110
  ammannioides, 110
Berkheya, 489
  spekeana, **487**, 489
Berula, 357
  erecta, 357
Bidens, 465
  angustata, 466
  biternata, **464**, 466
  cineroides, 466
  coriacea, 467, **468**
  elgonensis, 466
  grantii, 467
  incumbens, 466
  insignis, 467
  kilimandscharica, 467
  kirkii, 466
  lineata, 466
  meruensis, 467
  morotonensis, 466

Bidens–*continued*
  napierae, 467
  palustris, 466
  pilosa, **464**, 466
  rueppellii, 466
  rueppellioides, 466
  schimperi, 466
  sp. A, 466
  superba, **464**, 466
  ugandensis, 467, **468**
  ukambensis, 467
Biophytum, 149
  abyssinicum, **147**, 149
  petersianum, 149
Blaeria, 362
  filago, 362
  johnstonii, 362, **363**
Blainvillea, 460
  rhomboidea, 460
Blechnum, 58
  attenuatum, 58
  australe, 58
  ivohibense, 58
  tabulare, 58
Blepharis, 579
  fruticulosa, 579
  integrifolia, 579, **580**
  linariifolia, 579, **580**
  maderaspatensis, 579, **580**
  stuhlmannii, 579
Blepharispermum, 447
  fruticosum, 448
  sp. A, 447
  zanguebaricum, 448
Blotiella, 30
  glabra, 30, **31**
  sp. A, 30
  stipitata, 30, **31**
Blumea, 442
  aurita, 443
  caffra, 443
  perottetiana, 443
Boehmeria, 325
  platyphylla, 325
Boerhavia, 161
  coccinea, **160**, 162
  diffusa, 162
  erecta, 162
  repens, 162
Bolbitis, 52
  heudelotii, 52
Bolusiella, 790
  imbricata, **786**, 790
  iridifolia, 790
Bonatea, 744
  steudneri, 744, **745**
  tentaculifera, 744
  volkensiana, 744
Boöphone, 708
  disticha, 708, **710**
Boraginaceae, 517
Borreria, 407
  kotschyana, 409
  princei, 407
  scabra, **408**, 409

sp. A, **408**, 409
  stricta, **408**, 409
Bowiea, 685
  kilimandscharica, 685, **686**
  volubilis, 685
Brachycorythis, 729
  buchananii, **730**, 731
  kalbreyeri, **730**, 731
  ovata, **730**, 731
  pleistophylla, 731
  pubescens, 729, **730**
  tenuior, 729
Brachystelma, 392
  johnstonii, **386**, 392
  keniense, 393
  lineare, **386**, 393
  sp. A, 393
Brassica, 94
  campestris, 94
  integrifolia, 94
  napus, 94
  oleracea, 94
  rapa, 94
Brillantaisia, 581
  madagascariensis, 583
  nitens, 585
  nyanzarum, 583, **584**
Buchnera, 560
  capitata, 560, **561**
  hispida, 560, **561**
  nuttii, 560
  scabridula, 560
Bulbine, 674
  abyssinica, 674, **675**
Bulbophyllum, 760
  bequaertii, **762**, 763
  bifarium, 763
  cochleatum, **761**, 763
  encephalodes, 760, **762**
  falcatum, 763
  intertextum, 760, **761**
  oxypterum, 763
  schlechteri, 760, **761**
  sp. A, 763
  tentaculigerum, 763
Burnatia, 650
  enneandra, 650
Buttonia, 559
  hildebrandtii, 559

Cactaceae, 180
Caesalpinia, 236
  volkensii, 236
Caesalpiniaceae, 230
Cajanus, 282
  cajan, 282
Calanthe, 756
  volkensii, 756, **758**
Callitrichaceae, 158
Callitriche, 158
  stagnalis, 158
Calotropis, 380
  procera, 380
Camelina, 99
  alyssum, 99

Campanula, 509
  rigidipila, 509
  sp. A., 509
Campanulaceae, 509
Canarina, 509
  abyssinica, 509, **510**
  eminii, 509, **510**
Canavalia, 272
  ensiformis, 272
  virosa, 272
Capitanya, 632
  otostegioides, **629**, 632
Capparaceae, 90
Capparis, 92
Caprifoliaceae, 412
Capsella, 96
  bursa-pastoris, 96
Caralluma, 393
  dicapuae, **394**, 396
  dummeri, **394**, 396
  foetida, **395**, 396
  gracilipes, 396
  priogonum, 396
  russelliana, **395**, 396
  socotrana, 396
  speciosa, **395**, 396
  subterranea, 396
  vibratilis, **395**, 396
Cardamine, 96
  africana, 97, **98**
  hirsuta, 97
  obliqua, 97
  trichocarpa, 97, **98**
Cardiospermum, 347
  corindum, 347
  grandiflorum, 347
  halicacabum, 347
Carduus, 491
  afromontanus, 493
  chamaecephalus, 491, **492**
  keniensis, 491
  kikuyorum, 493
  millefolius, 491
  nyassanus, 491, **492**
  platyphyllus, 491
  sylvarum, 491
  theodori, 491
Carpolobia, 104
Caryophyllaceae, 110
Cassia, 231
  absus, 233
  bicapsularis, 233
  falcinella, 236
  fallacina, 233
  floribunda, 233
  grantii, 233
  hildebrandtii, **234**, 236
  italica, 233
  kirkii, **235**, 236
  mimosoides, 233, **235**
  nigricans, 236
  obtusifolia, 233
  occidentalis, 233, **234**
  parva, 233
  quarrei, 236

sp. B., 233
usambarensis, 233
Cassytha, 75
filiformis, 75
Catharanthus, 365
roseus, 365
Caucalis, 351
incognita, 355
melanantha, **354**, 355
pedunculata, 355
Caucanthus, 210
auriculatus, 210
Caylusea, 100
abyssinica, 100
Cayratia, 340
gracilis, 340
ibuensis, 341
Celastraceae, 325
Celosia, 131
anthelmintica, 132
argentea, 131
leptostachya, 132
schweinfurthiana, 132
trigyna, 132
Celsia, 550
brevipedicellata, 550
floccosa, 550, **552**
scrophulariaefolia, 550
Centaurea, 493
melitensis, 493
praecox, **492**, 494
Centella, 349
asiatica, 351
Centemopsis, 134
kirkii, 134
rubra, 134, **138**
Cephalaria, 414
pungens, 414, **415**
Cephalopentandra, 174
ecirrhosa, 174
Cephalostigma erectum, 511
Cerastium, 112
adnivale, 114
afromontanum, 112
indicum, 112, **113**
octandrum, 114
Ceratophyllaceae, 81
Ceratophyllum, 81
demersum, 81
submersum, 81
Ceratostigma, 508
abyssinicum, 508
Ceratotheca, 572
sesamoides, 572
Ceropegia, 389
abyssinica, **390**, 391
ballyana, **390**, 392
batesii, 391
brosima, 392
crassifolia, 392
cufodontii, **390**, 392
denticulata, **390**, 391
euryacme, 391
meyeri-johannis, **390**, 391
seticorona, 392

sp. A, 391
sp. B, 392
sp. C, 392
sp. D, 392
stenantha, 392
stenoloba, 391
succulenta, 392
Cestrum, 529
aurantiacum, 529
Ceterach, 69
cordatum, 69
Chamaeangis, 790
odoratissima, 790, **798**
orientalis, 790, **791**
vesicata, 790, **791**
Chascanum, 614
hildebrandtii, 614
Chaseella, 763
pseudohydra, 763
sp. A, 763
Chasmanthera, 83
dependens, 83
Cheilanthes, 35
bergiana, 37
farinosa, 37, **38**
hirta, 37, **38**
multifida, 37
sp. A, 37
sp. B, 37
Chenopodiaceae, 127
Chenopodium, 128
album, 128
ambrosioides, 129, **138**
carinatum, 129
fasciculosum, 129
murale, 128
opulifolium, 128
procerum, 129
pumilio, 129
schraderanum, 129
Chironia, 501
elgonensis, 501, **502**
Chlorophytum, 679
andongense, 683
bakeri, 683
blepharophyllum, **680**, 683
elgonense, 684
gallabatense, **682**, 683
limurense, 684
macrophyllum, **681**, 684
micranthum, 684
sp. A, 685
sp. B, 685
sparsiflorum, 684
tenuifolium, 684
tordense, 684
tuberosum, 684
viridescens, 683
Chrysanthellum, 465
americanum, **463**, 465
Chrysanthemoides, 486
monilifera, 486
Chrysocoma, 442
sp. A, 442
Cineraria, 475

grandiflora, 475
schimperi, 478
Cirsium, 493
buchwaldii, 493
vulgare, 493
Cissampelos, 83
friesiorum, 83
mucronata, 84
pareira, 84
Cissus, 341
aphyllantha, 341
cactiformis, 341, **342**
oliveri, 341
petiolata, 341
quadrangularis, 341
rotundifolia, 341, **342**
sp. A, 341
Cistanche, 567
tubulosa, **568**, 569
Clematis, 75
brachiata, 76
hirsuta, 76, **77**
simensis, 76, **77**
Clematopsis, 76
scabiosifolia, 76, **79**
Cleome, 90
allamanii, 92
angustifolia, 90
diandra, 90
hirta, 92, **93**
monophylla, 90, **91**
schimperi, 90
strigosa, 90, **91**
Clerodendrum, 614
buchholzii, 616
capitatum, 614
cephalanthum, 614
cordifolium, 614, **615**
discolor, 616
eriophyllum, 614
johnstonii, **615**, 616
melanocrater, 616
myricoides, 616
rotundifolium, 614
sp. A, 616
triplinerve, 616
ugandensis, 616
Cliffortia, 230
nitidula, **228**, 230
Clitoria, 268
ternata, 268, **269**
Clutia, 218
abyssinica, **217**, 219
mollis, 219
pedicellaris, 219
robusta, 219
Cluytiandra capillariformis, 213
Coccinia, 171
adoensis, 171, **172**
grandis, 173
microphylla, 173
trilobata, 173
Cocculus, 82
hirsutus, 83
pendulus, 82

Coldenia, 518
  procumbens, 518
Coleus,
  coeruleus, 638
  decumbens, 635
  edulis, 640
  ignarius, 638
  lactiflorus, 635
  lanuginosus, 638
  sylvaticus, 640
  tenuiflorus, 636
  tetensis, 635
Colutea, 316
  abyssinica, **274**, 316
  haleppica, 316
  istria, 316
Combretaceae, 183
Combretum, 183
  aculeatum, 183
  mossambicense, 183
  padoides, 183
  paniculatum, 183, **184**
Commelina, 654
  africana, 656, **658, 663**
  albescens, 657
  benghalensis, **658**, 660
  capitata, 657
  diffusa, 656
  eckloniana, 660
  elgonensis, **658**, 660
  erecta, 657, **659**
  foliacea, 657
  forskalaei, 657
  imberbis, **655**, 660
  kirkii, 656
  latifolia, **658**, 660
  lugardii, 657
  mannii, 656
  nudiflora, 656
  obscura, 656
  petersii, 660
  purpurea, 657
  reptans, 657
  sp. A, **655**, 660
  sp. B, 657, **665**
  sp. C, 657
  sp. D, 660
  sp. E, 657
  subulata, **655**, 657
  trilobosperma, 657
  velutina, 657, **659**
Commelinaceae, 653
Commicarpus, 162
  boissieri, 162
  pedunculosus, 162
  plumbagineus, 162
  stellatus, 162
Compositae, 416
Coniogramme, 32
  africana, 32
Conostomium, 398
  floribundum, 398
  keniense, 398
  quadrangulare, 398, **402**

Convolvulaceae, 530
Convolvulus, 534
  arvensis, 534
  farinosus, 535
  kilimandschari, **531**, 534
  sagittatus, 535
  siculus, 534
Conyza, 438
  aegyptiaca, 441
  bonariensis, 441
  floribunda, 442
  hochstetteri, **439**, 442
  hypoleuca, 440
  newii, **439**, 442
  pallidiflora, **437**, 442
  pedunculata, **437**, 440
  pyrifolia, **434**, 441
  pyrrhopappa, 441
  ruwenzoriensis, 441
  schimperi, **439**, 441
  sp. A, **437**, 440
  sp. B, 441
  sp. C, 442
  sp. D, 442
  sp. E, 442
  steudelii, 441
  stricta, 441
  subscaposa, **439**, 442
  theodori, 442
  tigrensis, 442
  vernonioides, 441
  volkensii, 441
  welwitschii, 441
Corallocarpus, 178
  boehmii, 178
  epigeus, 178
  schimperi, 178
Corbichonia, 119
  decumbens, 119
Corchorus, 187
  hochstetteri, 187
  olitorius, 187
  tridens, 187
  trilocularis, 188
Coreopsis,
  elgonensis, 466
  morotonensis, 466
Coriandrum, 351
  sativum, 351
Coronopus, 95
  didymus, 96
Corrigiola, 112
  litoralis, 112
Corydalis, 88
  mildbraedi, 88, **91**
Costus, 671
  spectabilis, **670**, 671
Cotula, 469
  abyssinica, **470**, 471
  anthemoides, 471
  cryptocephala, 469
Cotyledon, 104
  barbeyi, 104
Crabbea, 594
  velutina, 594, **595**

Crambe, 95
  abyssinica, 95
  hispanica, 95
Crassocephalum, 472
  bojeri, 472, **473**
  crepidioides, 472
  mannii, 472, **474**
  montuosum, 472, **473**
  picridifolium, **470**, 472
  rubens, **470**, 472
  vitellinum, 472
Crassula, 104
  alba, 104, **108**
  alsinoides, 105, **108**
  granvikii, 105, **108**
  nodulosa, 104
  pentandra, 105
  sp. A, 105
  sp. B, 105
  sp. C, 105
  volkensii, 104
Crassulaceae, 104
Craterostigma, 553
  hirsutum, **554**, 555
  lanceolatum, 555
  plantagineum, **554**, 555
  pumilum, **554**, 555
  sp. A, 555
  sp. B, 555
  sp. C, 555
Crepis, 500
  carbonaria, 500
  newii, 501
  oliverana, 500
  rueppellii, **495**, 500
Crinum, 708
  kirkii, **711**, 712
  sp. A, 712
Crossandra, 581
  friesiorum, 581
  mucronata, 581, **582**
  nilotica, 581
  stenostachya, 581
  subacaulis, 581, **582**
  tridentata, 581
Crotalaria, 290
  agatiflora, 296
  alexandri, 306
  anthyllopsis, 302
  axillaris, 303
  barkae, 298
  balbi, 300
  bogdaniana, 299
  bongensis, 303
  brevidens, 300, **304**
  burttii, 299
  cephalotes, **297**, 305
  chrysochlora, 300, **301**
  cleomifolia, 302
  comanestiana, 299
  cylindrica, **292**, 300
  cylindrocarpa, 298
  deflersii, 299
  deserticola, 305
  dewildemaniana, **297**, 300

emarginella, 303
fascicularis, 303
glauca, 299
goodiiformis, 296
goreensis, 298
greenwayi, 305
hyssopifolia, 306
imperialis, 296
incana, 298
jacksonii, 306
karagwensis, 305
keniensis, 303, **304**
laburnifolia, 296
lachnocarpoides, **292**, 298
lachnophora, **292**, 298
lanceolata, 300
lebrunii, 296
lotiformis, 302
lugardiorum, 305
massaiensis, 302
mauensis, 296
microcarpa, 303
natalitia, **292**, 298
ochroleuca, 300
ononoides, 299
oocarpa, 305
orthoclada, **292**, 299
pallida, 299
petitiana, 302
podocarpa, 298
polysperma, 296, **297**
pseudospartium, 296
pseudotenuirama, 306
pycnostachya, 299
quartiniana, 296
recta, **301**, 305
rhizoclada, 305
saxatilis, 296
scassellatii, **301**, 303
serengetiana, 296
shirensis, 303
spectabilis, 305
spinosa, **304**, 305
stolzii, 298
tabularis, 303
uguenensis, 302
ukambensis, 302
vallicola, **297**, 300
vasculosa, 302
vatkeana, 302
verdcourtii, 299
Cruciferae, 92
Cryptotaenia, 355
africana, 355
Ctenitis, 48
cirrhosa, 49
lanuginosa, 49
Cucumella, 175
engleri, 175
Cucumis, 174
aculeatus, 175
dipsaceus, 175
ficifolius, 175, **176**
figarei, 175, **179**
hirsutus, 175

humifructus, 175
prophetarum, 175
Cucurbitaceae, 166
Culcasia, 701
scandens, 701, **702**
Curroria, 369
volubilis, 369
Cuscuta, 532
australis, 532
campestris, 532
cassytoides, 532
epilinum, 533
hyalina, 532
kilimanjari, **531**, 532
planiflora, **531**, 532
suaveolens, 532
Cyanotis, 660
arachnoidea, 662
barbata, **659**, 662
caespitosa, **661**, 662
foecunda, **661**, 662
lanata, 662
longifolia, **661**, 662
paludosa, 662
Cyathea, 44
dregei, 45
manniana, 45
stuhlmannii, 44
Cyathula, 134
cylindrica, 135
erinacea, 135
mannii, 135
orthocantha, 135
polycephala, 135
schimperana, 135
sp. A, 135
uncinulata, 135
Cyclocheilon, 614
eriantherum, 614
Cyclosorus,
dentatus, 54, **55**
gongylodes, 54
interruptus, 54
madagascariensis, **26**, 54
patens, 54
quadrangularis, 54
sp. A, 54
striatus, 54
tottus, 54
Cycniopsis, 560
obtusifolia, 562, **566**
Cycnium, 560
adonense, 560, **566**
tomentosum, 560
Cynanchum, 385
abyssinicum, 385, **386**
altiscandens, 385
hastifolium, 385
sp. A, 387
tetrapterum, 385
validum, 387
Cynoglossum, 521
amplifolium, 521
coeruleum, 523
geometricum, 521, **522**

lanceolatum, 521
lancifolium, 521
sp. A, 521
sp. B, 521
Cynorkis, 731
anacamptoides, 731, **732**
kassnerana, 731, **732**
Cyphia, 513
glandulifera, 513, **514**
Cyphostemma, 341
adenocaule, 345
bambuseti, **343**, 345
braunii, 345
cyphopetala, 345
glandulosissima, 345
heterotrichum, 344
jatrophoides, 345, **346**
kilimandscharicum, 344
lentianum, 345
maranguense, **343**, 345
nierense, 344
nodiglandulosum, 345
orondo, 345, **346**
sesquipedale, 345
sp. A, 344
sp. B, 345
sp. C, 345
sp. D, 344
ukerewense, 345
Cyrtanthus, 712
salmonoides, 712
sanguineus, 712
sp. A, 712
Cyrtomium falcatum, 48
Cyrtorchis, 796
arcuata, **786**, 799
brownii, 799
praetermissa, **786**, 796
Cystopteris, 56
fragilis, 56

Dactyliandra, 174
nigrescens, 174
Dalbergia, 239
lactea, 241, **273**
melanoxylon, 241
Dalechampia, 218
ipomoeifolia, **217**, 218
scandens, 218
Dasysphaera, 136
prostrata, 136
Dasystachys
debilis, 683
gracilis, 683
Datura, 529
metel, 530
stramonium, 529
Davallia, 44
chaerophylloides, 44
Delosperma, 117
nakuruense, 117, **118**
Delphinium, 78
leroyi, **80**, 81
macrocentrum, 78, **80**
wellbyi, 81

Desmodium, 266
　barbatum, 267
　dregeanum, 267
　gangeticum, 267
　ramosissimum, 266
　repandum, **265**, 267
　salicifolium, 267
　setigerum, 266
　triflorum, 266
　velutinum, 267
Dianthoseris, 500
　schimperi, 500
Diaphananthe, 785
　fragrantissima, **787**, 788
　lorifolia, 788, **789**
　pulchella, 788, **800**
　quintasii, **787**, 788
　rutila, 788, **789**
　subsimplex, **787**, 788
　tenuicalcar, 790
　xanthopollinia, 788
Dibrachionostylus, 401
　kaessneri, 401
Dichondra, 533
　repens, 533
Dichrocephala, 436
　alpina, 436
　chrysanthemifolia, **434**, 436
　integrifolia, **434**, 436
Dicliptera, 607
　albicaulis, 609
　colorata, 607, **608**
　laxata, 607, **608**
　napierii, 609
　sp. A, 607
　sp. B, 609
　sp. C, 609
　verticillata, 607
Diclis, 551
　bambuseti, 551, **552**
　ovata, 551
Dicoma, 494
　tomentosa, 494
Dicranopteris, 27
　linearis, 27
Didymochlaena, 45
　truncatula, 45, **59**
Dierama, 716
　pendulum, 716
Dietes, 720
　prolongata, **719**, 720
Digera, 133
　muricata, 133
Dioscorea, 720
　dumetorum, 722
　praehensilis, 722
　quartiniana, **721**, 722
　schimperana, 720, **721**
Dioscoreaceae, 720
Dipcadi, 694
　arenarium, 694
　sp. A, 695
　viride, 694, **696**
Diplazium, 57
　hylophilum, 57

velaminosum, 57, **59**
　zanzibaricum, 57
Diplocyclos, 173
　palmatus, 173
　schliebenii, 173
Diplolophium, 357
　africanum, 357
Diplostigma, 387
　canescens, 387
Dipsacaceae, 414
Dipsacus, 414
　pinnatifidus, 414, **415**
Disa, 746
　concinna, 746, **747**
　deckenii, 746
　erubescens, 746, **748**
　hircicornis, 746, **747**
　ochrostachya, 746, **747**
　scutellifera, 749, **750**
　stairsii, 746, **750**
　welwitschii, **748**, 749
Discopodium, 528
　eremanthum, 528
　penninervum, 528
Disperis, 752
　anthoceros, **754**, 755
　aphylla, **754**, 755
　dicerochila, **754**, 755
　kilimanjarica, **754**, 755
　nemorosa, 755
　pusilla, 755
　reichenbachiana, **754**, 755
Disperma, 585
Dissotis, 181
　brazzae, 183
　canescens, 181, **182**
　debilis, 181
　incana, 181
　senegambiensis, 181, **182**
　speciosa, 181, **182**
Dolichos, 281
　compressus, **280**, 281
　kilimandscharicus, **280**, 281
　luticola, 281
　oliveri, 281
　sericeus, **280**, 281
　trilobus, 281
Dopatrium, 553
　dortmanna, 553
　junceum, 553
Dorstenia, 318
　afromontana, 318
　barnimiana, **319**, 320
　brownii, 318
　denticulata, 318, **319**
　foetida, 320
　scaphigera, 318
　schlechteri, 320
　zanzibarica, 320
Doryopteris, 37
　concolor, 39, **42**
　nicklesii, 39
Dracaena, 722
　laxissima, 722

Dregea, 388
　abyssinica, 389
　rubicunda, 389
　schimperi, **384**, 389
　stelostigma, 389
Drimia, 693
　congesta, 694
　elgonica, 694, **696**
　zombensis, 694
Drimiopsis, 697
　botryoides, 697
Droguetia, 325
　debilis, 327
　iners, 325
Drosera, 109
　burkeana, 109
　madagascariensis, 109
　pilosa, 109
Droseraceae, 109
Drymaria, 111
　cordata, 111, **113**
Drynaria, 70
　volkensii, 70
Dryoathyrium, 57
　boryanum, 57, **59**
Dryopteris, 45
　athamantica, 46, **47**
　callolepis, 46
　inaequalis, 46
　kilemensis, 46, **59**
　manniana, 46
　pentheri, 46
　schimperana, 46
　sp. A, 46
　squamiseta, 46
Dumasia, 268
　villosa, 268
Duosperma, 585
　eremophilum, 587
　kilimandscharicum, 587
　sp. A, 587
Duranta, 616
　repens, 616
Dyschoriste, 585
　hildebrandtii, 585
　perrottetii, 585
　procumbens, 585
　radicans, 585, **595**
　sp. A, 585
　thunbergiflora, 585
　trichocalyx, 585

Ecbolium, 599
　hamatum, 599
　revolutum, 599
Echidnopsis, 393
　dammiana, 393
Echinops, 489
　aberdaricus, 489
　amplexicaulis, 489, **490**
　angustilobus, 491
　eryngifolius, 489
　hispidus, **490**, 491
　hoehnelii, 489, **490**
　longifolius, 491

Echiochilon, 523
  lithospermoides, 523
Eclipta, 460
  alba, 460
Ectadiopsis, 369
  oblongifolia, 370, **372**
Edithcolea, 393
  grandis, 393, **394**
Elaphoglossum, 49
  acrostichoides, 51
  angulatum, 51
  aubertii, **26**, 51
  conforme, 51
  convolutum, 51
  deckenii, 52
  hybridum, 51
  lastii, 51
  mildbraedii, 52
  ruwenzorii, 52
  spathulatum, 51
  subcinnamomeum, 52
  tanganjicense, 52
  volkensii, 51
Elatinaceae, 110
Elatostema, 323
  orientale, 323, **324**
Elephantopus, 433
  scaber, 433
Elodea, 648
  densa, 649
Emex, 122
  australis, 122
  spinosus, 122
Emilia, 480
  coccinea, 480
  integrifolia, **482**, 483
  javanica, 480, **488**
  kikuyorum, 483, **488**
Endostemon, 630
  camporum, 630
  tereticaulis, **612**, 630
Englerastrum, 632
  scandens, 633
  schweinfurthii, 632
  sp. A, 632
Enicostema, 501
  axillare, 501
Enydra, 459
  fluctuans, 459
Epilobium, 155
  hirsutum, **152**, 156
  salignum, **152**, 156
  stereophyllum, 156
Epipactis, 755
  africana, 756, **757**
Epipogium, 755
  roseum, 755, **757**
Equisetum, 24
  ramosissimum, 24
Eremomastax, 587
  polysperma, **586**, 587
Erica, 362
  arborea, 364
  whyteana, **363**, 364
Ericaceae, 362

Erigeron, 438
  alpinus, 438
  bonariensis, 441
  floribundum, 442
  grantii, 436
Eriocaulaceae, 669
Eriocaulon, 669
  abyssinicum, 669
  schimperi, 669
  sp. A, 669
  volkensii, 669
Eriosema, 286
  bogdanii, 288
  buchananii, **287**, 288
  cordifolium, **287**, 290
  elliotii, 290
  flemingioides, 288
  glomeratum, 288
  jurionianum, 288, **289**
  macrostipulum, 288, **289**
  montanum, 288
  nutans, 288, **289**
  psoraleoides, 288
  rhodesicum, 290
  robustum, **287**, 288
  scioanum, **287**, 288
  shirense, 290
  sparsiflorum, **289**, 290
  vanderystii, 288
Eriospermum, 685
  abyssinicum, 685, **686**
  triphyllum, 685, **686**
Erlangea, 422
  amplifolia, 422
  boranensis, 424
  calycina, **421**, 422
  cordifolia, **421**, 424
  duemmeri, 422
  fusca, 424
  marginata, 424
  somalensis, 422
  sp. A, 424
  tomentosa, **423**, 424
Erucastrum, 94
  arabicum, 94
Erythrocephalum, 494
  microcephalum, 494
Erythrochlamys, 642
  spectabilis, 642
Erythroselinum, 360
  atropurpureum, 360
Ethulia, 420
  conyzoides, 420
  scheffleri, 420
  sp. A, 420
Eulophia, 772
  adenoglossa, **779**, 782
  angolensis, 776, **778**
  calantha, **779**, 780
  chlorotica, **774**, 782
  cristata, 780
  cucullata, **779**, 780
  galeoloides, **779**, 780
  grantii, 776
  horsfallii, **773**, 780

  latilabris, **778**, 780
  livingstoniana, 780, **781**
  montis-elgonis, **775**, 780
  orthoplectra, **773**, 776
  paivaeana, **775**, 776
  parvula, 776
  petersii, **774**, 776
  porphyroglossa, 780
  pyrophila, 776, **777**
  quartiniana, **777**, 780
  schimperana, 776
  shupangae, **781**, 782
  stachyodes, 782
  stenophylla, 776
  subulata, 782
  wakefieldii, **774**, 776
  warneckeana, 780, **781**,
  zeyheri, 780, **781**
Eulophidium, 782
  saundersianum, 782
Eupatorium, 433
  adenophorum, 433
  africanum, 433, **435**
Euphorbia, 219
  acalyphoides, 222
  agowensis, 222
  arabica, 221
  bongensis, **220**, 223
  brevitorta, 223
  buruana, 223
  crotonoides, 222, **224**
  cyparissoides, **220**, 223
  depauperata, 223, **224**
  engleri, 222
  geniculata, 222
  glochidiata, 223
  gossypina, 223
  graciliramea, 223
  granulata, 222
  heterochroma, **220**, 223, **224**
  hirta, 221, **224**
  inaequilatera, **220**, 221
  mossambicensis, 222
  polyantha, 223
  prostrata, **220**, 222
  pseudograntii, 222
  repetita, 222
  rivae, 221
  rubella, 221
  schimperana, **220**, 222
  sp. A, 223
  sp. B, 223
  systyloides, 222
  ugandensis, 223
  uhligiana, 223
  wellbyi, 222
  zambesiaca, 221
Euphorbiaceae, 210
Euryops, 484
  brownei, 484
  elgonensis, 484
  jacksonii, 486
Evolvulus, 533
  alsinoides, **531**, 533
  nummularius, 533

Exochaenium macranthum, 501

Fadogia, 405
  cienkowskii, 407, **408**
Fagonia, 140
  sp. A, 140
Fagopyrum, 126
  esculentum, 126
Falkia, 533
  canescens, 533
Farsetia, 96
  sp. A, 96
  stenoptera, 96
Felicia, 436
  abyssinica, **432**, 438
  grantii, 436
  muricata, 438
Ferula, 357
  communis, 358
  montis-elgonis, 358
Flabellaria, 209
  paniculata, 209
Flaveria, 467
  australasica, 469
Flemingia, 290
  grahamiana, 290
Fleurya, 321
  aestuans, 321
  interrupta, 321
  ovalifolia, 321
Floscopa, 664
  glomerata, **663**, 664
  rivularis, 664
Foeniculum, 357
  vulgare, 357
Fragaria, 227
  vesca, 227
Fuerstia, 648
  africana, 648
Fumaria, 88
  abyssinica, 89, **91**
Fumariaceae, 88

Galega, 314
  battiscombei, 314
  lindblomii, 314, **315**
Galinsoga, 467
  ciliata, 467
  parviflora, 467, **468**
Galium, 409
  aparinoides, 411
  chloroionanthum, 411
  kenyanum, 412
  glaciale, 411
  ossirwaense, 411
  ruwenzoriense, 411
  scioanum, **410**, 412
  simense, **410**, 411
  sp. A, 411
  spurium, 411
  thunbergianum, **410**, 411
Geigeria, 456
  acaulis, 456
  alata, 456

Geniosporum, 643
  hildebrandtii, 643
  paludosum, 643, **647**
Genlisea, 569
  hispidula, 569
Gentianaceae, 501
Geophila, 407
  repens, 407
Geraniaceae, 140
Geranium, 141
  aculeolatum, 141, **142**
  arabicum, 141, **142**
  elamellatum, 141, **142**
  kilimandscharicum, 141, **142**
  ocellatum, 141, **143**
  vagans, 141
Gerbera, 494
  piloselloides, 494
  viridifolia, 494, **495**
Gerrardanthus, 178
  lobatus, 178
Gesneriaceae, 571
Girardinia, 321
  bullosa, 323
  condensata, **319**, 323
Gisekia, 116
  pharnaceoides, 116, **118**
Gladiolus, 716
  natalensis, 716
  psittacinus, 716, **718**
  sp. A, **718**, 720
  watsonioides, 716
Gleichenia, 27
  elongata, 27
Glinus, 116
  lotoides, 116
  oppositifolius, 116
Gloriosa, 672
  simplex, 672, **673**
  virescens, 672
Glossonema, 373
  revoilii, 373
Glycine, 270
  wightii, **240**, 270
Gnaphalium, 455
  declinatum, **449**, 455
  luteo-album, 455
  purpureum, **446**, 455
  undulatum, 455
Gnidia, 159
  apiculata, 161
  buchananii, 161
  chrysantha, 159, **160**
  fastigiata, 161
  glauca, 159
  kraussiana, 159, **160**
  lamprantha, 159
  latifolia, 159
  macrorrhiza, **160**, 161
  subcordata, 161
Gomphocarpus, 377
  fruticosus, 377, **379**
  integer, 377
  kaessneri, 377
  physocarpus, 377, **379**

semilunatus, 377, **378**
  stenophyllus, **378**, 380
Gomphrena, 137
  celosioides, 139
Gongronema, 388
  angolense, 388
Gouania, 338
  longispicata, 338, **339**
Grammitis, 71
  sp. A, 71
Grangea, 436
  maderaspatana, 436
Guizotia, 462
  abyssinica, 465
  reptans, 462
  scabra, 462, **463**
Gunnera, 158
  perpensa, 158
Gutenbergia, 420
  fischeri, 422
  rueppellii, 420, **421**
Gymnema, 387
  sylvestre, 388
Gynandropsis, 92
  gynandra, 92, **93**
Gynura, 471,
  amplexicaulis, 471
  miniata, 471
  scandens, **470**, 471
  valeriana, 472

Habenaria, 731
  altior, 740
  attenuata, 737
  bracteosa, **734**, 737
  cavatibrachia, 739
  chirensis, **736**, 740
  chlorotica, 737, **738**
  cirrhata, 741
  cornuta, **736**, 739
  decorata, 739
  eggelingii, 737
  egregia, 739
  epipactidea, 737
  helicoplectrum, 741
  hologlossa, **733**, 737
  holubii, **734**, 741
  huillensis, 740
  humilior, **738**, 740
  keniensis, **738**, 739
  laurentii, **738**, 741
  lindblomii, **743**, 744
  linderi, 740
  macrantha, 739
  macrura, 741
  macruroides, 741, **743**
  malacophylla, **733**, 740
  ndiana, **733**, 740
  njamnjamica, 739
  peristyloides, 737, **742**
  petitiana, **733**, 737
  quartiniana, 739, **743**
  schimperana, **732**, 741
  splendens, **736**, 739
  thomsonii, 740

tweedieae, **733**, 739
vaginata, **738**, 741
walleri, 741, **742**
zambesina, 737, **742**
Haemanthus, 708
filiflorus, 708
multiflorus, 708, **709**
Halleria, 551
lucida, 551
Haloragaceae, 158
Haplocarpha, 486
scaposa, 486
schimperi, 486
rueppellii, **423**, 486
Haplosciadium, 355
abyssinicum, 355
Harpagocarpus, 123
snowdenii, 123
Harveya, 565
obtusifolia, 565
Haumaniastrum, 642
caeruleum, 643
galeopsifolius, 643
venosum, 643
Haydonia,
monophylla, 279
triphylla, 279
Hebenstretia, 567
dentata, 567, **612**
Helichrysum, 448
albiflorum, 452
amblyphyllum, 454
argyranthum, 455
brownei, **449**, 454
chionoides, 454
citrispinum, **453**, 454
cymosum, **449**, 454
ellipticifolium, 454
foetidum, **451**, 454
formosissimum, 455
gerberifolium, 452
globosum, 452, **453**
gloria-dei, 454
glumaceum, 452
guilelmi, 455
kilimanjari, 454
kirkii, 454
maranguense, **451**, 454
meyeri-johannis, 455
nandense, **451**, 455
newii, 454
nudifolium, 452
odoratissimum, **451**, 452
panduratum, **449**, 452
rhodolepis, 452
schimperi, 452, **453**
setosum, **453**, 454
sp. A, 452
Helinus, 340
integrifolius, 340
mystacinus, **337**, 340
Heliotropium, 518
albohispidum, 518
ovalifolium, **519**, 520
rariflorum, 518

scotteae, 520
sessilistigma, 518
somalense, 520
sp. A, 520
steudneri, **519**, 520
strigosum, 518
subulatum, **519**, 520
supinum, 520
undulatifolium, 520
Heracleum, 360
abyssinicum, **361**, 362
elgonense, 360
inexpectatum, 362
taylori, 362
Hermannia, 190
alhiensis, 191
exappendiculata, 191
kirkii, 191
oliveri, 191
sp. A, 191, **192**
uhligii, 191
viscosa, 191
Hernandiaceae, 75
Hesperantha, 716
petitiana, 716
Heteranthera, 700
callifolia, 700
Hewittia, 535
sublobata, 535
Hibiscus, 193
aethiopicus, **197**, 199
aponeurus, 196, **198**
articulatus, **198**, 199
calyphyllus, **194**, 196
cannabinus, **197**, 199
corymbosus, 199
diversifolius, **198**, 199
flavifolius, 196, **200**
fuscus, 196, **197**
greenwayi, 199
lunariifolius, 196
macranthus, 196
micranthus, 196, **198**
palmatus, 195
panduriformis, 199
sidiformis, 195
sp. A, 196
sp. B, 196
sp. C, 196, **197**
sp. D, 195
surattensis, 199
trionum, 195
vitifolius, **194**, 195
Hilleria, 127
latifolia, 127
Hippocratea, 326
africana, 326
goetzei, 326
indica, 326
Hirpicium, 486
diffusum, **488**, 489
Histiopteris, 30
incisa, 30
Hoehnelia, 420
vernonioides, 420, **421**

Holothrix, 727
aphylla, 729
arachnoidea, 729
elgonensis, **728**, 729
nyassae, 729
pentadactyla, **728**, 729
puberula, **728**, 729
Homalocheilos, 640
ramosissimum, 642
Hoslundia, 642
opposita, 642, **647**
Huernia, 396
aspera, 396
keniensis, **394**, 396
Hybanthus, 100
enneaspermus, 100
Hydnora, 84
abyssinica, 84
johannis, 84
Hydnoraceae, 84
Hydrilla, 649
verticillata, 649
Hydrocharitaceae, 648
Hydrocotyle, 349
mannii, 349
monticola, 349
ranunculoides, 349
sp. A, 349, **350**
Hygrophila, 581
auriculata, 583, **584**
pobeguinii, 583
sp. A, 583
spiciformis, 583
Hymenophyllum, 27
capillare, 28
kuhnii, 28
splendidum, 28
tunbrigense, 28
Hypericaceae, 183
Hypericum, 186
afromontanum, 186
annulatum, **185**, 186
conjunctum, 187
keniense, 186
kiboense, 186
lalandii, **185**, 186
lanceolatum, 186
peplidifolium, **185**, 187
quartinianum, 186
revolutum, 186
roeperianum, 186
scioanum, **185**, 187
Hypertelis, 117
bowkeriana, 117
Hypochoeris, 494
glabra, 496
Hypodematium, 46
crenatum, 48
Hypoestes, 609
aristata, 609, **610**
triflora, 609, **610**
verticillaris, **610**, 611
Hypolepis, 29
rugosula, 29, **31**
sparsisora, 30

Hypoxidaceae, 724
Hypoxis, 724
    angustifolia, 724, **725**
    kilimanjarica, 724
    multiflora, 724, **725**
    obtusa, 724, **725**
    villosa, 724
Hyptis, 628
    brevipes, 628
    pectinata, 628

Iboza, 642
    multiflora, 642
    riparia, 642
Icacinaceae, 326
Illigera, 75
    pentaphylla, 75
Ilysanthes, 556
    parviflora, **554**, 556
    pulchella, 556
    pusilla, **554**, 556
    rotundifolia, 556
    sp. A, 556
Impatiens, 149
    cruciata, 153
    elegantissima, **150**, 151
    eminii, 153
    fischeri, 151
    gilgii, 153
    hochstetteri, **152**, 153
    hohnellii, 153
    nana, 151
    niamniamensis, 151
    papilionacea, **150**, 153
    phlyctidoceras, 151
    rubromaculata, **152**, 153
    sodenii, 151
    stuhlmannii, 151
    telekii, 151
    tweediae, 151, **150**
Indigastrum macrostachyum, 259
Indigofera, 248
    alboglandulosa, 255
    ambelacensis, **249**, 252
    anabaptista, 251
    arrecta, **249**, 257
    asparagoides, 259
    astragalina, 258
    atriceps, **253**, 255
    baukeana, 258
    bogdanii, 257
    boranensis, 258
    brachynema, 255
    brevicalyx, 252, **253**
    brevipetiolata, 254
    capitata, 251
    carinata, 257
    circinella, **249**, 258
    cliffordiana, 257
    colutea, 254
    colutea, 255
    commiphoroides, 257
    congesta, 251
    conjugata, 258
    conradsii, 252

costata, 259
cufodontii, 259
deflexa, 259
demissa, 251
dendroides, 252
divaricata, 254
emarginella, 257
endecaphylla, 258
garckeana, 257
glabra, 252
goniocarpa, 257
goniodes, 259
hedyantha, 252
hendecaphylla, 258
hochstetteri, 251
homblei, 255, **256**
kaessneri, 255
longibarbata, 258
lupatana, 257
macrostachyum, 259
masaiensis, 255
mearnsii, 257
microcharoides, 259
mimosoides, **253**, 254
minimifolia, 252
monanthoides, 252
multifoliolata, 255
nairobiensis, 252
oblongifolia, 258
oliveri, 257
parviflora, 259
parvula, 258
pauciflora, 252
pentaphylla, 252
phillipsiae, 258
retroflexa, 257
rogersii, 254
scabra, 257
schimperi, 258
secundiflora, 255
semlikiensis, 254
setosissima, 255
shirensis, 254
spicata, **253**, 258
spinosa, 254
spirocarpa, 258
suaveolens, 252
subargentea, **253**, 254
subhirtella, 258
subulata, 257
swaziensis, 257
tanganyikensis, 252
tetragona, 257
tettensis, 258
thikaensis, 254
tinctoria, 258
trita, **249**, 257
uhehensis, 252
vicioides, 254
viscosa, 254, 255
vohemarensis, 252
volkensii, **256**, 258
wildemannii, 252
zenkeri, 255

Inula, 456
    decipiens, 456, **457**
    glomerata, 456
    mannii, 456
Iphigenia, 674
    oliveri, 674
Ipomoea, 539
    acuminata, 545
    alba, 547
    aquatica, 547
    arachnosperma, 545
    argyrophylla, 549
    batatas, 545
    blepharophylla, 542, **543**
    cairica, **546**, 547
    congesta, 545
    coscinosperma, 542
    crassipes, 544
    crepidiformis, 544
    eriocarpa, 542
    ficifolia, 545
    fulvicaulis, 542, **543**
    hartmannii, 548
    hederifolia, 547
    hildebrandtii, 548
    hochstetteri, 547
    involucrata, 544
    jaegeri, **538**, 549
    kituiensis, 548
    lapathifolia, 547
    lapidosa, 548
    learii, 545
    lilacina, 547
    longituba, 548
    mombassana, 544
    obscura, 545
    ochracea, 545, **546**
    oenotherae, 542, **543**
    pes-caprae, 547
    pes-tigridis, 545
    plebeia, 542
    polymorpha, 542, **543**
    purpurea, 545
    riparia, 547
    rubens, 547
    sinensis, 544
    sp. near cicatricosa, 549
    spathulata, 548
    tenuirostris, 544, **546**
    tricolor, 545
    wightii, 545, **546**
Iridaceae, 712
Isodictyophorus, 640
    defoliatus, 640, **641**
Isoetes, 24
    abyssinica, 24
    tenuifolia, 24
Isoglossa, 599
    gregorii, 599, **608**
    lactea, 599
    laxa, 599, **600**
    oerstediana, 599, **600**
    substrobilina, **600**, 601

Jacquemontia, 534
　ovalifolia, 534
Jasminum, 364
　abyssinicum, **363**, 365
　dichotomum, 364
　eminii, 364
　floribundum, **363**, 364
　fluminense, 365
　meyeri-johannis, 364
　parvifolium, 364
　pauciflorum, 364
　sp. A, 365
Jatropha, 218
　curcas, 218
　ferox, 218
　fissispina, 218
　parvifolia, 218
　spicata, 218
Juncaceae, 802
Juncus, 802
　bufonius, 802
　dregeanus, 803
　effusus, 803
　oxycarpus, 803
Jussiaea,
　perennis, 157
　repens, 156
　suffruticosa, 157
Justicia, 601
　anselliana, **602**, 603
　betonica, 603, **606**
　betonicoides, 604
　caerulea, 604, **606**
　cordata, 604
　diclipteroides, 605
　elliotii, 604
　exigua, **602**, 603
　extensa, 604
　fischeri, 604
　flava, **602**, 604
　glabra, 604
　heterocarpa, 605
　keniensis, 605
　leikipiensis, 605
　leptocarpa, 605
　matammensis, 603
　nyassana, 604
　odora, 604
　pinguior, 605, **606**
　ruwenzoriensis, 604
　sp. A, 603
　sp. C, 603
　sp. D, 604
　sp. E, 605
　striata, **602**, 605
　uncinulata, **602**, 603

Kaempferia, 671
　aethiopica, 671
Kalanchoe, 105
　citrina, 107
　densiflora, **106**, 107
　glaucescens, 107
　lanceolata, 107

lugardii, **106**, 107
marmorata, 107
pinnata, 105
rohlfsii, 107
sp. A, 107
sp. B, **106**, 107
Kanahia, 380
　laniflora, **376**, 380
Kedrostis, 177
　foetidissima, 178
　gijef, 177
　hirtella, 178
　pseudogijef, 177
Kleinia, 483
　barbertonicus, 483
　kleinioides, 483
　sp. A, 483
　sp. B, 483
　sp. C, 483
Kniphofia, 688
　rogersii, 688
　snowdenii, **687**, 688
　thomsonii, 688
Kochia, 130
　indica, 130
Kohautia, 398
　aspera, 398
　caespitosa, 398
　coccinea, 398, **399**
　virgata, 398
Kosteletskya, 199
　adoensis, 199, **200**
　begoniifolia, **200**, 201
Kotschya, 263
　aeschynomenoides, 263
　africana, 263
　capitulifera, 263
　recurvifolia, 263

Labiatae, 616
Lablab, 282
　purpureus, **269**, 282
Lactuca, 498
　capensis, **499**, 500
　glandulifera, **499**, 500
　paradoxa, 500
Lagarosiphon, 649
　hydrilloides, 649
　sp. A, 649
　tenuis, 649
Lagascea, 458
　mollis, 458
Lagenaria, 170
　abyssinica, 171
　breviflora, 171
　siceraria, 171
　sphaerica, 171
Laggera, 443
　alata, 443
　brevipes, 443, **444**
　elatior, 443, **444**
　pterodonta, 443, **444**
Landolphia, 365
　buchananii, 367
　kilimandscharica, 367

ugandensis, 367
Lantana, 613
Lapeyrousia, 716
　laxa, **716**, **718**
Laportea, 321
　alatipes, 321
Lathyrus, 316
　hygrophilus, **317**, 318
　sphaericus, **317**, 318
Launea, 496
　cornuta, 496, **497**
　hafunensis, 496
　intybacea, 496
　nana, 496
　nigricola, 496
Lauraceae, 75
Laurembergia, 158
　engleri, 158
Leea, 345
　guineensis, 347
Lefebvrea, 360
　abyssinica, 360
　brevipes, 360
Lemna, 706
　gibba, 707
　perpusilla, 707
　trisulca, 707
Lemnaceae, 706
Lentibulariaceae, 569
Leonotis, 619
　africana, 620
　elliottii, 620
　leonitis, 620
　mollissima, 620, **621**
　nepetifolia, 619
　velutina, 620
Lepidagathis, 596
　collina, **595**, 596
　scabra, 596
　scariosa, **595**, 596
Lepidium, 95
　africanum, 95
　bonariense, 95
　sativum, 95
Lepistemon, 537
　owariensis, **536**, 537
Lepistemonopsis, 537
　volkensii, 537
Leptadenia, 389
　hastata, **384**, 389
Leptogramma pozoi, 54
Leucas, 620
　bracteosa, 622
　calostachys, **612**, 623
　concinna, 622
　glabrata, 623
　jamesii, 622
　martinicensis, 622
　masaiensis, 623
　micrantha, 622
　mollis, 622
　neuflizeana, 623
　oligocephala, 623
　pododiskos, 622
　pratensis, 622

Leucas—*continued*
  schweinfurthii, 623
  sp. A, 622
  tricrenata, 623
  urticifolia, 622
  venulosa, 623
Lightfootia, 509
  abyssinica, 511, **512**
  cartilaginea, 511, **512**
  denticulata, 511
  glomerata, 511
  hirsuta, 511
  perotifolia, 511
  sp. A, 511
  sp. B, 511
  tanneri, 511
Liliaceae, 671
Limeum, 116
  viscosum, 116
Limosella, 553
  africana, 553
  aquatica, 553
  major, 553
  micrantha, 553
Linaceae, 139
Lindernia, 555
  abyssinica, **554**, 556
  diffusa, 556
  lobelioides, 556
  oliverana, **552**, 556
  sp. A, 556
  whytei, 556
Linum, 139
  keniense, 139
  usitatissimum, 139
  volkensii, 139, **145**
Liparis, 756
  deistelii, **759**, 760
  neglecta, 760
  odontochilus, 760
Lippia, 613
  grandiflora, 614
  javanica, 613
  somalensis, 613
  ukambensis, 613
  wilmsii, 613
Lithospermum, 523
  afromontanum, **522**, 523
Lobelia, 513
  aberdarica, 515, **516**
  anceps, **514**, 517
  bambuseti, 515
  baumanii, 515
  duripratii, 517
  elgonensis, 515
  gibberoa, 515, **516**
  holstii, **514**, 517
  keniensis, 515
  kinangopia, **514**, 517
  lindblomii, **514**, 517
  melleri var. *grossidens*, 517
  minutula, 517
  molleri, 517
  sattimae, 515
  telekii, 515

  welwitschii, 517
Loewia, 89
  tanaensis, 89
Lomariopsis, 52
  warneckei, 52
Lonchitis stipitata, 30
Loranthaceae, 326
Loranthus, 326
  acaciae, 330
  acacietorum, 332
  aurantiacus, 330
  braunii, 332, **333**
  brunneus, **331**, 334
  constrictiflorus, 332, **335**
  curviflorus, 330, **331**
  dschallensis, **329**, 330
  fischeri, **327**, 330
  heckmannianus, 330
  hildebrandtii, 330
  keudelii, 334
  kirkii, 330
  meridianum, 332
  oehleri, 334
  panganensis, 330, **333**
  platyphyllus, 330
  rufescens, **329**, 330
  sagittifolius, 330
  sp. B, 332
  sp. C, 332
  sp. D, 332
  stuhlmannii, 332
  sulphureus, 332
  ugogensis, 332
  ulugurense, 330, **335**
  woodfordioides, **331**, 332
  ziziphifolius, 332
Lotononis, 290
  angolensis, 290
  laxa, 290
  platycarpos, 290
Lotus, 313
  becquetii, **264**, 313
  corniculatus, 313
  discolor, 314
  friesiorum, 313
  goetzei, **264**, 314
  mearnsii, 313
  oehleri, 314
  tigrensis, 313
  tigrensis, 314
Loxogramme, 70
  lanceolata, 70
Ludwigia, 156
  abyssinica, 157
  erecta, 157
  jussiaeoides, 157
  leptocarpa, 156
  octovalvis, 157
  perennis, 157
  pubescens, 157
  stenorraphe, 157
  stolonifera, 156
Luffa, 173
  cylindrica, 173
Lupinus, 306

  albus, 306
  angustifolius, 306
  luteus, 306
  princei, 306, **307**
Luzula, 803
  abyssinica, 803
  campestris, 803
  johnstonii, 803
Lycium, 529
  europaeum, 529
Lycopodium, 22
  aberdaricum, 22
  cernuum, 22
  clavatum, 22
  dacrydioides, 23
  ophioglossoides, 23
  saururus, 23
  verticillatum, 23
Lysimachia, 506
  ruhmerana, 506, **507**
  volkensii, 506
Lythraceae, 153
Lythrum, 154
  rotundifolium, 154

Macrorungia, 607
  pubinervia, 607
Macrothelypteris aubertii, **31**, 54
Macrotyloma, 281
  africanum, 282
  axillare, **280**, 282
  daltonii, 282
  maranguense, 282
  stipulosum, 282
  uniflorum, 282
Maerua, 92
Malpighiaceae, 209
Malva, 205
  parviflora, 206
  verticillata, **202**, 205
Malvaceae, 193
Marattia, 25
  fraxinea, 25
Margaretta, 385
  rosea, **384**, 385
Marsilea, 72
  farinosa, 73
  gibba, 73
  macrocarpa, 73
  minuta, 73
Medicago, 313
  laciniata, 313
  lupulina, 313
  sativa, 313
Meineckia, 213
  phyllanthoides, 213
  sp. A, 213
Melanthera, 462
  albinervia, 462
  scandens, 462, **463**
Melastomataceae, 180
Melhania, 191
  ovata, 191
  velutina, 191, **192**
Melilotus, 312

alba, 313
indica, 312
officinalis, 312
suaveolens, 312
Melochia, 193
corchorifolia, 193
Menispermaceae, 82
Mentha, 628
aquatica, **627**, 628
longifolia, 628
sylvestris, 628
Merremia, 535
ampelophylla, 535
palmata, 537
pinnata, 535
pterygocaulos, 537
tridentata, 535
Micrargeria, 559
filiformis, 559
Micrococca, 213
holstii, 213
mercurialis, 213
Microcoelia, 785
guyoniana, 785, **786**
koehleri, 785, **786**
pachystemma, 785
smithii, 785
Microglossa oblongifolia, 441
Microlepia, 29
speluncae, 29
Microsorium, 71
punctatum, 71
Mikania, 436
cordata, 436
Mikaniopsis, 471
clematoides, 471
usambarensis, 471
Mimosa, 236
pigra, 237
pudica, 237
Mimosaceae, 236
Mimulopsis, 587
alpina, 587, **588**
arborescens, 587
solmsii, 587, **588**
Mimulus, 553
gracilis, 553
Mirabilis, 163
jalapa, 163
Misopates, 551
orontium, 551, **552**
Mitracarpum, 409
scaber, 409
verticillatum, 409
Moghania grahamiana, 290
Mohria, 27
caffrorum, 27
Mollugo, 116
cerviana, 117
nudicaulis, 117
Momordica, 168
boivinii, 170, **172**
calantha, 170
cissoides, 170
foetida, **169**, 170

friesiorum, **169**, 170
pterocarpa, 170
rostrata, 170
spinosa, 170
trifoliolata, 170
Monadenium, 225
invenustum, 225
montanum, 225
rhizophorum, 225
stapelioides, **224**, 225
trinerve, 225
yattanum, 225
Mondia, 370
ecornuta, 370
Monechma, 605
debile, 605, **606**
subsessilis, 605
Monopsis, 517
stellarioides, 517, **519**
Monothecium, 598
glandulosum, 598
Monsonia, 141
angustifolia, 141, **143**
glauca, 144
longipes, 144, **145**
ovata, 144
Montia, 121
fontana, 121
Moraceae, 318
Moraea, 720
carsonii, **719**, 720
thomsonii, **719**, 720
Mucuna, 270
gigantea, 270
poggei, **271**, 272
stans, 270
Mukia, 175
maderaspatana, 175, **176**
Murdannia, 667
clarkeana, 667
semiteres, 667, **668**
simplex, 667, **668**
Myosotis, 523
abyssinica, **522**, 523
keniensis, 523
vestergrenii, 523
Myriophyllum, 158
brasiliense, 158
Myrmecosicyos, 177
messorius, 177

Najadaceae, 652
Najas, 653
graminea, 653
pectinata, 653
Nasturtium officinale, 99
Neohyptis, 642
paniculata, 642
Neorautanenia, 282
mitis, 282
Nepeta, 617
azurea, 617, **618**
Nephrolepis, 43
biserrata, 43
cordifolia, 43

undulata, 43
Nervilia, 756
kotschyi, 756, **757**
Nesaea, 154
erecta, 154
floribunda, 154
lythroides, 154
schinzii, 155
Neuracanthus, 594
sp. A, 594
sp. C, 596
Nicandra, 529
physalodes, 529
Nicolasia nitens, 445
Nicotiana, 530
glauca, 530
tabacum, 530
Nidorella, 438
pedunculata, 440
resedifolia, 438
spartioides, **437**, 438
Notholaena, 35
inaequalis, 35, **38**
Nothosaerva, 136
brachiata, 136
Notonia, 483
abyssinica, 484, **485**
coccinea, 484
grantii, 484
gregorii, 484, **485**
hildebrandtii, 484
implexa, 484
petraea, 484, **485**
picticaulis, 484
schweinfurthii, 484
sp. A, 484
Nyctaginaceae, 161
Nymphaea, 81
caerulea, 81
capensis, 81
lotus, 81
Nymphaeaceae, 81
Nymphoides, 505
indica, 505

Oberonia, 756
disticha, 756
Ocimum, 643
americanum, 645
basilicum, 645
capitatum, 646
hadiense, 645
kilimandscharicum, **644**, 645
lamiifolium, **644**, 645
sp. A, 645
sp. B, 645
sp. C, 645
suave, **644**, 645
tomentosum. 645
Oenanthe, 357
palustris, 357
procumbens, 357
Oenostachys, 720
dichroa, 720

Oenothera, 157
  rosea, 157
Oldenlandia, 398
  acicularis, 401
  bullockii, 400
  caespitosa, 401
  corymbosa, **399, 401**
  fastigiata, 401
  friesiorum, 400
  goreensis, 400
  herbàcea, 401
  johnstonii, 400
  lancifolia, 400
  linearis, 401
  monanthos, **399**, 400
  scopulorum, 401
  verticillata, 400
  wiedemannii, 400
Oleaceae, 364
Oleandra, 44
  distenta, 44
Onagraceae, 155
Ophioglossum, 24
  lusoafricanum, 25
  polyphyllum, 25, **26**
  reticulatum, 25
  rubellum, 25
  sp. A, 25
  vulgatum, 25
Ophrestia, 270
  radicosa, 270
Opuntia, 180
  vulgaris, 180
Orchidaceae, 726
Oreophyton, 99
  falcatum, 99
Oreosyce, 175
  africana, 175, **176**
Ormocarpum, 260
  aromaticum, 260
  kirkii, 260
  mimosoides, 260
  trachycarpum, 260
  trichocarpum, 260, **262**
Ornithogalum, 695
  ecklonii, 697
  gracillimum, 695, **696**
  longibracteatum, 697
  sp. A, 697
Orobanchaceae, 567
Orobanche, 569
  cernua, 569
  minor, **568**, 590
  ramosa, 569
Orthosiphon, 646
  australis, 648
  hildebrandtii, **618**, 648
  parvifolius, **647**, 648
  rubicundus, **644**, 648
  somalensis, 648
  suffrutescens, 648
Osmunda, 25
  regalis, 27
Osteospermum, 486
  vaillantii, 486, **487**

Osyridicarpos, 334
  scandens, 336
Otomeria, 405
  elatior, 405
  oculata, 405
Ottelia, 649
  sp. A, 649
  ulvifolia, 649
Oxalidaceae, 144
Oxalis, 146
  anthelmintica, 146, **148**
  corniculata, 146, **147**
  latifolia, 146, **148**
  obliquifolia, 146, **147**
  radicosa, 146, **147**
  stricta, 146
Oxygonum, 126
  maculatum, 127
  sinuatum, **125**, 127
  sp. A, 126
  stuhlmannii, **118**, 127
Oxystelma, 373
  bornouense, 374

Pachycarpus, 380
  eximius, 380, **383**
  fulvus, 380
  grantii, 380
  lineolatus, **381**, 382
  rhinophyllus, 380
  schweinfurthii, 382, **383**
Paederia, 407
  pospischilii, 407
Pancratium, 712
  trianthum, 712, **717**
Papaveraceae, 88
Papilionaceae, 237
Paraknoxia, 405
  parviflora, 405, **406**
Parapentas, 397
  battiscombei, 398
Parietaria, 325
  debilis, 325
Parochetus, 312
  communis, 312
Parquetina, 370
  nigrescens, 370
Passiflora, 166
  eichlerana, 166
Passifloraceae, 163
Paullinia, 347
  pinnata, 348
Pavonia, 206
  arabica, 206
  elegans, 209
  grewioides, 206
  irakuensis, 209
  kilimandscharica, 209
  patens, 206, **208**
  propinqua, 206, **207**
  sp. A, 206
  urens, **208**, 209
  zeylanica, 206
Pedaliaceae, 572
Pegolettia, 456

senegalensis, 456
Pelargonium, 144
  alchemilloides, **143**, 144
  glechomoides, 144
  multibracteatum, 144
  quinquelobatum, 144, **145**
  whytei, 144
Pellaea, 39
  adiantoides, 40, **41**
  boivinii, 40
  calomelanos, 40, **41**
  doniana, 39
  involuta, 40
  longipilosa, 39, **41**
  quadripinnata, 40
  schweinfurthii, 40
  sp. A, 40
  viridis, 40, **42**
Pentamenes, 720
  sp. A, 720
Pentanisia, 405
  foetida, 405
  ouranogyne, 405, **406**
  schweinfurthii, 405, **406**
Pentarrhinum, 382
  abyssinicum, **366**, 385
  insipidum, **381**, 385
  sp. A, 385
Pentas, 401
  arvensis, 404
  decora, **399**, 404
  hindsioides, 404
  lanceolata, **403**, 404
  longiflora, **403**, 404
  parvifolia, **403**, 404
  pubiflora, 405, **406**
  schimperana, 404
  suswaensis, 404
  zanzibarica, 405
Pentodon, 401
  pentandrus, 401
Peperomia, 85
  abyssinica, 85, **87**
  arabica, 85
  bangroana, 85
  butaguensis, 85
  mannii, 85
  tetraphylla, 85, **87**
Peponium, 173
  vogelii, 173
Pergularia, 387
  daemia, **371**, 387
Periploca, 370
  linearifolia, **372**, 373
Peristrophe, 609
  bicalyculata, 609
Peucedanum, 358
  aberdarense, 358
  aculeolatum, 358, **361**
  canaliculatum, 358
  elgonense, **359**, 360
  friesiorum, 358
  kerstenii, 358
  linderi, 360
  sp. A, 358

Phanerophlebia, 48
  caryotidea, 48, **59**
  falcata, 48
Phaseolus,
  macrorhynchus, 279
  schimperi, 279
  stenocarpus, 279
Phaulopsis, 589
  imbricata, **586**, 589
Phyla, 613
  nodiflora, 613
Phyllanthus, 211
  amarus, 212
  capillaris, 212
  discoideus, 212
  fischeri, **207**, 213
  glaucophyllus, 212
  guineensis, 212
  inflatus, 212
  leucocalyx, 211
  maderaspatensis, 212
  meruensis, 213
  muelleranus, 212
  odontadenius, 212
  reticulatus, 212
  rotundifolius, 213
  sepialis, 213
  sp. A, 212
  sp. B, 212
  sp. C, 212
  suffrutescens, **207**, 212
Phymatodes, 70
  scolopendria, 70
Physalis, 528
  angulata, 529
  divaricata, 529
  ixocarpa, 529
  minima, 529
  peruviana, 529
Phytolacca, 127
  dodecandra, **125**, 127
  octandra, 127
Phytolaccaceae, 127
Pilea, 323
  ceratomera, 323
  johnstonii, 323
  tetraphylla, 323
  usambarensis, 323
  veronicifolia, 323
Piloselloides, 494
  hirsuta, **494**, **495**
Pimpinella, 356
  friesiorum, 356
  keniensis, **354**, 356
  kilimandscharica, 356
  peregrina, 356
  sp. A, 356
  volkensii, 356
Piper, 85
  capense, 88
  guineense, 88
  umbellatum, **86**, 88
Piperaceae, 84
Pisonia, 161
  aculeata, 161

Pistia, 706
  stratiotes, 706
Pityrogramma, 32
  aurantiaca, 32
Plantaginaceae, 508
Plantago, 508
  lanceolata, 509
  major, 509
  palmata, **507**, 508
Platostoma, 642
  africanum, 642
Platycerium, 69
  angolense, 69
Platycoryne, 744
  crocea, **728**, 744
Plectranthus, 633
  alboviolaceus, 638
  albus, 636
  assurgens, 636
  barbatus, **634**, 636
  caninus, **634**, 635
  coeruleus, 635
  comosus, 635
  cyaneus, 638
  cylindraceus, 635, **637**
  defoliatus, 640
  edulis, **639**, 640
  ignarius, 638
  kamerunensis, 638
  lactiflorus, **634**, 635
  lanuginosus, 638
  laxiflorus, 638, **639**
  longipes, 636
  luteus, 636
  marrubioides, 635, **637**
  masukensis, 636
  parvus, 638
  pauciflorus, 636
  prostratus, 638
  pubescens, 636
  sp. A, 635
  sp. B, 636, **641**
  sp. F, 640
  sp. G, 638
  sp. H, 638
  sylvestris, 636, **637**
  tenuiflorus, 636
  tetensis, 635
  zatarhendi, 640
Pleopeltis, 70
  excavata, 71
  macrocarpa, 71
  rotunda, **26**, 71
  schraderi, 71
Pluchea, 445
  bequaertii, 445
  dioscoridis, 445
  nitens, 445
  ovalis, 445
Plumbaginaceae, 508
Plumbago, 508
  montis-elgonis, 508
  zeylanica, **502**, 508
Podostemaceae, 109
Pollia, 664

condensata, 664
Pollichia, 111
  campestris, 111
Polycarpaea, 110
  corymbosa, 111
  eriantha, 111
Polycarpon, 111
  prostratum, 111
Polygala, 101
  abyssinica, 103
  albida, **102**, 103
  amboniensis, 101
  arenaria, 103
  erioptera, 103
  myriantha, 101
  ohlendorfiana, 103
  persicariifolia, 103
  petitiana, 101, **102**
  sadebeckiana, **102**, 103
  senensis, 103
  sphenoptera, **102**, 103
  ukirensis, 103
Polygalaceae, 101
Polygonaceae, 122
Polygonum, 124
  afromontanum, 124
  aviculare, 126
  baldschuanicum, 124
  capitatum, 124
  convolvulus, 124
  nepalense, 124
  pulchrum, 126
  salicifolium, **125**, 126
  senegalense, 126
  setulosum, **125**, 126
  strigosum, 126
Polystachya, 765
  adansoniae, 768, **770**
  albescens, 768
  bella, 768, **769**
  bicarinata, 766, **770**
  campyloglossa, 768, **769**
  confusa, 768
  cultriformis, 766, **769**
  eurychila, 766, **770**
  eurygnatha, 766, **771**
  fusiformis, 766, **767**
  golungensis, 768, **771**
  holstii, 768
  inconspicua, 766, **767**
  isochiloides, 768
  latilabris, 766, **767**
  lindblomii, 766, **770**
  shega, 768, **771**
  simplex, 766, **769**
  spatella, 766, **771**
  steudneri, **759**, 766
  stricta, **759**, 768
  tayloriana, 766
  tessellata, 768
  transvaalensis, **767**, 768
Polystichum, 48
  barbatum, 48
  fuscopaleaceum, 48
  magnificum, 48

Polystichum–*continued*
  volkensii, 48, **59**
Pontederiaceae, 700
Portulaca, 119
  foliosa, **120,** 121
  kermesina, 121
  oleracea, **120,** 121
  parensis, 121
  quadrifida, **120,** 121
  sp. A, 121
Portulacaceae, 119
Potamogeton, 652
  octandrus, 652
  pectinatus, 652
  richardii, 652
  schweinfurthii, 652
  trichoides, 652
Potamogetonaceae, 652
Potentilla, 227
  pensylvanica, 227
Pouzolzia, 325
  parasitica, 325
Premna, 614
Primulaceae, 505
Priva, 613
  cordifolia, 613
  curtisiae, **612,** 613
Pseudarthria, 267
  confertiflora, 267
  hookeri, 267
Pseuderanthemum, 598
  ludovicianum, 598
Pseudocarum, 356
  eminii, 356
Pseudosopubia, 560
  hildebrandtii, 560, **561**
  kituiensis, 560, 561
Pseudowolffia, 707
  hyalina, 707
Psiadia, 438
  arabica, 438
  punctulata, 438
Psilotrichum, 136
  elliottii, 137, **138**
  schimperi, 136
Psophocarpus, 272
  lancifolius, 272, **273**
Pteridium, 30
  aquilinum, 30
Pteris, 33
  buchananii, 35
  catoptera, 35, **36**
  cretica, 33, **34**
  dentata, 35
  intricata, 35
  mohasiensis, 35
  preussii, 35
  pteridioides, 35
  vittata, 33
Pterocephalus, 414
  frutescens, 416
Pterodiscus, 572
  ruspolii, 572
Pteroglossaspis, 782
  englerana, 782

eustachya, 782
  ruwenzoriensis, 783
Pterolobium, 236
  stellatum, **235,** 236
Pupalia, 135
  lappacea, 136
Pycnospora, 267
  lutescens, 267
Pycnostachys, 630
  coerulea, 632
  deflexifolia, **631,** 632
  eminii, 630
  meyeri, **631,** 632
  nepetifolia, 632
  niamniamensis, **631,** 632
  sp. A, 632
  speciosa, 632
  stuhlmannii, **631,** 632
  umbrosa, 630
Pyrenacantha, 326
  malvifolia, 326
Pyrrosia, 69
  schimperana, 70

Rangaeris, 796
  amaniensis, **795,** 796
  brachyceras, **795,** 796
  muscicola, 796, **797**
Ranunculaceae, 75
Ranunculus, 76
  aberdaricus, 78
  cryptanthus, 78
  keniensis, 78
  multifidus, 78, **79**
  oreophytus, 78, **79**
  sceleratus, 78
  stagnalis, 78
  volkensii, 78
Raphanus, 94
  raphanistrum, 95
  sativus, 95
Raphionacme, 370
  madiensis, 370, **371**
  splendens, 370
Reichardia, 500
  tingitana, 500
Renealmia, 671
  sp. A, 671
Resedaceae, 100
Rhamnaceae, 338
Rhamnus, 338
  prinoides, 338
Rhamphicarpa, 562
  ajugifolia, 564, **566**
  asperrima, 564
  fistulosa, 562
  herzfeldiana, **563,** 564
  heuglini, 564
  jamesii, 562, **563**
  meyeri-johannis, 562
  montana, 564, **566**
  recurva, 562, **563**
  sp. A, 562
  tenuisecta, 562
  tubulosa, **563,** 564

veronicifolia, 564
Rhinacanthus, 598
  nasutus, 598
  ndorensis, 598
Rhipsalis, 180
  baccifera, 180
Rhoicissus, 347
  revoilii, 347
  tridentata, 347, **350**
Rhynchosia, 282
  albiflora, 284
  albissima, 286
  alluaudii, 285
  densiflora, 285
  elegans, 285
  ferruginea, 285
  hirta, **283,** 284
  holstii, 286
  kilimandscharica, 286
  malacophylla, 286
  minima, **283,** 286
  nyasica, 285
  oblatifoliolata, 285
  orthobotrya, **283,** 285
  procurrens, 285
  pseudoviscosa, 285
  pulchra, 285
  resinosa, 285
  senaarensis, 286
  sublobata, 285
  totta, 285
  usambarensis, 285
Rhynchotropis curtisiae, 259
Richardia, 407
  braziliensis, **402,** 407
Ricinus, 218
  communis, 218
Roeperocharis, 744
  bennettiana, 744
Romulea, 714
  campanuloides, 714
  fischeri, 714, **715**
  keniensis, 714
Rorippa, 97
  cryptantha, 99
  madagascariensis, 99
  nasturtium-aquaticum, 99
  nudiuscula, 99
Rosaceae, 225
Rotala, 155
  repens, 155
  serpiculoides, 155
  tenella, 155
  urundiensis, 155
Rubia, 412
  cordifolia, **410,** 412
  longipetiolata, 412
Rubiaceae, 396
Rubus, 227
  adolfi-fredericii, 230
  apetalus, **229,** 230
  friesiorum, 230
  keniensis, 230
  pinnatus, 230
  rigidus, 230

rosifolius, 230
scheffleri, 230
steudneri, **229**, 230
volkensii, **228**, 230
Ruellia, 589
megachlamys, 589, **590**
patula, **582**, 589
prostrata, 589
Rumex, 123
abyssinicus, 123
acetosella, 123
anglocarpus, 123
bequaertii, 123
crispus, 124
ruwenzoriensis, 123
usambarensis, **118**, 123
Ruttya, 598
fruticosa, 598

Saba, 367
florida, **366**, 367
Sacleuxia, 369
tuberosa, 369
Sagina, 112
abyssinica, 112
afroalpina, 112
Salsola, 130
dendroides, 130
pestifera, 130
Salvia, 624
coccinea, 626
merjamie, **625**, 626
nilotica, **625**, 626
Salvinia, 73
auriculata, 73
Sambucus, 412
africana, 412, **413**
Sanicula, 351
elata, 351, **352**
Sansevieria, 722
conspicua, 722, **723**
ehrenbergii, **723**, 724
intermedia, 724
parva, 722
raffillii, 724
Santalaceae, 334
Sapindaceae, 347
Sarcophyte, 338
pirei, 338
Sarcostemma, 387
viminale, **386**, 387
Satureia, 626
abyssinica, 626, **627**
biflora, 626, **627**
kilimandschari, 626
pseudosimensis, 626, **627**
punctata, 626
simensis, 626
uhligii, 628
Satyrium, 749
carsonii, 752, **753**
cheirophorum, 752
coriophoroides, 752
crassicaule, **751**, 752
fimbriatum, 749, **751**

paludosum, 752
robustum, 752
sacculatum, **751**, 752
sceptrum, 752, **753**
schimperi, **750**, 752
volkensii, 749, **753**
Sauromatum, 706
venosum, **705**, 706
Saxymolbium, 374
heudelotanum, 374, **375**
sp. A, 374
Scabiosa, 416
columbaria, **415**, 416
Schimperella, 357
aberdarense, 357
Schizoglossum, 374
barbatum, 374
Schkuhria, 469
pinnata, 469
Scilla, 695,
indica, 695, **696**
kirkii, 695
sp. A, 695
Sclerocarpus, 460
africanus, 460
Scrophulariaceae, 549
Scutellaria, 619
paucifolia, **618**, 619
violascens, **618**, 619
Scutia, 340
myrtina, 340
Sebaea, 501
brachyphylla, 501
grandis, 501, **502**
microphylla, 501, **502**
Secamone, 373
africana, 373
parvifolia, 373
punctulata, 373
sp. A, 373
stuhlmannii, 373
Securidaca, 104
welwitschii, 104
Seddera, 533
hirsuta, 534
latifolia, 534
Sedum, 107
crassularia, 107
meyeri-johannis, 109
ruwenzoriense, **108**, 109
sp. A, 107
Selaginella, 23
abyssinica, 23
caffrorum, 23
dregei, 23
kraussiana, 24
phillipsiana, 23
yemensis, 23
Selago, 567
thomsonii, 567
Senecio, 475
abyssinicus, 478, **488**
aequinoctialis, 479
amblyphyllus, 480
barbatipes, 480

battiscombei, 480
brassica, 480
brassiciformis, 480
cheranganiensis, 480, **481**
coronopifolius, 479
cyanus, 478
discifolius, **477**, 478
elgonensis, 480
goetzei, 480
hageniae, 479
hochstetteri, 478, **482**
implexus, 484
jacksonii, 479
johnstonii, 480
keniodendron, 480
keniophytum, 479
lugardae, 478
lyratipartitus, 478
maranguensis, 479
moorei, 479
nandensis, 478
petitianus, 476, **477**
picticaulis, 484
purtschelleri, 479
rhammatophyllus, 479
roseiflorus, 478
ruwenzoriensis, 479, **482**
sarmentosus, 478
schweinfurthii, 479
snowdenii, 479
sotikensis, 478
sp. A, 478
sp. B, 478
sp. C, 479
sp. D, 480
sp. E, 480
sp. F, 480
stuhlmannii, 478
subsessilis, 480
syringifolius, 476, **477**
transmarinus, 479
trichopterygius, 480
ukambensis, 478
vulgaris, 480
Sericocomopsis, 134
hildebrandtii, 134
pallida, 134
Sericostachys, 134
scandens, 134
Sesamothamnus, 572
rivae, 572
Sesamum, 573
angolense, 573
angustifolium, 573
calycinum, **568**, 573
latifolium, 573
Sesbania, 259
dummeri, 260
goetzei, 260
keniensis, 260
macrantha, 260
quadrata, 260
sesban, 260
Sibthorpia, 556
europaea, 556

Sida, 201
  acuta, 203
  alba, 203
  cordifolia, 201
  cuneifolia, 201, **202**
  ovata, 203
  rhombifolia, **202,** 203
  sp. A, 203
  sp. B, 203
  ternata, 201, **202**
  urens, 201
  veronicifolia, 201
Sigesbeckia, 459
  abyssinica, **457,** 459
  orientalis, 459
Silene, 115
  burchellii, **113,** 115
  gallica, **113,** 115
  macrosolen, 115
Silybum, 493
  marianum, 493
Sisymbrium, 99
  erysimoides, 99
  officinale, 99
Smilacaceae, 700
Smilax, 700
  goetzeana, 700
  kraussiana, 700
Smithia, 263
  elliotii, 263, **264**
Solanaceae, 523
Solanum, 525
  aculeastrum, 528
  aculeatissimum, **527,** 528
  arundo, 528
  benderianum, 526
  dasyphyllum, 528
  dennekense, 528
  dubium, 528
  giganteum, 526
  hastifolium, 526, **527**
  incanum, **527,** 528
  indicum, 526
  mauense, **524,** 526
  mauritianum, 526
  nakurense, 526
  nigrum, 526, **527**
  renschii, 526
  richardii, 528
  schumannianum, 526
  sessilistellatum, **524,** 528
  setaceum, 526
  sp. A, 526
  sp. C, 528
  sp. J, 528
  taitense, 526
  terminale, **524,** 526
Solenostemon, 640
  latifolius, 640, **641**
  rotundifolius, **639,** 640
  sylvaticus, 640
  zambesiacus, 640
Sonchus, 496
  afromontanus, 498
  asper, **497,** 498

bipontini, 498
camporum, 498
luxurians, 498
oleraceus, 498
schweinfurthii, **497,** 498
stenophyllus, 498
Sopubia, 559
  ramosa, 559, **561**
  simplex, 559, **561**
  trifida, 559, **561**
  welwitschii, 559
Sparrmannia, 188
  ricinocarpa, 188, **189**
Spathionema, 279
  kilimandscharicum, 279
Spergula, 111
  arvensis, 111
Sphaeranthus, 445
  bullatus, 447
  confertifolius, 447
  cyathuloides, 447 /
  gomphrenoides, 447
  napierae, **447**
  suaveolens, **446,** 447
  ukambensis, **446,** 447
Sphaerocionium capillare, 28
Sphaerocodon, 388
  obtusifolium, 388
Sphaerothylax, 110
  abyssinica, 110
Sphenostylis, 279
  stenocarpa, 279
Spilanthes, 462
  mauritiana, 462, **463**
  oleracea, 462
Stachys, 623
  aculeolata, 624
  alpigena, 624
  bambuseti, 624
  hildebrandtii, 623
  lindblomiana, 624, **625**
  subrenifolia, 624
Stathmostelma, 382
  pedunculata, 382
  praetermissa, 382
  propinqua, 382
  rhacodes, **366,** 382
Stellaria, 114
  mannii, 114
  media, 114
  sennii, **113,** 114
Stemodiopsis, 551
  buchananii, 551
  humilis, 551
Stephania, 83
  abyssinica, 83
  cyanantha, 83
Sterculiaceae, 190
Stictocardia, 537
  beraviensis, **536,** 537
Stolzia, 772
  repens, **758,** 772
Streptocarpus, 571
  caulescens, 571
  glandulosissimus, 571

montanus, 572
Streptopetalum, 89
  hildebrandtii, 90
  serratum, 90
Striga, 564
  asiatica, 565, **568**
  baumannii, 565
  canescens, 565
  forbesii, 565, **568**
  gesnerioides, 565
  hermonthica, 565
  latericea, 565
  linearifolia, 565
Struthiola, 159
  thomsonii, 159, **160**
Stylochiton, 706
  angustifolius, 706
  salaamicus, 706
Stylosanthes, 263
  fruticosa, 263
Suaeda, 130
  monoica, 130
Subularia, 96
  monticola, 96
Swertia, 503
  calycina, **504,** 505
  crassiuscula, 503, **504**
  eminii, 505
  kilimandscharica, 503, **504**
  lugardae, 505
  parnassiflora, 503
  quartiniana, 503
  sattimae, 503
  scandens, 503
  stellarioides, 505
  subnivalis, 503
  tetrandra, **504,** 505
  uniflora, 503
  usambarensis, 505
  volkensis, 503
  welwitschii, 505

Tacazzea, 370
  apiculata, 370
  galactogoga, 370
Tagetes, 469
  minuta, 469
Talinum, 122
  caffrum, 122
  crispatulatum, 122
  portulacifolium, **120,** 122
Taraxacum, 496
  officinale, 496
Tectaria, 49
  gemmifera, 49, **50**
Tenaris, 389
  rostrata, 389
Tephrosia, 241
  aequilata, 248
  athiensis, 245
  atroviolacea, 247
  downsonii, 247
  drepanocarpa, 247
  elata, **242,** 247
  emeroides, **244,** 245

heckmanniana, 247
hildebrandtii, **242**, 245
holstii, 245, **246**
interrupta, **242**, 247
kassneri, 245
linearis, 245
longipes, 247
lortii, 245
lurida, 247
nana, 248
noctiflora, 245
nyikensis, 247
orientalis, 245
paniculata, 245
paniculata ssp. *holstii*, 245
pumila, **244**, 247
purpurea, 247
reptans, 247
rhodesica, 247
rigida, 247
subtriflora, 245
uniflora, 245
villosa, **246**, 247
vogelii, 248
Teramnus, 270
labialis, 270
uncinatus, **240**, 270
Tetragonia, 119
acanthocarpa, 119
tetragonioides, 119
Thalictrum, 76
rhynchocarpum, 76
Thelypteridaceae, 52
Thelypteris
bergiana, 56
chaseana, 56
confluens, 56
friesii, 56
gueintziana, **31**, 56
longicuspis, **31**, 56
strigosa, **31**, 56
zambesiaca, 56
Thesium, 336
kilimandscharica, 336
schweinfurthii, 336
sp. A, 336, **337**
sp. B, 338
stuhlmannii, 336
unyikense, 336, **337**
ussanguense, 336, **337**
Thlaspi, 96
alliaceum, 96
Thonningia, 338
sanguinea, 338
Thunbergia, 576
alata, **575**, 578
annua, 578
battiscombei, **575**, 578
elliotii, **575**, 578
fasciculata, 576
fischeri, 578, **590**
gibsonii, **577**, 578
gregorii, 578
holstii, 576, **577**
natalensis, 578

sp. C, 578
sp. D, 578
sp. E, 578
sp. F, 579
usambarensis, 578
Thymelaeaceae, 159
Tiliaceae, 187
Tiliacora, 82
funifera, 82
keniensis, 82
Tinnea, 619
aethiopica, 619, **621**
Tinospora, 83
caffra, 83
Tithonia, 460
diversifolia, 462
Tolpis, 494
capensis, **494**
Torenia, 555
thouarsii, 555
Torilis, 351
arvensis, 351, **353**
Trachyandra, 679
saltii, 679, **680**
Trachyspermum, 356
copticum, 356
Tragia, 216
brevipes, 216, **217**
insuavis, 216
scheffleri, 216
sp. A, 216
subsessilis, 216
Tragiella, 216
natalensis, 218
Trapa, 158
natans, 158
Trapaceae, 157
Trianthema, 117
ceratosepala, 117
triquetra, 117
Triaspis, 209
erlangeri, 210
niedenzuiana, 210
Tribulus, 140
cistoides, 140
terrestris, 140, **145**
Triceratorhynchus, 799
viridiflorus, **761**, 799
Trichodesma, 520
physaloides, 521, **522**
schimperi, 521
zeylanicum, 520
Trichomanes, 28
borbonicum, 29
chevalieri, 29
erosum, 28
giganteum, 28
mannii, 29
melanotrichum, 29
radicans, 28
sp. A, 29
Tridactyle, 799
anthomaniaca, **800**, 802
bicaudata, **801**, 802
cruciformis, 802

furcistipes, **801**, 802
scottellii, **800**, 802
tridentata, **762**, 802
Tridax, 467
procumbens, 467, **468**
Trifolium, 308
acaule, 312
baccarinii, **309**, 311
burchellianum, **264**, 311
cheranganiense, 311
cryptopodium, **309**, 310
elgonense, 312
goetzenii, 311
johnstonii, 311
kilimandscharicum, 310
lanceolatum, 311
lugardii, **309**, 312
multinerve, **309**, 312
polystachyum, **309**, 310
preussii, 311
repens, 311
rueppellianum, **309**, 311
var. *lanceolatum*, 311
semipilosum, **309**, 311
simense, **309**, 310
steudneri, **264**, 312
subrotundum, 311
tembense, 311
umbellulatum, 311
usambarense, 310
Triplocephalum, 447
holstii, 447
Tristemma, 183
incompletum, 183
Tristicha, 109
trifaria, 109
Triumfetta, 188
annua, 190
flavescens, 188
longicornuta, 188
macrophylla, 190
pentandra, 190
pilosa, 190
rhomboidea, **184**, 188, **189**
tomentosa, 190
Trochomeria, 174
macrocarpa, **172**, 174
Tryphostemma, 166
hanningtonianum, 166
longifolium, 166
sp. A, 166
Turbina, 549
stenosiphon, 549
Turneraceae, 89
Turritis glabra, 97
Tylophora, 388
lugardae, 388
sp. B, 388
sylvatica, 388
Tylophoropsis, 387
heterophylla, 387
Tylosema, 231
fassoglensis, 231, **232**
Typha, 707
domingensis, 707

Typha–*continued*
  latifolia, 708
Typhaceae, 707

Uebelinia, 114
  abyssinica, 115
  crassifolia, 115
  rotundifolia, 115
Umbelliferae, 348
Umbilicus, 109
  botryoides, **108**, 109
Urena, 206
  lobata, 206, **207**
Urera, 321
  cameroonensis, 321
  hypselodendra, 321, **322**
Urginea, 693
  altissima, **687**, 693
  indica, 693, **696**
Urtica, 320
  massaica, 321, **322**
Urticaceae, 320
Utricularia, 569
  arenaria, **570**, 571
  firmula, 571
  gibba, 571
  inflexa, **570**, 571
  livida, **570**, 571
  pentadactyla, 571
  prehensilis, **570**, 571
  reflexa, 571
  spiralis, 569

Valeriana, 412
  capensis, 414
  kilimandscharica, 412
  volkensii, **413**, 414
Valerianaceae, 412
Valerianella, 414
  microcarpa, 414
Vallisneria, 649
  spiralis, 649
Vanilla, 756
  polylepis, 756
Vatovaea, 272
  pseudolablab, 272
Vaupelia, 520
  hispida, 520
Ventilago, 340
  africana, 340
Verbascum, 550
  sinaiticum, 550
Verbena, 611
  bonariensis, 611
  officinalis, 611, **612**
  tenera, 611
Verbenaceae, 611
Vernonia, 424
  adoensis, 427
  aemulans, 427
  afromontana, 427
  amygdalina, 429
  auriculifera, 426
  brachycalyx, 427, **435**

chthonocephala, 426
cinerascens, 429
cinerea, 426
cistifolia, 431
colorata, 429
dumicola, 429
dummeri, 431, **435**
elliottii, 431
gerberiformis, 426
glabra, 431
hindii, 431
hochstetteri, 429
holstii, 429
hymenolepis, 427
jugalis, 429
karaguensis, **430**, 431
kraussii, 431
lasiopus, 429
pauciflora, 427, **428**
perottetii, 427
pteropoda, 429
pumila, 426, **430**
schweinfurthii, 431, **432**
seretii, 426
smithiana, **428**, 431
sp. B, 426
sp. C, 426
sp. D, 427
sp. E, 429
sp. F, 431
sp. G, 431
stenolepis, 427
subuligera, 426
syringifolia, 429, **432**
tufnellii, **428**, 429
turbinata, 431, **432**
undulata, 431
urticifolia, 429, **430**
violacea, 426
wakefieldii, 427
Veronica, 557
  abyssinica, 557, **558**
  anagallis-aquatica, 557, **558**
  glandulosa, 557
  gunae, 557
  javanica, 557, **558**
Vicia, 316
  benghalensis, 316
  hirsuta, 316, **317**
  paucifolia, 316
  sativa, 316, **317**
  villosa, 316
Vigna, 272
  abyssinica, 276
  ambacensis, 276
  bukobensis, 275
  caerulea, 278
  caesia, 276
  catjang, 278
  chiovendae, 276
  comosa, 276
  dekindtiana, 278
  esculenta, 278
  fischeri, 275

fragrans, 278
friesiorum, 278
frutescens, 278
gracilis, 276
heterophylla, **274**, 276
  var. *lanceolata*, 276
incana, 278
keniensis, 278
lancifolia, 276
leptodon, 276
luteola, 275
macrodon, 276
macrorhyncha, 279
maranguensis, 276
membranacea, 276, **277**
membranaceoides, 276
mensensis, 278
  var. *hastata*, 276
micrantha, 276
monophylla, **274**, 279
nilotica, 275
oblongifolia, 276
parkeri, 276, **277**
parviflora, 276
proboscidella, 279
pubigera, 276
pygmaea, 278
radiata, 279
reticulata, 278
schimperi, 275, **277**
sinensis, 278
sp. B, 278
stuhlmannii, 276
taubertii, 278
triphylla, 279
ulugurensis, 278
unguiculata, 278
vexillata, **277**, 279
Viola, 100
  abyssinica, **98**, 100
  duriprati, 100
  eminii, **98**, 100
Violaceae, 100
Viscum, 334
  fischeri, 334
  nervosum, 334
  schimperi, **327**, 334
  tuberculatum, **327**, 334
Vitaceae, 340
Vitex, 616
Vitis jatrophoides, 345
Vittaria, 72
  volkensii, 72
Volutaria, 493
  lippii, 493
  muricata, 493

Wahlenbergia, 511
  arabidifolia, **512**, 513
  kilimandscharica, **512**, 513
  pusilla, 513
  silenoides, 513
  sp. A, 513
  virgata, **512**, 513

Waltheria, 191
  indica, 191, **192**
Whitfieldia, 591
  elongata, 591
Wissadula, 209
  rostrata, 209
Withania, 529
  somnifera, 529
Wolffia, 707
  arrhiza, 707
Wormskioldia, 89
  lobata, 89
  pilosa, 89
Wurmbea, 674
  tenuis, 674, **675**

Xanthium, 459
  pungens, 459

Xiphopteris, 71
  flabelliformis, 72
  sp. B, 72
  strangeana, 72
Xyridaceae, 669
Xyris, 669
  capensis, 669, **670**
  rehmannii, 669, **670**
Xysmalobium, 374
  reticulatum, 374
  undulatum, 374, **375**

Ypsilopus, 796
  longifolia, 796, **798**

Zaleya, 117
  pentandra, 117

Zebrina, 662
  pendula, 664
Zehneria, 175
  minutiflora, 177
  oligosperma, 177
  scabra, **176**, 177
  sp. A, 177
Zephyranthes, 708
  grandiflora, 708
Zingiberaceae, 669
Zornia, 263
  albolutescens, 266
  apiculata, 266
  glochidiata, 266
  pratensis, **265**, 266
  setosa, **265**, 266
Zygophyllaceae, 139